RAND McNALLY

WORLD ATLAS

BARNES
&NOBLE
BOOKS
NEW YORK

**Chairman, President, and CEO,
Rand McNally and Company**

Henry J. Feinberg

**Vice President and General Manager,
Map & Atlas Publishing**

Jayne L. Fenton

Director, Reference Business

Kendra L. Ensor

Editors

Brett R. Gover
Ann T. Natunewicz

Art Direction and Design

John C. Nelson
Jamie O'Neal

Cartography (U.S.)

V. Patrick Healy
Jon M. Leverenz
Robert K. Argersinger
Barbara Benstead-Strassheim
Kerry B. Chambers
Marzee L. Eckhoff
Winifred V. Farbman
Susan K. Hudson
Gwynn A. Lloyd
Nina Lusterman
John M. McAvoy
Robert L. Merrill
Patty A. Porter
James A. Purvis
David R. Simmons
Thomas F. Vitacco

Cartography (U.K.)

Craig Asquith

Cartography (Italy)

Giovanni Baselli
Ubaldo Uberti

Manufacturing

Terry D. Rieger

Marketing

JoEllen A. Klein

Photo Research

Feldman and Associates, Inc.

Photo Credits

Jacket

© 1998 PhotoDisc Inc. (satellite photo)

Contents

© North Wind Picture Archives, iv (figures 4, 6, and 8)
© 1997 PhotoDisc Inc.: iii (t), vi (figure 3), viii (Energy)
Copyright © Corel Corp.: viii (Land, Population, and Population Growth)
Satellite photo, iv (figure 1), provided by Wally Jansen, WTJ Software Series

Rand McNally World Atlas

This edition published by Barnes & Noble, Inc., by arrangement with Rand McNally & Co.

Copyright © 1998 Rand McNally & Co.
1998 Barnes & Noble Books

www.randmcnally.com

M 10 9 8 7 6 5 4 3 2 1

ISBN 0-7607-1165-8

Published and printed in the United States of America

Rand McNally and Company.
      Rand McNally world atlas.
         p.   cm.
      Includes index.
      ISBN 0-7607-1165-8
      1. Atlases. I. Title.   II. Title: World Atlas
G1021 .R45   1997 <G&M>
912- - DC21   97-11900
                                                        CIP
                                                       MAPS

Contents

INTRODUCTORY SECTION

Understanding Maps & Atlases . . . . iv - v
How to Use the Atlas . . . . vi-vii
The World in Charts viii

MAPS

Index Map and Legend 1

World 2-5

World, Political 2-3
World, Physical 4-5

Europe 6-23

Europe, Political 6-7
Northern Europe 8-9
Scandinavia and the Baltic States 10-11
Northwest Europe 12-13
Mediterranean Lands 14-15
Southwest Europe 16-17
Southern Europe 18-19
Central and Eastern Europe 20-21
Eastern Europe 22-23

Asia 24-45

Asia, Political 24-25
Northern Eurasia 26-27
China, Mongolia, Korea, and Japan 28-29
Eastern China 30
Japan 31
Southeast Asia 32-33
Mainland Southeast Asia and the Philippines . . 34-35
Malaysia, Singapore, and Indonesia 36-37
Southwest Asia 38-39
India 40-41
The Middle East 42-43
Turkey and Transcaucasia 44-45

Africa 46-57

Africa, Political 46-47
Northern Africa 48-49

West Africa 50-51
Central and Southern Africa 52-53
Central Africa 54-55
Southern Africa and Madagascar 56-57

Australia and Oceania 58-63

Australia and Oceania, Political 58-59
Western Australia 60-61
Eastern Australia and New Zealand 62-63

Pacific and Indian Oceans 64-65
Atlantic Ocean 66

Antarctica 67

South America 68-74

South America, Political 68
Southern South America 69
Northern South America 70-71
Central South America 72-73
Northeast Brazil 74

North America 75-143

North America, Political 75
Mexico, Central America, and the Caribbean . . 76-77
Mexico 78-79
Central America and the Caribbean 80-81
Canada and Alaska 82-83
Canadian Province Maps 84-91
United States 92-93
U.S. State Maps 94-143

Arctic Region 144

INDEX

Index to the Reference Maps . . . . .I•1-I•80

Understanding Maps & Atlases

figure 1

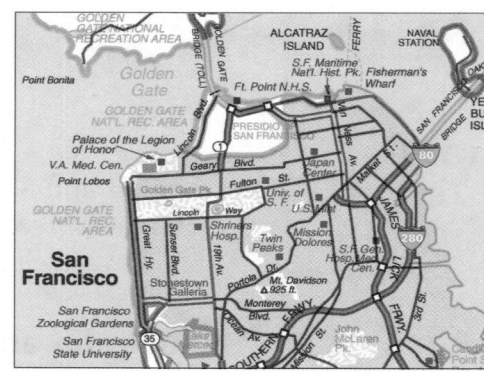

figure 2

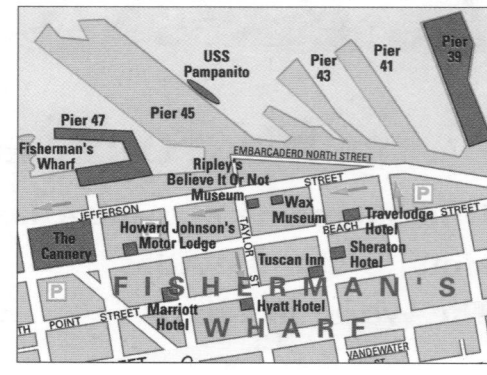

figure 3

What is a map?

A map is a representation, usually at a much-reduced size, of the location of things or places relative to one another. There are many different types of maps, including maps of the world, its regions or countries, cities, neighborhoods, and buildings. Figure 1 is a satellite image of California's San Francisco Bay area; figure 2 shows the same area represented on a road map; and figure 3 provides street-level detail of one of the city's neighborhoods.

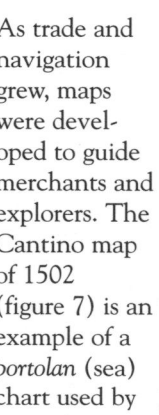

figure 4

A set of maps bound together is called an atlas. Abraham Ortelius' *Theatrum orbis terrarum*, published in 1570, is considered to be the first modern "atlas," although it was not referred to as such for almost 20 years. In 1589, Gerardus Mercator (figure 4) coined the term when he named his collection of maps after the mythological titan Atlas, who carried the Earth on his shoulders as punishment for warring against Zeus. Since then, the definition of "atlas" has been expanded, and atlases often include additional geographic information in diagrams, tables, and text.

History of Cartography

Around 500 B.C., on a tiny clay tablet the size of a hand, the Babylonians inscribed the Earth as a flat disk (figure 5) with Babylon at the center. Geographic knowledge was also highly developed among the Egyptians, who drew maps on papyrus and carved them into temple walls. Ancient Greek philosophers and scientists debated endlessly the nature of the Earth and its place in the universe; Ptolemy, the influential geographer and astronomer, made an early attempt to map the known world (figure 6). Roman maps most often depicted boundaries, physical features, and the infrastructure of the Roman Empire. Over the following centuries, territorial expansion directly increased geographic knowledge, which in turn greatly enhanced the cartography, or map-making, of the time.

figure 5

As trade and navigation grew, maps were developed to guide merchants and explorers. The Cantino map of 1502 (figure 7) is an example of a *portolan* (sea) chart used by mariners traveling to the newly discovered Americas. Information gained from the past expeditions of John Cabot, Christopher Columbus, and Ferdinand Magellan led to great advances in the content and structure of world maps. As a result, many maps produced between 1600 and 1800, including the colored woodcut shown in figure 8, were works of art as well as geographical representations.

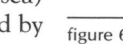

figure 6

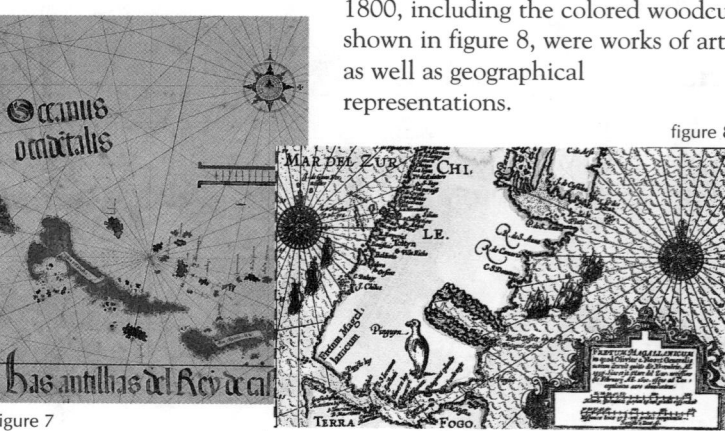

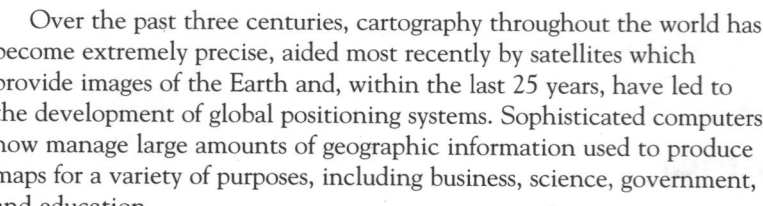

figure 8

figure 7

Over the past three centuries, cartography throughout the world has become extremely precise, aided most recently by satellites which provide images of the Earth and, within the last 25 years, have led to the development of global positioning systems. Sophisticated computers now manage large amounts of geographic information used to produce maps for a variety of purposes, including business, science, government, and education.

Latitude and Longitude

The imaginary horizontal line that circles the Earth exactly halfway between the North and South poles is called the Equator, which represents 0° latitude and lies 90° from either pole. The other lines of latitude, or parallels, measure the distance from the Equator, either north or south (figure 9). The imaginary vertical line that measures 0° longitude runs through the Greenwich Observatory in the United Kingdom, and is called the Prime Meridian. The other lines of longitude, or meridians, measure distances east and west of the Prime Meridian (figure 10), up to a maximum of 180°. Lines of latitude and longitude cross each other, forming a pattern called a grid system (figure 11). Any point on Earth can be located by its precise latitude and longitude coordinates.

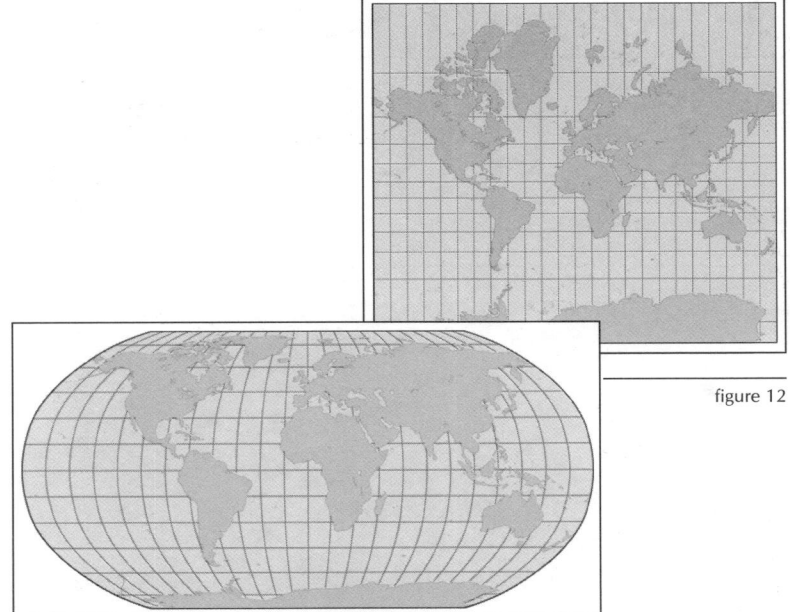

figure 12

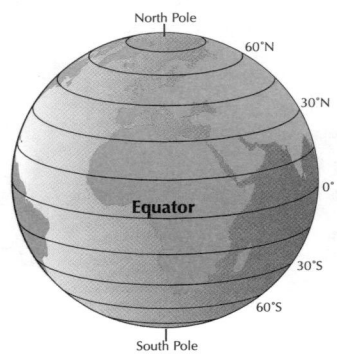

figure 9

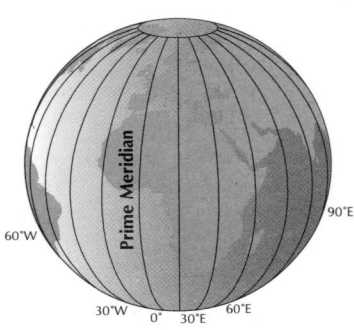

figure 10

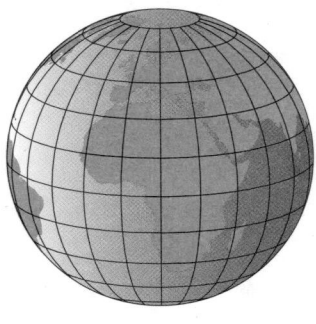

figure 11

figure 13

With the help of mathematics, cartographers are able to depict the curvature of the Earth on a two-dimensional surface. This process is called projecting a map, or creating a map projection. The size, shape, distance, area, and proportion of map features can be distorted, however, when the curves of a globe become the straight lines of a map. Distortion occurs because the Earth's spherical surface must be stretched and/or broken in places as it is flattened. Different map projections have specific properties that make them useful, and a cartographer must select the projection best-suited to the map's purpose.

The Mercator (figure 12) and the Robinson (figure 13) projections are commonly chosen for maps of the entire world. In this atlas, the Robinson is used along with four additional projections— the Lambert Azimuthal Equal Area, the Lambert Conformal Conic, the Sinusoidal, and the Azimuthal Equidisant.

Map scale

The scale of a map is the relationship between distances or areas shown on the map and the corresponding distances or areas on the Earth's surface. Large-scale maps generally show relatively small areas in greater detail than do small-scale maps, such as those of the world or the continents.

There are three different ways to express scale. Most often it is given as a fraction, such as 1:10,000,000, which means that the ratio of map distances to actual Earth distances is 1 to 10,000,000 (figure 14). Scale also can be expressed as a word phrase, such as, "One inch represents approximately 150 miles" (figure 15). Lastly, scale can be illustrated as a scale bar, labeled with miles on one side and kilometers on the other (figure 16). Any of these three scale expressions can be used to calculate distances on a map.

1:10 000 000

figure 14

One inch represents approximately 150 miles

figure 15

figure 16

Map projections

Spherical representations of the Earth are called globes, while flat representations are called maps. Because globes are round and three-dimensional, they can show the continents and oceans undistorted and unbroken; therefore, they represent the Earth and its various features more correctly than do maps. Maps, however, generally feature larger scales and higher levels of detail.

How to Use the Atlas

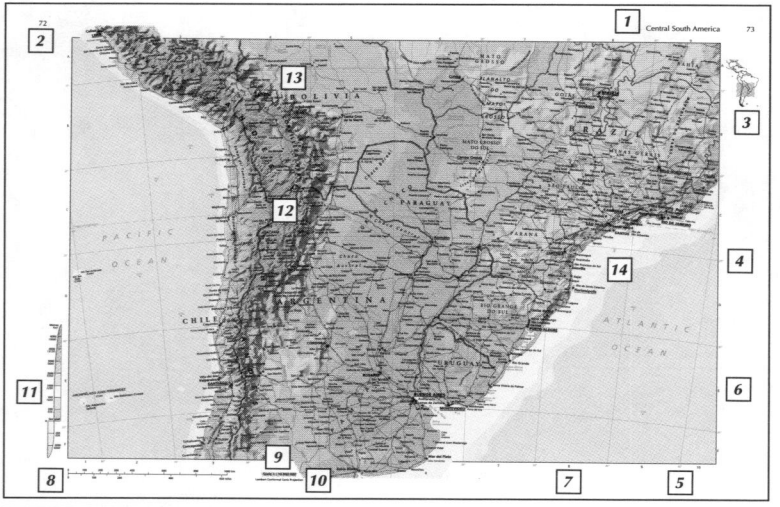

figure 1

[1] Map title
[2] Page number
[3] Locator map
[4] Latitude
[5] Longitude
[6] Index reference letter
[7] Index reference number
[8] Scale bar

[9] Scale ratio
[10] Map projection
[11] Hypsometric/bathymetric scale bar
[12] Shaded relief
[13] Hypsometric tints
    (to show elevation)
[14] Bathymetric tints
    (to show water depths)

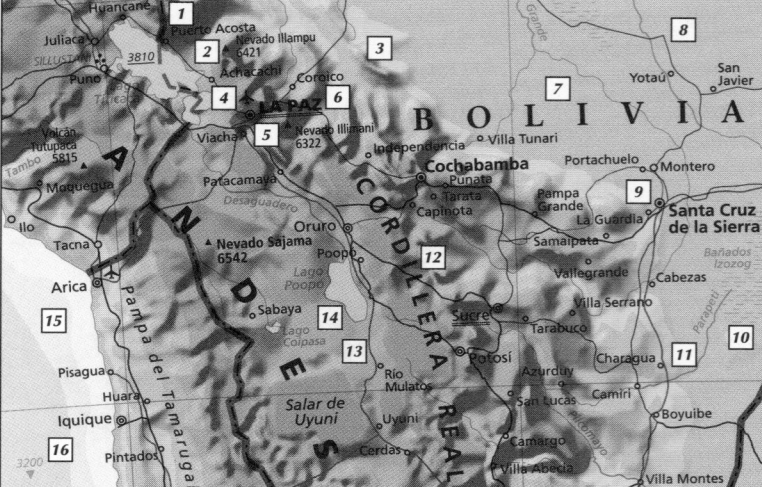

figure 2

[1] International boundary
[2] Mountain peak/elevation
[3] Hypsometric elevation tints
[4] International airport
[5] Urban area
[6] National capital
[7] Country name
[8] Road

[9] City/town
[10] Swamp
[11] River
[12] Mountain range
[13] Railroad
[14] Lake
[15] Bathymetric tints
[16] Depth of water (in meters)

What the Atlas Includes

At the core of the atlas is a collection of regional maps covering the entire world. The maps were designed to be as easy as possible to understand and use. Figure 1 is an example of a map spread contained in this atlas. The boxed numbers on this map, which correspond to items listed below it, highlight the features and information found on each map page—such as the map title, the locator map showing the area of the world depicted on the map, and the map scale.

Figure 2 is an enlarged section from the same map. As in figure 1, a few of the most common feature symbols have been highlighted. A more complete list of the map symbols used in this atlas can be found on page 1.

Following the regional maps are individual maps of each of the United States, and the Canadian provinces (figure 3).

The last section of the atlas is an 80-page index with entries for approximately 45,000 places and geographic features that appear on the maps.

Physical and Political Maps

The two main types of maps that appear in this atlas are physical maps and political maps. Physical maps, like the one shown in figure 4 (see next page), emphasize terrain, landforms, and elevation.

Political maps, as in figure 5, emphasize countries and

other political units over topography. The state and province maps found on pages 84-91 and pages 94-143 are both political and physical: they feature political coloration but also include shaded relief to depict landforms.

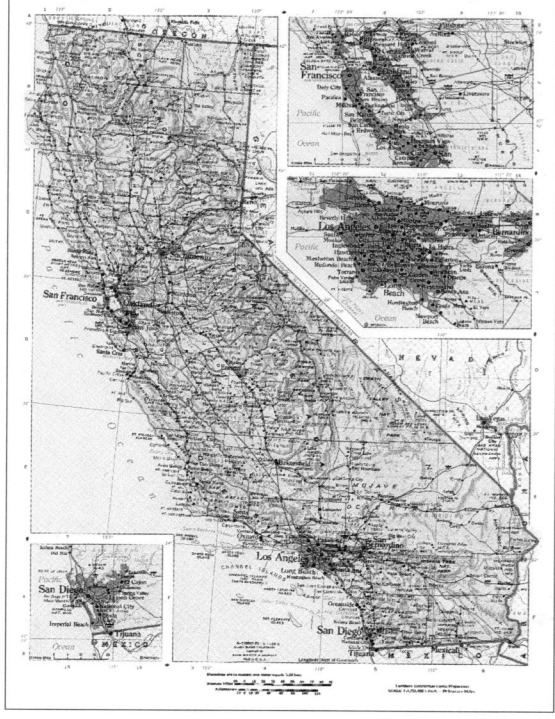

figure 3

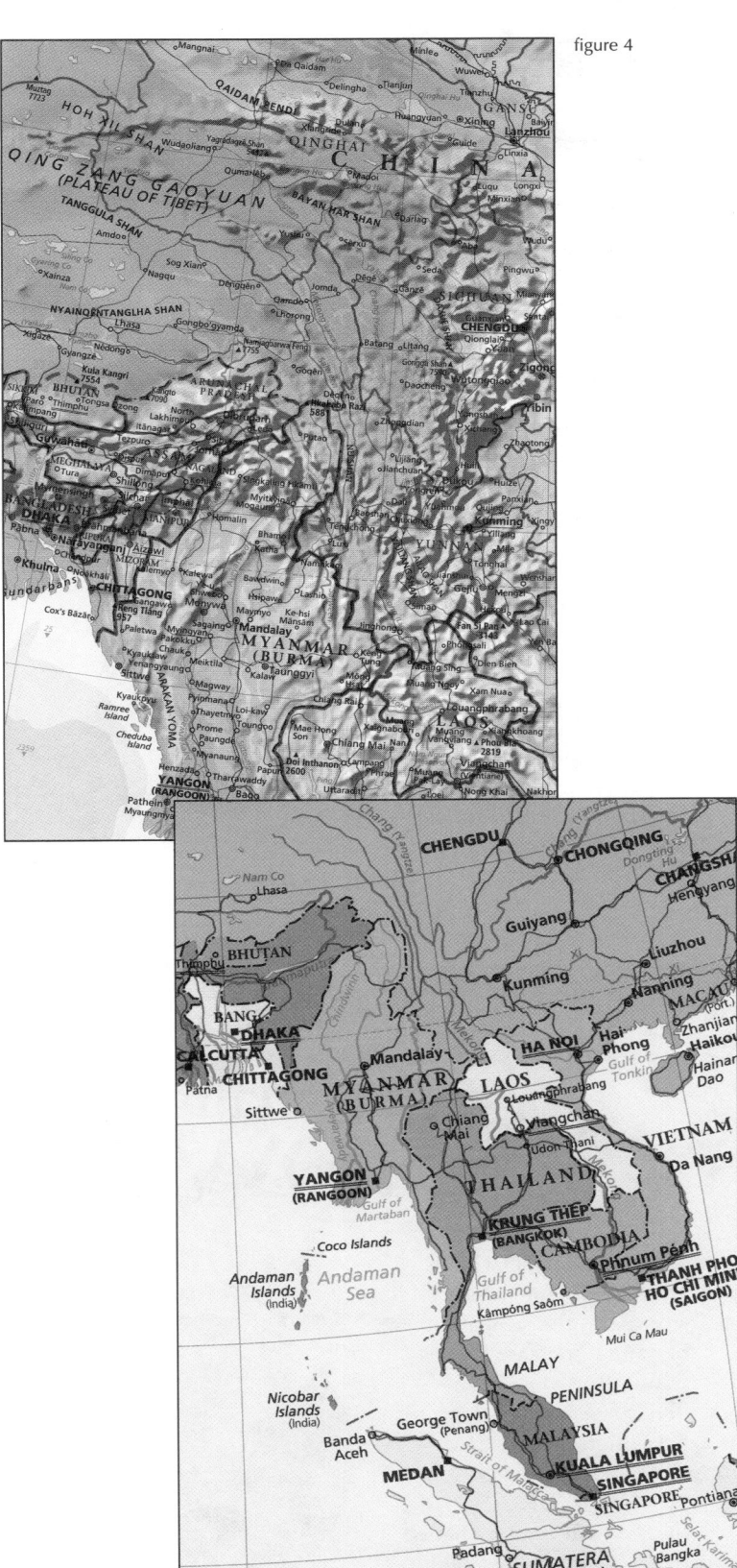

figure 4

figure 5

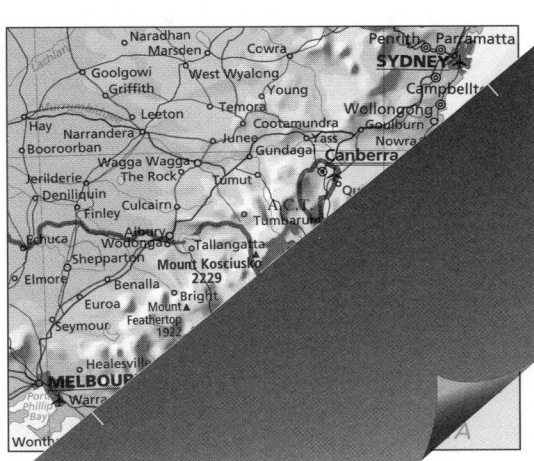

figure 6

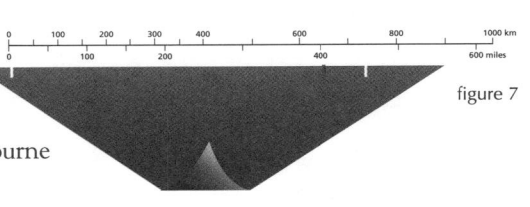

figure 7

between the 400-mile mark and the unlabeled 500-mile mark, indicating that the distance separating the two cities is approximately 450 miles (figure 7).

3) To confirm this measurement, make a third pencil mark (shown in red in figure 7) at the 400-mile mark. Slide the paper to the left so that the red mark lines up with 0. The white Sydney mark now falls very close to the 50-mile mark, which is unlabeled. Thus, Melbourne and Sydney are indeed approximately 450 (400 plus 50) miles apart.

Using the Index to Find Places

One of the most important purposes of an atlas is to help the reader locate places or features. In this atlas, each map is bordered by a letter and number grid. In the index, found in the back of the atlas on pages I•1 through I•80, every entry is assigned a map reference key, which consists of a letter and a number that correspond to a letter and a number on the grid. To locate places or features, follow the steps outlined in this example for Palembang, Indonesia:

P

Pālanpur, India	F5	40
Palaoa Point, C., Hi., U.S.	C4	104
Palapye, Bots.	F5	56
Palatine, Il., U.S.	A5	106
Palatka, Fl., U.S.	C5	102
Palau, ctry., Oc.	B8	37
Palawan, i., Phil.	B5	37
Pālayankottai, India	E8	41
Palembang, Indon.	D2	36
Palencia, Spain.	G6	17
Palermo, Italy	D5	18
Palestine, Ar., U.S.	C5	97
Palestine, Il., U.S.	D6	106
Palestine, Tx., U.S.	D5	136

figure 8

1) Look up Palembang in the index. The entry (figure 8) contains the following information: the feature name (Palembang), an abbreviation for the country (Indon.) in which Palembang is located, the map reference key (D2) that corresponds to Palembang's location on the map, and the page number (36) of the map on which Palembang can be found.

2) Turn to page 36. Look along either the left or right margin for the letter "D" —the letter code given for Palembang. The "D" denotes a narrow horizontal band, roughly 1½" wide, in which Palembang is located. Then, look along either the top or bottom margin for the number "2" —the numerical part of the code given for Palembang. The "2" denotes a narrow vertical band, also roughly 1½" wide, in which Palembang is located.

3) Using your finger, follow the "D" band and the "2" band to the area where they meet (figure 9). Palembang can be found within the darker shaded square where the bands overlap.

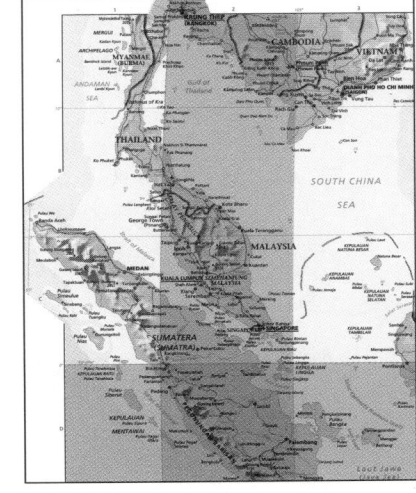

figure 9

Measuring Distances

Using a map scale bar, it is possible to calculate the distance between any two points on a map. To find the approximate distance between Melbourne and Sydney, Australia, for example, follow these steps:

1) Lay a piece of paper on the right-hand page of the "Eastern Australia and New Zealand" map found on pages 62-63, lining up its edge with the city dots for Melbourne and Sydney. Make a mark on the paper next to each dot (figure 6).

2) Place the paper along the scale bar found below the map, and position the first mark at 0. The second mark falls about halfway

Land

The Earth has a total surface area of 197 million square miles (510.2 million sq km). Water, including oceans, seas, lakes, and rivers, covers nearly three-quarters of this area; land only one-quarter.

The largest landmass is Eurasia, shared by the continents of Europe and Asia. Eurasia represents 36.5% of the Earth's total land area (but only 10.7% of the total surface area). The largest continent is Asia, which accounts for 30% of the total land area. Africa ranks second, with 20% of the total land area.

The smallest continent by far is Australia, which holds only 5.1% of the world's land. When it is grouped with New Zealand and the other islands of Oceania, the figure rises only slightly, to 5.7%.

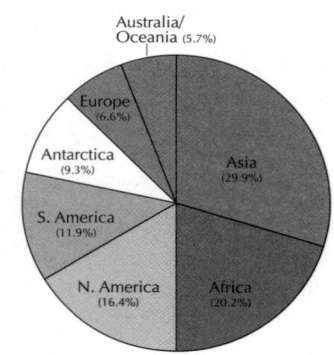

Percentage of world land area

Energy

A large percentage of the world's energy is used for manufacturing. This fact helps explain the great variances among the continents in the consumption of energy. Highly developed North America, with only 8% of the world's population, consumes nearly 30% of the world's energy, and more than five times as much as Africa and South America combined.

For two continents, energy consumption exceeds production: North America produces roughly nine-tenths of the energy it consumes, and Europe only three-fifths. In contrast, Africa consumes less than two-fifths of the energy it produces.

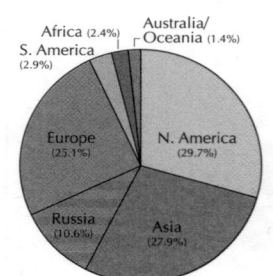

Percentage of world energy consumption

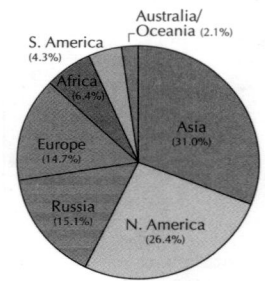

Percentage of world energy production

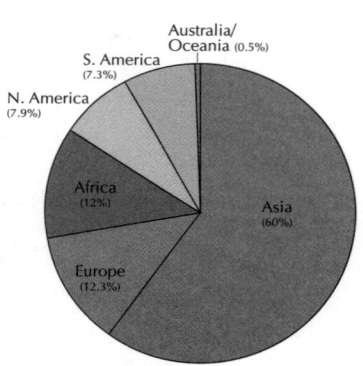

Population

Asia is the world's most populous continent, and has been for at least two millennia. Its current population of 3.5 billion represents an astonishing 60% of the world's people, nearly five times as much as any other continent. It is home to the world's two most populous countries: China, with nearly 1.2 billion people, and India, with 900 million. Four other Asian countries rank among the ten most populous in the world: Indonesia (4th), Pakistan (7th), Japan (8th), and Bangladesh (9th).

Europe and Africa each contain roughly 700 million people. Europe, however, has only one-third the land area of Africa, so its population density is three times greater. Antarctica has no permanent population and therefore does not appear on the graph.

Percentage of world population

population Growth

The world's population is growing at a rapid pace: at present, the annual rate of natural increase (births minus deaths) is 1.5%. Today, the world holds 5.8 billion people; some experts predict that by the year 2050 this number will have increased by two-thirds, to 9.8 billion.

The largest part of the growth is taking place in Asia, which already is home to three-fifths of the world's people. Of every hundred people added to the Earth's population each year, 65 are Asian. Africa is also gaining a larger share of the world total: the continent's current population represents 12% of the world total, but its growth accounts for more than 19% of the annual world increase.

Europe, on the other hand, is seeing its share of the world population erode. Although Europe is the second most populous continent, its annual growth represents less than 2% of the world total.

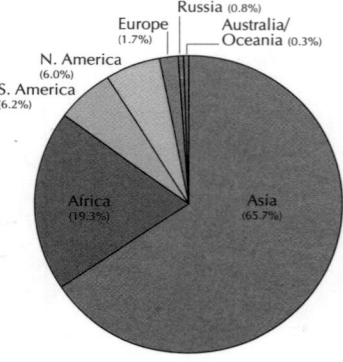

Percentage of world population growth

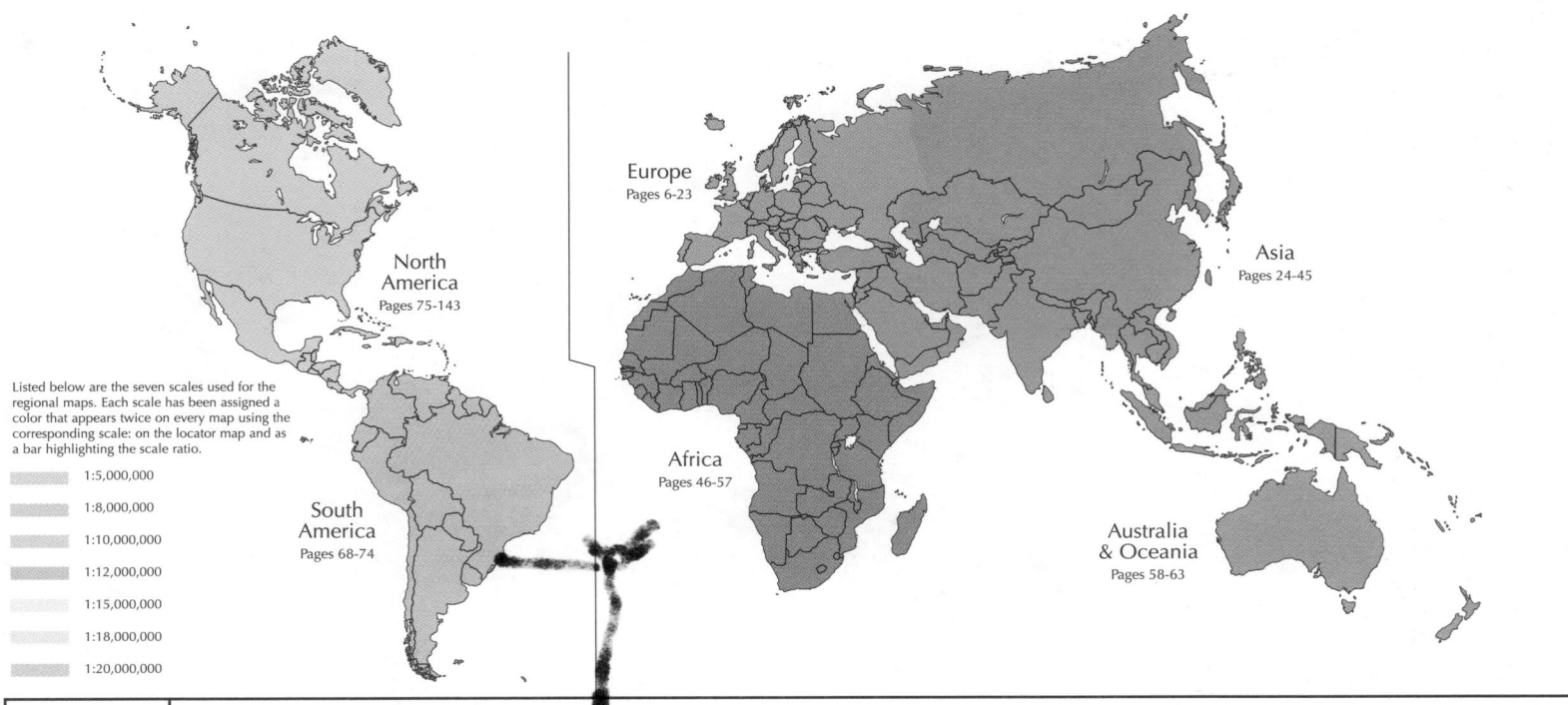

North America
Pages 75-143

Europe
Pages 6-23

Asia
Pages 24-45

South America
Pages 68-74

Africa
Pages 46-57

Australia & Oceania
Pages 58-63

Listed below are the seven scales used for the regional maps. Each scale has been assigned a color that appears twice on every map using the corresponding scale: on the locator map and as a bar highlighting the scale ratio.

1:5,000,000
1:8,000,000
1:10,000,000
1:12,000,000
1:15,000,000
1:18,000,000
1:20,000,000

Legend

World and Regional Maps

Hydrographic Features

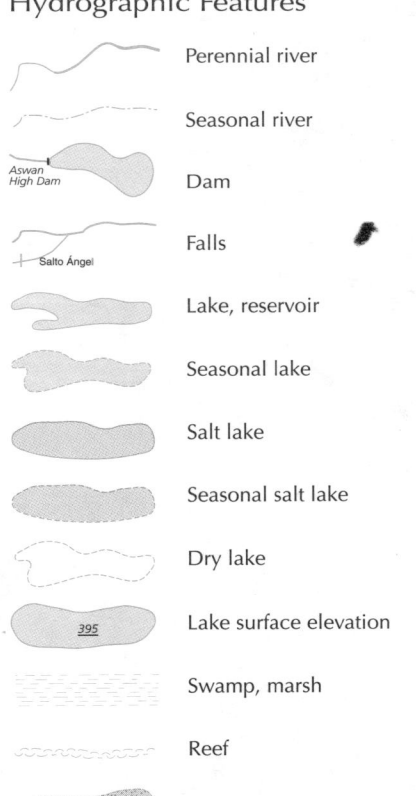

Perennial river

Seasonal river

Dam
Aswan High Dam

Falls
Salto Ángel

Lake, reservoir

Seasonal lake

Salt lake

Seasonal salt lake

Dry lake

Lake surface elevation
395

Swamp, marsh

Reef

Glacier/ice sheet

Topographic Features

Elevations and depths are given in meters.

764 Depth of water

▲ 2278 Elevation above sea level

▼ 1700 Elevation below sea level

≍ Mountain pass

Huo Shan 1774 Mountain peak/elevation

The highest elevation on each continent is underlined.
The highest elevation in each country is shown in boldface.

Transportation Features

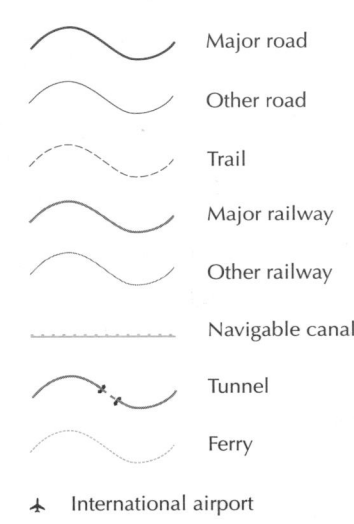

Major road

Other road

Trail

Major railway

Other railway

Navigable canal

Tunnel

Ferry

✈ International airport

✈ Other airport

Political Features

International Boundaries (First-order political unit)

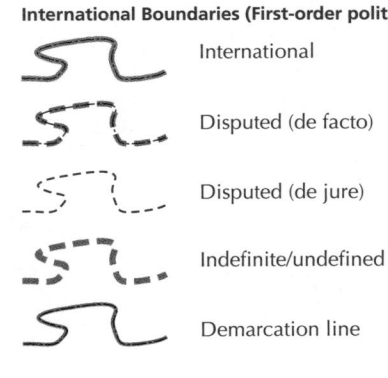

International

Disputed (de facto)

Disputed (de jure)

Indefinite/undefined

Demarcation line

Internal Boundaries

State/province

NORMANDIE Cultural/historic region
(Denmark) Administering country

Cities and Towns

The size of symbol and type indicates the relative importance of the locality.

■ **LONDON**

▣ **CHICAGO**

◉ **Milwaukee**

◎ Tacna

◉ Iquitos

○ Old Crow

▫ Mettawa

🦠 Urban area

Capitals

MEXICO CITY
Bonn — Country, dependency

RIO DE JANEIRO
Perth — State, province

MANCHESTER
Chester — County

Cultural Features

⬚ or ▪ National park

▪ Point of interest

⌇⌇⌇ Wall

∴ Ruins

State and Province Maps

Pages 84-91 and Pages 94-143

⊙ Capital

○ County seat

▲ Military installation

△ Point of interest

+ Mountain peak

International boundary

State/province boundary

County boundary

Road

Railroad

✖ Urban area

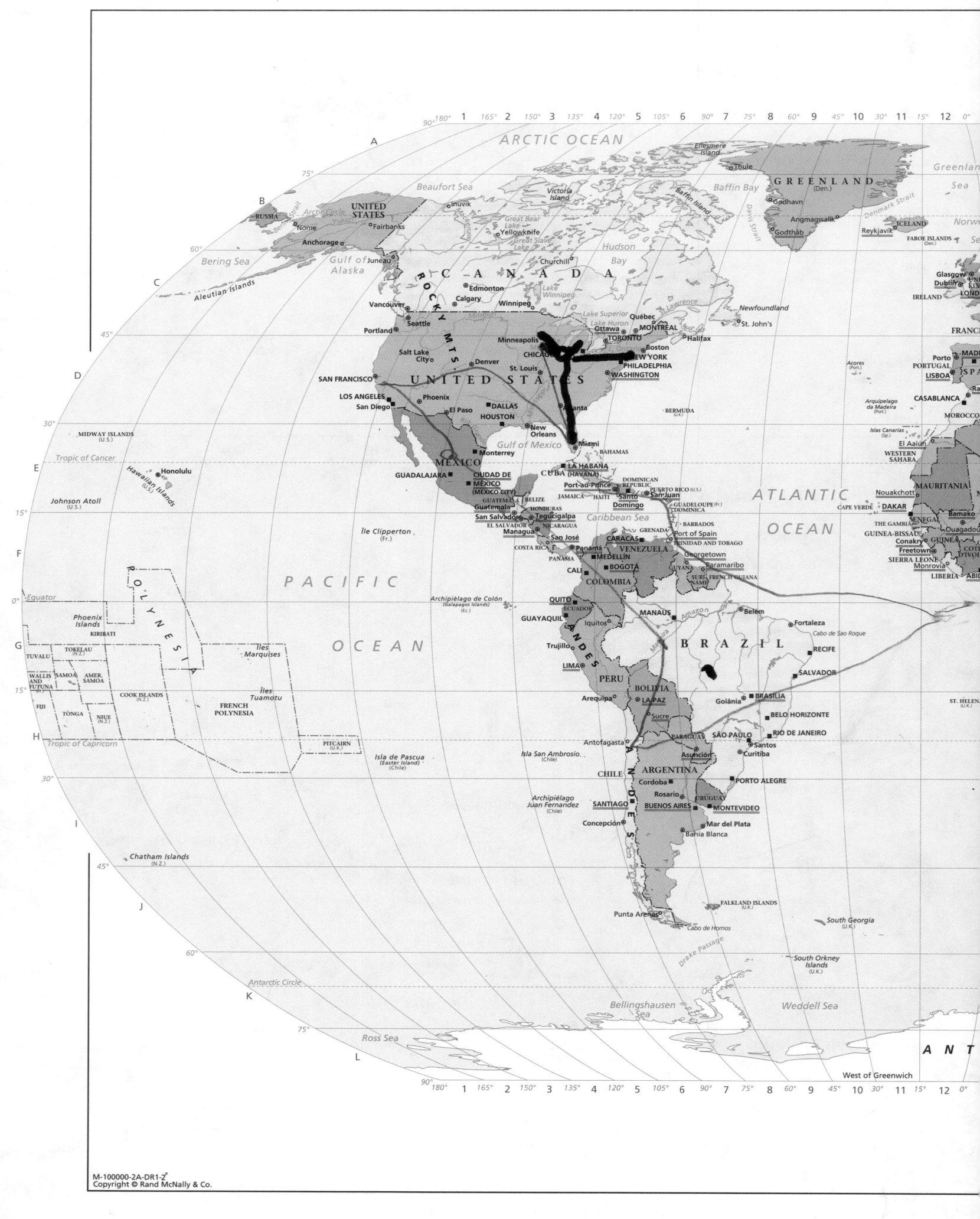

Scale 1 : 90 000 000

Robinson Projection

ARCTIC OCEAN

Spitsbergen   Zemlja Franca-Iosifa   A
VALBARD   Novosibirskie
(Nor.)   Barents Sea   ostrova
            more Laptevyh   Vostočno-Sibirskoe
    Novaja   more   75°
    Zemlja   Karskoe more   Tiksi   B
Narvik   Hammerfest   Murmansk   Vorkuta   Igarka   Lena   Arctic Circle   60°
WAY   SWEDEN   Arhangel'sk   Jakutsk   Magadan   Sea of   Bering Sea   C
slo   FINLAND   Ob'   R U S S I A   ostrov   Okhotsk   Kamčatka   Aleutian Is.
    Helsinki   Sahalin   (U.S.)
Stockholm   SANKT-PETERBURG   Perm'   Ekaterinburg   Krasnojarsk   Habarovsk   Petropavlovsk-
Kobenhavn   ESTONIA   NIŽNIJ   Čeljabinsk   Omsk   Novosibirsk   Irkutsk   Čita   Amur   Kamčatskij
NMARK   LATVIA   NOVGOROD   Samara   Akmola   Vladivostok   Kuril'skie   45°
BERLIN   MOSKVA   Volgograd   KAZAKSTAN   Ulaanbaatar   Sapporo   ostrova   D
GERMANY   LITH.   (MOSCOW)   Irtyš   Urümqi   BEIJING   SHENYANG   Hokkaidō
POLAND   BELARUS   KYIV   Aral   ALMATY   Hohhot   TIANJIN   Dalian   NORTH   Sea of   Sendai
WIEN   WARSZAWA   UKRAINE   Sea   MONGOLIA   GOBI   KOREA   Japan   Honshū   TOKYO
BUDAPEST   Black Sea   UZBEKISTAN   TIEN-SHAN   CHINA   SOUL   PUSAN   ŌSAKA   30°
ROMANIA   GEORGIA   TAŠKENT   KYRGYZSTAN   Xi'an   Qingdao   SOUTH   Fukuoka   PACIFIC
Beograd   BULGARIA   ARM. AZER.   TURKMENISTAN   TAJIKISTAN   Chengdu   Nanjing   SHANGHAI   KOREA   Yellow
ROMA   ISTANBUL   BAKI   Chongqing   WUHAN   Sea   Nansei-   OCEAN
ANKARA   TURKEY   KABOL   AFGHANISTAN   Lhasa   Changsha   shotō
AZAĪR   ATHÍNAI   Izmir   TEHRÁN   Esfahán   ISLAMABAD   HIMALAYAS   Kunming   GUANGZHOU   Tropic of Cancer
IERS)   GREECE   CYPRUS   SYRIA   Rawalpindi   Kathmandu   DHAKA   T'AIPEI   WAKE ISLAND
TUNISIA   LEBANON   BAGHDAD   IRAQ   IRAN   LAHORE   NEPAL   XIANGGANG   TAIWAN   (U.S.)
Tunis   ISRAEL   Amman   Abadan   PAKISTAN   DELHI   BANGL.   (HONG KONG)
Taråbulus   JORDAN   KUWAIT   QATAR   New   Ahmadábád   MYANMAR   Viangchan   Luzon   NORTHERN   15°
(Tripoli)   EL-ISKANDARIYA   AR-RIYÁD   Abú   Delhi   INDIA   (BURMA)   LAOS   PHILIPPINES   MARIANA
    (ALEXANDRIA)   (RIYADH)   Zaby   Masqat   HYDERABAD   YANGON   VIETNAM   ISLANDS   MARSHALL
GERIA   EL-QÁHIRA   SAUDI   U.A.E.   KARACHI   BANGALORE   (RANGOON)   THANH PHO   MANILA   (U.S.)   ISLANDS
    (CAIRO)   ARABIA   OMAN   MUMBAI   CHENNAI   KRUNG THEP   HO CHI MINH   Davao   GUAM
HARA   EGYPT   Red Sea   Pune   THAILAND   (BANGKOK)   CAMBODIA   Mindanao   (U.S.)
NIGER   CHAD   Al-Khartúm   San'a   Arabian   Bay of   Andaman   Phnum   FEDERATED STATES OF
    Lekci Chad   ERITREA   YEMEN   Sea   Bengal   Islands   Penh   BRUNEI   MICRONESIA   PALAU
amey   N'Djamena   Asmera   'Adan   Kochi   SRI LANKA   (India)   MALAYSIA
NIGERIA   SUDAN   DJIBOUTI   Djibouti   Gees Gwardafuy   Colombo   Nicobar   Medan   Kuala Lumpur
Kano   Abuja   ADĪS ÁBEBA   SOMALIA   MALDIVES   Islands   SINGAPORE   Borneo   PAPUA NEW   Equator   0°
orto-Novo   CENTRAL AFRICAN   ETHIOPIA   (India)   Banjarmasin   GUINEA
LAGOS   REPUBLIC   Muqdisho   Sumatera   INDONESIA   New   NAURU   KIRIBATI
CAMEROON   Bangui   UGANDA   KENYA   SEYCHELLES   Sulawesi   Guinea   SOLOMON
EQUAT.   Yaoundé   Kigali   KAMPALA   NAIROBI   Ujungpandang   Port Moresby   ISLANDS
GUIN.   GABON   DEM. REP. OF   RWANDA   JAKARTA   Surabaya   Cape York   TUVALU
Libreville   Brazzaville   THE CONGO   BURUNDI   TANZANIA   Jawa   Darwin   VANUATU   15°
    KINSHASA   (ZAIRE)   Bujumbura   Zanzibar   Cairns   FIJI   H
    LUANDA   Lubumbashi   Dodoma   Dar es Salaam   COMOROS   INDIAN   Coral   NEW   Suva
Lobito   ANGOLA   ZAMBIA   MALAWI   Lilongwe   MADAGASCAR   OCEAN   Sea   CALEDONIA   Nouméa
    NAMIBIA   BOTSWANA   ZIMBABWE   Hararé   Antananarivo   MAURITIUS   AUSTRALIA   Alice Springs   (Fr.)   Tropic of Capricorn
Windhoek   Gaborone   Pretoria   Maputo   REUNION   Brisbane   Rockhampton   30°
Walvis Bay   JOHANNESBURG   WAZILAND   (Fr.)   Perth   Darling   SYDNEY
    SOUTH   Durban   LESOTHO   Adelaide   Canberra   Tasman Sea
Cape Town   AFRICA   Port Elizabeth   MELBOURNE   Auckland   I
Cape of Good Hope   Íles Kerguélen   Tasmania   NEW ZEALAND   North Island   45°
                    (Fr.)   Hobart   Wellington
                                    South Island
SOUTHERN   OCEAN   Christchurch   J

            Antarctic Circle   60°
ENDERBY LAND   WILKES LAND   K   75°

CTICA   L
East of Greenwich
14 30° 15 45° 16 60° 17 75° 18 90° 19 105° 20 120° 21 135° 22 150° 23 165° 24 180° 90°

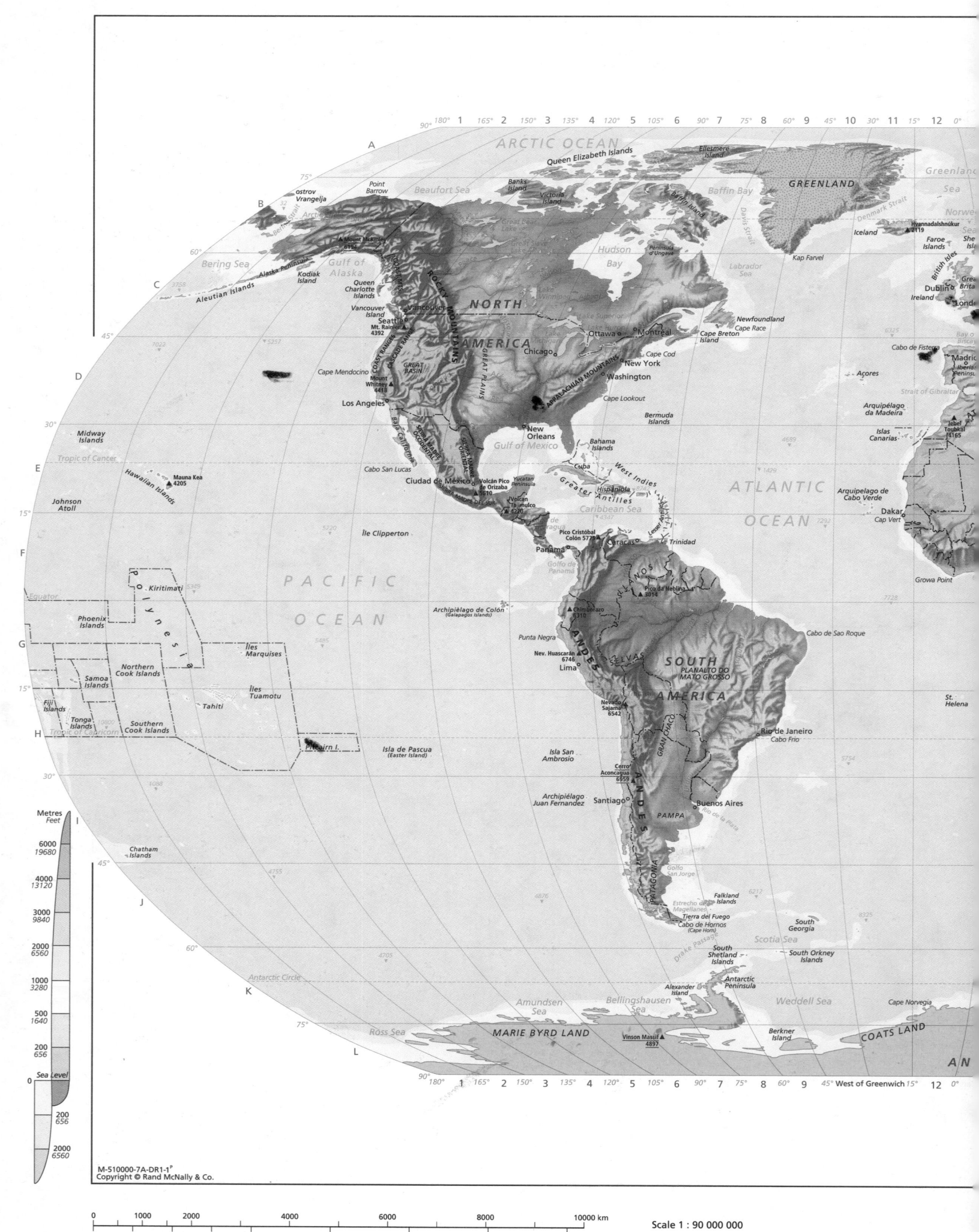

ARCTIC OCEAN

A

B

C

D

E

F

G

H

I

J

K

L

Queen Elizabeth Islands

Ellesmere Island

GREENLAND

Greenland Sea

Norwe

Point Barrow

Banks Island

Baffin Bay

Beaufort Sea

Victoria Island

Baffin Island

Davis Strait

Denmark Strait

Hvannadalshnúkur ▲2119

Iceland

Faroe Islands

She Isla

ostrov Vrangelja

Bering Strait

Arctic

Great Bear Lake

Peninsula d'Ungava

Hudson Bay

Kap Farvel

Labrador Sea

British Isles

Bering Sea

Alaska Peninsula

Gulf of Alaska

▲ Mount McKinley 6194

Great Slave Lake

NORTH

Lake Winnipeg

Lake Superior

Newfoundland Cape Race

Cape Breton Island

Dublin Ireland

Gre Brita

London

Aleutian Islands

Kodiak Island

Queen Charlotte Islands

Vancouver Island

Vancouver Seattle

Mt. Rainier 4392

AMERICA

Ottawa Montreal

Chicago

Cape Cod

New York

Washington

Cabo de Fisterra

Madrid Iberian Pen

Cape Mendocino

Mount Whitney ▲4418

GREAT BASIN

GREAT PLAINS

APPALACHIAN MOUNTAINS

Cape Lookout

Bermuda Islands

Açores

Strait of Gibraltar

Arquipélago da Madeira

Los Angeles

New Orleans

Gulf of Mexico

Bahama Islands

Jebel Toubkal ▲4165

Midway Islands

Tropic of Cancer

Cabo San Lucas

Cuba

West Indies

Islas Canarias

Mauna Kea ▲4205

Hawaiian Islands

Ciudad de México

Volcán Pico de Orizaba ▲5610

Yucatán Peninsula

Greater Antilles

Hispaniola

ATLANTIC

Arquipélago de Cabo Verde

Johnson Atoll

Volcán ▲ Tajumulco 4220

Caribbean Sea

OCEAN

Dakar Cap Vert

Île Clipperton

Pico Cristóbal Colón 5775

Lesser Antilles

Caracas Trinidad

Panamá Goffo de Panamá

Growa Point

PACIFIC

Polynesia Kiritimati

Archipiélago de Colón (Galapagos Islands)

LLANOS

Pico da Neblina ▲3014

OCEAN

Phoenix Islands

Punta Negra

Chimborazo ▲6310

ANDES

SOUTH

Cabo de São Roque

St. Helena

Iles Marquises

Nev. Huascarán ▲6746

Lima

SELVAS

AMERICA

PLANALTO DO MATO GROSSO

Samoa Islands

Northern Cook Islands

Iles Tuamotu

Nevado ▲ Sajama 6542

Fiji Islands

Tahiti

Rio de Janeiro

Cabo Frio

Tonga Islands

Southern Cook Islands

Tropic of Capricorn

Pitcairn I.

Isla de Pascua (Easter Island)

Isla San Ambrosio

GRAN CHACO

Cerro ▲ Aconcagua 6959

Archipiélago Juan Fernández

Santiago

PAMPA

Buenos Aires

Río de la Plata

PATAGONIA

ANDES

Chatham Islands

Golfo San Jorge

Falkland Islands

Tierra del Fuego

Cabo de Hornos (Cape Horn)

Estrecho de Magallanes

Drake Passage

South Georgia

Scotia Sea

South Orkney Islands

South Shetland Islands

Antarctic Circle

Amundsen Sea

Alexander Island

Antarctic Peninsula

Bellingshausen Sea

Weddell Sea

Cape Norvegia

Ross Sea

MARIE BYRD LAND

Vinson Massif ▲ 4897

Berkner Island

COATS LAND

AN

180° 165° 150° 135° 120° 105° 90° 75° 60° 45° West of Greenwich 15° 0°

Metres Feet

6000 19680

4000 13120

3000 9840

2000 6560

1000 3280

500 1640

200 656

Sea Level

200 656

2000 6560

M-510000-7A-DR1-1ᴾ
Copyright © Rand McNally & Co.

0   1000   2000   4000   6000   8000   10000 km

0   1000   2000   4000   6000 miles

Scale 1 : 90 000 000

Robinson Projection

14 *30°* 15 *45°* 16 *60°* 17 *75°* 18 *90°* 19 *105°* 20 *120°* 21 *135°* 22 *150°* 23 *165°* 24 *180°* *90°*

ARCTIC OCEAN

Zemlja Franca-Iosefa
Severnaja Zemlja
Novosibirskie ostrova
75°
A

itsbergen   *Barents Sea*   Novaja Zemlja   *Karskoe more*   *more Laptevyh*   *Vostočno-Sibirskoe more*
B
Nordkapp   Kol'skij poluostrov   gora Kamen 1701 ▲   gora Pobeda 3147 ▲   *60°*   *Bering Sea*

▲ Galdhøpiggen 2469   ZAPADNO-SIBIRSKAJA RAVNINA   SIBIR' (SIBERIA)   Kamčatka   C

Berlin   Moskva   Ekaterinberg   ASIA   Sea of Okhotsk
                    URAL'SKIE GORY   Irkutsk   ostrov Sahalin   mys Lopatka   *45°*
EUROPE   *Black Sea*   CAUCASUS   gora El'brus 5642   ozero Balhaš   ALTAJ 4374   Kuril'skie ostrova
APPENNINO   Balkan Peninsula   Koммунизма   Peak Pobedy 7439   TIEN SHAN   Ulaanbaatar   Hokkaidō   D
Roma   Istanbul   HINDU KUSH   KUNLUN SHAN   GOBI   Beijing   Honshū
Sardegna   Sicilia   Kriti   Cyprus   Qolleh-ye Damavand 5604   Qogir Feng 8611   Qing Zang Gaoyuan   Sea of Japan   Fuji-san 3776 ▲ Tōkyō
Corse   Tehran   DASHT-E KAVIR   HIMALAYAS   Bohng Shan   Shanghai   Shikoku Kyūshū   *30°*
Mediterranean Sea   KUHHA-YE ZAGROS   Delhi   ▲ Mount Everest 8848   Yellow Sea
     El-Qahira   Persian Gulf   East China Sea   Nansei-shotō
AHAGGAR   *Red Sea*   ARABIAN PENINSULA   Gulf of Oman   DECCAN   Taiwan   PACIFIC   *Tropic of Cancer*   E
Tahat 2908 ▲   TIBESTI   NUBIAN DESERT   AR-RUB' AL-KHALI   WESTERN GHATS   EASTERN GHATS   2359   Yu Shan 3997   OCEAN
SAHARA   ▲ Emi Koussi 3415   Mumbai   Bay of Bengal   Hainan Dao   Luzon   Mariana Islands   *15°*
AFRICA   Gulf of Aden   Suqutrá   Andaman Islands   Krung Thep   South China Sea   Manila   Philippine Sea   F
Lake Chad   SUDAN   ▲ Ras Dashen Terara 4620   Gees Gwardafuy   Pidurutalagala 2524   Nicobar Islands   INDOCHINA   Palawan   Philippine Islands   Marshall Islands
Lagos   ▲ Adis Abeba   Cape Comorin   Sri Lanka   5423   Andaman Sea   Gulf of Thailand   Gunong Kinabalu ▲ 4101   Mindanao   Palau Islands
Tomé   CONGO BASIN   Margherita Peak 5109 ▲   Maldive Islands   Sumatera   Malay Peninsula   BORNEO   Celebes Sea   Halmahera   Caroline Islands   Micronesia   *Equator*
Gulf of Guinea   ▲ Kirinyaga 5199   Seychelles   5340   MALAKA   Sulawesi   Seram   NEW GUINEA   New Britain   G
     Kilimanjaro 5895 ▲   Zanzibar   Les Amirantes   Greater Sunda Islands   Jakarta   Laut Jawa   Laut Banda   Mount Wilhelm 4509   Solomon Islands   8940
     RIFT VALLEY   Tanjona Bobaomby   INDIAN   6090   Jawa   Timor   Arafura Sea   Cape York   Melanesia   New Hebrides   *15°*
Cape Fria   Maromokotro 2875   OCEAN   1706   Timor Sea   Gulf of Carpentaria   Cape York Peninsula   Coral Sea   Fiji Islands   H
MADAGASCAR   Reunion   Mauritius   6658   Kimberley Plateau   Nouvelle-Calédonie   *Tropic of Capricorn*
KALAHARI DESERT   Tanjona Vohimena   North West Cape   Great Sandy Desert   AUSTRALIA   Sydney   5309
NAMIB DESERT   ▲ Thabana-Ntlenyana 3482   6400   Île Amsterdam   Mount Meharry 1253 ▲   GREAT VICTORIA DESERT   ▲ Mount Woodroffe 1435   GREAT DIVIDING RANGE   North Cape   *30°*
Cape Town   DRAKENSBERG   Cape Leeuwin   Great Australian Blight   Melbourne   ▲ Mount Kosciusko 2229   Tasman Sea   North Island   I
Cape of Good Hope   Mount Ossa 1617 ▲   Tasmania   Mount Ruapehu 2797 ▲   *45°*
5526   Prince Edward Islands 3079   Archipel Crozet   Îles Kerguélen   South East Cape   South Island   ▲ Mount Cook 3754
     Heard Island   SOUTHERN OCEAN   Macquarie Island   J
     6089   South West Cape
5124   4435   *60°*
Cape Poinsett   *Antarctic Circle*   K
ENDERBY LAND   WILKES LAND   VICTORIA LAND   Cape Adare   *75°*
JEEN MAUD LAND   Ross Sea
CTICA   L

East of Greenwich *45°* 16 *60°* 17 *75°* 18 *90°* 19 *105°* 20 *120°* 21 *135°* 22 *150°* 23 *165°* 24 *180°* *90°*

6

Scale 1 : 15 000 000

Equidistant Conic Projection

West of Greenwich   0°   East of Greenwich

| 0 | 200 | 400 | 800 | 1200 | 1600 km |

| 0 | 100 | 200 | 300 | 400 | 600 | 800 | 1000 miles |

D-550000-2A-DR1-1
Copyright © Rand McNally & Co.

ICELAND

ATLANTIC OCEAN

NORWEGIAN SEA

NORWAY

SWEDEN

FAROE ISLANDS (Den.)

SHETLAND ISLANDS

ORKNEY ISLANDS

SCOTLAND

HEBRIDES

NORTH SEA

DENMARK

GLASGOW
EDINBURGH

UNITED KINGDOM
NEWCASTLE UPON TYNE

IRELAND

NORTHERN IRELAND

DUBLIN
(BAILE ATHA CLIATH)

Belfast

LIVERPOOL
MANCHESTER
LEEDS
GREAT BRITAIN
ENGLAND

BIRMINGHAM
WALES

Swansea
Cardiff

CELTIC SEA

LONDON

ENGLISH CHANNEL

NETHERLANDS
AMSTERDAM
's-Gravenhage (The Hague)
ROTTERDAM

HAMBURG
BREMEN
BERLIN

GERMANY

ANTWERPEN
BRUXELLES (BRUSSELS)
LILLE
BELGIUM
DÜSSELDORF
ESSEN
KÖLN (COLOGNE)
BONN

STOCKHOLM
OSLO

KØBENHAVN (COPENHAGEN)

POMERANIA

POLAND

PARIS

FRANCE

NORMANDIE

BRETAGNE

LUXEMBOURG

FRANKFURT AM MAIN

MANNHEIM

STUTTGART

PRAHA (PRAGUE)

CZECH REPUBLIC

BOHEMIA

MÜNCHEN (MUNICH)

WIEN (VIENNA)

AUSTRIA

SWITZERLAND

BUDAPEST

Metres / Feet

4000 / 13120
3000 / 9840
2000 / 6560
1000 / 3280
500 / 1640
200 / 656
0 / Sea Level
200 / 656
2000 / 6560

D-559100-7A-DR1-1°
Copyright © Rand McNally & Co.

West of Greenwich 0° East of Greenwich

0   100   200   300   400   600   800   1000 km
0   100   200   400   600 miles

Scale 1 : 10 000 000

Lambert Conformal Conic Projection

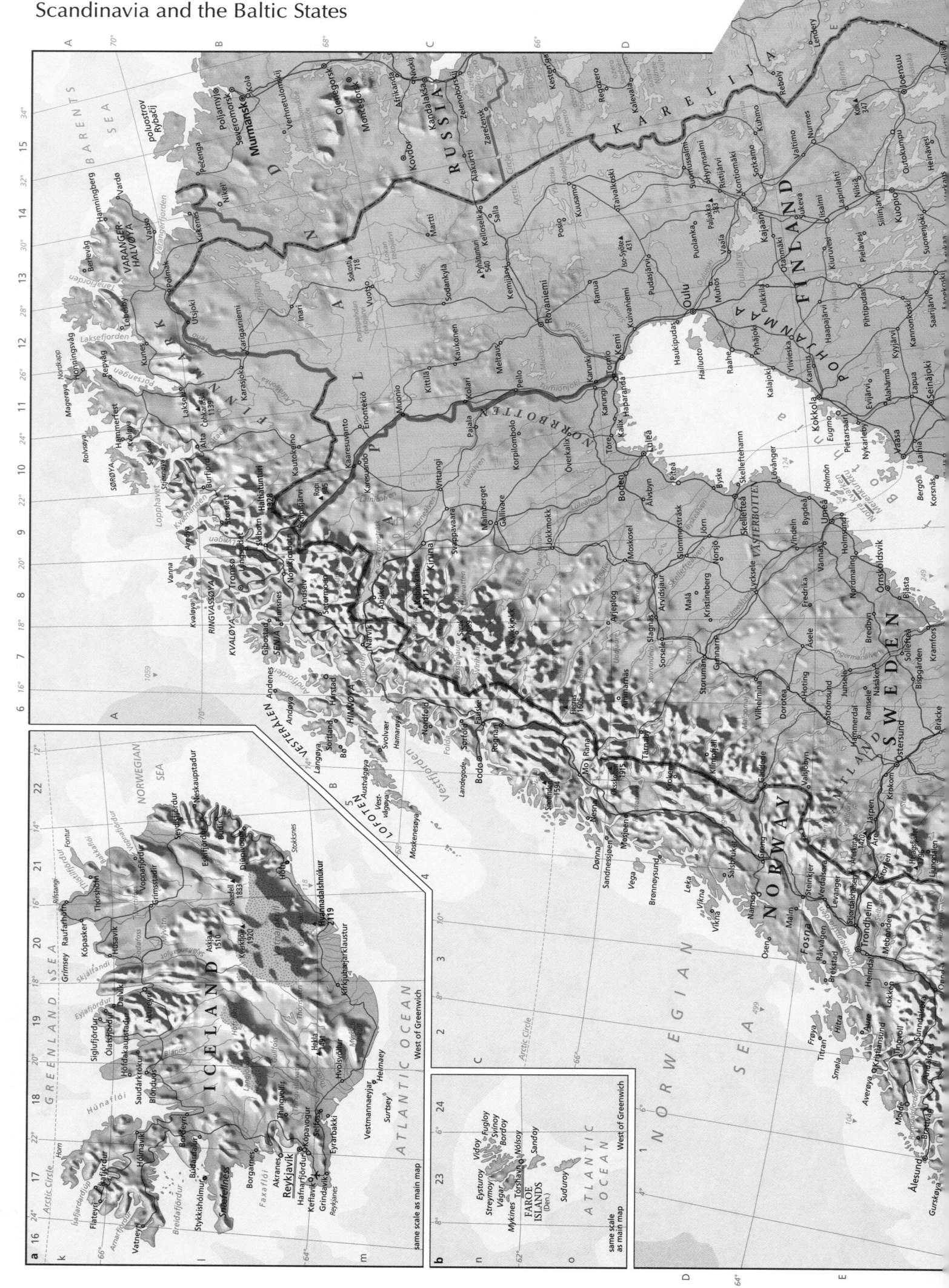

RUSSIA

SANKT-PETERBURG

F i n l a n d

HELSINKI (HELSINGFORS)

Tallinn

ESTONIA

LATVIA

RIGA

Gulf of Riga

LITHUANIA

Kaunas

Vilnius

Hrodna

BELARUS

MINSK

RUSSIA

Kaliningrad

Klaipėda

Gdańsk

Gdynia

Gulf of Gdansk

P O L A N D

SZCZECIN

Gulf of Finland

HIIUMAA

SAAREMAA

Ventspils

Liepāja

KIMITO

ÅLAND (AHVENANMAA)

Turku (Åbo)

Tampere

STOCKHOLM

UPPLAND

Uppsala

GOTLAND

Visby

ÖLAND

Kalmar

GOTSKA SANDÖN

BORNHOLM (Den.)

BLEKINGE

SMÅLAND

ÖSTERGÖTLAND

VÄSTERGÖTLAND

HALLAND

VÄRMLAND

DALARNA

HÄLSINGLAND

Vänern

Vättern

Göteborg (Gothenburg)

Malmö

Trelleborg

KØBENHAVN (COPENHAGEN)

DENMARK

Oslo

SJÆLLAND

FYN

JYLLAND

LANGELAND

LOLLAND

FALSTER

RÜGEN

USEDOM

Rostock

Lübeck

HAMBURG

Kiel

Flensburg

GERMANY

Schwerin

Neumünster

POMERANIA

Pomeranian Bay

B A L T I C   S E A

N O R T H   S E A

Skagerrak

Kattegat

The Sound

Bergen

Stavanger

Kristiansand

HARDANGER VIDDA

FRISIAN ISLANDS

OSTFRIESISCHE INSELN

NETH.

Wilhelmshaven

Emden

Bremerhaven

Cuxhaven

Helgoland

Deutsche Bucht

NORTH FRISIAN ISLANDS

To Harwich

To Aberdeen

To Newcastle

Scale 1 : 5 000 000

East of Greenwich

Lambert Conformal Conic Projection

Metres	Feet
2000	6560
1000	3280
500	1640
200	656
Sea Level	0
200	656
2000	6560

0   50 100 150 200 300 400 500 km

0   50 100 150 200 300 miles

12

Inset map (top left)

18   19

SHETLAND ISLANDS (U.K.)

Unst
Fetlar
Yell
Whalsay
St. Magnus Bay
MAINLAND
Foula   Lerwick
Bressay

To Torshavn

ATLANTIC OCEAN

NORTH SEA

Fair Isle

Westray
Rousay   Sanday
Stronsay
MAINLAND ORKNEY ISLANDS
Hoy   Kirkwall   South Ronaldsay
Thurso   Duncansby Head
John o' Groats

West of Greenwich

Main map

Flannan Islands
Butt of Lewis
Cape Wrath
Durness
John o' Groats
Duncansby Head
Thurso
Wick

MAINLAND
Stronsay
Hoy   Kirkwall   **ORKNEY ISLANDS**
To Lerwick

146

To Lerwick

OUTER HEBRIDES
ISLE OF LEWIS
Stornoway
Lochinver
Ben More Assynt 998
Helmsdale
Brora
Dornoch

North Uist
Benbecula
South Uist
Lochboisdale
The Little Minch
Portree
Kyle of Lochalsh
Dingwall
Moray Firth
Elgin
Portsoy
Fraserburgh
Kinnaird Head
Peterhead

St. Kilda
The Minch
ISLAND OF SKYE
Cam Eige 1182
Loch Ness
Inverness
Nairn

Barra
Rum
Eigg
Mallaig
SCOTLAND
Ben Macdui 1309
Aberdeen

Coll
Tobermory
Fort William
Ben Nevis 1343
BALMORAL
Stonehaven

Tiree
ISLAND OF MULL
Oban
Inveraray
GRAMPIAN MOUNTAINS
Montrose
Dundee
Arbroath

Colonsay
Firth of Lorn
Perth
Glenrothes
St. Andrews
Fife Ness

ISLAY
JURA
Greenock
Kirkcaldy
Dunfermline
Firth of Forth

Port Ellen
Kintyre
ISLAND OF ARRAN
GLASGOW
Motherwell
EDINBURGH
GREAT
Berwick-upon-Tweed

Malin Head
GIANT'S CAUSEWAY
Rathlin Island
Campbeltown
Kilmarnock
Ayr
SOUTHERN UPLANDS
Galashiels
Alnwick

Aran Island
Errigal Mountain 752
Buncrana
Coleraine
Larne
Girvan
843
Moffat
UNITED

Rocky Point
Londonderry
Ballymena
Dumfries
HADRIAN'S WALL
NEWCASTLE UPON TYNE

Donegal
Strabane
NORTHERN
Stranraer
Gatehouse of Fleet
Solway Firth
Carlisle
Penrith
Durham
Sunderland
Hartlepool

Donegal Bay
Omagh
IRELAND
Belfast
Bangor
Downpatrick
Whitehaven
Lake District
Middlesbrough

Erris Head
Sligo
Newry
Dundalk
ISLE OF MAN (U.K.)
Scafell Pikes 978
Kendal
Darlington
Scarborough
KINGDOM

Ballina
Carrick on Shannon
Ballyborough
Drogheda
Douglas
Barrow-in-Furness
Lancaster
Ripon
York
Bridlington

Achill Head
Castlebar
Longford
Dundalk Bay
Morecambe Bay
Blackpool
LEEDS
Kingston upon Hull

Clew Bay
Mweelrea 817
Roscommon
Athlone
IRISH SEA
Preston
Bradford
Huddersfield
BRITAIN

Clifden
CONNAUGHT
Liverpool
Bolton
MANCHESTER
Grimsby

Galway
Galway Bay
IRELAND
Kildare
DUBLIN (BAILE ÁTHA CLIATH)
ANGLESEY
Holyhead
Bangor
Wrexham
Chester
Sheffield
Mansfield
Lincoln
ENGLAND

ARAN ISLANDS
Port Laoise
LEINSTER
Dun Laoghaire
Caernarfon
Snowdon 1085
Stoke-on-Trent
Derby
Skegness

Ennistimon
CLIFFS OF MOHER
Wicklow Mountains 924
Wicklow
Pwllheli
CAMBRIAN MOUNTAINS
Stafford
Nottingham
Boston

Loop Head
Kilkee
Carlow
Arklow
Braich y Pwll
Stafford
Walsall
Leicester
Peterborough
King's Lynn
Cromer

Mouth of the Shannon
Limerick
Kilkenny
Cardigan Bay
Aberystwyth
Shrewsbury
Wolverhampton
BIRMINGHAM
Coventry
Northampton
Ely
Norwich
Great Yarmouth

Tralee
Newcastle West
Clonmel
Enniscorthy
Wexford
New Quay
Llandovery
CAMBRIAN MOUNTAINS
Dudley
Banbury
Bedford
Bury Saint Edmunds
Lowestoft

Caherciveen
Carrantoohil 1039
Mallow
Waterford
Rosslare
Carnsore Point
Cardigan
Builth Wells
Hereford
Worcester
Cambridge
Ipswich

Dingle Bay
Killarney
MUNSTER
Dungarvan
Youghal
Fishguard
St. David's Head
Carmarthen
WALES
Gloucester
Cheltenham
Milton Keynes
Luton
Colchester
Harwich

Kenmare
Cork
Kinsale
St. George's Channel
Milford Haven
Pembroke
Merthyr Tydfil
Newport
Oxford
LONDON
Clacton-on-Sea

Bantry Bay
Skull
Mizen Head
Old Head of Kinsale
CELTIC SEA
Swansea
Port Talbot
Cardiff
Bristol
Bath
Reading
Slough
Chelmsford
Southend-on-Sea

Lundy
Bristol Channel
Weston-super-Mare
Swindon
Basingstoke
Guildford
Reigate
Canterbury
Ramsgate

Barnstaple
Bridgwater
Taunton
Winchester
Crawley
Folkestone
Dover

Bude
CORNWALL
Exeter
Southampton
Worthing
Brighton
Hastings
Calais

Newquay
Redruth
Saint Austell
Bournemouth
Poole
Portsmouth
Eastbourne
Boulogne-sur-Mer
Berck

Penzance
Land's End
ISLES OF SCILLY
Plymouth
Torquay
Lyme Bay
Dorchester
Weymouth
Bill of Portland
ISLE OF WIGHT

Falmouth
Lizard Point
Start Point

English Channel

ATLANTIC OCEAN

Alderney
Cap de la Hague
Pointe de Barfleur
Baie de la Seine
Bolbec
Fécamp
Dieppe
Amiens
Saint-Quentin

GUERNSEY (U.K.)
St. Peter Port
Cherbourg
Yvetot
Neufchâtel-en-Bray
Beauvais
Chauny
Soiss
PICARDI

Sark
Le Havre
Rouen
Compiègne
Creil

CHANNEL ISLANDS
St. Helier
Carentan
Bayeux
NORMANDIE
Albert
Cambr

JERSEY (U.K.)
Sillon de Talbert
Coutances
Caen
Lisieux
Évreux
Saint-Denis
Versailles
PARIS
ÎLE-DE-FRANCE
Meaux
Corbeil-Essonnes

Île d'Ouessant
Lannion
Saint-Lô
Vire
Argentan
Dreux
Rambouillet
Étampes

Saint-Pol-de-Léon
Morlaix
Guingamp
Granville
Golfe de Saint-Malo
Saint-Malo
Dinan
Mayenne
Nogent-le-Rotrou
Chartres
Melun
Fontainebleau

Brest
Pointe de Saint-Mathieu
Landerneau
BRETAGNE
LE MONT-SAINT-MICHEL
Fougères
Alençon
Sens

Iroise
Douarnenez
Châteaulin
Loudéac
Vitré
Mamers
Le Mans
Vendôme
Orléans
Auxerre

Pointe du Raz
Quimper
Quimperlé
Rennes
Laval
Mayenne
Sablé-sur-Sarthe
La Flèche
Châteaudun
Gien

Concarneau
Hennebont
Redon
Châteaubriant
Segré
ANJOU
FRANCE

Pointe de Penmarc'h
Lorient
Île de Groix
Vannes
Muzillac
Blain
Angers
Saumur
TOURAINE
Tours
Romorantin-Lanthenay
Vierzon
Bourges

Quiberon
Le Palais
Carnac
Saint-Nazaire
Nantes
Rezé
Cholet
Thouars
Châtellerault
Liguel
Issoudun

Belle-Île
La Baule-Escoublac
Noirmoutier
Île de Noirmoutier
Mâchecoul
Saint-Jean-de-Monts
Bressuire
Châteauroux

Île d'Yeu

's-Grave... (The... RO...

Vlissingen
Oostende
Brug
RO...

Dunkerque
Roeselare
LILLE
BRU... (B...

Saint-Omer
Roubaix
Valenci
COLLINES DE L'ARTOIS
Lens
Arras
Maube...
Cambr...

Elevation scale (left margin)

Metres / Feet

3000 / 9840
2000 / 6560
1000 / 3280
500 / 1640
200 / 656
Sea Level
0
200 / 656
2000 / 6560

Scale bars (bottom)

0   50   100   150   200   300   400   500 km
0   50   100   200   300 miles

Scale 1 : 5 000 000
Lambert Conformal Conic Projection

West of Greenwich   0°   East of Greenwich

D-559594-7A-DR1-1°
Copyright © Rand McNally & Co.

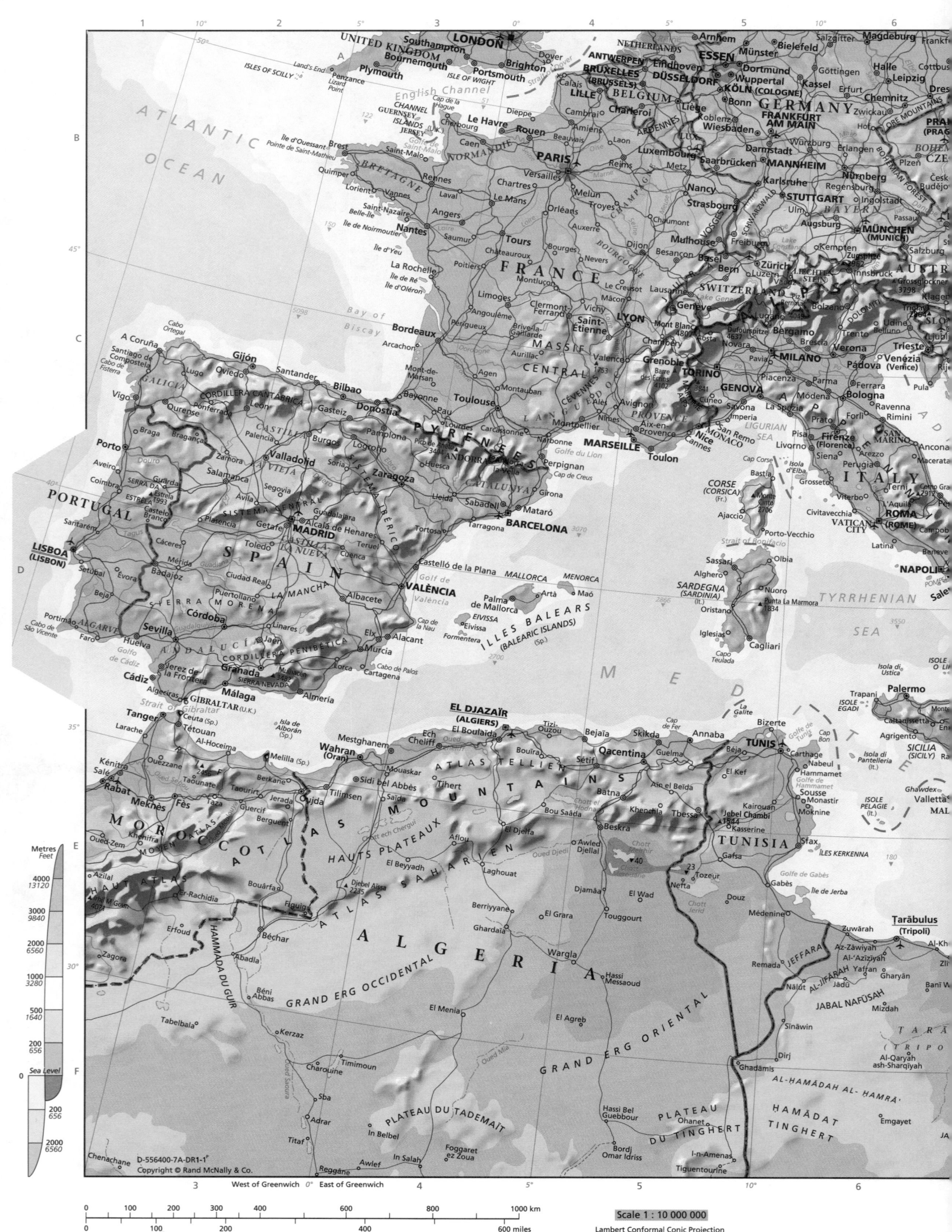

ATLANTIC OCEAN

UNITED KINGDOM
Southampton **LONDON**
ISLES OF SCILLY Land's End Bournemouth Brighton Dover
Penzance Plymouth Portsmouth
Lizard Point ISLE OF WIGHT
English Channel
122

Cap de la Hague Dieppe
Cherbourg Le Havre Rouen
Golfe de Saint-Malo Caen Beauvais
Saint-Malo NORMANDIE Amiens
Pointe de Saint-Mathieu Rennes **PARIS** Reims
Brest Laval Versailles Metz
BRETAGNE Angers Le Mans Chartres Troyes
Quimper Vannes Melun
Lorient Chaumont
Saint-Nazaire Saumur Orléans Auxerre
Nantes Tours Bourges Dijon
Île de Noirmoutier Châteauroux Nevers
Île d'Yeu Poitiers **FRANCE**
La Rochelle Montluçon Le Creusot
Île de Ré Angoulême Clermont- Mâcon
Île d'Oléron Limoges Ferrand Vichy

NETHERLANDS Arnhem Bielefeld Salzgitter Magdeburg Frankf
ANTWERPEN Eindhoven Münster
BRUXELLES Dortmund Göttingen Halle Leipzig
(BRUSSELS) **DÜSSELDORF** **ESSEN** Kassel Erfurt Chemnitz Dres
LILLE BELGIUM Wuppertal **KÖLN** (COLOGNE) **GERMANY** ORE MOUNTAINS PRAGUE
Calais Charleroi Liège Bonn Zwickau BOHEM
Cambrai Lille LUX. Koblenz **FRANKFURT** Hof CZE
Laon ARDENNES AM MAIN Würzburg Erlangen Bamberg BÖHMER
Nancy Luxembourg Saarbrücken Darmstadt **MANNHEIM** **NÜRNBERG** BOHMER FOREST
Strasbourg Karlsruhe Regensburg Budějo
VOSGES Stuttgart Ulm **BAYERN** Passau
Mulhouse Freiburg Augsburg **MÜNCHEN** (MUNICH) Salzburg
SCHWARZWALD Basel **ZÜRICH** Lake Kempten Zugspitze AUSTR
Besançon Bern Luzern LIECHT. Innsbruck
GENÈVE Pfz 3798 Grossglockner
Lausanne SWITZERLAND Bolzano 3564 Klagen
Mont Blanc 4045 DOLOMITI 3798
Grenoble 4802 Dufourspitze Bergamo Trento Belluno Udine SLO
1753 Barre 1637 Rosta Novara Brescia Trieste
Aurillac CENTRAL des Écrins Chambéry Pavia **MILANO** Verona Venézia
Valence 4102 3841 GENOVA Piacenza Pádova (Venice)
Briançon Cuneo Parma Ferrara Pula
Barre Savona La Spezia Módena Bologna Ravenna
Cannes Imperia LIGURIAN Pisa Firenze Forli Rimini
San Remo SEA Livorno (Florence) San A
MONACO Cap Corse Siena Arezzo SAN MARINO
Nice Isola Perúgia Macerata
CORSE d'Elba Grosseto Terni Monte Ancona
(CORSICA) Bastia Cimo 2912
(Fr.) Monte Civitavecchia L'Aquila
Cinto VATICAN **ROMA**
2706 Porto-Vecchio CITY (ROME)
Ajaccio Strait of Bonifacio Latina

O

Provence
Saint-Étienne **LYON**
MASSIF
Périgueux Le Puy
Arcachon Agen Montauban Avignon Aix-en-
Bordeaux Montpellier Nîmes Provence Toulon
Mont-de- Toulouse Narbonne PROVENCE
Marsan Carcassonne Golfe du Lion
Bayonne Pau Lourdes PYRÉNÉES
Donostia Pamplona Andorra 3404 Perpignan
Pico de Aneto La Vella Cap de Creus
Gijón Santander Bilbao Logroño Huesca Girona
A Coruña Oviedo Gasteiz Soria Lleida Sabadell
Santiago de León Burgos Zaragoza Mataró
Compostela Lugo Palencia **BARCELONA**
Cabo Ourense Valladolid Tarragona
Ortegal Ponferrada CASTILLE Segovia Tortosa
Cabo de Braga Bragança Zamora Guadalajara Teruel Castelló de la Plana MALLORCA MENORCA
Fisterra Vigo Salamanca Ávila Cuenca
Porto **MADRID** VALÈNCIA Palma Maó
PORTUGAL Guarda Plasencia Alcalá de Henares de Mallorca Artà
Coimbra SERRA DA Cáceres Toledo Albacete ILLES BALEARS
ESTRELA 1993 **SPAIN** Eivissa (BALEARIC ISLANDS)
Castelo Mérida Ciudad Real LA MANCHA Formentera (Sp.)
Branco Badajoz SIERRA MORENA Linares Cap de la Nau
LISBOA Évora Puertollano
(LISBON) Setúbal Córdoba Jaén Alacant Murcia
Beja ANDALUCÍA Elx
Sevilla Granada CORDILLERA PENIBÉTICA Cabo de Palos
Portimão Faro Huelva Mulhacén Orihuela Cartagena
Cabo de ALGARVE Jerez de 3482 Lorca
São Vicente Golfo la Frontera SIERRA NEVADA
de Cádiz Cádiz Málaga Almería
Algeciras GIBRALTAR (U.K.)
Tanger Ceuta (Sp.) Strait of Gibraltar
Larache Tétouan Isla de Alborán
Kénitra Al-Hoceima (Sp.)
Salé Melilla (Sp.)

SARDEGNA
(SARDINIA) Nuoro NAPOLI
(It.) Punta La Marmora POMP
Alghero 1834 TYRRHENIAN
Oristano SEA Sale
Iglesias Cagliari
Capo Isola di
Teulada Ustica Isola
O LIP

M E D I T E R R A N E A N S E A

MEDI Trapani Palermo
La ISOLE
Galite EGADI Caltanissetta
Bizerte SICILIA Agrigento
El Djazaïr (ALGIERS) Golfe de (SICILY)
El Boulaïda Tunis ISOLE
Tizi- **TUNIS** Béja Cap Bon Isola di PELAGIE
Ouzou Bejaïa Skikda Annaba Carthage Pantelleria Valletta
Ech Setif Guelma El Kef Nabeul (It.) MAL
Cheliff Bouïra Qacentina Hammamet Ghawdex Valletta
Mestghanem Oued Aïn el Beïda Sousse MALT
Wahran Tiaret Batna Kairouan Monastir
(Oran) ATLAS TELLIEN Khenchla Tbessa Jebel Chambi Moknine ISOLE PELAGIE
Mouaskar Bou Saâda Beskra 1544 Sfax (It.)
Sidi bel Abbès ATLAS Djelfa El Djem
Saïda Aflou MOUNTAINS TUNISIA
Tilimsen Chott el ÎLES KERKENNA
Oujda Hodna Gafsa
Taourirt HAUTS PLATEAUX Oued Djedi 40 180
Berkane El Beyyadh Laghouat 23
Taza Guercif El Wad Tozeur Gabès
Guercif Laghouat Nefta
Kenitra MOY Djebel Aïssa Djamáa El Wad Médenine Île de Jerba
Taza 2235 Chott
Jerada Berguent Djelfa Douz
Khenifra Oued-Zem SAHARIEN Ghardaïa ATLAS Tarâbulus
Zem Bouárfa Berriyane El Grara Touggourt Médenine (Tripoli)
Béchar HAMMADA DU GUIR Laghouat Zuwárah Az-Zâwiyah
Azilal Figuig ALGERIA Al-Aziziyah Al-Kh
HAUT Ghardaïa Wargla AL-JIFÁRAH Yaffran Zli
ATLAS Er-Rachidia Hassi Gharyan
M'Goun Béni Abbas GRAND ERG OCCIDENTAL Messaoud JEFFARA Remada Nálút Jádu JABAL NAFÚSAH Bani W
4071 Erfoud El Menia Sináwin Mizdah
Zagora Abadla El Agreb
GRAND ERG ORIENTAL TARÁ
Kerzaz (TRIPO
Tabelbala Dirj Al-Qaryah
El Menia ash-Sharqíyah
Ghadámis
AL-HAMÁDAH AL-HAMRÁ
Timimoun PLATEAU DU TADEMAÏT Ghadámis HAMÁDAT
Charouine Oued Mia PLATEAU TINGHERT
Sba GRAND ERG ORIENTAL DU TINGHERT
Adrar Hassi Bel HAMÁDAT
Guebbour Ohanet Emgayet
Titaf In Belbel In Salah Bordj TINGHERT
Chenachane Foggaret Omar Idriss
ez Zoua I-n-Amenas
Reggane Awlef Tiguentourine

Bay of Biscay
5098
5098

150

Dordogne

CÉVENNES

Metres/Feet
4000/13120
3000/9840
2000/6560
1000/3280
500/1640
200/656
0 Sea Level
200/656
2000/6560

West of Greenwich 0° East of Greenwich

Scale 1 : 10 000 000
Lambert Conformal Conic Projection

0 100 200 300 400 600 800 1000 km
0 100 200 400 600 miles

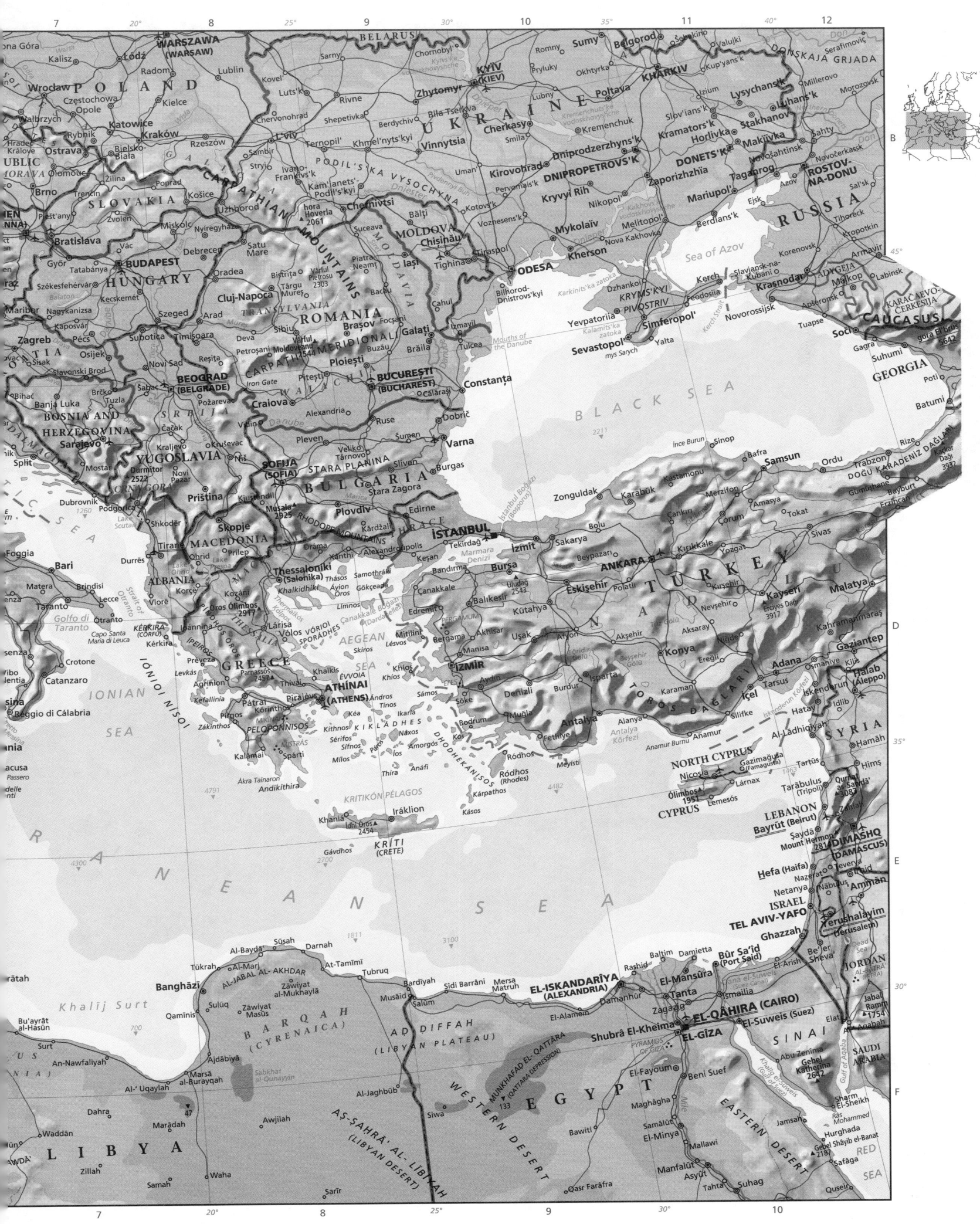

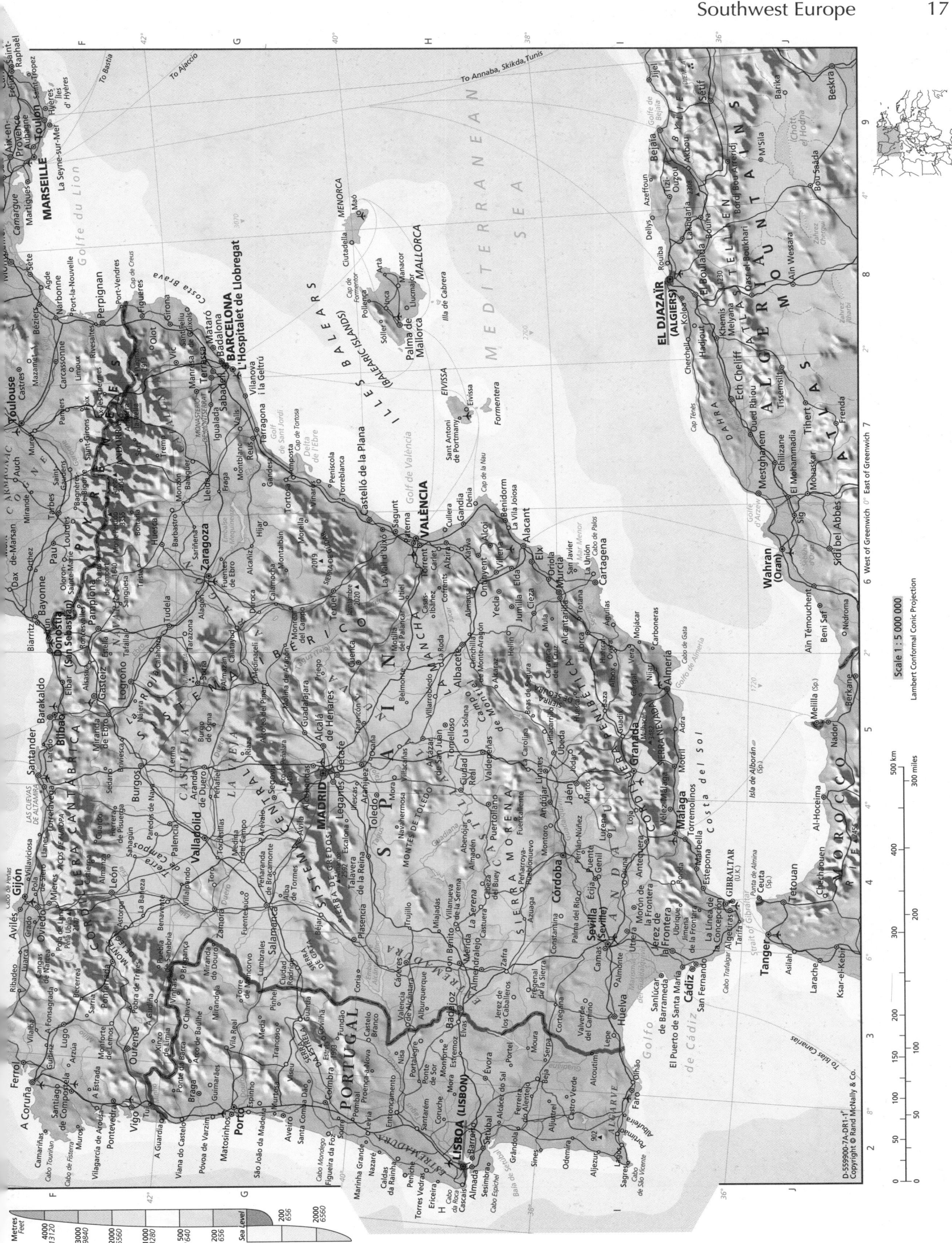

Scale 1 : 5 000 000

Lambert Conformal Conic Projection

D-559900-7A-DR1-1°
Copyright © Rand McNally & Co.

DENMARK

BALTIC SEA

LITHUANIA

RUSSIA

GERMANY

POLAND

BELOR

WARSZAWA
(WARSAW)

Berlin

CZECH REPUBLIC

PRAHA
(PRAGUE)

SLOVAKIA

L'viv

CARPATHIAN MOUNTAINS

AUSTRIA

WIEN
(VIENNA)

Bratislava

BUDAPEST

HUNGARY

ROMANIA

TRANSYLVANIA

SLOVENIA

Ljubljana

CROATIA

Zagreb

VOJVODINA

BANAT

Timișoara

ITALY

Trieste

ADRIATIC
SEA

BOSNIA AND
HERZEGOVINA

Sarajevo

SRBIJA
(SERBIA)

YUGOSLAVIA

BEOGRAD
(BELGRADE)

CARPATII MERIDIONALI

BUCUREȘTI
(BUCHAREST)

BULGARIA

Metres Feet	
2000 6560	
1000 3280	
500 1640	
200 656	
Sea Level 0	
200 656	
2000 6560	

D-559592-7A-DR1-1
Copyright © Rand McNally & Co.

0 50 100 150 200 300 400 500 km

0 50 100 200 300 miles

Scale 1 : 5 000 000

22° East of Greenwich

Lambert Conformal Conic Projection

A 11 32° 12 34° 13 36° 14 38° 15 40° 16 42°

V I A
ugavpils
Nevel'
Prečistoe
Gagarin
Naro-Fominsk
Kolomna
Kasimov

Mëry
Navapolack
Polack
Demidov
Tumanovo
Vjaz'ma
Obninsk
Stupino
Murmino
Sasovo

Hlybokae
Dajhinava
Vicebsk
Safonovo
Jarcevo
Dorogobuž
Znamenka
Malojaroslavec
Zarajsk
Rjazan'
Šilovo
Šack

Mjadzel
Bjahoml'
Lepel'
Sjanno
Smolensk
Miljatino
El'nja
Juhnov
Kaluga
Aleksin
Jasnogorsk
Zarajsk
Mihajlov
Rjazan'
Algasovo
B

Sredneruskaja Vozvyšennost'

ka
Dzjaninava
žynsk
Orša
Počinok
Kirov
Ljudinovo
Dubna
Tula
Ščekino
Uzlovaja
Bogorodick
Čaplygin
OKSKO-

MINSK
Žodzina
Barysau
Mar'ina Horka
Byhau
Roslavl'
Djat'kovo
Belëv
Plavsk
Tvarkovskij
Rjažsk
Mičurinsk
Tambov
C

žynsk
345
Červen'
Bobr
Mscislau
Kryčau
Žukovka
Bolhov
Arhangel'skoe
Efremov
Lebedjan'
Novomoskovsk

BELARUS
Asipovičy
Babrujsk
Žlobin
Kletnja
Brjansk
Karačev
Orel
Novosil'
Elec
Lipeck
Griazi
DONSKAJA

Y E
Sluck
Hlusk
Uneča
Počep
Navlja
Železnogorsk
Livny
Zadonsk
Usman'
Oktjabr'skoe
Mordovo
RAVNINA

Salihorsk
Svetlahorsk
Rečyca
Homel'
Starodub
Trubč'evsk
Komariči
Dimitrijev-
L'govskij
Ščigry
Kolpny
Semiluki
Voronež
Anna
Ertil'
D

Luninec
Mazyr
Hojniki
Novozybkov
Semenivka
Novhorod-
Sivers'kyi
Ryl'sk
L'gov
Kurčatov
Obojan'
Gubkin
Cernjanka
Ostrogožsk
Kamenka
Voroncovka

Stolin
El'sk
Horodnia
Shostka
Hlukhiv
Kursk
Staryj
Oskol
Bobrov
Liski
Buturlinovka

Berežove
Skarodnae
Chernihiv
Mena
Konotop
Bakhmach
Bilopillia
Sumy
Belgorod
Novyj Oskol
Alekseevka
Rossoš'
D

Olevsk
Ovruch
Chornobyl'
Chemer
Nizhyn
Romny
Lebedyn
Proletarskij
Šebekino
Valujki
Kantemirovka

Novohrad-
Volyns'kyi
Korosten'
Ivankiv
Malyn
Nosivka
Ichnia
Pryluky
Okhtyrka
Bohodukhiv
KHARKIV
Dvorichna

Slavuta
Cherniakhiv
Radomyshl'
Irpin'
KYÏV (KIEV)
Boryspil'
Pyriatyn
Lubny
Opishnia
Lyubotin
Chuhuïv
Kup'ians'k
Novopskov
E

Shepetivka
Polonne
Zhytomyr
Fastiv
Vasyl'kiv
Pereiaslav-
Khmel'nyts'kyi
Myrhorod
Merefa
Balakliia
Svatove
Starobil's'k

Berdychiv
Koziatyn
Skvyra
Bila Tserkva
Zolotonosha
Prydniprovs'ka
Nyzovyna
Poltava
Karlivka
Krasnohrad
Izium
Lysychans'k
Sieverodonets'k

Khmil'nyk
Bohuslav
Cherkasy
Smila
Krasnohrad
Lozova
Slov'ians'k
Kramators'k
Stakhanov
Luhans'k

Vinnytsia
Zhashkiv
Kremenchuk
Pavlysh
Aretemiv's'k
Alchevs'k
E

Zhmerynka
Khrystynivka
Tal'ne
Novomyrhorod
Znam'ianka
Oleksandriia
Novomoskovs'k
Kostiantynivka
Horlivka
Yenakiieve
Krasnyi
Luch

Uman
Mala
Vyska
Dniprodzerzhyns'k
DNIPROPETROVS'K
Pavlohrad
Krasnoarmiis'k
Makiivka
Torez

Bratslav
Tul'chyn
Haisyn
Vapniarka
Kirovohrad
Novoukrainka
Dolyns'ka
Slavorod
Donets'k
Novošahtinsk

Mohyliv-
Podil's'kyi
Bershad'
Balta
Kryvyi Rih
Kazanka
Ordzhonikidze
Marhanets'
Zaporizhzhia
Orikhiv
Polohy
Volnovakha
Dokuchaievs'k
Matveev
Kurgan
ROSTOV-
NA-DONÚ

kam'ianets'-
odil's'kyi
Soroca
Floreşti
Vradyivka
Yelanets'
Novyi Buh
Inhulets'
Apostolove
Nikopol'
Vasylivka
Tokmak
Chernihivka
Polohy
Pryazovs'ka
Vysochyna
Taganrog
Azov
F

Edinet
Bălţi
Răbniţa
Kotovs'k
Anan'iv
Troïts'ke
Voznesens'k
Snihurivka
Vesele
Molochans'k
Mariupol'
Novoazovs'k

Botoşani
MOLDOVA
Orhei
Dubăsari
Berezivka
Nova
Kakhovka
Melitopol'
Berdians'k
Gulf of Taganrog
Šabel'sk

Paşcani
Iaşi
Călăraşi
Chişinău
Tiraspol
Mykolaïv
Zhovtneve
Yakymivka
Prymors'k
Dolžanskaja
Starominskaja

Roman
Hânceşti
Tighina
Slobozia
ODESA
Kherson
Nova
Kakhovka
Primorsko-
Ahtarsk
Kanevskaja

Vaslui
Huşi
Comrat
Illichivs'k
Hola
Prystan'
Novotroïts'ke
Heniches'k
Sea of Azov
Timaševsk

Bacău
Bârlad
Artsyz
Bilhorod-
Dnistrovs'kyi
Kalanchak
Armians'k
Kosa
Arabats'ka
strilka
Brjuhoveckaja

Tecuci
Cahul
Tatarbunary
Skadovs'k
Krasno-
perekops'k
Dzhankoi
mys
Kazantyp
Temrjuk
RUSSIA
Slavjansk-
na-Kubáni
Krasnodar

Focşani
LOWER TRAJAN'S WALL
Chornomors'ke
KRYMS'KYI PIVOSTRIV
(CRIMEAN PENINSULA)
Soviets'kyi
Kerch
Varenikovskaja
Krymsk
Abinsk
ADYGEJA
G

Galaţi
Brăila
Izmaïl
Kiliia
mys
Tarkhankut
Yevpatoriia
Saky
Bilohirs'k
Feodosiia
Kerchens'kyi
pivostriv
Anapa
Novorossijsk
CAUCASUS
Gorjači
Ključ

Tulcea
Sulina
1259
KRYMS'KI HORY
mys
Mehanom
Kerch Strait
Gelendžik
Dzhubga

Urziceni
Ţăndărei
Mouths of
the Danube
Simferopol'
Alushta
Novomihajlovskij
Tuapse

Slobozia
Sevastopol'
mys Khersones
Yalta
Alupka
mys Sarych

Feteşti
Cernavodă
Constanţa

Silistra
Mangalia
B L A C K   S E A
H

'DOGORIE
Tervel
Dobrič

9 28° 10 30° 11 32° 12 34° 13 36° 14 38° 15

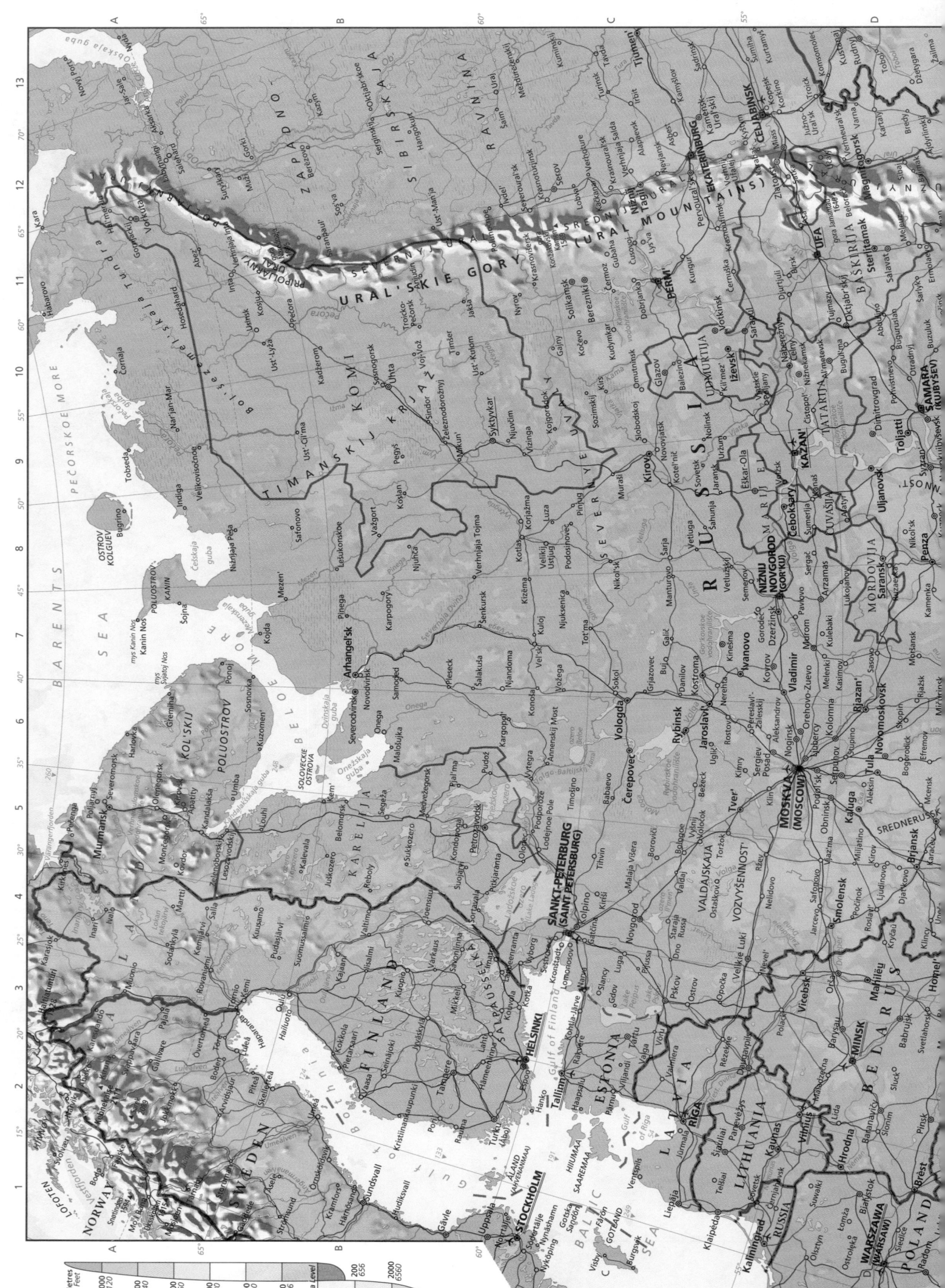

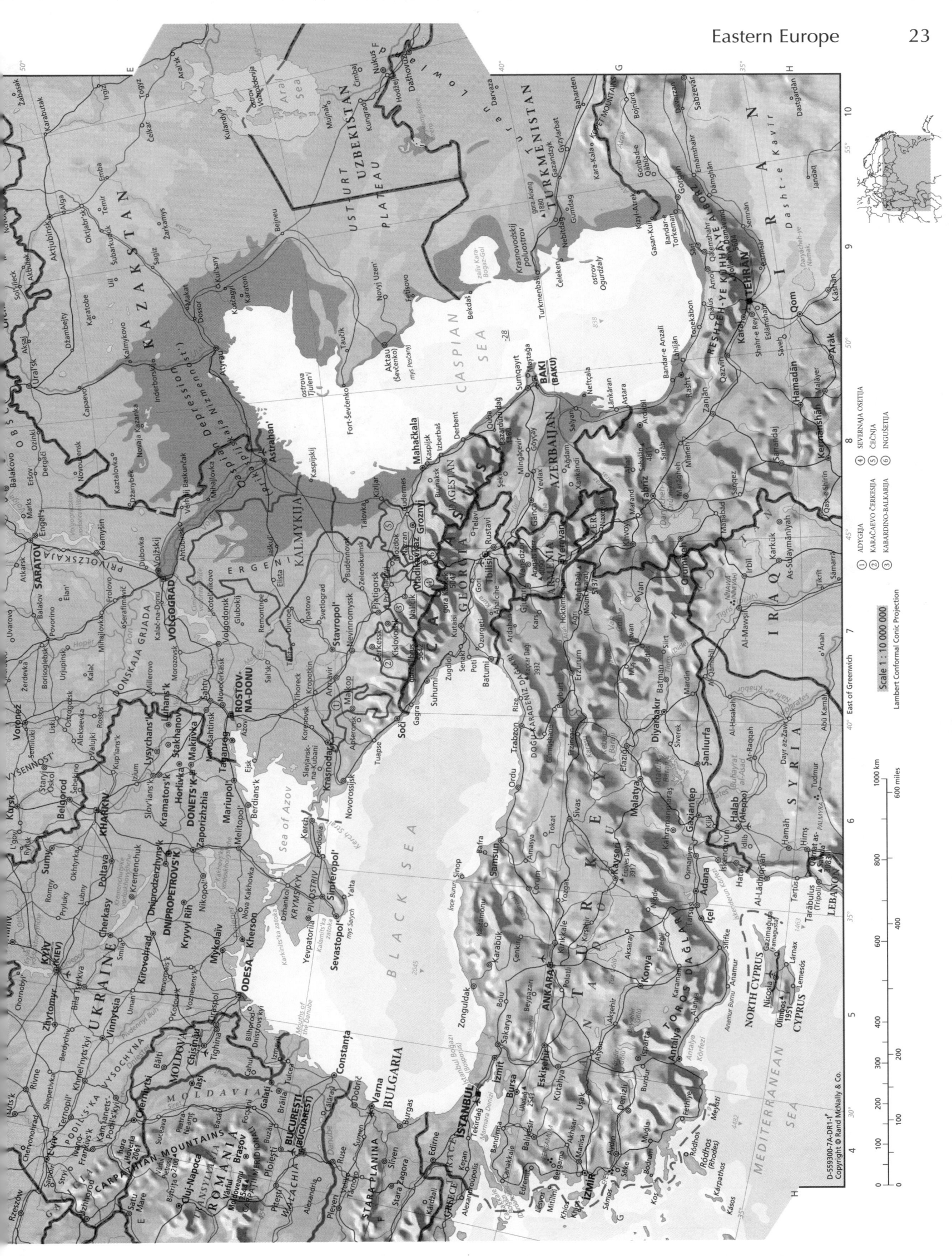

Scale 1 : 10 000 000

Lambert Conformal Conic Projection

D-5S9300-7A-DR1-1#
Copyright © Rand McNally & Co.

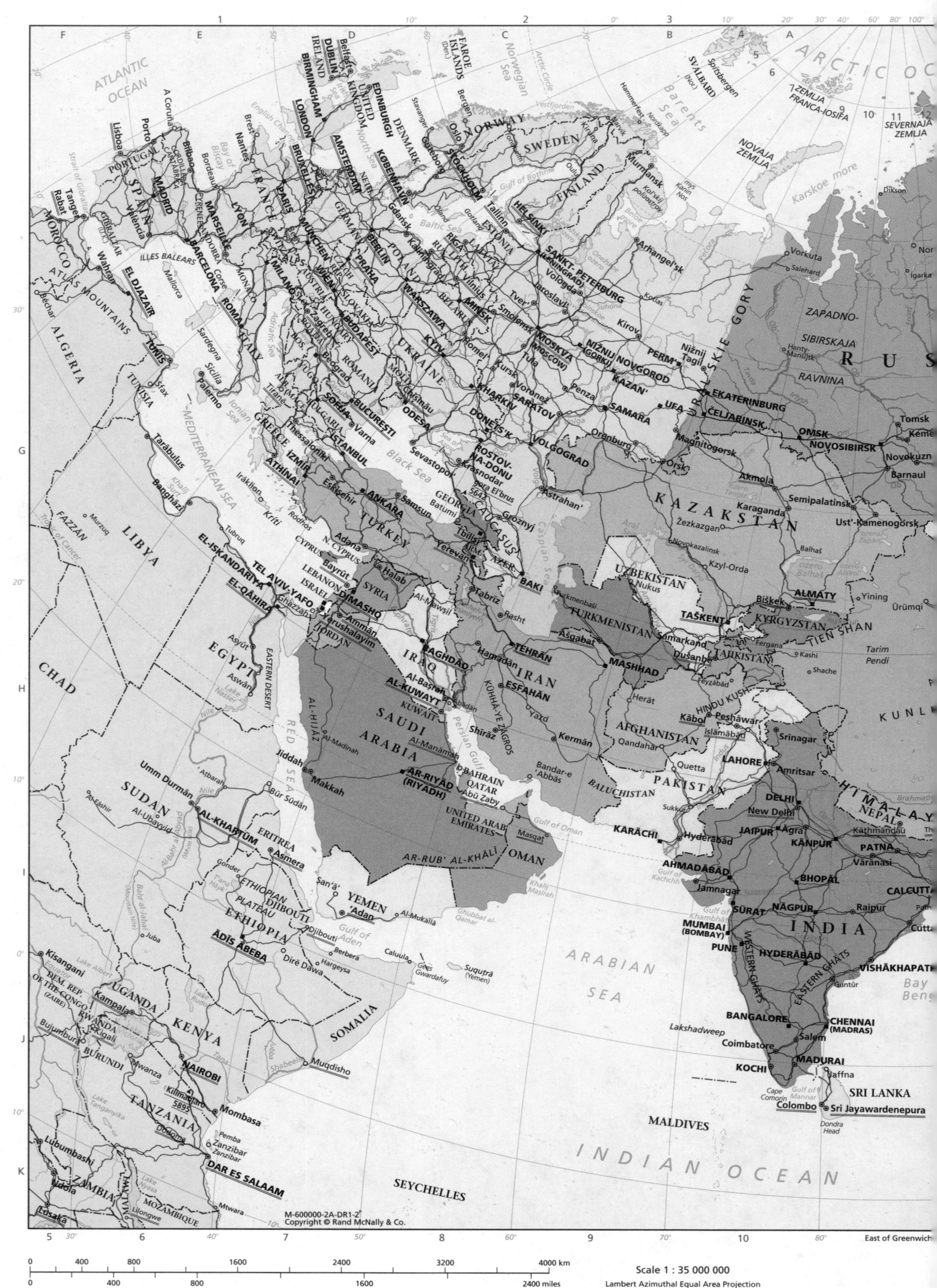

M-600000-2A-DR1-2
Copyright © Rand McNally & Co.

| 0 | 400 | 800 | 1600 | 2400 | 3200 | 4000 km |

| 0 | 400 | 800 | 1600 | 2400 miles |

Scale 1 : 35 000 000

Lambert Azimuthal Equal Area Projection

East of Greenwich

PACIFIC OCEAN

RUSSIA (SIBIR' / SIBERIA)

HREBET ČERSKOGO
VERHOJANSKIJ HREBET
STANOVOJ HREBET
SIHOTE-ALIN'

Hatanga
Tiksi
Kazače
Žigansk
Olenëk
Verhojansk
Srednekolymsk
Čerskij
mys Navarin
mys Oljutorskij
 Uelkal
Anadyr'
Markovo
POLUOSTROV KAMČATKA
Petropavlovsk-Kamčatskij
SREDINNYJ HREBET
Cape Attu
Attu Island
ALEUTIAN ISLANDS (U.S.)
Bering Sea

Lensk
Jakutsk
Tommot
Aldan
Skovorodino
Komsomol'sk-na-Amure
Nikolaevsk
Ohotsk
Ajan
mys Elizavety
Oha
ALEKSANDROVSK-Sahalinskij
OSTROV SAHALIN (SAKHALIN)
mys Terpenija
Južno-Sahalinsk
KURIL'SKIE OSTROVA (KURIL ISLANDS)
Sea of Okhotsk
mys Lopatka

EDNESIBIRSKOE PLOSKOGOR'E
Krasnojarsk
Angara
ozero Bajkal
Irkutsk
Ulan-Ude
Čita
Hailar
Jiamusi
Harbin
Vladivostok
Sapporo
HOKKAIDÔ
Asahikawa
Hakodate
Aomori
Sendai
HONSHÛ
Niigata
TÔKYÔ
YOKOHAMA
Kanazawa
Sea of Japan

MONGOLIA
HANGAYN NURUU
Hövsgöl nuur
Ulaanbaatar
Kerulen
GOBI
Hohhot
Zhangjiakou
BEIJING
Changchun
Shenyang
Fushun
Jilin
NORTH KOREA
Dandong
Pyongyang
SÔUL (SEOUL)
Taegu
PUSAN
SOUTH KOREA
Mokp'o
Cheju-do
KYÔTO
HIROSHIMA
OSAKA
NAGOYA
JAPAN
Shikoku
FUKUOKA
KYÛSHÛ
Kagoshima

CHINA
TAIYUAN
TIANJIN
DALIAN
Yinchuan
Lanzhou
SHIJIAZHUANG
JINAN
Qingdao
Xuzhou
Zhengzhou
Bo Hai
Yellow Sea
Korea Strait
NANSEI-SHOTÔ (RYUKYU ISLANDS)
Amami-o-shima
Okinawa-jima
Naha
East China Sea

CHENGDU
XI'AN
WUHAN
Hangzhou
CHONGQING
CHANGSHA
Nanchang
Hengyang
SHANGHAI
Ningbo
Wenzhou
Fuzhou
T'AIPEI
TAIWAN
Tainan
KAOHSIUNG

Guiyang
Kunming
Nanning
Liuzhou
GUANGZHOU
XIANGGANG (HONG KONG)
MACAU (Port.)
Zhanjiang
Luzon Strait

Qinghai Hu
Lhasa

Farallon de Pajaros
Agrihan
NORTHERN MARIANA ISLANDS (U.S.)
Anatahan
Saipan
Rota
Asana
GUAM (U.S.)
Philippine Sea
FEDERATED STATES OF MICRONESIA

DHAKA
CHITTAGONG
MYANMAR (BURMA)
Mandalay
LAOS
Louangphrabang
Chiang Mai
Vangchan
Udon Thani
VIETNAM
HA NOI
Hai Phong
Gulf of Tonkin
Haikou
Hainan Dao
Da Nang
South China Sea
LUZON
Baguio
Quezon City
PHILIPPINES
MANILA
Naga
Masbate
Samar
Mindoro
Panay
Iloilo
Negros
Cebu
MINDANAO
Davao
Cape San Agustin
Zamboanga
Moro Gulf
Tinaca Point
Koror
PALAU
New Ireland
Kavieng
Rabaul
New Britain
Bismarck Sea
Madang
Wewak

YANGON (RANGOON)
Gulf of Martaban
KRUNG THÊP (BANGKOK)
THAILAND
CAMBODIA
Phnum Pénh
THANH PHO HO CHI MINH (SAIGON)
Kâmpóng Saôm
Gulf of Thailand
Mui Ca Mau
Coco Islands
Andaman Islands (India)
Andaman Sea

MALAY PENINSULA
Bandar Seri Begawan
BRUNEI
Gunong Kinabalu 4101
MALAYSIA
Kuching
BORNEO (KALIMANTAN)
Pontianak
Celebes Sea
Manado
HALMAHERA
Morotai
Biak
Jayapura
Puncak Jaya 5030
NEW GUINEA
PAPUA NEW GUINEA
Port Moresby
Gulf of Papua

Nicobar Islands (India)
Banda Aceh
George Town (Penang)
MALAYSIA
KUALA LUMPUR
MEDAN
SINGAPORE
Strait of Malacca
Padang
Pulau Siberut
SUMATERA (SUMATRA)
Palembang
Tanjungkarang-Telukbetung
Pulau Bangka
Belitung
Banjarmasin
Balikpapan
SULAWESI (CELEBES)
Ujungpandang
Pulau Buton
Buru
Seram (Ceram)
Laut Seram
Laut Maluku
Laut Banda
Pulau Yos Sudarso
Arafura Sea
Cape Wessel
Cape Arnhem
Gulf of Carpentaria
CAPE YORK PENINSULA
Darwin
Melville Island
Cape York

JAKARTA
BANDUNG
SURABAYA
JAWA (JAVA)
Madura
Bali
Lombok
Sumbawa
Sumba
Flores
Laut Flores
Laut Sawu
Timor
Dili
Timor Sea
Kupang
INDONESIA
AUSTRALIA
Cairns
Coral Sea

Scale 1 : 20 000 000

M-700000-7A-DR1-2°
Copyright © Rand McNally & Co.

| 0 | 200 | 400 | 600 | 800 | 1200 | 1600 km |

| 0 | 200 | 400 | 800 miles |

Lambert Conformal Conic Projection

A B

OCEAN

UNITED STATES
ALASKA
Bering Strait
mys Dežneva

CHUKCHI SEA

International Date Line

ostrov Vrangelja

proliv Longa

BERING SEA

St. Lawrence Island
St. Matthew Island
Nunivak Island
Pribilof Islands

SEVERNAJA ZEMLJA
ostrov Bol'ševik
mys Čeljuskin

NOVOSIBIRSKE OSTROVA
ostrov Novaja Sibir'
LIAHOVSKIE OSTROVA
ostrov Bol'šoj Liahovskij

MORE LAPTEVYH
VOSTOČNO-SIBIRSKOE MORE
MEDVEŽI OSTROVA

ČUKOTSKIJ POLUOSTROV
Anadyr

KORIAKSKOE NAGORJE

ALEUTIAN ISLANDS
Attu Island

POLUOSTROV TAJMYR
Y BYRRANGA

KOMANDORSKIE OSTROVA

Hatanga

HREBET ČERSKOGO
MOMSKIJ HREBET

SREDINNYJ HREBET
POLUOSTROV KAMČATKA

Petropavlovsk-Kamčatskij

SREDNE-SIBIRSKOE PLOSKOGORJE

VERHOJANSKIJ HREBET

HREBET SUNTAR HOYATA

SEA OF OKHOTSK

Jakutsk

ALDANSKOE NAGORJE

HREBET DŽUGDŽUR

Šantarskie ostrova

OSTROV SAHALIN

KURIL'SKIE OSTROVA (KURIL ISLANDS)

Bratsk
Irkutsk
Angarsk
Ulan-Ude

STANOVOE NAGORIE
STANOVOJ HREBET

BUREINSKIJ HREBET

Komsomol'sk-na-Amure

Habarovsk

SIHOTE-ALIN

HOKKAIDO
Sapporo

BURJATIJA

JABLONOVIJ HREBET

XIAO HINGGAN LING

Vladivostok

SEA OF JAPAN

Aomori

MONGOLIA
HANGAYN NURUU
Ulaanbaatar

DA HINGGAN LING

MANCHURIA

HARBIN
CHANGCHUN
SHENYANG FUSHUN

NORTH KOREA
P'yŏngyang

HONSHŪ
Niigata
TOKYO
KAWASAKI
YOKOHAMA

NAGOYA
KYOTO
OSAKA
KOBE

JAPAN

CHINA

Beijing
TIANJIN
DALIAN

SOUTH KOREA
SŎUL
INCH'ŎN
PUSAN

HIROSHIMA

KITAKYŪSHŪ
FUKUOKA

KYŪSHŪ
SHIKOKU

Nagasaki
Kagoshima

YELLOW SEA

Qingdao

Baotou
Datong
Baoding
Shijiazhuang

Bo Hai

PACIFIC OCEAN

IZU-SHOTO

Metres	Feet
6000	19680
4000	13120
3000	9840
2000	6560
1000	3280
500	1640
200	656
Sea Level	0
200	656
2000	6560

100° East of Greenwich 12   110° 13   120° 14   130° 15

① ADYGEJA
② KARAČAEVO - ČERKESIJA
③ KABARDINO-BALKARIJA
④ SEVERNAJA OSETIJA
⑤ ČEČNJA
⑥ INGUŠETIJA

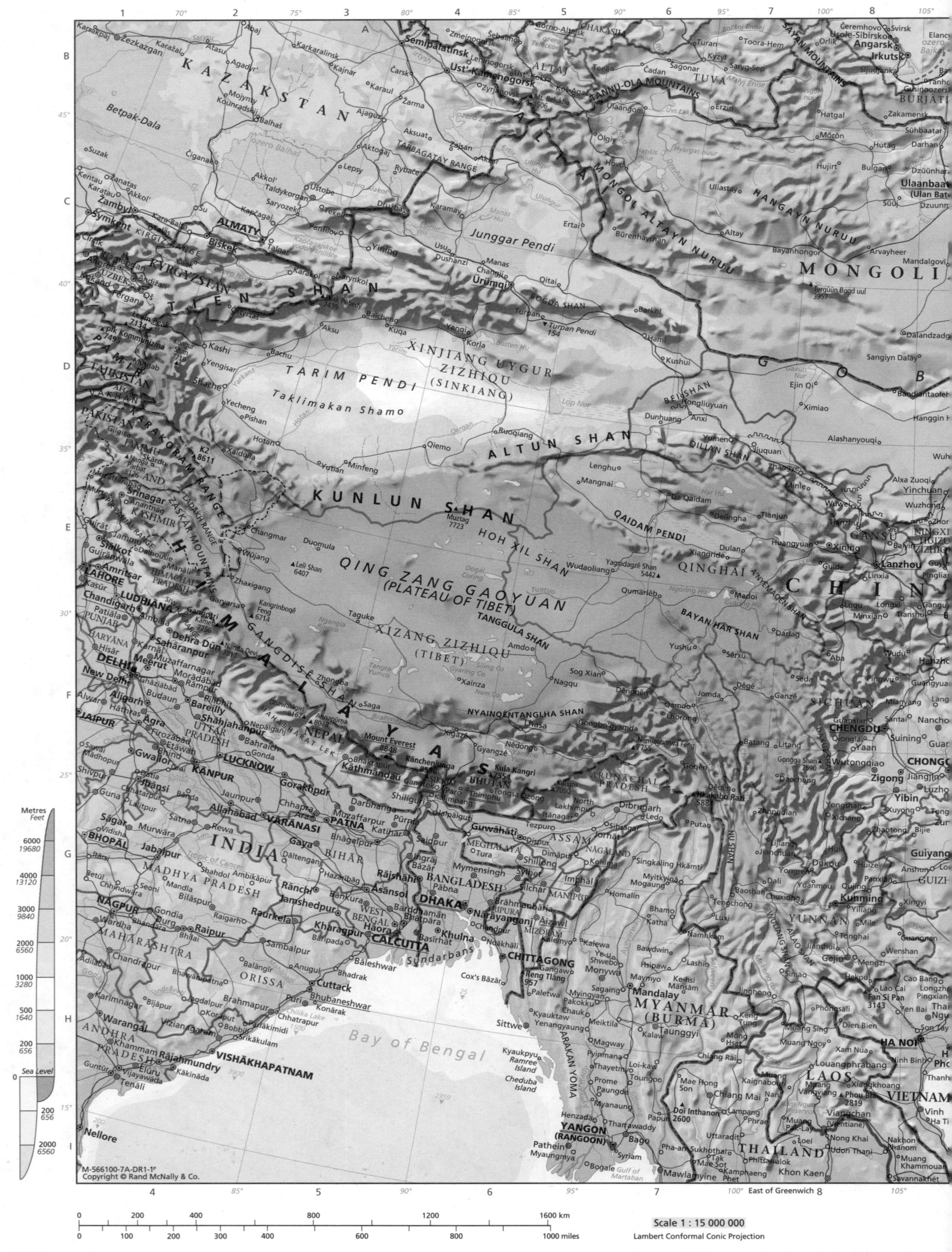

Scale 1 : 15 000 000

Lambert Conformal Conic Projection

RUSSIA

SIBIR'

DA HINGGAN LING

NEI MONGGOL ZIZHIQU
(INNER MONGOLIA)

MANCHURIA

HEILONGJIANG

XIAO HINGGAN LING

HARBIN

JILIN

CHANGCHUN

SHENYANG   FUSHUN

LIAONING

NORTH
KOREA

DALIAN

HEBEI

BEIJING

TIANJIN

TAIYUAN

SHANXI

SHAANXI

SHANDONG

JINAN

Qingdao

YELLOW SEA

SOUL
(SEOUL)

INCH'ON   SOUTH
KOREA

PUSAN

SEA OF JAPAN
(EAST SEA)

HONSHŪ

JAPAN

TŌKYŌ

YOKOHAMA

KAWASAKI

NAGOYA

KYŌTO   OSAKA

KŌBE

HIROSHIMA

KITAKYŪSHŪ
FUKUOKA

SHIKOKU

KYŪSHŪ

Nagasaki

OSTROV SAHALIN

Sea of
Okhotsk

KURIL'SKIE OSTROVA
(KURIL ISLANDS)

HOKKAIDŌ

Sapporo

HENAN

ANHUI   NANJING

WUHAN

HUBEI

SHANGHAI

Hangzhou

ZHEJIANG

JIANGXI

CHANGSHA

HUNAN

FUJIAN   Fuzhou

GUANGDONG

GUANGZHOU

MACAU
(Port.)

XIANGGANG
(HONG KONG)

HAINAN DAO

NANSEI-SHOTŌ (RYUKYU ISLANDS)

EAST CHINA SEA

Tropic of Cancer

TAIWAN

T'AIPEI

KAOHSIUNG

Taiwan Strait

Luzon
Strait

BATAN
ISLANDS

BABUYAN ISLANDS

SOUTH CHINA SEA

PHILIPPINE
SEA

PACIFIC
OCEAN

LUZON

PHILIPPINES

Okino-Tori-
shima
(Japan)

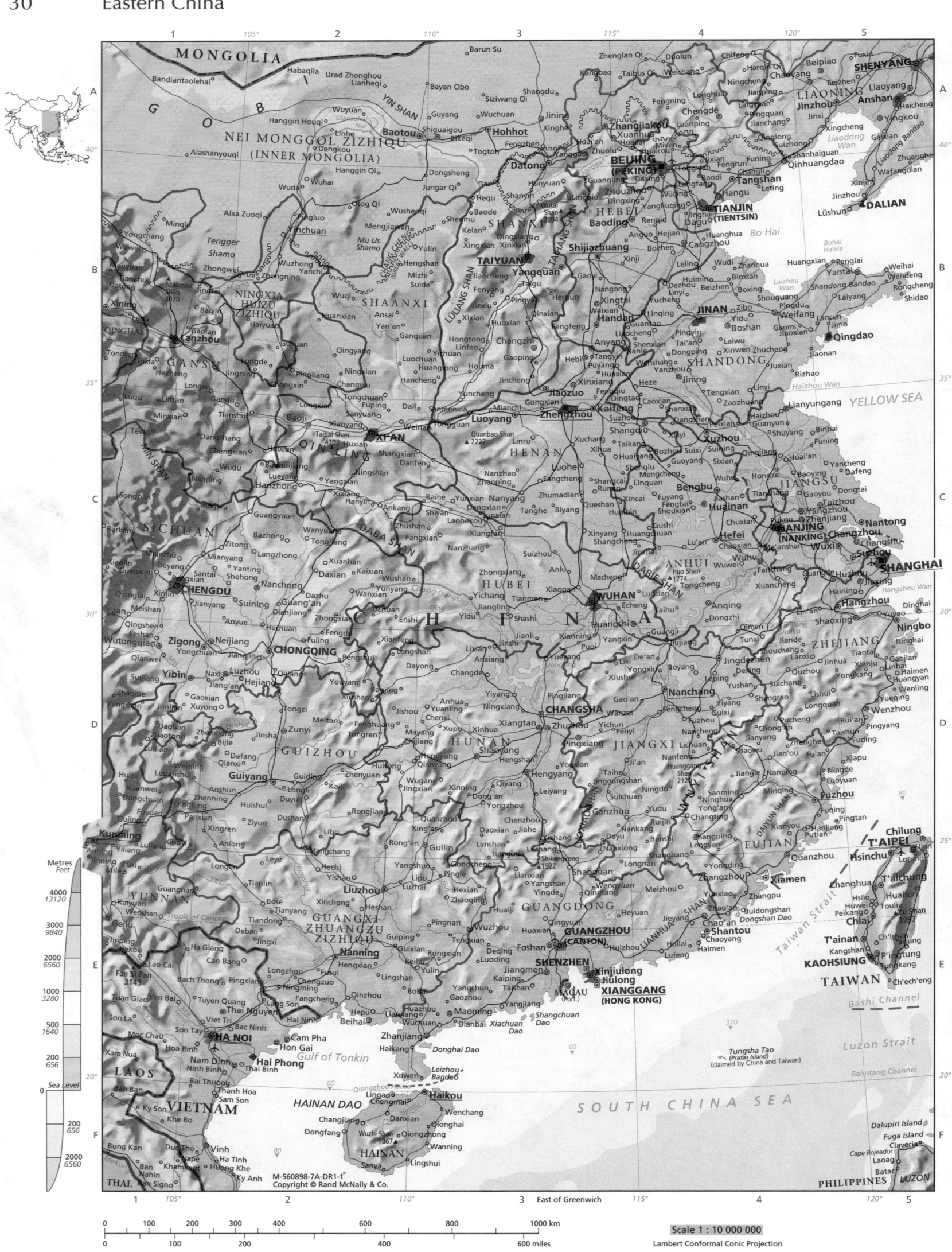

Metres
Feet

4000
13120

3000
9840

2000
6560

1000
3280

500
1640

200
656

Sea Level

0

200
656

2000
6560

M-600098-7A-DR1-2°
Copyright © Rand McNally & Co.

0   200   400   800   1200   1600 km
0   100 200   300   400   500   600   700   800   1000 miles

Scale 1 : 15 000 000

Sinusoidal Projection

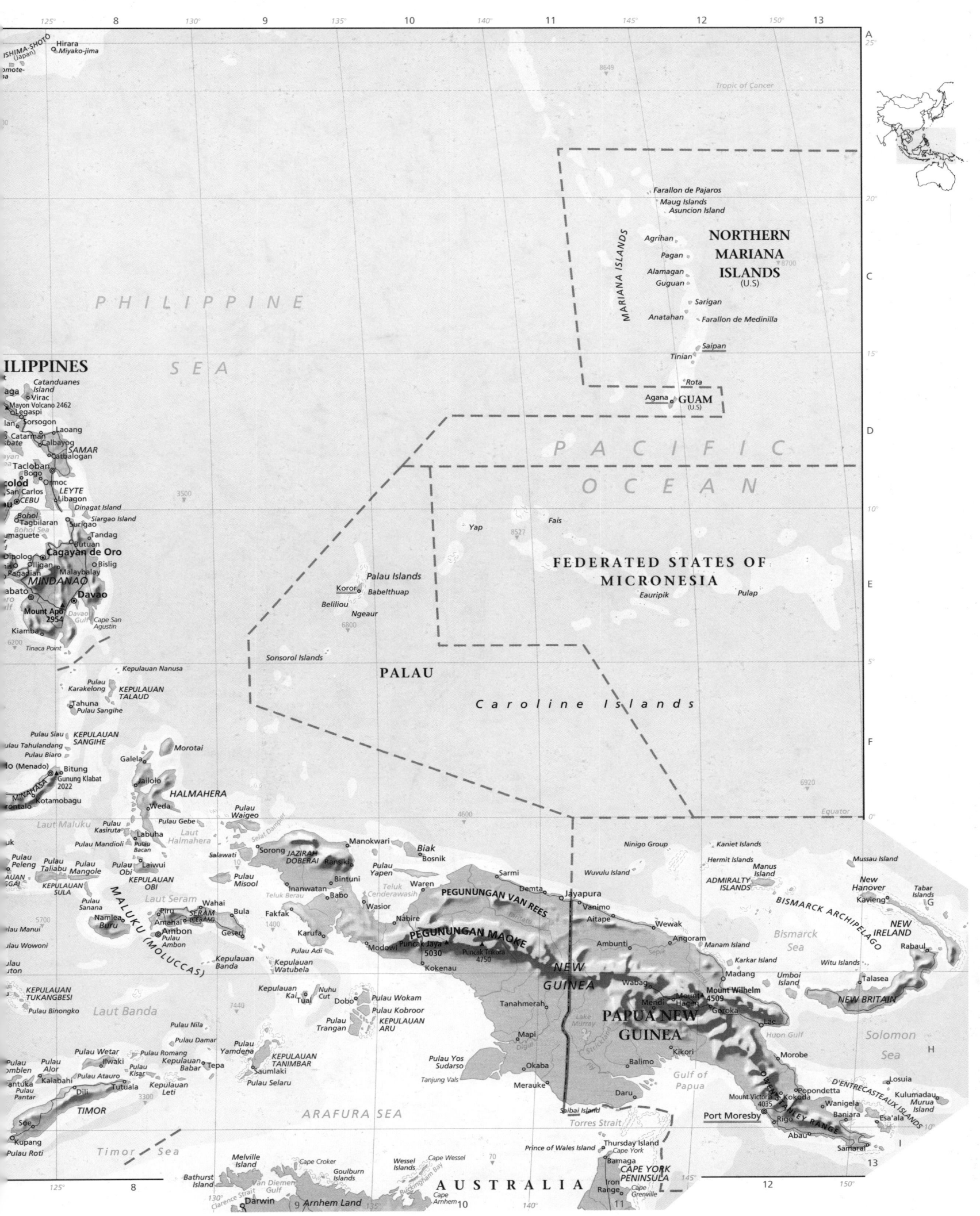

PHILIPPINE

SEA

PACIFIC

OCEAN

PHILIPPINES

Catanduanes
Island
Virac
Mayon Volcano 2462
Legaspi
Sorsogon
Laoang
Catarman
Calbayog
SAMAR
Tacloban
Catbalogan
Bogo
Ormoc
colod
San Carlos
LEYTE
Libagon
CEBU
Dinagat Island
Bohol
Tagbilaran
Siargao Island
Bohol Sea
Surigao
umaguete
Tandag
Dipolog
Cagayan de Oro
Butuan
Iligan
Bislig
Pagadian
Malaybalay
MINDANAO
Davao
 abato
Davao
Mount Apo
2954
Gulf
Cape San
Agustin
Kiamba
6200
Tinaca Point

Kepulauan Nanusa

Pulau
Karakelong   KEPULAUAN
TALAUD
Tahuna
Pulau Sangihe

Pulau Siau   KEPULAUAN
SANGIHE
Pulau Tahulandang
Pulau Biaro
Morotai
o (Menado)
Bitung
Galela
MINAHASA   Gunung Klabat
2022
Jailolo
ontalo   Kotamobagu   HALMAHERA
Laut Maluku   Pulau   Weda
Kasiruta   Pulau Gebe
Labuha
Pulau Waigeo
Pulau Mandioli   Laut
Pulau   Halmahera
Pulau   Bacan
Pulau   Salawati   Manokwari
Peleng   Pulau   JAZIRAH   Biak
Pulau   Obi   DOBERAI   Bosnik
Taliabu   Mangole   Laiwui   Sorong   Rangki
Pulau   KEPULAUAN   Pulau   Pulau
AUAN   OBI   Obi   Misool   Pulau
GAI   KEPULAUAN   Inanwatan   Yapen
SULA   Laut Seram   Wahai   Babo   Waren
Pulau   SERAM (CERAM)   Teluk Berau
Sanana   Bula   Fakfak   Teluk
5700   Namlea   Amahai   Cenderawasih
Baru   Piru   Geser   Nabire
au Manui   Pulau   Karufa   Modowi
au Wowoni   Ambon   Pulau Adi
Ambon
uton   Kepulauan
Banda   Pulau   Kokenau
KEPULAUAN   Kepulauan   Watubela
TUKANGBESI   Kai   Nuhu
Pulau Binongko   Laut Banda   Tual   Cut   Dobo   Pulau Wokam
7440   KEPULAUAN
Pulau Nila   ARU
Pulau Damar   Pulau   Tanahmerah
Pulau   Yamdena
Pulau Wetar   Pulau Romang   KEPULAUAN   Mapi
Pulau   Ilwaki   Pulau   TANIMBAR
omblen   Alor   Kisar   Tepa   Saumlaki   Pulau Yos
antuka   Pulau   Kepulauan   Sudarso
Pantar   Kalabahi   Pulau Atauro   Leti   Pulau Selaru   Tanjung Vals   Okaba   Merauke
Sge   Dili   Tutuala   3300
Kupang   TIMOR   ARAFURA SEA
Pulau Roti   Timor   Sea

8649

Tropic of Cancer

Farallon de Pajaros
Maug Islands
Asuncion Island

MARIANA ISLANDS   Agrihan
Pagan   NORTHERN
MARIANA
Alamagan   ISLANDS
Guguan   (U.S)
8700
Sarigan
Anatahan   Farallon de Medinilla

Saipan
Tinian
Rota
Agana   GUAM
(U.S)

Yap   Fais
8527

FEDERATED STATES OF
MICRONESIA
Palau Islands   Eauripik   Pulap
Koror   Babelthuap
Beliliou   Ngeaur   6800

Sonsorol Islands
PALAU
Caroline Islands

6920

Equator

Kaniet Islands
Ninigo Group   Hermit Islands   Mussau Island
Wuvulu Island   Manus   New
Sarmi   ADMIRALTY   Hanover
Demta   Vanimo   ISLANDS   Kavieng
Jayapura   Wewak   Karkar Island   NEW
PEGUNUNGAN VAN REES   Aitape   Angoram   Manam Island   IRELAND
Tanjak   Ambunti   Madang   Umboi   Rabaul
PEGUNUNGAN MAOKE   Sepik   Mount   Island   Witu Islands
Puncak Jaya   Wabag   Hagen   Talasea
5030   Puncak Trikora   NEW   Goroka   Mount Wilhelm   NEW BRITAIN
4750   GUINEA   Mendi   4509   Lae
Lake   Mount   Huon Gulf
PAPUA NEW   Murray   Hagen   Solomon
GUINEA   Goroka   Sea
Strickland   Kikori   Morobe
Balimo   Gulf of
Papua   D'ENTRECASTEAUX ISLANDS
Digul   Kumadau
Daru   Mount Victoria   Kokoda   Losuia
4035   Popondetta   Murua
Saibai Island   Port Moresby   Rigo   Island
Torres Strait   Banaro   Wanigela   Baniara
Thursday Island   Abau   Esa'ala
Prince of Wales Island   Cape York   STANLEY RANGE   Samarai
Bamaga   CAPE YORK
Iron   PENINSULA
Range   Cape
Grenville
Melville   Cape Croker   Wessel   Cape Wessel
Island   Goulburn   Islands
Bathurst   Islands
Island   Van Diemen   Buckingham Bay
Clarence Strait   Darwin   Arnhem Land   Cape
Arnhem

A U S T R A L I A

Bismarck
Sea

BISMARCK ARCHIPELAGO

Tabar
Islands

Scale 1 : 10 000 000

Lambert Conformal Conic Projection

M-569891-7A-DR1-1
Copyright © Rand McNally & Co.

EAST CHINA SEA

Tokuno-shima

NANSEI-SHOTO (RYUKYU ISLANDS)
(Japan)

Okino-Erabu-shima

Okinawa-jima
Kume-jima   Nago
Ishikawa
Naha

Hirara *Miyako-jima*

Yaeyama-rettō *Ishigaki*

Iriomote-jima

Tropic of Cancer

PACIFIC
OCEAN

Luzon Strait   BATAN
ISLANDS

Tungsha Tao
(Pratas Island)
(claimed by
China and Taiwan)

Balintang Channel

BABUYAN
ISLANDS   *Babuyan Island*

Dalupiri Island   *Calayan Island*   *Camiguin Island*

Fuga Island   Babuyan Channel
Claveria   Escarpada Point

Cape Bojeador   Aparri

HAINAN DAO

Pattle Island

Xisha Qundao
(Paracel Islands)
(claimed by China,
Taiwan, and Vietnam)

PHILIPPINE
SEA

Laoag
Batac   Tuguegarao City

Vigan

San Fernando   Bontoc
Ilagan
Lagawe
Solano

Lingayen   Casiguran
Gulf   Palanan Point

Rena Point   Bayombong
Bolinao   Baguio
Lingayen   Dagupan   Baler

Caiman Point   San Carlos

PHILIPPINES

Iba   Cabanatuan   Gapan
Angeles San Fernando
Olongapo   Polillo
Malolos   Calagua Islands
MANILA Quezon City
Cavite   Lamon
Bacoor   Bay   Daet   Caramoan   Catanduanes
Tagaytay   San Pablo   Island
Lucena   Naga Virac
SOUTH CHINA SEA   Lipa   Lucena
Lubang   Batangas   Mayon
Islands   Calapan Marinduque Volcano   Legaspi
Mount Halcon   Santa Cruz 2462   Sorsogon
2585   Bulan   Irosin
MINDORO   Burias   Laoang
Mamburao   Island Bulan Catarman
Bongabong   Tablas Sibuyan   Calbayog
Central   Island Sea Mandaon Placer SAMAR
Calamian   Masbate Masbate   Catbalogan
Group   Busuanga   Naval Borongan
Island   Kalibo   Visayan   Tacloban
Linapacan Strait   Roxas Sea Bogo Ormoc   Guiuan
Libro Point   PANAY   Camotes
El Nido   Cuyo   Victorias Cadiz Sea LEYTE
Taytay   Islands Sagay   Sogod
Guimaras San   Camotes   Dinagat Island
Roxas   Dumaran Ilollo Carlos Cebu
Bacungan   Island   Bacolod La Carlota CEBU Libagon
Puerto Princesa Cagayan Islands Guimaras Bohol Surigao
Inagahuan   Cavili Island   Island NEGROS Tagbilaran Siargao Island
Arena   Sipalay Bais Santander
PALAWAN   Island   Hinoba-an Camiguin Cabadbaran
Dumaguete   Siquijor Island Tandag
SPRATLY ISLANDS Siquijor Bohol Gingoog Butuan
(claimed by Brunei, China, Malaysia, Island Sea Prosperidad Lianga
Philippines, Taiwan and Vietnam) Dipolog Oroquieta Cagayan de Oro Bislig
Mount Mantalingajan Ozami Iligan Malaybalay Cateel
2085   Brooke's Point Liloy Kabasalan Marawi Kalatungan Mountain
Sulu Sea   Pagadian Parang MINDANAO Bagangao
Bugsuk Island   Siocon Pagadian Cotabato Mount Apo Davao
Balabac Island   Balabac Zamboanga 2954 Digos
San Miguel Islands Peninsula Tacurong Davao
Zamboanga   Moro Gulf Gulf
Pulau   Cagayan Sulu Kotonadal Mati
Balambangan Pulau Banggi Island Kiamba
Kota Belud   Pangutaran Group Tinaca Point Cape San
Senaja   Sarangani Island Agustin
Kudat   Jolo Jolo Island
Gunong Kinabalu Sandakan Pulau
4101   Ranau   Karakaralong
Kota Kinabalu   Sukau Tawitawi Tapul Group KEPULAUAN
Papar Beaufort Group   TALAUD
Pulau Labuan MALAYSIA Lahad Datu SULU ARCHIPELAGO INDONESIA
Labuan SABAH   Sibutu Pulau Sangihe Tahuna
Bandar Seri Begawan Semporna CELEBES SEA
BRUNEI Lawas   Kalabakan Tawau
Seri   Limbang Sebatik Island
Miri   Gunong Mulu BORNEO
2377

36

MERGUI
ARCHIPELAGO

Myinmoletkat Taung
2075

Nakhon Pathom
Chachoengsao
Samut Prakan
Samut
Sakhon
**KRUNG THEP
(BANGKOK)**

ANGKOR
WAT

Lumphät

Song Cau
Tuy Hoa

Palaw
Kadan Kyun

Phetchaburi
Cha-am
Hua Hin

Rayong
Chanthaburi

Bätdâmbâng

Kâmpóng
Thum
Pouthisat

CAMBODIA

Krâchéh
Phumï Dâk
Dâm

Buon Ma Thuot

Kâmpóng Cham

VIETNAM

MYANMAR
(BURMA)

Bentinck Island
Letsôk-aw
Kyun

Kanmaw
Kyun

Prachuap
Khiri Khan

Trat
Ko Chang
Ko Kut

Phnum Âoral
1813

Krông Kaôh Kóng

Phumï
Kaôh Kông

**Phnum Pénh
(Phnom Penh)**

Phumï Châmbâk
Svay Riêng

Loc Ninh

Tay Ninh

Da Lat

Bao Loc

Nha Trang

Cam Ranh

ANDAMAN

Lanbi Kyun

SEA

Chumphon

Isthmus of Kra

Ranong

Ko Tao

Ko Phangan

Ko Samui

Surat Thani

Kâmpóng Saôm
Kâmpôt

Kaôh Kông

Long Xuyen

Dao Phu Quoc

Rach Gia

Sa Dec
Can Tho

My Tho
Vinh Long

Vung Tau

Tra Vinh
Soc Trang

Bien Hoa

Phan Thiet

**THANH PHO HO CHI MINH
(SAIGON)**

Phan Rang

Îles Catwick

THAILAND

Phangnga

Nakhon Si Thammarat

Pak Phanang

Ca Mau

Bac Lieu

Mui Ca Mau

Hon Khoai

Con Son

SPRATLY ISLANDS

SOUTH CHINA

Ko Phuket
Phuket

Trang

Kantang

Phatthalung

Songkhla

Quan Dao Nam Du

SEA

Hat Yai
Satun

Pattani
Yala

Narathiwat

Pulau We
Banda Aceh

Lhokseumawe

Kangar
Pulau Langkawi
Alor Setar

MALAY PENINSULA

Sungai Kolok
Betong
Pasir Mas
Kota Bharu
Kuala Krai

Kuala Terengganu

Langsa

Gunung Abongabong
2985

Gunung
Bandahara
3012

Sungai Petani
George Town
(Penang)
Butterworth

Taiping
Ipoh
Kampar

Kuala Kangsar
Gunung Tahan
2187

Kuala Lipis

Cukai

MALAYSIA

Pulau Laut

KEPULAUAN
NATUNA BESAR

Natuna Besar

BRU

Miri

Niah

MALAYSIA

SARAWA

Meulaboh

Gunung Leuser
3381

Binjai
MEDAN
Tebingtinggi

Tapaktuan
Gunung Sinabung
2451
Pematangsiantar

Teluk Intan
Raub
Bentung
Gunung Benum
2107

Kuantan

KUALA LUMPUR
Shah Alam

SEMENANJUNG
MALAYSIA

Mukah

Bintulu

Pulau
Simeulue

Tanjungbalai
Kisaran

Klang
Seremban
Kajang
Kuala Pilah
Segamat

Labis

Mersing

Pulau Tioman

KEPULAUAN
ANAMBAS

Pulau
Midai
Pulau Subi

KEPULAUAN
NATUNA
SELATAN

Sibu

Sarikei

Betong

PEG. KAPUAS HULU

Sinabang

Tarutung

Bagansiapiapi
Rantauprapat

Pulau Rupat
Melaka

Muar
Pulau
Bengkalis
Batu Pahat

Keluang

Pulau Jemaja

Pulau Serasan

Kuching

Serian

Pulau Babi
Pulau
Tuangku

Sibolga
Padangsidempuan

Dumai

Johor Bahru

Tanjung
Datu

Sambas

Singkawang

Semitau

Bukit Raya
2278

Putussibau

Pulau
Nias

Gunungsitoli

SINGAPORE
Pulau
Batam
Pulau
Kundur

Pulau Bintan
Tanjungpinang

KEPULAUAN
TAMBELAN

Mempawah

PEGUNUNGAN

Pulau
Mursala

Pekanbaru

Pulau
Tebingtinggi
Padang

KEPULAUAN RIAU

Pontianak

Sanggau

Sintang

BORNEO
(KALIMANTA

Bangkinang

Pulau Pini

Equator

Talu

Pulau Pejantan

Gunung Saran
1758

KEPULAUAN BATU
Pulau Tanahmasa
Pulau Tanahbala

Bukittinggi
Padangpanjang
Pariaman

Payakumbuh
Taluk

Rengat

Tembilahan

Pulau Basu
Pulau Lingga

KEPULAUAN
LINGGA

Telukbatang

Sukadana

Pulau
Siberut

Padang
Painan

Sungaidareh

Pulau Singkep

Selat Berhala

Pulau
Karimata

Nangatayap

Ketapang

**SUMATERA
(SUMATRA)**

Muarabungo

Bangko

Tanjung Jabung

Sukaraja

Palangkaraya

KEPULAUAN
Pulau Sipura
MENTAWAI
Pulau Pagai
Utara

Mukomuko

Surulangun

Gunung Kerinci
3800

Jambi

Muntok

Pangkalpinang
Pulau
Bangka

Kendawangan

Kumai

Sampit

Pulau Pagai
Selatan

Lubuklinggau

Gresik

Tanjungpandan
Manggar
Belitung

Tanjung Sambar

Pangkalanbuun

Kualakap

Lais

Perabumulih
Muaraenim
Lahat
Gunung Dempo
3159

Palembang
Kayuagung

Pulau
Lepar

Tanjung Lumut

Banjar

Bengkulu

Baturaja

Menggala

Pulau
Enggano

Manna
Martapura

Kotabumi

Laut Jawa (Java Sea)

G R E A T E R   S U M

Tanjung Puting

Tanjung

Bintuhan

Metro

Krui

Tanjungkarang-Telukbetung
Panjang

I N D O N

INDIAN OCEAN

Kotaagung

Tanjung Cina

Selat Sunda

Serang

Bekasi
Karawang
Indramayu

Pulau
Masalembu
Besar

Pulau
Bawean

Tanjung Cangkuang

JAKARTA

Bogor
Cianjur

Purwakarta

Sumedang

Cirebon

Pekalongan

Kudus
Rembang

Tuban

MADURA

Bangkalan

Pameka

Sukabumi
BANDUNG

Garut

Tegal
Batang

SEMARANG
Gunung Slamet
3428
Purwokerto
Magelang

Surakarta
SURABAYA

Ujunggenteng

Sindangbarang

Cilacap

Gunung Lawu
3265

Kediri

Pasuruan

Selat Madura

Yogyakarta

Tulungagung

Blitar

Malang

Jember

Probolingo

JAWA (JAVA)

CHRISTMAS ISLAND
(Austl.)

Metres
Feet

3000
9840

2000
6560

1000
3280

500
1640

200
656

Sea Level

0

200
656

2000
6560

M-566700-7A-DR1-1º
Copyright © Rand McNally & Co.

East of Greenwich

Scale 1 : 10 000 000

Sinusoidal Projection

0 100 200 300 400 600 800 1000 km

0 100 200 300 400 500 600 miles

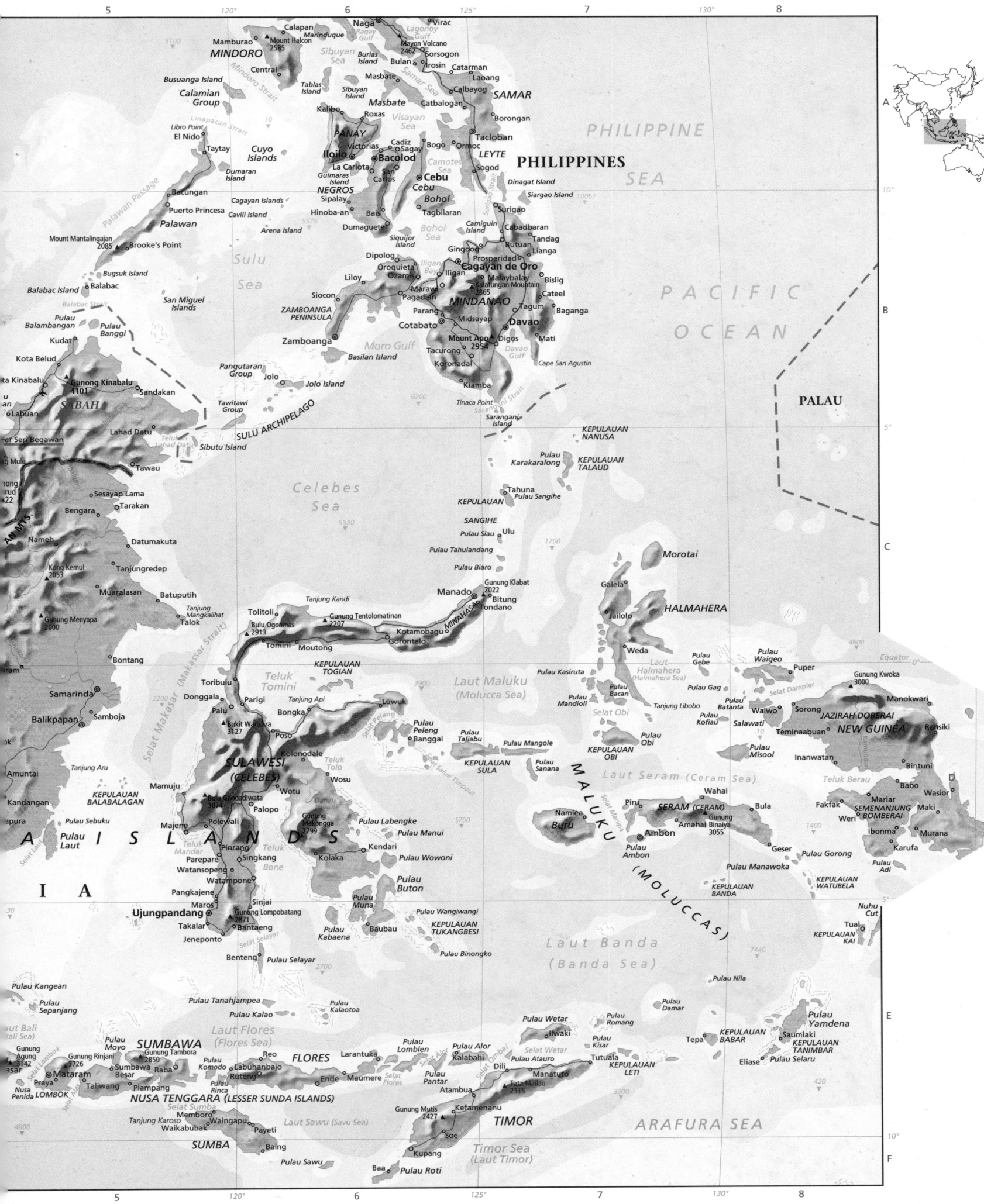

Metres
Feet

6000
19680

4000
13120

3000
9840

2000
6560

1000
3280

500
1640

200
656

0
Sea Level

200
656

2000
6560

| 0 | 200 | 400 | 800 | 1200 | 1600 km |

| 0 | 100 | 200 | 300 | 400 | 600 | 800 | 1000 miles |

Scale 1 : 15 000 000

Lambert Conformal Conic Projection

55° East of Greenwich 7

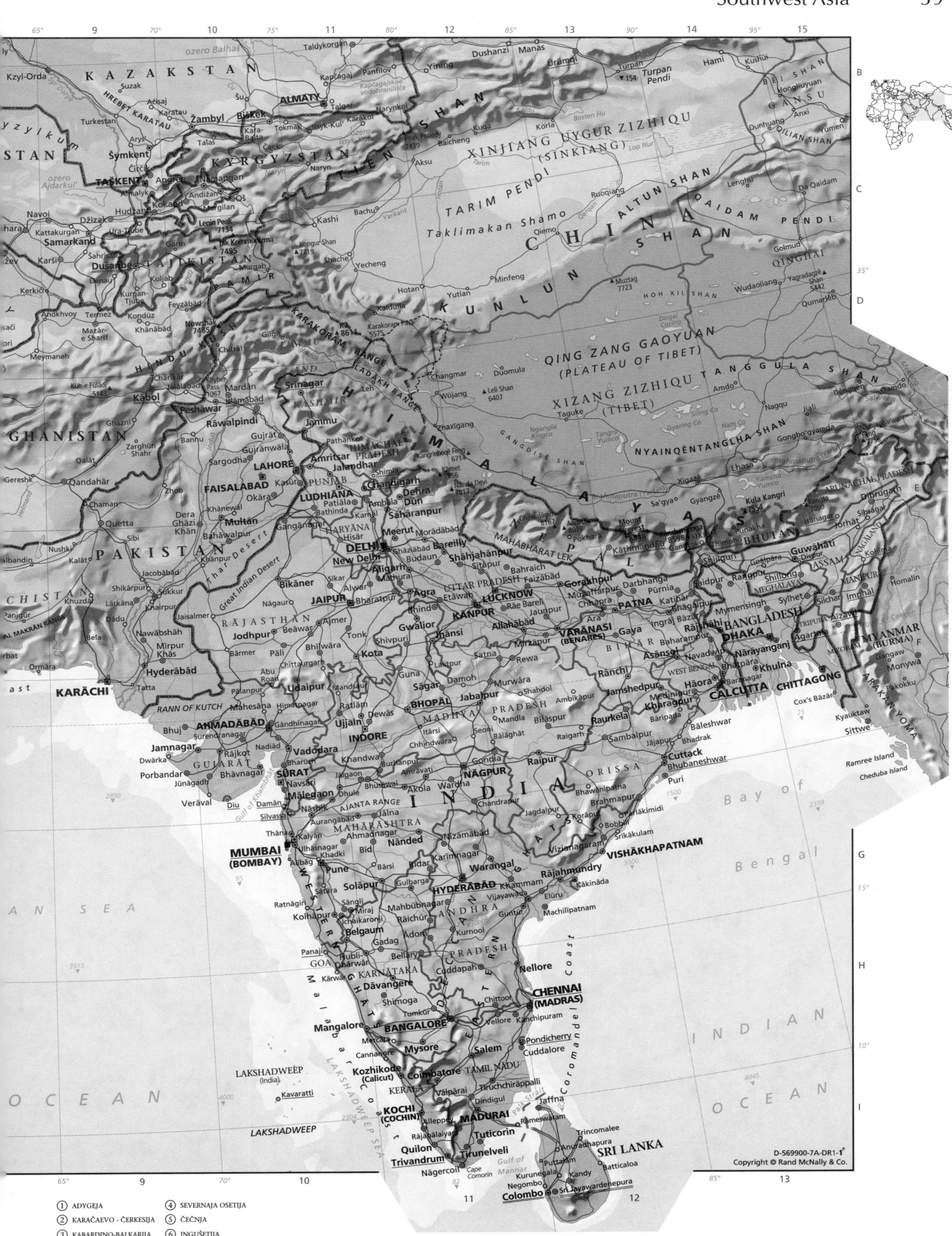

KAZAKSTAN

Kzyl-Orda   Suzak   Taldykorgan   Panfilov   Yining   Dushanzi   Manas   Hami   Kušuj

yzylkum   Arys   Kapčagaj   154   Honglituyuan   Honglituan   G A N S U

STAN   Turkestan   Karatau   HREBET KARATAU   Zambyl   Biškek   Naryn   Kuqa   TURPAN   Turpan Pendi   Anxi

ozero Balhas   ALMATY   Talgar   Narynkol   Kongur Shan   Urumqi   Dunhuang   Yumen   QILIAN SHAN

ozero Ajdarkul'   TASKENT   Almalyk   Naryn   Baicheng   XINJIANG UYGUR ZIZHIQU   (SINKIANG)   Lop Nur   QAIDAM PENDI

Šymkent   KYRGYZSTAN   Kashi   TARIM PENDI   ALTUN SHAN   Lenghu   Da Qaidam

Samarkand   Hudžand   Lenin Peak 7134   Yarkant   Taklimakan Shamo   C H I N A   QINGHAI

Karši   TADŽIKISTAN   Pik Kommunizma 7495   Shache   Yecheng   Muztag 7723   Wudaoliang   Yagradagzê 5442   Golmud

Dušanbe   PAMIR   Murgab   Hotan   HOH XIL SHAN   Qumarlêb

GHANISTAN   Feyzabad   Gilgit   KARAKORAM   Karakoram Pass   KUNLUN   SHAN   Dogai Coring   Qumarlêb

Kabol   HINDU KUSH   Chitral   JAMMU AND KASHMIR   LADAKH RANGE   Changmar   QING ZANG GAOYUAN   TANGGULA SHAN

Peshawar   Srinagar   Leh   Leli Shan 6407   (PLATEAU OF TIBET)   Amdo

Rawalpindi   Jammu   KASHMIR   XIZANG ZIZHIQU   (TIBET)   Nagqu   Jali

LAHORE   HIMACHAL PRADESH   Shimla   Taguke   NYAINQENTANGLHA SHAN   Lhasa

PAKISTAN   Amritsar   Jalandhar   H I M A L A Y A   Mount Everest   BHUTAN   ARUNACHAL PRADESH

FAISALABAD   PUNJAB   Chandigarh   Dehra Dun   NEPAL   Kathmandu   Thimphu   ASSAM

LUDHIANA   Patiala   Ambala   Saharanpur   MAHABHARAT LEK   Pokhara   Shiliguri   MEGHALAYA   NAGALAND

Multan   HARYANA   Meerut   Moradabad   Gorakhpur   Rajshahi   Shillong   MANIPUR

DELHI   Bareilly   Shahjahanpur   Muzaffarpur   Darbhanga   BANGLADESH   Imphal

New Delhi   Aligarh   Budaun   Sitapur   Bahraich   PATNA   DHAKA   MIZORAM   Homalin

JAIPUR   Mathura   UTTAR PRADESH   LUCKNOW   Faizabad   Gaya   Asansol   Khulna   MYANMAR (BURMA)

RAJASTHAN   Agra   KANPUR   Allahabad   VARANASI (BENARES)   BIHAR   CALCUTTA   CHITTAGONG   ARAKAN YOMA

Jodhpur   Gwalior   Jhansi   Satna   Rewa   Ranchi   Jamshedpur   Kharagpur   Cox's Bazar   Sittwe

Udaipur   BHOPAL   Jabalpur   MADHYA   PRADESH   Raurkela   WEST BENGAL   Haora

AHMADABAD   INDORE   Ujjain   Sagar   Damoh   Bilaspur   Sambalpur   Cuttack   Bhubaneshwar   Ramree Island

Jamnagar   GUJARAT   Vadodara   Baroda   NAGPUR   ORISSA   Puri   Cheduba Island

SURAT   AJANTA RANGE   I N D I A   Raipur   Brahmapur

MUMBAI (BOMBAY)   Nashik   MAHARASHTRA   Nanded   VISHAKHAPATNAM   Bay of

Pune   Solapur   HYDERABAD   Warangal   Rajahmundry   Bengal

Kolhapur   Belgaum   ANDHRA   Vijayawada   Machilipatnam

GOA   KARNATAKA   PRADESH   Nellore   CHENNAI (MADRAS)

Mangalore   BANGALORE   Salem   Pondicherry   INDIAN

LAKSHADWEEP (India)   Mysore   TAMIL NADU   Coromandel Coast

Kavaratti   Kozhikode (Calicut)   Coimbatore   OCEAN

LAKSHADWEEP   KOCHI (COCHIN)   MADURAI   Jaffna

OCEAN   Quilon   Tuticorin   Trincomalee

Trivandrum   Tirunelveli   SRI LANKA   Batticaloa

Nagercoil   Cape Comorin   Colombo   Sri Jayawardenepura   Kandy

D-569900-7A-DR1-1
Copyright © Rand McNally & Co.

① ADYGEJA   ④ SEVERNAJA OSETIJA
② KARAČAEVO - ČERKESIJA   ⑤ ČEČNJA
③ KABARDINO-BALKARIJA   ⑥ INGUŠETIJA

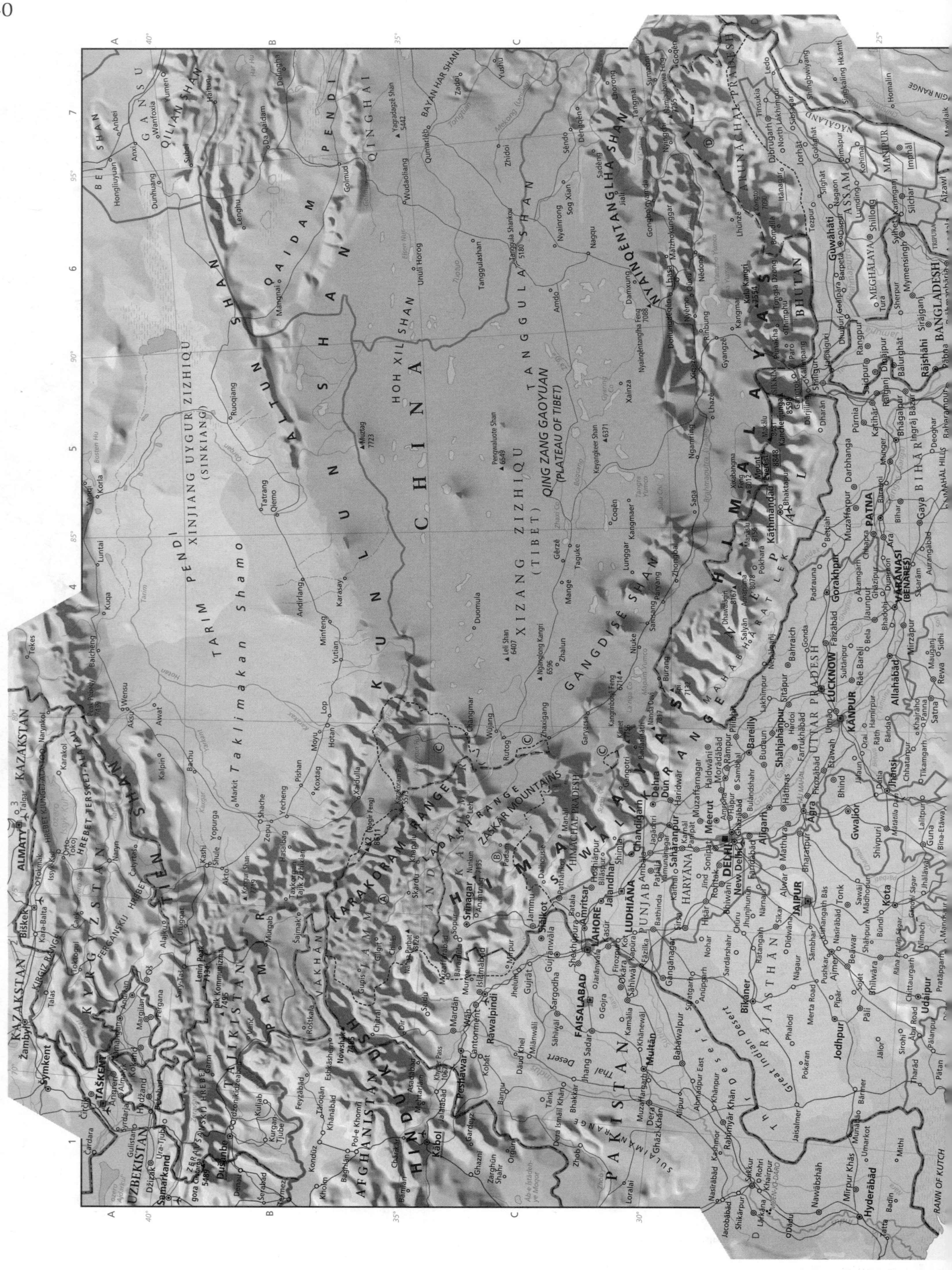
CHINA
XIZANG ZIZHIQU
(TIBET)
QING ZANG GAOYUAN
(PLATEAU OF TIBET)
XINJIANG UYGUR ZIZHIQU
(SINKIANG)
TARIM PENDI
Taklimakan Shamo
KUNLUN SHAN
ALTUN SHAN
QAIDAM PENDI
QINGHAI
GANSU
QILIAN SHAN
HOH XIL SHAN
TANGGULA SHAN
NYAINQÊNTANGLHA SHAN
GANGDISÊ SHAN
HIMALAYAS
KARAKORAM RANGE
HINDU KUSH
PAMIR
TIEN SHAN
KAZAKSTAN
KYRGYZSTAN
TAJIKISTAN
UZBEKISTAN
AFGHANISTAN
PAKISTAN
INDIA
NEPAL
BHUTAN
BANGLADESH
PUNJAB
HARYANA
HIMACHAL PRADESH
UTTAR PRADESH
RAJASTHAN
BIHAR
ASSAM
MEGHALAYA
ARUNACHAL PRADESH
NAGALAND
MANIPUR
Great Indian Desert
Thal Desert
ZASKAR MOUNTAINS
LADAKH RANGE
SULAIMAN RANGE
RANN OF KUTCH
DELHI
New Delhi
LAHORE
FAISALABAD
Rawalpindi
Islāmābād
Peshāwar
Kābol
Dušanbe
TAŠKENT
ALMATY
Biškek
Samarkand
Kāthmāndau
Lhasa
JAIPUR
KANPUR
LUCKNOW
PATNA
VĀRĀNASI
(BENARES)
Mount Everest
8848

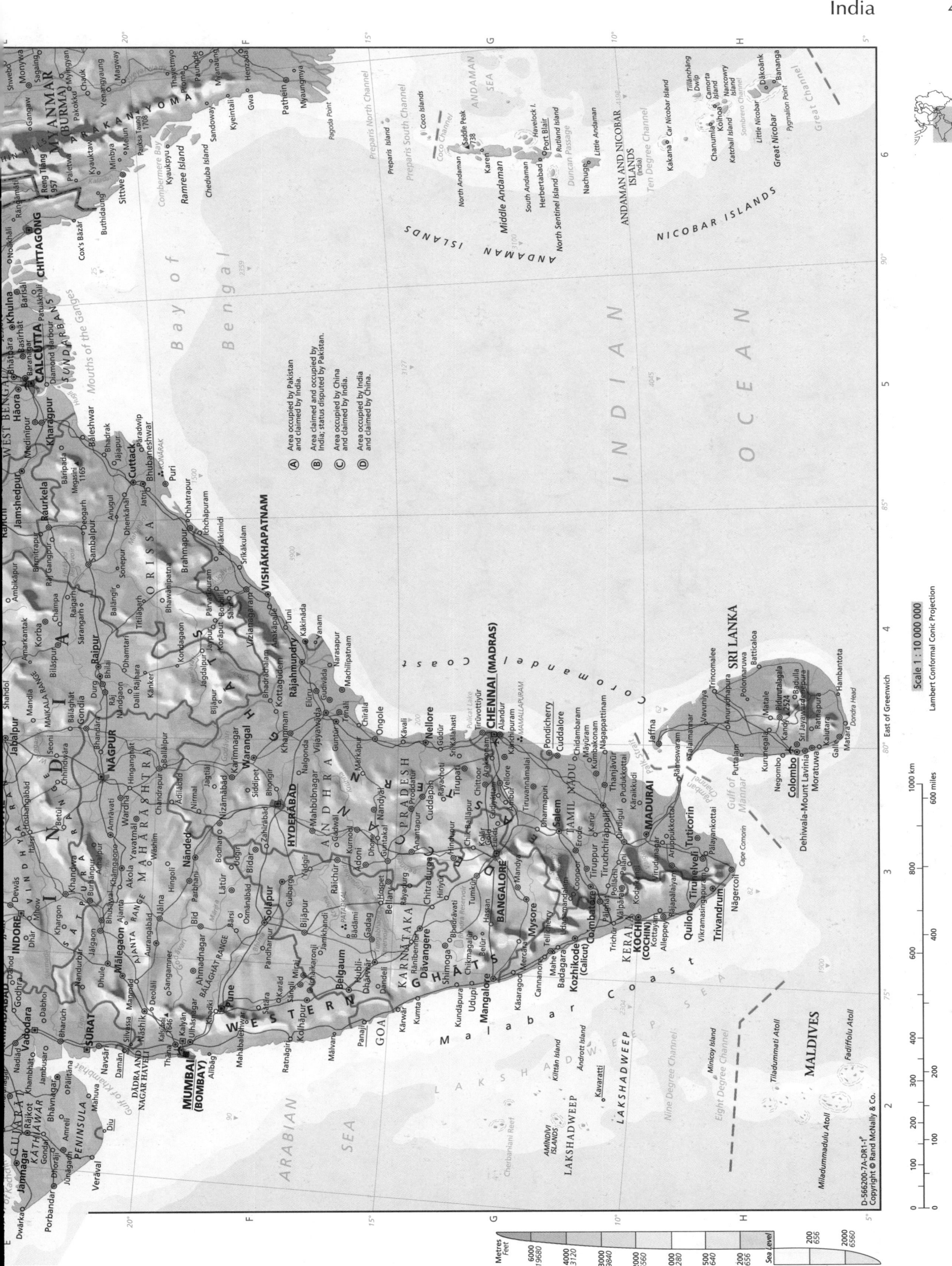

Area occupied by Pakistan and claimed by India.

Area claimed and occupied by India; status disputed by Pakistan.

Area occupied by China and claimed by India.

Area occupied by India and claimed by China.

Scale 1 : 10 000 000

Lambert Conformal Conic Projection

East of Greenwich

Metres / Feet
6000 / 19680
4000 / 13120
3000 / 9840
2000 / 6560
1000 / 3280
500 / 1640
200 / 656
Sea level
200 / 656
2000 / 6560

D-566200-7A-DR1-1°
Copyright © Rand McNally & Co.

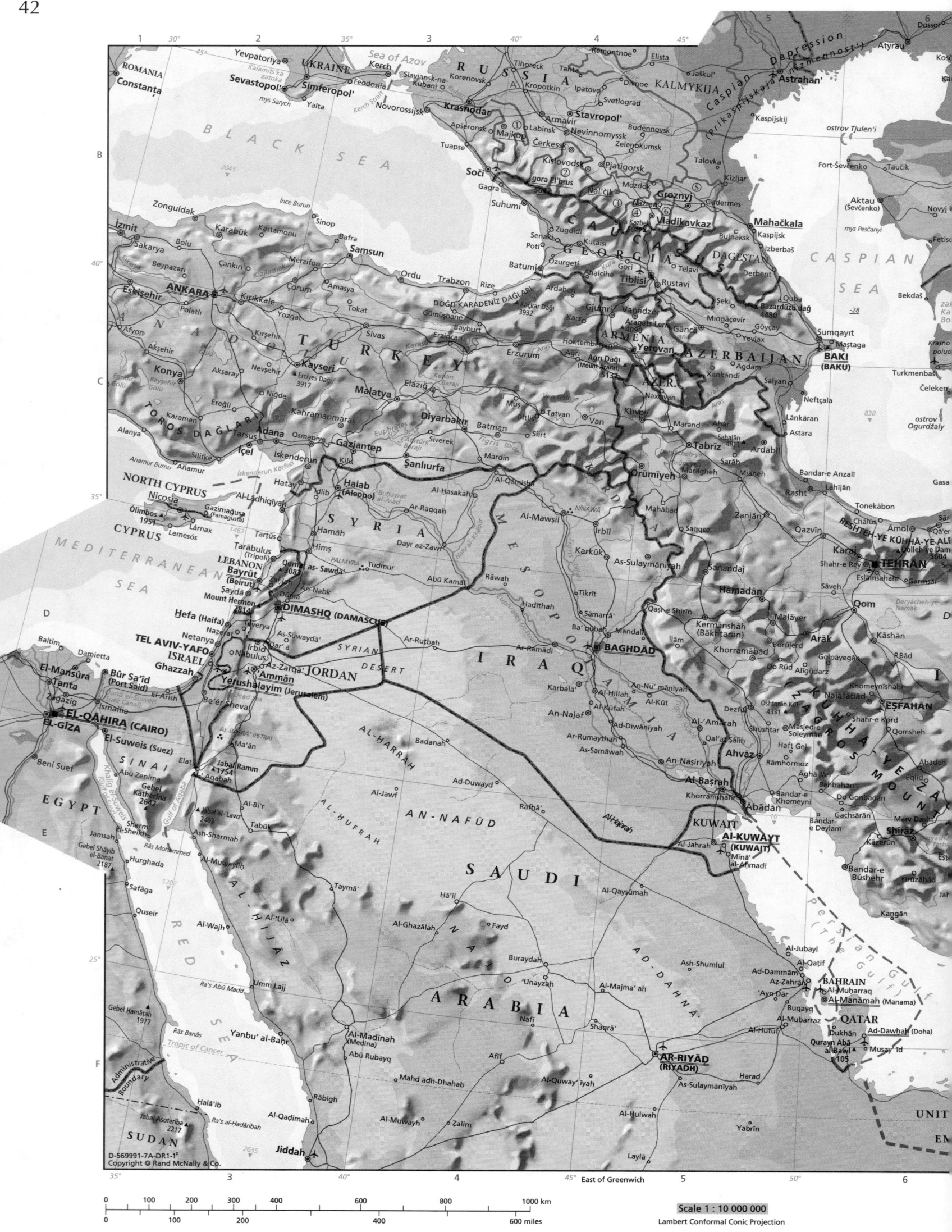

Scale 1 : 10 000 000

Lambert Conformal Conic Projection

KAZAKSTAN

Aral Sea

UST-URT PLATEAU

KYZYLKUM

UZBEKISTAN

TURKMENISTAN

GARAGUMY

KYRGYZSTAN

TIEN SHAN

CHINA

TAJIKISTAN

PAMIR

KARAKORAM RANGE

HINDU KUSH

JAMMU AND KASHMIR

AFGHANISTAN

PAKISTAN

BALUCHISTAN

CENTRAL MAKRAN RANGE

KIRTHAR RANGE

TOBA KAKAR RA.

SULAIMAN RANGE

Thal Desert

Thar Desert

Great Indian Desert

INDIA

RAJASTHAN

GUJARAT

KATHIAWAR PENINSULA

RANN OF KUTCH

OMAN

AL JABAL AL-AKHDAR

Gulf of Oman

Makran Coast

ARABIAN SEA

Strait of Hormuz

Tropic of Cancer

Selected cities and towns:

ALMATY, Biškek, TAŠKENT, Žambyl, Šymkent, Kzyl-Orda, Nukus, Dašhovuz, Urgenč, Hiva, Buhara, Samarkand, Dušanbe, Ašgabat, MASHHAD, Neyšābūr, Herāt, KĀBOL, Peshāwar, Rāwalpindi, Islāmābād, Srīnagar, LAHORE, FAISALĀBĀD, Amritsar, Siālkot, Multan, Qandahār, Quetta, Zāhedān, Kermān, Bam, KARĀCHI, Hyderābād, Sukkur, Bīkāner, Jodhpur, AHMADĀBĀD, Vadodara, SŪRAT, Masqat, Dubayy (Dubai), Bandar-e 'Abbās

Elevation scale:

Metres	Feet
6000	19680
4000	13120
3000	9840
2000	6560
1000	3280
500	1640
200	656
Sea Level	0
200	656
2000	6560

① ADYGEJA   ④ SEVERNAJA OSETIJA
② KARAČAEVO-ČERKESIJA   ⑤ ČEČNJA
③ KABARDINO-BALKARIJA   ⑥ INGUŠETIJA

BLACK SEA

BULGARIA

STARA PLANINA

Sliven
Aitos
Jambol
Nesebår
Pomorie
Burgas
Burgaski Zaliv
Sozopol
Elhovo
Rezovo

Komotiní
Kırklareli
İğneada
Kıyıköy
Edirne
Babaeski
Lüleburgaz
Saray
Karaköy
Uzunköprü
Hayrabolu
Çorlu
İSTANBUL
Şile
Ağva
Karasu
Alexandroúpolis
Ipsala
Malkara
Tekirdağ
Şilivri
Yeşilköy
Gebze
İzmit
Hendek
Keşan
Enez
Kadıköy
Marmara Denizi
Yalova
Gölcük
Sakarya
Düzce
Mengen
Samothráki
Gelibolu
Şarköy
Marmara Adası
İzmit Körfezi
Gemlik
Gemlik Körfezi
Yenişehir
Bolu
Gökçeada
İmroz
Eceabat
Lâpseki
Biga
Bandırma
Karacabey
Bursa
İnegöl
Bilecik
Göynük
Mudurnu

KÜRE DAĞLARI
Kerempe Burnu
İnebolu
Ayancık
Sinop
İnce Burun
Kurucaşile
Cide
Bafra Burnu
Gerze
Zonguldak
Kilimli
Azdavay
Taşköprü
Alaçam
Bafra
Samsun
Ereğli
Devrek
Karabük
Ilgaz
Kastamonu
Boyabat
Duragan
Çarşamba
Ünye
Fatsa
Akçakoca
Safranbolu
Araç
Kargı
Vezirköprü
Havza
Terme
Osmancık
Amasya
Merzifon
Niksar
Reşadiye

MEDITERRANEAN SEA

In November 1983 Turkish Cypriots unilaterally declared their independence as the Turkish Republic of Northern Cyprus. A United Nations buffer zone now runs across the island.

NORTH CYPRUS

CYPRUS

Area occupied by Israel since June 1967
(A) Golan Heights: occupied by Israel
(B) West Bank: parts occupied by Israel

Scale 1 : 5 000 000
Lambert Conformal Conic Projection

D-563700-7A-DR1-1"
Copyright © Rand McNally & Co.

CASPIAN SEA

Countries
RUSSIA
GEORGIA
ARMENIA
AZERBAIJAN
IRAN
IRAQ
SYRIA / SYRIAN DESERT
SAUDI ARABIA

Regions / Features
KARAÇAEVO-ÇERKESIJA
KABARDINO-BALKARIJA
SEVERNAJA OSETIJA
INGUŠETIJA
ČEČNJA
DAGESTAN
CAUCASUS
LESSER CAUCASUS
DOĞU KARADENİZ DAĞLARI
REŞEN DAĞ
MUNZUR DAĞLARI
BİNGÖL DAĞLARI
HACREŞ DAĞLARI
KEŞİŞ DAĞLARI
MESOPOTAMIA
JABAL SINJÂR
JABAL 'ABD AL-'AZÎZ
JABAL BISHRÎ
KÛHHÂ-YE TÂVÂLEŞ
KÛHHÂ-YE ZAGROS
KABÎR KÛH
Van Gölü
Atatürk Baraj
NINAWÁ (NINEVEH)

Cities and towns
Soči, Adler, Gagra, Gudauta, Suhumi, Očamčira, Gali, Zugdidi, Senaki, Poti, Sapitredia, Ozurgeti, Batumi, Hopa, Kutaisi, Tkibuli, Čiatura, Zestafoni, Gori, Tbilisi, Rustavi, Telavi, Kvareli, Gurdžaani, Kaspi, Dušeti, Ahalcihe, Bakuriani, Boržomi, Hašuri, Ahalkalaki, Posof, Bolnisi, Dmanisi, Zemo-Kedi, Dedoplis Ckaro, Signaği

Nal'čik, Terek, Beslan, Nazran', Vladikavkaz, Alagir, Itum-Kale, Botlih, Bujnaksk, Mahačkala, Kaspijsk, Izberbaš, Levaši, Sergokala, Gunib, Bežta, Vači, Madžalis, Derbent, Kasumkent, Rutul, Usuhčaj, Jalama, Xaçmaz, Quba, Qonaqkänd, Siyäzän, Altiağac, İsmayıllı, Oğuz, Şäki, Zaqatala, Qäbälä, Göyçay, Mingäçevir, Şämkir, Gäncä, Yevlax, Bärdä, Tärtär, Ağdam, Kürdämir, Sabirabad, İmişli, Saatlı, Äli Bayramlı, Füzuli, Xankändi, Qazımämmäd, Qobustan, Salyan, Biläsuvar, Neftçala, Bilä Su var, Garmi, Bälän Şafar 'Ali, Yardımlı, Länkäran, Astara, Namin, Ästärä, Ardabīl, Havīq, Sumqayıt, Maştağa, BAKI (BAKU), Suiti burnu

Trabzon, Rize, Pazar, Ardeşen, Artvin, Yusufeli, Şavşat, Ardahan, Çıldır, Tirebolu, Akçaabat, Of, Maçka, Gümüşhane, Bayburt, Oltu, Göle, Kars, Sarıkamış, Arpaçay, Gjumri, Artik, Vanadzor, Sevan, Şamkir, Mescit Tepe, Kelkit, Refahiye, Erzincan, Tercan, Aşkale, Erzurum, Narman, Pasinler, Horasan, Ağrı, Tutak, Kağızman, Iğdır, Hoktemberjan, Yerevan, Artashat, Ararat, Ashtarak, Aragats Lerr, Kamo, Martuni, Naxçıvan, Culfa, Kapan, Meghri, Ahar, Kaleybar, Meshgīn Shahr, Şabälän, Khalkhāl, Bandar-e Anzalī, Fowman

Gevaş, Van, Tatvan, Ahlat, Adilcevaz, Muş, Bulanık, Malazgirt, Erciş, Muradiye, Zūrābād, Qoṭūr, Khvoy, Marand, Sūfīān, Oşkū, Tabrīz, Sarāb, Āzar Shahr, Kūh-e Sahand, Ajab Shir, Marāgheh, Mīāneh, Bonāb, Malek Kandi, Mīāndoāb, Naqadeh, Mahābād, Sardasht, Sa'īn Dezh, Şāh Īndarjān, Ş Zanjān, Takāb, Saqqez, Baneh, Qeydār, Abhar

Diyarbakır, Bismil, Batman, Kurtalan, Siirt, Pervari, Çukurca, Hakkâri, Çatak, Başkale, Oromīyeh, Silvāneh, Piranşahr, Rāniyah, Bitlis, Hazro, Silvan, Kulp, Lice, Genç, Palu, Maden, Ergani, Elazığ, Hankendi, Hilvan, Siverek, Viranşehir, Çınar, Savur, Midyat, Mardin, Kızıltepe, Nusaybin, Derik, Findik, Şırnak, Cizre, İdil, Zakho, Al-'Amādīyah, Dahūk, 'Aqrah, Rawāndūz, Şanlıurfa, Sürüç, Akçakale, Ceylanpınar, Ra's al-'Ayn, 'Āmūdah, Al-Qāmishlī, Tall Kūjik, Tall Tamir, Al-Hasakah, Ash Shaddādah, Sinjār, Tall 'Afar, Al-Mawṣil (Mosul), Irbīl, As-Sulaymānīyah, Halabjah, Pāveh, Ar-Raqqah, Suwaydah, As-Suwār, Dayr az-Zawr, Al-Mayādīn, Abū Kamāl, Al Qā'im, Akāshāt, Ar-Ruṭbah, Ḥadīthah, 'Ānah, Būşayrah, Ash-Sharqāt, Al-Hadr, Tāwūq, Karkūk, Kifrī, Tuz, Tikrīt, Sāmarrā', Khānaqīn, Jalūlā', Qasr-e Shīrīn, Gīlān-e Gharb, Sūmār, Eslāmābād, Kermānshāh (Bākhtarān), Harsin, Sanandaj, Qorveh, Bījār, Ḥoseynābād, Divāndarreh, Kabūdarāhang, Bahār, Hamadān, Asadābād, Tūyserkān, Nahāvand, Malāyer, Kangāvar, Sahneh, Songor

Balad, Al-Khāliṣ, Ba'qūbah, Al Miqdādīyah, Mandalī, Mehrān, Ābdānān, Īlām, Kūhdasht, Khorramābād, Borūjerd, Dehlorān, Andimeshk, Dezfūl, Shūsh, Gatvand, Shūshtar, Hūzgān, Ahvāz

BAGHDAD, Ar-Ramādī, Al-Fallūjah, Karbalā', Al-Musayyab, ATLĀL BĀBIL (BABYLON), Al-Hindīyah, Al-Hillah, Al-Kifl, Ash-Shāmīyah, An-Nu'mānīyah, Al-Kūt, Shaykh Sa'd, 'Alī al-Gharbī, Al-'Amārah, Qal'at Sālih, Shithāthah, An Nukhayb, Al-Kūfah, An-Najaf, Ad-Dīwānīyah, Ar-Rumaythah, Ash-Shināfīyah, As-Samāwah, Qal'at Sukkar, Ash-Shaṭrah, An-Nāṣirīyah, Al-Qurnah, Al-Ḥalfāyah, Bostān, Sūsangerd

Jabal 'Unayzah 940, Al-Hamād, Al-Jalāmīd, Suwār

Elevations
gora El'brus 5642, gora Šhara 5068, gora Tebulosmta 4492, gori Karbek 5047, perevali Mamisonskij 2829, perevali Krestovyj 2379, Bazardüzü dağ 4480, Aragats Lerr 4090, Gämiş dağ 3724, Kaçkar Dağı 3932, Süphan Dağı 4058, Tendürek Dağı 3533, Ağrı Dağı (Mount Ararat) 5137, Aşağı Dağı 3275, Kuh-e Sahand 3712, Qazangöldağ 3829, Şabälän 4814, Cilo Dağı 4168, Karaca Dağ 1957, Kop Geçidi 2430, Keşiş Dağları 3230

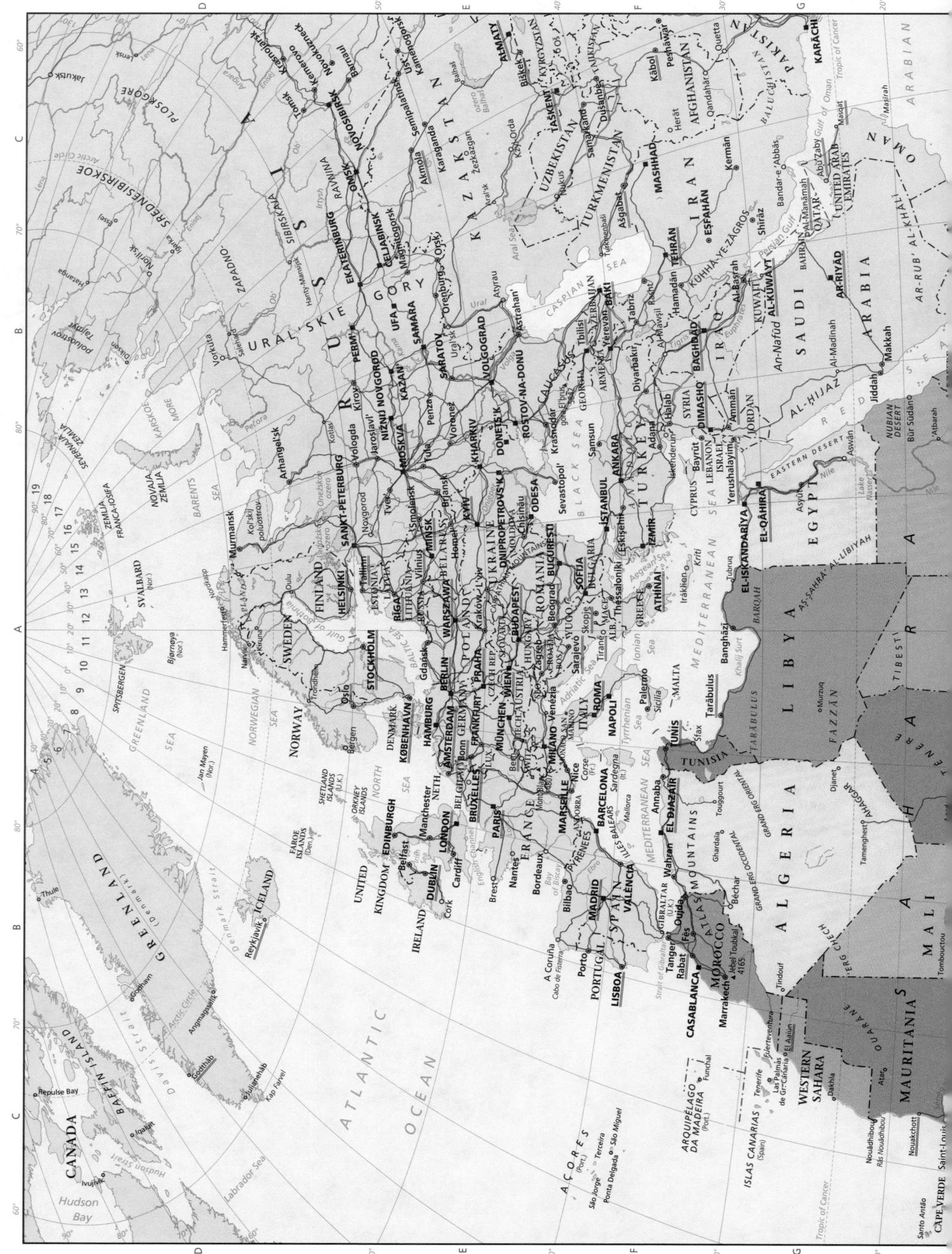

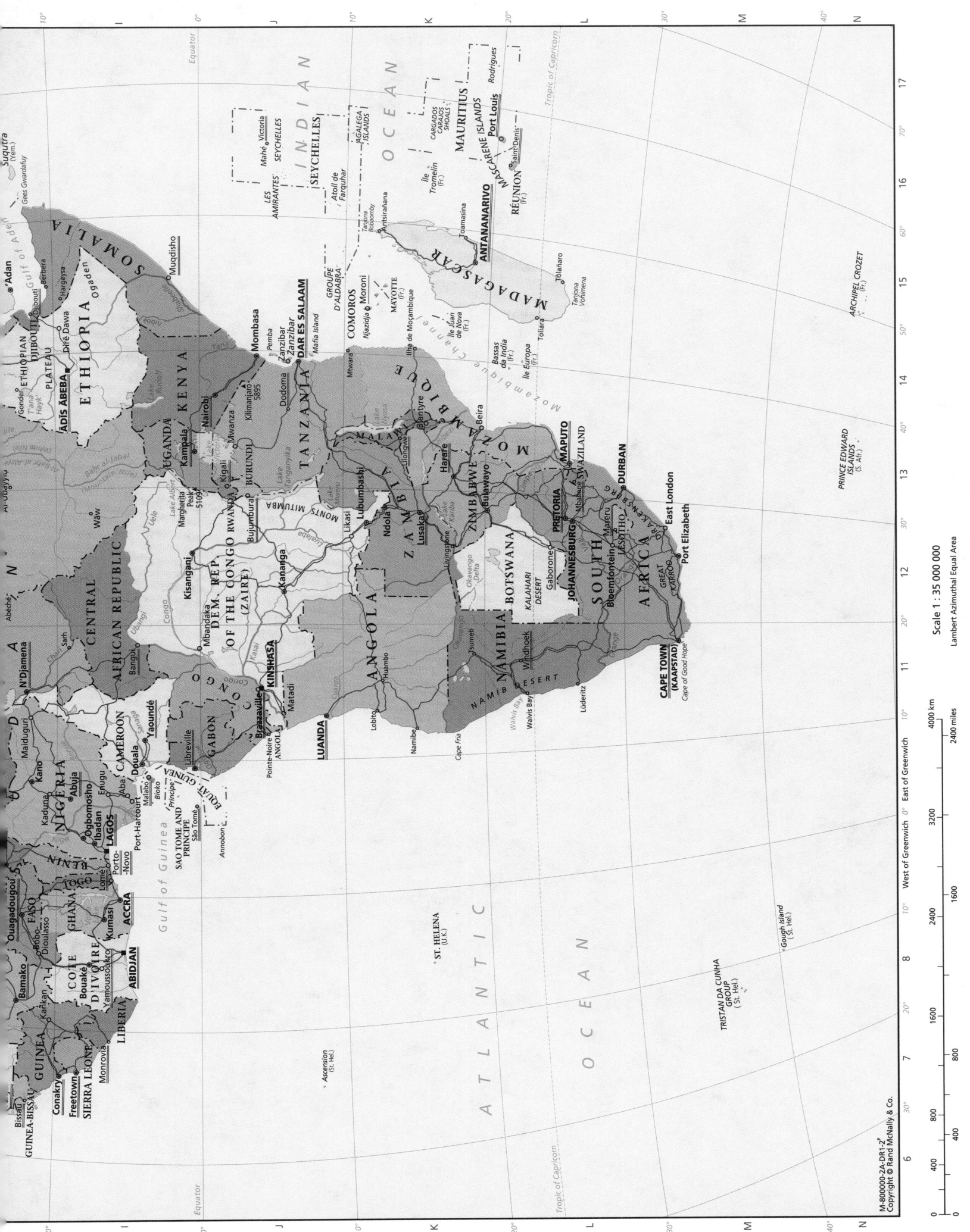

Scale 1 : 35 000 000
Lambert Azimuthal Equal Area

M-800000-2A-DR1-2
Copyright © Rand McNally & Co.

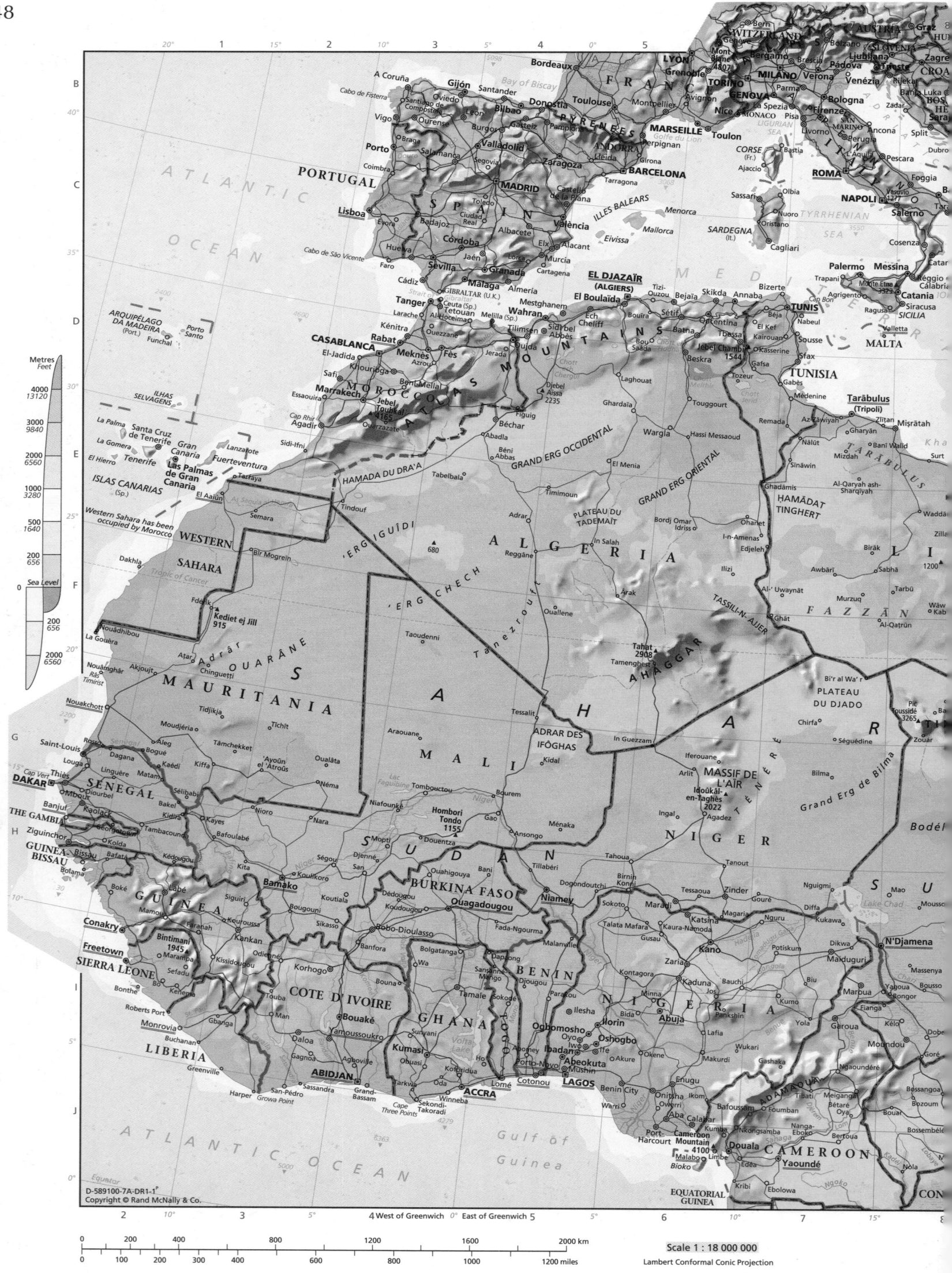

ATLANTIC OCEAN

PORTUGAL

Lisboa

SPAIN

MADRID

Barcelona

PYRENEES

FRANCE

LYON

TORINO

MILANO

GENOVA

MARSEILLE

CORSE (Fr.)

ROMA

NAPOLI

SARDEGNA (It.)

ILLES BALEARS

MEDITERRANEAN

TYRRHENIAN SEA

Palermo

SICILIA

Catania

MALTA

TUNIS

TUNISIA

Tarābulus (Tripoli)

TARĀBULUS

EL DJAZAÏR (ALGIERS)

ATLAS MOUNTAINS

CASABLANCA

Rabat

MOROCCO

Marrakech

Agadir

ALGERIA

GRAND ERG OCCIDENTAL

GRAND ERG ORIENTAL

PLATEAU DU TADEMAÏT

HAMĀDAT TINGHERT

FAZZĀN

WESTERN SAHARA

Western Sahara has been occupied by Morocco

El Aaiún

Tropic of Cancer

Dakhla

MAURITANIA

OUARÂNE

Nouakchott

ADRAR

Nouâdhibou

S A H A R A

AHAGGAR

Tahat 2908

PLATEAU DU DJADO

MALI

ADRAR DES IFÔGHAS

DAKAR

SENEGAL

THE GAMBIA

GUINEA-BISSAU

GUINEA

Conakry

Freetown

SIERRA LEONE

Bamako

S U D A N

BURKINA FASO

Ouagadougou

NIGER

Niamey

N'Djamena

Lake Chad

LIBERIA

Monrovia

COTE D'IVOIRE

Bouaké

Yamoussoukro

ABIDJAN

GHANA

Kumasi

ACCRA

Lomé

BENIN

Porto-Novo

Cotonou

LAGOS

NIGERIA

Abuja

Kano

Kaduna

CAMEROON

Yaoundé

Douala

EQUATORIAL GUINEA

ATLANTIC OCEAN

Gulf of Guinea

Equator

D-589100-7A-DR1-1
Copyright © Rand McNally & Co.

Metres / Feet
4000 / 13120
3000 / 9840
2000 / 6560
1000 / 3280
500 / 1640
200 / 656
Sea Level
200 / 656
2000 / 6560

Scale 1 : 18 000 000
Lambert Conformal Conic Projection

0   200   400   800   1200   1600   2000 km
0   100   200   300   400   600   800   1000   1200 miles

West of Greenwich   East of Greenwich

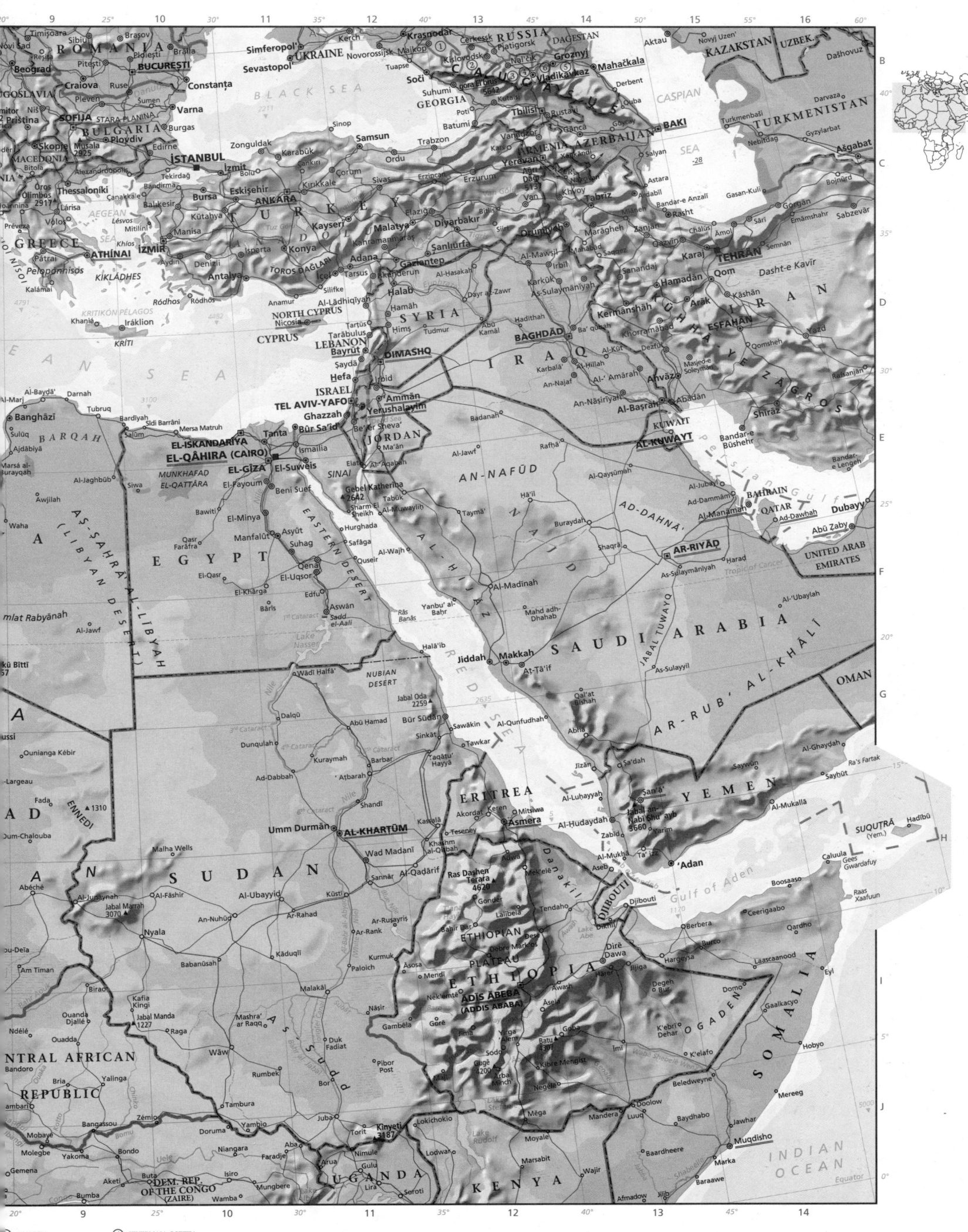

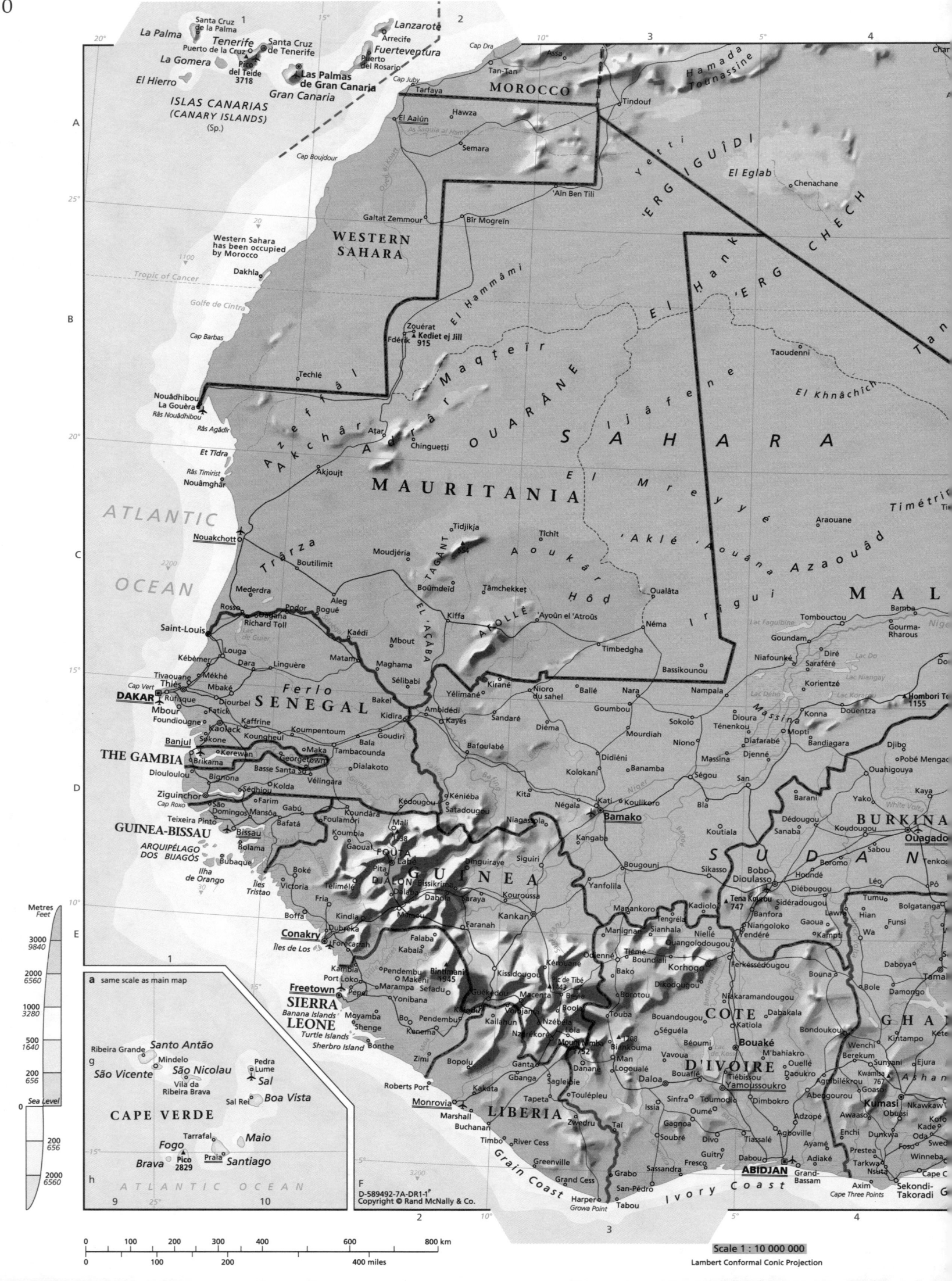

A

B

C

D

E

F

ATLANTIC

OCEAN

Santa Cruz
de la Palma
La Palma
Tenerife
Puerto de la Cruz
Santa Cruz
de Tenerife
La Gomera
Pico
del Teide
3718
Las Palmas
de Gran Canaria
El Hierro
Gran Canaria

ISLAS CANARIAS
(CANARY ISLANDS)
(Sp.)

Lanzarote
Arrecife
Fuerteventura
Puerto
del Rosario

Cap Dra

MOROCCO

Hamada
Tounassine

Assa

Tan-Tan

Cap Juby
Tarfaya

Hawza

Semara

'ERG IGUÎDI

El Eglab

Chenachane

Cap Boujdour

Western Sahara
has been occupied
by Morocco

Dakhla

Tropic of Cancer

Golfe de Cintra

Cap Barbas

**WESTERN
SAHARA**

Tindouf

Yetti

Galtat Zemmour

Bir Mogreïn

'Aïn Ben Tili

El Hank

Taoudenni

'ERG CHECH

El Khnâchich

Techlé

Zouérat
Fdérik
Kediet ej Jill
915

El Ḥammâmi

Adrâr Maqţeir

Nouâdhibou
La Goüèra
Râs Nouâdhibou

Azefâl

Akchâr

OUARÂNE

Ijâfene

Araouane

S A H A R A

Timétrine

Râs Agâdir

Et Tidra

Atar
Chinguetti

El Mreyyé

'Aklé 'Aouâna Azaouâd

Râs Timirist
Nouâmghâr

Akjoujt

Irrgui

M A L

Tidjikja

Tichît

Aoukâr

Araouane

Nouakchott

Trârza

Boutilimit

Moudjéria

Ḥôḍ

Oualâta

Gourma-
Rharous

Niger

Bamba

Mederdra

Aleg
Boghé

Kiffa

Ayoûn el 'Atroûs

Néma

Tombouctou

Goundam

Rosso
Dagana
Richard Toll
Lac
de Guier

Podor

Kaédi

EL 'ACÂBA

Timbedgha

Niafounké
Diré
Saraféré

Lac Do

Saint-Louis

Louga
Dara
Linguère

Mbout

Maghama

Sélibabi

Bassikounou

Lac Débo
Lac Niangay

Lac Korarou

Kébèmer

Matam

Kirané

Nampala

Massina

Hombori
1155

Tivaouane
Cap Vert
Thiès
DAKAR
Rufisque
Diourbel
Mbaké

Mékhé

Ferlo

Bakel

Yélimané

Nioro
du sahel

Ballé

Nara

Goumbou

Konna

Douentza

Mbour
Fatick

Fandougoune
Kaolack

SENEGAL

Kidira

Ambidédi
Kayes

Sandaré

Diéma

Sokoto

Ténenkou

Mopti

Bandiagara

Kaffrine

Koumpentoum

Goudiri

Mourdiah

Niono

Diafarabé

Djibo

Pobé Mengao

Banjul
Sokone
Kerewan
THE GAMBIA
Brikama

Koungheul
Maka
Georgetown
Basse Santa Su

Bala
Tambacounda
Dialakoto
Vélingara

Bafoulabé

Kolokani
Banamba

Massina
Djenné

Ségou
San

Barani

Ouahigouya

Yako

Kaya

Dioulouloi
Bignona

Ziguinchor
Cap Roxo
Séo
Teixeira Pinto
São
Domingos Mansôa

Sédhiou
Kolda

Farim
Gabú

Koundara
Foulamôri

Kédougou
Satadougou

Kita

Négala
Kati
Koulikoro

Bla

Dédougou

Koudougou

BURKINA

Ouagado

Bafatá

Koumbia

Mali
158

Niagassola

Bamako

Koutiala
Sanaba

GUINEA-BISSAU

Bolama

ARQUIPÉLAGO
DOS BIJAGÓS
Ilha
de Orango

Gaoual

Boké

FOUTA
DJALON
Pita
Dalaba

Dinguiraye

Siguiri

Kangaba

Bougouni

Sikasso

Bobo-
Dioulasso

Houndé

Boromo

Léo

Pô

Bubaque

Îles
Tristao

Victoria

Télimélé

Bissikrima

Dabola

Koussa

Kankan

Maganboro

Kadiolo
Tena Kourou
747

Sidéradougou
Diébougou

SUDAN

Tumu

Bolgatanga

Boffa

Fria

Kindia

Mamou

Faranah

Kouroussa

Yanfolila

Banfora

Niangoloko
Pendéré

Lawra
Hian

Funsi

Conakry
Îles de Los

Dubréka
Forécariah

Falaba

Kabala

Kérouané

Odienné
Tiémé
Boundiali

Ouangolodougou

Gaoua
Kampti

Wa

Kambia
Port Loko
Marampa

Pendembu
Makeni
Sefadu

Kissidougou

Pic de Tibé
1973

Bako

Korhogo

Ferkéssédougou

Bouna

Daboya

Freetown
**SIERRA
LEONE**
Banana Islands
Turtle Islands
Sherbro Island

Moyamba
Shenge
Bonthe

Yonibana
Bo
Kenema

Pendembu

Guéckédou
Macenta

Beyla

Borotou

Bouandougou

Niakaramandougou

Dikodougou

Katiola

Bondoukou

Bole

Damongo

Zimi

Bopolu

Ganta

Nzérékoré
Mount Nimba
1752

Touba

COTE

Séguéla

Vavoua

Bouaké
M'Bahiakro

Wenchi

Kintampo

Ejura

Roberts Port

Gbanga

Danané
Logoualé
Man

Bouaflé

Daoukro

Kwamé
767

Sunyani

Berekum

Goas

Monrovia
Marshall

LIBERIA
Buchanan

Kakata
Tapeta

Toulépleu
Gagnoa

D'IVOIRE
Yamoussoukro
Tiébissou

Sinfra
Toumodi

Oumé

Issia

Daloa

Divo

Abengourou

Agnibilékrou

Adzopé

Kumasi
Obuasi

Nkawkaw

Koforidua
Kade
Dunkwa

Timbo

River Cess

Greenville

Zwedru

Tai

Sassandra

Soubré

Guitry

Tiassalé

Dabou

Ayamé

Aboisso

Prestea
Tarkwa

Oda

Winneba

Cape Coast

Sekondi-
Takoradi

Grand Cess

Grabo

Grand-
Bassam

Axim
Cape Three Points

Harper
Growa Point

San-Pédro

ABIDJAN

Tabou

Grain Coast

Ivory Coast

D-589492-7A-DR1-1
Copyright © Rand McNally & Co.

Metres
Feet
3000
9840
2000
6560
1000
3280
500
1640
200
656
0
Sea Level
200
656
2000
6560

a same scale as main map

Ribeira Grande
Santo Antão
Mindelo
São Vicente
São Nicolau
Pedra
Lume
Sal
Vila da
Ribeira Brava
Sal Rei
Boa Vista

CAPE VERDE

Tarrafal
Fogo
Maio
Brava
Pico
2829
Praia
Santiago

ATLANTIC OCEAN

0 100 200 300 400 600 800 km

0 100 200 400 miles

Scale 1 : 10 000 000

Lambert Conformal Conic Projection

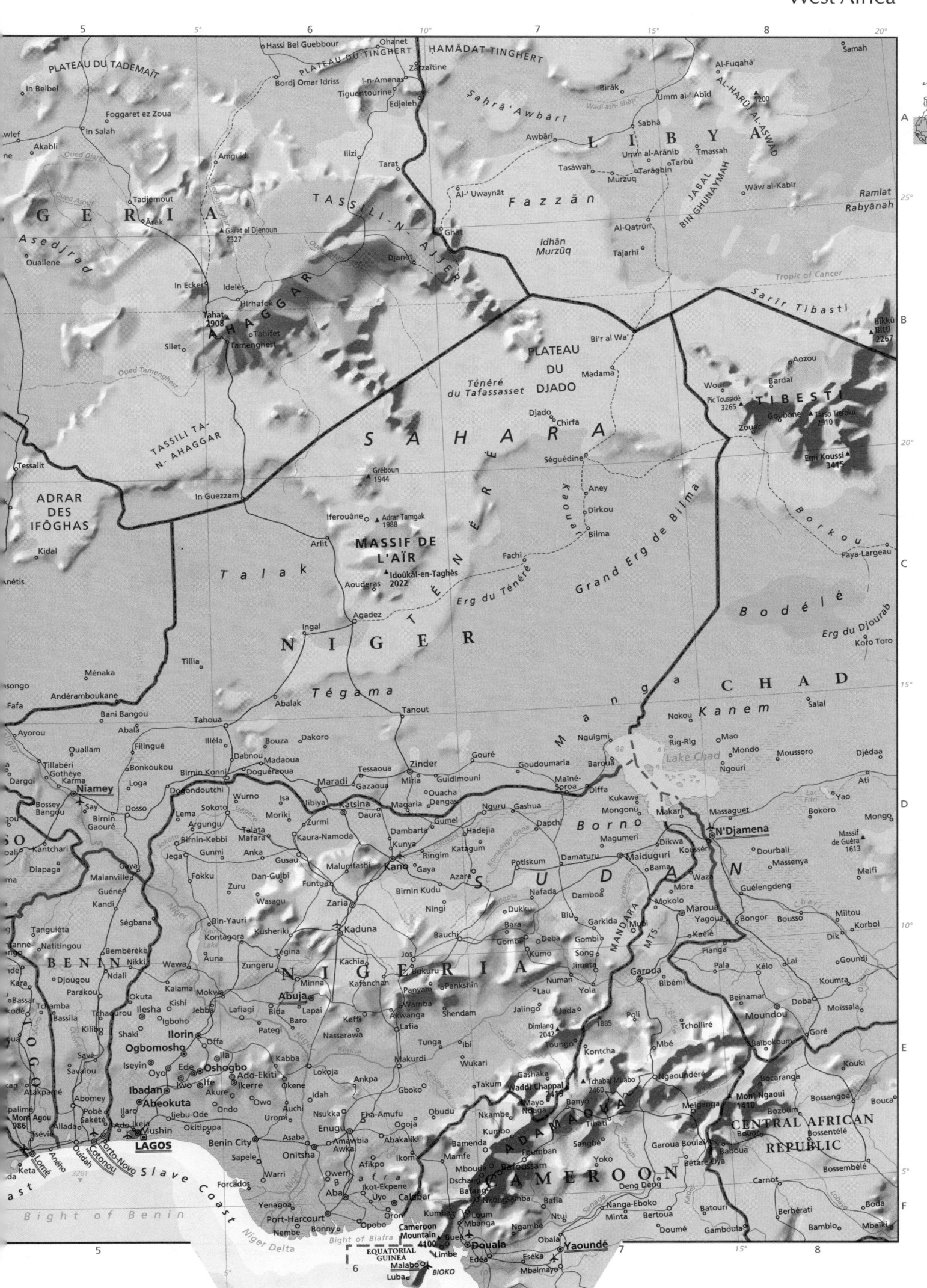

ATLANTIC

OCEAN

Tropic of Capricorn

Metres	Feet
4000	13120
3000	9840
2000	6560
1000	3280
500	1640
200	656
0	Sea Level
200	656
2000	6560

NIGERIA
CAMEROON
CENTRAL AFRICAN REPUBLIC
SUDAN
UGANDA
EQUATORIAL GUINEA
SAO TOME AND PRINCIPE
GABON
CONGO
DEM. REP. OF THE CONGO (ZAIRE)
RWANDA
BURUNDI
TANZANIA
ANGOLA
ZAMBIA
MALAWI
MOZAMBIQUE
NAMIBIA
ZIMBABWE
BOTSWANA
KALAHARI DESERT
SOUTH AFRICA
LESOTHO
SWAZILAND
MAPUTO
PRETORIA
JOHANNESBURG
CAPE TOWN (KAAPSTAD)

D-589200-7A-DR1-1°
Copyright © Rand McNally & Co.

| 0 | 200 | 400 | 800 | 1200 | 1600 | 2000 km |
| 0 | 100 | 200 | 400 | 600 | 800 | 1000 | 1200 miles |

East of Greenwich

Scale 1 : 18 000 000
Lambert Conformal Conic Projection

ETHIOPIA

Kibre Mengist
Imi
K'elafo
Negele
Gaalkacyo
Doolow
Beledweyne
Hobyo
Mandera
Luuq
SOMALIA
Mereeg
Baydhabo
Jawhar
Muqdisho
Wajir
Marka
Afmadow
Jilib
Baraawe
Mado Gashi
Jamaame
Garissa
Kismaayo

Buur Gaabo

Garsen
Lamu

Voi
Malindi

Mombasa

INDIAN

Chake Chake
Pemba
Zanzibar
Zanzibar

DAR ES SALAAM

OCEAN

Mafia Island
Kilindoni

SEYCHELLES
Praslin
Victoria   Mahé
LES
AMIRANTES
Poivre
Atoll
Île
Plate

Kilwa Kivinje

Lindi

Alphonse
Coëtivy

Masasi

SEYCHELLES

Palma

Mocimboa
da Praia
GROUPE
D'ALDABRA
Île au Cerf

ATOLL DE
COSMOLEDO
Atoll de
Farquhar

Njazidja
COMOROS
ÎLES GLORIEUSES
(Fr.)
Tanjona
Bobaomby
AGALEGA
ISLANDS

Pemba
Moroni
Nzwani
Mutsamudu
Antsiranana

Lhrio
Mwali
Dzaoudzi
MAYOTTE
(Fr.)

Nacala-a-Velha
Ambilobe

ARCHIPEL DES COMORES
Ambanja
Maromokotro
2876

Ilha de
Moçambique
Analalava
Bealanana
Sambava

Mogincual

Antsohihy
Antalaha

Angoche
Mahajanga
Maroantsetra

Moma
Mampikony
Mananara Avaratra

Île Juan
de Nova
(Fr.)
Besalampy
Soalala
Tsaratanana
Nosy
Sainte Marie

Île Tromelin
(Fr.)

CARGADOS
CARAJOS
SHOALS

Maevatanana

Maintirano
Moratenobe
Ambatondrazaka

MADAGASCAR
Toamasina

Baixo
da India
(Fr.)
Tsiroanomandidy
ANTANANARIVO

MAURITIUS

Miandrivazo
Ambatolampy
Vatomandry

Morondava
Antsirabe
Mahanoro

MASCARENE   ISLANDS
Rodrigues

Île Europa
(Fr.)
Ambositra

Mandabe
Saint-Denis
Port Louis
Manja
Fianarantsoa
Mananjary
Mauritius

Morombe
Ambalavao
Manakara
RÉUNION
(Fr.)
Saint-Pierre

Ankazoabo
Ihosy

Farafangana

Toliara
Betroka

Bekily

Ampanihy
Tôlañaro

Tsiombe
Ambovombe
Tanjona
Vohimena

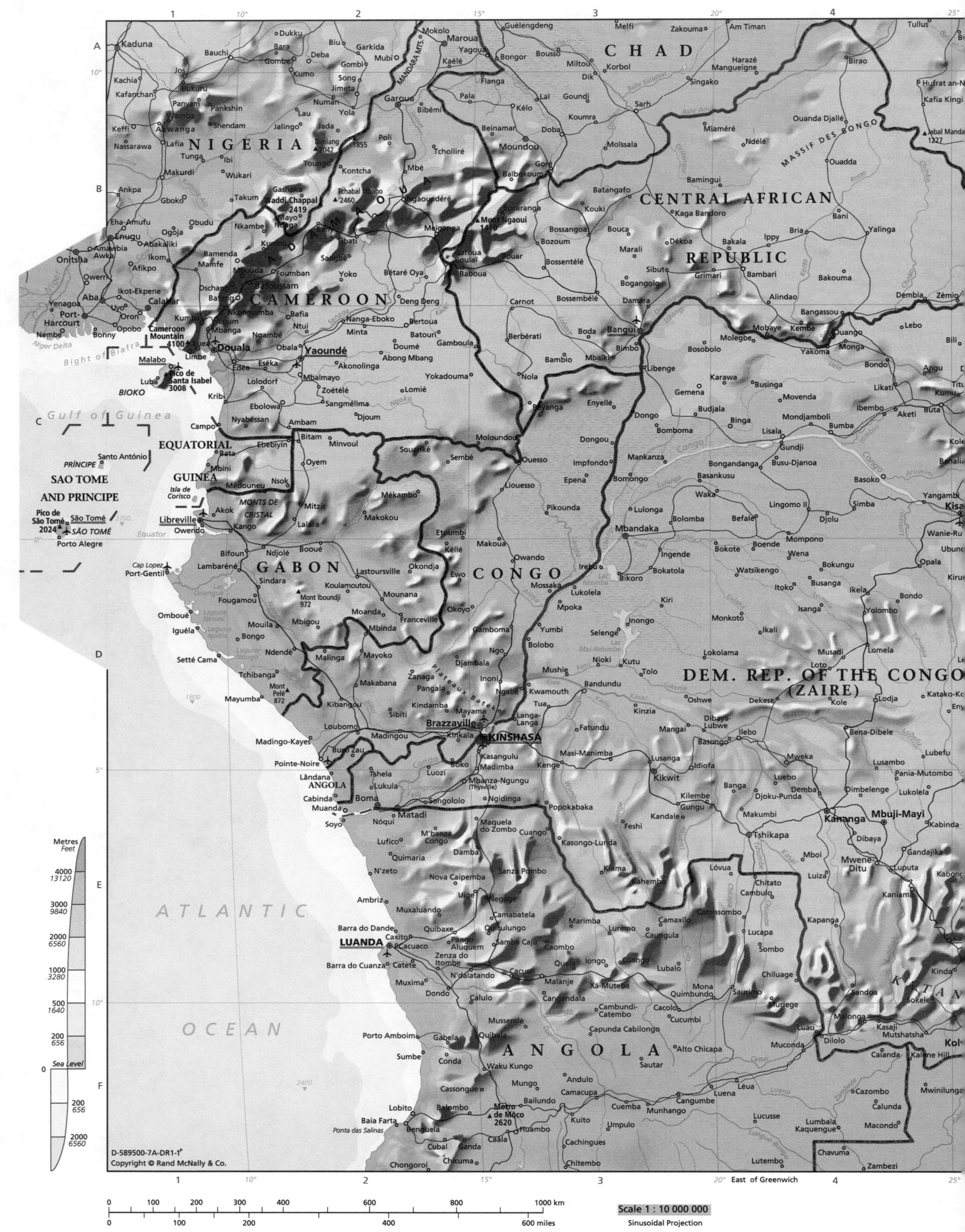

54

CHAD

CENTRAL AFRICAN

REPUBLIC

NIGERIA

CAMEROON

EQUATORIAL GUINEA

SAO TOME AND PRINCIPE

Gulf of Guinea

GABON

CONGO

DEM. REP. OF THE CONGO (ZAIRE)

ATLANTIC

OCEAN

ANGOLA

Metres
Feet

4000
13120

3000
9840

2000
6560

1000
3280

500
1640

200
656

Sea Level

200
656

2000
6560

D-589500-7A-DR1-1ª
Copyright © Rand McNally & Co.

| 0 | 100 | 200 | 300 | 400 | 600 | 800 | 1000 km |

| 0 | 100 | 200 | 400 | 600 miles |

Scale 1 : 10 000 000
Sinusoidal Projection

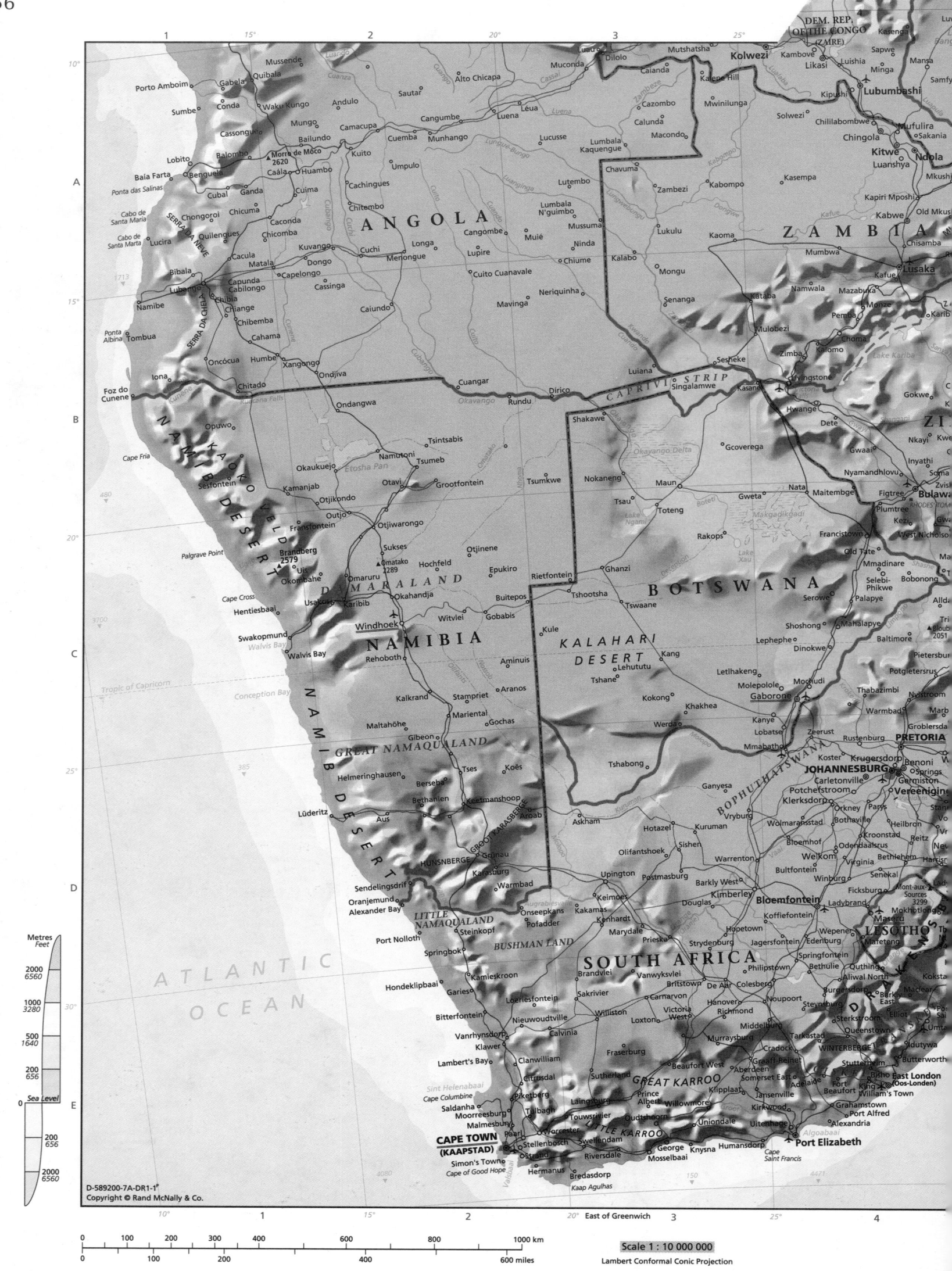

Metres Feet

2000 6560
1000 3280
500 1640
200 656
0 Sea Level
200 656
2000 6560

ATLANTIC
OCEAN

ANGOLA

ZAMBIA

NAMIBIA

BOTSWANA

SOUTH AFRICA

LESOTHO

KALAHARI DESERT

NAMIB DESERT

KAOKOVELD

DAMARALAND

GREAT NAMAQUALAND

LITTLE NAMAQUALAND

BUSHMAN LAND

GREAT KARROO

DEM. REP.
OF THE CONGO
(ZAIRE)

CAPRIVI STRIP

Tropic of Capricorn

Kolwezi
Lubumbashi
Kitwe
Ndola
Lusaka

Windhoek
Walvis Bay
Swakopmund

Gaborone
PRETORIA
JOHANNESBURG
Vereeniging
Bloemfontein
Maseru

CAPE TOWN
(KAAPSTAD)
Port Elizabeth
East London
(Oos-Londen)
Cape of Good Hope
Kaap Agulhas

D-589200-7A-DR1-1*
Copyright © Rand McNally & Co.

East of Greenwich

0 100 200 300 400 600 800 1000 km
0 100 200 400 600 miles

Scale 1 : 10 000 000
Lambert Conformal Conic Projection

TANZANIA

Kasama · Isoka · Chilumba
Chinsali · NYIKA PLATEAU 2606 · Manda · Lindi
Mpika · Livingstonia · Nyamtumbo · Nachingwea · Mtama · Mikindani
Mpika · Mzuzu · Rumphi · Mbamba Bay · Songea · Masasi · Newala · Mtwara
Mzimba · Nkhata Bay · Chamba · Tunduru · Cabo Delgado · Palma

ATOLL DE COSMOLEDO (Sey.)

Lundazi · Olivença · Mecula · Diaca · Quiterajo
Cóbuè · Mueda · Mucojo

Mpika · Nkhotakota · Metangula · Nantulo · Macomia · Quissanga
Chipata · MALAWI · Mchinji · Lichinga · Marrupa · Montepuez · Ancuabe · Pemba
Katete · Salima · Catur · Mada · Balama

COMOROS
Moroni · Njazidja · Kartala 2361 · ÎLES GLORIEUSES (Fr.)
Mwali · Nzwani · Mutsamudu
Fomboni
Mamoudzou · MAYOTTE (Fr.)

Vila Gamito · Lilongwe · Belém · Mandimba · Namapa · Memba
Mangochi · Cuamba · Muite · Nacala-a-Velha
Furancungo · Ulónguè · Malema · Ribauè · Mecubúri · Nacala
Zâmbuè · Fingoè · Kazula · Zomba · Namarrói · Alto Molócuè · Monapo · Lumbo
Uwonde · SERRA NAMULI · Murrupula · Nampula · Ilha do Moçambique
Blantyre · Sapitwa 3002 · Milange · Nametil · Mogincual

Tanjona Bobaomby
Antsiranana
Nosy Be · Ambohitra 1475
Andoany · Ambilobe · Iharaña
Ambanja · Maromokotro 2876 · Sambava
Maromandia · TSARATANANA · Antalaha
Analalava · Antsohihy · Andapa · Maroantsetra
Cap Masoala

Moatize · Tete · Thyolo · Chromo · Lugela · Mulevala · Angoche
Chioco · Chiperone 2054 · Nsanje · Mocuba · Larde
MAVURADONHA MTS. · Tambara · Doá · Mocubela · Moma
Shamva · Changara · Chemba · Morrumbala · Pebane
Bindura · Vila de Sena · Namacurra
MOZAMBIQUE · Vila Fontes · Mopeia · Quelimane
Mahajanga
Tanjona Vilanandro · Soalala · Marovoay · Mandritsara · Mananara Avaratra
Besalampy · Madirovalo · Mampikony
Bekodoka · Mahabe · Maevatanana · Tsaratanana · Nosy Sainte Marie
Mutare · Morafenobe · Kandreho · Andriamena · Ambodifototra
Manica · Nosy Barren · Maintirano · Fenoarivo Atsinanana
Chimoio · Monte Binga 2437 · Antsalova · Ankavandra · Ambatondrazaka
Dondo · Beira · Belo Tsiribihina · Miandrivazo · Tsiroanomandidy · Arivonimamo · Toamasina
Chibabava · Sofala · ANTANANARIVO · Moramanga
Espungabera · Manankandriana
Mahabo · Malaimbandy · Tsiafajavona 2642 · Ambatolampy · Vatomandry
Morondava · Ambositra · Mahanoro
Belo sur Mer · Ambatofinandrahana · Antsirabe
Nova Mambone · Andranopasy · Mandabe · Ambohimahasoa · Nosy-Varika
Inhassoro · Morombe · Manja · Fianarantsoa
Ilha do Bazaruto · Befandriana Atsimo · Ifanadiana
Vilankulo · Beroroha · Ambalavao · Manakara
Mapinhane · Ankazoabo · Ihosy · Pic Boby 2658 · Ivohibe · Vohipeno
Massinga · Manombo Atsimo · Sakaraha · Ranohira · Farafangana
Morrumbene · Sakaraha · Ivohibe · Vondrozo
Maxixe · Ponta da Barra · Toliara · Bezaha · Betroka · Vangaindrano
Inhambane · Ejeda · Bekily · Beraketa · Midongy Atsimo
Itampolo · Ampanihy · Manantenina
Androka · Amboasary
Tsiombe · Ambovombe · Tôlañaro
Tanjona Vohimena

INDIAN OCEAN

Bassas da India (Fr.)

Île Europa (Fr.)

Mozambique Channel

Île Juan de Nova (Fr.)

ARCHIPEL DES COMORES

MADAGASCAR

MAPUTO · Ilha da Inhaca
Bela Vista · Zitundo
SWAZILAND · Maputo
Lavumisa
Vryheid · Nongoma · Mtubatuba
Ulundi · Cape Saint Lucia · Lake Saint Lucia
Empangeni · Richards Bay
DURBAN · Pinetown
Umzinto
Port Shepstone

a
INDIAN OCEAN
Port Louis · MAURITIUS
Piton de la Petite Rivière Noire 828 · Curepipe · Mahébourg
Saint-Denis · Piton des Neiges 3070 · RÉUNION (Fr.)
Saint-Paul · Saint-Pierre
MASCARENE ISLANDS

b
INDIAN OCEAN
SEYCHELLES
Saint Pierre
GROUP D'ALDABRA · ATOLL DE COSMOLEDO
Astove · ATOLL DE FARQUHAR
AGALEGA ISLANDS (Maur.)

Praslin · La Digue
Silhouette · Victoria · Mahé
SEYCHELLES
Poivre Atoll · Desroches · Île Plate
LES AMIRANTES
Alphonse · Coëtivy Island

East of Greenwich

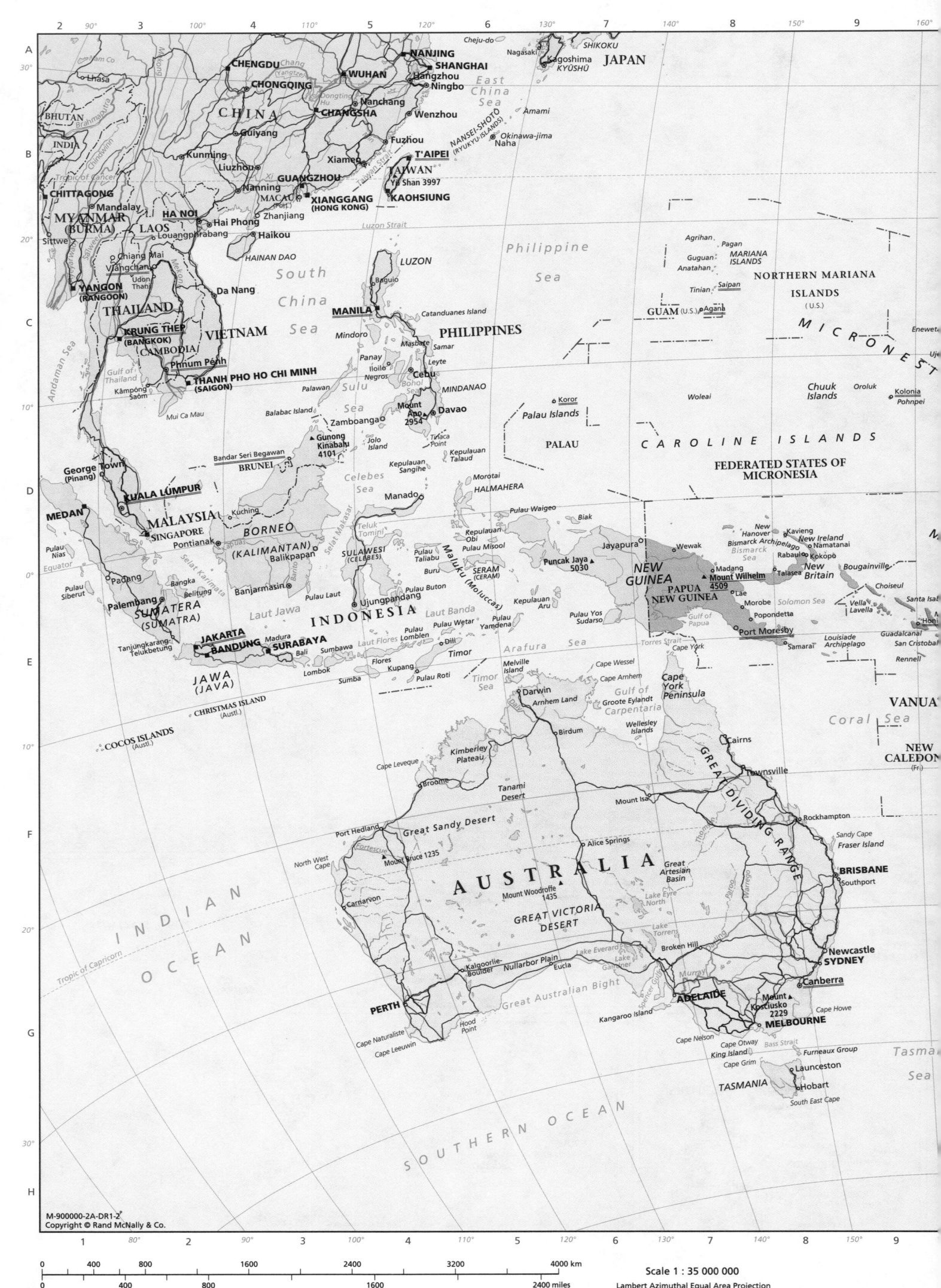

0	400	800	1600	2400	3200	4000 km

0	400	800	1600	2400 miles

Scale 1 : 35 000 000

Lambert Azimuthal Equal Area Projection

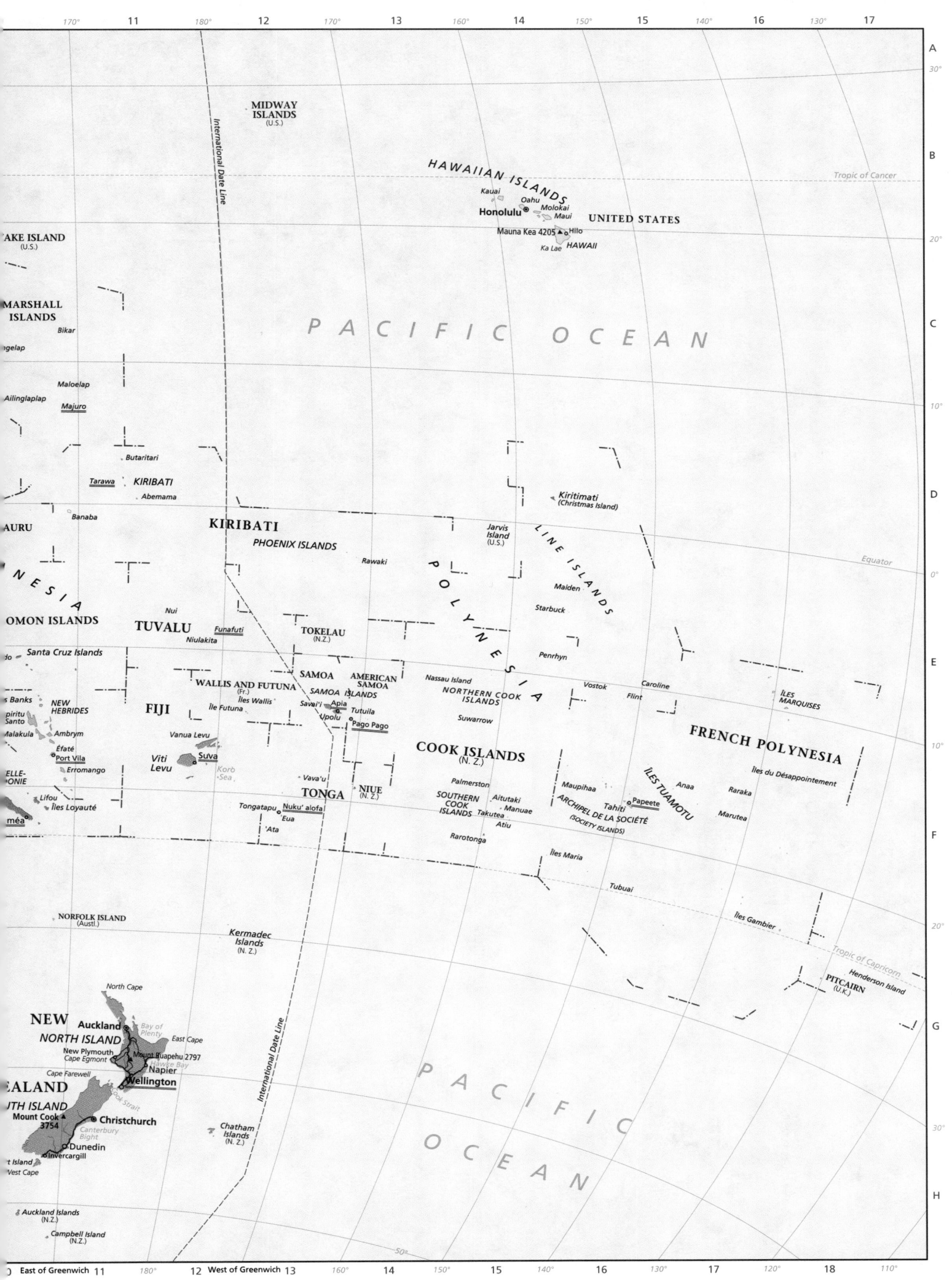

International Date Line

MIDWAY
ISLANDS
(U.S.)

HAWAIIAN ISLANDS

Tropic of Cancer

Kauai
Oahu
Molokai
Honolulu ⊙   Maui
Mauna Kea 4205 ▲ ⊙ Hilo
Ka Lae   HAWAII   UNITED STATES

AKE ISLAND
(U.S.)

PACIFIC   OCEAN

MARSHALL
ISLANDS

Bikar

ngelap

Maloelap

Ailinglaplap

Majuro

Butaritari

Tarawa   KIRIBATI

Abemama

Kiritimati
(Christmas Island)

AURU

Banaba

KIRIBATI

PHOENIX ISLANDS

Jarvis
Island
(U.S.)

LINE ISLANDS

Rawaki

Maiden

Equator

Starbuck

NESIA

Nui

OMON ISLANDS

TUVALU   Funafuti

Niulakita

TOKELAU
(N.Z.)

Penrhyn

P
O
L
Y
N
E
S
I
A

Santa Cruz Islands

do

Banks

NEW
HEBRIDES

piritu
Santo

Malakula   Ambrym

SAMOA   AMERICAN
SAMOA
WALLIS AND FUTUNA   ISLANDS
(Fr.)
Îles Wallis

FIJI   Île Futuna

Savai'i
Apia
Upolu   Tutuila

Pago Pago

Nassau Island

NORTHERN COOK
ISLANDS

Suwarrow

Vostok   Caroline

Flint

ÎLES
MARQUISES

FRENCH POLYNESIA

Vanua Levu

Éfaté
ELLE-   Port Vila
ONIE   Erromango

Viti
Levu   Suva

Koro
Sea

Maupihaa

Anaa

Îles du Désappointement

Raraka

COOK ISLANDS
(N.Z.)

ÎLES TUAMOTU

méa

Lifou   Îles Loyauté

Vava'u

NIUE
(N.Z.)

TONGA

Palmerston

Aitutaki
Manuae

SOUTHERN
COOK
ISLANDS   Takutea
Atiu

Tahiti
Papeete

ARCHIPEL DE LA SOCIÉTÉ
(SOCIETY ISLANDS)

Marutea

Tongatapu   Nuku' alofa

'Eua

'Ata

Rarotonga

Îles Maria

Tubuai

Îles Gambier

NORFOLK ISLAND
(Austl.)

Kermadec
Islands
(N.Z.)

Tropic of Capricorn

Henderson Island

PITCAIRN
(U.K.)

International Date Line

NEW   Auckland

NORTH ISLAND   Bay of
Plenty   East Cape

New Plymouth
Cape Egmont   Mount Ruapehu 2797
Napier   Hawke Bay

EALAND   Wellington

UTH ISLAND   Cook Strait

Mount Cook ▲
3754   Christchurch

Canterbury
Bight

Dunedin

t Island   Invercargill

West Cape

Chatham
Islands
(N.Z.)

PACIFIC

OCEAN

Auckland Islands
(N.Z.)

Campbell Island
(N.Z.)

ARAFURA SEA

TIMOR SEA

INDIAN OCEAN

NEW GUINEA

INDONESIA

SULAWESI (CELEBES)

JAWA (JAVA)

MADURA

LOMBOK

SUMBAWA

FLORES

TIMOR

SUMBA

Nusa Tenggara (Lesser Sunda Islands)

Laut Banda

Laut Flores

Laut Sawu

Laut Bali

AUSTRALIA

NORTHERN TERRITORY

Arnhem Land

Barkly Tableland

Kimberley Plateau

Great Sandy Desert

Tanami Desert

KING LEOPOLD RANGES

EDGAR RANGES

FREDERICK HILLS

Gulf of Carpentaria

Van Diemen Gulf

Beagle Gulf

Joseph Bonaparte Gulf

Darwin

Katherine

Port Hedland

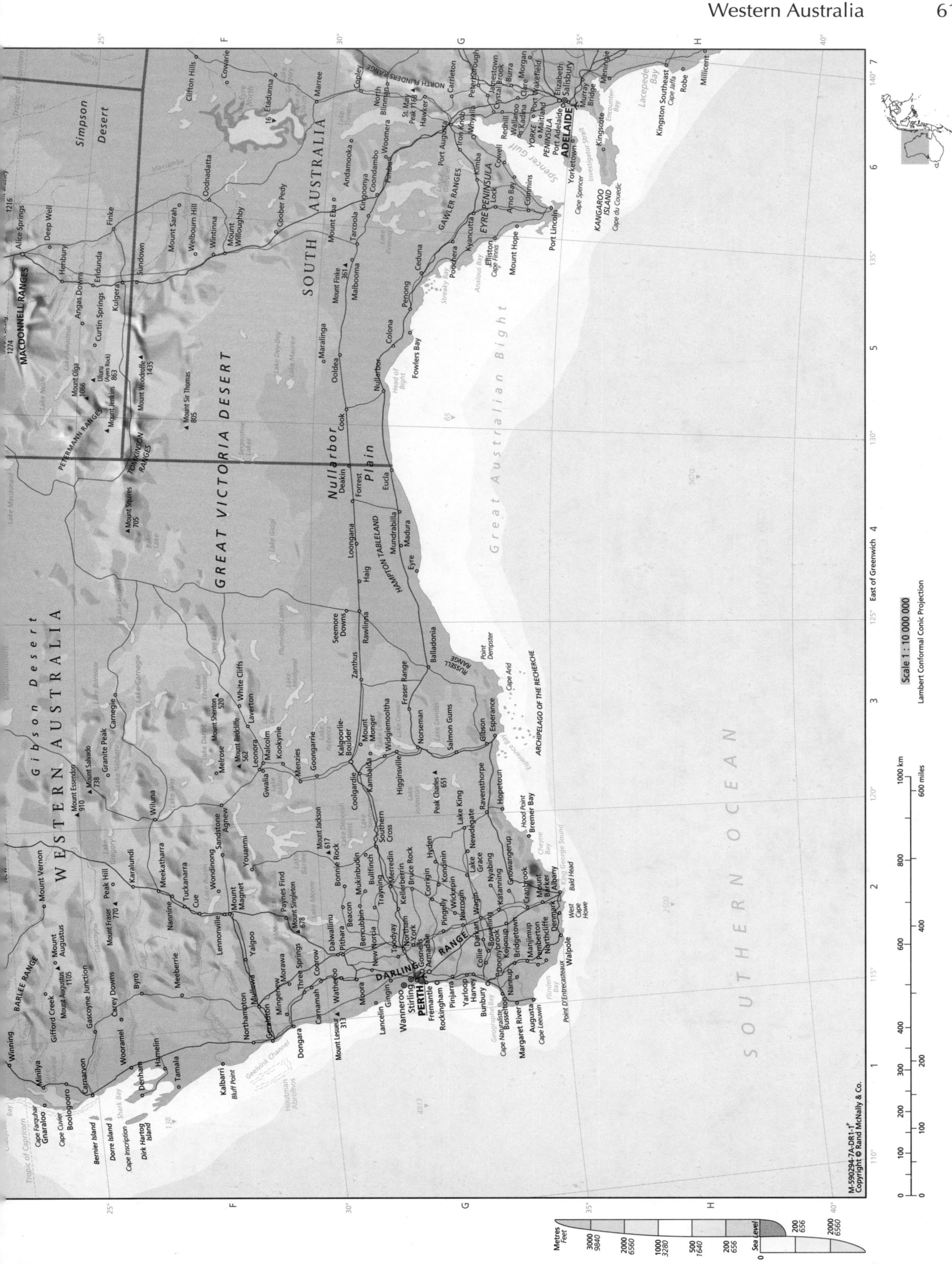

Scale 1 : 10 000 000

Lambert Conformal Conic Projection

M-590294-7A-DR1-1°
Copyright © Rand McNally & Co.

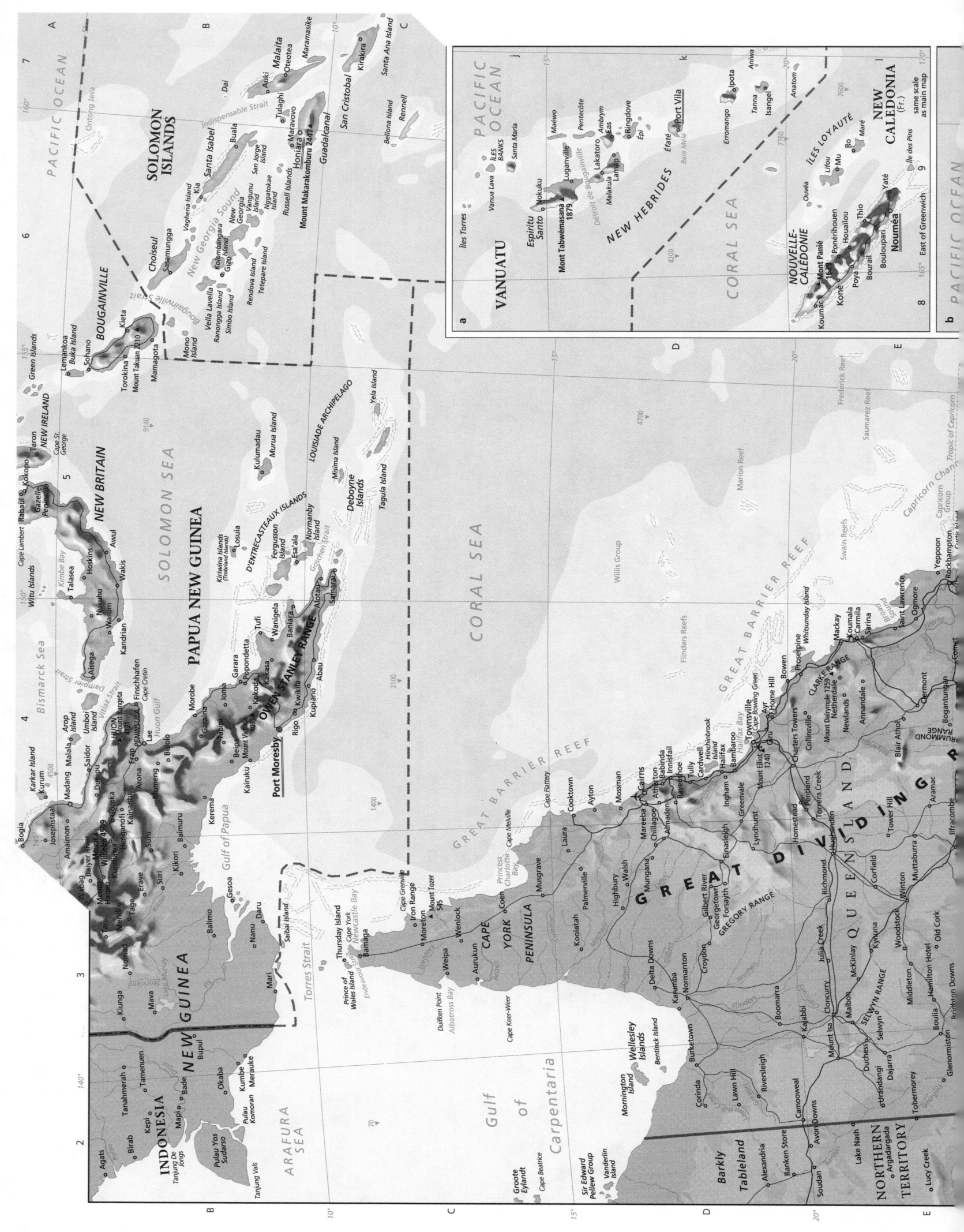

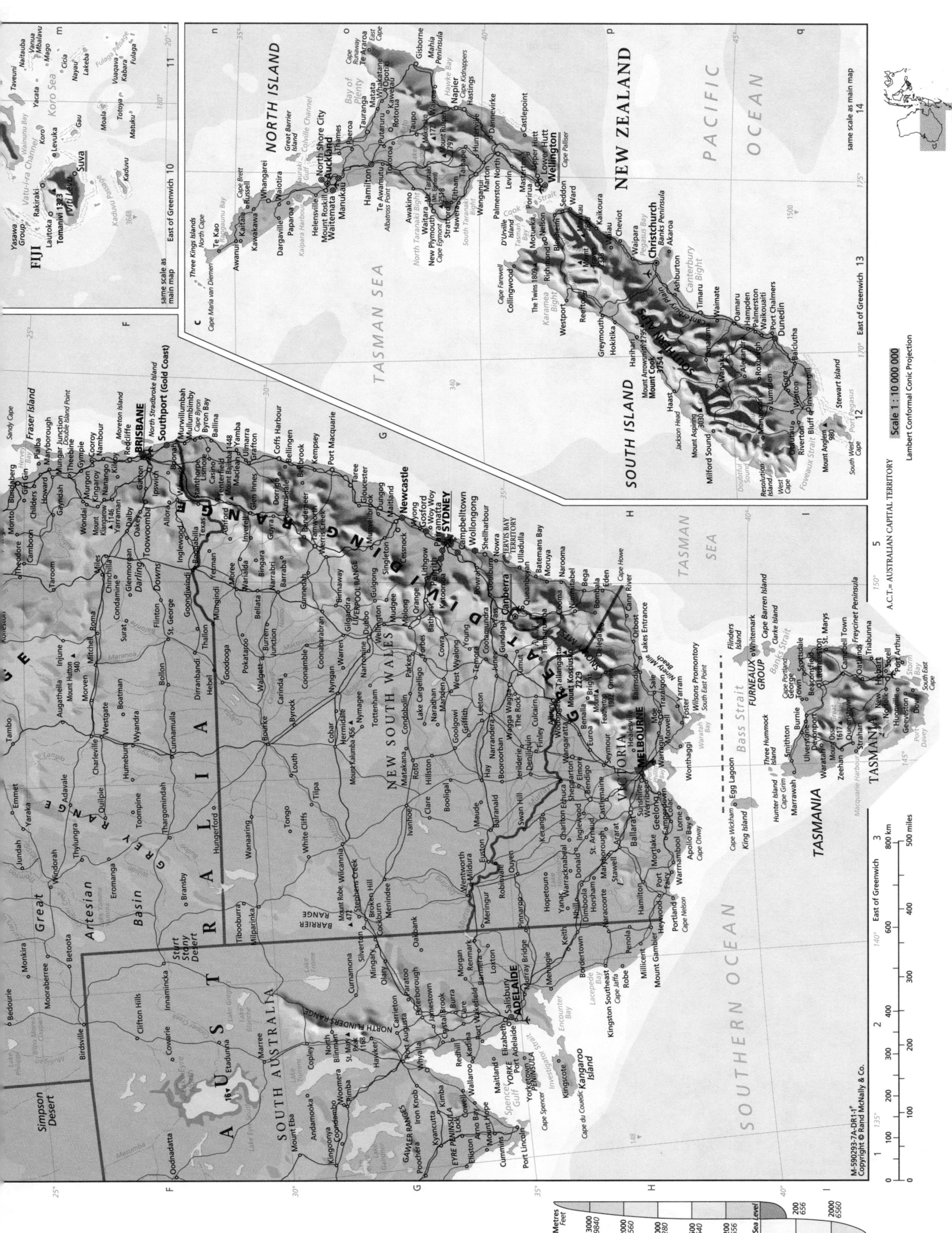

NORTH ISLAND

NEW ZEALAND

SOUTH ISLAND

TASMAN SEA

PACIFIC OCEAN

FIJI

Suva

Three Kings Islands
North Cape
Te Kao
Awanui
Kaitaia
Kawakawa
Cape Brett
Russell
Whangarei
Dargaville
Paparoa
Helensville
Mount Roskill
Waitemata
AUCKLAND
North Shore City
Manukau
Hamilton
Te Awamutu
Thames
Tauranga
Matata
Whakatane
Opotiki
Rotorua
Taupo
Waihi
Te Aroha
Morrinsville
Cambridge
Putaruru
Te Kuiti
Awakino
Cape Egmont
New Plymouth
Stratford
Hawera
Wanganui
Marton
Palmerston North
Levin
Lower Hutt
Porirua
WELLINGTON
Cape Palliser
Gisborne
Mahia Peninsula
Hawke Bay
Napier
Hastings
Waipukurau
Dannevirke
Masterton
Castlepoint
Cape Farewell
Collingwood
Westport
Reefton
Greymouth
Hokitika
Harihari
Haast
Jackson Head
Mount Aspiring 3035
Milford Sound
Doubtful Sound
Resolution Island
West Cape
South West Cape
Te Anau
Lumsden
Invercargill
Riverton
Bluff
Stewart Island
Mount Anglem 980
Gore
Mataura
Balclutha
Dunedin
Port Chalmers
Palmerston
Oamaru
Waikouaiti
Waimate
Timaru
Ashburton
Christchurch
Banks Peninsula
Akaroa
Cheviot
Kaikoura
Waiau
Wairau
Ward
Seddon
Blenheim
Picton
Nelson
Richmond
Motueka
D'Urville Island

Cook Strait

Mount Cook 3764

SOUTHERN ALPS

Canterbury Bight

Pegasus Bay

Tasman Bay

Golden Bay

Karamea Bight

Scale 1 : 10 000 000
Lambert Conformal Conic Projection

A.C.T. = AUSTRALIAN CAPITAL TERRITORY

QUEENSLAND

Sandy Cape
Fraser Island
Bundaberg
Maryborough
Hervey Bay
Gympie
Nambour
BRISBANE
Ipswich
Southport (Gold Coast)
North Stradbroke Island
Moreton Island
Redcliffe
Toowoomba
Warwick
Stanthorpe
Lismore
Casino
Grafton
Coffs Harbour
Kempsey
Port Macquarie
Taree
Newcastle
Gosford
Wyong
SYDNEY
Parramatta
Campbelltown
Wollongong
Nowra
Ulladulla
Batemans Bay
Moruya
Narooma
Bega
Eden
Cape Howe

NEW SOUTH WALES

CANBERRA
A.C.T.

Broken Hill

VICTORIA
MELBOURNE
Geelong
Ballarat
Bendigo
Shepparton
Warrnambool
Portland

Bass Strait
King Island
Flinders Island
Cape Barren Island

TASMANIA
Burnie
Devonport
Launceston
HOBART
Port Arthur

SOUTH AUSTRALIA
ADELAIDE
Murray Bridge
Spencer Gulf
Gulf St Vincent
Yorke Peninsula
Eyre Peninsula
Kangaroo Island
Port Lincoln
Port Augusta
Whyalla

GREAT DIVIDING RANGE

Great Artesian Basin

Simpson Desert

Strzelecki Desert

SOUTHERN OCEAN

M-590293-7A-DR1-1°
Copyright © Rand McNally & Co.

Metres   Feet
3000   9840
2000   6560
1000   3280
500   1640
200   656
Sea Level
200   656
2000   6560

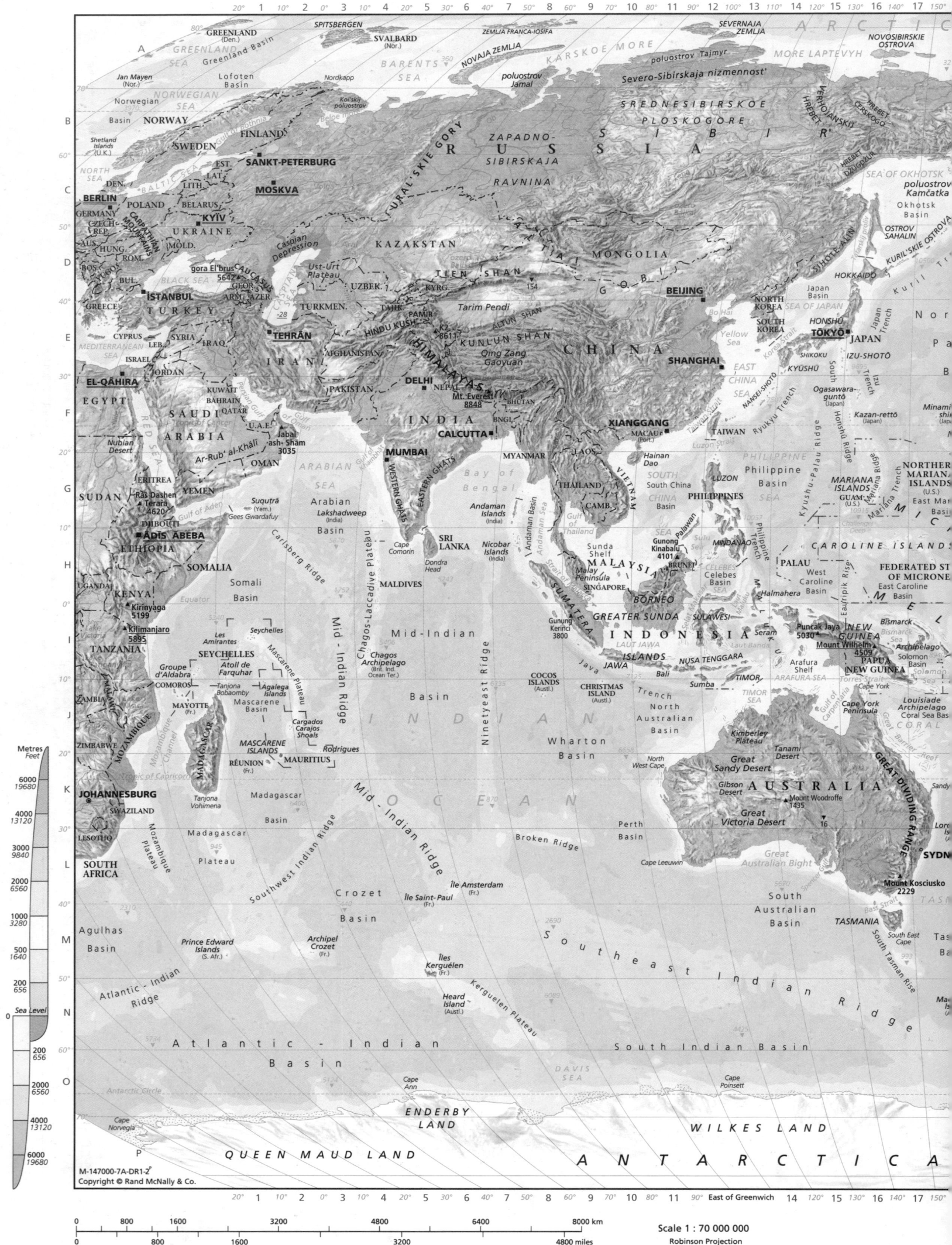

Metres
Feet

6000
19680

4000
13120

3000
9840

2000
6560

1000
3280

500
1640

200
656

Sea Level
0

200
656

2000
6560

4000
13120

6000
19680

M-147000-7A-DR1-2
Copyright © Rand McNally & Co.

0	800	1600	3200	4800	6400	8000 km

0	800	1600	3200	4800 miles

Scale 1 : 70 000 000

Robinson Projection

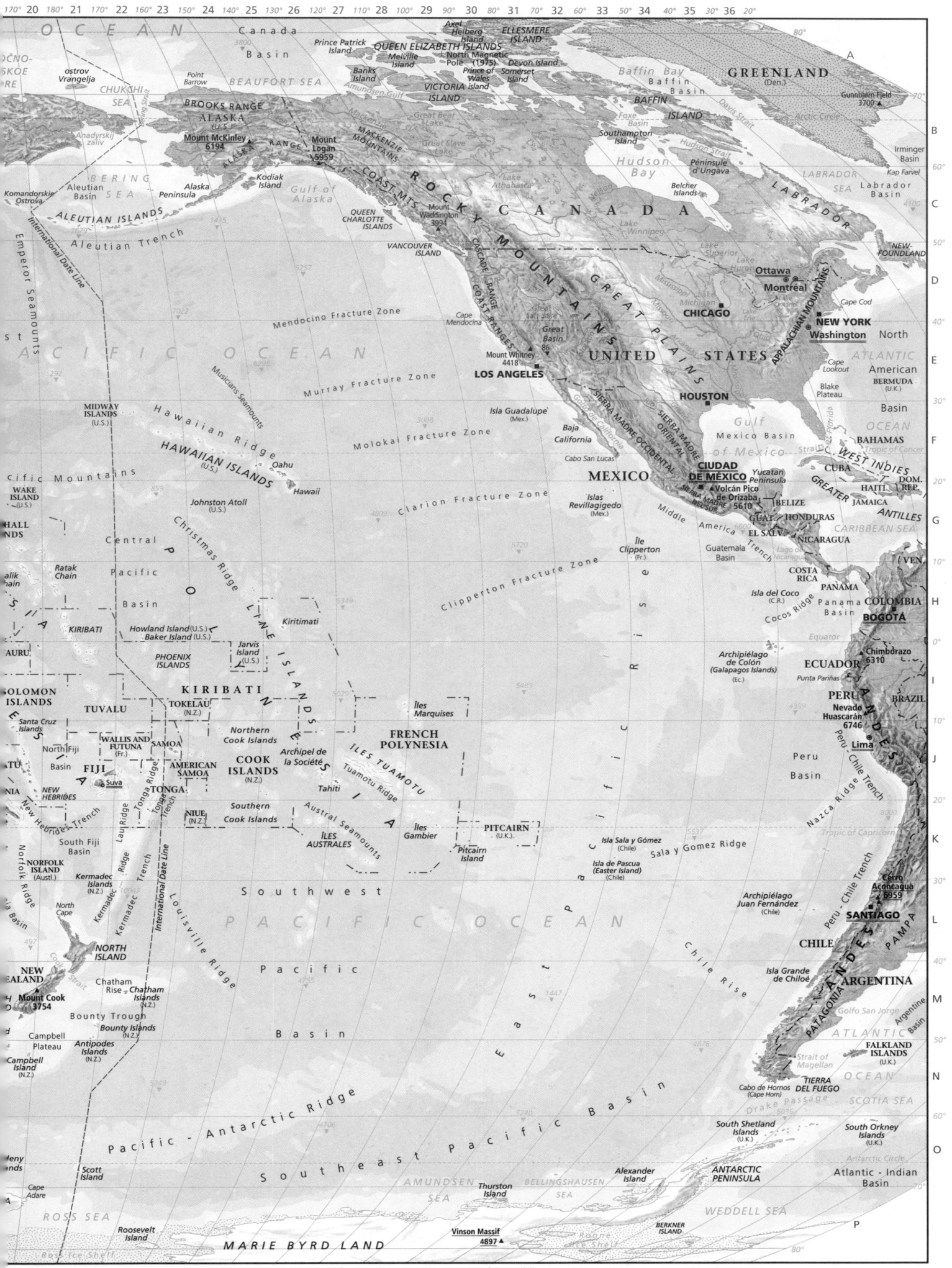

O C E A N
Canada
ОČNO-
SКОЕ
ostrov
Vrangelja
CHUKCHI
SEA
Anadyrskij
zaliv

Komandorskie
Ostrova

Aleutian
Basin

BERING
SEA

ALEUTIAN ISLANDS

Aleutian Trench

Point
Barrow

Prince Patrick
Island

Banks
Island

Prince
of
Wales
Island

Axel
Heiberg
Island

Melville
Island

Devon Island

Somerset
Island

ELLESMERE
ISLAND

GREENLAND
(Den.)

QUEEN ELIZABETH ISLANDS

North Magnetic
Pole (1975)

Baffin Bay

Baffin
Basin

Gunnbjørn Field
3700

Arctic Circle

BEAUFORT SEA

BROOKS RANGE

ALASKA

Mount McKinley
6194

Kodiak
Island

Alaska
Peninsula

Kodiak
Island

Gulf of
Alaska

QUEEN
CHARLOTTE
ISLANDS

VANCOUVER
ISLAND

Mackenzie

MACKENZIE
MOUNTAINS

Mount
Logan
5959

ALASKA RANGE

COAST MTS.

ROCKY MOUNTAINS

Great Bear
Lake

Great Slave
Lake

Lake
Athabasca

Amundsen Gulf

VICTORIA
ISLAND

Southampton
Island

Hudson Strait

Foxe
Basin

Baffin
ISLAND

Hudson
Bay

Belcher
Islands

Péninsule
d'Ungava

LABRADOR
SEA

Labrador
Basin

Kap Farvel

Irminger
Basin

BAFFIN

Davis Strait

CANADA

Lake
Winnipeg

Lake
Superior

Lake
Huron

Lake
Michigan

Lake
Erie

NEW-
FOUNDLAND

Emperor Seamounts

International Date Line

Emperor Seamounts

Mount
Waddington
3994

CASCADE RANGE

COAST RANGES

Cape
Mendocino

Mendocino Fracture Zone

GREAT PLAINS

Ottawa

Montréal

Cape Cod

CHICAGO

NEW YORK

Washington

North

P A C I F I C   O C E A N

Mount Whitney
4418

Great
Basin

Great
Salt
Lake

UNITED STATES

APPALACHIAN MOUNTAINS

Cape
Lookout

ATLANTIC

American

BERMUDA
(U.K.)

Murray Fracture Zone

LOS ANGELES

HOUSTON

SIERRA MADRE ORIENTAL

Cape
Lookout

Blake
Plateau

Basin

MIDWAY
ISLANDS
(U.S.)

Hawaiian Ridge

Musicians Seamounts

Isla Guadalupe
(Mex.)

Molokai Fracture Zone

Baja
California

Gulf of
Mexico

Mexico Basin

Tropic of Cancer

OCEAN

BAHAMAS

HAWAIIAN ISLANDS
(U.S.)

Oahu

Hawaii

Cabo San Lucas

CIUDAD
DE MÉXICO

Yucatán
Peninsula

WEST INDIES

CUBA

GREATER

HAITI

DOM.
REP.

cific Mountains

WAKE
ISLAND
(U.S.)

Johnston Atoll
(U.S.)

Clarion Fracture Zone

MEXICO

Volcán Pico
de Orizaba
5610

SIERRA MADRE DEL SUR

BELIZE

GUAT.

HONDURAS

JAMAICA

ANTILLES

HALL
NDS

Central

Islas
Revillagigedo
(Mex.)

Middle

America

EL SALV.

NICARAGUA

CARIBBEAN SEA

Pacific

Basin

Ratak
Chain

Ìle
Clipperton
(Fr.)

Guatemala
Basin

Trench

COSTA
RICA

Lago de
Nicaragua

VEN.

alik
hain

KIRIBATI

Howland Island (U.S.)
Baker Island (U.S.)

Jarvis
Island
(U.S.)

Kiritimati

Isla del Coco
(C.R.)

Cocos Ridge

PANAMA

Panama
Basin

COLOMBIA

AURU

PHOENIX
ISLANDS

BOGOTÁ

SOLOMON
ISLANDS

TUVALU

KIRIBATI

TOKELAU
(N.Z.)

Îles
Marquises

Archipiélago
de Colón
(Galapagos Islands)
(Ec.)

Equator

ECUADOR

Chimborazo
6310

Santa Cruz
Islands

Northern
Cook Islands

FRENCH
POLYNESIA

Punta Pariñas

PERU

BRAZIL

North Fiji
Basin

WALLIS AND
FUTUNA
(Fr.)

SAMOA

Archipel de
la Société

ÎLES TUAMOTU

Nevado
Huascarán
6746

TU

FIJI

AMERICAN
SAMOA

COOK
ISLANDS
(N.Z.)

Tuamotu Ridge

Peru - Chile Trench

NIA

Suva

TONGA

Tahiti

Peru

Basin

Lima

NEW
HEBRIDES

Lau Ridge

Tonga Ridge

NIUE
(N.Z.)

Southern
Cook Islands

Austral Seamounts

Îles
Gambier

PITCAIRN
(U.K.)

Nazca Ridge

South Fiji
Basin

ÎLES
AUSTRALES

Pitcairn
Island

Isla Sala y Gómez
(Chile)

Sala y Gomez Ridge

Tropic of Capricorn

NORFOLK
ISLAND
(Austl.)

Kermadec
Islands
(N.Z.)

International Date Line

Southwest

Isla de Pascua
(Easter Island)
(Chile)

Cerro
Aconcagua
6959

la
Basin

North
Cape

PACIFIC OCEAN

Archipiélago
Juan Fernández
(Chile)

SANTIAGO

Louisville Ridge

Pacific

CHILE

Chile Rise

PAMPA

NORTH
ISLAND

Chatham
Rise

Chatham
Islands
(N.Z.)

Isla Grande
de Chiloé

ARGENTINA

NEW
EALAND

Mount Cook
3754

Bounty Trough

Bounty Islands
(N.Z.)

Basin

ATLANTIC

PATAGONIA

Golfo San Jorge

Argentine
Basin

Campbell
Plateau

Antipodes
Islands
(N.Z.)

FALKLAND
ISLANDS
(U.K.)

Campbell
Island
(N.Z.)

Strait of
Magellan

TIERRA
DEL FUEGO

OCEAN

SCOTIA SEA

Pacific - Antarctic Ridge

Southeast Pacific Basin

Cabo de Hornos
(Cape Horn)

Drake Passage

South Shetland
Islands
(U.K.)

South Orkney
Islands
(U.K.)

Antarctic Circle

eny
Cape
Adare

Scott
Island

AMUNDSEN
SEA

Thurston
Island

BELLINGSHAUSEN
SEA

Alexander
Island

ANTARCTIC
PENINSULA

Atlantic - Indian
Basin

ROSS SEA

Roosevelt
Island

MARIE BYRD LAND

Vinson Massif
4897

Ronne
Ice Shelf

BERKNER
ISLAND

WEDDELL SEA

West of Greenwich

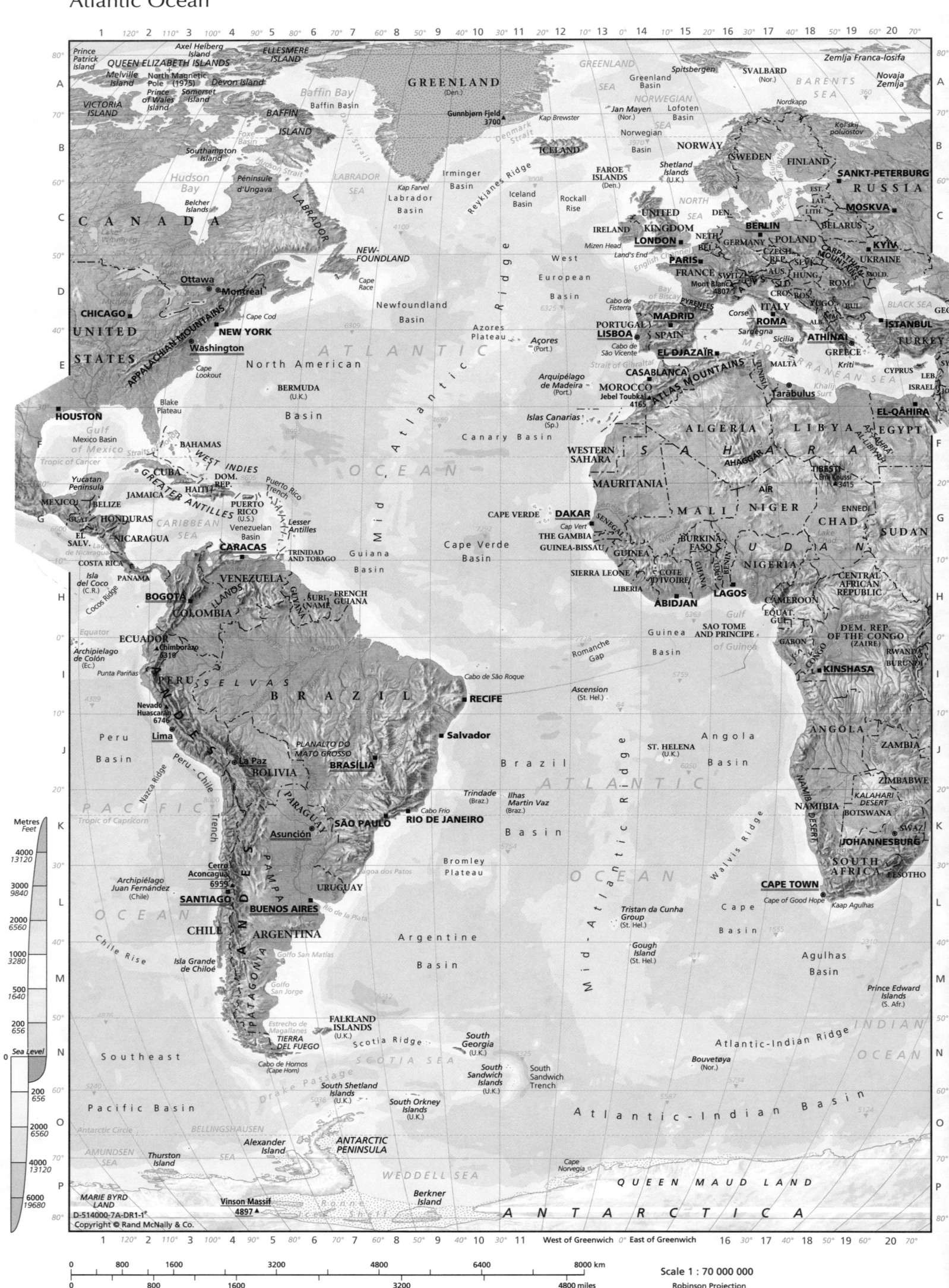

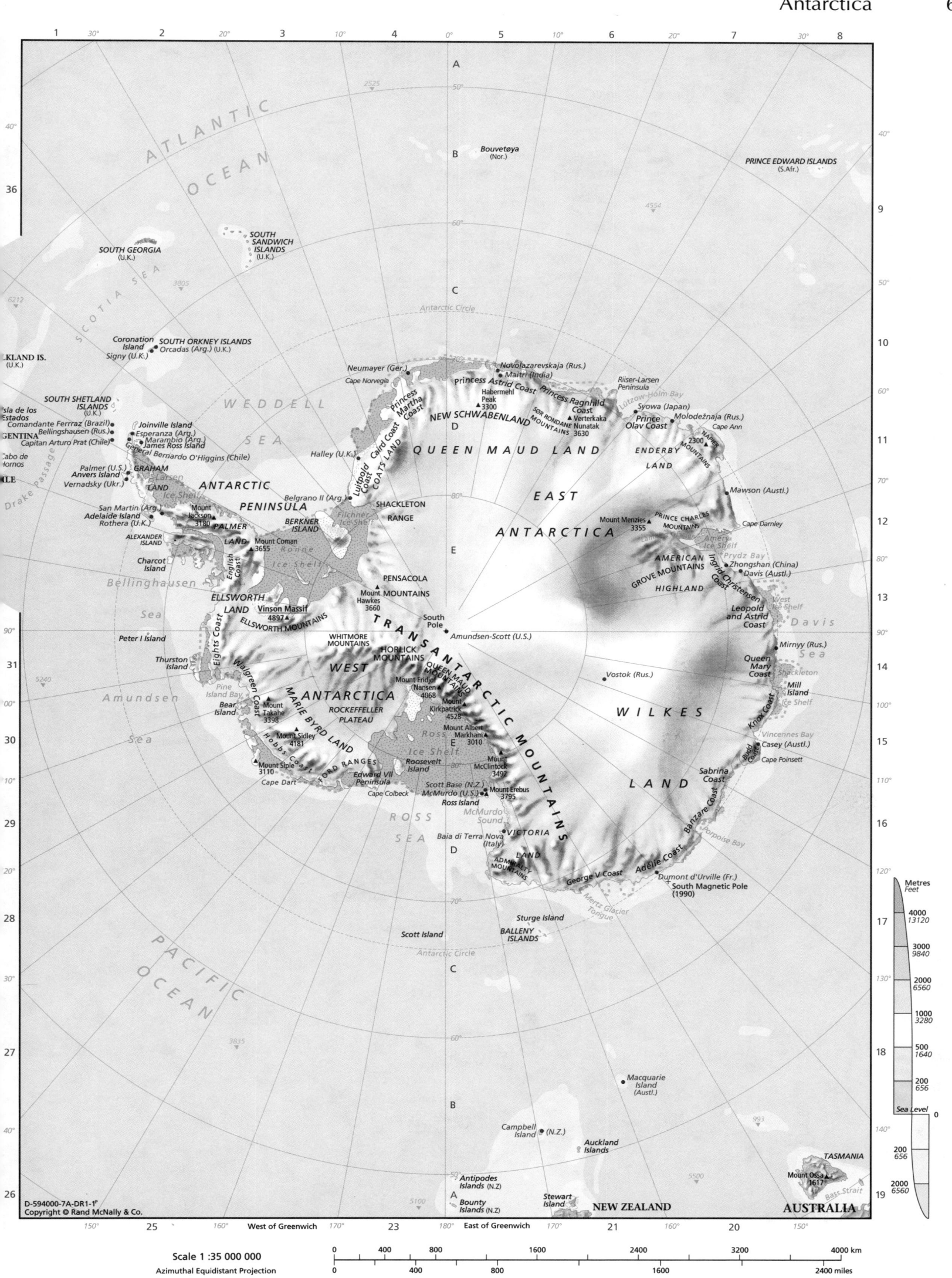

Scale 1:35 000 000

Azimuthal Equidistant Projection

D-594000-7A-DR1-1"
Copyright © Rand McNally & Co.

Scale 1 : 35 000 000
Lambert Azimuthal Equal Area Projection

M-540000-2A-DR1-1
Copyright © Rand McNally & Co.

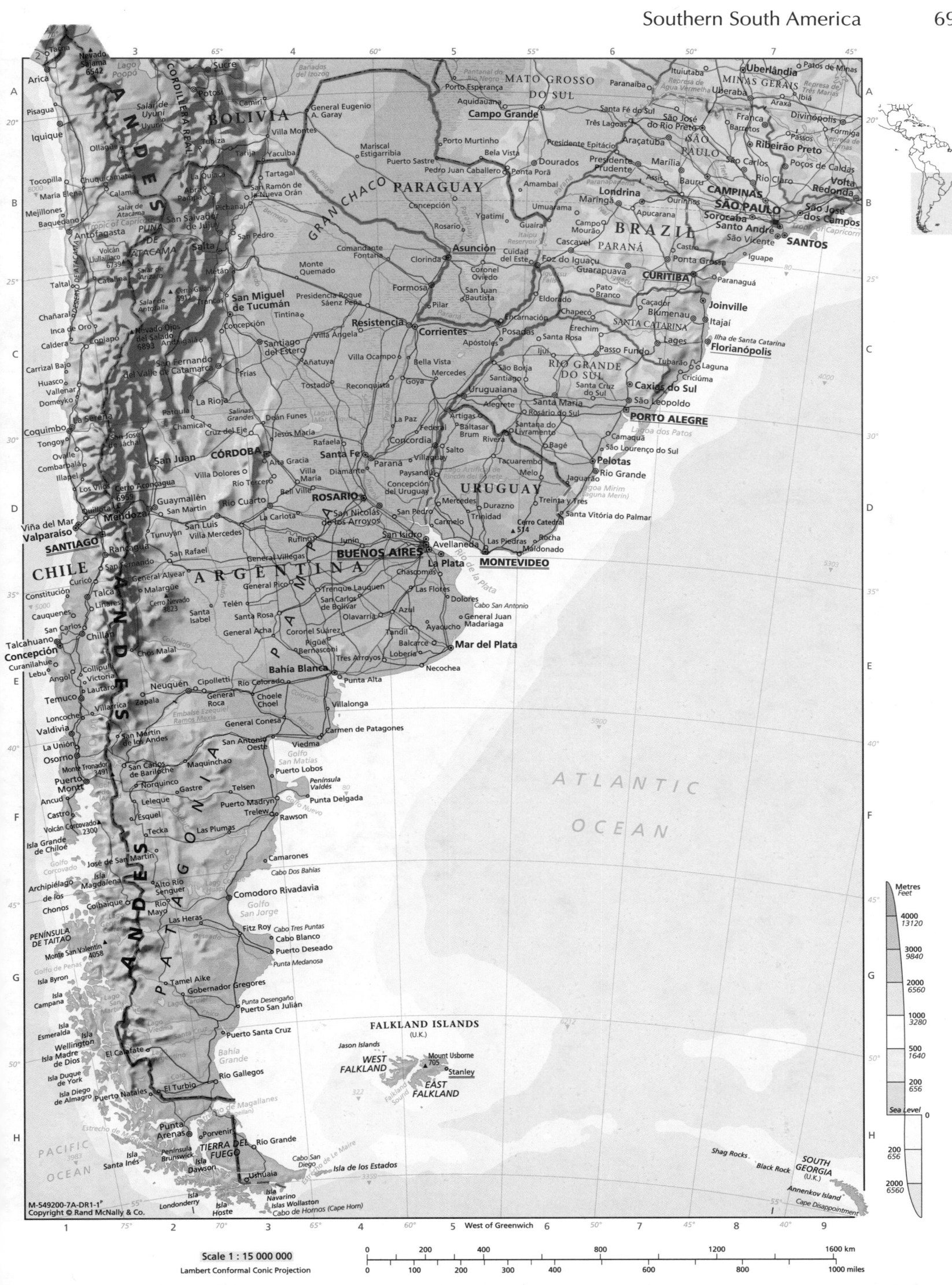

Scale 1 : 15 000 000
Lambert Conformal Conic Projection

West of Greenwich

Metres / Feet
6000 / 19680
4000 / 13120
3000 / 9840
2000 / 6560
1000 / 3280
500 / 1640
200 / 656
Sea Level
200 / 656
2000 / 6560

M-549100-7A-DR1-1ᴾ
Copyright © Rand McNally & Co.

Scale 1 : 15 000 000
Sinusoidal Projection

0   200   400   800   1200   1600 km
0   100   200   300   400   600   800   1000 miles

ATLANTIC

OCEAN

GRENADA
George's
Scarborough
Tobago
Port of Spain
TRINIDAD AND TOBAGO
Fernando
Trinidad

Morawhanna

Charity
Spring Garden
Parika   Georgetown
Bartica   New Amsterdam
Rockstone   Corriverton
Linden   Nieuw
Nickerie   Saint-Laurent
Kwakoegron   du Maroni   Île du Diable
Brokopondo   Kourou
Mount Roraima   Brokopondo Stuwmeer   Saint-Élie   Cayenne
2875   SURINAME   FRENCH   Régina   Cabo Orange
GUYANA   Juliana Top   GUIANA   Saint-Georges
Lethem   1230   Saül   Oiapoque

Cunani
Calçoene
Amapá
AMAPÁ   Ilha de Maracá

Caracaraí   Serra do
Navio   Equator

Prainha Nova

ACARAÍ MTS.   TUMUCHUMAC MTS.   Ilha Janaucu
Ilha Caviana de Fora
Macapá   Ilha Mexiana

ANAUS   Oriximiná   Ilha   ILHA DE   Bragança
Alenquer   Grande   MARAJÓ   Carutapera
Faro   Óbidos   Porto   do Gurupá   BELÉM   Cururupu
Parintins   de Moz   Breves   São Luís
Carreiro   Monte Alegre   Portel   Cametá   Camiranga   Pinheiro   Rosário   Parnaíba   Acaraú
Itacoatiara   Santarém   Abaetetuba   Viana   Itapecuru-Mirim   Camocim
Maués   Altamira   Monção   Sobral   FORTALEZA
Borba   Tucuruí   Bacabal   Brejo   Ipu   Maranguape   Baturité
Novo Aripuanã   Codó   Barras   Aracati
Manicoré   PARÁ   Marabá   Pedreiras   CEARÁ   Quixadá   Areia Branca
São João do   Imperatriz   Caxias   Campo   Crateús   Mossoró   Ceará-Mirim
Araguaia   MARANHÃO   Barra do Corda   Maior   RIO GRANDE   Natal
SERRA DOS CARAJÁS   Araguatins   Grajaú   Teresina   Senador   DO NORTE   Currais Novos
Carajás   Tocantinópolis   Colinas   Amarante   Iguatu   Pompeu   Caicó   Rio Tinto
Gradaús   Carolina   Mirador   Floriano   Picos   Juazeiro   João Pessoa
BRAZIL   Conceição do Araguaia   Loreto   Oeiras   do Norte   PARAÍBA   Patos   Campina Grande
SERRA DO CACHIMBO   Balsas   Benedito Leite   PIAUÍ   Sertânia   Olinda
Araguacema   Paulistana   São Raimundo   Serra   PERNAMBUCO   Caruaru   RECIFE
SERRA DOS APIACÁS   Pedro Aforso   Alto Parnaíba   Nonato   Talhada   Garanhuns   Barreiros
Tocantínia   Santa Filomena   Petrolina   Paulo Afonso   ALAGOAS   Maceió
SERRA FORMOSA   Pium   Gilbués   Juazeiro   Jeremoabo   Arapiraca
Prainha Nova   Palmas   Remanso   Senhor do Bonfim   SERGIPE   Propriá
Cristalândia   Porto Nacional   Parnaguá   Xique-Xique   Tucano   Itabaiana   Aracaju
Ilha do   TOCANTINS   Morro do Chapéu   Jacobina   Estância
MATO GROSSO   Bananal   Dianópolis   Barra   Serrinha   Inhambupe
Gurupi   Natividade   Represa de   Feira de Santana   Alagoinhas
PLANALTO DO   Paraná   Sobradinho   Candeias   Santo Amaro
MATO GROSSO   Arraias   Barreiras   Santo Antônio   SALVADOR
Diamantino   São Miguel   Posse   BAHIA   de Jesus   Valença
Utiariti   do Araguaia   Porangatu   Bom Jesus   Paramirim   Mucujê
Rosário Oeste   da Lapa   Guanambi   Caetité   Jequié   Ilhéus
Porto Esperidião   GOIÁS   Formosa   Januária   Vitória da   Itabuna
Cuiabá   Aruanã   DISTRITO   São Francisco   Conquista   Ibicaraí   Itapetinga   Canavieiras
Poxoréu   FEDERAL   Pedra Azul   Belmonte
San Ignacio   Aragarças   Goiás   BRASÍLIA   Montes Claros   Almenara   Porto Seguro
de Velasco   Rondonópolis   Iporá   Anápolis   Luziânia   Pirapora   Araçuaí   Prado
San José   Alto Araguaia   Pires do Rio   Diamantina   Alcobaça
de Chiquitos   Jataí   Rio Verde   Araguari   SERRA DO ESPINHAÇO   Governador   Nanuque   Caravelas
Roboré   MATO GROSSO   Morrinhos   Corinto   Valadares   São Mateus
DO SUL   Coxim   Itumbiara   Curvelo   ESPÍRITO
Puerto Suárez   Catalão   MINAS   GERAIS   Sete Lagoas   Caratinga   SANTO   Aracruz
Corumbá   Paranaíba   Araguari   Ibiá   Colatina
Porto   Uberlândia   Araxá   Pará   BELO   Ponte Nova   Vitória
Esperança   Campo Grande   Santa Fé do Sul   Ituiutaba   HORIZONTE   Itaguaçu   Vila Velha
Aquidauana   São José   Uberaba   Divinópolis   Itabira   Cachoeiro de Itapemirim
do Rio Preto   Barretos   Formiga   Itaúna   Lafaiete
PARAGUAY   Porto Murtinho   Bela Vista   França   Passos   Cabo de São Tomé
Pedro Juan   Dourados   Araçatuba   Poços de   Guaxupé   Juiz de   Campos
Caballero   Presidente   Marília   Ribeirão   Caldas   Fora
Ponta Porã   Prudente   Preto   SÃO PAULO   RIO DE JANEIRO
GRAN CHACO   Amambaí   Bauru   Rio Claro   Volta Redonda   Nova Iguaçu
Umuarama   PARANÁ   São José dos   Niterói
Concepción   Maringá   Apucarana   Campos   RIO DE JANEIRO
Londrina   Sorocaba   SÃO PAULO   Tropic of Capricorn

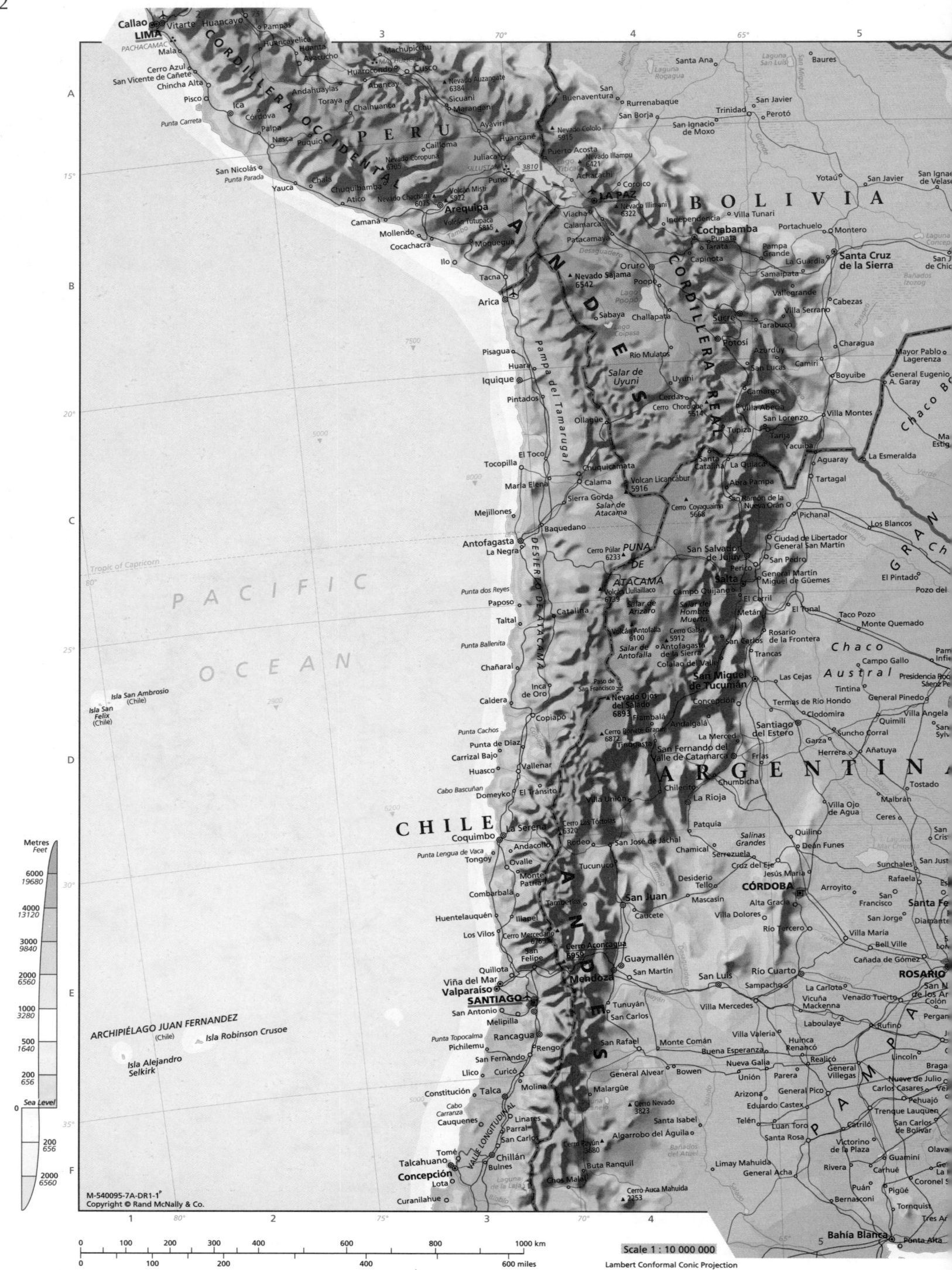

72

CORDILLERA OCCIDENTAL
PERU
BOLIVIA
ANDES
CORDILLERA REAL
PUNA DE ATACAMA
CHILE
ARGENTINA
PAMPA

PACIFIC OCEAN

Callao · **LIMA**
PACHACAMAC
Vitarte · Huancayo · Pampas
Mala · Huancavelica · Huanta · Ayacucho · Machupicchu
Cerro Azul · Andahuaylas · Abancay · Cusco · Nevado Auzangate 6384 · Sicuani · Marangani
San Vicente de Cañete · Toraya · Chalhuanca
Chincha Alta
Pisco · Ica · Córdova · Palpa · Ayaviri · Huancané
Punta Carreta · Nasca · Puquio · Caylloma · Juliaca · *ILLUSTA* · *3810* · Puerto Acosta · Nevado Illampu 6421 · Achacachi
San Nicolás · Chala · Chuquibamba · Nevado Coropuna 6305 · Volcán Misti 5822 · Puno · Coroico · **LA PAZ**
Punta Parada · Yauca · Atico · Nevado Chachani 6075 · **Arequipa** · Viacha · Nevado Illimani 6322 · Independencia · Villa Tunari
Camaná · Volcán Tutupaca 5815 · Calamarca · Patacamaya · **Cochabamba** · Punata · Portachuelo · Montero
Mollendo · Moquegua · Oruro · Pampa Grande · La Guardia · **Santa Cruz de la Sierra**
Cocachacra · Tacna · Nevado Sajama 6542 · Poopó · Samaipata
Ilo · Arica · Sabaya · Challapata · Sucre · Vallegrande · Villa Serrano · Cabezas
Lago Poopó · Tarabuco · Charagua
Pisagua · *Salar de Coipasa* · Río Mulatos · Potosí · Azurduy · Camiri · Mayor Pablo Lagerenza
Huara · Uyuni · San Lucas · Villa Abecia · Boyuibe · General Eugenio A. Garay
Iquique · *Salar de Uyuni* · Cerdas · Cerro Chorolque 5614 · Camargo · San Lorenzo · Villa Montes
Pintados · Ollagüe · Cerro Coyaguaima 5668 · Tupiza · Tarija · Yacuiba · La Esmeralda
El Toco · Chuquicamata · Volcán Licancabur 5916 · San Ramón de la Nueva Orán · Aguaray · La Quiaca · Abra Pampa · Tartagal
Tocopilla · Calama · Santa Catalina · La Quiaca · Pichanal · Los Blancos
María Elena · Sierra Gorda · *Salar de Atacama* · Ciudad de Libertador General San Martín
Mejillones · Baquedano · Cerro Púlar 6233 · San Salvador de Jujuy · San Pedro · General Martín Miguel de Güemes · El Pintado
Antofagasta · La Negra · **Salta** · Perico · Pozo del
Tropic of Capricorn · El Corril · General Martín Miguel de Güemes
Volcán Llullaillaco 6739 · Campo Quijano
Punta dos Reyes · Paposo · Catalina · Volcán Antofalla 6100 · *Salar de Arizaro* · *Salar del Hombre Muerto* · El Tunal · Metán · Taco Pozo · Monte Quemado
Taltal · Cerro Galán 5912 · Rosario de la Frontera · Chaco Austral
Punta Ballenita · *Salar de Antofalla* · Antofagasta de la Sierra · San Carlos · Trancas · Campo Gallo
Chañaral · Colalao del Valle · Las Cejas · Tintina · General Pinedo
Inca de Oro · Paso de San Francisco · **San Miguel de Tucumán** · Termas de Río Hondo · Villa Angela
Caldera · Nevado Ojos del Salado 6893 · Concepción · Clodomira · Quimili
Copiapó · Fiambalá · Andalgalá · Santiago del Estero · Suncho Corral
Punta Cachos · Cerro Bonete Grande 6872 · La Merced · Garza · Añatuya
La Merced · Tinogasta · San Fernando del Valle de Catamarca · Frías · Herrera
Punta de Díaz · Chumbicha · Tostado
Carrizal Bajo · Vallenar · Chilecito · La Rioja · Malbrán
Huasco · Villa Unión · La Rioja · Ceres
Cabo Bascuñán · Domeyko · El Tránsito · Patquía · Villa Ojo de Agua
Coquimbo · **La Serena** · Cerro Las Tórtolas 6320 · Salinas Grandes · Quilino · San Just
Punta Lengua de Vaca · Andacollo · Rodeo · San José de Jáchal · Chamical · Dean Funes · Sunchales
Tongoy · Ovalle · Tucunuco · Serrezuela · Cruz del Eje · Jesús María · Rafaela
Monte Patria · Desiderio Tello · **CÓRDOBA** · Arroyito · San Francisco · **Santa Fe**
Combarbalá · Tamberías · Mascasín · Alta Gracia · San Jorge · Diamante
Huentelauquén · Illapel · San Juan · Villa Dolores · Río Tercero · Villa María · Bell Ville
Los Vilos · Cerro Mercedario 6770 · Caucete · Cañada de Gómez
Cerro Aconcagua 6959 · San Felipe · Guaymallén · San Luis · Río Cuarto · **ROSARIO**
Quillota · Mendoza · San Martín · La Carlota · La Laguna
Viña del Mar · **Mendoza** · Sampacho · Vicuña Mackenna · Venado Tuerto · Colón
Valparaíso · San Antonio · Tunuyán · San Carlos · Villa Mercedes · Laboulaye · Rufino
SANTIAGO · Melipilla · Rancagua · Villa Valeria · Huinca Renancó · Lincoln
Punta Topocalma · Pichilemu · San Rafael · Monte Comán · Nueva Galia · General Villegas · Braga
San Fernando · Rengo · Buena Esperanza · Realicó · Nueve de Julio
Llico · Curicó · Molina · General Alvear · Bowen · Unión · Parera · Carlos Casares · Pehuajó
Constitución · Talca · Malargüe · Arizona · General Pico · Eduardo Castex · Trenque Lauquen
Cabo Carranza · Cerro Nevado 3823 · Santa Isabel · Telén · Catriló · San Carlos de Bolívar
Linares · Luan Toro · Santa Rosa · Olava
Parral · Limay Mahuida · General Acha · Guamini
Cauquenes · Cerro Payún 3680 · Rivera · La
Tomé · San Carlos · Puán · Coronel S
Talcahuano · Chillán · Buta Ranquil · Carhué
Concepción · Bulnes · Chos Malal · Tornquist
Lota · Laguna de la Laja · Bernasconi
Curanilahue · Cerro Auca Mahuida 2253 · **Bahía Blanca** · Punta Alta

Isla San Ambrosio (Chile)
Isla San Félix (Chile)

ARCHIPIÉLAGO JUAN FERNANDEZ (Chile) · *Isla Robinson Crusoe*
Isla Alejandro Selkirk

Metres / Feet
6000 / 19680
4000 / 13120
3000 / 9840
2000 / 6560
1000 / 3280
500 / 1640
200 / 656
0 / Sea Level
200 / 656
2000 / 6560

M-540095-7A-DR1-1"
Copyright © Rand McNally & Co.

Scale 1 : 10 000 000
Lambert Conformal Conic Projection

0 100 200 300 400 600 800 1000 km
0 100 200 400 600 miles

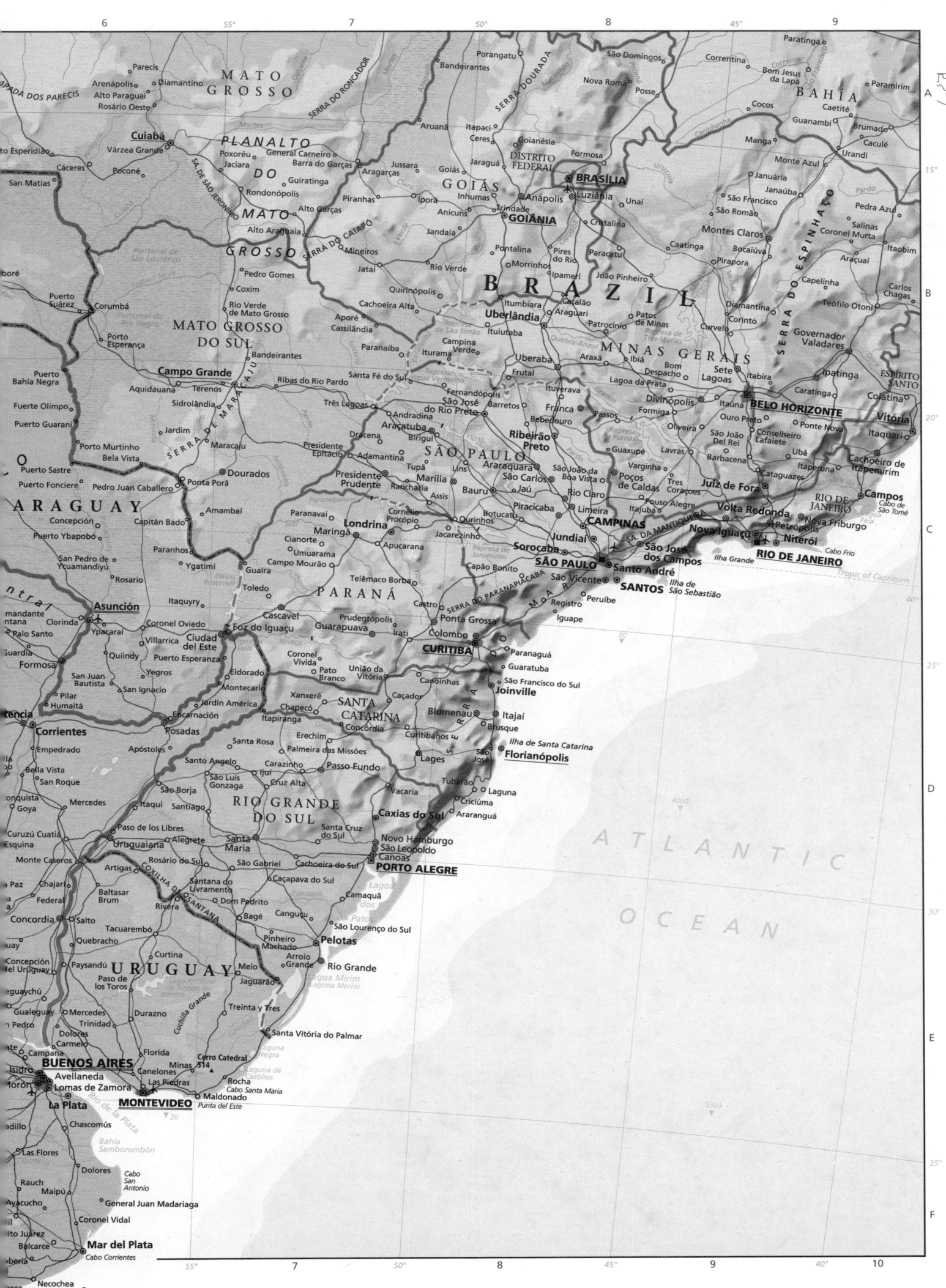

MATO GROSSO

Parecis
Arenápolis
Alto Paraguai
Diamantino
Rosário Oeste

PLANALTO
DO
MATO
GROSSO

Cuiabá
Várzea Grande
Poconé
Poxoréu
Jaciara
General Carneiro
Barra do Garças
Guiratinga
Rondonópolis
Alto Garças
Alto Araguaia
Pedro Gomes
Coxim

SA. DE SÃO JERÔNIMO
SERRA DO RONCADOR

Porangatu
Bandeirantes
São Domingos
Nova Roma
Posse
Correntina

Bom Jesus
da Lapa
Paratinga
Paramirim

BAHÍA
Cocos
Guanambi
Caetité
Brumado
Manga
São Francisco
São Romão
Monte Azul
Januária
Janaúba
Pedra Azul
Urandi
Caculé
Coronel Murta
Salinas
Itaobim
Araçuaí

Aruana
Itapaci
Ceres
Jussara
Goiás
Jaraguá
Goianésia
Formosa
Anápolis
Luziânia

DISTRITO
FEDERAL
BRASÍLIA

GOIÁS
Inhumas
Trindade
GOIÂNIA
Anicuns
Jandaia
Cristalina
Caatinga
Bocaiúva
Pirapora

BRAZIL
MINAS GERAIS

Montes Claros
Diamantina
Capelinha
Teófilo Otoni

SERRA DO ESPINHAÇO

Governador
Valadares
Ipatinga

ESPÍRITO
SANTO
Caratinga
Colatina
Vitória
Itaquari

Pontalina
Pires
do Rio
Morrinhos
Paracatu
João Pinheiro
Caatinga
Patos
de Minas
Curvelo
Três Marias

Itumbiara
Uberlândia
Araguari
Catalão
Patrocínio
Araxá
Ibiá
Bom
Despacho

Sete
Lagoas
Itabira
BELO HORIZONTE
Ouro Preto
Conselheiro
Lafaiete
Ponte Nova

Rio Verde
Quirinópolis
Cachoeira Alta
Aporé
Cassilândia
Paranaíba
Ituiutaba
Frutal
Ituverava
Franca
Passos
Formiga
Divinópolis
Oliveira
Lavras
Barbacena
Cataguazes
Itaperuna

Cachoeiro de
Itapemirim
Campos
Cabo de
São Tomé

MATO GROSSO
DO SUL

Puerto
Suárez
Corumbá
Porto
Esperança
Puerto
Bahía Negra
Fuerte Olimpo
Puerto Guaraní

Campo Grande
Aquidauana
Terenos
Sidrolândia
Jardim

Ribas do Rio Pardo
Santa Fé do Sul
Bandeirantes
Campina
Verde
Iturama

Fernandópolis
São José
do Rio Preto
Barretos
Bebedouro
São João da
Boa Vista
Poços
de Caldas
Guaxupé
Varginha
Três
Corações
Pouso Alegre
Volta Redonda
Nova Iguaçu
RIO DE
JANEIRO
Niterói
Nova Friburgo
Petrópolis

Três Lagoas
Andradina
Araçatuba
Birigui
Dracena
Adamantina
Tupã
Presidente
Epitácio
Presidente
Prudente
Rancharia
Marília
Assis
Bauru

SÃO PAULO
Araraquara
São Carlos
Jaú
Rio Claro
Limeira
Piracicaba
Botucatu
CAMPINAS
Jundiaí
Sorocaba
SÃO PAULO
Santo André
Santos
São Vicente
Ilha de
São Sebastião
Peruíbe
Registro
Iguape

Ribeirão
Preto

Puerto
Sastre
Puerto
Fonciere
Pedro Juan Caballero
Ponta Porã
Dourados
Amambaí
Capitán Bado

PARAGUAY
Concepción
Puerto Ybapobó
San Pedro de
Ycuamandiyú
Rosario
Ygatimí

Asunción

Clorinda
Palo Santo
Formosa
San Juan
Bautista
Pilar
Humaitá

Corrientes
Empedrado
Bella Vista
San Roque
Mercedes
Goya
Curuzú Cuatiá
Esquina

Villarrica
Coronel Oviedo
Ciudad
del Este
Puerto Esperanza
Yegros
Quiindy
Ypacaraí

Villa Rica
Encarnación
Posadas
Apóstoles
Santa Rosa
São Luís
Gonzaga
Santo Ángelo

Paranavaí
Cianorte
Umuarama
Campo Mourão
Guaíra
Toledo
Cascavel
Foz do Iguaçu
Eldorado
Montecarlo
Jardim América
Xanxerê
Itapiranga
Chapecó
Concórdia

Maringá
Londrina
Apucarana
Telêmaco Borba

PARANÁ
Ponta Grossa
Guarapuava
Prudentópolis
Irati
Coronel
Vivida
Pato
Branco
União da
Vitória
Caçador

Castro
Colombo
CURITIBA
Paranaguá
Guaratuba
São Francisco do Sul
Joinville

Cornélio
Procópio
Jacarezinho
Quirinos
Capão Bonito

SERRA DO PARANAPIACABA
São José
dos Campos

Ilha Grande
RIO DE JANEIRO
Cabo Frio
Tropic of Capricorn

Caçapava
Canoinhas

SANTA
CATARINA
Blumenau
Brusque
Itajaí
Ilha de Santa Catarina
Florianópolis

Santa Rosa
Erechim
Palmeira das Missões
Carazinho
Passo Fundo
Curitibanos
Lages
São José

Cruz Alta
Ijuí
São Borja
Santiago
Itaqui
Santo Ángelo

RIO GRANDE
DO SUL

Uruguaiana
Alegrete
Santa
Maria
Santa Cruz
do Sul
São Gabriel
Vacaria
Caxias do Sul
Araranguá
Criciúma
Tubarão
Laguna

Paso de los Libres
Rosário do Sul
Cachoeira do Sul
Novo Hamburgo
São Leopoldo
Canoas
PORTO ALEGRE

Monte Caseros
Artigas
Santana do
Livramento
Rivera
Dom Pedrito
Bagé
Caçapava do Sul

ATLANTIC

OCEAN

4000

URUGUAY

Chajarí
Federal
Concordia
Salto
Paysandú
Concepción
del Uruguay
Gualeguay
Mercedes
Trinidad

Baltasar
Brum
Tacuarembó
Quebracho
Curtina
Paso de
los Toros
Durazno
Florida

Pinheiro
Machado
Canguçu
São Lourenço do Sul
Camaquã
Pelotas
Arroio
Grande
Rio Grande

Melo
Jaguarão

Lagoa
dos
Patos

Lagoa Mirim
Laguna Merín

Santa Vitória do Palmar

Treinta y Tres

3303

Cerro Catedral
514
Minas
Rocha
Maldonado
Punta del Este

BUENOS AIRES
Avellaneda
Lomas de Zamora
La Plata

Canelones
Las Piedras
MONTEVIDEO
Cabo Santa María

Rio de la Plata

Chascomús

Bahía
Samborombón

Las Flores
Dolores
Rauch
Maipú
General Juan Madariaga
Coronel Vidal
Mar del Plata
Cabo Corrientes

Necochea

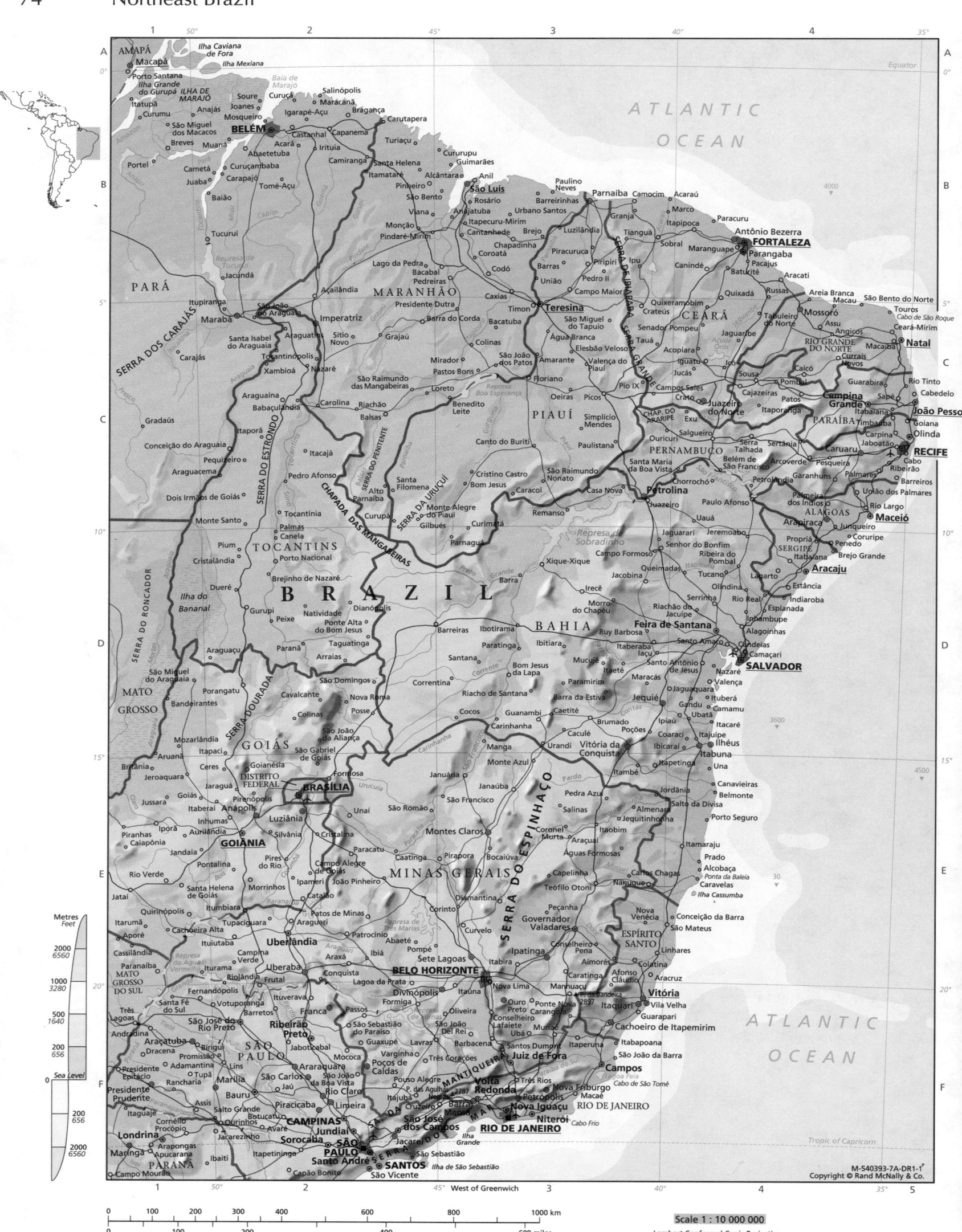

Scale 1 : 10 000 000

Lambert Conformal Conic Projection

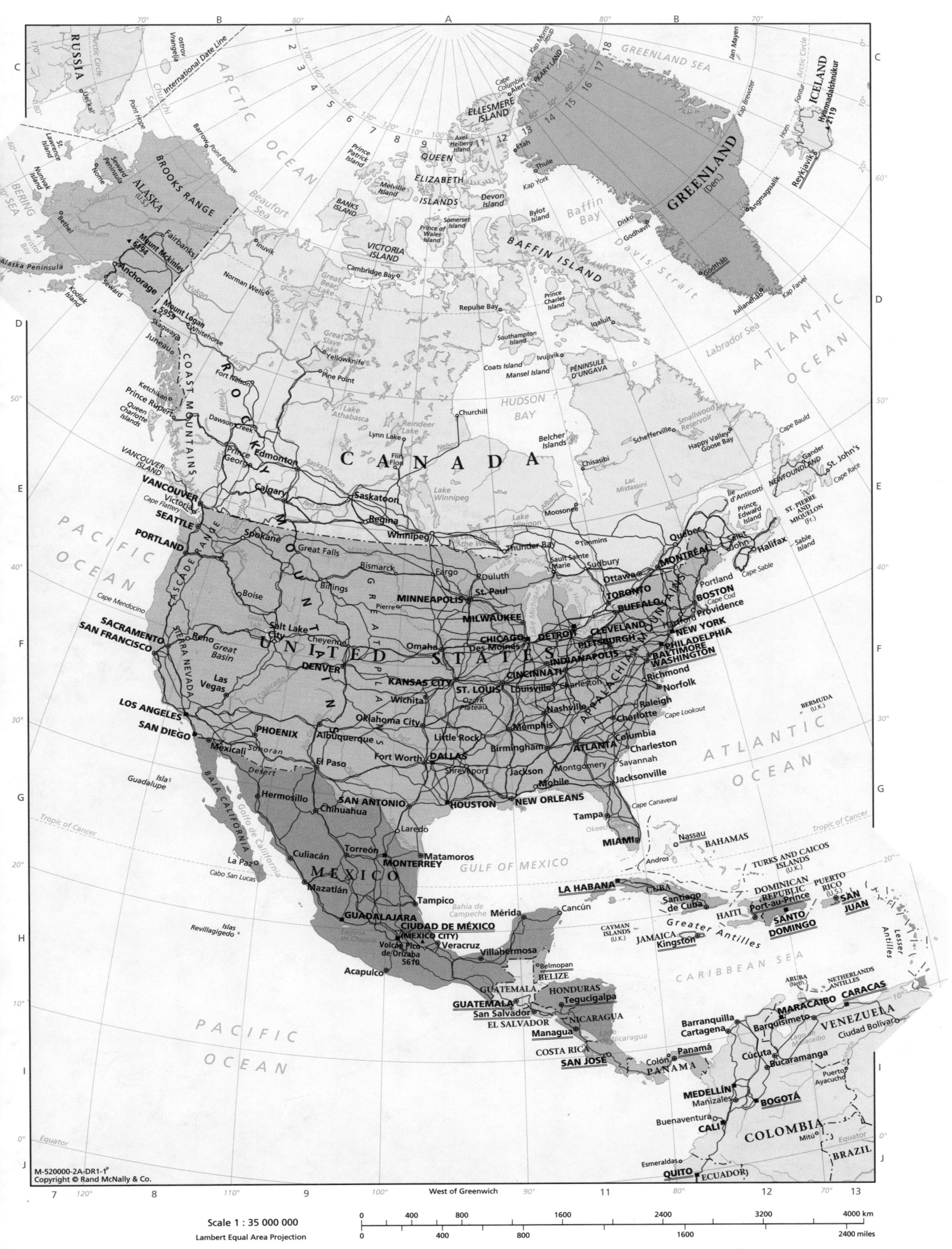

Scale 1 : 35 000 000

Lambert Equal Area Projection

| 0 | 400 | 800 | 1600 | 2400 | 3200 | 4000 km |

| 0 | 400 | 800 | 1600 | 2400 miles |

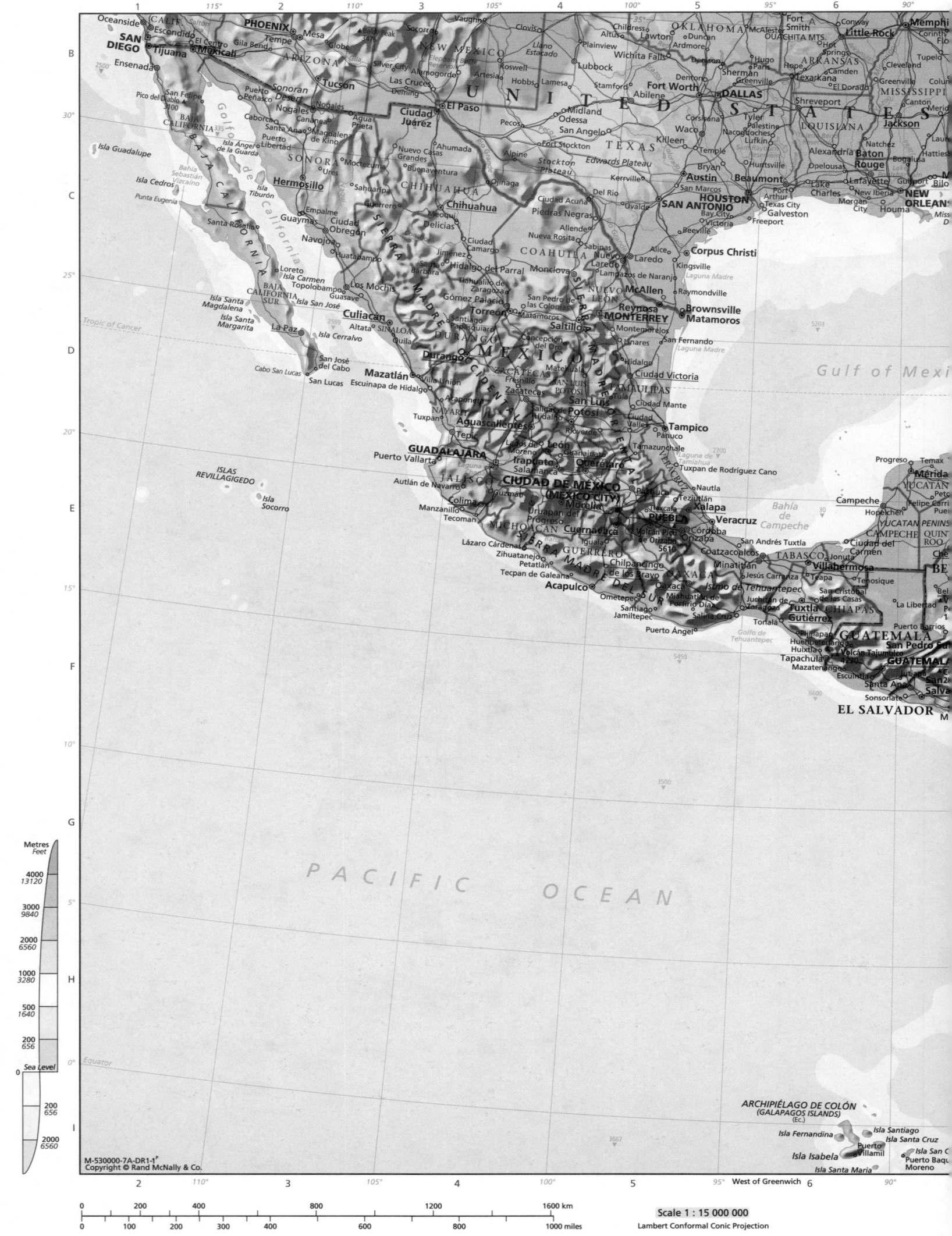

PACIFIC OCEAN

Metres
Feet
4000
13120
3000
9840
2000
6560
1000
3280
500
1640
200
656
Sea Level
0
200
656
2000
6560

M-530000-7A-DR1-1
Copyright © Rand McNally & Co.

0   200   400   800   1200   1600 km
0   100   200   300   400   600   800   1000 miles

Scale 1 : 15 000 000
Lambert Conformal Conic Projection

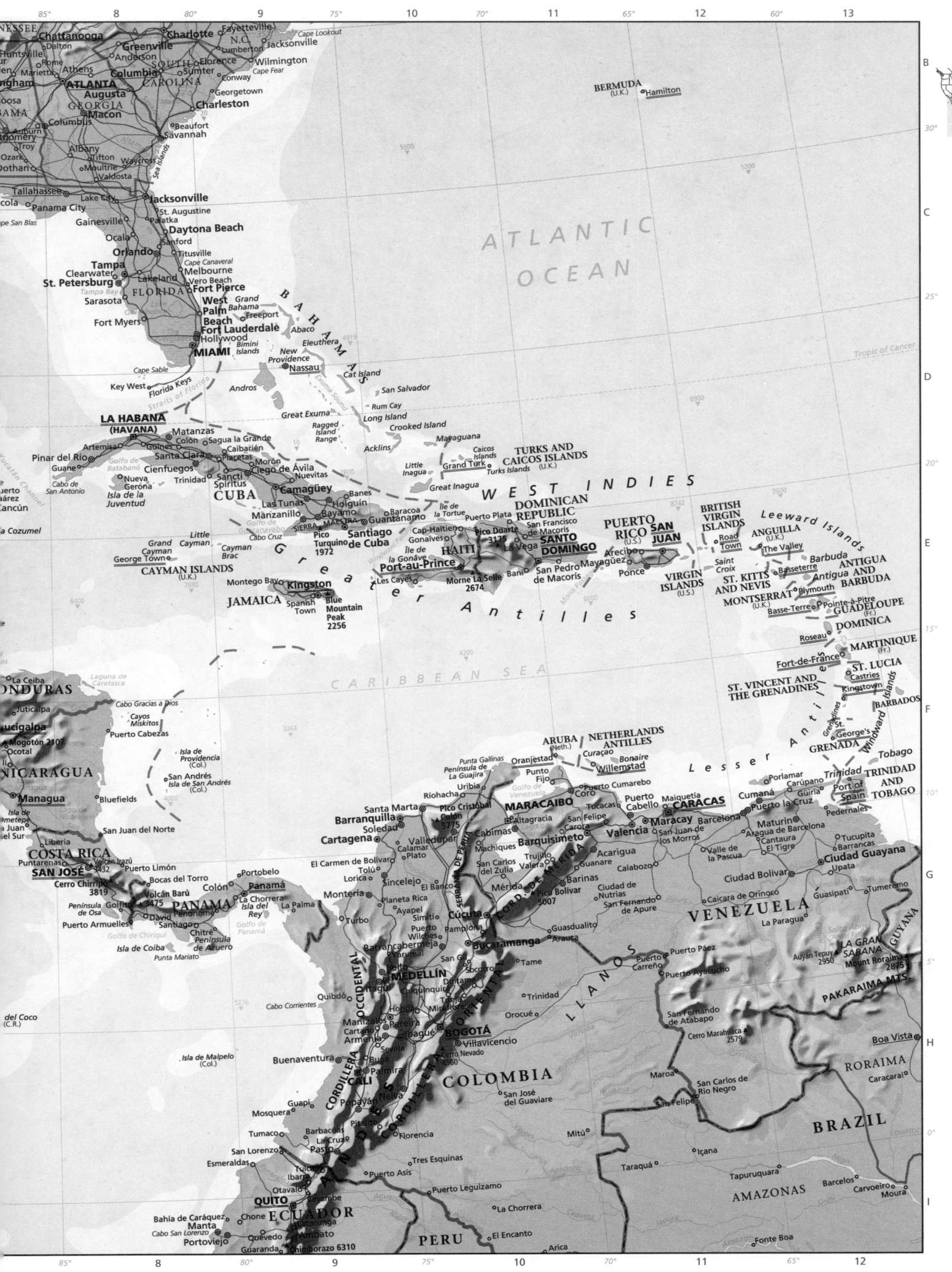

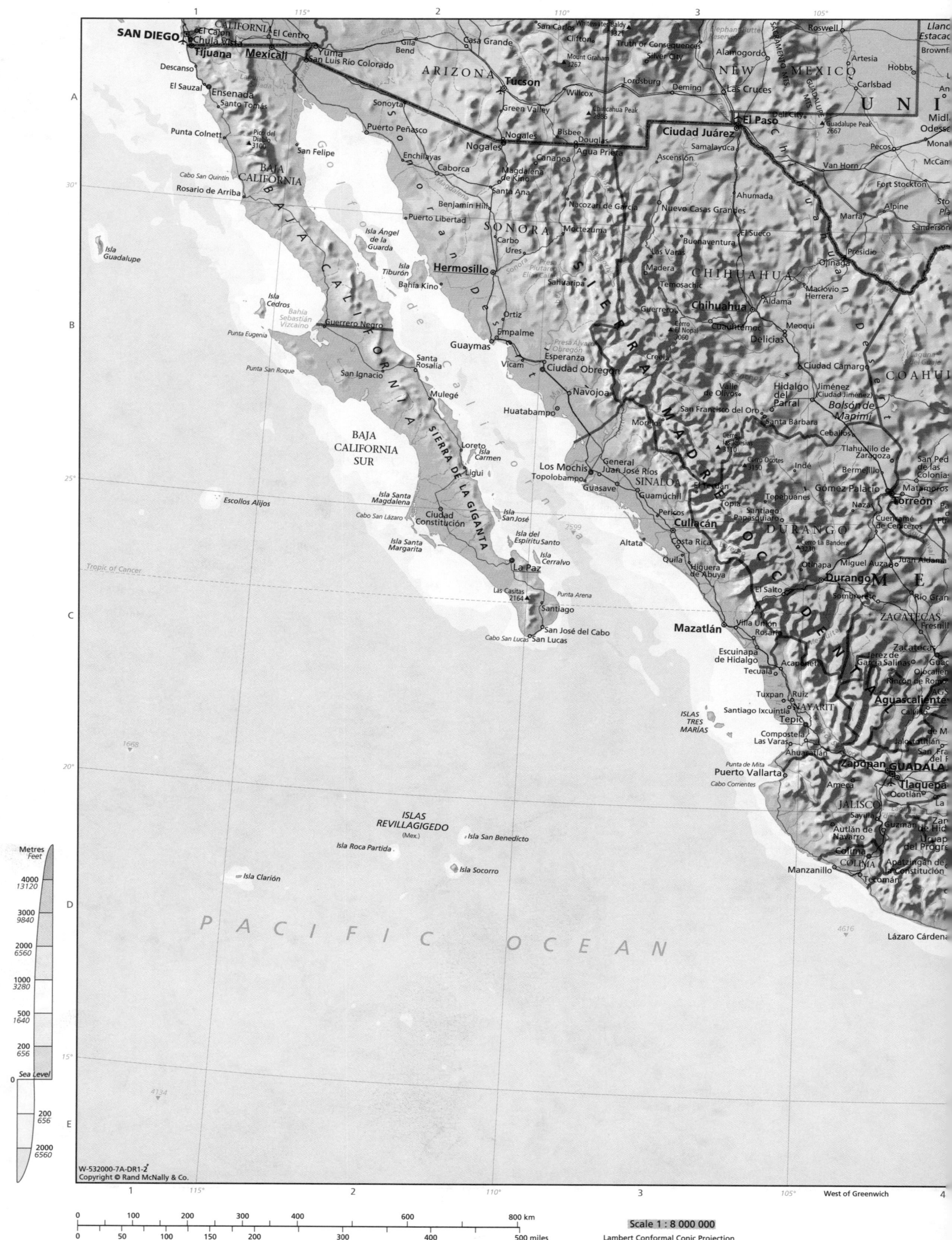

Scale 1 : 8 000 000
Lambert Conformal Conic Projection

West of Greenwich

Mexican State Abbreviations
AGS = AGUASCALIENTES
TLAX = TLAXCALA
D.F. = DISTRITO FEDERAL

GULF OF MEXICO

PACIFIC OCEAN

CARIBBEAN

MEXICO

YUCATAN PENINSULA

GUATEMALA

BELIZE

HONDURAS

EL SALVADOR

NICARAGUA

COSTA RICA

PANAMA

CUBA

JAMAICA

CAYMAN ISLANDS (U.K.)

LA HABANA (HAVANA)

Kingston

Metres Feet
4000 13120
3000 9840
2000 6560
1000 3280
500 1640
200 656
0 Sea Level
200 656
2000 6560

W-530093-7A-DR1-2
Copyright © Rand McNally & Co.

Scale 1 : 8 000 000
Lambert Conformal Conic Projection

West of Greenwich

0 100 200 300 400 600 800 km
0 50 100 150 200 300 400 500 miles

ATLANTIC OCEAN

Tropic of Cancer

6900

BAHAMAS
Crooked Island
Little Inagua
Acklins
Mayaguana
Samana Cay
North Caicos
Middle Caicos
East Caicos
Caicos Islands
Grand Turk
Turks Islands
TURKS AND CAICOS ISLANDS (U.K.)
Matthew Town
Great Inagua
Baracoa
Punta de Quemado
Île de la Tortue
Cap à Foux

W I N D W A R D   P A S S A G E

HISPANIOLA
Cabo Isabela
Manzanillo Bay
Limbé
Cap-Haïtien
Puerto Plata
Cabo Francés Viejo
Gonaïves
Mao
Santiago de los Caballeros
Moca
San Francisco de Macorís
Cabo Samaná
Sánchez
La Vega
HAITI
Pico Duarte 3175
Saint-Marc
San Juan de la Maguana
Pétion-Ville
Port-au-Prince
Morne La Selle 2674
Jérémie
Les Cayes
Jacmel
Pointe Abacou
Île de la Gonâve
Golfe de la Gonâve
Golfe de Gonâve
Canal du Sud
Alto Bandera 2630
Azua
Baní
San Cristóbal
San Pedro de Macorís
La Romana
Higüey
Cabo Engaño
Isla Saona
Cerro de Punta 1338
DOMINICAN REPUBLIC
Enriquillo
Isla Beata
Cabo Beata
Barahona
Bahía de Ocoa
Isla de Mona
Cabo Rojo
Mona Passage
Mayagüez
Ponce
PUERTO RICO (U.S.)
SAN JUAN
Arecibo
Bayamón
Caguas
Charlotte Amalie
St. Thomas
St. John
VIRGIN ISLANDS (U.S.)
Virgin Islands
St. Croix
Isla de Vieques

LESSER ANTILLES

BRITISH VIRGIN ISLANDS
Anegada
Virgin Gorda
Road Town
ANGUILLA (U.K.)
The Valley
Saint Martin (Fr.-Neth.)
Sabá (Neth.)
St. Christopher (St. Kitts)
Basseterre
ST. KITTS AND NEVIS
Nevis
MONTSERRAT (U.K.)
Plymouth
Barbuda
ANTIGUA AND BARBUDA
St. John's
Antigua
Anegada Passage
LEEWARD ISLANDS
Guadeloupe Passage
Grande-Terre
Basse-Terre
Soufrière 1467
Pointe-à-Pitre (Fr.)
GUADELOUPE
Marie Galante
Basse-Terre
Morne Diablotins 1447
DOMINICA
Roseau
Martinique Passage
Montagne Pelée 1397
Fort-de-France
MARTINIQUE (Fr.)
St. Lucia Channel
Mount Gimie 950
Castries
ST. LUCIA
St. Vincent Passage
Soufrière 1234
St. Vincent
ST. VINCENT AND THE GRENADINES
Kingstown
Mount Hillaby 340
Bridgetown
BARBADOS
Grenadines

C A R I B B E A N   S E A

6000
4200

A N T I L L E S

G R E A T E R   A N T I L L E S

ARUBA (Neth.)
Oranjestad
NETHERLANDS ANTILLES
Curaçao
Bonaire
Kralendijk
Willemstad
Punta Gallinas
Cabo San Román
Punta Espada
Península de La Guajira
Cabo de La Vela
Puerto Bolívar
Uribia
Maicao
Ríohacha
Santa Marta
Barranquilla
Isla La Orchila
Isla Blanquilla
Isla de Aves
Islas Los Roques
Isla La Tortuga
LESSER ANTILLES
St. George's
GRENADA
WINDWARD ISLANDS
Tobago
Scarborough
Isla de Margarita
La Asunción
Porlamar
Pen. de Paria
Punta Peñas
Carúpano
Güiria
Port of Spain
Arima
Trinidad
San Fernando
TRINIDAD AND TOBAGO
Río Claro
Point Fortin
Gulf of Paria
Boca de la Serpiente

Punto Fijo
Core
Puerto Cumarebo
Churuguara
Tucacas
Maiquetía
CARACAS
Guarenas
Cumaná
Barcelona
Pozuelos
Puerto la Cruz
Carúpano
Maturín
Pedernales
Isla Tobejuba
Boca Grande
Corocoro Island
Morawhanna
Dabajuro
San Rafael
Altagracia
Santa Rita
MARACAIBO
La Concepción
Cabimas
Ciudad Ojeda
Cerro 1990
Carora
Machiques
Mene Grande
Lago de Maracaibo
BARQUISIMETO
Puerto Cabello
San Felipe
Valencia
MARACAY
Chivacoa
Tinaquillo
San Carlos
La Victoria
Cua
Ocumare del Tuy
San Juan de los Morros
Chaguaramas
El Sombrero
Valle de la Pascua
Aragua de Barcelona
Anaco
Cantaura
Guanipa
Tigre
El Tigre
San José de Guanipa
Tucupita
Temblador
Barrancas
DELTA DEL ORINOCO
Pico Cristóbal Colón 5775
Valledupar
Agustín Codazzi
Santa Bárbara
Trujillo
Boconó
Guanare
Acarigua
San Carlos
Valera
Mérida
Pico Bolívar 5007
Barinas
Ciudad de Nutrias
San Fernando de Apure
Calabozo
El Tigre
Ciudad Bolívar
Upata
Ciudad Guayana
Embalse del Gurí
Cerro Bolívar 802
Ciudad Piar
Cerro Mato 1863
La Paragua
El Dorado
Guasipati
Tumeremo
Matthews Ridge
GUYANA
VENEZUELA
Maicao
Gamarra
Aguachica
Simití
El Banco
Ocaña
San Juan de Colón
Cúcuta
San Cristóbal
Pamplona
Bucaramanga
Floridablanca
Piedecuesta
Málaga
San Gil
Socorro
Guasdualito
Arauca
Arauquita
Elorza
Santa Rosa
La Urbana
Cabruta
Caicara de Orinoco
Puerto Páez
Puerto Carreño
Nueva Antioquia
Tame
COLOMBIA
L L A N O S
Puerto Wilches
Río Negro
Barbosa
Chiquinquirá
Dorada
Villavicencio
Puerto López
BOGOTÁ
Cerro Nevado 4560
San Martín
Granada
Tunja
Duitama
Sogamoso
Yopal
Miraflores
Trinidad
Orocué
Puerto Rondón
Cravo Norte
Cerro Yaví 2441
Puerto Ayacucho
Arabelo
Canaima
Auyán Tepuy 2950
La Gran Sabana
Mount Roraima 2875
El Callao
RORAIMA
B R A Z I L
Iru Tepuy
Salto Ángel
PAKARAIMA MOUNTAINS
Cerro Uquía 2500
San Fernando de Atabapo
Puerto Inírida
Puerto Nariño
Orinoco

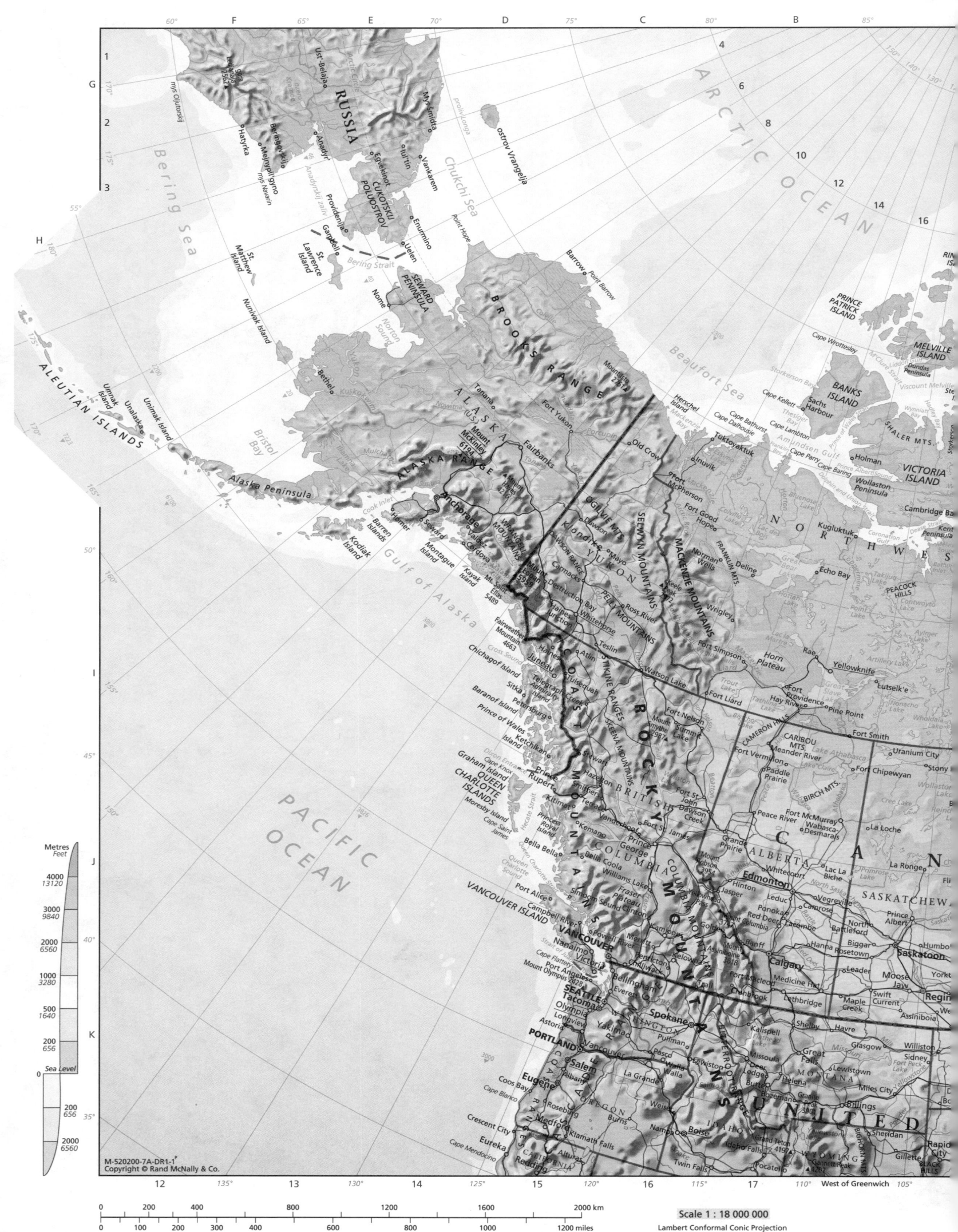

Metres
Feet

4000
13120

3000
9840

2000
6560

1000
3280

500
1640

200
656

Sea Level

200
656

2000
6560

M-520200-7A-DR1-1°
Copyright © Rand McNally & Co.

0   200   400   800   1200   1600   2000 km
0   100 200 300   400   500   600   700   800   1200 miles

Scale 1 : 18 000 000
Lambert Conformal Conic Projection

FAROE ISLANDS (Den.)
Tórshavn

ICELAND
Ísafjördur
Seydisfjördur
Akureyri
Reykjavik
Keflavik
Vestmannaeyjar
Hvannadalshnúkur 2119

GREENLAND (Den.)

Greenland Sea
Denmark Strait
Kap Brewster
Kap Gustav Holm
Mont Forel ▲3360
Angmagssalik
Jens Munks Ø
Kap Mösting
Kap Cort Adelaer
Kap Farvel
Julianehåb
Wigtut
Frederikshåb
Godthåb (Nuuk)
Sukkertoppen
Holsteinsborg
Sondre Stromfjord
Egedesminde
Godhavn
Disko
Qutdligssat
Jakobshavn
Umanak
Upernavik
Thule (Qaanaaq)
Etah
Kap York
Kap Sherard
Philpots Island
Coburg Island
Peary Land
Kap Morris Jesup
Kap Bridgman
Lincoln Sea
Cape Columbia
Barbeau Peak ▲2616
Alert
Cape Parker

ATLANTIC OCEAN

Baffin Bay
Davis Strait
Labrador Sea

ELLESMERE ISLAND
AXEL HEIBERG ISLAND
DEVON ISLAND
Jones Sound
Lady Ann Strait
Cornwallis Island
SOMERSET ISLAND
Resolute
Barrow Strait
Lancaster Sound
Arctic Bay
Brodeur Peninsula
Borden Peninsula
BAFFIN ISLAND
Pond Inlet
Bylot Island
Cape Adair
Clyde River
Cape Dyer
Home Bay
Cumberland Peninsula
Pangnirtung
Cumberland Sound
Cape Mercy
Loks Land
Resolution Island
Frobisher Bay
Iqaluit
Kimmirut
Hall Peninsula
META INCOGNITA PENINSULA
Hoare Bay

BOOTHIA PENINSULA
Gulf of Boothia
Taloyoak
Prince of Wales Island
Franklin
PRINCE OF WALES ISLAND
MELVILLE PENINSULA
Prince Charles Island
Air Force Island
Cape Wilson
Repulse Bay
Lyon Inlet
Vansittart Island
Cape Dorchester
Foxe Channel
Foxe Basin
Igloolik
Cape Chapman
Hall Haven
William Island

TERRITORIES
NORTHWEST TERRITORIES
Baker Lake
Aberdeen Lake
Franklin Lake
Rankin Inlet
Arviat
Wathkyed Lake
Kaminak Lake
Nueltin Lake

FOXE PENINSULA
Cape Dorset
Fair Ness
Foxe Peninsula
Nottingham Island
Salluit
Cap de Nouvelle-France
Ivujivik
Akpatok Island
Killiniq Island
Kangiqsujuaq
Cratère du Nouveau-Québec
Ungava Bay
PÉNINSULE D'UNGAVA
Kangirsuk
Mont d'Iberville
Mount Caubvick ▲1652
Hebron
Cape Chidley
Nain
Hopedale
South Aulatsivik Island
Tunungayualok Island

Kangiqsualujjuaq
Povungnituk
Kuujjuaq
Lac Payne
Ottawa Islands
Hopewell Islands
Inukjuak
King George Islands
Belcher Islands
Cape Henrietta Maria
Sanikiluaq

Hudson Bay
James Bay

SOUTHAMPTON ISLAND
Coral Harbour
Seahorse Point
Cape Pembroke
Coats Island
Mansel Island
Cape Southampton
Cape Low
Cape Kendall
Evans Strait
Fisher Strait

All islands within Hudson Bay, James Bay, and Ungava Bay lie within Northwest Territories.

Churchill
Cape Churchill
York Factory
Cape Tatnam
Fort Severn
Winisk
Southern Indian Lake
South Indian Lake
Gillam
Thompson
Wabowden
Sipiwesk Lake
MANITOBA
Norway House
Grand Rapids
Berens River
Gimli
Selkirk
WINNIPEG
Lake Winnipeg
Lake of the Woods
Portage la Prairie
Altona
Devils Lake
Grand Forks
Bemidji
Moorhead
Fargo
Aberdeen
Huron
Sioux Falls
Brookings
SOUTH DAKOTA
MINNEAPOLIS
St. Cloud
St. Paul
MINNESOTA
Duluth
Superior
Rochester
La Crosse
Madison
WISCONSIN
Eau Claire
Wausau
Green Bay
Appleton
Sheboygan
MILWAUKEE
CHICAGO
Rockford
Elgin
Gary

NEW FOUNDLAND
Labrador
Happy Valley-Goose Bay
Cape Harrison
Cartwright
Rigolet
Melville
Smallwood Reservoir
Schefferville
Cape Bauld
St. Anthony
Grey Islands
Battle Harbour
Belle Isle
Strait of Belle Isle
LONG RANGE MOUNTAINS
NEWFOUNDLAND
Springdale
Gander
Bonavista
Fogo Island
Carbonear
St. John's
Cape Race
Grand Bank
Channel-Port aux Basques
Cape Ray
Stephenville
Corner Brook
Gulf of St. Lawrence
SAINT PIERRE AND MIQUELON (Fr.)
CAPE BRETON ISLAND
Sydney
Glace Bay
Mont Jacques-Cartier ▲1268
Gaspé
Détroit de Jacques-Cartier
ÎLE D'ANTICOSTI
Pointe de l'Est
Havre-Saint-Pierre
Sept-Îles
Baie-Comeau
Port-Cartier
Natashquan
Blanc-Sablon
Saint-Augustin

QUÉBEC
MONTS OTISH
Lac Mistassini
Gagnon
Lac Manouane
Réservoir Manicouagan
Chibougamau
Matagami
La Sarre
Rouyn-Noranda
Val-d'Or
Amos
Senneterre
Chisasibi
Eastmain
Waskaganish
Rupert
Lac Evans
AKIMISKI ISLAND
Charlton Island
Attawapiskat
Fort Albany
Moosonee
Winisk

ONTARIO
Fort Severn
Pickle Lake
Big Trout Lake
Red Lake
Sioux Lookout
Armstrong
Atikokan
Thunder Bay
Nipigon
Geraldton
Hornepayne
Marathon
Hearst
Kapuskasing
Cochrane
Timmins
Chapleau
Wawa
Isle Royale
Sault Sainte Marie
Sudbury
Elliot Lake
North Bay
Pembroke
Bancroft
Barrie
Orillia
Peterborough
Belleville
Kitchener
London
Sarnia
Windsor
Chatham
Hamilton
TORONTO
OTTAWA
Hull

Trois-Rivières
Shawinigan
Joliette
Drummondville
MONTREAL
Québec
Lévis
Rivière-du-Loup
Rimouski
Matane
Chicoutimi
Jonquière
Alma
Saint-Félicien
La Tuque
Maniwaki
LES LAURENTIDES
APPALACHIAN MOUNTAINS
Sherbrooke

NEW BRUNSWICK
Edmundston
Campbellton
Bathurst
Fredericton
Moncton
Saint John
NOVA SCOTIA
Halifax
Dartmouth
Liverpool
Yarmouth
Digby
Truro
New Glasgow
Amherst
PRINCE EDWARD ISLAND
Charlottetown
Summerside
Îles de la Madeleine

Gulf of Maine
ATLANTIC OCEAN
Cape Cod
Sable Island

MAINE
Bangor
Augusta
Portland
Portsmouth
NEW HAMPSHIRE
Lewiston
Burlington
Montpelier
VERMONT
Concord
MASS.
BOSTON
Providence
New Haven
NEW YORK
Albany
Syracuse
Rochester
Buffalo
Binghamton
Scranton
PENNSYLVANIA
Watertown
NEW YORK
Newark
NEW JERSEY
Trenton
PHILADELPHIA

DETROIT
Flint
Lansing
Grand Rapids
Kalamazoo
Saginaw
Bay City
Traverse City
Petoskey
Alpena
Marquette
Escanaba
Menominee
Lake Michigan
Lake Huron
Lake Erie
Lake Ontario
Lake Superior
MICHIGAN
Ironwood
Hibbing
Ironton
Midland
Owosso
London

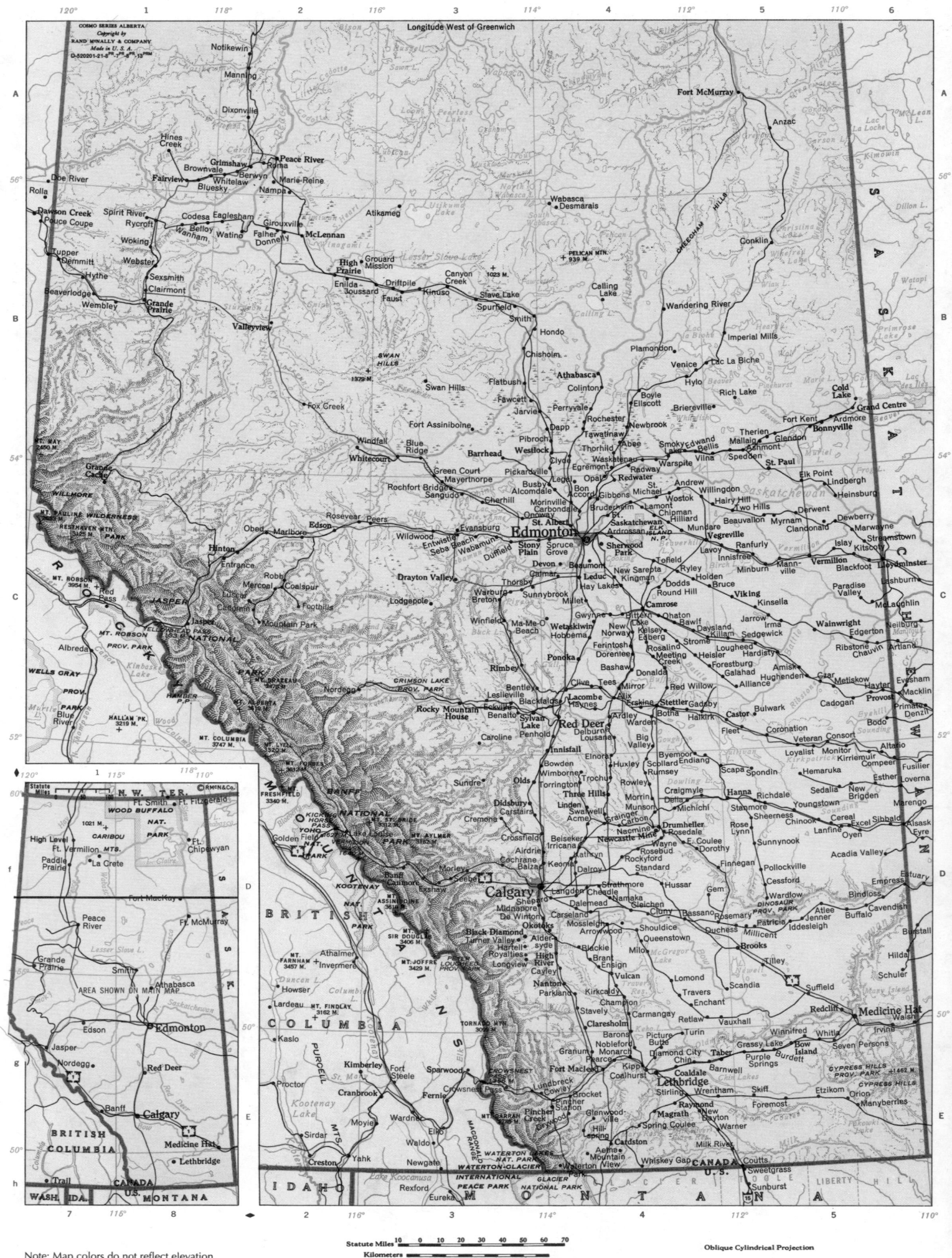

Note: Map colors do not reflect elevation.

Statute Miles 10 0 10 20 30 40 50 60 70

Kilometers 10 0 10 20 40 60 80 100

Oblique Cylindrical Projection

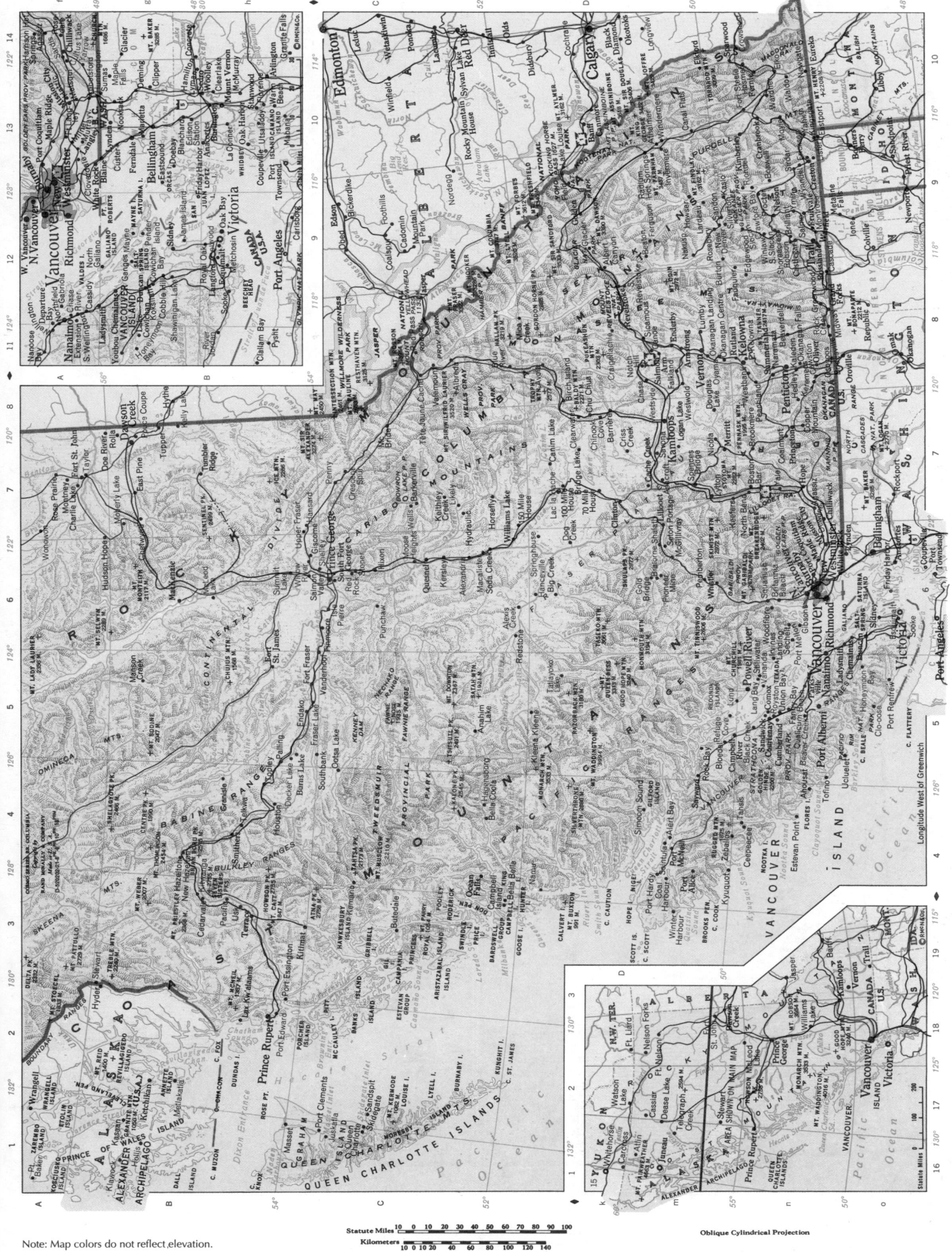

Note: Map colors do not reflect elevation.

Statute Miles 10 0 10 20 30 40 50 60 70 80 90 100

Kilometers 10 0 10 20   40   60   80   100   120   140

Oblique Cylindrical Projection

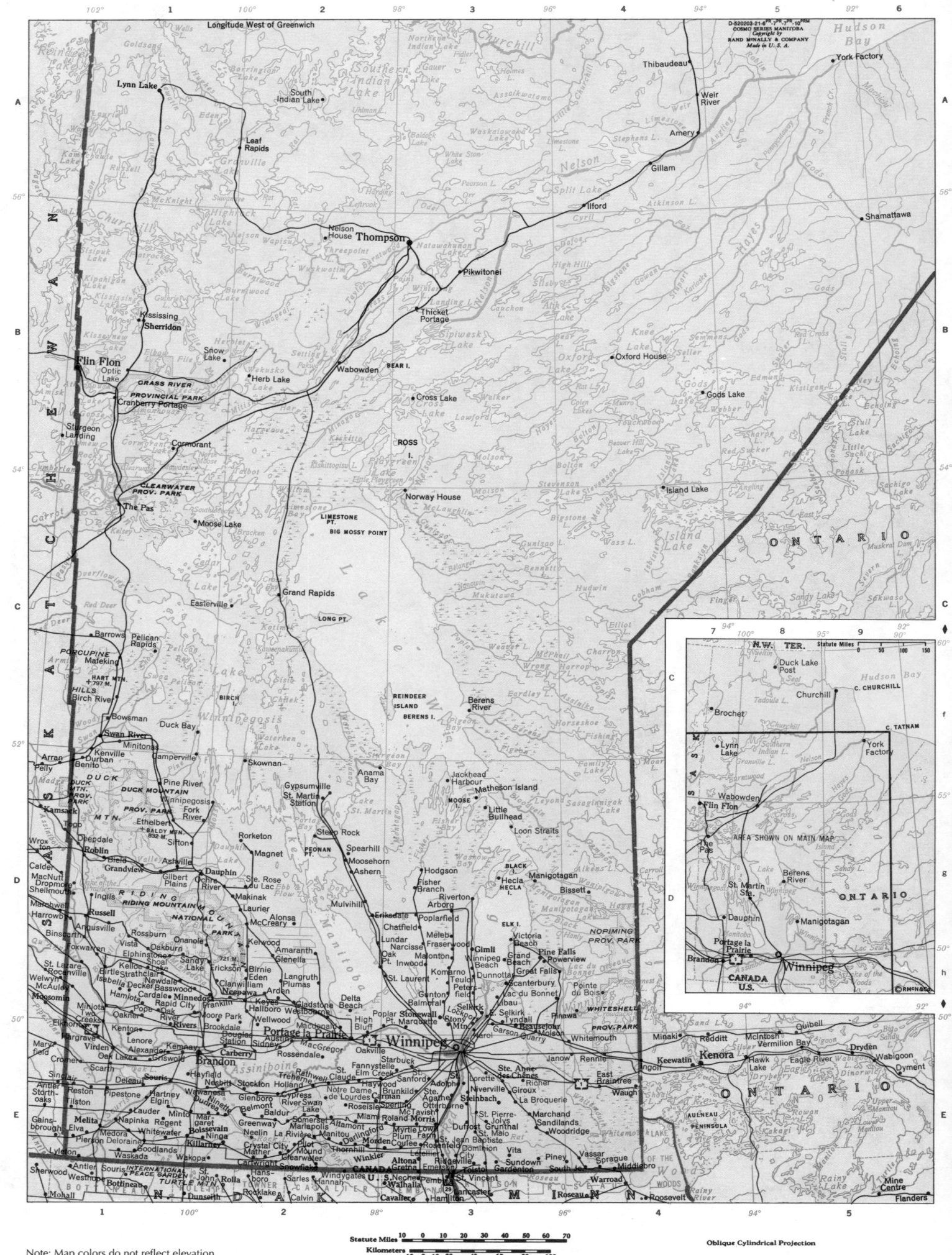

Longitude West of Greenwich

Note: Map colors do not reflect elevation.

Statute Miles
Kilometers

Oblique Cylindrical Projection

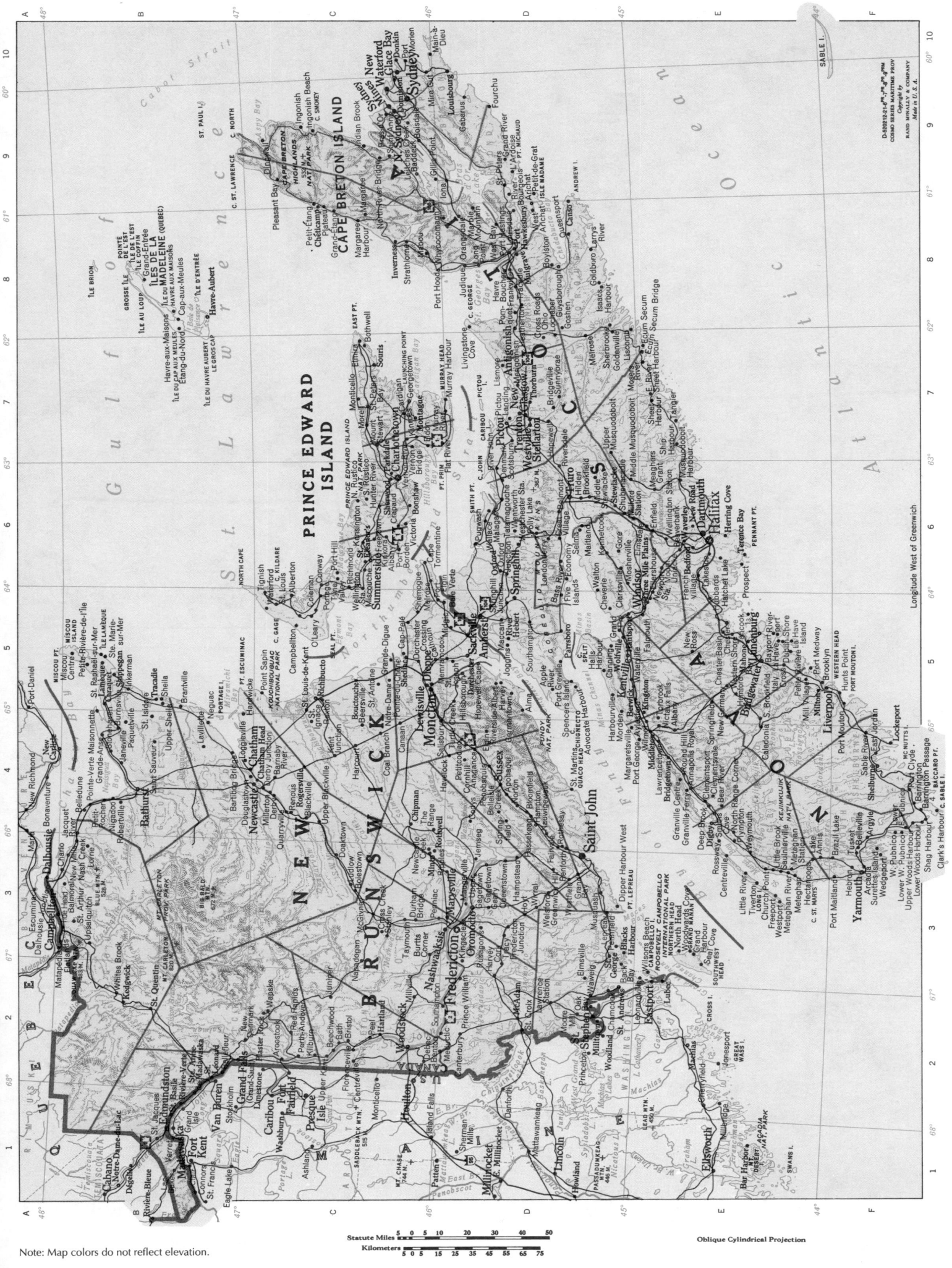

PRINCE EDWARD ISLAND

CAPE BRETON ISLAND

NEW BRUNSWICK

NOVA SCOTIA

QUEBEC

MAINE

Gulf of St. Lawrence

Cabot Strait

Atlantic Ocean

Bay of Fundy

Northumberland Strait

Saint John

Fredericton

Moncton

Halifax

Dartmouth

Sydney

Charlottetown

Summerside

Note: Map colors do not reflect elevation.

Statute Miles 5 0 5 10 20 30 40 50
Kilometers 5 0 5 15 25 35 45 55 65 75

Oblique Cylindrical Projection

Longitude West of Greenwich

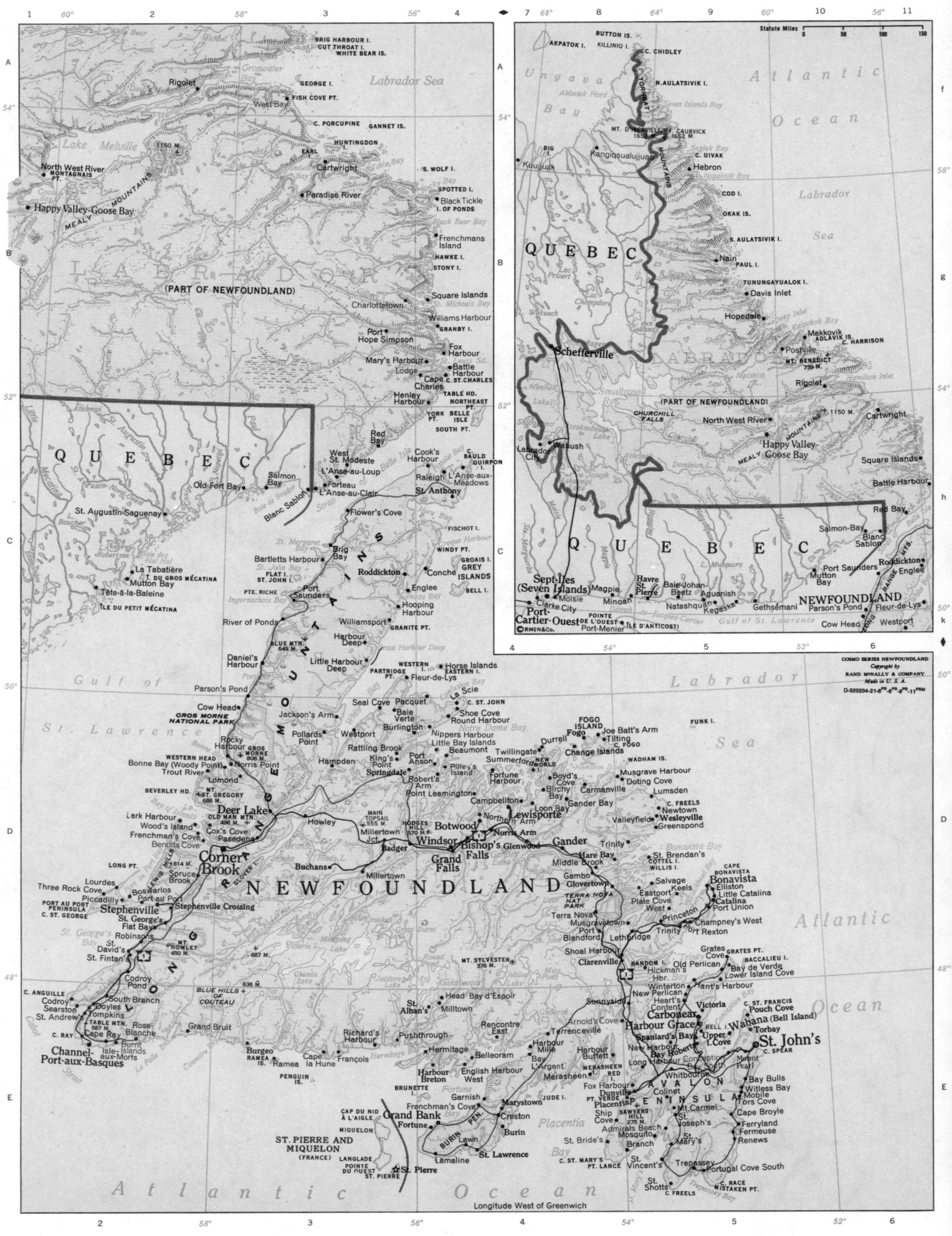

Note: Map colors do not reflect elevation.

Statute Miles   5 0 5 10   20   30   40   50   60

Kilometers   5 0 5 10   20   30   40   50   60   70   80

Lambert Conformal Conic Projection

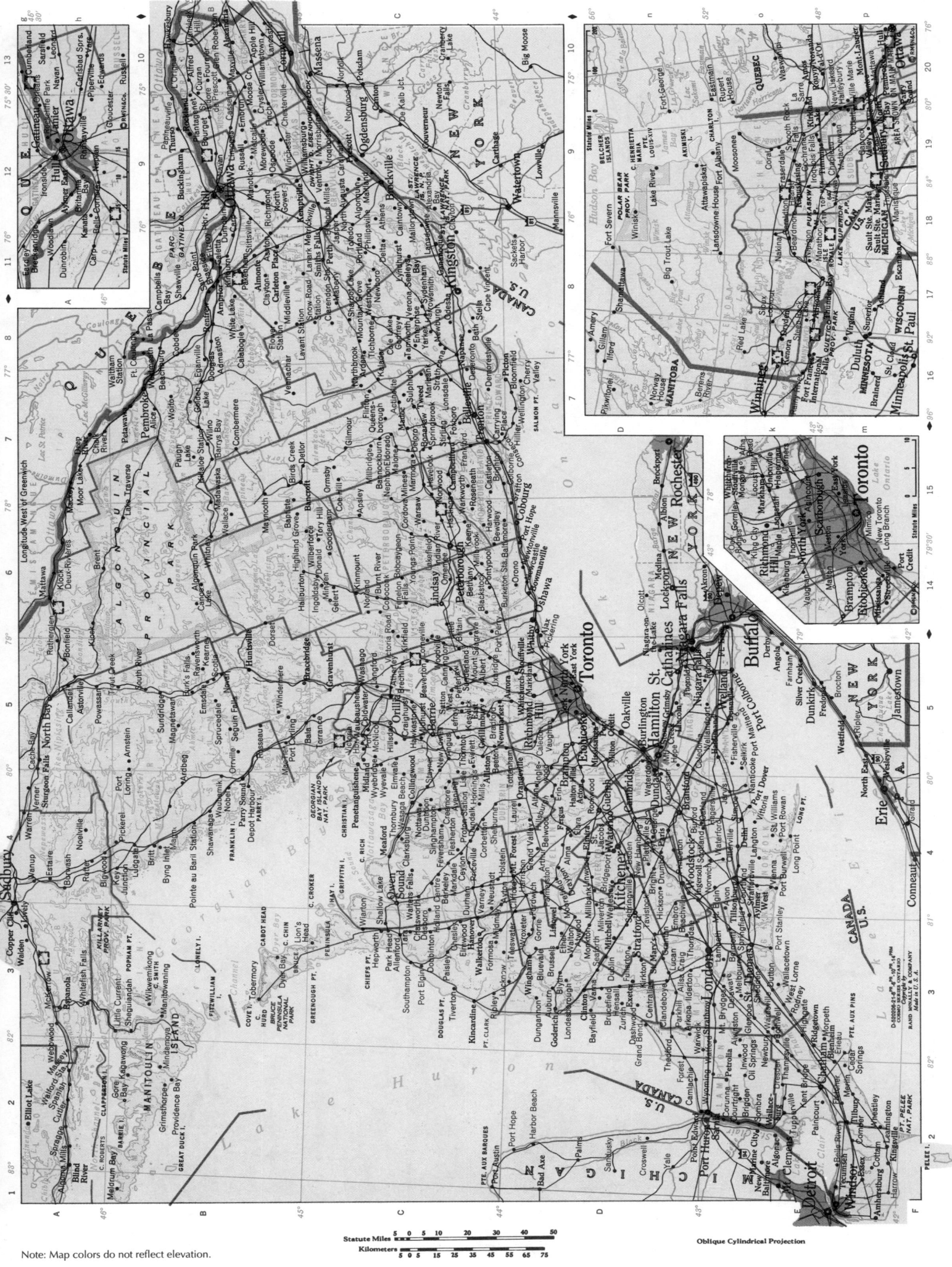

Note: Map colors do not reflect elevation.

Statute Miles 5 0 5 10   20   30   40   50

Kilometers
5 0 5 15 25 35 45 55 65 75

Oblique Cylindrical Projection

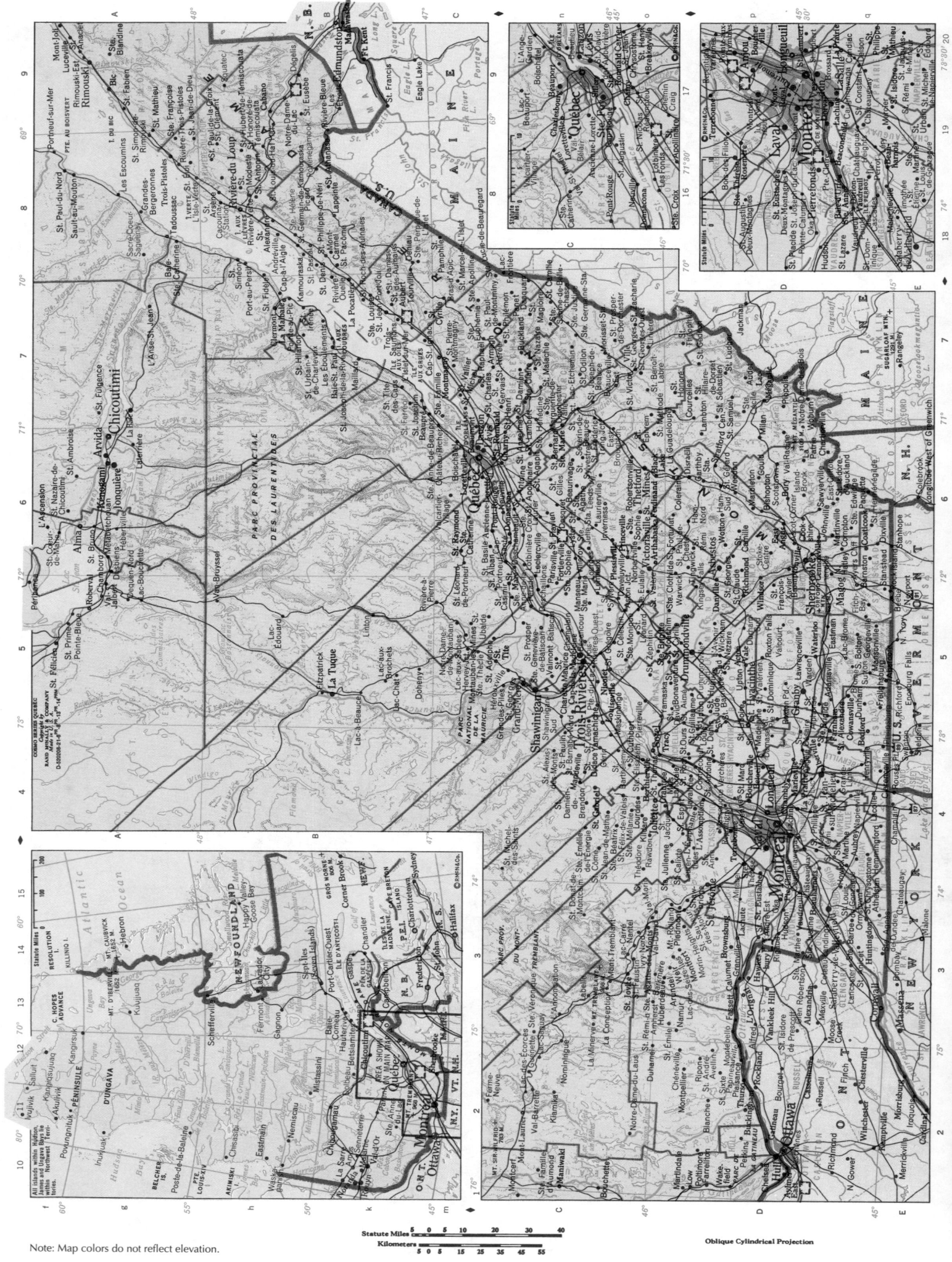

Note: Map colors do not reflect elevation.

Statute Miles 5 0 5   10   20   30   40

Kilometers 5 0 5   15   25   35   45   55

Oblique Cylindrical Projection

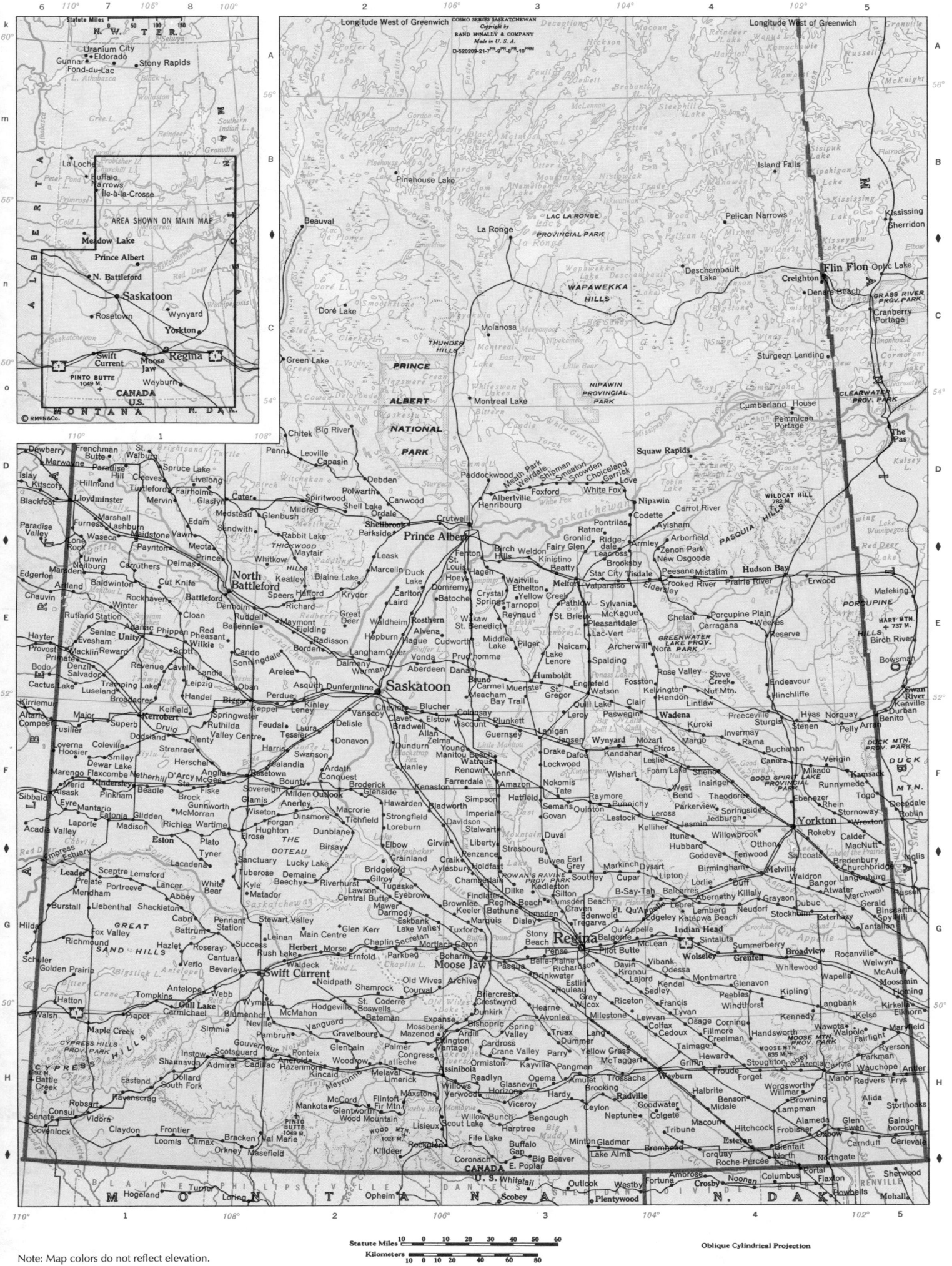

Note: Map colors do not reflect elevation.

Statute Miles 10 0 10 20 30 40 50 60
Kilometers 10 0 10 20 40 60 80

Oblique Cylindrical Projection

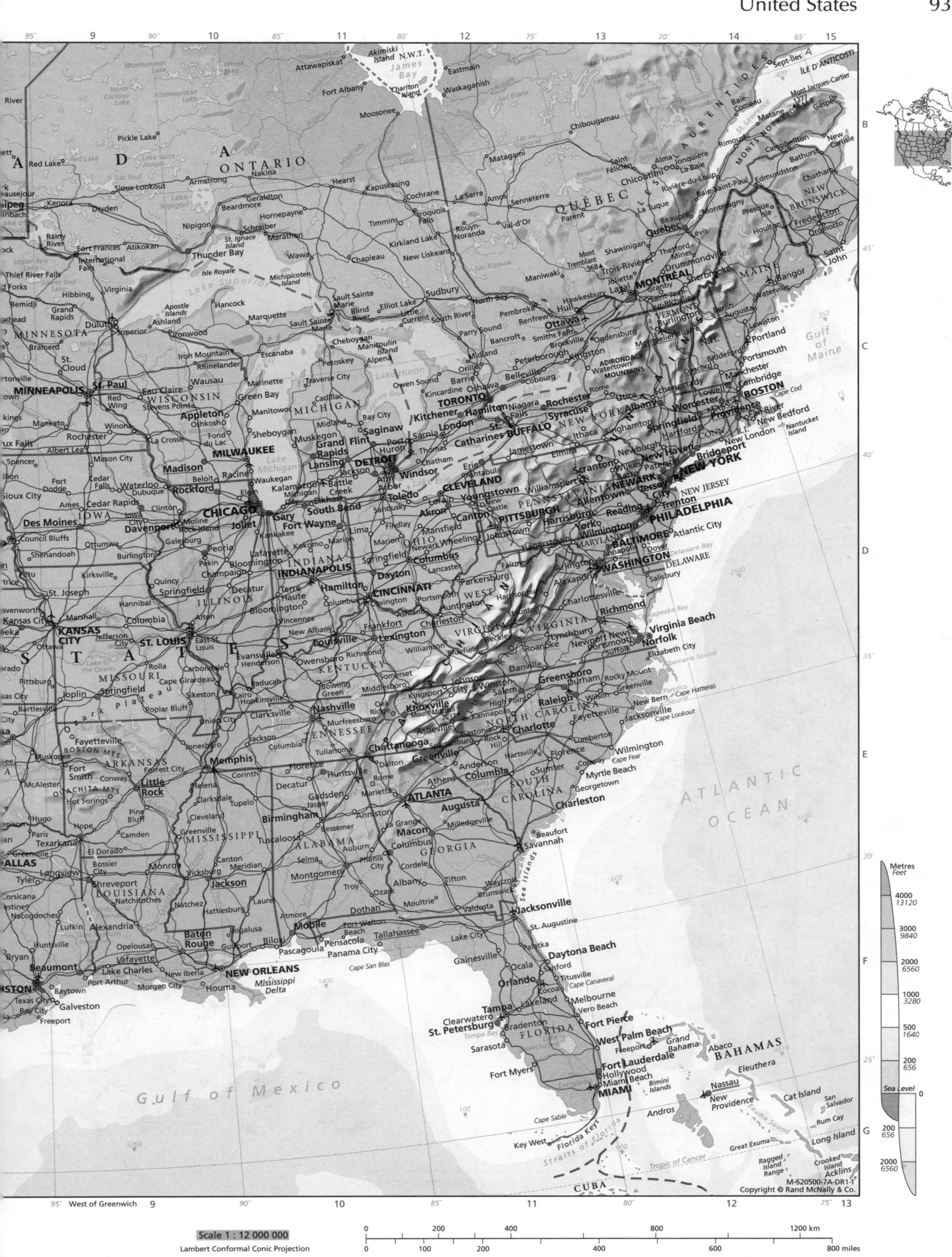

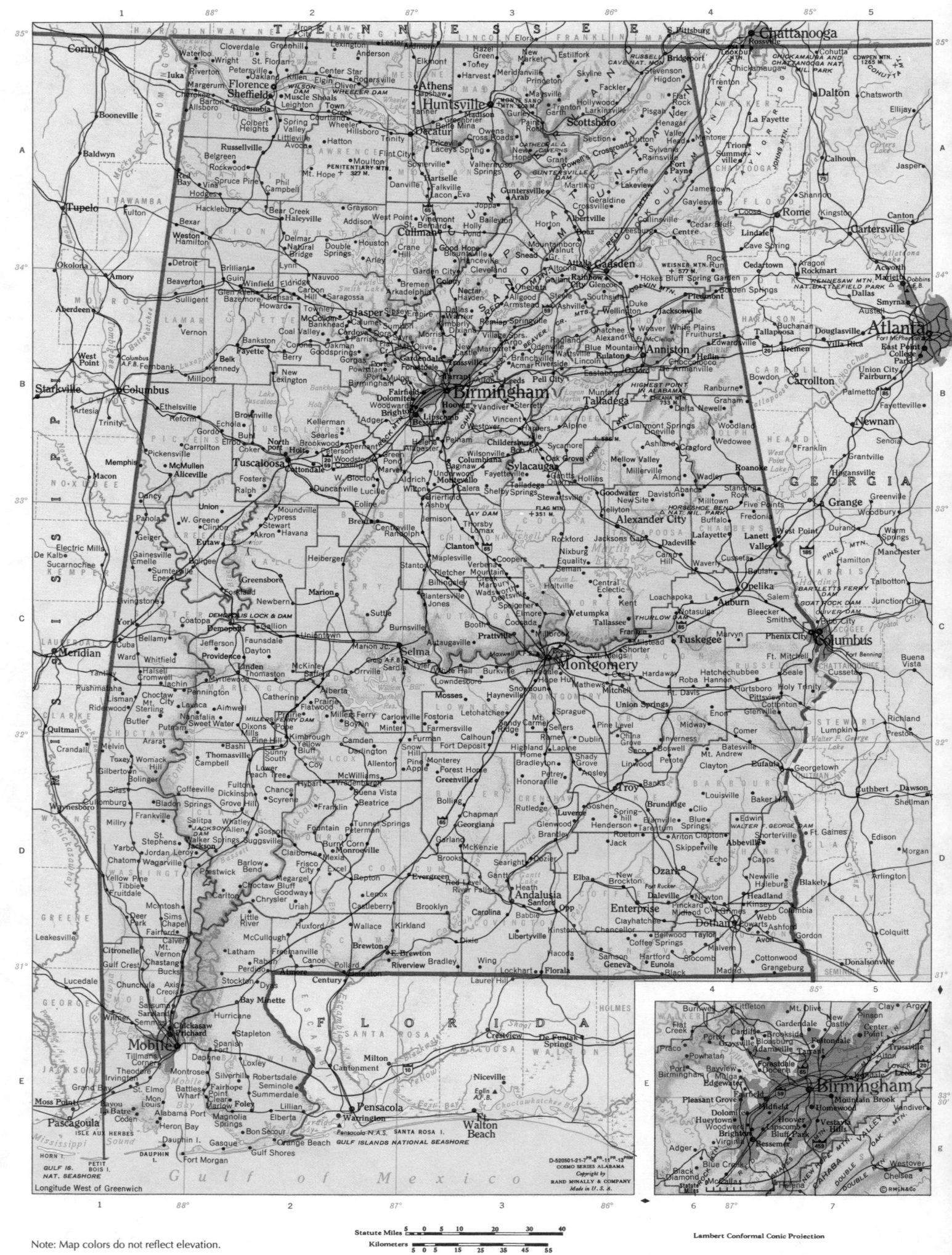

Note: Map colors do not reflect elevation.

Longitude West of Greenwich

Statute Miles
Kilometers

Lambert Conformal Conic Projection

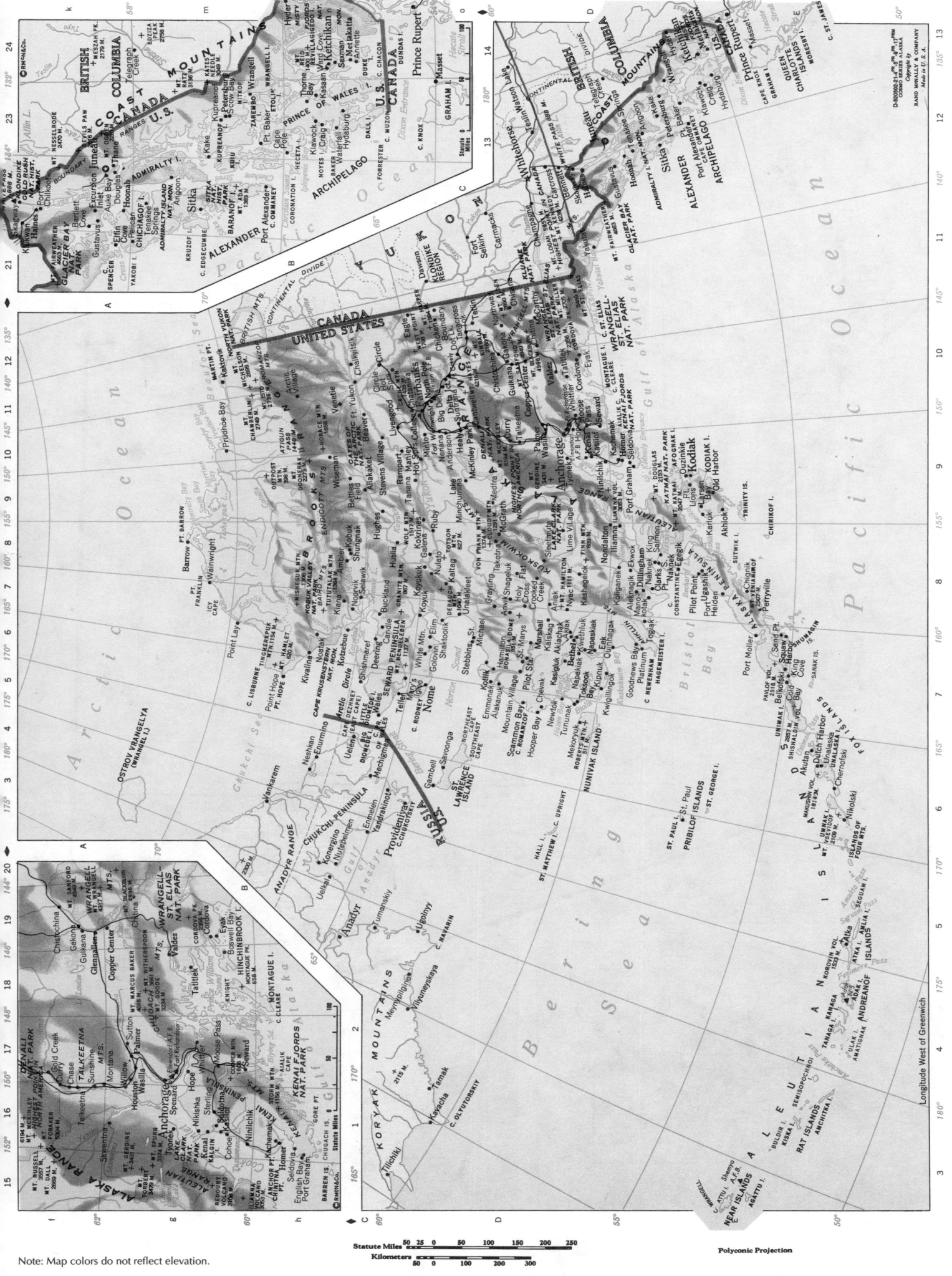

Note: Map colors do not reflect elevation.

Statute Miles 50 25 0   50   100   150   200   250
Kilometers   50 0   100   200   300

Polyconic Projection

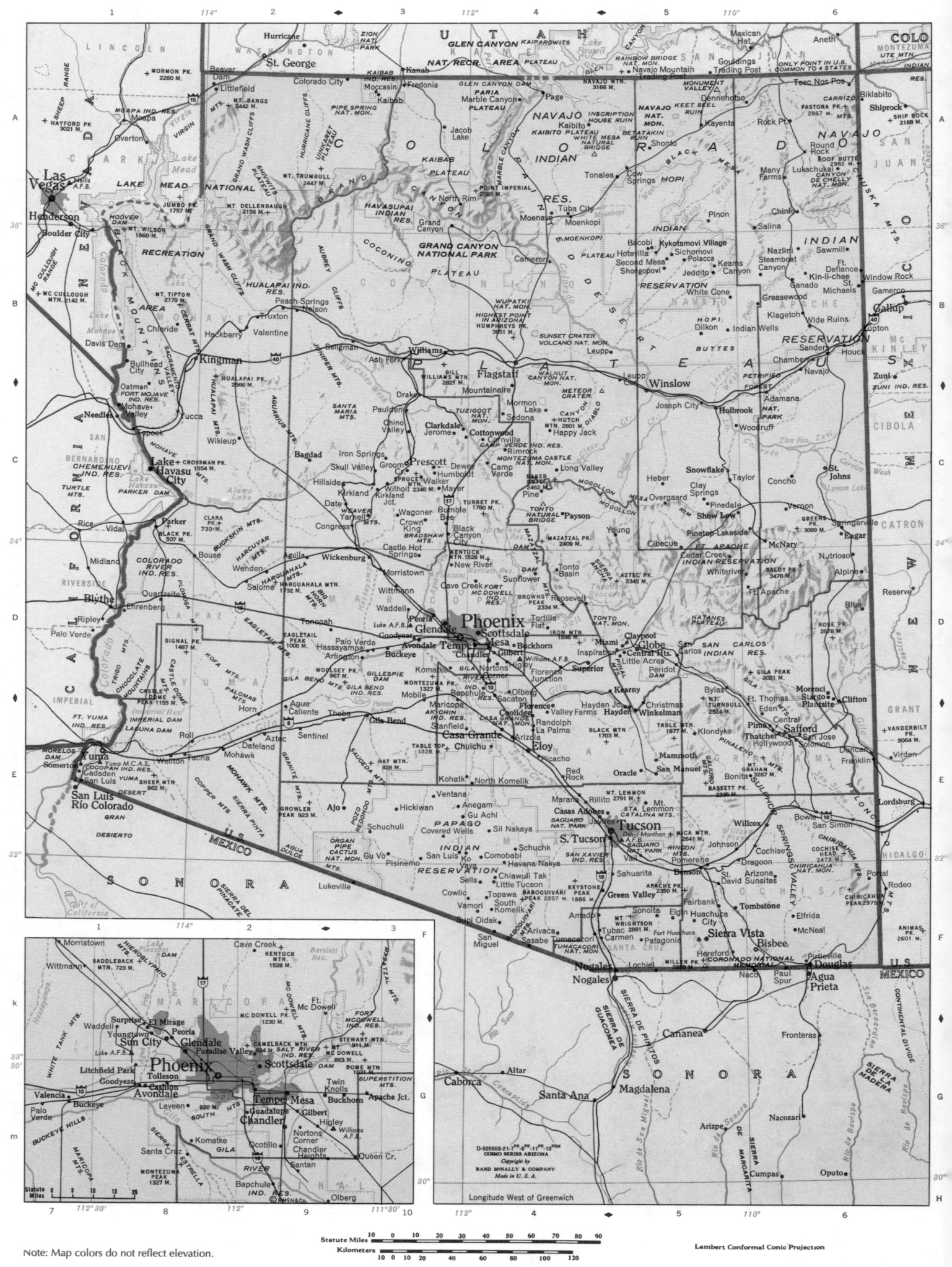

Note: Map colors do not reflect elevation.

Statute Miles
Kilometers

Lambert Conformal Conic Projection

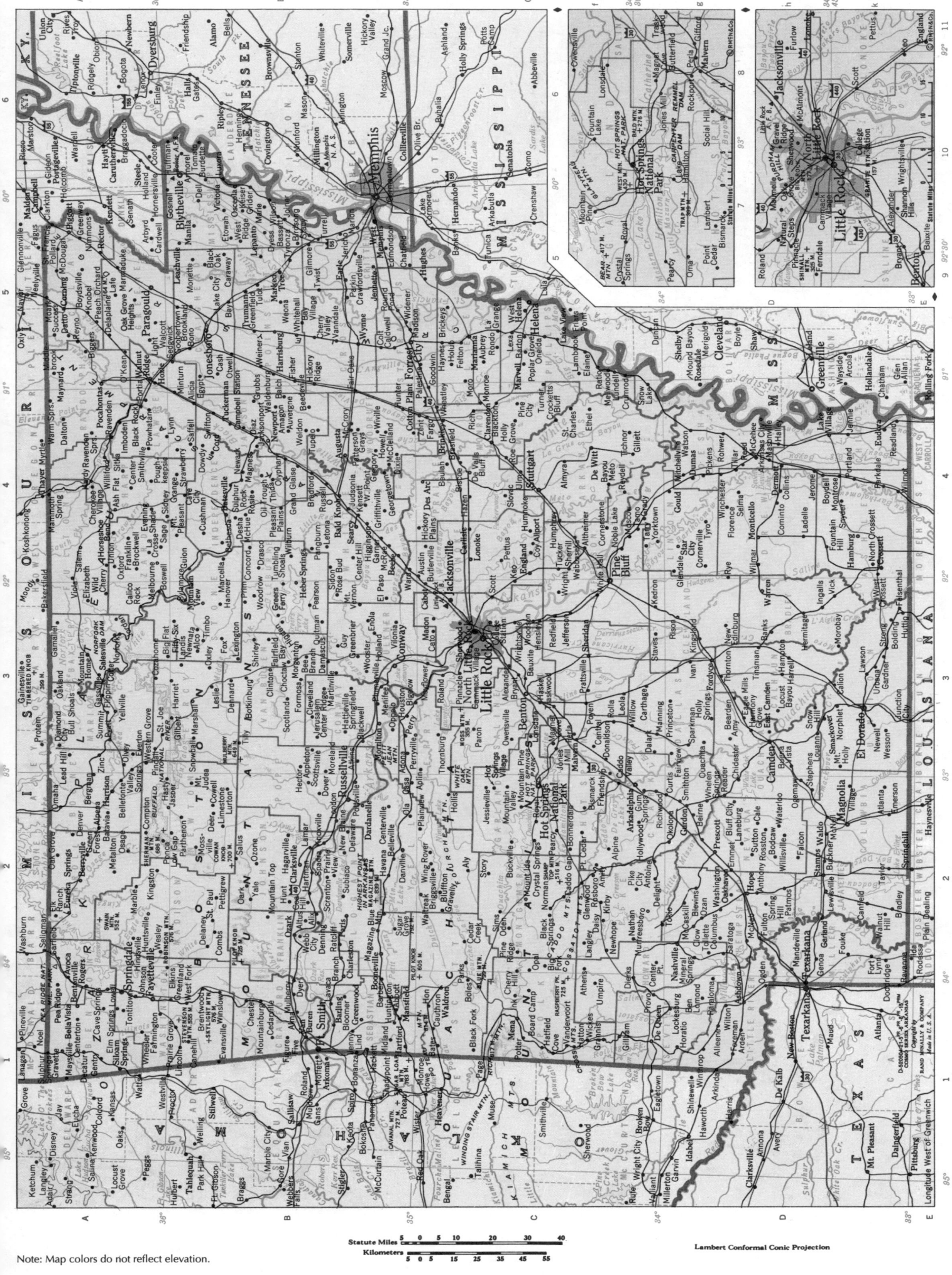

Note: Map colors do not reflect elevation.

Statute Miles 5 0 5 10 20 30 40
Kilometers 5 0 5 15 25 35 45 55

Lambert Conformal Conic Projection

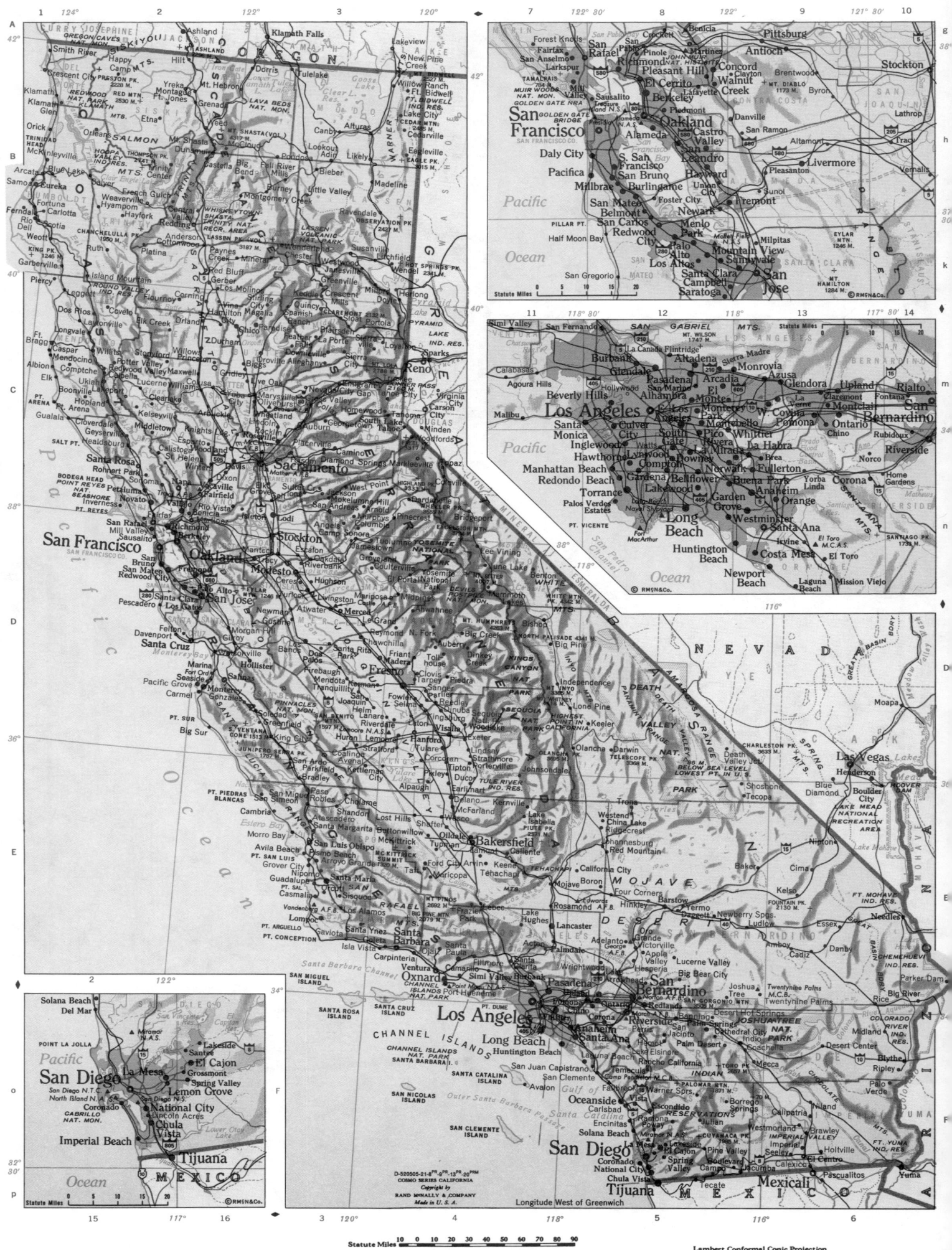

Note: Map colors do not reflect elevation.

Statute Miles
Kilometers

Lambert Conformal Conic Projection

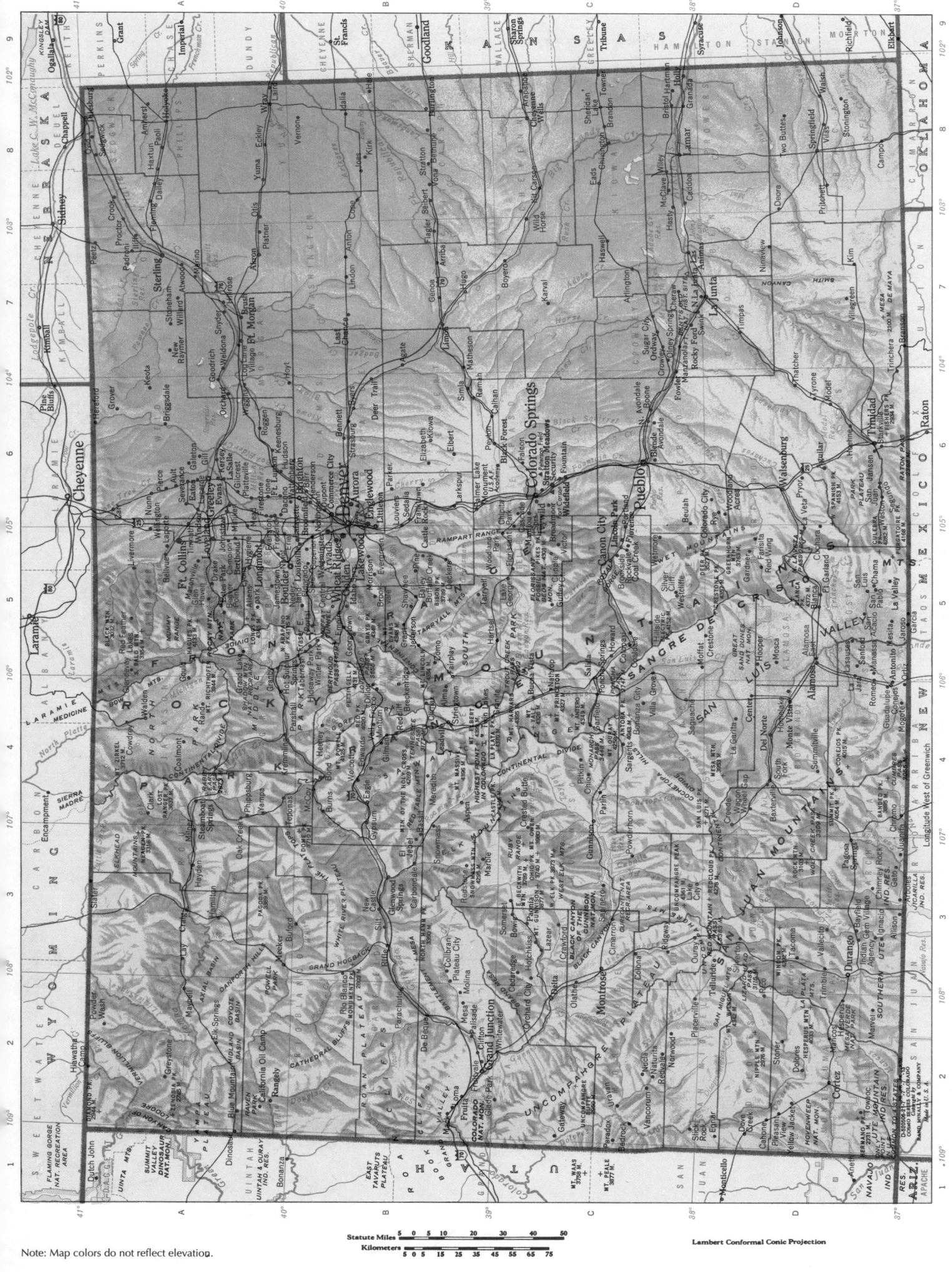

Note: Map colors do not reflect elevation.

Statute Miles 5 0 5 10   20   30   40   50
Kilometers 5 0 5 15 25 35 45 55 65 75

Lambert Conformal Conic Projection

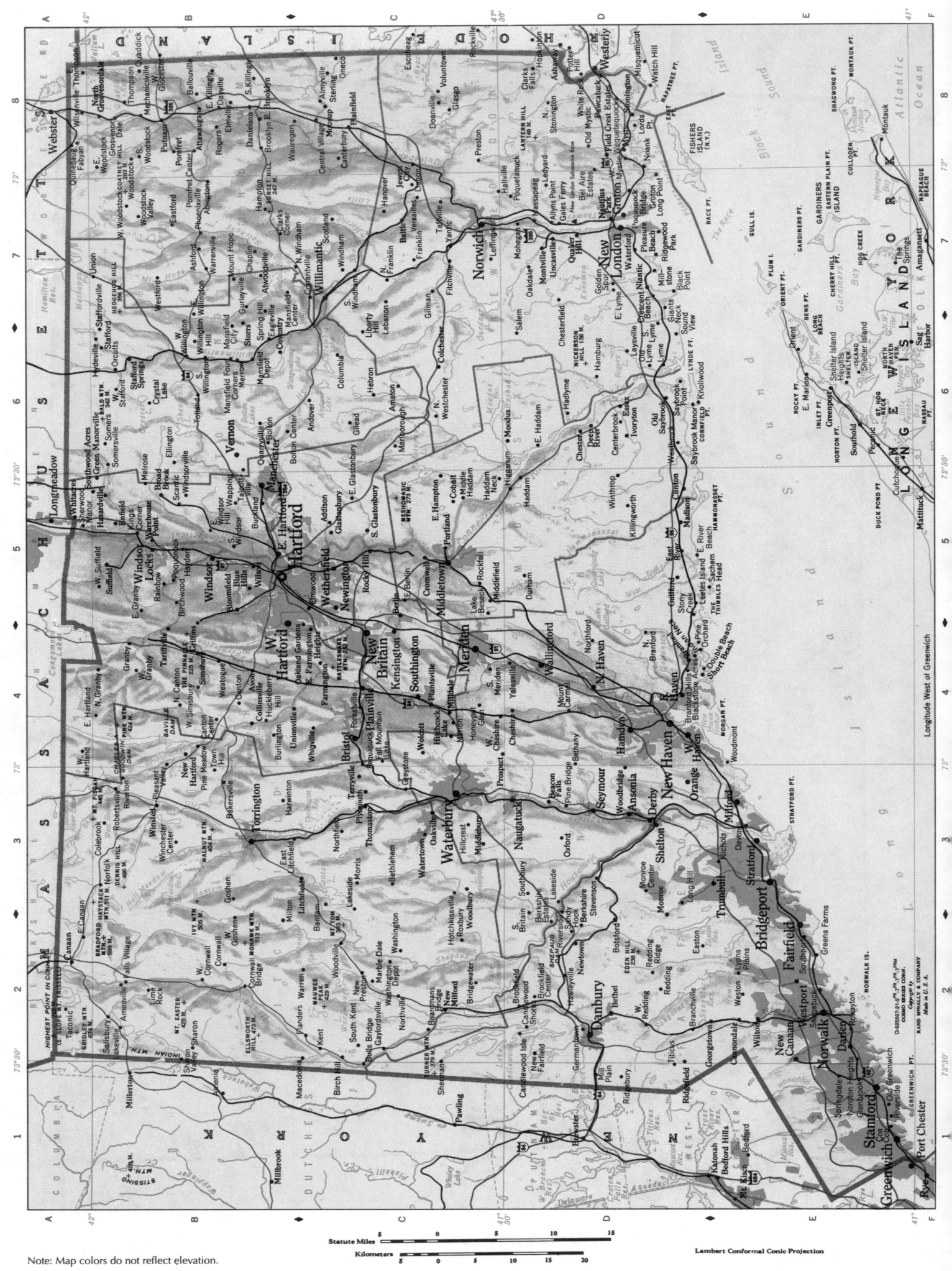

Note: Map colors do not reflect elevation.

Statute Miles

0   5   10   15

Kilometers

5   0   5   10   15   20

Lambert Conformal Conic Projection

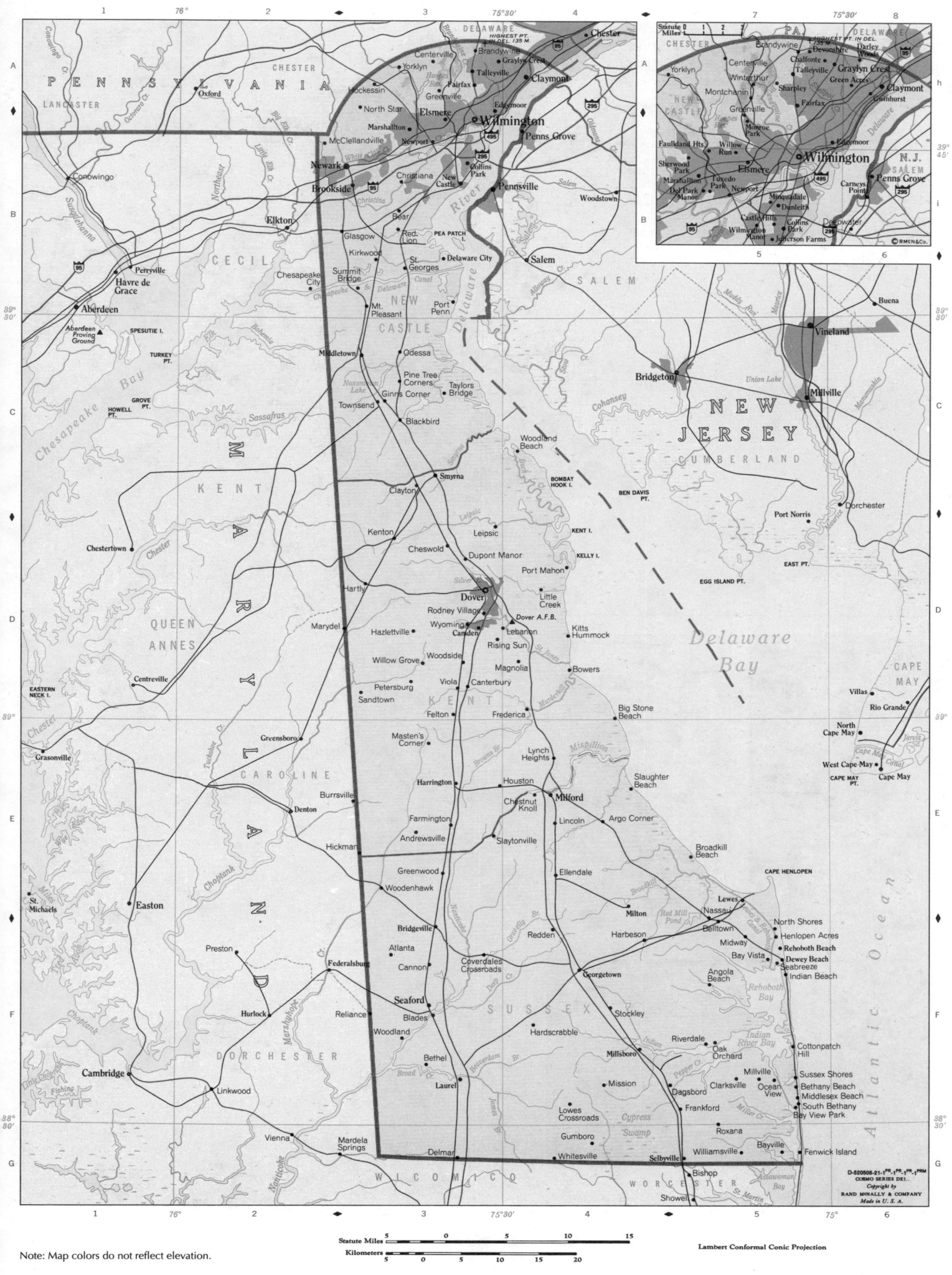

Note: Map colors do not reflect elevation.

Statute Miles
Kilometers

Lambert Conformal Conic Projection

D-520508-21-1ᴾᴸ-1ᴾᴸ-1ᵀᴿ-1ᴾᴿᴹ
COSMO SERIES DEL.
Copyright by
RAND McNALLY & COMPANY
Made in U.S.A.

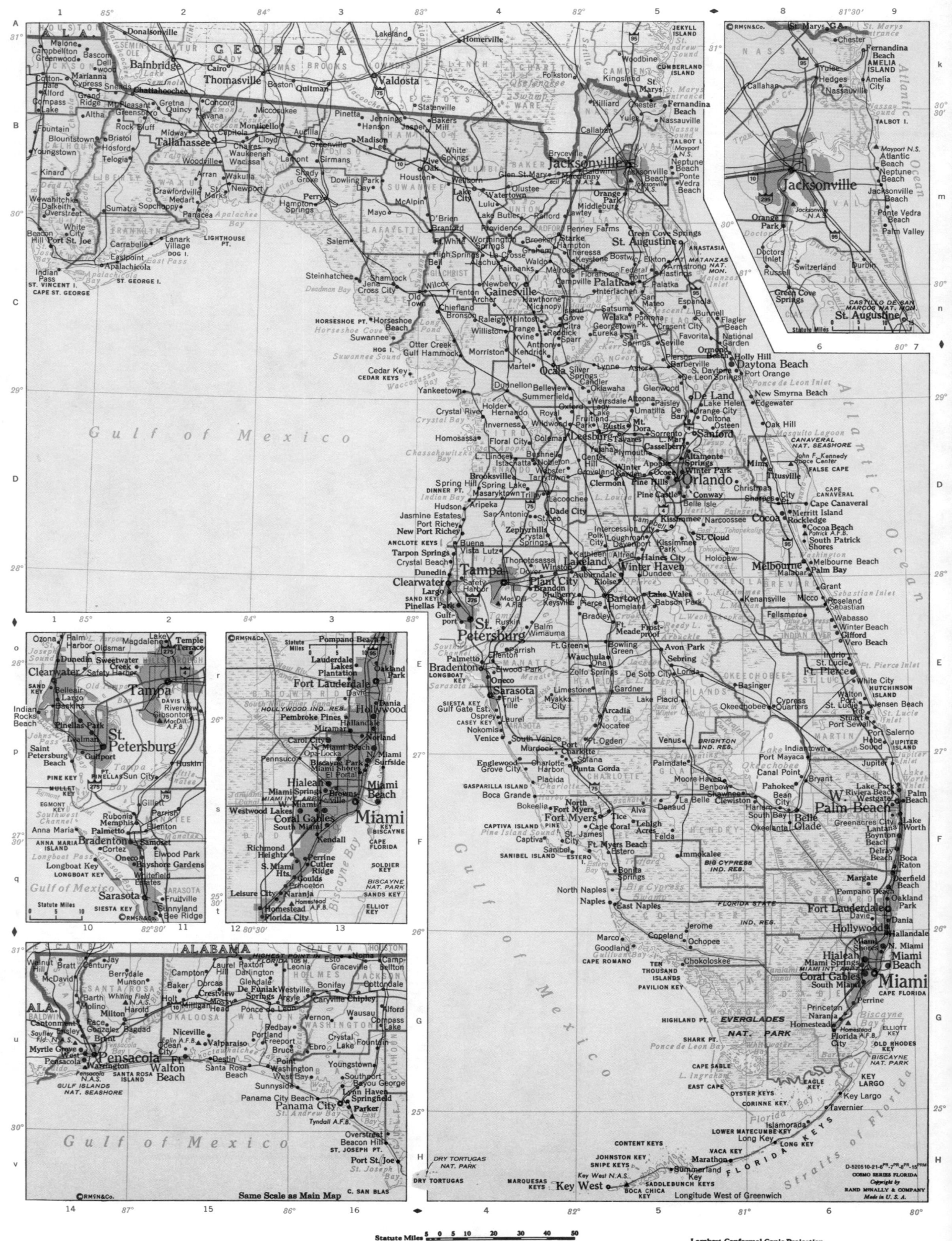

Note: Map colors do not reflect elevation.

Statute Miles
Kilometers

Lambert Conformal Conic Projection

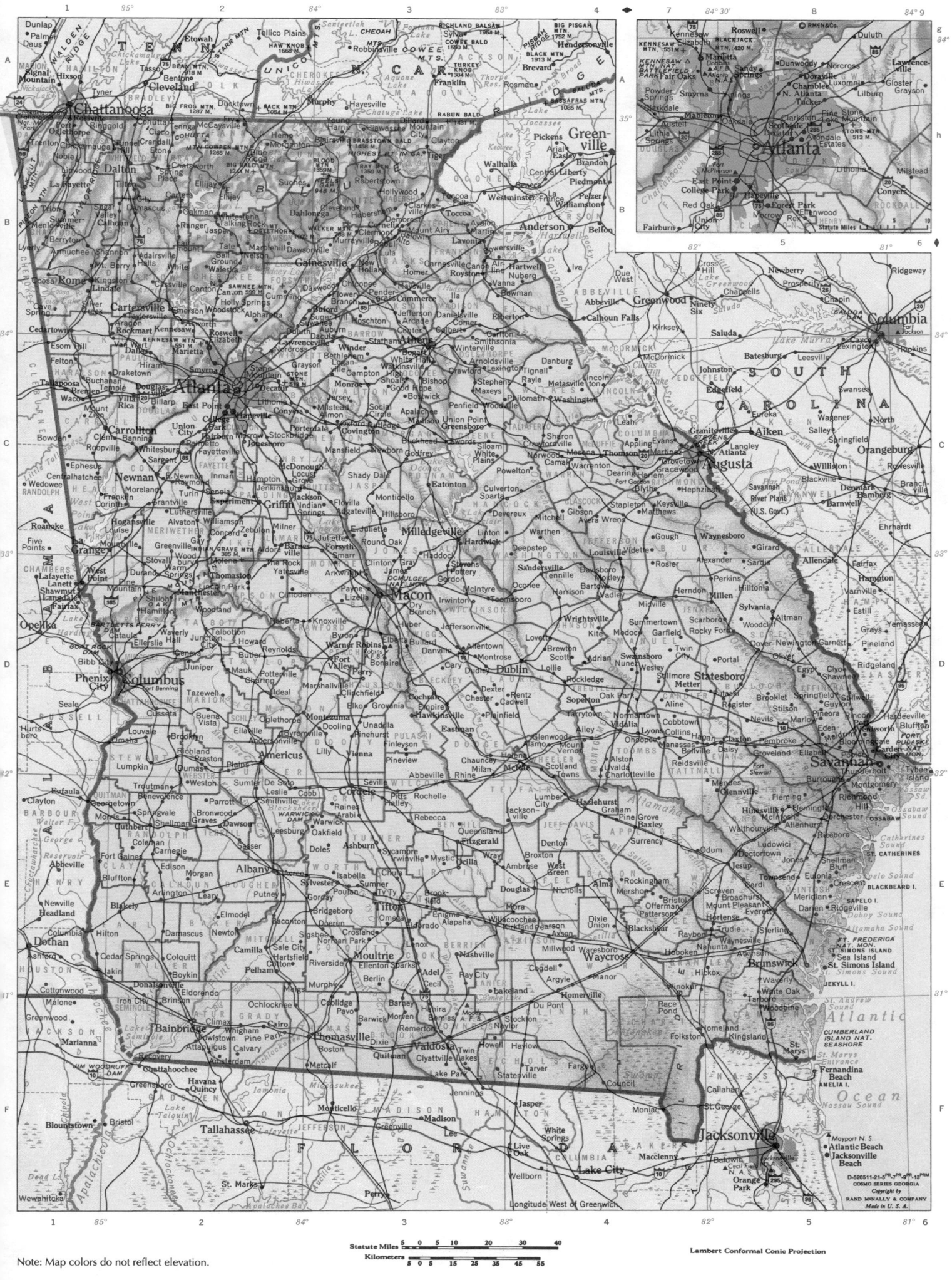

Note: Map colors do not reflect elevation.

Statute Miles 5 0 5 10 20 30 40
Kilometers 5 0 5 15 25 35 45 55

Lambert Conformal Conic Projection

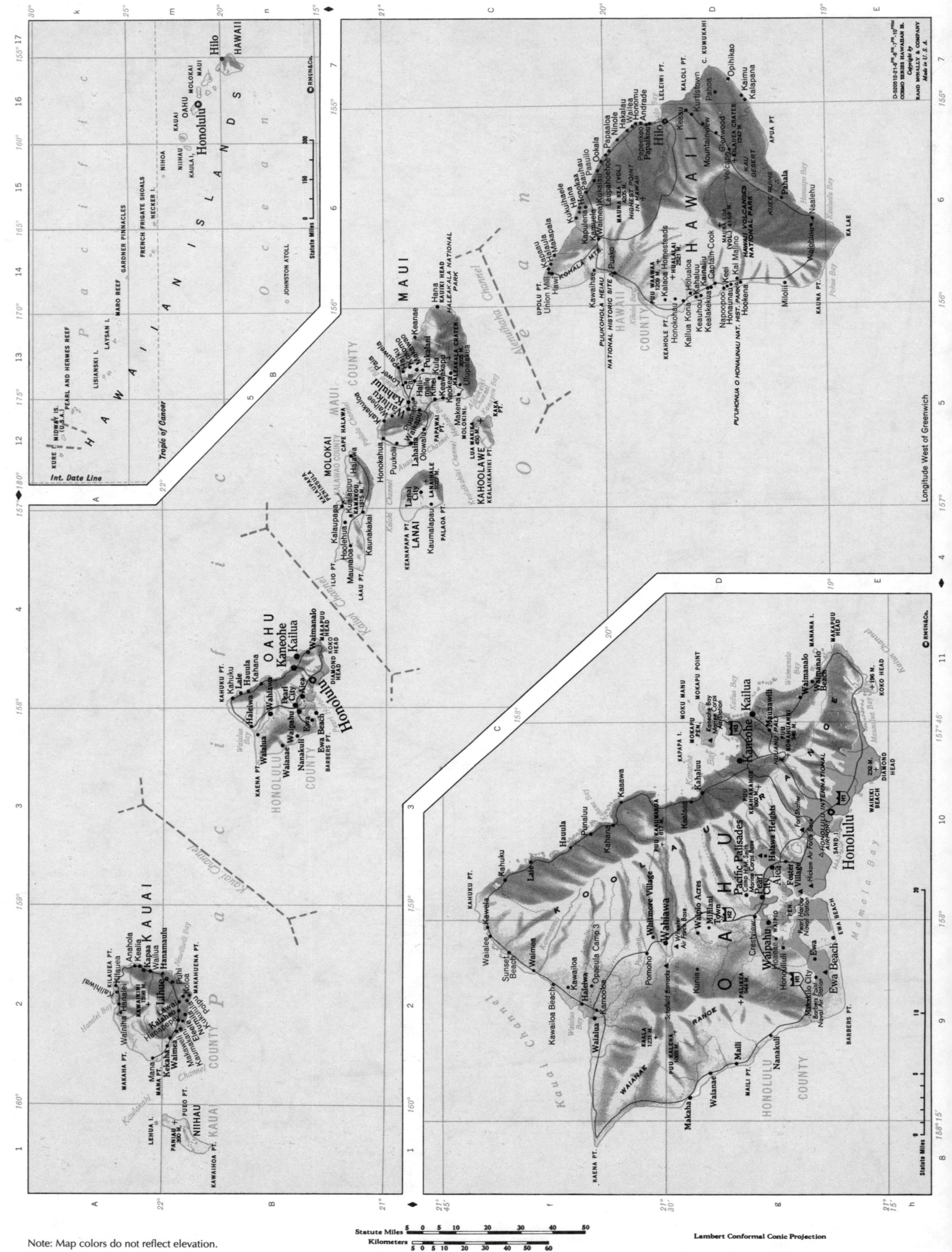

Note: Map colors do not reflect elevation.

Statute Miles
Kilometers

Lambert Conformal Conic Projection

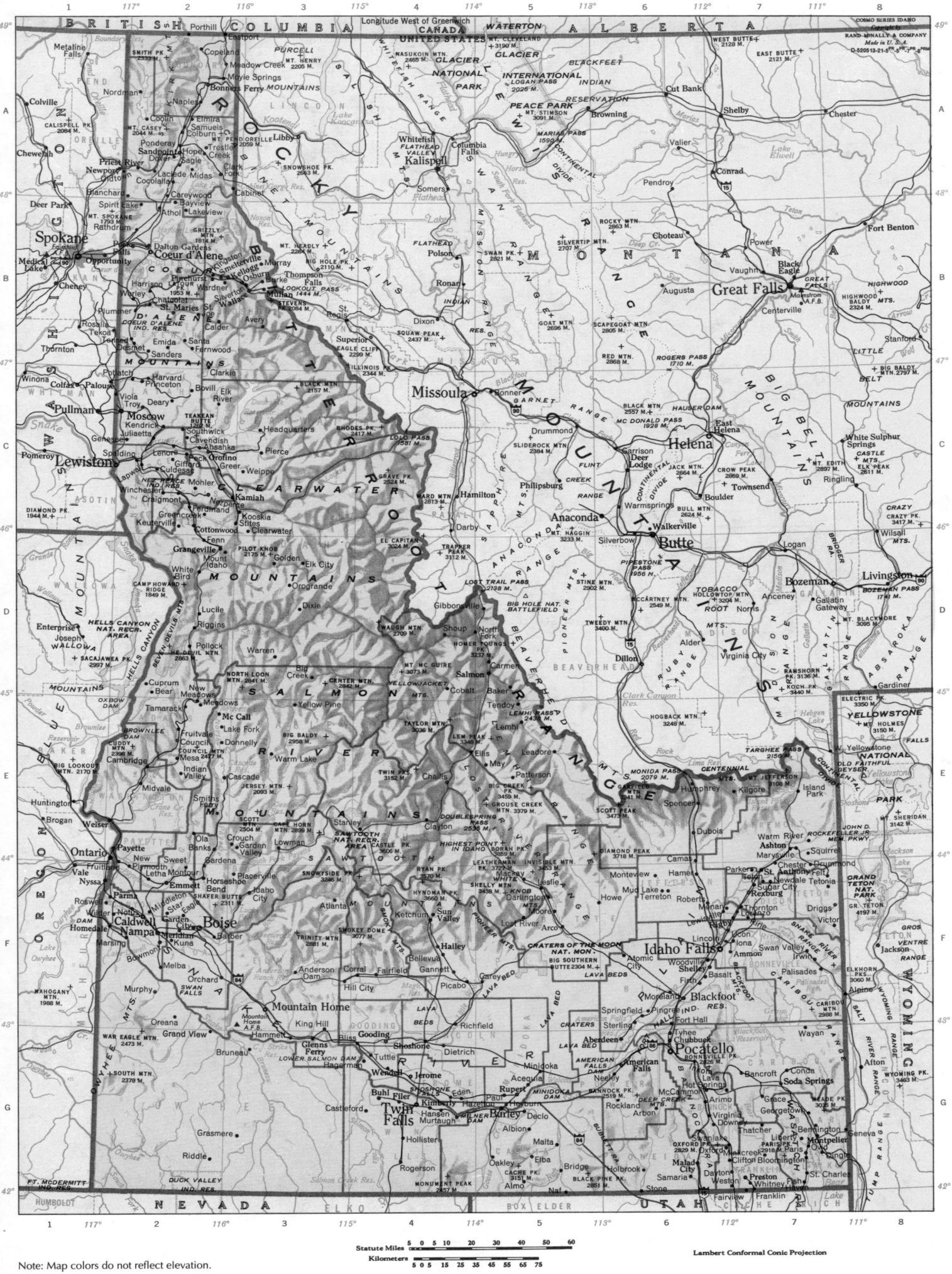

Note: Map colors do not reflect elevation.

Statute Miles 5 0 5 10   20   30   40   50   60
Kilometers   5 0 5 15 25 35 45 55 65 75

Lambert Conformal Conic Projection

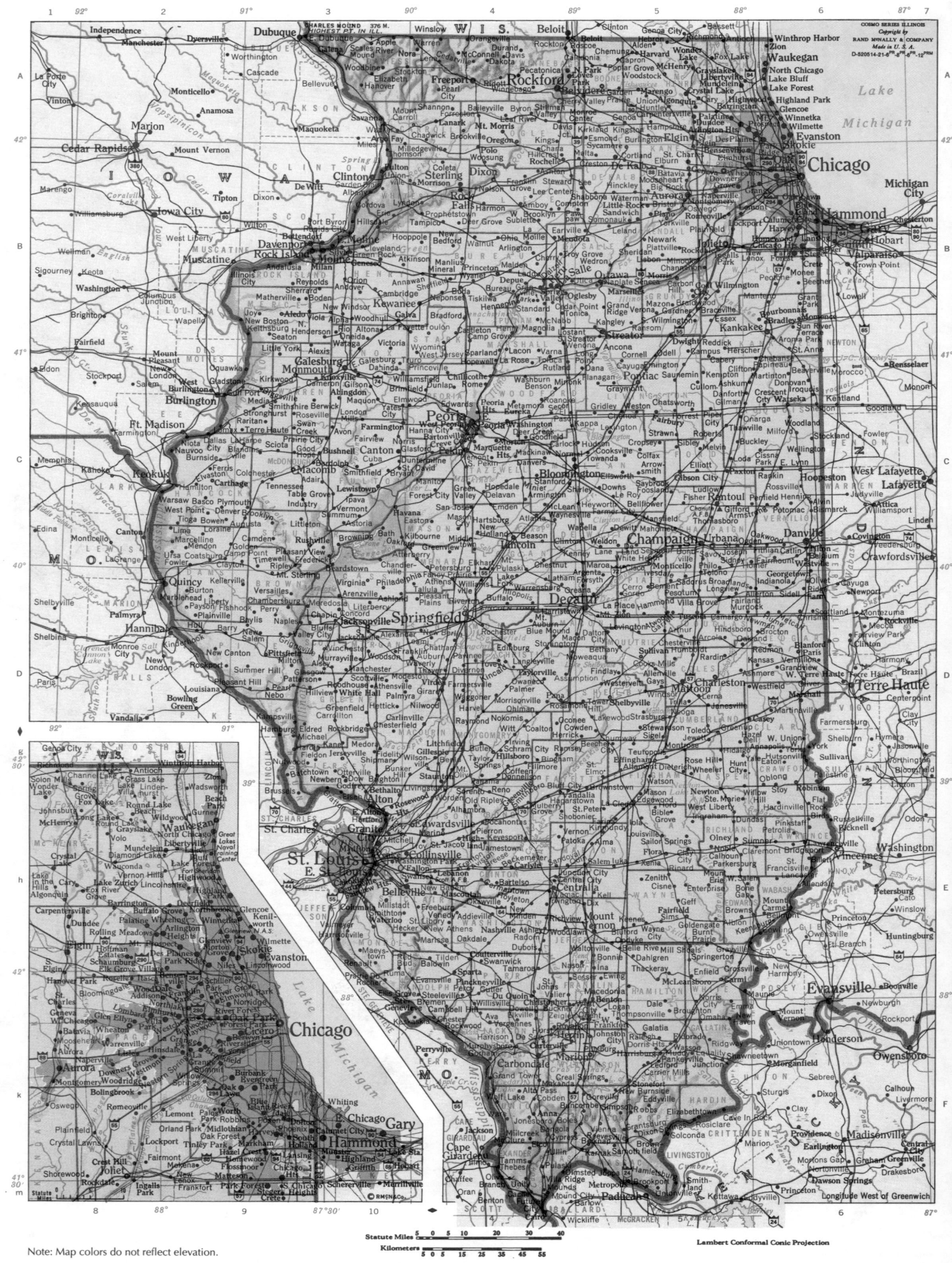

Note: Map colors do not reflect elevation.

Statute Miles 5 0 5 10 20 30 40

Kilometers 5 0 5 15 25 35 45 55

Lambert Conformal Conic Projection

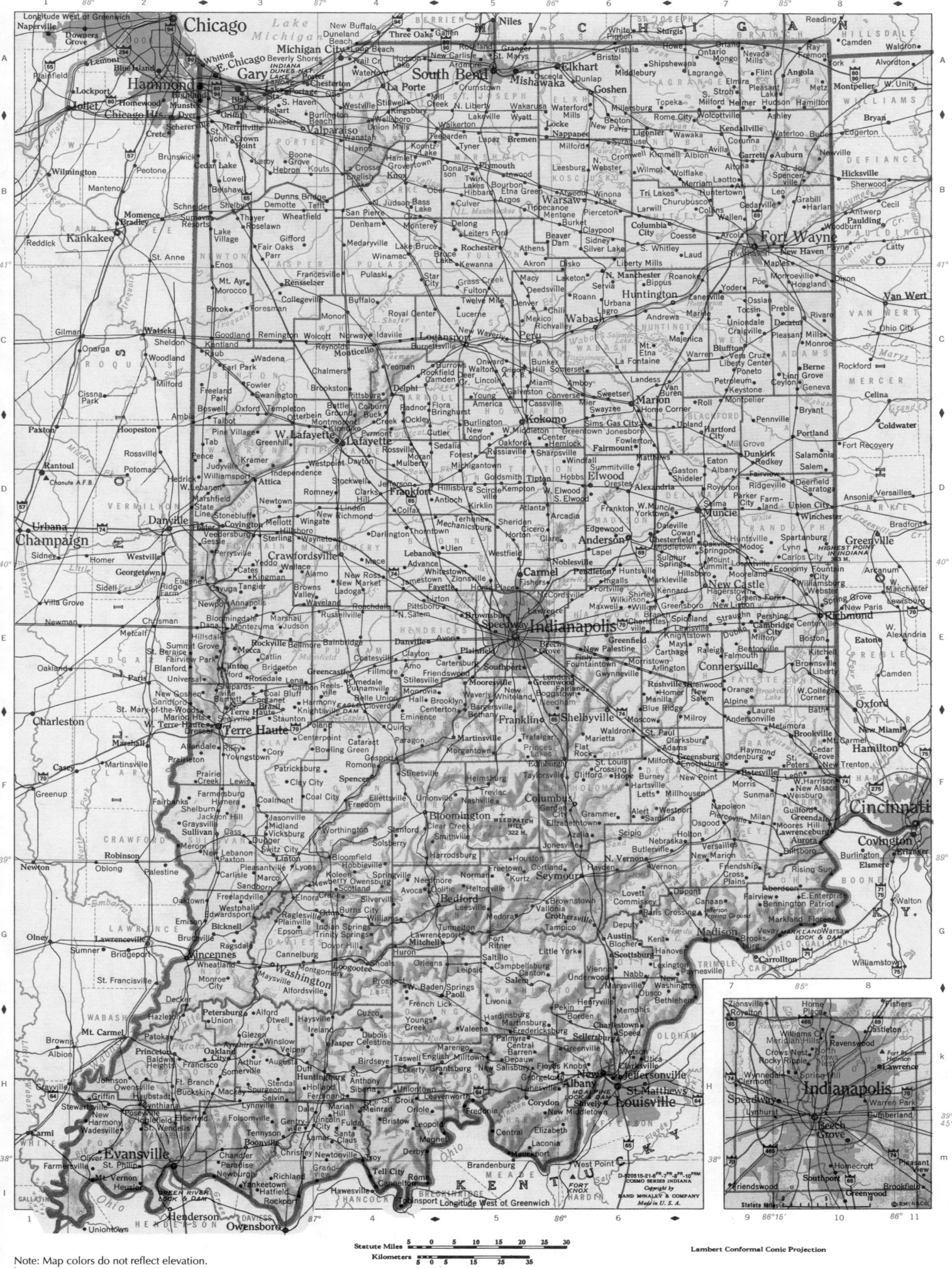

Note: Map colors do not reflect elevation.

Statute Miles 5 0 5 10 15 20 25 30
Kilometers 5 0 5 15 25 35

Lambert Conformal Conic Projection

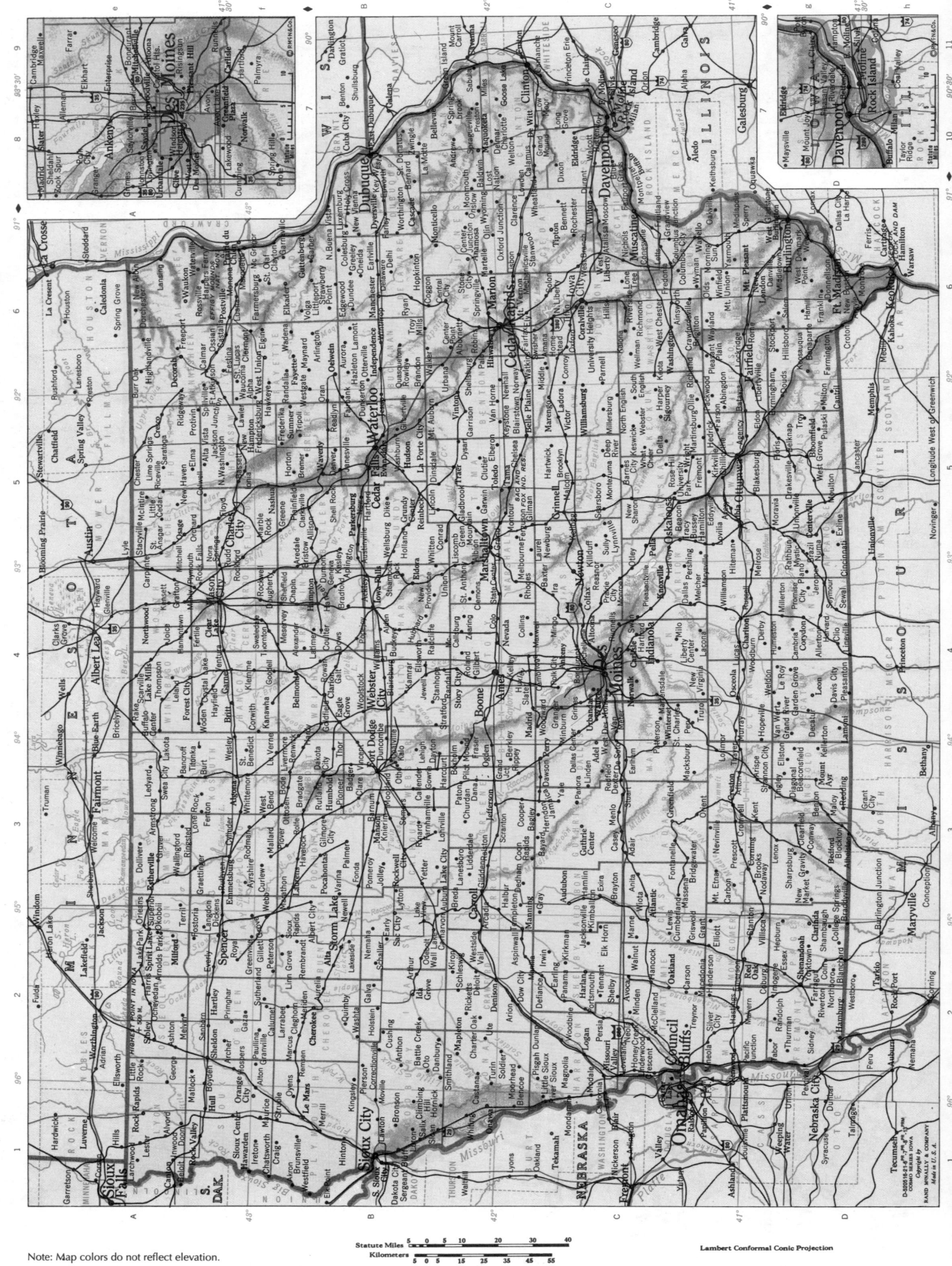

Note: Map colors do not reflect elevation.

Statute Miles

Kilometers

Lambert Conformal Conic Projection

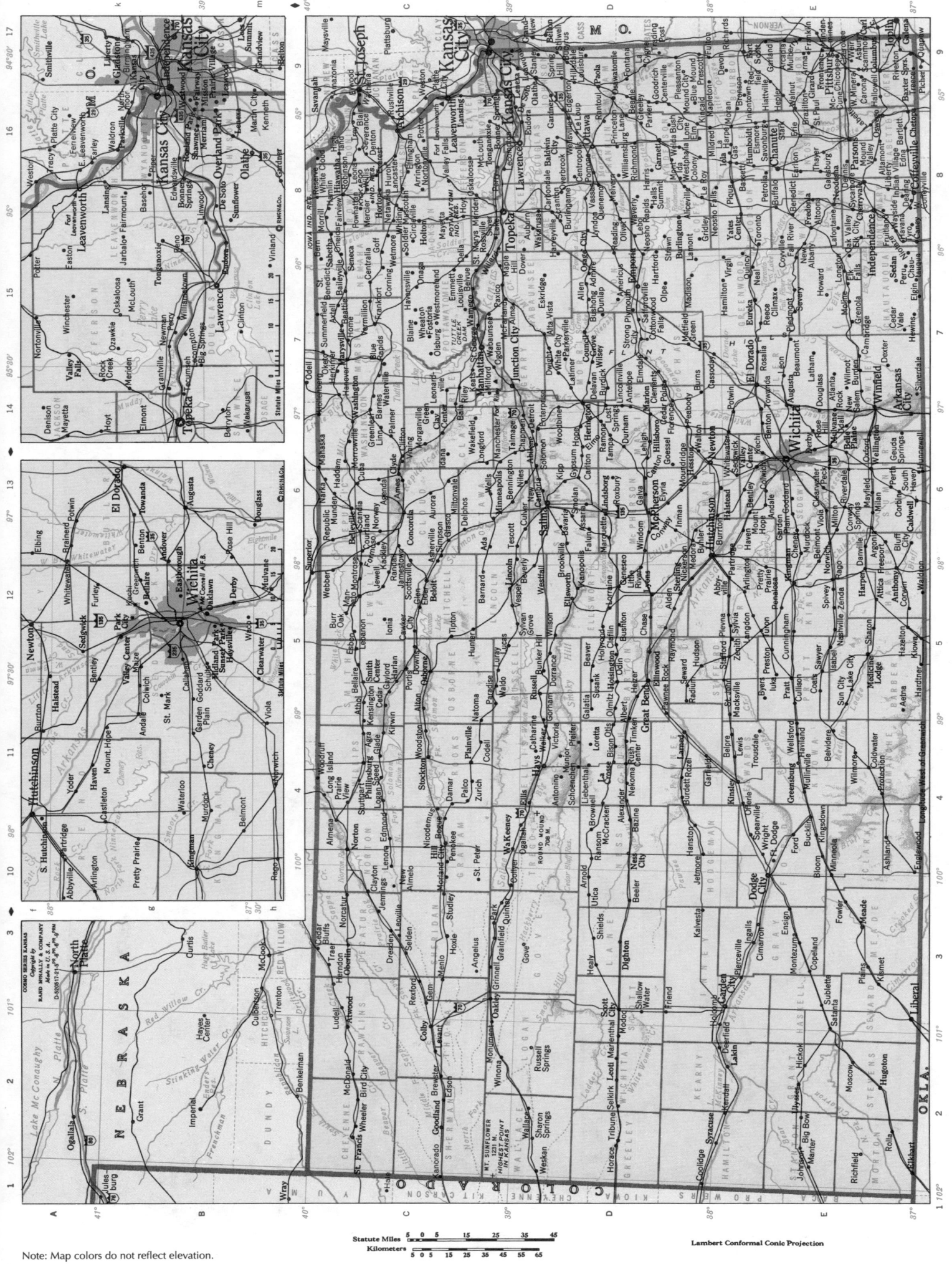

Note: Map colors do not reflect elevation.

Statute Miles   5 0 5   15   25   35   45
Kilometers   5 0 5   15   25   35   45   55   65

Lambert Conformal Conic Projection

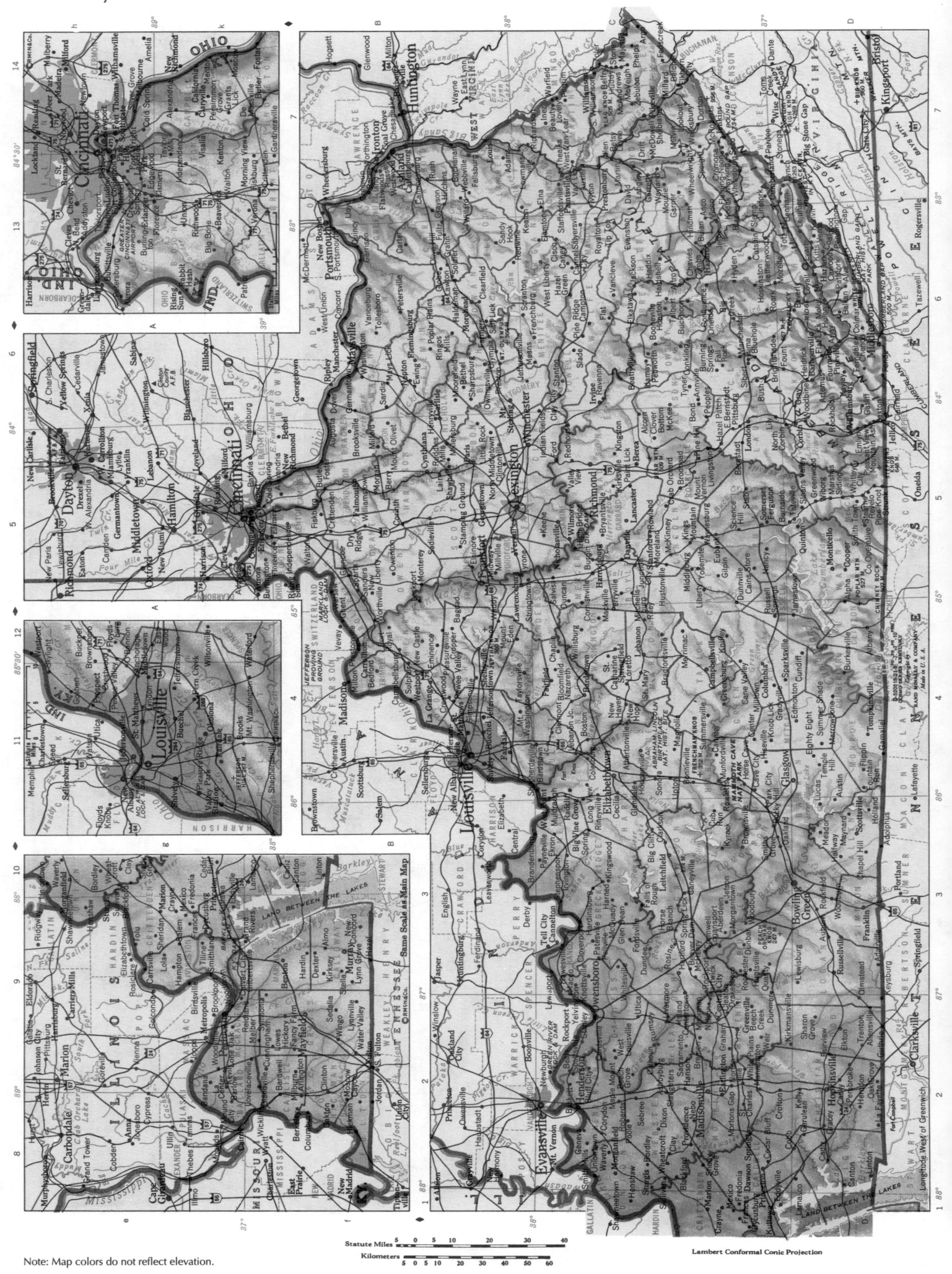

Note: Map colors do not reflect elevation.

Statute Miles
Kilometers

Lambert Conformal Conic Projection

Note: Map colors do not reflect elevation.

Statute Miles 5 0 5 10   20   30   40
Kilometers 5 0 5 15 25 35 45 55

Lambert Conformal Conic Projection

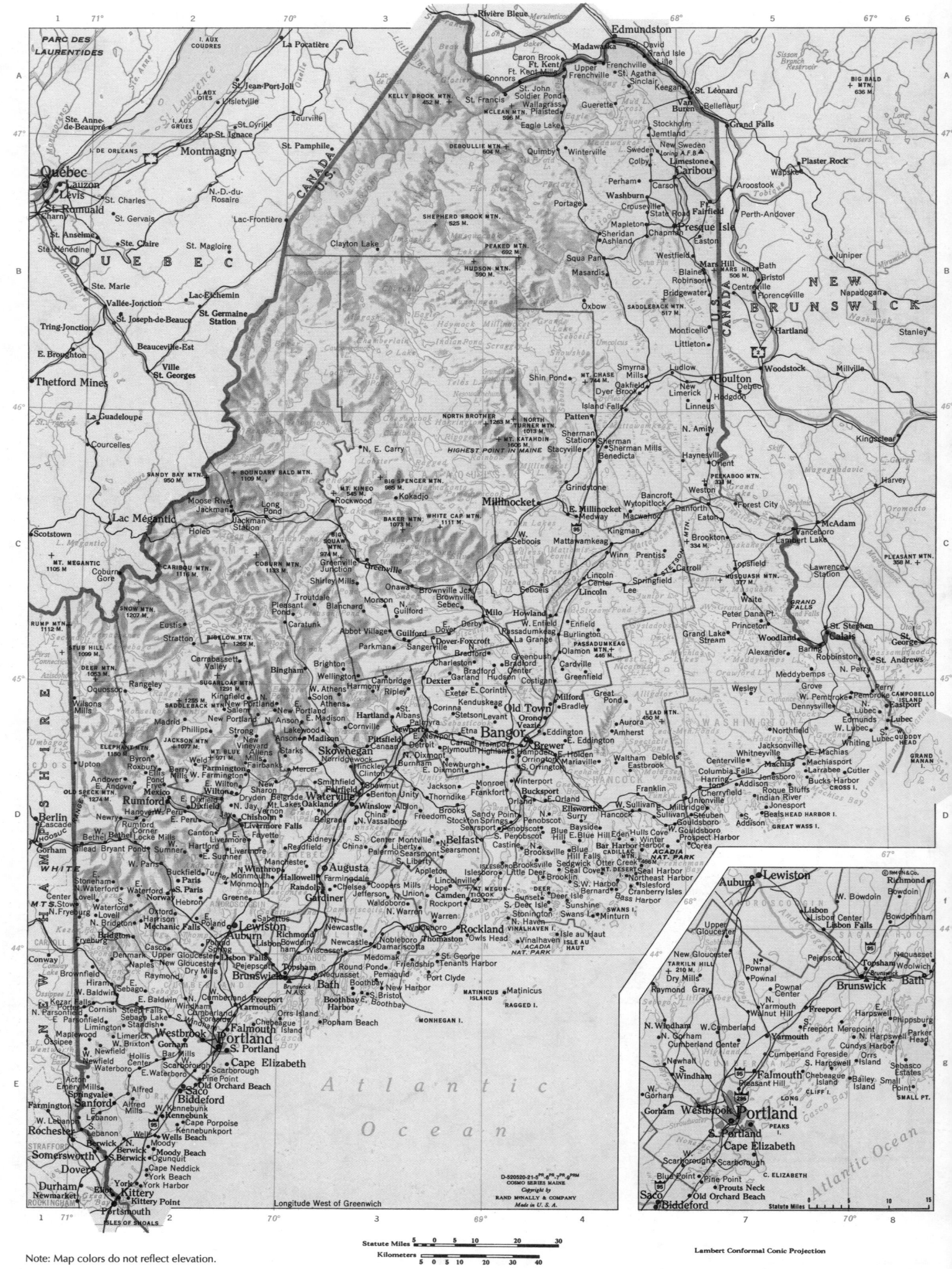

Note: Map colors do not reflect elevation.

Statute Miles
Kilometers

Lambert Conformal Conic Projection

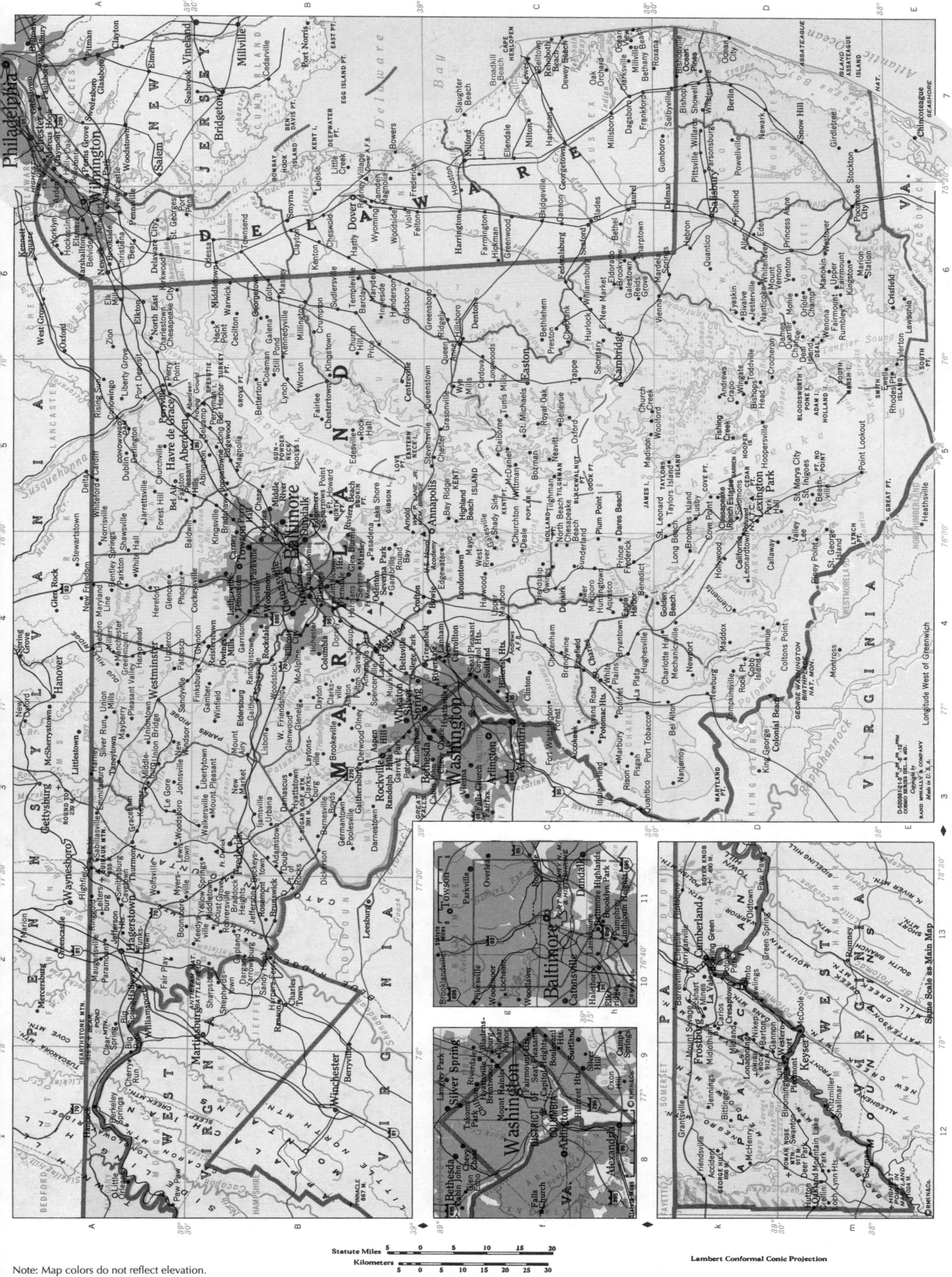

Note: Map colors do not reflect elevation.

Statute Miles 5 0 5 10 15 20
Kilometers 5 0 5 10 15 20 25 30

Lambert Conformal Conic Projection

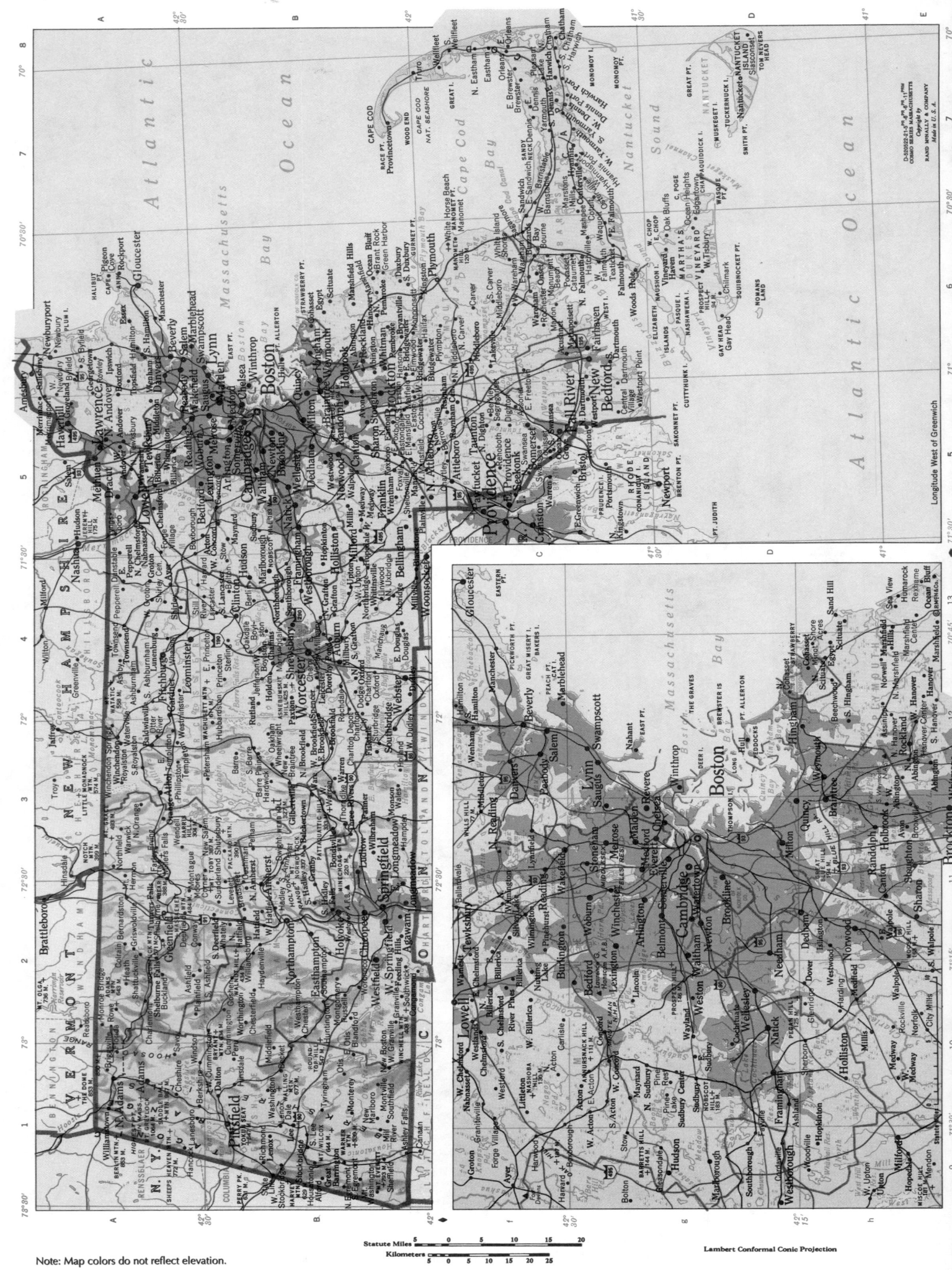

Note: Map colors do not reflect elevation.

Statute Miles   5   0   5   10   15   20
Kilometers   5   0   5   10   15   20   25

Lambert Conformal Conic Projection

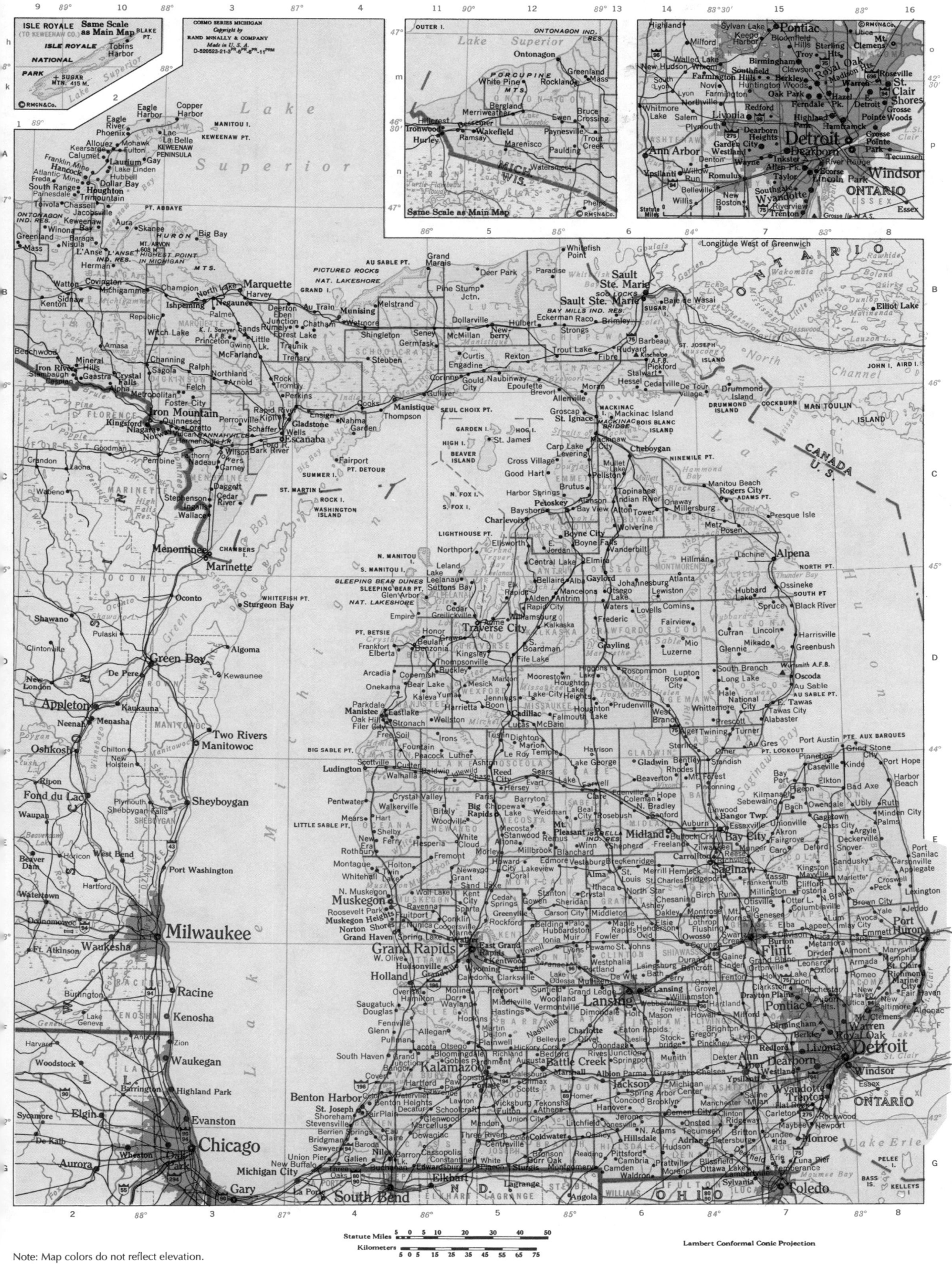

Note: Map colors do not reflect elevation.

Statute Miles 5 0 5 10 20 30 40 50
Kilometers
5 0 5 15 25 35 45 55 65 75

Lambert Conformal Conic Projection

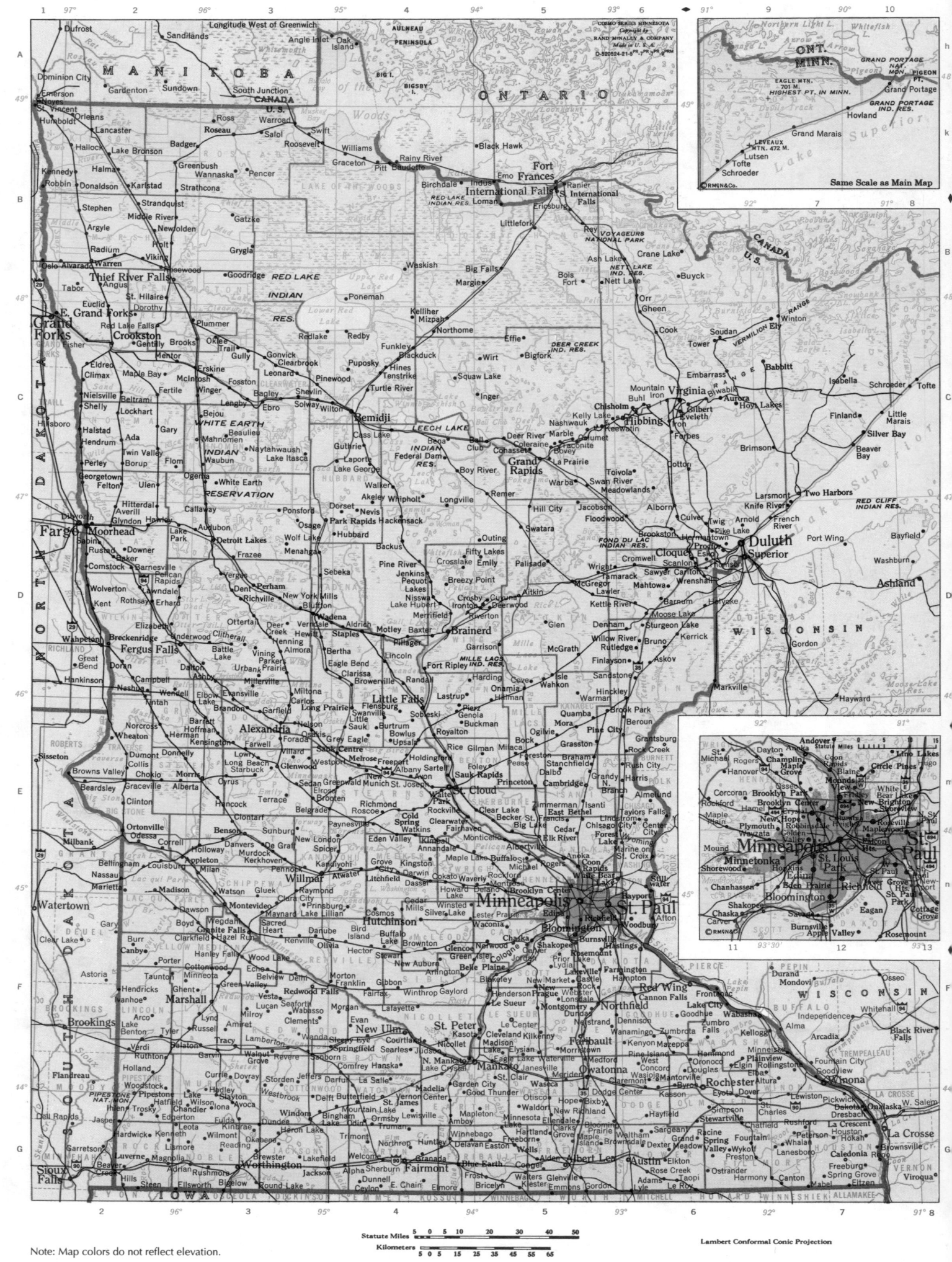

Note: Map colors do not reflect elevation.

Statute Miles 5 0 5 10   20   30   40   50

Kilometers 5 0 5 15 25 35 45 55 65

Lambert Conformal Conic Projection

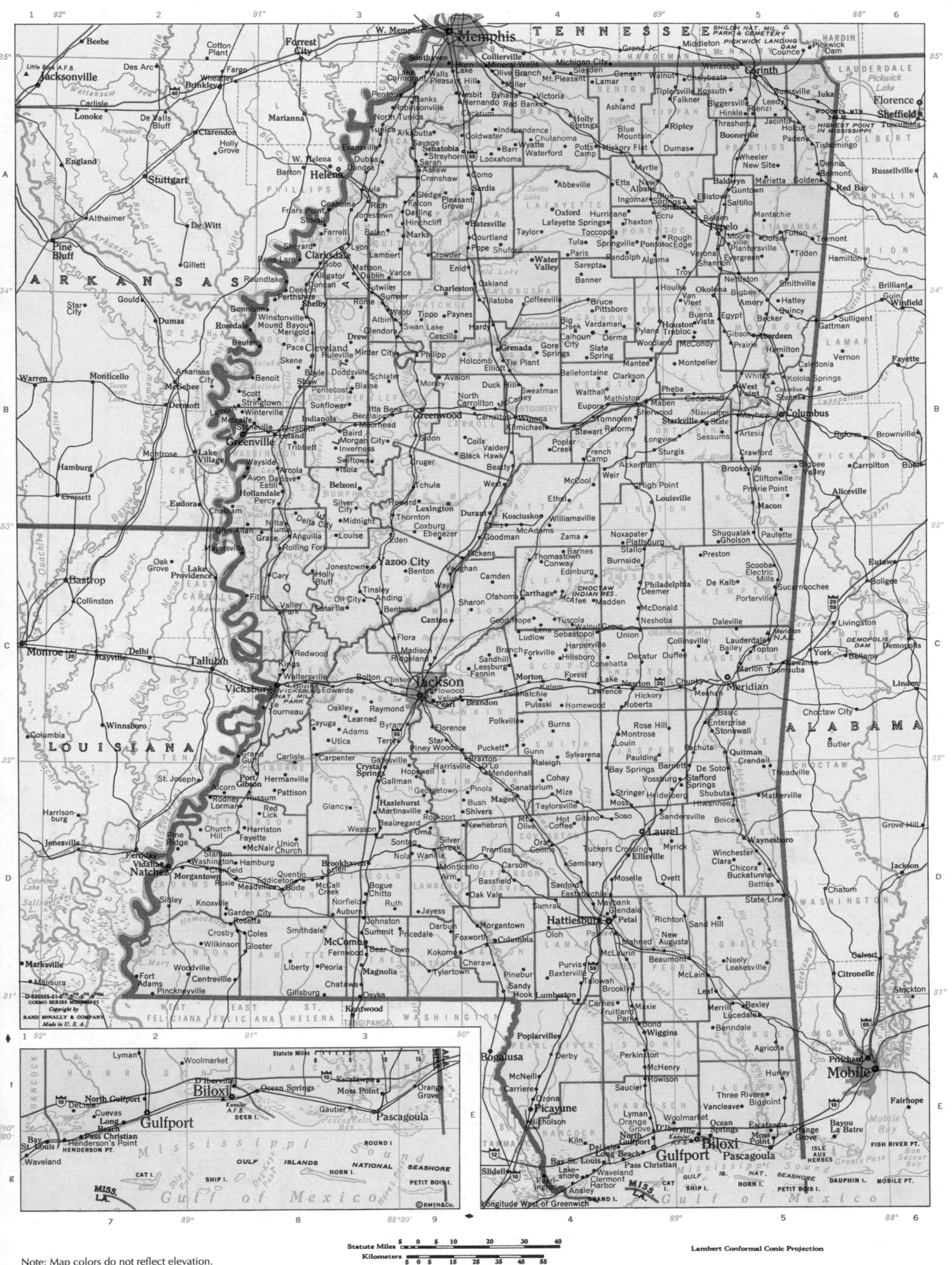

Note: Map colors do not reflect elevation.

Statute Miles
Kilometers

Lambert Conformal Conic Projection

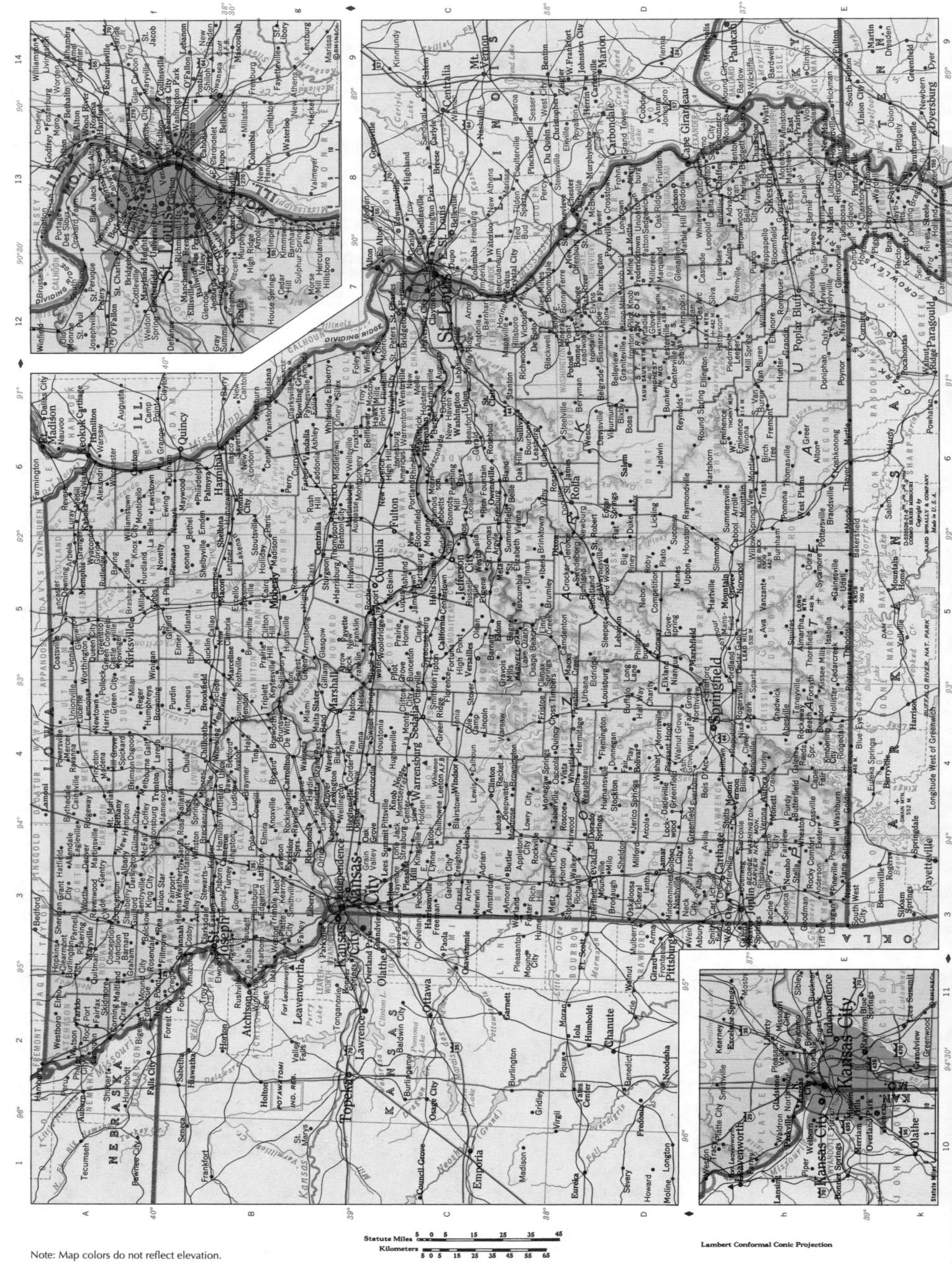

Note: Map colors do not reflect elevation.

Statute Miles 5 0 5   15   25   35   45
Kilometers 5 0 5 15 25 35 45 55 65

Lambert Conformal Conic Projection

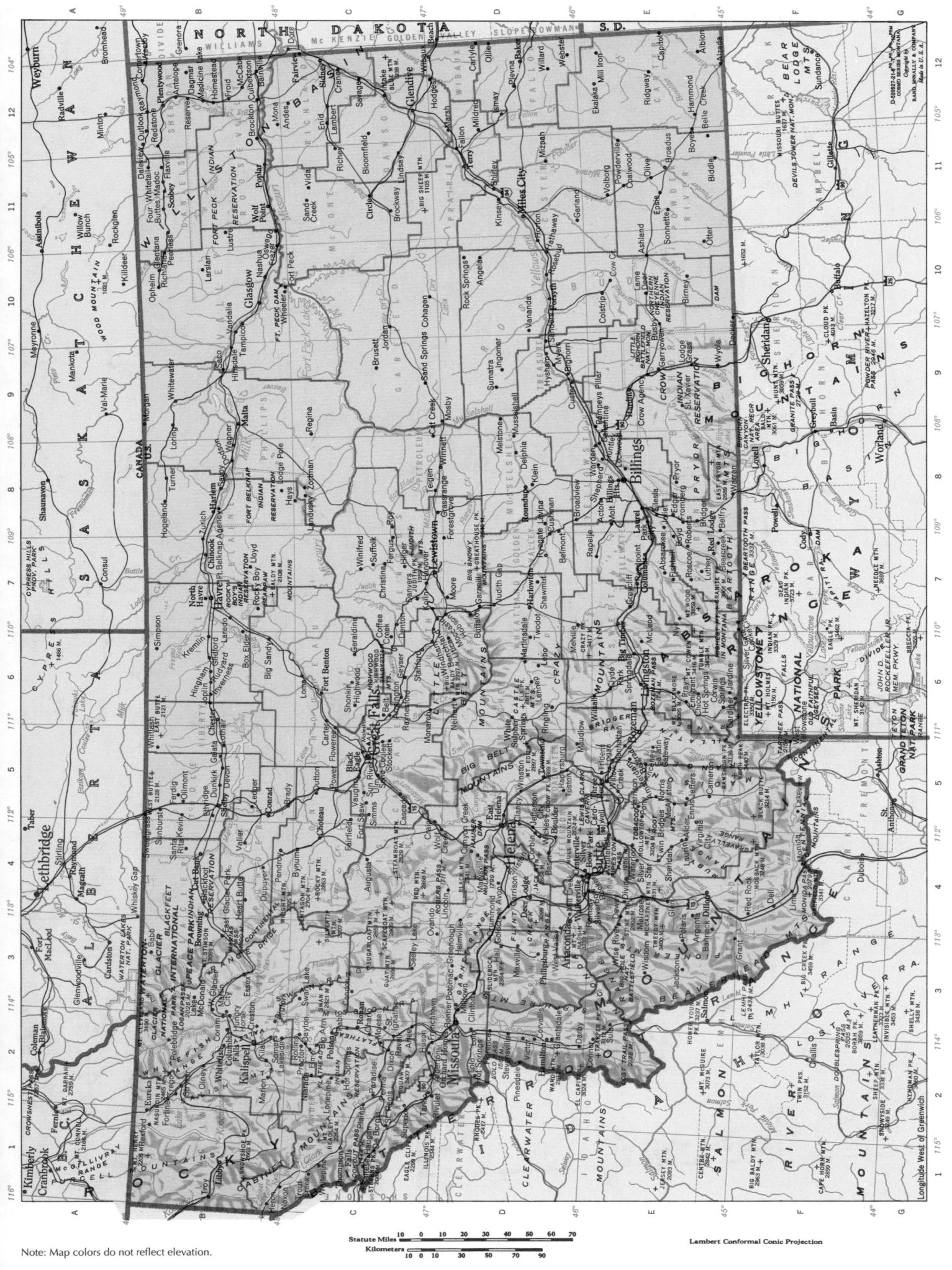

Note: Map colors do not reflect elevation.

Statute Miles
10 0 10 20 30 40 50 60 70
Kilometers
10 0 10   30   50   70   90

Lambert Conformal Conic Projection

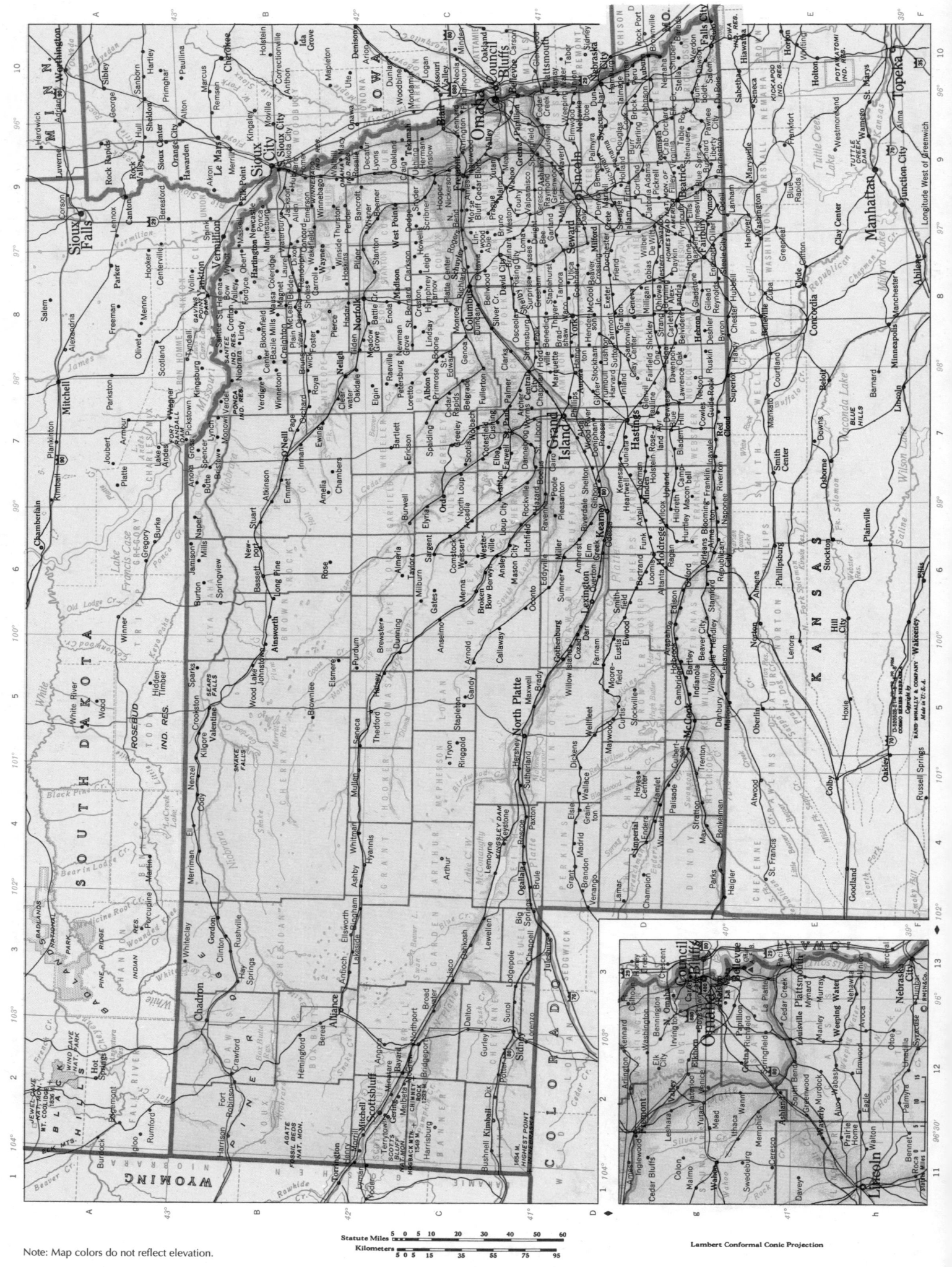

Note: Map colors do not reflect elevation.

Statute Miles 5 0 5 10   20   30   40   50   60

Kilometers 5 0 5 15   35   55   75   95

Lambert Conformal Conic Projection

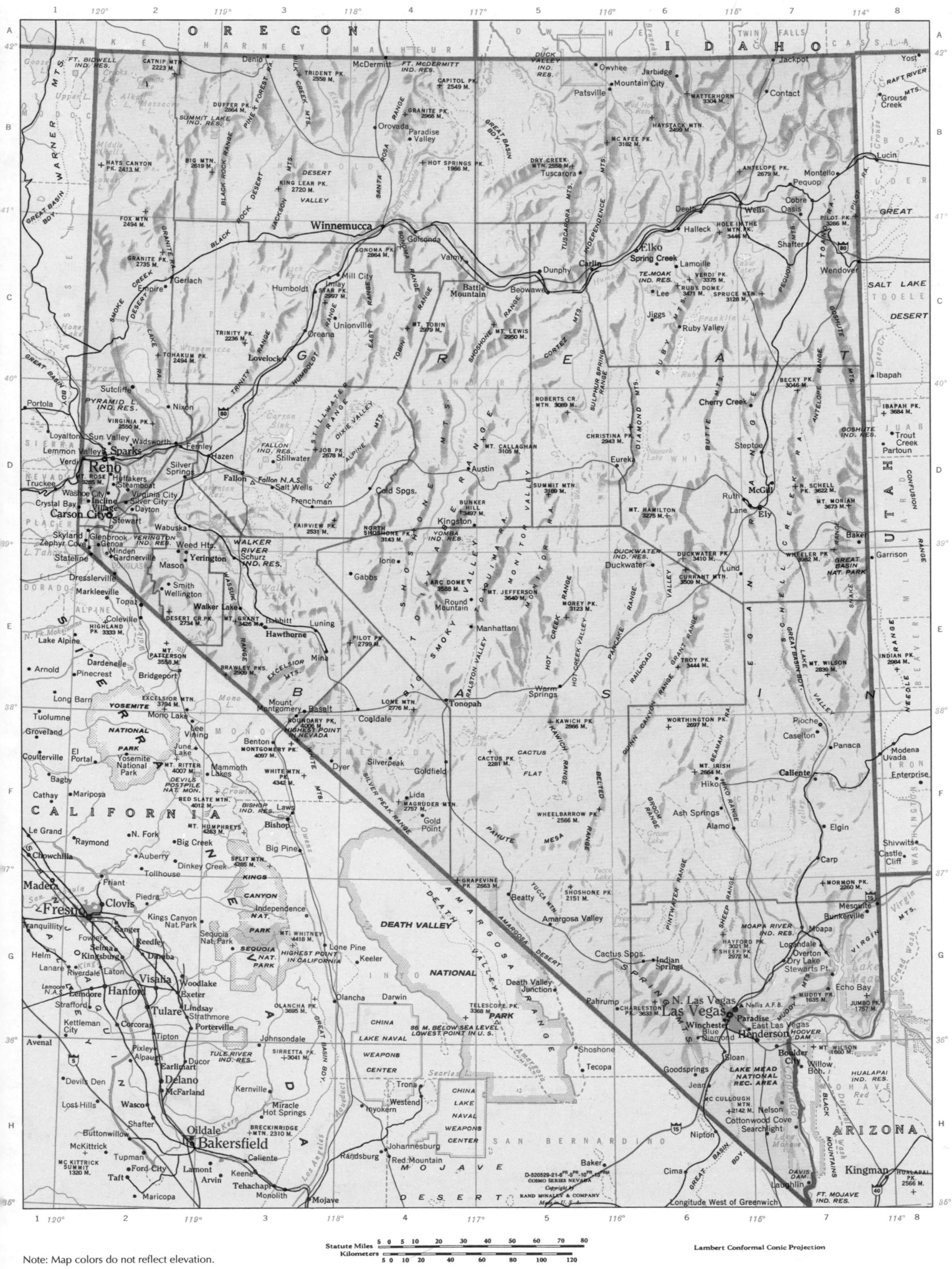

Note: Map colors do not reflect elevation.

Statute Miles
5 0 5 10   20   30   40   50   60   70   80
Kilometers
5 0 10 20   40   60   80   100   120

Lambert Conformal Conic Projection

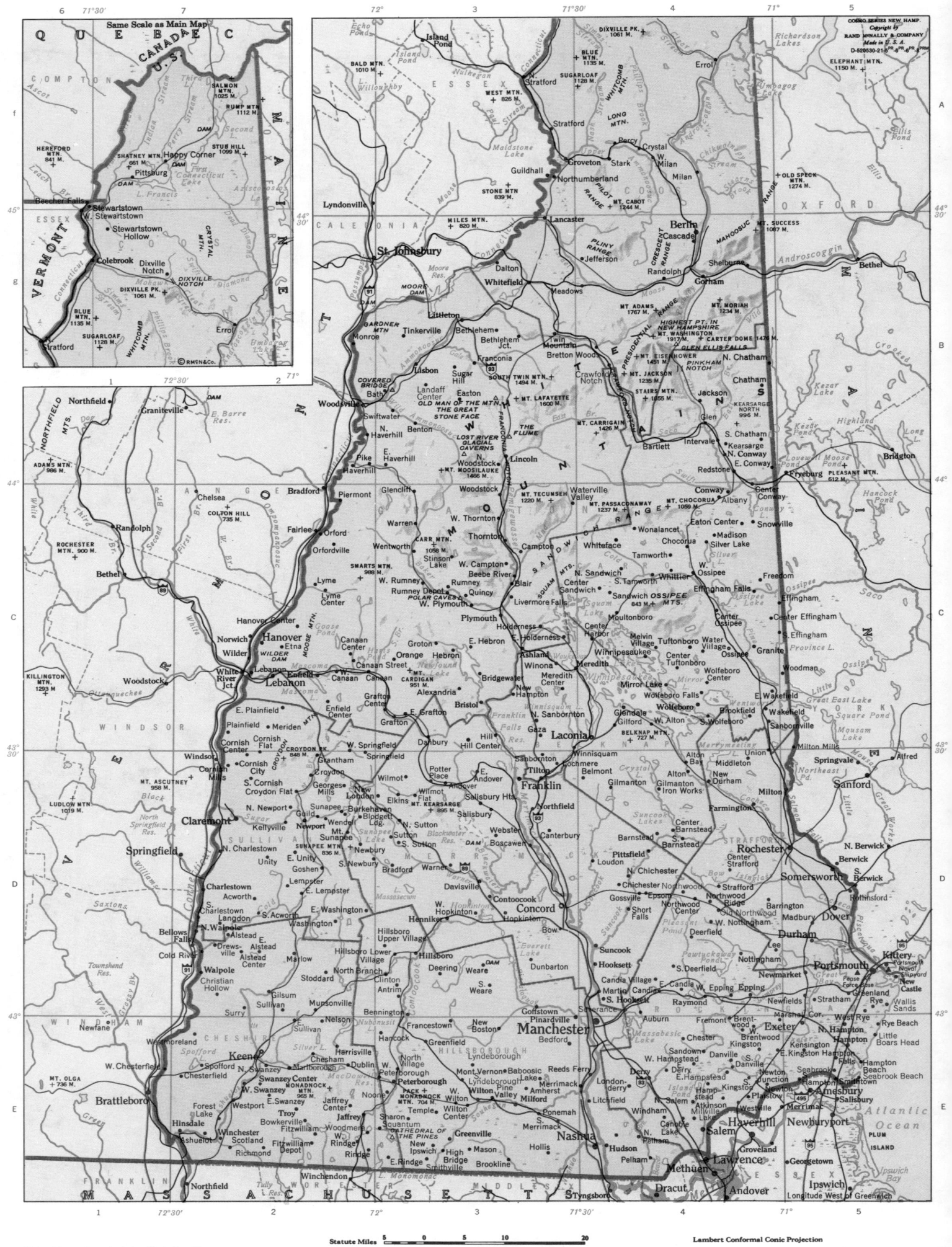

Note: Map colors do not reflect elevation.

Statute Miles 5 0 5 10 20

Kilometers 5 0 5 10 15 20 25

Lambert Conformal Conic Projection

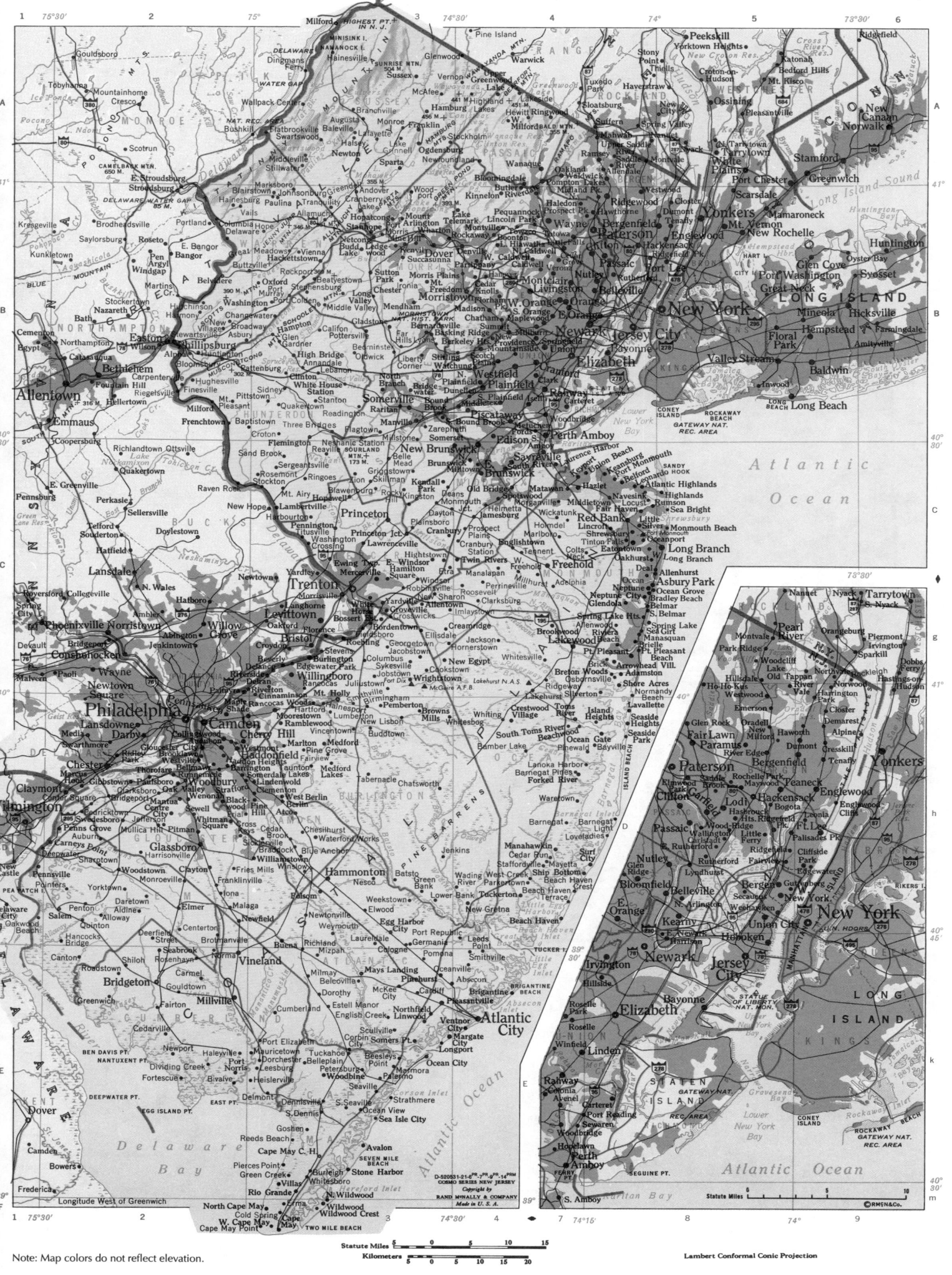

Note: Map colors do not reflect elevation.

Longitude West of Greenwich

Statute Miles
Kilometers

D-520531-21-6
COSMO SERIES NEW JERSEY
Copyright by
RAND M9NALLY & COMPANY
Made in U.S.A.

Statute Miles

Lambert Conformal Conic Projection

©RM&N&Co.

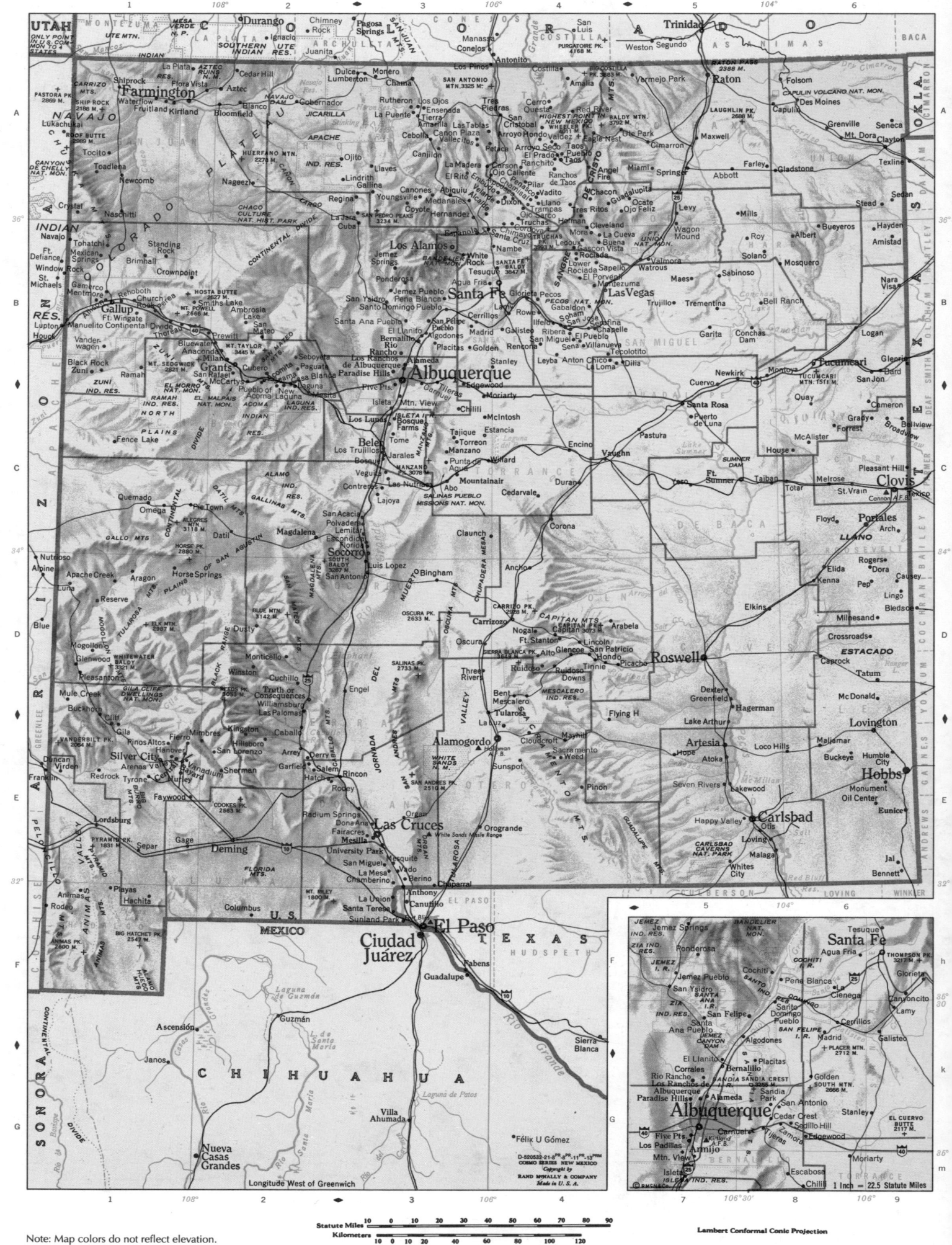

Note: Map colors do not reflect elevation.

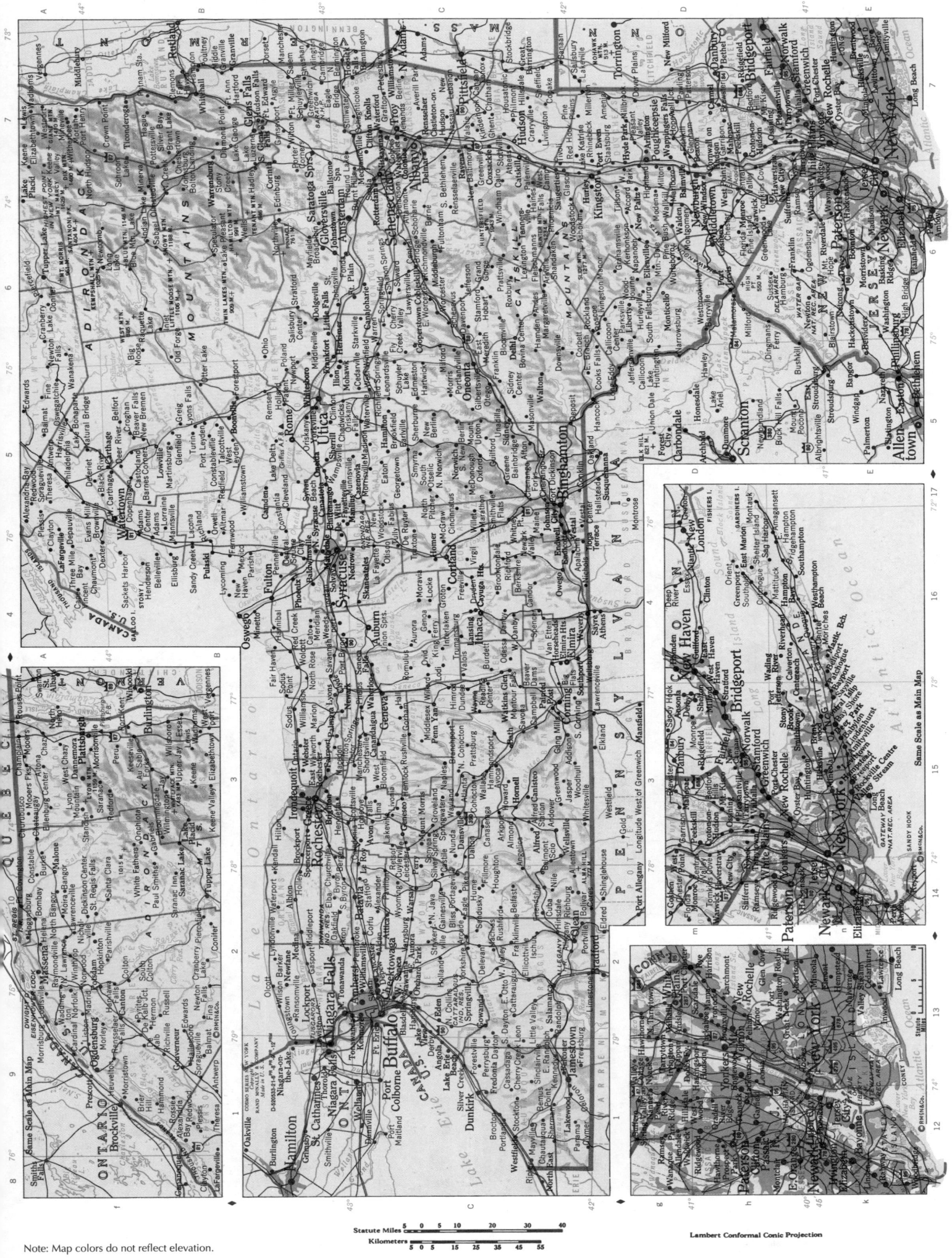

Note: Map colors do not reflect elevation.

Statute Miles 5 0 5 10   20   30   40
Kilometers 5 0 5 15 25 35 45 55

Lambert Conformal Conic Projection

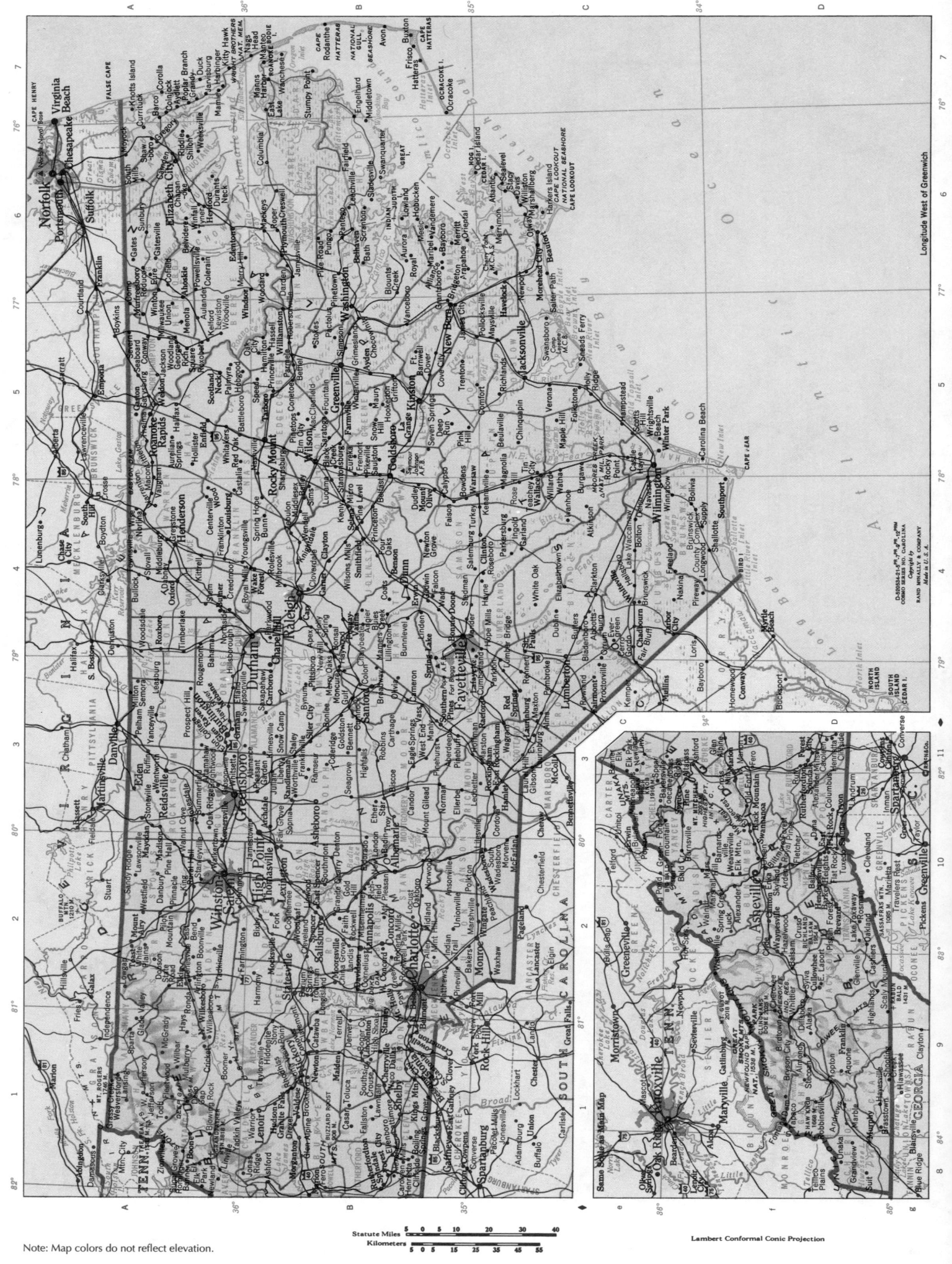

Note: Map colors do not reflect elevation.

Statute Miles
5 0 5 10   20   30   40
Kilometers
5 0 5 15 25 35 45 55

Same Scale as Main Map

Lambert Conformal Conic Projection

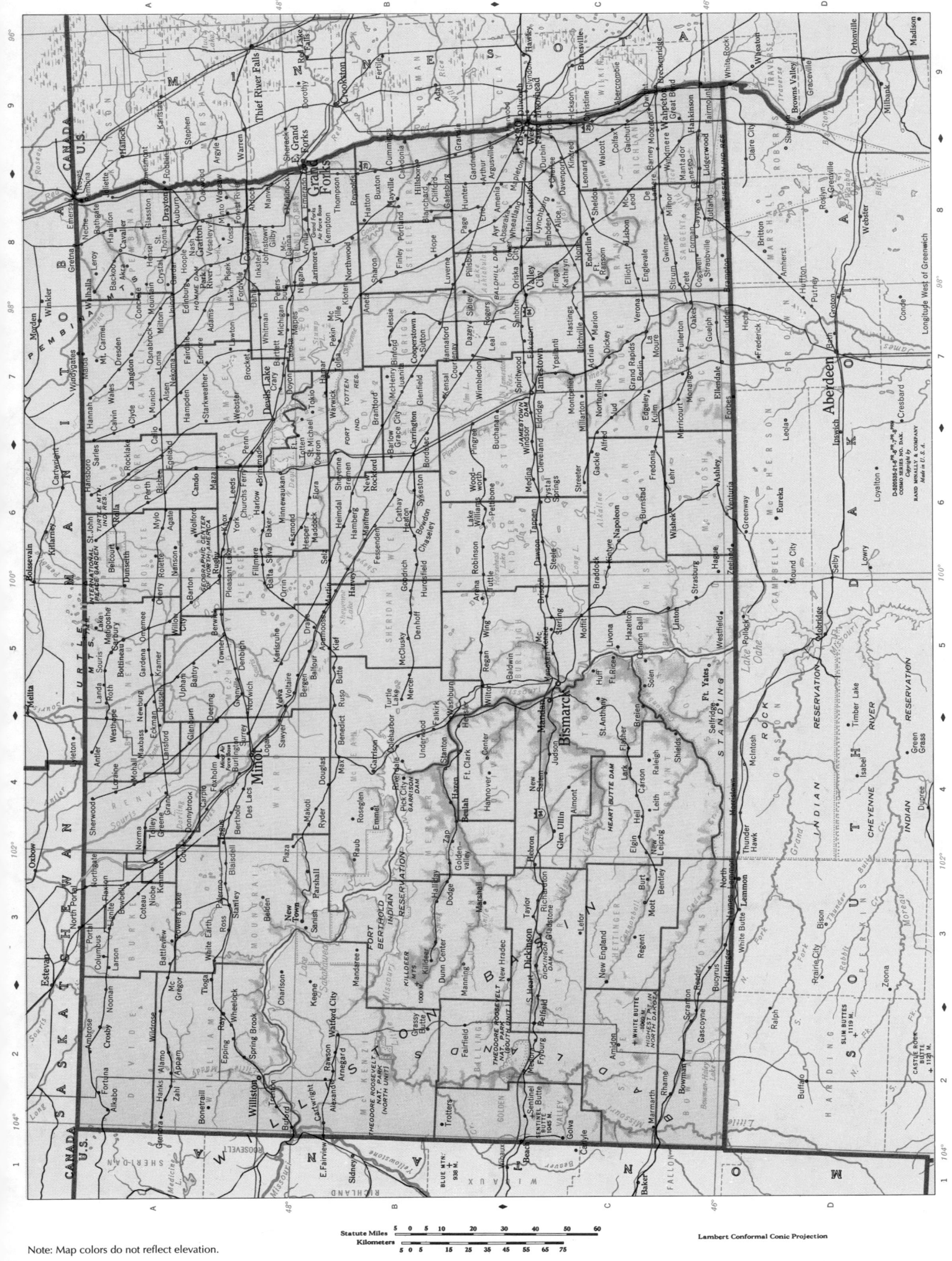

Note: Map colors do not reflect elevation.

Statute Miles 5 0 5 10 20 30 40 50 60
Kilometers 5 0 5 15 25 35 45 55 65 75

Lambert Conformal Conic Projection

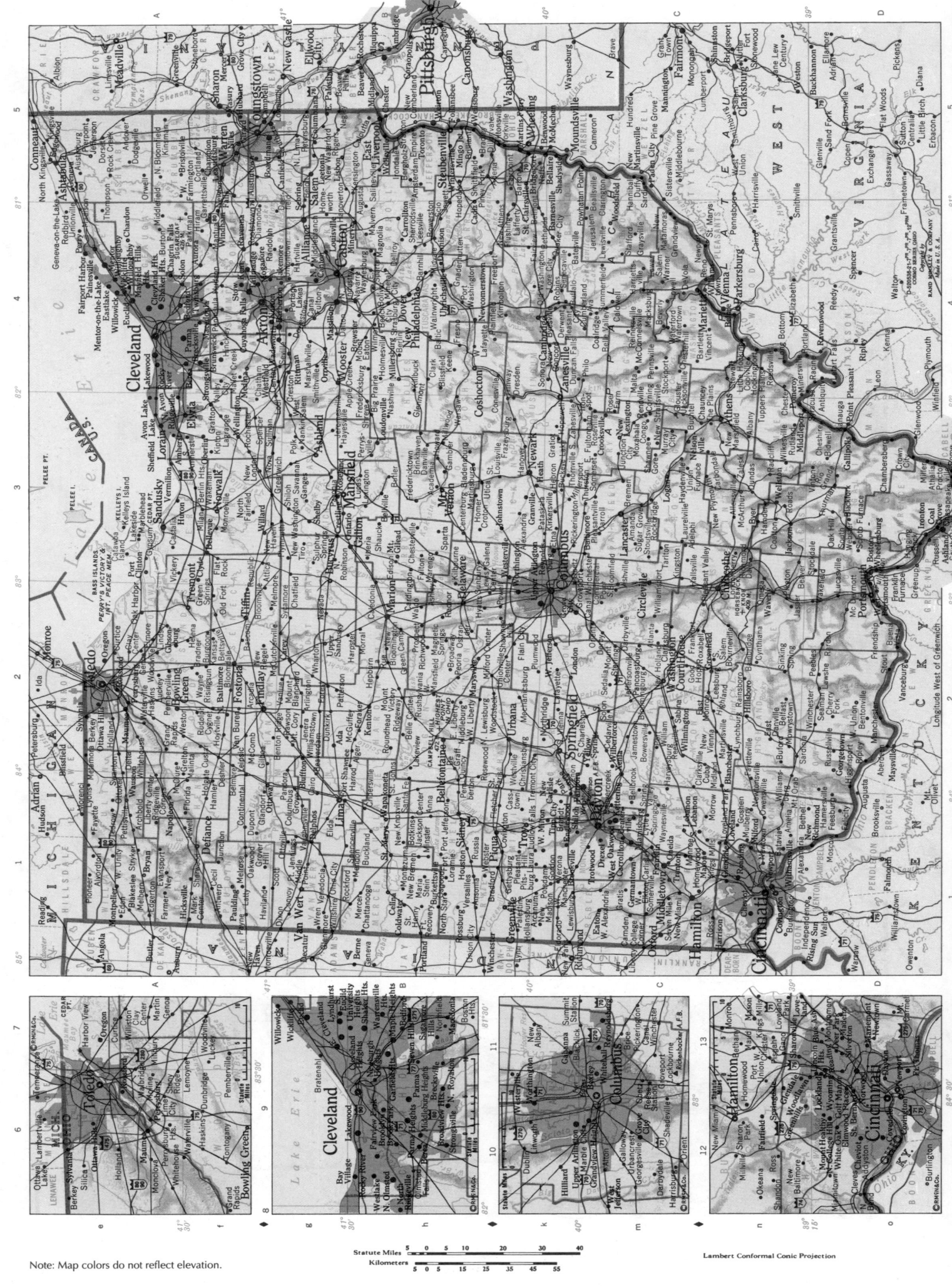

Note: Map colors do not reflect elevation.

Statute Miles 5 0 5 10   20   30   40
Kilometers 5 0 5   15   25   35   45   55

Lambert Conformal Conic Projection

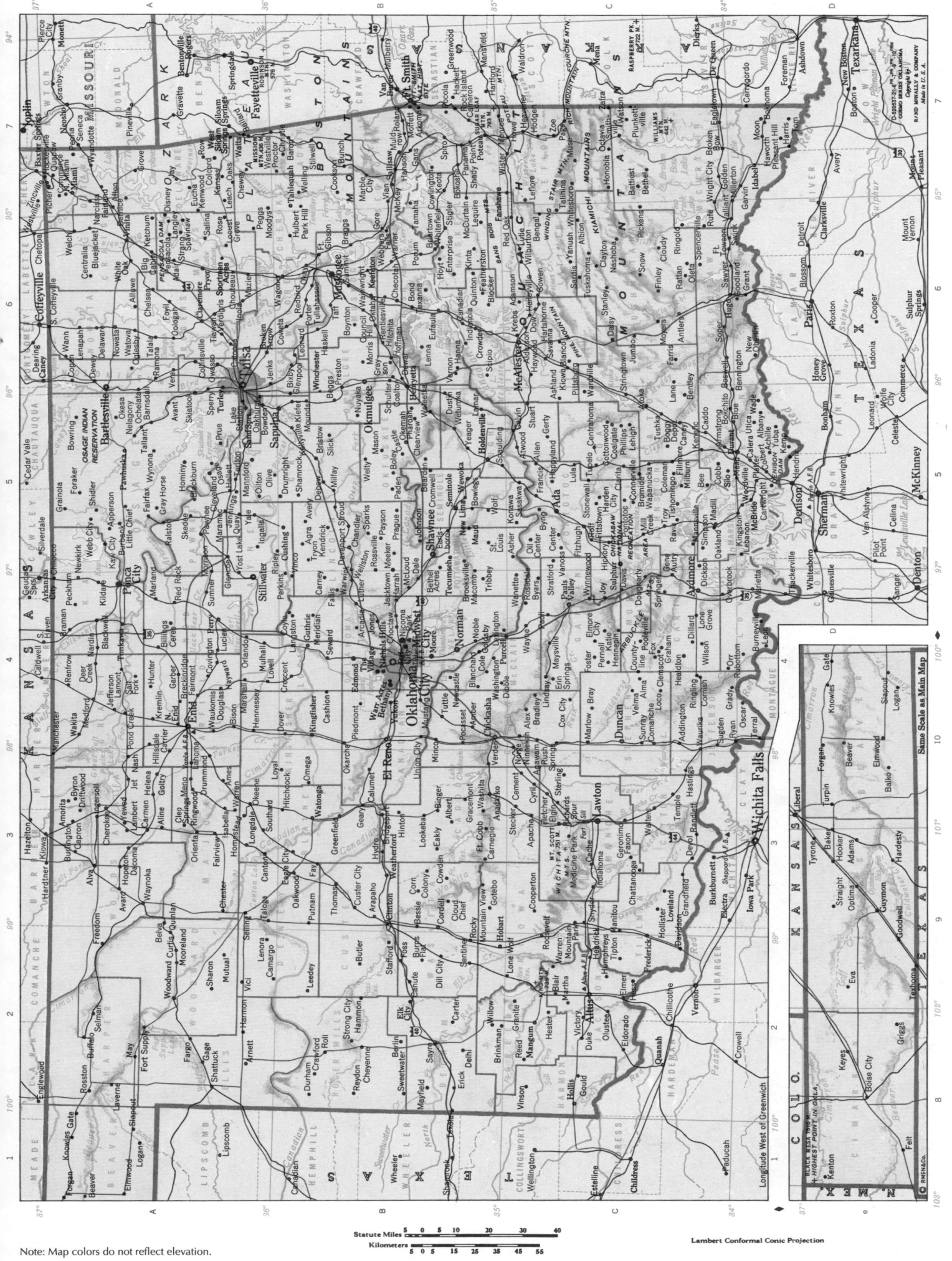

Note: Map colors do not reflect elevation.

Statute Miles 5 0 5   10   20   30   40
Kilometers 5 0 5   15   25   35   45   55

Lambert Conformal Conic Projection

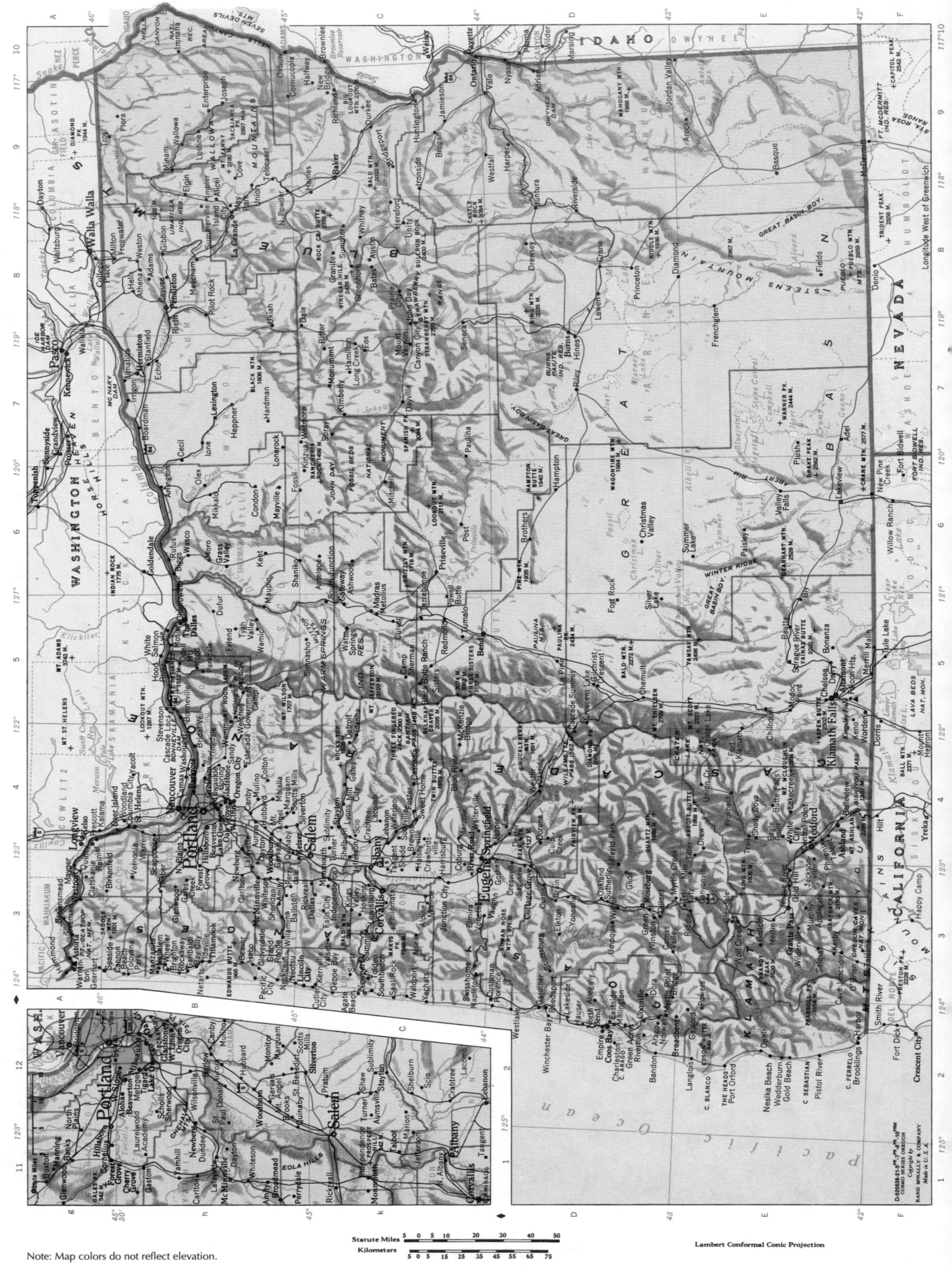

Note: Map colors do not reflect elevation.

Statute Miles
Kilometers

Lambert Conformal Conic Projection

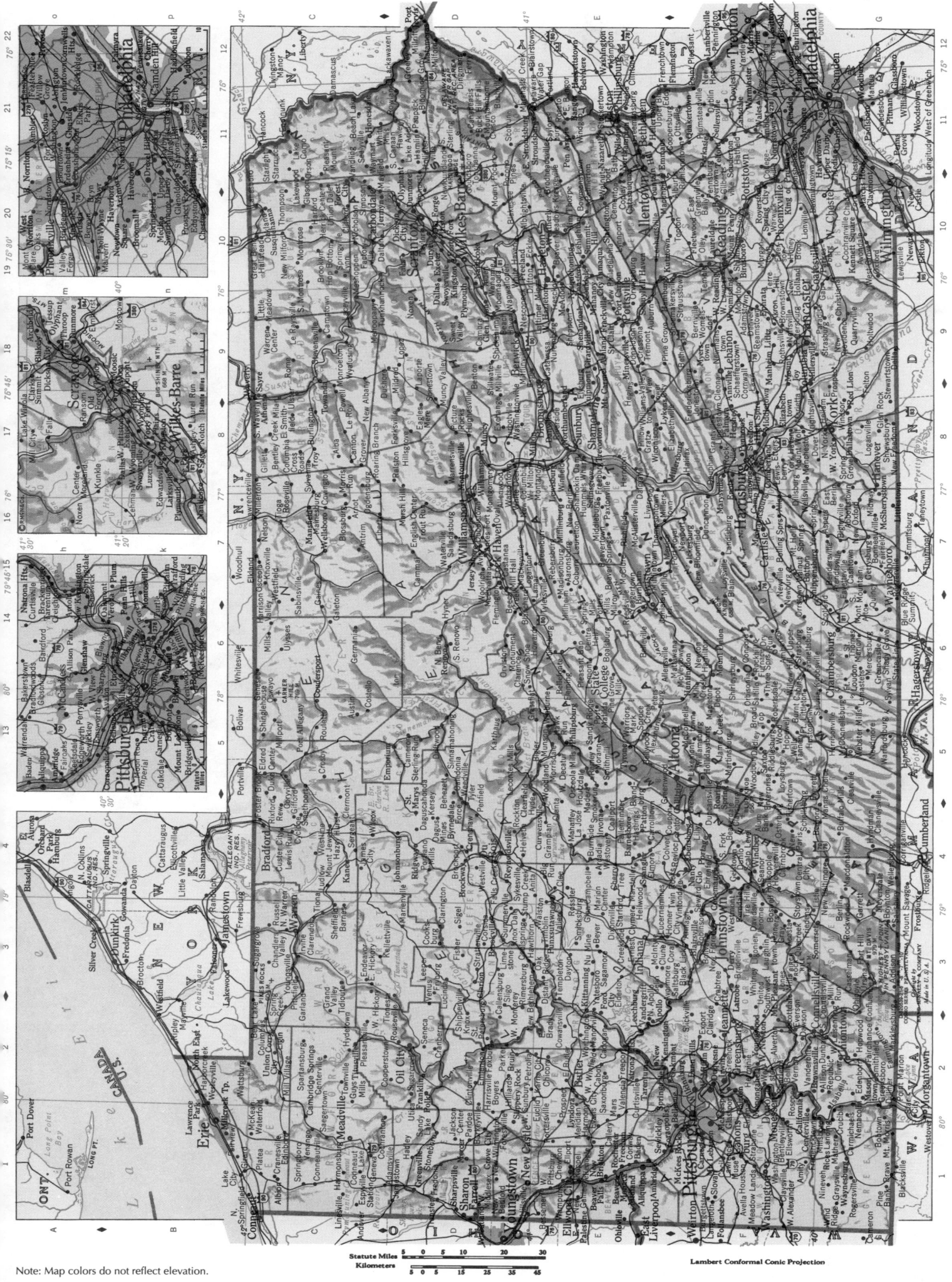

Note: Map colors do not reflect elevation.

Statute Miles
Kilometers

Lambert Conformal Conic Projection

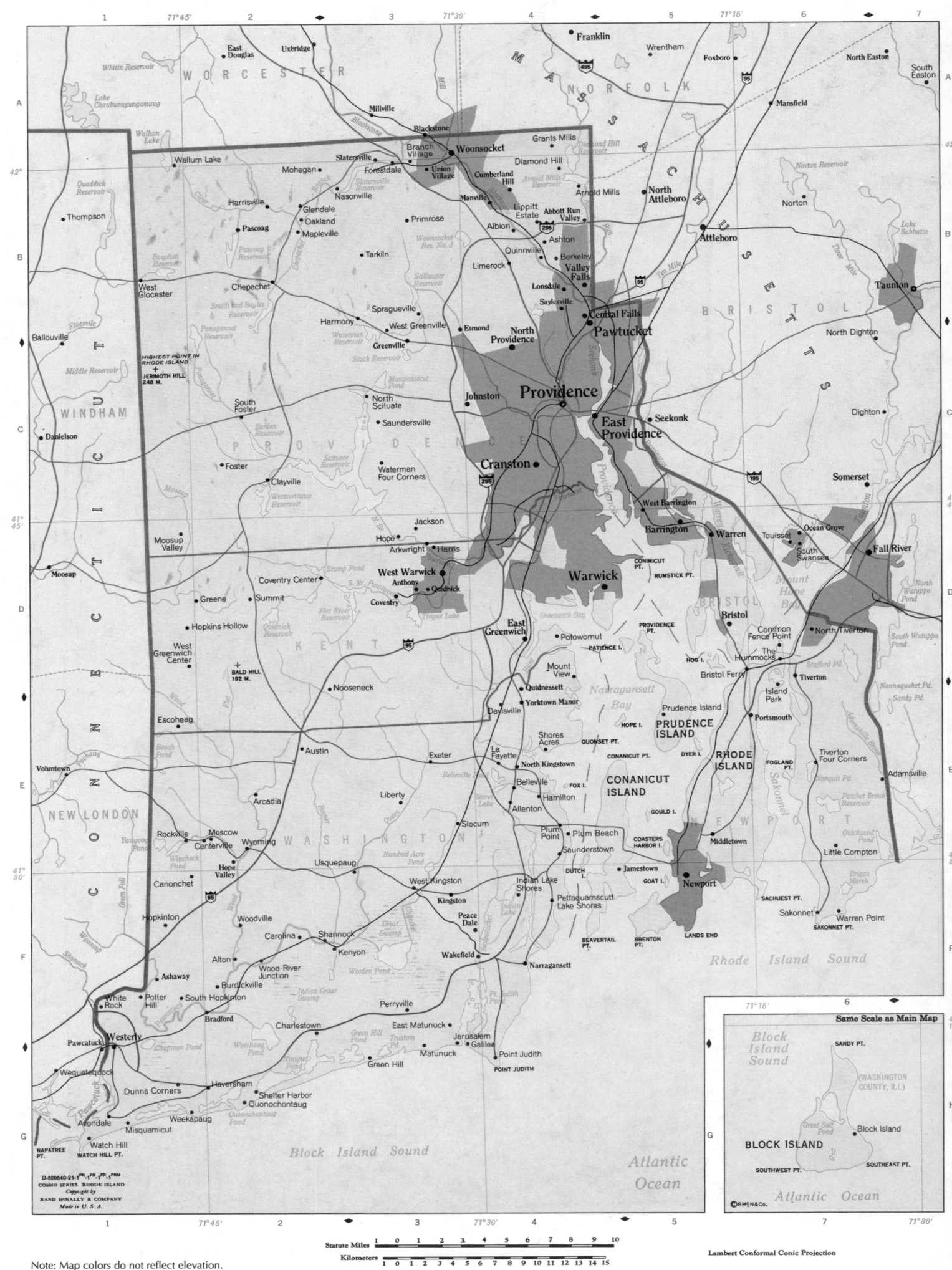

Note: Map colors do not reflect elevation.

Statute Miles 1 0 1 2 3 4 5 6 7 8 9 10

Kilometers 1 0 1 2 3 4 5 6 7 8 9 10 11 12 13 14 15

Lambert Conformal Conic Projection

BLOCK ISLAND

Same Scale as Main Map

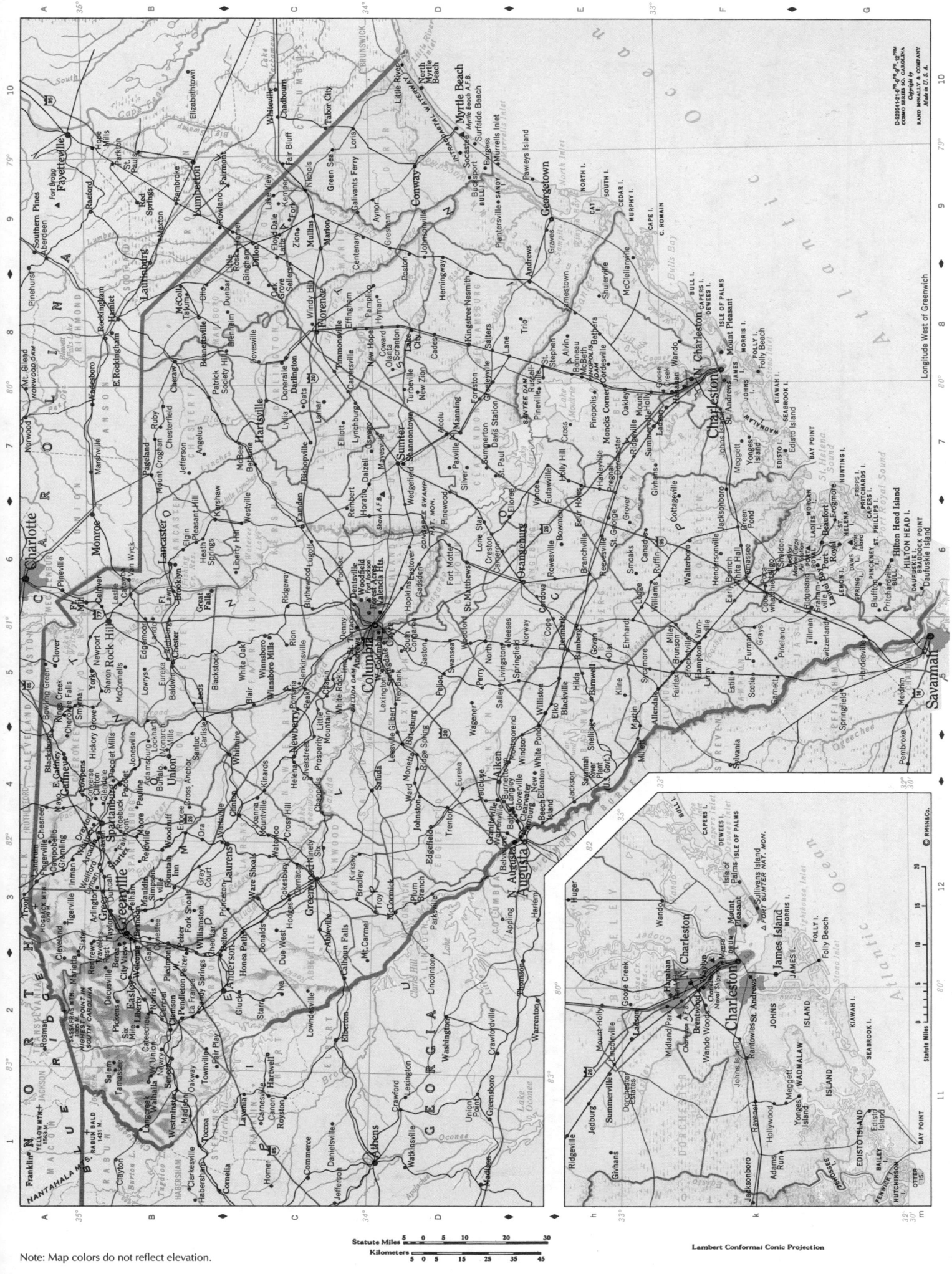

Note: Map colors do not reflect elevation.

Statute Miles   5 0 5   10   20   30
Kilometers   5 0 5   15   25   35   45

Lambert Conformal Conic Projection

Note: Map colors do not reflect elevation.

Statute Miles 5 0 5 10 20 30 40 50 60
Kilometers 5 0 5 15 25 35 45 55 65 75

Lambert Conformal Conic Projection

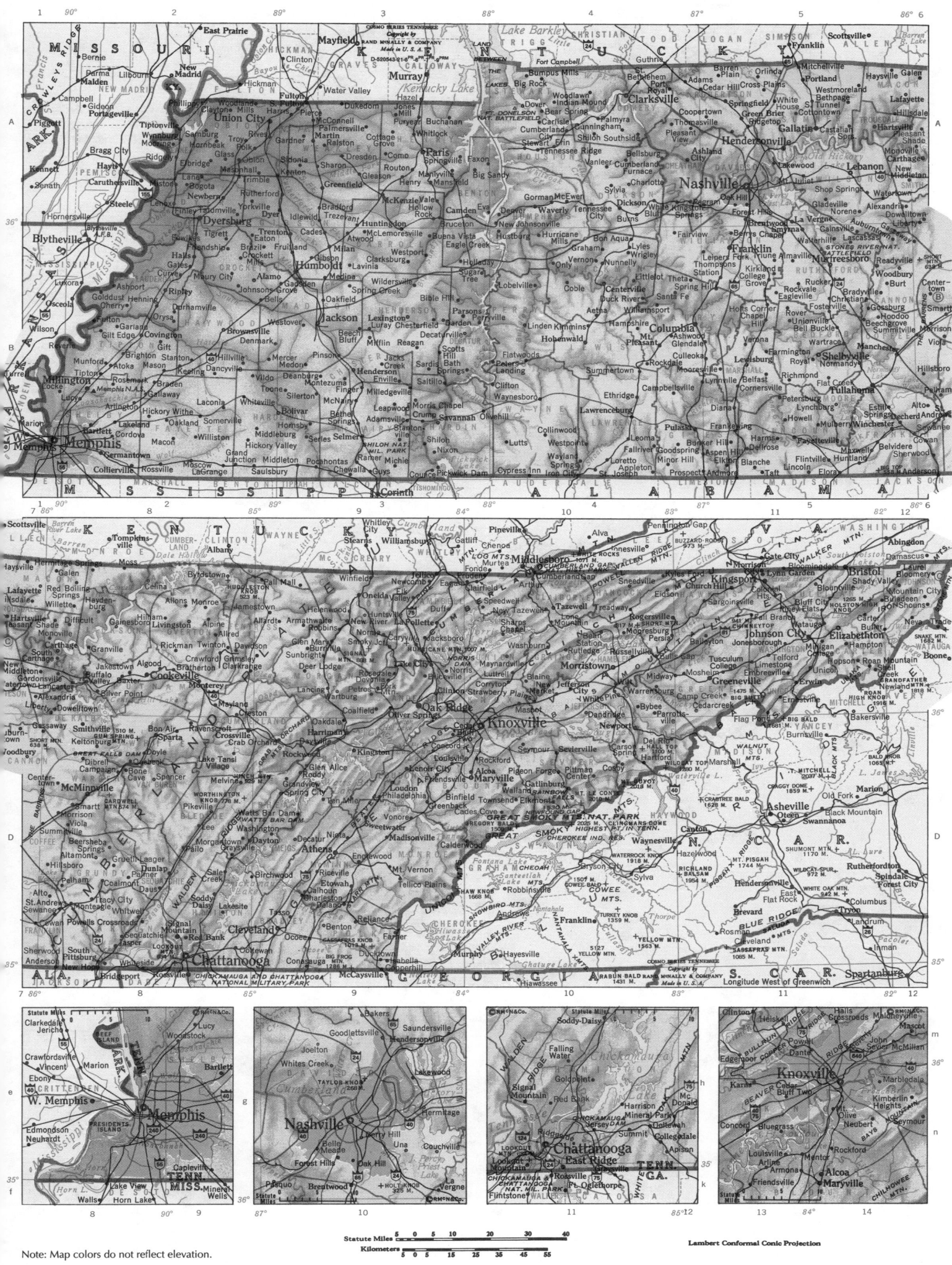

Note: Map colors do not reflect elevation.

Statute Miles 5 0 5 10 20 30 40
Kilometers 5 0 5 15 25 35 45 55

Lambert Conformal Conic Projection

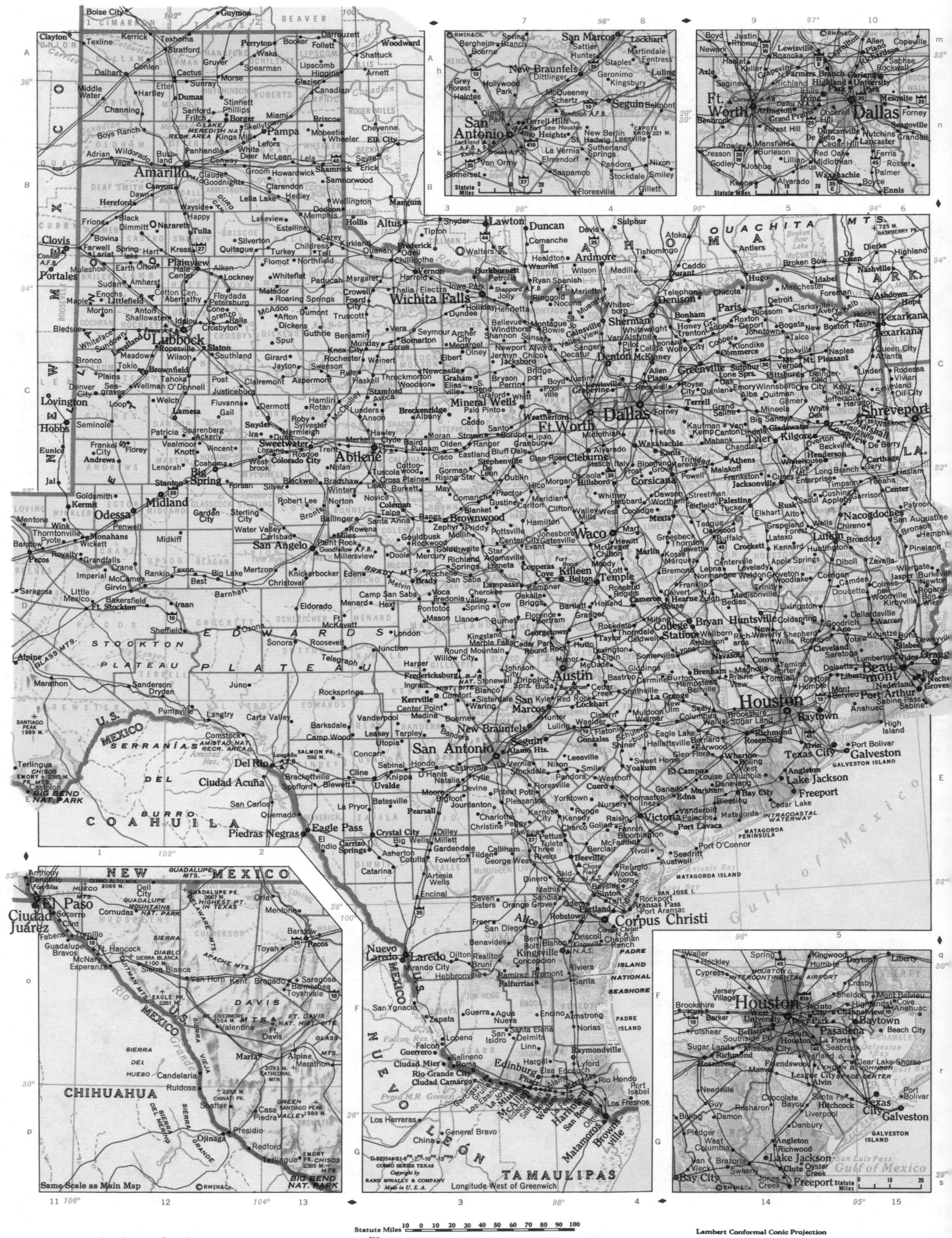

Note: Map colors do not reflect elevation.

Statute Miles   10 0 10 20 30 40 50 60 70 80 90 100

Kilometers   10 0 10 20 40 60 80 100 120 140

Lambert Conformal Conic Projection

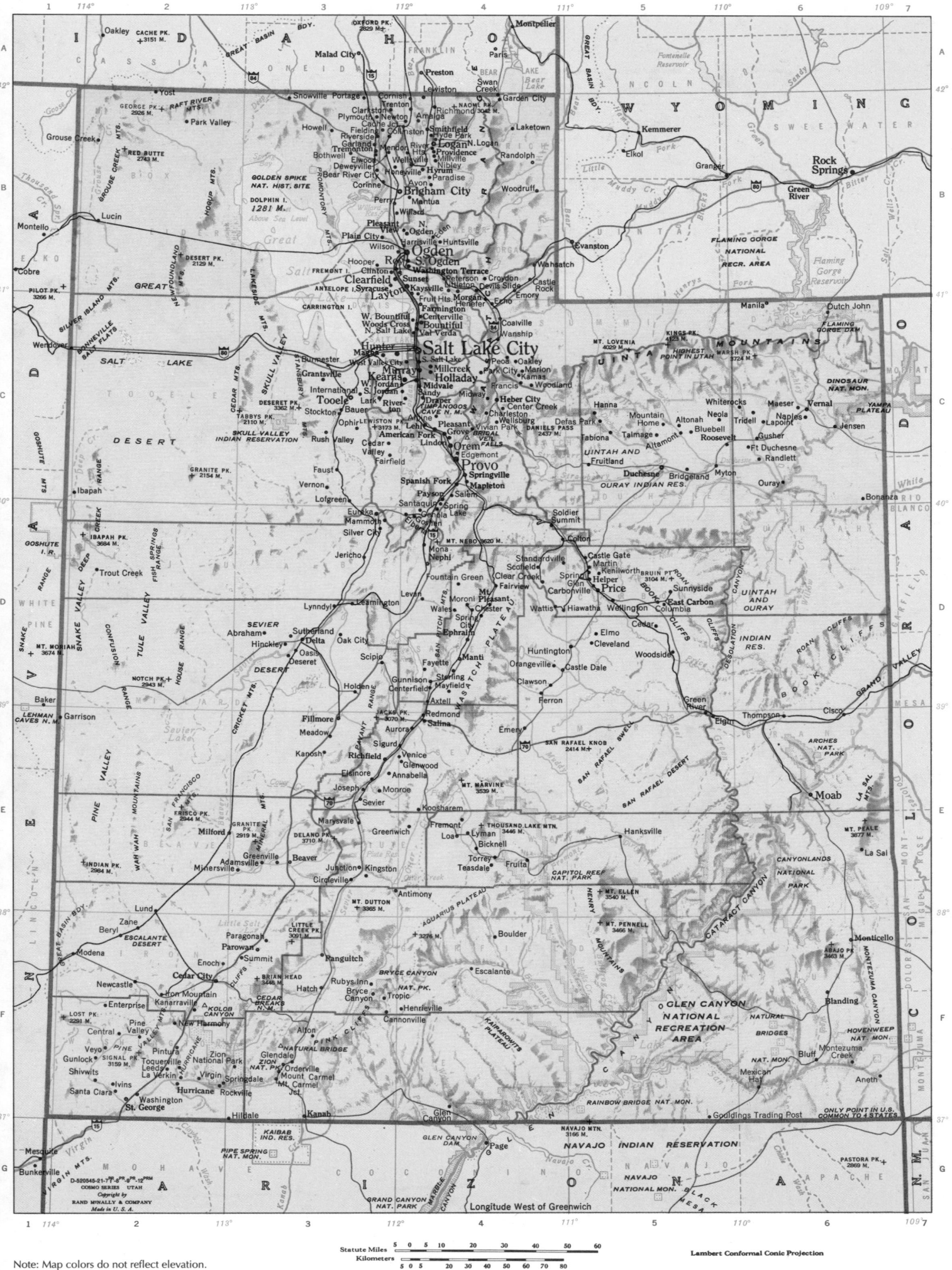

Note: Map colors do not reflect elevation.

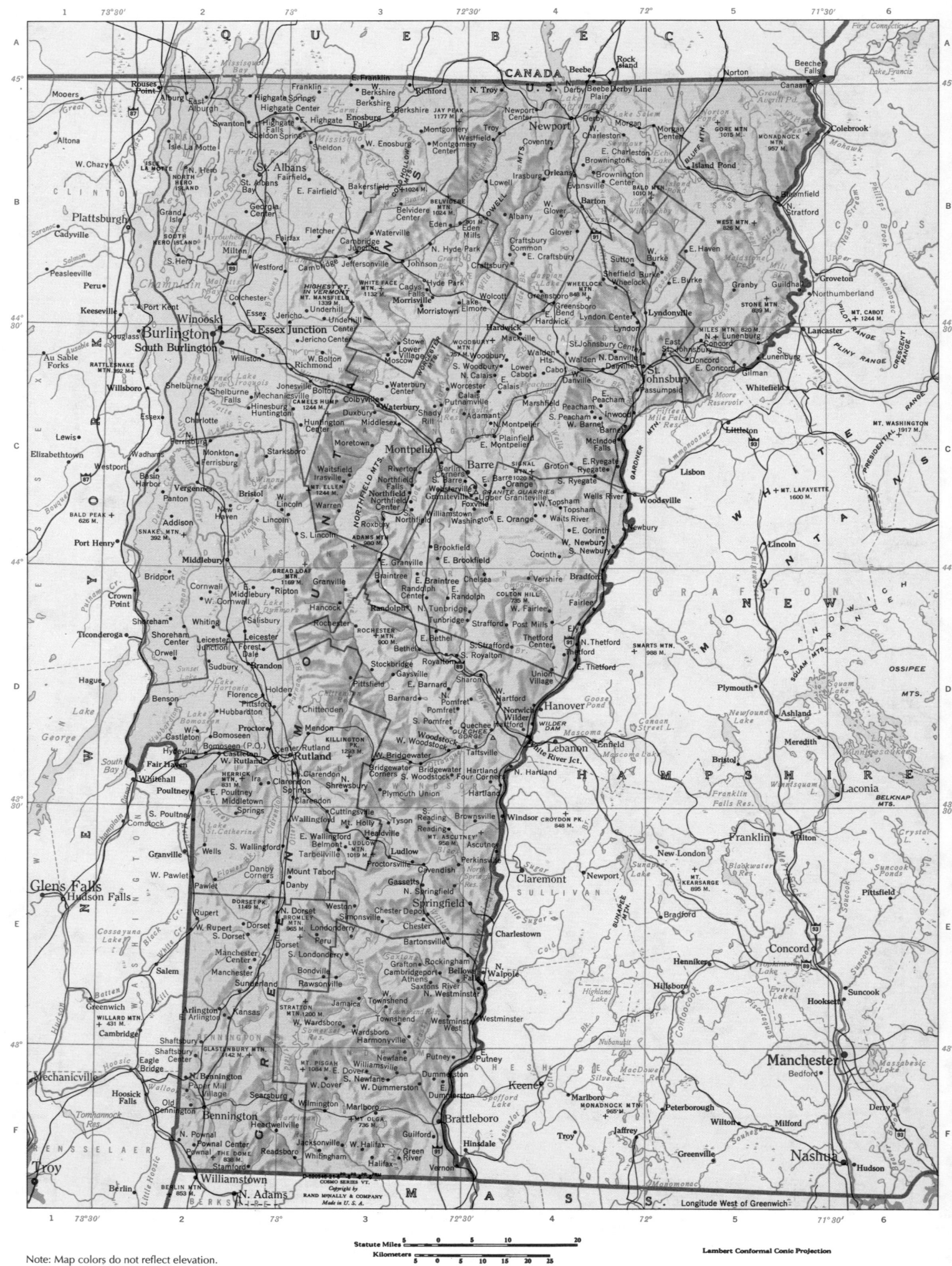

Note: Map colors do not reflect elevation.

Statute Miles
Kilometers

Lambert Conformal Conic Projection

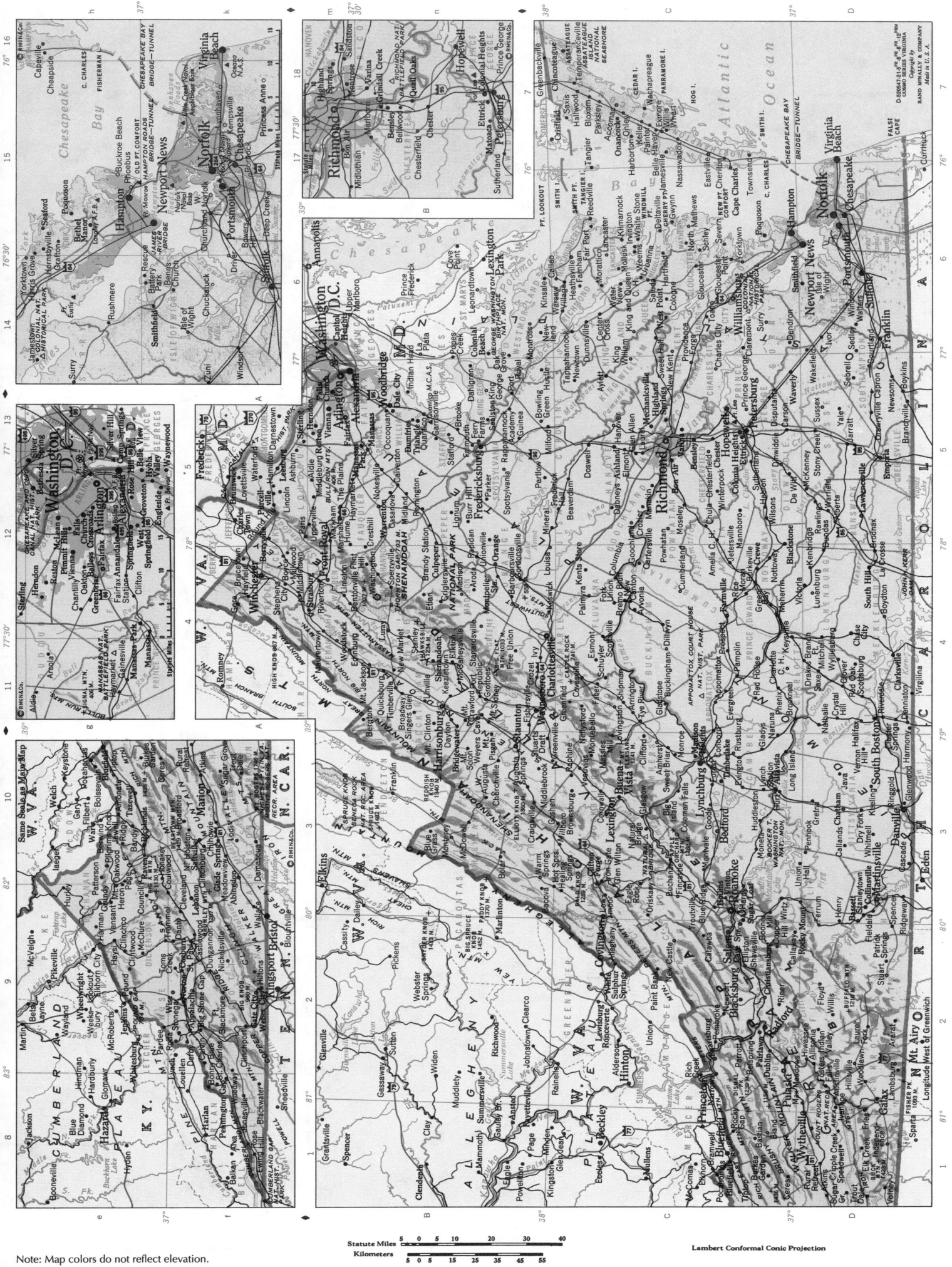

Note: Map colors do not reflect elevation.

Statute Miles
Kilometers

Lambert Conformal Conic Projection

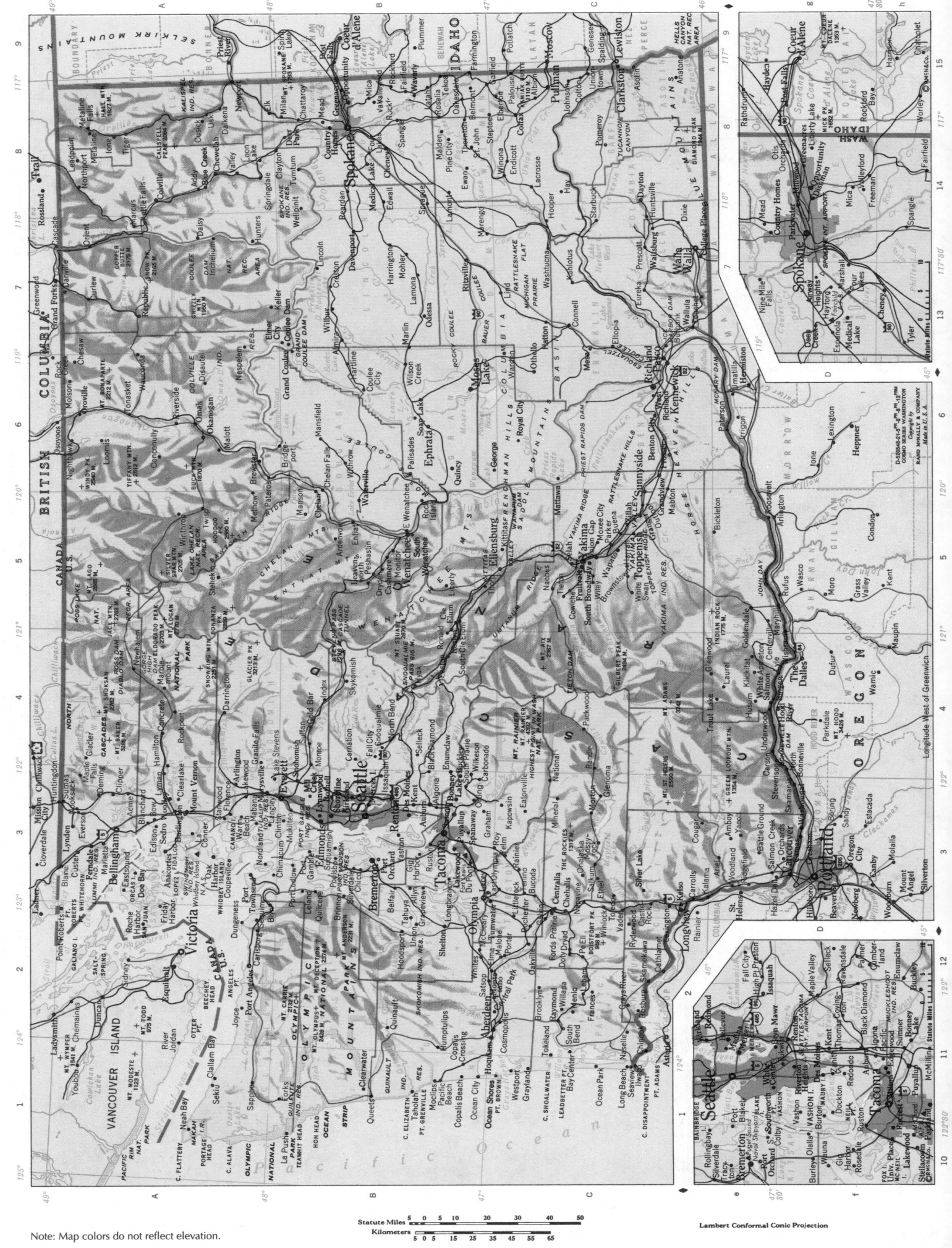

Note: Map colors do not reflect elevation.

Statute Miles 5   0   5   10   20   30   40   50
Kilometers 5 0 5   15   25   35   45   55   65

Lambert Conformal Conic Projection

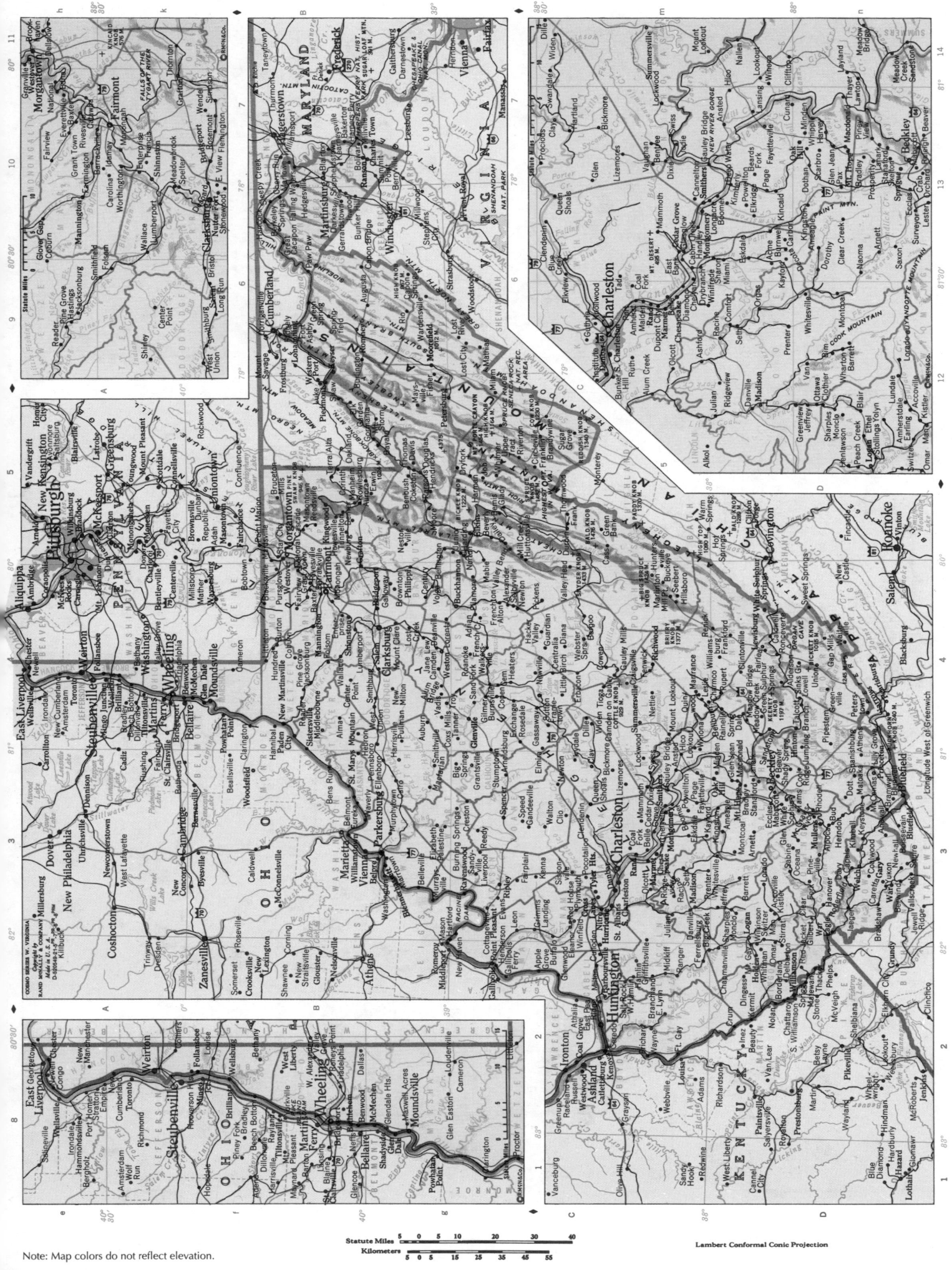

Note: Map colors do not reflect elevation.

Statute Miles 5 0 5 10   20   30   40
Kilometers 5 0 15   25   35   45   55

Lambert Conformal Conic Projection

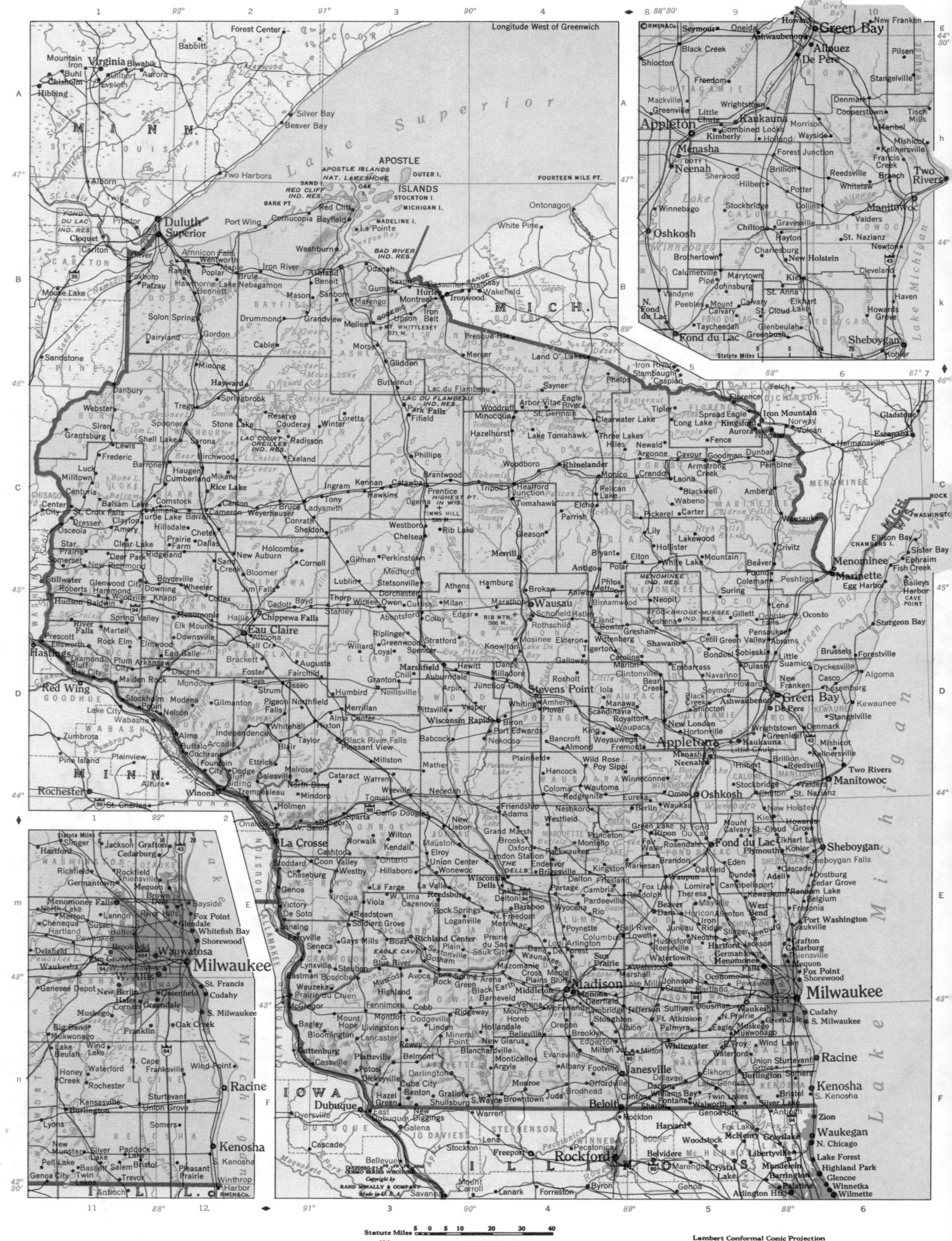

Note: Map colors do not reflect elevation.

Statute Miles

Kilometers

Lambert Conformal Conic Projection

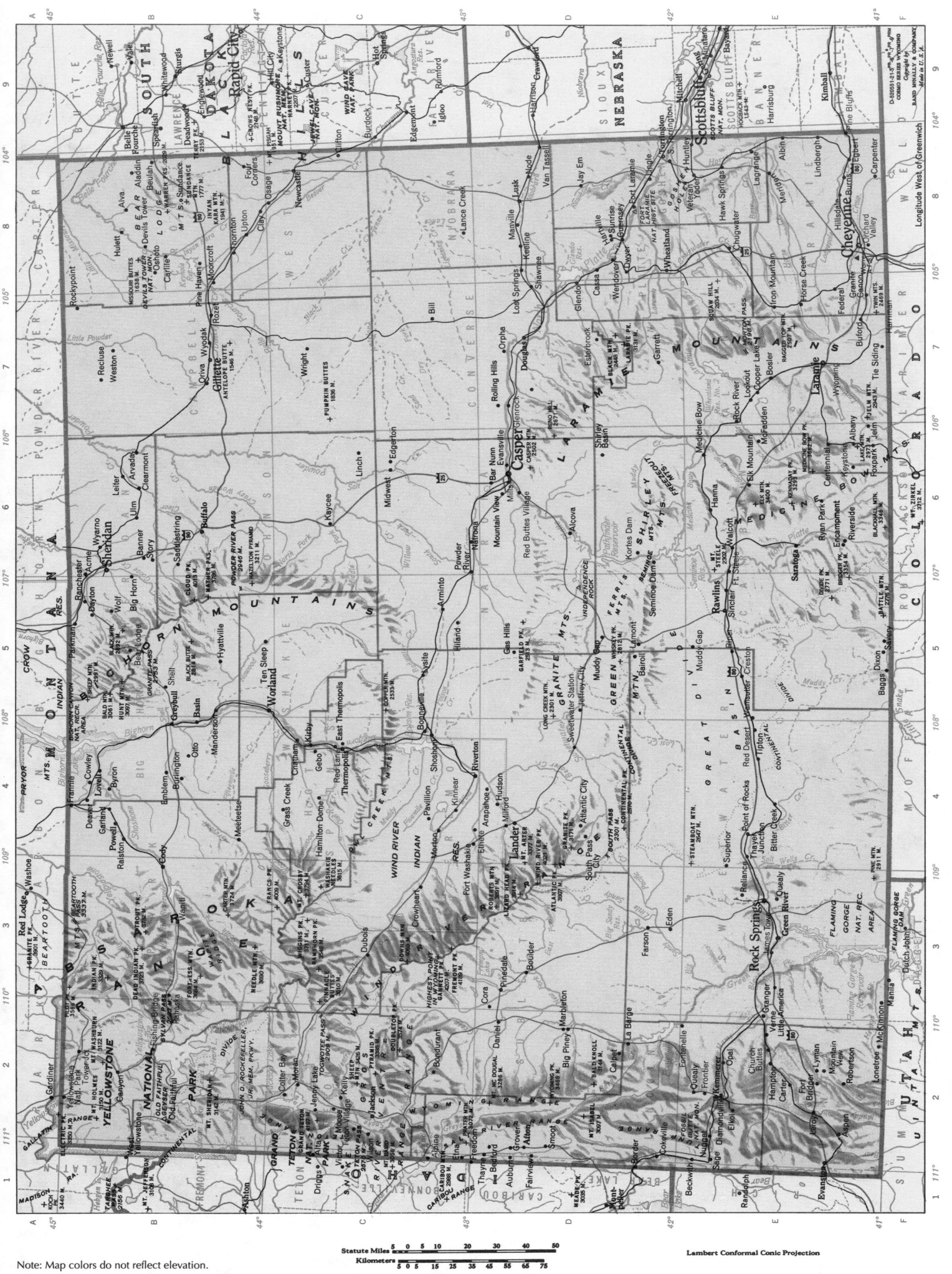

Note: Map colors do not reflect elevation.

Statute Miles   5 0 5 10   20   30   40   50
Kilometers   5 0 5   15   25   35   45   55   75

Lambert Conformal Conic Projection

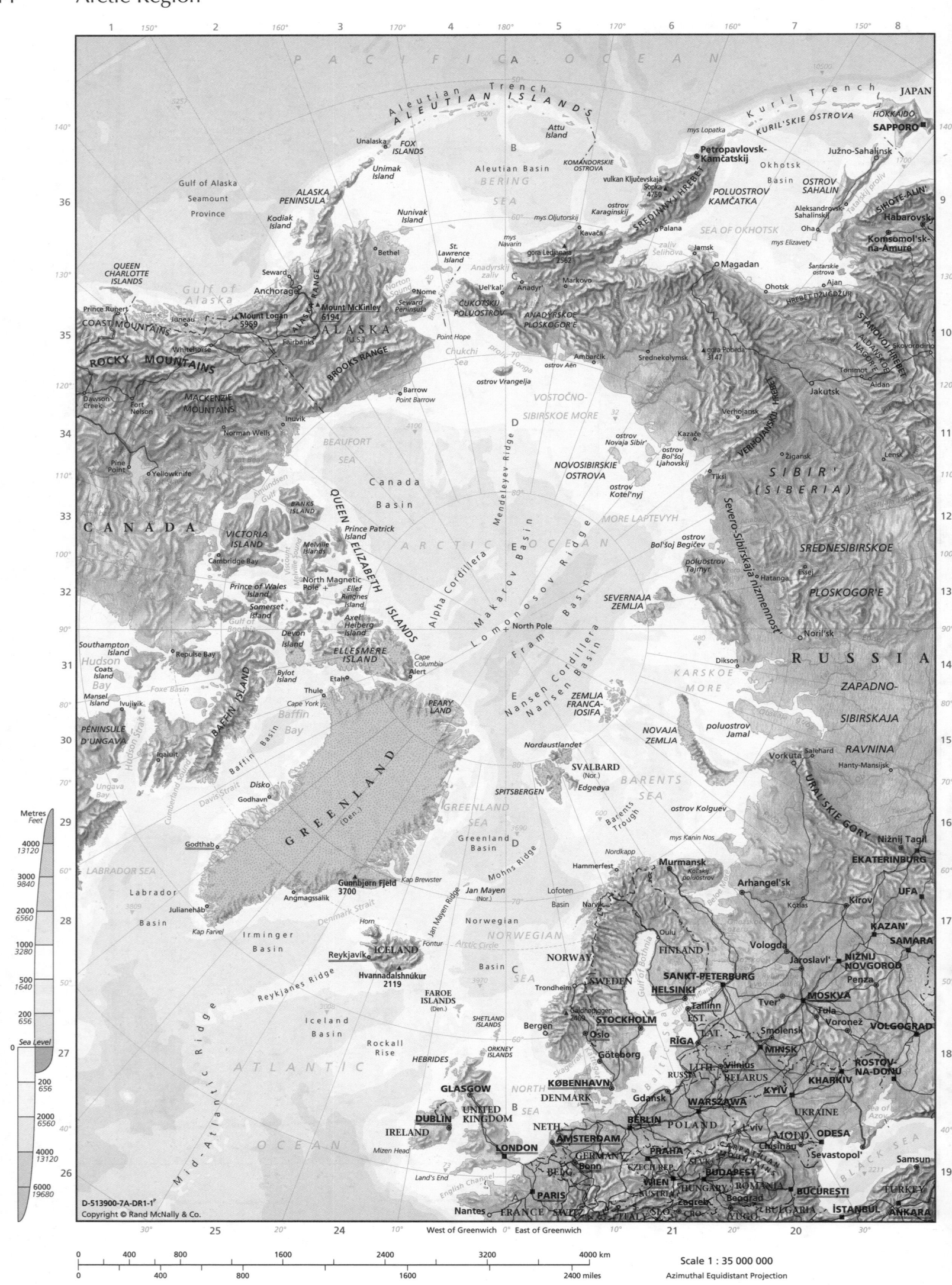

Metres
Feet
4000
13120

3000
9840

2000
6560

1000
3280

500
1640

200
656

Sea Level
0

200
656

2000
6560

4000
13120

6000
19680

D-513900-7A-DR1-1°
Copyright © Rand McNally & Co.

0   400   800   1600   2400   3200   4000 km
0   400   800   1600   2400 miles

Scale 1 : 35 000 000
Azimuthal Equidistant Projection

Index to World Reference Maps

Introduction to the Index

This index includes in a single alphabetical list approximately 45,000 names of features that appear on the reference maps. Each name is followed by the name of the country or continent in which it is located, a map reference key, and a page reference.

Names The names of cities appear in the index in regular type. The names of all other features appear in *italics*, followed by descriptive terms (hill, mtn., state) to indicate their nature.

Abbreviations of names on the maps have been standardized as much as possible. Names that are abbreviated on the maps are generally spelled out in full in the index.

Country names and names of features that extend beyond the boundaries of one country are followed by the name of the continent in which each is located. Country designations follow the names of all other places in the index. The locations of places in the United States, Canada, and the United Kingdom are further defined by abbreviations that indicate the state, province, or political division in which each is located.

All abbreviations used in the index are defined in the List of Abbreviations below.

Alphabetization Names are alphabetized in the order of the letters of the English alphabet. Spanish *ll* and *ch*, for example, are not treated as distinct letters. Furthermore, diacritical marks are disregarded in alphabetization—German or Scandinavian *ä* or *ö* are treated as *a* or *o*.

The names of physical features may appear inverted, since they are always alphabetized under the proper, not the generic, part of the name, thus: "Gibraltar, Strait of". Otherwise every entry, whether consisting of one word or more, is alphabetized as a single continuous entity. "Lakeland", for example, appears after "La Crosse" and before "La Salle". Names beginning with articles (Le Havre, Den Helder, Al-Manāmah) are not inverted. Names beginning "St.", "Ste." and "Sainte" are alphabetized as though spelled "Saint".

In the case of identical names, towns are listed first, then political divisions, then physical features. Entries that are completely identical are listed alphabetically by country name.

Map Reference Keys and Page References The map reference keys and page references are found in the last two columns of each entry.

Each map reference key consists of a letter and number. The letters appear along the sides of the maps. Lowercase letters indicate reference to inset maps. Numbers appear across the tops and bottoms of the maps.

Map reference keys for point features, such as cities and mountain peaks, indicate the locations of the symbols. For other features, such as countries, mountain ranges, or rivers, locations are given for the names.

The page number generally refers to the main map for the country in which the feature is located. Page references to two-page maps always refer to the left-hand page.

List of Abbreviations

Abbreviation	Meaning	Abbreviation	Meaning
Ab., Can.	Alberta, Can.	ctry.	independent country
Afg.	Afghanistan	Cuba	Cuba
Afr.	Africa	C.V.	Cape Verde
Ak., U.S.	Alaska, U.S.	Cyp.	Cyprus
Al., U.S.	Alabama, U.S.	Czech Rep.	Czech Republic
Alb.	Albania	D.C., U.S.	District of Columbia, U.S.
Alg.	Algeria	De., U.S.	Delaware, U.S.
Am. Sam.	American Samoa	Den.	Denmark
And.	Andorra	*dep.*	dependency, colony
anch.	anchorage	*depr.*	depression
Ang.	Angola	*dept.*	department, district
Anguilla	Anguilla	*des.*	desert
Ant.	Antarctica	Dji.	Djibouti
Antig.	Antigua and Barbuda	Dom.	Dominica
Ar., U.S.	Arkansas, U.S.	Dom. Rep.	Dominican Republic
Arg.	Argentina	D.R.C.	Democratic Republic of the Congo
Arm.	Armenia	Ec.	Ecuador
Aruba	Aruba	Egypt	Egypt
Asia	Asia	El Sal.	El Salvador
Aus.	Austria	Eng., U.K.	England, U.K.
Austl.	Australia	Eq. Gui.	Equatorial Guinea
Az., U.S.	Arizona, U.S.	Erit.	Eritrea
Azer.	Azerbaijan	Est.	Estonia
b.	bay, gulf, inlet, lagoon	*est.*	estuary
Bah.	Bahamas	Eth.	Ethiopia
Bahr.	Bahrain	Eur.	Europe
Barb.	Barbados	Falk. Is.	Falkland Islands
B.C., Can.	British Columbia, Can.	Far. Is.	Faroe Islands
Bdi.	Burundi	Fiji	Fiji
Bel.	Belgium	Fin.	Finland
Belize	Belize	Fl., U.S.	Florida, U.S.
Bela.	Belarus	*for.*	forest, moor
Benin	Benin	Fr.	France
Ber.	Bermuda	Fr. Gu.	French Guiana
Bhu.	Bhutan	Fr. Poly.	French Polynesia
B.I.O.T.	British Indian Ocean Territory	Ga., U.S.	Georgia, U.S.
Bngl.	Bangladesh	Gabon	Gabon
Bol.	Bolivia	Gam.	Gambia
Bos.	Bosnia and Herzegovina	Gaza Str.	Gaza Strip
Bots.	Botswana	Geor.	Georgia
Braz.	Brazil	Ger.	Germany
Br. Vir. Is.	British Virgin Islands	Ghana	Ghana
Bru.	Brunei	Gib.	Gibraltar
Bul.	Bulgaria	Golan Hts.	Golan Heights
Burkina	Burkina Faso	Grc.	Greece
c.	cape, point	Gren.	Grenada
Ca., U.S.	California, U.S.	Grnld.	Greenland
Camb.	Cambodia	Guad.	Guadeloupe
Cam.	Cameroon	Guam	Guam
Can.	Canada	Guat.	Guatemala
C.A.R.	Central African Republic	Guernsey	Guernsey
Cay. Is.	Cayman Islands	Gui.	Guinea
Chad	Chad	Gui.-B.	Guinea-Bissau
Chile	Chile	Guy.	Guyana
China	China	Haiti	Haiti
Christ. I.	Christmas Island	Hi., U.S.	Hawaii, U.S.
C. Iv.	Cote d'Ivoire	*hist.*	historic site, ruins
clf.	cliff, escarpment	*hist. reg.*	historic region
Co., U.S.	Colorado, U.S.	Hond.	Honduras
co.	county, parish	Hung.	Hungary
Cocos Is.	Cocos (Keeling) Islands	*i.*	island
Col.	Colombia	Ia., U.S.	Iowa, U.S.
Com.	Comoros	Ice.	Iceland
Congo	Congo	*ice*	ice feature, glacier
cont.	continent	Id., U.S.	Idaho, U.S.
Cook Is.	Cook Islands	Il., U.S.	Illinois, U.S.
C.R.	Costa Rica	In., U.S.	Indiana, U.S.
crat.	crater	India	India
Cro.	Croatia	Indon.	Indonesia
Ct., U.S.	Connecticut, U.S.	I. of Man	Isle of Man
		Iran	Iran
		Iraq	Iraq
		Ire.	Ireland
		Isr.	Israel

Abbreviation	Meaning	Abbreviation	Meaning
is.	islands	N.H., U.S.	New Hampshire, U.S.
Italy	Italy	Nic.	Nicaragua
Jam.	Jamaica	Nig.	Nigeria
Japan	Japan	Niger	Niger
Jersey	Jersey	N. Ire., U.K.	Northern Ireland, U.K.
Jer.	Jericho Area	Niue	Niue
Jord.	Jordan	N.J., U.S.	New Jersey, U.S.
Kaz.	Kazakhstan	N. Kor.	Korea, North
Kenya	Kenya	N.M., U.S.	New Mexico, U.S.
Kir.	Kiribati	N. Mar. Is.	Northern Mariana Islands
Ks., U.S.	Kansas, U.S.	Nmb.	Namibia
Kuw.	Kuwait	Nor.	Norway
Ky., U.S.	Kentucky, U.S.	Norf. I.	Norfolk Island
Kyrg.	Kyrgyzstan	N.S., Can.	Nova Scotia, Can.
l.	lake, pond	N.T., Can.	Northwest Territories, Can.
La., U.S.	Louisiana, U.S.	Nv., U.S.	Nevada, U.S.
Laos	Laos	N.Y., U.S.	New York, U.S.
Lat.	Latvia	N.Z.	New Zealand
Leb.	Lebanon	Oc.	Oceania
Leso.	Lesotho	Oh., U.S.	Ohio, U.S.
Lib.	Liberia	Ok., U.S.	Oklahoma, U.S.
Libya	Libya	Oman	Oman
Liech.	Liechtenstein	On., Can.	Ontario, Can.
Lith.	Lithuania	Or., U.S.	Oregon, U.S.
Lux.	Luxembourg	Pa., U.S.	Pennsylvania, U.S.
Ma., U.S.	Massachusetts, U.S.	Pak.	Pakistan
Macau	Macau	Palau	Palau
Mac.	Macedonia	Pan.	Panama
Madag.	Madagascar	Pap. N. Gui.	Papua New Guinea
Malay.	Malaysia	Para.	Paraguay
Mald.	Maldives	P.E., Can.	Prince Edward Island, Can.
Mali	Mali	*pen.*	peninsula
Malta	Malta	Peru	Peru
Marsh. Is.	Marshall Islands	Phil.	Philippines
Mart.	Martinique	Pit.	Pitcairn
Maur.	Mauritania	*pl.*	plain, flat
May.	Mayotte	*plat.*	plateau, highland
Mb., Can.	Manitoba, Can.	Pol.	Poland
Md., U.S.	Maryland, U.S.	Port.	Portugal
Me., U.S.	Maine, U.S.	P.Q., Can.	Quebec, Can.
Mex.	Mexico	P.R.	Puerto Rico
Mi., U.S.	Michigan, U.S.	*prov.*	province, region
Micron.	Micronesia, Federated States of	Qatar	Qatar
Mid. Is.	Midway Islands	Reu.	Reunion
mil.	military installation	*reg.*	physical region
Mn., U.S.	Minnesota, U.S.	*res.*	reservoir
Mo., U.S.	Missouri, U.S.	*rf.*	reef, shoal
Mol.	Moldova	R.I., U.S.	Rhode Island, U.S.
Mon.	Monaco	Rom.	Romania
Mong.	Mongolia	Russia	Russia
Monts.	Montserrat	Rw.	Rwanda
Mor.	Morocco	S.A.	South America
Moz.	Mozambique	S. Afr.	South Africa
Mrts.	Mauritius	Sau. Ar.	Saudi Arabia
Ms., U.S.	Mississippi, U.S.	S.C., U.S.	South Carolina, U.S.
Mt., U.S.	Montana, U.S.	*sci.*	scientific station
mth.	river mouth or channel	Scot., U.K.	Scotland, U.K.
mtn.	mountain	S.D., U.S.	South Dakota, U.S.
mts.	mountains	Sen.	Senegal
Mwi.	Malawi	Sey.	Seychelles
Myan.	Myanmar	S. Geor.	South Georgia and the South Sandwich Islands
N.A.	North America	Sing.	Singapore
Nauru	Nauru	Sk., Can.	Saskatchewan, Can.
N.B., Can.	New Brunswick, Can.	S. Kor.	Korea, South
N.C., U.S.	North Carolina, U.S.	S.L.	Sierra Leone
N. Cal.	New Caledonia	Slvk.	Slovakia
N. Cyp.	Cyprus, North	Slvn.	Slovenia
N.D., U.S.	North Dakota, U.S.	S. Mar.	San Marino
Ne., U.S.	Nebraska, U.S.	Sol. Is.	Solomon Islands
Nepal	Nepal		
Neth.	Netherlands		
Neth. Ant.	Netherlands Antilles		
Nf., Can.	Newfoundland, Can.		

Som.	Somalia
Spain	Spain
Sp. N. Afr.	Spanish North Africa
Sri L.	Sri Lanka
state	state, republic, canton
St. Hel.	St. Helena
St. K./N.	St. Kitts and Nevis
St. Luc.	St. Lucia
stm.	stream (river, creek)
St. P./M.	St. Pierre and Miquelon
strt.	strait
S. Tom./P.	Sao Tome and Principe
St. Vin.	St. Vincent and the Grenadines
Sudan	Sudan
Sur.	Suriname
Swaz.	Swaziland
sw.	swamp, marsh
Swe.	Sweden
Switz.	Switzerland
Syria	Syria
Tai.	Taiwan
Taj.	Tajikistan
Tan.	Tanzania
T./C. Is.	Turks and Caicos Islands
ter.	territory
Thai.	Thailand
Tn., U.S.	Tennessee, U.S.
Togo	Togo
Tok.	Tokelau
Tonga	Tonga
Trin.	Trinidad and Tobago
Tun.	Tunisia
Tur.	Turkey
Turk.	Turkmenistan
Tuvalu	Tuvalu
Tx., U.S.	Texas, U.S.
U.A.E.	United Arab Emirates
Ug.	Uganda
U.K.	United Kingdom
Ukr.	Ukraine
Ur.	Uruguay
U.S.	United States
Ut., U.S.	Utah, U.S.
Uzb.	Uzbekistan
Va., U.S.	Virginia, U.S.
val.	valley, watercourse
Vanuatu	Vanuatu
Vat.	Vatican City
Ven.	Venezuela
Viet.	Vietnam
V.I.U.S.	Virgin Islands (U.S.)
vol.	volcano
Vt., U.S.	Vermont, U.S.
Wa., U.S.	Washington, U.S.
Wake I.	Wake Island
Wales, U.K.	Wales, U.K.
Wal./F.	Wallis and Futuna
W.B.	West Bank
Wi., U.S.	Wisconsin, U.S.
W. Sah.	Western Sahara
W. Sam.	Western Samoa
wtfl.	waterfall
W.V., U.S.	West Virginia, U.S.
Wy., U.S.	Wyoming, U.S.
Yemen	Yemen
Yk., Can.	Yukon Territory, Can.
Yugo.	Yugoslavia
Zam.	Zambia
Zimb.	Zimbabwe

Name	Map Ref.	Page
A		
Aachen, Ger.	E10	12
Aali, Sadd el-, Egypt	F11	48
Äänekoski, Fin.	E11	10
Aba, China	E8	28
Aba, Nig.	E6	50
Abaco, i., Bah.	C9	76
Ābādān, Iran	D5	42
Ābādeh, Iran	D6	42
Abadla, Alg.	D4	48
Abaetê, Braz.	E2	74
Abaetetuba, Braz.	B2	74
Abag Qi, China	C10	28
Abaj, Kaz.	B2	28
Abajo Peak, mtn., Ut., U.S.	F6	137
Abakaliki, Nig.	E6	50
Abakan, Russia	D11	26
Abala, Niger	D5	50
Abancay, Peru	F5	70
Abashiri, Japan	B4	31
Abau, Pap. N. Gui.	I12	32
Ābay see Blue Nile, stm., Afr.	H11	48
Ābaya Hāyk', l., Eth.	B7	54
Abaza, Russia	D11	26
Abbaye, Point, c., Mi., U.S.	B2	115
Abbeville, Fr.	B7	16
Abbeville, Al., U.S.	D4	94
Abbeville, Ga., U.S.	E3	103
Abbeville, La., U.S.	E3	111
Abbeville, S.C., U.S.	C3	133
Abbeville, co., S.C., U.S.	C3	133
Abbotsford, Wi., U.S.	D3	142
Abbott Butte, mtn., Or., U.S.	E4	130
Abbott Run, stm., U.S.	B4	132
Abbott Run Valley, R.I., U.S.	B4	132
Ābdānān, Iran	F12	44
Abdulino, Russia	D9	22
Abe, Lake, l., Afr.	H13	48
Abéché, Chad	H9	48
Abengourou, C. Iv.	E4	50
Abenrå, Den.	I3	10
Abeokuta, Nig.	E5	50
Aberdeen, Scot., U.K.	B5	12
Aberdeen, Id., U.S.	G6	105
Aberdeen, Md., U.S.	A5	113
Aberdeen, Ms., U.S.	B5	117
Aberdeen, N.C., U.S.	B3	126
Aberdeen, Oh., U.S.	D2	128
Aberdeen, S.D., U.S.	B7	134
Aberdeen, Wa., U.S.	C2	140
Aberdeen Lake, l., N.T., Can.	E20	82
Abernathy, Tx., U.S.	C2	136
Abert, Lake, l., Or., U.S.	E6	130
Abert Rim, clf, Or., U.S.	E6	130
Aberystwyth, Wales, U.K.	D4	12
Abez', Russia	A11	22
Abhā, Sau. Ar.	G4	38
Abhar, Iran	D13	44
Abidjan, C. Iv.	E4	50
Abilene, Ks., U.S.	D6	109
Abilene, Tx., U.S.	C3	136
Abingdon, Il., U.S.	C3	106
Abingdon, Md., U.S.	B5	113
Abingdon, Va., U.S.	f10	139
Abington, Ma., U.S.	B6	114
Abington [Township], Pa., U.S.	o21	131
Abinsk, Russia	G15	20
Abisko, Swe.	B8	10
Abita Springs, La., U.S.	D5	111
Abitibi, stm., On., Can.	H23	82
Åbo see Turku, Fin.	F10	10
Abomey, Benin	E5	50
Abongabong, Gunung, mtn., Indon.	C1	36
Abong Mbang, Cam.	C2	54
Abou-Deïa, Chad	H8	48
Abraham Lake, res., Ab., Can.	C2	84
Abraham Lincoln Birthplace National Historic Site, hist., Ky., U.S.	C4	110
Abra Pampa, Arg.	C4	72
Absaroka Range, mts., U.S.	F7	143
Absarokee, Mt., U.S.	E7	119
Absecon, N.J., U.S.	E4	123
Absecon Inlet, b., N.J., U.S.	E4	123
Abu Dhabi see Abū Ẓaby, U.A.E.	F6	42
Abū Ḥamad, Sudan	G11	48
Abuja, Nig.	E6	50
Abū Kamāl, Syria	C9	44
Abū Madd, Ra's, c., Sau. Ar.	F3	42
Abū Maṭāriq, Sudan	A5	54
Abunã, Braz.	E6	70
Abū Road, India	E2	40
Abū Ẓaby (Abu Dhabi), U.A.E.	F6	42
Abu Zenîma, Egypt	F10	14
Abyaḍ, Al-Baḥr al- (White Nile), stm., Sudan	H11	48
Abyei, Sudan	B5	54
Academia, Oh., U.S.	B3	128
Acadia, co., La., U.S.	D3	111
Acadia National Park, Me., U.S.	D4	112
Açailândia, Braz.	B2	74
Acámbaro, Mex.	C4	78
Acaponeta, Mex.	D5	78
Acarai Mountains, mts., S.A.	C8	70
Acaraú, Braz.	B3	74
Acarigua, Ven.	B6	70
Acayucan, Mex.	D6	78
Accomack, co., Va., U.S.	C7	139
Accoville, W.V., U.S.	D3	141
Accra, Ghana	E4	50
Achacachi, Bol.	B4	72
Achalpur, India	E3	40
Acheng, China	B13	28
Acı Göl, l., Tur.	D3	44
Ačinsk, Russia	D11	26
Acireale, Italy	F5	18
Ačisaj, Kaz.	B9	42
Ackerman, Ms., U.S.	B4	117
Ackley, Ia., U.S.	B4	108
Acklins, i., Bah.	D10	76
Acoma Indian Reservation, N.M., U.S.	C2	124
Aconcagua, Cerro, mtn., Arg.	E4	72
Acopiara, Braz.	C4	74
Açores, is., Port.	F7	46
A Coruña, Spain	F2	16
Acre, state, Braz.	E5	70
Acton, Ma., U.S.	B5	114
Acton Vale, P.Q., Can.	D5	90
Acushnet, Ma., U.S.	C6	114
Acworth, Ga., U.S.	B2	103
Ada, Ghana	E5	50
Ada, Mn., U.S.	C2	116
Ada, Oh., U.S.	B2	128
Ada, Ok., U.S.	C5	129
Ada, co., Id., U.S.	F2	105
Ada, Mount, mtn., Ak., U.S.	m22	95
Adair, Ok., U.S.	A6	129
Adair, co., Ia., U.S.	C3	108
Adair, co., Ky., U.S.	C4	110
Adair, co., Mo., U.S.	A5	118
Adair, co., Ok., U.S.	B7	129
Adairsville, Ga., U.S.	B2	103
Adairville, Ky., U.S.	D3	110
Adak Island, i., Ak., U.S.	E4	95
Adak Naval Station, mil., Ak., U.S.	E4	95
Adam, Oman	F7	38
Adamantina, Braz.	F1	74
Adamaoua, prov., Cam.	E7	50
Adamaoua, mts., Afr.	B2	54
Adamawa see Adamaoua, mts., Afr.	B2	54
Adam Island, i., Md., U.S.	D5	113
Adams, Ma., U.S.	A1	114
Adams, Mn., U.S.	G6	116
Adams, N.Y., U.S.	B4	125
Adams, Wi., U.S.	E4	142
Adams, co., Co., U.S.	B6	99
Adams, co., Ia., U.S.	C3	108
Adams, co., Id., U.S.	E2	105
Adams, co., Il., U.S.	D2	106
Adams, co., In., U.S.	C8	107
Adams, co., Ms., U.S.	D2	117
Adams, co., N.D., U.S.	C3	127
Adams, co., Ne., U.S.	D7	120
Adams, co., Oh., U.S.	D2	128
Adams, co., Pa., U.S.	G7	131
Adams, co., Wa., U.S.	B7	140
Adams, co., Wi., U.S.	D4	142
Adams, Mount, mtn., N.H., U.S.	B4	122
Adams, Mount, mtn., Wa., U.S.	C4	140
Adams Point, c., Mi., U.S.	C7	115
Adams Run, S.C., U.S.	k11	133
Adamstown, Pa., U.S.	F9	131
Adamsville, Al., U.S.	f7	94
Adamsville, R.I., U.S.	E6	132
Adamsville, Tn., U.S.	B3	135
Adamsville Brook, stm., R.I., U.S.	E6	132
'Adan (Aden), Yemen	H5	38
Adana, Tur.	D6	44
Adare, Cape, c., Ant.	D22	67
Adda, stm., Italy	B2	18
Ad-Dabbah, Sudan	G11	48
Ad-Dahnā', des., Sau. Ar.	E5	38
Ad-Dāmir, Sudan	G2	48
Ad-Dammām, Sau. Ar.	E5	38
Ad-Dawhah (Doha), Qatar	E6	42
Ad-Diffah (Libyan Plateau), plat., Afr.	E9	14
Addis, La., U.S.	D4	111
Addis Ababa see Ādīs Ābeba, Eth.	B7	54
Addison, Al., U.S.	A2	94
Addison, Ct., U.S.	C5	100
Addison, Il., U.S.	k8	106
Addison, N.Y., U.S.	C3	125
Addison, Vt., U.S.	C2	138
Ad-Dīwānīyah, Iraq	D5	42
Addyston, Oh., U.S.	o12	128
Adel, Ga., U.S.	E3	103
Adel, Ia., U.S.	C3	108
Adelaide, Austl.	G2	62
Adelaide, S. Afr.	E4	56
Adelaide Island, i., Ant.	C33	67
Adelaide River, Austl.	C5	60
Adelanto, Ca., U.S.	E5	98
Adèle Island, i., Austl.	D3	60
Adelie Coast, Ant.	C19	67
Aden see 'Adan, Yemen	H5	38
Aden, Gulf of, b.	H5	38
Adi, Pulau, i., Indon.	D8	36
Adiaké, C. Iv.	E4	50
Adige, stm., Italy	B3	18
Ādīgrat, Eth.	H3	38
Ādilābād, India	F3	40
Adimi, Russia	B15	28
Adirondack Mountains, mts., N.Y., U.S.	A6	125
Ādīs Ābeba (Addis Ababa), Eth.	B7	54
Adıyaman, Tur.	D8	44
Adjuntas, Presa de las see Vicente Guerrero, Presa, res., Mex.	C5	78
Adler, Russia	A8	44
Admiralty Bay, b., Ak., U.S.	A9	95
Admiralty Gulf, b., Austl.	C4	60
Admiralty Inlet, b., N.T., Can.	D22	82
Admiralty Island, i., Ak., U.S.	m22	95
Admiralty Islands, is., Pap. N. Gui.	G12	32
Admiralty Mountains, mts., Ant.	D21	67
Ado, Nig.	E5	50
Adobe Creek Reservoir, res., Co., U.S.	C7	99
Ado-Ekiti, Nig.	E6	50
Adoni, India	F3	40
Adour, stm., Fr.	F6	16
Adra, Spain	I5	16
Adrar, Alg.	E4	48
Adrâr, reg., Maur.	B2	50
Adrian, Ga., U.S.	D4	103
Adrian, Mi., U.S.	G6	115
Adrian, Mn., U.S.	G3	116
Adrian, Mo., U.S.	C3	118
Adrianople see Edirne, Tur.	B2	44
Adriatic Sea, Eur.	C5	18
Adusa, D.R.C.	C5	54
Advance, Mo., U.S.	D8	118
Ādwa, Eth.	H12	48
Adygeja, state, Russia	E5	26
Adzopé, C. Iv.	E4	50
Aegean Sea	E10	18
Aën, ostrov, i., Russia	C18	26
A Estrada, Spain	F2	16
Afadjoto, mtn., Ghana	E5	50
Afars and Issas see Djibouti, ctry., Afr.	H13	48
Afghanistan, ctry., Asia	D8	42
Afgooye, Som.	C9	54
Afikpo, Nig.	E6	50
Aflou, Alg.	E4	14
Afmadow, Som.	J13	48
Afognak Island, i., Ak., U.S.	D9	95
Africa	E14	4
Afşin, Tur.	C7	44
Afton, Ia., U.S.	C3	108
Afton, Mn., U.S.	F6	116
Afton, Ok., U.S.	A7	129
Afton, Wy., U.S.	D2	143
Afyon, Tur.	C4	44
Agadez, Niger	C6	50
Agadir, Mor.	D2	48
Agagy, Kaz.	E9	26
Agalak, Sudan	A6	54
Agalega Islands, is., Mrts.	E11	52
Agana, Guam	D11	32
Agartala, India	E6	40
Agate Fossil Beds National Monument, Ne., U.S.	B2	120
Agattu Island, i., Ak., U.S.	E2	95
Agawam, Ma., U.S.	B2	114
Agboville, C. Iv.	E4	50
Ağdam, Azer.	C12	44
Agde, Fr.	F8	16
Agen, Fr.	E7	16
Agency, Ia., U.S.	D5	108
Agency, Mo., U.S.	B3	118
Āghā Jārī, Iran	D5	42
Aginskoe, Russia	D13	26
Agnew, Austl.	F3	60
Agnibilékrou, C. Iv.	E4	50
Agou, Mont, mtn., Togo	E5	50
Agoura Hills, Ca., U.S.	m11	98
Āgra, India	D3	40
Ağrı, Tur.	C10	44
Ağrı Dağı, mtn., Tur.	C11	44
Agrigento, Italy	F4	18
Agrihan, i., N. Mar. Is.	C12	32
Agrínion, Grc.	E8	18
Agrópoli, Italy	D5	18
Água Branca, Braz.	C3	74
Aguachica, Col.	D5	80
Aguadas, Col.	D4	80
Aguadulce, Pan.	D3	80
Agua Fria, N.M., U.S.	B3	124
Agua Fria, stm., Az., U.S.	D3	96
Aguán, stm., Hond.	B2	80
Agua Prieta, Mex.	A3	78
A Guardia, Spain	G2	16
Aguarico, stm., S.A.	D4	70
Aguascalientes, Mex.	C4	78
Aguascalientes, state, Mex.	C4	78
Águas Formosas, Braz.	E3	74
Água Vermelha, Represa de, res., Braz.	G9	70
Aguelhok, Mali	C5	50
Aguila, Az., U.S.	D2	96
Águilas, Spain	I6	16
Agulhas, Kaap, c., S. Afr.	E3	56
Agulhas Basin	M15	66
Agustín Codazzi, Col.	C5	80
Ahaggar, mts., Alg.	F6	48
Ahaggar, Tassili ta-n-, plat., Alg.	B5	50
Ahalcihe, Geor.	B10	44
Ahalkalaki, Geor.	B10	44
Ahar, Iran	C5	42
Ahklun Mountains, mts., Ak., U.S.	D7	95
Ahlat, Tur.	C10	44
Ahmadābād, India	E2	40
Ahmadnagar, India	F2	40
Ahmadpur East, Pak.	E10	42
Ahmar Mountains, mts., Eth.	B8	54
Ahoskie, N.C., U.S.	A6	126
Ahtanum Creek, stm., Wa., U.S.	C5	140
Ahtubinsk, Russia	E6	26
Ahuacatlán, Mex.	C4	78
Ahumada, Mex.	A3	78
Ahvāz, Iran	D5	42
Ahvenanmaa see Åland, is., Fin.	G9	10
Aialik, Cape, c., Ak., U.S.	D10	95
Aiea, Hi., U.S.	B4	104
Aiken, S.C., U.S.	D4	133
Aiken, co., S.C., U.S.	D4	133
Ailao Shan, mts., China	G8	28
Aileron, Austl.	D6	60
Ailinglaplap, atoll, Marsh. Is.	D10	58
Ailsa Craig, On., Can.	D3	89
Aim, Russia	D15	26
Aimorés, Braz.	E3	74
Aïn el Beïda, Alg.	D5	14
Ainslie Lake, l., N.S., Can.	C8	87
Ainsworth, Ne., U.S.	B6	120
Aïn Témouchent, Alg.	J6	16
Aïn Wessara, Alg.	J8	16
Aïr, Massif de l', mts., Niger	C6	50
Airdrie, Ab., Can.	D3	84
Aïssa, Djebel, mtn., Alg.	D4	48
Aitape, Pap. N. Gui.	G11	32
Aitkin, Mn., U.S.	D5	116
Aitkin, co., Mn., U.S.	D5	116
Aitutaki, atoll, Cook Is.	F14	58
Aiud, Rom.	F7	20
Aix, Mount, mtn., Wa., U.S.	C4	140
Aix-en-Provence, Fr.	F9	16
Aix-les-Bains, Fr.	E9	16
Aíyina, i., Grc.	F9	18
Aíyion, Grc.	E9	18
Āīzawl, India	E6	40
Aizu-wakamatsu, Japan	D16	28
'Ajab Shīr, Iran	D11	44
Ajaccio, Fr.	D2	18
Ajaguz, Kaz.	E9	26
Ajan, Russia	D15	26
Ajanta, India	E3	40
Ajanta Range, mts., India	E3	40
Ajax, On., Can.	D6	89
Ajdābiyā, Libya	D9	48
Ajdarkul', ozero, l., Uzb.	B9	42
Ajdyrlinskij, Russia	D10	22
Ajjer, Tassili-n-, plat., Alg.	E6	48
Ajmer, India	D2	40
Ajo, Az., U.S.	E3	96
Āk'ak'ī Besek'a, Eth.	B7	54
'Akāshāt, Iraq	F8	44
Akbou, Alg.	I9	16
Akbulak, Russia	D10	22
Akçaabat, Tur.	C7	44
Akçadağ, Tur.	C7	44
Akçakale, Tur.	D8	44
Akçakoca, Tur.	B4	44
Akchâr, reg., Maur.	C1	50
Ak-Chin Indian Reservation, Az., U.S.	E3	96
Akdağmadeni, Tur.	C6	44
Aketi, D.R.C.	C4	54
Akhḍar, Al-Jabal al-, mts., Oman	F7	42
Akhisar, Tur.	C2	44
Akiachak, Ak., U.S.	C7	95
Akita, Japan	D16	28
Akjoujt, Maur.	C2	50
Akkajaure, l., Swe.	C7	10
Akkol', Kaz.	E9	26
Akkol', Kaz.	B10	42
'Aklé ('Aouâna), reg., Afr.	C3	50
Akmola, Kaz.	D9	26
Akok, Gabon	C1	54
Akola, India	E3	40
Akonolinga, Cam.	C2	54
Akordat, Erit.	G12	48
Akranes, Ice.	I17	10a
Akron, Co., U.S.	A7	99
Akron, In., U.S.	B5	107
Akron, Ia., U.S.	B1	108
Akron, N.Y., U.S.	B2	125
Akron, Oh., U.S.	A4	128
Akron, Pa., U.S.	F9	131
Aksaj, Kaz.	D9	22
Aksaray, Tur.	C6	44
Aksarka, Russia	A12	22
Akşehir, Tur.	C4	44
Akşehir Gölü, l., Tur.	C4	44
Akseki, Tur.	D4	44
Aksu, China	C4	28
Aksuat, Kaz.	E10	26
Aktau, Kaz.	E7	26
Aktjubinsk, Kaz.	D7	26
Akto, China	B3	40
Aktogaj, Kaz.	E9	26
Akune, Japan	D1	31
Akure, Nig.	E6	50
Akureyri, Ice.	I19	10a
Akwanga, Nig.	E6	50
Akžar, Kaz.	B4	28
Alabama, state, U.S.	C3	94
Alabaster, Al., U.S.	B3	94
Alaca, Tur.	B6	44
Alaçam, Tur.	B6	44
Alacant, Spain	H6	16
Alachua, Fl., U.S.	C4	102
Alachua, co., Fl., U.S.	C4	102
Aladža manastir, Bul.	C12	18
Alagir, Russia	A11	44
Alagoas, state, Braz.	C4	74
Alagoinhas, Braz.	B4	74
Alagón, Spain	G6	16
Alahärmä, Fin.	E10	10
Alajuela, C.R.	C3	80
Alakanuk, Ak., U.S.	C7	95
Alakol', ozero, l., Kaz.	E10	26
Alalakeiki Channel, strt., Hi., U.S.	C5	104
Al-'Amādīyah, Iraq	D10	44
Alamagan, i., N. Mar. Is.	C12	32
Alamance, co., N.C., U.S.	B3	126
Al-'Amārah, Iraq	D5	42
Alameda, Ca., U.S.	h8	98
Alameda, N.M., U.S.	B3	124
Alameda, co., Ca., U.S.	D3	98
Alameda Naval Air Station, mil., Ca., U.S.	h8	98
Alamito Creek, stm., Tx., U.S.	p12	136
Alamo, Ga., U.S.	D4	103
Alamo, Nv., U.S.	F6	121
Alamo, Tn., U.S.	B2	135
Alamo, Tx., U.S.	F3	136
Alamogordo, N.M., U.S.	E4	124
Alamo Heights, Tx., U.S.	E3	136
Alamo Hueco Mountains, mts., N.M., U.S.	F1	124
Alamo Indian Reservation, N.M., U.S.	C2	124
Alamo Lake, res., Az., U.S.	C2	96
Alamosa, Co., U.S.	D5	99
Alamosa, co., Co., U.S.	D5	99
Alamosa, stm., Co., U.S.	D4	99
Alamosa Creek, stm., N.M., U.S.	D2	124
Alamosa East, Co., U.S.	D5	99
Åland, is., Fin.	G9	10
Ålands hav, Eur.	F8	10
Alandur, India	G4	40
Alanya, Tur.	D4	44
Alapaevsk, Russia	C11	22
Alapaha, Ga., U.S.	E3	103
Alapaha, stm., U.S.	E3	103
Al-'Aqabah, Jord.	E3	42
Alas, Selat, strt., Indon.	E5	36
Alaşehir, Tur.	C3	44
Alashanyouqi, China	C8	28
Alaska, state, U.S.	C9	95
Alaska, Gulf of, b., Ak., U.S.	D10	95
Alaska Peninsula, pen., Ak., U.S.	D8	95
Alaska Range, mts., Ak., U.S.	C9	95
Alatna, stm., Ak., U.S.	B9	95
Alatyr', Russia	D8	22
Alava, Cape, c., Wa., U.S.	A1	140
Alavus, Fin.	E10	10
Al-'Ayn, U.A.E.	F7	42
Al-'Azīzīyah, Libya	E6	14
Alba, Italy	B2	18
Al-Bāb, Syria	D7	44
Albacete, Spain	H6	16
Alba Iulia, Rom.	F7	20
Albania, ctry., Eur.	D7	18
Albano Laziale, Italy	D3	18
Albany, Austl.	G2	60
Albany, Ga., U.S.	E2	103
Albany, Il., U.S.	B3	106
Albany, In., U.S.	D7	107
Albany, Ky., U.S.	D5	110
Albany, La., U.S.	g10	111
Albany, Mn., U.S.	E4	116
Albany, Mo., U.S.	A3	118
Albany, N.Y., U.S.	C7	125
Albany, Or., U.S.	C3	130
Albany, Tx., U.S.	C3	136
Albany, Wi., U.S.	F4	142
Albany, co., N.Y., U.S.	C6	125
Albany, co., Wy., U.S.	E7	143
Albany, stm., On., Can.	o18	89
Al-Baṣrah, Iraq	D5	42
Al-Batrā' (Petra), hist., Jord.	D3	42
Al-Batrūn, Leb.	E6	44
Al-Baydā', Libya	D9	48
Albemarle, N.C., U.S.	B2	126
Albemarle, co., Va., U.S.	C4	139
Albemarle Island see Isabela, Isla, i., Ec.	D1	70
Albemarle Lake, l., Ms., U.S.	C2	117
Albemarle Sound, strt., N.C., U.S.	A6	126
Albert, Fr.	B8	16
Albert, Lake, l., Afr.	C6	54
Alberta, prov., Can.	C4	84
Alberta, Mount, mtn., Ab., Can.	C2	84
Albert City, Ia., U.S.	B3	108
Albert Lea, Mn., U.S.	G5	116
Albert Markham, Mount, mtn., Ant.	E22	67
Albert Nile, stm., Afr.	C6	54
Alberton, P.E., Can.	C5	87
Albertson, N.Y., U.S.	k13	125
Albertville see Kalemie, D.R.C.	E5	54
Albertville, Fr.	E10	16
Albertville, Al., U.S.	A3	94
Albertville, Mn., U.S.	E5	116
Albi, Fr.	F5	16
Albia, Ia., U.S.	C5	108
Albion, Il., U.S.	E5	106
Albion, In., U.S.	B7	107
Albion, Mi., U.S.	F6	115
Albion, Ne., U.S.	C7	120
Albion, N.Y., U.S.	B2	125
Albion, Pa., U.S.	C1	131
Albion, R.I., U.S.	B4	132
Albion, Wa., U.S.	C8	140
Al-Biqā', val., Leb.	F6	44
Alborán, Isla de, i., Spain	J5	16
Ålborg, Den.	H3	10
Alborz, Reshteh-ye Kūhhā-ye, mts., Iran	C6	42
Albox, Spain	I5	16

Name	Map Ref.	Page

Ālbū Gharz, Sabkhat, pl., Asia E9 44
Albuquerque, N.M., U.S. . . B3 124
Alburquerque, Spain H3 16
Alburtis, Pa., U.S. F10 131
Albury, Austl. H4 62
Alcalá de Henares, Spain . . G5 16
Alcalde, N.M., U.S. A3 124
Alcamo, Italy F4 18
Alcañiz, Spain G6 16
Alcántara Uno, Embalse de, res., Spain H3 16
Alcantarilla, Spain I6 16
Alcázar de San Juan, Spain . H5 16
Alcazarquivir see Er-Rachidia, Mor. E3 14
Alcester, S.D., U.S. D9 134
Alchevs'k, Ukr. E15 20
Alcoa, Tn., U.S. D10 135
Alcobaça, Braz. G12 70
Alcobendas, Spain G5 16
Alcoi, Spain H6 16
Alcolu, S.C., U.S. D7 133
Alcona, co., Mi., U.S. D7 115
Alcorn, co., Ms., U.S. A5 117
Aldabra, Groupe d', i., Sey. i11 57b
Aldama, Mex. B3 78
Aldan, Russia D14 26
Aldan, stm., Russia C15 26
Aldan Plateau see Aldanskoe nagor'e, plat., Russia D14 26
Aldanskoe nagor'e, plat., Russia D14 26
Alden, Ia., U.S. B4 108
Alden, Mn., U.S. G5 116
Alden, N.Y., U.S. C2 125
Alder Brook, stm., Vt., U.S. B4 138
Alderney, i., Guernsey F5 12
Alderson, W.V., U.S. D4 141
Aldrich, Al., U.S. B3 94
Aledo, Il., U.S. B3 106
Aleg, Maur. C2 50
Alegres Mountain, mtn., N.M., U.S. C2 124
Alegrete, Braz. D6 72
Alejandro Selkirk, Isla, i., Chile E1 72
Alejsk, Russia D10 26
Aleksandrov, Russia C6 22
Aleksandrovsk-Sahalinskij, Russia D16 26
Alekseevka, Russia D15 20
Aleksin, Russia B14 20
Aleksinac, Yugo. C8 18
Alençon, Fr. C7 16
Alenquer, Braz. D9 70
Alenuihaha Channel, strt., Hi., U.S. C5 104
Aleppo see Halab, Syria . . . D7 44
Alert Bay, B.C., Can. D4 85
Alès, Fr. E9 16
Alessándria, Italy B2 18
Ålesund, Nor. E2 10
Aleutian Basin B4 144
Aleutian Islands, is., Ak., U.S. E3 95
Aleutian Range, mts., Ak., U.S. D9 95
Aleutian Trench B4 144
Aleutka, Russia B18 26
Alex, Ok., U.S. C4 129
Alexander, co., Il., U.S. F4 106
Alexander, co., N.C., U.S. . . B1 126
Alexander, Lake, l., Mn., U.S. D4 116
Alexander Archipelago, is., Ak., U.S. D12 95
Alexander Bay, S. Afr. D2 56
Alexander City, Al., U.S. . . . C4 94
Alexander Island, i., Ant. . . C33 67
Alexandra, N.Z. q12 63c
Alexandretta see İskenderun, Tur. D7 44
Alexandria, Ont., Can. B10 89
Alexandria see El-Iskandarīya, Egypt E9 48
Alexandria, Rom. H8 20
Alexandria, S. Afr. E4 56
Alexandria, In., U.S. D6 107
Alexandria, Ky., U.S. B5 110
Alexandria, La., U.S. C3 111
Alexandria, Mn., U.S. E3 116
Alexandria, Tn., U.S. A5 135
Alexandria, Va., U.S. B5 139
Alexandroúpolis, Grc. D10 18
Alexis, Il., U.S. B3 106
Alfalfa, co., Ok., U.S. A3 129
Al-Fallūjah, Iraq F10 44
Al-Fāshir, Sudan H10 48
Alföld, pl., Hung. F6 20
Alfred, Ont., Can. B10 89
Alfred, N.Y., U.S. C3 125
Al-Fujayrah, U.A.E. E7 42
Al-Furāt see Euphrates, stm., Asia D4 42
Alga, Kaz. E10 22
Algarrobo del Águila, Arg. . F4 72
Algarve, hist. reg., Port. . . . I2 16
Algeciras, Spain I4 16
Alger, Oh., U.S. B2 128
Alger, co., Mi., U.S. B4 115
Algeria, ctry., Afr. E5 48
Al-Ghaydah, Yemen G6 38
Al-Ghazālah, Sau. Ar. E4 42

Alghero, Italy D2 18
Algiers see El Djazaïr, Alg. . C5 48
Algoabaai, b., S. Afr. E4 56
Algoma, Wi., U.S. D6 142
Algoma, Wa., U.S. B3 140
Algonac, Mi., U.S. F8 115
Algonquin, Il., U.S. A5 106
Algonquin Provincial Park, On., Can. B6 89
Algood, Tn., U.S. C8 135
Al-Hajarah, reg., Asia E5 42
Al-Halfāyah, Iraq G12 44
Al-Hamād, pl., Sau. Ar. G8 44
Al-Harrah, Sau. Ar. D3 42
Al-Harrah, reg., Asia D3 42
Al-Harūj al-Aswad, hills, Libya A8 50
Al-Hasakah, Syria D9 44
Al-Hawrah, Yemen H5 38
Al-Hayy, Iraq F12 44
Al-Hijāz, reg., Sau. Ar. E3 38
Al-Hillah, Iraq D4 42
Al-Hoceima, Mor. C4 48
Al-Hudaydah, Yemen H4 38
Al-Hufrah, reg., Sau. Ar. . . . E3 42
Al-Hufūf, Sau. Ar. E5 38
Al-Hulwah, Sau. Ar. F5 38
Aliağo, Tur. C2 44
Alībāg, India F2 40
'Alī al-Gharbī, Iraq F12 44
Alibunar, Yugo. D4 18
Alicante see Alacant, Spain H6 16
Alice, Tx., U.S. F3 136
Alice Lake, l., Mn., U.S. C7 116
Alice Springs, Austl. E5 60
Aliceville, Al., U.S. B1 94
Aligarh, India D3 40
Alingsås, Swe. H5 10
Alīpur, Pak. E10 42
Aliquippa, Pa., U.S. E1 131
Aliwal North, S. Afr. E4 56
Alix, Ab., Can. C4 84
Al-Jaghbūb, Libya E9 48
Al-Jahrah, Kuw. E5 42
Al-Jalāmīd, Sau. Ar. G9 44
Al-Jawārah, Oman G7 38
Al-Jawf, Libya F9 48
Al-Jawf, Sau. Ar. E3 38
Al-Jubayl, Sau. Ar. E5 38
Al-Junaynah, Sudan H9 48
Aljustrel, Port. I2 16
Alkali Lake, l., Nv., U.S. B2 121
Alkali Lake, l., Or., U.S. E6 130
Alkaline Lake, l., N.D., U.S. C6 127
Al-Karak, Jord. G6 44
Al-Khābūrah, Oman F7 38
Al-Khalīl (Hebron), W.B. . . . G6 44
Al-Khartūm, Sudan G11 48
Al-Khasab, Oman E7 42
Al-Khums, Libya E6 14
Al-Kifl, Iraq F11 44
Alkmaar, Neth. D9 12
Al-Kūfah, Iraq D4 42
Al-Kūt, Iraq D5 42
Al-Kuwayt (Kuwait), Kuw. . . E5 42
Al-Lādhiqīyah, Syria E6 44
Allagash, stm., Me., U.S. . . . B3 112
Allagash Lake, l., Me., U.S. . B3 112
Allahābād, India D4 40
Allah-Jun', Russia C15 26
Allamakee, co., Ia., U.S. . . . A6 108
Allan, Sk., Can. F2 91
Allanmyo, Myan. C3 34
Allardt, Tn., U.S. C9 135
Allatoona Lake, res., Ga., U.S. B2 103
Alldays, S. Afr. C4 56
Allegan, Mi., U.S. F5 115
Allegan, co., Mi., U.S. F5 115
Allegany, N.Y., U.S. C2 125
Allegany, co., Md., U.S. k13 113
Allegany, co., N.Y., U.S. . . . C2 125
Allegany Indian Reservation, N.Y., U.S. C2 125
Alleghany, co., N.C., U.S. . . A1 126
Alleghany, co., Va., U.S. . . . C2 139
Allegheny, co., Pa., U.S. . . . E2 131
Allegheny, stm., U.S. C2 131
Allegheny Reservoir, res., U.S. B4 131
Allemands, Lac Des, l., La., U.S. E5 111
Allemands, Lac Des, l., La., U.S. E5 111
Allen, co., In., U.S. B7 107
Allen, co., Ks., U.S. E8 109
Allen, co., Ky., U.S. D3 110
Allen, co., La., U.S. D3 111
Allen, Mount, mtn., Ak., U.S. C11 95
Allendale, N.J., U.S. A4 123
Allendale, S.C., U.S. E5 133
Allendale, co., S.C., U.S. . . . F5 133
Allende, Mex. B4 78
Allen Park, Mi., U.S. p15 115
Allenton, R.I., U.S. E4 132
Allenton, Wi., U.S. E5 142
Allentown, Pa., U.S. E11 131
Alleppey, India H3 40
Allerton, Point, c., Ma., U.S. B6 114
Alliance, Ne., U.S. B3 120
Alliance, Oh., U.S. B4 128
Allier, stm., Fr. D8 16

Alligator, stm., N.C., U.S. . . B6 126
Alligator Lake, l., Me., U.S. . D4 112
Allison, Ia., U.S. B5 108
Allison, Pa., U.S. G2 131
Allison Park, Pa., U.S. h14 131
Alliston [Beeton Tecumseh and Tottenham], On., Can. C5 89
Al-Līth, Sau. Ar. F4 38
Allouez, Wi., U.S. h9 142
Alloway Creek, stm., N.J., U.S. D2 123
Al-Luhayyah, Yemen G4 38
Allumette Lake, l., Can. B7 89
Allyn, Wa., U.S. B3 140
Alma, P.Q., Can. A6 90
Alma, Ar., U.S. B1 97
Alma, Ga., U.S. E4 103
Alma, Ks., U.S. C7 109
Alma, Mi., U.S. E6 115
Alma, Ne., U.S. D6 120
Alma, Wi., U.S. D2 142
Alma-Ata see Almaty, Kaz. . E9 26
Almada, Port. H2 16
Almadén, Spain H4 16
Al-Madīnah (Medina), Sau. Ar. F3 38
Al-Mafraq, Jord. F7 44
Almalyk, Uzb. E8 26
Al-Manāmah (Manama), Bahr. E6 42
Almanor, Lake, l., Ca., U.S. B3 98
Almansa, Spain H6 16
Al-Marj, Libya D9 48
Almaty, Kaz. E9 26
Al-Mawsil, Iraq C4 42
Al-Mayādīn, Syria E9 44
Almelo, Neth. D10 12
Almenara, Braz. E3 74
Almendralejo, Spain H3 16
Almería, Spain I5 16
Almería, Golfo de, b., Spain I5 16
Al'metevsk, Russia D7 26
Al-Mijlad, Sudan A5 54
Al-Miqdādīyah, Iraq F11 44
Almirante, Pan. D3 80
Almont, Mi., U.S. F7 115
Almonte, On., Can. B8 89
Almonte, Spain I3 16
Al-Mubarraz, Sau. Ar. F5 38
Al-Mubarraz, Sau. Ar. E5 42
Al-Muharraq, Bahr. E6 42
Al-Mukallā, Yemen H5 38
Al-Mukhā, Yemen H4 38
Al-Muwaylih, Sau. Ar. E3 38
Alnön, i., Swe. E7 10
Alnwick, Eng., U.K. C6 12
Aloha, Or., U.S. h12 130
Alor, Pulau, i., Indon. E6 36
Alor Setar, Malay. B2 36
Alpena, Mi., U.S. C7 115
Alpena, co., Mi., U.S. D7 115
Alpha Cordillera E33 144
Alpharetta, Ga., U.S. B2 103
Alphonse, i., Sey. i12 57b
Alpine, Az., U.S. D6 96
Alpine, Tx., U.S. D1 136
Alpine, Ut., U.S. C4 137
Alpine, co., Ca., U.S. C4 98
Alps, mts., Eur. B5 14
Al-Qadārif, Sudan H12 48
Al-Qā'im, Iraq E9 44
Al-Qāmishlī, Syria D9 44
Al-Qaryah ash-Sharqīyah, Libya D7 48
Al-Qaryatayn, Syria E7 44
Al-Qatīf, Sau. Ar. E6 38
Al-Qatrūn, Libya F7 48
Al-Qaysūmah, Sau. Ar. E5 38
Al-Quds see Jerusalem, Isr. G6 44
Al-Qunaytirah, Syria F6 44
Al-Qunfudhah, Sau. Ar. G4 38
Al-Qurnah, Iraq G12 44
Al-Qutayfah, Syria F7 44
Als, i., Den. I3 10
Alsace, hist. reg., Fr. C10 16
Alsasua, Spain F5 16
Alta, Nor. B10 10
Alta, Ia., U.S. B2 108
Altadena, Ca., U.S. m12 98
Alta Gracia, Arg. F5 72
Altagracia, Ven. C5 80
Altai, mts., Asia B5 28
Altaj, state, Russia A5 28
Altamaha, stm., Ga., U.S. . . E4 103
Altamira, Braz. D9 70
Altamont, Il., U.S. D5 106
Altamont, Ks., U.S. E8 109
Altamont, Or., U.S. E5 130
Altamont, Tn., U.S. D8 135
Altamonte Springs, Fl., U.S. D5 102
Altamura, Italy D6 18
Altata, Mex. C3 78
Altavista, Va., U.S. C3 139
Altay, Mong. B7 28
Altay Mountains see Altai, mts., Asia B5 28
Altevatnet, l., Nor. B8 10
Altheimer, Ar., U.S. C4 97
Alto, Ga., U.S. B3 103
Alto, N.M., U.S. D4 124
Alto Araguaia, Braz. C1 70
Alto Garças, Braz. B7 72
Alton, Ia., U.S. B2 108
Alton, Il., U.S. E3 106

Alton, Mo., U.S. E6 118
Alton, N.H., U.S. D4 122
Altona, Mb., Can. E3 86
Alton Bay, N.H., U.S. D4 122
Altoona, Al., U.S. A3 94
Altoona, Fl., U.S. D5 102
Altoona, Ia., U.S. C4 108
Altoona, Pa., U.S. E5 131
Altoona, Wi., U.S. D2 142
Alturas, Ca., U.S. B3 98
Altus, Ok., U.S. C2 129
Altus Air Force Base, mil., Ok., U.S. C2 129
Altus Reservoir, res., Ok., U.S. C2 129
Al-'Ubaylah, Sau. Ar. F6 38
Al-Ubayyid, Sudan H10 48
Alucra, Tur. B8 44
Alum Bank, Pa., U.S. F4 131
Alum Creek, stm., Oh., U.S. k11 128
Alupka, Ukr. G13 20
Al-'Uqaylah, Libya E7 14
Alushta, Ukr. G13 20
Al-'Uwaynāt, Libya E7 48
Alva, Fl., U.S. F5 102
Alva, Ok., U.S. A3 129
Alvarado, Mex. D5 78
Alvarado, Tx., U.S. C4 136
Álvaro Obregón, Presa, res., Mex. B3 78
Älvdalen, Swe. F6 10
Alvin, Tx., U.S. E5 136
Alvinston, On., Can. E3 89
Alvord Lake, l., Or., U.S. . . . E8 130
Al-Wajh, Sau. Ar. E3 38
Alwar, India D3 40
Alxa Zuoqi, China D9 28
Alzira, Spain H6 16
Ama, La., U.S. k11 111
Amacuro, stm., S.A. D7 80
Amadeus, Lake, l., Austl. . . . D5 60
Amador, co., Ca., U.S. C3 98
Amagansett, N.Y., U.S. n16 125
Amahai, Indon. D7 36
Amakusa-nada, Japan D1 31
Amakusa Sea see Amakusa-nada, Japan D1 31
Åmål, Swe. G5 10
Amalfi, Col. D4 80
Amalfi, Italy D5 18
Amaliás, Grc. F8 18
Amambaí, Braz. H8 70
Amami-Ō-shima, i., Japan . . E1 31
Amami-shotō, is., Japan . . . g6 31a
Amana, Ia., U.S. C6 108
Amaná, Braz. C9 70
Amapá, state, Braz. C9 70
Amarante, Braz. E11 70
Amarapura, Myan. B3 34
Amargosa, stm., U.S. G5 98
Amargosa Desert, des., U.S. G5 121
Amargosa Range, mts., U.S. G5 121
Amargosa Valley, Nv., U.S. . G5 121
Amarillo, Tx., U.S. B2 136
Amarkantak, India E4 40
Amasya, Tur. B6 44
Amatignak Island, i., Ak., U.S. E4 95
Amawbia Awka, Nig. E6 50
Amazon (Solimões) (Amazonas), stm., S.A. . D9 70
Amazonas see Amazon, stm., S.A. D9 70
Ambāla, India C3 40
Ambalavao, Madag. C8 56
Ambanja, Madag. A8 56
Ambarčik, Russia C18 26
Ambato, Ec. D4 70
Ambatofinandrahana, Madag. C8 56
Ambatolampy, Madag. B8 56
Ambatondrazaka, Madag. . . B8 56
Amberg, Ger. F12 12
Ambikāpur, India E4 40
Ambilobe, Madag. A8 56
Ambler, Pa., U.S. F11 131
Amboasary, Madag. D8 56
Ambodifototra, Madag. B8 56
Ambon, Indon. D7 36
Ambon, Pulau, i., Indon. . . . D7 36
Ambositra, Madag. C8 56
Ambovombe, Madag. D8 56
Amboy, Il., U.S. B4 106
Ambridge, Pa., U.S. E1 131
Ambriz, Ang. E2 54
Ambrym, i., Vanuatu k9 62a
Ambunti, Pap. N. Gui. G11 32
Āmbūr, India G4 40
Amchitka Island, i., Ak., U.S. E3 95
Amchitka Pass, strt., Ak., U.S. E4 95
Amderma, Russia C8 26
Amdo, China E6 28
Ameca, Mex. C4 78
Amelia, La., U.S. E4 111
Amelia, Oh., U.S. C1 128
Amelia, co., Va., U.S. C4 139
Amelia Court House, Va., U.S. C5 139

Amelia Island, i., Fl., U.S. . . k9 102
American, stm., Ca., U.S. . . . C3 98
American Falls, Id., U.S. G6 105
American Falls Dam, Id., U.S. G6 105
American Falls Reservoir, res., Id., U.S. F5 105
American Fork, Ut., U.S. . . . C4 137
American Highland, plat., Ant. D12 67
American Samoa, dep., Oc. F12 58
Americus, Ga., U.S. D2 103
Americus, Ks., U.S. D7 109
Amersfoort, Neth. D9 12
Amery, Wi., U.S. C1 142
Amery Ice Shelf, Ant. C17 67
Ames, Ia., U.S. B4 108
Amesbury, Ma., U.S. A6 114
Amfílokhía, Grc. E8 18
Amga, Russia C15 26
Amga, stm., Russia C14 26
Amgun', stm., Russia D15 26
Amherst, Ma., U.S. B2 114
Amherst, N.H., U.S. E3 122
Amherst, N.Y., U.S. C2 125
Amherst, Oh., U.S. A3 128
Amherst, Va., U.S. C3 139
Amherst, Wi., U.S. D4 142
Amherst, co., Va., U.S. C3 139
Amherstburg, On., Can. E1 89
Amherstdale, W.V., U.S. . . . n12 141
Amiens, Fr. C8 16
Aminuis, Nmb. C3 56
Amirantes, Les, is., Sey. . . . i12 57b
Amisk Lake, l., Sk., Can. . . . C4 91
Amistad, Presa de la (Amistad Reservoir), res., N.A. B4 78
Amistad National Recreation Area, Tx., U.S. E2 136
Amistad Reservoir (Amistad, Presa de la), res., N.A. . B4 78
Amite, La., U.S. D5 111
Amite, co., Ms., U.S. D3 117
Amite, stm., La., U.S. D5 111
Amity, Or., U.S. B3 130
Amityville, N.Y., U.S. E7 125
Amlia Island, i., Ak., U.S. . . E5 95
'Ammān, Jord. D3 44
Ammon, Id., U.S. F7 105
Ammonoosuc, stm., N.H., U.S. B3 122
Āmol, Iran C6 42
Amorgós, i., Grc. F10 18
Amory, Ms., U.S. B5 117
Amos, P.Q., Can. k11 90
Åmot, Nor. G2 10
Amoy see Xiamen, China . . G11 28
Ampanihy, Madag. C7 56
Ampasimanolotra, Madag. . B8 56
Amposta, Spain G7 16
Amrāvati, India E3 40
Amreli, India E2 40
Amritsar, India C2 40
Amroha, India D3 40
Amsterdam, Neth. D9 12
Amsterdam, N.Y., U.S. C6 125
Amstetten, Aus. F14 12
Am Timan, Chad A4 54
Amu Darya, stm., Asia B8 42
Amukta Pass, strt., Ak., U.S. E5 95
Amundsen Gulf, b., N.T., Can. D15 82
Amundsen Sea, Ant. C30 67
Amuntai, Indon. D5 36
Amur (Heilong), stm., Asia . D16 26
Amvrakikós Kólpos, b., Grc. E8 18
Anaa, atoll, Fr. Poly. F15 58
Anaco, Ven. D7 80
Anacoco, La., U.S. C2 111
Anaconda, Mt., U.S. D4 119
Anaconda Range, mts., Mt., U.S. E3 119
Anacortes, Wa., U.S. A3 140
Anacostia, stm., U.S. C4 113
Anacostia, Northwest Branch, stm., Md., U.S. B3 113
Anadarko, Ok., U.S. B3 129
Anadolu, hist. reg., Tur. C6 44
Anadyr', Russia C19 26
Anadyr', stm., Russia C19 26
Anadyr, Gulf of see Anadyrskij zaliv, b., Russia C20 26
Anadyrskij zaliv, b., Russia . C20 26
'Ānah, Iraq E9 44
Anaheim, Ca., U.S. F5 98
Anahola, Hi., U.S. A2 104
Anahuac, Tx., U.S. E5 136
Anakāpalle, India F4 40
Analalava, Madag. A8 56
Ana María, Golfo de, b., Cuba A4 80
Anambas, Kepulauan, is., Indon. C3 36
Anamosa, Ia., U.S. B6 108
Anamur, Tur. D3 44
Anan, Japan D2 31
Anan'īv, Ukr. F11 20
Anantapur, India G3 40
Anantnāg, India C3 40
Anapa, Russia G14 20
Anápolis, Braz. E2 74
Anastasia Island, i., Fl., U.S. C5 102
Anatahan, i., N. Mar. Is. . . . C12 32

Name	Map Ref.	Page

Anatolia see Anadolu, hist. reg., Tur. C6   44
Anatom, i., Vanuatu I9   62a
Añatuya, Arg. D5   72
Anbei, China A7   40
Ancaster, On., Can. D4   89
Ancha, Sierra, mts., Az., U.S. D4   96
Anchorage, Ak., U.S. . . . C10   95
Anchorage, Ky., U.S. . . . g11   110
Anchor Point, Ak., U.S. . . D9   95
Anchor Point, c., Ak., U.S. . h15   95
Ancienne-Lorette, P.Q., Can. C6   90
Anclote Keys, is., Fl., U.S. . D4   102
Ancona, Italy C4   18
Ancud, Chile F2   69
Anda, China B13   28
Andacollo, Chile E3   72
Andalgalá, Arg. D4   72
Åndalsnes, Nor. E2   10
Andalucía, hist. reg., Spain . I4   16
Andalusia, Al., U.S. D3   94
Andalusia, Il., U.S. B3   106
Andaman and Nicobar Islands, ter., India G6   40
Andaman Basin H12   64
Andaman Islands, is., India . G6   40
Andaman Sea, Asia E3   34
Andamooka, Austl. G2   62
Andapa, Madag. A8   56
Andéramboukane, Mali . . . C5   50
Anderson, Ak., U.S. C10   95
Anderson, Ca., U.S. B2   98
Anderson, In., U.S. D6   107
Anderson, Mo., U.S. E3   118
Anderson, S.C., U.S. B2   133
Anderson, co., Ks., U.S. . . D8   109
Anderson, co., Ky., U.S. . . C4   110
Anderson, co., S.C., U.S. . . B2   133
Anderson, co., Tn., U.S. . . C9   135
Anderson, co., Tx., U.S. . . D5   136
Anderson, stm., N.T., Can. . E14   82
Anderson, stm., U.S. H4   107
Anderson, Mount, mtn., Wa., U.S. B2   140
Anderson Ranch Reservoir, res., Id., U.S. F3   105
Andes, mts., S.A. B4   72
Andes, Lake, l., S.D., U.S. . D7   134
Andfjorden, strt., Nor. . . . B7   10
Andhra Pradesh, prov., India F3   40
Andīmeshk, Iran F13   44
Andirlang, China B4   40
Andižan, Uzb. E9   26
Andkhvoy, Afg. C9   42
Andoany, Madag. A8   56
Andong, S. Kor. D13   28
Andorra, ctry., Eur. F7   16
Andorra-la-Vella, And. . . . F7   16
Andover, Ks., U.S. g12   109
Andover, Ma., U.S. A5   114
Andover, Mn., U.S. m12   116
Andover, Oh., U.S. A5   128
Andover Lake, res., Ct., U.S. C6   100
Andøya, i., Nor. B6   10
Andradina, Braz. F1   74
Andreanof Islands, is., Ak., U.S. E4   95
Andrew, co., Mo., U.S. . . . B3   118
Andrew Island, i., N.S., Can. D9   87
Andrews, In., U.S. C6   107
Andrews, N.C., U.S. f9   126
Andrews, S.C., U.S. E8   133
Andrews, Tx., U.S. C1   136
Andrews, co., Tx., U.S. . . . C1   136
Andrews Air Force Base, mil., Md., U.S. C4   113
Andria, Italy D6   18
Andriamena, Madag. B8   56
Androka, Madag. D7   56
Andropov see Rybinsk, Russia D5   26
Andros, i., Bah. D9   76
Ándros, i., Grc. F10   18
Androscoggin, co., Me., U.S. D2   112
Androscoggin, stm., Me., U.S. D2   112
Androscoggin Lake, l., Me., U.S. D2   112
Āndrott Island, i., India . . G2   40
Andudu, D.R.C. C5   54
Andújar, Spain H4   16
Andulo, Ang. F3   54
Anegada, i., Br. Vir. Is. . . B7   80
Anegada Passage, strt., N.A. B7   80
Aného, Togo E5   50
Aneto, mtn., Spain F7   16
Aney, Niger C7   50
Ang'angxi, China B12   28
Angara, stm., Russia D11   26
Angarsk, Russia D12   26
Ånge, Swe. E6   10
Ángel, Salto (Angel Falls), wtfl., Ven. B7   70
Ángel de la Guarda, Isla, i., Mex. B2   78
Angeles, Phil. C8   34
Angeles Point, c., Wa., U.S. A2   140
Angel Falls see Ángel, Salto, wtfl., Ven. B7   70
Ängelholm, Swe. H5   10
Angelina, co., Tx., U.S. . . D5   136

Angels Camp, Ca., U.S. . . C3   98
Ångermanälven, stm., Swe. E7   10
Angers, Fr. D6   16
Angier, N.C., U.S. B4   126
Angkor Wat, hist., Camb. . D4   34
Anglesey, i., Wales, U.K. . D4   12
Angleton, Tx., U.S. E5   136
Angmagssalik, Grnld. E32   82
Ango, D.R.C. C5   54
Angoche, Moz. B6   56
Angol, Chile E2   69
Angola, In., U.S. A8   107
Angola, N.Y., U.S. C1   125
Angola, ctry., Afr. F3   54
Angola Basin J14   66
Angola Swamp, sw., N.C., U.S. C5   126
Angoon, Ak., U.S. D13   95
Angora see Ankara, Tur. . . C5   44
Angoram, Pap. N. Gui. . . . G11   32
Angostura see Ciudad Bolívar, Ven. B7   70
Angostura, Presa de la, res., Mex. D6   78
Angostura Reservoir, res., S.D., U.S. D2   134
Angoulême, Fr. E7   16
Angren, Uzb. E9   26
Angu, D.R.C. C4   54
Anguilla, Ms., U.S. C3   117
Anguilla, dep., N.A. E12   76
Anguille, Cape, c., Nf., Can. E2   88
Anguo, China B4   30
Anholt, i., Den. H4   10
Anhua, China D3   30
Anhui, state, China E11   28
Aniak, Ak., U.S. C8   95
Anil, Braz. B3   74
Animas, stm., U.S. D3   99
Animas Mountains, mts., N.M., U.S. F1   124
Animas Peak, mtn., N.M., U.S. F2   124
Animas Valley, val., N.M., U.S. F1   124
Anina, Rom. G6   20
Anita, Ia., U.S. C3   108
Aniva, zaliv, b., Russia . . B16   28
Anjār, India E2   40
Anjou, P.Q., Can. p19   90
Anjou, hist. reg., Fr. D6   16
Anjouan see Nzwani, i., Com. A7   56
Anjudin, Russia B10   22
Ankang, China E8   28
Ankara, Tur. C5   44
Ankavandra, Madag. B8   56
Ankazoabo, Madag. C7   56
Ankazobe, Madag. B8   56
Ankeny, Ia., U.S. C4   108
Anking see Anqing, China . E11   28
Ankoro, D.R.C. E5   54
Anlong, China D2   30
Anlu, China E10   28
Ann, Cape, c., Ma., U.S. . . A6   114
Anna, Russia D16   20
Anna, Il., U.S. F4   106
Anna, Oh., U.S. B1   128
Anna, Lake, res., Va., U.S. . B5   139
Annaba, Alg. C6   48
An-Nabk, Syria E7   44
An-Nafūd, des., Sau. Ar. . . E4   38
An-Najaf, Iraq D4   42
An-Najaf, state, Iraq G11   44
Anna Maria, Fl., U.S. p10   102
Anna Maria Island, i., Fl., U.S. q10   102
Annandale, Mn., U.S. E4   116
Annandale, Va., U.S. g12   139
Anna Plains, Austl. D3   60
Annapolis, Md., U.S. C5   113
Annapolis, stm., N.S., Can. E4   87
Annapolis Junction, Md., U.S. B4   113
Annapolis Royal, N.S., Can. E4   87
Annapūrna, mtn., Nepal . . D4   40
Ann Arbor, Mi., U.S. F7   115
An-Nāṣirīyah, Iraq D5   42
Annawan, Il., U.S. B4   106
Anne Arundel, co., Md., U.S. B4   113
Annecy, Fr. E10   16
Annenkov Island, i., S. Geor. H9   69
Annette, Ak., U.S. n24   95
An Nhon, Viet. D4   34
Anning, China E1   30
Anniston, Al., U.S. B4   94
Annobón, i., Eq. Gui. . . . C1   52
An-Nuhūd, Sudan H10   48
An Nukhayb, Iraq C4   42
An-Nu'māniyah, Iraq D5   42
Annville, Pa., U.S. F8   131
Anoka, Mn., U.S. E5   116
Anoka, co., Mn., U.S. . . . E5   116
Anori, Braz. D7   70
Anqing, China E11   28
Ansai, China B2   30
Ansbach, Ger. F12   12
Anshan, China C12   28
Anshun, China F9   28
Anson, Me., U.S. D3   112
Anson, Tx., U.S. C3   136
Anson, co., N.C., U.S. . . . B2   126

Ansongo, Mali C5   50
Ansonia, Ct., U.S. D3   100
Ansonia, Oh., U.S. B1   128
Ansted, W.V., U.S. C3   141
Antalaha, Madag. A9   56
Antalya, Tur. D4   44
Antalya, Gulf of see Antalya Körfezi, b., Tur. D4   44
Antalya Körfezi, b., Tur. . . D4   44
Antananarivo, Madag. . . . B8   56
Antarctica L13   4
Antarctic Peninsula, pen., Ant. D35   67
Antelope, co., Ne., U.S. . . B7   120
Antelope Creek, stm., Wy., U.S. C7   143
Antelope Island, i., Ut., U.S. B3   137
Antelope Peak, mtn., Nv., U.S. B7   121
Antelope Range, mts., Nv., U.S. D7   121
Antelope Reservoir, res., Or. E9   130
Antelope Wash, val., Nv., U.S. D5   121
Antequera, Spain I4   16
Antero, Mount, mtn., Co., U.S. C4   99
Antero Reservoir, res., Co., U.S. C5   99
Anthon, Ia., U.S. B2   108
Anthony, Fl., U.S. C4   102
Anthony, Ks., U.S. E5   109
Anthony, N.M., U.S. F3   124
Anthony, R.I., U.S. D3   132
Anthony, Tx., U.S. o11   136
Anthony Creek, stm., W.V., U.S. D4   141
Antibes, Fr. F10   16
Anticosti, Île d', i., P.Q., Can. k14   90
Antietam National Battlefield, hist., Md., U.S. B2   113
Antigo, Wi., U.S. C4   142
Antigua, i., Antig. B7   80
Antigua and Barbuda, ctry., N.A. E12   76
Antioch see Hatay, Tur. . . D7   44
Antioch, Ca., U.S. h9   98
Antioch, Il., U.S. A5   106
Antioquia, Col. D4   80
Antipodes Islands, is., N.Z. . N20   64
Antlers, Ok., U.S. C6   129
Antofagasta, Chile D2   69
Antofalla, Salar de, pl., Arg. D4   72
Anton, Tx., U.S. C1   136
Antongila, Helodrano, b., Madag. B8   56
Antônio Bezerra, Braz. . . . B4   74
Antonito, Co., U.S. D5   99
Antora Peak, mtn., Co., U.S. C4   99
Antrim, N.H., U.S. D3   122
Antrim, co., Mi., U.S. . . . C5   115
Antsalova, Madag. B7   56
Antsirabe, Madag. B8   56
Antsirañana, Madag. A8   56
Antsohihy, Madag. A8   56
Antwerp see Antwerpen, Bel. E9   12
Antwerp, Oh., U.S. A1   128
Antwerpen (Antwerp), Bel. E9   12
Anugul, India E5   40
Anūpgarh, India D2   40
Anuradhapura, Sri L. H4   40
Anxi, China C7   28
Anxiang, China D3   30
Anyang, China D10   28
A'nyêmaqên Shan, mts., China D7   28
Anyue, China C2   30
Anžero-Sudžensk, Russia . . D10   26
Anzio, Italy D4   18
Aoga-shima, i., Japan E15   28
Aoji-ri, N. Kor. B2   31
Aomori, Japan C16   28
Aoral, Mount see Aôral, Phnum, mtn., Camb. . . D4   34
Aôral, Phnum, mtn., Camb. D4   34
Aosta, Italy B1   18
'Aouâna ('Aklé), reg., Afr. . C3   50
Aouderas, Niger C6   50
Aouk, Bahr, stm., Afr. . . . I9   48
Aoukâr, reg., Maur. C3   50
Aozou, Chad B8   50
Apache, Ok., U.S. C3   129
Apache, co., Az., U.S. . . . B6   96
Apache Junction, Az., U.S. . m9   96
Apache Peak, mtn., Az., U.S. F5   96
Apalachee Bay, b., Fl., U.S. B2   102
Apalachicola, Fl., U.S. . . . C2   102
Apalachicola, stm., Fl., U.S. B1   102
Apalachicola Bay, b., Fl., U.S. C2   102
Apaporis, stm., S.A. C5   70
Aparri, Phil. C8   34
Apartadó, Col. D4   80
Apatity, Russia C5   26
Apatzingán de la Constitución, Mex. D4   78
Apeldoorn, Neth. D9   12
Apennines see Appennino, mts., Italy C4   18
Apex, N.C., U.S. B4   126

Apia, Samoa F12   58
Apiacás, Serra dos, plat., Braz. E8   70
Apishapa, stm., Co., U.S. . D6   99
Aplington, Ia., U.S. B5   108
Apo, Mount, mtn., Phil. . . E9   34
Apollo, Pa., U.S. E2   131
Apopka, Fl., U.S. D5   102
Apopka, Lake, l., Fl., U.S. . D5   102
Apostle Islands, is., Wi., U.S. A3   142
Apostle Islands National Lakeshore, Wi., U.S. . . A3   142
Apóstoles, Arg. D6   72
Apostolove, Ukr. F12   20
Appalachia, Va., U.S. f9   139
Appalachian Mountains, mts., N.A. D11   92
Appanoose, co., Ia., U.S. . D5   108
Appennino, mts., Italy . . . C4   18
Appennino Ligure, mts., Italy B2   18
Apple, state, Wi., U.S. . . . C1   142
Apple Creek, Oh., U.S. . . . B4   128
Applegate, Or., U.S. E3   130
Applegate, stm., Or., U.S. . E3   130
Appleton, Mn., U.S. E2   116
Appleton, Wi., U.S. D5   142
Appleton City, Mo., U.S. . . C3   118
Apple Valley, Ca., U.S. . . . E5   98
Apple Valley, Mn., U.S. . . n12   116
Appling, co., Ga., U.S. . . . E4   103
Appomattox, Va., U.S. . . . C4   139
Appomattox, co., Va., U.S. . C4   139
Appomattox, stm., Va., U.S. C4   139
Appomattox Court House National Historical Park, Va., U.S. C4   139
Apšeronsk, Russia B3   42
Apua Point, c., Hi., U.S. . . D6   104
Apucarana, Braz. F1   74
Apure, stm., Ven. B6   70
Apurímac, stm., Peru F5   70
Aqaba, Gulf of, b. E2   42
'Aqrah, Iraq D10   44
Aquarius Mountains, mts., Az., U.S. C2   96
Aquidauana, Braz. H8   70
Ara, India D4   40
Arab, Al., U.S. A3   94
'Arab, Bahr al-, stm., Sudan A4   54
Arabi, La., U.S. k11   111
Arabian Basin G9   64
Arabian Desert see Eastern Desert, des., Egypt . . . E11   48
Arabian Gulf see Persian Gulf, b., Asia E6   42
Arabian Sea G8   38
Aracaju, Braz. D4   74
Aracati, Braz. B4   74
Araçatuba, Braz. F1   74
Aracruz, Braz. E3   74
Araçuaí, Braz. E3   74
Arad, Rom. F6   20
Arafura Sea E7   58
Arafura Shelf I16   64
Aragac, gora see Aragats Lerr, mtn., Arm. B11   44
Aragarças, Braz. G9   70
Aragats Lerr, mtn., Arm. . . B11   44
Arago, Cape, c., Or., U.S. . D2   130
Aragon, Ga., U.S. B1   103
Aragón, hist. reg., Spain . . G6   16
Araguacema, Braz. E10   70
Aragua de Barcelona, Ven. B7   70
Araguaia, stm., Braz. E10   70
Araguaína, Braz. C2   74
Araguari, Braz. E2   74
Araguatins, Braz. C2   74
Ārāk, Alg. E5   48
Arāk, Iran D5   42
Arakan Yoma, mts., Myan. . B2   34
Arakkonam, India G3   40
Araks (Aras) (Araz), stm., Asia B10   44
Aral see Aral'sk, Kaz. E8   26
Aral Sea, Asia B7   42
Aral'sk, Kaz. E8   26
Aranda de Duero, Spain . . G5   16
Aranjuez, Spain G5   16
Aranos, Nmb. C2   56
Aransas, co., Tx., U.S. . . . E4   136
Aransas Bay, b., Tx., U.S. . E4   136
Aransas Pass, Tx., U.S. . . . F4   136
Aranyaprathet, Thai. D4   34
Araouane, Mali C4   50
Arapaho, Ok., U.S. B3   129
Arapahoe, Ne., U.S. D6   120
Arapahoe, co., Co., U.S. . . B6   99
Arapiraca, Braz. C4   74
Arapkir, Tur. C8   44
Arapongas, Braz. F1   74
Araranguá, Braz. D8   72
Araraquara, Braz. F2   74
Ararat, Arm. C11   44
Ararat, Austl. H3   62
Ararat, Mount see Ağrı Dağı, mtn., Tur. C11   44
Aras (Araks) (Araz), stm., Asia C12   44
Arauca, Col. D5   80
Arauquita, Col. D5   80
Araxá, Braz. E2   74
Araz (Araks) (Aras), stm., Asia C12   44

Ārba Minch', Eth. B7   54
Arboga, Swe. G6   10
Arborg, Mb., Can. D3   86
Arbroath, Scot., U.K. B5   12
Arbuckle, Lake, l., Fl., U.S. E5   102
Arbuckle Mountains, mts., Ok., U.S. C4   129
Arbuckles, Lake of the, res., Ok., U.S. C5   129
Arcachon, Fr. E6   16
Arcade, Ga., U.S. B3   103
Arcade, N.Y., U.S. C2   125
Arcadia, Ca., U.S. m12   98
Arcadia, Fl., U.S. E5   102
Arcadia, In., U.S. D5   107
Arcadia, La., U.S. B3   111
Arcadia, Mo., U.S. D7   118
Arcadia, S.C., U.S. B4   133
Arcadia, Wi., U.S. D2   142
Arcanum, Oh., U.S. C1   128
Arcata, Ca., U.S. B1   98
Arc Dome, mtn., Nv., U.S. . E4   121
Archangel see Arhangel'sk, Russia C6   26
Archbald, Pa., U.S. m18   131
Archbold, Oh., U.S. A1   128
Archdale, N.C., U.S. B3   126
Archer, co., Tx., U.S. C4   102
Archer, co., Tx., U.S. C3   136
Archer City, Tx., U.S. C3   136
Arches National Park, Ut., U.S. E6   137
Archie, Mo., U.S. C3   118
Archuleta, co., Co., U.S. . . D3   99
Arco, Id., U.S. F5   105
Arcola, Il., U.S. D5   106
Arcoverde, Braz. C4   74
Arctic Ocean E36   144
Ardabīl, Iran C5   42
Ardahan, Tur. B10   44
Ardakān, Iran D6   42
Årdalstangen, Nor. F2   10
Ardennes, reg., Eur. B9   16
Ardeşen, Tur. B9   44
Ardmore, Al., U.S. A3   94
Ardmore, In., U.S. A5   107
Ardmore, Ok., U.S. C4   129
Ardmore, Tn., U.S. B5   135
Ardsley, N.Y., U.S. g13   125
Arecibo, P.R. B6   80
Areia Branca, Braz. B4   74
Arena, Point, c., Ca., U.S. . C2   98
Arena, Punta, c., Mex. . . . C3   78
Arenac, co., Mi., U.S. . . . D7   115
Arenápolis, Braz. A6   72
Arenas, Cayo, i., Mex. . . . C6   78
Arendal, Nor. G3   10
Arequipa, Peru G4   70
Arévalo, Spain G4   16
Arezzo, Italy C3   18
Argenta, Il., U.S. D5   106
Argentan, Fr. C6   16
Argentina, ctry., S.A. E3   69
Argentine Basin L9   66
Argentino, Lago, l., Arg. . . H2   69
Argeș, stm., Rom. G8   20
Arghandāb, stm., Afg. . . . D9   42
Argolikós Kólpos, b., Grc. . F9   18
Argonne, reg., Fr. C9   16
Árgos, Grc. F9   18
Argos, In., U.S. B5   107
Argostólion, Grc. E8   18
Argun' (Ergun), stm., Asia . A12   28
Argungu, Nig. D5   50
Argyle, Mn., U.S. B2   116
Argyle, Wi., U.S. F4   142
Arhangel'sk, Russia C6   26
Arhangel'skoe, Russia . . . C14   20
Arhéa Epídavros, hist., Grc. F9   18
Århus, Den. H4   10
Arica, Chile A2   69
Arica, Col. D5   70
Arichat, N.S., Can. D8   87
Arid, Cape, c., Austl. G3   60
Arīḥā (Jericho), Gaza Str. . G6   44
Arikaree, stm., U.S. B8   99
Arima, Trin. C7   80
Arinos, stm., Braz. F8   70
Ariquemes, Braz. E7   70
Aristazabal Island, i., B.C., Can. C3   85
Ariton, Al., U.S. D4   94
Arivonimamo, Madag. . . . B8   56
Arizaro, Salar de, pl., Arg. . D4   72
Arizona, Arg. F4   72
Arizona, state, U.S. C4   96
Arizona Sunsites, Az., U.S. F6   96
Arjay, Ky., U.S. D6   110
Arjeplog, Swe. C7   10
Arjona, Col. C4   80
Arka, Russia C16   26
Arkabutla Lake, res., Ms., U.S. A4   117
Arkadelphia, Ar., U.S. . . . C2   97
Arkalyk, Kaz. D8   26
Arkansas, co., Ar., U.S. . . . C4   97
Arkansas, state, U.S. C3   97
Arkansas, stm., U.S. E9   92
Arkansas City, Ks., U.S. . . E6   109
Arkoma, Ok., U.S. B7   129
Arktičeskogo Instituta, ostrova, is., Russia . . . B10   26
Arles, Fr. F9   16
Arlington, Ga., U.S. E2   103
Arlington, Ma., U.S. B5   114

Name	Map Ref.	Page

Arlington, Mn., U.S. F4 116
Arlington, N.C., U.S. A2 126
Arlington, Ne., U.S. C9 120
Arlington, N.Y., U.S. D7 125
Arlington, Oh., U.S. B2 128
Arlington, S.C., U.S. B3 133
Arlington, S.D., U.S. C8 134
Arlington, Tn., U.S. B2 135
Arlington, Tx., U.S. n9 136
Arlington, Va., U.S. B5 139
Arlington, Vt., U.S. E2 138
Arlington, Wa., U.S. A3 140
Arlington, co., Va., U.S. . . g12 139
Arlington, Lake, res., Tx.,
   U.S. n9 136
Arlington Heights, Il., U.S. . A5 106
Arlit, Niger C6 50
Arlon, Bel. F9 12
Arma, Ks., U.S. E9 109
Armada, Mi., U.S. F8 115
Armadale, Austl. G2 60
Armagh, P.Q., Can. C7 90
Armagnac, hist. reg., Fr. . . F7 16
Armavir, Russia B4 42
Armenia, Col. C4 70
Armenia, ctry., Asia B11 44
Armians'k, Ukr. F12 20
Armidale, Austl. G5 62
Armijo, N.M., U.S. k7 124
Armour, S.D., U.S. D7 134
Armstrong, B.C., Can. D8 85
Armstrong, Ia., U.S. A3 108
Armstrong, co., Pa., U.S. . . E2 131
Armstrong, co., Tx., U.S. . . B2 136
Armstrong Creek, stm.,
   W.V., U.S. m13 141
Arnaudville, La., U.S. D4 111
Arnett, W.V., U.S. D3 141
Arnhem, Neth. E10 12
Arnhem, Cape, c., Austl. . . C6 60
Arnhem Bay, b., Austl. . . . C6 60
Arnhem Land, reg., Austl. . C5 60
Arno, stm., Italy C3 18
Arnold, Mn., U.S. D6 116
Arnold, Mo., U.S. C7 118
Arnold, Ne., U.S. C5 120
Arnold, Pa., U.S. h14 131
Arnold Mills, R.I., U.S. . . . B4 132
Arnold Mills Reservoir, res.,
   R.I., U.S. B4 132
Arnold's Cove, Nf., Can. . . E4 88
Arnolds Park, Ia., U.S. . . . A2 108
Arnøya, Nor. A9 10
Arnprior, On., Can. B8 89
Aroab, Nmb. D2 56
Aroostook, co., Me., U.S. . . B4 112
Ar-Rahad, Sudan H11 48
Arraias, Braz. F10 70
Ar-Ramādī, Iraq D4 42
Arran, Island of, i., Scot.,
   U.K. C4 12
Ar-Rank, Sudan H11 48
Ar-Raqqah, Syria E8 44
Arras, Fr. B8 16
Arrecife, Spain A2 50
Arriaga, Mex. D6 78
Ar-Riyāḍ (Riyadh), Sau. Ar. F5 38
Arroio Grande, Braz. E7 72
Arrowhead Mountain Lake,
   res., Vt., U.S. B2 138
Arrowrock Reservoir, res.,
   Id., U.S. F3 105
Arrowwood Lake, res.,
   N.D., U.S. B7 127
Arroyito, Arg. E5 72
Arroyo Grande, Ca., U.S. . . E3 98
Ar-Rub' al-Khālī, des., Asia G6 38
Ar-Rumaythah, Iraq D4 42
Ar-Ruṣayriṣ, Sudan H11 48
Ar-Ruṭbah, Iraq D4 42
Arsenev, Russia C14 28
Árta, Grc. E8 18
Artà, Spain H8 16
Artašat (Artashat), Arm. . . C11 44
Artashat (Artašat), Arm. . . C11 44
Art'em, Russia C14 28
Artemisa, Cuba A3 80
Artemivs'k, Ukr. E14 20
Artëmovsk, Russia D11 26
Artemus, Ky., U.S. D6 110
Arter, Mount, mtn., Wy.,
   U.S. D4 143
Artesia, N.M., U.S. E5 124
Arthabaska, P.Q., Can. . . . C6 90
Arthur, On., Can. D4 89
Arthur, Il., U.S. D5 106
Arthur, co., Ne., U.S. C4 120
Arthur, Lake, l., La., U.S. . D3 111
Arthur, Lake, res., Pa., U.S. E1 131
Arthur Kill, stm., N.J., U.S. k8 123
Artigas, Ur. E6 72
Artik, Arm. B10 44
Artsyz, Ukr. F10 20
Artvin, Tur. B9 44
Aru, Kepulauan, is., Indon. H10 32
Aru, Tanjung, c., Indon. . . D5 36
Arua, Ug. C6 54
Aruanã, Braz. G9 70
Aruba, dep., N.A. C6 80
Arunāchal Pradesh, prov.,
   India D6 40
Aruppukkottai, India H3 40
Arusha, Tan. D7 54
Aruwimi, stm., D.R.C. . . . C4 54
Arvada, Co., U.S. B5 99

Arvayheer, Mong. B8 28
Arvidsjaur, Swe. D8 10
Arvika, Swe. G5 10
Arvin, Ca., U.S. E4 98
Arvon, Mount, mtn., Mi.,
   U.S. B2 115
Arvonia, Va., U.S. C4 139
Arxan, China B11 28
Arys', Kaz. E8 26
Arzamas, Russia C7 22
Arzew, Golfe d', b., Alg. . . J6 16
Aša, Russia D10 22
Asaba, Nig. E6 50
Asad, Buḥayrat al-, res.,
   Syria D8 44
Asad, Lake see Asad,
   Buḥayrat al-, res., Syria D8 44
Asadābād, Afg. C10 42
Asadābād, Iran E13 44
Asahi-dake, vol., Japan . . . B4 28
Asahikawa, Japan C16 28
Āsānsol, India E5 40
Asbest, Russia C11 22
Asbestos, P.Q., Can. D6 90
Asbury Park, N.J., U.S. . . . C4 123
Ascensión, Mex. A3 78
Ascension, co., La., U.S. . . D5 111
Ascension, i., St. Hel. J8 46
Ascoli Piceno, Italy C4 18
Aseb, Erit. H13 48
Åseda, Swe. H6 10
Āsela, Eth. B7 54
Åsele, Swe. D7 10
Ašgabat, Turk. F7 26
Ashanti, prov., Ghana E4 50
Ashaway, R.I., U.S. F1 132
Ashburn, Ga., U.S. E3 103
Ashburton, N.Z. p13 63c
Ashburton, stm., Austl. . . . E2 60
Ashcroft, B.C., Can. D7 85
Ashdod, Isr. G6 44
Ashdown, Ar., U.S. D1 97
Ashe, co., N.C., U.S. A1 126
Asheboro, N.C., U.S. B3 126
Ashepoo, stm., S.C., U.S. . . F6 133
Ashern, Mb., U.S. D2 86
Asherton, Tx., U.S. E3 136
Asheville, N.C., U.S. f10 126
Ash Flat, Ar., U.S. A4 97
Ashford, Al., U.S. D4 94
Ashford, W.V., U.S. m12 141
Ash Grove, Mo., U.S. D4 118
Ashikaga, Japan C3 31
Ashkhabad see Ašgabat,
   Turk. F7 26
Ashland, Al., U.S. B4 94
Ashland, Il., U.S. D3 106
Ashland, Ks., U.S. E4 109
Ashland, Ky., U.S. B7 110
Ashland, Ma., U.S. g10 114
Ashland, Me., U.S. B4 112
Ashland, Mo., U.S. C5 118
Ashland, Ne., U.S. C9 120
Ashland, N.H., U.S. C3 122
Ashland, Oh., U.S. B3 128
Ashland, Or., U.S. E4 130
Ashland, Pa., U.S. E9 131
Ashland, Va., U.S. C5 139
Ashland, Wi., U.S. B3 142
Ashland, co., Oh., U.S. . . . B3 128
Ashland, co., Wi., U.S. . . . B3 142
Ashland, Mount, mtn., Or.,
   U.S. E4 130
Ashland City, Tn., U.S. . . . A4 135
Ashland Reservoir, res., Ma.,
   U.S. h10 114
Ashley, In., U.S. A7 107
Ashley, N.D., U.S. C6 127
Ashley, Oh., U.S. B3 128
Ashley, Pa., U.S. n17 131
Ashley, co., Ar., U.S. D4 97
Ashley, stm., S.C., U.S. . . . F7 133
Ashley Creek, stm., Ut.,
   U.S. C6 137
Ashmore, P.Q., Can. D5 106
Ashmore Islands, is., Austl. C3 60
Ashokan Reservoir, res.,
   N.Y., U.S. D6 125
Ash-Shaddādah, Syria D9 44
Ash-Shāmīyah, Iraq F11 44
Ash-Shāriqah, U.A.E. E7 42
Ash-Sharqāt, Iraq E10 44
Ash-Shaṭrah, Iraq G12 44
Ash-Shiḥr, Yemen H5 38
Ash-Shināfīyah, Iraq G11 44
Ashtabula, Oh., U.S. A5 128
Ashtabula, co., Oh., U.S. . . A5 128
Ashtabula, Lake, res., N.D.,
   U.S. B8 127
Ashtarak, Arm. B11 44
Ashton, Id., U.S. E7 105
Ashton, Il., U.S. B4 106
Ashton, Md., U.S. B3 113
Ashton, R.I., U.S. B4 132
Ashuanipi Lake, l., Nf., Can. h8 88
Ashuelot, stm., N.H., U.S. . E2 122
Ashville, Al., U.S. B3 94
Ashville, Oh., U.S. C3 128
Ashwaubenon, Wi., U.S. . . D5 142
Asi, stm., Asia D7 44
Asia C19 4
Asilah, Mor. J3 16
Asinara, Golfo dell', b., Italy D2 18
Asinara, Isola, i., Italy D2 18
Asino, Russia D10 26

Asipovičy, Bela. C10 20
'Asīr, reg., Sau. Ar. G4 38
Aşkale, Tur. C9 44
Askersund, Swe. G6 10
Askham, S. Afr. D3 56
Asmara see Asmera, Erit. . G12 48
Asmera, Erit. G12 48
Āsosa, Eth. A6 54
Asotin, Wa., U.S. C8 140
Asotin, co., Wa., U.S. C8 140
Asotin Creek, stm., Wa.,
   U.S. C8 140
Aspen, Co., U.S. B4 99
Aspen Butte, mtn., Or., U.S. E4 130
Aspermont, Tx., U.S. C2 136
Aspendos, hist., Tur. D4 44
Aspinwall, Pa., U.S. k14 131
Aspy Bay, b., N.S., Can. . . C9 87
Assa, Mor. A3 50
Assabet, stm., Ma., U.S. . . g9 114
As-Safīrah, Syria D7 44
As-Salṭ, Jord. F6 44
Assam, prov., India D6 40
As-Samāwah, Iraq D5 42
Assateague Island, i., U.S. . D7 113
Assateague Island National
   Seashore, U.S. D7 113
Assawoman Bay, b., Md.,
   U.S. D7 113
Assiniboine, stm., Can. . . . E2 86
Assiniboine, Mount, mtn.,
   Can. D3 84
Assis, Braz. F1 74
Assu, Braz. C4 74
As-Sudd, reg., Sudan I11 48
As-Sulaymānīyah, Iraq . . . C5 42
As-Sulaymānīyah, Sau. Ar. F5 38
As-Sulayyil, Sau. Ar. F5 38
As-Sumayh, Sudan B5 54
As-Suwaydā', Syria F7 44
Astara, Azer. C13 44
Āstārā, Iran C13 44
Asti, Italy B2 18
Astipálaia, i., Grc. F11 18
Astorga, Spain F3 16
Astoria, Il., U.S. C3 106
Astoria, Or., U.S. A3 130
Astove, i., Sey. j11 57b
Astrahan', Russia E6 26
Asunción, Para. D6 72
Asuncion Island, i., N. Mar.
   Is. C12 32
Aswân, Egypt F11 48
Aswan High Dam see Aali,
   Sadd el-, Egypt F11 48
Asyûṭ, Egypt E11 48
'Ata, i., Tonga G12 58
Atacama, Desierto de, des.,
   Chile C2 69
Atacama, Puna de, plat.,
   S.A. C4 72
Atacama, Salar de, pl., Chile B3 69
Atakpamé, Togo E5 50
Atambua, Indon. E6 36
Aṭar, Maur. B2 50
Atascadero, Ca., U.S. E3 98
Atascosa, co., Tx., U.S. . . . E3 136
Atasu, Kaz. E9 26
Atatürk Baraji, res., Tur. . . D8 44
Atauro, Pulau, i., Indon. . . E7 36
'Aṭbarah, Sudan G11 48
Atbasar, Kaz. D8 26
Atchafalaya, La., U.S. D4 111
Atchafalaya Bay, b., La.,
   U.S. E4 111
Atchison, Ks., U.S. C8 109
Atchison, co., Ks., U.S. . . . C8 109
Atchison, co., Mo., U.S. . . A2 118
Athabasca, Ab., Can. B4 84
Athabasca, stm., Ab., Can. G17 82
Athabasca, Lake, l., Can. . G17 82
Athena, Or., U.S. B8 130
Athens see Athínai, Grc. . . E9 18
Athens, Al., U.S. A3 94
Athens, Ga., U.S. C3 103
Athens, Il., U.S. C4 106
Athens, Mi., U.S. F5 115
Athens, N.Y., U.S. C7 125
Athens, Oh., U.S. C3 128
Athens, Pa., U.S. C8 131
Athens, Tn., U.S. D9 135
Athens, Tx., U.S. C5 136
Athens, W.V., U.S. D3 141
Athens, Wi., U.S. D3 142
Athens, co., Oh., U.S. C3 128
Atherton, Austl. D4 62
Athi, stm., Kenya D7 54
Athínai (Athens), Grc. E9 18
Athol, Ma., U.S. A3 114
Athos, mtn., Grc. D10 18
Ati, Chad D8 50
Atiak, Ug. C6 54
Atik Lake, l., Mb., Can. . . . B4 86
Atikokan, Nf., Can. h8 88
Atikonak Lake, l., Nf., Can. h8 88
Atiu, i., Cook Is. G14 58
Atka, Russia C17 26
Atka Island, i., Ak., U.S. . . E5 95
Atkarsk, Russia D8 22
Atkins, Ar., U.S. B3 97
Atkins, Va., U.S. D1 139
Atkinson, Il., U.S. B3 106
Atkinson, Ne., U.S. B7 120

Atkinson, N.H., U.S. E4 122
Atkinson, co., Ga., U.S. . . . E4 103
Atlanta, Ga., U.S. C2 103
Atlanta, Il., U.S. C4 106
Atlanta, In., U.S. D5 107
Atlanta, Mi., U.S. C6 115
Atlanta, Tx., U.S. C5 136
Atlantic, Ia., U.S. C2 108
Atlantic, N.C., U.S. C6 126
Atlantic, co., N.J., U.S. . . . E3 123
Atlantic Beach, Fl., U.S. . . m9 102
Atlantic City, N.J., U.S. . . . E4 123
Atlantic Highlands, N.J.,
   U.S. C4 123
Atlantic-Indian Basin O12 66
Atlantic-Indian Ridge N14 66
Atlantic Ocean E9 66
Atlantic Peak, mtn., Wy.,
   U.S. D3 143
Atlas Mountains, mts., Afr. D4 48
Atlas Saharien, mts., Alg. . E3 14
Atlas Tellien, mts., Alg. . . D4 14
Atlin Lake, l., Can. G13 82
Atmore, Al., U.S. D2 94
Atna Peak, mtn., B.C., Can. C3 85
Atoka, Ok., U.S. C5 129
Atoka, Tn., U.S. B2 135
Atoka, co., Ok., U.S. C5 129
Atoka Reservoir, res., Ok.,
   U.S. C5 129
Atrak (Atrek), stm., Asia . . C7 42
Atrato, stm., Col. B4 70
Atrek (Atrak), stm., Asia . . C6 42
Aṭ-Ṭā'if, Sau. Ar. F4 38
Attala, co., Ms., U.S. B4 117
Attalla, Al., U.S. A3 94
Attapu, Laos D5 34
Attawapiskat, stm., On.,
   Can. n18 89
Attica, In., U.S. D3 107
Attica, Ks., U.S. E5 109
Attica, N.Y., U.S. C2 125
Attica, Oh., U.S. A3 128
Attleboro, Ma., U.S. C5 114
Attu Island, i., Ak., U.S. . . E2 95
Atuel, Bañados del, sw.,
   Arg. F4 72
Åtvidaberg, Swe. G7 10
Atwater, Ca., U.S. D3 98
Atwater, Mn., U.S. E4 116
Atwood, On., Can. D3 89
Atwood, Il., U.S. D5 106
Atwood, Ks., U.S. C2 109
Atwood, Tn., U.S. B3 135
Atwood Lake, res., Oh.,
   U.S. B4 128
Atyrau, Kaz. E7 26
Auau Channel, strt., Hi.,
   U.S. C5 104
Aubagne, Fr. F9 16
Auberry, Ca., U.S. D4 98
Auburn, Al., U.S. C4 94
Auburn, Ca., U.S. C3 98
Auburn, Ga., U.S. B3 103
Auburn, Il., U.S. D4 106
Auburn, In., U.S. B7 107
Auburn, Ks., U.S. D8 109
Auburn, Ky., U.S. D3 110
Auburn, Ma., U.S. B4 114
Auburn, Mi., U.S. E6 115
Auburn, Ne., U.S. D10 120
Auburn, N.Y., U.S. C4 125
Auburn, Wa., U.S. B3 140
Auburndale, Fl., U.S. D5 102
Auburn Heights, Mi., U.S. . F7 115
Aubusson, Fr. E8 16
Auch, Fr. F7 16
Auchi, Nig. E6 50
Aucilla, stm., Fl., U.S. B3 102
Auckland, N.Z. o13 63c
Auckland Islands, is., N.Z. . J10 58
Audrain, co., Mo., U.S. . . . B6 118
Audubon, Ia., U.S. C3 108
Audubon, N.J., U.S. D2 123
Audubon, co., Ia., U.S. . . . C2 108
Augathela, Austl. F4 62
Auglaize, co., Oh., U.S. . . . B1 128
Auglaize, stm., Oh., U.S. . . A1 128
Augrabiesvalle, wtfl, S. Afr. D3 56
Au Gres, Mi., U.S. D7 115
Augsburg, Ger. F12 12
Augusta, Austl. G1 60
Augusta, Italy F5 18
Augusta, Ar., U.S. B4 97
Augusta, Ga., U.S. C5 103
Augusta, Ks., U.S. E7 109
Augusta, Ky., U.S. B6 110
Augusta, Me., U.S. D3 112
Augusta, Mi., U.S. F5 115
Augusta, Wi., U.S. D2 142
Augusta, co., Va., U.S. B3 139
Augustów, Pol. C7 20
Augustus, Mount, mtn.,
   Austl. E2 60
Aulander, N.C., U.S. A5 126
Aulneau Peninsula, pen.,
   On., Can. E4 86
Ault, Co., U.S. A6 99
Aumsville, Or., U.S. k12 130
Aurangābād, India F3 40
Aurangābād, India E4 40
Aure, Nor. E3 10
Aurelia, Ia., U.S. B2 108
Aurich, Ger. D10 12

Aurillac, Fr. E8 16
Aurora, On., Can. C5 89
Aurora, Co., U.S. B6 99
Aurora, Il., U.S. B5 106
Aurora, In., U.S. F8 107
Aurora, Mn., U.S. C6 116
Aurora, Mo., U.S. E4 118
Aurora, Ne., U.S. D7 120
Aurora, Oh., U.S. A4 128
Aurora, S.D., U.S. C9 134
Aurora, Ut., U.S. E4 137
Aurora, co., S.D., U.S. D7 134
Aus, Nmb. D2 56
Au Sable, Mi., U.S. D7 115
Au Sable, stm., Mi., U.S. . . D6 115
Ausable, stm., N.Y., U.S. . . f11 125
Au Sable Forks, N.Y., U.S. . f11 125
Au Sable Point, c., Mi., U.S. D7 115
Au Sable Point, c., Mi., U.S. B4 115
Austell, Ga., U.S. h7 103
Austin, In., U.S. G6 107
Austin, Mn., U.S. G6 116
Austin, Nv., U.S. D4 121
Austin, Tx., U.S. D4 136
Austin, co., Tx., U.S. E4 136
Austintown, Oh., U.S. A5 128
Austinville, Va., U.S. D2 139
Australia, ctry., Oc. G7 58
Australia, i., Austl. H21 4
Australian Capital Territory,
   ter., Austl. H4 62
Austral Seamounts K23 64
Austria, ctry., Eur. G14 12
Autauga, co., Al., U.S. C3 94
Autaugaville, Al., U.S. C3 94
Autlán de Navarro, Mex. . . D4 78
Auvergne, hist. reg., Fr. . . E8 16
Auxerre, Fr. D8 16
Auxier, Ky., U.S. C7 110
Auxvasse, Mo., U.S. B6 118
Auyán Tepuy, mtn., Ven. . . B7 70
Auzangate, Nevado, mtn.,
   Peru F5 70
Ava, Mo., U.S. E5 118
Avallon, Fr. D8 16
Avalon, Ca., U.S. F4 98
Avalon, Pa., U.S. h13 131
Avalon, Lake, res., N.M.,
   U.S. E5 124
Avalon Peninsula, pen., Nf.,
   Can. E5 88
Avaré, Braz. F2 74
Aveiro, Port. G2 16
Avella, Pa., U.S. F1 131
Avellaneda, Arg. E6 72
Avellino, Italy D5 18
Avenal, Ca., U.S. E3 98
Avery, co., N.C., U.S. e11 126
Avesta, Swe. F7 10
Avezzano, Italy C4 18
Avignon, Fr. F9 16
Ávila, Spain G4 16
Avilés, Spain F4 16
Avilla, In., U.S. B7 107
Avis, Pa., U.S. D7 131
Aviston, Il., U.S. E4 106
Avoca, Ia., U.S. C2 108
Avoca, Pa., U.S. m18 131
Avola, Italy F5 18
Avon, Ct., U.S. B4 100
Avon, Il., U.S. C3 106
Avon, Ma., U.S. B5 114
Avon, Mn., U.S. E4 116
Avon, N.Y., U.S. C3 125
Avon, Oh., U.S. A3 128
Avondale, Az., U.S. D3 96
Avondale, Co., U.S. C6 99
Avondale, Pa., U.S. G10 131
Avondale Estates, Ga., U.S. h8 103
Avon Lake, Ia., U.S. e8 108
Avon Lake, Oh., U.S. A3 128
Avonmore, Pa., U.S. E3 131
Avon Park, Fl., U.S. E5 102
Avoyelles, co., La., U.S. . . . C3 111
Awaaso, Ghana E4 50
Āwarē, Eth. B8 54
Āwasa, Eth. B7 54
Āwash, Eth. B8 54
Āwash, stm., Eth. H13 48
Awbārī, Libya E7 48
Awbārī, Ṣaḥrā', reg., Libya A7 50
Awjilah, Libya E9 48
Awled Djellal, Alg. E5 14
Awlef, Alg. F4 14
Axim, Ghana F4 50
Axiós (Vardar), stm., Eur. . D9 18
Axis, Al., U.S. E1 94
Axtell, Ne., U.S. D6 120
Ayacucho, Arg. F6 72
Ayacucho, Peru F5 70
Ayamé, C. Iv. E4 50
Ayancık, Tur. B6 44
Ayapel, Col. D4 80
Ayaviri, Peru F5 70
Ayden, N.C., U.S. B5 126
Aydın, Tur. D2 44
Ayer, Ma., U.S. A4 114
Ayers Cliff, P.Q., Can. D5 90
Ayeyarwady, stm., Myan. . C3 34
Áyios Nikólaos, Grc. G10 18
Áyiou Óros, Kólpos, b.,
   Grc. D10 18
Aylesford, N.S., Can. D5 87

Name	Map Ref.	Page
Aylmer, Mount, mtn., Ab., Can.	D3	84
Aylmer East, P.Q., Can.	D2	90
Aylmer West, On., Can.	E4	89
'Ayn Dār, Sau. Ar.	E5	42
Ayorou, Niger	D5	50
'Ayoûn el 'Atroûs, Maur.	C3	50
Ayr, Austl.	D4	62
Ayr, Scot., U.K.	C4	12
Ayvalık, Tur.	C2	44
Āzamgarh, India	D4	40
Azaouâd, reg., Mali	C4	50
Azare, Nig.	D7	50
Āžar Shahr, Iran	D11	44
Azdavay, Tur.	B5	44
Azeffâl, dunes, Maur.	B2	50
Azerbaijan, ctry., Asia	B12	44
Azilal, Mor.	E2	14
Aziscohos Lake, l., Me., U.S.	C1	112
Azle, Tx., U.S.	n9	136
Azogues, Ec.	D4	70
Azores see Açores, is., Port.	F7	46
Azores Plateau	D10	66
Azov, Russia	F15	20
Azov, Sea of, Eur.	F14	20
Azraq, Al-Baḥr al- see Blue Nile, stm., Afr.	H11	48
Azrou, Mor.	D3	48
Aztec, N.M., U.S.	A2	124
Aztec Peak, mtn., Az., U.S.	D5	96
Aztec Ruins National Monument, N.M., U.S.	A1	124
Azua, Dom. Rep.	B5	80
Azuaga, Spain	H4	16
Azuero, Península de, pen., Pan.	D3	80
Azul, Arg.	F6	72
Azurduy, Bol.	B5	72
Azusa, Ca., U.S.	m13	98
Az-Zahrān, Sau. Ar.	E5	42
Az-Zarqā', Jord.	D3	42
Az-Zāwiyah, Libya	D7	48

B

Name	Map Ref.	Page
Baa, Indon.	F6	36
Baardheere, Som.	J13	48
Babadag, Rom.	G10	20
Babaeski, Tur.	B2	44
Babaevo, Russia	C6	22
Babanūsah, Sudan	H10	48
Babar, Kepulauan, is., Indon.	E7	36
Babb Creek, stm., Pa., U.S.	C7	131
Babbitt, Mn., U.S.	C7	116
Babbitt, Nv., U.S.	E3	121
Bab el Mandeb see Mandeb, Bab el, strt.	H4	38
Babelthuap, i., Palau	E9	32
Bābil, Aṭlāl (Babylon), hist., Iraq	F11	44
Babine, stm., B.C., Can.	B4	85
Babine Lake, l., B.C., Can.	B5	85
Babine Range, mts., B.C., Can.	B4	85
Babo, Indon.	D8	36
Baboquivari Mountains, mts., Az., U.S.	F4	96
Baboquivari Peak, mtn., Az., U.S.	F4	96
Babrujsk, Bela.	C10	20
Babuškin, Russia	A9	28
Babuyan Channel, strt., Phil.	C8	34
Babuyan Island, i., Phil.	C8	34
Babuyan Islands, is., Phil.	C8	34
Babylon, N.Y., U.S.	n15	125
Babylon see Bābil, Aṭlāl, hist., Iraq	F11	44
Baca, co., Co., U.S.	D8	99
Bacabal, Braz.	B3	74
Bacan, Pulau, i., Indon.	D7	36
Bacău, Rom.	F9	20
Bachu, China	D3	28
Back, stm., N.T., Can.	h12	133
Bačka Palanka, Yugo.	B7	18
Backbone Mountain, mtn., U.S.	m12	113
Bac Lieu, Viet.	E5	34
Bac Ninh, Viet.	B5	34
Bacolod, Phil.	D8	34
Bacon, co., Ga., U.S.	E4	103
Baconton, Ga., U.S.	E2	103
Bacoor, Phil.	D8	34
Bād, Iran	D6	42
Bad, stm., S.D., U.S.	C5	134
Bad, stm., Wi., U.S.	B3	142
Badagara, India	G3	40
Badajoz, Spain	H3	16
Badalona, Spain	G8	16
Bādāmi, India	F3	40
Badanah, Sau. Ar.	A4	38
Bad Axe, Mi., U.S.	E8	115
Baddeck, N.S., Can.	C9	87
Baden, Aus.	G14	12
Baden, On., Can.	D4	89
Baden, Pa., U.S.	E1	131
Baden-Baden, Ger.	F11	12
Badger, Nf., Can.	D3	88
Bad Hersfeld, Ger.	E11	12
Badīn, Pak.	F9	42
Badin, N.C., U.S.	B2	126
Badin Lake, res., N.C., U.S.	B2	126
Bad Kreuznach, Ger.	F10	12
Badlands, hills, S.D., U.S.	D3	134
Badlands, reg., U.S.	C2	127
Badlands National Park, S.D., U.S.	D3	134
Bad Reichenhall, Ger.	G13	12
Bad River Indian Reservation, Wi., U.S.	B3	142
Bad Tölz, Ger.	G12	12
Badulla, Sri L.	H4	40
Badwater Creek, stm., Wy., U.S.	C5	143
Bafang, Cam.	B2	54
Bafatá, Gui.-B.	D2	50
Baffin Basin	C29	144
Baffin Bay, b., N.A.	D26	82
Baffin Bay, b., Tx., U.S.	E4	136
Baffin Bugt see Baffin Bay, b., N.A.	D26	82
Baffin Island, i., N.T., Can.	D24	82
Bafia, Cam.	C2	54
Bafing, stm., Afr.	D2	50
Bafoulabé, Mali	D2	50
Bafoussam, Cam.	B2	54
Bafra, Tur.	B6	44
Bafwasende, D.R.C.	C5	54
Bagaces, C.R.	C2	80
Bagamoyo, Tan.	E7	54
Baganga, Phil.	E9	34
Bagansiapiapi, Indon.	C2	36
Bagdad see Baghdād, Iraq	D4	42
Bagdad, Az., U.S.	C2	96
Bagdad, Fl., U.S.	u14	102
Bagdarin, Russia	D13	26
Bagé, Braz.	F2	72
Baggs, Wy., U.S.	E5	143
Baghdād, Iraq	D4	42
Bagheria, Italy	E4	18
Baghlān, Afg.	C9	42
Bagley, Mn., U.S.	C3	116
Bagnères-de-Bigorre, Fr.	F7	16
Bago, Myan.	C3	34
Baguio, Phil.	C8	34
Bahamas, ctry., N.A.	C9	76
Bahār, Iran	E13	44
Baharampur, India	E5	40
Baharden, Turk.	C7	42
Bahardok, Turk.	C7	42
Bahāwalpur, Pak.	E10	42
Bahçe, Tur.	D7	44
Bahia, state, Braz.	D3	74
Bahía, Islas de la, is., Hond.	B2	80
Bahía Blanca, Arg.	F5	72
Bahir Dar, Eth.	H12	48
Bahraich, India	D4	40
Bahrain, ctry., Asia	E6	42
Bahta, Russia	C10	26
Bāhū Kalāt, Iran	E8	42
Baía Farta, Ang.	F2	54
Baia Mare, Rom.	F7	20
Baicheng, China	B12	28
Baicheng, China	C4	28
Baidoa see Baydhabo, Som.	J13	48
Baie-Comeau, P.Q., Can.	k13	90
Baie-d'Urfé, P.Q., Can.	q19	90
Baie-Saint-Paul, P.Q., Can.	B7	90
Baie Verte, Nf., Can.	D3	88
Baihe, China	C3	30
Baikal, Lake see Bajkal, ozero, l., Russia	D12	26
Baile Átha Cliath see Dublin, Ire.	D3	12
Băilești, Rom.	G7	20
Bailey, co., Tx., U.S.	B1	136
Bailey Island, Me., U.S.	g8	112
Bailey Island, i., S.C., U.S.	k11	133
Baileys Crossroads, Va., U.S.	g12	139
Bailundo, Ang.	F3	54
Bainbridge, Ga., U.S.	F2	103
Bainbridge, In., U.S.	E4	107
Bainbridge, Oh., U.S.	C2	128
Bainbridge Island, i., Wa., U.S.	e10	140
Baing, Indon.	F6	36
Baird, Tx., U.S.	C3	136
Bairdford, Pa., U.S.	h14	131
Baird Inlet, b., Ak., U.S.	C7	95
Baird Mountains, mts., Ak., U.S.	B7	95
Bairin Zuoqi, China	C11	28
Bairnsdale, Austl.	H4	62
Bais, Phil.	E8	34
Baishuijiang, China	C2	30
Baitou Shan see Paektu, Mount, mtn., Asia	C13	28
Baiyin, China	D8	28
Baja, Hung.	F5	20
Baja California, state, Mex.	A1	78
Baja California, pen., Mex.	B2	78
Baja California Norte see Baja California, state, Mex.	A1	78
Baja California Sur, state, Mex.	B2	78
Bajestān, Iran	D7	42
Bajkal, ozero, l., Russia	D12	26
Bajkit, Russia	C11	26
Bajkonur, Kaz.	E8	26
Bajmak, Russia	D10	22
Bajo Boquete, Pan.	D3	80
Bajramaly, Turk.	C8	42
Bakala, C.A.R.	B4	54
Bakanas, Kaz.	B11	42
Bakel, Sen.	D2	50
Baker, La., U.S.	D4	111
Baker, Mt., U.S.	D12	119
Baker, Or., U.S.	C9	130
Baker, co., Fl., U.S.	B4	102
Baker, co., Ga., U.S.	E2	103
Baker, co., Or., U.S.	C9	130
Baker, stm., N.H., U.S.	C3	122
Baker, Mount, mtn., Wa., U.S.	A4	140
Baker Air Force Base, mil., Ar., U.S.	B6	97
Baker Butte, mtn., Az., U.S.	C4	96
Baker Island, i., Oc.	H21	64
Baker Island, i., Ak., U.S.	n22	95
Baker Lake, l., Austl.	F4	60
Baker Lake, l., Me., U.S.	B3	112
Baker Lake, res., Wa., U.S.	A4	140
Bakersfield, Ca., U.S.	E4	98
Bakers Island, i., Ma., U.S.	f12	114
Bakerstown, Pa., U.S.	h14	131
Bakhmach, Ukr.	D12	20
Bakı (Baku), Azer.	B13	44
Bako, Eth.	B7	54
Bakouma, C.A.R.	B4	54
Baku see Bakı, Azer.	B13	44
Bala, Sen.	D2	50
Balabac Island, i., Phil.	E7	34
Balabac Strait, strt., Asia	E7	34
Ba'labakk, Leb.	F7	44
Baladēk, Russia	D15	26
Bālāghāt, India	E4	40
Balaguer, Spain	G7	16
Balakliia, Ukr.	E14	20
Balakovo, Russia	D6	26
Balama, Moz.	A6	56
Balambangan, Pulau, i., Malay.	B5	36
Bālā Morghāb, Afg.	C8	42
Balāngīr, India	E4	40
Balašov, Russia	D6	26
Balassagyarmat, Hung.	F5	20
Balaton, Mn., U.S.	F3	116
Balaton, l., Hung.	F4	20
Balbina, Represa, res., Braz.	D8	70
Balcad, Som.	C9	54
Balcarce, Arg.	F6	72
Balcarres, Sk., Can.	G4	91
Balclutha, N.Z.	p12	63c
Bald Eagle Lake, l., Mn., U.S.	C7	116
Bald Eagle Lake, l., Mn., U.S.	m12	116
Baldhill Dam, N.D., U.S.	B7	127
Bald Knob, Ar., U.S.	B4	97
Bald Knoll, mtn., Wy., U.S.	D2	143
Bald Mountain, mtn., Or., U.S.	C9	130
Bald Mountain, mtn., Or., U.S.	D5	130
Bald Mountain, mtn., Wy., U.S.	B5	143
Bald Mountains, mts., N.C., U.S.	f10	126
Baldwin, Fl., U.S.	B5	102
Baldwin, Ga., U.S.	B3	103
Baldwin, La., U.S.	E4	111
Baldwin, Mi., U.S.	E5	115
Baldwin, Pa., U.S.	k14	131
Baldwin, S.C., U.S.	B5	133
Baldwin, Wi., U.S.	D1	142
Baldwin, co., Al., U.S.	E2	94
Baldwin, co., Ga., U.S.	C3	103
Baldwin City, Ks., U.S.	D8	109
Baldwinsville, N.Y., U.S.	B4	125
Baldwinville, Ma., U.S.	A3	114
Baldwyn, Ms., U.S.	A5	117
Baldy Mountain, mtn., B.C., Can.	D7	85
Baldy Mountain, mtn., Mb., Can.	D1	86
Baldy Mountain, mtn., Mt., U.S.	B7	119
Baldy Mountain, mtn., N.M., U.S.	A4	124
Baldy Peak, mtn., Az., U.S.	D6	96
Balearic Islands see Balears, Illes, is., Spain	H7	16
Balears, Illes (Balearic Islands), is., Spain	H7	16
Baleia, Ponta da, c., Braz.	E4	74
Baleine, Rivière à la, stm., P.Q., Can.	g13	90
Balej, Russia	D13	26
Baler, Phil.	C8	34
Bāleshwar, India	E5	40
Balezino, Russia	C9	22
Balfate, Hond.	B2	80
Balfour, N.C., U.S.	f10	126
Balhaš, Kaz.	E9	26
Balhaš, ozero, l., Kaz.	E9	26
Bali, i., Indon.	E5	36
Bali, Laut (Bali Sea), Indon.	E5	36
Balıkesir, Tur.	C2	44
Balikpapan, Indon.	D5	36
Balimo, Pap. N. Gui.	H11	32
Balintang Channel, strt., Phil.	C8	34
Bali Sea see Bali, Laut, Indon.	E5	36
Balkan Mountains see Stara Planina, mts., Eur.	C9	18
Balkaria see Kabardino-Balkarija, state, Russia	E6	26
Balkh, Afg.	C9	42
Balkhash, Lake see Balhaš, ozero, l., Kaz.	E9	26
Ball, La., U.S.	C3	111
Balladonia, Austl.	G3	60
Ballālpur, India	F3	40
Ballarat, Austl.	H3	62
Ballard, co., Ky., U.S.	e8	110
Ball Club Lake, l., Mn., U.S.	C5	116
Balleny Islands, is., Ant.	C21	67
Ball Ground, Ga., U.S.	B2	103
Ballina, Austl.	F5	62
Ballina, Ire.	C2	12
Ballinger, Tx., U.S.	D3	136
Ball Mountain Lake, res., Vt., U.S.	E3	138
Ballston Spa, N.Y., U.S.	B7	125
Ballwin, Mo., U.S.	f12	118
Bally, Pa., U.S.	F10	131
Ballymena, N. Ire., U.K.	C3	12
Balmoral, N.B., Can.	B3	87
Balmoral Castle, hist., Scot., U.K.	C5	12
Balmville, N.Y., U.S.	D6	125
Balombo, Ang.	F2	54
Balqash Köli see Balhaš, ozero, l., Kaz.	E9	26
Balş, Rom.	G8	20
Balsam Lake, Wi., U.S.	C1	142
Balsam Lake, l., Wi., U.S.	C1	142
Balsas, Braz.	E10	70
Balsas, stm., Mex.	D4	78
Balta, Ukr.	F10	20
Baltasar Brum, Ur.	E6	72
Bălți, Mol.	F9	20
Baltic, Ct., U.S.	C7	100
Baltic, S.D., U.S.	D9	134
Baltic Sea, Eur.	I7	10
Baltijsk, Russia	B5	20
Baltim, Egypt	E10	14
Baltimore, Md., U.S.	B4	113
Baltimore, Oh., U.S.	C3	128
Baltimore, co., Md., U.S.	B4	113
Baltimore Highlands, Md., U.S.	h11	113
Baluchistan, hist. reg., Asia	E8	42
Bālurghāt, India	D5	40
Balygyčan, Russia	C17	26
Bam, Iran	E7	42
Bama, Nig.	D7	50
Bamako, Mali	C4	50
Bamba, Mali	C4	50
Bambari, C.A.R.	B4	54
Bamberg, Ger.	F12	12
Bamberg, S.C., U.S.	E5	133
Bamberg, co., S.C., U.S.	E5	133
Bambesi, Eth.	B6	54
Bamenda, Cam.	B2	54
Bāmīān, Afg.	D9	42
Bamingui, C.A.R.	B4	54
Bampūr, Iran	E8	42
Banaba, i., Kir.	E10	58
Banalia, D.R.C.	C5	54
Banamba, Mali	D3	50
Bananal, Ilha do, i., Braz.	D1	74
Banana River, b., Fl., U.S.	D6	102
Bananga, India	H6	40
Banās, Rās, c., Egypt	F12	48
Banat, hist. reg., Eur.	G6	20
Banaz, Tur.	C3	44
Banbury, Eng., U.K.	D6	12
Bancroft, On., Can.	B7	89
Bancroft, Ia., U.S.	A3	108
Bancroft see Chililabombwe, Zam.	A4	56
Bānda, India	D4	40
Banda, Kepulauan, is., Indon.	D7	36
Banda, Laut (Banda Sea), Indon.	E7	36
Banda Aceh, Indon.	B1	36
Bandama, stm., C. Iv.	E4	50
Bandar Beheshtī, Iran	E8	42
Bandar-e 'Abbās, Iran	E7	42
Bandar-e Anzalī, Iran	C5	42
Bandar-e Deylam, Iran	E6	42
Bandar-e Khomeynī, Iran	D5	42
Bandar-e Lengeh, Iran	E6	42
Bandar-e Torkeman, Iran	C6	42
Bandar Seri Begawan, Bru.	C4	36
Banda Sea see Banda, Laut, Indon.	E7	36
Banded Peak, mtn., Co., U.S.	D4	99
Bandeira, Pico da, mtn., Braz.	F3	74
Bandeirantes, Braz.	B7	72
Bandelier National Monument, N.M., U.S.	B3	124
Bandera, co., Tx., U.S.	E3	136
Bandiagara, Mali	D4	50
Bandiantaolehai, China	C8	28
Bandırma, Tur.	B2	44
Ban Don, Ao, b., Thai.	E3	34
Bandundu, D.R.C.	D3	54
Bandung, Indon.	E3	36
Bāneh, Iran	E11	44
Banes, Cuba	A4	80
Banff National Park, Ab., Can.	D2	84
Banfora, Burkina	D4	50
Bangalore, India	G3	40
Bangassou, C.A.R.	C4	54
Banggai, Indon.	D6	36
Banggai, Kepulauan, is., Indon.	G7	32
Banggi, Pulau, i., Malay.	B5	36
Banghāzī, Libya	D9	48
Bangka, Pulau, i., Indon.	D3	36
Bangka, Selat, strt., Indon.	D3	36
Bangkalan, Indon.	E4	36
Bangkinang, Indon.	C2	36
Bangko, Indon.	D2	36
Bangkok see Krung Thep, Thai.	D4	34
Bangladesh, ctry., Asia	B2	34
Bang Mun Nak, Thai.	C4	34
Ban Gnômmarat Kèo, Laos	C5	34
Bangor, N. Ire., U.K.	C4	12
Bangor, Wales, U.K.	D4	12
Bangor, Me., U.S.	D4	112
Bangor, Mi., U.S.	F4	115
Bangor, Pa., U.S.	E11	131
Bangor, Wi., U.S.	E3	142
Bangor Township, Mi., U.S.	E7	115
Bangs, Tx., U.S.	D3	136
Bangs, Mount, mtn., Az., U.S.	A2	96
Bangui, C.A.R.	C3	54
Bangweulu, Lake, l., Zam.	A4	56
Ban Houayxay, Laos	B4	34
Bani, Burkina	D4	50
Baní, Dom. Rep.	B5	80
Baniara, Pap. N. Gui.	B4	62
Banister, stm., Va., U.S.	D4	139
Banī Walīd, Libya	D7	48
Bāniyās, Syria	E6	44
Banja Luka, Bos.	B6	18
Banjarmasin, Indon.	D4	36
Banjul, Gam.	D1	50
Banka Banka, Austl.	D5	60
Bankhead Lake, res., Al., U.S.	B2	94
Banks, co., Ga., U.S.	B3	103
Banks, Îles, is., Vanuatu	j9	62a
Banks Island, i., B.C., Can.	C2	85
Banks Lake, res., Wa., U.S.	B6	140
Banks Strait, strt., Austl.	I4	62
Bānkura, India	E5	40
Ban Nalè, Laos	C4	34
Banner, co., Ne., U.S.	C2	120
Banner Elk, N.C., U.S.	A1	126
Banning, Ca., U.S.	F5	98
Bannock, co., Id., U.S.	G6	105
Bannock Peak, mtn., Id., U.S.	F6	105
Bannock Range, mts., Id., U.S.	G6	105
Bannu, Pak.	D10	42
Ban Pong, Thai.	D3	34
Ban Signo, Laos	C5	34
Banská Bystrica, Slvk.	E5	20
Bānswāra, India	E2	40
Bantaeng, Indon.	E6	36
Bantam, stm., Ct., U.S.	B3	100
Bantam Lake, l., Ct., U.S.	C3	100
Banyo, Cam.	B2	54
Banyuwangi, Indon.	E4	36
Banzare Coast, Ant.	C17	67
Baode, China	D10	28
Baodi, China	B4	30
Baoding, China	D11	28
Bao Ha, Viet.	B4	34
Baoji, China	E9	28
Baojing, China	D2	30
Bao Loc, Viet.	D5	34
Baoqing, China	A2	31
Baoshan, China	F7	28
Baoting, China	H9	30
Baotou, China	C9	28
Baoying, China	E11	28
Ba'qūbah, Iraq	D4	42
Baquedano, Chile	B2	69
Bara, Nig.	D7	50
Baraawe, Som.	J13	48
Baraboo, Wi., U.S.	E4	142
Baraboo, stm., Wi., U.S.	E3	142
Baracoa, Cuba	A5	80
Baraga, Mi., U.S.	B2	115
Baraga, co., Mi., U.S.	B2	115
Barahona, Dom. Rep.	B5	80
Barakaldo, Spain	F5	16
Baram, stm., Malay.	C4	36
Bāramūla, India	C2	40
Baranagar, India	E5	40
Baranavičy, Bela.	C9	20
Barani, Burkina	D4	50
Baranof Island, i., Ak., U.S.	m22	95
Barataria, La., U.S.	E5	111
Barataria Bay, b., La., U.S.	E6	111
Barauni, India	D5	40
Barbacena, Braz.	F3	74
Barbacoas, Col.	C4	70
Barbados, ctry., N.A.	F12	76
Barbar, Sudan	G11	48
Barbas, Cap, c., W. Sah.	B1	50
Barbastro, Spain	F7	16
Barber, co., Ks., U.S.	E5	109
Barbers Point, c., Hi., U.S.	g9	104
Barbers Point Naval Air Station, Hi., U.S.	g9	104
Barberton, S. Afr.	D5	56
Barberton, Oh., U.S.	A4	128
Barbour, co., Al., U.S.	D4	94
Barbour, co., W.V., U.S.	B4	141
Barboursville, W.V., U.S.	C2	141
Barbourville, Ky., U.S.	D6	110
Barbuda, i., Antig.	B7	80
Barcaldine, Austl.	E4	62
Barcelona, Spain	G8	16
Barcelona, Ven.	B6	70
Barcelos, Braz.	D7	70

Name	Map Ref.	Page

Barcroft, Lake, res., Va., U.S. — g12 — 139
Bǎrdä, Azer. — B12 — 44
Bardaï, Chad — B8 — 50
Bardawīl, Sabkhet el-, b., Egypt — G5 — 44
Bardejov, Slvk. — E6 — 20
Barden Reservoir, res., R.I., U.S. — C2 — 132
Bardīyah, Libya — D10 — 48
Bardstown, Ky., U.S. — C4 — 110
Bardwell, Ky., U.S. — f9 — 110
Bardwell Lake, res., Tx., U.S. — C4 — 136
Bareilly, India — D3 — 40
Barents Sea, Eur. — B6 — 26
Barents Trough — D20 — 144
Bargersville, In., U.S. — E5 — 107
Bar Harbor, Me., U.S. — D4 — 112
Bari, Italy — D6 — 18
Barika, Alg. — J9 — 16
Barillas, Guat. — B1 — 80
Barīm, i., Yemen — H4 — 38
Barinas, Ven. — B6 — 70
Bāripada, India — E5 — 40
Bârîs, Egypt — F11 — 48
Barisāl, Bngl. — E6 — 40
Barisan, Pegunungan, mts., Indon. — D2 — 36
Barkam, China — C1 — 30
Barker Heights, N.C., U.S. — f10 — 126
Barkhamsted Reservoir, res., Ct., U.S. — B3 — 100
Barkley, Lake, res., U.S. — f10 — 110
Barkley Sound, strt., B.C., Can. — E5 — 85
Barkly East, S. Afr. — E4 — 56
Barkly Tableland, plat., Austl. — D6 — 60
Barkol, China — C6 — 28
Bark Point, c., Wi., U.S. — B2 — 142
Barksdale Air Force Base, mil., La., U.S. — B2 — 111
Bârlad, Rom. — F9 — 20
Barlee, Lake, l., Austl. — F2 — 60
Barletta, Italy — D6 — 18
Barling, Ar., U.S. — B1 — 97
Barlow, Ky., U.S. — e8 — 110
Bärmer, India — D2 — 40
Barmera, Austl. — G3 — 62
Barnaul, Russia — D10 — 26
Barnegat Bay, b., N.J., U.S. — D4 — 123
Barnegat Inlet, b., N.J., U.S. — D4 — 123
Barnes, co., N.D., U.S. — B7 — 127
Barnesboro, Pa., U.S. — E4 — 131
Barnes Sound, strt., Fl., U.S. — G6 — 102
Barnesville, Ga., U.S. — C2 — 103
Barnesville, Mn., U.S. — D2 — 116
Barnesville, Oh., U.S. — C4 — 128
Barnhart, Mo., U.S. — C7 — 118
Barnsdall, Ok., U.S. — A5 — 129
Barnstable, Ma., U.S. — C7 — 114
Barnstable, co., Ma., U.S. — C7 — 114
Barnstaple, Eng., U.K. — E4 — 12
Barnwell, S.C., U.S. — E5 — 133
Barnwell, co., S.C., U.S. — E5 — 133
Baro, Nig. — E6 — 50
Barpeta, India — D6 — 40
Barqah (Cyrenaica), hist. reg., Libya — E8 — 14
Barques, Pointe aux, c., Mi., U.S. — D8 — 115
Barquisimeto, Ven. — A6 — 70
Barra, Braz. — D3 — 74
Barra, i., Scot., U.K. — B3 — 12
Barra, Ponta da, c., Moz. — C6 — 56
Barrackville, W.V., U.S. — B4 — 141
Barra do Corda, Braz. — C2 — 74
Barra do Cuanza, Ang. — E2 — 54
Barra do Dande, Ang. — E2 — 54
Barra do Garças, Braz. — B7 — 72
Barra Mansa, Braz. — F3 — 74
Barranca, Peru — F4 — 70
Barrancabermeja, Col. — B5 — 70
Barrancas, Ven. — D7 — 80
Barranquilla, Col. — A5 — 70
Barras, Braz. — B3 — 74
Barre, Vt., U.S. — C4 — 138
Barre, Lake, l., La., U.S. — E5 — 111
Barre Falls Reservoir, res., Ma., U.S. — B4 — 114
Barreiras, Braz. — D3 — 74
Barreiro, Port. — H2 — 16
Barreiros, Braz. — C4 — 74
Barren, co., Ky., U.S. — D4 — 110
Barren, stm., Ky., U.S. — C3 — 110
Barren, Nosy, i., Madag. — B7 — 56
Barren Island, i., Md., U.S. — D5 — 113
Barren Islands, is., Ak., U.S. — h15 — 95
Barren River Lake, res., Ky., U.S. — D3 — 110
Barretos, Braz. — F2 — 74
Barrett, W.V., U.S. — D3 — 141
Barrhead, Ab., Can. — B3 — 84
Barrie, On., Can. — C5 — 89
Barrie Island, i., On., Can. — B2 — 89
Barrière, Fr. — D7 — 85
Barrier Range, mts., Austl. — G3 — 62
Barrington, Il., U.S. — A5 — 106
Barrington, N.J., U.S. — D2 — 123
Barrington, R.I., U.S. — D5 — 132
Barrington, stm., R.I., U.S. — C5 — 132
Barron, Wi., U.S. — C2 — 142
Barron, co., Wi., U.S. — C2 — 142
Barron Lake, Mi., U.S. — G4 — 115

Barrow, Ak., U.S. — A8 — 95
Barrow, co., Ga., U.S. — B3 — 103
Barrow, Point, c., Ak., U.S. — A8 — 95
Barrow Creek, Austl. — E5 — 60
Barrow-in-Furness, Eng., U.K. — C5 — 12
Barrow Island, i., Austl. — E2 — 60
Barry, Il., U.S. — D2 — 106
Barry, co., Mi., U.S. — F5 — 115
Barry, co., Mo., U.S. — E4 — 118
Barrys Bay, On., Can. — B7 — 89
Bārsi, India — F3 — 40
Barstow, Ca., U.S. — E5 — 98
Bartholomew, co., In., U.S. — F6 — 107
Bartholomew, Bayou, stm., U.S. — D4 — 97
Bartica, Guy. — B8 — 70
Bartın, Tur. — B5 — 44
Bartlesville, Ok., U.S. — A6 — 129
Bartlett, N.H., U.S. — B4 — 122
Bartlett, Tn., U.S. — B2 — 135
Bartlett, Tx., U.S. — D4 — 136
Bartlett Reservoir, res., Az., U.S. — D4 — 96
Bartletts Ferry Dam, U.S. — C4 — 94
Barton, Oh., U.S. — B5 — 128
Barton, Vt., U.S. — B4 — 138
Barton, co., Ks., U.S. — D5 — 109
Barton, co., Mo., U.S. — D3 — 118
Barton, stm., Vt., U.S. — B4 — 138
Bartonville, Il., U.S. — C4 — 106
Bartow, Fl., U.S. — E5 — 102
Bartow, co., Ga., U.S. — B2 — 103
Barú, Volcán, vol., Pan. — D3 — 80
Barun Su, China — A3 — 30
Baruun-Urt, Mong. — B10 — 28
Barysaŭ, Bela. — B10 — 20
Basalt, Co., U.S. — B3 — 99
Basankusu, D.R.C. — C3 — 54
Bascuñán, Cabo, c., Chile — D3 — 72
Basehor, Ks., U.S. — k16 — 109
Basel, Switz. — G10 — 12
Bashan Lake, l., Ct., U.S. — D6 — 100
Bashaw, Ab., Can. — C4 — 84
Bashi Channel, strt., Asia — B8 — 34
Basilan Island, i., Phil. — E8 — 34
Basile, La., U.S. — D3 — 111
Basin, Wy., U.S. — B4 — 143
Basingstoke, Eng., U.K. — E6 — 12
Basīrhāt, India — E5 — 40
Baskahegan Lake, l., Me., U.S. — C5 — 112
Başkale, Tur. — C10 — 44
Basking Ridge, N.J., U.S. — B3 — 123
Baškirija, state, Russia — D7 — 26
Basoko, D.R.C. — C4 — 54
Basra see Al-Baṣrah, Iraq — D5 — 42
Bassano, Ab., Can. — D4 — 84
Bassar, Togo — E5 — 50
Bassein see Pathein, Myan. — C2 — 34
Basse Santa Su, Gam. — D2 — 50
Basse-Terre, Guad. — B7 — 80
Basseterre, St. K./N. — B7 — 80
Basse-Terre, i., Guad. — B7 — 80
Bassett, Ne., U.S. — B6 — 120
Bassett, Va., U.S. — D3 — 139
Bassett Peak, mtn., Az., U.S. — E5 — 96
Bassikounou, Maur. — C3 — 50
Bass Islands, is., Oh., U.S. — A3 — 128
Bass Lake, In., U.S. — B4 — 107
Bass Strait, strt., Austl. — H4 — 62
Basswood Lake, l., Mn., U.S. — B7 — 116
Båstad, Swe. — H5 — 10
Bastia, Fr. — C2 — 18
Bastrop, La., U.S. — B4 — 111
Bastrop, Tx., U.S. — D4 — 136
Bastrop, co., Tx., U.S. — D4 — 136
Basu, Pulau, i., Indon. — D2 — 36
Basutoland see Lesotho, ctry., Afr. — D4 — 56
Bata, Eq. Gui. — C1 — 54
Batabanó, Golfo de, b., Cuba — A3 — 80
Batac, Phil. — C8 — 34
Batagaj, Russia — C15 — 26
Batala, India — C3 — 40
Batamaj, Russia — C14 — 26
Batang, China — E7 — 28
Batang, Indon. — E3 — 36
Batangafo, C.A.R. — B3 — 54
Batangas, Phil. — D8 — 34
Batan Islands, is., Phil. — B8 — 34
Batanta, Pulau, i., Indon. — D8 — 36
Batavia see Jakarta, Indon. — E3 — 36
Batavia, Il., U.S. — B5 — 106
Batavia, N.Y., U.S. — C2 — 125
Batavia, Oh., U.S. — C1 — 128
Batchelor, Austl. — C5 — 60
Batchelor Bay, b., N.C., U.S. — B6 — 126
Bătdâmbâng, Camb. — D4 — 34
Batemans Bay, Austl. — H5 — 62
Bates, co., Mo., U.S. — C3 — 118
Batesburg, S.C., U.S. — D4 — 133
Batesville, Ar., U.S. — B4 — 97
Batesville, In., U.S. — F7 — 107
Batesville, Ms., U.S. — A4 — 117
Bath, N.B., Can. — C2 — 87
Bath, On., Can. — C8 — 89
Bath, Eng., U.K. — E5 — 12
Bath, Me., U.S. — E3 — 112
Bath, N.Y., U.S. — C3 — 125
Bath, Pa., U.S. — E11 — 131
Bath, S.C., U.S. — D4 — 133

Bath, co., Ky., U.S. — B6 — 110
Bath, co., Va., U.S. — B3 — 139
Bathinda, India — C3 — 40
Bathurst, Austl. — G4 — 62
Bathurst, N.B., Can. — B4 — 87
Bathurst see Banjul, Gam. — D1 — 50
Bathurst Island, i., Austl. — C5 — 60
Batiscan, stm., P.Q., Can. — B5 — 90
Batman, Tur. — D9 — 44
Batna, Alg. — C6 — 48
Baton Rouge, La., U.S. — D4 — 111
Batouri, Cam. — C2 — 54
Batsto, stm., N.J., U.S. — D3 — 123
Batticaloa, Sri L. — H4 — 40
Battle, Can. — H17 — 82
Battle Creek, Ia., U.S. — B2 — 108
Battle Creek, Mi., U.S. — F5 — 115
Battle Creek, Ne., U.S. — C8 — 120
Battle Ground, In., U.S. — C4 — 107
Battle Ground, Wa., U.S. — D3 — 140
Battle Lake, Mn., U.S. — D3 — 116
Battle Mountain, Nv., U.S. — C5 — 121
Battle Mountain, mtn., Wy., U.S. — E5 — 143
Batu, mtn., Eth. — B7 — 54
Batu, Kepulauan, is., Indon. — D1 — 36
Batumi, Geor. — B9 — 44
Batu Pahat, Malay. — C2 — 36
Baturaja, Indon. — D2 — 36
Baturité, Braz. — B4 — 74
Baubau, Indon. — E6 — 36
Bauchi, Nig. — D6 — 50
Baudette, Mn., U.S. — B4 — 116
Bauld, Cape, c., Nf., Can. — C4 — 88
Baures, Bol. — A5 — 72
Bauru, Braz. — F2 — 74
Bauska, Lat. — H11 — 10
Bautzen, Ger. — E14 — 12
Bavispe, stm., Mex. — A3 — 78
Bawdwin, Myan. — B3 — 34
Bawean, Pulau, i., Indon. — E4 — 36
Bawiti, Egypt — E10 — 48
Baxley, Ga., U.S. — E4 — 103
Baxter, Ia., U.S. — C4 — 108
Baxter, Mn., U.S. — D4 — 116
Baxter, Tn., U.S. — C8 — 135
Baxter, co., Ar., U.S. — A3 — 97
Baxter Springs, Ks., U.S. — E9 — 109
Bay, Ar., U.S. — B5 — 97
Bay, co., Fl., U.S. — u16 — 102
Bay, co., Mi., U.S. — E6 — 115
Bayamo, Cuba — A4 — 80
Bayamón, P.R. — B6 — 80
Bayan Har Shan, mts., China — E7 — 28
Bayanhongor, Mong. — B8 — 28
Bayano, Lago, res., Pan. — D4 — 80
Bayan Obo, China — C10 — 28
Bayard, Ne., U.S. — C2 — 120
Bayard, N.M., U.S. — E1 — 124
Bayboro, N.C., U.S. — B6 — 126
Bayburt, Tur. — B9 — 44
Bay City, Mi., U.S. — E7 — 115
Bay City, Or., U.S. — B3 — 130
Bay City, Tx., U.S. — E5 — 136
Bay de Verde, Nf., Can. — D5 — 88
Baydhabo, Som. — J13 — 48
Bayeux, Fr. — C6 — 16
Bayfield, On., Can. — D3 — 89
Bayfield, Co., U.S. — D3 — 99
Bayfield, Wi., U.S. — B3 — 142
Bayfield, co., Wi., U.S. — B2 — 142
Baylor, co., Tx., U.S. — C3 — 136
Bay Mills Indian Reservation, Mi., U.S. — B6 — 115
Bay Minette, Al., U.S. — E2 — 94
Bayombong, Phil. — C8 — 34
Bayonne, Fr. — F6 — 16
Bayonne, N.J., U.S. — B4 — 123
Bayou Bodcau Reservoir, res., La., U.S. — B2 — 111
Bayou D'Arbonne Lake, res., La., U.S. — B3 — 111
Bayou George, Fl., U.S. — u16 — 102
Bayou Goula, La., U.S. — D4 — 111
Bayou La Batre, Al., U.S. — E1 — 94
Bayovar, Peru — E3 — 70
Bay Point, c., S.C., U.S. — G7 — 133
Bayport, Mn., U.S. — E6 — 116
Bayport, N.Y., U.S. — n15 — 125
Bayreuth, Ger. — F12 — 12
Bay Ridge, Md., U.S. — C5 — 113
Bay Roberts, Nf., Can. — E5 — 88
Bayrūt (Beirut), Leb. — F6 — 44
Bays, Lake of, l., On., Can. — B5 — 89
Bay Saint Louis, Ms., U.S. — E4 — 117
Bay Shore, N.Y., U.S. — n15 — 125
Bayshore Gardens, Fl., U.S. — q10 — 102
Bayside, Wi., U.S. — m12 — 142
Bay Springs, Ms., U.S. — D4 — 117
Bayt Laḥm, W.B. — G6 — 44
Baytown, Tx., U.S. — E5 — 136
Bayview, Al., U.S. — f7 — 94
Bay Village, Oh., U.S. — h9 — 128
Baza, Spain — I5 — 16
Bazardjuzju, gora see Bazardüzü daǧ, mtn., Azer. — B12 — 44
Bazardüzü daǧ, mtn., Azer. — B12 — 44
Bazaruto, Ilha do, i., Moz. — C6 — 56
Bazhong, China — C2 — 30
Be, Nosy, i., Madag. — A8 — 56
Beach, Il., U.S. — h9 — 106

Beach, N.D., U.S. — C1 — 127
Beachburg, On., Can. — B8 — 89
Beach City, Oh., U.S. — B4 — 128
Beach Haven Inlet, b., N.J., U.S. — D4 — 123
Beach Pond, res., U.S. — C8 — 100
Beachville, On., Can. — D4 — 89
Beachwood, N.J., U.S. — D4 — 123
Beacon, Austl. — G2 — 60
Beacon, N.Y., U.S. — D7 — 125
Beacon Falls, Ct., U.S. — D3 — 100
Beaconsfield, P.Q., Can. — q19 — 90
Beadle, co., S.D., U.S. — C7 — 134
Beagle Gulf, b., Austl. — C4 — 60
Bealanana, Madag. — A8 — 56
Beale, Cape, c., B.C., Can. — E5 — 85
Beale Air Force Base, mil., Ca., U.S. — C3 — 98
Bear, De., U.S. — B3 — 101
Bear, stm., U.S. — B3 — 137
Bear Creek, Al., U.S. — A2 — 94
Bear Creek, stm., Or., U.S. — E4 — 130
Bear Creek, stm., Wy., U.S. — E8 — 143
Bear Creek, stm., U.S. — E2 — 109
Bearden, Ar., U.S. — D3 — 97
Beardstown, Il., U.S. — C3 — 106
Bear Inlet, b., N.C., U.S. — C5 — 126
Bear Island see Bjørnøya, i., Nor. — B3 — 26
Bear Lake, co., Id., U.S. — G7 — 105
Bear Lake, l., Wi., U.S. — C2 — 142
Bear Lake, l., U.S. — C5 — 92
Bear Lake, l., U.S. — A4 — 137
Bear Lodge Mountains, mts., Wy., U.S. — B8 — 143
Bear Mountain, mtn., Or., U.S. — D4 — 130
Bearpaw Mountains, mts., Mt., U.S. — B7 — 119
Bear River, N.S., Can. — E4 — 87
Bear River City, Ut., U.S. — B3 — 137
Beartooth Pass, Wy., U.S. — B3 — 143
Beartooth Range, mts., U.S. — E7 — 119
Bear Town, Ms., U.S. — D3 — 117
Beās, stm., India — C3 — 40
Beata, Isla, i., Dom. Rep. — B5 — 80
Beatrice, Ne., U.S. — D9 — 120
Beatrice, Cape, c., Austl. — C2 — 62
Beatty, Nv., U.S. — G5 — 121
Beattyville, Ky., U.S. — C6 — 110
Beaufort, N.C., U.S. — C6 — 126
Beaufort, S.C., U.S. — G6 — 133
Beaufort, co., N.C., U.S. — B5 — 126
Beaufort, co., S.C., U.S. — G6 — 133
Beaufort Marine Corps Air Station, mil., S.C., U.S. — F6 — 133
Beaufort Sea, N.A. — D12 — 82
Beaufort West, S. Afr. — E3 — 56
Beau Lake, l., Me., U.S. — A3 — 112
Beaumont, Ab., Can. — C4 — 84
Beaumont, Ms., U.S. — D5 — 117
Beaumont, Tx., U.S. — D5 — 136
Beaune, Fr. — D9 — 16
Beauport, P.Q., Can. — n17 — 90
Beaupré, P.Q., Can. — B7 — 90
Beauregard, co., La., U.S. — D2 — 111
Beausejour, Mb., Can. — D3 — 86
Beauvais, Fr. — C8 — 16
Beauval, Sk., Can. — B2 — 91
Beaver, Ok., U.S. — A1 — 129
Beaver, Pa., U.S. — E1 — 131
Beaver, Ut., U.S. — E3 — 137
Beaver, W.V., U.S. — D3 — 141
Beaver, co., Ok., U.S. — e10 — 129
Beaver, co., Pa., U.S. — E1 — 131
Beaver, co., Ut., U.S. — E2 — 137
Beaver, stm., Can. — B2 — 91
Beaver, stm., N.Y., U.S. — B6 — 125
Beaver, stm., R.I., U.S. — E2 — 132
Beaver, stm., Ut., U.S. — E2 — 137
Beaver, stm., U.S. — A2 — 129
Beaverbank, N.S., Can. — E6 — 87
Beaver Brook, stm., U.S. — E4 — 122
Beaver City, Ne., U.S. — D6 — 120
Beavercreek, Oh., U.S. — C1 — 128
Beaver Creek, stm., N.D., U.S. — C1 — 127
Beaver Creek, stm., N.D., U.S. — C5 — 127
Beaver Creek, stm., Ok., U.S. — C3 — 129
Beaver Creek, stm., Tn., U.S. — m13 — 135
Beaver Creek, stm., Wy., U.S. — D4 — 143
Beaver Creek, stm., U.S. — E4 — 120
Beaver Creek, stm., U.S. — C8 — 143
Beaverdale, Pa., U.S. — F4 — 131
Beaver Dam, Ky., U.S. — C3 — 110
Beaver Dam, Wi., U.S. — E5 — 142
Beaverdam Branch, stm., De., U.S. — F3 — 101
Beaverdam Lake, res., Wi., U.S. — E5 — 142
Beaverhead, co., Mt., U.S. — E3 — 119
Beaverhead, stm., Mt., U.S. — E4 — 119
Beaverhead Mountains, mts., U.S. — D5 — 105
Beaver Falls, Pa., U.S. — E1 — 131
Beaverhead, co., Mt., U.S. — E3 — 119
Beaver Island, i., Mi., U.S. — C5 — 115
Beaver Lake, res., Ar., U.S. — A2 — 97
Beaverlodge, Ab., Can. — B1 — 84
Beaver Meadows, Pa., U.S. — E10 — 131

Beaver Run Reservoir, res., Pa., U.S. — F2 — 131
Beavertail Point, c., R.I., U.S. — F4 — 132
Beaverton, Mi., U.S. — E6 — 115
Beaverton, Or., U.S. — B4 — 130
Beāwar, India — D2 — 40
Bebedouro, Braz. — C8 — 72
Bécancour, P.Q., Can. — C5 — 90
Bečej, Yugo. — B8 — 18
Béchar, Alg. — D4 — 48
Becharof Lake, l., Ak., U.S. — D8 — 95
Bechuanaland see Botswana, ctry., Afr. — C3 — 56
Beckemeyer, Il., U.S. — E4 — 106
Becker, Mn., U.S. — E5 — 116
Becker, co., Mn., U.S. — D3 — 116
Beckham, co., Ok., U.S. — B2 — 129
Beckley, W.V., U.S. — D3 — 141
Becky Peak, mtn., Nv., U.S. — D7 — 121
Bedelē, Eth. — B7 — 54
Bedford, P.Q., Can. — D5 — 90
Bedford, Eng., U.K. — D6 — 12
Bedford, Ia., U.S. — D3 — 108
Bedford, In., U.S. — G5 — 107
Bedford, Ky., U.S. — B4 — 110
Bedford, Ma., U.S. — B5 — 114
Bedford, N.H., U.S. — E3 — 122
Bedford, Oh., U.S. — A4 — 128
Bedford, Pa., U.S. — F4 — 131
Bedford, Va., U.S. — C3 — 139
Bedford, co., Pa., U.S. — G4 — 131
Bedford, co., Tn., U.S. — B5 — 135
Bedford, co., Va., U.S. — C3 — 139
Bedford Hills, N.Y., U.S. — D7 — 125
Bee, co., Tx., U.S. — E4 — 136
Beebe, P.Q., Can. — D5 — 90
Beebe, Ar., U.S. — B4 — 97
Beecher, Il., U.S. — B6 — 106
Beech Fork, stm., Ky., U.S. — C4 — 110
Beech Grove, In., U.S. — E5 — 107
Beech Island, S.C., U.S. — E4 — 133
Beemer, Ne., U.S. — C9 — 120
Bee Ridge, Fl., U.S. — q11 — 102
Beersheba see Be'ér Sheva', Isr. — D2 — 42
Be'ér Sheva', Isr. — D2 — 42
Beeton (part of Alliston Beeton Tecumseth and Tottenham), On., Can. — C5 — 89
Beeville, Tx., U.S. — E4 — 136
Befale, D.R.C. — C4 — 54
Befandriana Atsimo, Madag. — C7 — 56
Bega, Austl. — H4 — 62
Beggs, Ok., U.S. — B5 — 129
Behbahān, Iran — D6 — 42
Behm Canal, strt., Ak., U.S. — n24 — 95
Bei'an, China — B13 — 28
Beigi, Eth. — B6 — 54
Beihai, China — G9 — 28
Beijing, China — D11 — 28
Beiliu, China — E3 — 30
Beipiao, China — C12 — 28
Beira, Moz. — B5 — 56
Beirut see Bayrūt, Leb. — F6 — 44
Bei Shan, mts., China — C7 — 28
Beitbridge, Zimb. — C5 — 56
Beizhen, China — A5 — 30
Beizhen, China — B4 — 30
Beja, Port. — I3 — 16
Béja, Tun. — C6 — 48
Bejaïa, Alg. — C6 — 48
Bejaïa, Golfe de, b., Alg. — I9 — 16
Béjar, Spain — G4 — 16
Bejneu, Kaz. — E7 — 26
Bekabad, Uzb. — B9 — 42
Bekasi, Indon. — E3 — 36
Bekdaš, Turk. — B6 — 42
Békéscsaba, Hung. — F6 — 20
Bekily, Madag. — C8 — 56
Bekodoka, Madag. — B8 — 56
Bela, India — D4 — 40
Bela, Pak. — E9 — 42
Bela Crkva, Yugo. — B8 — 18
Bel Air, Md., U.S. — A5 — 113
Bel Alton, Md., U.S. — D4 — 113
Belarus, ctry., Eur. — C9 — 20
Belau see Palau, ctry., Oc. — F10 — 32
Bela Vista, Braz. — H8 — 70
Bela Vista, Moz. — D5 — 56
Belcamp, Md., U.S. — B5 — 113
Belchatów, Pol. — D5 — 20
Belchertown, Ma., U.S. — B3 — 114
Belcourt, N.D., U.S. — A6 — 127
Belden, Ms., U.S. — A5 — 117
Belding, Mi., U.S. — E5 — 115
Beledweyne, Som. — J13 — 48
Belém, Braz. — D9 — 74
Belém, Moz. — A6 — 56
Belém de São Francisco, Braz. — C4 — 74
Belen, N.M., U.S. — C3 — 124
Belëv, Russia — C14 — 20
Belfair, Wa., U.S. — B3 — 140
Belfast, N. Ire., U.K. — C4 — 12
Belfast, Me., U.S. — D3 — 112
Belfield, N.D., U.S. — C2 — 127
Belford, N.J., U.S. — C4 — 123
Belfort, Fr. — D10 — 16
Belfry, Ky., U.S. — C7 — 110
Belgaum, India — F2 — 40
Belgium, Wi., U.S. — E6 — 142

Name	Map Ref.	Page
Belgium, ctry., Eur.	B9	16
Belgorod, Russia	D5	26
Belgrade, Mn., U.S.	E3	116
Belgrade, Mt., U.S.	E5	119
Belgrade see Beograd, Yugo.	B8	18
Belhaven, N.C., U.S.	B6	126
Beliliou, i., Palau	E9	32
Belington, W.V., U.S.	B5	141
Belitung, i., Indon.	D3	36
Belize, ctry., N.A.	B2	80
Belize City, Belize	B2	80
Belknap, co., N.H., U.S.	C3	122
Belknap Crater, crat., Or., U.S.	C5	130
Bell, co., Ky., U.S.	D6	110
Bell, co., Tx., U.S.	D4	136
Bella Coola, stm., B.C., Can.	C4	84
Bellaire, Ks., U.S.	g12	109
Bellaire, Mi., U.S.	D5	115
Bellaire, Oh., U.S.	C5	128
Bellaire, Tx., U.S.	r14	136
Bellamy, Al., U.S.	C1	94
Bellary, India	F3	40
Bella Vista, Arg.	D6	72
Bellavista, Peru	E4	70
Bella Vista, Ar., U.S.	A1	97
Bellbrook, Oh., U.S.	C1	128
Belle, Mo., U.S.	C6	118
Belle, W.V., U.S.	C3	141
Belle, stm., La., U.S.	k9	111
Belleair, Fl., U.S.	p10	102
Belle Bay, b., Nf., Can.	E4	88
Belle Chasse, La., U.S.	E5	111
Bellefontaine, Oh., U.S.	B2	128
Bellefonte, Pa., U.S.	E6	131
Belle Fourche, S.D., U.S.	C2	134
Belle Fourche, stm., U.S.	C3	134
Belle Fourche Reservoir, res., S.D., U.S.	C2	134
Belle Glade, Fl., U.S.	F6	102
Belle-Île, i., Fr.	D5	16
Belle Isle, Fl., U.S.	D5	102
Belle Isle, i., Nf., Can.	C4	88
Belle Isle, Strait of, strt., Nf., Can.	C3	88
Belle Meade, Tn., U.S.	g10	135
Belle Plaine, Ks., U.S.	E6	109
Belle Plaine, Mn., U.S.	F5	116
Belle River, On., Can.	E2	89
Belle Rose, La., U.S.	D4	111
Belle Vernon, Pa., U.S.	F2	131
Belleview, Fl., U.S.	C4	102
Belle View, Va., U.S.	g12	139
Belleville, On., Can.	C7	89
Belleville, Il., U.S.	E4	106
Belleville, Ks., U.S.	C6	109
Belleville, Mi., U.S.	p15	115
Belleville, N.J., U.S.	B4	123
Belleville, Pa., U.S.	E6	131
Belleville, Wi., U.S.	F4	142
Belleville Pond, l., R.I., U.S.	E4	132
Bellevue, Ia., U.S.	B7	108
Bellevue, Id., U.S.	F4	105
Bellevue, Ky., U.S.	h13	110
Bellevue, Mi., U.S.	F5	115
Bellevue, Ne., U.S.	C10	120
Bellevue, Oh., U.S.	A3	128
Bellevue, Pa., U.S.	F1	131
Bellevue, Wa., U.S.	e11	140
Bellflower, Ca., U.S.	n12	98
Bellingham, Ma., U.S.	B5	114
Bellingham, Wa., U.S.	A3	140
Bellingshausen Sea, Ant.	C32	67
Bell Island, i., Nf., Can.	C4	88
Bellmawr, N.J., U.S.	D2	123
Bello, Col.	B4	70
Bellows Falls, Vt., U.S.	E4	138
Bellport, N.Y., U.S.	n16	125
Bells, Tn., U.S.	B2	135
Bells Creek, stm., W.V., U.S.	m13	141
Belluno, Italy	A4	18
Bell Ville, Arg.	E5	72
Bellville, Oh., U.S.	B3	128
Bellville, Tx., U.S.	E4	136
Bellwood, Il., U.S.	k9	106
Bellwood, Pa., U.S.	E5	131
Bellwood, Va., U.S.	n18	139
Belmar, N.J., U.S.	C4	123
Belmond, Ia., U.S.	B4	108
Belmont, On., Can.	E3	89
Belmont, Ca., U.S.	h8	98
Belmont, Ma., U.S.	g11	114
Belmont, Ms., U.S.	A5	117
Belmont, N.C., U.S.	B1	126
Belmont, N.H., U.S.	D4	122
Belmont, W.V., U.S.	B3	141
Belmont, Wi., U.S.	F3	142
Belmont, co., Oh., U.S.	B5	128
Belmonte, Braz.	G12	70
Belmopan, Belize	B2	80
Bel-Nor, Mo., U.S.	f13	118
Beloe, ozero, l., Russia	C5	26
Beloeil, P.Q., Can.	D4	90
Beloe more, Russia	C5	26
Belogorsk, Russia	D14	26
Belo Horizonte, Braz.	E3	74
Beloit, Ks., U.S.	C5	109
Beloit, Oh., U.S.	B5	128
Beloit, Wi., U.S.	F4	142
Belomorsk, Russia	C5	26
Beloreck, Russia	D10	22
Belorussia see Belarus, ctry., Eur.	C9	20
Belo Tsiribihina, Madag.	B7	56
Belpre, Oh., U.S.	C4	128
Belt, Mt., U.S.	C6	119
Belted Range, mts., Nv., U.S.	F5	121
Belton, Mo., U.S.	C3	118
Belton, S.C., U.S.	B3	133
Belton, Tx., U.S.	D4	136
Belton Lake, res., Tx., U.S.	D4	136
Beltrami, co., Mn., U.S.	B3	116
Beltsville, Md., U.S.	B4	113
Beluha, gora, mtn., Asia	B5	28
Belūr, India	G3	40
Belvedere, S.C., U.S.	D4	133
Belvidere, Il., U.S.	A5	106
Belvidere, N.J., U.S.	B2	123
Belyj, ostrov, i., Russia	B8	26
Belyj Jar, Russia	D10	26
Belzoni, Ms., U.S.	B3	117
Bembèrèkè, Benin	D5	50
Bement, Il., U.S.	D5	106
Bemidji, Mn., U.S.	C4	116
Bemidji, Lake, l., Mn., U.S.	C4	116
Benāb, Iran	D11	44
Bena-Dibele, D.R.C.	D4	54
Benalla, Austl.	H4	62
Benares see Vārānasi, India	D4	40
Benavente, Spain	F4	16
Benavides, Tx., U.S.	F3	136
Benbecula, i., Scot., U.K.	B3	12
Benbrook Lake, res., Tx., U.S.	n9	136
Bencubbin, Austl.	G2	60
Bend, Or., U.S.	C5	130
Ben Davis Point, c., N.J., U.S.	E2	123
Bendeleben, Mount, mtn., Ak., U.S.	B7	95
Bendigo, Austl.	H3	62
Benedict, Md., U.S.	C4	113
Benedito Leite, Braz.	E11	70
Benevento, Italy	D5	18
Benewah, co., Id., U.S.	B2	105
Bengal, Bay of, b., Asia	F5	40
Bengbu, China	E11	28
Benghazi see Banghāzī, Libya	D9	48
Bengkalis, Pulau, i., Indon.	C2	36
Bengkulu, Indon.	D2	36
Bengtsfors, Swe.	G5	10
Benguela, Ang.	F2	54
Bengweulu Swamps, sw., Zam.	A5	56
Benham, Ky., U.S.	D7	110
Ben Hill, co., Ga., U.S.	E3	103
Beni, D.R.C.	C5	54
Beni, stm., Bol.	F6	70
Béni Abbas, Alg.	D4	48
Benicia, Ca., U.S.	C2	98
Beni-Mellal, Mor.	D3	48
Benin, ctry., Afr.	D5	50
Benin, Bight of, b., Afr.	E6	50
Benin City, Nig.	E6	50
Beni Saf, Alg.	J6	16
Beni Suef, Egypt	E11	48
Benito Juárez, Arg.	F6	72
Benjamin Constant, Braz.	D5	70
Benkelman, Ne., U.S.	D4	120
Benld, Il., U.S.	D4	106
Bennett, Co., U.S.	B6	99
Bennett, co., S.D., U.S.	D4	134
Bennettsville, S.C., U.S.	B8	133
Bennington, Ne., U.S.	g12	120
Bennington, N.H., U.S.	D3	122
Bennington, Vt., U.S.	F2	138
Bennington, co., Vt., U.S.	E2	138
Benoit, Ms., U.S.	B2	117
Benoni, S. Afr.	D4	56
Bénoué see Benue, stm., Afr.	E6	50
Bensenville, Il., U.S.	B6	106
Bensheim, Ger.	F11	12
Bensley, Va., U.S.	C5	139
Benson, Az., U.S.	F5	96
Benson, Mn., U.S.	E3	116
Benson, N.C., U.S.	B4	126
Benson, co., N.D., U.S.	A6	127
Benteng, Indon.	E6	36
Bentinck Island, i., Austl.	D2	62
Bentinck Island, i., Myan.	D3	34
Bentley, Ab., Can.	C3	84
Bentleyville, Pa., U.S.	F1	131
Benton, Ar., U.S.	C3	97
Benton, Il., U.S.	E5	106
Benton, Ks., U.S.	E6	109
Benton, Ky., U.S.	f9	110
Benton, La., U.S.	B2	111
Benton, Pa., U.S.	D9	131
Benton, Tn., U.S.	D9	135
Benton, Wi., U.S.	F3	142
Benton, co., Ar., U.S.	A1	97
Benton, co., Ia., U.S.	B5	108
Benton, co., In., U.S.	C3	107
Benton, co., Mn., U.S.	E4	116
Benton, co., Ms., U.S.	A4	117
Benton, co., Mo., U.S.	C4	118
Benton, co., Or., U.S.	C3	130
Benton, co., Tn., U.S.	A3	135
Benton, co., Wa., U.S.	C6	140
Benton City, Wa., U.S.	C6	140
Benton Harbor, Mi., U.S.	F4	115
Benton Heights, Mi., U.S.	F4	115
Bentonville, Ar., U.S.	A1	97
Ben Tre, Viet.	D5	34
Bent's Old Fort National Historic Site, hist., Co., U.S.	C7	99
Bentung, Malay.	C2	36
Benue, stm., Afr.	E6	50
Benwood, W.V., U.S.	f8	141
Benxi, China	C12	28
Benzie, co., Mi., U.S.	D4	115
Beogr025 (Belgrade), Yugo.	B8	18
Béoumi, C. Iv.	E3	50
Beowawe, Nv., U.S.	C5	121
Beppu, Japan	D2	31
Beraketa, Madag.	C8	56
Berat, Alb.	D7	18
Berau, Teluk, b., Indon.	D8	36
Berazino, Bela.	C10	20
Berbera, Som.	H14	48
Berbérati, C.A.R.	C3	54
Berck, Fr.	B7	16
Berdians'k, Ukr.	F14	20
Berdigestjah, Russia	C14	26
Berdyčiv, Ukr.	E10	20
Berea, Ky., U.S.	C5	110
Berea, Oh., U.S.	A4	128
Berea, S.C., U.S.	B3	133
Berehove, Ukr.	E7	20
Berekum, Ghana	E4	50
Berens, stm., Can.	C3	86
Beresford, S.D., U.S.	D9	134
Berettyóújfalu, Hung.	F6	20
Berezhany, Ukr.	E8	20
Berezivka, Ukr.	F11	20
Berezniki, Russia	D7	26
Berëzovo, Russia	C8	26
Berg, Swe.	F7	10
Bergama, Tur.	C2	44
Bergamo, Italy	B2	18
Bergen, Ger.	D12	12
Bergen, Nor.	F1	10
Bergen, co., N.J., U.S.	A4	123
Bergenfield, N.J., U.S.	B4	123
Bergerac, Fr.	E7	16
Bergland, Mi., U.S.	m12	115
Berguent, Mor.	E3	14
Berhala, Selat, strt., Indon.	D2	36
Beringa, ostrov, i., Russia	D18	26
Beringov proliv see Bering Strait, strt.	F6	82
Beringovskij, Russia	C19	26
Bering Sea	G3	82
Bering Strait, strt.	F6	82
Berkakit, Russia	D14	26
Berkane, Mor.	E3	14
Berkeley, Ca., U.S.	D2	98
Berkeley, Mo., U.S.	f13	118
Berkeley, R.I., U.S.	B4	132
Berkeley, co., S.C., U.S.	E8	133
Berkeley, co., W.V., U.S.	B6	141
Berkeley Heights, N.J., U.S.	B4	123
Berkeley Springs, W.V., U.S.	B6	141
Berkley, Mi., U.S.	F7	115
Berks, co., Pa., U.S.	F9	131
Berkshire, co., Ma., U.S.	B1	114
Berkshire Hills, hills, Ma., U.S.	B1	114
Berlevåg, Nor.	A13	10
Berlin, Ger.	D13	12
Berlin, Ct., U.S.	C5	100
Berlin, Md., U.S.	D7	113
Berlin, N.H., U.S.	B4	122
Berlin, N.J., U.S.	D3	123
Berlin, Pa., U.S.	G4	131
Berlin, Wi., U.S.	E5	142
Berlin Lake, res., Oh., U.S.	A4	128
Bermejo, stm., S.A.	C5	72
Bermuda, dep., N.A.	B12	76
Bern, Switz.	A1	18
Bernalillo, N.M., U.S.	B3	124
Bernalillo, co., N.M., U.S.	C3	124
Bernardsville, N.J., U.S.	B3	123
Bernasconi, Arg.	F5	72
Berne, see Bern, Switz.	A1	18
Berne, In., U.S.	C8	107
Berner Alpen, mts., Switz.	A1	18
Bernese Alps see Berner Alpen, mts., Switz.	A1	18
Bernice, La., U.S.	B3	111
Bernie, Mo., U.S.	E8	118
Bernier Island, i., Austl.	E1	60
Bernina, Piz, mtn., Eur.	A2	18
Beroroha, Madag.	C8	56
Berrien, co., Ga., U.S.	E3	103
Berrien, co., Mi., U.S.	F4	115
Berrien Springs, Mi., U.S.	G4	115
Berry, Al., U.S.	B2	94
Berry, hist. reg., Fr.	D7	16
Berryessa, Lake, res., Ca., U.S.	C2	98
Berry Hill, Tn., U.S.	g10	135
Berryville, Ar., U.S.	A2	97
Berryville, Va., U.S.	A5	139
Berseba, Nmb.	D2	56
Bershad', Ukr.	E10	20
Berthierville, P.Q., Can.	C4	90
Berthoud, Co., U.S.	A5	99
Berthoud Pass, Co., U.S.	B5	99
Bertie, co., N.C., U.S.	A5	126
Bertrand, Mo., U.S.	E8	118
Bertrand, Ne., U.S.	D6	120
Bertoua, Cam.	C2	54
Berwick, Ia., U.S.	e8	108
Berwick, La., U.S.	E4	111
Berwick, Me., U.S.	E2	112
Berwick, Pa., U.S.	D9	131
Berwick-upon-Tweed, Eng., U.K.	C6	12
Berwyn, Ab., Can.	A2	84
Berwyn, Il., U.S.	k9	106
Berwyn, Pa., U.S.	o20	131
Besalampy, Madag.	B7	56
Besançon, Fr.	D9	16
Beskids, mts., Eur.	E5	20
Beskra, Alg.	D6	48
Beslan, Russia	A11	44
Besni, Tur.	D7	44
Bessemer, Al., U.S.	B3	94
Bessemer, Mi., U.S.	n11	115
Bessemer, Pa., U.S.	E1	131
Bessemer City, N.C., U.S.	B1	126
Bétaré Oya, Cam.	B2	54
Betatakin Ruin, hist., Az., U.S.	A5	96
Bethalto, Il., U.S.	E3	106
Bethanien, Nmb.	D2	56
Bethany, Ct., U.S.	D4	100
Bethany, Il., U.S.	D5	106
Bethany, Mo., U.S.	A3	118
Bethany, Ok., U.S.	B4	129
Bethany, W.V., U.S.	A4	141
Bethany Beach, De., U.S.	F5	101
Bethel, Ak., U.S.	C7	95
Bethel, Ct., U.S.	D2	100
Bethel, Me., U.S.	D2	112
Bethel, N.C., U.S.	B5	126
Bethel, Oh., U.S.	D1	128
Bethel, Vt., U.S.	D3	138
Bethel Park, Pa., U.S.	k14	131
Bethel Springs, Tn., U.S.	B3	135
Bethesda, Md., U.S.	C3	113
Bethesda, Oh., U.S.	B4	128
Bethlehem, S. Afr.	D4	56
Bethlehem, Ct., U.S.	C3	100
Bethlehem, N.H., U.S.	B3	122
Bethlehem, Pa., U.S.	E11	131
Bethlehem see Bayt Laḥm, W.B.	G6	44
Bethulie, S. Afr.	E4	56
Betong, Malay.	C4	36
Betong, Thai.	E4	34
Betoota, Austl.	F3	62
Betpak-Dala, des., Kaz.	E8	26
Betroka, Madag.	C8	56
Betsiboka, stm., Madag.	B8	56
Betsie, Point, c., Mi., U.S.	D4	115
Betsy Layne, Ky., U.S.	C7	110
Bettendorf, Ia., U.S.	C7	108
Bettiah, India	D4	40
Betūl, India	E3	40
Betwa, stm., India	D3	40
Betzdorf, Ger.	E10	12
Beulah, Co., U.S.	C6	99
Beulah, N.D., U.S.	B4	127
Beulah, Lake, l., Ms., U.S.	B3	117
Beulaville, N.C., U.S.	C5	126
Beuthen see Bytom, Pol.	D5	20
B. Everett Jordan Lake, res., N.C., U.S.	B3	126
Beverley Head, c., Nf., Can.	D2	88
Beverly, Ma., U.S.	A6	114
Beverly, N.J., U.S.	C3	123
Beverly, Oh., U.S.	C4	128
Beverly, W.V., U.S.	C5	141
Beverly Hills, Ca., U.S.	m12	98
Beverly Shores, In., U.S.	A4	107
Bexar, co., Tx., U.S.	E3	136
Bexley, Oh., U.S.	m11	128
Beya, Gui.	E3	50
Beypazarı, Tur.	B4	44
Beyşehir, Tur.	D4	44
Beyşehir Gölü, l., Tur.	D4	44
Bežeck, Russia	C6	22
Béziers, Fr.	F8	16
Bhadohi, India	D4	40
Bhadrachalam, India	F4	40
Bhadrak, India	E5	40
Bhadra Reservoir, res., India	G3	40
Bhadrāvati, India	G3	40
Bhāgalpur, India	D5	40
Bhāgīrathi see Ganges, stm., India	D5	40
Bhakkar, Pak.	D10	42
Bhaktapur, Nepal	D5	40
Bhamo, Myan.	B3	34
Bhandāra, India	E3	40
Bharatpur, India	D3	40
Bharūch, India	E2	40
Bhātpāra, India	E5	40
Bhāvnagar, India	E2	40
Bhawānipatna, India	F4	40
Bhilai, India	E4	40
Bhīlwāra, India	D2	40
Bhīma, stm., India	F3	40
Bhind, India	D3	40
Bhiwāni, India	D3	40
Bhongīr, India	F3	40
Bhopāl, India	E3	40
Bhubaneshwar, India	E5	40
Bhuj, India	E1	40
Bhusāwal, India	E3	40
Bhutan, ctry., Asia	D6	40
Bia, Mount see Bia, Phou, mtn., Laos	C4	34
Bia, Phou, mtn., Laos	C4	34
Biafra, Bight of, b., Afr.	C1	54
Biak, i., Indon.	G10	32
Biała Podlaska, Pol.	D7	20
Białogard, Pol.	B4	20
Białystok, Pol.	C7	20
Bianco, Monte (Blanc, Mont), mtn., Eur.	B1	18
Biankouma, C. Iv.	E3	50
Biaora, India	E3	40
Biaro, Pulau, i., Indon.	C7	36
Biarritz, Fr.	F6	16
Bibala, Ang.	A1	56
Bibb, co., Al., U.S.	C2	94
Bibb, co., Ga., U.S.	D3	103
Bibémi, Cam.	B2	54
Biberach an der Riss, Ger.	F11	12
Bic, P.Q., Can.	A9	90
Bic, Île du, i., P.Q., Can.	A9	90
Biche, Lac la, l., Ab., Can.	B4	84
Bicknell, In., U.S.	G3	107
Bīd, India	F3	40
Bida, Nig.	E6	50
Bīdar, India	F3	40
Biddeford, Me., U.S.	E2	112
Bidwell, Mount, mtn., Ca., U.S.	B3	98
Biel, Switz.	A1	18
Bielefeld, Ger.	E11	12
Biella, Italy	B2	18
Bielsko-Biała, Pol.	E5	20
Bielsk Podlaski, Pol.	C7	20
Bien Hoa, Viet.	D5	34
Bienville, co., La., U.S.	B2	111
Bienville, Lac, l., P.Q., Can.	g12	90
Big, stm., Mo., U.S.	c7	118
Biga, Tur.	B2	44
Big Bald, mtn., Ga., U.S.	B2	103
Big Bald Mountain, mtn., N.B., Can.	B3	87
Big Baldy, mtn., Id., U.S.	E3	105
Big Baldy Mountain, mtn., Mt., U.S.	D6	119
Big Bay De Noc, b., Mi., U.S.	C4	115
Big Bear City, Ca., U.S.	E5	98
Big Belt Mountains, mts., Mt., U.S.	D5	119
Big Bend, Wi., U.S.	n11	142
Big Bend Dam, S.D., U.S.	C6	134
Big Bend National Park, Tx., U.S.	E1	136
Big Birch Lake, l., Mn., U.S.	E4	116
Big Black, stm., Me., U.S.	B3	112
Big Black, stm., Ms., U.S.	C3	117
Big Blue, stm., In., U.S.	E6	107
Big Burro Mountains, mts., N.M., U.S.	E1	124
Big Cabin Creek, stm., Ok., U.S.	A6	129
Big Coal, stm., W.V., U.S.	C3	141
Big Costilla Peak, mtn., N.M., U.S.	A4	124
Big Creek, stm., Tn., U.S.	e8	135
Big Creek Lake, res., Al., U.S.	E1	94
Big Creek Peak, mtn., Id., U.S.	E5	105
Big Cypress Indian Reservation, Fl., U.S.	F5	102
Big Cypress Swamp, sw., Fl., U.S.	F5	102
Big Darby Creek, stm., Oh., U.S.	C2	128
Big Delta, Ak., U.S.	C10	95
Big Duke Dam, N.C., U.S.	B2	126
Big Eau Pleine, stm., Wi., U.S.	D3	142
Big Eau Pleine Reservoir, res., Wi., U.S.	D4	142
Big Escambia Creek, stm., U.S.	D2	94
Big Flats, N.Y., U.S.	C4	125
Bigfork, Mt., U.S.	B2	119
Big Fork, stm., Mn., U.S.	B5	116
Biggs, Ca., U.S.	C3	98
Big Hatchet Peak, mtn., N.M., U.S.	F1	124
Big Hole, stm., Mt., U.S.	E4	119
Big Hole National Battlefield, hist., Mt., U.S.	E3	119
Big Horn, co., Mt., U.S.	E9	119
Big Horn, co., Wy., U.S.	B4	143
Bighorn Canyon National Recreation Area, U.S.	F8	119
Bighorn Lake, res., U.S.	E8	119
Big Horn Mountains, mts., Az., U.S.	D2	96
Bighorn Mountains, mts., U.S.	C6	92
Bighorn Mountains, mts., U.S.	B5	143
Bight, Head of, b., Austl.	G5	60
Big Kandiyohi Lake, l., Mn., U.S.	F4	116
Big Lake, Mn., U.S.	E5	116
Big Lake, Tx., U.S.	D2	136
Big Lake, l., Me., U.S.	C5	112
Biglerville, Pa., U.S.	G7	131
Big Lookout Mountain, mtn., Or., U.S.	C9	130
Big Lost, stm., Id., U.S.	F5	105
Big Mossy Point, c., Mb., Can.	C2	86
Big Mountain, mtn., Nv., U.S.	B2	121
Big Muddy, stm., Il., U.S.	F4	106
Big Nemaha, stm., Ne., U.S.	D10	120
Bignona, Sen.	D1	50

Name	Map Ref.	Page

Big Otter, stm., Va., U.S. — C3 — 139
Big Pine Lake, l., Mn., U.S. — D3 — 116
Big Pine Mountain, mtn., Ca., U.S. — E4 — 98
Big Piney, Wy., U.S. — D2 — 143
Big Piney, stm., Mo., U.S. — D5 — 118
Bigpoint, Ms., U.S. — E5 — 117
Big Rapids, Mi., U.S. — E5 — 115
Big Rib, stm., Wi., U.S. — C3 — 142
Big River, Sk., Can. — D2 — 91
Big Sable Point, c., Mi., U.S. — D4 — 115
Big Sandy, Mt., U.S. — B6 — 119
Big Sandy, Tx., U.S. — C5 — 136
Big Sandy, stm., Az., U.S. — C2 — 96
Big Sandy, stm., Tn., U.S. — B3 — 135
Big Sandy, stm., Wy., U.S. — D3 — 143
Big Sandy, stm., U.S. — C2 — 141
Big Sandy Creek, stm., W.V., U.S. — C3 — 141
Big Sandy Lake, l., Mn., U.S. — D5 — 116
Big Sandy Reservoir, res., Wy., U.S. — D3 — 143
Big Sheep Mountain, mtn., Mt., U.S. — C11 — 119
Big Sioux, stm., U.S. — E9 — 134
Big Smoky Valley, val., Nv., U.S. — E4 — 121
Big Snowy Mountains, mts., Mt., U.S. — D7 — 119
Big Southern Butte, mtn., Id., U.S. — F5 — 105
Big South Fork, stm., Ky., U.S. — k13 — 110
Big Spring, Tx., U.S. — C2 — 136
Big Stone, co., Mn., U.S. — E2 — 116
Big Stone City, S.D., U.S. — B9 — 134
Big Stone Gap, Va., U.S. — f9 — 139
Big Stone Lake, l., U.S. — E2 — 116
Big Sunflower, stm., Ms., U.S. — B3 — 117
Big Thompson, stm., Co., U.S. — A5 — 99
Big Timber, Mt., U.S. — E7 — 119
Big Trout Lake, l., On., Can. — n17 — 89
Big Walnut Creek, stm., Oh., U.S. — m11 — 128
Big Wood, stm., Id., U.S. — F4 — 105
Bihać, Bos. — B5 — 18
Bihar, India — D5 — 40
Bihār, prov., India — E5 — 40
Biharamulo, Tan. — D6 — 54
Bijagós, Arquipélago dos, is., Gui.-B. — D1 — 50
Bijāpur, India — F3 — 40
Bījār, Iran — E12 — 44
Bijeljina, Bos. — B7 — 18
Bijie, China — F9 — 28
Bijsk, Russia — D10 — 26
Bīkāner, India — D2 — 40
Bikar, atoll, Marsh. Is. — C10 — 58
Bikeqi, China — C10 — 28
Bikin, Russia — B14 — 28
Bikini, atoll, Marsh. Is. — C10 — 58
Bīkkū Bīttī, mtn., Libya — F8 — 48
Bikoro, D.R.C. — D3 — 54
Bilāspur, India — C3 — 40
Bilāspur, India — E4 — 40
Biläsuvar, Azer. — C13 — 44
Bila Tserkva, Ukr. — E11 — 20
Bilauktaung Range, mts., Asia — D3 — 34
Bilbao, Spain — F5 — 16
Bilecik, Tur. — B4 — 44
Bilgoraj, Pol. — D7 — 20
Bili, D.R.C. — C5 — 54
Bilhorod-Dnistrovs'kyi, Ukr. — F11 — 20
Bilk Creek Mountains, mts., Nv., U.S. — B3 — 121
Billerica, Ma., U.S. — A5 — 114
Billings, Mo., U.S. — D4 — 118
Billings, Mt., U.S. — E8 — 119
Billings, co., N.D., U.S. — B2 — 127
Billings Heights, Mt., U.S. — E8 — 119
Bill Williams, stm., Az., U.S. — C1 — 96
Bill Williams Mountain, mtn., Az., U.S. — B3 — 96
Bilma, Niger — C7 — 50
Bilohirs'k, Ukr. — D13 — 20
Bilopillia, Ukr. — D13 — 20
Biloxi, Ms., U.S. — E5 — 117
Biloxi, stm., Ms., U.S. — E4 — 117
Biloxi Bay, b., Ms., U.S. — f8 — 117
Biltmore Forest, N.C., U.S. — f10 — 126
Bimbo, C.A.R. — C3 — 54
Bimini Islands, is., Bah. — C9 — 76
Bīna-Etāwa, India — E3 — 40
Bindura, Zimb. — B5 — 56
Binga, D.R.C. — C4 — 54
Binga, Monte, mtn., Afr. — B5 — 56
Bingamon Creek, stm., W.V., U.S. — k10 — 141
Bingara, Austl. — F5 — 62
Bingen, Wa., U.S. — D4 — 140
Binger, Ok., U.S. — B3 — 129
Bingham, Me., U.S. — C3 — 112
Bingham, co., Id., U.S. — F6 — 105
Binghamton, N.Y., U.S. — C5 — 125
Bingöl, Tur. — C9 — 44
Binhai, China — E12 — 28
Binh Son, Viet. — C5 — 34
Binjai, Indon. — C1 — 36
Binongko, Pulau, i., Indon. — E6 — 36
Bintan, Pulau, i., Indon. — C2 — 36
Bintimani, mtn., S.L. — E2 — 50
Bintuhan, Indon. — D2 — 36

Bintulu, Malay. — C4 — 36
Bintuni, Indon. — D8 — 36
Binxian, China — B4 — 30
Binyang, China — B5 — 34
Bin-Yauri, Nig. — D5 — 50
Binzert see Bizerte, Tun. — C6 — 48
Biobío, stm., Chile — F3 — 72
Bioko, i., Eq. Gui. — C1 — 54
Birāk, Libya — E7 — 48
Bi'r al Wa'r, Libya — F7 — 48
Birao, C.A.R. — A4 — 54
Birch, stm., W.V., U.S. — C4 — 141
Birch Island, i., Mb., Can. — C2 — 86
Birch Lake, l., Mn., U.S. — C7 — 116
Birch River, Mb., Can. — C1 — 86
Birch Run, Mi., U.S. — E7 — 115
Birchy Bay, Nf., Can. — D4 — 88
Bird Creek, stm., Ok., U.S. — A6 — 129
Bird Island, Mn., U.S. — F4 — 116
Bird Island, i., N.C., U.S. — D4 — 126
Birdsboro, Pa., U.S. — F10 — 131
Birdum, Austl. — D5 — 60
Birecik, Tur. — D8 — 44
Birigui, Braz. — F1 — 74
Birmingham, Eng., U.K. — D6 — 12
Birmingham, Al., U.S. — B3 — 94
Birmingham, Mi., U.S. — F7 — 115
Birmitrapur, India — E4 — 40
Bīrjand, Iran — D7 — 42
Birnin-Kebbi, Nig. — D5 — 50
Birnin Konni, Niger — D6 — 50
Birnin Kudu, Nig. — D6 — 50
Birobidžan, Russia — E15 — 26
Biron, Wi., U.S. — D4 — 142
Birsk, Russia — C10 — 22
Birtle, Mb., Can. — D1 — 86
Biržai, Lith. — H11 — 10
Bisbee, Az., U.S. — F6 — 96
Biscay, Bay of (Gascogne, Golfe de), b., Eur. — E5 — 16
Biscayne, Key, i., Fl., U.S. — s13 — 102
Biscayne Bay, b., Fl., U.S. — G6 — 102
Biscayne National Monument, Fl., U.S. — G6 — 102
Biscayne Park, Fl., U.S. — s13 — 102
Biscoe, N.C., U.S. — B3 — 126
Bishkek see Biškek, Kyrg. — E9 — 26
Bishop, Ca., U.S. — D4 — 98
Bishop, Tx., U.S. — F4 — 136
Bishop's Falls, Nf., Can. — D4 — 88
Bishopville, S.C., U.S. — C7 — 133
Biškek, Kyrg. — E9 — 26
Bislig, Phil. — D8 — 34
Bismarck, Il., U.S. — C6 — 106
Bismarck, Mo., U.S. — D7 — 118
Bismarck, N.D., U.S. — C5 — 127
Bismarck Archipelago, is., Pap. N. Gui. — G12 — 32
Bismarck Range, mts., Pap. N. Gui. — H11 — 32
Bismarck Sea, Pap. N. Gui. — G12 — 32
Bismil, Tur. — D9 — 44
Bison Peak, mtn., Co., U.S. — B5 — 99
Bissau, Gui.-B. — D1 — 50
Bissikrima, Gui. — D2 — 50
Bistineau, Lake, res., La., U.S. — B2 — 111
Bistrița, Rom. — F8 — 20
Bitam, Gabon — C2 — 54
Bitlis, Tur. — C10 — 44
Bitola, Mac. — D8 — 18
Bitou, Burkina — D4 — 50
Bitterfontein, S. Afr. — E2 — 56
Bitter Creek, stm., Wy., U.S. — E4 — 143
Bitter Lake, l., S.D., U.S. — B8 — 134
Bitterroot, stm., Mt., U.S. — D2 — 119
Bitterroot Range, mts., U.S. — B4 — 92
Bitterroot Range, mts., U.S. — B3 — 105
Bitung, Indon. — C7 — 36
Biu, Nig. — D7 — 50
Biwabik, Mn., U.S. — C6 — 116
Biwa-ko, l., Japan — C3 — 31
Bixby, Ok., U.S. — B6 — 129
Biyang, China — C3 — 30
Bizerte, Tun. — C6 — 48
Bjala, Bul. — C10 — 18
Bjarèzina, stm., Bela. — C10 — 20
Bjelovar, Cro. — B6 — 18
Bjørnøya, i., Nor. — B3 — 26
Bla, Mali — D3 — 50
Black, stm., Asia — B4 — 34
Black, stm., Ar., U.S. — B4 — 97
Black, stm., Az., U.S. — D5 — 96
Black, stm., La., U.S. — C4 — 111
Black, stm., Mi., U.S. — E8 — 115
Black, stm., N.C., U.S. — C4 — 126
Black, stm., N.Y., U.S. — B4 — 125
Black, stm., S.C., U.S. — D8 — 133
Black, stm., Vt., U.S. — E3 — 138
Black, stm., Wi., U.S. — D3 — 142
Black Bear Creek, stm., Ok., U.S. — A4 — 129
Blackbeard Island, i., Ga., U.S. — E5 — 103
Blackburn, Mount, mtn., Ak., U.S. — C11 — 95
Black Butte Lake, res., Ca., U.S. — C2 — 98
Black Canyon, val., Co., U.S. — C3 — 99
Black Canyon City, Az., U.S. — C3 — 96

Black Canyon of the Gunnison National Monument, Co., U.S. — C3 — 99
Black Creek, B.C., Can. — E5 — 85
Black Creek, Wi., U.S. — D5 — 142
Black Creek, stm., S.C., U.S. — B7 — 133
Black Creek, stm., U.S. — B1 — 124
Black Diamond, Ab., Can. — D3 — 84
Black Diamond, Wa., U.S. — B4 — 140
Blackduck, Mn., U.S. — C4 — 116
Black Eagle, Mt., U.S. — C5 — 119
Black Earth, Wi., U.S. — E4 — 142
Blackfalds, Ab., Can. — C4 — 84
Blackfeet Indian Reservation, Mt., U.S. — B4 — 119
Blackfoot, Id., U.S. — F6 — 105
Blackfoot, stm., Mt., U.S. — C3 — 119
Blackfoot Mountains, mts., Id., U.S. — F7 — 105
Blackfoot Reservoir, res., Id., U.S. — G7 — 105
Blackford, co., In., U.S. — D7 — 107
Black Forest, Co., U.S. — C6 — 99
Black Forest see Schwarzwald, mts., Ger. — F11 — 12
Blackhall Mountain, mtn., Wy., U.S. — E6 — 143
Black Hawk, S.D., U.S. — C2 — 134
Black Hawk, co., Ia., U.S. — B5 — 108
Black Hills, mts., U.S. — C2 — 134
Blackjack Mountain, mtn., Ga., U.S. — h8 — 103
Black Lake, P.Q., Can. — C6 — 90
Black Lake, l., Mi., U.S. — C6 — 115
Black Lake, l., N.Y., U.S. — f9 — 125
Black Lick, Pa., U.S. — F3 — 131
Black Mingo Creek, stm., S.C., U.S. — D9 — 133
Blackmore, Mount, mtn., Mt., U.S. — E6 — 119
Black Mountain, N.C., U.S. — f10 — 126
Black Mountain, mtn., Az., U.S. — E4 — 96
Black Mountain, mtn., Co., U.S. — A5 — 99
Black Mountain, mtn., Id., U.S. — C3 — 105
Black Mountain, mtn., Mt., U.S. — D4 — 119
Black Mountain, mtn., Or., U.S. — B7 — 130
Black Mountain, mtn., Wy., U.S. — B5 — 143
Black Mountain, mtn., Wy., U.S. — D7 — 143
Black Mountain, mtn., U.S. — D7 — 110
Black Mountains, mts., Az., U.S. — B1 — 96
Black Peak, mtn., Az., U.S. — C1 — 96
Black Pine Peak, mtn., Id., U.S. — G5 — 105
Blackpool, Eng., U.K. — D5 — 12
Black Range, mts., N.M., U.S. — D2 — 124
Black River Falls, Wi., U.S. — D3 — 142
Black Rock, Ar., U.S. — A4 — 97
Black Rock, N.M., U.S. — B1 — 124
Black Rock, rock, S. Geor. — H8 — 69
Black Rock Desert, des., Nv., U.S. — B3 — 121
Black Rock Range, mts., Nv., U.S. — B3 — 121
Blacksburg, S.C., U.S. — A4 — 133
Blacksburg, Va., U.S. — C2 — 139
Black Sea — F5 — 22
Blacks Fork, stm., U.S. — E3 — 143
Blackshear, Ga., U.S. — E4 — 103
Blackstone, Ma., U.S. — B4 — 114
Blackstone, Va., U.S. — C5 — 139
Blackstone, stm., R.I., U.S. — B4 — 132
Black Thunder Creek, stm., Wy., U.S. — C8 — 143
Blackville, N.B., Can. — C4 — 87
Blackville, S.C., U.S. — E5 — 133
Black Volta, stm., Afr. — D4 — 50
Blackwalnut Point, c., Md., U.S. — C5 — 113
Black Warrior, stm., Al., U.S. — C2 — 94
Blackwater, stm., Ire. — D2 — 12
Blackwater, stm., Fl., U.S. — u15 — 102
Blackwater, stm., Md., U.S. — D5 — 113
Blackwater, stm., N.H., U.S. — D3 — 122
Blackwater, stm., Va., U.S. — D6 — 139
Blackwater Reservoir, res., N.H., U.S. — D3 — 122
Blackwell, Ok., U.S. — A4 — 129
Blackwood, N.J., U.S. — D2 — 123
Bladen, co., N.C., U.S. — C4 — 126
Bladenboro, N.C., U.S. — C4 — 126
Bladensburg, Md., U.S. — f9 — 113
Blades, De., U.S. — F3 — 101
Blagoevgrad, Bul. — D9 — 18
Blagoveščensk, Russia — D14 — 26
Blaine, Me., U.S. — B5 — 112
Blaine, Mn., U.S. — m12 — 116
Blaine, Tn., U.S. — C10 — 135
Blaine, Wa., U.S. — A3 — 140
Blaine, co., Id., U.S. — F4 — 105
Blaine, co., Mt., U.S. — B7 — 119
Blaine, co., Ne., U.S. — C6 — 120
Blaine, co., Ok., U.S. — B3 — 129

Blaine Lake, Sk., Can. — E2 — 91
Blair, Ne., U.S. — C9 — 120
Blair, Ok., U.S. — C2 — 129
Blair, W.V., U.S. — n12 — 141
Blair, Wi., U.S. — D2 — 142
Blair, co., Pa., U.S. — E5 — 131
Blairstown, Ia., U.S. — C5 — 108
Blairsville, Pa., U.S. — F3 — 131
Blake Island, i., Wa., U.S. — e11 — 140
Blakely, Ga., U.S. — E2 — 103
Blakely, Pa., U.S. — m18 — 131
Blake Plateau — E6 — 66
Blake Point, c., Mi., U.S. — h10 — 115
Blanc, Cap see Nouâdhibou, Râs, c., Afr. — B1 — 50
Blanc, Mont (Bianco, Monte), mtn., Eur. — B1 — 18
Blanca Peak, mtn., Co., U.S. — D5 — 99
Blanchard, La., U.S. — B2 — 111
Blanchard, Ok., U.S. — B4 — 129
Blanchard, stm., Oh., U.S. — A1 — 128
Blanchardville, Wi., U.S. — F4 — 142
Blanchester, Oh., U.S. — C2 — 128
Blanco, Tx., U.S. — D3 — 136
Blanco, co., Tx., U.S. — D3 — 136
Blanco, Cape, c., Or., U.S. — E2 — 130
Bland, Mo., U.S. — C6 — 118
Bland, co., Va., U.S. — C1 — 139
Blanding, Ut., U.S. — F6 — 137
Blandinsville, Il., U.S. — C3 — 106
Blanquilla, Isla, i., Ven. — C7 — 80
Blantyre, Mwi. — B5 — 56
Blasdell, N.Y., U.S. — C2 — 125
Blawnox, Pa., U.S. — k14 — 131
Bleckley, co., Ga., U.S. — D3 — 103
Bledsoe, co., Tn., U.S. — D8 — 135
Blekinge, hist. reg., Swe. — H6 — 10
Blende, Co., U.S. — C6 — 99
Blenheim, On., Can. — E3 — 89
Blenheim, N.Z. — p13 — 63c
Blennerhassett, W.V., U.S. — B3 — 141
Blind, stm., La., U.S. — h10 — 111
Blind River, On., Can. — A2 — 89
Blissfield, Mi., U.S. — G7 — 115
Blitar, Indon. — E4 — 36
Block Island, R.I., U.S. — h7 — 132
Block Island, i., R.I., U.S. — h7 — 132
Block Island Sound, strt., U.S. — G2 — 132
Bloemfontein, S. Afr. — E4 — 56
Bloemhof, S. Afr. — D4 — 56
Blois, Fr. — D7 — 16
Blommestein Meer see Brokopondo Stuwmeer, res., Sur. — C8 — 70
Blönduós, Ice. — l18 — 10a
Blood Mountain, mtn., Ga., U.S. — B3 — 103
Bloodsworth Island, i., Md., U.S. — D5 — 113
Bloodvein, stm., Can. — D3 — 86
Bloomer, Wi., U.S. — C2 — 142
Bloomfield, On., Can. — D7 — 89
Bloomfield, Ct., U.S. — B5 — 100
Bloomfield, Ia., U.S. — D5 — 108
Bloomfield, In., U.S. — F4 — 107
Bloomfield, Ky., U.S. — C4 — 110
Bloomfield, Mo., U.S. — E8 — 118
Bloomfield, N.J., U.S. — h8 — 123
Bloomfield, N.M., U.S. — A2 — 124
Bloomfield Hills, Mi., U.S. — o15 — 115
Bloomingdale, Ga., U.S. — D5 — 103
Bloomingdale, Il., U.S. — k8 — 106
Bloomingdale, N.J., U.S. — A4 — 123
Bloomingdale, Tn., U.S. — C11 — 135
Blooming Prairie, Mn., U.S. — G5 — 116
Bloomington, Il., U.S. — C4 — 106
Bloomington, In., U.S. — F4 — 107
Bloomington, Mn., U.S. — F5 — 116
Bloomington, Tx., U.S. — E4 — 136
Bloomington, Wi., U.S. — F3 — 142
Bloomington, Lake, res., Il., U.S. — C5 — 106
Bloomsburg, Pa., U.S. — E9 — 131
Bloomville, Oh., U.S. — A2 — 128
Blossburg, Pa., U.S. — C7 — 131
Blossom, Tx., U.S. — C5 — 136
Blount, co., Al., U.S. — B3 — 94
Blount, co., Tn., U.S. — D10 — 135
Blountstown, Fl., U.S. — B1 — 102
Blountsville, Al., U.S. — A3 — 94
Blountville, Tn., U.S. — C11 — 135
Blowing Rock, N.C., U.S. — A1 — 126
Blue, stm., Co., U.S. — B4 — 99
Blue, stm., In., U.S. — H5 — 107
Blue, stm., Mo., U.S. — k10 — 118
Blue, stm., Ok., U.S. — C5 — 129
Blue Ash, Oh., U.S. — o13 — 128
Blue Buck Point, c., La., — E2 — 111
Blue Creek, W.V., U.S. — m13 — 141
Blue Creek, stm., W.V., U.S. — m13 — 141
Blue Cypress Lake, l., Fl., U.S. — E6 — 102
Blue Diamond, Nv., U.S. — G6 — 121
Blue Earth, Mn., U.S. — G4 — 116
Blue Earth, co., Mn., U.S. — G4 — 116
Blue Earth, stm., Mn., U.S. — G4 — 116
Bluefield, Va., U.S. — C1 — 139
Bluefield, W.V., U.S. — D3 — 141
Bluefields, Nic. — C3 — 80
Blue Grass, Ia., U.S. — C7 — 108
Blue Hill, Me., U.S. — D4 — 112

Blue Hill, Ne., U.S. — D7 — 120
Blue Hill Range, hills, Ma., U.S. — h11 — 114
Blue Hills, Ct., U.S. — B5 — 100
Blue Hills, Il., U.S. — B6 — 106
Bluejoint Lake, l., Or., U.S. — E7 — 130
Blue Lake, Ca., U.S. — B2 — 98
Blue Mesa Reservoir, res., Co., U.S. — C3 — 99
Blue Mound, Il., U.S. — D4 — 106
Blue Mound, Ms., U.S. — A4 — 117
Blue Mountain, mtn., Mt., U.S. — C12 — 119
Blue Mountain, mtn., N.M., U.S. — D2 — 124
Blue Mountain, mtn., Pa., U.S. — F6 — 131
Blue Mountain Lake, res., Ar., U.S. — B2 — 97
Blue Mountain Peak, mtn., Jam. — E4 — 80
Blue Mountains, mts., U.S. — B4 — 92
Blue Nile, stm., Afr. — H11 — 48
Blue Point, Me., U.S. — g7 — 112
Blue Rapids, Ks., U.S. — C7 — 109
Blue Ridge, Va., U.S. — C3 — 139
Blue Ridge, mts., U.S. — D11 — 92
Blue Ridge Summit, Pa., U.S. — G7 — 131
Blue Springs, Mo., U.S. — h11 — 118
Bluestone, stm., W.V., U.S. — D3 — 141
Bluestone Lake, res., W.V., U.S. — D4 — 141
Bluewell, W.V., U.S. — D3 — 141
Bluff, N.Z. — q12 — 63c
Bluff City, Tn., U.S. — C11 — 135
Bluff Creek, stm., Ok., U.S. — A4 — 129
Bluff Lake, res., Ms., U.S. — B5 — 117
Bluff Park, Al., U.S. — g7 — 94
Bluffs, Il., U.S. — D3 — 106
Bluffton, In., U.S. — C7 — 107
Bluffton, Oh., U.S. — B2 — 128
Bluffton, S.C., U.S. — G6 — 133
Blumenau, Braz. — D8 — 72
Bly, Or., U.S. — E5 — 130
Blying Sound, strt., Ak., U.S. — h17 — 95
Blyth, On., Can. — D3 — 89
Blythe, Ca., U.S. — F6 — 98
Blytheville, Ar., U.S. — B6 — 97
Bo, S.L. — E2 — 50
Boaco, Nic. — C2 — 80
Boa Esperança, Represa, res., Braz. — E11 — 70
Boalsburg, Pa., U.S. — E6 — 131
Boardman, Oh., U.S. — A5 — 128
Boardman, Or., U.S. — B7 — 130
Boa Vista, Braz. — C7 — 70
Boa Vista, i., C.V. — g10 — 50a
Boaz, Al., U.S. — A3 — 94
Bobai, China — E2 — 30
Bobaomby, Tanjona, c., Madag. — A8 — 56
Bobbili, India — F4 — 40
Bobcaygeon, On., Can. — C6 — 89
Bobo-Dioulasso, Burkina — D4 — 50
Bobonong, Bots. — C4 — 56
Bobrov, Russia — D16 — 20
Bobrynets', Ukr. — E12 — 20
Bobtown, Pa., U.S. — G2 — 131
Boby, mtn., Madag. — C8 — 56
Boca Chica Key, i., Fl., U.S. — H5 — 102
Boca Ciega Bay, b., Fl., U.S. — p10 — 102
Boca do Acre, Braz. — E6 — 70
Boca Grande, Fl., U.S. — F4 — 102
Bocaiúva, Braz. — E3 — 74
Bocaranga, C.A.R. — B3 — 54
Boca Raton, Fl., U.S. — F6 — 102
Bocas del Toro, Pan. — D3 — 80
Bochnia, Pol. — E6 — 20
Bochum, Ger. — E10 — 12
Boconó, Ven. — D5 — 80
Bocşa, Rom. — G6 — 20
Bodajbo, Russia — D13 — 26
Bodega Head, c., Ca., U.S. — C2 — 98
Bodélé, reg., Chad — C8 — 50
Boden, Swe. — D9 — 10
Bodhan, India — F3 — 40
Bodie Island, i., N.C., U.S. — B7 — 126
Bodkin Point, c., Md., U.S. — B5 — 113
Bodø, Nor. — C6 — 10
Bodrum, Tur. — D2 — 44
Boende, D.R.C. — D4 — 54
Boerne, Tx., U.S. — E3 — 136
Boeuf, stm., La., U.S. — C4 — 111
Boeuf, Lake, l., La., U.S. — k10 — 111
Boffa, Gui. — D2 — 50
Bogale, Myan. — C3 — 34
Bogalusa, La., U.S. — D6 — 111
Bogangolo, C.A.R. — B3 — 54
Bogart, Ga., U.S. — C3 — 103
Bogata, Tx., U.S. — C5 — 136
Boğazlıyan, Tur. — C6 — 44
Bogda Shan, mts., China — C5 — 28
Boger City, N.C., U.S. — B1 — 126
Bogo, Phil. — D8 — 34
Bogor, Indon. — E3 — 36
Bogorodsk, Russia — C15 — 20
Bogotá, Col. — C5 — 70
Bogota, N.J., U.S. — h8 — 123
Bogué, Maur. — C2 — 50
Bogue Chitto, Ms., U.S. — D3 — 117
Bogue Chitto, stm., U.S. — D5 — 111
Bogue Inlet, b., N.C., U.S. — C5 — 126
Bogue Phalia, stm., Ms., U.S. — B3 — 117
Bo Hai, b., China — D11 — 28

Name	Map Ref.	Page
Bohai Haixia, strt., China	D12	28
Bohemia, hist. reg., Czech Rep.	E3	20
Bohodukhiv, Ukr.	D13	20
Bohol, i., Phil.	E8	34
Bohol Sea, Phil.	E8	34
Bohuslav, Ukr.	E11	20
Boiling Springs, N.C., U.S.	B1	126
Boiling Springs, Pa., U.S.	F7	131
Bois Blanc Island, i., Mi., U.S.	C6	115
Bois Brule, stm., Wi., U.S.	B2	142
Boischâtel, P.Q., Can.	C6	90
Bois-des-Filion, P.Q., Can.	p19	90
Bois de Sioux, stm., Mn., U.S.	E2	116
Boise, Id., U.S.	F2	105
Boise, co., Id., U.S.	F3	105
Boise City, Ok., U.S.	e8	129
Boissevain, Mb., Can.	E1	86
Boissevain, Va., U.S.	e10	139
Boistfort Peak, mtn., Wa., U.S.	C2	140
Bojeador, Cape, c., Phil.	C8	34
Bojnūrd, Iran	C7	42
Boké, Gui.	D2	50
Boknafjorden, strt., Nor.	G1	10
Boko, Congo	D2	54
Bokoro, Chad	D8	50
Bokungu, D.R.C.	D4	54
Bolama, Gui.-B.	D1	50
Bolbec, Fr.	C7	16
Bole, Ghana	E4	50
Bolesławiec, Pol.	D3	20
Boley, Ok., U.S.	B5	129
Bolgatanga, Ghana	D4	50
Bolhov, Russia	C14	20
Boli, China	B14	30
Bolingbrook, Il., U.S.	k8	106
Bolivar, Mo., U.S.	D4	118
Bolivar, Oh., U.S.	B4	128
Bolivar, Tn., U.S.	B3	135
Bolivar, W.V., U.S.	B7	141
Bolivar, co., Ms., U.S.	B3	117
Bolívar, Cerro, mtn., Ven.	B6	70
Bolivar, Lake, l., Ms., U.S.	B3	117
Bolívar, Pico, mtn., Ven.	B5	70
Bolivia, ctry., S.A.	G7	70
Bollinger, co., Mo., U.S.	D7	118
Bollnäs, Swe.	F7	10
Bolnisi, Geor.	B11	44
Bolobo, D.R.C.	D3	54
Bologna, Italy	B3	18
Bologoe, Russia	C5	22
Bolomba, D.R.C.	C3	54
Bol'šaja Murta, Russia	D11	26
Bolsena, Lago di, l., Italy	C3	18
Bol'šereck, Russia	D17	26
Bol'ševik, ostrov, i., Russia	B12	26
Bol'šezemel'skaja Tundra, reg., Russia	A9	22
Bol'šoj Begičev, ostrov, i., Russia	B13	26
Bol'šoj Enisej, stm., Russia	A7	28
Bol'šoj Kamen', Russia	B2	31
Bol'šoj Ljahovskij, ostrov, i., Russia	B16	26
Bolton, Eng., U.K.	D5	12
Bolton, Ms., U.S.	C3	117
Bolton Lakes, l., Ct., U.S.	B6	100
Bolton Landing, N.Y., U.S.	B7	125
Bolu, Tur.	B4	44
Bolvadin, Tur.	C4	44
Bolzano, Italy	A3	18
Boma, D.R.C.	E2	54
Bombay see Mumbai, India	F2	40
Bombay Hook Island, i., De., U.S.	C4	101
Bomberai, Semenanjung, pen., Indon.	D8	36
Bom Despacho, Braz.	B8	72
Bomdila, India	D6	40
Bom Jesus da Lapa, Braz.	D3	74
Bomongo, D.R.C.	C3	54
Bomoseen, Lake, l., Vt., U.S.	D2	138
Bomu, stm., Afr.	C4	54
Bon, Cap, c., Tun.	C7	48
Bon Accord, Ab., Can.	C4	84
Bon Air, Va., U.S.	C5	139
Bonaire, Ga., U.S.	D3	103
Bonaire, i., Neth. Ant.	C6	80
Bonanza Peak, mtn., Wa., U.S.	A5	140
Bonasila Dome, mtn., Ak., U.S.	C7	95
Bonaventure, P.Q., Can.	A4	87
Bonavista, Nf., Can.	D5	88
Bonavista, Cape, c., Nf., Can.	D5	88
Bonavista Bay, b., Nf., Can.	D5	88
Bond, co., Il., U.S.	E4	106
Bondo, D.R.C.	C4	54
Bondo, D.R.C.	D4	54
Bondoukou, C. Iv.	E4	50
Bondsville, Ma., U.S.	B3	114
Bonduel, Wi., U.S.	D5	142
Bondurant, Ia., U.S.	C4	108
Bône see Annaba, Alg.	C6	48
Bone, Gulf of see Bone, Teluk, b., Indon.	D6	36
Bone, Teluk, b., Indon.	D6	36
Bone Lake, l., Wi., U.S.	C1	142
Bongandanga, D.R.C.	C4	54
Bongka, Indon.	D6	36
Bongo, Massif des, mts., C.A.R.	B4	54
Bongor, Chad	D8	50
Bonham, Tx., U.S.	C4	136
Bonifacio, Strait of, strt., Eur.	D2	18
Bonifay, Fl., U.S.	u16	102
Bonin Islands see Ogasawara-guntō, is., Japan	F16	64
Bonita Springs, Fl., U.S.	F5	102
Bonkoukou, Niger	D5	50
Bonn, Ger.	E10	12
Bonneauville, Pa., U.S.	G7	131
Bonne Bay, b., Nf., Can.	D3	88
Bonner, co., Id., U.S.	A2	105
Bonners Ferry, Id., U.S.	A2	105
Bonner Springs, Ks., U.S.	C9	109
Bonnet Carre Floodway, La., U.S.	h11	111
Bonne Terre, Mo., U.S.	D7	118
Bonneville, co., Id., U.S.	F7	105
Bonneville Dam, U.S.	B4	130
Bonneville Peak, mtn., Id., U.S.	F6	105
Bonneville Salt Flats, pl., Ut., U.S.	C2	137
Bonney Lake, Wa., U.S.	B3	140
Bonnie Doone, N.C., U.S.	B4	126
Bonnie Rock, Austl.	F3	60
Bonny, Nig.	F6	50
Bonny Reservoir, res., Co., U.S.	B8	99
Bonnyville, Ab., Can.	B5	84
Bono, Ar., U.S.	B5	97
Bon Secour, Al., U.S.	E2	94
Bonthe, S.L.	E2	50
Bontoc, Phil.	C8	34
Booker, Tx., U.S.	A2	136
Booker T. Washington National Monument, Va., U.S.	C3	139
Boola, Gui.	E3	50
Boolaloo, Austl.	E2	60
Boomer, W.V., U.S.	C3	141
Boone, Ia., U.S.	B4	108
Boone, N.C., U.S.	A1	126
Boone, co., Ar., U.S.	A3	97
Boone, co., Ia., U.S.	B3	108
Boone, co., Il., U.S.	A5	106
Boone, co., In., U.S.	D4	107
Boone, co., Ky., U.S.	B5	110
Boone, co., Mo., U.S.	B5	118
Boone, co., Ne., U.S.	C7	120
Boone, co., W.V., U.S.	C3	141
Boone, stm., Ia., U.S.	B4	108
Boone Lake, res., Tn., U.S.	C11	135
Booneville, Ar., U.S.	B2	97
Booneville, Ms., U.S.	A5	117
Boonsboro, Md., U.S.	A2	113
Boonton, N.J., U.S.	B4	123
Boonville, In., U.S.	H3	107
Boonville, Mo., U.S.	C5	118
Boonville, N.C., U.S.	A2	126
Boonville, N.Y., U.S.	B5	125
Boosaaso, Som.	H14	48
Boothbay Harbor, Me., U.S.	E3	112
Boothia, Gulf of, b., N.T., Can.	D21	82
Booths Creek, stm., W.V., U.S.	h11	141
Boothville, La., U.S.	E6	111
Booué, Gabon	D2	54
Bophuthatswana, hist. reg., S. Afr.	D4	56
Bopolu, Lib.	E2	50
Bor, Sudan	I11	48
Bor, Tur.	D6	44
Bor, Yugo.	B9	18
Borah Peak, mtn., Id., U.S.	E5	105
Borås, Swe.	H5	10
Borba, Braz.	D8	72
Bordeaux, Fr.	E6	16
Borden, co., Tx., U.S.	C2	136
Bordentown, N.J., U.S.	C3	123
Bordj Bou Arreridj, Alg.	J9	48
Bordj Omar Idriss, Alg.	E6	48
Bordoy, i., Far. Is.	n23	10b
Borgarnes, Ice.	l17	10a
Borger, Tx., U.S.	B2	136
Borgholm, Swe.	H7	10
Borgne, Lake, b., La., U.S.	D6	111
Borisoglebsk, Russia	D7	22
Borken, Ger.	E10	12
Borkou, reg., Chad	C8	50
Borlänge, Swe.	F6	10
Borneo (Kalimantan), i., Asia	D4	36
Bornholm, i., Den.	I6	10
Borno, prov., Nig.	D7	50
Borogoncy, Russia	C15	26
Boromo, Burkina	D4	50
Boron, Ca., U.S.	E5	98
Borongan, Phil.	D9	34
Boroviči, Russia	C16	22
Borrego Springs, Ca., U.S.	F5	98
Borroloola, Austl.	D6	60
Borşa, Rom.	F8	20
Borūjerd, Iran	D5	42
Boryslav, Ukr.	E7	20
Boryspil', Ukr.	D11	20
Borzja, Russia	D13	26
Boržomi, Geor.	B10	44
Bosanski Novi, Bos.	B6	18
Boscobel, Wi., U.S.	E3	142
Bose, China	G9	28
Boshan, China	D11	28
Bosna, stm., Bos.	B6	18
Bosnia and Herzegovina, ctry., Eur.	B6	18
Bosnik, Indon.	G10	32
Bosobolo, D.R.C.	C3	54
Bosporus see İstanbul Boğazı, strt., Tur.	B3	44
Bosque, co., Tx., U.S.	D4	136
Bossangoa, C.A.R.	B3	54
Bossembélé, C.A.R.	B3	54
Bossentélé, C.A.R.	B3	54
Bossier, co., La., U.S.	B2	111
Bossier City, La., U.S.	B2	111
Bostān, Iran	G13	44
Bosten Hu, l., China	C5	28
Boston, Eng., U.K.	D6	12
Boston, Ga., U.S.	F3	103
Boston, Ma., U.S.	B5	114
Boston Bay, b., Ma., U.S.	B6	114
Boston Mountains, mts., U.S.	B2	97
Boswell, In., U.S.	C3	107
Boswell, Ok., U.S.	C6	129
Boswell, Pa., U.S.	F3	131
Botetourt, co., Va., U.S.	C3	139
Bothell, Wa., U.S.	B3	140
Bothnia, Gulf of, b., Eur.	F8	10
Bothwell, On., Can.	E3	89
Botkins, Oh., U.S.	B1	128
Botlih, Russia	A12	44
Botoşani, Rom.	F9	20
Botswana, ctry., Afr.	C3	56
Bottineau, N.D., U.S.	A5	127
Bottineau, co., N.D., U.S.	A4	127
Botucatu, Braz.	F2	74
Botwood, Nf., Can.	D4	88
Bouaflé, C. Iv.	E3	50
Bouaké, C. Iv.	E3	50
Bouar, C.A.R.	B3	54
Bouarfa, Mor.	E3	14
Bouca, C.A.R.	B3	54
Boucherville, P.Q., Can.	D4	90
Bouctouche, N.B., Can.	C5	87
Boudreaux, Lake, l., La., U.S.	E5	111
Bougainville, i., Pap. N. Gui.	B6	62
Bougainville, Détroit de, strt., Vanuatu	k9	62a
Bougie see Bejaïa, Alg.	C6	48
Bougouni, Mali	D3	50
Bouïra, Alg.	C5	48
Boujdour, Cap, c., W. Sah.	A2	50
Boulder, Co., U.S.	A5	99
Boulder, Mt., U.S.	D4	119
Boulder, co., Co., U.S.	A5	99
Boulder City, Nv., U.S.	H7	121
Boulevard Heights, Md., U.S.	f9	113
Boulia, Austl.	E2	62
Boulogne-sur-Mer, Fr.	B7	16
Boulsa, Burkina	D4	50
Bouna, C. Iv.	E4	50
Boundary, co., Id., U.S.	A2	105
Boundary Bay, b., Wa., U.S.	A3	140
Boundary Peak, mtn., Nv., U.S.	F3	121
Bound Brook, N.J., U.S.	B3	123
Boundiali, C. Iv.	E3	50
Bountiful, Ut., U.S.	C4	137
Bounty Islands, is., N.Z.	M21	64
Bounty Trough	M20	64
Bourail, N. Cal.	l9	62a
Bourbeuse, stm., Mo., U.S.	C6	118
Bourbon, In., U.S.	B5	107
Bourbon, Mo., U.S.	C6	118
Bourbon, co., Ks., U.S.	E9	109
Bourbon, co., Ky., U.S.	B5	110
Bourbonnais, Il., U.S.	B6	106
Bourem, Mali	C4	50
Bourg, La., U.S.	E5	111
Bourg-en-Bresse, Fr.	D9	16
Bourges, Fr.	D8	16
Bourgogne, hist. reg., Fr.	D9	16
Bourke, Austl.	G4	62
Bournemouth, Eng., U.K.	E5	12
Bou Saâda, Alg.	C5	48
Bouse, Az., U.S.	D2	96
Bousso, Chad	D8	50
Boutilimit, Maur.	C2	50
Boutte, La., U.S.	k11	111
Bouvetøya, i., Ant.	B5	67
Bouza, Niger	D6	50
Bovey, Mn., U.S.	C5	116
Bovina, Tx., U.S.	B1	136
Bow, N.H., U.S.	D3	122
Bow, stm., Ab., Can.	D4	84
Bowden, Ab., Can.	D4	84
Bowdish Reservoir, res., R.I., U.S.	B1	132
Bowdon, Ga., U.S.	C1	103
Bowen, Arg.	F4	72
Bowen, Austl.	D9	62
Bowie, Az., U.S.	E6	96
Bowie, Md., U.S.	C4	113
Bowie, Tx., U.S.	C4	136
Bowie, co., Tx., U.S.	C5	136
Bow Island, Ab., Can.	E5	84
Bow Lake, l., N.H., U.S.	D4	122
Bowling Green, Fl., U.S.	E5	102
Bowling Green, Ky., U.S.	D3	110
Bowling Green, Mo., U.S.	B6	118
Bowling Green, Oh., U.S.	A2	128
Bowling Green, S.C., U.S.	A5	133
Bowling Green, Va., U.S.	B5	139
Bowling Green, Cape, c., Austl.	D4	62
Bowman, Ga., U.S.	B3	103
Bowman, N.D., U.S.	C2	127
Bowman, S.C., U.S.	E6	133
Bowman, co., N.D., U.S.	C2	127
Bowman Creek, stm., Pa., U.S.	m16	131
Bowman-Haley Lake, res., N.D., U.S.	C2	127
Bowral, Austl.	G5	62
Bowron, stm., B.C., Can.	C7	85
Bowstring Lake, l., Mn., U.S.	C5	116
Boxboro, Ma., U.S.	A6	114
Boxing, China	B4	30
Boyabat, Tur.	B6	44
Boyang, China	D4	30
Boyce, La., U.S.	C3	111
Boyceville, Wi., U.S.	C1	142
Boyd, Tx., U.S.	C4	136
Boyd, co., Ky., U.S.	B7	110
Boyd, co., Ne., U.S.	B7	120
Boyden, Ia., U.S.	A2	108
Boyd Lake, l., Me., U.S.	C4	112
Boyer, stm., Ia., U.S.	C2	108
Boyertown, Pa., U.S.	F10	131
Boykins, Va., U.S.	D5	139
Boyle, Ab., Can.	B4	84
Boyle, Ms., U.S.	B3	117
Boyle, co., Ky., U.S.	C5	110
Boyne City, Mi., U.S.	C6	115
Boynton Beach, Fl., U.S.	F6	102
Boyoma Falls see Stanley Falls, wtfl., D.R.C.	C5	54
Boysen Reservoir, res., Wy., U.S.	C4	143
Boys Town, Ne., U.S.	g12	120
Bozeman, Mt., U.S.	E5	119
Bozeman Pass, Mt., U.S.	E6	119
Bozhen, China	D11	28
Bozhou, China	C4	30
Bozova, Tur.	D8	44
Bozüyük, Tur.	C3	44
Bra, Italy	B1	18
Bracebridge, On., Can.	B5	89
Bräcke, Swe.	E6	10
Bracken, co., Ky., U.S.	B5	110
Brackenridge, Pa., U.S.	h15	131
Brackettville, Tx., U.S.	E2	136
Brad, Rom.	F7	20
Braddock, Pa., U.S.	k14	131
Braddock Heights, Md., U.S.	B2	113
Braddock Point, c., S.C., U.S.	G6	133
Bradenton, Fl., U.S.	E4	102
Bradenville, Pa., U.S.	F3	131
Bradford, Eng., U.K.	D5	12
Bradford, Ar., U.S.	B4	97
Bradford, Oh., U.S.	B1	128
Bradford, Pa., U.S.	C4	131
Bradford, R.I., U.S.	F2	132
Bradford, Tn., U.S.	A3	135
Bradford, Vt., U.S.	D4	138
Bradford, co., Fl., U.S.	C4	102
Bradford, co., Pa., U.S.	C8	131
Bradford [West Gwillimbury], On., Can.	C5	89
Bradfordwoods, Pa., U.S.	h13	131
Bradley, Il., U.S.	B6	106
Bradley, Me., U.S.	D4	112
Bradley, W.V., U.S.	D3	141
Bradley, co., Ar., U.S.	D3	97
Bradley, co., Tn., U.S.	D9	135
Bradley Beach, N.J., U.S.	C4	123
Bradner, Oh., U.S.	A2	128
Bradshaw, Md., U.S.	B5	113
Bradshaw Mountains, mts., Az., U.S.	C3	96
Brady, Tx., U.S.	D3	136
Braga, Port.	G2	16
Bragado, Arg.	F5	72
Bragança, Braz.	B2	74
Bragança, Port.	G3	16
Brahmanbaria, Bngl.	E6	40
Brahmapur, India	F4	40
Brahmaputra (Yarlung), stm., Asia	D6	40
Braidwood, Il., U.S.	B5	106
Brăila, Rom.	G9	20
Brainerd, Mn., U.S.	D4	116
Braintree, Ma., U.S.	B5	114
Brampton, On., Can.	D5	89
Bramwell, W.V., U.S.	D3	141
Branch, co., Mi., U.S.	G5	115
Branch, stm., R.I., U.S.	B3	132
Branch, stm., Wi., U.S.	h10	142
Branch Lake, l., Me., U.S.	D4	112
Branch Village, R.I., U.S.	B3	132
Branchville, S.C., U.S.	E6	133
Brandon, Mb., Can.	E2	86
Brandon, Fl., U.S.	E4	102
Brandon, Ms., U.S.	C4	117
Brandon, S.C., U.S.	B3	133
Brandon, S.D., U.S.	D9	134
Brandon, Vt., U.S.	D2	138
Brandon, Wi., U.S.	E5	142
Brandvlei, S. Afr.	E3	56
Brandy Peak, mtn., Or., U.S.	E3	130
Brandywine, Md., U.S.	C4	113
Brandywine Creek, stm., U.S.	A3	101
Branford, Ct., U.S.	D4	100
Branford Hills, Ct., U.S.	D4	100
Branson, Mo., U.S.	E4	118
Brantford, On., Can.	D4	89
Brantley, Al., U.S.	D3	94
Brantley, co., Ga., U.S.	E4	103
Brant Rock, Ma., U.S.	B6	114
Brantville, N.B., Can.	B5	87
Bras d'Or Lake, l., N.S., Can.	D9	87
Brasil, ctry., S.A.	D2	74
Brasiléia, Braz.	F6	70
Brasília, Braz.	E2	74
Braşov, Rom.	G8	20
Brasstown Bald, mtn., Ga., U.S.	B3	103
Brassua Lake, res., Me., U.S.	C3	112
Bratenahl, Oh., U.S.	g9	128
Bratislava, Slvk.	E4	20
Bratsk, Russia	D12	26
Bratskoe vodohranilišče, res., Russia	D12	26
Bratsk Reservoir see Bratskoe vodohranilišče, res., Russia	D12	26
Brattleboro, Vt., U.S.	F3	138
Braunau am Inn, Aus.	F13	12
Braunschweig, Ger.	D12	12
Brava, i., C.V.	h10	50a
Bravo (Rio Grande), stm., N.A.	B5	78
Brawley, Ca., U.S.	F6	98
Brawley Peaks, mts., Nv., U.S.	E3	121
Braxton, co., W.V., U.S.	C4	141
Bray, Ok., U.S.	C4	129
Braymer, Mo., U.S.	B4	118
Brazeau, stm., Ab., Can.	C2	84
Brazil, In., U.S.	E3	107
Brazil, ctry., S.A.	D5	68
Brazil Basin	J11	66
Brazoria, Tx., U.S.	r14	136
Brazoria, co., Tx., U.S.	E5	136
Brazos, co., Tx., U.S.	D4	136
Brazos, stm., Tx., U.S.	D4	136
Brazzaville, Congo	D3	54
Brčko, Bos.	B7	18
Brea, Ca., U.S.	n13	98
Breakenridge, Mount, mtn., B.C., Can.	E7	85
Breathitt, co., Ky., U.S.	C6	110
Breaux Bridge, La., U.S.	D4	111
Breckenridge, Co., U.S.	B4	99
Breckenridge, Mi., U.S.	E6	115
Breckenridge, Mn., U.S.	D2	116
Breckenridge, Tx., U.S.	C3	136
Breckinridge, co., Ky., U.S.	C3	110
Brecksville, Oh., U.S.	A4	128
Břeclav, Czech Rep.	E4	20
Breda, Neth.	E9	12
Bredasdorp, S. Afr.	E3	56
Bredy, Russia	D11	22
Breese, Il., U.S.	E4	106
Breiðafjörður, b., Ice.	l17	10a
Brejo, Braz.	D10	74
Bremen, Ger.	D11	12
Bremen, Ga., U.S.	C1	103
Bremen, In., U.S.	B5	107
Bremen, Oh., U.S.	C3	128
Bremer, co., Ia., U.S.	B5	108
Bremer Bay, Austl.	G2	60
Bremerhaven, Ger.	D11	12
Bremerton, Wa., U.S.	B3	140
Bremond, Tx., U.S.	D4	136
Brenham, Tx., U.S.	D4	136
Brenner Pass, Eur.	A3	18
Brent, Al., U.S.	C2	94
Brent, Fl., U.S.	u14	102
Brenton Point, c., R.I., U.S.	F5	132
Brentwood, Ca., U.S.	h9	98
Brentwood, Md., U.S.	f9	113
Brentwood, Mo., U.S.	f13	118
Brentwood, N.Y., U.S.	E7	125
Brentwood, Pa., U.S.	k14	131
Brentwood, S.C., U.S.	k11	133
Brentwood, Tn., U.S.	A5	135
Brescia, Italy	B1	18
Breslau see Wrocław, Pol.	D4	20
Bressuire, Fr.	D6	16
Brèst, Bela.	C7	20
Brest, Fr.	C4	16
Bretagne, hist. reg., Fr.	C5	16
Breton, Pertuis, strt., Fr.	D6	16
Breton Islands, is., La., U.S.	E6	111
Breton Sound, strt., La., U.S.	E6	111
Breueh, Pulau, i., Indon.	E1	32
Brevard, N.C., U.S.	f10	126
Brevard, co., Fl., U.S.	E6	102
Breves, Braz.	B1	74
Brevoort Lake, l., Mi., U.S.	B6	115
Brewer, Me., U.S.	D4	112
Brewster, Ma., U.S.	C7	114

Name	Map Ref.	Page

Brewster, N.Y., U.S. D7 125
Brewster, Oh., U.S. B4 128
Brewster, Wa., U.S. A6 140
Brewster, co., Tx., U.S. . . . E1 136
Brewster, Kap, c., Grnld. . . D35 82
Brewster Islands, is., Ma.,
    U.S. g12 114
Brewton, Al., U.S. D2 94
Brezhnev see Naberežnye
    Čelny, Russia D7 26
Bria, C.A.R. B4 54
Brian Boru Peak, mtn., B.C.,
    Can. B4 85
Brian Head, mtn., Ut., U.S. F3 137
Briceville, Tn., U.S. C9 135
Brick [Township], N.J., U.S. C4 123
Bridal Veil Falls, wtfl, Ut.,
    U.S. C4 137
Bridgehampton, N.Y., U.S. . n16 125
Bridgeport, Al., U.S. A4 94
Bridgeport, Ct., U.S. E3 100
Bridgeport, Il., U.S. E6 106
Bridgeport, Mi., U.S. E7 115
Bridgeport, Ne., U.S. C2 120
Bridgeport, Oh., U.S. B5 128
Bridgeport, Pa., U.S. o20 131
Bridgeport, Tx., U.S. C4 136
Bridgeport, W.V., U.S. B4 141
Bridgeport, Wa., U.S. B6 140
Bridger, Mt., U.S. E8 119
Bridger Peak, mtn., Wy.,
    U.S. E5 143
Bridger Range, mts., Mt.,
    U.S. E6 119
Bridgeton, Mo., U.S. C7 118
Bridgeton, N.J., U.S. E2 123
Bridgetown, Austl. G2 60
Bridgetown, Barb. C7 80
Bridgetown, N.S., Can. E4 87
Bridgeville, De., U.S. F3 101
Bridgeville, Pa., U.S. k13 131
Bridgewater, Ma., U.S. C6 114
Bridgewater, N.J., U.S. B3 123
Bridgewater, Va., U.S. B4 139
Bridgman, Mi., U.S. G4 115
Bridgton, Me., U.S. D2 112
Bridgwater, Eng., U.K. E5 12
Bridlington, Eng., U.K. C6 12
Brielle, N.J., U.S. C4 123
Brigantine, N.J., U.S. E4 123
Brigantine Beach, N.J., U.S. E4 123
Brigden, On., Can. E2 89
Briggs Marsh, sw., R.I., U.S. F6 132
Brigham City, Ut., U.S. B3 137
Bright, Austl. H4 62
Brighton, On., Can. C7 89
Brighton, Eng., U.K. E6 12
Brighton, Al., U.S. B3 94
Brighton, Co., U.S. B6 99
Brighton, Ia., U.S. C6 108
Brighton, Il., U.S. D3 106
Brighton, Mi., U.S. F7 115
Brighton, N.Y., U.S. B3 125
Brighton, Tn., U.S. B2 135
Brighton Indian Reservation,
    Fl., U.S. E5 102
Brikama, Gam. D1 50
Brilliant, Al., U.S. A2 94
Brilliant, Oh., U.S. B5 128
Brillion, Wi., U.S. D5 142
Brimfield, Il., U.S. C4 106
Brindisi, Italy D6 18
Brinkley, Ar., U.S. C4 97
Brinnon, Wa., U.S. B3 140
Brisbane, Austl. F5 62
Briscoe, co., Tx., U.S. B2 136
Bristol, N.B., Can. C2 87
Bristol, Eng., U.K. E5 12
Bristol, Ct., U.S. C4 100
Bristol, In., U.S. A6 107
Bristol, N.H., U.S. C3 122
Bristol, R.I., U.S. D5 132
Bristol, Tn., U.S. C11 135
Bristol, Va., U.S. f9 139
Bristol, Vt., U.S. C2 138
Bristol, co., Ma., U.S. C5 114
Bristol, co., R.I., U.S. D5 132
Bristol Bay, b., Ak., U.S. . . D7 95
Bristol Channel, strt., U.K. E5 12
Bristol [Township], Pa., U.S. F12 131
Bristow, Ok., U.S. B5 129
British Columbia, prov.,
    Can. C6 85
British Guiana see Guyana,
    ctry., S.A. B8 70
British Honduras see Belize,
    ctry., N.A. B2 80
British Indian Ocean
    Territory, dep., Afr. . . . I10 64
British Isles, is., Eur. C12 4
British Virgin Islands, dep.,
    N.A. E12 76
Britstown, S. Afr. E3 56
Britt, Ia., U.S. A4 108
Brittany see Bretagne, hist.
    reg., Fr. C5 16
Britton, S.D., U.S. B8 134
Brive-la-Gaillarde, Fr. E7 16
Brjansk, Russia D5 26
Brjuhoveckaja, Russia G15 20
Brno, Czech Rep. E4 20
Broad, stm., S.C., U.S. C5 133
Broad Brook, Ct., U.S. B5 100
Broadkill, stm., De., U.S. . . E4 101
Broadkill Beach, De., U.S. . E5 101

Broad Run, stm., Va., U.S. . g11 139
Broad Sound, b., Austl. . . . E4 62
Broadus, Mt., U.S. E11 119
Broadview Heights, Oh.,
    U.S. h9 128
Broadwater, co., Mt., U.S. . D5 119
Broadway, N.C., U.S. B3 126
Broadway, Va., U.S. B4 139
Brockman, Mount, mtn.,
    Austl. E2 60
Brockport, N.Y., U.S. B3 125
Brockton, Ma., U.S. B5 114
Brockton Reservoir, res.,
    Ma., U.S. h11 114
Brockville, On., Can. C9 89
Brockway, Pa., U.S. D4 131
Brodhead, Ky., U.S. C5 110
Brodhead, Wi., U.S. F4 142
Brodheadsville, Pa., U.S. . . E11 131
Brodnica, Pol. C5 20
Brody, Ukr. D8 20
Broken Arrow, Ok., U.S. . . . A6 129
Broken Bow, Ne., U.S. C6 120
Broken Bow, Ok., U.S. C7 129
Broken Bow Lake, res., Ok.,
    U.S. C7 129
Broken Hill, Austl. G3 62
Broken Hill see Kabwe,
    Zam. A4 56
Broken Ridge L12 64
Brokopondo, Sur. C8 70
Brokopondo Stuwmeer,
    res., Sur. C8 70
Brome, Lac, l., P.Q., Can. . . D5 90
Bromley Plateau K10 66
Bromptonville, P.Q., Can. . . D6 90
Bronson, Mi., U.S. G5 115
Bronx, N.Y., U.S. E7 125
Bronxville, N.Y., U.S. h13 125
Brook, In., U.S. C3 107
Brooke, co., W.V., U.S. A4 141
Brookfield, N.S., Can. D6 87
Brookfield, Ct., U.S. D2 100
Brookfield, Il., U.S. k9 106
Brookfield, Mo., U.S. B4 118
Brookfield, Wi., U.S. m11 142
Brookfield Center, Ct., U.S. D2 100
Brookhaven, Ms., U.S. D3 117
Brookhaven, W.V., U.S. h11 141
Brookings, Or., U.S. E2 130
Brookings, S.D., U.S. C9 134
Brookings, co., S.D., U.S. . . C9 134
Brookland, Ar., U.S. B5 97
Brooklandville, Md., U.S. . . g10 113
Brooklet, Ga., U.S. D5 103
Brookline, Ma., U.S. B5 114
Brooklyn, N.S., Can. E5 87
Brooklyn, Ct., U.S. B8 100
Brooklyn, Ia., U.S. C5 108
Brooklyn, In., U.S. E5 107
Brooklyn, Mi., U.S. F6 115
Brooklyn, Ms., U.S. D4 117
Brooklyn, Oh., U.S. h9 128
Brooklyn, S.C., U.S. B6 133
Brooklyn, Wi., U.S. F4 142
Brooklyn Center, Mn., U.S. E5 116
Brooklyn Park, Md., U.S. . . h11 113
Brooklyn Park, Mn., U.S. . . m12 116
Brookneal, Va., U.S. C4 139
Brook Park, Oh., U.S. h9 128
Brookport, Il., U.S. F5 106
Brooks, Ab., Can. D5 84
Brooks, Ky., U.S. g11 110
Brooks, co., Ga., U.S. F3 103
Brooks, co., Tx., U.S. F3 136
Brooks Air Force Base, mil.,
    Tx., U.S. k7 136
Brookshire, Tx., U.S. E5 136
Brookside, Al., U.S. f7 94
Brookside, De., U.S. B3 101
Brooks Range, mts., Ak.,
    U.S. B9 95
Brookston, In., U.S. C4 107
Brooksville, Fl., U.S. D4 102
Brooksville, Ky., U.S. B5 110
Brooksville, Ms., U.S. B5 117
Brookville, In., U.S. F8 107
Brookville, Oh., U.S. C1 128
Brookville, Pa., U.S. D3 131
Brookville Lake, res., In.,
    U.S. E7 107
Brookwood, Al., U.S. B2 94
Brookwood, N.J., U.S. C4 123
Broomall, Pa., U.S. p20 131
Broome, Austl. D3 60
Broome, co., N.Y., U.S. C5 125
Broomfield, Co., U.S. B5 99
Brossard, P.Q., Can. q20 90
Broussard, La., U.S. D4 111
Browerville, Mn., U.S. D4 116
Brown, co., Il., U.S. D3 106
Brown, co., In., U.S. F5 107
Brown, co., Ks., U.S. C8 109
Brown, co., Mn., U.S. F4 116
Brown, co., Ne., U.S. B6 120
Brown, co., Oh., U.S. D2 128
Brown, co., S.D., U.S. B7 134
Brown, co., Tx., U.S. D3 136
Brown, co., Wi., U.S. D6 142
Brown, Point, c., Wa., U.S. . C1 140
Brown City, Mi., U.S. E8 115
Brown Deer, Wi., U.S. m12 142
Brownfield, Tx., U.S. C1 136
Browning, Mt., U.S. B3 119

Brownlee Dam, U.S. E2 105
Brownlee Reservoir, res.,
    U.S. C10 130
Browns, stm., Vt., U.S. B2 138
Browns Branch, stm., De.,
    U.S. E3 101
Brownsburg, P.Q., Can. . . . D3 90
Brownsburg, In., U.S. E5 107
Brownsdale, Mn., U.S. G6 116
Browns Inlet, b., N.C., U.S. C5 126
Browns Mills, N.J., U.S. . . . D3 123
Browns Peak, mtn., Az.,
    U.S. D4 96
Brownstown, In., U.S. G5 107
Browns Valley, Mn., U.S. . . E2 116
Brownsville, Fl., U.S. s13 102
Brownsville, Ky., U.S. C3 110
Brownsville, Or., U.S. C4 130
Brownsville, Pa., U.S. F2 131
Brownsville, Tn., U.S. B2 135
Brownsville, Tx., U.S. G4 136
Brownton, Mn., U.S. F4 116
Brownville Junction, Me.,
    U.S. C3 112
Brownwood, Tx., U.S. D3 136
Brownwood, Lake, res., Tx.,
    U.S. D3 136
Broxton, Ga., U.S. E4 103
Bruce, Ms., U.S. B4 117
Bruce, Wi., U.S. C2 142
Bruce, Mount, mtn., Austl. E2 60
Bruce National Park, On.,
    Can. B3 89
Bruce Peninsula, pen., On.,
    Can. B3 89
Bruce Rock, Austl. G2 60
Bruceton, Tn., U.S. A3 135
Bruderheim, Ab., Can. C4 84
Bruin Point, mtn., Ut., U.S. D5 137
Brule, co., S.D., U.S. D6 134
Brule, stm., U.S. C5 142
Brule Lake, l., Mn., U.S. . . . k9 116
Brumado, Braz. D3 74
Brundidge, Al., U.S. D4 94
Bruneau, stm., U.S. G3 105
Brunei see Bandar Seri
    Begawan, Bru. C4 36
Brunei, ctry., Asia F6 34
Bruno, Sk., Can. E3 91
Brunswick see
    Braunschweig, Ger. . . . D12 12
Brunswick, Ga., U.S. E5 103
Brunswick, Md., U.S. B2 113
Brunswick, Me., U.S. E3 112
Brunswick, Mo., U.S. B4 118
Brunswick, Oh., U.S. A4 128
Brunswick, co., N.C., U.S. . C4 126
Brunswick, co., Va., U.S. . . D5 139
Brunswick, Península, pen.,
    Chile H2 69
Brunswick Naval Air Station,
    mil., Me., U.S. E3 112
Brush, Co., U.S. A7 99
Brushy Mountains, mts.,
    N.C., U.S. B1 126
Brusly, La., U.S. D4 111
Brusque, Braz. D8 72
Brussels see Bruxelles, Bel. E9 12
Brussels, On., Can. D3 89
Bruxelles (Brussels), Bel. . . E9 12
Bryan, Oh., U.S. A1 128
Bryan, Tx., U.S. D4 136
Bryan, co., Ga., U.S. D5 103
Bryan, co., Ok., U.S. D5 129
Bryans Road, Md., U.S. . . . C3 113
Bryant, Ar., U.S. C3 97
Bryantville, Ma., U.S. B6 114
Bryce Canyon National
    Park, rec., Ut., U.S. . . . F3 137
Bryn Mawr, Wa., U.S. e11 140
Bryson City, N.C., U.S. f9 126
Brzeg, Pol. D4 20
Bua Yai, Thai. C4 34
Bu'ayrat al-Hasun, Libya . . B2 14
Bubaque, Gui.-B. D1 50
Bucak, Tur. D4 44
Bucaramanga, Col. B5 70
Buccaneer Archipelago, is.,
    Austl. D3 60
Buchanan, Lib. E2 50
Buchanan, Ga., U.S. C1 103
Buchanan, Mi., U.S. G4 115
Buchanan, Va., U.S. C3 139
Buchanan, co., Ia., U.S. . . . B6 108
Buchanan, co., Mo., U.S. . . B3 118
Buchanan, co., Va., U.S. . . . e9 139
Buchans, Nf., Can. D3 88
Bucharest see București,
    Rom. G9 20
Buckatunna, Ms., U.S. D5 117
Buckeye, Az., U.S. D3 96
Buckeye Lake, Oh., U.S. . . . C3 128
Buckhannon, W.V., U.S. . . . C4 141
Buck Hill Falls, Pa., U.S. . . D11 131
Buckhorn Lake, res., Ky.,
    U.S. C6 110
Buckingham, P.Q., Can. . . . D2 90
Buckingham, co., Va., U.S. C4 139
Buckley, Wa., U.S. B3 140
Bucklin, Ks., U.S. E4 109
Bucklin, Mo., U.S. B5 118
Buck Mountain, mtn., Wa.,
    U.S. A6 140
Buckner, Mo., U.S. h11 118

Bucks, co., Pa., U.S. F11 131
Buckskin Mountains, mts.,
    Az., U.S. C2 96
Bucksport, Me., U.S. D4 112
Bucksport, S.C., U.S. D9 133
Buco Zau, Ang. D2 54
București (Bucharest), Rom. G9 20
Bucyrus, Oh., U.S. B3 128
Buda, Tx., U.S. D4 136
Budapest, Hung. F5 20
Budaun, India D3 40
Budd Lake, l., N.J., U.S. . . . B3 123
Bude, Ms., U.S. D3 117
Budënnovsk, Russia B4 42
Búðir, Ice. I21 10a
Budjala, D.R.C. C3 54
Buea, Cam. C1 54
Buechel, Ky., U.S. B4 110
Buena, N.J., U.S. D3 123
Buena, Wa., U.S. C5 140
Buena Esperanza, Arg. E4 72
Buena Park, Ca., U.S. n12 98
Buenaventura, Col. C4 70
Buenaventura, Mex. B3 78
Buena Vista, Co., U.S. C4 99
Buena Vista, Fl., U.S. D4 102
Buena Vista, Ga., U.S. D2 103
Buena Vista, Va., U.S. C3 139
Buena Vista, co., Ia., U.S. . B2 108
Buenos Aires, Arg. E6 72
Buffalo, Ia., U.S. C7 108
Buffalo, Mn., U.S. E5 116
Buffalo, Mo., U.S. D4 118
Buffalo, N.Y., U.S. C2 125
Buffalo, Ok., U.S. A2 129
Buffalo, S.C., U.S. B4 133
Buffalo, Tx., U.S. D5 136
Buffalo, W.V., U.S. C3 141
Buffalo, Wi., U.S. D2 142
Buffalo, Wy., U.S. B6 143
Buffalo, co., Ne., U.S. D6 120
Buffalo, co., S.D., U.S. C6 134
Buffalo, co., Wi., U.S. D2 142
Buffalo, stm., Ar., U.S. B3 97
Buffalo, stm., Mn., U.S. . . . D2 116
Buffalo, stm., Tn., U.S. B4 135
Buffalo, stm., Wi., U.S. D2 142
Buffalo Bill Reservoir, res.,
    Wy., U.S. B3 143
Buffalo Center, Ia., U.S. . . . A4 108
Buffalo Creek, stm., W.V.,
    U.S. h10 141
Buffalo Creek, stm., W.V.,
    U.S. n12 141
Buffalo Creek, stm., W.V. . . f8 141
Buffalo Grove, Il., U.S. h9 106
Buffalo Lake, Mn., U.S. . . . F4 116
Buffalo Lake, l., Ab., Can. . C4 84
Buffalo Lake, res., Tx., U.S. B1 136
Buffalo Lake, res., Wi., U.S. E4 142
Buffumville Lake, res., Ma.,
    U.S. B4 114
Buford, Ga., U.S. B2 103
Bug, stm., Eur. C6 20
Buga, Col. C4 70
Bugsuk Island, i., Phil. E7 34
Bugt, China B12 28
Bugul'ma, Russia D9 22
Buguruslan, Russia D9 22
Buhara, Uzb. F8 26
Buhl, Id., U.S. G4 105
Buhl, Mn., U.S. C6 116
Buhler, Ks., U.S. D6 109
Buies Creek, N.C., U.S. . . . B4 126
Buitepos, Nmb. C2 56
Buj, Russia C7 22
Bujnaksk, Russia A12 31
Bujumbura, Bdi. D5 54
Bukačača, Russia D13 26
Bukama, D.R.C. E5 54
Bukavu, D.R.C. C5 54
Bukeya, D.R.C. F5 54
Būkān, Iran D12 44
Bukittinggi, Indon. D2 36
Bukoba, Tan. D6 54
Bula, Indon. D8 36
Bulan, Phil. D8 34
Bulan, Ky., U.S. C6 110
Bulancak, Tur. B8 44
Bulandshahr, India D3 40
Bulanık, Tur. C10 44
Bulawayo, Zimb. C4 56
Buldan, Tur. C3 44
Bulgan, Mong. B8 28
Bulgaria, ctry., Eur. C10 18
Bulkley, stm., B.C., Can. . . B4 85
Bullaxaar, Som. A8 54
Bull Creek, stm., S.D., U.S. B2 134
Bullfinch, Austl. G2 60
Bullfrog Creek, stm., Ut.,
    U.S. F5 137
Bullhead City, Az., U.S. . . . B1 96
Bull Island, i., S.C., U.S. . . D9 133
Bull Island, i., S.C., U.S. . . F8 133
Bull Island, i., S.C., U.S. . . G6 133
Bullitt, co., Ky., U.S. C4 110
Bull Mountain, mtn., Mt.,
    U.S. D4 119
Bulloch, co., Ga., U.S. D5 103
Bullock, co., Al., U.S. C4 94
Bullock Creek, Mi., U.S. . . . E6 115
Bull Run, stm., Va., U.S. . . g11 139
Bulls Bay, b., S.C., U.S. . . . F8 133

Bulls Gap, Tn., U.S. C10 135
Bull Shoals, Ar., U.S. A3 97
Bull Shoals Lake, res., U.S. D9 92
Bull Shoals Lake, res., U.S. A3 97
Bully Creek Reservoir, res.,
    Or., U.S. C9 130
Bultfontein, S. Afr. D4 56
Bumba, D.R.C. C4 54
Bumping, stm., Wa., U.S. . . C4 140
Buna, Tx., U.S. D6 136
Bunbury, Austl. G2 60
Buncombe, co., N.C., U.S. . f10 126
Bundaberg, Austl. E5 62
Bündi, India D3 40
Bungoma, Kenya C6 54
Bungo-suidō, strt., Japan . . E14 28
Bunia, D.R.C. C6 54
Bunker Hill, Il., U.S. D4 106
Bunker Hill, In., U.S. C5 107
Bunker Hill, W.V., U.S. m12 141
Bunker Hill, mtn., Nv., U.S. D4 121
Bunkerville, Nv., U.S. G7 121
Bunkie, La., U.S. D3 111
Bunnell, Fl., U.S. C5 102
Buntok, Indon. D4 36
Bünyan, Tur. C6 44
Buolkalah, Russia B13 26
Buon Ma Thuot, Viet. D5 34
Buor-Haja, guba, b., Russia B15 26
Buqayq, Sau. Ar. E5 42
Bura, Kenya D7 54
Burang, China D4 40
Buras, La., U.S. E6 111
Buraydah, Sau. Ar. E4 38
Burbank, Ca., U.S. m12 98
Burbank, Il., U.S. k9 106
Burbank, Wa., U.S. C7 140
Burco, Som. I14 48
Burdickville, R.I., U.S. F2 132
Burdur, Tur. D4 44
Burdur Gölü, l., Tur. D4 44
Bureau, co., Il., U.S. B4 106
Bureinskij hrebet, mts.,
    Russia D15 26
Bürenhayrhan, Mong. B6 28
Burfjord, Nor. B10 10
Burgas, Bul. C11 18
Burgaski Zaliv, b., Bul. C11 18
Burgaw, N.C., U.S. C5 126
Burgeo, Nf., Can. E3 88
Burgersdorp, S. Afr. E4 56
Burgettstown, Pa., U.S. . . . F1 131
Burgin, Ky., U.S. C5 110
Burgo de Osma, Spain G5 16
Burgos, Spain F5 16
Burgundy see Bourgogne,
    hist. reg., Fr. D9 16
Burhaniye, Tur. C2 44
Burhānpur, India E3 40
Burias Island, i., Phil. D8 34
Burin, Nf., Can. E4 88
Burin Peninsula, pen., Nf.,
    Can. E4 88
Buri Ram, Thai. C4 34
Burjatija, state, Russia D13 26
Burkburnett, Tx., U.S. B3 136
Burke, S.D., U.S. D6 134
Burke, co., Ga., U.S. C4 103
Burke, co., N.C., U.S. B1 126
Burke, co., N.D., U.S. A3 127
Burke Channel, strt., B.C.,
    Can. C4 85
Burkesville, Ky., U.S. D4 110
Burketown, Austl. D2 62
Burkina Faso, ctry., Afr. . . . D4 50
Burk's Falls, On., Can. B5 89
Burleigh, co., N.D., U.S. . . . C5 127
Burleson, Tx., U.S. n9 136
Burleson, co., Tx., U.S. D4 136
Burley, Id., U.S. G5 105
Burlingame, Ca., U.S. h8 98
Burlingame, Ks., U.S. D8 109
Burlington, On., Can. D5 89
Burlington, Co., U.S. B8 99
Burlington, Ia., U.S. D6 108
Burlington, Ks., U.S. D8 109
Burlington, Ky., U.S. A5 110
Burlington, Ma., U.S. f11 114
Burlington, N.C., U.S. A3 126
Burlington, N.D., U.S. A4 127
Burlington, N.J., U.S. C3 123
Burlington, Vt., U.S. C2 138
Burlington, Wa., U.S. A3 140
Burlington, Wi., U.S. F5 142
Burlington, co., N.J., U.S. . . D3 123
Burlington Junction, Mo.,
    U.S. A2 118
Burlit, Russia A2 31
Burma see Myanmar, ctry.,
    Asia B3 34
Burnaby, B.C., Can. E6 85
Burnet, Tx., U.S. D3 136
Burnet, co., Tx., U.S. D3 136
Burnett, co., Wi., U.S. C1 142
Burney, Ca., U.S. B3 98
Burnham, Pa., U.S. E6 131
Burnie, Austl. I4 62
Burns, Or., U.S. D7 130
Burns, Tn., U.S. A4 135
Burns, Wy., U.S. E8 143
Burns Flat, Ok., U.S. B2 129
Burnside, Ky., U.S. D5 110
Burns Lake, B.C., Can. B5 85

Name	Map Ref.	Page

Burns Paiute Indian Reservation, Or., U.S. — D7 130
Burnsville, Mn., U.S. — F5 116
Burnsville, Ms., U.S. — A5 117
Burnsville, N.C., U.S. — f10 126
Burnsville Lake, res., W.V., U.S. — C4 141
Burnt Islands, Nf., Can. — E2 88
Burnt Mills, Lake, l., Va., U.S. — k14 139
Burntside Lake, l., Mn., U.S. — C6 116
Burntwood, stm., Mb., Can. — B2 86
Burra, Austl. — G2 62
Burrel, Alb. — D8 18
Burr Oak, Mi., U.S. — G5 115
Burr Oak Reservoir, res., Oh., U.S. — C3 128
Burrton, Ks., U.S. — D6 109
Bursa, Tur. — B3 44
Būr Sa'īd, Egypt — D11 48
Būr Sūdān, Sudan — G12 48
Burt, co., Ne., U.S. — C9 120
Burt Lake, l., Mi., U.S. — C6 115
Burton, Mi., U.S. — F7 115
Burton, Oh., U.S. — A4 128
Burtts Corner, N.B., Can. — C3 87
Buru, i., Indon. — D7 36
Burullus, Buheirat el-, l., Egypt — G4 44
Burundi, ctry., Afr. — D5 54
Burwell, Ne., U.S. — C6 120
Bury Saint Edmunds, Eng., U.K. — D7 12
Busanga, D.R.C. — D4 54
Bushman Land, hist. reg., S. Afr. — D2 56
Bushnell, Fl., U.S. — D4 102
Bushnell, Il., U.S. — C3 106
Bush River, b., Md., U.S. — B5 113
Busia, Ug. — C6 54
Businga, D.R.C. — C4 54
Busira, stm., D.R.C. — D3 54
Busko-Zdrój, Pol. — D6 20
Buṣrá ash-Shām, Syria — F7 44
Busselton, Austl. — G2 60
Busu-Djanoa, D.R.C. — C4 54
Buta, D.R.C. — C4 54
Butare, Rw. — D5 54
Butaritari, atoll, Kir. — D11 58
Bute Inlet, b., B.C., Can. — D5 85
Butembo, D.R.C. — C5 54
Butere, Kenya — C6 54
Buthidaung, Myan. — B2 34
Butiaba, Ug. — C6 54
Butler, Al., U.S. — C1 94
Butler, Ga., U.S. — D2 103
Butler, In., U.S. — B8 107
Butler, Ky., U.S. — B5 110
Butler, Mo., U.S. — C3 118
Butler, N.J., U.S. — B4 123
Butler, Oh., U.S. — B3 128
Butler, Pa., U.S. — E2 131
Butler, Wi., U.S. — m11 142
Butler, co., Al., U.S. — D3 94
Butler, co., Ia., U.S. — B5 108
Butler, co., Ks., U.S. — E7 109
Butler, co., Ky., U.S. — C3 110
Butler, co., Mo., U.S. — E7 118
Butler, co., Ne., U.S. — C8 120
Butler, co., Oh., U.S. — C1 128
Butler, co., Pa., U.S. — E2 131
Butner, N.C., U.S. — A4 126
Buton, Pulau, i., Indon. — D6 36
Butrint, hist., Alb. — E8 18
Buttahatchee, stm., U.S. — B5 117
Butte, Mt., U.S. — E4 119
Butte, co., Ca., U.S. — C3 98
Butte, co., Id., U.S. — F5 105
Butte, co., S.D., U.S. — C2 134
Butte des Morts, Lake, l., Wi., U.S. — D5 142
Butte Mountains, mts., Nv., U.S. — D6 121
Butternut Lake, l., Wi., U.S. — C5 142
Butterworth, Malay. — B2 36
Buttonwillow, Ca., U.S. — E4 98
Butts, co., Ga., U.S. — C3 103
Butuan, Phil. — E9 34
Buturlinovka, Russia — D16 20
Buulobarde, Som. — C9 54
Buur Gaabo, Som. — D8 54
Buxton, N.C., U.S. — B7 126
Büyük Ağrı Dağı see Ağrı Dağı, mtn., Tur. — C11 44
Büyükmenderes, stm., Tur. — D2 44
Buzuluk, Russia — D9 22
Buzzards Bay, Ma., U.S. — C6 114
Buzzards Bay, b., Ma., U.S. — C6 114
Bwendi, D.R.C. — C5 54
Bydgoszcz, Pol. — C5 20
Byelorussia see Belarus, ctry., Eur. — C9 20
Byers, Co., U.S. — B6 99
Byesville, Oh., U.S. — C4 128
Byhalia, Ms., U.S. — A4 117
Byhaŭ, Bela. — C11 20
Bylas, Az., U.S. — D5 96
Byng, Ok., U.S. — C5 129
Byrdstown, Tn., U.S. — C8 135
Byro, Austl. — F2 60
Byron, Ga., U.S. — D3 103
Byron, Il., U.S. — A4 106
Byron, Mn., U.S. — F6 116
Byron, Wy., U.S. — B4 143

Byron, Cape, c., Austl. — F5 62
Byron Bay, Austl. — F5 62
Byrranga, gory, mts., Russia — B12 26
Bytom, Pol. — D5 20
Bytów, Pol. — B4 20
Byzantium see İstanbul, Tur. — B3 44

C

Caála, Ang. — F3 54
Caatinga, Braz. — B8 72
Cabadbaran, Phil. — E9 34
Cabaiguán, Cuba — A4 80
Caballo Mountains, mts., N.M., U.S. — E2 124
Caballo Reservoir, res., N.M., U.S. — E2 124
Cabanatuan, Phil. — C8 34
Cabano, P.Q., Can. — B9 90
Cabarrus, co., N.C., U.S. — B2 126
Cabbage Swamp, sw., Fl., U.S. — m9 102
Cabedelo, Braz. — C5 74
Cabell, co., W.V., U.S. — C2 141
Cabeza del Buey, Spain — H4 16
Cabimas, Ven. — A5 70
Cabin Creek, W.V., U.S. — m13 141
Cabin Creek, stm., W.V., U.S. — m13 141
Cabinda, Ang. — E2 54
Cabinet Gorge Reservoir, res., U.S. — B1 119
Cabinet Mountains, mts., Mt., U.S. — B1 119
Cabin John, Md., U.S. — C3 113
Cabo, Braz. — C4 74
Cabo Blanco, Arg. — G3 69
Cabonga, Réservoir, res., P.Q., Can. — I24 82
Cabool, Mo., U.S. — D5 118
Caborca, Mex. — C2 78
Cabot, Ar., U.S. — C3 97
Cabot, Mount, mtn., N.H., U.S. — A4 122
Cabot Head, c., On., Can. — B3 89
Cabrayil, Azer. — C12 44
Cabri, Sk., Can. — G1 91
Cabrillo National Monument, Ca., U.S. — o15 98
Caçador, Braz. — D7 72
Čačak, Yugo. — C8 18
Caçapava do Sul, Braz. — E7 72
Cacapon, stm., W.V., U.S. — B6 141
Cáceres, Braz. — G8 70
Cáceres, Spain — H3 16
Cache, Ok., U.S. — C3 129
Cache, co., Ut., U.S. — B4 137
Cache, stm., Ar., U.S. — C5 97
Cache, stm., Il., U.S. — F4 106
Cache Bay, On., Can. — A5 89
Cache Creek, B.C., Can. — D7 85
Cache la Poudre, stm., Co., U.S. — A5 99
Cache Mountain, mtn., Ak., U.S. — B10 95
Cache Peak, mtn., Id., U.S. — G5 105
Cachimbo, Serra do, mts., Braz. — E8 70
Cachingues, Ang. — F3 54
Cachoeira do Sul, Braz. — E7 72
Cachoeiro de Itapemirim, Braz. — E8 74
Cacolo, Ang. — F3 54
Caconda, Ang. — A2 56
Cactus Flat, pl., Nv., U.S. — F5 121
Cactus Peak, mtn., Nv., U.S. — F5 121
Cacuaco, Ang. — E2 54
Caçulé, Braz. — A9 72
Čadan, Russia — D11 26
Caddo, Ok., U.S. — C5 129
Caddo, co., La., U.S. — B2 111
Caddo, co., Ok., U.S. — B3 129
Caddo, stm., Ar., U.S. — C2 97
Caddo Creek, stm., Ok., U.S. — C4 129
Caddo Lake, res., U.S. — B2 111
Cadillac, Mi., U.S. — D5 115
Cadillac Mountain, mtn., Me., U.S. — D4 112
Cadiz, Phil. — D8 34
Cádiz, Spain — I3 16
Cadiz, Ky., U.S. — D2 110
Cadiz, Oh., U.S. — B4 128
Cádiz, Golfo de, b., Eur. — I3 16
Cadiz, Gulf of see Cádiz, Golfo de, b., Eur. — I3 16
Cadott, Wi., U.S. — D2 142
Čaek, Kyrg. — A2 40
Caen, Fr. — C6 16
Caernarfon, Wales, U.K. — D4 12
Caesar Creek Lake, res., Oh., U.S. — C2 128
Caetité, Braz. — D3 74
Cagayan de Oro, Phil. — E8 34
Cagayan Islands, is., Phil. — E8 34
Cagayan Sulu Island, i., Phil. — E7 34
Čagda, Russia — D15 26
Cagles Mill Lake, res., In., U.S. — F4 107
Cagliari, Italy — E2 18
Cagliari, Golfo di, b., Italy — E2 18
Caguas, P.R. — B6 80
Cahaba, stm., Al., U.S. — C2 94
Cahama, Ang. — B1 56
Cahokia, Il., U.S. — E3 106

Cahora Bassa, Albufeira, res., Moz. — B5 56
Cahors, Fr. — E7 16
Cahul, Mol. — G10 20
Caiapó, Serra do, mts., Braz. — B7 72
Caibarién, Cuba — A4 80
Caicara de Orinoco, Ven. — D6 80
Caicó, Braz. — C4 74
Caicos Islands, is., T./C. Is. — A5 80
Caicos Passage, strt., N.A. — A5 80
Cailloma, Peru — B3 72
Caillou Bay, b., La., U.S. — E5 111
Caillou Lake, l., La., U.S. — E5 111
Caimanera, Cuba — B4 80
Cairnbrook, Pa., U.S. — F4 131
Cairns, Austl. — D4 62
Cairo see El-Qâhira, Egypt — D11 48
Cairo, Ga., U.S. — F2 103
Cairo, Il., U.S. — F4 106
Cairo, Ne., U.S. — D7 120
Caiundo, Ang. — B2 56
Cajamarca, Peru — E4 70
Cajazeiras, Braz. — C4 74
Calabar, Nig. — F6 50
Calabozo, Ven. — B6 70
Calagua Islands, is., Phil. — D8 34
Calahorra, Spain — F6 16
Calais, Fr. — B7 16
Calais, Me., U.S. — C5 112
Calama, Chile — A3 69
Calamian Group, is., Phil. — D7 34
Calamus, stm., Ne., U.S. — B6 120
Calapan, Phil. — D8 34
Călărași, Mol. — F10 20
Călăraşi, Rom. — G9 20
Calatayud, Spain — G6 16
Calaveras, co., Ca., U.S. — C3 98
Calayan Island, i., Phil. — C8 34
Calbayog, Phil. — D8 34
Calcasieu, co., La., U.S. — D2 111
Calcasieu, stm., La., U.S. — D2 111
Calcasieu Lake, l., La., U.S. — E2 111
Calcasieu Pass, strt., La., U.S. — E2 111
Calçoene, Braz. — C9 70
Calcutta, India — E5 40
Calcutta, Oh., U.S. — B5 128
Calcutta Lake, l., Nv., U.S. — B2 121
Caldas da Rainha, Port. — H2 16
Caldera, Chile — C2 69
Calderwood, Tn., U.S. — D10 135
Caldron Falls Reservoir, res., Wi., U.S. — C5 142
Caldwell, Id., U.S. — F2 105
Caldwell, Ks., U.S. — E6 109
Caldwell, N.J., U.S. — B4 123
Caldwell, Oh., U.S. — C4 128
Caldwell, Tx., U.S. — D4 136
Caldwell, co., Ky., U.S. — C2 110
Caldwell, co., La., U.S. — B3 111
Caldwell, co., Mo., U.S. — B3 118
Caldwell, co., N.C., U.S. — B1 126
Caldwell, co., Tx., U.S. — E4 136
Caledon, On., Can. — D5 89
Caledonia, Mi., U.S. — F5 115
Caledonia, Mn., U.S. — G7 116
Caledonia, Ms., U.S. — B5 117
Caledonia, N.Y., U.S. — C3 125
Caledonia, co., Vt., U.S. — C4 138
Calera, Al., U.S. — B3 94
Calera, Ok., U.S. — D5 129
Calexico, Ca., U.S. — F6 98
Calgary, Ab., Can. — D3 84
Calhoun, Ga., U.S. — B2 103
Calhoun, Ky., U.S. — C2 110
Calhoun, co., Al., U.S. — B4 94
Calhoun, co., Ar., U.S. — D3 97
Calhoun, co., Fl., U.S. — B1 102
Calhoun, co., Ga., U.S. — E2 103
Calhoun, co., Ia., U.S. — B3 108
Calhoun, co., Il., U.S. — D3 106
Calhoun, co., Mi., U.S. — F5 115
Calhoun, co., Ms., U.S. — B4 117
Calhoun, co., S.C., U.S. — D6 133
Calhoun, co., Tx., U.S. — E4 136
Calhoun, co., W.V., U.S. — C3 141
Calhoun City, Ms., U.S. — B4 117
Calhoun Falls, S.C., U.S. — C2 133
Cali, Col. — C4 70
Calico Rock, Ar., U.S. — A3 97
Calicut see Kozhikode, India — G3 40
Caliente, Nv., U.S. — F7 121
California, Mo., U.S. — C5 118
California, Pa., U.S. — F2 131
California, state, U.S. — D4 98
California, Golfo de, b., Mex. — B2 78
California, Gulf of see California, Golfo de, b., Mex. — B2 78
California Aqueduct, Ca., U.S. — E4 98
Calipatria, Ca., U.S. — F6 98
Calispell Peak, mtn., Wa., U.S. — A8 140
Calistoga, Ca., U.S. — C2 98
Callaghan, Mount, mtn., Nv., U.S. — D5 121
Callahan, co., Tx., U.S. — C3 136
Callao, Peru — F4 70
Callaway, co., Mo., U.S. — C6 118
Calling Lake, l., Ab., Can. — B4 84
Calloway, co., Ky., U.S. — f9 110
Calmar, Ab., Can. — C4 84

Calmar, Ia., U.S. — A6 108
Caloosahatchee, stm., Fl., U.S. — F5 102
Caltanissetta, Italy — F4 18
Calulo, Ang. — E2 54
Calumet, P.Q., Can. — D3 90
Calumet, Mi., U.S. — A2 115
Calumet, co., Wi., U.S. — D5 142
Calumet, Lake, l., Il., U.S. — k9 106
Calumet City, Il., U.S. — B6 106
Calunda, Ang. — F4 54
Caluula, Som. — H15 48
Calvert, Tx., U.S. — D4 136
Calvert, co., Md., U.S. — C4 113
Calvert City, Ky., U.S. — e9 110
Calverton Park, Mo., U.S. — f13 118
Calvillo, Mex. — C4 78
Calvinia, S. Afr. — E2 56
Camabatela, Ang. — E3 54
Camaçari, Braz. — D4 74
Camacupa, Ang. — F3 54
Camagüey, Cuba — A4 80
Camaná, Peru — G5 70
Camanche, Ia., U.S. — C7 108
Camano Island, i., Wa., U.S. — A3 140
Camaquã, Braz. — E7 72
Camará, Braz. — D7 70
Camargo, Bol. — C4 72
Camargue, reg., Fr. — F9 16
Camarones, Arg. — F3 69
Camas, Spain — I3 16
Camas, Wa., U.S. — D3 140
Camas, co., Id., U.S. — F4 105
Ca Mau, Viet. — E5 34
Ca Mau, Mui, c., Viet. — E4 34
Cambodia, ctry., Asia — D4 34
Cambrai, Fr. — B8 16
Cambria, Ca., U.S. — E3 98
Cambria, Wi., U.S. — E4 142
Cambria, co., Pa., U.S. — E4 131
Cambridge, On., Can. — D4 89
Cambridge, Eng., U.K. — D7 12
Cambridge, Ia., U.S. — C4 108
Cambridge, Il., U.S. — B3 106
Cambridge, Ma., U.S. — B5 114
Cambridge, Md., U.S. — C5 113
Cambridge, Mn., U.S. — E5 116
Cambridge, Ne., U.S. — D5 120
Cambridge, N.Y., U.S. — B7 125
Cambridge, Oh., U.S. — B4 128
Cambridge, Wi., U.S. — F4 142
Cambridge City, In., U.S. — E7 107
Cambridge Reservoir, res., Ma., U.S. — g10 114
Cambridge Springs, Pa., U.S. — C1 131
Cambulo, Ang. — E4 54
Cambundi-Catembo, Ang. — F3 54
Camden, Al., U.S. — D2 94
Camden, Ar., U.S. — D3 97
Camden, De., U.S. — D3 101
Camden, In., U.S. — C4 107
Camden, Me., U.S. — D3 112
Camden, N.J., U.S. — D2 123
Camden, N.Y., U.S. — B5 125
Camden, Oh., U.S. — C1 128
Camden, S.C., U.S. — C6 133
Camden, Tn., U.S. — A3 135
Camden, co., Ga., U.S. — F5 103
Camden, co., Mo., U.S. — C5 118
Camden, co., N.C., U.S. — A6 126
Camden, co., N.J., U.S. — D3 123
Camdenton, Mo., U.S. — D5 118
Camelback Mountain, mtn., Az., U.S. — k9 96
Cameron, Az., U.S. — B4 96
Cameron, La., U.S. — E2 111
Cameron, Mo., U.S. — B3 118
Cameron, Tx., U.S. — D4 136
Cameron, W.V., U.S. — B4 141
Cameron, Wi., U.S. — C2 142
Cameron, co., La., U.S. — E2 111
Cameron, co., Pa., U.S. — D5 131
Cameron, co., Tx., U.S. — F4 136
Cameron Hills, hills, Can. — G16 82
Cameroon, ctry., Afr. — J7 48
Cameroon Mountain, vol., Cam. — C1 54
Cametá, Braz. — B2 74
Çamiçi Gölü, l., Tur. — D2 44
Camiguin Island, i., Phil. — C8 34
Camiguin Island, i., Phil. — E8 34
Camilla, Ga., U.S. — E2 103
Camino, Ca., U.S. — C3 98
Camiranga, Braz. — D10 70
Camiri, Bol. — C5 72
Camissombo, Ang. — E4 54
Cammack Village, Ar., U.S. — C3 97
Camocim, Braz. — B3 74
Camooweal, Austl. — D2 62
Camorta Island, i., India — H6 40
Camotes Sea, Phil. — D8 34
Campana, Arg. — E6 72
Campbell, Fl., U.S. — D5 102
Campbell, Mo., U.S. — E7 118
Campbell, Oh., U.S. — A5 128
Campbell, co., Ky., U.S. — B5 110
Campbell, co., S.D., U.S. — B5 134
Campbell, co., Tn., U.S. — C9 135
Campbell, co., Va., U.S. — C3 139
Campbell, co., Wy., U.S. — B7 143
Campbellford, On., Can. — C7 89

Campbell Hill, hill, Oh., U.S. — B2 128
Campbell Island, i., N.Z. — J10 58
Campbell Lake, l., Or., U.S. — E7 130
Campbell Plateau — M20 64
Campbellsburg, In., U.S. — G5 107
Campbellsburg, Ky., U.S. — B4 110
Campbells Creek, stm., W.V., U.S. — m13 141
Campbellsport, Wi., U.S. — E5 142
Campbellsville, Ky., U.S. — C4 110
Campbellton, N.B., Can. — A3 87
Campbellton, Nf., Can. — D4 88
Campbelltown, Austl. — G5 62
Campbeltown, Scot., U.K. — C4 12
Campeche, Mex. — D6 78
Campeche, state, Mex. — D6 78
Campeche, Bahía de, b., Mex. — D6 78
Campeche, Gulf of see Campeche, Bahía de, b., Mex. — D6 78
Camperdown, Austl. — H3 62
Camperville, Mb., Can. — D1 86
Cam Pha, Viet. — B5 34
Camp Hill, Al., U.S. — C4 94
Camp Hill, Pa., U.S. — F8 131
Camp H. M. Smith Marine Corps Base, mil., Hi., U.S. — g10 104
Camp Howard Ridge, mtn., Id., U.S. — D2 105
Câmpina, Rom. — G8 20
Campina Grande, Braz. — C4 74
Campinas, Braz. — F2 74
Campina Verde, Braz. — E2 74
Camp Lejeune Marine Corps Base, mil., N.C., U.S. — C5 126
Campo, Cam. — C1 54
Campobasso, Italy — D5 18
Campobello Island, i., N.B., Can. — E3 87
Campo de la Cruz, Col. — C5 80
Campo Formoso, Braz. — D3 74
Campo Gallo, Arg. — D5 72
Campo Grande, Braz. — H9 70
Campo Maior, Braz. — B3 74
Campo Mourão, Braz. — F1 74
Campos, Braz. — F3 74
Campos Sales, Braz. — C3 74
Camp Pendleton Marine Corps Base, mil., Ca., U.S. — F5 98
Camp Point, Il., U.S. — C2 106
Camp Springs, Md., U.S. — f9 113
Campti, La., U.S. — C2 111
Campton, N.H., U.S. — C3 122
Câmpulung, Rom. — G8 20
Câmpulung Moldovenesc, Rom. — F8 20
Camp Verde, Az., U.S. — C4 96
Camp Verde Indian Reservation, Az., U.S. — C4 96
Cam Ranh, Viet. — D5 34
Camrose, Ab., Can. — C4 84
Çan, Tur. — B2 44
Canaan, Ct., U.S. — A2 100
Canaan, N.H., U.S. — C2 122
Canaan, stm., N.B., Can. — C4 87
Canada, ctry., N.A. — G17 82
Canada Basin — D1 144
Canada Bay, b., Nf., Can. — C3 88
Cañada de Gómez, Arg. — E5 72
Canada Falls Lake, res., Me., U.S. — C2 112
Canadensis, Pa., U.S. — D11 131
Canadian, Tx., U.S. — B2 136
Canadian, co., Ok., U.S. — B3 129
Canadian, stm., U.S. — D7 92
Canaima, Ven. — D7 80
Canajoharie, N.Y., U.S. — C6 125
Çanakkale, Tur. — B2 44
Çanakkale Boğazı (Dardanelles), strt., Tur. — C1 44
Canal Flats, B.C., Can. — D10 85
Canal Fulton, Oh., U.S. — B4 128
Canal Winchester, Oh., U.S. — C3 128
Canandaigua, N.Y., U.S. — C3 125
Canandaigua Lake, l., N.Y., U.S. — C3 125
Cananea, Mex. — A2 78
Canarias, Islas (Canary Islands), is., Spain — A1 50
Canary Basin — F10 66
Canary Islands see Canarias, Islas, is., Spain — A1 50
Cañasgordas, Col. — D4 80
Canastota, N.Y., U.S. — B5 125
Canaveral, Cape, c., Fl., U.S. — D6 102
Canaveral National Seashore, Fl., U.S. — D6 102
Canavieiras, Braz. — E4 74
Canberra, Austl. — H4 62
Canby, Mn., U.S. — F2 116
Canby, Or., U.S. — B4 130
Cancún, Mex. — C7 78
Candeias, Braz. — D4 74
Candia see Iráklion, Grc. — G10 18
Candiac, P.Q., Can. — q19 90
Candle Lake, l., Sk., Can. — D3 91
Candler, co., Ga., U.S. — D4 103
Candlewood, Lake, l., Ct., U.S. — D1 100

Name	Map Ref.	Page

Candlewood Isle, Ct., U.S. . **D2** 100
Candlewood Shores, Ct., U.S. . **D2** 100
Cando, N.D., U.S. . **A6** 127
Candor, N.C., U.S. . **B3** 126
Cane, Ia., U.S. . **C2** 111
Canelones, Ur. . **E6** 72
Caney, Ks., U.S. . **E8** 109
Caney, stm., Ok., U.S. . **A5** 129
Caney Creek, stm., Tx., U.S.**r14** 136
Caney Fork, stm., Tn., U.S. **C5** 135
Canfield, Oh., U.S. . **A5** 128
Cangas de Narcea, Spain . **F3** 16
Cangkuang, Tanjung, c., Indon. . **E3** 36
Cangombe, Ang. . **A2** 56
Canguçu, Braz. . **E7** 72
Cangumbe, Ang. . **F3** 54
Cangyuan, China . **B3** 34
Cangzhou, China . **D11** 28
Caniapiscau, stm., P.Q., Can. . **g13** 90
Canicattì, Italy . **F4** 18
Canindé, Braz. . **B4** 74
Canistear Reservoir, res., N.J., U.S. . **A4** 123
Canisteo, N.Y., U.S. . **C3** 125
Canisteo, stm., N.Y., U.S. . **C3** 125
Canistota, S.D., U.S. . **D8** 134
Çankırı, Tur. . **B5** 44
Canmore, Ab., Can. . **D5** 84
Cannanore, India . **G3** 40
Cannelton, In., U.S. . **I4** 107
Cannes, Fr. . **F10** 16
Canning, N.S., Can. . **D5** 87
Cannon, Tn., U.S. . **B5** 135
Cannon, stm., Mn., U.S. . **F5** 116
Cannon Air Force Base, mil., N.M., U.S. . **C6** 124
Cannonball, stm., N.D., U.S.**C5** 127
Cannon Beach, Or., U.S. . **B3** 130
Cannondale, Ct., U.S. . **E2** 100
Cannon Falls, Mn., U.S. . **F6** 116
Cannonsburg, Ky., U.S. . **B7** 110
Cannonsville Reservoir, res., N.Y., U.S. . **C5** 125
Canoas, Braz. . **D7** 72
Canoinhas, Braz. . **D7** 72
Canon, Ga., U.S. . **B3** 103
Canon City, Co., U.S. . **C5** 99
Canonsburg, Pa., U.S. . **F1** 131
Cantabrian Mountains see Cantábrica, Cordillera, mts., Spain . **F4** 16
Cantábrica, Cordillera, mts., Spain . **F4** 16
Cantaura, Ven. . **B7** 70
Canterbury, Eng., U.K. . **E7** 12
Canterbury, De., U.S. . **D3** 101
Canterbury Bight, b., N.Z. . **p13** 63c
Can Tho, Viet. . **E5** 34
Canton see Guangzhou, China . **E3** 30
Canton, Ct., U.S. . **B4** 100
Canton, Ga., U.S. . **B2** 103
Canton, Il., U.S. . **C3** 106
Canton, Ks., U.S. . **D6** 109
Canton, Ma., U.S. . **B5** 114
Canton, Mo., U.S. . **A6** 118
Canton, Ms., U.S. . **C3** 117
Canton, N.C., U.S. . **f10** 126
Canton, N.Y., U.S. . **f9** 125
Canton, Oh., U.S. . **B4** 128
Canton, Ok., U.S. . **A3** 129
Canton, Pa., U.S. . **C8** 131
Canton, S.D., U.S. . **D9** 134
Canton, Tx., U.S. . **C5** 136
Canton Lake, res., Ok., U.S.**A3** 129
Cantonment, Fl., U.S. . **u14** 102
Canutama, Braz. . **E6** 70
Canutillo, Tx., U.S. . **o11** 136
Čany, ozero, l., Russia . **D9** 26
Canyon, Tx., U.S. . **B2** 136
Canyon, co., Id., U.S. . **F2** 105
Canyon City, Or., U.S. . **C8** 130
Canyon de Chelly National Monument, Az., U.S. . **A6** 96
Canyon Ferry Lake, res., Mt., U.S. . **D5** 119
Canyon Lake, Tx., U.S. . **E3** 136
Canyon Lake, res., Tx., U.S. **E3** 136
Canyonlands National Park, Ut., U.S. . **E6** 137
Canyonville, Or., U.S. . **E3** 130
Cao Bang, Viet. . **B5** 34
Caoxian, China . **C4** 30
Čapac, Mi., U.S. . **F8** 115
Čapaevo, Kaz. . **D9** 22
Cap-à-l'Aigle, P.Q., Can. . **B7** 90
Capanema, Braz. . **B2** 74
Capão Bonito, Braz. . **F2** 74
Cap-aux-Meules, P.Q., Can. **B8** 87
Cap-de-la-Madeleine, P.Q., Can. . **C5** 90
Cape Barren Island, i., Austl.**I4** 62
Cape Basin . **L14** 66
Cape Breton Highlands National Park, N.S., Can. . **C9** 87
Cape Breton Island, i., N.S., Can. . **C9** 87
Cape Broyle, Nf., Can. . **E5** 88
Cape Canaveral, Fl., U.S. . **D6** 102
Cape Charles, Va., U.S. . **C6** 139
Cape Coast

Cape Cod Bay, b., Ma., U.S.**C7** 114
Cape Cod Canal, Ma., U.S. . **C6** 114
Cape Cod National Seashore, Ma., U.S. . **C7** 114
Cape Coral, Fl., U.S. . **F5** 102
Cape Elizabeth, Me., U.S. . **E2** 112
Cape Fear, stm., N.C., U.S. **C4** 126
Cape Girardeau, Mo., U.S. . **D8** 118
Cape Girardeau, co., Mo., U.S. . **D8** 118
Cape Hatteras National Seashore, N.C., U.S. . **B7** 126
Cape Horn Mountain, mtn., Id., U.S. . **E3** 105
Cape Island, i., S.C., U.S. . **E9** 133
Capelinha, Braz. . **E3** 74
Capelongo, Ang. . **A2** 56
Cape Lookout National Seashore, N.C., U.S. . **C6** 126
Cape May, N.J., U.S. . **F3** 123
Cape May, co., N.J., U.S. . **E3** 123
Cape May Court House, N.J., U.S. . **E3** 123
Capers Inlet, b., S.C., U.S. . **k12** 133
Capers Island, i., S.C., U.S. **F8** 133
Capers Island, i., S.C., U.S. **G6** 133
Cape Sable Island, i., N.S., Can. . **F4** 87
Cape Town (Kaapstad), S. Afr. . **E2** 56
Cape Verde Basin . **G10** 66
Cape Verde, ctry., Afr. . **g9** 50a
Cape York Peninsula, pen., Austl. . **C3** 62
Cap-Haïtien, Haiti . **B5** 80
Capinota, Bol. . **B4** 72
Capitan, N.M., U.S. . **D4** 124
Capitan Mountains, mts., N.M., U.S. . **D4** 124
Capitan Peak, mtn., N.M., U.S. . **D4** 124
Capitol Heights, Ia., U.S. . **e8** 108
Capitol Heights, Md., U.S. . **C4** 113
Capitol Peak, mtn., Nv., U.S. . **B4** 121
Capitol Reef National Park, Ut., U.S. . **E4** 137
Čaplygin, Russia . **C15** 20
Cap-Pelé, N.B., Can. . **C5** 87
Capreol, On., Can. . **p19** 89
Capri, Isola di, i., Italy . **D5** 18
Capricorn Channel, strt., Austl. . **E5** 62
Capricorn Group, is., Austl. **E5** 62
Caprivi Strip, hist. reg., Nmb. . **B3** 56
Cap-Rouge, P.Q., Can. . **n17** 90
Cap-Saint-Ignace, P.Q., Can.**B7** 90
Captain Cook, Hi., U.S. . **D6** 104
Captiva, Fl., U.S. . **F4** 102
Captiva Island, i., Fl., U.S. . **F4** 102
Capulin Volcano National Monument, N.M., U.S. . **A6** 124
Capunda Cabilongo, Ang. . **F2** 54
Caquetá (Japurá), stm., S.A. **D5** 70
Čara, Russia . **D13** 26
Caracal, Rom. . **G8** 20
Caracaraí, Braz. . **C7** 70
Caracas, Ven. . **A6** 70
Carajás, Braz. . **E9** 70
Carajás, Serra dos, hills, Braz. . **E9** 70
Carangola, Braz. . **F3** 74
Caransebeş, Rom. . **G7** 20
Caraquet, N.B., Can. . **B5** 87
Caratasca, Laguna de, b., Hond. . **B3** 80
Caratinga, Braz. . **E3** 74
Carauari, Braz. . **D6** 70
Caravaca de la Cruz, Spain. **H6** 16
Caravelas, Braz. . **G12** 70
Caraway, Ar., U.S. . **B5** 97
Carazinho, Braz. . **D7** 72
Carberry, Mb., Can. . **E2** 86
Carbon, co., Mt., U.S. . **E7** 119
Carbon, co., Pa., U.S. . **E10** 131
Carbon, co., Ut., U.S. . **D5** 137
Carbon, co., Wy., U.S. . **E5** 143
Carbondale, Co., U.S. . **B3** 99
Carbondale, Il., U.S. . **F4** 106
Carbondale, Ks., U.S. . **D8** 109
Carbondale, Pa., U.S. . **C10** 131
Carbonear, Nf., Can. . **E5** 88
Carbonia, Italy . **E2** 18
Carcassonne, Fr. . **F8** 16
Čardara, Kaz. . **B9** 42
Cárdenas, Cuba . **A3** 80
Cárdenas, Mex. . **D6** 78
Cardiff, Wales, U.K. . **E5** 12
Cardigan, Wales, U.K. . **D4** 12
Cardigan Bay, b., P.E., Can. **C7** 87
Cardigan Bay, b., Wales, U.K. . **D4** 12
Cardinal, On., Can. . **C9** 89
Cardington, Oh., U.S. . **B3** 128
Cardston, Ab., Can. . **E4** 84
Cardwell, Mo., U.S. . **E7** 118
Čardžev, Turk. . **F8** 26
Carei, Rom. . **F7** 20
Careiro, Braz. . **D8** 70
Carelia see Karelia, hist. reg., Eur. . **C12** 6
Carencro, La., U.S. . **D3** 111

Caretta, W.V., U.S. . **D3** 141
Carey, Id., U.S. . **F5** 105
Carey, Oh., U.S. . **B2** 128
Carey Downs, Austl. . **F2** 60
Cargados Carajos Shoals, is., Mrts. . **F11** 52
Caribbean Sea . **C4** 80
Cariboo Mountains, mts., B.C., Can. . **C7** 85
Caribou, Me., U.S. . **B5** 112
Caribou, co., Id., U.S. . **G7** 105
Caribou Island, i., N.S., Can.**D7** 87
Caribou Lake, l., Me., U.S. . **C3** 112
Caribou Mountain, mtn., Id., U.S. . **F7** 105
Caribou Mountains, mts., Ab., Can. . **f7** 84
Caribou Range, mts., Id., U.S. . **F7** 105
Caripito, Ven. . **C7** 80
Carl Blackwell, Lake, res., Ok., U.S. . **A4** 129
Carlet, Spain . **H6** 16
Carleton, Mi., U.S. . **F7** 115
Carleton, Mount, mtn., N.B., Can. . **B3** 87
Carleton Place, On., Can. . **B8** 89
Carletonville, S. Afr. . **D4** 56
Carlin, Nv., U.S. . **C5** 121
Carlinville, Il., U.S. . **D4** 106
Carlisle, Eng., U.K. . **C5** 12
Carlisle, Ar., U.S. . **C4** 97
Carlisle, Ia., U.S. . **C4** 108
Carlisle, In., U.S. . **G3** 107
Carlisle, Ky., U.S. . **B5** 110
Carlisle, Oh., U.S. . **C1** 128
Carlisle, Pa., U.S. . **F7** 131
Carlisle, co., Ky., U.S. . **f8** 110
Carl Junction, Mo., U.S. . **D3** 118
Carlos Casares, Arg. . **F5** 72
Carlos Chagas, Braz. . **E3** 74
Carlow, Ire. . **I3** 12
Carlsbad see Karlovy Vary, Czech Rep. . **D2** 20
Carlsbad, Ca., U.S. . **F5** 98
Carlsbad, N.M., U.S. . **E5** 124
Carlsbad Caverns National Park, N.M., U.S. . **E5** 124
Carlsberg Ridge . **H8** 64
Carlstadt, N.J., U.S. . **h8** 123
Carlton, Mn., U.S. . **D6** 116
Carlton, Or., U.S. . **B3** 130
Carlton, co., Mn., U.S. . **D6** 116
Carlyle, Il., U.S. . **E4** 106
Carlyle Lake, res., Il., U.S. . **E4** 106
Carman, Mb., Can. . **E2** 86
Carmanville, Nf., Can. . **D4** 88
Carmarthen, Wales, U.K. . **E4** 12
Carmaux, Fr. . **E8** 16
Carmel, Ca., U.S. . **D3** 98
Carmel, In., U.S. . **E5** 107
Carmel, N.Y., U.S. . **D7** 125
Carmelo, Ur. . **E6** 72
Carmen, Isla, i., Mex. . **D4** 78
Carmen, Isla del, i., Mex. . **D6** 78
Carmen de Patagones, Arg. **F4** 69
Carmi, Il., U.S. . **E5** 106
Carmi, Lake, l., Vt., U.S. . **B3** 138
Carnamah, Austl. . **F2** 60
Carnarvon, Austl. . **E1** 60
Carnarvon, S. Afr. . **E3** 56
Carnation, Wa., U.S. . **B4** 140
Carnegie, Ok., U.S. . **B3** 129
Carnegie, Pa., U.S. . **F1** 131
Carnegie, Lake, l., Austl. . **F3** 60
Carneys Point, N.J., U.S. . **D2** 123
Carnic Alps, mts., Eur. . **A4** 18
Car Nicobar Island, i., India **H6** 40
Carnot, C.A.R. . **G3** 54
Caro, Mi., U.S. . **E7** 115
Carol City, Fl., U.S. . **s13** 102
Caroleen, N.C., U.S. . **B1** 126
Carolina, Braz. . **C2** 74
Carolina, R.I., U.S. . **F2** 132
Carolina, W.V., U.S. . **k10** 141
Carolina Beach, N.C., U.S. . **C5** 126
Caroline, co., Md., U.S. . **C6** 113
Caroline, co., Va., U.S. . **C5** 139
Caroline, atoll, Kir. . **E15** 58
Caroline Islands, is., Oc. . **D8** 58
Caroní, stm., Ven. . **C7** 70
Carora, Ven. . **C5** 80
Carpathian Mountains, mts., Eur. . **E6** 20
Carpaţii Meridionali, mts., Rom. . **G7** 20
Carpentaria, Gulf of, b., Austl. . **F7** 58
Carpenter Dam, Ar., U.S. . **g7** 97
Carpentersville, Il., U.S. . **A5** 106
Carpentras, Fr. . **E9** 16
Carpina, Braz. . **C4** 74
Carpinteria, Ca., U.S. . **E4** 98
Carrabelle, Fl., U.S. . **C2** 102
Carranza, Cabo, c., Chile . **F3** 72
Carrara, Italy . **B3** 18
Carrauntoohil, mtn., Ire. . **D2** 12
Carrboro, N.C., U.S. . **B3** 126
Carreta, Punta, c., Peru . **F4** 70
Carrick on Shannon, Ire. . **I3** 12
Carrie, Mount, mtn., Wa., U.S. . **B2** 140
Carriere, Ms., U.S. . **E4** 117
Carrier Mills, Il., U.S. . **F5** 106
Carrington, N.D., U.S. . **B6** 127

Carrington Island, i., Ut., U.S. . **C3** 137
Carrizal Bajo, Chile . **C2** 69
Carrizo Creek, stm., U.S. . **A1** 136
Carrizo Mountain, mtn., N.M., U.S. . **D4** 124
Carrizo Mountains, mts., U.S. . **A6** 96
Carrizozo, N.M., U.S. . **D4** 124
Carroll, Ia., U.S. . **B3** 108
Carroll, co., Ar., U.S. . **A2** 97
Carroll, co., Ga., U.S. . **C1** 103
Carroll, co., Ia., U.S. . **B3** 108
Carroll, co., Il., U.S. . **A4** 106
Carroll, co., In., U.S. . **C4** 107
Carroll, co., Ky., U.S. . **B4** 110
Carroll, co., Md., U.S. . **A3** 113
Carroll, co., Mo., U.S. . **B4** 118
Carroll, co., Ms., U.S. . **B4** 117
Carroll, co., N.H., U.S. . **C4** 122
Carroll, co., Oh., U.S. . **B4** 128
Carroll, co., Tn., U.S. . **B3** 135
Carroll, co., Va., U.S. . **D2** 139
Carrollton, Al., U.S. . **B1** 94
Carrollton, Ga., U.S. . **C1** 103
Carrollton, Il., U.S. . **D3** 106
Carrollton, Ky., U.S. . **B4** 110
Carrollton, Mi., U.S. . **E7** 115
Carrollton, Mo., U.S. . **B4** 118
Carrollton, Oh., U.S. . **B4** 128
Carrollton, Pa., U.S. . **E4** 131
Carrot, stm., Can. . **D4** 91
Carry Falls Reservoir, res., N.Y., U.S. . **f10** 125
Çarşamba, Tur. . **B7** 44
Čarsk, Kaz. . **B4** 28
Carson, Ia., U.S. . **C2** 108
Carson, Wa., U.S. . **D4** 140
Carson, co., Tx., U.S. . **B2** 136
Carson, stm., Nv., U.S. . **D2** 121
Carson City, Mi., U.S. . **E6** 115
Carson City, Nv., U.S. . **D2** 121
Carson Lake, l., Nv., U.S. . **D3** 121
Carson Sink, l., Nv., U.S. . **D3** 121
Carson Spring, Tn., U.S. . **D10** 135
Carstairs, Ab., Can. . **D3** 84
Cartagena, Col. . **A4** 70
Cartagena, Spain . **I6** 16
Cartago, C.R. . **D3** 80
Cartago, Col. . **A4** 70
Carter, co., Ky., U.S. . **B6** 110
Carter, co., Mo., U.S. . **E7** 118
Carter, co., Mt., U.S. . **E12** 119
Carter, co., Ok., U.S. . **C4** 129
Carter, co., Tn., U.S. . **C11** 135
Carter Lake, Ia., U.S. . **C2** 108
Carter Mountain, mtn., Wy., U.S. . **B3** 143
Carters Lake, res., Ga., U.S. **B2** 103
Cartersville, Ga., U.S. . **B2** 103
Carterville, Il., U.S. . **F4** 106
Carterville, Mo., U.S. . **D3** 118
Carthage, Tun. . **F3** 18
Carthage, Il., U.S. . **C2** 106
Carthage, In., U.S. . **E6** 107
Carthage, Mo., U.S. . **D3** 118
Carthage, Ms., U.S. . **C4** 117
Carthage, N.C., U.S. . **B3** 126
Carthage, N.Y., U.S. . **B5** 125
Carthage, Tn., U.S. . **C8** 135
Carthage, Tx., U.S. . **C5** 136
Carthage, hist., Tun. . **F3** 18
Cartier Islands, is., Austl. . **C3** 60
Cartwright, Nf., Can. . **B3** 88
Cartwright, Ok., U.S. . **D5** 129
Caruaru, Braz. . **C4** 74
Carúpano, Ven. . **A7** 70
Carutapera, Braz. . **D10** 70
Caruthersville, Mo., U.S. . **E8** 118
Carver, Ma., U.S. . **C6** 114
Carver, Mn., U.S. . **F5** 116
Carver, co., Mn., U.S. . **F5** 116
Carville, La., U.S. . **h9** 111
Carvoeiro, Braz. . **D7** 70
Cary, Il., U.S. . **A5** 106
Cary, N.C., U.S. . **B4** 126
Caryville, Tn., U.S. . **C9** 135
Casablanca, Mor. . **D3** 48
Casa Grande, Az., U.S. . **E4** 96
Casa Grande National Monument, Az., U.S. . **E4** 96
Casale Monferrato, Italy . **B2** 18
Casa Nova, Braz. . **C3** 74
Casas Adobes, Az., U.S. . **E5** 96
Cascade, Co., U.S. . **C6** 99
Cascade, Ia., U.S. . **B6** 108
Cascade, Id., U.S. . **E2** 105
Cascade, Mt., U.S. . **C5** 119
Cascade, co., Mt., U.S. . **C5** 119
Cascade Locks, Or., U.S. . **B5** 130
Cascade Range, mts., N.A. . **C3** 92
Cascade Reservoir, res., Id., U.S. . **E3** 105
Cascade Tunnel, Wa., U.S. . **B4** 140
Cascais, Port. . **H2** 16
Cascavel, Braz. . **D7** 72
Casco Bay, b., Me., U.S. . **E3** 112
Caserta, Italy . **D5** 18
Caseville, Mi., U.S. . **E7** 115
Casey, Il., U.S. . **D6** 106
Casey, co., Ky., U.S. . **C5** 110
Casey, Mount, mtn., Id., U.S. . **A2** 105
Casey Key, i., Fl., U.S. . **E4** 102

Cashion, Az., U.S. . **m8** 96
Cashmere, Wa., U.S. . **B5** 140
Cashton, Wi., U.S. . **E3** 142
Casino, Austl. . **F5** 62
Casper, Wy., U.S. . **D6** 143
Casper Mountain, mtn., Wy., U.S. . **D6** 143
Caspian, Mi., U.S. . **B2** 115
Caspian Depression (Prikaspijskaja nizmennost'), pl. . **E8** 22
Caspian Lake, l., Vt., U.S. . **B4** 138
Caspian Sea . **F9** 22
Cass, co., Ia., U.S. . **C3** 108
Cass, co., Il., U.S. . **D3** 106
Cass, co., In., U.S. . **C5** 107
Cass, co., Mi., U.S. . **G4** 115
Cass, co., Mn., U.S. . **D4** 116
Cass, co., Mo., U.S. . **C3** 118
Cass, co., N.D., U.S. . **C8** 127
Cass, co., Ne., U.S. . **D9** 120
Cass, co., Tx., U.S. . **C5** 136
Cass, stm., Mi., U.S. . **E7** 115
Cassai (Kasai), stm., Afr. . **F4** 54
Cass City, Mi., U.S. . **E7** 115
Casselberry, Fl., U.S. . **D5** 102
Casselman, On., Can. . **B9** 89
Casselman, stm., U.S. . **k12** 113
Casselton, N.D., U.S. . **C8** 127
Cassia, co., Id., U.S. . **G5** 105
Cassiar, B.C., Can. . **m17** 85
Cassilândia, Braz. . **E1** 74
Cassinga, Ang. . **B2** 56
Cassino, Italy . **D4** 18
Cass Lake, Mn., U.S. . **C4** 116
Cass Lake, l., Mn., U.S. . **C4** 116
Cassongue, Ang. . **F2** 54
Cassopolis, Mi., U.S. . **G4** 115
Cassumba, Ilha, i., Braz. . **E4** 74
Cassville, Ga., U.S. . **B2** 103
Cassville, Mo., U.S. . **E4** 118
Cassville, Wi., U.S. . **F3** 142
Castalia, Oh., U.S. . **A3** 128
Castanea, Pa., U.S. . **D7** 131
Castanhal, Braz. . **B2** 74
Castellammare, Golfo di, b., Italy . **E4** 18
Castelló de la Plana, Spain . **H6** 16
Castelo Branco, Port. . **H3** 16
Castelsarrasin, Fr. . **F7** 16
Castelvetrano, Italy . **F4** 18
Castilla, Peru . **E3** 70
Castilla la Nueva, hist. reg., Spain . **H4** 16
Castilla la Vieja, hist. reg., Spain . **G5** 16
Castillo de San Marcos National Monument, Fl., U.S. . **n9** 102
Castine, Me., U.S. . **D4** 112
Castlebar, Ire. . **I2** 12
Castleberry, Al., U.S. . **D2** 94
Castle Dale, Ut., U.S. . **D4** 137
Castle Dome Mountains, mts., Az., U.S. . **D1** 96
Castle Dome Peak, mtn., Az., U.S. . **D1** 96
Castlegar, B.C., Can. . **E9** 85
Castle Hayne, N.C., U.S. . **C5** 126
Castle Hills, De., U.S. . **i7** 101
Castlemaine, Austl. . **H3** 62
Castle Mountains, mts., Mt., U.S. . **D6** 119
Castle Peak, mtn., Co., U.S. **B4** 99
Castle Peak, mtn., Id., U.S. . **E4** 105
Castle Point, Mo., U.S. . **f13** 118
Castle Rock, Co., U.S. . **B6** 99
Castle Rock, Wa., U.S. . **C3** 140
Castle Rock, mtn., Or., U.S. **C8** 130
Castle Rock Lake, res., Wi., U.S. . **E4** 142
Castleton, Vt., U.S. . **D2** 138
Castlewood, Va., U.S. . **f9** 139
Castor, Ab., Can. . **C5** 84
Castor, stm., Mo., U.S. . **D7** 118
Castres, Fr. . **F8** 16
Castries, St. Luc. . **C7** 80
Castro, Braz. . **C7** 72
Castro, Chile . **E2** 69
Castro, co., Tx., U.S. . **B1** 136
Castro Valley, Ca., U.S. . **h8** 98
Castrovillari, Italy . **E6** 18
Castroville, Ca., U.S. . **D3** 98
Castroville, Tx., U.S. . **E3** 136
Castuera, Spain . **H4** 16
Caswell, co., N.C., U.S. . **A3** 126
Cataguazes, Braz. . **C9** 72
Catahoula, co., La., U.S. . **C4** 111
Catahoula Lake, l., La., U.S. **C3** 111
Catalão, Braz. . **E2** 74
Catalina, Nf., Can. . **D5** 88
Catalina, Chile . **C3** 69
Catalunya, hist. reg., Spain . **D13** 16
Catanduanes Island, i., Phil. **D8** 34
Catania, Italy . **F5** 18
Catanzaro, Italy . **E6** 18
Cataouatche, Lake, l., La., U.S. . **k11** 111
Catarino Rodríguez, Mex. . **C4** 78
Catarman, Phil. . **D8** 34
Catasauqua, Pa., U.S. . **E11** 131
Cataumet, Ma., U.S. . **C6** 114
Catawba, co., N.C., U.S. . **B1** 126
Catawba, stm., S.C., U.S. . **B6** 133
Catawba, South Fork, stm., N.C., U.S. . **B1** 126

Name	Map Ref.	Page

Catawissa, Pa., U.S. **E9** 131
Catbalogan, Phil. **D8** 34
Catete, Ang. **E2** 54
Cathance, Lake, l., Me.,
  U.S. **D5** 112
Cathedral City, Ca., U.S. . . **F5** 98
Cathedral of the Pines,
  N.H., U.S. **E3** 122
Catherine, Lake, res., Ar.,
  U.S. **C3** 97
Cat Island, i., Bah. **D9** 76
Cat Island, i., Ma., U.S. . . **f12** 114
Cat Island, i., Ms., U.S. . . **E4** 117
Cat Island, i., Ms., U.S. . . **E4** 117
Cat Island, i., S.C., U.S. . . **E9** 133
Catlettsburg, Ky., U.S. **B7** 110
Catlin, Il., U.S. **C6** 106
Catnip Mountain, mtn., Nv.,
  U.S. **B2** 121
Catoche, Cabo, c., Mex. . . **C7** 78
Catonsville, Md., U.S. **B4** 113
Catoosa, Ok., U.S. **A6** 129
Catoosa, co., Ga., U.S. . . . **B1** 103
Catrilό, Arg. **F5** 72
Catron, co., N.M., U.S. . . . **D1** 124
Catskill, N.Y., U.S. **C7** 125
Catskill Mountains, mts.,
  N.Y., U.S. **C6** 125
Catt, Mount, mtn., B.C.,
  Can. **B3** 85
Cattaraugus, co., N.Y., U.S. **C2** 125
Cattaraugus Creek, stm.,
  N.Y., U.S. **C2** 125
Cattaraugus Indian
  Reservation, N.Y., U.S. **C2** 125
Čatyrtaš, Kyrg. **A3** 40
Caubvick, Mount (Iberville,
  Mont d'), mtn., Can. . . **f9** 88
Cauca, stm., Col. **B5** 70
Caucasia, Col. **D4** 80
Caucasus, mts. **A10** 44
Caucete, Arg. **E4** 72
Caucomgomoc Lake, l.,
  Me., U.S. **B3** 112
Caungula, Ang. **E3** 54
Cauquenes, Chile **E2** 69
Caura, stm., Ven. **B7** 70
Cavalier, N.D., U.S. **A8** 127
Cavalier, co., N.D., U.S. . . **A7** 127
Cave City, Ar., U.S. **B4** 97
Cave City, Ky., U.S. **C4** 110
Cave Creek, Az., U.S. **D4** 96
Cave Junction, Or., U.S. . . **E3** 130
Cave Point, c., Wi., U.S. . . **D6** 142
Cave Run Lake, res., Ky.,
  U.S. **B6** 110
Cave Spring, Ga., U.S. . . . **B1** 103
Cave Spring, Va., U.S. . . . **C2** 139
Cavetown, Md., U.S. **A2** 113
Caviana de Fora, Ilha, i.,
  Braz. **A2** 74
Cavite, Phil. **D8** 34
Cawood, Ky., U.S. **D6** 110
Cawston, B.C., Can. **E8** 85
Caxias, Braz. **B3** 74
Caxias do Sul, Braz. **D7** 72
Caxito, Ang. **E2** 54
Cayambe, vol., Ec. **C4** 70
Cayce, S.C., U.S. **D5** 133
Cayenne, Fr. Gu. **C9** 70
Cayman Brac, i., Cay. Is. . . **B4** 80
Cayman Islands, dep., N.A. **E8** 76
Cayuga, In., U.S. **E3** 107
Cayuga, co., N.Y., U.S. . . . **C4** 125
Cayuga Heights, N.Y., U.S. **C4** 125
Cayuga Lake, l., N.Y., U.S. **C4** 125
Cazenovia, N.Y., U.S. **C5** 125
Cazombo, Ang. **F4** 54
Ceará, state, Braz. **C4** 74
Ceará-Mirim, Braz. **C4** 74
Ceballos, Mex. **B4** 78
Čeboksary, Russia **D6** 26
Cebu, Phil. **D8** 34
Cebu, i., Phil. **D8** 34
Cecil, co., Md., U.S. **A6** 113
Cecil Field Naval Air
  Station, mil., Fl., U.S. . . **B5** 102
Cecilia, Ky., U.S. **C4** 110
Cecina, Italy **C3** 18
Čečnja, state, Russia **E6** 26
Cedar, co., Ia., U.S. **C6** 108
Cedar, co., Mo., U.S. **D4** 118
Cedar, co., Ne., U.S. **B8** 120
Cedar, stm., Ne., U.S. **B7** 120
Cedar, stm., Wa., U.S. . . . **B4** 140
Cedar, stm., U.S. **C6** 108
Cedar Bluff, Al., U.S. **A4** 94
Cedar Bluff Reservoir, res.,
  Ks., U.S. **D4** 109
Cedar Bluff Two, Tn., U.S. **D9** 135
Cedar Breaks National
  Monument, Ut., U.S. . . **F3** 137
Cedarburg, Wi., U.S. **E6** 142
Cedar City, Ut., U.S. **F2** 137
Cedar Creek, stm., N.D.,
  U.S. **C3** 127
Cedar Creek, stm., N.J.,
  U.S. **D4** 123
Cedar Creek, stm., Oh.,
  U.S. **e7** 128
Cedar Creek Lake, res., Tx.,
  U.S. **C4** 136
Cedar Crest, N.M., U.S. . . **k8** 124
Cedaredge, Co., U.S. **C3** 99
Cedar Falls, Ia., U.S. **B5** 108
Cedar Grove, N.J., U.S. . . **B4** 123

Cedar Grove, W.V., U.S. . . **C3** 141
Cedar Grove, Wi., U.S. . . . **E6** 142
Cedar Hill, Mo., U.S. **g12** 118
Cedar Hill, Tx., U.S. **n10** 136
Cedarhurst, N.Y., U.S. . . . **k13** 125
Cedar Island, i., N.C., U.S. **C6** 126
Cedar Island, i., S.C., U.S. **E9** 133
Cedar Island, i., Va., U.S. **C7** 139
Cedar Key, Fl., U.S. **C3** 102
Cedar Keys, is., Fl., U.S. . . **C3** 102
Cedar Lake, In., U.S. **B3** 107
Cedar Lake, res., Mb., Can. **C1** 86
Cedar Lake, res., Il., U.S. **F4** 106
Cedar Mountain, mtn., Ca.,
  U.S. **B3** 98
Cedar Point, c., Md., U.S. **D5** 113
Cedar Point, c., Oh., U.S. **A3** 128
Cedar Point, c., Oh., U.S. **e7** 128
Cedar Rapids, Ia., U.S. . . . **C6** 108
Cedar Springs, Mi., U.S. . . **E5** 115
Cedartown, Ga., U.S. **B1** 103
Cedar Vale, Ks., U.S. **E7** 109
Cedarville, Oh., U.S. **C2** 128
Cedros, Isla, i., Mex. **B1** 78
Ceduna, Austl. **G5** 60
Ceerigaabo, Som. **H14** 48
Cefalonia see Kefallinía, i.,
  Grc. **E8** 18
Cefalù, Italy **F5** 18
Čegdomyn, Russia **D15** 26
Cegléd, Hung. **F5** 20
Čehov, Russia **B14** 20
Čehov, Russia **A4** 31
Çekerek, Tur. **B6** 44
Çekerek, stm., Tur. **C6** 44
Celaya, Mex. **C4** 78
Celebes see Sulawesi, i.,
  Indon. **D6** 36
Celebes Basin **H15** 64
Celebes Sea, Asia **C6** 36
Čeleken, Turk. **C6** 42
Celina, Oh., U.S. **B1** 128
Celina, Tn., U.S. **C8** 135
Celina, Tx., U.S. **C4** 136
Čeljabinsk, Russia **D8** 26
Celje, Slvn. **A5** 18
Čelkar, Kaz. **E7** 26
Celle, Ger. **D11** 12
Celtic Sea, Eur. **B3** 16
Cement, Ok., U.S. **C3** 129
Cementon, Pa., U.S. **E10** 131
Cenderawasih, Teluk, b.,
  Indon. **G10** 32
Cenderawasih Bay see
  Cenderawasih, Teluk,
  b., Indon. **G10** 32
Centennial Mountains, mts.,
  Id., U.S. **E7** 105
Center, Co., U.S. **D4** 99
Center, N.D., U.S. **B4** 127
Center, Tx., U.S. **D5** 136
Centerbrook, Ct., U.S. . . . **D6** 100
Centerburg, Oh., U.S. **B3** 128
Centereach, N.Y., U.S. . . . **n15** 125
Centerfield, Ut., U.S. **D4** 137
Center Hill Lake, res., Tn.,
  U.S. **C8** 135
Center Moriches, N.Y., U.S. **n16** 125
Center Mountain, mtn., Id.,
  U.S. **D3** 105
Center Point, Al., U.S. . . . **f7** 94
Center Point, Ia., U.S. . . . **B6** 108
Centerville, Ia., U.S. **D5** 108
Centerville, In., U.S. **E8** 107
Centerville, La., U.S. **E4** 111
Centerville, Ma., U.S. **C7** 114
Centerville, Oh., U.S. **C1** 128
Centerville, Pa., U.S. **F2** 131
Centerville, S.D., U.S. **D9** 134
Centerville, Tn., U.S. **B4** 135
Centerville, Ut., U.S. **C4** 137
Central, Phil. **D8** 34
Central, N.M., U.S. **E1** 124
Central, S.C., U.S. **B2** 133
Central, Cordillera, mts.,
  Col. **E4** 80
Central, Cordillera, mts.,
  Peru **E4** 70
Central, Massif, mts., Fr. . . **E8** 16
Central, Sistema, mts., Spain **G4** 16
Central African Republic,
  ctry., Afr. **B3** 54
Central City, Co., U.S. . . . **B5** 99
Central City, Ia., U.S. **B6** 108
Central City, Il., U.S. **E4** 106
Central City, Ky., U.S. . . . **C2** 110
Central City, Ne., U.S. . . . **C7** 120
Central City, Pa., U.S. **F4** 131
Central Falls, R.I., U.S. . . . **B4** 132
Central Heights, Az., U.S. **D5** 96
Centralia, Il., U.S. **E4** 106
Centralia, Mo., U.S. **B5** 118
Centralia, Wa., U.S. **C3** 140
Central Islip, N.Y., U.S. . . **n15** 125
Central Lake, Mi., U.S. . . . **C5** 115
Central Makrān Range, mts.,
  Pak. **E8** 42
Central Pacific Basin **G21** 64
Central Park, Wa., U.S. . . . **C2** 140
Central Point, Or., U.S. . . . **E4** 130
Central Siberian Uplands
  see Srednesibirskoe
  ploskogor'e, plat.,
  Russia **C12** 26

Central Square, N.Y., U.S. **B4** 125
Central Valley, Ca., U.S. . . **B2** 98
Central Valley, N.Y., U.S. . . **D6** 125
Central Village, Ct., U.S. . . **C8** 100
Centre, Al., U.S. **A4** 94
Centre, co., Pa., U.S. **E6** 131
Centre Hall, Pa., U.S. **E6** 131
Centreville, Al., U.S. **C2** 94
Centreville, Il., U.S. **E3** 106
Centreville, Md., U.S. **B5** 113
Centreville, Mi., U.S. **G5** 115
Centreville, Ms., U.S. **D2** 117
Centuria, Wi., U.S. **C1** 142
Century, Fl., U.S. **u14** 102
Ceos see Kéa, i., Grc. **F10** 18
Ceram see Seram, i., Indon. **D7** 36
Ceram Sea see Seram, Laut,
  Indon. **D7** 36
Cerbat Mountains, mts., Az.,
  U.S. **B1** 96
Cerdas, Bol. **C4** 72
Ceredo, W.V., U.S. **C2** 141
Čeremhovo, Russia **D12** 26
Čerepovec, Russia **D5** 26
Ceres, Arg. **D5** 72
Ceres, Braz. **E2** 74
Ceres, Ca., U.S. **D3** 98
Ceresco, Ne., U.S. **C9** 120
Cerignola, Italy **D5** 18
Čerkessk, Russia **E6** 26
Čerlak, Russia **D9** 26
Čermoz, Russia **C10** 22
Cernavodă, Rom. **G10** 20
Černjahovsk, Russia **B6** 20
Černjanka, Russia **D14** 20
Černobyl', Ukr. **D11** 20
Černuška, Russia **C10** 22
Černyševskij, Russia **C13** 26
Cerralvo, Isla, i., Mex. . . . **C3** 78
Cerritos, Mex. **C4** 78
Cerro Azul, Peru **A2** 72
Cerro de Pasco, Peru **F4** 70
Cerro Gordo, Il., U.S. **D5** 106
Cerro Gordo, co., Ia., U.S. **A4** 108
Čerskij, Russia **C18** 26
Čerskogo, hrebet, mts.,
  Russia **C15** 26
Červen', Bela. **C10** 20
Cervino see Matterhorn,
  mtn., Eur. **A1** 18
Cesena, Italy **B4** 18
Cēsis, Lat. **H11** 10
České Budějovice, Czech
  Rep. **E3** 20
Çeşme, Tur. **C2** 44
Česskaja guba, b., Russia . **A8** 22
Cessnock, Austl. **G5** 62
Cetinje, Yugo. **C7** 18
Ceuta, Sp. N. Afr. **J4** 16
Cévennes, reg., Fr. **E8** 16
Ceyhan, Tur. **D6** 44
Ceyhan, stm., Tur. **D6** 44
Ceylanpınar, Tur. **D9** 44
Ceylon see Sri Lanka, ctry.,
  Asia **H4** 40
Cha-am, Thai. **D3** 34
Chachani, Nevado, vol.,
  Peru **G5** 70
Chachapoyas, Peru **E4** 70
Chachoengsao, Thai. **D4** 34
Chaco, stm., N.M., U.S. . . **A1** 124
Chaco Austral, reg., Arg. . . **D5** 72
Chaco Boreal, reg., Para. . **C5** 72
Chaco Central, reg., Arg. . **C5** 72
Chaco Culture National
  Historic Park, N.M.,
  U.S. **A2** 124
Chacon, Cape, c., Ak., U.S. **n24** 95
Chad, ctry., Chad **G8** 48
Chad, Lake, l., Afr. **D7** 50
Chadbourn, N.C., U.S. . . . **C4** 126
Chadds Ford, Pa., U.S. . . **G10** 131
Chadron, Ne., U.S. **B3** 120
Chadwicks, N.Y., U.S. . . . **B5** 125
Chaffee, Mo., U.S. **D8** 118
Chaffee, co., Co., U.S. . . . **C4** 99
Chaffin, Ma., U.S. **B4** 114
Chaghcharān, Afg. **D9** 42
Chagos Archipelago, is.,
  B.I.O.T. **I10** 64
Chagos-Laccadive Plateau **I10** 64
Chagrin Falls, Oh., U.S. . . **A4** 128
Chaguaramas, Ven. **D6** 80
Chahār Borjak, Afg. **D8** 42
Chai Nat, Thai. **C4** 34
Chaiyaphum, Thai. **C4** 34
Chajari, Arg. **E6** 72
Chakachamna Lake, l., Ak.,
  U.S. **g15** 95
Chakari, Zimb. **B4** 56
Chakasija, state, Russia . . . **A5** 28
Chala, Peru **B3** 72
Chalatenango, El Sal. **C2** 80
Chalbi Desert, des., Kenya **C7** 54
Chalcidice see Khalkidhikí,
  hist. reg., Grc. **D9** 18
Chalcis see Khalkís, Grc. . . **E9** 18
Chaleur Bay, b., Can. **B4** 87
Chalfonte, De., U.S. **h7** 101
Chalk River, On., Can. . . . **A7** 90
Challapata, Bol. **B4** 72
Challenger Deep **G17** 64
Challis, Id., U.S. **E4** 105
Chalmette, La., U.S. **E6** 111
Châlons-en-Champagne, Fr. **C9** 16

Chalon-sur-Saône, Fr. **D9** 16
Chālūs, Iran **C6** 42
Chama, N.M., U.S. **A3** 124
Chama, Rio, stm., N.M.,
  U.S. **A3** 124
Chaman, Pak. **D9** 42
Chambal, stm., India **D3** 40
Chamberlain, S.D., U.S. . . **D6** 134
Chamberlain Lake, l., Me.,
  U.S. **B3** 112
Chamberlin, Mount, mtn.,
  Ak., U.S. **B10** 95
Chambers, co., Al., U.S. . . **C4** 94
Chambers, co., Tx., U.S. . . **E5** 136
Chambersburg, Pa., U.S. . . **G6** 131
Chambers Island, i., Wi.,
  U.S. **C6** 142
Chambéry, Fr. **E9** 16
Chambi, Jebel, mtn., Tun. **C6** 48
Chamblee, Ga., U.S. **h8** 103
Chambly, P.Q., Can. **D4** 90
Chamical, Arg. **E4** 72
Chamisal, N.M., U.S. **A4** 124
Chāmpa, India **E4** 40
Champagne, hist. reg., Fr. **C9** 16
Champaign, Il., U.S. **C5** 106
Champaign, co., Il., U.S. **C5** 106
Champaign, co., Oh., U.S. **B2** 128
Champasak, Laos **D5** 34
Champion, Oh., U.S. **A5** 128
Champlain, Lake, l., N.A. **C13** 92
Champlin, Mn., U.S. **m12** 116
Champotón, Mex. **D6** 78
Chañaral, Chile **C2** 69
Chance, Md., U.S. **D6** 113
Chanchelulla Peak, mtn.,
  Ca., U.S. **B2** 98
Chandalar, stm., Ak., U.S. **B10** 95
Chandeleur Islands, is., La.,
  U.S. **E7** 111
Chandeleur Sound, strt.,
  La., U.S. **E6** 111
Chandīgarh, India **C3** 40
Chandler, P.Q., Can. **k14** 90
Chandler, Az., U.S. **D4** 96
Chandler, In., U.S. **H3** 107
Chandler, Ok., U.S. **B5** 129
Chandler, Tx., U.S. **C5** 136
Chandler Heights, Az., U.S. **m9** 96
Chāndpur, Bngl. **E6** 40
Chandrapur, India **F3** 40
Chang (Yangtze), stm.,
  China **E9** 28
Chang, Ko, i., Thai. **D4** 34
Changane, stm., Moz. . . . **C5** 56
Changara, Moz. **B5** 56
Chang Cheng (Great Wall),
  China **B2** 30
Changchun, China **C13** 28
Changde, China **F10** 28
Changhua, Tai. **E5** 30
Changji, China **C5** 28
Changjiang, China **H9** 28
Changli, China **B4** 30
Changmar, China **E3** 28
Changning, China **B3** 34
Changsha, China **F10** 28
Changshu, China **C5** 30
Changting, China **F11** 28
Changwu, China **B2** 30
Changzhi, China **D10** 28
Changzhou, China **E12** 28
Chanhassen, Mn., U.S. . . **n11** 116
Channahon, Il., U.S. **B5** 106
Channel Islands, is., Eur. . **C5** 16
Channel Islands National
  Park, Ca., U.S. **F4** 98
Channel Lake, Il., U.S. . . **H8** 106
Channel-Port-aux-Basques,
  Nf., Can. **E2** 88
Channelview, Tx., U.S. . . . **r14** 136
Chanthaburi, Thai. **D4** 34
Chantilly, Va., U.S. **g12** 139
Chanute, Ks., U.S. **E8** 109
Chao'an, China **G11** 28
Chao Hu, l., China **E11** 28
Chaoxian, China **C4** 30
Chaoyang, China **C12** 28
Chaoyang, China **E4** 30
Chapadinha, Braz. **B3** 74
Chapala, Laguna de, l.,
  Mex. **C4** 78
Chaparral, Col. **E4** 80
Chapecó, Braz. **D7** 72
Chapel Hill, N.C., U.S. . . . **B3** 126
Chapel Hill, Tn., U.S. **B5** 135
Chaplin, stm., Ky., U.S. . . **C4** 110
Chaplin Lake, l., Sk., Can. **G2** 91
Chaplynka, Ukr. **F12** 20
Chapman, Ks., U.S. **D6** 109
Chapman Pond, l., R.I., U.S. **F1** 132
Chapmanville, W.V., U.S. **D2** 141
Chappaquiddick Island, i.,
  Ma., U.S. **D7** 114
Chappell, Ne., U.S. **C3** 120
Charagua, Bol. **B5** 72
Charcas, Mex. **C4** 78
Chardon, Oh., U.S. **A4** 128
Charenton, La., U.S. **E4** 111
Chari, stm., Afr. **H8** 48
Chārīkār, Afg. **C9** 42
Chariton, Ia., U.S. **C4** 108
Chariton, co., Mo., U.S. . . **B4** 118
Chariton, stm., U.S. **A5** 118
Charity, Guy. **B8** 70

Charleroi, Bel. **E9** 12
Charleroi, Pa., U.S. **F2** 131
Charles, co., Md., U.S. . . . **C3** 113
Charles, stm., Ma., U.S. . . **B5** 114
Charles, Cape, c., Va., U.S. **C6** 139
Charles A. Goodwin Dam,
  Ct., U.S. **B3** 100
Charlesbourg, P.Q., Can. . **n17** 90
Charles City, Ia., U.S. **A5** 108
Charles City, co., Va., U.S. **C5** 139
Charles Mill Lake, res., Oh.,
  U.S. **B3** 128
Charles Mix, co., S.D., U.S. **D7** 134
Charles Mound, hill, Il., U.S. **A3** 106
Charleston, Ar., U.S. **B1** 97
Charleston, Il., U.S. **D5** 106
Charleston, Mo., U.S. **E8** 118
Charleston, Ms., U.S. **A3** 117
Charleston, Or., U.S. **D2** 130
Charleston, S.C., U.S. **F8** 133
Charleston, Tn., U.S. **D9** 135
Charleston, W.V., U.S. . . . **C3** 141
Charleston, co., S.C., U.S. **F8** 133
Charleston Air Force Base,
  mil., S.C., U.S. **k11** 133
Charleston Naval Shipyard,
  mil., S.C., U.S. **k12** 133
Charleston Peak, mtn., Nv.,
  U.S. **G6** 121
Charlestown, In., U.S. **H6** 107
Charlestown, N.H., U.S. . . **D2** 122
Charlestown, R.I., U.S. . . . **F2** 132
Charles Town, W.V., U.S. **B7** 141
Charleville, Austl. **F4** 62
Charleville-Mézières, Fr. . . **C9** 16
Charlevoix, Mi., U.S. **C5** 115
Charlevoix, co., Mi., U.S. **C5** 115
Charlevoix, Lake, l., Mi.,
  U.S. **C5** 115
Charlo, N.B., Can. **B3** 87
Charlotte, Mi., U.S. **F6** 115
Charlotte, N.C., U.S. **B2** 126
Charlotte, Tn., U.S. **A4** 135
Charlotte, Tx., U.S. **E3** 136
Charlotte, co., Fl., U.S. . . . **F5** 102
Charlotte, co., Va., U.S. . . **C4** 139
Charlotte Amalie, V.I.U.S. **B6** 80
Charlotte Hall, Md., U.S. . **D4** 113
Charlotte Harbor, Fl., U.S. **F4** 102
Charlotte Harbor, b., Fl.,
  U.S. **F4** 102
Charlottesville, Va., U.S. . . **B4** 139
Charlottetown, P.E., Can. **C6** 87
Charlton, co., Ga., U.S. . . **F4** 103
Charmco, W.V., U.S. **C4** 141
Charny, P.Q., Can. **C6** 90
Charters Towers, Austl. . . **E4** 62
Chartres, Fr. **C7** 16
Chascomús, Arg. **F6** 72
Chase, B.C., Can. **D8** 85
Chase, Md., U.S. **B5** 113
Chase, co., Ks., U.S. **D7** 109
Chase, co., Ne., U.S. **D4** 120
Chase City, Va., U.S. **D4** 139
Chaska, Mn., U.S. **F5** 116
Chassahowitzka Bay, b., Fl.,
  U.S. **D4** 102
Chassell, Mi., U.S. **B2** 115
Châteaubriant, Fr. **D6** 16
Châteaudun, Fr. **C7** 16
Châteauguay, P.Q., Can. . **D4** 90
Château-Richer, P.Q., Can. **C6** 90
Châteauroux, Fr. **D7** 16
Châtellerault, Fr. **D7** 16
Chatfield, Mn., U.S. **G6** 116
Chatham, N.B., Can. **B4** 87
Chatham, On., Can. **E2** 89
Chatham, Il., U.S. **D4** 106
Chatham, La., U.S. **B3** 111
Chatham, Ma., U.S. **C8** 114
Chatham, N.J., U.S. **B4** 123
Chatham, N.Y., U.S. **C7** 125
Chatham, Va., U.S. **D3** 139
Chatham, co., Ga., U.S. . . **E5** 103
Chatham, co., N.C., U.S. . **B3** 126
Chatham Islands, is., N.Z. **I12** 58
Chatham Rise **M21** 64
Chatham Strait, strt., Ak.,
  U.S. **m22** 95
Châtillon-sur-Seine, Fr. . . . **D9** 16
Chatom, Al., U.S. **D1** 94
Chatsworth, Ga., U.S. . . . **B2** 103
Chatsworth, Il., U.S. **C5** 106
Chatsworth Reservoir, res.,
  Ca., U.S. **m11** 98
Chattahoochee, Fl., U.S. . **B2** 102
Chattahoochee, co., Ga.,
  U.S. **D2** 103
Chattahoochee, stm., U.S. **E1** 103
Chattanooga, Tn., U.S. . . **D8** 135
Chattaroy, W.V., U.S. . . . **D2** 141
Chattooga, co., Ga., U.S. **B1** 103
Chattooga, stm., U.S. . . . **B1** 133
Chatuge Lake, res., U.S. . . **g9** 126
Chaudière, stm., P.Q., Can. **C7** 90
Chauk, Myan. **B2** 34
Chaumont, Fr. **C9** 16
Chauncey, Oh., U.S. **C3** 128
Chauny, Fr. **C8** 16
Chautauqua, co., Ks., U.S. **E7** 109
Chautauqua, co., N.Y., U.S. **C1** 125
Chautauqua Lake, l., N.Y.,
  U.S. **C1** 125
Chauvin, La., U.S. **E5** 111
Chaves, Port. **G3** 12

Name	Map Ref.	Page
Chaves, co., N.M., U.S.	D5	124
Cheaha Mountain, mtn., Al., U.S.	B4	94
Cheat, Shavers Fork, stm., W.V., U.S.	B5	141
Cheatham, co., Tn., U.S.	A4	135
Cheb, Czech Rep.	D2	20
Chebanse, Il., U.S.	C6	106
Cheboygan, Mi., U.S.	C6	115
Cheboygan, co., Mi., U.S.	C6	115
Chech, 'Erg, des., Afr.	E5	50
Chechaouen, Mor.	J4	16
Chechnya see Čečnja, state, Russia	E6	26
Checotah, Ok., U.S.	B6	129
Chedabucto Bay, b., N.S., Can.	D8	87
Cheduba Island, i., Myan.	C2	34
Cheeseman Lake, res., Co., U.S.	B5	99
Chehalem Mountains, mts., Or., U.S.	h12	130
Chehalis, Wa., U.S.	C3	140
Chehalis, stm., Wa., U.S.	C2	140
Cheju, S. Kor.	E13	28
Cheju-do, i., S. Kor.	E13	28
Chekhov see Čehov, Russia	B14	20
Chekhov see Čehov, Russia	A4	31
Chelan, Wa., U.S.	B5	140
Chelan, co., Wa., U.S.	B4	140
Chelan, Lake, l., Wa., U.S.	A5	140
Chelan Mountains, mts., Wa., U.S.	A5	140
Chelif, Oued, stm., Alg.	D4	14
Chełm, Pol.	D7	20
Chełmno, Pol.	C5	20
Chelmsford, Eng., U.K.	E7	12
Chelmsford, Ma., U.S.	A5	114
Chelsea, P.Q., Can.	D2	90
Chelsea, Al., U.S.	g7	94
Chelsea, Ma., U.S.	B5	114
Chelsea, Mi., U.S.	F6	115
Chelsea, Ok., U.S.	A6	129
Cheltenham, Eng., U.K.	E5	12
Cheltenham, Md., U.S.	C4	113
Chelyabinsk see Čeljabinsk, Russia	D8	26
Chelyan, W.V., U.S.	C3	141
Chemba, Moz.	B5	56
Chemehuevi Indian Reservation, Ca., U.S.	E6	98
Chemnitz, Ger.	E13	12
Chemquasabamticook Lake (Ross Lake), l., Me., U.S.	B3	112
Chemung, co., N.Y., U.S.	C4	125
Chemung, stm., Pa., U.S.	C8	131
Chemung Lake, l., On., Can.	C6	89
Chenāb, stm., Asia	C2	40
Chenango, co., N.Y., U.S.	C5	125
Chenango, stm., N.Y., U.S.	C5	125
Chenango Bridge, N.Y., U.S.	C5	125
Chenes, River Aux, b., La., U.S.	k12	111
Chénéville, P.Q., Can.	D2	90
Cheney, Ks., U.S.	E6	109
Cheney, Wa., U.S.	B8	140
Cheney Reservoir, res., Ks., U.S.	E6	109
Cheneyville, La., U.S.	C3	111
Chengde, China	C11	28
Chengdu, China	E8	28
Chengmai, China	F2	30
Chengshan Jiao, c., China	D12	28
Chengxian, China	C2	30
Chennai (Madras), India	G4	40
Chenoa, Il., U.S.	C5	106
Chenoweth, Or., U.S.	B5	130
Chenxi, China	D3	30
Chenzhou, China	F10	28
Chepachet, R.I., U.S.	B2	132
Chepachet, stm., R.I., U.S.	B2	132
Chequamegon Bay, b., Wi., U.S.	B3	142
Cher, stm., Fr.	D7	16
Cheraw, S.C., U.S.	B8	133
Cherbaniani Reef, rf., India	G2	40
Cherbourg, Fr.	C6	16
Cherchell, Alg.	I8	16
Chergui, Chott ech, l., Alg.	D5	48
Cherkasy, Ukr.	E11	20
Cherkessia see Karačaevo-Čerkesija, state, Russia	E6	26
Cherniakhiv, Ukr.	D10	20
Chernihiv, Ukr.	D11	20
Chernivtsi, Ukr.	E8	20
Chernobyl see Černobyl', Ukr.	D11	20
Cherokee, Al., U.S.	A2	94
Cherokee, Ia., U.S.	B2	108
Cherokee, Ks., U.S.	E9	109
Cherokee, Ok., U.S.	A3	129
Cherokee, co., Al., U.S.	A4	94
Cherokee, co., Ga., U.S.	B2	103
Cherokee, co., Ia., U.S.	B2	108
Cherokee, co., Ks., U.S.	E9	109
Cherokee, co., N.C., U.S.	f8	126
Cherokee, co., Ok., U.S.	A4	133
Cherokee, co., Tx., U.S.	D5	136
Cherokee Indian Reservation, N.C., U.S.	f9	126
Cherokee Lake, res., Tn., U.S.	C10	135
Cherokees, Lake O' The, res., Ok., U.S.	A7	129
Cherokee Village, Ar., U.S.	A4	97
Cherry, co., Ne., U.S.	B4	120
Cherry Creek, stm., S.D., U.S.	C3	134
Cherry Hill, N.J., U.S.	D2	123
Cherry Point, c., Va., U.S.	C6	139
Cherry Point Marine Corps Air Station, mil., N.C., U.S.	C6	126
Cherryvale, Ks., U.S.	E8	109
Cherry Valley, Ar., U.S.	B5	97
Cherry Valley, Il., U.S.	A5	106
Cherryville, N.C., U.S.	B1	126
Cherskiy Mountains see Čerskogo, hrebet, mts., Russia	C15	26
Chervonohrad, Ukr.	D8	20
Chesaning, Mi., U.S.	E6	115
Chesapeake, Oh., U.S.	D3	128
Chesapeake, Va., U.S.	D6	139
Chesapeake, W.V., U.S.	C3	141
Chesapeake and Delaware Canal, U.S.	B3	101
Chesapeake Bay, b., U.S.	D12	92
Chesapeake Bay Bridge-Tunnel, Va., U.S.	D7	139
Chesapeake Beach, Md., U.S.	C4	113
Chesapeake City, Md., U.S.	A6	113
Chesdin, Lake, res., Va., U.S.	C5	139
Chesha Bay see Češskaja guba, b., Russia	A8	22
Cheshire, Ct., U.S.	D4	100
Cheshire, co., N.H., U.S.	E2	122
Cheshire Reservoir, res., Ma., U.S.	A1	114
Chesley, On., Can.	C3	89
Chesnee, S.C., U.S.	A4	133
Chester, Eng., U.K.	D5	12
Chester, Ca., U.S.	B3	98
Chester, Ct., U.S.	D6	100
Chester, Ga., U.S.	D3	103
Chester, Il., U.S.	F4	106
Chester, Md., U.S.	C5	113
Chester, Mt., U.S.	B6	119
Chester, N.H., U.S.	E4	122
Chester, N.Y., U.S.	D6	125
Chester, Pa., U.S.	G11	131
Chester, S.C., U.S.	B5	133
Chester, Va., U.S.	C5	139
Chester, Vt., U.S.	E3	138
Chester, W.V., U.S.	A4	141
Chester, co., Pa., U.S.	G10	131
Chester, co., S.C., U.S.	B5	133
Chester, co., Tn., U.S.	B3	135
Chester, stm., Md., U.S.	B5	113
Chester Basin, N.S., Can.	E5	87
Chester Depot, Vt., U.S.	E3	138
Chesterfield, In., U.S.	D6	107
Chesterfield, S.C., U.S.	B7	133
Chesterfield, co., S.C., U.S.	B7	133
Chesterfield, co., Va., U.S.	C5	139
Chesterton, In., U.S.	A3	107
Chestertown, Md., U.S.	B5	113
Chesterville, On., Can.	B9	89
Chesuncook Lake, l., Me., U.S.	C3	112
Cheswick, Pa., U.S.	h14	131
Cheswold, De., U.S.	D3	101
Cheta see Heta, stm., Russia	B11	26
Chetac, Lake, l., Wi., U.S.	C2	142
Chetco, stm., Or., U.S.	E2	130
Chetek, Wi., U.S.	C2	142
Chetek, Lake, l., Wi., U.S.	C2	142
Chetopa, Ks., U.S.	E8	109
Chetumal, Mex.	D7	78
Chetumal, Bahia, b., N.A.	B2	80
Chetwynd, B.C., Can.	B7	85
Chevak, Ak., U.S.	C6	95
Cheviot, Oh., U.S.	C1	128
Chevreuil, Point, c., La., U.S.	E4	111
Chevy Chase, Md., U.S.	C3	113
Chewack, stm., Wa., U.S.	A5	140
Chewelah, Wa., U.S.	A8	140
Cheyenne, Ok., U.S.	B2	129
Cheyenne, Wy., U.S.	E8	143
Cheyenne, co., Co., U.S.	C8	99
Cheyenne, co., Ks., U.S.	C2	109
Cheyenne, co., Ne., U.S.	C2	120
Cheyenne, stm., U.S.	C7	92
Cheyenne, stm., U.S.	C4	134
Cheyenne, Dry Fork, stm., Wy., U.S.	C7	143
Cheyenne River Indian Reservation, S.D., U.S.	B4	134
Cheyenne Wells, Co., U.S.	C8	99
Chhapra, India	D4	40
Chhatarpur, India	E3	40
Chhatrapur, India	F5	40
Chhindwāra, India	E3	40
Chi, stm., Thai.	C4	34
Chiai, Tai.	E5	30
Chiange, Ang.	B1	56
Chiang Kham, Thai.	C4	34
Chiang Khan, Thai.	C4	34
Chiang Mai, Thai.	C3	34
Chiang Rai, Thai.	C3	34
Chiapas, state, Mex.	D6	78
Chiba, Japan	C4	31
Chiblow Lake, l., On., Can.	A1	89
Chibougamau, P.Q., Can.	k12	90
Chibuto, Moz.	C5	56
Chicago, Il., U.S.	B6	106
Chicago Heights, Il., U.S.	B6	106
Chicago Sanitary and Ship Canal, Il., U.S.	k8	106
Chicamacomico, stm., Md., U.S.	D6	113
Chicapa, stm., Afr.	E4	54
Chichagof Island, i., Ak., U.S.	m22	95
Chichén Itzá, hist., Mex.	C7	78
Chickahominy, stm., Va., U.S.	C5	139
Chickamauga, Ga., U.S.	B1	103
Chickamauga and Chattanooga National Military Park, U.S.	k11	135
Chickamauga Dam, Tn., U.S.	h11	135
Chickamauga Lake, res., Tn., U.S.	D8	135
Chickasaw, Al., U.S.	E1	94
Chickasaw, co., Ia., U.S.	A5	108
Chickasaw, co., Ms., U.S.	B5	117
Chickasawhay, stm., Ms., U.S.	D5	117
Chickasaw National Recreation Area, Ok., U.S.	C5	129
Chickasha, Ok., U.S.	B4	129
Chickasha, Lake, res., Ok., U.S.	B3	129
Chickwolnepy Stream, stm., N.H., U.S.	A4	122
Chiclayo, Peru	E4	70
Chico, Ca., U.S.	C3	98
Chico, stm., Arg.	F3	69
Chicoma, Ang.	A1	56
Chicopee, Ga., U.S.	B3	103
Chicopee, Ma., U.S.	B2	114
Chicora, Pa., U.S.	E2	131
Chicot, Lake, l., Ar., U.S.	D4	97
Chicot Island, i., La., U.S.	E6	111
Chicoutimi, P.Q., Can.	A6	90
Chicoutimi, stm., P.Q., Can.	A6	90
Chidambaram, India	G3	40
Chiefland, Fl., U.S.	C4	102
Chieti, Italy	C5	18
Chifeng, China	C11	28
Chignecto, Cape, c., N.S., Can.	D5	87
Chignecto Bay, b., Can.	D5	87
Chigubo, Moz.	C5	56
Chihli, Gulf of see Bo Hai, b., China	D11	28
Chihuahua, Mex.	B3	78
Chihuahua, state, Mex.	B3	78
Chihuahuan Desert, des., N.A.	A3	78
Chikaskia, stm., U.S.	A4	129
Chik Ballāpur, India	G3	40
Chikmagalūr, India	G3	40
Chilās, Pak.	C10	42
Childersburg, Al., U.S.	B3	94
Childress, Tx., U.S.	B2	136
Childress, co., Tx., U.S.	B2	136
Chile, ctry., S.A.	D2	69
Chilecito, Arg.	D4	72
Chile Rise	L29	64
Chilhowie, Va., U.S.	f10	139
Chililabombwe, Zam.	A4	56
Chilko, stm., B.C., Can.	D6	85
Chilko Lake, l., B.C., Can.	D5	85
Chillán, Chile	E2	69
Chillicothe, Il., U.S.	C4	106
Chillicothe, Mo., U.S.	B4	118
Chillicothe, Oh., U.S.	C3	128
Chilliwack, B.C., Can.	E7	85
Chillum, Md., U.S.	f9	113
Chiloé, Isla Grande de, i., Chile	F2	69
Chiloquin, Or., U.S.	E5	130
Chilpancingo de los Bravo, Mex.	D5	78
Chilton, Wi., U.S.	D5	142
Chilton, co., Al., U.S.	C3	94
Chiluage, Ang.	E4	54
Chilung, Tai.	D5	30
Chimacum, Wa., U.S.	A3	140
Chimaltenango, Guat.	C4	124
Chimayo, N.M., U.S.	A4	124
Chimborazo, vol., Ec.	D4	70
Chimbote, Peru	E4	70
Chimney Rock, mtn., Ne., U.S.	C2	120
Chimoio, Moz.	B5	56
China, ctry., Asia	D8	28
China Grove, N.C., U.S.	B2	126
China Lake, l., Me., U.S.	D3	112
Chinandega, Nic.	C2	80
Chincha Alta, Peru	F4	70
Chinchilla, Austl.	F5	62
Chincoteague, Va., U.S.	C7	139
Chincoteague Bay, b., U.S.	D7	113
Chinde, Moz.	B6	56
Chindwin, stm., Myan.	A3	34
Chingola, Zam.	A4	56
Chinguetti, Maur.	B2	50
Chin Hills, hills, Myan.	B2	34
Chinhoyi, Zimb.	A5	56
Chinitna Point, c., Ak., U.S.	h15	95
Chinju, S. Kor.	D13	28
Chinle, Az., U.S.	A6	96
Chino, Ca., U.S.	F5	98
Chinook, Mt., U.S.	B7	119
Chinook, Wa., U.S.	C2	140
Chinook, Lake, res., Or., U.S.	C5	130
Chino Valley, Az., U.S.	C3	96
Chinsali, Zam.	A5	56
Chinvali, Geor.	A10	44
Chioco, Moz.	B5	56
Chioggia, Italy	B4	18
Chios see Khíos, Grc.	E11	18
Chipata, Zam.	A5	56
Chipita Park, Co., U.S.	C6	99
Chipley, Fl., U.S.	u16	102
Chipola, stm., Fl., U.S.	B1	102
Chipman, N.B., Can.	C4	87
Chippewa, co., Mi., U.S.	B6	115
Chippewa, co., Mn., U.S.	E3	116
Chippewa, co., Wi., U.S.	C2	142
Chippewa, stm., Mn., U.S.	E3	116
Chippewa, stm., Wi., U.S.	D2	142
Chippewa, Lake, l., Wi., U.S.	C2	142
Chippewa Falls, Wi., U.S.	D2	142
Chipuxet, stm., R.I., U.S.	F3	132
Chiquimula, Guat.	C2	80
Chiquinquirá, Col.	B5	70
Chīrāla, India	G3	40
Chirfa, Niger	B7	50
Chiricahua Mountains, mts., Az., U.S.	E6	96
Chiricahua National Monument, Az., U.S.	F6	96
Chiricahua Peak, mtn., Az., U.S.	F6	96
Chirikof Island, i., Ak., U.S.	D8	95
Chiriquí, Golfo de, b., Pan.	D3	80
Chiriquí, Laguna de, b., Pan.	D3	80
Chiromo, Mwi.	B6	56
Chirripó, Cerro, mtn., C.R.	D3	80
Chisago, co., Mn., U.S.	E6	116
Chisago City, Mn., U.S.	E6	116
Ch'ishan, Tai.	E5	30
Chisholm, Me., U.S.	D2	112
Chisholm, Mn., U.S.	C6	116
Chishui, stm., China	D2	30
Chişinău, Mol.	F10	20
Chisos Mountains, mts., Tx., U.S.	E1	136
Chita see Čita, Russia	D13	26
Chitado, Ang.	B1	56
Chitato, Ang.	E4	54
Chitembo, Ang.	F3	54
Chitina, stm., Ak., U.S.	g19	95
Chitose, Japan	B4	31
Chitradurga, India	G3	40
Chitrāl, Pak.	C10	42
Chitré, Pan.	D3	80
Chittagong, Bngl.	E6	40
Chittaurgarh, India	E2	40
Chittenango, N.Y., U.S.	B5	125
Chittenden, co., Vt., U.S.	C2	138
Chittenden Reservoir, res., Vt., U.S.	D3	138
Chittoor, India	G3	40
Chitungwiza, Zimb.	B5	56
Chiumbe (Tshumbe), stm., Afr.	E4	54
Chiume, Ang.	B3	56
Chivacoa, Ven.	C6	80
Chivilcoy, Arg.	E5	72
Chŏăm Khsant, Camb.	D4	34
Chocolate Mountains, mts., U.S.	E6	98
Chocope, Peru	E4	70
Choctaw, Ok., U.S.	B4	129
Choctaw, co., Al., U.S.	C1	94
Choctaw, co., Ms., U.S.	B4	117
Choctaw, co., Ok., U.S.	C6	129
Choctawhatchee Bay, b., Fl., U.S.	u15	102
Choctaw Indian Reservation, Ms., U.S.	C4	117
Choele Choel, Arg.	E3	69
Chojnice, Pol.	C4	20
Chókwe, Moz.	C5	56
Cholet, Fr.	D6	16
Choluteca, Hond.	C2	80
Choluteca, stm., Hond.	C2	80
Choma, Zam.	B4	56
Chomutov, Czech Rep.	D2	20
Chon Buri, Thai.	D4	34
Chone, Ec.	D3	70
Chong'an, China	D9	28
Ch'ŏngjin, N. Kor.	C13	28
Ch'ŏngju, S. Kor.	D13	28
Chongqing, China	F9	28
Chongxin, China	B2	30
Chongzuo, China	D9	28
Chŏnju, S. Kor.	D13	28
Chonos, Archipiélago de los, is., Chile	G2	69
Choptank, stm., Md., U.S.	C6	113
Chornomors'ke, Ukr.	G12	20
Chortkiv, Ukr.	E8	20
Chōshi, Japan	D6	31
Chos Malal, Arg.	F3	72
Choteau, Mt., U.S.	C4	119
Chouteau, Mt., U.S.	A6	129
Chouteau, co., Mt., U.S.	C6	119
Chowan, co., N.C., U.S.	A6	126
Chowan, stm., N.C., U.S.	A6	126
Chowchilla, Ca., U.S.	D3	98
Choybalsan, Mong.	B10	28
Choyr, Mong.	B9	28
Chrisman, Il., U.S.	D6	106
Christchurch, N.Z.	p13	63c
Christian, co., Il., U.S.	D4	106
Christian, co., Ky., U.S.	D2	110
Christian, co., Mo., U.S.	E4	118
Christiana, De., U.S.	B3	101
Christiana, Pa., U.S.	G9	131
Christiansburg, Va., U.S.	C2	139
Christian Sound, strt., Ak., U.S.	n22	95
Christina, stm., Ab., Can.	A5	84
Christina, stm., De., U.S.	B3	101
Christina, Lake, l., Mn., U.S.	D3	116
Christina Peak, mtn., Nv., U.S.	D6	121
Christmas, Fl., U.S.	D5	102
Christmas Island, dep., Oc.	I4	32
Christmas Island, i., Christ. I.	F4	58
Christmas Island see Kiritimati, atoll, Kir.	D14	58
Christmas Lake, l., Or., U.S.	D6	130
Christmas Ridge	G22	64
Christopher, Il., U.S.	F4	106
Chubbuck, Id., U.S.	G6	105
Chubut, stm., Arg.	F3	69
Chugach Islands, is., Ak., U.S.	h16	95
Chugach Mountains, mts., Ak., U.S.	g18	95
Chugwater, Wy., U.S.	E8	143
Chugwater Creek, stm., Wy., U.S.	E8	143
Chuhuïv, Ukr.	E14	20
Chukchi Sea	E5	82
Chukotsk Peninsula see Čukotskij poluostrov, pen., Russia	C20	26
Chula Vista, Ca., U.S.	F5	98
Chulucanas, Peru	E3	70
Chumbicha, Arg.	D4	72
Chumphon, Thai.	D3	34
Chum Saeng, Thai.	C4	34
Chunchula, Al., U.S.	E1	94
Chungking see Chongqing, China	F9	28
Chuntuquí, Guat.	B1	80
Chupadera Mesa, mtn., N.M., U.S.	D3	124
Chuquibamba, Peru	B3	72
Chuquicamata, Chile	B3	69
Chur, Switz.	A2	18
Church Hill, Tn., U.S.	C11	135
Churchill, Mb., Can.	f9	86
Churchill, co., Nv., U.S.	D3	121
Churchill, stm., Can.	G21	82
Churchill, stm., Nf., Can.	h9	88
Churchill, Cape, c., Mb., Can.	f9	86
Churchill, Mount, mtn., B.C., Can.	E6	85
Churchill Falls, wtfl, Nf., Can.	h8	88
Churchill Lake, l., Sk., Can.	m7	91
Churchill Lake, l., Me., U.S.	B3	112
Church Point, La., U.S.	D3	111
Church Rock, N.M., U.S.	B1	124
Churchton, Md., U.S.	C4	113
Churchville, N.Y., U.S.	B3	125
Chūru, India	D2	40
Churubusco, In., U.S.	B7	107
Chuska Mountains, mts., Az., U.S.	A6	96
Chuuk Islands, is., Micron.	D9	58
Chuvashia see Čuvašija, state, Russia	D6	26
Chuxian, China	C4	30
Chuxiong, China	F8	28
Cianjur, Indon.	E3	36
Cianorte, Braz.	C7	72
Čiatura, Geor.	A10	44
Cibecue, Az., U.S.	C5	96
Cibola, co., N.M., U.S.	C1	124
Cibolo Creek, stm., Tx., U.S.	h7	136
Cicero, Il., U.S.	B6	106
Cicero, In., U.S.	D5	107
Cide, Tur.	B5	44
Ciechanów, Pol.	C6	20
Ciego de Ávila, Cuba	A4	80
Cienfuegos, Cuba	A3	80
Cieza, Spain	H6	16
Çifteler, Tur.	C4	44
Çiganak, Kaz.	E9	26
Çihanbeyli, Tur.	C5	44
Çiili, Tur.	B9	42
Čikoj, stm., Asia	D12	26
Cilacap, Indon.	E3	36
Çildır Gölü, l., Tur.	B10	44
Çilik, Kaz.	B11	29
Cimarron, Ks., U.S.	E3	109
Cimarron, N.M., U.S.	A5	124
Cimarron, co., Ok., U.S.	e8	129
Cimarron, stm., U.S.	D8	92
Čimbaj, Uzb.	B7	42
Cimljanskoe vodohranilišče, res., Russia	E7	22
Cina, Tanjung, c., Indon.	E2	36
Çınar, Tur.	D9	44
Cincinnati, Oh., U.S.	C1	128
Çine, Tur.	D3	44
Cinnaminson, N.J., U.S.	D3	123
Cintalapa, Mex.	D6	78
Cinto, Monte, mtn., Fr.	C2	18

Name	Map Ref.	Page
Cintra, Golfe de, b., W. Sah.	B1	50
Cipolletti, Arg.	E3	69
Čirčik, Uzb.	E8	26
Circle, Ak., U.S.	B11	95
Circle, Mt., U.S.	C11	119
Circle Pines, Mn., U.S.	m12	116
Circleville, Oh., U.S.	C3	128
Cirebon, Indon.	E3	36
Cirò Marina, Italy	E6	18
Cisco, Tx., U.S.	C3	136
Ciskei, hist. reg., S. Afr.	E4	56
Cisnădie, Rom.	G8	20
Cispus, stm., Wa., U.S.	C4	140
Cissna Park, Il., U.S.	C6	106
Čistopol', Russia	C9	22
Čita, Russia	D13	26
Citlaltépetl, Volcán see Pico de Orizaba, Volcán, vol., Mex.	D5	78
Citra, Fl., U.S.	C4	102
Citronelle, Al., U.S.	D1	94
Citrus, co., Fl., U.S.	D4	102
City of Refuge National Historical Park, Hi., U.S.	D5	104
City View, S.C., U.S.	B3	133
Ciudad Acuña, Mex.	B4	78
Ciudad Anáhuac, Mex.	B4	78
Ciudad Bolívar, Ven.	B7	70
Ciudad Camargo, Mex.	C2	78
Ciudad Camargo, Mex.	B3	78
Ciudad Constitución, Mex.	C2	78
Ciudad del Carmen, Mex.	D6	78
Ciudad del Este, Para.	D7	72
Ciudad de Libertador General San Martín, Arg.	C5	72
Ciudad de México (Mexico City), Mex.	D5	78
Ciudad de Nutrias, Ven.	D6	70
Ciudad Guayana, Ven.	B7	70
Ciudad Juárez, Mex.	A3	78
Ciudad Madero, Mex.	C5	78
Ciudad Mante, Mex.	C5	78
Ciudad Miguel Alemán, Mex.	B5	78
Ciudad Netzahualcóyotl, Mex.	D5	78
Ciudad Obregón, Mex.	B3	78
Ciudad Ojeda, Ven.	C5	80
Ciudad Real, Spain	H5	16
Ciudad Rodrigo, Spain	G3	16
Ciudad Valles, Mex.	C5	78
Ciudad Victoria, Mex.	C5	78
Ciutadella, Spain	G8	16
Civitanova Marche, Italy	C4	18
Civitavecchia, Italy	C3	18
Çivril, Tur.	C3	44
Cizre, Tur.	D10	44
C.J. Strike Reservoir, res., Id., U.S.	G3	105
Clackamas, Or., U.S.	h12	130
Clackamas, co., Or., U.S.	B4	130
Clacton-on-Sea, Eng., U.K.	E7	12
Claflin, Ks., U.S.	D5	109
Claiborne, co., La., U.S.	B2	111
Claiborne, co., Ms., U.S.	D3	117
Claiborne, co., Tn., U.S.	C10	135
Claiborne, Lake, res., La., U.S.	B3	111
Clair, N.B., Can.	B1	87
Claire, Lake, l., Ab., Can.	f8	84
Clair Engle Lake, res., Ca., U.S.	B2	98
Clairton, Pa., U.S.	F2	131
Clallam, co., Wa., U.S.	B1	140
Clallam Bay, Wa., U.S.	A1	140
Clam Lake, l., Wi., U.S.	C1	142
Clan Alpine Mountains, mts., Nv., U.S.	D4	121
Clanton, Al., U.S.	C3	94
Clanwilliam, S. Afr.	E2	56
Clara City, Mn., U.S.	F3	116
Clara Peak, mtn., Az., U.S.	C2	96
Clare, Mi., U.S.	E6	115
Clare, co., Mi., U.S.	E6	115
Claremont, Ca., U.S.	m13	98
Claremont, N.C., U.S.	B1	126
Claremont, N.H., U.S.	D2	122
Claremont, mtn., Ca., U.S.	C3	98
Claremore, Ok., U.S.	A6	129
Clarence, Ia., U.S.	C6	108
Clarence, Mo., U.S.	B5	118
Clarence Strait, strt., Austl.	C5	60
Clarence Strait, strt., Ak., U.S.	n23	95
Clarendon, Ar., U.S.	C4	97
Clarendon, Tx., U.S.	B2	136
Clarendon, co., S.C., U.S.	D7	133
Clarendon, stm., Vt., U.S.	E2	138
Clarendon Hills, Il., U.S.	k9	106
Clarenville, Nf., Can.	D4	88
Claresholm, Ab., Can.	D4	84
Clarinda, Ia., U.S.	D2	108
Clarion, Ia., U.S.	B4	108
Clarion, Pa., U.S.	D3	131
Clarion, co., Pa., U.S.	D3	131
Clarion, stm., Pa., U.S.	D3	131
Clarión, Isla, i., Mex.	D2	78
Clarion Fracture Zone	G25	64
Clarissa, Mn., U.S.	D4	116
Clark, N.J., U.S.	B4	123
Clark, S.D., U.S.	C8	134
Clark, co., Ar., U.S.	C2	97
Clark, co., Id., U.S.	E6	105
Clark, co., Il., U.S.	D6	106
Clark, co., In., U.S.	H6	107
Clark, co., Ks., U.S.	E4	109
Clark, co., Ky., U.S.	C5	110
Clark, co., Mo., U.S.	A6	118
Clark, co., Nv., U.S.	G6	121
Clark, co., Oh., U.S.	C2	128
Clark, co., S.D., U.S.	C8	134
Clark, co., Wa., U.S.	D3	140
Clark, co., Wi., U.S.	D3	142
Clark, Lake, l., Ak., U.S.	C9	95
Clark, Point, c., On., Can.	C3	89
Clarkdale, Az., U.S.	C3	96
Clarkdale, Ga., U.S.	h7	103
Clarke, co., Al., U.S.	D2	94
Clarke, co., Ga., U.S.	C3	103
Clarke, co., Ia., U.S.	D4	108
Clarke, co., Ms., U.S.	C5	117
Clarke, co., Va., U.S.	A4	139
Clarke Island, i., Austl.	I4	62
Clarkesville, Ga., U.S.	B3	103
Clarkfield, Mn., U.S.	F3	116
Clark Fork, stm., U.S.	C1	119
Clarks, La., U.S.	B3	111
Clarks, stm., Ky., U.S.	f9	110
Clarksburg, Md., U.S.	B3	113
Clarksburg, W.V., U.S.	B4	141
Clarksdale, Ms., U.S.	A3	117
Clarks Grove, Mn., U.S.	G5	116
Clark's Harbour, N.S., Can.	F4	87
Clarks Hill, In., U.S.	D4	107
Clarks Hill Lake, res., U.S.	E11	92
Clarkson, Ky., U.S.	C3	110
Clarkson, Ne., U.S.	C8	120
Clarks Summit, Pa., U.S.	m18	131
Clarkston, Ga., U.S.	h8	103
Clarkston, Mi., U.S.	F7	115
Clarkston, Ut., U.S.	B3	137
Clarkston, Wa., U.S.	C8	140
Clarksville, Ar., U.S.	B2	97
Clarksville, De., U.S.	F5	101
Clarksville, Ia., U.S.	B5	108
Clarksville, In., U.S.	H6	107
Clarksville, Tn., U.S.	A4	135
Clarksville, Tx., U.S.	C5	136
Clarksville, Va., U.S.	D4	139
Clarkton, Mo., U.S.	E8	118
Clarkton, N.C., U.S.	C4	126
Clatskanie, Or., U.S.	A3	130
Clatsop, co., Or., U.S.	A3	130
Claude, Tx., U.S.	B2	136
Clawson, Mi., U.S.	o15	115
Claxton, Ga., U.S.	D5	103
Clay, Ky., U.S.	C2	110
Clay, co., Al., U.S.	B4	94
Clay, co., Ar., U.S.	A5	97
Clay, co., Fl., U.S.	B5	102
Clay, co., Ga., U.S.	E2	103
Clay, co., Ia., U.S.	A2	108
Clay, co., Il., U.S.	E5	106
Clay, co., In., U.S.	F3	107
Clay, co., Ks., U.S.	C6	109
Clay, co., Ky., U.S.	C6	110
Clay, co., Mn., U.S.	D2	116
Clay, co., Mo., U.S.	B3	118
Clay, co., Ms., U.S.	B5	117
Clay, co., N.C., U.S.	f9	126
Clay, co., Ne., U.S.	D7	120
Clay, co., S.D., U.S.	E8	134
Clay, co., Tn., U.S.	C8	135
Clay, co., Tx., U.S.	C3	136
Clay, co., W.V., U.S.	C3	141
Clay Center, Ks., U.S.	C6	109
Clay Center, Ne., U.S.	D7	120
Clay City, Il., U.S.	E5	106
Clay City, In., U.S.	F3	107
Clay City, Ky., U.S.	C6	110
Clay Creek, stm., S.D., U.S.	D8	134
Claymont, De., U.S.	A4	101
Clayoquot Sound, strt., B.C., Can.	E4	85
Claypool, Az., U.S.	D5	96
Claysburg, Pa., U.S.	F5	131
Claysville, Pa., U.S.	F1	131
Clayton, Al., U.S.	D4	94
Clayton, De., U.S.	C3	101
Clayton, Ga., U.S.	B3	103
Clayton, In., U.S.	E4	107
Clayton, La., U.S.	C4	111
Clayton, Mo., U.S.	f13	118
Clayton, N.C., U.S.	B4	126
Clayton, N.J., U.S.	D2	123
Clayton, N.M., U.S.	A6	124
Clayton, N.Y., U.S.	A4	125
Clayton, Ok., U.S.	C6	129
Clayton, co., Ga., U.S.	C2	103
Clayton, co., Ia., U.S.	B6	108
Claytor Lake, res., Va., U.S.	C2	139
Clear, stm., R.I., U.S.	B2	132
Clear Boggy Creek, stm., Ok., U.S.	C5	129
Clear Creek, co., Co., U.S.	B5	99
Clear Creek, stm., Tn., U.S.	C9	135
Clear Creek, stm., Wy., U.S.	B6	143
Cleare, Cape, c., Ak., U.S.	D10	95
Clearfield, Ky., U.S.	B6	110
Clearfield, Pa., U.S.	D5	131
Clearfield, Ut., U.S.	B3	137
Clearfield, co., Pa., U.S.	D5	131
Clear Fork, stm., W.V., U.S.	n13	141
Clear Fork, stm., W.V., U.S.	D3	141
Clearlake, Ca., U.S.	C2	98
Clear Lake, Ia., U.S.	A4	108
Clear Lake, S.D., U.S.	C9	134
Clearlake, Wa., U.S.	A3	140
Clear Lake, Wi., U.S.	C1	142
Clear Lake, l., Ia., U.S.	A4	108
Clear Lake, l., Ut., U.S.	D3	137
Clear Lake, res., Ca., U.S.	B3	98
Clear Lake Reservoir, res., Ca., U.S.	B3	98
Clear Lake Shores, Tx., U.S.	r15	136
Clear Stream, stm., N.H., U.S.	g7	122
Clearwater, B.C., Can.	D7	85
Clearwater, Fl., U.S.	E4	102
Clearwater, Ks., U.S.	E6	109
Clearwater, S.C., U.S.	E4	133
Clearwater, co., Id., U.S.	C3	105
Clearwater, co., Mn., U.S.	C3	116
Clearwater, stm., Can.	A5	84
Clearwater, stm., Id., U.S.	C2	105
Clearwater, stm., Mn., U.S.	C3	116
Clearwater Lake, res., Mo., U.S.	D7	118
Clearwater Mountains, mts., Id., U.S.	C2	105
Cleburne, Tx., U.S.	C4	136
Cleburne, co., Al., U.S.	B4	94
Cleburne, co., Ar., U.S.	B3	97
Cle Elum, Wa., U.S.	B5	140
Cle Elum, stm., Wa., U.S.	B4	140
Cle Elum Lake, res., Wa., U.S.	B4	140
Clementon, N.J., U.S.	D3	123
Clemmons, N.C., U.S.	A2	126
Clemson, S.C., U.S.	B2	133
Clendenin, W.V., U.S.	C3	141
Clendening Lake, res., Oh., U.S.	B4	128
Cleona, Pa., U.S.	F9	131
Clermont, Austl.	E4	62
Clermont, P.Q., Can.	B7	90
Clermont, Fl., U.S.	D5	102
Clermont, co., Oh., U.S.	C1	128
Clermont-Ferrand, Fr.	E8	16
Cleveland, Ga., U.S.	B3	103
Cleveland, Mn., U.S.	F5	116
Cleveland, Ms., U.S.	B3	117
Cleveland, N.C., U.S.	B2	126
Cleveland, Oh., U.S.	A4	128
Cleveland, Ok., U.S.	A5	129
Cleveland, Tn., U.S.	D9	135
Cleveland, Tx., U.S.	D5	136
Cleveland, Wi., U.S.	k10	142
Cleveland, co., Ar., U.S.	D3	97
Cleveland, co., N.C., U.S.	B1	126
Cleveland, co., Ok., U.S.	B4	129
Cleveland, Mount, mtn., Mt., U.S.	B3	119
Cleveland Heights, Oh., U.S.	A4	128
Cleves, Oh., U.S.	o12	128
Clew Bay, b., Ire.	D2	12
Clewiston, Fl., U.S.	F6	102
Cliff Island, i., Me., U.S.	g7	112
Clifford, On., Can.	D4	89
Cliffside, N.C., U.S.	B1	126
Cliffside Park, N.J., U.S.	h9	123
Clifton, Az., U.S.	D6	96
Clifton, Co., U.S.	B2	99
Clifton, Il., U.S.	C6	106
Clifton, N.J., U.S.	B4	123
Clifton, S.C., U.S.	B4	133
Clifton, Tn., U.S.	B4	135
Clifton, Tx., U.S.	D4	136
Clifton Forge, Va., U.S.	C3	139
Clifton Knolls, N.Y., U.S.	C7	125
Clifton Springs, N.Y., U.S.	C3	125
Clinch, co., Ga., U.S.	F4	103
Clinch, stm., U.S.	D9	135
Clinch Mountain, mtn., U.S.	C10	135
Clingmans Dome, mtn., U.S.	D10	135
Clinton, B.C., Can.	D7	85
Clinton, On., Can.	D3	89
Clinton, Ar., U.S.	B3	97
Clinton, Ct., U.S.	D5	100
Clinton, Ia., U.S.	C7	108
Clinton, Il., U.S.	C5	106
Clinton, In., U.S.	E3	107
Clinton, Ky., U.S.	f9	110
Clinton, La., U.S.	D4	111
Clinton, Ma., U.S.	B4	114
Clinton, Md., U.S.	C4	113
Clinton, Me., U.S.	D3	112
Clinton, Mi., U.S.	F7	115
Clinton, Mo., U.S.	C4	118
Clinton, Ms., U.S.	C3	117
Clinton, N.C., U.S.	C4	126
Clinton, N.Y., U.S.	B5	125
Clinton, Ok., U.S.	B3	129
Clinton, S.C., U.S.	C4	133
Clinton, Tn., U.S.	C9	135
Clinton, Ut., U.S.	B3	137
Clinton, Wa., U.S.	B3	140
Clinton, Wi., U.S.	F5	142
Clinton, co., Ia., U.S.	C7	108
Clinton, co., Il., U.S.	E4	106
Clinton, co., In., U.S.	D4	107
Clinton, co., Ky., U.S.	D4	110
Clinton, co., Mi., U.S.	F6	115
Clinton, co., Mo., U.S.	B3	118
Clinton, co., N.Y., U.S.	f11	125
Clinton, co., Oh., U.S.	C2	128
Clinton, co., Pa., U.S.	D6	131
Clinton, Lake, res., Il., U.S.	C5	106
Clinton Lake, res., Ks., U.S.	m15	109
Clinton Reservoir, res., N.J., U.S.	A4	123
Clintonville, Wi., U.S.	D5	142
Clintwood, Va., U.S.	e9	139
Clio, Al., U.S.	D4	94
Clio, Mi., U.S.	E7	115
Clio, S.C., U.S.	B8	133
Clipperton, Île, atoll, Oc.	G28	64
Clipperton Fracture Zone	H25	64
Clive, Ia., U.S.	e8	108
Clodomira, Arg.	D5	72
Cloncurry, Austl.	E3	62
Clonmel, Ire.	D3	12
Cloquet, Mn., U.S.	D6	116
Cloquet, stm., Mn., U.S.	C6	116
Clorinda, Arg.	D6	72
Closter, N.J., U.S.	B5	123
Clothier, W.V., U.S.	n12	141
Cloud, co., Ks., U.S.	C6	109
Cloudcroft, N.M., U.S.	E4	124
Cloud Peak, mtn., Wy., U.S.	B5	143
Clover, S.C., U.S.	A5	133
Cloverdale, Al., U.S.	A2	94
Cloverdale, Ca., U.S.	C2	98
Cloverdale, In., U.S.	E4	107
Cloverport, Ky., U.S.	C3	110
Clovis, Ca., U.S.	D4	98
Clovis, N.M., U.S.	C6	124
Cluj-Napoca, Rom.	F7	20
Clute, Tx., U.S.	r14	136
Clyde, Ks., U.S.	C6	109
Clyde, N.C., U.S.	f10	126
Clyde, N.Y., U.S.	B4	125
Clyde, Oh., U.S.	A3	128
Clyde, Tx., U.S.	C3	136
Clyde, Firth of, b., Scot., U.K.	C4	12
Clymer, Pa., U.S.	E3	131
Cnossus see Knossós, hist., Grc.	G10	18
Coachella, Ca., U.S.	F5	98
Coachella Canal, Ca., U.S.	F6	98
Coahoma, Tx., U.S.	C2	136
Coahoma, co., Ms., U.S.	A3	117
Coahuila, state, Mex.	B4	78
Coal, co., Ok., U.S.	C5	129
Coal, stm., W.V., U.S.	C3	141
Coal Branch, N.B., Can.	C4	87
Coal City, Il., U.S.	B5	106
Coal Creek, stm., Ok., U.S.	B6	129
Coaldale, Ab., Can.	E4	84
Coal Fork, W.V., U.S.	C3	141
Coal Fork, stm., W.V., U.S.	m13	141
Coalgate, Ok., U.S.	C5	129
Coal Grove, Oh., U.S.	D3	128
Coal Hill, Ar., U.S.	B2	97
Coalhurst, Ab., Can.	E4	84
Coalinga, Ca., U.S.	D3	98
Coalmont, Tn., U.S.	D8	135
Coalville, Ut., U.S.	C4	137
Coalwood, W.V., U.S.	D3	141
Coaraci, Braz.	D4	74
Coari, Braz.	D7	70
Coast Mountains, mts., N.A.	G13	82
Coast Ranges, mts., U.S.	C3	92
Coatesville, Pa., U.S.	G10	131
Coaticook, P.Q., Can.	D6	90
Coats, N.C., U.S.	B4	126
Coats Land, reg., Ant.	D2	67
Coatzacoalcos, Mex.	D6	78
Cobalt, On., Can.	p19	89
Cobán, Guat.	B1	80
Cobar, Austl.	G4	62
Cobb, co., Ga., U.S.	C2	103
Cobb, stm., Mn., U.S.	G5	116
Cobble Mountain Reservoir, res., Ma., U.S.	B2	114
Cobbosseecontee Lake, l., Me., U.S.	D3	112
Cobden, On., Can.	B8	89
Cobden, Il., U.S.	F4	106
Cobequid Mountains, mts., N.S., Can.	D5	87
Cobham, stm., Can.	C4	86
Cobija, Bol.	F6	70
Cobleskill, N.Y., U.S.	C6	125
Cobourg, On., Can.	D6	89
Cobourg Peninsula, pen., Austl.	C5	60
Cóbuè, Moz.	A5	56
Cobun Creek, stm., W.V., U.S.	h11	141
Coburg, Ger.	E12	12
Coburg, Or., U.S.	C3	130
Cocachacra, Peru	B3	72
Cochabamba, Bol.	B4	72
Cocheco, stm., N.H., U.S.	D5	122
Cochin see Kochi, India	H3	40
Cochise, co., Az., U.S.	F5	96
Cochise Head, mtn., Az., U.S.	E6	96
Cochiti Indian Reservation, N.M., U.S.	h8	124
Cochiti Reservoir, res., N.M., U.S.	B3	124
Cochituate, Ma., U.S.	g10	114
Cochituate, Lake, l., Ma., U.S.	g10	114
Cochran, Ga., U.S.	D3	103
Cochran, co., Tx., U.S.	C1	136
Cochrane, Ab., Can.	D3	84
Cochrane, On., Can.	o19	89
Cochranton, Pa., U.S.	C1	131
Cocke, co., Tn., U.S.	D10	135
Cockeysville, Md., U.S.	B4	113
Cockrell Hill, Tx., U.S.	n10	136
Coco, stm., N.A.	F8	76
Coco, Cayo, i., Cuba	A4	80
Coco, Isla del, i., C.R.	D2	80
Cocoa, Fl., U.S.	D6	102
Cocoa Beach, Fl., U.S.	D6	102
Coco Channel, strt., Asia	D2	34
Coco Islands, is., Myan.	D2	34
Coconino, co., Az., U.S.	B3	96
Cocopah Indian Reservation, Az., U.S.	E1	96
Cocos Islands, dep., Oc.	F3	58
Cocos Ridge	H5	66
Cod, Cape, c., Ma., U.S.	C7	114
Codajás, Braz.	D7	70
Coden, Al., U.S.	E1	94
Codington, co., S.D., U.S.	C8	134
Codó, Braz.	B3	74
Cody, Wy., U.S.	B3	143
Coeburn, Va., U.S.	f9	139
Coen, Austl.	C3	62
Coeroeni (Corentyne), stm., S.A.	C8	70
Coëtivy, i., Sey.	i13	57b
Coeur d'Alene, Id., U.S.	B2	105
Coeur d'Alene, stm., Id., U.S.	B2	105
Coeur d'Alene Indian Reservation, Id., U.S.	B2	105
Coeur d'Alene Lake, res., Id., U.S.	B2	105
Coeur d'Alene Mountains, mts., Id., U.S.	B2	105
Coffee, co., Al., U.S.	D3	94
Coffee, co., Ga., U.S.	E4	103
Coffee, co., Tn., U.S.	B5	135
Coffeeville, Ms., U.S.	B4	117
Coffey, co., Ks., U.S.	D8	109
Coffeyville, Ks., U.S.	E8	109
Coffs Harbour, Austl.	G5	62
Coggon, Ia., U.S.	B6	108
Cognac, Fr.	E6	16
Cohansey, stm., N.J., U.S.	E2	123
Cohasset, Ma., U.S.	B6	114
Cohasset, Mn., U.S.	C5	116
Cohocton, stm., N.Y., U.S.	C3	125
Cohoes, N.Y., U.S.	C7	125
Cohoon, Lake, res., Va., U.S.	k14	139
Cohutta Mountain, mtn., Ga., U.S.	B2	103
Coiba, Isla de, i., Pan.	D3	80
Coihaique, Chile	G2	69
Coimbatore, India	G4	40
Coimbra, Port.	G2	16
Coipasa, Lago, l., Bol.	B4	72
Cojutepeque, El Sal.	C2	80
Cokato, Mn., U.S.	E4	116
Coke, co., Tx., U.S.	D2	136
Cokeville, Wy., U.S.	D2	143
Čokurdah, Russia	B16	26
Colac, Austl.	H3	62
Colatina, Braz.	E3	74
Colbeck, Cape, c., Ant.	D25	67
Colbert, Ok., U.S.	D5	129
Colbert, co., Al., U.S.	A2	94
Colborne, On., Can.	C7	89
Colby, Ks., U.S.	C2	109
Colby, Wi., U.S.	D3	142
Colchester, Eng., U.K.	E7	12
Colchester, Ct., U.S.	C6	100
Colchester, Il., U.S.	C3	106
Colcord, Ok., U.S.	A7	129
Cold, stm., N.H., U.S.	D2	122
Cold, stm., N.H., U.S.	C4	122
Cold Bay, Ak., U.S.	E7	95
Cold Lake, Ab., Can.	B5	84
Cold Spring, Ky., U.S.	A5	110
Cold Spring, Mn., U.S.	E4	116
Coldwater, On., Can.	C5	89
Coldwater, Ks., U.S.	E4	109
Coldwater, Mi., U.S.	G5	115
Coldwater, Ms., U.S.	A4	117
Coldwater, Oh., U.S.	B1	128
Coldwater, stm., Ms., U.S.	A3	117
Coldwater Creek, stm., U.S.	e9	129
Cole, co., Mo., U.S.	C5	118
Colebrook, N.H., U.S.	g7	122
Colebrook River Lake, res., Ct., U.S.	A3	100
Cole Camp, Mo., U.S.	C4	118
Coleen, stm., Ak., U.S.	B11	95
Coleman, Mi., U.S.	E6	115
Coleman, Tx., U.S.	D3	136
Coleman, Wi., U.S.	C5	142
Coleman, co., Tx., U.S.	D3	136
Coleraine, N. Ire., U.K.	C3	12
Coleraine, Mn., U.S.	C5	116
Coles, co., Il., U.S.	D5	106
Colesberg, S. Afr.	E4	56
Colfax, Ca., U.S.	C3	98
Colfax, Ia., U.S.	C4	108
Colfax, Il., U.S.	C5	106
Colfax, In., U.S.	D4	107
Colfax, La., U.S.	C3	111
Colfax, Wa., U.S.	C8	140
Colfax, Wi., U.S.	D2	142
Colfax, co., Ne., U.S.	C8	120
Colfax, co., N.M., U.S.	A5	124
Colhué Huapi, Lago, l., Arg.	G3	69
Colima, Mex.	D4	78

Name	Map Ref.	Page
Colima, state, Mex.	D4	78
Colinas, Braz.	C3	74
Coll, i., Scot., U.K.	B3	12
College, Ak., U.S.	B10	95
Collegedale, Tn., U.S.	h11	135
College Park, Ga., U.S.	C2	103
College Park, Md., U.S.	C4	113
College Place, Wa., U.S.	C7	140
College Station, Ar., U.S.	C3	97
College Station, Tx., U.S.	D4	136
Collegeville, In., U.S.	C3	107
Collegeville, Pa., U.S.	F11	131
Colleton, co., S.C., U.S.	F6	133
Collie, Austl.	G2	60
Collier, co., Fl., U.S.	F5	102
Colliers, W.V., U.S.	f8	141
Collierville, Tn., U.S.	B2	135
Collin, co., Tx., U.S.	C4	136
Collingdale, Pa., U.S.	p20	131
Collingswood, N.J., U.S.	D2	123
Collingsworth, co., Tx., U.S.	B2	136
Collingwood, On., Can.	C4	89
Collins, Ms., U.S.	D4	117
Collins Park, De., U.S.	B3	101
Collinsville, Al., U.S.	A4	94
Collinsville, Ct., U.S.	B4	100
Collinsville, Il., U.S.	E4	106
Collinsville, Ms., U.S.	C5	117
Collinsville, Ok., U.S.	A6	129
Collinwood, Tn., U.S.	B4	135
Collipulli, Chile	E2	69
Colmar, Fr.	C10	16
Colmar Manor, Md., U.S.	f9	113
Colo, Ia., U.S.	B4	108
Cologne see Köln, Ger.	E10	12
Coloma, Mi., U.S.	F4	115
Colombia, ctry., S.A.	C5	70
Colombo, Braz.	D8	72
Colombo, Sri L.	H3	40
Colón, Arg.	E5	72
Colón, Cuba	A3	80
Colón, Pan.	D3	80
Colon, Mi., U.S.	G5	115
Colón, Archipiélago de (Galapagos Islands), is., Ec.	C2	70
Colonial Beach, Va., U.S.	B6	139
Colonial Heights, Tn., U.S.	C11	135
Colonial Heights, Va., U.S.	C5	139
Colonial National Historical Park, Va., U.S.	C6	139
Colonie, N.Y., U.S.	C7	125
Colorado, co., Tx., U.S.	E4	136
Colorado, state, U.S.	B5	99
Colorado, stm., Arg.	E4	69
Colorado, stm., N.A.	E5	92
Colorado, stm., Tx., U.S.	D3	136
Colorado City, Az., U.S.	A3	96
Colorado City, Co., U.S.	D6	99
Colorado City, Tx., U.S.	C2	136
Colorado City, Lake, res., Tx., U.S.	C2	136
Colorado National Monument, Co., U.S.	B2	99
Colorado River Aqueduct, Ca., U.S.	F6	98
Colorado River Indian Reservation, U.S.	D1	96
Colorado Springs, Co., U.S.	C6	99
Colquitt, Ga., U.S.	E2	103
Colquitt, co., Ga., U.S.	E3	103
Colstrip, Mt., U.S.	E10	119
Colton, S.D., U.S.	D9	134
Coltons Point, Md., U.S.	D4	113
Columbia, Al., U.S.	D4	94
Columbia, Il., U.S.	E3	106
Columbia, Ky., U.S.	C4	110
Columbia, Md., U.S.	B4	113
Columbia, Mo., U.S.	C5	118
Columbia, Ms., U.S.	D4	117
Columbia, N.C., U.S.	B6	126
Columbia, Pa., U.S.	F9	131
Columbia, S.C., U.S.	C5	133
Columbia, Tn., U.S.	B4	135
Columbia, co., Ar., U.S.	D2	97
Columbia, co., Fl., U.S.	B4	102
Columbia, co., Ga., U.S.	C4	103
Columbia, co., N.Y., U.S.	C7	125
Columbia, co., Or., U.S.	B3	130
Columbia, co., Pa., U.S.	D9	131
Columbia, co., Wa., U.S.	C7	140
Columbia, co., Wi., U.S.	E4	142
Columbia, stm., N.A.	B3	92
Columbia, Mount, mtn., Can.	C2	84
Columbia City, In., U.S.	B7	107
Columbia City, Or., U.S.	B4	130
Columbia Falls, Mt., U.S.	B2	119
Columbia Heights, Mn., U.S.	m12	116
Columbia Lake, res., Ct., U.S.	C6	100
Columbia Mountains, mts., B.C., Can.	C7	85
Columbia Mountains, mts., N.A.	H15	82
Columbiana, Al., U.S.	B3	94
Columbiana, Oh., U.S.	B5	128
Columbiana, co., Oh., U.S.	B5	128
Columbiaville, Mi., U.S.	E7	115
Columbus, Ga., U.S.	D2	103
Columbus, In., U.S.	F6	107
Columbus, Ks., U.S.	E9	109
Columbus, Ms., U.S.	B5	117
Columbus, Mt., U.S.	E7	119
Columbus, N.C., U.S.	f10	126
Columbus, Ne., U.S.	C8	120
Columbus, N.M., U.S.	F2	124
Columbus, Oh., U.S.	C2	128
Columbus, Tx., U.S.	E4	136
Columbus, Wi., U.S.	E4	142
Columbus, co., N.C., U.S.	C4	126
Columbus Air Force Base, mil., Ms., U.S.	B5	117
Columbus Grove, Oh., U.S.	B1	128
Columbus Junction, Ia., U.S.	C6	108
Columbus Lake, res., Ms., U.S.	B5	117
Colusa, Ca., U.S.	C2	98
Colusa, co., Ca., U.S.	C2	98
Colver, Pa., U.S.	E4	131
Colville, Wa., U.S.	A8	140
Colville, stm., Ak., U.S.	B9	95
Colville, stm., Wa., U.S.	A8	140
Colville Indian Reservation, Wa., U.S.	A6	140
Colvos Passage, strt., Wa., U.S.	f10	140
Colwich, Ks., U.S.	E6	109
Colwood, B.C., Can.	h12	85
Comacchio, Italy	B4	18
Comacchio, Valli di, l., Italy	B4	18
Comal, co., Tx., U.S.	E3	136
Comalcalco, Mex.	D6	78
Coman, Mount, mtn., Ant.	D34	67
Comanche, Ok., U.S.	C4	129
Comanche, Tx., U.S.	D3	136
Comanche, co., Ks., U.S.	E4	109
Comanche, co., Ok., U.S.	C3	129
Comanche, co., Tx., U.S.	D3	136
Comandante Fontana, Arg.	D6	72
Comayagua, Hond.	C2	80
Combahee, stm., S.C., U.S.	F6	133
Combarbalá, Chile	D2	69
Comber, On., Can.	E2	89
Combermere Bay, b., Myan.	D2	34
Combined Locks, Wi., U.S.	h9	142
Combs, Ky., U.S.	C6	110
Comer, Ga., U.S.	B3	103
Comfort, Tx., U.S.	E3	136
Comilla, Bngl.	E6	40
Comitán, Mex.	D6	78
Comite, stm., La., U.S.	D4	111
Commerce, Ga., U.S.	B3	103
Commerce, Ok., U.S.	A7	129
Commerce, Tx., U.S.	C5	136
Commerce City, Co., U.S.	B6	99
Committee Bay, b., N.T., Can.	E22	82
Common Fence Point, R.I., U.S.	D6	132
Communism Peak see Kommunizma, pik, mtn., Taj.	F9	26
Como, Italy	B2	18
Como, Ms., U.S.	A4	117
Como, Lago di, l., Italy	B2	18
Comodoro Rivadavia, Arg.	G3	69
Comores, Archipel des, is., Afr.	A7	56
Comorin, Cape, c., India	H3	40
Comoros, ctry., Afr.	A7	56
Comox, B.C., Can.	E5	85
Compiègne, Fr.	C8	16
Compostela, Mex.	C4	78
Compton, P.Q., Can.	D6	90
Compton, Ca., U.S.	n12	98
Comrat, Mol.	F10	20
Comstock, Mi., U.S.	F5	115
Conakry, Gui.	E2	50
Conanicut Island, i., R.I., U.S.	E5	132
Conanicut Point, c., R.I., U.S.	E5	132
Concarneau, Fr.	D5	16
Conceição da Barra, Braz.	E4	74
Conceição do Araguaia, Braz.	C2	74
Concepción, Arg.	D4	72
Concepción, Chile	E2	69
Concepción, Para.	C6	72
Concepción del Oro, Mex.	C4	78
Concepción del Uruguay, Arg.	E6	72
Conception, Point, c., Ca., U.S.	E3	98
Conception Bay, b., Nf., Can.	E5	88
Conception Bay South, Nf., Can.	E5	88
Conchas Lake, res., N.M., U.S.	B5	124
Concho, co., Tx., U.S.	D3	136
Concho, stm., Tx., U.S.	D2	136
Conchos, stm., Mex.	B3	78
Concord, Ca., U.S.	h8	98
Concord, Ma., U.S.	B5	114
Concord, Mi., U.S.	F6	115
Concord, Mo., U.S.	g13	118
Concord, N.C., U.S.	B2	126
Concord, N.H., U.S.	D3	122
Concord, stm., Ma., U.S.	A5	114
Concordia, Arg.	E6	72
Concórdia, Braz.	D7	72
Concordia, Ks., U.S.	C6	109
Concordia, Mo., U.S.	C4	118
Concordia, co., La., U.S.	C4	111
Concrete, Wa., U.S.	A4	140
Conda, Ang.	F2	54
Condobolin, Austl.	G4	62
Condon, Or., U.S.	B6	130
Condoto, Col.	D4	80
Conecuh, co., Al., U.S.	D2	94
Conecuh, stm., U.S.	D3	94
Conejos, co., Co., U.S.	D4	99
Conejos, stm., Co., U.S.	D4	99
Conejos Peak, mtn., Co., U.S.	D4	99
Conemaugh, Pa., U.S.	F4	131
Conemaugh River Lake, res., Pa., U.S.	F3	131
Congamond Lakes, l., U.S.	A4	100
Congaree, stm., S.C., U.S.	D6	133
Congaree Swamp National Monument, S.C., U.S.	D6	133
Congo, ctry., Afr.	D3	54
Congo (Zaïre), stm., Afr.	D2	54
Congo, Democratic Republic of the, ctry., Afr.	D4	54
Congress, Az., U.S.	C3	96
Conimicut Point, c., R.I., U.S.	D5	132
Conklin, N.Y., U.S.	C5	125
Connaught, hist. reg., Ire.	D2	12
Conneaut, Oh., U.S.	A5	128
Conneaut Creek, stm., Oh., U.S.	A5	128
Conneaut Lake, l., Pa., U.S.	C1	131
Connecticut, state, U.S.	C5	100
Connecticut, stm., U.S.	C5	100
Connell, Wa., U.S.	C7	140
Connellsville, Pa., U.S.	F2	131
Connersville, In., U.S.	E7	107
Conover, N.C., U.S.	B1	126
Conowingo, Md., U.S.	A5	113
Conrad, Ia., U.S.	B5	108
Conrad, Mt., U.S.	B5	119
Conroe, Tx., U.S.	D5	136
Conselheiro Lafaiete, Braz.	F3	74
Conselheiro Pena, Braz.	E8	74
Conshohocken, Pa., U.S.	F11	131
Consolación del Sur, Cuba	A3	80
Consort, Ab., Can.	C5	84
Constance see Konstanz, Ger.	G11	12
Constance, Lake, l., Eur.	A2	18
Constanța, Rom.	G10	20
Constantina, Spain	I4	16
Constantine see Qacentina, Alg.	C6	48
Constantine, Mi., U.S.	G5	115
Constantine, Cape, c., Ak., U.S.	D8	95
Constantinople see İstanbul, Tur.	B3	44
Constitución, Chile	E2	69
Contas, stm., Braz.	D3	74
Content Keys, is., Fl., U.S.	H5	102
Continental, Oh., U.S.	A1	128
Continental Peak, mtn., Wy., U.S.	D4	143
Continental Reservoir, res., Co., U.S.	D3	99
Contoocook, N.H., U.S.	D3	122
Contoocook, stm., N.H., U.S.	D3	122
Contra Costa, co., Ca., U.S.	D3	98
Contrecoeur, P.Q., Can.	D4	90
Converse, In., U.S.	C6	107
Converse, S.C., U.S.	B4	133
Converse, co., Wy., U.S.	C7	143
Convoy, Oh., U.S.	B1	128
Conway, Ar., U.S.	B3	97
Conway, Fl., U.S.	D5	102
Conway, Mo., U.S.	D5	118
Conway, N.C., U.S.	A5	126
Conway, N.H., U.S.	C4	122
Conway, Pa., U.S.	E1	131
Conway, S.C., U.S.	D9	133
Conway, co., Ar., U.S.	B3	97
Conway, Lake, res., Ar., U.S.	B3	97
Conway Lake, l., N.H., U.S.	C4	122
Conway Springs, Ks., U.S.	E6	109
Conyers, Ga., U.S.	C2	103
Coober Pedy, Austl.	F5	60
Cook, Mn., U.S.	C6	116
Cook, co., Ga., U.S.	E3	103
Cook, co., Il., U.S.	B6	106
Cook, co., Mn., U.S.	k9	116
Cook, Cape, c., B.C., Can.	D4	85
Cook, Mount, mtn., N.Z.	p12	63c
Cooke, co., Tx., U.S.	C4	136
Cookes Peak, mtn., N.M., U.S.	E2	124
Cookeville, Tn., U.S.	C8	135
Cook Inlet, b., Ak., U.S.	D9	95
Cook Islands, dep., Oc.	F13	58
Cook Point, c., Md., U.S.	C5	113
Cookshire, P.Q., Can.	D6	90
Cookson, Ok., U.S.	B7	129
Cooktown, Austl.	D4	62
Cooleemee, N.C., U.S.	B2	126
Coolgardie, Austl.	G3	60
Coolidge, Az., U.S.	E4	96
Coolidge, Ga., U.S.	E3	103
Cooma, Austl.	H4	62
Coonabarabran, Austl.	G4	62
Coonamble, Austl.	G4	62
Coonoor, India	G3	40
Coon Rapids, Ia., U.S.	C3	108
Coon Rapids, Mn., U.S.	E5	116
Coon Valley, Wi., U.S.	E2	142
Cooper, Tx., U.S.	C5	136
Cooper, co., Mo., U.S.	C5	118
Cooper, stm., S.C., U.S.	F8	133
Cooper Creek, stm., Austl.	F2	62
Cooper Mountain, mtn., Ak., U.S.	g17	95
Coopersburg, Pa., U.S.	F11	131
Cooperstown, N.D., U.S.	B7	127
Cooperstown, N.Y., U.S.	C6	125
Coopersville, Mi., U.S.	E5	115
Coorow, Austl.	F2	60
Coos, co., N.H., U.S.	A4	122
Coos, co., Or., U.S.	D2	130
Coos, stm., Or., U.S.	D2	130
Coosa, co., Al., U.S.	C3	94
Coosa, stm., U.S.	C3	94
Coosada, Al., U.S.	C3	94
Coosawhatchie, stm., S.C., U.S.	F5	133
Coos Bay, Or., U.S.	D2	130
Cootamundra, Austl.	G4	62
Copalis Beach, Wa., U.S.	B1	140
Copan, Oh., U.S.	A6	129
Copan Reservoir, res., Ok., U.S.	A6	129
Copenhagen see København, Den.	I5	10
Copiah, co., Ms., U.S.	D3	117
Copiapó, Chile	C2	69
Coplay, Pa., U.S.	E10	131
Copper, stm., Ak., U.S.	C11	95
Copperas Cove, Tx., U.S.	D4	136
Copper Butte, mtn., Wa., U.S.	A7	140
Copper Mountain, mtn., Wy., U.S.	C5	143
Copper Mountains, mts., Az., U.S.	E2	96
Coquille, Or., U.S.	D2	130
Coquimbo, Chile	C2	69
Corabia, Rom.	H8	20
Coral Gables, Fl., U.S.	G6	102
Coral Sea, Oc.	F9	58
Coral Sea Basin,	J18	64
Coralville, Ia., U.S.	C6	108
Coralville Lake, res., Ia., U.S.	C5	108
Coraopolis, Pa., U.S.	E1	131
Corbeil-Essonnes, Fr.	C8	16
Corbin, Ky., U.S.	D5	110
Corcoran, Ca., U.S.	D4	98
Corcoran, Mn., U.S.	m11	116
Corcovado, Golfo de, Chile	F2	69
Corcovado, Volcán, vol., Chile	F2	69
Cordele, Ga., U.S.	E3	103
Cordell, Ok., U.S.	B3	129
Cordell Hull Lake, res., Tn., U.S.	C8	135
Córdoba, Arg.	E5	72
Córdoba, Mex.	D5	78
Córdoba, Spain	I4	16
Córdova, Peru	A2	72
Cordova see Córdoba, Spain	I4	16
Cordova, Ak., U.S.	C10	95
Cordova, Al., U.S.	B2	94
Cordova, N.C., U.S.	C3	126
Cordova, N.M., U.S.	A4	124
Cordova Peak, mtn., Ak., U.S.	C10	95
Corentyne (Coeroeni), stm., S.A.	C8	70
Corfu see Kérkira, Grc.	E7	18
Corfu see Kérkira, i., Grc.	E7	18
Coria, Spain	H3	16
Corinna, Me., U.S.	D3	112
Corinne, Ut., U.S.	B3	137
Corinne Key, i., Fl., U.S.	G6	102
Corinth see Kórinthos, Grc.	F9	18
Corinth, Ms., U.S.	A5	117
Corinth, N.Y., U.S.	B7	125
Corinth, Gulf of see Korinthiakós Kólpos, b., Grc.	E9	18
Corinto, Braz.	E3	74
Corisco, Isla de, i., Eq. Gui.	C1	54
Cork, Ire.	E2	12
Çorlu, Tur.	B2	44
Cormorant Lake, l., Mb., Can.	B1	86
Cornelia, Ga., U.S.	B3	103
Cornélio Procópio, Braz.	F1	74
Cornelius, N.C., U.S.	B2	126
Cornelius, Or., U.S.	g11	130
Cornell, Wi., U.S.	C2	142
Corner Brook, Nf., Can.	D3	88
Cornersville, Tn., U.S.	B5	135
Cornfield Point, c., Ct., U.S.	D6	100
Cornie Bayou, stm., U.S.	D3	97
Corning, Ar., U.S.	A5	97
Corning, Ca., U.S.	C2	98
Corning, Ia., U.S.	D3	108
Corning, N.Y., U.S.	C3	125
Cornish, Me., U.S.	E2	112
Corno Grande, mtn., Italy	C4	18
Cornville, Az., U.S.	C4	96
Cornwall, On., Can.	B10	89
Cornwall, Pa., U.S.	F9	131
Cornwall, hist. reg., Eng., U.K.	E4	12
Cornwall on Hudson, N.Y., U.S.	D6	125
Coroatá, Braz.	B3	74
Corocoro Island, i., S.A.	D7	80
Čoroh, stm., Asia	B9	44
Coroico, Bol.	B4	72
Coromandel Coast, India	G4	40
Corona, Ca., U.S.	F5	98
Coronado, Ca., U.S.	F5	98
Coronado, Bahía de, b., C.R.	D3	80
Coronado National Memorial, Az., U.S.	F5	96
Coronation, Ab., Can.	C5	84
Coronation Gulf, b., N.T., Can.	E17	82
Coronation Island, i., Ant.	B36	67
Coronation Island, i., Ak., U.S.	n22	95
Coronel Murta, Braz.	B9	72
Coronel Oviedo, Para.	D6	72
Coronel Suárez, Arg.	F5	72
Coronel Vivida, Braz.	D7	72
Coropuna, Nevado, vol., Peru	G5	70
Corozal, Belize	B2	80
Corozal, Col.	D4	80
Corpus Christi, Tx., U.S.	F4	136
Corpus Christi Naval Air Station, mil., Tx., U.S.	F4	136
Correctionville, Ia., U.S.	B2	108
Correntina, Braz.	A9	72
Corrib, Lough, l., Ire.	D2	12
Corrientes, Arg.	D6	72
Corrientes, Cabo, c., Col.	B4	70
Corrientes, Cabo, c., Mex.	C3	78
Corrigan, Tx., U.S.	D5	136
Corriganville, Md., U.S.	k13	113
Corrigin, Austl.	G2	60
Corriverton, Guy.	B8	70
Corry, Pa., U.S.	C2	131
Corse (Corsica), i., Fr.	C2	18
Corse, Cap, c., Fr.	C2	18
Corsica, S.D., U.S.	D7	134
Corsica see Corse, i., Fr.	C2	18
Corsicana, Tx., U.S.	C4	136
Corson, co., S.D., U.S.	B4	134
Corson Inlet, b., N.J., U.S.	E3	123
Cort Adelaer, Kap, c., Grnld.	F31	82
Corte, Fr.	C2	18
Cortés, Mar de see California, Golfo de, b., Mex.	B2	78
Cortez, Co., U.S.	D2	99
Cortez, Fl., U.S.	q10	102
Cortez, Sea of see California, Golfo de, b., Mex.	B2	78
Cortez Mountains, mts., Nv., U.S.	C5	121
Cortland, Il., U.S.	B5	106
Cortland, N.Y., U.S.	C4	125
Cortland, Oh., U.S.	A5	128
Cortland, co., N.Y., U.S.	C4	125
Çorum, Tur.	B6	44
Çorumbá, Braz.	G8	70
Corunna see A Coruña, Spain	F2	16
Corunna, Mi., U.S.	F6	115
Coruripe, Braz.	D4	74
Corvallis, Or., U.S.	C3	130
Corydon, Ia., U.S.	D4	108
Corydon, In., U.S.	H5	107
Corydon, Ky., U.S.	C2	110
Coryell, co., Tx., U.S.	D4	136
Cos see Kos, i., Grc.	F11	18
Cosenza, Italy	E6	18
Coshocton, Oh., U.S.	B4	128
Coshocton, co., Oh., U.S.	B4	128
Cosmoledo, Atoll de, i., Sey.	i11	57b
Cosmopolis, Wa., U.S.	C2	140
Cosmos, Mn., U.S.	F4	116
Cosne-sur-Loire, Fr.	D8	16
Cossatot, stm., Ar., U.S.	C1	97
Costa Mesa, Ca., U.S.	n13	98
Costa Rica, Mex.	C3	78
Costa Rica, ctry., N.A.	F8	76
Costilla, co., Co., U.S.	D5	99
Coswig, Ger.	E13	12
Cotabato, Phil.	E8	34
Cote d'Ivoire, ctry., Afr.	E3	50
Cotonou, Benin	E5	50
Cotopaxi, vol., Ec.	D4	70
Cottage Grove, Mn., U.S.	n13	116
Cottage Grove, Or., U.S.	D3	130
Cottage Grove Reservoir, res., Or., U.S.	D3	130
Cottam, On., Can.	E2	89
Cottbus, Ger.	E14	12
Cotter, Ar., U.S.	A3	97
Cottle, co., Tx., U.S.	B2	136
Cottleville, Mo., U.S.	f12	118
Cotton, co., Ok., U.S.	C3	129
Cottondale, Al., U.S.	B2	94
Cotton Plant, Ar., U.S.	B4	97
Cottonport, La., U.S.	C3	111
Cotton Valley, La., U.S.	B2	111
Cottonwood, Al., U.S.	D4	94
Cottonwood, Az., U.S.	C3	96
Cottonwood, Ca., U.S.	B2	98
Cottonwood, Id., U.S.	C2	105
Cottonwood, Mn., U.S.	F3	116
Cottonwood, co., Mn., U.S.	F3	116
Cottonwood, stm., Ks., U.S.	D7	109

Name	Map Ref.	Page

Cottonwood, stm., Mn., U.S. F3   116
Cottonwood Creek, stm., Wy., U.S. C4   143
Cottonwood Falls, Ks., U.S.   D7   109
Cotuit, Ma., U.S. C7   114
Cotulla, Tx., U.S. E3   136
Coudersport, Pa., U.S. . . . C5   131
Cougar Reservoir, res., Or., U.S. C4   130
Coulee Creek, stm., Wa., U.S. g13   140
Coulee Dam, Wa., U.S. . . . B7   140
Coulee Dam National Recreation Area, Wa., U.S. A7   140
Coulterville, Il., U.S. E4   106
Counce, Tn., U.S. B3   135
Council, Id., U.S. E2   105
Council Bluffs, Ia., U.S. . . . C2   108
Council Grove, Ks., U.S. . . D7   109
Council Grove Lake, res., Ks., U.S. D7   109
Council Mountain, mtn., Id., U.S. E2   105
Country Homes, Wa., U.S. B8   140
Coupeville, Wa., U.S. A3   140
Courland Lagoon, b., Eur. B6   20
Courtenay, B.C., Can. E5   85
Courte Oreilles, Lac, l., Wi., U.S. C2   142
Courtland, On., Can. E4   89
Courtland, Al., U.S. A2   94
Courtland, Va., U.S. D5   139
Coushatta, La., U.S. B2   111
Cove Creek, stm., Ut., U.S. E3   137
Covedale, Oh., U.S. o12   128
Coventry, Eng., U.K. D6   12
Coventry, Ct., U.S. B6   100
Coventry, R.I., U.S. D3   132
Cove Point, c., Md., U.S. . . D5   113
Covilhã, Port. G3   16
Covina, Ca., U.S. m13   98
Covington, Ga., U.S. C3   103
Covington, In., U.S. D3   107
Covington, Ky., U.S. A10   110
Covington, La., U.S. D5   111
Covington, Oh., U.S. B1   128
Covington, Tn., U.S. B2   135
Covington, Va., U.S. C3   139
Covington, co., Al., U.S. . . D3   94
Covington, co., Ms., U.S. . . D4   117
Cowan, Tn., U.S. B5   135
Cowansville, P.Q., Can. . . . D5   90
Cowarts, Al., U.S. D4   94
Cow Creek, stm., Wa., U.S. C7   140
Cowee Mountains, mts., N.C., U.S. f9   126
Cowell, Austl. G2   62
Cowen, Mount, mtn., Mt., U.S. E6   119
Coweta, Ok., U.S. B6   129
Coweta, co., Ga., U.S. C2   103
Cow Head, Nf., Can. D3   88
Cowichan Bay, B.C., Can. . g12   85
Cow Lakes, l., Or., U.S. . . . D9   130
Cowley, Wy., U.S. B4   143
Cowley, co., Ks., U.S. E7   109
Cowlington, Ok., U.S. B7   129
Cowlitz, co., Wa., U.S. . . . C2   140
Cowlitz, stm., Wa., U.S. . . . C3   140
Cowpasture, stm., Va., U.S. B3   139
Cowpen Mountain, mtn., Ga., U.S. B2   103
Cowpens, S.C., U.S. A4   133
Cowra, Austl. G4   62
Coxim, Braz. G9   70
Coxsackie, N.Y., U.S. C7   125
Cox's Bāzār, Bngl. E6   40
Cox's Cove, Nf., Can. D2   88
Coyuca de Catalán, Mex. . . D4   78
Cozad, Ne., U.S. D6   120
Cozumel, Mex. C7   78
Cozumel, Isla, i., Mex. C7   78
Crab Creek, stm., Wa., U.S. B7   140
Crab Creek, stm., Wa., U.S. C6   140
Crab Orchard, Ky., U.S. . . . C5   110
Crab Orchard, Tn., U.S. . . . D9   135
Crab Orchard, W.V., U.S. . . n13   141
Crab Orchard Lake, res., Il., U.S. F4   106
Crabtree, Pa., U.S. F3   131
Crabtree Mills, P.Q., Can. . . D4   90
Cracow see Kraków, Pol. . . D5   20
Cradock, S. Afr. E4   56
Crafton, Pa., U.S. k13   131
Craig, Ak., U.S. D13   95
Craig, Co., U.S. A3   99
Craig, co., Ok., U.S. A6   129
Craig, co., Va., U.S. C2   139
Craig Air Force Base, mil., Al., U.S. C3   94
Craig Creek, stm., Va., U.S. C2   139
Craighead, co., Ar., U.S. . . B5   97
Craigsville, Va., U.S. B3   139
Craigsville, W.V., U.S. C4   141
Craiova, Rom. G7   20
Cramerton, N.C., U.S. B1   126
Cranberry Lake, l., N.Y., U.S. A6   125
Cranberry Portage, Mb., Can. B1   86
Cranbrook, Austl. G2   60
Cranbrook, B.C., Can. E10   85
Crandall, Tx., U.S. n10   136

Crandon, Wi., U.S. C5   142
Crane, Mo., U.S. E4   118
Crane, Tx., U.S. D1   136
Crane, co., Tx., U.S. D1   136
Crane Creek, stm., Oh., U.S. e7   128
Crane Creek Reservoir, res., Id., U.S. E2   105
Crane Lake, l., Il., U.S. C3   106
Crane Lake, l., Mn., U.S. . . B6   116
Crane Mountain, mtn., Or., U.S. E6   130
Crane Prairie Reservoir, res., Or., U.S. D5   130
Cranford, N.J., U.S. B4   123
Cranston, R.I., U.S. C4   132
Crater Lake, l., Or., U.S. . . E4   130
Crater Lake National Park, Or., U.S. E4   130
Craters of the Moon National Monument, Id., U.S. F5   105
Crateús, Braz. C3   74
Crato, Braz. C4   74
Craven, co., N.C., U.S. . . . B5   126
Crawford, Ga., U.S. C3   103
Crawford, Ms., U.S. B5   117
Crawford, Ne., U.S. B2   120
Crawford, co., Ar., U.S. . . . B1   97
Crawford, co., Ga., U.S. . . D3   103
Crawford, co., Ia., U.S. . . . B2   108
Crawford, co., Il., U.S. D6   106
Crawford, co., In., U.S. . . . H4   107
Crawford, co., Ks., U.S. . . . E9   109
Crawford, co., Mi., U.S. . . . D6   115
Crawford, co., Mo., U.S. . . D6   118
Crawford, co., Oh., U.S. . . B3   128
Crawford, co., Pa., U.S. . . . C1   131
Crawford, co., Wi., U.S. . . . E3   142
Crawford Lake, l., Me., U.S. C5   112
Crawford Notch State Park, N.H., U.S. B4   122
Crawfordsville, Ar., U.S. . . . B5   97
Crawfordsville, In., U.S. . . . D4   107
Crawfordville, Fl., U.S. B2   102
Crawley, Eng., U.K. E6   12
Crazy Mountains, mts., Mt., U.S. D6   119
Crazy Peak, mtn., Mt., U.S. D6   119
Crazy Woman Creek, stm., Wy., U.S. B6   143
Creal Springs, Il., U.S. F5   106
Creedmoor, N.C., U.S. A4   126
Creek, co., Ok., U.S. B5   129
Cree Lake, l., Sk., Can. . . . m7   91
Creemore, On., Can. C4   89
Creighton, Ne., U.S. B8   120
Creighton, Pa., U.S. h14   131
Creil, Fr. C5   16
Crema, Italy B2   18
Cremona, Italy B3   18
Crenshaw, Ms., U.S. A3   117
Crenshaw, co., Al., U.S. . . . D3   94
Creola, Al., U.S. E1   94
Cres, Otok, i., Cro. B5   18
Cresaptown, Md., U.S. k13   113
Crescent, Ok., U.S. B4   129
Crescent, Or., U.S. D5   130
Crescent Lake, l., Wa., U.S. A2   140
Crescent City, Ca., U.S. . . . B1   98
Crescent City, Fl., U.S. C5   102
Crescent Lake, l., Fl., U.S. . C5   102
Crescent Lake, l., Or., U.S. . D5   130
Crescent Springs, Ky., U.S. . h13   110
Cresco, Ia., U.S. A5   108
Cresskill, N.J., U.S. h9   123
Cresson, Pa., U.S. F4   131
Cressona, Pa., U.S. E9   131
Crested Butte, Co., U.S. . . C4   99
Crest Hill, Il., U.S. k8   106
Crestline, Oh., U.S. B3   128
Creston, B.C., Can. E9   85
Creston, Ia., U.S. C3   108
Creston, Oh., U.S. B4   128
Crestone Peak, mtn., Co., U.S. D5   99
Crestview, Fl., U.S. u15   102
Crestview, Hi., U.S. g10   104
Crestwood, Ky., U.S. B4   110
Crestwood Village, N.J., U.S. D4   123
Creswell, Or., U.S. D3   130
Crete, Il., U.S. B6   106
Crete, Ne., U.S. D9   120
Crete see Kríti, i., Grc. G10   18
Crete, Sea of see Kritikón Pélagos, Grc. G10   18
Creve Coeur, Il., U.S. C4   106
Crewe, Eng., U.K. D5   12
Crewe, Va., U.S. C4   139
Criciúma, Braz. D8   72
Cricket, N.C., U.S. A1   126
Cridersville, Oh., U.S. B1   128
Crimean Mountains see Kryms'ki hory, mts., Ukr. G13   20
Crimean Peninsula see Kryms'kyi pivostriv, pen., Ukr. G12   20
Crisfield, Md., U.S. E6   113
Crisp, co., Ga., U.S. E3   103
Cristalândia, Braz. F10   70
Cristalina, Braz. E2   74
Cristóbal Colón, Pico, mtn., Col. A5   70
Crittenden, Ky., U.S. B5   110

Crittenden, co., Ar., U.S. . . B5   97
Crittenden, co., Ky., U.S. . . e9   110
Crivitz, Wi., U.S. C6   142
Crna Gora (Montenegro), prov., Yugo. C7   18
Croatia, ctry., Eur. B5   18
Crocker, Mo., U.S. D5   118
Crockett, Ca., U.S. g8   98
Crockett, Tx., U.S. D5   136
Crockett, co., Tn., U.S. . . . B2   135
Crockett, co., Tx., U.S. . . . D2   136
Crofton, Ky., U.S. C2   110
Crofton, Md., U.S. B4   113
Crofton, Ne., U.S. B8   120
Croix, Lac la, l., Mn., U.S. . B6   116
Croker, Cape, c., Austl. . . . C6   60
Croker, Cape, c., On., Can. C4   89
Croker Island, i., Austl. C5   60
Cromona, Ky., U.S. C7   110
Cromwell, Ct., U.S. C5   100
Cromwell, Ia., U.S. C3   108
Crook, co., Or., U.S. C6   130
Crook, co., Wy., U.S. B8   143
Crooked, stm., Or., U.S. . . C6   130
Crooked Creek, stm., Pa., U.S. C7   131
Crooked Creek, stm., Il., U.S. E3   109
Crooked Creek Lake, res., Pa., U.S. E3   131
Crooked Island, i., Bah. . . . D10   76
Crooked Island Passage, strt., Bah. A5   80
Crooked Lake, l., Fl., U.S. . . E5   102
Crooked Lake, l., Mn., U.S. B7   116
Crooks, S.D., U.S. D9   134
Crooks Lake, l., Nv., U.S. . . B2   121
Crookston, Mn., U.S. C2   116
Crooksville, Oh., U.S. C3   128
Crosby, Mn., U.S. D5   116
Crosby, N.D., U.S. A2   127
Crosby, Tx., U.S. r14   136
Crosby, co., Tx., U.S. C2   136
Crosby, Mount, mtn., Wy., U.S. C3   143
Crosbyton, Tx., U.S. C2   136
Cross, co., Ar., U.S. B5   97
Cross Creek, stm., W.V., U.S. f8   141
Crossett, Ar., U.S. D4   97
Crossfield, Ab., Can. D3   84
Cross Island, i., Me., U.S. . . D5   112
Cross Lake, Mb., Can. B3   86
Crosslake, Mn., U.S. D4   116
Cross Lake, l., Me., U.S. . . A4   112
Cross Lake, res., La., U.S. . B2   111
Cross Lanes, W.V., U.S. . . . C3   141
Crossman Peak, mtn., Az., U.S. C1   96
Cross Plains, Tn., U.S. A5   135
Cross Plains, Tx., U.S. C3   136
Cross Plains, Wi., U.S. E4   142
Cross Sound, strt., Ak., U.S. k21   95
Crossville, Al., U.S. A4   94
Crossville, Il., U.S. E5   106
Crossville, Tn., U.S. D8   135
Croswell, Mi., U.S. E8   115
Crothersville, In., U.S. G6   107
Crotone, Italy E6   18
Croton-on-Hudson, N.Y., U.S. D7   125
Crouse, N.C., U.S. B1   126
Crow, stm., Mn., U.S. E4   116
Crow Agency, Mt., U.S. . . . E9   119
Crow Creek, stm., U.S. . . . A6   99
Crow Creek Indian Reservation, S.D., U.S. C6   134
Crowder, Ms., U.S. A3   117
Crowell, Tx., U.S. C3   136
Crow Indian Reservation, Mt., U.S. E9   119
Crowley, La., U.S. D3   111
Crowley, Tx., U.S. n9   136
Crowley, co., Co., U.S. . . . C7   99
Crowley, Lake, res., Ca., U.S. D4   98
Crowleys Ridge, mtn., U.S. B5   97
Crown Point, In., U.S. B3   107
Crown Point, La., U.S. k11   111
Crownpoint, N.M., U.S. . . . B1   124
Crown Peak, mtn., Mt., U.S. D5   119
Crowsnest Pass, Ab., Can. . E3   84
Crowsnest Pass, Can. E3   84
Crow Wing, co., Mn., U.S. . D4   116
Crow Wing, stm., Mn., U.S. D4   116
Crozet, Va., U.S. B4   139
Crozet, Archipel, is., Afr. . . N15   46
Crozet Basin L9   64
Cruces, Cuba A3   80
Crump Lake, l., Or., U.S. . . E7   130
Cruz, Cabo, c., Cuba B4   80
Cruz Alta, Braz. D7   72
Cruz del Eje, Arg. E5   72
Cruzeiro, Braz. F2   74
Cruzeiro do Sul, Braz. E5   70
Crystal, Mn., U.S. m12   116
Crystal, stm., Co., U.S. . . . B3   99
Crystal Bay, Nv., U.S. D1   121
Crystal Bay, b., Fl., U.S. . . . D4   102
Crystal Beach, Fl., U.S. . . . D4   102
Crystal City, Mb., Can. E2   86
Crystal City, Mo., U.S. C7   118
Crystal City, Tx., U.S. E3   136
Crystal Falls, Mi., U.S. B2   115
Crystal Lake, Ct., U.S. B6   100

Crystal Lake, Fl., U.S. u16   102
Crystal Lake, Il., U.S. A5   106
Crystal Lake, l., Ct., U.S. . . B6   100
Crystal Lake, l., Mi., U.S. . . D4   115
Crystal Lake, l., N.H., U.S. . D4   122
Crystal Lake, l., Vt., U.S. . . B4   138
Crystal Lawns, Il., U.S. . . . k8   106
Crystal Pond, res., Ct., U.S. B7   100
Crystal River, Fl., U.S. D4   102
Crystal Springs, Ms., U.S. . D3   117
Čū, stm., Asia B10   42
Cúa, Ven. C6   80
Cuamba, Moz. A6   56
Cuando (Kwando), stm., Afr. B3   56
Cuangar, Ang. B2   56
Cuango, Ang. E3   54
Cuango, Ang. E3   54
Cuango (Kwango), stm., Afr. E3   54
Cuanza, stm., Ang. E3   52
Cuauhtémoc, Mex. B3   78
Cuba, Il., U.S. C3   106
Cuba, Mo., U.S. C6   118
Cuba, N.M., U.S. A3   124
Cuba, N.Y., U.S. C2   125
Cuba, ctry., N.A. D9   76
Cuba City, Wi., U.S. F3   142
Cubal, Ang. F2   54
Cubango (Okavango), stm., Afr. B2   56
Cubero, N.M., U.S. B2   124
Cucharas, stm., Co., U.S. . . D6   99
Cúcuta, Col. B5   70
Cudahy, Wi., U.S. F6   142
Cuddalore, India G3   40
Cuddapah, India G3   40
Cuddy Mountain, mtn., Id., U.S. E2   105
Cue, Austl. F2   60
Cuenca, Ec. D4   70
Cuenca, Spain G5   16
Cuencamé de Ceniceros, Mex. C4   78
Cuernavaca, Mex. D5   78
Cuero, Tx., U.S. E4   136
Cuiabá, Braz. G8   70
Cuilo (Kwilu), stm., Afr. . . . E3   54
Cuima, Ang. A2   56
Cuíto, stm., Ang. B2   56
Cuito Cuanavale, Ang. B2   56
Cuitzeo, Laguna de, l., Mex. D4   78
Cuivre, West Fork, stm., Mo., U.S. B6   118
Čukai, Malay. C2   36
Čukotskij poluostrov, pen., Russia C20   26
Čulakkurgan, Kaz. B9   42
Culberson, co., Tx., U.S. . . o12   136
Culbertson, Mt., U.S. B12   119
Culbertson, Ne., U.S. D5   120
Culebra Peak, mtn., Co., U.S. D5   99
Culfa, Azer. C11   44
Culiacán, Mex. C3   78
Cullen, La., U.S. B2   111
Cullera, Spain H6   16
Cullman, Al., U.S. A3   94
Cullman, co., Al., U.S. A3   94
Culloden, W.V., U.S. C2   141
Cullowhee, N.C., U.S. f9   126
Čul'man, Russia D14   26
Culpeper, Va., U.S. B4   139
Culpeper, co., Va., U.S. . . . B5   139
Culver, In., U.S. B5   107
Culver City, Ca., U.S. m12   98
Culvers Lake, l., N.J., U.S. . A3   123
Čulym, Russia D10   26
Čulym, stm., Russia D10   26
Cumaná, Ven. A7   70
Cumberland, B.C., Can. . . . E5   85
Cumberland, Ky., U.S. D7   110
Cumberland, Md., U.S. . . . k13   113
Cumberland, Wi., U.S. C2   142
Cumberland, co., Il., U.S. . . D5   106
Cumberland, co., Ky., U.S. . D4   110
Cumberland, co., Me., U.S. E2   112
Cumberland, co., N.C., U.S. C4   126
Cumberland, co., N.J., U.S. E2   123
Cumberland, co., Pa., U.S. . F7   131
Cumberland, co., Tn., U.S. . D8   135
Cumberland, co., Va., U.S. . C4   139
Cumberland, stm., U.S. . . . D4   110
Cumberland, Lake, res., Ky., U.S. D5   110
Cumberland Center, Me., U.S. g7   112
Cumberland Foreside, Me., U.S. E2   112
Cumberland Gap, U.S. D6   110
Cumberland Gap National Historical Park, U.S. . . . D6   110
Cumberland Hill, R.I., U.S. . B4   132
Cumberland Island National Seashore, Ga., U.S. . . . F5   103
Cumberland Lake, l., Sk., Can. C4   91
Cumbres Pass, Co., U.S. . . D4   99
Cuming, co., Ne., U.S. C9   120
Cumming, Ga., U.S. B2   103
Çumra, Tur. D5   44
Čunani, Braz. C9   70
Čundža, Kaz. B11   42
Cunene (Kunene), stm., Afr. B1   56
Cuneo, Italy B1   18

Čunja, stm., Russia C11   26
Cunnamulla, Austl. F4   62
Cunningham, Ky., U.S. f9   110
Cupar, Sk., Can. G3   91
Curaçao, i., Neth. Ant. C6   80
Curanilahue, Chile E2   69
Čurapča, Russia C15   26
Curecanti National Recreation Area, Co., U.S. C3   99
Curepipe, Mrts. g10   57a
Curicó, Chile D2   69
Curitiba, Braz. D8   72
Curitibanos, Braz. D7   72
Curlew Creek, stm., Wa., U.S. A7   140
Curlew Lake, l., Wa., U.S. . A7   140
Currais Novos, Braz. C4   74
Currant Mountain, mtn., Nv., U.S. E6   121
Current, stm., U.S. A5   97
Currituck, co., N.C., U.S. . . A6   126
Curry, co., N.M., U.S. C6   124
Curry, co., Or., U.S. E2   130
Curtea de Argeş, Rom. . . . G8   20
Curtin Springs, Austl. F5   60
Curtis, Ne., U.S. D5   120
Curtis Island, i., Austl. E5   62
Curtisville, Pa., U.S. E2   131
Cururupu, Braz. B3   74
Curuzú Cuatiá, Arg. D6   72
Curvelo, Braz. E3   74
Curwensville, Pa., U.S. . . . E4   131
Curwensville Lake, res., Pa., U.S. E4   131
Curwood, Mount, mtn., Mi., U.S. B2   115
Cusco, Peru F5   70
Cushing, Ok., U.S. B5   129
Cushman, Lake, res., Wa., U.S. B2   140
Čusovoj, Russia C10   22
Cusseta, Ga., U.S. D2   103
Custer, S.D., U.S. D2   134
Custer, co., Co., U.S. C5   99
Custer, co., Id., U.S. E4   105
Custer, co., Mt., U.S. D11   119
Custer, co., Ne., U.S. C6   120
Custer, co., Ok., U.S. B2   129
Custer, co., S.D., U.S. D2   134
Custer Battlefield National Monument, Mt., U.S. . . . E9   119
Cut, Nuhu, i., Indon. E8   36
Cut Bank, Mt., U.S. B4   119
Cut Bank Creek, stm., N.D., U.S. A4   127
Cutchogue, N.Y., U.S. m16   125
Cuthbert, Ga., U.S. E2   103
Cutler Ridge, Fl., U.S. s13   102
Cut Off, La., U.S. E5   111
Cuttack, India E5   40
Cuttyhunk Island, i., Ma., U.S. D6   114
Čuvašija, state, Russia D6   26
Cuvier, Cape, c., Austl. . . . E1   60
Cuxhaven, Ger. D11   12
Cuyahoga, co., Oh., U.S. . . A4   128
Cuyahoga, stm., Oh., U.S. . A4   128
Cuyahoga Falls, Oh., U.S. . A4   128
Cuyama, stm., Ca., U.S. . . E4   98
Cuyamaca Peak, mtn., Ca., U.S. F5   98
Cuyo Islands, is., Phil. D8   34
Cuyuni, stm., S.A. D7   80
C.W. McConaughy, Lake, res., Ne., U.S. C4   120
Cyclades see Kikládhes, is., Grc. F10   18
Cynthiana, In., U.S. H2   107
Cynthiana, Ky., U.S. B5   110
Cypress Creek, stm., Tx., U.S. r14   136
Cypress Hills Provincial Park, Sk., Can. H1   91
Cypress Lake, l., Fl., U.S. . . D5   102
Cypress Quarters, Fl., U.S. . E6   102
Cypress Swamp, sw., U.S. . F4   101
Cyprus, ctry., Asia E5   44
Cyprus, North see North Cyprus, ctry., Asia E5   44
Cyrenaica see Barqah, hist. reg., Libya E8   14
Cyril, Ok., U.S. C3   129
Cythera see Kíthira, i., Grc. F9   18
Cythnos see Kíthnos, i., Grc. F10   18
Czech Republic, ctry., Eur. . E3   20
Częstochowa, Pol. D5   20

D

Dabajuro, Ven. C5   80
Dabeiba, Col. D4   80
Dabhoi, India E2   40
Dabie Shan, mts., China . . E5   28
Dabola, Gui. D2   50
Dabou, C. Iv. E4   50
Daboya, Ghana E4   50
Dacca see Dhaka, Bngl. . . . E6   40
Dacono, Co., U.S. A6   99
Dacula, Ga., U.S. C3   103
Dade, co., Fl., U.S. G6   102
Dade, co., Ga., U.S. B1   103

Name	Map Ref.	Page
Dade, co., Mo., U.S.	D4	118
Dade City, Fl., U.S.	D4	102
Dadeville, Al., U.S.	C4	94
Dādra and Nagar Haveli, prov., India	E2	40
Dādu, Pak.	E9	42
Daet, Phil.	D8	34
Dafang, China	D2	30
Dafeng, China	C5	30
Daga Medo, Eth.	B8	54
Dagana, Sen.	C1	50
Dagestan, state, Russia	E6	26
Dagestan see Altaj, state, Russia	A5	28
Daggett, co., Ut., U.S.	C6	137
Dagsboro, De., U.S.	F5	101
Dagu, China	B4	30
Daguan, China	D1	30
Dagupan, Phil.	C8	34
Da Hinggan Ling, mts., China	B12	28
Dahlak Archipelago, is., Erit.	G4	38
Dahlonega, Ga., U.S.	B3	103
Dāhod, India	E2	40
Dahomey see Benin, ctry., Afr.	D5	50
Dahra, Libya	E8	48
Dahūk, Iraq	D10	44
Dailing, China	A1	31
Daingerfield, Tx., U.S.	C5	136
Dairen see Dalian, China	D12	28
Dakar, Sen.	D1	50
Dakhla, W. Sah.	B1	50
Dākoānk, India	H6	40
Dakoro, Niger	D6	50
Dakota, co., Mn., U.S.	F5	116
Dakota, co., Ne., U.S.	B9	120
Dakota City, Ia., U.S.	B3	108
Dakota City, Ne., U.S.	B9	120
Đakovica, Yugo.	C8	18
Đakovo, Cro.	B7	18
Dalaba, Gui.	D2	50
Dalälven, stm., Swe.	F7	10
Dalandzadgad, Mong.	C8	28
Dalarna, hist. reg., Swe.	F6	10
Da Lat, Viet.	D5	34
Dālbandin, Pak.	E8	42
Dalby, Austl.	F5	62
Dale, In., U.S.	H4	107
Dale, co., Al., U.S.	D4	94
Dale City, Va., U.S.	B5	139
Dale Hollow Lake, res., U.S.	C8	135
Daleville, Al., U.S.	D4	94
Daleville, In., U.S.	D6	107
Dalhart, Tx., U.S.	A1	136
Dalhousie, N.B., Can.	A3	87
Dalhousie, India	C3	40
Dali, China	F8	28
Dali, China	C2	30
Dalian, China	D12	28
Dall, Mount, mtn., Ak., U.S.	f15	95
Dallam, co., Tx., U.S.	A1	136
Dallas, Ga., U.S.	C2	103
Dallas (part of Melcher), Ia., U.S.	C4	108
Dallas, N.C., U.S.	B1	126
Dallas, Or., U.S.	C3	130
Dallas, Pa., U.S.	D10	131
Dallas, Tx., U.S.	C4	136
Dallas, co., Al., U.S.	C2	94
Dallas, co., Ar., U.S.	D3	97
Dallas, co., Ia., U.S.	C3	108
Dallas, co., Mo., U.S.	D4	118
Dallas, co., Tx., U.S.	C4	136
Dallas Center, Ia., U.S.	C4	108
Dallas City, Il., U.S.	C2	106
Dallas Naval Air Station, mil., Tx., U.S.	n9	136
Dallastown, Pa., U.S.	G8	131
Dalli Rājhara, India	E4	40
Dall Island, i., Ak., U.S.	n23	95
Dalmacija, hist. reg., Eur.	C6	18
Dalmatia see Dalmacija, hist. reg., Eur.	C6	18
Dal'negorsk, Russia	E15	26
Dal'nerečensk, Russia	B14	28
Daloa, C. Iv.	E3	50
Dalqū, Sudan	F11	48
Dāltenganj, India	E4	40
Dalton, Ga., U.S.	B2	103
Dalton, Ma., U.S.	B1	114
Dalton, Oh., U.S.	B4	128
Dalton, Pa., U.S.	C10	131
Dalton Gardens, Id., U.S.	B2	105
Dalupiri Island, i., Phil.	C8	34
Dalvík, Ice.	l19	10a
Dalwallinu, Austl.	G2	60
Daly, stm., Austl.	C5	60
Daly City, Ca., U.S.	h8	98
Daly Waters, Austl.	D5	60
Damān, India	E2	40
Damanhūr, Egypt	E10	14
Damaraland, hist. reg., Nmb.	C2	56
Damariscotta, Me., U.S.	D3	112
Damariscotta Lake, l., Me., U.S.	D3	112
Damascus see Dimashq, Syria	F7	44
Damascus, Md., U.S.	B3	113
Damascus, Va., U.S.	f10	139
Damaturu, Nig.	D7	50
Damāvand, Qolleh-ye, vol., Iran	C6	42
Damba, Ang.	E3	54
Dambarta, Nig.	D6	50
Dāmghān, Iran	C6	42
Damietta, Egypt	E10	14
Damoh, India	E3	40
Damongo, Ghana	E4	50
Dampier, Austl.	E2	60
Dampier, Selat, strt., Indon.	D8	36
Dan, stm., U.S.	D3	139
Dana, In., U.S.	E3	107
Danakil, reg., Afr.	H13	48
Da Nang, Viet.	C5	34
Danané, C. Iv.	E3	50
Danbury, Ct., U.S.	D2	100
Danbury, Tx., U.S.	r14	136
Dandeli, India	F2	40
Dandong, China	C12	28
Dandridge, Tn., U.S.	C10	135
Dane, co., Wi., U.S.	E4	142
Danfeng, China	C3	30
Dangchang, China	C1	30
Dangriga, Belize	B2	80
Dangshan, China	C4	30
Dania, Fl., U.S.	F6	102
Daniels, co., Mt., U.S.	B11	119
Danielson, Ct., U.S.	B8	100
Daniels Pass, Ut., U.S.	C4	137
Danilov, Russia	C7	22
Danlí, Hond.	C2	80
Dannemora, N.Y., U.S.	f11	125
Dannevirke, N.Z.	p14	63c
Dansville, N.Y., U.S.	C3	125
Dante, Va., U.S.	f9	139
Danube, stm., Eur.	C9	14
Danube, Mouths of the, mth., Eur.	G10	20
Danvers, Il., U.S.	C4	106
Danvers, Ma., U.S.	A6	114
Danville, P.Q., Can.	D5	90
Danville, Ar., U.S.	B2	97
Danville, Ca., U.S.	h9	98
Danville, Ia., U.S.	D6	108
Danville, Il., U.S.	C6	106
Danville, In., U.S.	E4	107
Danville, Ky., U.S.	C5	110
Danville, Oh., U.S.	B3	128
Danville, Pa., U.S.	E8	131
Danville, Va., U.S.	D3	139
Danxian, China	F2	30
Danzig see Gdańsk, Pol.	B5	20
Daocheng, China	F8	28
Daokro, C. Iv.	E4	50
Daoxian, China	D3	30
Dapaong, Togo	D5	50
Dapchi, Nig.	D7	50
Daphne, Al., U.S.	E2	94
Da Qaidam, China	D7	28
Dar'ā, Syria	F7	44
Dārāb, Iran	E6	42
Darabani, Rom.	E9	20
Dāraiyyā, Syria	F7	44
Darbhanga, India	D5	40
Darby, Mt., U.S.	D2	119
Darby, Pa., U.S.	G11	131
Dardanelle, Ar., U.S.	B2	97
Dardanelle Lake, res., Ar., U.S.	B2	97
Dardanelles see Çanakkale Boğazı, strt., Tur.	C1	44
Dare, co., N.C., U.S.	B7	126
Darende, Tur.	C7	44
Dar es Salaam, Tan.	E7	54
Dargan-Ata, Turk.	B8	42
Dargaville, N.Z.	o13	63c
Darhan, Mong.	B9	28
Darien, Ct., U.S.	E2	100
Darien, Ga., U.S.	E5	103
Darien, Wi., U.S.	F5	142
Dārjiling, India	D5	40
Darke, co., Oh., U.S.	B1	128
Darlag, China	E7	28
Darley Woods, De., U.S.	h8	101
Darling, stm., Austl.	G3	62
Darling, Lake, res., N.D., U.S.	A4	127
Darling Range, mts., Austl.	G2	60
Darlington, Eng., U.K.	C6	12
Darlington, Md., U.S.	A5	113
Darlington, S.C., U.S.	C8	133
Darlington, Wi., U.S.	F3	142
Darlington, co., S.C., U.S.	C8	133
Darłowo, Pol.	B4	20
Darmstadt, Ger.	F11	12
Darnah, Libya	D9	48
Darnley, Cape, c., Ant.	C12	67
Darrah, Mount, mtn., Can.	E3	84
Darreh Gaz, Iran	C7	42
Darrington, Wa., U.S.	A4	140
Dart, Cape, c., Ant.	D27	67
Daru, Pap. N. Gui.	H11	32
Darvaza, Turk.	E7	26
Darwin, Austl.	C5	60
Dašhovuz, Turk.	E7	26
Dassel, Mn., U.S.	E4	116
Dastgardān, Iran	D7	42
Date, Japan	B4	31
Datia, India	D3	40
Datil Mountains, mts., N.M., U.S.	C2	124
Datong, China	C10	28
Datong, China	B1	30
Datu, Tanjung, c., Asia	C3	36
Daufuskie Island, i., S.C., U.S.	G6	133
Daung Kyun, i., Myan.	D3	34
Dauphin, Mb., Can.	D1	86
Dauphin, co., Pa., U.S.	F8	131
Dauphin, stm., Mb., Can.	D2	86
Dauphin Island, Al., U.S.	E1	94
Dauphin Island, i., Al., U.S.	E1	94
Dauphin Lake, l., Mb., Can.	D2	86
Dāvangere, India	G3	40
Davao, Phil.	E9	34
Davao Gulf, b., Phil.	E9	34
Dāvarzan, Iran	C7	42
Daveluyville, P.Q., Can.	C5	90
Davenport, Fl., U.S.	D5	102
Davenport, Ia., U.S.	C7	108
Davenport, Ok., U.S.	B5	129
Davenport, Wa., U.S.	B7	140
David, Pan.	D3	80
David City, Ne., U.S.	C8	120
Davidson, N.C., U.S.	B2	126
Davidson, co., N.C., U.S.	B2	126
Davidson, co., Tn., U.S.	A5	135
Davidsville, Pa., U.S.	F4	131
Davie, Fl., U.S.	F6	102
Davie, co., N.C., U.S.	B2	126
Daviess, co., In., U.S.	G3	107
Daviess, co., Ky., U.S.	C2	110
Daviess, co., Mo., U.S.	B3	118
Davis, Ca., U.S.	C3	98
Davis, Ok., U.S.	C4	129
Davis, W.V., U.S.	B5	141
Davis, co., Ia., U.S.	D5	108
Davis, co., Ut., U.S.	C3	137
Davis, Mount, mtn., Pa., U.S.	G3	131
Davis Creek, stm., W.V., U.S.	m12	141
Davis Dam, U.S.	H7	121
Davis Islands, is., Fl., U.S.	p11	102
Davis Lake, l., Or., U.S.	E5	130
Davis-Monthan Air Force Base, mil., Az., U.S.	E5	96
Davison, Mi., U.S.	E7	115
Davison, co., S.D., U.S.	D7	134
Davis Sea, Ant.	C13	67
Davisstrædet see Davis Strait, strt., N.A.	E28	82
Davis Strait, strt., N.A.	E28	82
Davisville, R.I., U.S.	E4	132
Dawa, stm., Afr.	C7	54
Dawei, Myan.	D3	34
Dawes, co., Ne., U.S.	B2	120
Dawna Range, mts., Myan.	C3	34
Daws Island, i., S.C., U.S.	G6	133
Dawson, Ga., U.S.	E2	103
Dawson, Mn., U.S.	F2	116
Dawson, co., Ga., U.S.	B2	103
Dawson, co., Mt., U.S.	C11	119
Dawson, co., Ne., U.S.	D6	120
Dawson, co., Tx., U.S.	C1	136
Dawson, Isla, i., Chile	H2	69
Dawson, Mount, mtn., B.C., Can.	D9	85
Dawson Creek, B.C., Can.	B7	85
Dawson Springs, Ky., U.S.	C2	110
Dax, Fr.	F6	16
Daxian, China	E9	28
Daxing, China	B4	30
Daxue Shan, mts., China	E8	28
Day, co., S.D., U.S.	B8	134
Dayao, China	A4	34
Dayong, China	D3	30
Dayr az-Zawr, Syria	E9	44
Daysland, Ab., Can.	C4	84
Dayton, Ia., U.S.	B3	108
Dayton, In., U.S.	D4	107
Dayton, Ky., U.S.	h14	110
Dayton, Md., U.S.	B4	113
Dayton, Mn., U.S.	m12	116
Dayton, Nv., U.S.	D2	121
Dayton, Oh., U.S.	C1	128
Dayton, Or., U.S.	B3	130
Dayton, Tn., U.S.	D8	135
Dayton, Tx., U.S.	D5	136
Dayton, Va., U.S.	B4	139
Dayton, Wa., U.S.	B8	140
Dayton, Wy., U.S.	B5	143
Daytona Beach, Fl., U.S.	C5	102
Dayu, China	F10	28
Dayville, Ct., U.S.	B8	100
Dazhu, China	C2	30
De Aar, S. Afr.	E3	56
Dead, North Branch, stm., Me., U.S.	C2	112
Dead, South Branch, stm., Me., U.S.	C2	112
Dead Creek, stm., Vt., U.S.	C2	138
Dead Diamond, stm., N.H., U.S.	g7	122
Dead Indian Peak, mtn., Wy., U.S.	B3	143
Dead Lake, l., Mn., U.S.	D3	116
Dead Lakes, l., Fl., U.S.	B1	102
Deadman Bay, b., Fl., U.S.	C3	102
Deadman Creek, stm., Wa., U.S.	g14	140
Dead Sea, l., Asia	G6	44
Deadwood, S.D., U.S.	C2	134
Deadwood Reservoir, res., Id., U.S.	E3	105
Deaf Smith, co., Tx., U.S.	B1	136
Deakin, Austl.	G4	60
Deale, Md., U.S.	C4	113
Deal Island, Md., U.S.	D6	113
Deal Island, i., Md., U.S.	D6	113
De'an, China	D4	30
Dean, stm., B.C., Can.	C4	85
Dean Channel, strt., B.C., Can.	C4	85
Deán Funes, Arg.	E5	72
Dearborn, Mi., U.S.	F7	115
Dearborn, co., In., U.S.	F7	107
Dearborn Heights, Mi., U.S.	p15	115
Death Valley, val., Ca., U.S.	D5	98
Death Valley National Park, U.S.	D5	98
Deba, China	D7	50
De Baca, co., N.M., U.S.	C5	124
Debao, China	E2	30
De Bary, Fl., U.S.	D5	102
Debauch Mountain, mtn., Ak., U.S.	C8	95
Dęblin, Pol.	D6	20
Debre Birhan, Eth.	B7	54
Debre Mark'os, Eth.	A7	54
Debrecen, Hung.	F6	20
Debre Tabor, Eth.	H3	38
Debre Zeyit, Eth.	B7	54
De Cade, Lake, l., La., U.S.	E5	111
Decatur, Al., U.S.	A3	94
Decatur, Ga., U.S.	C2	103
Decatur, Il., U.S.	D5	106
Decatur, In., U.S.	C8	107
Decatur, Ms., U.S.	C4	117
Decatur, Ne., U.S.	B9	120
Decatur, Tn., U.S.	D9	135
Decatur, Tx., U.S.	C4	136
Decatur, co., Ga., U.S.	F2	103
Decatur, co., Ia., U.S.	D4	108
Decatur, co., In., U.S.	F6	107
Decatur, co., Ks., U.S.	C3	109
Decatur, co., Tn., U.S.	B3	135
Decatur, Lake, res., Il., U.S.	D5	106
Decaturville, Tn., U.S.	B3	135
Deccan, plat., India	G3	40
Deception, Mount, mtn., Wa., U.S.	B2	140
Decherd, Tn., U.S.	B5	135
Děčín, Czech Rep.	D3	20
Decize, Fr.	D8	16
Deckerville, Mi., U.S.	E8	115
Decorah, Ia., U.S.	A6	108
Dedham, Ma., U.S.	B5	114
Dedoplis Ckaro, Geor.	B12	44
Dédougou, Burkina	D4	50
Deep, stm., N.C., U.S.	B3	126
Deep Creek, stm., Ut., U.S.	F3	137
Deep Creek, stm., Ut., U.S.	B3	137
Deep Creek, stm., Ut., U.S.	C2	137
Deep Creek, stm., Wa., U.S.	g13	140
Deep Creek Lake, res., Md., U.S.	K12	113
Deep Creek Mountains, mts., Id., U.S.	G6	105
Deep Fork, stm., Ok., U.S.	B5	129
Deep Inlet, b., Nf., Can.	g10	88
Deep Red Creek, stm., Ok., U.S.	C3	129
Deep River, On., Can.	A7	89
Deep River, Ct., U.S.	D6	100
Deer Creek, stm., Oh., U.S.	C2	128
Deer Creek Indian Reservation, Mn., U.S.	C5	116
Deerfield, Il., U.S.	h9	106
Deerfield, Ks., U.S.	E2	109
Deerfield, Ma., U.S.	A2	114
Deerfield, Mi., U.S.	G7	115
Deerfield, Wi., U.S.	E4	142
Deerfield, stm., U.S.	A2	114
Deerfield Beach, Fl., U.S.	F6	102
Deer Island, pen., Ma., U.S.	g12	114
Deer Island, i., Ms., U.S.	f8	117
Deer Isle, i., Me., U.S.	D4	112
Deer Lake, Nf., Can.	D3	88
Deer Lake, l., Nf., Can.	D3	88
Deer Lake, l., Mn., U.S.	C5	116
Deer Lodge, Mt., U.S.	D4	119
Deer Lodge, co., Mt., U.S.	E3	119
Deer Park, N.Y., U.S.	n15	125
Deer Park, Oh., U.S.	o13	128
Deer Park, Wa., U.S.	B8	140
Deer River, Mn., U.S.	C5	116
Defiance, Oh., U.S.	A1	128
Defiance, co., Oh., U.S.	A1	128
Defiance, Mount, mtn., Or., U.S.	B5	130
De Forest, Wi., U.S.	E4	142
De Funiak Springs, Fl., U.S.	u15	102
Dêgê, China	D2	30
Degeh Bur, Eth.	B8	54
Dégelis, P.Q., Can.	B9	90
Degerfors, Swe.	G6	10
De Graff, Oh., U.S.	B2	128
De Gray Lake, res., Ar., U.S.	C3	97
Dehiwala-Mount Lavinia, Sri L.	H3	40
Dehlorān, Iran	F12	44
Dehra Dūn, India	C3	40
Dehui, China	C13	28
Dej, Rom.	F7	20
Dejnau, Turk.	C8	42
De Kalb, Il., U.S.	B5	106
De Kalb, Ms., U.S.	C5	117
De Kalb, Tx., U.S.	C5	136
De Kalb, co., Al., U.S.	A4	94
De Kalb, co., Ga., U.S.	C2	103
De Kalb, co., Il., U.S.	B5	106
De Kalb, co., In., U.S.	B7	107
De Kalb, co., Mo., U.S.	B3	118
De Kalb, co., Tn., U.S.	D8	135
Dekese, D.R.C.	D4	54
Delafield, Wi., U.S.	m11	142
Delanco, N.J., U.S.	C3	123
De Land, Fl., U.S.	C5	102
Delano, Ca., U.S.	E4	98
Delano, Mn., U.S.	E5	116
Delano Peak, mtn., Ut., U.S.	E3	137
Delārām, Afg.	D8	42
Delaronde Lake, l., Sk., Can.	C2	91
Delavan, Il., U.S.	C4	106
Delavan, Wi., U.S.	F5	142
Delaware, Oh., U.S.	B2	128
Delaware, co., Ia., U.S.	B6	108
Delaware, co., In., U.S.	D7	107
Delaware, co., N.Y., U.S.	C5	125
Delaware, co., Oh., U.S.	B2	128
Delaware, co., Ok., U.S.	A7	129
Delaware, co., Pa., U.S.	G11	131
Delaware, state, U.S.	D3	101
Delaware, stm., Ks., U.S.	C8	109
Delaware, stm., U.S.	G11	131
Delaware, East Branch, stm., N.Y., U.S.	C5	125
Delaware Bay, b., U.S.	D13	92
Delaware City, De., U.S.	B3	101
Delaware Lake, res., Oh., U.S.	B3	128
Delaware Water Gap, N.J., U.S.	B2	123
Delaware Water Gap National Recreation Area, U.S.	B2	123
Delbarton, W.V., U.S.	D2	141
Delcambre, La., U.S.	E4	111
Del City, Ok., U.S.	B4	129
De Leon, Tx., U.S.	C3	136
De Leon Springs, Fl., U.S.	C5	102
Delfzijl, Neth.	D10	12
Delgado, Cabo, c., Moz.	A7	56
Delhi, India	D3	40
Delhi, La., U.S.	B4	111
Delhi, N.Y., U.S.	C6	125
Delice, stm., Tur.	B6	44
Delicias, Mex.	B3	78
Delingde, Russia	B13	26
Delingha, China	D7	28
De Lisle, Ms., U.S.	E4	117
Dellenbaugh, Mount, mtn., Az., U.S.	A2	96
Dell Rapids, S.D., U.S.	D9	134
Dellys, Alg.	I8	16
Del Mar, Ca., U.S.	o15	98
Delmar, De., U.S.	G3	101
Delmar, Md., U.S.	D6	113
Delmar, N.Y., U.S.	C7	125
Delmenhorst, Ger.	D11	12
Del Norte, Co., U.S.	D4	99
Del Norte, co., Ca., U.S.	B2	98
Deloraine, Mb., Can.	E1	86
Delos see Dhílos, hist., Grc.	F10	18
Del Park Manor, De., U.S.	i7	101
Delphi, In., U.S.	C4	107
Delphi see Dhelfoí, hist., Grc.	E9	18
Delphos, Oh., U.S.	B1	128
Delran, N.J., U.S.	C3	123
Delray Beach, Fl., U.S.	F6	102
Del Rio, Tx., U.S.	E2	136
Delson, P.Q., Can.	q19	90
Delta, Co., U.S.	C2	99
Delta, Oh., U.S.	A2	128
Delta, Ut., U.S.	D3	137
Delta, co., Co., U.S.	C3	99
Delta, co., Mi., U.S.	C3	115
Delta, co., Tx., U.S.	C5	136
Delta, reg., Ms., U.S.	B3	117
Delta Junction, Ak., U.S.	C10	95
Delta Peak, mtn., B.C., Can.	A3	85
Delta Reservoir, res., N.Y., U.S.	B5	125
Deltaville, Va., U.S.	C6	139
Deltona, Fl., U.S.	D5	102
Del Verme Falls, wtfl, Eth.	B8	54
Demarest, N.J., U.S.	h9	123
Demba, D.R.C.	E4	54
Dembia, C.A.R.	B4	54
Dembī Dolo, Eth.	B6	54
Demidov, Russia	B11	20
Deming, N.M., U.S.	E2	124
Demirci, Tur.	C3	44
Demjanskoe, Russia	D8	26
Demmin, Ger.	D13	12
Democratic Republic of the Congo see Congo, Democratic Republic of the, ctry., Afr.	D4	52
Demopolis, Al., U.S.	C2	94
Demorest, Ga., U.S.	B3	103
Demotte, In., U.S.	B3	107
Dempo, Gunung, vol., Indon.	D2	36
Demta, Indon.	G11	32
Denakil see Danakil, reg., Afr.	H13	48
Denali National Park, Ak., U.S.	C9	95
Denan, Eth.	B8	54
Denare Beach, Sk., Can.	C4	91

Name	Map Ref.	Page

Denau, Uzb. — F8 — 26
Dengas, Niger — D6 — 50
Dengkou, China — A2 — 30
Dêngqên, China — E7 — 28
Dengxian, China — C3 — 30
Denham, Austl. — F1 — 60
Denham, Mount, mtn., Jam. — B4 — 80
Denham Springs, La., U.S. — D5 — 111
Den Helder, Neth. — D9 — 12
Dénia, Spain — H7 — 16
Deniliquin, Austl. — H4 — 62
Denison, Ia. — B2 — 108
Denison, Tx., U.S. — C4 — 136
Denison Dam, U.S. — D5 — 129
Denizli, Tur. — D3 — 44
Denmark, Austl. — G2 — 60
Denmark, S.C., U.S. — E5 — 133
Denmark, Wi., U.S. — D6 — 142
Denmark, ctry., Eur. — I4 — 10
Denmark Strait, strt. — E34 — 82
Dennehotso, Az., U.S. — A6 — 96
Dennis, Ma., U.S. — C7 — 114
Dennison, Oh., U.S. — B4 — 128
Dennis Port, Ma., U.S. — C7 — 114
Denny Terrace, S.C., U.S. — C5 — 133
Denpasar, Indon. — E5 — 36
Dent, co., Mo., U.S. — D6 — 118
Denton, Md., U.S. — C6 — 113
Denton, N.C., U.S. — B2 — 126
Denton, Tx., U.S. — C4 — 136
Denton, co., Tx., U.S. — C4 — 136
D'Entrecasteaux, Point, c., Austl. — G2 — 60
D'Entrecasteaux Islands, is., Pap. N. Gui. — H13 — 32
Dentsville, S.C., U.S. — C6 — 133
Denver, Co., U.S. — B6 — 99
Denver, Ia., U.S. — B5 — 108
Denver, Pa., U.S. — F9 — 131
Denver, co., Co., U.S. — B6 — 99
Denver City, Tx., U.S. — C1 — 136
Denville, N.J., U.S. — B4 — 123
Deoghar, India — E5 — 40
Deolāli, India — F2 — 40
De Pere, Wi., U.S. — D5 — 142
Depew, N.Y., U.S. — C2 — 125
Depoe Bay, Or., U.S. — C2 — 130
Deposit, N.Y., U.S. — C5 — 125
Depue, Il., U.S. — B4 — 106
Dêqên, China — F7 — 28
Deqing, China — E3 — 30
De Queen, Ar., U.S. — C1 — 97
De Queen Reservoir, res., Ar., U.S. — C1 — 97
De Quincy, La., U.S. — D2 — 111
Dera Ghāzi Khān, Pak. — E10 — 42
Dera Ismāīl Khān, Pak. — D10 — 42
Derbent, Russia — E6 — 26
Derby, Austl. — D3 — 60
Derby, Eng., U.K. — D6 — 12
Derby, Ct., U.S. — D3 — 100
Derby, Ks., U.S. — E6 — 109
Derby, Vt., U.S. — B4 — 138
Derby Line, Vt., U.S. — A4 — 138
Derg, Lough, l., Ire. — D2 — 12
Dergači, Russia — D8 — 22
De Ridder, La., U.S. — D2 — 111
Derik, Tur. — D9 — 44
Derma, Ms., U.S. — B4 — 117
Dermott, Ar., U.S. — D4 — 97
Dernieres, Isles, is., La., U.S. — E5 — 111
Derry see Londonderry, N. Ire., U.K. — C3 — 12
Derry, N.H., U.S. — E4 — 122
Derry, Pa., U.S. — F3 — 131
Derventa, Bos. — B6 — 18
Derwood, Md., U.S. — B3 — 113
Des Allemands, La., U.S. — E5 — 111
Désappointement, Îles du, is., Fr. Poly. — F15 — 58
Des Arc, Ar., U.S. — C4 — 97
Desbiens, P.Q., Can. — A6 — 90
Descanso, Mex. — A1 — 78
Deschaillons [-sur-Saint-Laurent], P.Q., Can. — C5 — 90
Deschambault, P.Q., Can. — C6 — 90
Deschambault Lake, l., Sk., Can. — C4 — 91
Deschutes, co., Or., U.S. — D5 — 130
Deschutes, stm., Or., U.S. — B6 — 130
Desē, Eth. — H12 — 48
Deseado, stm., Arg. — G3 — 69
Desengaño, Punta, c., Arg. — G3 — 69
Deseret Peak, mtn., Ut., U.S. — C3 — 137
Deseronto, On., Can. — C7 — 89
Desert Creek Peak, mtn., Nv., U.S. — E2 — 121
Desert Hot Springs, Ca., U.S. — F5 — 98
Desert Peak, mtn., Ut., U.S. — B2 — 137
Desert Valley, val., Nv., U.S. — B3 — 121
Desha, Ar., U.S. — B4 — 97
Desha, co., Ar., U.S. — D4 — 97
Deshler, Ne., U.S. — D8 — 120
Deshler, Oh., U.S. — A2 — 128
Des Lacs, stm., N.D., U.S. — A4 — 127
Desloge, Mo., U.S. — D7 — 118
De Smet, S.D., U.S. — C8 — 134
Des Moines, Ia., U.S. — C4 — 108
Des Moines, Wa., U.S. — B3 — 140
Des Moines, co., Ia., U.S. — D6 — 108
Des Moines, stm., U.S. — D5 — 108
Desna, stm., Eur. — D11 — 20
De Soto, Ia. — C3 — 108

De Soto, Il., U.S. — F4 — 106
De Soto, Ks., U.S. — D9 — 109
De Soto, Mo., U.S. — C7 — 118
De Soto, co., Fl., U.S. — E5 — 102
De Soto, co., La., U.S. — B2 — 111
De Soto, co., Ms., U.S. — A3 — 117
Despard, W.V., U.S. — k10 — 141
Des Peres, Mo., U.S. — f13 — 118
Des Plaines, Il., U.S. — A6 — 106
Des Plaines, stm., U.S. — k8 — 106
Desroches, i., Sey. — i12 — 57b
Dessau, Ger. — E13 — 12
Destin, Fl., U.S. — u15 — 102
Destrehan, La., U.S. — E5 — 111
Detour, Point, c., Mi., U.S. — C4 — 115
Detroit, Mi., U.S. — F7 — 115
Detroit Lake, res., Or., U.S. — C4 — 130
Detroit Lakes, Mn., U.S. — D3 — 116
Dettifoss, wtfl, Ice. — l20 — 10a
Deuel, co., Ne., U.S. — C3 — 120
Deuel, co., S.D., U.S. — C9 — 134
Deutsche Bucht, b., Ger. — C10 — 12
Deux-Montagnes, P.Q., Can. — p19 — 90
Deux Montagnes, Lac des, l., P.Q., Can. — q19 — 90
Deva, Rom. — G7 — 20
De Valls Bluff, Ar., U.S. — C4 — 97
Develi, Tur. — C6 — 44
Deventer, Neth. — D10 — 12
DeView, Bayou, stm., Ar., U.S. — B4 — 97
Devils Island see Diable, Île du, i., Fr. Gu. — B9 — 70
Devils Lake, N.D., U.S. — A7 — 127
Devils Lake, l., N.D., U.S. — A6 — 127
Devils Paw, mtn., Ak., U.S. — k23 — 95
Devils Postpile National Monument, Ca., U.S. — D4 — 98
Devils Tower National Monument, Wy., U.S. — B8 — 143
Devil Track Lake, l., Mn., U.S. — k9 — 116
Devine, Tx., U.S. — E3 — 136
DeVola, Oh., U.S. — C4 — 128
Devon, Ab., Can. — C4 — 84
Devonport, Austl. — I4 — 62
Devonshire, De., U.S. — h7 — 101
Dewar, Ok., U.S. — B6 — 129
Dewās, India — I7 — 40
Dewees Inlet, b., S.C., U.S. — k12 — 133
Dewees Island, i., S.C., U.S. — F8 — 133
Dewey, Az., U.S. — C3 — 96
Dewey, Ok., U.S. — A6 — 129
Dewey, co., Ok., U.S. — B2 — 129
Dewey, co., S.D., U.S. — B4 — 134
Dewey Beach, De., U.S. — F5 — 101
Dewey Lake, res., Ky., U.S. — C7 — 110
Deweyville, Tx., U.S. — D6 — 136
De Witt, Ar., U.S. — C4 — 97
De Witt, Ia., U.S. — C7 — 108
De Witt, Mi., U.S. — F6 — 115
De Witt, N.Y., U.S. — B4 — 125
De Witt, co., Il., U.S. — C4 — 106
De Witt, co., Tx., U.S. — E4 — 136
Dexing, China — D4 — 30
Dexter, Ia., U.S. — C3 — 108
Dexter, Me., U.S. — C3 — 112
Dexter, Mi., U.S. — F7 — 115
Dexter, Mo., U.S. — E8 — 118
Dexter, N.M., U.S. — D5 — 124
Dexter, Lake, l., Fl., U.S. — C5 — 102
Dezfūl, Iran — D5 — 42
Dezhou, China — D11 — 28
Dezhneva, mys, c., Russia — C21 — 26
Dhahran see Az-Zahrān, Sau. Ar. — D5 — 42
Dhaka, Bngl. — E6 — 40
Dhamtari, India — E4 — 40
Dhanbād, India — E5 — 40
Dhār, India — E3 — 40
Dhārān, Nepal — D5 — 40
Dharmapuri, India — G3 — 40
Dhawalāgiri, mtn., Nepal — D4 — 40
Dhenkānāl, India — E5 — 40
Dhílos, hist., Grc. — F10 — 18
Dhodhekánisos, is., Grc. — F11 — 18
Dhone, India — F3 — 40
Dhoomadheere, Som. — C8 — 54
Dhoraji, India — E2 — 40
Dhubri, India — D5 — 40
Dhule, India — E2 — 40
Diable, Île du, i., Fr. Gu. — B9 — 70
Diablo, Canyon, val., Az., U.S. — C4 — 96
Diablo, Mount, mtn., Ca., U.S. — h9 — 98
Diablo, Pico del, mtn., Mex. — A1 — 78
Diablo Dam, Wa., U.S. — A4 — 140
Diablo Lake, res., Wa., U.S. — A4 — 140
Diablo Range, mts., Ca., U.S. — D3 — 98
Diablotins, Morne, vol., Dom. — B7 — 80
Diaca, Moz. — A6 — 56
Dialakoto, Sen. — D2 — 50
Diamante, Arg. — E5 — 72
Diamantina, Braz. — E6 — 74
Diamantina, stm., Austl. — E3 — 62
Diamantino, Braz. — F8 — 70
Diamond Harbour, India — E5 — 40
Diamond Head, crat., Hi., U.S. — B4 — 104

Diamond Hill, R.I., U.S. — B4 — 132
Diamond Hill Reservoir, res., R.I., U.S. — A4 — 132
Diamond Lake, Il., U.S. — h9 — 106
Diamond Lake, l., Or., U.S. — D4 — 130
Diamond Mountains, mts., Nv., U.S. — D6 — 121
Diamond Peak, mtn., Co., U.S. — A2 — 99
Diamond Peak, mtn., Id., U.S. — E5 — 105
Diamond Peak, mtn., Or., U.S. — D4 — 130
Diamond Peak, mtn., Wa., U.S. — C8 — 140
Diamondville, Wy., U.S. — E2 — 143
Dianbai, China — E3 — 30
Dianjiang, China — C2 — 30
Dianópolis, Braz. — F10 — 70
Diapaga, Burkina — D5 — 50
Diaz, Ar., U.S. — B4 — 97
Dibaya, D.R.C. — E4 — 54
D'Iberville, Ms., U.S. — E5 — 117
Diboll, Tx., U.S. — D5 — 136
Dibrugarh, India — D6 — 40
Dickens, co., Tx., U.S. — C2 — 136
Dickenson, co., Va., U.S. — e9 — 139
Dickerson, Md., U.S. — B3 — 113
Dickey, co., N.D., U.S. — C7 — 127
Dickeyville, Wi., U.S. — F3 — 142
Dickinson, N.D., U.S. — C3 — 127
Dickinson, co., Ia., U.S. — A2 — 108
Dickinson, co., Ks., U.S. — D6 — 109
Dickinson, co., Mi., U.S. — B3 — 115
Dickinson Dam, N.D., U.S. — C3 — 127
Dickson, Ok., U.S. — C5 — 129
Dickson, Tn., U.S. — A4 — 135
Dickson, co., Tn., U.S. — A4 — 135
Dickson City, Pa., U.S. — D10 — 131
Dicle see Tigris, stm., Asia — D5 — 42
Didao, China — A2 — 30
Didbiran, Russia — D15 — 26
Didsbury, Ab., Can. — D3 — 84
Dīdwāna, India — D2 — 40
Diefenbaker, Lake, res., Sk., Can. — F2 — 91
Diego de Almagro, Isla, i., Chile — H1 — 69
Diégo-Suarez see Antsirañana, Madag. — A8 — 56
Diéma, Mali — D3 — 50
Dien Bien, Viet. — B4 — 34
Diepholz, Ger. — D11 — 12
Dieppe, N.B., Can. — C5 — 87
Dieppe, Fr. — C7 — 16
Dierks, Ar., U.S. — C1 — 97
Di'er Songhua see Songhua, stm., China — B14 — 28
Dif, Kenya — C8 — 54
Diffa, Niger — D7 — 50
Dighton, Ks., U.S. — D3 — 109
Digne, Fr. — E10 — 16
Digos, Phil. — E9 — 34
Digul, stm., Indon. — H10 — 32
Diinsor, Som. — C8 — 54
Dijlah see Tigris, stm., Asia — D5 — 42
Dijon, Fr. — D9 — 16
Dike, Ia., U.S. — B5 — 108
Dikhil, Dji. — H13 — 48
Dikili, Tur. — C2 — 44
Dikson, Russia — B10 — 26
Dikwa, Nig. — D7 — 50
Dīla, Eth. — B7 — 54
Dili, Indon. — E7 — 36
Dillard, Or., U.S. — D3 — 130
Dill City, Ok., U.S. — B2 — 129
Dilley, Tx., U.S. — E3 — 136
Dillingham, Ak., U.S. — D8 — 95
Dillon, Mt., U.S. — E4 — 119
Dillon, S.C., U.S. — C9 — 133
Dillon, co., S.C., U.S. — C9 — 133
Dillon Lake, res., Oh., U.S. — B3 — 128
Dillon Reservoir, res., Co., U.S. — B4 — 99
Dillonvale, Oh., U.S. — B5 — 128
Dillsboro, In., U.S. — F7 — 107
Dillsburg, Pa., U.S. — F7 — 131
Dilworth, Mn., U.S. — D2 — 116
Dimāpur, India — D6 — 40
Dimashq (Damascus), Syria — F7 — 44
Dimbokro, C. Iv. — E4 — 50
Dimitrovgrad, Bul. — C10 — 18
Dimitrovgrad, Russia — D6 — 26
Dimling, mtn., Nig. — E7 — 50
Dimmit, co., Tx., U.S. — E3 — 136
Dimmitt, Tx., U.S. — B1 — 136
Dimondale, Mi., U.S. — F6 — 115
Dinagat Island, i., Phil. — D9 — 34
Dinājpur, Bngl. — D5 — 40
Dinan, Fr. — C5 — 16
Dinar, Tur. — C4 — 44
Dinaric Alps, mts., Eur. — G4 — 20
Dindigul, India — G3 — 40
Dinghai, China — E12 — 28
Dingle Bay, b., Ire. — D1 — 12
Dingmans Ferry, Pa., U.S. — D12 — 131
Dingolfing, Ger. — F13 — 12
Dingtao, China — B4 — 30
Dinguiraye, Gui. — D2 — 50
Dingxiang, China — B3 — 30
Dingxing, China — B4 — 30
Dinner Point, c., Fl., U.S. — D4 — 102
Dinokwe, Bots. — C4 — 56

Dinosaur National Monument, U.S. — C6 — 137
Dinuba, Ca., U.S. — D4 — 98
Dinwiddie, co., Va., U.S. — C5 — 139
Dioura, Mali — D3 — 50
Diourbel, Sen. — D1 — 50
Dipolog, Phil. — E8 — 34
Dīr, Pak. — C10 — 42
Diré, Mali — C4 — 50
Diré Dawa, Eth. — B8 — 54
Dirico, Ang. — B3 — 56
Dirj, Libya — E6 — 14
Dirk Hartog Island, i., Austl. — F1 — 60
Dirkou, Niger — C7 — 50
Dirty Devil, stm., Ut., U.S. — E5 — 137
Disappointment, Cape, c., S. Geor. — H9 — 69
Disappointment, Cape, c., Wa., U.S. — C1 — 140
Disappointment, Lake, l., Austl. — E3 — 60
Dishman, Wa., U.S. — g14 — 140
Disko, i., Grnld. — E28 — 82
Dismal, stm., Ne., U.S. — C5 — 120
Dispur, India — D6 — 40
Disraëli, P.Q., Can. — D6 — 90
District of Columbia, dept., U.S. — f8 — 113
Distrito Federal, state, Braz. — E2 — 74
Distrito Federal, state, Mex. — D5 — 78
Diu, India — E2 — 40
Dīvāndarreh, Iran — E12 — 44
Divernon, Il., U.S. — D4 — 106
Divide, co., N.D., U.S. — A2 — 127
Divide Peak, mtn., Wy., U.S. — E5 — 143
Divinópolis, Braz. — F3 — 74
Divisor, Serra do, plat., S.A. — E5 — 70
Divnoe, Russia — A4 — 42
Divo, C. Iv. — E3 — 50
Divriği, Tur. — C8 — 44
Dix, stm., Ky., U.S. — C5 — 110
Dixfield, Me., U.S. — D2 — 112
Dixie, co., Fl., U.S. — C3 — 102
Dixie, co., N.D., U.S. — A2 — 127
Dixie Valley, val., Nv., U.S. — D4 — 121
Dixon, Ca., U.S. — C3 — 98
Dixon, Il., U.S. — B4 — 106
Dixon, Mo., U.S. — D5 — 118
Dixon, N.M., U.S. — A4 — 124
Dixon, co., Ne., U.S. — B9 — 120
Dixon Entrance, strt., N.A. — H13 — 82
Dixonville, Pa., U.S. — E3 — 131
Diyarbakır, Tur. — D9 — 44
Djado, Plateau du, plat., Niger — B7 — 50
Djamâa, Alg. — E5 — 14
Djambala, Congo — D2 — 54
Djanet, Alg. — B6 — 50
Djat'kovo, Russia — C13 — 20
Djelfa, Alg. — A5 — 50
Djemila, hist., Alg. — I9 — 16
Djenné, Mali — D4 — 50
Djibo, Burkina — D4 — 50
Djibouti, Dji. — H13 — 48
Djibouti, ctry., Afr. — H13 — 48
Djoku-Punda, D.R.C. — E4 — 54
Djougou, Benin — E5 — 50
Djoum, Cam. — C2 — 54
Djugu, D.R.C. — C6 — 54
Djurtjuli, Russia — C9 — 22
Dmitrija Lapteva, proliv, strt., Russia — B16 — 26
Dmitrijev-L'govskij, Russia — C13 — 20
Dnepropetrovsk see Dnipropetrovs'k, Ukr. — E13 — 20
Dnestr see Dniester, stm., Eur. — F11 — 20
Dnieper (Dnepr) (Dnipro), stm., Eur. — F12 — 20
Dniester (Nistru) (Dnister), stm., Eur. — F11 — 20
Dniprodzerzhyns'k, Ukr. — E13 — 20
Dniprodzerzhyns'ke vodoskhovyshche, res., Ukr. — E13 — 20
Dnipropetrovs'k, Ukr. — E13 — 20
Dnister see Dniester, stm., Eur. — F11 — 20
Dno, Russia — C5 — 22
Dôa, Moz. — B5 — 56
Doaktown, N.B., Can. — C3 — 87
Doba, Chad — E8 — 50
Dobbs Ferry, N.Y., U.S. — g13 — 125
Dobele, Lat. — H10 — 10
Doberai, Jazirah, pen., Indon. — D8 — 32
Dobo, Indon. — H9 — 32
Doboj, Bos. — B7 — 18
Dobrič, Bul. — C11 — 18
Dobrjanka, Russia — C10 — 22
Dobruja, hist. reg., Eur. — H9 — 20
Dobson, N.C., U.S. — A2 — 126
Doce, stm., Braz. — E3 — 74
Docena, Al., U.S. — f7 — 94
Doctors Lake, l., Fl., U.S. — m8 — 102
Doddridge, co., W.V., U.S. — B4 — 141
Dodecanese see Dhodhekánisos, is., Grc. — F11 — 18
Dodge, Ne., U.S. — C9 — 120
Dodge, co., Ga., U.S. — D3 — 103
Dodge, co., Mn., U.S. — G6 — 116
Dodge, co., Ne., U.S. — C9 — 120
Dodge, co., Wi., U.S. — E5 — 142
Dodge Center, Mn., U.S. — F6 — 116
Dodge City, Ks., U.S. — E3 — 109

Dodgeville, Wi., U.S. — F3 — 142
Dodoma, Tan. — E7 — 54
Doerun, Ga., U.S. — E3 — 103
Doe Run, Mo., U.S. — D7 — 118
Dog, stm., Vt., U.S. — C3 — 138
Dogai Coring, l., China — E5 — 28
Dog Island, i., Fl., U.S. — C2 — 102
Dog Keys Pass, strt., Ms., U.S. — g8 — 117
Dog Lake, l., Mb., Can. — D2 — 86
Do Gonbadān, Iran — D9 — 42
Dogondoutchi, Niger — D5 — 50
Doğubayazıt, Tur. — C11 — 44
Doğu Karadeniz Dağları, mts., Tur. — B8 — 44
Doha see Ad-Dawḥah, Qatar — E6 — 42
Dokka, Nor. — F4 — 10
Dokuchaievs'k, Ukr. — F14 — 20
Dolbeau, P.Q., Can. — k12 — 90
Dole, Fr. — D9 — 16
Dolgeville, N.Y., U.S. — B6 — 125
Dolinsk, Russia — B16 — 28
Dollar Bay, Mi., U.S. — A2 — 115
Dolomite, Al., U.S. — B3 — 94
Dolomites see Dolomiti, mts., Italy — A3 — 18
Dolomiti, mts., Italy — A3 — 18
Dolores, Arg. — E6 — 72
Dolores, Co., U.S. — D2 — 99
Dolores, Ur. — C5 — 72
Dolores, co., Co., U.S. — D2 — 99
Dolores, stm., U.S. — E7 — 137
Dolphin Island, i., Ut., U.S. — B3 — 137
Dolton, Il., U.S. — k9 — 106
Dolyns'ka, Ukr. — E12 — 20
Dombås, Nor. — E3 — 10
Dome Mountain, mtn., Az., U.S. — k9 — 96
Dome Peak, mtn., Co., U.S. — B3 — 99
Domeyko, Chile — C3 — 69
Dominica, ctry., N.A. — E12 — 76
Dominican Republic, ctry., N.A. — H12 — 75
Dominique, Canal de la see Martinique Passage, strt., N.A. — B7 — 80
Domo, Eth. — I14 — 48
Dom Pedrito, Braz. — E7 — 72
Don, stm., Russia — E6 — 26
Dona Ana, N.M., U.S. — E3 — 124
Dona Ana, co., N.M., U.S. — E2 — 124
Donaldsonville, La., U.S. — D4 — 111
Donalsonville, Ga., U.S. — E2 — 103
Donau see Danube, stm., Eur. — C9 — 14
Donauwörth, Ger. — F12 — 12
Don Benito, Spain — H4 — 16
Dondo, Ang. — B2 — 56
Dondo, Moz. — B5 — 56
Dondra Head, c., Sri L. — H4 — 40
Donegal, Ire. — C2 — 12
Donegal Bay, b., Ire. — C2 — 12
Doneraile, S.C., U.S. — C8 — 133
Donets'k, Ukr. — F14 — 20
Dong, stm., China — B7 — 34
Dong'an, China — D3 — 30
Dongara, Austl. — F1 — 60
Dongchuan, China — D1 — 30
Dongfang, China — H9 — 28
Donggala, Indon. — D5 — 36
Donghai Dao, i., China — G10 — 28
Dong Hoi, Viet. — B4 — 34
Dongjingcheng, China — B1 — 31
Dongo, Ang. — A2 — 56
Dongping, China — B4 — 30
Dongsheng, China — B3 — 30
Dongtai, China — C5 — 30
Dongting Hu, l., China — F10 — 28
Dongzhi, China — E7 — 30
Doniphan, Mo., U.S. — E7 — 118
Doniphan, Ne., U.S. — D7 — 120
Doniphan, co., Ks., U.S. — C8 — 109
Donkey Creek, stm., Wy., U.S. — E5 — 143
Donkin, N.S., Can. — C10 — 87
Donley, co., Tx., U.S. — B2 — 136
Dønna, Nor. — C5 — 10
Donna, Tx., U.S. — F3 — 136
Donnacona, P.Q., Can. — C6 — 90
Donnellson, Ia., U.S. — D6 — 108
Donner Pass, Ca., U.S. — C3 — 98
Donnybrook, Austl. — G2 — 60
Donora, Pa., U.S. — F2 — 131
Donostia (San Sebastián), Spain — F6 — 16
Donskaja grjada, hills, Eur. — E7 — 22
Don Upland see Donskaja grjada, hills, Eur. — E7 — 22
Doolow, Som. — J13 — 48
Dooly, co., Ga., U.S. — D3 — 103
Doonerak, Mount, mtn., Ak., U.S. — B9 — 95
Door, co., Wi., U.S. — D6 — 142
Dora, Al., U.S. — B2 — 94
Doraville, Ga., U.S. — h8 — 103
Dorcheat, Bayou, stm., U.S. — B2 — 111
Dorchester, N.B., Can. — D5 — 87
Dorchester, Eng., U.K. — E5 — 12
Dorchester, co., Md., U.S. — D5 — 113
Dorchester, co., S.C., U.S. — E7 — 133
Dordogne, stm., Fr. — E7 — 16
Dordrecht, Neth. — E9 — 12
Doré Lake, l., Sk., Can. — C2 — 91

Name	Map Ref.	Page
Dorena Lake, res., Or., U.S.	D3	130
Dori, Burkina	D4	50
Dorion-Vaudreuil, P.Q., Can.	q18	90
Dormont, Pa., U.S.	k13	131
Dornbirn, Aus.	G11	12
Dorogobuž, Russia	B12	20
Dorohoi, Rom.	F9	20
Dorothy Pond, Ma., U.S.	B4	114
Dorr, Mi., U.S.	F5	115
Dorre Island, i., Austl.	F1	60
Dorset, Vt., U.S.	E2	138
Dorsey, Md., U.S.	B4	113
Dortmund, Ger.	E10	12
Dorton, Ky., U.S.	C7	110
Dörtyol, Tur.	D7	44
Do Rūd, Iran	D5	42
Doruma, D.R.C.	C5	54
Dorval, P.Q., Can.	q19	90
Dosatuj, Russia	D13	26
Dos Bahías, Cabo, c., Arg.	G3	69
Dosso, Niger	D5	50
Dossor, Kaz.	E9	22
Dothan, Al., U.S.	D4	94
Douala, Cam.	C1	54
Douarnenez, Fr.	C4	16
Double Beach, Ct., U.S.	D4	100
Double Island Point, c., Austl.	F5	62
Doublespring Pass, Id., U.S.	E5	105
Double Springs, Al., U.S.	A2	94
Doubletop Peak, mtn., Wy., U.S.	C2	143
Doubs, stm., Eur.	D9	16
Douentza, Mali	C4	50
Dougherty, co., Ga., U.S.	E2	103
Douglas, I. of Man	C4	12
Douglas, S. Afr.	D3	56
Douglas, Az., U.S.	F6	96
Douglas, Ga., U.S.	E4	103
Douglas, Mi., U.S.	F4	115
Douglas, Wy., U.S.	D7	143
Douglas, co., Co., U.S.	B6	99
Douglas, co., Ga., U.S.	C2	103
Douglas, co., Il., U.S.	D5	106
Douglas, co., Ks., U.S.	D8	109
Douglas, co., Mn., U.S.	E3	116
Douglas, co., Mo., U.S.	E5	118
Douglas, co., Ne., U.S.	C9	120
Douglas, co., Nv., U.S.	E2	121
Douglas, co., Or., U.S.	D3	130
Douglas, co., S.D., U.S.	D7	134
Douglas, co., Wa., U.S.	B6	140
Douglas, co., Wi., U.S.	B2	142
Douglas, Mount, mtn., Ak., U.S.	D9	95
Douglas Channel, strt., B.C., Can.	C3	85
Douglas Lake, l., Mi., U.S.	C6	115
Douglas Lake, res., Tn., U.S.	D10	135
Douglass, Ks., U.S.	E7	109
Douglastown, N.B., Can.	B4	87
Douglasville, Ga., U.S.	C2	103
Dourados, Braz.	H9	70
Dourbali, Chad	D8	50
Douro (Duero), stm., Eur.	G2	16
Dousman, Wi., U.S.	E5	142
Dove Creek, Co., U.S.	D2	99
Dover, Eng., U.K.	E7	12
Dover, Ar., U.S.	B2	97
Dover, De., U.S.	D3	101
Dover, Fl., U.S.	D4	102
Dover, Ma., U.S.	h10	114
Dover, N.H., U.S.	D5	122
Dover, N.J., U.S.	B3	123
Dover, Oh., U.S.	B4	128
Dover, Pa., U.S.	F8	131
Dover, Tn., U.S.	A4	135
Dover, Strait of, strt., Eur.	B7	16
Dover Air Force Base, mil., De., U.S.	D4	101
Dover-Foxcroft, Me., U.S.	C3	112
Dover Plains, N.Y., U.S.	D7	125
Dowagiac, Mi., U.S.	G4	115
Dowlatābād, Iran	E7	42
Downers Grove, Il., U.S.	B5	106
Downey, Ca., U.S.	n12	98
Downey, Id., U.S.	G6	105
Downingtown, Pa., U.S.	F10	131
Downpatrick, N. Ire., U.K.	C4	12
Downs, Ks., U.S.	C5	109
Downs Mountain, mtn., Wy., U.S.	C3	143
Downton, Mount, mtn., B.C., Can.	C5	85
Dows, Ia., U.S.	B4	108
Doylestown, Oh., U.S.	B4	128
Doylestown, Pa., U.S.	F11	131
Doyline, La., U.S.	B2	111
Dra'a, Hamada du, des., Alg.	E3	48
Dracena, Braz.	F1	74
Dracut, Ma., U.S.	A5	114
Drăgăşani, Rom.	E8	20
Dragør, Den.	I5	10
Drain, Or., U.S.	D3	130
Drakensberg, mts., Afr.	D4	56
Drake Passage, strt.	B33	67
Drake Peak, mtn., Or., U.S.	E6	130
Dráma, Grc.	D10	18
Drammen, Nor.	G4	10
Draper, Ut., U.S.	C4	137
Drau (Dráva), stm., Eur.	F2	20
Dráva (Drau), stm., Eur.	G4	20
Drayton, On., Can.	D4	89
Drayton, N.D., U.S.	A8	127
Drayton, S.C., U.S.	B4	133
Drayton Plains, Mi., U.S.	F7	115
Drayton Valley, Ab., Can.	C3	84
Dresden, On., Can.	E2	89
Dresden, Ger.	E13	12
Dresden, Oh., U.S.	B3	128
Dresden, Tn., U.S.	A3	135
Dresslerville, Nv., U.S.	E2	121
Dreux, Fr.	C7	16
Drew, Ms., U.S.	B3	117
Drew, co., Ar., U.S.	D4	97
Drews Reservoir, res., Or., U.S.	E6	130
Drexel, Mo., U.S.	C3	118
Drexel, N.C., U.S.	B1	126
Drexel, Oh., U.S.	C1	128
Drift, Ky., U.S.	C7	110
Driggs, Id., U.S.	F7	105
Drinit, Gjiri i, b., Alb.	D7	18
Driskill Mountain, hill, La., U.S.	B3	111
Drobeta-Turnu Severin, Rom.	G7	20
Drogheda, Ire.	D3	12
Drohobych, Ukr.	E7	20
Drumheller, Ab., Can.	D4	84
Drum Island, i., S.C., U.S.	k12	133
Drummond, Lake, l., Va., U.S.	D6	139
Drummond, Mi., U.S.	C7	115
Drummond Island, i., Mi., U.S.	C7	115
Drummondville, P.Q., Can.	D5	90
Drumright, Ok., U.S.	B5	129
Druskininkai, Lith.	I11	10
Družba, Kaz.	B4	28
Drybranch, W.V., U.S.	m13	141
Dry Cimarron, stm., U.S.	A6	124
Dry Creek Mountain, mtn., Nv., U.S.	B5	121
Dryden, On., Can.	o16	89
Dryden, N.Y., U.S.	C4	125
Dry Fork, stm., Mo., U.S.	D6	118
Dry Fork, stm., W.V., U.S.	D3	141
Dry Fork, stm., W.V., U.S.	B5	141
Dry Ridge, Ky., U.S.	B5	110
Dry Tortugas, is., Fl., U.S.	H5	102
Dschang, Cam.	B1	54
Duarte, Pico, mtn., Dom. Rep.	B5	80
Dubach, La., U.S.	B3	111
Dubai see Dubayy, U.A.E.	E7	42
Dubăsari, Mol.	F10	20
Du Bay, Lake, res., Wi., U.S.	D4	142
Dubayy (Dubai), U.A.E.	E7	42
Dubbo, Austl.	G4	62
Dublin (Baile Átha Cliath), Ire.	D3	12
Dublin, Ga., U.S.	D4	103
Dublin, In., U.S.	E7	107
Dublin, N.H., U.S.	E2	122
Dublin, Oh., U.S.	k10	128
Dublin, Pa., U.S.	F11	131
Dublin, Tx., U.S.	C3	136
Dublin, Va., U.S.	C2	139
Dubno, Ukr.	D8	20
Dubois, In., U.S.	H4	107
Du Bois, Pa., U.S.	D4	131
Dubois, Wy., U.S.	C3	143
Dubois, co., In., U.S.	H4	107
Duboistown, Pa., U.S.	D7	131
Dubovka, Russia	E7	22
Dubréka, Gui.	E2	50
Dubrovnik, Cro.	C7	18
Dubrovytsia, Ukr.	D9	20
Dubuque, Ia., U.S.	B7	108
Dubuque, co., Ia., U.S.	B7	108
Duchesne, Ut., U.S.	C5	137
Duchesne, co., Ut., U.S.	C5	137
Duchesne, stm., Ut., U.S.	C5	137
Duck, stm., Tn., U.S.	B4	135
Duck Bay, Mb., Can.	C1	86
Duck Creek, stm., Oh., U.S.	C4	128
Duck Creek, stm., Wi., U.S.	h9	142
Duck Lake, Sk., Can.	E2	91
Duck Lake, l., Me., U.S.	C4	112
Duck Mountain Provincial Park, Ie., Can.	F5	91
Duck Valley Indian Reservation, U.S.	B5	121
Duckwater Indian Reservation, Nv., U.S.	E6	121
Duckwater Peak, mtn., Nv., U.S.	E6	121
Du Couedic, Cape, c., Austl.	H2	62
Dudinka, Russia	C10	26
Dudley, Eng., U.K.	D5	12
Dudley, Ma., U.S.	B4	114
Duenweg, Mo., U.S.	D3	118
Duero (Douro), stm., Eur.	G4	16
Due West, S.C., U.S.	C3	133
Duffer Peak, mtn., Nv., U.S.	B3	121
Dufourspitze, mtn., Eur.	B1	18
Dugdemona, stm., La., U.S.	B3	111
Dugger, In., U.S.	F3	107
Dugi Otok, i., Cro.	C5	18
Duifken Point, c., Austl.	C3	62
Duisburg, Ger.	E10	12
Duitama, Col.	B5	70
Duke Island, i., Ak., U.S.	n24	95
Dukes, co., Ma., U.S.	D6	114
Duk Fadiat, Sudan	I11	48
Dukhān, Qatar	E6	42
Dukku, Nig.	D7	50
Dukou, China	F8	28
Dulan, China	D7	28
Dulce, N.M., U.S.	A2	124
Dulce, stm., Arg.	E5	72
Dul'durga, Russia	D13	26
Dūmā, Syria	F7	44
Dumaguete, Phil.	E8	34
Dumai, Indon.	C2	36
Dumaran Island, i., Phil.	D7	34
Dumas, Ar., U.S.	D4	97
Dumas, Tx., U.S.	B2	136
Dumfries, Scot., U.K.	C5	12
Dumfries, Va., U.S.	B5	139
Dumont, Ia., U.S.	B5	108
Dumont, N.J., U.S.	B5	123
Dumraon, India	D4	40
Duna see Danube, stm., Eur.	C9	14
Dunai see Danube, stm., Eur.	C9	14
Dunaïvtsi, Ukr.	E9	20
Dunaj see Danube, stm., Eur.	C9	14
Dunărea see Danube, stm., Eur.	C9	14
Dunaújváros, Hung.	F5	20
Dunav see Danube, stm., Eur.	C9	14
Dunay see Danube, stm., Eur.	C9	14
Dunbar, Pa., U.S.	G2	131
Dunbar, W.V., U.S.	C3	141
Duncan, B.C., Can.	E6	85
Duncan, Az., U.S.	E6	96
Duncan, Ok., U.S.	C4	129
Duncan, S.C., U.S.	B3	133
Duncan Falls, Oh., U.S.	C4	128
Duncan Lake, res., B.C., Can.	D9	85
Duncannon, Pa., U.S.	F7	131
Duncan Passage, strt., India	G6	40
Duncansville, Pa., U.S.	F5	131
Duncanville, Tx., U.S.	n10	136
Dundalk, On., Can.	C4	89
Dundalk, Ire.	C3	12
Dundalk, Md., U.S.	B4	113
Dundalk Bay, b., Ire.	D3	12
Dundas, On., Can.	D5	89
Dundee, S. Afr.	D5	56
Dundee, Scot., U.K.	B5	12
Dundee, Fl., U.S.	D5	102
Dundee, Il., U.S.	A5	106
Dundee, Mi., U.S.	G7	115
Dundee, N.Y., U.S.	C4	125
Dundee, Or., U.S.	h11	130
Dundy, co., Ne., U.S.	D4	120
Dunedin, N.Z.	q13	63c
Dunedin, Fl., U.S.	D4	102
Dunellen, N.J., U.S.	B4	123
Dunfermline, Scot., U.K.	B5	12
Düngarpur, India	E2	40
Dungarvan, Ire.	D3	12
Dungeness, stm., Wa., U.S.	A2	140
Dungu, D.R.C.	C5	54
Dunham, P.Q., Can.	D5	90
Dunhuang, China	C6	28
Dunkard Creek, stm., U.S.	A4	141
Dunkerque, Fr.	B8	16
Dunkerton, Ia., U.S.	B5	108
Dunkirk see Dunkerque, Fr.	B8	16
Dunkirk, In., U.S.	D7	107
Dunkirk, N.Y., U.S.	C1	125
Dunkirk, Oh., U.S.	B2	128
Dunklin, co., Mo., U.S.	E7	118
Dunkwa, Ghana	E4	50
Dún Laoghaire, Ire.	D3	12
Dunlap, Ia., U.S.	C2	108
Dunlap, Il., U.S.	C4	106
Dunlap, In., U.S.	A6	107
Dunlap, Tn., U.S.	D8	135
Dunleary see Dún Laoghaire, Ire.	D3	12
Dunleith, De., U.S.	i7	101
Dunloup Creek, stm., W.V., U.S.	n13	141
Dunmore, Pa., U.S.	D10	131
Dunmore, Lake, l., Vt., U.S.	D2	138
Dunn, N.C., U.S.	B4	126
Dunn, co., N.D., U.S.	B3	127
Dunn, co., Wi., U.S.	D2	142
Dunnellon, Fl., U.S.	C4	102
Dunnville, On., Can.	E5	89
Dunqulah, Sudan	G11	48
Dunseith, N.D., U.S.	A5	127
Dunsmuir, Ca., U.S.	B2	98
Dunville, Nf., Can.	E5	88
Dunwoody, Ga., U.S.	h8	103
Duolun, China	C11	28
Duomula, China	E4	28
Du Page, co., Il., U.S.	B5	106
Du Page, stm., Il., U.S.	k8	106
Duplin, co., N.C., U.S.	C5	126
Dupnica, Bul.	G8	18
Dupont, Co., U.S.	B6	99
Dupont, In., U.S.	n18	107
Dupont City, W.V., U.S.	m12	141
Dupont Manor, De., U.S.	D3	101
Duque de York, Isla, i., Chile	H1	69
Duquesne, Pa., U.S.	F2	·131
Du Quoin, Il., U.S.	E4	106
Durand, Il., U.S.	A4	106
Durand, Mi., U.S.	F6	115
Durand, Wi., U.S.	D2	142
Durango, Mex.	E8	78
Durango, Co., U.S.	D3	99
Durango, state, Mex.	E8	78
Durant, Ia., U.S.	C7	108
Durant, Ms., U.S.	B4	117
Durant, Ok., U.S.	D5	129
Durazno, Ur.	E6	72
Durban, S. Afr.	D5	56
Durg, India	E4	40
Durgāpur, India	E5	40
Durham, On., Can.	C4	89
Durham, Eng., U.K.	C6	12
Durham, Ca., U.S.	C3	98
Durham, Ct., U.S.	D5	100
Durham, N.C., U.S.	B4	126
Durham, N.H., U.S.	D5	122
Durham, co., N.C., U.S.	A4	126
Durmitor, mtn., Yugo.	C7	18
Durrell, Nf., Can.	D4	88
Durrës, Alb.	D7	18
Dursunbey, Tur.	C3	44
D'Urville Island, i., N.Z.	p13	63c
Duryea, Pa., U.S.	D10	131
Dušanbe, Taj.	F8	26
Dušekan, Russia	C12	26
Dushan, China	F9	28
Dushanbe see Dušanbe, Taj.	F8	26
Dushanzi, China	C4	28
Duson, La., U.S.	D3	111
Düsseldorf, Ger.	E10	12
Dutchess, co., N.Y., U.S.	D7	125
Dutch Island, i., R.I., U.S.	F4	132
Dutton, On., Can.	E3	89
Dutton, Mount, mtn., Ut., U.S.	E3	137
Duval, co., Fl., U.S.	B5	102
Duval, co., Tx., U.S.	F3	136
Duxbury, Ma., U.S.	B6	114
Duyun, China	F9	28
Düzce, Tur.	B4	44
Dvina Bay see Dvinskaja guba, b., Russia	A6	22
Dvinskaja guba, b., Russia	A6	22
Dwārka, India	E1	40
Dwight, Il., U.S.	B5	106
Dwight D. Eisenhower Lock, N.Y., U.S.	f9	125
Dworshak Reservoir, res., Id., U.S.	C3	105
Dyer, In., U.S.	A2	107
Dyer, Tn., U.S.	A3	135
Dyer, co., Tn., U.S.	A2	135
Dyer Island, i., R.I., U.S.	E5	132
Dyersburg, Tn., U.S.	A2	135
Dyersville, Ia., U.S.	B6	108
Dyess Air Force Base, mil., Tx., U.S.	C3	136
Dysart, Ia., U.S.	B5	108
Džalinda, Russia	A12	28
Džambejty, Kaz.	D9	22
Džanybek, Kaz.	E8	22
Džardžan, Russia	C14	26
Dzaudzhikau see Vladikavkaz, Russia	E6	26
Dzerzhinsk see Dzjaržynsk, Bela.	C9	20
Dzerzhinsk see Dzeržinsk, Russia	C7	22
Dzeržinsk, Russia	C7	22
Dzětygara, Kaz.	D8	26
Dzhambul see Žambyl, Kaz.	E9	26
Dzhankoi, Ukr.	G13	20
Dzierżoniów, Pol.	D4	20
Džizak, Uzb.	E8	26
Dzjaržynsk, Bela.	C9	20
Dzjubga, Russia	G15	20
Džugdžur, hrebet, mts., Russia	D15	26
Dzungarian Basin see Junggar Pendi, China	B5	28
Džusaly, Kaz.	A8	42
Dzüünharaa, Mong.	B9	28
Dzuunmod, Mong.	B9	28
E		
Eads, Co., U.S.	C8	99
Eagan, Mn., U.S.	n12	116
Eagar, Az., U.S.	C6	96
Eagle, Co., U.S.	B4	99
Eagle, Id., U.S.	F2	105
Eagle, Ne., U.S.	h12	120
Eagle, Wi., U.S.	F5	142
Eagle, co., Co., U.S.	B4	99
Eagle, stm., Nf., Can.	B2	88
Eagle Creek Reservoir, res., In., U.S.	E5	107
Eagle Grove, Ia., U.S.	B4	108
Eagle Key, i., Fl., U.S.	G6	102
Eagle Lake, Ca., U.S.	A4	112
Eagle Lake, Mn., U.S.	F5	116
Eagle Lake, Tx., U.S.	E4	136
Eagle Lake, l., Ca., U.S.	B3	98
Eagle Lake, l., Me., U.S.	B3	112
Eagle Lake, l., Me., U.S.	A4	112
Eagle Lake, l., Ms., U.S.	C3	117
Eagle Lake, l., Wi., U.S.	C4	142
Eagle Mountain, mtn., Mn., U.S.	k9	116
Eagle Mountain Lake, res., Tx., U.S.	m9	136
Eagle Nest Lake, l., N.M., U.S.	A4	124
Eagle Pass, Tx., U.S.	E2	136
Eagle Peak, mtn., Ca., U.S.	B3	98
Eagle Point, Or., U.S.	E4	130
Eagle River, Wi., U.S.	C4	142
Eagletail Mountains, mts., Az., U.S.	D2	96
Eagletail Peak, mtn., Az., U.S.	D2	96
Eagletown, Ok., U.S.	C7	129
Earle, Ar., U.S.	B5	97
Earlham, Ia., U.S.	C3	108
Earlimart, Ca., U.S.	E4	98
Earlington, Ky., U.S.	C2	110
Earlville, Ia., U.S.	B6	108
Earlville, Il., U.S.	B5	106
Early, Ia., U.S.	B2	108
Early, co., Ga., U.S.	E2	103
Earth, Tx., U.S.	B1	136
Easley, S.C., U.S.	B2	133
East, stm., Ct., U.S.	D5	100
East, stm., N.Y., U.S.	k13	125
East, stm., Wi., U.S.	h9	142
East Alton, Il., U.S.	E3	106
East Angus, P.Q., Can.	D6	90
East Arlington, Vt., U.S.	E2	138
East Aurora, N.Y., U.S.	C2	125
East Bangor, Pa., U.S.	E11	131
East Bank, W.V., U.S.	m13	141
East Barre, Vt., U.S.	C4	138
East Baton Rouge, co., La., U.S.	D4	111
East Bay, b., Fl., U.S.	u16	102
East Bay, b., Tx., U.S.	R15	136
East Beckwith Mountain, mtn., Co., U.S.	C3	99
East Berlin, Ct., U.S.	C5	100
East Berlin, Pa., U.S.	G8	131
East Bernard, Tx., U.S.	E4	136
East Bernstadt, Ky., U.S.	C5	110
East Bethel, Mn., U.S.	E5	116
East Billerica, Ma., U.S.	f11	114
Eastborough, Ks., U.S.	g12	109
Eastbourne, Eng., U.K.	E7	12
East Brady, Pa., U.S.	E2	131
East Branch Clarion River Lake, res., Pa., U.S.	C4	131
East Brewton, Al., U.S.	D2	94
East Bridgewater, Ma., U.S.	B6	114
East Brimfield Lake, res., Ma., U.S.	B3	114
East Brooklyn, Ct., U.S.	B8	100
East Broughton, P.Q., Can.	C6	90
East Brunswick, N.J., U.S.	C4	123
East Butte, mtn., Mt., U.S.	B5	119
East Cache Creek, stm., Ok., U.S.	C3	129
East Caicos, i., T./C. Is.	A5	80
East Cape, c., N.Z.	o14	63c
East Cape, c., Fl., U.S.	G5	102
East Carbon, Ut., U.S.	D5	137
East Caroline Basin	H17	64
East Carroll, co., La., U.S.	B4	111
East Chicago, In., U.S.	A3	107
East China Sea, Asia	F12	28
East Chop, c., Ma., U.S.	D6	114
East Cleveland, Oh., U.S.	g9	128
East Cote Blanche Bay, b., La., U.S.	E4	111
East Dennis, Ma., U.S.	C7	114
East Derry, N.H., U.S.	E4	122
East Detroit, Mi., U.S.	p16	115
East Douglas, Ma., U.S.	B4	114
East Dubuque, Il., U.S.	A3	106
Eastend, Sk., Can.	H1	91
Easter Island see Pascua, Isla de, i., Chile	K28	64
Eastern Bay, b., Md., U.S.	C5	113
Eastern Desert, des., Egypt	C11	48
Eastern Ghāts, mts., India	G3	40
Eastern Neck Island, i., Md., U.S.	B5	113
Eastern Point, c., Ma., U.S.	f13	114
Eastern Sayans see Vostočnyj Sajan, mts., Russia	D11	26
Easterville, Mb., Can.	C2	86
East Falkland, i., Falk. Is.	H5	69
East Falmouth, Ma., U.S.	C6	114
East Feliciana, co., La., U.S.	D4	111
East Flat Rock, N.C., U.S.	f10	126
East Fork, stm., Wy., U.S.	D3	143
East Fork Lake, res., Oh., U.S.	C1	128
East Frisian Islands see Ostfriesische Inseln, is., Ger.	D10	12
East Gaffney, S.C., U.S.	A4	133
East Galesburg, Il., U.S.	C3	106
East Granby, Ct., U.S.	B5	100
East Grand Forks, Mn., U.S.	C2	116
East Grand Rapids, Mi., U.S.	F5	115
East Greenville, Pa., U.S.	F10	131
East Greenwich, R.I., U.S.	D4	132
East Gwillimbury, On., Can.	C5	89
East Hampstead, N.H., U.S.	E4	122
East Hampton, Ct., U.S.	C5	100
East Hampton, N.Y., U.S.	n16	125
Easthampton, Ma., U.S.	B2	114
East Hartford, Ct., U.S.	B5	100
East Hartland, Ct., U.S.	B4	100
East Haven, Ct., U.S.	D4	100
East Helena, Mt., U.S.	D5	119
East Jordan, Mi., U.S.	C5	115
Eastlake, Oh., U.S.	A4	128

Name	Map Ref.	Page

East Lake Tohopekaliga, l., Fl., U.S. D5 102
Eastland, Tx., U.S. C3 136
Eastland, co., Tx., U.S. C3 136
East Lansing, Mi., U.S. . . F6 115
East Las Vegas, Nv., U.S. . . G6 121
East Liverpool, Oh., U.S. . . B5 128
East London (Oos-Londen), S. Afr. E4 56
East Longmeadow, Ma., U.S. B2 114
East Los Angeles, Ca., U.S. . . m12 98
East Lyme, Ct., U.S. . . D7 100
East Lynn Lake, res., W.V., U.S. C2 141
Eastmain-Opinaca, Réservoir, res., P.Q., Can. h11 90
Eastman, P.Q., Can. D5 90
Eastman, Ga., U.S. D3 103
East Mariana Basin G18 64
East Matunuck, R.I., U.S. . . F3 132
East Middlebury, Vt., U.S. . . D2 138
East Millinocket, Me., U.S. . . C4 112
East Moline, Il., U.S. B3 106
East Montpelier, Vt., U.S. . . C4 138
East Naples, Fl., U.S. F5 102
East Newnan, Ga., U.S. . . . C2 103
East Nishnabotna, stm., Ia., U.S. C2 108
East Norriton, Pa., U.S. . . o20 131
East Olympia, Wa., U.S. . . . C3 140
Easton, Md., U.S. C5 113
Easton, Pa., U.S. E11 131
Easton Reservoir, res., Ct., U.S. E2 100
East Orange, N.J., U.S. B4 123
East Orleans, Ma., U.S. . . . C8 114
Eastover, S.C., U.S. D6 133
East Pacific Rise M27 64
East Pakistan see Bangladesh, ctry., Asia . B2 34
East Palatka, Fl., U.S. C5 102
East Palestine, Oh., U.S. . . . B5 128
East Pass, strt., Fl., U.S. . . . C2 102
East Pea Ridge, W.V., U.S. . . C2 141
East Peoria, Il., U.S. C4 106
East Pepperell, Ma., U.S. . . . A4 114
East Petersburg, Pa., U.S. . . F9 131
East Pittsburgh, Pa., U.S. . . k14 131
Eastpoint, Fl., U.S. C2 102
East Point, Ga., U.S. C2 103
East Point, c., P.E., Can. . . . C8 87
East Point, c., Ma., U.S. . . . B6 114
East Point, c., N.J., U.S. . . . E2 123
Eastport, Nf., Can. D5 88
Eastport, Me., U.S. D6 112
East Prairie, Mo., U.S. E8 118
East Providence, R.I., U.S. . . C4 132
East Pryor Mountain, mtn., Mt., U.S. E8 119
East Quogue, N.Y., U.S. . . . n16 125
East Range, mts., Nv., U.S. . . C4 121
East Ridge, Tn., U.S. h11 135
East River, Ct., U.S. D5 100
East Rochester, N.Y., U.S. . . B3 125
East Rockingham, N.C., U.S. C3 126
East Rutherford, N.J., U.S. . . h8 123
East Saint Louis, Il., U.S. . . E3 106
East Sea see Japan, Sea of, Asia C14 28
East Selkirk, Mb., Can. D3 86
East Siberian Sea see Vostočno-Sibirskoe more, Russia B17 26
Eastsound, Wa., U.S. A3 140
East Spencer, N.C., U.S. . . . B2 126
East Stroudsburg, Pa., U.S. . . D11 131
East Tawas, Mi., U.S. D7 115
East Troy, Wi., U.S. F5 142
East Vestal, N.Y., U.S. C4 125
East View, W.V., U.S. k10 141
East Walker, stm., U.S. E2 121
East Walpole, Ma., U.S. . . . h11 114
East Wareham, Ma., U.S. . . . C6 114
East Washington, Pa., U.S. . . F1 131
East Wenatchee, Wa., U.S. . . B5 140
East Windsor, N.J., U.S. . . . C3 123
East York, On., Can. D5 89
Eaton, Co., U.S. A6 99
Eaton, In., U.S. D7 107
Eaton, Oh., U.S. C1 128
Eaton, co., Mi., U.S. F6 115
Eaton Rapids, Mi., U.S. F6 115
Eatonton, Ga., U.S. C3 103
Eatontown, N.J., U.S. C4 123
Eatonville, Wa., U.S. C3 140
Eau Claire, Wi., U.S. D2 142
Eau Claire, co., Wi., U.S. . . . D2 142
Eau Claire, stm., Wi., U.S. . . D2 142
Eau Claire, Lac à l', l., P.Q., Can. g11 90
Eauripik Rise H17 64
Ebano, Mex. C5 78
Ebebiyin, Eq. Gui. C2 54
Ebensburg, Pa., U.S. F4 131
Eber Gölü, l., Tur. C4 44
Eberswalde-Finow, Ger. D13 12
Ebetsu, Japan B4 31
Ebinur Hu, l., China B4 28
Ebolowa, Cam. C2 54
Ebre see Ebro, stm., Spain . G7 16
Ebre, Delta de l', Spain G7 16
Ebro, stm., Spain G7 16
Eccles, W.V., U.S. n13 141

Ech Cheliff, Alg. C5 48
Echeng, China C3 30
Echo Bay, Nv., U.S. G7 121
Echo Lake, l., Me., U.S. D3 112
Echo Lake, l., Vt., U.S. B5 138
Eckerö, i., Fin. F8 10
Eckhart Mines, Md., U.S. . . . k13 113
Eckville, Ab., Can. C3 84
Eclectic, Al., U.S. C3 94
Econfina, stm., Fl., U.S. B3 102
Écorces, Rivière aux, stm., P.Q., Can. A6 90
Ecorse, Mi., U.S. p15 115
Ecru, Ms., U.S. A4 117
Ector, co., Tx., U.S. D1 136
Ecuador, ctry., S.A. D4 70
Edcouch, Tx., U.S. F4 136
Eddy, co., N.D., U.S. B7 127
Eddy, co., N.M., U.S. E5 124
Eddystone, Pa., U.S. p20 131
Eddyville, Ia., U.S. C5 108
Eddyville, Ky., U.S. e9 110
Ede, Neth. C5 12
Edéa, Cam. C2 54
Eden, Ga., U.S. D5 103
Eden, Md., U.S. D6 113
Eden, N.C., U.S. A3 126
Eden, N.Y., U.S. C2 125
Eden, Tx., U.S. D3 136
Edenburg, S. Afr. D4 56
Eden Prairie, Mn., U.S. n12 116
Edenton, N.C., U.S. A6 126
Eden Valley, Mn., U.S. E4 116
Edfu, Egypt F11 48
Edgar, Ne., U.S. D8 120
Edgar, Wi., U.S. D4 142
Edgar, co., Il., U.S. D6 106
Edgard, La., U.S. D5 111
Edgartown, Ma., U.S. D6 114
Edgecombe, co., N.C., U.S. B5 126
Edgecombe, Cape, c., Ak., U.S. m21 95
Edgefield, S.C., U.S. D4 133
Edgefield, co., S.C., U.S. . . . D4 133
Edgeley, N.D., U.S. C7 127
Edgemere, Md., U.S. B5 113
Edgemont, S.D., U.S. D2 134
Edgemoor, De., U.S. A3 101
Edgeøya, i., Nor. B4 26
Edgerton, Ks., U.S. D8 109
Edgerton, Mn., U.S. G2 116
Edgerton, Oh., U.S. A1 128
Edgerton, Wi., U.S. F4 142
Edgerton, Wy., U.S. C6 143
Edgewater, Al., U.S. f7 94
Edgewater, Fl., U.S. D6 102
Edgewater, Md., U.S. C4 113
Edgewater, N.J., U.S. h9 123
Edgewater Park, N.J., U.S. . . C3 123
Edgewood, Ia., U.S. B6 108
Edgewood, In., U.S. D6 107
Edgewood, Ky., U.S. h13 110
Edgewood, Md., U.S. B5 113
Edgewood, N.M., U.S. B3 124
Edgewood, Oh., U.S. A5 128
Edgewood, Pa., U.S. k14 131
Edgewood, Wa., U.S. f11 140
Edgeworth, Pa., U.S. h13 131
Édhessa, Grc. D9 18
Edina, Mn., U.S. n12 116
Edina, Mo., U.S. A5 118
Edinboro, Pa., U.S. C1 131
Edinburg, Il., U.S. D4 106
Edinburg, Tx., U.S. F3 136
Edinburg, Va., U.S. B4 139
Edinburgh, Scot., U.K. C5 12
Edinburgh, In., U.S. F6 107
Edineţ, Mol. E9 20
Edirne, Tur. B2 44
Edison, Ga., U.S. E2 103
Edison, N.J., U.S. B4 123
Edisto, stm., S.C., U.S. E6 133
Edisto Island, i., S.C., U.S. . . F7 133
Edith, Mount, mtn., Mt., U.S. D5 119
Edjeleh, Alg. E6 48
Edmond, Ok., U.S. B4 129
Edmonds, Wa., U.S. B3 140
Edmonson, co., Ky., U.S. . . . C3 110
Edmonton, Ab., Can. C4 84
Edmonton, Ky., U.S. D4 110
Edmore, Mi., U.S. E5 115
Edmunds, co., S.D., U.S. . . . B6 134
Edmundston, N.B., Can. B1 87
Edna, Tx., U.S. E4 136
Edon, Oh., U.S. A1 128
Édouard, Lac, l., P.Q., Can. B5 90
Edremit, Tur. C2 44
Edremit Körfezi, b., Tur. . . . C2 44
Edson, Ab., Can. C2 84
Eduardo Castex, Arg. F5 72
Edward, Lake, l., Afr. B5 54
Edwards, Ms., U.S. C3 117
Edwards, co., Il., U.S. E5 106
Edwards, co., Ks., U.S. E4 109
Edwards, co., Tx., U.S. E2 136
Edwards Air Force Base, mil., Ca., U.S. E5 98
Edwardsburg, Mi., U.S. G4 115
Edwards Butte, mtn., Or., U.S. B3 130

Edwardsville, Il., U.S. E4 106
Edwardsville, Ks., U.S. k16 109
Edwardsville, Pa., U.S. n17 131
Edward VII Peninsula, pen., Ant. D25 67
El Cuervo Butte, mtn., N.M., U.S. k9 124
Eel, stm., Ca., U.S. B2 98
Eel, stm., In., U.S. C6 107
Eel, stm., In., U.S. F3 107
Éfaté, i., Vanuatu k9 62a
Efes (Ephesus), hist., Tur. . . D2 44
Effigy Mounds National Monument, Ia., U.S. . . . A6 108
Effingham, Il., U.S. D5 106
Effingham, co., Ga., U.S. . . . D5 103
Effingham, co., Il., U.S. D5 106
Efland, N.C., U.S. A3 126
Efremov, Russia C15 20
Egadi, Isole, is., Italy E4 18
Egan Range, mts., Nv., U.S. . E7 121
Eganville, On., Can. B7 89
Egedesminde, Grnld. E29 82
Eger, Hung. F6 20
Eggenfelden, Ger. F13 12
Egg Harbor City, N.J., U.S. . . D3 123
Egg Island Point, c., N.J., U.S. E2 123
Egijn, stm., Mong. A8 28
Eglin Air Force Base, mil., Fl., U.S. u15 102
Egmont, Cape, c., N.Z. o13 63c
Egmont, Mount see Taranaki, Mount, vol., N.Z. o13 63c
Egmont Bay, b., P.E., Can. . . C5 87
Egmont Channel, strt., Fl., U.S. p10 102
Egmont Key, i., Fl., U.S. . . . p10 102
Egvekinot, Russia C20 26
Egypt, ctry., Afr. E10 48
Egypt, Lake of, res., Il., U.S. F5 106
Eha-Amufu, Nig. E6 50
Ehrenberg, Az., U.S. D1 96
Eibar, Spain F5 16
Eielson Air Force Base, mil., Ak., U.S. C10 95
Eigersund, Nor. G2 10
Eight Degree Channel, strt., Asia H2 40
Eights Coast, Ant. D31 67
Eighty Mile Beach, Austl. . . . D3 60
Eindhoven, Neth. E9 12
Eirunepé, Braz. E6 70
Eisenach, Ger. E12 12
Eisenerz, Aus. G14 12
Eisenhower, Mount, mtn., N.H., U.S. B4 122
Eisenhüttenstadt, Ger. D14 12
Eisenstadt, Aus. G15 12
Eivissa, Spain H7 16
Eivissa (Ibiza), i., Spain . . . H7 16
Ejin Qi, China C8 28
Ejsk, Russia F15 20
Ejura, Ghana E4 50
Ekaterinburg, Russia D8 26
Ekibastuz, Kaz. D9 26
Ekimčan, Russia D15 26
Ekonda, Russia C12 26
Ela, Myan. C3 34
El Aaiún, W. Sah. A2 50
Elaine, Ar., U.S. C5 97
El-Alamein, Egypt E9 14
Elan', Russia D7 22
Elancy, Russia D12 26
El-Arish, Egypt E10 14
Elat, Isr. E2 42
Elat, Gulf of see Aqaba, Gulf of, b. E2 42
Elath see Elat, Isr. E2 42
Elazığ, Tur. C8 44
Elba, Al., U.S. D3 94
Elba, Isola d', i., Italy C3 18
El Banco, Col. D5 80
Elbasan, Alb. D7 18
Elbe see Labe, stm., Eur. . . . E14 12
Elberfeld, In., U.S. H3 107
Elbert, co., Co., U.S. B6 99
Elbert, co., Ga., U.S. B4 103
Elbert, Mount, mtn., Co., U.S. B4 99
Elberta, Ga., U.S. D3 103
Elberton, Ga., U.S. B4 103
El Beyyadh, Alg. E4 14
Elbistan, Tur. C7 44
Elbląg, Pol. B5 20
El Boulaïda, Alg. C5 48
Elbow, stm., Ab., Can. D3 84
Elbow Lake, Mn., U.S. E3 116
El'brus, gora, mtn., Russia . . E6 26
Elbrus, Mount see El'brus, gora, mtn., Russia E6 26
Elburz Mountains see Alborz, Reshteh-ye Kūhhā-ye, mts., Iran . C6 42
El Cajon, Ca., U.S. F5 98
El Calafate, Arg. H2 69
El Callao, Ven. D7 80
El Campo, Tx., U.S. E4 136
El Capitan, mtn., Mt., U.S. . . D2 119
El Capitan Reservoir, res., Ca., U.S. o16 98
El Carmen de Bolívar, Col. . B4 70
El Centro, Ca., U.S. F6 98

El Cerrito, Ca., U.S. h8 98
Elcho Island, i., Austl. C6 60
El Djazaïr (Algiers), Alg. . . . C5 48
El Djelfa, Alg. E4 14
Eldon, Ia., U.S. D5 108
Eldon, Mo., U.S. C5 118
Eldora, Ia., U.S. B4 108
Eldorado, Arg. D7 72
El Dorado, Ar., U.S. D3 97
Eldorado, Il., U.S. F5 106
El Dorado, Ks., U.S. E7 109
Eldorado, Tx., U.S. D2 136
El Dorado, Ven. D7 80
El Dorado, co., Ca., U.S. . . C3 98
Eldorado Peak, mtn., Wa., U.S. A4 140
Eldorado Springs, Co., U.S. . B5 99
El Dorado Springs, Mo., U.S. D3 118
Eldoret, Kenya C7 54
Eldridge, Ia., U.S. C7 108
Eleanor, W.V., U.S. C3 141
Elec, Russia D5 26
Electra, Tx., U.S. C3 136
Electra Lake, res., Co., U.S. . D3 99
Electric Peak, mtn., Co., U.S. C5 99
Electric Peak, mtn., Mt., U.S. E6 119
Elefantes (Olifants), stm., Afr. C5 56
El Encanto, Col. D5 70
Elephant Butte Reservoir, res., N.M., U.S. D2 124
Eleuthera, i., Bah. C9 76
Eleven Mile Canyon Reservoir, res., Co., U.S. C5 99
Eleven Point, stm., U.S. A4 97
El-Fayoum, Egypt E11 48
Elgin, Scot., U.K. B5 12
Elgin, Ia., U.S. B6 108
Elgin, Il., U.S. A5 106
Elgin, Mn., U.S. F6 116
Elgin, N.D., U.S. C4 127
Elgin, Ne., U.S. C7 120
Elgin, Ok., U.S. C3 129
Elgin, Or., U.S. B9 130
Elgin, S.C., U.S. B6 133
Elgin, Tx., U.S. D4 136
Elgon, Mount, mtn., Afr. . . . C6 54
El Grara, Alg. E4 14
El Hammâmi, reg., Maur. . . B2 50
El Hank, clf., Afr. B3 50
El Hierro, i., Spain A1 50
Elhovo, Bul. C11 18
Eliase, Indon. E8 36
Elida, Oh., U.S. B1 128
El-Iskandarîya, Egypt D10 48
Elista, Russia E6 26
Elizabeth, Austl. G2 62
Elizabeth, Co., U.S. B6 99
Elizabeth, N.J., U.S. B4 123
Elizabeth, W.V., U.S. B3 141
Elizabeth, Cape, c., Wa., U.S. B1 140
Elizabeth City, N.C., U.S. . . A6 126
Elizabeth Islands, is., Ma., U.S. D6 114
Elizabethton, Tn., U.S. C11 135
Elizabethtown, Ky., U.S. . . . C4 110
Elizabethtown, N.C., U.S. . . . C4 126
Elizabethtown, Pa., U.S. . . . F8 131
Elizabethville, Pa., U.S. E8 131
Elizavety, mys, c., Russia . . . D16 26
El Jebel, Co., U.S. B3 99
El-Jadida, Mor. D3 48
Ełk, Pol. C7 20
Elk, co., Ks., U.S. E7 109
Elk, co., Pa., U.S. D4 131
Elk, stm., Co., U.S. A4 99
Elk, stm., Ks., U.S. E7 109
Elk, stm., W.V., U.S. C3 141
Elk, stm., Wi., U.S. C3 142
Elk, stm., U.S. A2 94
Elkader, Ia., U.S. B6 108
Elk City, Id., U.S. D3 105
Elk City, Ok., U.S. B2 129
Elk City Lake, res., Ks., U.S. E7 109
Elk Creek, stm., Ok., U.S. . . B2 129
Elk Creek, stm., S.D., U.S. . . C3 134
El Kef, Tun. C6 48
El Kere, Eth. B8 54
Elkford, B.C., Can. D10 85
Elk Grove, Ca., U.S. C3 98
Elk Grove Village, Il., U.S. . . h9 106
El-Khârga, Egypt E11 48
Elkhart, Ks., U.S. E2 109
Elkhart, co., In., U.S. A6 107
Elkhart, stm., In., U.S. A6 107
Elkhart Lake, Wi., U.S. E5 142
El Khroub, Alg. B6 48
Elkhorn, Mb., Can. E1 86
Elk Horn, Ia., U.S. C2 108
Elkhorn, Ne., U.S. g12 120
Elkhorn, Wi., U.S. F5 142
Elkhorn, stm., Ne., U.S. B7 120

Elkhorn City, Ky., U.S. C7 110
Elkhorn Peaks, mts., Id., U.S. F7 105
Elkin, N.C., U.S. A2 126
Elkins, Ar., U.S. A1 97
Elkins, W.V., U.S. C5 141
Elkland, Pa., U.S. C7 131
Elk Mills, Md., U.S. A6 113
Elk Mound, Wi., U.S. D2 142
Elk Mountain, Wy., U.S. E6 143
Elk Mountain, mtn., N.M., U.S. D1 124
Elk Mountain, mtn., Wy., U.S. E6 143
Elk Mountains, mts., Co., U.S. B3 99
Elk Mountains, mts., U.S. . . D1 134
Elko, Nv., U.S. C6 121
Elko, co., Nv., U.S. B6 121
Elk Peak, mtn., Mt., U.S. . . . D6 119
Elk Point, Ab., Can. C5 84
Elk Point, S.D., U.S. E9 134
Elk Rapids, Mi., U.S. D5 115
Elkridge, Md., U.S. B4 113
Elk River, Mn., U.S. E5 116
Elkton, Ky., U.S. D2 110
Elkton, Md., U.S. A6 113
Elkton, Mi., U.S. E7 115
Elkton, S.D., U.S. C9 134
Elkton, Va., U.S. B4 139
Elkview, W.V., U.S. m13 141
Elkville, Il., U.S. F4 106
Ellaville, Ga., U.S. D2 103
Ellen, Mount, mtn., Ut., U.S. E5 137
Ellendale, De., U.S. E4 101
Ellendale, N.D., U.S. C7 127
Ellensburg, Wa., U.S. C5 140
Ellenton, Fl., U.S. E4 102
Ellenville, N.Y., U.S. D6 125
Ellerbe, N.C., U.S. B3 126
Ellerslie, Md., U.S. k13 113
Ellesmere Island, i., N.T., Can. B24 82
Ellettsville, In., U.S. F4 107
Ellice Islands see Tuvalu, ctry., Oc. E11 58
Ellicott City, Md., U.S. B4 113
Ellijay, Ga., U.S. B2 103
Ellington, Ct., U.S. B6 100
Ellington, Mo., U.S. D7 118
Ellinwood, Ks., U.S. D5 109
Elliot, S. Afr. E4 56
Elliot Lake, On., Can. A2 89
Elliott, Ms., U.S. B4 117
Elliott, co., Ky., U.S. B6 110
Elliott Bay, b., Wa., U.S. . . . e11 140
Elliott Key, i., Fl., U.S. G6 102
Ellis, Ks., U.S. D4 109
Ellis, co., Ks., U.S. D4 109
Ellis, co., Ok., U.S. A2 129
Ellis, co., Tx., U.S. C4 136
Ellis, stm., N.H., U.S. B4 122
Elliston, Va., U.S. C2 139
Ellisville, Mo., U.S. f12 118
Ellisville, Ms., U.S. D4 117
Ellore see Elūru, India F4 40
Elloree, S.C., U.S. D6 133
Ellport, Pa., U.S. E1 131
Ellsworth, Ks., U.S. D5 109
Ellsworth, Me., U.S. D4 112
Ellsworth, Pa., U.S. F1 131
Ellsworth, Wi., U.S. D1 142
Ellsworth, co., Ks., U.S. D5 109
Ellsworth Air Force Base, mil., S.D., U.S. C2 134
Ellsworth Land, reg., Ant. . . D32 67
Ellsworth Mountains, mts., Ant. D32 67
Ellwood City, Pa., U.S. E1 131
Elm, stm., N.D., U.S. B8 127
Elma, Ia., U.S. A5 108
Elma, Wa., U.S. C2 140
Elmadağ, Tur. C5 44
El-Mahalla el-Kubra, Egypt . G4 44
Elmalı, Tur. D3 44
El-Mansûra, Egypt E10 14
Elm City, N.C., U.S. B5 126
Elm Creek, Ne., U.S. D6 120
Elmendorf Air Force Base, mil., Ak., U.S. C10 95
El Menia, Alg. D5 48
Elm Grove, Wi., U.S. m11 142
Elmhurst, Il., U.S. B6 106
Elmhurst, Pa., U.S. D10 131
El-Minya, Egypt E11 48
Elmira, N.Y., U.S. C4 125
El Mirage, Az., U.S. k8 96
Elmira Heights, N.Y., U.S. . . C4 125
El Mohammadia, Alg. J7 16
Elmont, N.Y., U.S. k13 125
Elmora, Pa., U.S. E4 131
Elmore, Mn., U.S. G4 116
Elmore, Oh., U.S. A2 128
Elmore, co., Al., U.S. C3 94
Elmore, co., Id., U.S. F3 105
El Morro National Monument, N.M., U.S. . B1 124
El Mreyyé, reg., Maur. C3 50
Elmsdale, N.S., Can. E6 87
Elmshorn, Ger. D11 12
Elm Springs, Ar., U.S. A1 97
Elmvale, On., Can. C5 89
Elmwood, Il., U.S. C3 106
Elmwood, Wi., U.S. D1 142
Elmwood Park, Il., U.S. k9 106

Name	Map Ref.	Page
Elmwood Park, N.J., U.S.	h8	123
Elmwood Place, Oh., U.S.	o13	128
Elnora, Il., U.S.	G3	107
Eloise, Fl., U.S.	E5	102
Elon College, N.C., U.S.	A3	126
Elora, On., Can.	D4	89
Elorza, Ven.	D6	80
Éloten, Turk.	C8	42
Eloy, Az., U.S.	E4	96
El Paso, Il., U.S.	C4	106
El Paso, Tx., U.S.	o11	136
El Paso, co., Co., U.S.	C6	99
El Paso, co., Tx., U.S.	o11	136
El Pital, Cerro, mtn., N.A.	C2	80
El Portal, Fl., U.S.	s13	102
El Prado, N.M., U.S.	A4	124
El Progreso, Hond.	B2	80
El Puerto de Santa María, Spain	I3	16
El-Qâhira (Cairo), Egypt	D10	48
El-Qasr, Egypt	E10	48
El Reno, Ok., U.S.	B4	129
Elrose, Sk., Can.	F1	91
Elroy, Wi., U.S.	E3	142
Elsa, Tx., U.S.	F3	136
Elsah, Il., U.S.	E3	106
El Salto, Mex.	C3	78
El Salvador, ctry., N.A.	C2	80
El Sauzal, Mex.	A1	78
Elsberry, Mo., U.S.	B7	118
Elsie, Mi., U.S.	E6	115
Elsinore, Ut., U.S.	E3	137
El'sk, Bela.	D10	20
Elsmere, De., U.S.	B3	101
Elsmere, Ky., U.S.	B5	110
El Sueco, Mex.	B3	78
El-Suweis, Egypt	E11	48
Eltham, N.Z.	o13	63c
Elton, La., U.S.	D3	111
El Toro Marine Corps Air Station, mil., Ca., U.S.	n13	98
El Turbio, Arg.	H2	69
El-Uqsor, Egypt	E11	48
Elūru, India	F4	40
El Vado Reservoir, res., N.M., U.S.	A3	124
Elvas, Port.	H3	16
Elvins, Mo., U.S.	D7	118
El Wad, Alg.	E5	14
El Wak, Kenya	C8	54
Elwell, Lake, res., Mt., U.S.	B5	119
Elwha, stm., Wa., U.S.	A2	140
Elwood, In., U.S.	D6	107
Elwood, Ks., U.S.	C9	109
Elwood, Ne., U.S.	D6	120
Elx, Spain	H6	16
Ely, Eng., U.K.	D7	12
Ely, Mn., U.S.	C7	116
Ely, Nv., U.S.	D7	121
Elyria, Oh., U.S.	A3	128
Elysburg, Pa., U.S.	E8	131
Emämshahr, Iran	C7	42
Emanuel, co., Ga., U.S.	D4	103
Emba, Kaz.	E10	22
Emba, stm., Kaz.	E7	26
Embarras, stm., Il., U.S.	E6	106
Embarrass, stm., Wi., U.S.	D5	142
Embro, On., Can.	D4	89
Embu, Kenya	D7	54
Emden, Ger.	D10	12
Emerald, Austl.	E4	62
Emerson, Mb., Can.	E3	86
Emerson, Ga., U.S.	B2	103
Emerson, Ne., U.S.	B9	120
Emerson, N.J., U.S.	h8	123
Emery, co., Ut., U.S.	E5	137
Emet, Tur.	C3	44
Emiliano Zapata, Mex.	D6	78
Emily, Mn., U.S.	D5	116
Emily, Lake, l., Mn., U.S.	E3	116
Eminence, Ky., U.S.	B4	110
Emirdağ, Tur.	C4	44
Emmaus, Pa., U.S.	E11	131
Emmen, Neth.	D10	12
Emmet, co., Ia., U.S.	A3	108
Emmet, co., Mi., U.S.	C6	115
Emmetsburg, Ia., U.S.	A3	108
Emmett, Id., U.S.	F2	105
Emmitsburg, Md., U.S.	A3	113
Emmonak, Ak., U.S.	C7	95
Emmons, co., N.D., U.S.	C5	127
Emory Peak, mtn., Tx., U.S.	E1	136
Empalme, Mex.	B2	78
Empangeni, S. Afr.	D5	56
Empedrado, Arg.	D6	72
Emperor Seamounts	D19	64
Empire, La., U.S.	E6	111
Empire, Nv., U.S.	C2	121
Empoli, Italy	C3	18
Emporia, Ks., U.S.	D7	109
Emporia, Va., U.S.	D5	139
Emporium, Pa., U.S.	D5	131
Empty Quarter see Ar-Rub' al-Khālī, des., Asia	G6	38
Emsworth, Pa., U.S.	h13	131
Encampment, Wy., U.S.	E6	143
Encarnación, Para.	D6	72
Enchilayas, Mex.	A2	78
Encinitas, Ca., U.S.	h5	98
Encontrados, Ven.	D5	80
Encounter Bay, b., Austl.	H2	62
Ende, Indon.	E6	36
Enderby, B.C., Can.	D8	85
Enderby Land, reg., Ant.	D9	67
Enderlin, N.D., U.S.	C8	127
Enders Reservoir, res., Ne., U.S.	D4	120
Endicott, N.Y., U.S.	C4	125
Endicott Mountains, mts., Ak., U.S.	B9	95
Endless Lake, l., Me., U.S.	C4	112
Endwell, N.Y., U.S.	C4	125
Enewetak, atoll, Marsh. Is.	C10	58
Enfield (Thompsonville), Ct., U.S.	B5	100
Enfield, N.C., U.S.	A5	126
Enfield, N.H., U.S.	C2	122
Engel's, Russia	D6	26
Enggano, Pulau, i., Indon.	E2	36
England, Ar., U.S.	C4	97
England, prov., U.K.	D6	12
Englee, Nf., Can.	C3	88
Engleside, Va., U.S.	g12	139
Englewood, Co., U.S.	B6	99
Englewood, Fl., U.S.	F4	102
Englewood, N.J., U.S.	B5	123
Englewood, Oh., U.S.	C1	128
Englewood, Tn., U.S.	D9	135
Englewood Cliffs, N.J., U.S.	h9	123
English, In., U.S.	H5	107
English Bāzār see Ingrāj Bāzār, India	E5	40
English Channel, strt., Eur.	C5	16
English Coast, Ant.	D33	67
Enid, Ok., U.S.	A4	129
Enid Lake, res., Ms., U.S.	A4	117
Enigma, Ga., U.S.	E3	103
Enisej (Yenisey), stm., Russia	C10	26
eNjesuthi, mtn., Afr.	D4	56
Enka, N.C., U.S.	f10	126
Enköping, Swe.	G7	10
Enna, Italy	F5	18
Ennedi, plat., Chad	G9	48
Ennis, Mt., U.S.	E5	119
Ennis, Tx., U.S.	C4	136
Enoch, Ut., U.S.	F2	137
Enola, Pa., U.S.	F8	131
Enontekiö, Fin.	B10	10
Enoree, S.C., U.S.	B4	133
Enoree, stm., S.C., U.S.	B3	133
Enosburg Falls, Vt., U.S.	B3	138
Enriquillo, Lago, l., Dom. Rep.	B5	80
Enschede, Neth.	D10	12
Ensenada, Mex.	A1	78
Enshi, China	E9	28
Enshu Bay see Enshū-nada, Japan	D3	31
Enshū-nada, Japan	D3	31
Ensley, Fl., U.S.	u14	102
Entebbe, Ug.	C6	54
Enterprise, Al., U.S.	D4	94
Enterprise, Ks., U.S.	D6	109
Enterprise, Or., U.S.	B9	130
Enterprise, Ut., U.S.	F2	137
Enterprise, W.V., U.S.	B4	141
Entiat, stm., Wa., U.S.	B5	140
Entiat, Lake, l., Wa., U.S.	B5	140
Entiat Mountains, mts., Wa., U.S.	B5	140
Entroncamento, Port.	H2	16
Enugu, Nig.	E6	50
Enumclaw, Wa., U.S.	B4	140
Enyamba, D.R.C.	D5	54
Eola Hills, hills, Or., U.S.	h11	130
Epena, Congo	C3	54
Épernay, Fr.	C8	16
Ephesus see Efes, hist., Tur.	D2	44
Ephraim, Ut., U.S.	D4	137
Ephrata, Pa., U.S.	F9	131
Ephrata, Wa., U.S.	B6	140
Épi, i., Vanuatu	I9	62a
Épinal, Fr.	C10	16
Epirus see Ípeiros, hist. reg., Grc.	E8	18
Epping, N.H., U.S.	D4	122
Epukiro, Nmb.	C2	56
Epworth, Ia., U.S.	B7	108
Eqlīd, Iran	D6	42
Equatorial Guinea, ctry., Afr.	C1	54
Erath, La., U.S.	E3	111
Erath, co., Tx., U.S.	C3	136
Erbaa, Tur.	B7	44
Erciş, Tur.	C10	44
Erciyes Dağı, vol., Tur.	C6	44
Érd, Hung.	F5	20
Erdek, Tur.	B2	44
Erdemli, Tur.	D6	44
Erdene see Ulaan-Uul, Mong.	C10	28
Erebus, Mount, mtn., Ant.	D21	67
Erechim, Braz.	D7	72
Ereğli, Tur.	D5	44
Ereğli, Tur.	B4	44
Erenhot, China	C10	28
Erfoud, Mor.	E3	14
Erfurt, Ger.	E12	12
Ergani, Tur.	C8	44
Ergel, Mong.	C9	28
Ergene, stm., Tur.	B2	44
Ergeni, hills, Russia	D6	26
Ergun see Argun', stm., Asia	D14	26
Erick, Ok., U.S.	B2	129
Erickson, Mb., Can.	D2	86
Erie, Co., U.S.	A5	99
Erie, Il., U.S.	B3	106
Erie, Ks., U.S.	E8	109
Erie, Mi., U.S.	G7	115
Erie, Pa., U.S.	B1	131
Erie, co., N.Y., U.S.	C2	125
Erie, co., Oh., U.S.	A3	128
Erie, co., Pa., U.S.	C1	131
Erie, Lake, l., N.A.	C11	92
Erie Canal, N.Y., U.S.	B5	125
Erimo-misaki, c., Japan	C16	28
Erin, On., Can.	D4	89
Erin, Tn., U.S.	A4	135
Eritrea, ctry., Afr.	G12	48
Erlangen, Ger.	F12	12
Erlanger, Ky., U.S.	A5	110
Erling, Lake, res., Ar., U.S.	D2	97
Ermelo, S. Afr.	D4	56
Ermenek, Tur.	D5	44
Ermolaevo, Russia	D10	22
Ermoúpolis, Grc.	F10	18
Erne, Lower Lough, l., N. Ire., U.K.	C3	12
Erne, Upper Lough, l., Eur.	C3	12
Erode, India	G3	40
Erofej Pavlovič, Russia	D14	26
Eropol, Russia	C18	26
Er-Rachidia, Mor.	E3	14
Errego, Moz.	B6	56
Erromango, i., Vanuatu	I9	62a
Eršov, Russia	D8	22
Ertai, China	B6	28
Ertil', Russia	D16	20
Ertis see Irtysh, stm., Asia	D8	26
Ertix see Irtysh, stm., Asia	D8	26
Erwin, N.C., U.S.	B4	126
Erwin, Tn., U.S.	C11	135
Eryuan, China	A3	34
Erzgebirge, mts., Eur.	E9	8
Erzin, Russia	D11	26
Erzincan, Tur.	C8	44
Erzurum, Tur.	C9	44
Esa'ala, Pap. N. Gui.	H13	32
Esbjerg, Den.	I3	10
Escalante, Ut., U.S.	F4	137
Escalante, stm., Ut., U.S.	F4	137
Escalon, Ca., U.S.	D3	98
Escambia, co., Al., U.S.	D2	94
Escambia, co., Fl., U.S.	u14	102
Escambia, stm., Fl., U.S.	u14	102
Escanaba, Mi., U.S.	C3	115
Escanaba, stm., Mi., U.S.	B3	115
Escárcega, Mex.	D6	78
Escarpada Point, c., Phil.	C8	34
Escatawpa, Ms., U.S.	E5	117
Escatawpa, stm., U.S.	D5	117
Escondido, Ca., U.S.	F5	98
Escondido, stm., Nic.	C3	80
Escoumins, Rivière des, stm., P.Q., Can.	A8	90
Escuinapa de Hidalgo, Mex.	C3	78
Escuintla, Guat.	C1	80
Escuminac, Point, c., N.B., Can.	B5	87
Eséka, Cam.	C2	54
Eşfahān, Iran	D6	42
Esil', Kaz.	D8	26
Eškar-Ola, Russia	D6	26
Eskilstuna, Swe.	G7	10
Eskimo Lakes, l., N.T., Can.	E13	82
Eskişehir, Tur.	C4	44
Esla, stm., Spain	G4	16
Eslāmābād, Iran	E12	44
Eslāmshahr, Iran	C6	42
Eşme, Tur.	C3	44
Esmeralda, co., Nv., U.S.	F4	121
Esmeraldas, Ec.	C4	70
Esmond, R.I., U.S.	B4	132
Espanola, On., Can.	A3	89
Espanola, N.M., U.S.	B3	124
Esparto, Ca., U.S.	C2	98
Esperança, Braz.	B3	70
Esperance, Austl.	G3	60
Esperance Bay, b., Austl.	G3	60
Esperanza, Arg.	E5	72
Esperanza, Mex.	B3	78
Espinhaço, Serra do, mts., Braz.	E3	74
Espinho, Port.	G2	16
Espírito Santo, state, Braz.	E3	74
Espiritu Santo, i., Vanuatu	j9	62a
Espíritu Santo, Isla del, i., Mex.	C2	78
Esplanada, Braz.	D4	74
Espoo, Fin.	F11	10
Espungabera, Moz.	C5	56
Espy, Pa., U.S.	D9	131
Esquel, Arg.	F2	69
Esquimalt, B.C., Can.	E6	85
Esquina, Arg.	D6	72
Essaouira, Mor.	D3	48
Essen, Ger.	E10	12
Essendon, Mount, mtn., Austl.	E3	60
Essequibo, stm., Guy.	C8	70
Essex, On., Can.	E2	89
Essex, Ia., U.S.	D2	108
Essex, Ma., U.S.	A6	114
Essex, Md., U.S.	B5	113
Essex, co., Ma., U.S.	A5	114
Essex, co., N.J., U.S.	B4	123
Essex, co., N.Y., U.S.	B7	125
Essex, co., Va., U.S.	C6	139
Essex, co., Vt., U.S.	B5	138
Essex Junction, Vt., U.S.	C2	138
Essexville, Mi., U.S.	E7	115
Esslingen am Neckar, Ger.	F11	12
Estacada, Or., U.S.	B4	130
Estacado, Llano, pl., U.S.	C1	136
Estados, Isla de los, i., Arg.	H4	69
Eṣṭahbān, Iran	E6	42
Estância, Braz.	D4	74
Estancia, N.M., U.S.	C3	124
Estcourt, S. Afr.	D4	56
Estelí, Nic.	C2	80
Estella, Spain	F5	16
Estelline, S.D., U.S.	C9	134
Estepona, Spain	I4	16
Estero Bay, b., Ca., U.S.	E3	98
Estero Bay, b., Fl., U.S.	F5	102
Estero Island, i., Fl., U.S.	F5	102
Estes Park, Co., U.S.	A5	99
Estherville, Ia., U.S.	A3	108
Estherwood, La., U.S.	D3	111
Estill, S.C., U.S.	F5	133
Estill, co., Ky., U.S.	C6	110
Estill Springs, Tn., U.S.	B5	135
Estonia, ctry., Eur.	G11	10
Estremadura, hist. reg., Port.	H2	16
Esztergom, Hung.	F5	20
Etah, Grnld.	C25	82
Étampes, Fr.	C8	16
Étang-du-Nord, P.Q., Can.	B8	87
Etāwa, India	D3	40
Ethel, W.V., U.S.	n12	141
Ethel Creek, Austl.	E3	60
Ethiopia, ctry., Afr.	I12	48
Etna, Pa., U.S.	k14	131
Etna, Monte, vol., Italy	F5	18
Etobicoke, On., Can.	D5	89
Etolin Island, i., Ak., U.S.	m23	95
Etolin Strait, strt., Ak., U.S.	C6	95
Etosha Pan, pl., Nmb.	B2	56
Etowah, Tn., U.S.	D9	135
Etowah, co., Al., U.S.	A3	94
Etowah, stm., Ga., U.S.	B2	103
Et Tīdra, i., Maur.	C1	50
Ettrick, Va., U.S.	C5	139
Eua, i., Tonga	G12	58
Euboea see Évvoia, i., Grc.	E9	18
Euboea, Gulf of see Vórios Evvoïkós Kólpos, b., Grc.	E9	18
Eucla, Austl.	G4	60
Euclid, Oh., U.S.	A4	128
Eudora, Ar., U.S.	D4	97
Eudora, Ks., U.S.	D8	109
Eufaula, Al., U.S.	D4	94
Eufaula, Ok., U.S.	B6	129
Eufaula Lake, res., Ok., U.S.	B6	129
Eugene, Or., U.S.	C3	130
Eugenia, Punta, c., Mex.	B1	78
Eugmo, i., Fin.	E10	10
Eunice, La., U.S.	D3	111
Eunice, N.M., U.S.	E6	124
Euphrates (Al-Furāt), stm., Asia	D4	42
Eupora, Ms., U.S.	B4	117
Eureka, Ca., U.S.	B1	98
Eureka, Il., U.S.	C4	106
Eureka, Ks., U.S.	E7	109
Eureka, Mo., U.S.	f12	118
Eureka, Mt., U.S.	B1	119
Eureka, Nv., U.S.	D6	121
Eureka, S.C., U.S.	B5	133
Eureka, S.D., U.S.	B6	134
Eureka, co., Nv., U.S.	D5	121
Eureka Springs, Ar., U.S.	A2	97
Euroa, Austl.	H4	62
Europe	C13	4
Eustis, Fl., U.S.	D5	102
Eutaw, Al., U.S.	C2	94
Eutsuk Lake, l., B.C., Can.	C5	85
Evangeline, co., La., U.S.	D3	111
Evans, Co., U.S.	A6	99
Evans, Ga., U.S.	C4	103
Evans, W.V., U.S.	C3	141
Evans, co., Ga., U.S.	D5	103
Evans, Mount, mtn., Co., U.S.	B5	99
Evansburg, Ab., Can.	C3	84
Evans City, Pa., U.S.	E1	131
Evansdale, Ia., U.S.	B5	108
Evanston, Il., U.S.	A6	106
Evanston, Wy., U.S.	E2	143
Evansville, Il., U.S.	E4	106
Evansville, In., U.S.	I2	107
Evansville, Wi., U.S.	F4	142
Evansville, Wy., U.S.	D6	143
Eva Perón see La Plata, Arg.	F5	72
Evart, Mi., U.S.	E5	115
Evarts, Ky., U.S.	D6	110
Eveleth, Mn., U.S.	C6	116
Evensk, Russia	C17	26
Everest, Mount, mtn., Asia	D6	40
Everett, Ma., U.S.	g11	114
Everett, Pa., U.S.	F5	131
Everett, Wa., U.S.	B3	140
Everett Lake, res., N.H., U.S.	D3	122
Everglades National Park, Fl., U.S.	G5	102
Evergreen, Al., U.S.	D3	94
Evergreen, Co., U.S.	B5	99
Evergreen Park, Il., U.S.	k9	106
Everly, Ia., U.S.	A2	108
Everson, Wa., U.S.	A3	140
Evje, Nor.	G2	10
Évora, Port.	H3	16
Évreux, Fr.	C7	16
Évros (Marica) (Meriç), stm., Eur.	D11	18
E.V. Spence Reservoir, res., Tx., U.S.	D2	136
Évvoia, i., Grc.	E9	18
Ewa, Hi., U.S.	B3	104
Ewa Beach, Hi., U.S.	B3	104
Ewa Beach, Hi., U.S.	g9	104
Ewing Township, N.J., U.S.	C3	123
Ewo, Congo	D2	54
Excelsior Mountain, mtn., Ca., U.S.	C4	98
Excelsior Mountains, mts., Nv., U.S.	E3	121
Excelsior Springs, Mo., U.S.	B3	118
Exeter, On., Can.	D3	89
Exeter, Eng., U.K.	E5	12
Exeter, Ca., U.S.	D4	98
Exeter, Ne., U.S.	D8	120
Exeter, N.H., U.S.	E5	122
Exeter, Pa., U.S.	D10	131
Exeter, stm., N.H., U.S.	E5	122
Exira, Ia., U.S.	C3	108
Exmore, Va., U.S.	C7	139
Exmouth, Austl.	E1	60
Exmouth Gulf, b., Austl.	E1	60
Experiment, Ga., U.S.	C2	103
Exploits, stm., Nf., Can.	D3	88
Exploits, Bay of, b., Nf., Can.	D4	88
Export, Pa., U.S.	F2	131
Extremadura, hist. reg., Spain	H3	16
Exuma Cays, is., Bah.	A4	80
Exuma Sound, strt., Bah.	D9	76
Eyasi, Lake, l., Tan.	D7	54
Eyl, Som.	I14	48
Eylar Mountain, mtn., Ca., U.S.	D3	98
Eyota, Mn., U.S.	G6	116
Eyre, Austl.	G4	60
Eyre North, Lake, l., Austl.	F2	62
Eyre Peninsula, pen., Austl.	G6	60
Ezequiel Ramos Mexía, Embalse, res., Arg.	E3	69
Ezine, Tur.	C2	44

F

Name	Map Ref.	Page
Fabens, Tx., U.S.	o11	136
Fabius, stm., Mo., U.S.	A6	118
Fabriano, Italy	C4	18
Fachi, Niger	C7	50
Factoryville, Pa., U.S.	C10	131
Fada, Chad	G9	48
Fada-Ngourma, Burkina	D5	50
Faenza, Italy	B3	18
Faeroe Islands see Faroe Islands, is., Far. Is.	B12	4
Făgăraş, Rom.	G8	20
Fagernes, Nor.	F3	10
Fagersta, Swe.	G6	10
Fairacres, N.M., U.S.	E3	124
Fairbank, Ia., U.S.	B5	108
Fairbanks, Ak., U.S.	C10	95
Fair Bluff, N.C., U.S.	C3	126
Fairborn, Oh., U.S.	C1	128
Fairburn, Ga., U.S.	C2	103
Fairbury, Il., U.S.	C5	106
Fairbury, Ne., U.S.	D8	120
Fairchance, Pa., U.S.	G2	131
Fairchild Air Force Base, mil., Wa., U.S.	g13	140
Fairdale, Ky., U.S.	B4	110
Fairfax, Ca., U.S.	C2	98
Fairfax, De., U.S.	A3	101
Fairfax, Ia., U.S.	C6	108
Fairfax, Mn., U.S.	F4	116
Fairfax, Mo., U.S.	A2	118
Fairfax, Ok., U.S.	A5	129
Fairfax, S.C., U.S.	F5	133
Fairfax, Va., U.S.	B5	139
Fairfax, co., Va., U.S.	B5	139
Fairfield, Al., U.S.	B3	94
Fairfield, Ca., U.S.	C2	98
Fairfield, Ct., U.S.	E2	100
Fairfield, Il., U.S.	E5	106
Fairfield, Ia., U.S.	C6	108
Fairfield, Me., U.S.	D3	112
Fairfield, Oh., U.S.	n12	128
Fairfield, Tx., U.S.	D4	136
Fairfield, co., Ct., U.S.	D2	100
Fairfield, co., Oh., U.S.	C3	128
Fairfield, co., S.C., U.S.	C5	133
Fairfield Bay, Ar., U.S.	B3	97
Fairfield Pond, l., Vt., U.S.	B3	138
Fair Grove, Mo., U.S.	D4	118
Fair Grove, N.C., U.S.	B2	126
Fairhaven, Ma., U.S.	C6	114
Fair Haven, Mi., U.S.	F8	115
Fair Haven, N.J., U.S.	C4	123
Fair Haven, Vt., U.S.	D2	138
Fairhope, Al., U.S.	E2	94
Fair Isle, i., Scot., U.K.	i19	12a
Fairland, In., U.S.	E6	107
Fairland, Ok., U.S.	A7	129
Fair Lawn, N.J., U.S.	h8	123
Fairlawn, Va., U.S.	C2	139
Fairlea, W.V., U.S.	D4	141
Fairmont, Il., U.S.	C6	106
Fairmont, Mn., U.S.	G4	116
Fairmont, N.C., U.S.	C3	126
Fairmont, Ne., U.S.	D8	120
Fairmont, W.V., U.S.	B4	141

Name	Map Ref.	Page

Fairmount, Ga., U.S. **B2** 103
Fairmount, In., U.S. . . . **D6** 107
Fairmount Heights, Md.,
U.S. **f9** 113
Fair Oaks, Ga., U.S. **h7** 103
Fairoaks, Pa., U.S. . . . **h13** 131
Fair Plain, Mi., U.S. **F4** 115
Fairport, N.Y., U.S. **B3** 125
Fairport Harbor, Oh., U.S. . **A4** 128
Fairvale, N.B., Can. **D4** 87
Fairview, Ab., Can. **A1** 84
Fairview, Mt., U.S. **C12** 119
Fairview, N.J., U.S. **h8** 123
Fairview, Ok., U.S. **A3** 129
Fairview, Pa., U.S. **B1** 131
Fairview, Tn., U.S. **B4** 135
Fairview, Ut., U.S. **D4** 137
Fairview Heights, Il., U.S. . . **E3** 106
Fairview Park, In., U.S. . . . **E3** 107
Fairview Park, Oh., U.S. . . **g9** 128
Fairview Peak, mtn., Nv.,
U.S. **D3** 121
Fairview Peak, mtn., Or.,
U.S. **D4** 130
Fairway, Ks., U.S. **k16** 109
Fairweather Mountain, mtn.,
N.A. **G12** 82
Fais, i., Micron. **E11** 32
Faisalabad, Pak. **D10** 42
Faison, N.C., U.S. **B4** 126
Faizābād, India **D4** 40
Fakfak, Indon. **D8** 36
Fakse Bugt, b., Den. **I5** 10
Faku, China **C12** 28
Falaba, S.L. **E2** 50
Falam, Myan. **B2** 34
Falconer, N.Y., U.S. **C1** 125
Falcon Heights, Mn., U.S. . **n12** 116
Falcon Heights, Or., U.S. . . **E5** 130
Fălești, Mol. **F9** 20
Falfurrias, Tx., U.S. **F3** 136
Falher, Ab., Can. **B2** 84
Falkenberg, Swe. **H5** 10
Falkland Islands, dep., S.A. . **H4** 69
Falkland Islands, is., Falk. Is. **J9** 4
Falkland Sound, strt., Falk.
Is. **H4** 69
Falköping, Swe. **G5** 10
Falkville, Al., U.S. **A3** 94
Fall, stm., Ks., U.S. **E7** 109
Fall Branch, Tn., U.S. . . . **C11** 135
Fallbrook, Ca., U.S. **F5** 98
Fall City, Wa., U.S. **B4** 140
Fall Creek, Wi., U.S. **D2** 142
Falling Creek, stm., Va., U.S. **n17** 139
Falling Rock Creek, stm.,
W.V., U.S. **m13** 141
Fall Mountain Lake, Ct.,
U.S. **C4** 100
Fallon, Nv., U.S. **D3** 121
Fallon, co., Mt., U.S. **D12** 119
Fallon Indian Reservation,
Nv., U.S. **D3** 121
Fallon Naval Air Station,
mil., Nv., U.S. **D3** 121
Fall River, Ma., U.S. **C5** 114
Fall River, Wi., U.S. **E4** 142
Fall River, co., S.D., U.S. . . **D2** 134
Fall River Lake, res., Ks.,
U.S. **E7** 109
Falls, co., Tx., U.S. **D4** 136
Falls Church, Va., U.S. . . . **g12** 139
Falls City, Ne., U.S. **D10** 120
Falls City, Or., U.S. **C3** 130
Falls Creek, Pa., U.S. **D4** 131
Fallston, Md., U.S. **A5** 113
Falmouth, N.S., Can. **E5** 87
Falmouth, Eng., U.K. **E4** 12
Falmouth, Ky., U.S. **B5** 110
Falmouth, Ma., U.S. **C6** 114
Falmouth, Me., U.S. **E2** 112
Falmouth, Va., U.S. **B5** 139
False Bay see Valsbaai, b.,
S. Afr. **E2** 56
False Cape, c., Fl., U.S. . . . **D6** 102
False Cape, c., Va., U.S. . . **D7** 139
Falster, i., Den. **I5** 10
Fălticeni, Rom. **F9** 20
Falun, Swe. **F6** 10
Fanchang, China **C4** 30
Fancy Farm, Ky., U.S. **f9** 110
Fangak, Sudan **B6** 54
Fangcheng, China **E2** 30
Fangcheng, China **C3** 30
Fangxian, China **C3** 30
Fangzheng, China **A1** 31
Fannin, co., Ga., U.S. **B2** 103
Fannin, co., Tx., U.S. **C4** 136
Fanny, Mount, mtn., Or.,
U.S. **B9** 130
Fano, Italy **C4** 18
Fan Si Pan, mtn., Viet. . . . **B4** 34
Faradje, D.R.C. **C5** 54
Faradofay see Tôlañaro,
Madag. **D8** 56
Farafangana, Madag. **C8** 56
Farāh, Afg. **D8** 42
Farallon de Medinilla, i., N.
Mar. Is. **C12** 32
Farallon de Pajaros, i., N.
Mar. Is. **B12** 32
Faranah, Gui. **E2** 50
Farasān, Jazā'ir, is., Sau. Ar. **G4** 38
Farewell, Cape, c., N.Z. . . . **p13** 63c
Fargo, Ga., U.S. **F4** 103

Fargo, N.D., U.S. **C9** 127
Faribault, Mn., U.S. **F5** 116
Faribault, co., Mn., U.S. . . **G4** 116
Farīdābād, India **D3** 40
Farīdkot, India **D3** 40
Farley, Ia., U.S. **B6** 108
Farmer City, Il., U.S. **C5** 106
Farmers Branch, Tx., U.S. . **n10** 136
Farmersburg, In., U.S. . . . **F3** 107
Farmerville, La., U.S. **B3** 111
Farmingdale, Me., U.S. . . . **D3** 112
Farmington, Ar., U.S. **A1** 97
Farmington, Ct., U.S. **C4** 100
Farmington, Ia., U.S. **D6** 108
Farmington, Il., U.S. **C3** 106
Farmington, Me., U.S. **D2** 112
Farmington, Mi., U.S. **p15** 115
Farmington, Mn., U.S. **F5** 116
Farmington, Mo., U.S. **D7** 118
Farmington, N.H., U.S. . . . **D4** 122
Farmington, N.M., U.S. . . . **A1** 124
Farmington, Ut., U.S. **C4** 137
Farmington, stm., Ct., U.S. . **B4** 100
Farmington Hills, Mi., U.S. . **o15** 115
Farmland, In., U.S. **D7** 107
Farmville, N.C., U.S. **B5** 126
Farmville, Va., U.S. **C4** 139
Farnham, P.Q., Can. **D5** 90
Faro, Braz. **D8** 70
Faro, Port. **I3** 16
Faroe Islands, dep., Eur. . . **o23** 10b
Faroe Islands, is., Far. Is. . . **B12** 4
Fårön, i., Swe. **H8** 10
Fårösund, Swe. **H8** 10
Farquhar, Atoll de, is., Sey. . **j12** 57b
Farrell, Pa., U.S. **D1** 131
Farrukhābād, India **D3** 40
Fartak, Ra's, c., Yemen . . . **G6** 38
Farvel, Kap, c., Grnld. . . . **G31** 82
Farwell, Mi., U.S. **E6** 115
Farwell, Tx., U.S. **B1** 136
Fasā, Iran **E6** 42
Fastiv, Ukr. **D10** 20
Fatick, Sen. **D1** 50
Fatsa, Tur. **B7** 44
Faulk, co., S.D., U.S. **B6** 134
Faulkland Heights, De., U.S. **i7** 101
Faulkner, co., Ar., U.S. . . . **B3** 97
Faulkton, S.D., U.S. **B6** 134
Fauquier, co., Va., U.S. . . . **B5** 139
Fauske, Nor. **C6** 10
Fawnie Nose, mtn., B.C.,
Can. **C5** 85
Faxaflói, b., Ice. **l17** 10a
Faya-Largeau, Chad **C8** 50
Fayd, Sau. Ar. **E4** 42
Fayette, Al., U.S. **B2** 94
Fayette, Ia., U.S. **B6** 108
Fayette, Mo., U.S. **B5** 118
Fayette, Ms., U.S. **D2** 117
Fayette, Oh., U.S. **A1** 128
Fayette, co., Al., U.S. **B3** 94
Fayette, co., Ga., U.S. **C2** 103
Fayette, co., Ia., U.S. **B6** 108
Fayette, co., Il., U.S. **D5** 106
Fayette, co., In., U.S. **E7** 107
Fayette, co., Ky., U.S. **B5** 110
Fayette, co., Oh., U.S. **C2** 128
Fayette, co., Pa., U.S. **G2** 131
Fayette, co., Tn., U.S. **B2** 135
Fayette, co., Tx., U.S. **E4** 136
Fayette, co., W.V., U.S. . . . **C3** 141
Fayetteville, Ar., U.S. **A1** 97
Fayetteville, Ga., U.S. **C2** 103
Fayetteville, N.C., U.S. . . . **B4** 126
Fayetteville, Pa., U.S. **G6** 131
Fayetteville, Tn., U.S. **B5** 135
Fayetteville, W.V., U.S. . . . **C3** 141
Fāzilka, India **C2** 40
Fazzān, hist. reg., Libya . . **A7** 50
Fdérik, Maur. **B2** 50
Fear, Cape, c., N.C., U.S. . . **D5** 126
Feather, stm., Ca., U.S. . . . **C3** 98
Fécamp, Fr. **C7** 16
Federal, Arg. **E6** 72
Federalsburg, Md., U.S. . . . **C6** 113
Federated States of
Micronesia see
Micronesia, Federated
States of, ctry., Oc. . . . **D8** 58
Feeding Hills, Ma., U.S. . . . **B2** 114
Fehmarn, i., Ger. **C12** 12
Feijó, Braz. **E5** 70
Feira de Santana, Braz. . . . **D4** 74
Felipe Carrillo Puerto, Mex. **D7** 78
Fellsmere, Fl., U.S. **E6** 102
Felton, Ca., U.S. **D2** 98
Felton, De., U.S. **D3** 101
Femunden, l., Nor. **E4** 10
Fence, stm., Mi., U.S. **B2** 115
Fence Lake, l., Wi., U.S. . . **C4** 142
Fenelon Falls, On., Can. . . **C6** 89
Fengcheng, China **F11** 28
Fengcheng, China **C8** 28
Fengdu, China **F9** 28
Fengfeng, China **D3** 30
Fenghuang, China **D2** 30
Fengning, China **A4** 30
Fengqing, China **B3** 34
Fengqiu, China **B3** 30
Fengrun, China **B4** 30
Fengtai, China **C4** 30
Fengzhen, China **A3** 30
Fenimore Pass, strt., Ak.,
U.S. **E4** 95
Fennimore, Wi., U.S. **F3** 142
Fennville, Mi., U.S. **F4** 115

Fenoarivo Atsinanana,
Madag. **B8** 56
Fenton, Mi., U.S. **F7** 115
Fentress, co., Tn., U.S. . . . **C9** 135
Fenwick Island, i., S.C., U.S. **k11** 133
Fenyang, China **D10** 28
Fenyi, China **D3** 30
Feodosiia, Ukr. **G13** 20
Fer, Point au, c., La., U.S. . . **E4** 111
Ferdinand, In., U.S. **H4** 107
Ferdows, Iran **D7** 42
Fergana, Uzb. **E9** 26
Fergana Mountains see
Ferganskij hrebet, mts.,
Kyrg. **A2** 40
Ferganskij hrebet, mts.,
Kyrg. **A2** 40
Fergus, On., Can. **D4** 89
Fergus, co., Mt., U.S. **C7** 119
Fergus Falls, Mn., U.S. . . . **D2** 116
Ferguson, Ky., U.S. **C5** 110
Ferguson, Mo., U.S. **C7** 118
Ferkéssédougou, C. Iv. . . . **E3** 50
Ferlo, reg., Sen. **C2** 50
Ferme-Neuve, P.Q., Can. . . **C2** 90
Fermo, Italy **C4** 18
Fermont, P.Q., Can. **h13** 90
Fernandina Beach, Fl., U.S. **B5** 102
Fernandópolis, Braz. **F1** 74
Fernando Póo see Bioko, i.,
Eq. Gui. **C1** 54
Fernán-Núñez, Spain **I4** 16
Fern Creek, Ky., U.S. **g11** 110
Ferndale, Ca., U.S. **B1** 98
Ferndale, Md., U.S. **B4** 113
Ferndale, Mi., U.S. **p15** 115
Ferndale, Pa., U.S. **F4** 131
Ferndale, Wa., U.S. **A3** 140
Fernie, B.C., Can. **E10** 85
Fernley, Nv., U.S. **D2** 121
Fern Ridge Lake, res., Or.,
U.S. **C3** 130
Fernwood, Id., U.S. **B2** 105
Fernwood, Ms., U.S. **D3** 117
Feroe Islands see Faroe
Islands, dep., Far. Is. . . **C5** 8
Ferrara, Italy **B3** 18
Ferrelo, Cape, c., Or., U.S. . **E2** 130
Ferriday, La., U.S. **C4** 111
Ferris, Tx., U.S. **C4** 136
Ferris Mountains, mts., Wy.,
U.S. **D5** 143
Ferro see El Hierro, i., Spain **A1** 50
Ferrol, Spain **F2** 16
Ferron, Ut., U.S. **D4** 137
Ferrum, Va., U.S. **D2** 139
Ferry, co., Wa., U.S. **A7** 140
Ferry Farms, Va., U.S. . . . **B5** 139
Ferryland, Nf., Can. **E5** 88
Ferry Point, c., N.J., U.S. . . **k7** 123
Fertile, Mn., U.S. **C2** 116
Fès, Mor. **D4** 48
Feshi, D.R.C. **E3** 54
Fessenden, N.D., U.S. . . . **B6** 127
Festus, Mo., U.S. **C7** 118
Fetești, Rom. **G9** 20
Fethiye, Tur. **D3** 44
Fetisovo, Kaz. **B6** 42
Feuilles, Rivière aux, stm.,
P.Q., Can. **g12** 90
Feyzābād, Afg. **C10** 42
Fianarantsoa, Madag. **C8** 56
Fianga, Chad **E8** 50
Fichē, Eth. **B7** 54
Ficksburg, S. Afr. **D4** 56
Fidalgo Island, i., Wa., U.S. **A3** 140
Fieldale, Va., U.S. **D3** 139
Fields, Lake, l., Fl., U.S. . . **B3** 102
Fields, Lake, l., La., U.S. . . **k10** 111
Fier, Alb. **D7** 18
Fifteenmile Creek, stm.,
Wy., U.S. **B4** 143
Fifteen Mile Falls Reservoir,
res., U.S. **C5** 138
Fifth Cataract, wtfl, Sudan . **G11** 48
Figtree, Zimb. **C4** 56
Figueira da Foz, Port. **G2** 16
Figueres, Spain **F8** 16
Figuig, Mor. **D4** 48
Fiji, ctry., Oc. **m10** 63b
Filchner Ice Shelf, Ant. . . . **D1** 67
Filer, Id., U.S. **G4** 105
Filingué, Niger **D5** 50
Filippoi, hist., Grc. **D10** 18
Fillmore, Ca., U.S. **E4** 98
Fillmore, Ut., U.S. **E3** 137
Fillmore, co., Mn., U.S. . . . **G6** 116
Fillmore, co., Ne., U.S. . . . **D8** 120
Fimi, stm., D.R.C. **D3** 54
Findlay, Il., U.S. **D5** 106
Findlay, Oh., U.S. **A2** 128
Fingoè, Moz. **B5** 56
Finike, Tur. **D4** 44
Finke, Austl. **F5** 60
Finland, ctry., Eur. **E12** 10
Finland, Gulf of, b., Eur. . . **G10** 10
Finley, Austl. **H4** 62
Finley, Tn., U.S. **A2** 135
Finney, co., Ks., U.S. **D3** 109
Finn Mountain, mtn., Ak.,
U.S. **C8** 95
Fins, Oman **F7** 42
Finspång, Swe. **G6** 10
Fircrest, Wa., U.S. **f10** 140

Firebaugh, Ca., U.S. **D3** 98
Firenze (Florence), Italy . . . **C3** 18
Firestone, Co., U.S. **A6** 99
Fīrozābād, India **D3** 40
Fīrozpur, India **C2** 40
First Cataract, wtfl, Egypt . **F11** 48
First Connecticut Lake, l.,
N.H., U.S. **f7** 122
Fīrūzābād, Iran **E6** 42
Fish, stm., Al., U.S. **E2** 94
Fish, stm., Me., U.S. **A4** 112
Fish Creek, stm., W.V., U.S. **g8** 141
Fisher, Il., U.S. **C5** 106
Fisher, co., Tx., U.S. **C2** 136
Fisher Bay, b., Mb., Can. . . **D3** 86
Fishermans Island, i., Va.,
U.S. **h15** 139
Fishers, In., U.S. **E5** 107
Fishers Island, i., N.Y., U.S. **m16** 125
Fishers Peak, mtn., Co., U.S. **D6** 99
Fishersville, Va., U.S. **B4** 139
Fishing Bay, b., Md., U.S. . **D5** 113
Fishing Creek, Md., U.S. . . **D5** 113
Fishing Creek, stm., N.C.,
U.S. **A5** 126
Fishing Creek, stm., S.C.,
U.S. **B5** 133
Fishing Creek, stm., W.V.,
U.S. **B4** 141
Fishing Creek Reservoir,
res., S.C., U.S. **B6** 133
Fishkill, N.Y., U.S. **D7** 125
Fish Lake, l., Ut., U.S. **E4** 137
Fish River Lake, l., Me., U.S. **B4** 112
Fishtrap Lake, res., Ky., U.S. **C7** 110
Fiskdale, Ma., U.S. **B3** 114
Fisterra, Cabo de, c., Spain **F2** 16
Fitchburg, Ma., U.S. **A4** 114
Fitri, Lac, l., Chad **D8** 50
Fitzgerald, Ga., U.S. **E3** 103
Fitz Roy, Arg. **G3** 69
Fitzroy, stm., Austl. **D3** 60
Fitzroy Crossing, Austl. . . . **D4** 60
Fitzwilliam, N.H., U.S. **E2** 122
Fitzwilliam Island, i., On.,
Can. **B3** 89
Fiume see Rijeka, Cro. . . . **B5** 18
Five Island Lake, l., Ia., U.S. **A3** 108
Fivemile Creek, stm., Wy.,
U.S. **C4** 143
Five Points, N.M., U.S. . . . **B3** 124
Fizi, D.R.C. **D5** 54
Flagler, co., Fl., U.S. **C5** 102
Flagler Beach, Fl., U.S. . . . **C5** 102
Flagstaff, Az., U.S. **B4** 96
Flagstaff Lake, l., Or., U.S. . **E7** 130
Flambeau, stm., Wi., U.S. . **C3** 142
Flaming Gorge Dam, Ut.,
U.S. **C6** 137
Flaming Gorge National
Recreation Area, U.S. . . **E3** 143
Flaming Gorge Reservoir,
res., U.S. **C6** 92
Flaming Gorge Reservoir,
res., U.S. **E3** 143
Flanagan, Il., U.S. **C5** 106
Flandreau, S.D., U.S. **C9** 134
Flandreau Indian
Reservation, S.D., U.S. **C9** 134
Flat, stm., Mi., U.S. **E5** 115
Flat, stm., N.C., U.S. **A4** 126
Flat, stm., R.I., U.S. **E2** 132
Flat Brook, stm., N.J., U.S. . **A3** 123
Flathead, co., Mt., U.S. . . . **B2** 119
Flathead, South Fork, stm.,
Mt., U.S. **C3** 119
Flathead Indian Reservation,
Mt., U.S. **C2** 119
Flathead Lake, l., Mt., U.S. . **C2** 119
Flathead Valley, val., Mt.,
U.S. **C2** 119
Flat Lake, l., La., U.S. **k9** 111
Flat Lick, Ky., U.S. **D6** 110
Flat River, Mo., U.S. **D7** 118
Flat River Reservoir, res.,
R.I., U.S. **D3** 132
Flat Rock, Mi., U.S. **F7** 115
Flat Rock, In., U.S. **F6** 107
Flat Rock, N.C., U.S. **f10** 126
Flattery, Cape, c., Austl. . . **C4** 62
Flattery, Cape, c., Wa., U.S. **A1** 140
Flatwoods, Ky., U.S. **B7** 110
Fleetwood, Pa., U.S. **F10** 131
Fleming, co., Ky., U.S. **B6** 110
Fleming-Neon, Ky., U.S. . . **C7** 110
Flemingsburg, Ky., U.S. . . **B6** 110
Flemington, N.J., U.S. **B3** 123
Flemington, Pa., U.S. **D7** 131
Flen, Swe. **G7** 10
Flensburg, Ger. **C11** 12
Fletcher, N.C., U.S. **f10** 126
Fletcher, Ok., U.S. **C3** 129
Flin Flon, Mb., Can. **B1** 86
Flinders, stm., Austl. **D3** 62
Flinders Bay, b., Austl. . . . **G2** 60
Flinders Island, i., Austl. . . **H4** 62
Flinders Reefs, rf., Austl. . . **D4** 62
Flint, Mi., U.S. **E7** 115
Flint, i., Kir. **F14** 58
Flint, stm., Ga., U.S. **E2** 103
Flint City, Al., U.S. **A3** 94
Flint Creek Range, mts.,
Mt., U.S. **D3** 119
Flint Run, stm., W.V., U.S. . **k9** 141

Flippin, Ar., U.S. **A3** 97
Flisa, Nor. **F5** 10
Flomaton, Al., U.S. **D2** 94
Flora, Il., U.S. **E5** 106
Flora, In., U.S. **C4** 107
Flora, Ms., U.S. **C3** 117
Florala, Al., U.S. **D3** 94
Floral City, Fl., U.S. **D4** 102
Florence see Firenze, Italy . **C3** 18
Florence, Al., U.S. **A2** 94
Florence, Az., U.S. **D4** 96
Florence, Co., U.S. **C5** 99
Florence, Ks., U.S. **D7** 109
Florence, Ky., U.S. **A5** 110
Florence, Ms., U.S. **C3** 117
Florence, N.J., U.S. **C3** 123
Florence, Or., U.S. **D2** 130
Florence, S.C., U.S. **C8** 133
Florence, co., S.C., U.S. . . **C8** 133
Florence, co., Wi., U.S. . . . **C5** 142
Florenceville, N.B., Can. . . **C2** 87
Florencia, Col. **C4** 70
Flores, i., Indon. **E6** 36
Flores, Laut (Flores Sea),
Indon. **E6** 36
Flores Sea see Flores, Laut,
Indon. **E6** 36
Florești, Mol. **F10** 20
Floresville, Tx., U.S. **E3** 136
Florham Park, N.J., U.S. . . **B4** 123
Floriano, Braz. **E3** 74
Florianópolis, Braz. **D8** 72
Florida, Cuba **A4** 80
Florida, N.Y., U.S. **D6** 125
Florida, Ur. **E6** 72
Florida, state, U.S. **E5** 102
Florida, Cape, c., Fl., U.S. . **G6** 102
Florida, Straits of, strt., N.A. **G11** 92
Florida Bay, b., Fl., U.S. . . **H6** 102
Florida Keys, is., Fl., U.S. . **H6** 102
Florida Mountains, mts.,
N.M., U.S. **E2** 124
Florida State Indian
Reservation, Fl., U.S. . . **F5** 102
Florien, La., U.S. **C2** 111
Flórina, Grc. **D8** 18
Florissant, Mo., U.S. **f13** 118
Florissant Fossil Beds
National Monument,
Co., U.S. **C5** 99
Florø, Nor. **F1** 10
Flossmoor, Il., U.S. **k9** 106
Flovilla, Ga., U.S. **C3** 103
Flower Brook, stm., Vt., U.S. **E2** 138
Flowery Branch, Ga., U.S. . **B3** 103
Flowood, Ms., U.S. **C3** 117
Floyd, co., Ga., U.S. **B1** 103
Floyd, co., Ia., U.S. **A5** 108
Floyd, co., In., U.S. **H6** 107
Floyd, co., Ky., U.S. **C7** 110
Floyd, co., Tx., U.S. **B2** 136
Floyd, co., Va., U.S. **D2** 139
Floyd, stm., Ia., U.S. **B1** 108
Floydada, Tx., U.S. **C2** 136
Floyds Fork, stm., Ky., U.S. **B4** 110
Floyds Knobs, In., U.S. . . . **H6** 107
Flushing see Vlissingen,
Neth. **E8** 12
Flushing, Mi., U.S. **E7** 115
Flushing, Oh., U.S. **B4** 128
Fluvanna, co., Va., U.S. . . **C4** 139
Foard, co., Tx., U.S. **B3** 136
Foča, Bos. **C7** 18
Focșani, Rom. **D5** 20
Foggia, Italy **D5** 18
Fogland Point, c., R.I., U.S. **E6** 132
Fogo, Nf., Can. **D4** 88
Fogo, i., C.V. **g10** 50a
Fogo, co., Can., Nf., Can. . **D5** 88
Fogo Island, i., Nf., Can. . . **D4** 88
Foix, Fr. **F7** 16
Fokku, Nig. **D5** 50
Folda, b., Nor. **C6** 10
Foley, Al., U.S. **E2** 94
Foley, Mn., U.S. **E5** 116
Foligno, Italy **C4** 18
Folkestone, Eng., U.K. . . . **E7** 12
Folkston, Ga., U.S. **F4** 103
Follansbee, W.V., U.S. . . . **A4** 141
Folly Beach, S.C., U.S. . . . **F8** 133
Folly Island, i., S.C., U.S. . **F8** 133
Folsom, Ca., U.S. **C3** 98
Fomboni, Com. **A7** 56
Fonda, Ia., U.S. **B3** 108
Fond du Lac, Wi., U.S. . . . **E5** 142
Fond du Lac, co., Wi., U.S. **E5** 142
Fond du Lac Indian
Reservation, Mn., U.S. **D6** 116
Fonseca, Golfo de, b., N.A. **C2** 80
Fontainebleau, Fr. **C8** 16
Fontana, Ca., U.S. **m14** 98
Fontana, Wi., U.S. **F5** 142
Fontana Lake, res., N.C.,
U.S. **f9** 126
Fontanelle, Ia., U.S. **C3** 108
Fonte Boa, Braz. **D6** 70
Fontenay-le-Comte, Fr. . . . **D6** 16
Fontenelle Reservoir, res.,
Wy., U.S. **D2** 143
Fontur, c., Ice. **k21** 10a
Foochow see Fuzhou,
China **F11** 28
Footville, Wi., U.S. **F4** 142

Name	Map Ref.	Page

Foraker, Mount, mtn., Ak., U.S. — f16 — 95
Forbes, Austl. — G4 — 62
Forbes, Mount, mtn., Ab., Can. — D2 — 84
Forcados, Nig. — E6 — 50
Forchheim, Ger. — F12 — 12
Ford, co., Il., U.S. — C5 — 106
Ford, co., Ks., U.S. — E4 — 109
Ford, stm., Mi., U.S. — C3 — 115
Ford City, Ca., U.S. — E4 — 98
Ford City, Pa., U.S. — E2 — 131
Fordoche, La., U.S. — D4 — 111
Fords Prairie, Wa., U.S. — C2 — 140
Fordyce, Ar., U.S. — D3 — 97
Forécariah, Gui. — E2 — 50
Foreman, Ar., U.S. — D1 — 97
Forest, On., Can. — D2 — 89
Forest, Ms., U.S. — C4 — 117
Forest, Oh., U.S. — B2 — 128
Forest, co., Pa., U.S. — C3 — 131
Forest, co., Wi., U.S. — C5 — 142
Forest, stm., N.D., U.S. — A8 — 127
Forest Acres, S.C., U.S. — C6 — 133
Forestburg, Ab., Can. — C4 — 84
Forest City, Ia., U.S. — A4 — 108
Forest City, N.C., U.S. — B1 — 126
Forest City, Pa., U.S. — C11 — 131
Forestdale, R.I., U.S. — B3 — 132
Forest Dale, Vt., U.S. — D2 — 138
Forest Glen, La., U.S. — h12 — 111
Forest Grove, Or., U.S. — B3 — 130
Forest Hill, Md., U.S. — A5 — 113
Forest Hills, Pa., U.S. — k14 — 131
Forest Knolls, Ca., U.S. — g7 — 98
Forest Lake, Mn., U.S. — E6 — 116
Forest Park, Ga., U.S. — h8 — 103
Forest Park, Il., U.S. — k9 — 106
Forillon, Parc National de, P.Q., Can. — k14 — 90
Fork Creek, stm., W.V., U.S. — m12 — 141
Forked Deer, stm., Tn., U.S. — B2 — 135
Forkland, Al., U.S. — C2 — 94
Forks, Wa., U.S. — B1 — 140
Forlì, Italy — B4 — 18
Formentera, i., Spain — H7 — 16
Formia, Italy — D4 — 18
Formiga, Braz. — F2 — 74
Formosa, Arg. — D6 — 72
Formosa, Braz. — E2 — 74
Formosa see Taiwan, ctry., Asia — B8 — 34
Formosa, Serra, plat., Braz. — F9 — 70
Formosa Strait see Taiwan Strait, strt., Asia — E4 — 30
Forney, Tx., U.S. — C4 — 136
Forrest, Austl. — G4 — 60
Forrest, Il., U.S. — C5 — 106
Forrest, co., Ms., U.S. — D4 — 117
Forrest City, Ar., U.S. — B5 — 97
Forrester Island, i., Ak., U.S. — n23 — 95
Forreston, Il., U.S. — A4 — 106
Forsayth, Austl. — D3 — 62
Forst, Ger. — E14 — 12
Forsyth, Ga., U.S. — C3 — 103
Forsyth, Il., U.S. — D5 — 106
Forsyth, Mo., U.S. — E4 — 118
Forsyth, Mt., U.S. — D10 — 119
Forsyth, co., Ga., U.S. — B2 — 103
Forsyth, co., N.C., U.S. — A2 — 126
Fortaleza, Braz. — B4 — 74
Fort Apache Indian Reservation, Az., U.S. — D5 — 96
Fort-Archambault see Sarh, Chad — B3 — 54
Fort Ashby, W.V., U.S. — B6 — 141
Fort Atkinson, Wi., U.S. — F5 — 142
Fort Beaufort, S. Afr. — E4 — 56
Fort Belknap Indian Reservation, Mt., U.S. — B8 — 119
Fort Belvoir, mil., Va., U.S. — g12 — 139
Fort Bend, co., Tx., U.S. — E5 — 136
Fort Benjamin Harrison, mil., In., U.S. — k10 — 107
Fort Benning, mil., Ga., U.S. — D2 — 103
Fort Benton, Mt., U.S. — C6 — 119
Fort Berthold Indian Reservation, N.D., U.S. — B3 — 127
Fort Bidwell Indian Reservation, Ca., U.S. — B3 — 98
Fort Bliss, mil., Tx., U.S. — o11 — 136
Fort Bragg, Ca., U.S. — C2 — 98
Fort Bragg, mil., N.C., U.S. — B3 — 126
Fort Branch, In., U.S. — H2 — 107
Fort Calhoun, Ne., U.S. — C9 — 120
Fort Campbell, mil., U.S. — A4 — 135
Fort Carson, mil., Co., U.S. — C6 — 99
Fort Chipewyan, Ab., Can. — f8 — 84
Fort Clatsop National Memorial, hist., Or., U.S. — A3 — 130
Fort Cobb, Ok., U.S. — B3 — 129
Fort Cobb Reservoir, res., Ok., U.S. — B3 — 129
Fort Collins, Co., U.S. — A5 — 99
Fort Coulonge, P.Q., Can. — B8 — 89
Fort-Dauphin see Tôlañaro, Madag. — D8 — 56
Fort Davis National Historic Site, hist., Tx., U.S. — o13 — 136
Fort Defiance, Az., U.S. — B6 — 96
Fort-de-France, Mart. — C7 — 80
Fort Deposit, Al., U.S. — D3 — 94

Fort Detrick, mil., Md., U.S. — B3 — 113
Fort Dix, mil., N.J., U.S. — C3 — 123
Fort Dodge, Ia., U.S. — B3 — 108
Fort Donelson National Battlefield, Tn., U.S. — A4 — 135
Fort Edward, N.Y., U.S. — B7 — 125
Fort Erie, On., Can. — E6 — 89
Fort Eustis, mil., Va., U.S. — h14 — 139
Fort Fairfield, Me., U.S. — B5 — 112
Fort Frances, On., Can. — o16 — 89
Fort Gaines, Ga., U.S. — E1 — 103
Fort Gay, W.V., U.S. — C2 — 141
Fort Gibson, Ok., U.S. — B6 — 129
Fort Gibson Lake, res., Ok., U.S. — A6 — 129
Fort Gordon, mil., Ga., U.S. — C4 — 103
Fort Greely, mil., Ak., U.S. — C10 — 95
Forth, Firth of, b., Scot., U.K. — B5 — 12
Fort Hall, Id., U.S. — F6 — 105
Fort Hall Indian Reservation, Id., U.S. — F6 — 105
Fort Hood, mil., Tx., U.S. — D4 — 136
Fort Howard, Md., U.S. — B5 — 113
Fort Huachuca, mil., Az., U.S. — F5 — 96
Fort Jackson, mil., S.C., U.S. — C6 — 133
Fort Jefferson National Monument, Fl., U.S. — H4 — 102
Fort Kent, Me., U.S. — A4 — 112
Fort Knox, mil., Ky., U.S. — B4 — 110
Fort-Lamy see N'Djamena, Chad — D8 — 50
Fort Laramie, Wy., U.S. — D8 — 143
Fort Laramie National Historic Site, hist., Wy., U.S. — D8 — 143
Fort Lauderdale, Fl., U.S. — F6 — 102
Fort Lawn, S.C., U.S. — B6 — 133
Fort Leavenworth, mil., Ks., U.S. — C9 — 109
Fort Lee, N.J., U.S. — B5 — 123
Fort Lee, mil., Va., U.S. — C5 — 139
Fort Leonard Wood, mil., Mo., U.S. — D5 — 118
Fort Lewis, mil., Wa., U.S. — B3 — 140
Fort Loramie, Oh., U.S. — B1 — 128
Fort Loudon, Pa., U.S. — G6 — 131
Fort Loudoun Lake, res., Tn., U.S. — D9 — 135
Fort Lupton, Co., U.S. — A6 — 99
Fort MacArthur, mil., Ca., U.S. — n12 — 98
Fort Macleod, Ab., Can. — E4 — 84
Fort Madison, Ia., U.S. — D6 — 108
Fort Matanzas National Monument, Fl., U.S. — C5 — 102
Fort McClellan, mil., Al., U.S. — B4 — 94
Fort McDermitt Indian Reservation, U.S. — B4 — 121
Fort McDowell Indian Reservation, Az., U.S. — D4 — 96
Fort McHenry National Monument And Historic Shrine, Md., U.S. — g11 — 113
Fort McMurray, Ab., Can. — A5 — 84
Fort Meade, Fl., U.S. — E5 — 102
Fort Meade, mil., Md., U.S. — B4 — 113
Fort Meadow Reservoir, res., Ma., U.S. — g9 — 114
Fort Mill, S.C., U.S. — A6 — 133
Fort Mitchell, Al., U.S. — C4 — 94
Fort Mitchell, Ky., U.S. — h13 — 110
Fort Mojave Indian Reservation, U.S. — C1 — 96
Fort Monmouth, mil., N.J., U.S. — C4 — 123
Fort Monroe, mil., Va., U.S. — h15 — 139
Fort Morgan, Co., U.S. — A7 — 99
Fort Myer, mil., Va., U.S. — g12 — 139
Fort Myers, Fl., U.S. — F5 — 102
Fort Myers Beach, Fl., U.S. — F5 — 102
Fort Nelson, B.C., Can. — m18 — 85
Fort Oglethorpe, Ga., U.S. — B1 — 103
Fort Payne, Al., U.S. — A4 — 94
Fort Peck Indian Reservation, Mt., U.S. — B11 — 119
Fort Peck Lake, res., Mt., U.S. — C9 — 119
Fort Pierce, Fl., U.S. — E6 — 102
Fort Pierce Inlet, b., Fl., U.S. — E6 — 102
Fort Pierre, S.D., U.S. — C5 — 134
Fort Plain, N.Y., U.S. — C6 — 125
Fort Polk, mil., La., U.S. — C2 — 111
Fort Portal, Ug. — A6 — 54
Fort Randall Dam, S.D., U.S. — D7 — 134
Fort Recovery, Oh., U.S. — B1 — 128
Fortress Mountain, mtn., Wy., U.S. — B3 — 143
Fort Richardson, mil., Ak., U.S. — C10 — 95
Fort Riley, mil., Ks., U.S. — C7 — 109
Fort Ritchie, mil., Md., U.S. — A3 — 113
Fort Rucker, mil., Al., U.S. — D4 — 94
Fort Saint James, B.C., Can. — B5 — 85
Fort Saint John, B.C., Can. — A7 — 85
Fort Sam Houston, mil., Tx., U.S. — k7 — 136
Fort Saskatchewan, Ab., Can. — C4 — 84
Fort Scott, Ks., U.S. — E9 — 109
Fort-Ševčenko, Kaz. — E7 — 26
Fort Shafter, mil., Hi., U.S. — g10 — 104

Fort Shawnee, Oh., U.S. — B1 — 128
Fort Sill, mil., Ok., U.S. — C3 — 129
Fort Smith, Ar., U.S. — B1 — 97
Fort Stewart, mil., Ga., U.S. — D5 — 103
Fort Stockton, Tx., U.S. — D1 — 136
Fort Sumner, N.M., U.S. — C5 — 124
Fort Sumter National Monument, S.C., U.S. — k12 — 133
Fort Supply Lake, res., Ok., U.S. — A2 — 129
Fort Thomas, Ky., U.S. — h14 — 110
Fort Totten, N.D., U.S. — B7 — 127
Fort Totten Indian Reservation, N.D., U.S. — B7 — 127
Fortuna, Ca., U.S. — B1 — 98
Fortune, Nf., Can. — E4 — 88
Fortune Bay, b., Nf., Can. — E4 — 88
Fort Union National Monument, N.M., U.S. — B5 — 124
Fort Valley, Ga., U.S. — D3 — 103
Fort Vermilion, Ab., Can. — f7 — 84
Fortville, In., U.S. — E6 — 107
Fort Wainwright, mil., Ak., U.S. — C10 — 95
Fort Walton Beach, Fl., U.S. — u15 — 102
Fort Washington Forest, Md., U.S. — C4 — 113
Fort Wayne, In., U.S. — B7 — 107
Fort William, Scot., U.K. — B4 — 12
Fort Wingate, N.M., U.S. — B1 — 124
Fort Worth, Tx., U.S. — C4 — 136
Fort Wright, Ky., U.S. — h13 — 110
Fort Yukon, Ak., U.S. — B10 — 95
Fort Yuma Indian Reservation, Ca., U.S. — F6 — 98
Foshan, China — G10 — 28
Foso, Ghana — E4 — 50
Fossano, Italy — B1 — 18
Fossil Butte National Monument, Wy., U.S. — E2 — 143
Fossil Lake, l., Or., U.S. — D6 — 130
Foss Reservoir, res., Ok., U.S. — B2 — 129
Fosston, Mn., U.S. — C3 — 116
Foster, Or., U.S. — C4 — 130
Foster, co., N.D., U.S. — B6 — 127
Foster Village, Hi., U.S. — g10 — 104
Fostoria, Oh., U.S. — A2 — 128
Fougamou, Gabon — D2 — 54
Fougères, Fr. — C6 — 16
Fouke, Ar., U.S. — D2 — 97
Foulamôri, Gui. — D2 — 50
Foumban, Cam. — B2 — 54
Foundiougne, Sen. — D1 — 50
Fountain, Co., U.S. — C6 — 99
Fountain, co., In., U.S. — D3 — 107
Fountain City, In., U.S. — E8 — 107
Fountain City, Wi., U.S. — D2 — 142
Fountain Hill, Pa., U.S. — E11 — 131
Fountain Inn, S.C., U.S. — B3 — 133
Fountain Peak, mtn., Ca., U.S. — E6 — 98
Fourche LaFave, stm., Ar., U.S. — C2 — 97
Fourche Maline, stm., Ok., U.S. — C6 — 129
Four Mountains, Islands of, is., Ak., U.S. — E6 — 95
Four Oaks, N.C., U.S. — B4 — 126
Fourth Cataract, wtfl, Sudan — G11 — 48
Fouta Djalon, reg., Gui. — D2 — 50
Foveaux Strait, strt., N.Z. — q12 — 63c
Fowler, co., Ca., U.S. — D4 — 98
Fowler, Co., U.S. — C6 — 99
Fowler, In., U.S. — C3 — 107
Fowler, Mi., U.S. — E6 — 115
Fowlerville, Mi., U.S. — F6 — 115
Fowman, Iran — D13 — 44
Fox, stm., Mb., Can. — B4 — 86
Fox, stm., Mi., U.S. — B4 — 115
Fox, stm., Wi., U.S. — D5 — 142
Fox, stm., U.S. — B5 — 106
Fox, stm., U.S. — A6 — 118
Foxboro, On., Can. — C7 — 89
Foxboro, Ma., U.S. — B5 — 114
Fox Creek, Ab., Can. — B2 — 84
Foxe Basin, b., N.T., Can. — E24 — 82
Fox Island, i., R.I., U.S. — E4 — 132
Fox Island, i., Wa., U.S. — f10 — 140
Fox Islands, is., Ak., U.S. — E6 — 95
Fox Lake, Il., U.S. — A5 — 106
Fox Lake, Wi., U.S. — E5 — 142
Fox Lake, l., Il., U.S. — h8 — 106
Fox Mountain, mtn., Nv., U.S. — B2 — 121
Fox Point, Wi., U.S. — E6 — 142
Fox River Grove, Il., U.S. — h8 — 106
Foxworth, Ms., U.S. — D4 — 117
Foz do Cunene, Ang. — B1 — 56
Foz do Iguaçu, Braz. — D7 — 72
Frackville, Pa., U.S. — E9 — 131
Fraga, Spain — G7 — 16
Fram Basin — E22 — 144
Framingham, Ma., U.S. — B5 — 114
Franca, Braz. — F2 — 74
Franca-Iosifa, Zemlja, is., Russia — B7 — 26
Francis, Lake, l., N.H., U.S. — f7 — 122
Francis Case, Lake, l., S.D., U.S. — D6 — 134
Francistown, Bots. — C4 — 56

Franconia, N.H., U.S. — B3 — 122
Franconia Notch, N.H., U.S. — B3 — 122
Francs Peak, mtn., Wy., U.S. — C3 — 143
Franken, hist. reg., Ger. — E11 — 12
Frankenmuth, Mi., U.S. — E7 — 115
Frankford, On., Can. — C7 — 89
Frankford, De., U.S. — F5 — 101
Frankfort, Il., U.S. — m9 — 106
Frankfort, In., U.S. — D4 — 107
Frankfort, Ks., U.S. — C7 — 109
Frankfort, Ky., U.S. — B5 — 110
Frankfort, Mi., U.S. — D4 — 115
Frankfort, N.Y., U.S. — B5 — 125
Frankfort, Oh., U.S. — C2 — 128
Frankfurt, Ger. — D14 — 12
Frankfurt am Main, Ger. — E11 — 12
Franklin, Ga., U.S. — C1 — 103
Franklin, In., U.S. — F5 — 107
Franklin, Ky., U.S. — D3 — 110
Franklin, La., U.S. — E4 — 111
Franklin, Ma., U.S. — B5 — 114
Franklin, N.C., U.S. — f9 — 126
Franklin, N.H., U.S. — D3 — 122
Franklin, N.J., U.S. — A3 — 123
Franklin, Oh., U.S. — C1 — 128
Franklin, Pa., U.S. — D2 — 131
Franklin, Tn., U.S. — B5 — 135
Franklin, Tx., U.S. — D4 — 136
Franklin, Va., U.S. — D6 — 139
Franklin, W.V., U.S. — C5 — 141
Franklin, Wi., U.S. — n11 — 142
Franklin, co., Al., U.S. — A2 — 94
Franklin, co., Ar., U.S. — B2 — 97
Franklin, co., Fl., U.S. — C2 — 102
Franklin, co., Ga., U.S. — B3 — 103
Franklin, co., Ia., U.S. — B4 — 108
Franklin, co., Id., U.S. — G7 — 105
Franklin, co., Il., U.S. — E4 — 106
Franklin, co., In., U.S. — F7 — 107
Franklin, co., Ks., U.S. — D8 — 109
Franklin, co., Ky., U.S. — B5 — 110
Franklin, co., La., U.S. — B4 — 111
Franklin, co., Ma., U.S. — A2 — 114
Franklin, co., Me., U.S. — C2 — 112
Franklin, co., Mo., U.S. — C6 — 118
Franklin, co., Ms., U.S. — D3 — 117
Franklin, co., N.C., U.S. — A4 — 126
Franklin, co., Ne., U.S. — D7 — 120
Franklin, co., N.Y., U.S. — f10 — 125
Franklin, co., Oh., U.S. — B2 — 128
Franklin, co., Pa., U.S. — G6 — 131
Franklin, co., Tn., U.S. — B5 — 135
Franklin, co., Tx., U.S. — C5 — 136
Franklin, co., Va., U.S. — D3 — 139
Franklin, co., Vt., U.S. — B2 — 138
Franklin, co., Wa., U.S. — C6 — 140
Franklin, Point, c., Ak., U.S. — A8 — 95
Franklin D. Roosevelt Lake, res., Wa., U.S. — B7 — 140
Franklin Falls Reservoir, res., N.H., U.S. — C3 — 122
Franklin Grove, Il., U.S. — B4 — 106
Franklin Lake, l., Nv., U.S. — C6 — 121
Franklin Park, Il., U.S. — k9 — 106
Franklinton, La., U.S. — D5 — 111
Franklinton, N.C., U.S. — A4 — 126
Franklinville, N.Y., U.S. — C2 — 125
Frankston, Tx., U.S. — C5 — 136
Frankton, In., U.S. — D6 — 107
Fransfontein, Nmb. — C2 — 56
Franz Josef Land see Franca-Iosifa, Zemlja, is., Russia — B7 — 26
Fraser, stm., B.C., Can. — E7 — 85
Fraser, stm., Nf., Can. — g9 — 88
Fraser, Mount, mtn., Can. — C8 — 85
Fraserburg, S. Afr. — E3 — 56
Fraserburgh, Scot., U.K. — B5 — 12
Fraser Island, i., Austl. — F5 — 62
Fraser Lake, B.C., Can. — B5 — 85
Fraser Plateau, plat., B.C., Can. — D6 — 85
Frazee, Mn., U.S. — D3 — 116
Frazeysburg, Oh., U.S. — B3 — 128
Frazier Park, Ca., U.S. — E4 — 98
Frederic, Wi., U.S. — C1 — 142
Frederica, De., U.S. — D4 — 101
Fredericia, Den. — I3 — 10
Frederick, Co., U.S. — A6 — 99
Frederick, Md., U.S. — B3 — 113
Frederick, Ok., U.S. — C2 — 129
Frederick, co., Md., U.S. — B3 — 113
Frederick, co., Va., U.S. — A4 — 139
Fredericksburg, Ia., U.S. — B5 — 108
Fredericksburg, Tx., U.S. — D3 — 136
Fredericksburg, Va., U.S. — B5 — 139
Frederick Sound, strt., Ak., U.S. — m23 — 95
Fredericktown, Mo., U.S. — D7 — 118
Fredericktown, Oh., U.S. — B3 — 128
Fredericktown, Pa., U.S. — F1 — 131
Fredericton, N.B., Can. — D3 — 87
Fredericton Junction, N.B., Can. — D3 — 87
Frederikshåb, Grnld. — F29 — 82
Frederikshavn, Den. — H4 — 10
Fredonia, Az., U.S. — A3 — 96
Fredonia, Ks., U.S. — E8 — 109
Fredonia, N.Y., U.S. — C1 — 125
Fredonia, Wi., U.S. — E6 — 142
Fredrikstad, Nor. — G4 — 10
Freeborn, co., Mn., U.S. — G5 — 116
Freeburg, Il., U.S. — E4 — 106

Freedom, Pa., U.S. — E1 — 131
Freedom, Wy., U.S. — D2 — 143
Freehold, N.J., U.S. — C4 — 123
Freeland, Mi., U.S. — E6 — 115
Freeland, Pa., U.S. — D10 — 131
Freelandville, In., U.S. — G3 — 107
Freel Peak, mtn., Ca., U.S. — C4 — 98
Freels, Cape, c., Nf., Can. — E5 — 88
Freels, Cape, c., Nf., Can. — D5 — 88
Freeman, S.D., U.S. — D8 — 134
Freeman, Lake, l., In., U.S. — C4 — 107
Freemansburg, Pa., U.S. — E11 — 131
Freemason Island, i., La., U.S. — E7 — 111
Freeport, Bah. — C9 — 76
Freeport, Il., U.S. — A4 — 106
Freeport, Me., U.S. — E2 — 112
Freeport, N.Y., U.S. — n15 — 125
Freeport, Pa., U.S. — E2 — 131
Freeport, Tx., U.S. — E5 — 136
Freer, Tx., U.S. — F3 — 136
Freestone, co., Tx., U.S. — D4 — 136
Freetown, S.L. — E2 — 50
Freetown, In., U.S. — G5 — 107
Freezeout Mountains, mts., Wy., U.S. — D6 — 143
Fregenal de la Sierra, Spain — H3 — 16
Freiburg, Ger. — G10 — 12
Freising, Ger. — F12 — 12
Freistadt, Aus. — F14 — 12
Fréjus, Fr. — F10 — 16
Fremantle, Austl. — G2 — 60
Fremont, Ca., U.S. — D2 — 98
Fremont, Ia., U.S. — C5 — 108
Fremont, In., U.S. — A8 — 107
Fremont, Mi., U.S. — E5 — 115
Fremont, N.C., U.S. — B5 — 126
Fremont, Ne., U.S. — C9 — 120
Fremont, Oh., U.S. — A2 — 128
Fremont, co., Co., U.S. — C5 — 99
Fremont, co., Ia., U.S. — D2 — 108
Fremont, co., Id., U.S. — E7 — 105
Fremont, co., Wy., U.S. — C4 — 143
Fremont, stm., Ut., U.S. — E4 — 137
Fremont Island, i., Ut., U.S. — B3 — 137
Fremont Lake, l., Wy., U.S. — D3 — 143
Fremont Peak, mtn., Wy., U.S. — C3 — 143
French Broad, stm., U.S. — D10 — 135
Frenchburg, Ky., U.S. — C6 — 110
French Creek, stm., Pa., U.S. — C2 — 131
French Frigate Shoals, rf., Hi., U.S. — m14 — 104
French Guiana, dep., S.A. — C9 — 70
French Lick, In., U.S. — G4 — 107
Frenchman Bay, b., Me., U.S. — D4 — 112
Frenchman Creek, stm., U.S. — D4 — 120
Frenchman Hills, hills, Wa., U.S. — C6 — 140
Frenchman Lake, l., Nv., U.S. — G6 — 121
French Polynesia, dep., Oc. — F15 — 58
French Settlement, La., U.S. — D5 — 111
French Somaliland see Djibouti, ctry., Afr. — H13 — 48
Frenda, Alg. — J7 — 16
Freshfield, Mount, mtn., Can. — D2 — 84
Fresnillo, Mex. — C4 — 78
Fresno, Ca., U.S. — D4 — 98
Fresno, co., Ca., U.S. — D4 — 98
Fresno Reservoir, res., Mt., U.S. — B6 — 119
Frewsburg, N.Y., U.S. — C1 — 125
Freycinet Peninsula, pen., Austl. — I4 — 62
Fria, Gui. — D2 — 50
Fria, Cape, c., Nmb. — B1 — 56
Friars Point, Ms., U.S. — A3 — 117
Frías, Arg. — D4 — 72
Fribourg, Switz. — A1 — 18
Friday Harbor, Wa., U.S. — A2 — 140
Fridley, Mn., U.S. — m12 — 116
Fridtjof Nansen, Mount, mtn., Ant. — E25 — 67
Friedrichshafen, Ger. — G11 — 12
Friend, Ne., U.S. — D8 — 120
Friendsville, Tn., U.S. — D9 — 135
Fries, Va., U.S. — D2 — 139
Frio, co., Tx., U.S. — E3 — 136
Frio, stm., Tx., U.S. — E3 — 136
Frio, Cabo, c., Braz. — F4 — 74
Friona, Tx., U.S. — B1 — 136
Fripps Island, i., S.C., U.S. — G7 — 133
Frisco, Co., U.S. — B4 — 99
Frisco City, Al., U.S. — D2 — 94
Frisco Peak, mtn., Ut., U.S. — E2 — 137
Frisian Islands, is., Eur. — D9 — 12
Frissell, Mount, mtn., U.S. — A2 — 100
Fritch, Tx., U.S. — B2 — 136
Friza, proliv, strt., Russia — B17 — 28
Frobisher Bay, b., N.T., Can. — F26 — 82
Frobisher Lake, l., Sk., Can. — m7 — 91
Frolovo, Russia — E7 — 22
Frome, Lake, l., Austl. — G3 — 62
Frontenac, Ks., U.S. — E9 — 109
Frontera, Mex. — D6 — 78
Frontera, Mex. — B4 — 78
Frontier, co., Ne., U.S. — D5 — 120
Front Range, mts., Co., U.S. — A5 — 99
Front Royal, Va., U.S. — B4 — 139
Frosinone, Italy — D4 — 18

Name	Map Ref.	Page

Frostburg, Md., U.S. k13 113
Frostproof, Fl., U.S. E5 102
Frøya, i., Nor. D3 10
Fruita, Co., U.S. B2 99
Fruit Heights, Ut., U.S. B4 137
Fruitland, Id., U.S. F2 105
Fruitland, Md., U.S. . . . D6 113
Fruitland, N.M., U.S. . . . A1 124
Fruitland Park, Fl., U.S. . . D5 102
Fruitport, Mi., U.S. E4 115
Fruitvale, B.C., Can. E9 85
Fruitvale, Co., U.S. . . . B2 99
Fruitvale, Wa., U.S. . . . C5 140
Fruitville, Fl., U.S. E4 102
Frunze see Biškek, Kyrg. . E9 26
Frutal, Braz. E2 74
Fryeburg, Me., U.S. D2 112
Fu'an, China D4 30
Fuding, China D5 30
Fuerte, stm., Mex. B3 78
Fuerte Olimpo, Para. C6 72
Fuerteventura, i., Spain . . A2 50
Fuga Island, i., Phil. B3 34
Fuji, Japan C3 31
Fuji, Mount see Fuji-san,
  vol., Japan D15 28
Fujian, state, China F11 28
Fujin, China B14 28
Fuji-san, vol., Japan . . . D15 28
Fujiyama see Fuji-san, vol.,
  Japan D15 28
Fukui, Japan D15 28
Fukuoka, Japan E14 28
Fukushima, Japan C4 31
Fukuyama, Japan D2 31
Fūlādī, Kūh-e, mtn., Afg. . D9 42
Fulaga Passage, i., Fiji . . . m11 63b
Fulda, Ger. E11 12
Fulda, Mn., U.S. G3 116
Fuling, China D2 30
Fullerton, Ca., U.S. n13 98
Fullerton, Ne., U.S. C8 120
Fulton, Il., U.S. B3 106
Fulton, Ky., U.S. f9 110
Fulton, Md., U.S. B4 113
Fulton, Mo., U.S. C6 118
Fulton, Ms., U.S. A5 117
Fulton, N.Y., U.S. B4 125
Fulton, co., Ar., U.S. . . . A4 97
Fulton, co., Ga., U.S. . . . C2 103
Fulton, co., Il., U.S. C3 106
Fulton, co., In., U.S. B5 107
Fulton, co., Ky., U.S. . . . f8 110
Fulton, co., N.Y., U.S. . . B6 125
Fulton, co., Oh., U.S. . . . A1 128
Fulton, co., Pa., U.S. . . . G5 131
Fultondale, Al., U.S. f7 94
Funafuti, i., Tuvalu E11 58
Funchal, Port. D1 48
Fundy, Bay of, b., Can. . . D4 87
Fundy National Park, N.B.,
  Can. D4 87
Funhalouro, Moz. C5 56
Funing, China B4 30
Funing, China C4 30
Funkstown, Md., U.S. . . . A2 113
Funsi, Ghana D4 50
Funtua, Nig. D6 50
Fuping, China C2 30
Fuqing, China D4 30
Fuquay-Varina, N.C., U.S. . B4 126
Furnace Brook, stm., Vt.,
  U.S. D3 138
Furnas, co., Ne., U.S. . . . D6 120
Furnas, Represa de, res.,
  Braz. F2 74
Furneaux Group, is., Austl. . I4 62
Fürstenwalde, Ger. D14 12
Furudal, Swe. F6 10
Fushun, China C12 28
Fusui, China G9 28
Futuna, Île, i., Wal./F. . . . F12 58
Fuxin, China A5 30
Fuyang, China E11 28
Fuyu, China B12 28
Fuyuan, China D1 30
Fuzhou, China F11 28
Fuzhou, China F11 28
Füzuli, Azer. C12 44
Fyffe, Al., U.S. A4 94
Fyn, i., Den. I4 10

G

Gaalkacyo, Som. I14 48
Gabbs, Nv., U.S. E4 121
Gabela, Ang. F2 54
Gaberones see Gaborone,
  Bots. C4 56
Gabès, Tun. D7 48
Gabon, ctry., Afr. D2 54
Gaborone, Bots. C4 56
Gabriola, B.C., Can. f12 85
Gabrovo, Bul. C10 18
Gabú, Gui.-B. D2 50
Gachsārān, Iran D6 42
Gadag, India F3 40
Gäddede, Swe. D6 10
Gadsden, Al., U.S. A3 94
Gadsden, co., Fl., U.S. . . . B2 102
Gadwāl, India F3 40
Gaeta, Italy D4 18
Gaeta, Golfo di, b., Italy . D4 18
Gaffney, S.C., U.S. A4 133
Gafsa, Tun. D6 48

Gag, Pulau, i., Indon. . . . D7 36
Gagarin, Russia B13 20
Gage, co., Ne., U.S. D9 120
Gagetown, N.B., Can. . . . D3 87
Gagnoa, C. Iv. E3 50
Gagra, Geor. A9 44
Gahanna, Oh., U.S. k11 128
Gaillard, Lake, l., Ct., U.S. . D5 100
Gaines, co., Tx., U.S. . . . C1 136
Gainesboro, Tn., U.S. . . . C8 135
Gaines Creek, stm., Ok.,
  U.S. C6 129
Gainesville, Fl., U.S. C4 102
Gainesville, Ga., U.S. . . . B3 103
Gainesville, Mo., U.S. . . . E5 118
Gainesville, Tx., U.S. . . . C4 136
Gainesville, Va., U.S. . . . g11 139
Gairdner, Lake, l., Austl. . G2 62
Gaithersburg, Md., U.S. . . B3 113
Gaixian, China C12 28
Gaizina Kalns, hill, Lat. . . H11 10
Gajny, Russia B9 22
Galán, Cerro, mtn., Arg. . . D4 72
Galapagos Islands see
  Colón, Archipiélago de,
  is., Ec. C2 70
Galashiels, Scot., U.K. . . . C5 12
Galați, Rom. G9 20
Galatia, Il., U.S. F5 106
Galax, Va., U.S. D2 139
Galdhøpiggen, mtn., Nor. . F3 10
Galela, Indon. C7 36
Galena, Ak., U.S. C8 95
Galena, Il., U.S. A3 106
Galena, Ks., U.S. E9 109
Galesburg, Il., U.S. C3 106
Galesburg, Mi., U.S. F5 115
Galesville, Md., U.S. C4 113
Galesville, Wi., U.S. D2 142
Galeton, Pa., U.S. C6 131
Gali, Geor. A9 44
Galič, Russia C7 22
Galicia, hist. reg., Eur. . . . E7 20
Galilee, Sea of, l., Isr. . . . F6 44
Galion, Oh., U.S. B3 128
Galisteo Creek, stm., N.M.,
  U.S. k8 124
Galiuro Mountains, mts.,
  Az., U.S. E5 96
Gallant, Al., U.S. A3 94
Gallatin, Mo., U.S. B4 118
Gallatin, Tn., U.S. A5 135
Gallatin, co., Il., U.S. . . . F5 106
Gallatin, co., Ky., U.S. . . . B5 110
Gallatin, co., Mt., U.S. . . . E5 119
Gallatin, stm., Mt., U.S. . . E5 119
Gallatin Range, mts., Mt.,
  U.S. E5 119
Gallaway, Tn., U.S. B2 135
Galle, Sri L. H4 40
Gallia, co., Oh., U.S. D3 128
Galliano, La., U.S. E5 111
Gallinas, Punta, c., Col. . . A5 70
Gallinas Mountains, mts.,
  N.M., U.S. C2 124
Gallipoli, Italy D6 18
Gallipoli see Gelibolu, Tur. . B2 44
Gallipolis, Oh., U.S. D3 128
Gallitzin, Pa., U.S. F4 131
Gallo Mountains, mts.,
  N.M., U.S. C1 124
Galloo Island, i., N.Y., U.S. . B4 125
Gallup, N.M., U.S. B1 124
Galt, Ca., U.S. C3 98
Galtat Zemmour, W. Sah. . A2 50
Galva, Il., U.S. B3 106
Galva, Ks., U.S. D6 109
Galveston, In., U.S. C5 107
Galveston, Tx., U.S. E5 136
Galveston, co., Tx., U.S. . . E5 136
Galveston Bay, b., Tx., U.S. . E5 136
Galveston Island, i., Tx.,
  U.S. E5 136
Galway, Ire. D2 12
Galway Bay, b., Ire. D2 12
Gamarra, Col. B5 70
Gambēla, Eth. B6 54
Gambell, Ak., U.S. C5 95
Gambia, stm., Afr. D2 50
Gambia, The, ctry., Afr. . . D1 50
Gambier, Oh., U.S. B3 128
Gambier, Îles, is., Fr. Poly. . G16 58
Gambo, Nf., Can. D4 88
Gamboma, Congo D3 54
Gamboula, C.A.R. H9 54
Gambrills, Md., U.S. B4 113
Gan, stm., China D4 30
Ganado, Az., U.S. B6 96
Ganado, Tx., U.S. E4 136
Gananoque, On., Can. . . . C8 89
Gäncä, Azer. B12 44
Gand see Gent, Bel. E8 12
Ganda, Ang. F2 54
Gandajika, D.R.C. E4 54
Gandak, stm., Asia D4 40
Gander, Nf., Can. D4 88
Gander, stm., Nf., Can. . . D4 88
Gander Lake, l., Nf., Can. . D4 88
Gandesa, Spain G7 16
Gāndhīnagar, India E2 40
Gandhi Reservoir see
  Gāndhi Sāgar, res.,
  India E3 40

Gāndhi Sāgar, res., India . . E3 40
Gandia, Spain H6 16
Gandu, Braz. D4 74
Ganga see Ganges, stm.,
  Asia D5 40
Gangānagar, India D2 40
Gangaw, Myan. B2 34
Gangdisê Shan, mts., China . E4 28
Ganges, B.C., Can. g12 85
Ganges (Ganga), stm., Asia . D5 40
Ganges, Mouths of the,
  mth., Asia B1 34
Gang Mills, N.Y., U.S. . . . C3 125
Gangtok, India D5 40
Gangu, China E9 28
Gannett Peak, mtn., Wy.,
  U.S. C3 143
Ganquan, China B2 30
Gansu, state, China D8 28
Gantt, S.C., U.S. B3 133
Gantt Lake, res., Al., U.S. . D3 94
Ganzê, China E8 28
Ganzhou, China F10 28
Gao, Mali C4 50
Gao'an, China D4 30
Gaolan, China B1 30
Gaomi, China B4 30
Gaoping, China B3 30
Gaoua, Burkina D4 50
Gaoual, Gui. D2 50
Gaoxian, China D1 30
Gaoyi, China B3 30
Gaoyou, China C4 30
Gaoyou Hu, l., China C4 30
Gaozhou, China E3 30
Gap, Fr. E10 16
Gap, Pa., U.S. G9 131
Gapan, Phil. C8 34
Garagumskij kanal imeni
  Prezidenta
  Turkmenistana S.A.
  Nijazova (Kara-Kum
  Canal), Turk. C8 42
Garagumy, des., Turk. . . . F7 26
Garanhuns, Braz. C4 74
Garber, Ok., U.S. A4 129
Garberville, Ca., U.S. B2 98
Garda, Lago di, l., Italy . . B3 18
Garden, co., Ne., U.S. . . . C3 120
Gardena, Ca., U.S. n12 98
Garden City, Ga., U.S. . . . D5 103
Garden City, Id., U.S. . . . F2 105
Garden City, Ks., U.S. . . . E3 109
Garden City, Mi., U.S. . . . p15 115
Garden City, Mo., U.S. . . . C3 118
Gardendale, Al., U.S. B3 94
Garden Grove, Ca., U.S. . . n13 98
Garden Island, i., Mi., U.S. . C5 115
Garden Plain, Ks., U.S. . . . E6 109
Gardeyz, Afg. D9 42
Gardiner, Me., U.S. D3 112
Gardiner, Mt., U.S. E6 119
Gardiner, Or., U.S. D2 130
Gardiners Island, i., N.Y.,
  U.S. m16 125
Gardner, Il., U.S. B5 106
Gardner, Ks., U.S. D9 109
Gardner, Ma., U.S. A4 114
Gardner Canal, strt., B.C.,
  Can. C3 85
Gardner Lake, l., Ct., U.S. . C6 100
Gardner Lake, l., Me., U.S. . D5 112
Gardner Pinnacles, Hi., U.S. . k14 104
Gardnerville, Nv., U.S. . . . E2 121
Garfield, N.J., U.S. h8 123
Garfield, co., Co., U.S. . . . B2 99
Garfield, co., Mt., U.S. . . . C9 119
Garfield, co., Ne., U.S. . . . C6 120
Garfield, co., Ok., U.S. . . . A4 129
Garfield, co., Ut., U.S. . . . F4 137
Garfield, co., Wa., U.S. . . . C8 140
Garfield Heights, Oh., U.S. . h9 128
Garfield Mountain, mtn.,
  Mt., U.S. F4 119
Garfield Peak, mtn., Wy.,
  U.S. D5 143
Garibaldi, Or., U.S. B3 130
Garibaldi, Mount, mtn.,
  B.C., Can. E6 85
Garies, S. Afr. E2 56
Garissa, Kenya D7 54
Garland, N.C., U.S. C4 126
Garland, Tx., U.S. n10 136
Garland, Ut., U.S. B3 137
Garland, co., Ar., U.S. . . . C2 97
Garland, co., Oh., U.S. . . . A4 128
Garm, Taj. C10 42
Garmī, Iran C13 44
Garmisch-Partenkirchen,
  Ger. G12 12
Garmsār, Iran C6 42
Garnavillo, Ia., U.S. B6 108
Garner, Ia., U.S. A4 108
Garner, N.C., U.S. B4 126
Garnet Range, mts., Mt.,
  U.S. D3 119
Garnett, Ks., U.S. D8 109
Garnish, Nf., Can. E4 88
Garonne, stm., Eur. E6 16
Garoua, Cam. B2 54
Garoua Boulaï, Cam. B2 54
Garrard, co., Ky., U.S. . . . C5 110
Garretson, S.D., U.S. D9 134
Garrett, In., U.S. B7 107
Garrett, co., Md., U.S. . . . k12 113

Garrett Park, Md., U.S. . . . B3 113
Garrettsville, Oh., U.S. . . . A4 128
Garrison, Ky., U.S. B6 110
Garrison, Md., U.S. B4 113
Garrison, N.D., U.S. B4 127
Garrison Dam, N.D., U.S. . B4 127
Garsen, Kenya D8 54
Garut, Indon. E3 36
Garvin, co., Ok., U.S. C4 129
Garwolin, Pol. D6 20
Gary, In., U.S. A3 107
Gary, W.V., U.S. D3 141
Garyarsa, China E4 28
Garysburg, N.C., U.S. . . . A5 126
Garyville, La., U.S. D5 111
Garza, co., Tx., U.S. C2 136
Garza-Little Elm Reservoir,
  res., Tx., U.S. C4 136
Gasan-Kuli, Turk. C6 42
Gas City, In., U.S. D6 107
Gascogne, hist. reg., Fr. . . F7 16
Gasconade, co., Mo., U.S. . C6 118
Gasconade, stm., Mo., U.S. . C6 118
Gascony see Gascogne,
  hist. reg., Fr. F7 16
Gascoyne, stm., Austl. . . . E2 60
Gascoyne Junction, Austl. . F2 60
Gashaka, Nig. E7 50
Gashua, Nig. D7 50
Gasparilla Island, i., Fl., U.S. . F4 102
Gaspé, P.Q., Can. k14 90
Gaspé, Péninsule de la,
  pen., P.Q., Can. k13 90
Gaspésie, Péninsule de la,
  pen., P.Q., Can. k13 90
Gassaway, W.V., U.S. C4 141
Gassville, Ar., U.S. A3 97
Gasteiz, Spain F5 16
Gaston, In., U.S. D7 107
Gaston, N.C., U.S. A5 126
Gaston, S.C., U.S. D5 133
Gaston, co., N.C., U.S. . . . B1 126
Gaston, Lake, res., U.S. . . A5 126
Gaston Dam, N.C., U.S. . . A5 126
Gastonia, N.C., U.S. B1 126
Gastre, Arg. F3 69
Gatčina, Russia C5 22
Gate City, Va., U.S. f9 139
Gates, Tn., U.S. B2 135
Gates, co., N.C., U.S. A6 126
Gates of the Arctic National
  Park, Ak., U.S. B9 95
Gatesville, Tx., U.S. D4 136
Gatineau, P.Q., Can. D2 90
Gatineau, stm., P.Q., Can. . D2 90
Gatineau, Parc de la, P.Q.,
  Can. D2 90
Gatlinburg, Tn., U.S. D10 135
Gatton, Austl. F5 62
Gauley, stm., W.V., U.S. . . C3 141
Gauley Bridge, W.V., U.S. . C3 141
Gaustatoppen, mtn., Nor. . G3 10
Gautier, Ms., U.S. f8 117
Gävdhos, i., Grc. G10 18
Gavins Point Dam, U.S. . . B8 120
Gawler, Austl. F2 62
Gawler Ranges, mts., Austl. . G2 62
Gaya, India E5 40
Gaya, Nig. D6 50
Gaya, Niger D5 50
Gay Head, c., Ma., U.S. . . D6 114
Gaylord, Mi., U.S. C6 115
Gaylord, Mn., U.S. F4 116
Gayndah, Austl. F5 62
Gaza see Ghazzah, Gaza
  Str. G6 44
Gazandzyk, Turk. C7 42
Gazaoua, Niger D6 50
Gaza Strip, Asia G6 44
Gaziantep, Tur. D7 44
Gazimağusa (Famagusta), N.
  Cyp. E5 44
Gazimağusa Körfezi, b., N.
  Cyp. E6 44
Gazipaşa, Tur. D5 44
Gbanga, Lib. E3 50
Gboko, Nig. E6 50
Gdańsk, Pol. B5 20
Gdov, Russia G12 10
Gdynia, Pol. B5 20
Gearhart, Or., U.S. A3 130
Gearhart Mountain, mtn.,
  Or., U.S. E6 130
Geary, N.B., Can. D3 87
Geary, Ok., U.S. B3 129
Geary, co., Ks., U.S. D7 109
Geauga, co., Oh., U.S. . . . A4 128
Gebe, Pulau, i., Indon. . . . D7 36
Gebze, Tur. B3 44
Gediz, Tur. C3 44
Geelong, Austl. H3 62
Geesthacht, Ger. D12 12
Geilo, Nor. F3 10
Geistown, Pa., U.S. F4 131
Geist Reservoir, res., In.,
  U.S. E6 107
Geita, Tan. D6 54
Gejiu, China G8 28
Gela, Italy F5 18
Gelasa, Selat, strt., Indon. . D3 36
Gelendžik, Russia G15 20
Gelibolu, Tur. B2 44
Gelsenkirchen, Ger. E10 12
Gem, co., Id., U.S. E2 105
Gemena, D.R.C. C3 54
Gemlik, Tur. B3 44
Gemlik Körfezi, b., Tur. . . . B3 44

Genalē (Jubba), stm., Afr. . B8 54
Genç, Tur. C9 44
General Acha, Arg. F5 72
General Alvear, Arg. F4 72
General Carneiro, Braz. . . B7 72
General Carrera, Lago, l.,
  S.A. G2 69
General Conesa, Arg. F4 69
General Eugenio A. Garay,
  Para. C5 72
General Juan José Ríos,
  Mex. B3 78
General Juan Madariaga,
  Arg. F6 72
General La Madrid, Arg. . . F5 72
General Pico, Arg. F5 72
General Pinedo, Arg. D5 72
General Roca, Arg. E3 69
General Villegas, Arg. . . . F5 72
Genesee, Id., U.S. C2 105
Genesee, Mi., U.S. E7 115
Genesee, co., Mi., U.S. . . . E7 115
Genesee, co., N.Y., U.S. . . B2 125
Genesee, stm., N.Y., U.S. . C2 125
Geneseo, Il., U.S. B3 106
Geneseo, N.Y., U.S. C3 125
Geneva see Genève, Switz. . A1 18
Geneva, Al., U.S. D4 94
Geneva, Il., U.S. B5 106
Geneva, In., U.S. C8 107
Geneva, Ne., U.S. D8 120
Geneva, N.Y., U.S. C4 125
Geneva, Oh., U.S. A5 128
Geneva, co., Al., U.S. D4 94
Geneva, Lake, l., Eur. A1 18
Geneva, Lake, l., Fl., U.S. . F5 142
Geneva-on-the-Lake, Oh.,
  U.S. A5 128
Genève (Geneva), Switz. . . A1 18
Gengma, China B3 34
Genoa see Genova, Italy . . B2 18
Genoa, Il., U.S. A5 106
Genoa, Ne., U.S. C8 120
Genoa, Nv., U.S. D2 121
Genoa, Oh., U.S. A2 128
Genoa, Gulf of see Genova,
  Golfo di, b., Italy B2 18
Genoa City, Wi., U.S. F5 142
Genola, Ut., U.S. D4 137
Genova, Italy B2 18
Genova, Golfo di, b., Italy . B2 18
Gent, Bel. E8 12
Gentry, Ar., U.S. A1 97
Gentry, co., Mo., U.S. . . . A3 118
Geographe Bay, b., Austl. . G2 60
George, S. Afr. E3 56
George, Ia., U.S. A2 108
George, co., Ms., U.S. . . . E5 117
George, stm., P.Q., Can. . . g13 84
George, Cape, c., N.S., Can. . D8 87
George, Lake, l., Fl., U.S. . C5 102
George, Lake, l., N.Y., U.S. . B7 125
George B. Stevenson
  Reservoir, res., Pa., U.S. . D6 131
George Peak, mtn., Ut.,
  U.S. B2 137
George Town, Austl. I4 62
Georgetown, Austl. D3 62
Georgetown, P.E.I., Can. . . C7 87
George Town, Cay. Is. . . . B3 80
Georgetown, Gam. D2 50
Georgetown, Guy. B8 70
George Town (Penang),
  Malay. B2 36
Georgetown, Ca., U.S. . . . C3 98
Georgetown, Co., U.S. . . . B5 99
Georgetown, Ct., U.S. . . . D2 100
Georgetown, De., U.S. . . . F4 101
Georgetown, Ga., U.S. . . . E1 103
Georgetown, Il., U.S. D6 106
Georgetown, In., U.S. H6 107
Georgetown, Ky., U.S. . . . B5 110
Georgetown, Ma., U.S. . . . A6 114
Georgetown, Oh., U.S. . . . D2 128
Georgetown, S.C., U.S. . . . E9 133
Georgetown, Tx., U.S. . . . D4 136
Georgetown, co., S.C., U.S. . E9 133
George V Coast, Ant. C20 67
George Washington
  Birthplace National
  Monument, Va., U.S. . . . B6 139
George Washington Carver
  National Monument,
  Mo., U.S. E3 118
George West, Tx., U.S. . . . E3 136
Georgia, ctry., Asia A10 44
Georgia, state, U.S. D3 103
Georgiana, Al., U.S. D3 94
Georgian Bay, b., On., Can. . B3 89
Georgina, stm., Austl. . . . D2 62
Gera, Ger. E13 12
Gerald, Mo., U.S. C6 118
Geraldine, Al., U.S. A4 94
Geraldton, Austl. F1 60
Geraldton, On., Can. o18 89
Gerber Reservoir, res., Or.,
  U.S. E5 130
Gerdine, Mount, mtn., Ak.,
  U.S. C9 95
Gerede, Tur. B4 44
Gereshk, Afg. D8 42
Gering, Ne., U.S. C2 120
Gerlach, Nv., U.S. C2 121
Gerlachovský štít, mtn.,
  Slvk. E6 20

Name	Map Ref.	Page

Germantown, Il., U.S. — E4 106
Germantown, Md., U.S. — B3 113
Germantown, Oh., U.S. — C1 128
Germantown, Tn., U.S. — B2 135
Germantown, Wi., U.S. — E5 142
Germany, ctry., Eur. — E12 12
Germiston, S. Afr. — D4 56
Gerona see Girona, Spain — G8 16
Geronimo, Ok., U.S. — C3 129
Gervais, Or., U.S. — B4 130
Gêrzê, China — C4 40
Geser, Indon. — D8 36
Getafe, Spain — G5 16
Gettysburg, Pa., U.S. — G7 131
Gettysburg, S.D., U.S. — C6 134
Geyve, Tur. — B4 44
Ghadāmis, Libya — E6 48
Ghāghara, stm., Asia — D4 40
Ghana, ctry., Afr. — E4 50
Ghanzi, Bots. — C3 56
Ghardaïa, Alg. — D5 48
Gharyān, Libya — D7 48
Ghāt, Libya — F7 48
Ghawdex, i., Malta — F5 18
Ghazāl, Bahr al-, stm., Sudan — B5 54
Ghāziābād, India — D3 40
Ghāzīpur, India — D4 40
Ghaznī, Afg. — D9 42
Ghazzah, Gaza Str. — G6 44
Gheen, Mn., U.S. — C6 116
Gheorgheni, Rom. — F8 20
Gherla, Rom. — F7 20
Ghilizane, Alg. — J7 16
Ghūrīān, Afg. — D8 42
Gianitsá, Grc. — D9 18
Giant's Causeway, N. Ire., U.K. — C3 12
Giants Neck, Ct., U.S. — D7 100
Gibara, Cuba — A4 80
Gibbon, Mn., U.S. — F4 116
Gibbon, Ne., U.S. — D7 120
Gibbons, Ab., Can. — C4 84
Gibb River, Austl. — D4 60
Gibbstown, N.J., U.S. — D2 123
Gibeon, Nmb. — D2 56
Gibraltar, dep., Eur. — I4 16
Gibraltar, Strait of, strt. — J4 16
Gibsland, La., U.S. — B2 111
Gibson, Ga., U.S. — C4 103
Gibson, co., In., U.S. — H2 107
Gibson, co., Tn., U.S. — A3 135
Gibsonburg, Oh., U.S. — A2 128
Gibson City, Il., U.S. — C5 106
Gibson Desert, des., Austl. — E3 60
Gibsonia, Pa., U.S. — h14 131
Gibson Island, i., Md., U.S. — B5 113
Gibsons, B.C., Can. — E6 85
Gibsonton, Fl., U.S. — p11 102
Gibsonville, N.C., U.S. — A3 126
Giddings, Tx., U.S. — D4 136
Gideon, Mo., U.S. — E8 118
Gien, Fr. — D8 16
Giessen, Ger. — E11 12
Gifford, Fl., U.S. — E6 102
Gifford, Il., U.S. — C5 106
Gifford Creek, Austl. — E2 60
Gifu, Japan — D15 28
Gig Harbor, Wa., U.S. — B3 140
Giglio, Isola del, i., Italy — C3 18
Gihon, stm., Vt., U.S. — B3 138
Gijón, Spain — F4 16
Gila, co., Az., U.S. — D5 96
Gila, stm., U.S. — E5 92
Gila Bend, Az., U.S. — E3 96
Gila Bend Indian Reservation, Az., U.S. — D3 96
Gila Bend Mountains, mts., Az., U.S. — D2 96
Gila Cliff Dwellings National Monument, N.M., U.S. — D1 124
Gila Mountains, mts., Az., U.S. — D6 96
Gila Peak, mtn., Az., U.S. — D6 96
Gila River Indian Reservation, Az., U.S. — D4 96
Gilbert, Az., U.S. — D4 96
Gilbert, Ia., U.S. — B4 108
Gilbert, La., U.S. — B4 111
Gilbert, Mn., U.S. — C6 116
Gilbert Islands see Kiribati, is., Kir. — D11 58
Gilbert Peak, mtn., Wa., U.S. — C4 140
Gilbert Plains, Mb., Can. — D1 86
Gilbertsville, Ky., U.S. — f9 110
Gilbertsville, Pa., U.S. — F10 131
Gilbertville, Ma., U.S. — B5 114
Gilbués, Braz. — E10 70
Gilchrist, Or., U.S. — D5 130
Gilchrist, co., Fl., U.S. — C4 102
Gilcrest, Co., U.S. — A6 99
Giles, co., Tn., U.S. — B4 135
Giles, co., Va., U.S. — C2 139
Gilford Island, i., B.C., Can. — B4 85
Gilgandra, Austl. — G4 62
Gilgil, Kenya — D7 54
Gilgit, Pak. — C10 42
Gillam, Mb., Can. — A4 86
Gillespie, Il., U.S. — D4 106
Gillespie, co., Tx., U.S. — D3 136
Gillespie Dam, Az., U.S. — D3 96
Gillett, Ar., U.S. — C4 97
Gillett, Wi., U.S. — D5 142
Gillette, Wy., U.S. — B7 143

Gilliam, co., Or., U.S. — B6 130
Gilman, Il., U.S. — C5 106
Gilman, Vt., U.S. — C5 138
Gilmanton, N.H., U.S. — D4 122
Gilmer, Tx., U.S. — C5 136
Gilmer, co., Ga., U.S. — B2 103
Gilmer, co., W.V., U.S. — C4 141
Gilpin, co., Co., U.S. — B5 99
Gilroy, Ca., U.S. — D3 98
Gīmbī, Eth. — B7 54
Gimie, Mount, vol., St. Luc. — C7 80
Gimli, Mb., Can. — D3 86
Gingoog, Phil. — E9 34
Giralia, Austl. — E1 60
Girard, Il., U.S. — D4 106
Girard, Ks., U.S. — E9 109
Girard, Oh., U.S. — A5 128
Girard, Pa., U.S. — B1 131
Girardot, Col. — E5 80
Girardville, Pa., U.S. — E9 131
Giresun, Tur. — B8 44
Girona, Spain — G8 16
Gironde, est., Fr. — E6 16
Girvan, Scot., U.K. — C4 12
Gisborne, N.Z. — o14 63c
Gitarama, Rw. — D5 54
Gitega, Bdi. — D5 54
Giurgiu, Rom. — H8 20
Giyon, Eth. — B7 54
Giza see El-Gîza, Egypt — E11 48
Giza, Pyramids of, Egypt — F10 14
Gizduvan, Uzb. — B8 42
Gižiga, Russia — C18 26
Giżycko, Pol. — B6 20
Gjirokastër, Alb. — D8 18
Gjøvik, Nor. — F4 10
Gjumri, Arm. — B10 44
Glacier, co., Mt., U.S. — B3 119
Glacier Bay, b., Ak., U.S. — k21 95
Glacier Bay National Park, Ak., U.S. — D12 95
Glacier National Park, B.C., Can. — D9 85
Glacier National Park, Mt., U.S. — B2 119
Glacier Peak, mtn., Wa., U.S. — A4 140
Gladbrook, Ia., U.S. — B5 108
Glade Creek, stm., W.V., U.S. — n13 141
Glade Creek, stm., W.V., U.S. — n14 141
Glade Creek, stm., Wa., U.S. — C6 140
Glades, co., Fl., U.S. — F5 102
Glade Spring, Va., U.S. — f10 139
Gladewater, Tx., U.S. — C5 136
Gladstone, Austl. — E5 62
Gladstone, Mb., Can. — D2 86
Gladstone, Mi., U.S. — C4 115
Gladstone, Mo., U.S. — h10 118
Gladstone, Or., U.S. — B4 130
Gladwin, Mi., U.S. — E6 115
Gladwin, co., Mi., U.S. — D6 115
Glåma, stm., Nor. — F4 10
Glascock, co., Ga., U.S. — C4 103
Glasford, Il., U.S. — C4 106
Glasgow, Scot., U.K. — C4 12
Glasgow, Ky., U.S. — C4 110
Glasgow, Mo., U.S. — B5 118
Glasgow, Mt., U.S. — B10 119
Glasgow, Va., U.S. — C3 139
Glasgow, W.V., U.S. — m13 141
Glassboro, N.J., U.S. — D2 123
Glassport, Pa., U.S. — F2 131
Glastonbury, Ct., U.S. — C5 100
Glazier Lake, l., Me., U.S. — A3 112
Glazov, Russia — D7 26
Gleason, Tn., U.S. — A3 135
Glen Allan, Ms., U.S. — B2 117
Glen Allen, Va., U.S. — C5 139
Glenboro, Mb., Can. — E2 86
Glenbrook, Nv., U.S. — D2 121
Glen Burnie, Md., U.S. — B4 113
Glen Canyon Dam, Az., U.S. — A4 96
Glen Canyon National Recreation Area, U.S. — F5 137
Glencoe, On., Can. — E3 89
Glencoe, Al., U.S. — B4 94
Glencoe, Il., U.S. — A6 106
Glencoe, Mn., U.S. — F4 116
Glendale, Az., U.S. — D3 96
Glendale, Ca., U.S. — m12 98
Glendale, Ms., U.S. — D4 117
Glendale, Oh., U.S. — C1 128
Glendale, Or., U.S. — E3 130
Glendale, R.I., U.S. — B2 132
Glendale, S.C., U.S. — B4 133
Glendale, Wi., U.S. — m12 142
Glendale Heights, W.V., U.S. — g8 141
Glendive, Mt., U.S. — C12 119
Glendo, Wy., U.S. — D7 143
Glendora, Ca., U.S. — m13 98
Glendo Reservoir, res., Wy., U.S. — D8 143
Glenelg, Md., U.S. — B4 113
Glen Ellis Falls, wtfl, N.H., U.S. — B4 122
Glen Ellyn, Il., U.S. — k8 106

Glenham, N.Y., U.S. — D7 125
Glen Innes, Austl. — F5 62
Glen Jean, W.V., U.S. — D3 141
Glen Lake, l., Mi., U.S. — D5 115
Glen Lyon, Pa., U.S. — D9 131
Glenmora, La., U.S. — D3 111
Glenn, co., Ca., U.S. — C2 98
Glennallen, Ak., U.S. — f19 95
Glenns Ferry, Id., U.S. — G3 105
Glennville, Ga., U.S. — E5 103
Glenolden, Pa., U.S. — p20 131
Glenpool, Ok., U.S. — B5 129
Glen Raven, N.C., U.S. — A3 126
Glen Ridge, N.J., U.S. — h8 123
Glen Rock, N.J., U.S. — h8 123
Glen Rock, Pa., U.S. — G8 131
Glenrock, Wy., U.S. — D7 143
Glenrothes, Scot., U.K. — B5 12
Glenroy, Austl. — E1 60
Glens Falls, N.Y., U.S. — B7 125
Glen Ullin, N.D., U.S. — C4 127
Glenview, Il., U.S. — h9 106
Glenville, Mn., U.S. — G5 116
Glenville, W.V., U.S. — C4 141
Glenwood, Nf., Can. — D4 88
Glenwood, Ar., U.S. — C2 97
Glenwood, Ga., U.S. — D4 103
Glenwood, Ia., U.S. — C2 108
Glenwood, Mn., U.S. — E3 116
Glenwood, Va., U.S. — D3 139
Glenwood City, Wi., U.S. — C1 142
Glenwood Springs, Co., U.S. — B3 99
Glidden, Ia., U.S. — B3 108
Glide, Or., U.S. — D3 130
Glittertinden, mtn., Nor. — F3 10
Globe, Az., U.S. — D5 96
Głogów, Pol. — D4 20
Gloster, Ms., U.S. — D2 117
Gloucester, Eng., U.K. — E5 12
Gloucester, Ma., U.S. — A6 114
Gloucester, Va., U.S. — C6 139
Gloucester, co., N.J., U.S. — D2 123
Gloucester, co., Va., U.S. — C6 139
Gloucester City, N.J., U.S. — D2 123
Gloucester Point, Va., U.S. — C6 139
Glouster, Oh., U.S. — C3 128
Glover Island, i., Nf., Can. — D3 88
Gloversville, N.Y., U.S. — B6 125
Glovertown, Nf., Can. — D4 88
Gloverville, S.C., U.S. — E4 133
Glubokij, Russia — E7 22
Głuchołazy, Pol. — D4 20
Gluck, S.C., U.S. — C2 133
Glyndon, Md., U.S. — B4 113
Glyndon, Mn., U.S. — D2 116
Glynn, co., Ga., U.S. — E5 103
Gmünd, Aus. — F14 12
Gmunden, Aus. — G13 12
Gnadenhutten, Oh., U.S. — B4 128
Gnarp, Swe. — E7 10
Gniezno, Pol. — C4 20
Gnowangerup, Austl. — G2 60
Goa, prov., India — F2 40
Goālpāra, India — D6 40
Goat Island, i., R.I., U.S. — F5 132
Goat Mountain, mtn., Mt., U.S. — C3 119
Goat Rock Dam, U.S. — C4 94
Goba, Eth. — B7 54
Gobabis, Nmb. — C2 56
Gobi, des., Asia — C7 28
Gobles, Mi., U.S. — F5 115
Gobō, Japan — H9 31
Godāfoss, wtfl, Ice. — l20 10a
Godāvari, stm., India — F3 40
Goddard, Ks., U.S. — E6 109
Goderich, On., Can. — D3 89
Godfrey, Il., U.S. — E3 106
Godhavn, Grnld. — E29 82
Godhra, India — E2 40
Gödöllő, Hung. — F5 20
Gods, stm., Mb., Can. — A5 86
Gods Lake, l., Mb., Can. — B4 86
Godthåb (Nuuk), Grnld. — F29 82
Goff Creek, stm., Ok., U.S. — e9 129
Goffstown, N.H., U.S. — D3 122
Gogebic, co., Mi., U.S. — n12 115
Gogebic, Lake, l., Mi., U.S. — m12 115
Goiana, Braz. — C5 74
Goianésia, Braz. — E2 74
Goiânia, Braz. — E2 74
Goiás, Braz. — E1 74
Goiás, state, Braz. — F10 70
Gojra, Pak. — D10 42
Gök, stm., Tur. — B6 44
Gökçeada, i., Tur. — B1 44
Gökova Körfezi, b., Tur. — D2 44
Göksun, Tur. — C7 44
Gokwe, Zimb. — B4 56
Golāghāt, India — D6 40
Golconda, Il., U.S. — F5 106
Golconda, Nv., U.S. — C4 121
Gölcük, Tur. — B3 44
Gold Bar, Wa., U.S. — B4 140
Gold Beach, Or., U.S. — E2 130
Gold Coast see Southport, Austl. — F5 62
Golden, B.C., Can. — D9 85
Golden, Co., U.S. — B5 99
Golden City, Mo., U.S. — D3 118

Goldendale, Wa., U.S. — D5 140
Golden Gate Bridge, Ca., U.S. — h7 98
Golden Gate National Recreation Area, Ca., U.S. — h7 98
Golden Hinde, mtn., B.C., Can. — E5 85
Golden Meadow, La., U.S. — E5 111
Golden Spike National Historic Site, hist., Ut., U.S. — B3 137
Golden Valley, Mn., U.S. — n12 116
Golden Valley, co., Mt., U.S. — D7 119
Golden Valley, co., N.D., U.S. — B2 127
Goldfield, Ia., U.S. — B4 108
Goldfield, Nv., U.S. — F4 121
Gold Hill, Or., U.S. — E3 130
Goldsboro, N.C., U.S. — B5 126
Goldsby, Ok., U.S. — B4 129
Goldsworthy, Austl. — E2 60
Goldthwaite, Tx., U.S. — D3 136
Goleniów, Pol. — C3 20
Goleta, Ca., U.S. — E4 98
Golfito, C.R. — D3 80
Golf Manor, Oh., U.S. — o13 128
Gölhisar, Tur. — D3 44
Golmud, China — B6 40
Golpāyegān, Iran — D6 42
Goma, D.R.C. — D5 54
Gomati, stm., India — D4 40
Gombe, Nig. — D7 50
Gombi, Nig. — D7 50
Gomel see Homel', Bela. — C11 20
Gómez Palacio, Mex. — B4 78
Gonaïves, Haiti — B5 80
Gonam, Russia — D15 26
Gonâve, Golfe de la, b., Haiti — B5 80
Gonâve, Île de la, i., Haiti — B5 80
Gonbad-e Qābūs, Iran — C7 42
Gonda, India — D4 40
Gondal, India — E2 40
Gonder, Eth. — H12 48
Gondia, India — E4 40
Gönen, Tur. — B2 44
Gongbo'gyamda, China — E6 28
Gongcheng, China — B3 30
Gongga Shan, mtn., China — F8 28
Gongxian, China — C3 30
Gongzhuling, China — C12 28
Gonzales, Ca., U.S. — D3 98
Gonzales, La., U.S. — D5 111
Gonzales, Tx., U.S. — E4 136
Gonzales, co., Tx., U.S. — E4 136
González, Mex. — C5 78
Gonzalez, Fl., U.S. — u14 102
Goochland, co., Va., U.S. — C5 139
Goode, Mount, mtn., Ak., U.S. — g18 95
Goodfellow Air Force Base, mil., Tx., U.S. — D2 136
Good Hope, Cape of, c., S. Afr. — E2 56
Good Hope Mountain, mtn., B.C., Can. — D5 85
Goodhue, co., Mn., U.S. — F6 116
Gooding, Id., U.S. — G4 105
Gooding, co., Id., U.S. — F4 105
Goodland, In., U.S. — C3 107
Goodland, Ks., U.S. — C2 109
Goodlettsville, Tn., U.S. — g10 135
Goodman, Mo., U.S. — E3 118
Goodman, Ms., U.S. — C4 117
Good Pine, La., U.S. — C3 111
Goodsprings, Nv., U.S. — H6 121
Goodview, Mn., U.S. — F7 116
Goodwater, Al., U.S. — B3 94
Goodwell, Ok., U.S. — e9 129
Goodyear, Az., U.S. — D3 96
Goondiwindi, Austl. — F5 62
Goose, stm., N.D., U.S. — B8 127
Goose Bay, b., Nf., Can. — B1 88
Gooseberry Creek, stm., Wy., U.S. — B4 143
Goose Creek, S.C., U.S. — F7 133
Goose Creek, stm., Va., U.S. — C3 139
Goose Creek, stm., U.S. — G5 105
Goose Creek Reservoir, res., S.C., U.S. — k11 133
Goose Lake, l., U.S. — C3 92
Goose Lake, l., U.S. — B3 98
Goose Pond, l., N.H., U.S. — C2 122
Gordo, Al., U.S. — B2 94
Gordon, Ga., U.S. — D3 103
Gordon, Ne., U.S. — B3 120
Gordon, co., Ga., U.S. — B2 103
Gordon Downs, Austl. — D4 60
Gordonsville, Tn., U.S. — C8 135
Gordonsville, Va., U.S. — B4 139
Goré, Chad — E8 50
Gorê, Eth. — B7 54
Gore, N.Z. — q12 63c
Gore, Ok., U.S. — B6 129
Gore Bay, On., Can. — B2 89

Gore Point, c., Ak., U.S. — h16 95
Gore Range, mts., Co., U.S. — B4 99
Goreville, Il., U.S. — F5 106
Gorgān, Iran — C6 42
Gorge High Dam, Wa., U.S. — A4 140
Gorham, Me., U.S. — E2 112
Gorham, N.H., U.S. — B4 122
Gori, Geor. — A11 44
Gorizia, Italy — B4 18
Gor'kij see Nižnij Novgorod, Russia — D6 26
Gorkiy Reservoir see Gor'kovskoe vodohranilišče, res., Russia — C7 22
Gor'kovskoe vodohranilišče, res., Russia — C7 22
Görlitz, Ger. — E14 12
Gorlovka see Horlivka, Ukr. — E15 20
Gorman, Tx., U.S. — C3 136
Gorna Orjahovica, Bul. — C10 18
Gornjackij, Russia — A11 22
Gorno-Altajsk, Russia — D10 26
Gornozavodsk, Russia — B16 28
Gorodec, Russia — C7 22
Goroka, Pap. N. Gui. — H12 32
Gorong, Pulau, i., Indon. — D8 36
Gorontalo, Indon. — C6 36
Gorzów Wielkopolski, Pol. — C3 20
Gosford, Austl. — G5 62
Goshen, In., U.S. — A6 107
Goshen, N.Y., U.S. — D6 125
Goshen, Oh., U.S. — C1 128
Goshen, co., Wy., U.S. — D8 143
Goshute Indian Reservation, U.S. — D7 121
Goshute Lake, l., Nv., U.S. — C7 121
Goshute Mountains, mts., Nv., U.S. — C7 121
Goslar, Ger. — E12 12
Gosnells, Austl. — G2 60
Gosper, co., Ne., U.S. — D6 120
Gosport, In., U.S. — F4 107
Gossinga, Sudan — B5 54
Gostivar, Mac. — D8 18
Gostyń, Pol. — D4 20
Gostynin, Pol. — C5 20
Göteborg (Gothenburg), Swe. — H4 10
Gothenburg see Göteborg, Swe. — H4 10
Gothenburg, Ne., U.S. — D5 120
Gotland, i., Swe. — H8 10
Gotō-rettō, is., Japan — E13 28
Gotska Sandön, i., Swe. — G8 10
Göttingen, Ger. — E11 12
Goubone, Chad — B8 50
Goudoumaria, Niger — D7 50
Gough Island, i., St. Hel. — N9 46
Gouin, Réservoir, res., P.Q., Can. — I25 82
Goulburn, Austl. — G4 62
Goulburn Islands, is., Austl. — C5 60
Gould, Ar., U.S. — D4 97
Goulding, Fl., U.S. — u14 102
Gould Island, i., R.I., U.S. — E5 132
Goulds, Fl., U.S. — s13 102
Goundam, Mali — E8 50
Goundi, Chad — E8 50
Gouré, Niger — D7 50
Gouverneur, N.Y., U.S. — f9 125
Gove, co., Ks., U.S. — D3 109
Governador Valadares, Braz. — E3 74
Govind Ballabh Pant Reservoir see Govind Ballabh Pant Sāgar, res., India — E4 40
Govind Ballabh Pant Sāgar, res., India — E4 40
Gowanda, N.Y., U.S. — C2 125
Gower, Mo., U.S. — B3 118
Gowrie, Ia., U.S. — B3 108
Goya, Arg. — D6 72
Göyçay, Azer. — B12 44
Gozo see Ghawdex, i., Malta — F5 18
Graaff-Reinet, S. Afr. — E3 56
Grabill, In., U.S. — B8 107
Grabo, C. Iv. — F3 50
Grace, Id., U.S. — G7 105
Graceville, Fl., U.S. — u16 102
Graceville, Mn., U.S. — E2 116
Gracewood, Ga., U.S. — C4 103
Gracias a Dios, Cabo, c., N.A. — F8 76
Gradaús, Braz. — E9 74
Grady, co., Ga., U.S. — F2 103
Grady, co., Ok., U.S. — C4 129
Graettinger, Ia., U.S. — A3 108
Grafton, Austl. — F5 62
Grafton, Il., U.S. — E3 106
Grafton, Ma., U.S. — B4 114
Grafton, N.D., U.S. — A8 127
Grafton, Oh., U.S. — A3 128
Grafton, Va., U.S. — h15 139
Grafton, W.V., U.S. — B4 141
Grafton, Wi., U.S. — E6 142
Grafton, co., N.H., U.S. — C3 122
Graham, N.C., U.S. — A3 126
Graham, Tx., U.S. — C3 136
Graham, co., Az., U.S. — E5 96
Graham, co., Ks., U.S. — C4 109
Graham, co., N.C., U.S. — f9 126

Name	Map Ref.	Page
Graham, Lake, res., Tx., U.S.	C3	136
Graham, Mount, mtn., Az., U.S.	E6	96
Graham Island, i., B.C., Can.	C1	85
Graham Lake, l., Me., U.S.	D4	112
Graham Land, reg., Ant.	C34	67
Grahamstown, S. Afr.	E4	56
Grahn, Ky., U.S.	B6	110
Grainger, co., Tn., U.S.	C10	135
Grain Valley, Mo., U.S.	h3	118
Grajaú, Braz.	C2	74
Grajewo, Pol.	C7	20
Grambling, La., U.S.	B3	111
Gramercy, La., U.S.	h10	111
Granada, Col.	E5	80
Granada, Nic.	C2	80
Granada, Spain	I5	16
Granbury, Tx., U.S.	C4	136
Granby, P.Q., Can.	D5	90
Granby, Co., U.S.	A5	99
Granby, Ct., U.S.	B4	100
Granby, Mo., U.S.	E3	118
Granby, Lake, res., Co., U.S.	A5	99
Gran Canaria, i., Spain	A1	50
Gran Chaco, reg., S.A.	C5	72
Grand, co., Co., U.S.	A4	99
Grand, co., Ut., U.S.	E6	137
Grand, stm., On., Can.	D4	89
Grand, stm., Mi., U.S.	E5	115
Grand, stm., Mo., U.S.	A3	118
Grand, stm., Oh., U.S.	A4	128
Grand, stm., S.D., U.S.	B4	134
Grand Bahama, i., Bah.	C9	76
Grand Bank, Nf., Can.	E4	88
Grand-Bassam, C. Iv.	E4	50
Grand Bay, N.B., Can.	D3	87
Grand Bay, Al., U.S.	E1	94
Grand Bend, On., Can.	D3	89
Grand Blanc, Mi., U.S.	F7	115
Grand Caillou, La., U.S.	E5	111
Grand Canal see Da Yunhe, China	D11	28
Grand Canyon, Az., U.S.	A3	96
Grand Canyon, val., Az., U.S.	A3	96
Grand Canyon National Park, Az., U.S.	B3	96
Grand Cayman, i., Cay. Is.	B3	80
Grand Centre, Ab., Can.	B5	84
Grand Cess, Lib.	F3	50
Grand Coteau, La., U.S.	D3	111
Grand Coulee, Wa., U.S.	B6	140
Grand Coulee Dam, Wa., U.S.	B6	140
Grande, stm., Bol.	G7	70
Grande, stm., Braz.	F1	74
Grande, stm., Ven.	D7	80
Grande, Bahía, b., Arg.	H3	69
Grande, Boca, mth., Ven.	D7	80
Grande, Ilha, i., Braz.	F3	74
Grande, Rio see Rio Grande, stm., N.A.	B5	78
Grande-Anse, N.B., Can.	B4	87
Grande Cache, Ab., Can.	C1	84
Grande Comore see Njazidja, i., Com.	A7	56
Grande de Matagalpa, stm., Nic.	C3	80
Grande de Santiago, stm., Mex.	C4	78
Grande do Gurupá, Ilha, i., Braz.	B1	74
Grand-Entrée, P.Q., Can.	B8	87
Grande Prairie, Ab., Can.	B1	84
Grand Erg de Bilma, des., Niger	C7	50
Grand Erg Occidental, des., Alg.	D5	48
Grand Erg Oriental, des., Alg.	D6	48
Grande rivière de la Baleine, stm., P.Q., Can.	g11	90
Grande Ronde, stm., U.S.	C8	140
Grandes, Salinas, pl., Arg.	E4	72
Grandes-Bergeronnes, P.Q., Can.	A8	90
Grande-Terre, i., Guad.	B7	80
Grand Falls (Grand-Sault), N.B., Can.	B2	87
Grand Falls, wtfl, Me., U.S.	C5	112
Grand Falls [-Windsor], Nf., Can.	D4	88
Grandfather Mountain, mtn., N.C., U.S.	A1	126
Grandfield, Ok., U.S.	C3	129
Grand Forks, B.C., Can.	E8	85
Grand Forks, N.D., U.S.	B8	127
Grand Forks, co., N.D., U.S.	B8	127
Grand Forks Air Force Base, mil., N.D., U.S.	B8	127
Grand Harbour, N.B., Can.	E3	87
Grand Haven, Mi., U.S.	E4	115
Grand Island, Ne., U.S.	D7	120
Grand Island, i., La., U.S.	D6	111
Grand Island, i., Mi., U.S.	B4	115
Grand Isle, La., U.S.	E6	111
Grand Isle, co., Vt., U.S.	B2	138
Grand Isle, i., U.S.	E6	111
Grand Junction, Co., U.S.	B2	99
Grand Junction, Ia., U.S.	B3	108
Grand Lake, l., N.B., Can.	D3	87
Grand Lake, l., Nf., Can.	D3	88
Grand Lake, l., La., U.S.	E6	111
Grand Lake, l., La., U.S.	E3	111
Grand Lake, l., Mi., U.S.	C7	115
Grand Lake, l., Oh., U.S.	B5	128
Grand Lake, l., Oh., U.S.	B1	128
Grand Lake Matagamon, l., Me., U.S.	B4	112
Grand Lake Seboeis, l., Me., U.S.	B4	112
Grand Ledge, Mi., U.S.	F6	115
Grand Manan Island, i., N.B., Can.	E3	87
Grand Marais, Mn., U.S.	k9	116
Grand Meadow, Mn., U.S.	G6	116
Grand-Mère, P.Q., Can.	C5	90
Grand Mound, Ia., U.S.	C7	108
Grand Portage Indian Reservation, Mn., U.S.	k10	116
Grand Portage National Monument, Mn., U.S.	h10	116
Grand Prairie, Tx., U.S.	n10	136
Grand Rapids, Mi., U.S.	F5	115
Grand Rapids, Mn., U.S.	C5	116
Grand Rapids, Oh., U.S.	f6	128
Grand Saline, Tx., U.S.	C5	136
Grand Terre Islands, is., La., U.S.	E6	111
Grand Teton, mtn., Wy., U.S.	C2	143
Grand Teton National Park, Wy., U.S.	C2	143
Grand Tower, Il., U.S.	F4	106
Grand Traverse, co., Mi., U.S.	D5	115
Grand Traverse Bay, b., Mi., U.S.	C5	115
Grand Turk, T./C. Is.	A5	80
Grand Valley, On., Can.	D4	89
Grandview, Mb., Can.	D1	86
Grandview, In., U.S.	I4	107
Grandview, Mo., U.S.	C3	118
Grandview, Wa., U.S.	C6	140
Grandview Heights, Oh., U.S.	m10	128
Grandville, Mi., U.S.	F5	115
Grandy, N.C., U.S.	A7	126
Granger, Ia., U.S.	C4	108
Granger, In., U.S.	A5	107
Granger, Tx., U.S.	D4	136
Granger, Wa., U.S.	C5	140
Grängesberg, Swe.	F6	10
Grangeville, Id., U.S.	D2	105
Granisle, B.C., Can.	B4	85
Granite, Ok., U.S.	C2	129
Granite, co., Mt., U.S.	D3	119
Granite City, Il., U.S.	E3	106
Granite Falls, Mn., U.S.	F3	116
Granite Falls, N.C., U.S.	B1	126
Granite Falls, Wa., U.S.	A4	140
Granite Lake, res., Nf., Can.	D3	88
Granite Mountain, mtn., Ak., U.S.	B7	95
Granite Mountains, mts., Az., U.S.	E2	96
Granite Mountains, mts., Wy., U.S.	D5	143
Granite Pass, Wy., U.S.	B5	143
Granite Peak, mtn., Mt., U.S.	E7	119
Granite Peak, mtn., Nv., U.S.	C2	121
Granite Peak, mtn., Nv., U.S.	B4	121
Granite Peak, mtn., Ut., U.S.	E3	137
Granite Peak, mtn., Ut., U.S.	C2	137
Granite Peak, mtn., Wy., U.S.	D4	143
Granite Quarry, N.C., U.S.	B2	126
Granite Range, mts., Nv., U.S.	C2	121
Graniteville, S.C., U.S.	D4	133
Graniteville, Vt., U.S.	C4	138
Granja, Braz.	B3	74
Grant, Al., U.S.	A3	94
Grant, Mi., U.S.	E5	115
Grant, Ne., U.S.	D4	120
Grant, co., Ar., U.S.	C3	97
Grant, co., In., U.S.	D6	107
Grant, co., Ks., U.S.	E2	109
Grant, co., Ky., U.S.	B5	110
Grant, co., La., U.S.	C3	111
Grant, co., Mn., U.S.	E2	116
Grant, co., N.D., U.S.	C4	127
Grant, co., Ne., U.S.	C4	120
Grant, co., N.M., U.S.	E1	124
Grant, co., Ok., U.S.	A4	129
Grant, co., Or., U.S.	C7	130
Grant, co., S.D., U.S.	B8	134
Grant, co., W.V., U.S.	B5	141
Grant, co., Wa., U.S.	B6	140
Grant, co., Wi., U.S.	F3	142
Grant, Mount, mtn., Nv., U.S.	E3	121
Grant City, Mo., U.S.	A3	118
Grant Park, Il., U.S.	B6	106
Grant Range, mts., Nv., U.S.	E6	121
Grants, N.M., U.S.	B2	124
Grantsburg, Wi., U.S.	C1	142
Grants Pass, Or., U.S.	E3	130
Grantsville, Ut., U.S.	C3	137
Grantsville, W.V., U.S.	C3	141
Grant Town, W.V., U.S.	B4	141
Granville, Ga., U.S.	C2	103
Granville, Fr.	C6	16
Granville, Il., U.S.	B4	106
Granville, N.Y., U.S.	B7	125
Granville, Oh., U.S.	B3	128
Granville, W.V., U.S.	h11	141
Granville, co., N.C., U.S.	A4	126
Granville Lake, l., Mb., Can.	A1	86
Grapeland, Tx., U.S.	D5	136
Grapeview, Wa., U.S.	B3	140
Grapevine, Tx., U.S.	C4	136
Grapevine Lake, res., Tx., U.S.	n9	136
Grapevine Peak, mtn., Nv., U.S.	G4	121
Gräsö, i., Swe.	F8	10
Grasonville, Md., U.S.	C5	113
Grass, stm., Mb., Can.	B2	86
Grass, stm., N.Y., U.S.	f9	125
Grasse, Fr.	F10	16
Grass Lake, Il., U.S.	h8	106
Grass Lake, Mi., U.S.	F6	115
Grass Lake, l., Il., U.S.	h8	106
Grass Valley, Ca., U.S.	C3	98
Grassy Brook, stm., Vt., U.S.	E3	138
Grassy Lake, l., La., U.S.	k9	111
Grates Point, c., Nf., Can.	D5	88
Gratiot, co., Mi., U.S.	E6	115
Gratis, Oh., U.S.	C1	128
Grave Creek, stm., W.V., U.S.	g8	141
Gravelly Branch, stm., De., U.S.	F4	101
Gravelly Range, mts., Mt., U.S.	E4	119
Gravenhage, 's- see 's-Gravenhage, Neth.	D8	12
Gravenhurst, On., Can.	C5	89
Grave Peak, mtn., Id., U.S.	C4	105
Graves, co., Ky., U.S.	f9	110
Gravette, Ar., U.S.	A1	97
Gray, Fr.	D9	16
Gray, Ga., U.S.	C3	103
Gray, Ky., U.S.	D5	110
Gray, La., U.S.	k10	111
Gray, Me., U.S.	g7	112
Gray, co., Ks., U.S.	E3	109
Gray, co., Tx., U.S.	B2	136
Grayback Mountain, mtn., Or., U.S.	E3	130
Gray Court, S.C., U.S.	B3	133
Grayland, Wa., U.S.	C1	140
Grayling, Mi., U.S.	D6	115
Graylyn Crest, De., U.S.	A3	101
Grays Harbor, co., Wa., U.S.	B2	140
Grays Harbor, b., Wa., U.S.	C1	140
Grayslake, Il., U.S.	A5	106
Grays Lake, sw., Id., U.S.	F7	105
Grayson, Ky., U.S.	B7	110
Grayson, co., Ky., U.S.	C3	110
Grayson, co., Tx., U.S.	C4	136
Grayson, co., Va., U.S.	D1	139
Grayson Lake, res., Ky., U.S.	B7	110
Grays Peak, mtn., Co., U.S.	B5	99
Gray Summit, Mo., U.S.	g12	118
Graysville, Al., U.S.	f7	94
Graysville, Tn., U.S.	D8	135
Grayville, Il., U.S.	E5	106
Graz, Aus.	G14	12
Great Alfold see Alföld, pl., Hung.		20
Great Artesian Basin, Austl.	F3	62
Great Australian Bight, b., Austl.	G4	60
Great Averill Pond, l., Vt., U.S.	B5	138
Great Barrier Island, i., N.Z.	o14	63c
Great Barrier Reef, rf., Austl.	D4	62
Great Barrington, Ma., U.S.	B1	114
Great Basin, U.S.	C4	92
Great Basin National Park, Nv., U.S.	E7	121
Great Bay, b., N.H., U.S.	D5	122
Great Bay, b., N.J., U.S.	D4	123
Great Bear Lake, l., N.T., Can.	E15	82
Great Belt see Storebælt, strt., Den.	I4	10
Great Bend, Ks., U.S.	D5	109
Great Britain see United Kingdom, ctry., Eur.	C6	12
Great Captain Island, i., Ct., U.S.	F1	100
Great Channel, strt., Asia	E2	34
Great Dismal Swamp, sw., U.S.	D6	139
Great Divide Basin, Wy., U.S.	E4	143
Great Dividing Range, mts., Austl.	H4	62
Great East Lake, l., U.S.	C5	122
Great Egg Harbor, stm., N.J., U.S.	D3	123
Greater Antilles, is., N.A.	E9	76
Greater Khingan Range see Da Hinggan Ling, mts., China	B12	28
Greater Sunda Islands, is., Asia	D3	36
Great Exuma, i., Bah.	D9	76
Great Falls, Mt., U.S.	C5	119
Great Falls, S.C., U.S.	B6	133
Great Falls, wtfl, Md., U.S.	B3	113
Great Falls Dam, Tn., U.S.	D6	135
Greathouse Peak, mtn., Mt., U.S.	D7	119
Great Inagua, i., Bah.	D10	76
Great Indian Desert (Thar Desert), des., Asia	D2	40
Great Island, spit, Ma., U.S.	C7	114
Great Island, i., N.C., U.S.	B6	126
Great Karroo, plat., S. Afr.	E3	56
Great Lakes Naval Training Center, mil., Il., U.S.	h9	106
Great Miami, stm., U.S.	C1	128
Great Misery Island, i., Ma., U.S.	f12	114
Great Moose Lake, l., Me., U.S.	D3	112
Great Namaqualand, hist. reg., Nmb.	D2	56
Great Neck, N.Y., U.S.	h13	125
Great Nicobar, i., India	H6	40
Great Ouse, stm., Eng., U.K.	D7	12
Great Pee Dee, stm., U.S.	D9	133
Great Plains, pl., N.A.	E9	75
Great Point, c., Ma., U.S.	D7	114
Great Ruaha, stm., Tan.	E7	54
Great Sacandaga Lake, l., N.Y., U.S.	C6	125
Great Salt Lake, l., Ut., U.S.	B3	137
Great Salt Lake Desert, des., Ut., U.S.	C2	137
Great Salt Plains Lake, res., Ok., U.S.	A3	129
Great Salt Pond, b., R.I., U.S.	h7	132
Great Sand Dunes National Monument, Co., U.S.	D5	99
Great Sandy Desert, des., Austl.	E3	60
Great Slave Lake, l., N.T., Can.	F17	82
Great Smoky Mountains, mts., U.S.	B8	135
Great Smoky Mountains National Park, U.S.	B8	135
Great Swamp, sw., R.I., U.S.	F3	132
Great Victoria Desert, des., Austl.	F4	60
Great Village, N.S., Can.	D6	87
Great Wall see Chang Cheng, hist., China	B2	30
Great Wass Island, i., Me., U.S.	D5	112
Great Yarmouth, Eng., U.K.	D7	12
Great Zab, stm., Asia	D10	44
Gréboun, mtn., Niger	C6	50
Greece, N.Y., U.S.	B3	125
Greece, ctry., Eur.	E8	18
Greeley, Co., U.S.	A6	99
Greeley, Pa., U.S.	D12	131
Greeley, co., Ks., U.S.	D2	109
Greeley, co., Ne., U.S.	C7	120
Green, Or., U.S.	D3	130
Green, co., Ky., U.S.	C4	110
Green, co., Wi., U.S.	F4	142
Green, stm., Il., U.S.	B4	106
Green, stm., Ky., U.S.	C2	110
Green, stm., Wa., U.S.	B3	140
Green, stm., U.S.	D6	92
Green, stm., U.S.	F3	138
Green Acres, De., U.S.	h8	101
Greenacres, Wa., U.S.	B8	140
Greenacres City, Fl., U.S.	F6	102
Greenback, Tn., U.S.	D9	135
Green Bay, Wi., U.S.	D6	142
Green Bay, b., B10		92
Green Bay, b., U.S.	D3	115
Greenbelt, Md., U.S.	C4	113
Greenbrier, Ar., U.S.	B3	97
Greenbrier, Tn., U.S.	A5	135
Greenbrier, co., W.V., U.S.	D4	141
Greenbrier, stm., W.V., U.S.	D4	141
Greenbush, Mn., U.S.	B2	116
Greencastle, In., U.S.	E4	107
Greencastle, Pa., U.S.	G6	131
Green City, Mo., U.S.	A5	118
Green Cove Springs, Fl., U.S.	C5	102
Greendale, In., U.S.	F8	107
Greendale, Wi., U.S.	F6	142
Greene, Ia., U.S.	B5	108
Greene, N.Y., U.S.	C5	125
Greene, co., Al., U.S.	C1	94
Greene, co., Ar., U.S.	A5	97
Greene, co., Ga., U.S.	C3	103
Greene, co., Ia., U.S.	B3	108
Greene, co., Il., U.S.	D3	106
Greene, co., In., U.S.	F4	107
Greene, co., Mo., U.S.	D4	118
Greene, co., Ms., U.S.	D5	117
Greene, co., N.C., U.S.	B5	126
Greene, co., N.Y., U.S.	C6	125
Greene, co., Oh., U.S.	C2	128
Greene, co., Pa., U.S.	G1	131
Greene, co., Tn., U.S.	C11	135
Greene, co., Va., U.S.	B4	139
Greeneville, Tn., U.S.	C11	135
Green Fall, stm., U.S.	F1	132
Greenfield, Ca., U.S.	D3	98
Greenfield, Ia., U.S.	C3	108
Greenfield, Il., U.S.	D3	106
Greenfield, In., U.S.	E6	107
Greenfield, Ma., U.S.	A2	114
Greenfield, Mo., U.S.	D4	118
Greenfield, N.H., U.S.	E3	122
Greenfield, Oh., U.S.	C2	128
Greenfield, Tn., U.S.	A3	135
Greenfield, Wi., U.S.	n12	142
Greenfield Plaza, Ia., U.S.	e8	108
Green Forest, Ar., U.S.	A2	97
Green Harbor, Ma., U.S.	B6	114
Green Hill Pond, l., R.I., U.S.	G3	132
Greenhills, Oh., U.S.	n12	128
Green Lake, Wi., U.S.	E5	142
Green Lake, co., Wi., U.S.	E4	142
Green Lake, l., Me., U.S.	D4	112
Green Lake, l., Wi., U.S.	E5	142
Greenland, Ar., U.S.	B1	97
Greenland, N.H., U.S.	D5	122
Greenland, dep., N.A.	D30	82
Greenland Basin	D23	144
Greenland Sea	B9	46
Greenlee, co., Az., U.S.	D6	96
Green Lookout Mountain, mtn., Wa., U.S.	D3	140
Green Mountain, mtn., Wy., U.S.	D5	143
Green Mountain Reservoir, res., Co., U.S.	B4	99
Green Mountains, mts., Vt., U.S.	F2	138
Greenock, Scot., U.K.	C4	12
Greenock, Pa., U.S.	F2	131
Green Peter Lake, res., Or., U.S.	C4	130
Green Pond, Al., U.S.	B2	94
Green Pond, l., N.J., U.S.	A4	123
Greenport, N.Y., U.S.	m16	125
Green River, Ut., U.S.	E5	137
Green River, Wy., U.S.	E3	143
Green River Lake, res., Ky., U.S.	C4	110
Green River Lock and Dam, U.S.	I2	107
Green River Reservoir, res., Vt., U.S.	B3	138
Green Rock, Il., U.S.	B3	106
Greensboro, Al., U.S.	C2	94
Greensboro, Ga., U.S.	C3	103
Greensboro, Md., U.S.	C6	113
Greensboro, N.C., U.S.	A3	126
Greensburg, In., U.S.	F7	107
Greensburg, Ks., U.S.	E4	109
Greensburg, Ky., U.S.	C4	110
Greensburg, Pa., U.S.	F2	131
Greens Peak, mtn., Az., U.S.	C6	96
Greensville, co., Va., U.S.	D5	139
Green Swamp, sw., N.C., U.S.	C4	126
Greentown, In., U.S.	D6	107
Greenup, Il., U.S.	D5	106
Greenup, Ky., U.S.	B7	110
Greenup, co., Ky., U.S.	B7	110
Green Valley, Az., U.S.	F5	96
Greenview, Il., U.S.	C4	106
Greenville, Lib.	E3	50
Greenville, Al., U.S.	D3	94
Greenville, Ca., U.S.	B3	98
Greenville, De., U.S.	A3	101
Greenville, Ga., U.S.	C2	103
Greenville, Il., U.S.	E4	106
Greenville, Ky., U.S.	C2	110
Greenville, Me., U.S.	C3	112
Greenville, Mi., U.S.	E5	115
Greenville, Ms., U.S.	B2	117
Greenville, N.C., U.S.	B5	126
Greenville, N.H., U.S.	E3	122
Greenville, Oh., U.S.	B1	128
Greenville, Pa., U.S.	D1	131
Greenville, R.I., U.S.	C3	132
Greenville, S.C., U.S.	B3	133
Greenville, Tx., U.S.	C4	136
Greenville, co., S.C., U.S.	B3	133
Greenville Creek, stm., Oh., U.S.	B1	128
Greenville Junction, Me., U.S.	C3	112
Greenwich, Ct., U.S.	E1	100
Greenwich, N.Y., U.S.	B7	125
Greenwich, Oh., U.S.	A3	128
Greenwich Bay, b., R.I., U.S.	D4	132
Greenwich Point, c., Ct., U.S.	E1	100
Greenwood, B.C., Can.	E8	85
Greenwood, Ar., U.S.	B1	97
Greenwood, De., U.S.	E3	101
Greenwood, In., U.S.	E5	107
Greenwood, La., U.S.	B2	111
Greenwood, Mo., U.S.	k11	118
Greenwood, Ms., U.S.	B3	117
Greenwood, Pa., U.S.	E5	131
Greenwood, S.C., U.S.	C3	133
Greenwood, Wi., U.S.	D3	142
Greenwood, co., Ks., U.S.	E7	109
Greenwood, co., S.C., U.S.	C3	133
Greenwood, Lake, res., In., U.S.	G4	107
Greenwood, Lake, res., S.C., U.S.	C3	133
Greenwood Lake, N.Y., U.S.	D6	125
Greenwood Lake, l., Mn., U.S.	C7	116
Greenwood Lake, l., U.S.	A4	123
Greer, S.C., U.S.	B3	133
Greer, co., Ok., U.S.	C2	129
Greers Ferry Lake, res., Ar., U.S.	B3	97
Greeson, Lake, res., Ar., U.S.	C2	97
Gregg, co., Tx., U.S.	C5	136

Name	Map Ref.	Page
Gregory, S.D., U.S.	D6	134
Gregory, co., S.D., U.S.	D6	134
Gregory Range, mts., Austl.	D3	62
Greifswald, Ger.	C13	12
Greilickville, Mi., U.S.	D5	115
Gremiha, Russia	E6	26
Grenada, Ms., U.S.	B4	117
Grenada, co., Ms., U.S.	B4	117
Grenada, ctry., N.A.	F12	76
Grenada Lake, res., Ms., U.S.	B4	117
Grenadines, is., N.A.	F12	76
Grenen, c., Den.	H4	10
Grenoble, Fr.	E9	16
Grenville, P.Q., Can.	D3	90
Grenville, Cape, c., Austl.	C3	62
Grenville, Point, c., Wa., U.S.	B1	140
Gresham, Or., U.S.	B4	130
Gresik, Indon.	E4	36
Gresik, Indon.	D2	36
Gretna, Mb., Can.	E3	86
Gretna, Fl., U.S.	B2	102
Gretna, La., U.S.	E5	111
Gretna, Ne., U.S.	C9	120
Gretna, Va., U.S.	D3	139
Grevená, Grc.	D8	18
Grey, stm., Nf., Can.	E3	88
Greybull, Wy., U.S.	B4	143
Greybull, stm., Wy., U.S.	B4	143
Greylock, Mount, mtn., Ma., U.S.	A1	114
Greymouth, N.Z.	p13	63c
Grey Range, mts., Austl.	F3	62
Greys, stm., Wy., U.S.	C2	143
Greytown, S. Afr.	D5	56
Gridley, Ca., U.S.	C3	98
Gridley, Il., U.S.	C5	106
Griffin, Ga., U.S.	C2	103
Griffiss Air Force Base, mil., N.Y., U.S.	B5	125
Griffith, Austl.	G4	62
Griffith, In., U.S.	A3	107
Grifton, N.C., U.S.	B5	126
Griggs, co., N.D., U.S.	B7	127
Griggsville, Il., U.S.	D3	106
Grim, Cape, c., Austl.	I3	62
Grimes, Ia., U.S.	C4	108
Grimes, co., Tx., U.S.	D4	136
Grimsby, On., Can.	D5	89
Grimsby, Eng., U.K.	D7	12
Grímsey, i., Ice.	k20	10a
Grimshaw, Ab., Can.	A2	84
Grimsley, Tn., U.S.	C9	135
Grímstaðir, Ice.	l20	10a
Grindall Creek, Va., U.S.	n18	139
Grinnell, Ia., U.S.	C5	108
Griswold, Ia., U.S.	C2	108
Grizzly Mountain, mtn., Id., U.S.	B2	105
Grizzly Mountain, mtn., Or., U.S.	C6	130
Grizzly Mountain, mtn., Wa., U.S.	A7	140
Grjazi, Russia	C15	20
Grjazovec, Russia	C7	22
Groais Island, i., Nf., Can.	C4	88
Groblersdal, S. Afr.	D4	56
Grodno see Hrodono, Bela.	C7	20
Groesbeck, Tx., U.S.	D4	136
Groningen, Neth.	D10	12
Groom Lake, l., Nv., U.S.	F6	121
Groom Range, mts., Nv., U.S.	F6	121
Groote Eylandt, i., Austl.	C6	60
Grootfontein, Nmb.	B2	56
Gros Morne National Park, Nf., Can.	D3	88
Grosse Isle Naval Air Station, mil., Mi., U.S.	p15	115
Grosse Pointe Park, Mi., U.S.	p16	115
Grosse Pointe Woods, Mi., U.S.	p16	115
Grosseto, Italy	C3	18
Grossglockner, mtn., Aus.	G13	12
Grossmont, Ca., U.S.	o16	98
Gros Ventre, stm., Wy., U.S.	C2	143
Gros Ventre Range, mts., Wy., U.S.	C2	143
Groswater Bay, b., Nf., Can.	H28	82
Groton, Ct., U.S.	D7	100
Groton, N.Y., U.S.	C4	125
Groton, S.D., U.S.	B7	134
Groton Long Point, Ct., U.S.	D7	100
Grottoes, Va., U.S.	B4	139
Grouse Creek, stm., Ut., U.S.	B2	137
Grouse Creek Mountain, mtn., Id., U.S.	E5	105
Grove, Ok., U.S.	A7	129
Grove City, Fl., U.S.	F4	102
Grove City, Oh., U.S.	C2	128
Grove City, Pa., U.S.	D1	131
Grove Hill, Al., U.S.	D2	94
Groveland, Fl., U.S.	D5	102
Groveland, Ma., U.S.	A5	114
Grove Mountains, mts., Ant.	D12	67
Grove Point, c., Md., U.S.	B5	113
Groveport, Oh., U.S.	C3	128
Grover City, Ca., U.S.	E3	98
Groves, Tx., U.S.	E6	136
Groveton, N.H., U.S.	A3	122
Groveton, Tx., U.S.	D5	136
Groveton, Va., U.S.	g12	139
Grovetown, Ga., U.S.	C4	103
Groveville, N.J., U.S.	C3	123
Growa Point, c., Lib.	F3	50
Growler Peak, mtn., Az., U.S.	E2	96
Groznyj, Russia	E6	26
Grudziądz, Pol.	C5	20
Gruetli-Laager, Tn., U.S.	D8	135
Grulla, Tx., U.S.	F3	136
Grünau, Nmb.	D2	56
Grundy, Va., U.S.	e9	139
Grundy, co., Ia., U.S.	B5	108
Grundy, co., Il., U.S.	B5	106
Grundy, co., Mo., U.S.	A4	118
Grundy, co., Tn., U.S.	D8	135
Grundy Center, Ia., U.S.	B5	108
Grunthal, Mb., Can.	E3	86
Gruver, Tx., U.S.	A2	136
Guacanayabo, Golfo de, b., Cuba	A4	80
Guadalajara, Mex.	C4	78
Guadalajara, Spain	G5	16
Guadalcanal, i., Sol. Is.	B6	62
Guadalquivir, stm., Spain	I4	16
Guadalquivir, Marismas del, sw., Spain	I3	16
Guadalupe, Mex.	C4	78
Guadalupe, Mex.	B4	78
Guadalupe, Az., U.S.	m9	96
Guadalupe, Ca., U.S.	E3	98
Guadalupe, co., N.M., U.S.	C5	124
Guadalupe, co., Tx., U.S.	E4	136
Guadalupe, Isla, i., Mex.	B1	78
Guadalupe Mountains, mts., U.S.	E5	124
Guadalupe Mountains National Park, Tx., U.S.	o12	136
Guadalupe Peak, mtn., Tx., U.S.	o12	136
Guadeloupe, dep., N.A.	E12	76
Guadeloupe Passage, strt., N.A.	B7	80
Guadiana, stm., Eur.	I5	16
Guadix, Spain	I5	16
Guaíra, Braz.	C7	72
Guajará-Mirim, Braz.	F6	70
Guaje, Laguna del, l., Mex.	B4	78
Gualeguay, Arg.	E6	72
Gualeguaychú, Arg.	E6	72
Guam, dep., Oc.	D12	32
Guaminí, Arg.	F5	72
Guamúchil, Mex.	B3	78
Guanaja, Isla de, i., Hond.	B2	80
Guanajuato, Mex.	C4	78
Guanajuato, state, Mex.	C4	78
Guanambi, Braz.	D3	74
Guanare, Ven.	B6	70
Guane, Cuba	A3	80
Guang'an, China	E9	28
Guangde, China	C4	30
Guangdong, state, China	G10	28
Guangji, China	D4	30
Guangling, China	B3	30
Guangnan, China	G8	28
Guangxi Zhuangzu Zizhiqu, state, China	G9	28
Guangyuan, China	E9	28
Guangzhou (Canton), China	E3	30
Guano Lake, l., Or., U.S.	E7	130
Guantánamo, Cuba	A4	80
Guantao, China	B4	30
Guanxian, China	E8	28
Guanyun, China	C4	30
Guapí, Col.	C4	70
Guápiles, C.R.	C3	80
Guaporé, stm., S.A.	F7	70
Guarabira, Braz.	C4	74
Guarapari, Braz.	F3	74
Guarapuava, Braz.	D7	72
Guaratuba, Braz.	D8	72
Guarda, Port.	G3	16
Guardafui, Cape see Gwardafuy, Gees, c., Som.	H15	48
Guardo, Spain	F4	16
Guarenas, Ven.	C6	80
Guárico, stm., Ven.	D6	80
Guasave, Mex.	B3	78
Guasdualito, Ven.	B5	70
Guasipati, Ven.	B7	70
Guatemala, Guat.	C1	80
Guatemala, ctry., N.A.	D6	78
Guatemala Basin	G29	64
Guaviare, stm., Col.	C6	70
Guaxupé, Braz.	F2	74
Guayana see Ciudad Guayana, Ven.	B7	70
Guayana see Guyana, ctry., S.A.	B8	70
Guayape, stm., Hond.	C2	80
Guayaquil, Ec.	D3	70
Guayaquil, Golfo de, b., S.A.	D3	70
Guaymallén, Arg.	E4	72
Guaymas, Mex.	B2	78
Gubaha, Russia	C10	22
Gubbio, Italy	C4	18
Guben, Ger.	E14	12
Guben (Gubin), Pol.	D3	20
Gubin (Guben), Pol.	D3	20
Gubkin, Russia	G5	20
Gudauta, Geor.	A9	44
Gudermes, Russia	B5	42
Gudivāda, India	F4	40
Gudiyāttam, India	G3	40
Gūdūr, India	G3	40
Guékédou, Gui.	E2	50
Guélengdeng, Chad	D8	50
Guelma, Alg.	D5	14
Guelph, On., Can.	D4	89
Guercif, Mor.	E3	14
Güere, stm., Ven.	D7	80
Guéret, Fr.	D7	16
Guernsey, Wy., U.S.	D8	143
Guernsey, co., Oh., U.S.	B4	128
Guernsey, dep., Eur.	F5	12
Guerrero, Mex.	B3	78
Guerrero, state, Mex.	D4	78
Guerrero Negro, Mex.	B2	78
Gueydan, La., U.S.	D3	111
Guga, Russia	D15	26
Gugē, mtn., Eth.	B7	54
Guguan, i., N. Mar. Is.	C12	32
Guiana Basin	G9	64
Guide, China	D8	28
Guiding, China	D2	30
Guildford, Eng., U.K.	E6	12
Guilford, Ct., U.S.	D5	100
Guilford, Me., U.S.	C3	112
Guilford, co., N.C., U.S.	A3	126
Guilin, China	F10	28
Guimarães, Port.	G2	16
Guimaras Island, i., Phil.	D8	34
Guin, Al., U.S.	B2	94
Guinea, ctry., Afr.	D2	50
Guinea, Gulf of, b., Afr.	I10	46
Guinea Basin	H13	66
Guinea-Bissau, ctry., Afr.	D1	50
Güines, Cuba	A3	80
Guingamp, Fr.	C5	16
Guiping, China	E3	30
Güira de Melena, Cuba	A3	80
Guiratinga, Braz.	B7	72
Güiria, Ven.	A7	70
Guitry, C. Iv.	E3	50
Guiuan, Phil.	D9	34
Guixi, China	D4	30
Guixian, China	G9	28
Guiyang, China	F9	28
Guizhou, state, China	F9	28
Gujarāt, prov., India	E2	40
Gujrānwāla, Pak.	D10	42
Gujrāt, Pak.	D10	42
Gulbarga, India	F3	40
Gulbene, Lat.	H12	10
Gulf, co., Fl., U.S.	C1	102
Gulf, The see Persian Gulf, b., Asia	E6	42
Gulf Gate Estates, Fl., U.S.	E4	102
Gulf Islands National Seashore, U.S.	E5	117
Gulf of Alaska Seamount Province	B1	144
Gulfport, Fl., U.S.	E4	102
Gulfport, Ms., U.S.	E4	117
Gulf Shores, Al., U.S.	E2	94
Gulgong, Austl.	G4	62
Gulian, China	A12	28
Gulistan, Uzb.	B9	42
Gullfoss, wtfl, Ice.	I19	10a
Gull Island, i., N.C., U.S.	B7	126
Gullivan Bay, b., Fl., U.S.	G5	102
Gull Lake, l., Ab., Can.	C4	84
Gull Lake, l., Mn., U.S.	D4	116
Güllük Körfezi, b., Tur.	D2	44
Gulu, Ug.	C6	54
Gumboro, De., U.S.	G4	101
Gumdag, Turk.	C6	42
Gumel, Nig.	D6	50
Gumi, Nig.	D6	50
Gummi, Nig.	D6	50
Gümüşhane, Tur.	B8	44
Guna, India	E3	40
Gundagai, Austl.	H4	62
Gundji, D.R.C.	C4	54
Gungu, D.R.C.	E3	54
Gunisao, stm., Mb., Can.	C3	86
Gunmi, Nig.	D6	50
Gunnbjørn Fjeld, mtn., Grnld.	E34	82
Gunnedah, Austl.	G5	62
Gunnison, Ms., U.S.	B3	117
Gunnison, Ut., U.S.	D4	137
Gunnison, co., Co., U.S.	C3	99
Gunnison, stm., Co., U.S.	C2	99
Gunnison, Mount, mtn., Co., U.S.	C3	99
Gunpowder Neck, c., Md., U.S.	B5	113
Gunpowder River, b., Md., U.S.	B5	113
Guntakal, India	F3	40
Gunter Air Force Base, mil., Al., U.S.	C3	94
Guntersville, Al., U.S.	A3	94
Guntersville Lake, res., Al., U.S.	A3	94
Guntown, Ms., U.S.	A5	117
Guntūr, India	F4	40
Gunungsitoli, Indon.	C1	36
Guoyang, China	C4	30
Gupis, Pak.	C10	42
Gurdon, Ar., U.S.	D2	97
Gurdžaani, Geor.	B11	44
Gurley, Al., U.S.	A3	94
Gurnee, Il., U.S.	h9	106
Gurnet Point, c., Ma., U.S.	B6	114
Gürün, Tur.	C7	44
Gurupi, Braz.	D2	74
Gurupi, stm., Braz.	B2	74
Gusau, Nig.	D6	50
Gusev, Russia	B7	20
Gușgy, Turk.	F8	26
Gushi, China	C4	30
Gusinoozersk, Russia	A9	28
Guspini, Italy	E2	18
Gustav Holm, Kap, c., Grnld.	E33	82
Gustine, Ca., U.S.	D3	98
Güstrow, Ger.	D13	12
Guthrie, Ky., U.S.	D2	110
Guthrie, Ok., U.S.	B4	129
Guthrie, W.V., U.S.	m12	141
Guthrie, co., Ia., U.S.	C3	108
Guthrie Center, Ia., U.S.	C3	108
Guttenberg, Ia., U.S.	B6	108
Guttenberg, N.J., U.S.	h8	123
Guwāhāti, India	D6	40
Guyana, ctry., S.A.	B8	70
Guyandotte, stm., W.V., U.S.	C2	141
Guyang, China	A3	30
Guymon, Ok., U.S.	e9	129
Guysborough, N.S., Can.	D8	87
Guyton, Ga., U.S.	D5	103
Guyuan, China	D9	28
Guzar, Uzb.	C9	42
Güzelyurt Körfezi, b., N. Cyp.	E5	44
Guzmán, Mex.	D4	78
Gwaai, Zimb.	B4	56
Gwādar, Pak.	E8	42
Gwalia, Austl.	F3	60
Gwalior, India	D3	40
Gwanda, Zimb.	C4	56
Gwardafuy, Gees, c., Som.	H15	48
Gwayi, stm., Zimb.	B4	56
Gweru, Zimb.	B4	56
Gweta, Bots.	C4	56
Gwinhurst, De., U.S.	h8	101
Gwinn, Mi., U.S.	B3	115
Gwinner, N.D., U.S.	C8	127
Gwinnett, co., Ga., U.S.	C2	103
Gwydyr Bay, b., Ak., U.S.	A10	95
Gwynns Falls, stm., Md., U.S.	g10	113
Gyangzê, China	F5	28
Gyaring Co, l., China	E5	28
Gyaring Hu, l., China	E7	28
Gyda, Russia	B9	26
Gydanskij poluostrov, pen., Russia	B9	26
Gyldenløves Fjord, b., Grnld.	F31	82
Gympie, Austl.	F5	62
Gyöngyös, Hung.	F5	20
Győr, Hung.	F4	20
Gypsum, Co., U.S.	B4	99
Gyzylarbat, Turk.	F7	26

H

Name	Map Ref.	Page
Haakon, co., S.D., U.S.	C4	134
Haapsalu, Est.	G10	10
Haarlem, Neth.	D9	12
Haast, N.Z.	p12	63c
Habarovo, Russia	A11	22
Habarovsk, Russia	E15	26
Ḥabbānīyah, Buḥayrat al-, res., Iraq	F10	44
Habersham, co., Ga., U.S.	B3	103
Hachijō-jima, i., Japan	E15	28
Hachinohe, Japan	C16	28
Hachiōji, Japan	C3	31
Hackberry, La., U.S.	E2	111
Hackensack, N.J., U.S.	B4	123
Hackensack, stm., N.J., U.S.	h8	123
Hackettstown, N.J., U.S.	B3	123
Hackleburg, Al., U.S.	A2	94
Haddam, Ct., U.S.	D5	100
Haddock, Ga., U.S.	C3	103
Haddonfield, N.J., U.S.	D2	123
Haddon Heights, N.J., U.S.	D2	123
Hadejia, Nig.	D7	50
Hadejia, stm., Nig.	D6	50
Hadera, Isr.	F6	44
Haderslev, Den.	I3	10
Hadībū, Yemen	H6	38
Ḥadīthah, Iraq	D4	42
Hadjout, Alg.	I8	16
Hadley Lake, l., Me., U.S.	D5	112
Hadrian's Wall, eng., U.K.	C5	12
Haeju, N. Kor.	D13	28
Hafik, Tur.	C7	44
Hafnarfjörður, Ice.	I17	10a
Haft Gel, Iran	D5	42
Hagan, La., U.S.	D5	103
Hagemeister Island, i., Ak., U.S.	D7	95
Hagerman, Id., U.S.	G4	105
Hagerman, N.M., U.S.	D5	124
Hagerstown, In., U.S.	E7	107
Hagerstown, Md., U.S.	A2	113
Hagfors, Swe.	F5	10
Haggin, Mount, mtn., Mt., U.S.	D3	119
Hagi, Japan	D2	31
Ha Giang, Viet.	B5	34
Hague, Neth.	D9	12
Hague, Sk., Can.	E2	91
Haguenau, Fr.	C10	16
Hagues Peak, mtn., Co., U.S.	A5	99
Ha! Ha!, Baie des, b., P.Q., Can.	C2	88
Hahira, Ga., U.S.	F3	103
Hahnville, La., U.S.	E5	111
Haicheng, China	A5	30
Hai Duong, Viet.	B5	34
Haifa see Ḥefa, Isr.	D2	42
Haig, Austl.	G4	60
Haikang, China	E3	30
Haikou, China	G10	28
Haiku, Hi., U.S.	C5	104
Ḥā'il, Sau. Ar.	E4	38
Hailar, China	B11	28
Hailey, Id., U.S.	F4	105
Haileybury, On., Can.	p20	89
Haileyville, Ok., U.S.	C6	129
Hailin, China	B1	31
Hailun, China	B13	28
Haimen, China	F12	28
Haimen, China	E4	30
Hainan, prov., China	H9	28
Hainan Dao, i., China	H9	28
Hainan Dao see Hainan Dao, i., China	H9	28
Haines, Ak., U.S.	D12	95
Haines City, Fl., U.S.	D5	102
Haining, China	C5	30
Hai Ninh, Viet.	B5	34
Hai Phong, Viet.	B5	34
Haisyn, Ukr.	E10	20
Haiti, ctry., N.A.	H12	75
Haitun, China	B7	40
Haiyang, China	B2	30
Haizhou, China	E11	28
Haizhou Wan, b., China	B4	30
Hajdúböszörmény, Hung.	F6	20
Hajnówka, Pol.	C7	20
Hakkâri, Tur.	D10	44
Hakodate, Japan	C16	28
Ḥalab (Aleppo), Syria	D7	44
Halachó, Mex.	C6	78
Halā'ib, Sudan	F12	48
Halawa, Cape, c., Hi., U.S.	B5	104
Halawa Heights, Hi., U.S.	g10	104
Halberstadt, Ger.	E12	12
Halden, Nor.	G4	10
Haldimand, On., Can.	E5	89
Haldwāni, India	D3	40
Hale, co., Al., U.S.	C2	94
Hale, co., Tx., U.S.	B2	136
Haleakala Crater, crat., Hi., U.S.	C5	104
Haleakala National Park, Hi., U.S.	C6	104
Hale Center, Tx., U.S.	B2	136
Haleiwa, Hi., U.S.	B3	104
Hales Corners, Wi., U.S.	n11	142
Halethorpe, Md., U.S.	B4	113
Haleyville, Al., U.S.	A2	94
Half Moon Bay, Ca., U.S.	k8	98
Halfway, Md., U.S.	A2	113
Haliburton, On., Can.	B6	89
Halibut Point, c., Ma., U.S.	A6	114
Halicarnassus, hist., Tur.	D2	44
Halifax, N.S., Can.	E6	87
Halifax, Va., U.S.	D4	139
Halifax, co., N.C., U.S.	A5	126
Halifax, co., Va., U.S.	D4	139
Haliimaile, Hi., U.S.	C5	104
Hall, co., Ga., U.S.	B3	103
Hall, co., Ne., U.S.	D7	120
Hall, co., Tx., U.S.	B2	136
Halla, Mount see Halla-san, mtn., S. Kor.	E13	28
Hallam Peak, mtn., B.C., Can.	C8	85
Hallandale, Fl., U.S.	G6	102
Ḥallānīyah, Juzur al-, is., Oman	G7	38
Halla-san, mtn., S. Kor.	E13	28
Halle, Ger.	E12	12
Hällefors, Swe.	F6	10
Hallein, Aus.	G13	12
Hallettsville, Tx., U.S.	E4	136
Hallie, Wi., U.S.	D2	142
Hall Island, i., Ak., U.S.	C5	95
Hall Meadow Brook Reservoir, res., Ct., U.S.	B3	100
Hall Mountain, mtn., Wa., U.S.	A8	140
Hallock, Mn., U.S.	B2	116
Hallowell, Me., U.S.	D3	112
Halls, Tn., U.S.	B2	135
Hallsberg, Swe.	G6	10
Halls Creek, Austl.	C4	60
Halls Creek, stm., Ut., U.S.	F5	137
Halls Crossroads, Tn., U.S.	m14	135
Halls Stream, stm., N.H., U.S.	f7	122
Hallstahammar, Swe.	G7	10
Hallstead, Pa., U.S.	C10	131
Hallsville, Mo., U.S.	B5	118
Hallsville, Tx., U.S.	C5	136
Halmahera, i., Indon.	C7	36
Halmahera, i., Indon. (Halmahera Sea), Indon.	D7	36
Halmahera Sea see Halmahera, Laut, Indon.	D7	36
Hal'mer-Ju, Russia	A11	22
Halmstad, Swe.	H5	10
Halsey, Or., U.S.	C3	130
Hälsingland, hist. reg., Swe.	F7	10
Halstad, Mn., U.S.	C2	116
Halstead, Ks., U.S.	E6	109

Name	Map Ref.	Page
Haltiatunturi, mtn., Eur.	B9	10
Halton Hills, On., Can.	D5	89
Hamada, Japan	D2	31
Hamadān, Iran	D5	42
Ḥamāh, Syria	E7	44
Ḥamāh, state, Syria	E7	44
Hamamatsu, Japan	E15	28
Hamar, Nor.	F4	10
Hamarøya, Nor.	B6	10
Hambantota, Sri L.	H4	40
Hamblen, co., Tn., U.S.	C10	135
Hamburg, Ger.	D12	12
Hamburg, Ar., U.S.	D4	97
Hamburg, Ia., U.S.	D2	108
Hamburg, N.Y., U.S.	C2	125
Hamburg, Pa., U.S.	E10	131
Hamden, Ct., U.S.	D4	100
Hamden, Oh., U.S.	C3	128
Hämeenlinna, Fin.	F11	10
Hamel, Mn., U.S.	m11	116
Hameln, Ger.	D11	12
Hamersley Range, mts., Austl.	E2	60
Hami, China	C6	28
Hamilton, Austl.	H3	62
Hamilton, Ber.	B12	76
Hamilton, N.Z.	o14	63c
Hamilton, Al., U.S.	A2	94
Hamilton, Il., U.S.	C2	106
Hamilton, In., U.S.	A8	107
Hamilton, Mi., U.S.	F4	115
Hamilton, Mo., U.S.	B3	118
Hamilton, Ms., U.S.	B5	117
Hamilton, Mt., U.S.	D2	119
Hamilton, N.Y., U.S.	C5	125
Hamilton, Oh., U.S.	C1	128
Hamilton, Tx., U.S.	D3	136
Hamilton, Va., U.S.	A5	139
Hamilton, co., Fl., U.S.	B3	102
Hamilton, co., Ia., U.S.	B4	108
Hamilton, co., Il., U.S.	E5	106
Hamilton, co., In., U.S.	D5	107
Hamilton, co., Ks., U.S.	E2	109
Hamilton, co., Ne., U.S.	D7	120
Hamilton, co., N.Y., U.S.	B6	125
Hamilton, co., Oh., U.S.	C1	128
Hamilton, co., Tn., U.S.	D8	135
Hamilton, co., Tx., U.S.	D3	136
Hamilton, Lake, res., Ar., U.S.	C2	97
Hamilton, Mount, mtn., Ak., U.S.	C8	95
Hamilton, Mount, mtn., Ca., U.S.	k9	98
Hamilton, Mount, mtn., Nv., U.S.	D6	121
Hamilton Inlet, b., Nf., Can.	A2	88
Hamilton Reservoir, res., Ma., U.S.	B3	114
Hamilton Sound, strt., Nf., Can.	D4	88
Hamilton Square, N.J., U.S.	C3	123
Hamina, Fin.	F12	10
Hamiota, Mb., Can.	D1	86
Hamīrpur, India	D4	40
Hamlet, In., U.S.	B4	107
Hamlet, N.C., U.S.	C3	126
Hamlet, Mount, mtn., Ak., U.S.	B6	95
Hamlin, Pa., U.S.	D11	131
Hamlin, Tx., U.S.	C2	136
Hamlin, W.V., U.S.	C2	141
Hamlin, co., S.D., U.S.	C8	134
Hamlin Lake, l., Mi., U.S.	D4	115
Hamm, Ger.	E10	12
Hammamet, Tun.	F3	18
Hammamet, Golfe de, b., Tun.	F3	18
Hammam Lif, Tun.	F3	18
Ḥammār, Hawr al-, l., Iraq	G12	44
Hammerfest, Nor.	A10	10
Hammon, Ok., U.S.	B2	129
Hammonasset, stm., Ct., U.S.	D5	100
Hammonasset Point, c., Ct., U.S.	E5	100
Hammond, In., U.S.	A2	107
Hammond, La., U.S.	D5	111
Hammond, Wi., U.S.	D1	142
Hammond Bay, b., Mi., U.S.	C6	115
Hammonton, N.J., U.S.	D3	123
Hamningberg, Nor.	A14	10
Hampden, Nf., Can.	D3	88
Hampden, Me., U.S.	D4	112
Hampden, co., Ma., U.S.	B2	114
Hampden Highlands, Me., U.S.	D4	112
Hampshire, Il., U.S.	A5	106
Hampshire, co., Ma., U.S.	B2	114
Hampshire, co., W.V., U.S.	B6	141
Hampstead, Md., U.S.	A4	113
Hampstead, N.C., U.S.	C5	126
Hampton, N.B., Can.	D4	87
Hampton, Ar., U.S.	D3	97
Hampton, Ga., U.S.	C2	103
Hampton, Ia., U.S.	B4	108
Hampton, N.H., U.S.	E5	122
Hampton, S.C., U.S.	F5	133
Hampton, Tn., U.S.	C11	135
Hampton, Va., U.S.	C6	139
Hampton, co., S.C., U.S.	F5	133
Hampton Bays, N.Y., U.S.	n16	125
Hampton Beach, N.H., U.S.	E5	122
Hampton Butte, mtn., Or., U.S.	D6	130
Hampton Roads, Va., U.S.	k15	139
Hampton Roads Bridge-Tunnel, Va., U.S.	k15	139
Ḥamrā', Al-Ḥamādah al-, des., Libya	F6	14
Hamra, As Saquia al, stm., W. Sah.	A2	50
Hams Fork, stm., Wy., U.S.	E2	143
Hamtramck, Mi., U.S.	p15	115
Ḥāmūn, Daryācheh-ye, l., Iran	D8	42
Han, stm., China	E9	28
Hana, Hi., U.S.	C6	104
Hanahan, S.C., U.S.	F7	133
Hanalei Bay, b., Hi., U.S.	A2	104
Hanamaki, Japan	D16	28
Hanamaulu, Hi., U.S.	B2	104
Hanapepe, Hi., U.S.	B2	104
Hânceşti, Mol.	F10	20
Hanceville, Al., U.S.	A3	94
Hancheng, China	D10	28
Hancock, Md., U.S.	A1	113
Hancock, Mi., U.S.	A2	115
Hancock, Mn., U.S.	E3	116
Hancock, co., Ga., U.S.	C3	103
Hancock, co., Ia., U.S.	A4	108
Hancock, co., Il., U.S.	C2	106
Hancock, co., In., U.S.	E6	107
Hancock, co., Ky., U.S.	C3	110
Hancock, co., Me., U.S.	D4	112
Hancock, co., Ms., U.S.	E4	117
Hancock, co., Oh., U.S.	A2	128
Hancock, co., Tn., U.S.	C10	135
Hancock, co., W.V., U.S.	A4	141
Hand, co., S.D., U.S.	C6	134
Handan, China	D10	28
Handyga, Russia	C15	26
Hanford, Ca., U.S.	D4	98
Hangayn nuruu, mts., Mong.	B7	28
Hangchow see Hangzhou, China	E12	28
Hanggin Houqi, China	C9	28
Hanggin Qi, China	D9	28
Hangman Creek, stm., Wa., U.S.	B8	140
Hangokurt, Russia	B11	22
Hangu, China	B4	30
Hangzhou, China	E12	28
Hangzhou Wan, b., China	C5	30
Hanjiang, China	F11	28
Hankinson, N.D., U.S.	C9	127
Hanko, Fin.	G10	10
Hanna, Ab., Can.	D5	84
Hanna, Wy., U.S.	E6	143
Hanna City, Il., U.S.	C4	106
Hannahville Indian Reservation, Mi., U.S.	C3	115
Hannibal, Mo., U.S.	B6	118
Hannover, Ger.	D11	12
Hanöbukten, b., Swe.	I6	10
Ha Noi, Viet.	B5	34
Hanover, On., Can.	C3	89
Hanover see Hannover, Ger.	D11	12
Hanover, Il., U.S.	A3	106
Hanover, In., U.S.	G7	107
Hanover, Ks., U.S.	C7	109
Hanover, Ma., U.S.	B6	114
Hanover, Mn., U.S.	m11	116
Hanover, N.H., U.S.	C2	122
Hanover, Pa., U.S.	G8	131
Hanover, co., Va., U.S.	C5	139
Hanover Park, Il., U.S.	k8	106
Hansen, Id., U.S.	G4	105
Hansford, co., Tx., U.S.	A2	136
Hanson, Ma., U.S.	B6	114
Hanson, co., S.D., U.S.	D8	134
Hanstholm, Den.	H3	10
Hanty-Mansijsk, Russia	C8	26
Hanyin, China	C2	30
Hanzhong, China	E9	28
Haora, India	E5	40
Haparanda, Swe.	D11	10
Hapčeranga, Russia	E13	26
Hapeville, Ga., U.S.	C2	103
Happy Valley, N.M., U.S.	E5	124
Happy Valley-Goose Bay, Nf., Can.	B1	88
Hāpur, India	D3	40
Harahan, La., U.S.	k11	111
Haralson, co., Ga., U.S.	C1	103
Harare, Zimb.	B5	56
Harazé Mangueigne, Chad	B4	54
Harbala, Russia	C14	26
Harbeson, De., U.S.	F4	101
Harbin, China	B13	28
Harbor, Or., U.S.	E2	130
Harbor Beach, Mi., U.S.	E8	115
Harborcreek, Pa., U.S.	B2	131
Harbor Springs, Mi., U.S.	C6	115
Harbour Breton, Nf., Can.	E4	88
Harbour Grace, Nf., Can.	E5	88
Harcuvar Mountains, mts., Az., U.S.	D2	96
Hardangerfjorden, b., Nor.	F2	10
Hardee, co., Fl., U.S.	E5	102
Hardeeville, S.C., U.S.	G5	133
Hardeman, co., Tn., U.S.	B2	135
Hardeman, co., Tx., U.S.	B3	136
Hardin, Il., U.S.	D3	106
Hardin, Mt., U.S.	E9	119
Hardin, co., Ia., U.S.	B4	108
Hardin, co., Il., U.S.	F5	106
Hardin, co., Ky., U.S.	C4	110
Hardin, co., Oh., U.S.	B2	128
Hardin, co., Tn., U.S.	B3	135
Hardin, co., Tx., U.S.	D5	136
Harding, S. Afr.	E4	56
Harding, co., N.M., U.S.	B5	124
Harding, co., S.D., U.S.	B2	134
Harding, Lake, res., U.S.	C4	94
Hardinsburg, Ky., U.S.	C3	110
Hardisty, Ab., Can.	C5	84
Hardoi, India	D4	40
Hardwick, Ga., U.S.	C3	103
Hardwick, Vt., U.S.	B4	138
Hardwood Ridge, mtn., Pa., U.S.	D11	131
Hardy, co., W.V., U.S.	B6	141
Hardy Lake, res., In., U.S.	G6	107
Hare Bay, Nf., Can.	D4	88
Hare Bay, b., Nf., Can.	C4	88
Hārer, Eth.	B8	48
Hargeysa, Som.	I13	48
Har Hu, l., China	D7	28
Hari, stm., Indon.	D2	36
Haridwār, India	D3	40
Harīrūd, stm., Asia	D8	42
Harkers Island, N.C., U.S.	C6	126
Harlan, Ia., U.S.	C2	108
Harlan, In., U.S.	B8	107
Harlan, Ky., U.S.	D6	110
Harlan, co., Ky., U.S.	D6	110
Harlan, co., Ne., U.S.	D6	120
Harlan County Lake, res., Ne., U.S.	E6	120
Harlem, Fl., U.S.	F6	102
Harlem, Ga., U.S.	C4	103
Harlem, Mt., U.S.	B8	119
Harleyville, S.C., U.S.	E7	133
Harlingen, Tx., U.S.	F4	136
Harlow, Eng., U.K.	E7	12
Harlowton, Mt., U.S.	D7	119
Harmånger, Swe.	F7	10
Harmanli, Bul.	D10	18
Harmon, co., Ok., U.S.	C2	129
Harmon Creek, stm., W.V., U.S.	f8	141
Harmony, In., U.S.	E3	107
Harmony, Mn., U.S.	G6	116
Harmony, Pa., U.S.	E1	131
Harmony, R.I., U.S.	B3	132
Harnett, co., N.C., U.S.	B4	126
Harney, co., Or., U.S.	D7	130
Harney, Lake, l., Fl., U.S.	D5	102
Harney Lake, l., Or., U.S.	D7	130
Harney Peak, mtn., S.D., U.S.	D2	134
Härnösand, Swe.	E7	10
Haro Strait, strt., Wa., U.S.	A2	140
Harper, Lib.	I3	50
Harper, Ks., U.S.	E5	109
Harper, co., Ks., U.S.	E5	109
Harper, co., Ok., U.S.	A2	129
Harper, Mount, mtn., Ak., U.S.	C11	95
Harpers Ferry, W.V., U.S.	B7	141
Harpers Ferry National Historical Park, W.V., U.S.	B7	141
Harpersville, Al., U.S.	B3	94
Harpeth, stm., Tn., U.S.	A5	135
Harqin Qi, China	A4	30
Harquahala Mountain, mtn., Az., U.S.	D2	96
Harquahala Mountains, mts., Az., U.S.	D2	96
Harrah, Ok., U.S.	B4	129
Harricana, stm., Can.	H24	82
Harriman, Tn., U.S.	D9	135
Harriman Reservoir, res., Vt., U.S.	F3	138
Harrington, De., U.S.	E3	101
Harrington Park, N.J., U.S.	h9	123
Harris, Mn., U.S.	E6	116
Harris, R.I., U.S.	D3	132
Harris, co., Ga., U.S.	D2	103
Harris, co., Tx., U.S.	E5	136
Harris, Lake, l., Fl., U.S.	D5	102
Harrisburg, Ar., U.S.	B5	97
Harrisburg, Il., U.S.	F5	106
Harrisburg, Or., U.S.	C3	130
Harrisburg, Pa., U.S.	F8	131
Harrisburg, S.D., U.S.	D9	134
Harrismith, S. Afr.	D4	56
Harrison, Ar., U.S.	A2	97
Harrison, Mi., U.S.	D6	115
Harrison, N.J., U.S.	k8	123
Harrison, N.Y., U.S.	h13	125
Harrison, Oh., U.S.	C1	128
Harrison, Tn., U.S.	h11	135
Harrison, co., Ia., U.S.	C2	108
Harrison, co., In., U.S.	H5	107
Harrison, co., Ky., U.S.	B5	110
Harrison, co., Mo., U.S.	A3	118
Harrison, co., Ms., U.S.	E4	117
Harrison, co., Oh., U.S.	B4	128
Harrison, co., Tx., U.S.	C5	136
Harrison, co., W.V., U.S.	B4	141
Harrison, Cape, c., Nf., Can.	g10	88
Harrison Bay, b., Ak., U.S.	A9	95
Harrisonburg, Va., U.S.	B4	139
Harrison Hot Springs, B.C., Can.	f14	85
Harrison Lake, l., B.C., Can.	E7	85
Harrisonville, Mo., U.S.	C3	118
Harriston, On., Can.	D4	89
Harristown, Il., U.S.	D4	106
Harrisville, R.I., U.S.	B2	132
Harrisville, Ut., U.S.	C4	137
Harrisville, W.V., U.S.	B3	141
Harrodsburg, Ky., U.S.	C5	110
Harrow, On., Can.	E2	89
Harry S. Truman Reservoir, res., Mo., U.S.	C4	118
Harry Strunk Lake, res., Ne., U.S.	D5	120
Harsīn, Iran	E12	44
Harstad, Nor.	B7	10
Hart, Mi., U.S.	E4	115
Hart, Tx., U.S.	B1	136
Hart, co., Ga., U.S.	B4	103
Hart, co., Ky., U.S.	C4	110
Hart, Lake, l., Fl., U.S.	D5	102
Hartford, Al., U.S.	D4	94
Hartford, Ct., U.S.	B5	100
Hartford, Ia., U.S.	C4	108
Hartford, Il., U.S.	E3	106
Hartford, Ky., U.S.	C3	110
Hartford, Mi., U.S.	F4	115
Hartford, S.D., U.S.	D9	134
Hartford, Vt., U.S.	D4	138
Hartford, Wi., U.S.	E5	142
Hartford, co., Ct., U.S.	B4	100
Hartford City, In., U.S.	D7	107
Hartington, Ne., U.S.	B8	120
Hart Lake, l., Or., U.S.	E7	130
Hartland, N.B., Can.	C2	87
Hartland, Me., U.S.	D3	112
Hartland, Wi., U.S.	E5	142
Hartley, Ia., U.S.	A2	108
Hartley, co., Tx., U.S.	B1	136
Hartselle, Al., U.S.	A3	94
Hartshorne, Ok., U.S.	C6	129
Hartsville, S.C., U.S.	C7	133
Hartsville, Tn., U.S.	A5	135
Hartville, Oh., U.S.	B4	128
Hartwell, Ga., U.S.	B4	103
Hartwell Lake, res., U.S.	B1	133
Harvard, Il., U.S.	A5	106
Harvard, Ne., U.S.	D7	120
Harvard, Mount, mtn., Co., U.S.	C4	99
Harvey, Il., U.S.	B6	106
Harvey, La., U.S.	E5	111
Harvey, Mi., U.S.	B3	115
Harvey, N.D., U.S.	B6	127
Harvey, co., Ks., U.S.	D6	109
Harvey Lake, res., Pa., U.S.	m16	131
Harveys Creek, stm., Pa., U.S.	n16	131
Harwich, Eng., U.K.	E7	12
Harwich Port, Ma., U.S.	C7	114
Haryāna, prov., India	D3	40
Hasalbag, China	B3	40
Hasbrouck Heights, N.J., U.S.	h8	123
Haskell, Ar., U.S.	C3	97
Haskell, Ok., U.S.	B6	129
Haskell, Tx., U.S.	C3	136
Haskell, co., Ks., U.S.	E3	109
Haskell, co., Ok., U.S.	B6	129
Haskell, co., Tx., U.S.	C3	136
Haskovo, Bul.	D10	18
Hassan, India	G3	40
Hassayampa, stm., Az., U.S.	D3	96
Hasselt, Bel.	E9	12
Hassi Messaoud, Alg.	D6	48
Hässleholm, Swe.	H5	10
Hastings, On., Can.	C7	89
Hastings, N.Z.	o14	63c
Hastings, Eng., U.K.	E7	12
Hastings, Mi., U.S.	F5	115
Hastings, Mn., U.S.	F6	116
Hastings, Ne., U.S.	D7	120
Hastings, Pa., U.S.	E4	131
Hastings-on-Hudson, N.Y., U.S.	h13	125
Hašuri, Geor.	B10	44
Hatanga, Russia	B12	26
Hatanga, stm., Russia	B12	26
Hatangskij zaliv, b., Russia	B12	26
Hatay (Antioch), Tur.	D7	44
Hatch, N.M., U.S.	E2	124
Hatchet Lake, N.S., Can.	E7	87
Hatchie, stm., Tn., U.S.	B2	135
Hatchineha, Lake, l., Fl., U.S.	D5	102
Hat Creek, stm., S.D., U.S.	E2	134
Hatfield, In., U.S.	I3	107
Hatfield, Pa., U.S.	F11	131
Hatgal, Mong.	A8	28
Hāthras, India	D3	40
Ha Tinh, Viet.	C5	34
Hat Mountain, mtn., Az., U.S.	E3	96
Hatteras, N.C., U.S.	B7	126
Hatteras, Cape, c., N.C., U.S.	B7	126
Hatteras Inlet, b., N.C., U.S.	B7	126
Hattiesburg, Ms., U.S.	D4	117
Hatton, N.D., U.S.	B8	127
Hat Yai, Thai.	E4	34
Hatyrka, Russia	C19	26
Haubstadt, In., U.S.	H2	107
Haugesund, Nor.	G1	10
Haughton, La., U.S.	B2	111
Haukeligrend, Nor.	G2	10
Haukivesi, l., Fin.	E13	10
Hauser, Or., U.S.	D2	130
Haut, Isle au, i., Me., U.S.	D4	112
Haut Atlas, mts., Mor.	E2	14
Hauula, Hi., U.S.	B4	104
Havana see La Habana, Cuba	A3	80
Havana, Fl., U.S.	B2	102
Havana, Il., U.S.	C3	106
Havasu, Lake, res., U.S.	C1	96
Havasupai Indian Reservation, Az., U.S.	A3	96
Havelock, On., Can.	C7	89
Havelock, N.C., U.S.	C6	126
Havelock Island, i., India	G6	40
Haven, Ks., U.S.	E6	109
Haverford [Township], Pa., U.S.	o20	131
Haverhill, Ma., U.S.	A5	114
Haverstraw, N.Y., U.S.	D7	125
Haviland, Ks., U.S.	E4	109
Havre, Mt., U.S.	B7	119
Havre de Grace, Md., U.S.	A5	113
Havre North, Mt., U.S.	B7	119
Havza, Tur.	B6	44
Haw, stm., N.C., U.S.	B3	126
Hawaii, co., Hi., U.S.	D6	104
Hawaii, state, U.S.	C5	104
Hawaii, i., Hi., U.S.	D6	104
Hawaii, is., Hi., U.S.	i17	92a
Hawaiian Islands, is., Hi., U.S.	m14	104
Hawaiian Ridge	F22	64
Hawaii Volcanoes National Park, Hi., U.S.	D6	104
Hawarden, Ia., U.S.	A1	108
Hawera, N.Z.	o13	63c
Hawesville, Ky., U.S.	C3	110
Hawi, Hi., U.S.	C6	104
Hawke Bay, b., N.Z.	o14	63c
Hawker, Austl.	G2	62
Hawkes, Mount, mtn., Ant.	E34	67
Hawkesbury, On., Can.	B10	89
Hawkesbury Island, i., B.C., Can.	C3	85
Hawkins, co., Tn., U.S.	C11	135
Hawkinsville, Ga., U.S.	D3	103
Hawley, Mn., U.S.	D2	116
Hawley, Pa., U.S.	D11	131
Haworth, N.J., U.S.	h9	123
Haw River, N.C., U.S.	A3	126
Hawthorne, Ca., U.S.	n12	98
Hawthorne, Fl., U.S.	C4	102
Hawthorne, N.J., U.S.	B4	123
Hawthorne, Nv., U.S.	E3	121
Hawthorne, N.Y., U.S.	g13	125
Hawza, W. Sah.	A2	50
Haxtun, Co., U.S.	A8	99
Hay, Austl.	G3	62
Hayden, Az., U.S.	E5	96
Hayden, Co., U.S.	A3	99
Hayden Lake, l., Id., U.S.	B2	105
Hayes, La., U.S.	D3	111
Hayes, co., Ne., U.S.	D4	120
Hayes, stm., Mb., Can.	B5	86
Hayes, Mount, mtn., Ak., U.S.	C10	95
Hayfield, Mn., U.S.	G6	116
Hayford Peak, mtn., Nv., U.S.	G6	121
Haymock Lake, l., Me., U.S.	B3	112
Haynesville, La., U.S.	B2	111
Hayneville, Al., U.S.	C3	94
Hayrabolu, Tur.	B2	44
Hays, Ks., U.S.	D4	109
Hays, N.C., U.S.	A1	126
Hays, co., Tx., U.S.	D3	136
Hays Canyon Peak, mtn., Nv., U.S.	B2	121
Hay Springs, Ne., U.S.	B3	120
Haystack Mountain, mtn., Nv., U.S.	B6	121
Haysville, Ks., U.S.	g12	109
Hayti, Mo., U.S.	E8	118
Hayti Heights, Mo., U.S.	E8	118
Hayward, Ca., U.S.	h8	98
Hayward, Wi., U.S.	B2	142
Haywood, co., N.C., U.S.	f9	126
Haywood, co., Tn., U.S.	B2	135
Hazard, Ky., U.S.	C6	110
Hazardville, Ct., U.S.	B5	100
Hazārībāg, India	E5	40
Hazel Dell, Wa., U.S.	D3	140
Hazel Green, Al., U.S.	A3	94
Hazel Green, Wi., U.S.	F3	142
Hazel Park, Mi., U.S.	p15	115
Hazelton Pyramid, mtn., Wy., U.S.	B5	143
Hazelwood, N.C., U.S.	f10	126
Hazen, Ar., U.S.	C4	97
Hazen, N.D., U.S.	B4	127
Hazen Bay, b., Ak., U.S.	C6	95
Hazlehurst, Ga., U.S.	E4	103
Hazlehurst, Ms., U.S.	D3	117
Hazlet, N.J., U.S.	C4	123
Hazleton, In., U.S.	H2	107
Hazleton, Pa., U.S.	E10	131
Head Harbor Island, i., Me., U.S.	D5	112

Name	Map Ref.	Page

Headland, Al., U.S. **D4** 94
Headley, Mount, mtn., Mt.,
U.S. **C1** 119
Healdsburg, Ca., U.S. **C2** 98
Healdton, Ok., U.S. **C4** 129
Healesville, Austl. **H4** 62
Healy, Ak., U.S. **C10** 95
Heard, co., Ga., U.S. **C1** 103
Hearne, Tx., U.S. **D4** 136
Hearst, On., Can. **o19** 89
Heart, stm., N.D., U.S. **C3** 127
Heart Butte Dam, N.D.,
U.S. **C4** 127
Heart Lake, l., Wy., U.S. . . . **B2** 143
Heart's Content, Nf., Can. . **E5** 88
Heath, Oh., U.S. **B3** 128
Heath Springs, S.C., U.S. . . **B6** 133
Heavener, Ok., U.S. **C7** 129
Hebbronville, Tx., U.S. **F3** 136
Hebei, state, China **D11** 28
Heber, Az., U.S. **C5** 96
Heber City, Ut., U.S. **C4** 137
Heber Springs, Ar., U.S. . . . **B3** 97
Hébertville, P.Q., Can. **A6** 90
Hebgen Lake, res., Mt., U.S **F5** 119
Hebi, China **D10** 28
Hebrides, is., Scot., U.K. . . **D4** 6
Hebrides, Sea of the, Scot.,
U.K. **B3** 12
Hebron, N.S., Can. **F3** 87
Hebron, Il., U.S. **A5** 106
Hebron, In., U.S. **B3** 107
Hebron, Ky., U.S. **h13** 110
Hebron, Md., U.S. **D6** 113
Hebron, N.D., U.S. **C3** 127
Hebron, Ne., U.S. **D8** 120
Hebron, Oh., U.S. **C3** 128
Hebron see Al-Khalīl, W.B. **G6** 44
Hecate Strait, strt., B.C.,
Can. **C2** 85
Hecelchakán, Mex. **D6** 78
Heceta Island, i., Ak., U.S. **n23** 95
Hechi, China **G9** 28
Hechuan, China **D2** 30
Hecla Island, i., Mb., Can. . **D3** 86
Hector, Mn., U.S. **F4** 116
Hedemora, Swe. **F6** 10
He Devil, mtn., Id., U.S. . . . **D2** 105
Hedrick, Ia., U.S. **C5** 108
Ḥefa (Haifa), Isr. **D2** 42
Hefei, China **E11** 28
Heflin, Al., U.S. **B4** 94
Hefner, Lake, res., Ok., U.S.**B4** 129
Hegang, China **B14** 28
Hegins, Pa., U.S. **E9** 131
Heide, Ger. **C11** 12
Heidelberg, Ger. **F11** 12
Heidelberg, Ms., U.S. **D5** 117
Heidrick, Ky., U.S. **D6** 110
Heilbron, S. Afr. **D4** 56
Heilbronn, Ger. **F11** 12
Heilong (Amur), stm., Asia **D14** 26
Heilongjiang, state, China . **B13** 28
Heilongjiang see Heilong,
stm., Asia **D16** 26
Heilongjiang see Amur,
stm., Asia **D16** 26
Heinävesi, Fin. **E13** 10
Hejaz see Al-Ḥijāz, reg.,
Sau. Ar. **E3** 38
Hejian, China **B4** 30
Hejiang, China **D2** 30
Hekimhan, Tur. **C7** 44
Hekla, vol., Ice. **l19** 10a
Hekou, China **G8** 28
Helagsfjället, mtn., Swe. . . . **E5** 10
Helena, Al., U.S. **B3** 94
Helena, Ar., U.S. **C5** 97
Helena, Ga., U.S. **D4** 103
Helena, Mt., U.S. **D4** 119
Helena, Ok., U.S. **A3** 129
Helensville, N.Z. **o13** 63c
Helgoländer Bucht, b., Ger. **C11** 12
Heli, China **A2** 31
Hellam, Pa., U.S. **G8** 131
Hellertown, Pa., U.S. **E11** 131
Hellín, Spain **H6** 16
Hells Canyon, val., U.S. . . **B10** 130
Hells Canyon National
Recreation Area, U.S. . **B10** 130
Hell-Ville see Andoany,
Madag. **A8** 56
Helmand, stm., Asia **D8** 42
Helmeringhausen, Nmb. . . **D2** 56
Helmstedt, Ger. **D12** 12
Helotes, Tx., U.S. **h7** 136
Helper, Ut., U.S. **D5** 137
Helsingborg, Swe. **H5** 10
Helsingfors see Helsinki,
Fin. **F11** 10
Helsingør, Den. **H5** 10
Helsinki (Helsingfors), Fin. . **F11** 10
Hematite, Mo., U.S. **C7** 118
Hemet, Ca., U.S. **F5** 98
Hemingford, Ne., U.S. **B2** 120
Hemingway, S.C., U.S. **D9** 133
Hemlock, Mi., U.S. **E6** 115
Hemlock Reservoir, res.,
Ct., U.S. **E2** 100
Hemmingford, P.Q., Can. . . **D4** 90
Hemphill, Tx., U.S. **D6** 136
Hemphill, co., Tx., U.S. . . . **B2** 136
Hempstead, N.Y., U.S. . . . **n15** 125
Hempstead, Tx., U.S. **D4** 136
Hempstead, co., Ar., U.S. . **D2** 97

Hemsön, i., Swe. **E8** 10
Henagar, Al., U.S. **A4** 94
Henan, state, China **E10** 28
Hendek, Tur. **B4** 44
Henderson, Ky., U.S. **C2** 110
Henderson, La., U.S. **D4** 111
Henderson, Mn., U.S. **F5** 116
Henderson, N.C., U.S. **A4** 126
Henderson, Ne., U.S. **D8** 120
Henderson, Nv., U.S. **G7** 121
Henderson, Tn., U.S. **B3** 135
Henderson, Tx., U.S. **C5** 136
Henderson, co., Il., U.S. . . . **C3** 106
Henderson, co., Ky., U.S. . . **C2** 110
Henderson, co., N.C., U.S. . **f10** 126
Henderson, co., Tn., U.S. . . **B3** 135
Henderson, co., Tx., U.S. . . **C5** 136
Henderson Island, i., Pit. . . **G17** 58
Henderson's Point, Ms.,
U.S. **g7** 117
Hendersonville, N.C., U.S. . **f10** 126
Hendersonville, Tn., U.S. . . **A5** 135
Hendricks, Mn., U.S. **F2** 116
Hendricks, co., In., U.S. . . . **E4** 107
Hendry, co., Fl., U.S. **F5** 102
Hengshan, China **D9** 28
Hengshan, China **D3** 30
Hengxian, China **E2** 30
Hengyang, China **F10** 28
Heniches'k, Ukr. **F13** 20
Henlawson, W.V., U.S. . . . **n12** 141
Henlopen, Cape, c., De.,
U.S. **E5** 101
Hennebont, Fr. **D5** 16
Hennepin, co., Mn., U.S. . . **E5** 116
Hennessey, Ok., U.S. **A4** 129
Henniker, N.H., U.S. **D3** 122
Henning, Mn., U.S. **D3** 116
Henning, Tn., U.S. **B2** 135
Henrico, co., Va., U.S. **C5** 139
Henrietta, N.C., U.S. **B1** 126
Henrietta, Tx., U.S. **C3** 136
Henrietta Maria, Cape, c.,
On., Can. **n19** 89
Henry, Il., U.S. **B4** 106
Henry, co., Al., U.S. **D4** 94
Henry, co., Ga., U.S. **C2** 103
Henry, co., Ia., U.S. **C6** 108
Henry, co., Il., U.S. **B3** 106
Henry, co., In., U.S. **E7** 107
Henry, co., Ky., U.S. **B4** 110
Henry, co., Mo., U.S. **C4** 118
Henry, co., Oh., U.S. **A1** 128
Henry, co., Tn., U.S. **A3** 135
Henry, co., Va., U.S. **D3** 139
Henry, Mount, mtn., Mt.,
U.S. **B1** 119
Henryetta, Ok., U.S. **B6** 129
Henrys Fork, stm., U.S. . . . **E2** 143
Henryville, P.Q., Can. **D4** 90
Henryville, In., U.S. **G6** 107
Hensall, On., Can. **D3** 89
Hentiesbaai, Nmb. **C1** 56
Henzada, Myan. **C3** 34
Hephzibah, Ga., U.S. **C4** 103
Heppner, Or., U.S. **B7** 130
Hepu, China **G9** 28
Hequ, China **B3** 30
Herāt, Afg. **D8** 42
Herbert G. West, Lake, res.,
Wa., U.S. **C7** 140
Herbes, Isle aux, i., Al., U.S.**E1** 94
Herculaneum, Mo., U.S. . . **C7** 118
Hereford, Eng., U.K. **D5** 12
Hereford, Md., U.S. **A4** 113
Hereford, Tx., U.S. **B1** 136
Hereford Inlet, b., N.J., U.S.**E3** 123
Herford, Ger. **D11** 12
Herington, Ks., U.S. **D7** 109
Herkimer, N.Y., U.S. **B6** 125
Herkimer, co., N.Y., U.S. . . **B5** 125
Hermann, Mo., U.S. **C6** 118
Hermano Peak, mtn., Co.,
U.S. **D2** 99
Hermantown, Mn., U.S. . . . **D6** 116
Hermanus, S. Afr. **E2** 56
Herminie, Pa., U.S. **F2** 131
Hermiston, Or., U.S. **B7** 130
Hermitage, Nf., Can. **E4** 88
Hermitage, Ar., U.S. **D3** 97
Hermitage Bay, b., Nf., Can.**E3** 88
Hermit Islands, is., Pap. N.
Gui. **G12** 32
Hermon, Mount, mtn., Asia **F6** 44
Hermosillo, Mex. **B2** 78
Hernando, Fl., U.S. **D4** 102
Hernando, Ms., U.S. **A4** 117
Hernando, co., Fl., U.S. . . . **D4** 102
Herndon, Va., U.S. **B5** 139
Herning, Den. **H3** 10
Heron Lake, Mn., U.S. **G3** 116
Herrera, Arg. **D5** 72
Herrin, Il., U.S. **F4** 106
Herring Bay, b., Md., U.S. . **C4** 113
Herring Cove, N.S., Can. . . **E6** 87
Herrington Lake, res., Ky.,
U.S. **C5** 110
Herscher, Il., U.S. **B5** 106
Hershey, Pa., U.S. **F8** 131
Hertford, N.C., U.S. **A6** 126
Hertford, co., N.C., U.S. . . . **A5** 126
Hervey Bay, b., Austl. **E5** 62
Heshan, China **E2** 30
Heshun, China **B3** 30
Hesperia, Ca., U.S. **E5** 98

Hesperia, Mi., U.S. **E4** 115
Hesperus Mountain, mtn.,
Co., U.S. **D2** 99
Hesston, Ks., U.S. **D6** 109
Heta, stm., Russia **B11** 26
Hettinger, N.D., U.S. **D3** 127
Hettinger, co., N.D., U.S. . . **C3** 127
Hexian, China **G10** 28
Heyburn, Id., U.S. **G5** 105
Heyuan, China **E3** 30
Heyworth, Il., U.S. **C5** 106
Heze, China **B4** 30
Hialeah, Fl., U.S. **G6** 102
Hiawatha, Ia., U.S. **B6** 108
Hiawatha, Ks., U.S. **C8** 109
Hibbing, Mn., U.S. **C6** 116
Hickam Air Force Base, mil.,
Hi., U.S. **g10** 104
Hickman, Ky., U.S. **f8** 110
Hickman, Ne., U.S. **D9** 120
Hickman, co., Ky., U.S. **f8** 110
Hickman, co., Tn., U.S. **B4** 135
Hickory, N.C., U.S. **B1** 126
Hickory, co., Mo., U.S. **D4** 118
Hicksville, N.Y., U.S. **E7** 125
Hicksville, Oh., U.S. **A1** 128
Hico, Tx., U.S. **D3** 136
Hico, W.V., U.S. **C3** 141
Hidalgo, Mex. **C5** 78
Hidalgo, Tx., U.S. **F3** 136
Hidalgo, state, Mex. **C5** 78
Hidalgo, co., N.M., U.S. . . . **F1** 124
Hidalgo, co., Tx., U.S. **F3** 136
Hidalgo del Parral, Mex. . . **B3** 78
Hiddenite, N.C., U.S. **B1** 126
Hieroglyphic Mountains,
mts., Az., U.S. **k8** 96
Higbee, Mo., U.S. **B5** 118
Higganum, Ct., U.S. **D5** 100
Higgins Lake, l., Mi., U.S. . **D6** 115
Higgins Millpond, res., Md.,
U.S. **C6** 113
Higginsville, Mo., U.S. **B4** 118
High Bridge, N.J., U.S. **B3** 123
High Falls Reservoir, res.,
Wi., U.S. **C5** 142
High Island, i., Mi., U.S. . . . **C5** 115
Highland, Il., U.S. **E4** 106
Highland, In., U.S. **A3** 107
Highland, Ks., U.S. **C8** 109
Highland, Mi., U.S. **o14** 115
Highland, N.Y., U.S. **D7** 125
Highland, Wi., U.S. **E3** 142
Highland, co., Oh., U.S. . . . **C2** 128
Highland, co., Va., U.S. . . . **B3** 139
Highland Lake, l., Me., U.S. **g7** 112
Highland Lakes, N.J., U.S. . **A4** 123
Highland Park, Il., U.S. **A6** 106
Highland Park, Mi., U.S. . . **p15** 115
Highland Park, Tx., U.S. . . **n10** 136
Highland Peak, mtn., Ca.,
U.S. **C4** 98
Highland Point, c., Fl., U.S. **G6** 102
Highlands, N.C., U.S. **f9** 126
Highlands, N.J., U.S. **C5** 123
Highlands, Tx., U.S. **r14** 136
Highlands, co., Fl., U.S. . . . **E5** 102
Highland Springs, Va., U.S. **C5** 139
High Level, Ab., Can. **F7** 84
Highmore, S.D., U.S. **C6** 134
High Point, N.C., U.S. **B2** 126
High Prairie, Ab., Can. **B2** 84
High Ridge, Mo., U.S. . . . **g12** 118
High River, Ab., Can. **D4** 84
Highrock Lake, l., Mb., Can.**B1** 86
High Rock Lake, l., N.C.,
U.S. **B2** 126
High Spire, Pa., U.S. **F8** 131
High Springs, Fl., U.S. **C4** 102
Hightown, N.J., U.S. **C3** 123
Highwood, Il., U.S. **A6** 106
Highwood Baldy, mtn., Mt.,
U.S. **C6** 119
Highwood Mountains, mts.,
Mt., U.S. **C6** 119
Higuera de Abuya, Mex. . . **C3** 78
Higüey, Dom. Rep. **B6** 80
Hiiumaa, i., Est. **G10** 10
Hiko Range, mts., Nv., U.S **F6** 121
Hilbert, Wi., U.S. **D5** 142
Hildale, Ut., U.S. **F3** 137
Hilden, N.S., Can. **D6** 87
Hildesheim, Ger. **D11** 12
Hill, co., Mt., U.S. **B6** 119
Hill, co., Tx., U.S. **D4** 136
Hillaby, Mount, mtn., Barb. **C8** 80
Hill City, Ks., U.S. **C4** 109
Hill City, S.D., U.S. **D2** 134
Hillcrest, Il., U.S. **B4** 106
Hillcrest Heights, Md., U.S. **C4** 113
Hillerød, Den. **I5** 10
Hilliard, Fl., U.S. **B5** 102
Hilliard, Oh., U.S. **k10** 128
Hills, Ia., U.S. **C6** 108
Hills, Mn., U.S. **G2** 116
Hillsboro, Il., U.S. **D4** 106
Hillsboro, Ks., U.S. **D6** 109
Hillsboro, Mo., U.S. **C7** 118
Hillsboro, N.D., U.S. **B8** 127
Hillsboro, Oh., U.S. **C2** 128
Hillsboro, Or., U.S. **B4** 130
Hillsboro, Tx., U.S. **C4** 136
Hillsboro, Wi., U.S. **E3** 142

Hillsboro Canal, Fl., U.S. . . **F6** 102
Hillsborough, N.B., Can. . . **D5** 87
Hillsborough, N.C., U.S. . . . **A3** 126
Hillsborough, co., Fl., U.S. . **E4** 102
Hillsborough, co., N.H.,
U.S. **E3** 122
Hillsborough Bay, b., P.E.,
Can. **C6** 87
Hillsburgh, On., Can. **D4** 89
Hills Creek Lake, res., Or.,
U.S. **D4** 130
Hillsdale, Mi., U.S. **G6** 115
Hillsdale, N.J., U.S. **g8** 123
Hillsdale, co., Mi., U.S. . . . **G6** 115
Hillside, N.J., U.S. **k8** 123
Hillsville, Pa., U.S. **D1** 131
Hillsville, Va., U.S. **D2** 139
Hilo, Hi., U.S. **D6** 104
Hilo Bay, b., Hi., U.S. **D6** 104
Hilok, Russia **D13** 26
Hilton, N.Y., U.S. **B3** 125
Hilton Head Island, S.C.,
U.S. **G6** 133
Hilton Head Island, i., S.C.,
U.S. **G6** 133
Hilvan, Tur. **D8** 44
Himāchal Pradesh, prov.,
India **C3** 40
Himalayas, mts., Asia **C3** 40
Himatnagar, India **E2** 40
Himeji, Japan **D2** 31
Ḥimş, Syria **E7** 44
Hinchinbrook Island, i.,
Austl. **D4** 62
Hinchinbrook Island, i., Ak.,
U.S. **g18** 95
Hinckley, Il., U.S. **B5** 106
Hinckley, Mn., U.S. **D6** 116
Hinckley, Ut., U.S. **D3** 137
Hinckley Reservoir, res.,
N.Y., U.S. **B5** 125
Hindman, Ky., U.S. **C7** 110
Hinds, co., Ms., U.S. **C3** 117
Hindu Kush, mts., Asia . . . **C1** 40
Hindupur, India **G3** 40
Hines, Or., U.S. **D7** 130
Hinesville, Ga., U.S. **E5** 103
Hinganghāt, India **E3** 40
Hingham, Ma., U.S. **B6** 114
Hingham Bay, b., Ma., U.S **g12** 114
Hingol, stm., Pak. **E9** 42
Hingoli, India **F3** 40
Hinis, Tur. **C9** 44
Hinnøya, i., Nor. **B6** 10
Hinsdale, Il., U.S. **k9** 106
Hinsdale, N.H., U.S. **E2** 122
Hinsdale, co., Co., U.S. . . . **D3** 99
Hinton, Ab., Can. **C2** 84
Hinton, Ia., U.S. **B1** 108
Hinton, Ok., U.S. **B3** 129
Hinton, W.V., U.S. **D4** 141
Hīrākud Reservoir, res.,
India **E4** 40
Hiram, Ga., U.S. **C2** 103
Hiram, Oh., U.S. **A4** 128
Hirara, Japan **B9** 34
Hirfanlı Barajı, res., Tur. . . . **C5** 44
Hiriyūr, India **G3** 40
Hirosaki, Japan **C16** 28
Hiroshima, Japan **E14** 28
Hirson, Fr. **C9** 16
Hirtshals, Den. **H3** 10
Hisār, India **D3** 40
Hispaniola, i., N.A. **A5** 80
Hita, Japan **D2** 31
Hitachi, Japan **D16** 28
Hitchcock, Tx., U.S. **r14** 136
Hitchcock, co., Ne., U.S. . . **D4** 120
Hitchcock Lake, Ct., U.S. . . **C4** 100
Hitoyoshi, Japan **D2** 31
Hitra, i., Nor. **E3** 10
Hiva, Uzb. **B8** 42
Hiwassee, stm., Tn., U.S. . . **D9** 135
Hiwassee Lake, res., N.C.,
U.S. **f8** 126
Hjälmaren, l., Swe. **G6** 10
Hjelmelandsvågen, Nor. . . . **G2** 10
Hjørring, Den. **H3** 10
Hkakabo Razi, mtn., Myan. **A3** 34
Hlukhiv, Ukr. **D12** 20
Hlusk, Bela. **C10** 20
Hlybokae, Bela. **B9** 20
Ho, Ghana **E5** 50
Hoa Binh, Viet. **B5** 34
Hoagland, In., U.S. **C8** 107
Hoback, stm., Wy., U.S. . . . **C2** 143
Hobart, Austl. **I4** 62
Hobart, In., U.S. **A3** 107
Hobart, Ok., U.S. **B2** 129
Hobbs, N.M., U.S. **E6** 124
Hobbs Coast, Ant. **D28** 67
Hobe Sound, Fl., U.S. **E6** 102
Hoboken, N.J., U.S. **k8** 123
Hobyo, Som. **I14** 48
Ho Chi Minh City see
Thanh Pho Ho Chi
Minh, Viet. **D5** 34
Hockessin, De., U.S. **A3** 101
Hocking, co., Oh., U.S. . . . **C3** 128
Hocking, stm., Oh., U.S. . . **C3** 128
Hockley, co., Tx., U.S. **C1** 136
Hōd, reg., Maur. **C3** 50
Hodeida see Al-Ḥudaydah,
Yemen **H4** 38
Hodgeman, co., Ks., U.S. . **D4** 109

Hodgenville, Ky., U.S. **C4** 110
Hodges Village Reservoir,
res., Ma., U.S. **B4** 114
Hódmezővásárhely, Hung. . **F6** 20
Hodna, Chott el, l., Alg. . . . **C5** 48
Hodonín, Czech Rep. **B1** 42
Hoeryŏng-ŭp, N. Kor. **B1** 31
Hof, Ger. **E12** 12
Höfdakaupstadur, Ice. . . . **l18** 10a
Hoffman Estates, Il., U.S. . **h8** 106
Hofors, Swe. **F7** 10
Hofsjökull, Ice. **l19** 10a
Hōfu, Japan **D2** 31
Höganäs, Swe. **H5** 10
Hogansville, Ga., U.S. **C2** 103
Hogback Mountain, mtn.,
Mt., U.S. **F4** 119
Hoggar see Ahaggar, mts.,
Alg. **F6** 48
Hog Island, i., Fl., U.S. . . . **C3** 102
Hog Island, i., Mi., U.S. . . . **C5** 115
Hog Island, i., N.C., U.S. . . **B6** 126
Hog Island, i., R.I., U.S. . . . **D5** 132
Hog Island, i., Va., U.S. . . . **C7** 139
Hoh, stm., Wa., U.S. **B1** 140
Hohenwald, Tn., U.S. **B4** 135
Hoh Head, c., Wa., U.S. . . **B1** 140
Hohhot, China **C10** 28
Hohoe, Ghana **E5** 50
Ho-Ho-Kus, N.J., U.S. **h8** 123
Hoh Xil Shan, mts., China **D5** 28
Hoi An, Viet. **C5** 34
Hoima, Ug. **C6** 54
Hoisington, Ks., U.S. **D5** 109
Hojniki, Bela. **D10** 20
Hokah, Mn., U.S. **G7** 116
Hoke, co., N.C., U.S. **B3** 126
Hokes Bluff, Al., U.S. **B4** 94
Hokitika, N.Z. **p13** 63c
Hokkaidō, i., Japan **C16** 28
Hoktemberjan, Arm. **B11** 44
Hola Prystan', Ukr. **F12** 20
Holbrook, Az., U.S. **C5** 96
Holbrook, Ma., U.S. **B5** 114
Holcomb, Ks., U.S. **E3** 109
Holden, Ma., U.S. **B4** 114
Holden, Mo., U.S. **C4** 118
Holden, W.V., U.S. **D2** 141
Holdenville, Ok., U.S. **B5** 129
Holdrege, Ne., U.S. **D6** 120
Hole in the Mountain Peak,
mtn., Nv., U.S. **C6** 121
Holgate, Oh., U.S. **A1** 128
Holguín, Cuba **A4** 80
Holland, In., U.S. **H3** 107
Holland, Mi., U.S. **F4** 115
Holland, Oh., U.S. **A2** 128
Holland, Tx., U.S. **D4** 136
Hollandale, Ms., U.S. **B3** 117
Hollandia see Jayapura,
Indon. **G11** 32
Holland Island, i., Md., U.S. **D5** 113
Holland Point, c., Md., U.S. **C4** 113
Holland Straits, strt., Md.,
U.S. **D5** 113
Holley, N.Y., U.S. **B2** 125
Holliday, Tx., U.S. **C3** 136
Hollidaysburg, Pa., U.S. . . . **F5** 131
Hollins, Va., U.S. **C3** 139
Hollis, Ok., U.S. **C2** 129
Hollister, Ca., U.S. **D3** 98
Hollister, Mo., U.S. **E4** 118
Holliston, Ma., U.S. **B5** 114
Holloman Air Force Base,
mil., N.M., U.S. **E3** 124
Hollow Rock, Tn., U.S. . . . **A3** 135
Hollowtop Mountain, mtn.,
Mt., U.S. **E4** 119
Holly, Co., U.S. **C8** 99
Holly, Mi., U.S. **F7** 115
Holly Grove, Ar., U.S. **C4** 97
Holly Hill, Fl., U.S. **C5** 102
Holly Hill, S.C., U.S. **E7** 133
Holly Pond, Al., U.S. **A3** 94
Holly Ridge, N.C., U.S. . . . **C5** 126
Holly Shelter Swamp, sw.,
N.C., U.S. **C5** 126
Holly Springs, Ga., U.S. . . . **B2** 103
Holly Springs, Ms., U.S. . . **A4** 117
Holly Springs, N.C., U.S. . . **B4** 126
Hollywood, Al., U.S. **A4** 94
Hollywood, Fl., U.S. **F6** 102
Hollywood, Md., U.S. **D5** 113
Hollywood, S.C., U.S. . . . **k11** 133
Hollywood Indian
Reservation, Fl., U.S. . . **r3** 102
Holmen, Wi., U.S. **E2** 142
Holmes, co., Fl., U.S. . . . **u16** 102
Holmes, co., Ms., U.S. . . . **B3** 117
Holmes, co., Oh., U.S. . . . **B4** 128
Holmes, Mount, mtn., Wy.,
U.S. **B2** 143
Holmsk, Russia **E16** 26
Holoby, Ukr. **D8** 20
Holstebro, Den. **H3** 10
Holstein, Ia., U.S. **B2** 108
Holsteinsborg, Grnld. . . . **E29** 82
Holston, stm., Tn., U.S. . . **C11** 135
Holston, Middle Fork, stm.,
Va., U.S. **f10** 139
Holston High Knob, mtn.,
Tn., U.S. **C11** 135
Holt, Al., U.S. **B2** 94

Name	Map Ref.	Page

Holt, Mi., U.S. F6 115
Holt, co., Mo., U.S. A2 118
Holt, co., Ne., U.S. B7 120
Holt Lake, res., Al., U.S. . . . B2 94
Holton, Ks., U.S. C8 109
Holtville, Ca., U.S. F6 98
Holualoa, Hi., U.S. D6 104
Holy Cross, Mountain of
the, mtn., Co., U.S. B4 99
Holyhead, Wales, U.K. D4 12
Holyoke, Co., U.S. A8 99
Holyoke, Ma., U.S. B2 114
Holyoke Range, hills, Ma.,
U.S. B2 114
Homalin, Myan. B2 34
Hombori Tondo, mtn., Mali C4 50
Hombre Muerto, Salar del,
pl., Arg. D4 72
Homecroft, In., U.S. m10 107
Homedale, Id., U.S. F2 105
Home Hill, Austl. D4 62
Homel', Bela. C11 20
Homeland, Ga., U.S. F4 103
Home Place, In., U.S. E5 107
Homer, Ak., U.S. D9 95
Homer, Ga., U.S. B3 103
Homer, Il., U.S. C6 106
Homer, La., U.S. B2 111
Homer, Mi., U.S. F6 115
Homer, N.Y., U.S. C4 125
Homer City, Pa., U.S. E3 131
Homerville, Ga., U.S. E4 103
Homer Youngs Peak, mtn.,
Mt., U.S. E3 119
Homestead, Fl., U.S. G6 102
Homestead, Pa., U.S. k14 131
Homestead National
Monument of America,
Ne., U.S. D9 120
Homewood, Al., U.S. g7 94
Homewood, Il., U.S. B6 106
Homewood, Oh., U.S. C1 128
Hominy, Ok., U.S. A5 129
Hominy Creek, stm., Ok.,
U.S. A5 129
Homme Dam, N.D., U.S. . . A8 127
Homochitto, stm., Ms., U.S. D2 117
Homosassa, Fl., U.S. D4 102
Homs see Al-Khums, Libya E6 14
Homs see Ḥimṣ, Syria E7 44
Honaker, Va., U.S. e10 139
Honan see Henan, state,
China E10 28
Honaunau, Hi., U.S. D6 104
Honda, Col. B5 70
Hondo, Tx., U.S. E3 136
Hondo, stm., N.A. B2 80
Hondo, Rio, stm., N.M.,
U.S. D4 124
Honduras, ctry., N.A. C2 80
Honduras, Gulf of, b., N.A. B2 80
Honea Path, S.C., U.S. . . . C3 133
Hønefoss, Nor. F4 10
Honeoye Falls, N.Y., U.S. . . C3 125
Honesdale, Pa., U.S. C11 131
Honey Brook, Pa., U.S. . . . F10 131
Honey Grove, Tx., U.S. . . . C5 136
Honey Lake, l., Ca., U.S. . . B3 98
Honeypot Glen, Ct., U.S. . . C4 100
Honeyville, Ut., U.S. B3 137
Hong, Song see Red, stm.,
Asia B4 34
Hon Gai, Viet. B5 34
Honga River, b., Md., U.S. . D5 113
Hongjiang, China F9 28
Hong Kong see Xianggang,
China E3 30
Hongliuyuan, China C7 28
Hongshui, stm., China G9 28
Hongtong, China B3 30
Hongze, China C4 30
Hongze Hu, l., China E11 28
Honiara, Sol. Is. B6 62
Honjō, Japan C3 31
Honokaa, Hi., U.S. C6 104
Honolulu, Hi., U.S. B4 104
Honolulu, co., Hi., U.S. . . . B3 104
Honolulu International
Airport, Hi., U.S. g10 104
Honomu, Hi., U.S. D6 104
Honouliuli, Hi., U.S. g9 104
Honshū, i., Japan D16 28
Honuapo Bay, b., Hi., U.S. D6 104
Honuu, Russia C16 26
Hood, co., Tx., U.S. C4 136
Hood, Mount, mtn., Or.,
U.S. B5 130
Hood Canal, b., Wa., U.S. . B2 140
Hoodoo Peak, mtn., Wa.,
U.S. A5 140
Hood Point, c., Austl. G2 60
Hood River, Or., U.S. B5 130
Hood River, co., Or., U.S. . B5 130
Hoodsport, Wa., U.S. B2 140
Hoogeveen, Neth. D10 12
Hooker, Ok., U.S. e9 129
Hooker, co., Ne., U.S. C4 120
Hooker Creek, Austl. D5 60
Hooksett, N.H., U.S. D4 122
Hoonah, Ak., U.S. D12 95
Hoopa Valley Indian
Reservation, Ca., U.S. . . B2 98
Hooper, Ne., U.S. C9 120
Hooper Bay, Ak., U.S. C6 95

Hooper Islands, is., Md.,
U.S. D5 113
Hooper Strait, strt., Md.,
U.S. D5 113
Hoopes Reservoir, res., De.,
U.S. A3 101
Hoopeston, Il., U.S. C6 106
Hoorn, Neth. D9 12
Hoosac Range, mts., U.S. . A1 114
Hoosic, stm., U.S. C7 125
Hoosick Falls, N.Y., U.S. . . C7 125
Hoover Dam, U.S. G7 121
Hoover Reservoir, res., Oh.,
U.S. B3 128
Hooverson Heights, W.V.,
U.S. f8 141
Hopa, Tur. B9 44
Hopatcong, N.J., U.S. B3 123
Hopatcong, Lake, l., N.J.,
U.S. A3 123
Hope, B.C., U.S. E7 85
Hope, Ar., U.S. D2 97
Hope, In., U.S. F6 107
Hope, R.I., U.S. D3 132
Hope, Point, c., Ak., U.S. . . B6 95
Hopedale, Il., U.S. C4 106
Hopedale, Ma., U.S. B4 114
Hope Island, i., R.I., U.S. . . E5 132
Hopelchén, Mex. D7 78
Hope Mills, N.C., U.S. C4 126
Hopër, stm., Russia D7 22
Hopes Advance, Cap, c.,
P.Q., Can. f13 90
Hopetoun, Austl. G3 60
Hopetown, S. Afr. D3 56
Hope Valley, R.I., U.S. E2 132
Hopewell, Va., U.S. C5 139
Hopewell Junction, N.Y.,
U.S. D7 125
Hopi Indian Reservation,
Az., U.S. A5 96
Hopkins, Mn., U.S. n12 116
Hopkins, S.C., U.S. D6 133
Hopkins, co., Ky., U.S. . . . C2 110
Hopkins, co., Tx., U.S. . . . C5 136
Hopkinsville, Ky., U.S. . . . D2 110
Hopkinton, Ia., U.S. B6 108
Hopkinton, Ma., U.S. B4 114
Hopkinton, R.I., U.S. F1 132
Hopkinton Lake, res., N.H.,
U.S. D3 122
Hopwood, Pa., U.S. G2 131
Hoquiam, Wa., U.S. C2 140
Hor, Russia A2 31
Horace, N.D., U.S. C9 127
Horace Mountain, mtn.,
Ak., U.S. B10 95
Horasan, Tur. B10 44
Horatio, Ar., U.S. D1 97
Horicon, Wi., U.S. E5 142
Horine, Mo., U.S. C7 118
Horlick Mountains, mts.,
Ant. E29 67
Horlivka, Ukr. E15 20
Hormuz, Strait of, strt., Asia E7 42
Horn, c., Ice. k17 10a
Horn, Cape see Hornos,
Cabo de, c., Chile I3 69
Hornavan, l., Swe. C7 10
Hornell, N.Y., U.S. C3 125
Hornersville, Mo., U.S. . . . E7 118
Horn Island, i., Ms., U.S. . . E5 117
Horn Island Pass, strt., Ms.,
U.S. g8 117
Horn Lake, Ms., U.S. A3 117
Hornos, Cabo de (Horn,
Cape), c., Chile I3 69
Horodenka, Ukr. E8 20
Horodnia, Ukr. D11 20
Horodok, Ukr. E7 20
Horqin Youyi Qianqi, China B12 28
Horry, co., S.C., U.S. D10 133
Horse, stm., Ct., U.S. C6 100
Horse Cave, Ky., U.S. C4 110
Horse Creek, stm., U.S. . . . E8 143
Horse Creek Reservoir, res.,
Co., U.S. C7 99
Horsehead Lake, l., N.D.,
U.S. B6 127
Horseheads, N.Y., U.S. . . . C4 125
Horse Heaven Hills, hills,
Wa., U.S. C6 140
Horsens, Den. I3 10
Horse Peak, mtn., N.M.,
U.S. D1 124
Horseshoe Bend, Id., U.S. . F2 105
Horseshoe Bend National
Military Park, Al., U.S. . C4 94
Horseshoe Cove, b., Fl.,
U.S. C3 102
Horseshoe Point, c., Fl.,
U.S. C3 102
Horseshoe Reservoir, res.,
Az., U.S. C4 96
Horsham, Austl. H3 62
Horten, Nor. G4 10
Horton, Ks., U.S. C8 109
Horton, stm., N.T., Can. . . E15 82
Hortonia, Lake, l., Vt., U.S. D2 138
Hortonville, Wi., U.S. D5 142
Horyn', stm., Eur. D9 20
Hosa'ina, Eth. B7 54
Hoschton, Ga., U.S. B3 103
Hosedahard, Russia A10 22
Hoshāb, Pak. E8 42

Hoshangābād, India E3 40
Hoshiārpur, India C3 40
Hospers, Ia., U.S. A2 108
Hospet, India F3 40
Hosta Butte, mtn., N.M.,
U.S. B1 124
Hotan, China D3 28
Hotan, stm., China A4 40
Hotazel, S. Afr. D3 56
Hotchkiss, Co., U.S. C3 99
Hot Creek Range, mts., Nv.,
U.S. E5 121
Hot Creek Valley, val., Nv.,
U.S. E5 121
Hot Spring, co., Ar., U.S. . . C2 97
Hot Springs, S.D., U.S. . . . D2 134
Hot Springs, co., Wy., U.S. C4 143
Hot Springs National Park,
Ar., U.S. C2 97
Hot Springs National Park,
Ar., U.S. C2 97
Hot Springs Peak, mtn., Ca.,
U.S. B3 98
Hot Springs Peak, mtn., Nv.,
U.S. B4 121
Houaïlou, N. Cal. l9 62a
Houghton, Mi., U.S. A2 115
Houghton, N.Y., U.S. C2 125
Houghton, co., Mi., U.S. . . B2 115
Houghton Lake, Mi., U.S. . D6 115
Houghton Lake, l., Mi., U.S. D6 115
Houghton Lake Heights,
Mi., U.S. D6 115
Houlton, Me., U.S. B5 112
Houma, China D10 28
Houma, La., U.S. E5 111
House Springs, Mo., U.S. . . g12 118
Houston, De., U.S. E3 101
Houston, Mn., U.S. G7 116
Houston, Mo., U.S. D6 118
Houston, Ms., U.S. B4 117
Houston, Pa., U.S. F1 131
Houston, Tx., U.S. E5 136
Houston, co., Al., U.S. . . . D4 94
Houston, co., Ga., U.S. . . . D3 103
Houston, co., Mn., U.S. . . . G7 116
Houston, co., Tn., U.S. . . . A4 135
Houston, co., Tx., U.S. . . . D5 136
Houston, stm., La., U.S. . . D2 111
Houston, Lake, res., Tx.,
U.S. r14 136
Houston Intercontinental
Airport, Tx., U.S. r14 136
Houtman Abrolhos, is.,
Austl. F1 60
Houtzdale, Pa., U.S. E5 131
Hovd, Mong. B6 28
Hovd, stm., Mong. B6 28
Hovenweep National
Monument, Ut., U.S. . . F6 137
Hoverla, hora, mtn., Ukr. . . E8 20
Hovmantorp, Swe. H6 10
Hövsgöl nuur, l., Mong. . . . A8 28
Howard, Ks., U.S. E7 109
Howard, S.D., U.S. C8 134
Howard, Wi., U.S. D5 142
Howard, co., Ar., U.S. C2 97
Howard, co., Ia., U.S. A5 108
Howard, co., In., U.S. C5 107
Howard, co., Md., U.S. . . . B4 113
Howard, co., Mo., U.S. . . . B5 118
Howard, co., Ne., U.S. . . . C7 120
Howard, co., Tx., U.S. C2 136
Howard City, Mi., U.S. . . . E5 115
Howard Hanson Reservoir,
res., Wa., U.S. B4 140
Howard Lake, Mn., U.S. . . E4 116
Howard Prairie Lake, res.,
Or., U.S. E4 130
Howards Grove-Millersville,
Wi., U.S. E6 142
Howe, Cape, c., Austl. H5 62
Howell, Mi., U.S. F7 115
Howell, co., Mo., U.S. E6 118
Howells, Ne., U.S. C8 120
Howe Sound, strt., B.C.,
Can. E6 85
Howick, P.Q., Can. D4 90
Howland, Me., U.S. C4 112
Howland Island, i., Oc. . . . H21 64
Hoxie, Ar., U.S. A5 97
Hoxie, Ks., U.S. C3 109
Hoyerswerda, Ger. E14 12
Hoyt Lakes, Mn., U.S. C6 116
Hradec Králové, Czech Rep. D3 20
Hrodnoo, Bela. C7 20
Hron, stm., Slvk. E5 20
Hsilo, Tai. E5 30
Hsinchu, Tai. E5 30
Hsipaw, Myan. B3 34
Huacho, Peru F4 70
Huachuca City, Az., U.S. . . F5 96
Hua Hin, Thai. D3 34
Huai'an, China E11 28
Huai'an, China A3 30
Huaibin, China C4 30
Huaiji, China E3 30
Huailai, China A4 30
Huainan, China E11 28
Huairou, China A4 30
Huaiyang, China E11 28
Huajuapan de León, Mex. . D5 78
Hualalai, vol., Hi., U.S. . . . D6 104

Hualapai Indian
Reservation, Az., U.S. . B2 96
Hualapai Mountains, mts.,
Az., U.S. C2 96
Hualapai Peak, mtn., Az.,
U.S. B2 96
Hualien, Tai. E5 30
Huallaga, stm., Peru E4 70
Huambo, Ang. F3 54
Huanan, China A2 31
Huancavelica, Peru F4 70
Huancayo, Peru F4 70
Huang (Yellow), stm., China D11 28
Huangchuan, China E11 28
Huangho see Huang, stm.,
China D11 28
Huanghua, China B4 30
Huanglong, China B2 30
Huangshi, China E11 28
Huangxian, China B5 30
Huangyan, China D5 30
Huangyuan, China D8 28
Huanta, Peru A3 72
Huanxian, China B2 30
Huaral, Peru F4 70
Huarocondo, Peru A3 72
Huascarán, Nevado, mtn.,
Peru E4 70
Huasco, Chile C2 69
Huatabampo, Mex. B3 78
Huauchinango, Mex. C5 78
Huaxian, China E3 30
Huaxian, China B3 30
Huazhou, China E3 30
Hubbard, Ia., U.S. B4 108
Hubbard, Oh., U.S. A5 128
Hubbard, Or., U.S. B4 130
Hubbard, Tx., U.S. D4 136
Hubbard, co., Mn., U.S. . . . C4 116
Hubbard Creek Lake, res.,
Tx., U.S. C3 136
Hubbard Lake, l., Mi., U.S. D7 115
Hubbardton, stm., Vt., U.S. D2 138
Hubbell, Mi., U.S. A2 115
Hubei, state, China E10 28
Hubli-Dhārwār, India F3 40
Huckleberry Mountain,
mtn., Or., U.S. D4 130
Huddersfield, Eng., U.K. . . D6 12
Hudiksvall, Swe. F7 10
Hudson, P.Q., Can. D3 90
Hudson, Co., U.S. A6 99
Hudson, Fl., U.S. D4 102
Hudson, Ia., U.S. B5 108
Hudson, Il., U.S. C5 106
Hudson, Ma., U.S. B4 114
Hudson, Mi., U.S. G6 115
Hudson, N.C., U.S. B1 126
Hudson, N.H., U.S. E4 122
Hudson, N.Y., U.S. C7 125
Hudson, Oh., U.S. A4 128
Hudson, Wi., U.S. D1 142
Hudson, Wy., U.S. D4 143
Hudson, co., N.J., U.S. . . . B4 123
Hudson, stm., U.S. E7 125
Hudson, Lake, res., Ok.,
U.S. A6 129
Hudson Bay, b., Can. G24 82
Hudson Falls, N.Y., U.S. . . B7 125
Hudson Hope, B.C., Can. . . A6 85
Hudson Lake, In., U.S. . . . A4 107
Hudson Strait, strt., Can. . . F25 82
Hudsonville, Mi., U.S. F5 115
Hudspeth, co., Tx., U.S. . . o12 136
Hudžand, Taj. E8 26
Hue, Viet. C5 34
Huehuetenango, Guat. . . . B1 80
Huelva, Spain I3 16
Huércal-Overa, Spain I6 16
Huerfano, co., Co., U.S. . . D5 99
Huerfano, stm., Co., U.S. . D6 99
Huerfano Mountain, mtn.,
N.M., U.S. A2 124
Huesca, Spain F6 16
Huéscar, Spain I5 16
Huetamo de Núñez, Mex. . D4 78
Hueytown, Al., U.S. g6 94
Huffakers, Nv., U.S. D2 121
Hufrat an-Nahās, Sudan . . B4 54
Hugh Butler Lake, res., Ne.,
U.S. D5 120
Hughenden, Austl. E3 62
Hughes, Ar., U.S. C5 97
Hughes, co., Ok., U.S. . . . B5 129
Hughes, co., S.D., U.S. . . . C5 134
Hughes, North Fork, stm.,
W.V., U.S. B3 141
Hughes, South Fork, stm.,
W.V., U.S. B3 141
Hughesville, Md., U.S. . . . C4 113
Hughesville, Pa., U.S. D8 131
Hugli, stm., India E5 40
Hugo, Co., U.S. B7 99
Hugo, Mn., U.S. m13 116
Hugo, Ok., U.S. C6 129
Hugo Lake, res., Ok., U.S. . C6 129
Hugoton, Ks., U.S. E2 109
Hŭich'ŏn, N. Kor. C13 28
Huilai, China E4 30
Huili, China F8 28
Huimin, China B4 30
Huinca Renancó, Arg. E5 72
Huishui, China D2 30
Huitong, China D2 30

Huixian, China C2 30
Huixtla, Mex. D6 78
Huize, China F8 28
Huizhou, China E3 30
Hujirt, Mong. B8 28
Hulah Lake, res., Ok., U.S. . A5 129
Hulett, Wy., U.S. B8 143
Hulin, China B14 28
Hull, P.Q., Can. D2 90
Hull, Ia., U.S. A1 108
Hull, Ma., U.S. B6 114
Huma, China A13 28
Humaitá, Braz. E7 70
Humaitá, Para. D6 72
Humansdorp, S. Afr. E3 56
Humansville, Mo., U.S. . . . D4 118
Humbe, Ang. B1 56
Humble, Tx., U.S. E5 136
Humboldt, Az., U.S. C3 96
Humboldt, Ia., U.S. B3 108
Humboldt, Ks., U.S. E8 109
Humboldt, Ne., U.S. D10 120
Humboldt, Tn., U.S. B3 135
Humboldt, co., Ca., U.S. . . B2 98
Humboldt, co., Ia., U.S. . . . B3 108
Humboldt, co., Nv., U.S. . . B3 121
Humboldt, stm., Nv., U.S. . C3 121
Humboldt Range, mts., Nv.,
U.S. C3 121
Humenné, Slvk. E6 20
Hummels Wharf, Pa., U.S. . E8 131
Humphrey, Ar., U.S. C4 97
Humphrey, Ne., U.S. C8 120
Humphreys, co., Ms., U.S. . B3 117
Humphreys, co., Tn., U.S. . A4 135
Humphreys, Mount, mtn.,
Ca., U.S. D4 98
Humphreys Peak, mtn., Az.,
U.S. B4 96
Humpty Doo, Austl. C5 60
Hūn, Libya F7 14
Hun, stm., China A5 30
Húnaflói, b., Ice. k18 10a
Hunan, state, China F10 28
Hunchun, China B2 31
Hundred Acre Pond, l., R.I.,
U.S. E3 132
Hunedoara, Rom. G7 20
Hungary, ctry., Eur. F5 20
Hŭngdŏki-dong, N. Kor. . . D13 28
Hungry Horse, Mt., U.S. . . B2 119
Hungry Horse Reservoir,
res., Mt., U.S. B3 119
Hunjiang, China C13 28
Hunsberge, mts., Nmb. . . . D2 56
Hunt, co., Tx., U.S. C4 136
Hunt, stm., R.I., U.S. D4 132
Hunter Island, i., Austl. . . . I3 62
Hunter Island, i., B.C., Can. D3 85
Huntertown, In., U.S. B7 107
Huntingburg, In., U.S. H4 107
Huntingdon, P.Q., Can. . . . D3 90
Huntingdon, Pa., U.S. F6 131
Huntingdon, Tn., U.S. A3 135
Huntingdon, co., Pa., U.S. . F5 131
Hunting Island, i., S.C., U.S. G7 133
Huntington, Ar., U.S. B1 97
Huntington, In., U.S. C7 107
Huntington, N.Y., U.S. . . . E7 125
Huntington, Tx., U.S. D5 136
Huntington, Ut., U.S. D5 137
Huntington, W.V., U.S. . . . C2 141
Huntington, co., In., U.S. . . C6 107
Huntington Beach, Ca., U.S. F4 98
Huntington Lake, res., In.,
U.S. C7 107
Huntington Woods, Mi.,
U.S. p15 115
Huntingtown, Md., U.S. . . . C4 113
Huntland, Tn., U.S. B5 135
Huntley, Il., U.S. A5 106
Hunt Mountain, mtn., Wy.,
U.S. B5 143
Huntsville, On., Can. B5 89
Huntsville, Al., U.S. A3 94
Huntsville, Ar., U.S. A2 97
Huntsville, Mo., U.S. B5 118
Huntsville, Tn., U.S. C9 135
Huntsville, Tx., U.S. D5 136
Hunucmá, Mex. C7 78
Hunyuan, China D10 28
Huon Gulf, b., Pap. N. Gui. H12 64
Huoxian, China B3 30
Hurd, Cape, c., On., Can. . B3 89
Hurghada, Egypt E11 48
Hurley, Ms., U.S. E5 117
Hurley, N.M., U.S. E1 124
Hurley, N.Y., U.S. D6 125
Hurley, Wi., U.S. B3 142
Hurlock, Md., U.S. C6 113
Huron, Oh., U.S. A3 128
Huron, S.D., U.S. C7 134
Huron, co., Mi., U.S. E7 115
Huron, co., Oh., U.S. A3 128
Huron, stm., Mi., U.S. p14 115
Huron, Lake, l., N.A. C11 92
Huron Mountains, hills, Mi.,
U.S. B3 115
Hurricane, Ut., U.S. F2 137
Hurricane, W.V., U.S. C2 141
Hurst, Il., U.S. F4 106
Hurt, Va., U.S. C3 139
Hurtsboro, Al., U.S. C4 94
Húsavík, Ice. k20 10a

Name	Map Ref.	Page
Huşi, Rom.	F10	20
Hustisford, Wi., U.S.	E5	142
Husum, Ger.	C11	12
Hutag, Mong.	B8	28
Hutchins, Tx., U.S.	n10	136
Hutchinson, Ks., U.S.	D6	109
Hutchinson, Mn., U.S.	F4	116
Hutchinson, co., S.D., U.S.	D8	134
Hutchinson, co., Tx., U.S.	B2	136
Hutchinson Island, i., Fl., U.S.	E6	102
Hutchinson Island, i., S.C., U.S.	k11	133
Hutch Mountain, mtn., Az., U.S.	C4	96
Huttig, Ar., U.S.	D3	97
Huwei, Tai.	E5	30
Huxian, China	C2	30
Huxley, Ia., U.S.	C4	108
Hūzgān, Iran	G13	44
Huzhou, China	E12	28
Hužir, Russia	A9	28
Hvannadalshnúkur, mtn., Ice.	m20	10a
Hwange, Zimb.	B4	56
Hwang Ho see Huang, stm., China	D11	28
Hyannis, Ma., U.S.	C7	114
Hyannis Port, Ma., U.S.	C7	114
Hyargas nuur, l., Mong.	B6	28
Hyattsville, Md., U.S.	C4	113
Hybla Valley, Va., U.S.	g12	139
Hyco, stm., Va., U.S.	D3	139
Hyco Lake, res., N.C., U.S.	A3	126
Hydaburg, Ak., U.S.	D13	95
Hyde, Pa., U.S.	D5	131
Hyde, co., N.C., U.S.	B6	126
Hyde, co., S.D., U.S.	C6	134
Hyden, Austl.	G2	60
Hyde Park, N.Y., U.S.	D7	125
Hyde Park, Ut., U.S.	B4	137
Hyder, Ak., U.S.	D13	95
Hyderābād, India	F3	40
Hyderābād, Pak.	E9	42
Hydeville, Vt., U.S.	D2	138
Hydra see Ídhra, i., Grc.	F9	18
Hydro, Ok., U.S.	B3	129
Hyères, Fr.	F10	16
Hyesan, N. Kor.	C13	28
Hymera, In., U.S.	F3	107
Hyndman, Pa., U.S.	G4	131
Hyndman Peak, mtn., Id., U.S.	F4	105
Hyrum, Ut., U.S.	B4	137
Hythe, Ab., Can.	B1	84
Hyvinkää, Fin.	F11	10

I

Name	Map Ref.	Page
Iaçu, Braz.	D3	74
Ialomița, stm., Rom.	G9	20
Iamonia, Lake, l., Fl., U.S.	B2	102
Iaşi, Rom.	F9	20
Iatt, Lake, res., La., U.S.	C3	111
Iba, Phil.	C7	34
Ibadan, Nig.	E5	50
Ibagué, Col.	C4	70
Ibaiti, Braz.	D7	72
Ibapah Peak, mtn., Ut., U.S.	D2	137
Ibarra, Ec.	C4	70
Ibembo, D.R.C.	C4	54
Iberia, Mo., U.S.	C5	118
Iberia, co., La., U.S.	E4	111
Iberian Mountains see Ibérico, Sistema, mts., Spain	G5	16
Ibérico, Sistema, mts., Spain	G5	16
Iberville, P.Q., Can.	D4	90
Iberville, co., La., U.S.	D4	111
Iberville, Mont d' (Caubvick, Mount), mtn., Can.	g14	90
Ibiá, Braz.	E2	74
Ibicaraí, Braz.	D4	74
Ibiza see Eivissa, i., Spain	H7	16
Ibonma, Indon.	D8	36
Ibotirama, Braz.	D3	74
'Ibrī, Oman	F7	42
Ica, Peru	F4	70
Içá (Putumayo), stm., S.A.	D6	70
Içana, Braz.	C6	70
Içana (Isana), stm., S.A.	C6	70
Ice Harbor Dam, Wa., U.S.	C7	140
Iceland, ctry., Eur.	I18	10a
Iceland Basin	B25	144
Ichaikaronji, India	F2	40
Ichchāpuram, India	F4	40
Ichnia, Ukr.	D12	20
Icicle Creek, stm., Wa., U.S.	B5	140
Ičinskaja Sopka, vulkan, vol., Russia	D17	26
Icó, Braz.	C4	74
Icy Cape, c., Ak., U.S.	A7	95
Icy Strait, strt., Ak., U.S.	k22	95
Ida, Mi., U.S.	G7	115
Ida, co., Ia., U.S.	B2	108
Ida, Lake, l., Mn., U.S.	D3	116
Idabel, Ok., U.S.	D7	129
Ida Grove, Ia., U.S.	B2	108
Idah, Nig.	E6	50
Idaho, co., Id., U.S.	D3	105
Idaho, state, U.S.	E3	105
Idaho Falls, Id., U.S.	F6	105
Idaho Springs, Co., U.S.	B5	99
Idalou, Tx., U.S.	C2	136
Idamay, W.V., U.S.	k10	141
Idaville, In., U.S.	C4	107
Ider, Al., U.S.	A4	94
Ídhi Óros, mtn., Grc.	G10	18
Ídhra, i., Grc.	F9	18
İdil, Tur.	D9	44
Idiofa, D.R.C.	D3	54
Idlib, state, Syria	E7	44
Idoûkâl-en-Taghès, mtn., Niger	C6	50
Idutywa, S. Afr.	E4	56
Ifakara, Tan.	E7	54
Ife, Nig.	E5	50
Iferouâne, Niger	C6	50
Ifôghas, Adrar des, mts., Afr.	C5	50
Iganga, Ug.	C6	54
Igarapé-Açu, Braz.	B2	74
Igarka, Russia	C10	26
Igboho, Nig.	E5	50
İğdir, Tur.	C11	44
Iglesias, Italy	E2	18
Ignacio, Co., U.S.	D3	99
Iguaçu, stm., S.A.	D7	72
Iguala, Mex.	D5	78
Igualada, Spain	G7	16
Iguassu Falls see Iguaçu, Cataratas do, wtfl, Braz.	D7	72
Iguatu, Braz.	C4	74
Iguazú see Iguaçu, stm., S.A.	D7	72
Iguéla, Gabon	D1	54
Iguîdi, 'Erg, dunes, Afr.	A3	50
Iharaña, Madag.	A8	56
Iheya-shima, i., Japan	g6	31a
Ihosy, Madag.	C8	56
Iisalmi, Fin.	E12	10
Iizuka, Japan	D2	31
Ijâfene, des., Maur.	B3	50
Ijebu-Ode, Nig.	E5	50
IJsselmeer, l., Neth.	D9	12
Ijuí, Braz.	D7	72
Ika, Russia	D12	26
Ikaría, i., Grc.	F11	18
Ikeja, Nig.	E5	50
Ikela, D.R.C.	D4	54
Ikerre, Nig.	E6	50
Ikom, Nig.	E6	50
Ikot-Ekpene, Nig.	E6	50
Ila, Nig.	E5	50
Ilagan, Phil.	C8	34
Ilām, Iran	D5	42
Ilan, Tai.	E5	30
Ilaro, Nig.	E5	50
Iława, Pol.	C5	20
Ilbenge, Russia	C14	26
Île-à-la-Crosse, Lac, l., Sk., Can.	B2	91
Ilebo, D.R.C.	D4	54
Île-de-France, hist. reg., Fr.	C8	16
Île-Perrot, P.Q., Can.	q19	90
Ilesha, Nig.	E5	50
Ilha de Moçambique, Moz.	B7	56
Ilhéus, Braz.	D4	74
Iliamna Lake, l., Ak., U.S.	D8	95
Iliamna Volcano, vol., Ak., U.S.	C9	95
Iligan, Phil.	E8	34
Iligan Bay, b., Phil.	E8	34
Ilion, N.Y., U.S.	B5	125
Ilio Point, c., Hi., U.S.	B4	104
Ilizi, Alg.	E6	48
Iljinskij, Russia	E16	26
Illampu, Nevado, mtn., Bol.	G6	70
Illana Bay, b., Phil.	E8	34
Illapel, Chile	D2	69
Illéla, Niger	D6	50
Illichivs'k, Ukr.	F11	20
Illimani, Nevado, mtn., Bol.	B4	72
Illinois, state, U.S.	C4	106
Illinois, stm., Il., U.S.	B5	106
Illinois, stm., Or., U.S.	E3	130
Illinois, stm., U.S.	A7	129
Illinois Peak, mtn., Id., U.S.	B3	105
Illiopolis, Il., U.S.	D4	106
Illmo, Mo., U.S.	D8	118
Il'men', ozero, l., Russia	C5	22
Ilo, Peru	G5	70
Iloilo, Phil.	D8	34
Ilorin, Nig.	E5	50
Ilovlja, Russia	F15	8
Ilwaco, Wa., U.S.	C1	140
Ilwaki, Indon.	E7	36
Imabari, Japan	D2	31
Imandra, ozero, l., Russia	C15	10
Imatra, Fin.	F13	10
Imboden, Ar., U.S.	A4	97
Īmī, Eth.	B8	54
İmişli, Azer.	C13	44
Imlay, Nv., U.S.	C3	121
Imlay City, Mi., U.S.	E7	115
Immokalee, Fl., U.S.	F5	102
Imola, Italy	B3	18
Imperatriz, Braz.	C2	74
Imperia, Italy	C2	18
Imperial, Ca., U.S.	F6	98
Imperial, Mo., U.S.	C7	118
Imperial, Ne., U.S.	D4	120
Imperial, Pa., U.S.	k13	131
Imperial, co., Ca., U.S.	F6	98
Imperial Beach, Ca., U.S.	o15	98
Imperial Dam, U.S.	E1	96
Imperial Reservoir, res., U.S.	E1	96
Imperial Valley, val., Ça., U.S.	F6	98
Impfondo, Congo	C3	54
Imphāl, India	E6	40
I-n-Amenas, Alg.	E6	48
Inanwatan, Indon.	D8	36
Inari, Fin.	B12	10
Inarijärvi, l., Fin.	B12	10
In Belbel, Alg.	F4	14
Inca, Spain	H8	16
Inca de Oro, Chile	C3	69
İnce Burun, c., Tur.	A6	44
Inch'ŏn, S. Kor.	D13	28
Incline Village, Nv., U.S.	D2	121
Indé, Mex.	B3	78
Independence, Ia., U.S.	B6	108
Independence, Ks., U.S.	E8	109
Independence, Ky., U.S.	B5	110
Independence, La., U.S.	D5	111
Independence, Mo., U.S.	B3	118
Independence, Or., U.S.	C3	130
Independence, Va., U.S.	D1	139
Independence, Wi., U.S.	D2	142
Independence, co., Ar., U.S.	B4	97
Independence, stm., N.Y., U.S.	B5	125
Independence Mountains, mts., Nv., U.S.	C5	121
Independence National Historical Park, Pa., U.S.	p21	131
Independence Rock, mtn., Wy., U.S.	D5	143
Inderborskij, Kaz.	E7	26
India, ctry., Asia	E3	40
Indian, stm., On., Can.	B7	89
Indian, stm., De., U.S.	F4	101
Indian, stm., Mi., U.S.	B4	115
Indian, stm., N.Y., U.S.	A5	125
Indiana, Pa., U.S.	E3	131
Indiana, co., Pa., U.S.	E3	131
Indiana, state, U.S.	E5	107
Indiana Dunes National Lakeshore, In., U.S.	A3	107
Indianapolis, In., U.S.	E5	107
Indian Bay, b., Fl., U.S.	D4	102
Indian Cedar Swamp, sw., R.I., U.S.	F2	132
Indian Creek, stm., Oh., U.S.	C1	128
Indian Creek, stm., S.D., U.S.	B2	134
Indian Creek, stm., Tn., U.S.	B3	135
Indian Creek, stm., W.V., U.S.	D4	141
Indian Creek, stm., W.V., U.S.	k9	141
Indian Head, Md., U.S.	C3	113
Indian Island, i., N.C., U.S.	B6	126
Indian Lake, l., Mi., U.S.	C4	115
Indian Lake, l., N.Y., U.S.	B6	125
Indian Lake, l., Oh., U.S.	B2	128
Indian Lake, l., R.I., U.S.	F2	132
Indian Neck, Ct., U.S.	D4	100
Indian Ocean	J11	64
Indianola, Ia., U.S.	C4	108
Indianola, Ms., U.S.	B3	117
Indianola, Ne., U.S.	D5	120
Indian Peak, mtn., Ut., U.S.	E2	137
Indian Peak, mtn., Wy., U.S.	B3	143
Indian Prairie Canal, Fl., U.S.	E5	102
Indian River, co., Fl., U.S.	E6	102
Indian River, b., Fl., U.S.	D6	102
Indian River Bay, b., De., U.S.	F5	101
Indian Rock, mtn., Wa., U.S.	D5	140
Indian Rocks Beach, Fl., U.S.	p10	102
Indian Springs, Nv., U.S.	G6	121
Indian Stream, stm., N.H., U.S.	f7	122
Indiantown, Fl., U.S.	E6	102
Indian Trail, N.C., U.S.	B2	126
Indiga, Russia	A8	22
Indigirka, stm., Russia	C16	26
Indio, Ca., U.S.	F5	98
Indochina, reg., Asia	C4	34
Indonesia, ctry., Asia	D4	36
Indore, India	E3	40
Indramayu, Indon.	E3	36
Indrāvati, stm., India	F4	40
Indus, stm., Asia	D1	40
İnegöl, Tur.	B3	44
Infiernillo, Presa del, res., Mex.	D4	78
Ingal, Niger	C6	50
Ingalls, In., U.S.	E6	107
Ingalls Park, Il., U.S.	B5	106
Ingende, D.R.C.	D3	54
Ingersoll, On., Can.	D4	89
Ingham, Austl.	D4	62
Ingham, co., Mi., U.S.	F6	115
Ingleside, Tx., U.S.	F4	136
Inglewood, Ca., U.S.	n12	98
Ingolstadt, Ger.	F12	12
Ingraham, Lake, l., Fl., U.S.	G5	102
Ingrāj Bāzār, India	E5	40
Ingram, Pa., U.S.	k13	131
Ingrid Christensen Coast, Ant.	D12	67
In Guezzam, Alg.	G6	48
Inguşetija, state, Russia	E6	26
Ingushetia see Inguşetija, state, Russia	E6	26
Inhaca, Ilha da, i., Moz.	D5	56
Inhambane, Moz.	C6	56
Inhambupe, Braz.	F12	70
Inhaminga, Moz.	B6	56
Inharrime, Moz.	C6	56
Inhassoro, Moz.	C6	56
Inhulets', Ukr.	F12	20
Inhumas, Braz.	E2	74
Inírida, stm., Col.	C6	70
Inkerman, N.B., Can.	B5	87
Inkom, Id., U.S.	G6	105
Inkster, Mi., U.S.	p15	115
Inland Sea see Seto-naikai, Japan	E14	28
Inman, Ks., U.S.	D6	109
Inman, S.C., U.S.	A3	133
Inn, stm., Eur.	G12	12
Inner Channel, strt., Belize	B2	80
Inner Hebrides, is., Scot., U.K.	B3	12
Inner Mongolia see Nei Monggol Zizhiqu, prov., China	C10	28
Innisfail, Austl.	D4	62
Innisfail, Ab., Can.	C4	84
Innsbruck, Aus.	G12	12
Inola, Ok., U.S.	A6	129
Inongo, D.R.C.	D3	54
Inowrocław, Pol.	C5	20
In Salah, Alg.	E5	48
Inscription House Ruin, hist., Az., U.S.	A5	96
Institute, W.V., U.S.	m12	141
Inta, Russia	C8	26
Interlachen, Fl., U.S.	C5	102
International Falls, Mn., U.S.	B5	116
Inthanon, Doi, mtn., Thai.	C3	34
Intracoastal Waterway, U.S.	E4	111
Inukjuak, P.Q., Can.	g11	90
Invercargill, N.Z.	q12	63c
Inverell, Austl.	F5	62
Inver Grove Heights, Mn., U.S.	n12	116
Invermere, B.C., Can.	D9	85
Inverness, Scot., U.K.	B4	12
Inverness, Ca., U.S.	C2	98
Inverness, Fl., U.S.	D4	102
Inverness, Ms., U.S.	B3	117
Inverway, Austl.	D4	60
Investigator Strait, strt., Austl.	H2	62
Invisible Mountain, mtn., Id., U.S.	F5	105
Inwood, Ia., U.S.	A1	108
Inwood, N.Y., U.S.	k13	125
Inwood, W.V., U.S.	B6	141
Inyan Kara Creek, stm., Wy., U.S.	B8	143
Inyan Kara Mountain, mtn., Wy., U.S.	B8	143
Inyo, co., Ca., U.S.	D5	98
Inyo, Mount, mtn., Ca., U.S.	D5	98
Inyo Mountains, mts., Ca., U.S.	D4	98
Ioánnina, Grc.	E8	18
Iola, Ks., U.S.	E8	109
Iola, Wi., U.S.	D4	142
Iona, Id., U.S.	F7	105
Ione, Ca., U.S.	C3	98
Iongo, Ang.	C3	54
Ionia, Mi., U.S.	F5	115
Ionia, co., Mi., U.S.	F5	115
Ionian Islands see Iónioi Nísoi, is., Grc.	E7	18
Ionian Sea, Eur.	E7	18
Iónioi Nísoi (Ionian Islands), is., Grc.	E7	18
Iony, ostrov, i., Russia	D16	26
Íos, i., Grc.	F10	18
Iosco, co., Mi., U.S.	D7	115
Iota, La., U.S.	D3	111
Iowa, La., U.S.	D2	111
Iowa, co., Ia., U.S.	C5	108
Iowa, co., Wi., U.S.	E3	142
Iowa, state, U.S.	C4	108
Iowa, stm., Ia., U.S.	C6	108
Iowa, West Branch, stm., Ia., U.S.	B4	108
Iowa City, Ia., U.S.	C6	108
Iowa Falls, Ia., U.S.	B4	108
Iowa Indian Reservation, U.S.	C8	109
Iowa Lake, l., U.S.	A3	108
Iowa Park, Tx., U.S.	C3	136
Iraan, Tx., U.S.	D2	136
Iráklion, Grc.	G10	18
Iran, ctry., Asia	D6	42
Iran Mountains, mts., Asia	C5	36
Trānshahr, Iran	E8	42
Irapuato, Mex.	C4	78
Iraq, ctry., Asia	D4	42
Irati, Braz.	D7	72
Irazú, Volcán, vol., C.R.	C3	80
Irbid, Jord.	D3	42
Irbīl, Iraq	C4	42
Irbit, Russia	C11	22
Irecê, Braz.	D3	74
Iredell, co., N.C., U.S.	B2	126
Ireland, ctry., Eur.	D2	12
Irgiz, Kaz.	E8	26
Irigui, reg., Afr.	C3	50
Iriklinskij, Russia	D10	22
Iringa, Tan.	E7	54
Iriomote-jima, i., Japan	B8	34
Irion, co., Tx., U.S.	D2	136
Iriri, stm., Braz.	D9	70
Irish, Mount, mtn., Nv., U.S.	F6	121
Irish Sea, Eur.	D4	12
Irkutsk, Russia	D12	26
Irminger Basin	C26	144
Irmo, S.C., U.S.	C5	133
Iroise, b., Fr.	C4	16
Iron, co., Mi., U.S.	B2	115
Iron, co., Mo., U.S.	D7	118
Iron, co., Ut., U.S.	F2	137
Iron, co., Wi., U.S.	B3	142
Irondale, Al., U.S.	f7	94
Irondequoit, N.Y., U.S.	B3	125
Iron Gate, val., Eur.	G7	20
Iron Gate Reservoir, res., Ca., U.S.	B2	98
Iron Knob, Austl.	G2	62
Iron Mountain, Mi., U.S.	C2	115
Iron Mountain, mtn., Az., U.S.	D4	96
Iron Mountains, mts., U.S.	D1	139
Iron Ridge, Wi., U.S.	E5	142
Iron River, Mi., U.S.	B2	115
Iron River, Wi., U.S.	B2	142
Ironton, Mo., U.S.	D7	118
Ironton, Oh., U.S.	D3	128
Ironwood, Mi., U.S.	n11	115
Iroquois, On., Can.	C9	89
Iroquois, co., Il., U.S.	C6	106
Iroquois, stm., U.S.	C6	106
Iroquois, Lake, l., Vt., U.S.	B2	138
Iroquois Falls, On., Can.	o19	89
Irosin, Phil.	D8	34
Irpin', Ukr.	D11	20
Irrawaddy see Ayeyarwady, stm., Myan.	C3	34
Irricana, Ab., Can.	D4	84
Irrigon, Or., U.S.	B7	130
Irtyš see Irtysh, stm., Asia	D8	26
Irtysh, stm., Asia	D8	26
Irtysj see Irtysh, stm., Asia	D8	26
Irtyšsk, Kaz.	D9	26
Irumu, D.R.C.	C5	54
Irún, Spain	F6	16
Iruña see Pamplona, Spain	F6	16
Irvine, Ca., U.S.	n13	98
Irvine, Ky., U.S.	C6	110
Irving, Tx., U.S.	n10	136
Irvington, Al., U.S.	E1	94
Irvington, Il., U.S.	E4	106
Irvington, Ky., U.S.	C3	110
Irvington, N.J., U.S.	k8	123
Irvington, N.Y., U.S.	g13	125
Irwin, Pa., U.S.	F2	131
Irwin, co., Ga., U.S.	E3	103
Irwinton, Ga., U.S.	D3	103
Isa, Nig.	D6	50
Isabel, Mount, mtn., Wy., U.S.	D2	143
Isabela, Isla, i., Ec.	D1	70
Isabella, co., Mi., U.S.	E6	115
Isabella Indian Reservation, Mi., U.S.	E6	115
Isabella Lake, l., Mn., U.S.	C7	116
Ísafjarðardjúp, Ice.	k17	10a
Ísafjörður, Ice.	k17	10a
Isana (Içana), stm., S.A.	C5	70
Isanga, D.R.C.	D4	54
Isangel, Vanuatu	k9	62a
Isanti, Mn., U.S.	E5	116
Isanti, co., Mn., U.S.	E5	116
Isar, stm., Eur.	F13	12
Ischia, Isola d', i., Italy	D4	18
Ise, Japan	D3	31
Isernia, Italy	D5	18
Iseyin, Nig.	E5	50
Isfahan see Eşfahān, Iran	D6	42
Ishigaki, Japan	B8	34
Ishikari, stm., Japan	B4	31
Ishikawa, Japan	A9	34
Ishinomaki, Japan	D16	28
Ishpeming, Mi., U.S.	B3	115
Išim, Russia	D8	26
Išim, stm., Asia	D9	26
Isinglass, stm., N.H., U.S.	D4	122
Isiolo, Kenya	C7	54
Isiro, D.R.C.	C5	54
Iskår, stm., Bul.	C10	18
İskenderun, Tur.	D7	44
İskenderun Körfezi, b., Tur.	D6	44
İskilip, Tur.	B6	44
Islāmābād, Pak.	D10	42
Islamorada, Fl., U.S.	H6	102

Name — Map Ref. — Page

Island, co., Wa., U.S. A3 140
Island Beach, N.J., U.S. D4 123
Island City, Or., U.S. B8 130
Island Falls, Me., U.S. B4 112
Island Lake, l., Mb., Can. C4 86
Island Park, R.I., U.S. E6 132
Island Park Reservoir, res., Id., U.S. E7 105
Island Pond, Vt., U.S. B5 138
Island Pond, l., N.H., U.S. E4 122
Islands, Bay of, b., Nf., Can. D2 88
Isla Vista, Ca., U.S. E4 98
Islay, i., Scot., U.K. C3 12
Isle-aux-Morts, Nf., Can. E2 88
Isle of Man, dep., Eur. C4 12
Isle of Palms, S.C., U.S. k12 133
Isle of Wight, co., Va., U.S. D6 139
Isle of Wight Bay, b., Md., U.S. D7 113
Isle Royale National Park, Mi., U.S. h9 115
Islesboro Island, i., Me., U.S. D4 112
Isleta, N.M., U.S. C3 124
Isleta Indian Reservation, N.M., U.S. C3 124
Islington, Ma., U.S. h11 114
Ismailia, Egypt D11 48
İsmayıllı, Azer. B13 44
Isoka, Zam. A5 56
Isola, Ms., U.S. B3 117
Isparta, Tur. D4 44
İspir, Tur. B9 44
Israel, ctry., Asia D2 42
Israel, stm., N.H., U.S. B3 122
Issaquah, Wa., U.S. B3 140
Issaquena, co., Ms., U.S. C2 117
Issia, C. Iv. E3 50
Issoire, Fr. E8 16
Issoudun, Fr. D8 16
Issyk-Kul', Kyrg. E9 26
Issyk-Kul', ozero, l., Kyrg. E9 26
İstanbul, Tur. B3 44
İstanbul Boğazı (Bosporus), strt., Tur. B3 44
Isto, Mount, mtn., Ak., U.S. B11 95
Istokpoga, Lake, l., Fl., U.S. E5 102
Itabaiana, Braz. D4 74
Itabaiana, Braz. C4 74
Itaberaba, Braz. D3 74
Itaberaí, Braz. E2 74
Itabira, Braz. E3 74
Itabuna, Braz. D4 74
Itacoatiara, Braz. D8 70
Itagüí, Col. B4 70
Itaipu Reservoir, res., S.A. C7 72
Itaituba, Braz. D8 70
Itajaí, Braz. D8 72
Itajubá, Braz. F2 74
Itajuípe, Braz. D4 74
Italy, Tx., U.S. C4 136
Italy, ctry., Eur. C4 18
Itamaraju, Braz. E4 74
Itambé, Braz. E3 74
Itānagar, India D6 40
Itaobim, Braz. E3 74
Itapecuru-Mirim, Braz. B3 74
Itaperuna, Braz. F3 74
Itapetinga, Braz. E3 74
Itapetininga, Braz. F2 74
Itapipoca, Braz. B4 74
Itapiranga, Braz. D7 72
Itaporanga, Braz. C4 74
Itaquari, Braz. F3 74
Itaqui, Braz. D6 72
Itārsi, India E3 40
Itasca, Il., U.S. k8 106
Itasca, Tx., U.S. C4 136
Itasca, co., Mn., U.S. C5 116
Itasca, Lake, l., Mn., U.S. C3 116
Itaúna, Braz. F3 74
Itawamba, co., Ms., U.S. A5 117
Itenes see Guaporé, stm., S.A. F7 70
Iténez see Guaporé, stm., S.A. F7 70
Ithaca, Mi., U.S. E6 115
Ithaca, N.Y., U.S. C4 125
Ithaca see Itháki, i., Grc. E8 18
Itháki, i., Grc. E8 18
Itimbiri, stm., D.R.C. C4 54
Itoigawa, Japan C3 31
Itoko, D.R.C. D4 54
Itta Bena, Ms., U.S. B3 117
Ituango, Col. D4 80
Ituberá, Braz. D4 74
Ituiutaba, Braz. E2 74
Itumbiara, Braz. E2 74
Iturama, Braz. E1 74
Iturup, ostrov, i., Russia E16 26
Ituverava, Braz. F2 74
Itzehoe, Ger. D11 12
Iuka, Ms., U.S. A5 117
Iul'tin, Russia C20 26
Iva, S.C., U.S. C2 133
Ivanava, Bela. C8 20
Ivangorod, Russia G13 10
Ivanhoe, Mn., U.S. F2 116
Ivankov, Ukr. D10 20
Ivano-Frankivs'k, Ukr. E8 20
Ivanovo, Russia D6 26
Ivdel', Russia C8 26
Ivigtut, Grnld. F30 82
Ivins, Ut., U.S. F2 137
Ivohibe, Madag. C8 56
Ivory Coast see Cote d'Ivoire, ctry., Afr. E3 50
Ivoryton, Ct., U.S. D6 100
Ivrea, Italy B1 18
Iwaki, Japan D16 28
Iwo, Nig. E5 50
Ixmiquilpan, Méx. C5 78
Ixtapa, Mex. D4 78
Ixtepec, Mex. D5 78
Izabal, Lago de, l., Guat. B2 80
Izamal, Mex. C7 78
Izard, co., Ar., U.S. A4 97
Izberbaš, Russia A12 44
Iževsk, Russia D7 26
Iziaslav, Ukr. D9 20
Izium, Ukr. E14 20
Ižma, stm., Russia A9 22
Izmaïl, Ukr. G10 20
İzmir, Tur. C2 44
İzmir Körfezi, b., Tur. C2 44
İzmit, Tur. B3 44
İzmit Körfezi, b., Tur. B3 44
İznik, Tur. B3 44
İznik Gölü, l., Tur. B3 44
Izucar de Matamoros, Mex. D5 78
Izu-shotō, is., Japan E15 28
Izu Trench F17 64

J

Jabal, Baḩr al- (Mountain Nile), stm., Sudan I11 48
Jabalpur, India E3 40
Jabiru, Austl. C5 60
Jablah, Syria E6 44
Jablonec nad Nisou, Czech Rep. D3 20
Jablonovyj hrebet, mts., Russia D13 26
Jaboatão, Braz. C4 74
Jaboticabal, Braz. F2 74
Jacareí, Braz. F2 74
Jacarezinho, Braz. F2 74
Jaciara, Braz. B7 72
Jacinto City, Tx., U.S. r14 136
Jack, co., Tx., U.S. C3 136
Jackfish Lake, l., Sk., Can. D1 91
Jackman, Me., U.S. C2 112
Jackman Station, Me., U.S. C2 112
Jack Mountain, mtn., Mt., U.S. D4 119
Jack Mountain, mtn., Wa., U.S. A5 140
Jackpot, Nv., U.S. B7 121
Jacksboro, Tn., U.S. C9 135
Jacksboro, Tx., U.S. C3 136
Jacks Mountain, mtn., Pa., U.S. E6 131
Jackson, Al., U.S. D2 94
Jackson, Ca., U.S. C3 98
Jackson, Ga., U.S. C3 103
Jackson, Ky., U.S. C6 110
Jackson, La., U.S. D4 111
Jackson, Mi., U.S. F6 115
Jackson, Mn., U.S. G4 116
Jackson, Mo., U.S. D8 118
Jackson, Ms., U.S. C3 117
Jackson, Oh., U.S. C3 128
Jackson, S.C., U.S. E4 133
Jackson, Tn., U.S. B3 135
Jackson, Wi., U.S. E5 142
Jackson, Wy., U.S. C2 143
Jackson, co., Al., U.S. A3 94
Jackson, co., Ar., U.S. B4 97
Jackson, co., Co., U.S. A4 99
Jackson, co., Fl., U.S. B1 102
Jackson, co., Ga., U.S. B3 103
Jackson, co., Ia., U.S. B7 108
Jackson, co., Il., U.S. F4 106
Jackson, co., In., U.S. G5 107
Jackson, co., Ks., U.S. C8 109
Jackson, co., Ky., U.S. C5 110
Jackson, co., La., U.S. B3 111
Jackson, co., Mi., U.S. F6 115
Jackson, co., Mn., U.S. G3 116
Jackson, co., Mo., U.S. B3 118
Jackson, co., Ms., U.S. E5 117
Jackson, co., N.C., U.S. f9 126
Jackson, co., Oh., U.S. C3 128
Jackson, co., Ok., U.S. C2 129
Jackson, co., Or., U.S. E4 130
Jackson, co., S.D., U.S. D4 134
Jackson, co., Tn., U.S. C8 135
Jackson, co., Tx., U.S. E4 136
Jackson, co., W.V., U.S. C3 141
Jackson, co., Wi., U.S. D3 142
Jackson, stm., Va., U.S. C3 139
Jackson, Lake, l., Fl., U.S. E5 102
Jackson, Lake, l., Fl., U.S. B2 102
Jackson, Mount, mtn., Ant. D34 67
Jackson, Mount, mtn., N.H., U.S. B4 122
Jackson Center, Oh., U.S. B1 128
Jackson Lake, res., Wy., U.S. C2 143
Jackson Mountains, mts., Nv., U.S. B3 121
Jackson's Arm, Nf., Can. D3 88
Jacksons Gap, Al., U.S. C4 94
Jacksonville, Al., U.S. B4 94
Jacksonville, Ar., U.S. C3 97
Jacksonville, Fl., U.S. B5 102
Jacksonville, Il., U.S. D3 106
Jacksonville, N.C., U.S. C5 126
Jacksonville, Or., U.S. E4 130
Jacksonville, Tx., U.S. D5 136
Jacksonville Beach, Fl., U.S. B5 102
Jacksonville Naval Air Station, mil., Fl., U.S. B5 102
Jacks Peak, mtn., Ut., U.S. E3 137
Jacmel, Haiti B5 80
Jacobābād, Pak. E9 42
Jacobina, Braz. D3 74
Jacques-Cartier, stm., P.Q., Can. B6 90
Jacques-Cartier, Détroit de, strt., P.Q., Can. I27 82
Jacquet River, N.B., Can. B4 87
Jacundá, Braz. B2 74
Jada, Nig. E7 50
Jaén, Peru E4 70
Jaén, Spain I5 16
Jaffa, Cape, c., Austl. H2 62
Jaffna, Sri L. H4 40
Jaffrey, N.H., U.S. E2 122
Jagādhri, India C3 40
Jagdalpur, India F4 40
Jagersfontein, S. Afr. D4 56
Jagodnoe, Russia C16 26
Jagtiāl, India F3 40
Jaguaquara, Braz. D4 74
Jaguarão, Braz. E7 72
Jaguaribe, Braz. C4 74
Jahrom, Iran E6 42
Jailolo, Indon. C7 36
Jaipur, India D3 40
Jaisalmer, India D2 40
Jājapur, India E5 40
Jakarta, Indon. E3 36
Jakobshavn, Grnld. E29 82
Jakša, Russia B10 22
Jakutija, state, Russia C14 26
Jakutsk, Russia C14 26
Jal, N.M., U.S. E6 124
Jalālābād, Afg. D10 42
Jalandhar, India C3 40
Jalapa see Xalapa, Mex. D5 78
Jālaun, India D3 40
Jālgaon, India E3 40
Jalingo, Nig. E7 50
Jalisco, state, Mex. C4 78
Jālna, India F3 40
Jālor, India D2 40
Jalostotitlán, Mex. C4 78
Jalpāiguri, India D5 40
Jalūlā', Iraq E11 44
Jamaica, ctry., N.A. E9 76
Jamaica Bay, b., N.Y., U.S. k13 125
Jamaica Channel, strt., N.A. B4 80
Jamal, poluostrov, pen., Russia B8 26
Jamantau, gora, mtn., Russia D7 26
Jambi, Indon. D2 36
Jambol, Bul. C11 18
Jambusar, India E2 40
James, stm., Mo., U.S. E4 118
James, stm., Va., U.S. C5 139
James, stm., U.S. C8 92
James, Lake, l., In., U.S. A7 107
James, Lake, res., N.C., U.S. B1 126
James Bay, b., Can. H23 82
James Branch, stm., De., U.S. F3 101
Jamesburg, N.J., U.S. C4 123
James City, N.C., U.S. B5 126
James City, co., Va., U.S. C6 139
James Island, S.C., U.S. k12 133
James Island, i., Md., U.S. C5 113
James Island, i., S.C., U.S. F8 133
James River Bridge, Va., U.S. k15 139
Jamestown, Austl. G2 62
Jamestown, In., U.S. E4 107
Jamestown, Ky., U.S. D4 110
Jamestown, N.C., U.S. B3 126
Jamestown, N.D., U.S. C7 127
Jamestown, N.Y., U.S. C1 125
Jamestown, Oh., U.S. C2 128
Jamestown, R.I., U.S. F5 132
Jamestown, Tn., U.S. C9 135
James Town, Wy., U.S. E3 143
Jamestown Dam, N.D., U.S. C7 127
Jamestown Reservoir, res., N.D., U.S. C7 127
Jamkhandi, India F3 40
Jammerbugten, b., Den. H3 10
Jammu, India C2 40
Jammu and Kashmir, hist. reg., Asia C10 38
Jamnagar, India E2 40
Jämsä, Fin. F11 10
Jamshedpur, India E5 40
Jamsk, Russia D17 26
Jämtland, hist. reg., Swe. E6 10
Jamuna, stm., Bngl. D5 40
Jana, stm., Russia C15 26
Janaúba, Braz. E3 74
Janaucu, Ilha, i., Braz. C10 70
Janesville, Ca., U.S. B3 98
Janesville, Ia., U.S. B5 108
Janesville, Mn., U.S. F5 116
Janesville, Wi., U.S. F4 142
Jan Mayen, i., Nor. D23 144
Jan Mayen Ridge C24 144
Jansenville, S. Afr. E3 56
Janskij, Russia C15 26
Janskij zaliv, b., Russia B15 26
Januária, Braz. E3 74
Jaora, India E3 40
Japan, ctry., Asia D15 28
Japan, Sea of (East Sea), Asia C14 28
Japan Basin D16 64
Japan Trench E17 64
Japurá (Caquetá), stm., S.A. D6 70
Jaraguá, Braz. E2 74
Jaransk, Russia C8 22
Jarānwāla, Pak. D10 42
Jarcevo, Russia B12 20
Jardim, Braz. C6 72
Jardín América, Arg. D6 72
Jari, stm., Braz. C9 70
Jarocin, Pol. D4 20
Jaroslavl', Russia D6 26
Jarosław, Pol. D7 20
Jarrettsville, Md., U.S. A5 113
Jar-Sale, Russia A13 22
Järva-Jaani, Est. G11 10
Järvenpää, Fin. F11 10
Jarvis Island, i., Oc. E13 58
Jasikan, Ghana E5 50
Jāsk, Iran E7 42
Jaškul', Russia A5 42
Jasło, Pol. E6 20
Jasmine Estates, Fl., U.S. D4 102
Jasnogorsk, Russia B14 20
Jason Islands, is., Falk. Is. H4 69
Jasonville, In., U.S. F3 107
Jasper, Al., U.S. B2 94
Jasper, Fl., U.S. B4 102
Jasper, Ga., U.S. B2 103
Jasper, In., U.S. H4 107
Jasper, Mo., U.S. D3 118
Jasper, Tn., U.S. D8 135
Jasper, Tx., U.S. D6 136
Jasper, co., Ga., U.S. C3 103
Jasper, co., Ia., U.S. C4 108
Jasper, co., Il., U.S. D5 106
Jasper, co., In., U.S. B3 107
Jasper, co., Mo., U.S. D3 118
Jasper, co., Ms., U.S. C4 117
Jasper, co., S.C., U.S. G5 133
Jasper, co., Tx., U.S. D5 136
Jasper National Park, Ab., Can. C1 84
Jataí, Braz. E1 74
Jatni, India E5 40
Jaú, Braz. F2 74
Jaunpur, India D4 40
Java see Jawa, i., Indon. E3 36
Javari (Yavarí), stm., S.A. D5 70
Java Sea see Jawa, Laut, Indon. D3 36
Java Trench I13 64
Jawa (Java), i., Indon. E3 36
Jawa, Laut (Java Sea), Indon. D3 36
Jawhar, Som. J14 48
Jay, Ok., U.S. A7 129
Jay, co., In., U.S. D7 107
Jaya, Puncak, mtn., Indon. G10 32
Jayapura, Indon. G11 32
Jaypur, India F4 40
Jaz Mūrīān, Hāmūn-e, l., Iran E7 42
J. B. Thomas, Lake, res., Tx., U.S. C2 136
Jean, Nv., U.S. H6 121
Jeanerette, La., U.S. E4 111
Jean Lafitte National Historical Park, La., U.S. k12 111
Jeannette, Pa., U.S. F2 131
Jebba, Nig. E5 50
Jeddore Lake, res., Nf., Can. D3 88
Jędrzejów, Pol. D6 20
Jeff Davis, co., Ga., U.S. E4 103
Jeff Davis, co., Tx., U.S. o12 136
Jefferson, Ga., U.S. B3 103
Jefferson, Ia., U.S. B3 108
Jefferson, La., U.S. k11 111
Jefferson, N.C., U.S. A1 126
Jefferson, Oh., U.S. A5 128
Jefferson, Or., U.S. C3 130
Jefferson, S.C., U.S. B7 133
Jefferson, Tx., U.S. C5 136
Jefferson, Wi., U.S. E5 142
Jefferson, co., Al., U.S. B3 94
Jefferson, co., Ar., U.S. C3 97
Jefferson, co., Co., U.S. B5 99
Jefferson, co., Fl., U.S. B3 102
Jefferson, co., Ga., U.S. C4 103
Jefferson, co., Ia., U.S. C5 108
Jefferson, co., Id., U.S. F6 105
Jefferson, co., Il., U.S. E5 106
Jefferson, co., In., U.S. G6 107
Jefferson, co., Ks., U.S. C8 109
Jefferson, co., Ky., U.S. B4 110
Jefferson, co., La., U.S. E5 111
Jefferson, co., Mo., U.S. C7 118
Jefferson, co., Ms., U.S. D2 117
Jefferson, co., Mt., U.S. D4 119
Jefferson, co., Ne., U.S. D8 120
Jefferson, co., N.Y., U.S. A5 125
Jefferson, co., Oh., U.S. B5 128
Jefferson, co., Ok., U.S. C4 129
Jefferson, co., Or., U.S. C5 130
Jefferson, co., Pa., U.S. D3 131
Jefferson, co., Tn., U.S. C10 135
Jefferson, co., Tx., U.S. E5 136
Jefferson, co., W.V., U.S. B7 141
Jefferson, co., Wa., U.S. B1 140
Jefferson, co., Wi., U.S. E5 142
Jefferson, stm., Mt., U.S. E5 119
Jefferson, Mount, mtn., Id., U.S. E7 105
Jefferson, Mount, mtn., Nv., U.S. E5 121
Jefferson, Mount, mtn., Or., U.S. C5 130
Jefferson City, Mo., U.S. C5 118
Jefferson City, Tn., U.S. C10 135
Jefferson Davis, co., La., U.S. D3 111
Jefferson Davis, co., Ms., U.S. D4 117
Jefferson Farms, De., U.S. i7 101
Jefferson Proving Ground, mil., In., U.S. G7 107
Jeffersontown, Ky., U.S. B4 110
Jeffersonville, Ga., U.S. D3 103
Jeffersonville, In., U.S. H6 107
Jeffersonville, Ky., U.S. C6 110
Jeffersonville, Oh., U.S. C2 128
Jeffrey, W.V., U.S. D3 141
Jeffrey City, Wy., U.S. D5 143
Jeffries Creek, stm., S.C., U.S. C8 133
Jega, Nig. D5 50
Jehossee Island, i., S.C., U.S. k11 133
Jēkabpils, Lat. H11 10
Jekyll Island, i., Ga., U.S. E5 103
Jelenia Góra, Pol. D3 20
Jelgava, Lat. H10 10
Jellico, Tn., U.S. C9 135
Jelm Mountain, mtn., Wy., U.S. E7 143
Jemaja, Pulau, i., Indon. C3 36
Jember, Indon. E4 36
Jemez, stm., N.M., U.S. k7 124
Jemez Canyon Dam, N.M., U.S. k7 124
Jemez Indian Reservation, N.M., U.S. h7 124
Jemez Pueblo, N.M., U.S. B3 124
Jemison, Al., U.S. C3 94
Jena, Ger. E12 12
Jena, La., U.S. C3 111
Jeneponto, Indon. E5 36
Jenkins, Ky., U.S. C7 110
Jenkins, co., Ga., U.S. D5 103
Jenkintown, Pa., U.S. o21 131
Jenks, Ok., U.S. A6 129
Jennings, La., U.S. D3 111
Jennings, Mo., U.S. f13 118
Jennings, co., In., U.S. G6 107
Jensen Beach, Fl., U.S. E6 102
Jens Munks Ø, i., Grnld. F32 82
Jequié, Braz. D3 74
Jequitinhonha, Braz. E3 74
Jequitinhonha, stm., Braz. E3 74
Jerada, Mor. D4 48
Jerauld, co., S.D., U.S. C7 134
Jérémie, Haiti B5 80
Jeremoabo, Braz. D4 74
Jerez de García Salinas, Mex. C4 78
Jerez de la Frontera, Spain I3 16
Jerez de los Caballeros, Spain H3 16
Jericho see Arīḩā, Gaza Str. G6 44
Jericho, Vt., U.S. B3 138
Jerid, Chott, l., Tun. D6 48
Jerimoth Hill, hill, R.I., U.S. C1 132
Jermyn, Pa., U.S. C10 131
Jerome, Id., U.S. G4 105
Jerome, Pa., U.S. F4 131
Jerome, co., Id., U.S. G4 105
Jersey, co., Il., U.S. D3 106
Jersey, dep., Eur. F5 12
Jersey City, N.J., U.S. B4 123
Jersey Mountain, mtn., Id., U.S. E3 105
Jersey Shore, Pa., U.S. D7 131
Jerseyville, Il., U.S. D3 106
Jerusalem see Yerushalayim, Isr. G6 42
Jervis Inlet, b., B.C., Can. D6 85
Jesi, Italy C4 18
Jessamine, co., Ky., U.S. C5 110
Jesselton see Kota Kinabalu, Malay. B5 36
Jessore, Bngl. E5 40
Jessup, Md., U.S. B4 113
Jessup, Pa., U.S. m18 131
Jesup, Ga., U.S. E5 103
Jesup, Ia., U.S. B5 108
Jesup, Lake, l., Fl., U.S. D5 102
Jésus, Île, i., P.Q., Can. p19 90
Jesús Carranza, Mex. D5 78
Jesús María, Arg. E5 72
Jetmore, Ks., U.S. D4 109
Jewel Cave National Monument, S.D., U.S. D2 134
Jewell, Ia., U.S. B4 108
Jewell, co., Ks., U.S. C5 109
Jewett City, Ct., U.S. C8 100
Jhālāwār, India E3 40
Jhang Sadar, Pak. D10 42
Jhānsi, India D3 40
Jhelum, Pak. D10 42
Jhunjhunūn, India D3 40
Jiahe, China D3 30
Jiali, China C6 40
Jialing, stm., China E8 28
Jiamusi, China B14 28
Ji'an, China D3 30
Jianchang, China A4 30
Jianchuan, China F8 28
Jiande, China D4 30

Name	Map Ref.	Page
Jiang'an, China	D2	30
Jiangcheng, China	B4	34
Jiangjin, China	F9	28
Jiangle, China	D4	30
Jiangling, China	C3	30
Jiangmen, China	G10	28
Jiangsu, state, China	E11	28
Jiangxi, state, China	F11	28
Jianli, China	D3	30
Jian'ou, China	F11	28
Jianping, China	A4	30
Jianshui, China	G8	28
Jianyang, China	D4	30
Jianyang, China	C1	30
Jiaocheng, China	B3	30
Jiaonan, China	B4	30
Jiaoxian, China	D12	28
Jiaozuo, China	D10	28
Jiashan, China	C4	30
Jibiya, Nig.	D6	50
Jicarilla Apache Indian Reservation, N.M., U.S.	A2	124
Jičín, Czech Rep.	D3	20
Jiddah, Sau. Ar.	F3	38
Jiexiu, China	B3	30
Jieyang, China	G11	28
Jihlava, Czech Rep.	E3	20
Jijel, Alg.	I9	16
Jijiga, Eth.	B8	54
Jilib, Som.	J13	48
Jilin, China	C13	28
Jilin, state, China	C13	28
Jill, Kediet ej, mtn., Maur.	B2	50
Jīma, Eth.	B7	54
Jimbolia, Rom.	G6	20
Jiménez (Ciudad Jiménez), Mex.	B4	78
Jimeta, Nig.	E7	50
Jim Hogg, co., Tx., U.S.	F3	136
Jim Lake, res., N.D., U.S.	B7	127
Jimo, China	B5	30
Jim Thorpe, Pa., U.S.	E10	131
Jim Wells, co., Tx., U.S.	F3	136
Jinan, China	D11	28
Jincheng, China	B3	30
Jīnd, India	D3	40
Jingdezhen, China	F11	28
Jinggangshan, China	F10	28
Jinghai, China	B4	30
Jinghong, China	G8	28
Jingning, China	B2	30
Jingxi, China	E2	30
Jingxian, China	D2	30
Jinhua, China	F11	28
Jining, China	D11	28
Jining, China	C10	28
Jinja, Ug.	C6	54
Jinning, China	E1	30
Jinsha, China	D2	30
Jinshi, China	F10	28
Jinzhai, China	C4	30
Jinzhou, China	C12	28
Jinzhou, China	D12	28
Ji-Paraná, Braz.	F7	70
Jishou, China	D2	30
Jisr ash-Shughūr, Syria	E7	44
Jiu, stm., Rom.	G7	20
Jiujiang, China	F11	28
Jiulong (Kowloon), China	E3	30
Jiuquan, China	D7	28
Jiutai, China	C13	28
Jixi, China	B14	28
Jixian, China	C11	28
Jīzān, Sau. Ar.	G4	38
Joanna, S.C., U.S.	C4	133
João Pessoa, Braz.	C5	74
João Pinheiro, Braz.	E2	74
Job Peak, mtn., Nv., U.S.	D3	121
Jocassee, Lake, res., U.S.	B1	133
Jódar, Spain	I5	16
Jo Daviess, co., Il., U.S.	A3	106
Jodhpur, India	D2	40
Joe Batt's Arm [-Barr'd Islands-Shoal Bay], Nf., Can.	D4	88
Joensuu, Fin.	E13	10
Joes Brook, stm., Vt., U.S.	C4	138
Joes Creek, stm., W.V., U.S.	m12	141
Joetsu, Japan	D15	28
Joffre, Mount, mtn., Can.	D3	84
Johannesburg, S. Afr.	D4	56
John, Cape, c., N.S., Can.	D6	87
John Day, Or., U.S.	C8	130
John Day, stm., Or., U.S.	B6	130
John Day, stm., U.S.	D5	140
John Day Fossil Beds National Monument, Or., U.S.	C6	130
John F. Kennedy Space Center, sci., Fl., U.S.	D6	102
John H. Kerr Dam, Va., U.S.	D4	139
John H. Kerr Reservoir, res., U.S.	D4	139
John Martin Reservoir, res., Co., U.S.	C7	99
John Muir National Historical Site, hist., Ca., U.S.	h8	98
John Redmond Reservoir, res., Ks., U.S.	D8	109
John Sevier, Tn., U.S.	m14	135
Johns Island, i., S.C., U.S.	F7	133
Johnson, Ks., U.S.	E2	109
Johnson, Vt., U.S.	B3	138
Johnson, co., Ar., U.S.	B2	97
Johnson, co., Ga., U.S.	D4	103
Johnson, co., Ia., U.S.	C6	108
Johnson, co., Il., U.S.	F5	106
Johnson, co., In., U.S.	F5	107
Johnson, co., Ks., U.S.	D9	109
Johnson, co., Ky., U.S.	C7	110
Johnson, co., Mo., U.S.	C4	118
Johnson, co., Ne., U.S.	D9	120
Johnson, co., Tn., U.S.	C12	135
Johnson, co., Tx., U.S.	C4	136
Johnson, co., Wy., U.S.	B6	143
Johnsonburg, Pa., U.S.	D4	131
Johnson City, N.Y., U.S.	C5	125
Johnson City, Tn., U.S.	C11	135
Johnson City, Tx., U.S.	D3	136
Johnson Creek, Wi., U.S.	E5	142
Johnsonville, S.C., U.S.	D9	133
Johns Pass, strt., Fl., U.S.	p10	102
Johnston, Ia., U.S.	e8	108
Johnston, R.I., U.S.	C4	132
Johnston, S.C., U.S.	D4	133
Johnston, co., N.C., U.S.	B4	126
Johnston, co., Ok., U.S.	C5	129
Johnston Atoll, atoll, Oc.	G22	64
Johnston City, Il., U.S.	F5	106
Johnston Key, i., Fl., U.S.	H5	102
Johnstown, Co., U.S.	A6	99
Johnstown, N.Y., U.S.	B6	125
Johnstown, Oh., U.S.	B3	128
Johnstown, Pa., U.S.	F4	131
John W. Flannagan Reservoir, res., Va., U.S.	e9	139
Johor Bahru, Malay.	C2	36
Joigny, Fr.	C8	16
Joiner, Ar., U.S.	B5	97
Joinville, Braz.	D8	72
Jokkmokk, Swe.	C8	10
Joliet, Il., U.S.	B5	106
Joliette, P.Q., Can.	C4	90
Jolo, Phil.	E8	34
Jolo Island, i., Phil.	E8	34
Jomda, China	E7	28
Jones, Ok., U.S.	B4	129
Jones, co., Ga., U.S.	C3	103
Jones, co., Ia., U.S.	B6	108
Jones, co., Ms., U.S.	D4	117
Jones, co., N.C., U.S.	B5	126
Jones, co., S.D., U.S.	D5	134
Jones, co., Tx., U.S.	C3	136
Jonesboro, Ar., U.S.	B5	97
Jonesboro, Ga., U.S.	C2	103
Jonesboro, Il., U.S.	F4	106
Jonesboro, In., U.S.	D6	107
Jonesboro, La., U.S.	B3	111
Jonesborough, Tn., U.S.	C11	135
Jonesburg, Mo., U.S.	C6	118
Jones Creek, Tx., U.S.	s14	136
Jones Mill, Ar., U.S.	C3	97
Jonesport, Me., U.S.	D5	112
Jonestown, Ms., U.S.	A3	117
Jonesville, La., U.S.	C4	111
Jonesville, Mi., U.S.	G6	115
Jonesville, N.C., U.S.	A2	126
Jonesville, S.C., U.S.	B4	133
Jonesville, Va., U.S.	f8	139
Joniškis, Lith.	H10	10
Jonquière, P.Q., Can.	A6	90
Jonuta, Mex.	D6	78
Joplin, Mo., U.S.	D3	118
Joppatowne, Md., U.S.	B5	113
Jordan, Mn., U.S.	F5	116
Jordan, ctry., Asia	D3	42
Jordan, stm., Asia	F6	44
Jordan, stm., Ut., U.S.	C4	137
Jordan Creek, stm., U.S.	E9	130
Jordan Lake, res., Al., U.S.	C3	94
Jorhāt, India	D6	40
Jornado del Muerto, des., N.M., U.S.	D3	124
Joroinen, Fin.	E12	10
Jos, Nig.	E6	50
José de San Martín, Arg.	F2	69
Joseph, Or., U.S.	B9	130
Joseph, Lac, l., Nf., Can.	h8	88
Joseph Bonaparte Gulf, b., Austl.	C4	60
Joseph City, Az., U.S.	C5	96
Josephine, co., Or., U.S.	E3	130
Joshua, Tx., U.S.	n9	136
Joshua Tree, Ca., U.S.	E5	98
Joshua Tree National Monument, Ca., U.S.	F6	98
Jostedalsbreen, Nor.	F2	10
Jourdanton, Tx., U.S.	E3	136
Jovellanos, Cuba	A3	80
J. Percy Priest Lake, res., U.S.	A5	135
Juab, co., Ut., U.S.	D2	137
Juan Aldama, Mex.	C4	78
Juan de Fuca, Strait of, strt., N.A.	B3	92
Juan Fernandez, Archipiélago, is., Chile	E1	72
Juanjuí, Peru	E4	70
Juazeiro, Braz.	C3	74
Juazeiro do Norte, Braz.	C4	74
Juba, Sudan	J11	48
Jubba (Genalē), stm., Afr.	C8	54
Juby, Cap, c., Mor.	A2	50
Júcar, stm., Spain	H6	16
Juchitán de Zaragoza, Mex.	D6	78
Judenau, Aus.	G14	12
Judith, stm., Mt., U.S.	C7	119
Judith, Point, c., R.I., U.S.	G4	101
Judith Basin, co., Mt., U.S.	C6	119
Judith Island, i., N.C., U.S.	B6	126
Judith Mountains, mts., Mt., U.S.	C7	119
Judith Peak, mtn., Mt., U.S.	C7	119
Judsonia, Ar., U.S.	B4	97
Juhnov, Russia	B13	20
Juidongshan, China	E4	30
Juiz de Fora, Braz.	F3	74
Jukta, Russia	C12	26
Julesburg, Co., U.S.	A8	99
Juliaca, Peru	G5	70
Julia Creek, Austl.	E3	62
Julian, Ca., U.S.	F5	98
Julian, W.V., U.S.	C3	141
Julian Alps, mts., Eur.	A4	18
Juliana Top, mtn., Sur.	C8	70
Julianehåb, Grnld.	F30	82
Jumba, Som.	D8	54
Jumbo Peak, mtn., Nv., U.S.	G7	121
Jumilla, Spain	H6	16
Jump, stm., Wi., U.S.	C3	142
Jūnāgadh, India	E2	40
Junction, Tx., U.S.	D3	136
Junction City, Ar., U.S.	D3	97
Junction City, Ks., U.S.	C7	109
Junction City, Ky., U.S.	C5	110
Junction City, La., U.S.	A3	111
Junction City, Or., U.S.	C3	130
Jundiaí, Braz.	F2	74
Juneau, Ak., U.S.	D13	95
Juneau, Wi., U.S.	E5	142
Juneau, co., Wi., U.S.	E3	142
Junee, Austl.	G4	62
June in Winter, Lake, l., Fl., U.S.	E5	102
Jungar Qi, China	D10	28
Junggar Pendi, China	B5	28
Juniata, Ne., U.S.	D7	120
Juniata, co., Pa., U.S.	F7	131
Juniata, stm., Pa., U.S.	F7	131
Junín, Arg.	A5	72
Junior Lake, l., Me., U.S.	C4	112
Juniper Mountains, mts., Az., U.S.	B2	96
Junipero Serra Peak, mtn., Ca., U.S.	D3	98
Jūniyah, Leb.	F6	44
Junlian, China	D1	30
Junxian, China	E10	28
Jupiter, Fl., U.S.	F6	102
Jupiter Inlet, b., Fl., U.S.	F6	102
Jupiter Island, i., Fl., U.S.	E6	102
Jur, Russia	D15	26
Jura, i., Scot., U.K.	C4	12
Jurga, Russia	D10	26
Jūrmala, Lat.	H10	10
Juruá, stm., S.A.	E6	70
Juruena, stm., Braz.	F8	70
Jurumirim, Represa, res., Braz.	C8	72
Juškozero, Russia	B5	22
Jussara, Braz.	B7	72
Justin, Tx., U.S.	C4	136
Jutaí, stm., Braz.	D6	70
Jutiapa, Guat.	C1	80
Juticalpa, Hond.	C2	80
Jutland see Jylland, reg., Den.	I3	10
Juventud, Isla de la, i., Cuba	A3	80
Juxian, China	B4	30
Južno-Sahalinsk, Russia	E16	26
Južno-Ural'sk, Russia	D11	22
Jylland, reg., Den.	I3	10
Jyväskylä, Fin.	E11	10

K

K2 (Qogir Feng), mtn., Asia	B3	40
Kaaawa, Hi., U.S.	f10	104
Kaahka, Turk.	C7	42
Kaala, mtn., Hi., U.S.	f9	104
Kaalualu Bay, b., Hi., U.S.	E6	104
Kaaumakua, Puu, mtn., Hi., U.S.	f10	104
Kabaena, Pulau, i., Indon.	E6	36
Kabala, S.L.	E2	50
Kabale, Ug.	D5	54
Kabalega Falls, wtfl, Ug.	C6	54
Kabalo, D.R.C.	D5	54
Kabambare, D.R.C.	D5	54
Kabardino-Balkarija, state, Russia	E6	26
Kabba, Nig.	E6	50
Kabetogama Lake, l., Mn., U.S.	B5	116
Kabinda, D.R.C.	D4	54
Kabīr Kūh, mts., Iran	F12	44
Kābol, Afg.	D9	42
Kabompo, stm., Zam.	A3	56
Kabongo, D.R.C.	E5	54
Kabūdarāhang, Iran	E13	44
Kābūd see Kābol, Afg.	D9	42
Kabwe, Zam.	A4	56
Kabylie, reg., Alg.	I9	16
Kachchh, Gulf of, b., India	E1	40
Kachess Lake, res., Wa., U.S.	B4	140
Kačkanar, Russia	C10	22
Kadan Kyun, i., Myan.	D4	34
Kade, Ghana	E4	50
Kadınhanı, Tur.	A4	44
Kadiolo, Mali	D3	50
Kadirli, Tur.	D7	44
Kadoka, S.D., U.S.	D4	134
Kadoma, Zimb.	B4	56
Kaduna, Nig.	D6	50
Kaduna, stm., Nig.	D6	50
Kāduqlī, Sudan	H10	48
Kadykčan, Russia	C16	26
Kadžerom, Russia	B10	22
Kaédi, Maur.	C2	50
Kaélé, Cam.	A2	54
Kaena Point, c., Hi., U.S.	B3	104
Kafanchan, Nig.	E6	50
Kaffrine, Sen.	D1	50
Kafia Kingi, Sudan	I9	48
Kafue, Zam.	B4	56
Kafue, stm., Zam.	A4	56
Kaga, Japan	C3	31
Kaga Bandoro, C.A.R.	B3	54
Kagera, stm., Afr.	D6	54
Kağızman, Tur.	B10	44
Kagoshima, Japan	E14	28
Kagul see Cahul, Mol.	G10	20
Kahaluu, Hi., U.S.	D6	104
Kahaluu, Hi., U.S.	g10	104
Kahama, Tan.	D6	54
Kahana Bay, b., Hi., U.S.	f10	104
Kahemba, D.R.C.	E3	54
Kahoka, Mo., U.S.	A6	118
Kahoolawe, i., Hi., U.S.	C5	104
Kahramanmaraş, Tur.	D7	44
Kahuku, Hi., U.S.	B4	104
Kahuku Point, c., Hi., U.S.	B4	104
Kahului, Hi., U.S.	C5	104
Kahului Bay, b., Hi., U.S.	C5	104
Kai, Kepulauan, is., Indon.	E8	36
Kaibab Indian Reservation, Az., U.S.	A3	96
Kaifeng, China	E10	28
Kaikoura, N.Z.	p13	63c
Kailahun, S.L.	E2	50
Kailas see Kangrinboqê Feng, mtn., China	E4	28
Kailas Range see Gangdisê Shan, mts., China	E4	28
Kaili, China	D2	30
Kailu, China	C12	28
Kailua, Hi., U.S.	B4	104
Kailua Bay, b., Hi., U.S.	g11	104
Kailua Kona, Hi., U.S.	D6	104
Kainji Lake, res., Nig.	D5	50
Kaiping, China	E3	30
Kairouan, Tun.	C7	48
Kaiserslautern, Ger.	F10	12
Kaitaia, N.Z.	o13	63c
Kaithal, India	D3	40
Kaiwi Channel, strt., Hi., U.S.	h17	92a
Kaiwi Channel, strt., Hi., U.S.	B4	104
Kaixian, China	C2	30
Kaiyuan, China	C12	28
Kaiyuan, China	E1	30
Kajaani, Fin.	D12	10
Kajakī, Band-e, res., Afg.	D9	42
Kajang, Malay.	C2	36
Kajiado, Kenya	D7	54
Kajnar, Kaz.	E9	26
Kaka, Sudan	A6	54
Kakamas, S. Afr.	D3	56
Kakamega, Kenya	C6	54
Kaka Point, c., Hi., U.S.	C5	104
Kakata, Lib.	E2	50
Kake, Ak., U.S.	D13	95
Kakhovka Reservoir see Kakhovs'ke vodoskhovyshche, res., Ukr.	F13	20
Kakhovs'ke vodoskhovyshche, res., Ukr.	F13	20
Kākināda, India	F4	40
Kalaa Kebira, Tun.	G3	18
Kalaallit Nunaat see Greenland, dep., N.A.	D30	82
Kalabahi, Indon.	E6	36
Kalabo, Zam.	B3	56
Kalač, Russia	D7	22
Kalač-na-Donu, Russia	E7	22
Kaladan, stm., Asia	B2	34
Kalahari Desert, des., Afr.	C3	56
Kalaheo, Hi., U.S.	B2	104
Kalajoki, Fin.	D10	10
Kalakan, Russia	D13	26
Kalama, Wa., U.S.	C3	140
Kalámai, Grc.	E8	18
Kalamazoo, Mi., U.S.	F5	115
Kalamazoo, co., Mi., U.S.	F5	115
Kalamazoo, stm., Mi., U.S.	F5	115
Kalamits'ka zatoka, b., Ukr.	G12	20
Kalanchak, Ukr.	F12	20
Kalao, Pulau, i., Indon.	E6	36
Kalaotoa, Pulau, i., Indon.	E6	36
Kalasin, Thai.	C4	34
Kalāt, Pak.	E9	42
Kalaupapa Peninsula, pen., Hi., U.S.	B5	104
Kalaw, Myan.	B3	34
Kalawao, co., Hi., U.S.	B5	104
Kalbarri, Austl.	F1	60
Kaleden, B.C., Can.	E8	85
Kalemie, D.R.C.	E5	54
Kalemyo, Myan.	B2	34
Kalena, Puu, mtn., Hi., U.S.	g9	104
Kalene Hill, Zam.	A3	56
Kalevala, Russia	D14	10
Kalewa, Myan.	B2	34
Kalgin Island, i., Ak., U.S.	g16	95
Kalgoorlie-Boulder, Austl.	G3	60
Kalibo, Phil.	D8	34
Kalima, D.R.C.	D5	54
Kalimantan see Borneo, i., Asia	D4	36
Kálimnos, Grc.	F11	18
Kálimnos, i., Grc.	F11	18
Kālimpang, India	D5	40
Kalinin see Tver', Russia	D5	26
Kaliningrad, Russia	D4	26
Kalinkavičy, Bela.	C10	20
Kalispel Indian Reservation, Wa., U.S.	A8	140
Kalispell, Mt., U.S.	B2	119
Kalisz, Pol.	D5	20
Kalixälven, stm., Swe.	C9	10
Kalkaska, Mi., U.S.	D5	115
Kalkaska, co., Mi., U.S.	D5	115
Kallavesi, l., Fin.	E12	10
Kalmar, Swe.	H7	10
Kalmarsund, strt., Swe.	H7	10
Kalmykija, state, Russia	E6	26
Kalohi Channel, strt., Hi., U.S.	C4	104
Kaloli Point, c., Hi., U.S.	D7	104
Kalomo, Zam.	B4	56
Kalona, Ia., U.S.	C6	108
Kalone Peak, mtn., B.C., Can.	C4	85
Kalpin, China	A3	40
Kalsūbai, mtn., India	F2	40
Kaluga, Russia	D5	26
Kalush, Ukr.	E8	20
Kalutara, Sri L.	H4	40
Kalyān, India	F2	40
Kama, D.R.C.	D5	54
Kama, stm., Russia	D7	26
Kamaishi, Japan	D16	28
Kamakou, mtn., Hi., U.S.	B5	104
Kamālia, Pak.	D10	42
Kaman, Tur.	C5	44
Kamarān, i., Yemen	G4	38
Kama Reservoir see Kamskoe vodohranilišče, res., Russia	C10	22
Kamas, Ut., U.S.	C4	137
Kambalda, Austl.	G3	60
Kambove, D.R.C.	F5	54
Kamčatka, poluostrov, pen., Russia	D17	26
Kamchatka Peninsula see Kamčatka, poluostrov, pen., Russia	D17	26
Kamen', gora, mtn., Russia	C11	26
Kamenka, Russia	D15	20
Kamenka, Russia	D7	22
Kamen'-na-Obi, Russia	D10	26
Kamenskoe, Russia	C18	26
Kamensk-Ural'skij, Russia	C11	22
Kāmet, mtn., Asia	C3	40
Kamiah, Id., U.S.	C2	105
Kamiak Butte, mtn., Wa., U.S.	C8	140
Kam'ianets'-Podil's'kyi, Ukr.	E9	20
Kamina, D.R.C.	E5	54
Kamloops, B.C., Can.	D7	85
Kamo, Arm.	B11	44
Kampala, Ug.	C6	54
Kampar, Malay.	C2	36
Kampen, Neth.	D9	12
Kampeska, Lake, l., S.D., U.S.	C8	134
Kamphaeng Phet, Thai.	C3	34
Kâmpóng Cham, Camb.	D5	34
Kâmpóng Chhnăng, Camb.	D4	34
Kâmpóng Saôm, Camb.	D4	34
Kâmpóng Thum, Camb.	D4	34
Kâmpôt, Camb.	D4	34
Kampti, Burkina	D4	50
Kampuchea see Cambodia, ctry., Asia	D4	34
Kamskoe vodohranilišče, res., Russia	C10	22
Kamuela (Waimea), Hi., U.S.	C6	104
Kamyšin, Russia	D6	26
Kamyšlov, Russia	C11	22
Kanab, Ut., U.S.	F3	137
Kanab Creek, stm., U.S.	A3	96
Kanabec, co., Mn., U.S.	E5	116
Kanaga Island, i., Ak., U.S.	E4	95
Kanairiktok, stm., Nf., Can.	g9	88
Kananga, D.R.C.	E4	54
Kanapou Bay, b., Hi., U.S.	C5	104
Kanaš, Russia	C8	22
Kanata, On., Can.	B9	89
Kanawha, Ia., U.S.	B4	108
Kanawha, co., W.V., U.S.	C3	141
Kanawha, stm., W.V., U.S.	C3	141
Kanazawa, Japan	D15	28
Kānchenjunga, mtn., Asia	D5	40
Kānchipuram, India	G3	40
Kandahar see Qandahār, Afg.	D9	42
Kandalaksha, Russia	C15	10
Kandalaksha Bay see Kandalakšskaja guba, b., Russia	A5	22

Name	Map Ref.	Page

Kandalakšskaja guba, b., Russia . . . . A5 — 22
Kandale, D.R.C. . . . . E3 — 54
Kandangan, Indon. . . . . . . D5 — 36
Kandi, Benin . . . . D5 — 50
Kandira, Tur. . . . . B4 — 44
Kandiyohi, co., Mn., U.S. . . E3 — 116
Kandy, Sri L. . . . . H4 — 40
Kane, Pa., U.S. . . . . C4 — 131
Kane, co., Il., U.S. . . . . B5 — 106
Kane, co., Ut., U.S. . . . . . . F3 — 137
Kanem, prov., Chad . . . . . D8 — 50
Kaneohe, Hi., U.S. . . . . . . B4 — 104
Kaneohe Bay, b., Hi., U.S. . g10 — 104
Kaneohe Bay Marine Corps Air Station, mil., Hi., U.S. . . . . g10 — 104
Kangaba, Mali . . . . D3 — 50
Kangal, Tur. . . . . C7 — 44
Kangān, Iran . . . . E6 — 42
Kangar, Malay. . . . . B2 — 36
Kangaroo Island, i., Austl. . H2 — 62
Kangāvar, Iran . . . . E12 — 44
Kangbao, China . . . . A3 — 30
Kangean, Pulau, i., Indon. . E5 — 36
Kanggye, N. Kor. . . . . C13 — 28
Kango, Gabon . . . . C2 — 54
Kangpu, China . . . . A3 — 34
Kangrinboqê Feng, mtn., China . . . . E4 — 28
Kangshan, Tai. . . . . E5 — 30
Kangto, mtn., Asia . . . . . . A2 — 34
Kaniama, D.R.C. . . . . E4 — 54
Kaniet Islands, is., Pap. N. Gui. . . . . G12 — 32
Kanin, poluostrov, pen., Russia . . . . C6 — 26
Kaningo, Kenya . . . . D7 — 54
Kanin Nos, Russia . . . . . . A7 — 22
Kanin Nos, mys, c., Russia C6 — 26
Kanjiža, Yugo. . . . . A8 — 18
Kankakee, Il., U.S. . . . . . . B6 — 106
Kankakee, co., Il., U.S. . . . . B6 — 106
Kankakee, stm., U.S. . . . . . B5 — 106
Kankan, Gui. . . . . D3 — 50
Känker, India . . . . E4 — 40
Kanmaw Kyun, i., Myan. . . . D3 — 34
Kannapolis, N.C., U.S. . . . . B2 — 126
Kannonkoski, Fin. . . . . . . E11 — 10
Kano, Nig. . . . . D6 — 50
Kanopolis, Ks., U.S. . . . . . D5 — 109
Kanopolis Lake, res., Ks., U.S. . . . . D5 — 109
Kanoya, Japan . . . . D2 — 31
Kānpur, India . . . . D4 — 40
Kansas, Il., U.S. . . . . D6 — 106
Kansas, state, U.S. . . . . . . D5 — 109
Kansas, stm., Ks., U.S. . . . C7 — 109
Kansas City, Ks., U.S. . . . . C9 — 109
Kansas City, Mo., U.S. . . . . B3 — 118
Kansk, Russia . . . . D11 — 26
Kantang, Thai. . . . . E3 — 34
Kantchari, Burkina . . . . . . D5 — 50
Kantemirovka, Russia . . . . E15 — 20
Kanye, Bots. . . . . D4 — 56
Kaohsiung, Tai. . . . . L9 — 30
Kaoko Veld, plat., Nmb. . . . B1 — 56
Kaolack, Sen. . . . . D1 — 50
Kaoma, Zam. . . . . A3 — 56
Kaouar, reg., Niger . . . . . . C7 — 50
Kapaa, Hi., U.S. . . . . A2 — 104
Kapaau, Hi., U.S. . . . . C6 — 104
Kapan, Arm. . . . . C12 — 44
Kapanga, D.R.C. . . . . E4 — 54
Kapapa Island, i., Hi., U.S. . g10 — 104
Kapčagaj, Kaz. . . . . B11 — 42
Kapčagajskoe vodohranilišče, res., Kaz. . . . . B11 — 42
Kapchagay Reservoir see Kapčagajskoe vodohranilišče, res., Kaz. . . . . B11 — 42
Kapfenberg, Aus. . . . . G14 — 12
Kapiri Mposhi, Zam. . . . . . A4 — 56
Kaplan, La., U.S. . . . . D3 — 111
Kapoeta, Sudan . . . . C6 — 54
Kaposvár, Hung. . . . . F4 — 20
Kaptai Lake see Karnaphuli Reservoir, res., Bngl. . . E6 — 40
Kapuas, stm., Indon. . . . . . D3 — 36
Kapuas, stm., Indon. . . . . . D4 — 36
Kapuas Hulu, Pegunungan (Kapuas Hulu, Pergunungan), mts., Asia . . . . C4 — 36
Kapuas Hulu, Pergunungan (Kapuas Hulu, Pegunungan), mts., Asia C4 — 36
Kapuskasing, On., Can. . . . o19 — 89
Kapuvár, Hung. . . . . F4 — 20
Kapyľ, Bela. . . . . C9 — 20
Kara, Russia . . . . A10 — 26
Kara-Balta, Kyrg. . . . . A2 — 40
Karabaš, Russia . . . . C11 — 22
Kara-Bogaz-Gol, zaliv, b., Turk. . . . . E7 — 26
Kara-Bogaz-Gol Gulf see Kara-Bogaz-Gol, zaliv, b., Turk. . . . . E7 — 26
Karabük, Tur. . . . . B5 — 44
Karabula, Russia . . . . D11 — 26
Karaburun, Tur. . . . . C2 — 44
Karabutak, Kaz. . . . . E11 — 22
Karacabey, Tur. . . . . B3 — 44

Karačaevo-Čerkesija, state, Russia . . . . E6 — 26
Karačev, Russia . . . . C13 — 20
Karáchi, Pak. . . . . F9 — 42
Karād, India . . . . F2 — 40
Karaganda, Kaz. . . . . E9 — 26
Karaginskij, ostrov, i., Russia D18 — 26
Karaginskij zaliv, b., Russia . D18 — 26
Kāraikkudi, India . . . . G3 — 40
Karaj, Iran . . . . C6 — 42
Karakaya Baraji, res., Tur. . . C8 — 44
Karakelong, Pulau, i., Indon. F8 — 32
Karakol, Kyrg. . . . . E9 — 26
Karakoram Pass, Asia . . . . B3 — 40
Karakoram Range, mts., Asia B3 — 40
Karakul', Uzb. . . . . C8 — 42
Kara-Kum Canal see Garagumskij kanal imeni Prezidenta Turkmenistana S.A. Nijazova, Turk. . . . . . C8 — 42
Karaman, Tur. . . . . D5 — 44
Karamay, China . . . . B4 — 28
Karamea Bight, b., N.Z. . . . p13 — 63c
Karapınar, Tur. . . . . D5 — 44
Karasay, China . . . . B4 — 40
Karasburg, Nmb. . . . . D2 — 56
Kara Sea see Karskoe more, Russia . . . . B8 — 26
Karasu, Tur. . . . . B4 — 44
Karasu, stm., Tur. . . . . C9 — 44
Karasuk, Russia . . . . D9 — 26
Karatau, Kaz. . . . . B10 — 42
Karatau, hrebet, mts., Kaz. . E8 — 26
Karatobe, Kaz. . . . . E9 — 22
Karaton, Kaz. . . . . A6 — 42
Karatsu, Japan . . . . D1 — 31
Karaul, Kaz. . . . . B3 — 28
Karaul, Russia . . . . B10 — 26
Karawang, Indon. . . . . E3 — 36
Karažal, Kaz. . . . . B2 — 28
Karbalā', Iraq . . . . D4 — 42
Karbalā', state, Iraq . . . . . . F10 — 44
Kårböle, Swe. . . . . F6 — 10
Karcag, Hung. . . . . F6 — 20
Kardeljevo, Cro. . . . . C6 — 18
Kardhítsa, Grc. . . . . E8 — 18
Kărdžali, Bul. . . . . D10 — 18
Karelia see Karelija, state, Russia . . . . C5 — 26
Karelia, hist. reg., Eur. . . . . C12 — 6
Karelija, state, Russia . . . . . C5 — 26
Karema, Tan. . . . . E6 — 54
Karesuando, Swe. . . . . B10 — 10
Kargopol', Russia . . . . C5 — 26
Kariba, Zimb. . . . . B4 — 56
Kariba, Lake, res., Afr. . . . . B4 — 56
Karibib, Nmb. . . . . C2 — 56
Karigasniemi, Fin. . . . . B11 — 10
Karimata, Selat (Karimata Strait), strt., Indon. . . . D3 — 36
Karimata Strait see Karimata, Selat, strt., Indon. . . . . D3 — 36
Karīmganj, India . . . . E6 — 40
Karīmnagar, India . . . . F3 — 40
Karimunjawa, Pulau, i., Indon. . . . . E4 — 36
Karisimbi, Volcan, vol., Afr. D5 — 54
Karkaralinsk, Kaz. . . . . B3 — 28
Karkar Island, i., Pap. N. Gui. . . . . G12 — 32
Karkheh, stm., Iran . . . . . . G12 — 44
Karkinits'ka zatoka, b., Ukr. G12 — 20
Karkūk, Iraq . . . . C4 — 42
Karlivka, Ukr. . . . . E13 — 20
Karl-Marx-Stadt see Chemnitz, Ger. . . . . E11 — 12
Karlovac, Cro. . . . . B5 — 18
Karlovy Vary, Czech Rep. . . D2 — 20
Karlshamn, Swe. . . . . H6 — 10
Karlskoga, Swe. . . . . G6 — 10
Karlskrona, Swe. . . . . H6 — 10
Karlsruhe, Ger. . . . . F11 — 12
Karlstad, Swe. . . . . G5 — 10
Karlstad, Mn., U.S. . . . . . . B2 — 116
Karma, Niger . . . . D5 — 50
Karnāl, India . . . . D3 — 40
Karnaphuli Reservoir, res., Bngl. . . . . E6 — 40
Karnātaka, prov., India . . . . G3 — 40
Karnes, co., Tx., U.S. . . . . . E4 — 136
Karnes City, Tx., U.S. . . . . . E4 — 136
Karns, Tn., U.S. . . . . n13 — 135
Kárpathos, i., Grc. . . . . G11 — 18
Karpogory, Russia . . . . B7 — 22
Karratha, Austl. . . . . E2 — 60
Kars, Tur. . . . . B10 — 44
Karsakpaj, Kaz. . . . . B1 — 28
Karši, Uzb. . . . . F8 — 26
Karskie Vorota, proliv, strt., Russia . . . . B7 — 26
Karskoe more, Russia . . . . B8 — 26
Kartaly, Russia . . . . D8 — 22
Karufa, Indon. . . . . D8 — 36
Kārūn, stm., Iran . . . . G13 — 44
Karūr, India . . . . G3 — 40
Karvina, Czech Rep. . . . . . E5 — 20
Kārwār, India . . . . G2 — 40
Karymskoe, Russia . . . . . . A10 — 28
Kasai (Cassai), stm., Afr. . . D3 — 54
Kasaji, D.R.C. . . . . F4 — 54
Kasama, Zam. . . . . A5 — 56
Kasane, Bots. . . . . B4 — 56
Kasanga, Tan. . . . . E6 — 54

Kasangulu, D.R.C. . . . . D3 — 54
Kāsaragod, India . . . . G3 — 40
Kasempa, Zam. . . . . A4 — 56
Kasenga, D.R.C. . . . . F5 — 54
Kasenye, D.R.C. . . . . C6 — 54
Kasese, D.R.C. . . . . D5 — 54
Kasese, Ug. . . . . C6 — 54
Kāshān, Iran . . . . D6 — 42
Kashgar see Kashi, China . . D3 — 28
Kashi, China . . . . D3 — 28
Kāshmar, Iran . . . . C7 — 42
Kasimov, Russia . . . . B16 — 20
Kasiruta, Pulau, i., Indon. . . D7 — 36
Kaslo, B.C., Can. . . . . E9 — 85
Kasongo, D.R.C. . . . . D5 — 54
Kasongo-Lunda, D.R.C. . . . E3 — 54
Kásos, i., Grc. . . . . G11 — 18
Kasota, Mn., U.S. . . . . F5 — 116
Kaspi, Geor. . . . . B11 — 44
Kaspijsk, Russia . . . . A12 — 44
Kaspijskij, Russia . . . . E6 — 26
Kassalā, Sudan . . . . G12 — 48
Kassandra, Gulf of see Kassándras, Kólpos, b., Grc. . . . . D9 — 18
Kassándras, Kólpos, b., Grc. D9 — 18
Kassel, Ger. . . . . E11 — 12
Kasserine, Tun. . . . . C6 — 48
Kasson, Mn., U.S. . . . . F6 — 116
Kastamonu, Tur. . . . . B5 — 44
Kastoría, Grc. . . . . D8 — 18
Kasulu, Tan. . . . . D6 — 54
Kasūr, Pak. . . . . D10 — 42
Kataba, Zam. . . . . B4 — 56
Katahdin, Mount, mtn., Me., U.S. . . . . C4 — 112
Katako-Kombe, D.R.C. . . . . D4 — 54
Katanga, hist. reg., D.R.C. . E4 — 54
Katangli, Russia . . . . D16 — 26
Katanning, Austl. . . . . G2 — 60
Katchall Island, i., India . . . H6 — 40
Kateríni, Grc. . . . . D9 — 18
Kates Needle, mtn., Ak., U.S. . . . . m24 — 95
Katha, Myan. . . . . B3 — 34
Katherîna, Gebel, mtn., Egypt . . . . E11 — 48
Katherine, Austl. . . . . C5 — 60
Kāthiāwār Peninsula, pen., India . . . . E2 — 40
Kathleen, Fl., U.S. . . . . D4 — 102
Kāthmāndau, Nepal . . . . . . D5 — 40
Kati, Mali . . . . D3 — 50
Katihār, India . . . . D5 — 40
Katiola, C. Iv. . . . . E3 — 50
Katmai, Mount, mtn., Ak., U.S. . . . . D9 — 95
Katmai National Park, Ak., U.S. . . . . D9 — 95
Kātmāndu see Kāthmāndau, Nepal . D5 — 40
Katompi, D.R.C. . . . . E5 — 54
Katoomba, Austl. . . . . G5 — 62
Katowice, Pol. . . . . D5 — 20
Katrineholm, Swe. . . . . G7 — 10
Katsina, Nig. . . . . D6 — 50
Kattakurgan, Uzb. . . . . C9 — 42
Kattegat, strt., Eur. . . . . . . B12 — 12
Katy, Tx., U.S. . . . . r14 — 136
Kauai, co., Hi., U.S. . . . . . . B1 — 104
Kauai, i., Hi., U.S. . . . . A2 — 104
Kauai Channel, strt., Hi., U.S. . . . . h17 — 92a
Kauai Channel, strt., Hi., U.S. . . . . B3 — 104
Kau Desert, des., Hi., U.S. . D6 — 104
Kaufbeuren, Ger. . . . . G12 — 12
Kaufman, Tx., U.S. . . . . . . C4 — 136
Kaufman, co., Tx., U.S. . . . C4 — 136
Kauiki Head, c., Hi., U.S. . . C6 — 104
Kaujuitoq see Resolute, N.T., Can. . . . . D20 — 82
Kaukauna, Wi., U.S. . . . . . D5 — 142
Kaula Island, i., Hi., U.S. . . m15 — 104
Kaulakahi Channel, strt., Hi., U.S. . . . . A2 — 104
Kaumakani, Hi., U.S. . . . . . B2 — 104
Kaunakakai, Hi., U.S. . . . . . B4 — 104
Kauna Point, c., Hi., U.S. . . D6 — 104
Kaura-Namoda, Nig. . . . . . D6 — 50
Kavača, Russia . . . . C19 — 26
Kavadarci, Mac. . . . . D8 — 18
Kavála, Grc. . . . . D10 — 18
Kavalerovo, Russia . . . . . . C15 — 28
Kāvali, India . . . . G4 — 40
Kavaratti, India . . . . G2 — 40
Kāveri, stm., India . . . . G3 — 40
Kavieng, Pap. N. Gui. . . . . G13 — 32
Kavīr, Dasht-e, des., Iran . . C7 — 42
Kawaihoa Point, c., Hi., U.S. B1 — 104
Kawaikini, mtn., Hi., U.S. . . A2 — 104
Kawambwa, Zam. . . . . E5 — 54
Kawasaki, Japan . . . . D15 — 28
Kawerau, N.Z. . . . . o14 — 63c
Kawich Peak, mtn., Nv., U.S. . . . . F5 — 121
Kawich Range, mts., Nv., U.S. . . . . F5 — 121
Kaw Lake, res., Ok., U.S. . . A5 — 129
Kaxgar, stm., China . . . . . . B3 — 40
Kay, co., Ok., U.S. . . . . A4 — 129
Kaya, Burkina . . . . D4 — 50
Kaycee, Wy., U.S. . . . . C6 — 143
Kayenta, Az., U.S. . . . . A5 — 96

Kayes, Mali . . . . D2 — 50
Kayseri, Tur. . . . . C6 — 44
Kaysville, Ut., U.S. . . . . . . B4 — 137
Kayuagung, Indon. . . . . . . D2 — 36
Kazače, Russia . . . . B15 — 26
Kazahskij melkosopočnik, hills, Kaz. . . . . D9 — 26
Kazakh Hills see Kazahskij melkosopočnik, hills, Kaz. . . . . D9 — 26
Kazakstan, ctry., Asia . . . . . E8 — 26
Kazalinsk, Kaz. . . . . A8 — 42
Kazan', Russia . . . . D6 — 26
Kazanka, Ukr. . . . . F12 — 20
Kazanlăk, Bul. . . . . C10 — 18
Kazan-rettō, is., Japan . . . . F17 — 64
Kazbek, gora, vol. . . . . A11 — 44
Kāzerūn, Iran . . . . E6 — 42
Kazincbarcika, Hung. . . . . . E8 — 20
Kaztalovka, Kaz. . . . . E8 — 22
Kazym, Russia . . . . B12 — 22
Kéa, i., Grc. . . . . F10 — 18
Keaau, Hi., U.S. . . . . D6 — 104
Keahiakahoe, Puu, mtn., Hi., U.S. . . . . g10 — 104
Keahole Point, c., Hi., U.S. . D5 — 104
Kealaikahiki Channel, strt., Hi., U.S. . . . . C5 — 104
Kealaikahiki Point, c., Hi., U.S. . . . . C5 — 104
Kealakekua, Hi., U.S. . . . . . D6 — 104
Kealia, Hi., U.S. . . . . A2 — 104
Keams Canyon, Az., U.S. . . B5 — 96
Keanapapa Point, c., Hi., U.S. . . . . C4 — 104
Keansburg, N.J., U.S. . . . . . C4 — 123
Kearney, Mo., U.S. . . . . . . B3 — 118
Kearney, Ne., U.S. . . . . D6 — 120
Kearney, co., Ne., U.S. . . . . D7 — 120
Kearns, Ut., U.S. . . . . C4 — 137
Kearny, Az., U.S. . . . . D5 — 96
Kearny, N.J., U.S. . . . . h8 — 123
Kearny, co., Ks., U.S. . . . . . D2 — 109
Keban Baraji, res., Tur. . . . . C8 — 44
Keban Reservoir see Keban Baraji, res., Tur. . . . . . C8 — 44
Kébèmèr, Sen. . . . . C1 — 50
Kebnekaise, mtn., Swe. . . . C8 — 10
K'ebrī Dehar, Eth. . . . . B8 — 54
Kecskemét, Hung. . . . . F5 — 20
Kedges Straits, strt., Md., U.S. . . . . D5 — 113
Kedgwick, N.B., Can. . . . . . B2 — 87
Kediri, Indon. . . . . E4 — 36
Kedon, Russia . . . . C17 — 26
Kédougou, Sen. . . . . D2 — 50
Keego Harbor, Mi., U.S. . . . o15 — 115
Keene, N.H., U.S. . . . . E2 — 122
Keene, Tx., U.S. . . . . n9 — 136
Keer-Weer, Cape, c., Austl. C3 — 62
Keeseville, N.Y., U.S. . . . . . f11 — 125
Keesler Air Force Base, mil., Ms., U.S. . . . . E5 — 117
Keetmanshoop, Nmb. . . . . D2 — 56
Keet Seel Ruin, hist., Az., U.S. . . . . A5 — 96
Keewatin, On., Can. . . . . . . E4 — 86
Keewatin, Mn., U.S. . . . . . . C5 — 116
Kefallinía, i., Grc. . . . . E8 — 18
Kefamenanu, Indon. . . . . . E6 — 36
Keffi, Nig. . . . . E6 — 50
Keflavík, Ice. . . . . m17 — 10a
Kegonsa, Lake, l., Wi., U.S. F4 — 142
Kehra, Est. . . . . G11 — 10
Ke-hsi Mānsām, Myan. . . . . B3 — 34
Keila, Est. . . . . G11 — 10
Keiser, Ar., U.S. . . . . B5 — 97
Keith, co., Ne., U.S. . . . . . . C4 — 120
Keizer, Or., U.S. . . . . C3 — 130
Kejimkujik National Park, N.S., Can. . . . . E4 — 87
Kekaha, Hi., U.S. . . . . B2 — 104
Kékes, mtn., Hung. . . . . . . F5 — 20
K'elafo, Eth. . . . . B8 — 54
Kelan, China . . . . B3 — 30
Kelantan, stm., Malay. . . . . B2 — 36
Kelibia, Tun. . . . . F3 — 18
Kelkit, Tur. . . . . B8 — 44
Kelkit, stm., Tur. . . . . B7 — 44
Keller, Tx., U.S. . . . . n9 — 136
Kellerberrin, Austl. . . . . . . G2 — 60
Kelleys Island, i., Oh., U.S. . A3 — 128
Kellogg, Ia., U.S. . . . . C5 — 108
Kellogg, Id., U.S. . . . . B2 — 105
Kelloselkä, Fin. . . . . C13 — 10
Kelowna, B.C., Can. . . . . . . E8 — 85
Kelso, Wa., U.S. . . . . C3 — 140
Keluang, Malay. . . . . C2 — 36
Kem', Russia . . . . C5 — 26
Kembé, C.A.R. . . . . C4 — 54
Kemerovo, Russia . . . . D10 — 26
Kemi, Fin. . . . . D11 — 10
Kemijärvi, Fin. . . . . C12 — 10
Kemijoki, stm., Fin. . . . . . . C11 — 10
Kemmerer, Wy., U.S. . . . . . E2 — 143
Kemp, Tx., U.S. . . . . C4 — 136
Kemp, Lake, res., Tx., U.S. . C3 — 136
Kemper, co., Ms., U.S. . . . . C5 — 117
Kempsey, Austl. . . . . G5 — 62
Kempten, Ger. . . . . G12 — 12

Kemptville, On., Can. . . . . . B9 — 89
Kemul, Kong, mtn., Indon. . C5 — 36
Kenai, Ak., U.S. . . . . C9 — 95
Kenai Fjords National Park, Ak., U.S. . . . . D10 — 95
Kenai Mountains, mts., Ak., U.S. . . . . h16 — 95
Kenai Peninsula, pen., Ak., U.S. . . . . h16 — 95
Kenansville, N.C., U.S. . . . . C5 — 126
Kenbridge, Va., U.S. . . . . . D4 — 139
Kendal, Eng., U.K. . . . . C5 — 12
Kendall, Fl., U.S. . . . . s13 — 102
Kendall, co., Il., U.S. . . . . . . B5 — 106
Kendall, co., Tx., U.S. . . . . . E3 — 136
Kendall Park, N.J., U.S. . . . C3 — 123
Kendallville, In., U.S. . . . . . B7 — 107
Kendari, Indon. . . . . D6 — 36
Kendawangan, Indon. . . . . D4 — 36
Kenedy, Tx., U.S. . . . . E4 — 136
Kenedy, co., Tx., U.S. . . . . . F4 — 136
Kenema, S.L. . . . . E2 — 50
Kenesaw, Ne., U.S. . . . . . . D7 — 120
Kenge, D.R.C. . . . . D3 — 54
Kêng Tung, Myan. . . . . B3 — 34
Kenhardt, S. Afr. . . . . D3 — 56
Kenilworth, Il., U.S. . . . . . . h9 — 106
Kénitra, Mor. . . . . D3 — 48
Kenly, N.C., U.S. . . . . B4 — 126
Kenmare, N.D., U.S. . . . . . A3 — 127
Kenmore, N.Y., U.S. . . . . . . C2 — 125
Kennaday Peak, mtn., Wy., U.S. . . . . E6 — 143
Kennebago Lake, l., Me., U.S. . . . . C2 — 112
Kennebec, co., Me., U.S. . . D3 — 112
Kennebec, stm., Me., U.S. . D3 — 112
Kennebunk, Me., U.S. . . . . E2 — 112
Kennebunkport, Me., U.S. . . E2 — 112
Kennedy, Cape see Canaveral, Cape, c., Fl., U.S. . . . . D6 — 102
Kennedy Entrance, strt., Ak., U.S. . . . . D9 — 95
Kenner, La., U.S. . . . . E5 — 111
Kennesaw, Ga., U.S. . . . . . B2 — 103
Kennesaw Mountain, mtn., Ga., U.S. . . . . C2 — 103
Kennett, Mo., U.S. . . . . E7 — 118
Kennett Square, Pa., U.S. . . G10 — 131
Kennewick, Wa., U.S. . . . . . C6 — 140
Keno, Or., U.S. . . . . E5 — 130
Kénogami, Lac, l., P.Q., Can. . . . . A6 — 90
Kenora, On., Can. . . . . o16 — 89
Kenosha, Wi., U.S. . . . . F6 — 142
Kenosha, co., Wi., U.S. . . . . F5 — 142
Kenova, W.V., U.S. . . . . . . C2 — 141
Kensett, Ar., U.S. . . . . B4 — 97
Kensico Reservoir, res., N.Y., U.S. . . . . g13 — 125
Kensington, P.E., Can. . . . . C6 — 87
Kensington, Ct., U.S. . . . . . C4 — 100
Kensington, Md., U.S. . . . . B3 — 113
Kent, Oh., U.S. . . . . A4 — 128
Kent, Wa., U.S. . . . . B3 — 140
Kent, co., De., U.S. . . . . . . D3 — 101
Kent, co., Md., U.S. . . . . . . B5 — 113
Kent, co., Mi., U.S. . . . . E5 — 115
Kent, co., R.I., U.S. . . . . . . D2 — 132
Kent, co., Tx., U.S. . . . . C2 — 136
Kentau, Kaz. . . . . B9 — 42
Kent City, Mi., U.S. . . . . . . E5 — 115
Kent Island, i., De., U.S. . . . D4 — 101
Kent Island, i., Md., U.S. . . . C5 — 113
Kentland, In., U.S. . . . . C3 — 107
Kenton, De., U.S. . . . . D3 — 101
Kenton, Oh., U.S. . . . . B2 — 128
Kenton, Tn., U.S. . . . . A2 — 135
Kenton, co., Ky., U.S. . . . . . B5 — 110
Kent Point, c., Md., U.S. . . . C5 — 113
Kentucky, state, U.S. . . . . . C4 — 110
Kentucky, stm., Ky., U.S. . . B5 — 110
Kentucky Lake, res., U.S. . . D10 — 92
Kentwood, La., U.S. . . . . . . D5 — 111
Kentwood, Mi., U.S. . . . . . . F5 — 115
Kenvil, N.J., U.S. . . . . B3 — 123
Kenvir, Ky., U.S. . . . . D6 — 110
Kenya, ctry., Afr. . . . . C7 — 54
Kenya, Mount see Kirinyaga, mtn., Kenya D7 — 54
Kenyon, Mn., U.S. . . . . F6 — 116
Kenyon, R.I., U.S. . . . . F2 — 132
Keokea, Hi., U.S. . . . . C5 — 104
Keokuk, Ia., U.S. . . . . D6 — 108
Keokuk, co., Ia., U.S. . . . . . C5 — 108
Keokuk Lock and Dam, U.S. D6 — 108
Keosauqua, Ia., U.S. . . . . . D6 — 108
Keota, Ia., U.S. . . . . C6 — 108
Keota, Ok., U.S. . . . . B7 — 129
Keowee, Lake, res., S.C., U.S. . . . . B2 — 133
Kępno, Pol. . . . . D4 — 20
Kerala, prov., India . . . . . . G3 — 40
Kerang, Austl. . . . . H3 — 62
Kerava, Fin. . . . . F11 — 10
Kerch, Ukr. . . . . G14 — 20
Kerch Strait, strt., Eur. . . . . G14 — 20
Keremeos, B.C., Can. . . . . . E8 — 85
Keren, Erit. . . . . G12 — 48
Kerguelen, Îles, is., Afr. . . . M10 — 64
Kerguelen Plateau . . . . N10 — 64
Kerhonkson, N.Y., U.S. . . . . D6 — 125
Kericho, Kenya . . . . D7 — 54

Name	Map Ref.	Page
Kerinci, Gunung, vol., Indon.	D2	36
Kerkhoven, Mn., U.S.	E3	116
Kerki, Turk.	C9	42
Kerkiči, Turk.	F8	26
Kérkira, Grc.	E7	18
Kérkira (Corfu), i., Grc.	E7	18
Kermadec Islands, is., N.Z.	G12	58
Kermadec Ridge	L20	64
Kermadec Trench	L21	64
Kermān, Iran	D7	42
Kermānshāh (Bākhtarān), Iran	D5	42
Kermit, Tx., U.S.	D1	136
Kermode, Mount, mtn., B.C., Can.	C2	85
Kern, co., Ca., U.S.	E4	98
Kern, stm., Ca., U.S.	E4	98
Kernersville, N.C., U.S.	A2	126
Kernville, Ca., U.S.	E4	98
Kérouané, Gui.	E3	50
Kerr, co., Tx., U.S.	D3	136
Kerr, Lake, l., Fl., U.S.	C5	102
Kerrville, Tx., U.S.	D3	136
Kersey, Co., U.S.	A6	99
Kershaw, S.C., U.S.	B6	133
Kershaw, co., S.C., U.S.	C6	133
Kerulen, stm., Asia	B10	28
Keşan, Tur.	B2	44
Kesennuma, Japan	D16	28
Keshena, Wi., U.S.	D5	142
Keskin, Tur.	C5	44
Kesten'ga, Russia	D14	10
Keszthely, Hung.	F4	20
Ket', stm., Russia	D10	26
Keta, Ghana	E5	50
Ketapang, Indon.	D3	36
Ketchikan, Ak., U.S.	D13	95
Ketchum, Id., U.S.	F4	105
Kete-Krachi, Ghana	E4	50
Kętrzyn, Pol.	B6	20
Kettering, Oh., U.S.	C1	128
Kettle, stm., Mn., U.S.	D6	116
Kettle Creek, stm., Pa., U.S.	D6	131
Kettle Creek Lake, res., Pa., U.S.	D6	131
Kettle Falls, Wa., U.S.	A7	140
Keuka Lake, l., N.Y., U.S.	C3	125
Kewanee, Il., U.S.	B4	106
Kewaskum, Wi., U.S.	E5	142
Kewaunee, Wi., U.S.	D6	142
Kewaunee, co., Wi., U.S.	D6	142
Keweenaw, co., Mi., U.S.	A2	115
Keweenaw Bay, b., Mi., U.S.	B2	115
Keweenaw Peninsula, pen., Mi., U.S.	A3	115
Keweenaw Point, c., Mi., U.S.	A3	115
Keya Paha, co., Ne., U.S.	B6	120
Keya Paha, stm., U.S.	A5	120
Keyhole Reservoir, res., Wy., U.S.	B8	143
Key Largo, Fl., U.S.	G6	102
Keyport, N.J., U.S.	C4	123
Keyser, W.V., U.S.	B6	141
Keystone, W.V., U.S.	D3	141
Keystone Heights, Fl., U.S.	C4	102
Keystone Lake, res., Ok., U.S.	A5	129
Keystone Peak, mtn., Az., U.S.	F4	96
Keysville, Va., U.S.	C4	139
Key West, Fl., U.S.	H5	102
Key West Naval Air Station, mil., Fl., U.S.	H5	102
Kezar Falls, Me., U.S.	E2	112
Kezar Lake, l., Me., U.S.	D2	112
Kezi, Zimb.	D12	26
Kežma, Russia	D12	26
Khābūr, Nahr al-, stm., Asia	E9	44
Khadki, India	F2	40
Khairpur, Pak.	F9	42
Khajrāho, India	E4	40
Khakhea, Bots.	C3	56
Khalkhāl, Iran	D13	44
Khalkidhikí, hist. reg., Grc.	D9	18
Khalkís, Grc.	E9	18
Khambhāt, India	E2	40
Khambhāt, Gulf of, b., India	E2	40
Khāmgaon, India	E3	40
Khammam, India	F4	40
Khānābād, Afg.	C9	42
Khān al-Baghdādī, Iraq	F10	44
Khānaqīn, Iraq	E11	44
Khandwa, India	E3	40
Khānewāl, Pak.	D10	42
Khaniá, Grc.	G9	18
Khanión, Kólpos, b., Grc.	G9	18
Khanka, Lake, l., Asia	C14	28
Khānpur, Pak.	E10	42
Kharagpur, India	E5	40
Khargon, India	E3	40
Kharkiv, Ukr.	E14	20
Khartoum see Al-Kharṭūm, Sudan	G11	48
Khāsh, Afg.	D8	42
Khāsh, Iran	E8	42
Khashm al-Qirbah, Sudan	H12	48
Khemis Melyana, Alg.	I8	16
Khenchla, Alg.	D5	14
Khenifra, Mor.	E2	14
Kherson, Ukr.	F12	20
Khmel'nyts'kyi, Ukr.	E9	20
Khmil'nyk, Ukr.	E9	20
Kholm, Afg.	C9	42
Khomeynīshahr, Iran	D6	42
Khong see Mekong, stm., Asia	C4	34
Khon Kaen, Thai.	C4	34
Khorramābād, Iran	D5	42
Khorramshahr, Iran	D5	42
Khotyn, Ukr.	E9	20
Khouribga, Mor.	D3	48
Khrystynivka, Ukr.	E10	20
Khulna, Bngl.	E5	40
Khust, Ukr.	E7	20
Khuzdār, Pak.	E9	42
Khvoy, Iran	C4	42
Khyber Pass, Asia	C2	40
Kiama, D.R.C.	E3	54
Kiamba, Phil.	E8	34
Kiamichi, stm., Ok., U.S.	C6	129
Kiamika, stm., P.Q., Can.	C2	90
Kiana, Ak., U.S.	B7	95
Kiangarow, Mount, mtn., Austl.	F5	62
Kiawah Island, i., S.C., U.S.	F7	133
Kibangou, Congo	D2	54
Kibombo, D.R.C.	D5	54
Kibondo, Tan.	D6	54
Kibre Mengist, Eth.	B7	54
Kičevo, Mac.	D8	18
Kickamuit, stm., R.I., U.S.	D5	132
Kickapoo, stm., Wi., U.S.	E3	142
Kickapoo, Lake, res., Tx., U.S.	C3	136
Kickapoo Indian Reservation, Ks., U.S.	C8	109
Kicking Horse Pass, Can.	D2	84
Kidal, Mali	C5	50
Kidatu, Tan.	E7	54
Kidder, co., N.D., U.S.	C6	127
Kidira, Sen.	D2	50
Kiefer, Ok., U.S.	B5	129
Kiel, Ger.	C12	12
Kiel, Wi., U.S.	E5	142
Kiel Bay see Kieler Bucht, b., Ger.	C12	12
Kiel Canal see Nord-Ostsee-Kanal, Ger.	C11	12
Kielce, Pol.	D6	20
Kieler Bucht, b., Ger.	C12	12
Kiester, Mn., U.S.	G5	116
Kiev see Kyïv, Ukr.	D11	20
Kiev Reservoir see Kyïvs'ke vodoskhovyshche, res., Ukr.	D11	20
Kiffa, Maur.	C2	50
Kigali, Rw.	D6	54
Kigoma, Tan.	D5	54
Kihčik, Russia	D17	26
Kihei, Hi., U.S.	C5	104
Kiholo Bay, b., Hi., U.S.	D5	104
Kii Strait see Kii-suidō, strt., Japan	E15	28
Kii-suidō, strt., Japan	E15	28
Kikinda, Yugo.	B8	18
Kikládhes, is., Grc.	F10	18
Kikori, Pap. N. Gui.	H11	32
Kikwit, D.R.C.	E3	54
Kil, Swe.	G5	10
Kilauea, Hi., U.S.	A2	104
Kilauea Crater, crat., Hi., U.S.	D6	104
Kilauea Point, c., Hi., U.S.	A2	104
Kilchu-ŭp, N. Kor.	B1	31
Kildurk, Austl.	D4	60
Kilgore, Tx., U.S.	C5	136
Kilibo, Benin	E5	50
Kiliia, Ukr.	G10	20
Kilimanjaro, mtn., Tan.	D7	54
Kilimli, Tur.	B4	44
Kilindoni, Tan.	E7	54
Kilis, Tur.	D7	44
Kilkenny, Ire.	D3	12
Kilkís, Grc.	D9	18
Killaloe Station, On., Can.	B7	89
Killam, Ab., Can.	C5	84
Killarney, Mb., Can.	E2	86
Killarney Provincial Park, On., Can.	A3	89
Killdeer, N.D., U.S.	B3	127
Killeen, Tx., U.S.	D4	136
Killen, Al., U.S.	A2	94
Killian, La., U.S.	h10	111
Killik, stm., Ak., U.S.	B9	95
Killiniq Island, i., Can.	F27	82
Killona, La., U.S.	h11	111
Kilmarnock, Scot., U.K.	C4	12
Kilmarnock, Va., U.S.	C6	139
Kilmichael, Ms., U.S.	B4	117
Kiln, Ms., U.S.	E4	117
Kilomines, D.R.C.	C6	54
Kilosa, Tan.	E7	54
Kilttān Island, i., India	G2	40
Kilwa, D.R.C.	E5	54
Kilwa Kivinje, Tan.	E7	54
Kimba, Austl.	G2	62
Kimball, Mn., U.S.	E4	116
Kimball, Ne., U.S.	C2	120
Kimball, S.D., U.S.	D7	134
Kimball, co., Ne., U.S.	C2	120
Kimball, Mount, mtn., Ak., U.S.	C11	95
Kimberley, B.C., Can.	E9	85
Kimberley, S. Afr.	D3	56
Kimberley Plateau, plat., Austl.	D4	60
Kimberlin Heights, Tn., U.S.	n14	135
Kimberly, Al., U.S.	B3	94
Kimberly, Id., U.S.	G4	105
Kimberly, W.V., U.S.	m13	141
Kimberly, Wi., U.S.	h9	142
Kimble, co., Tx., U.S.	D3	136
Kimch'aek, N. Kor.	C13	28
Kimito, i., Fin.	G10	10
Kimry, Russia	C6	22
Kinabalu, Gunong, mtn., Malay.	B5	36
Kinabatangan, stm., Malay.	B5	36
Kinbasket Lake, res., B.C., Can.	D8	85
Kincaid, Il., U.S.	D4	106
Kincaid, W.V., U.S.	m13	141
Kincaid, Lake, res., Il., U.S.	D4	106
Kincardine, On., Can.	C3	89
Kincheloe Air Force Base, mil., Mi., U.S.	B6	115
Kinda, D.R.C.	E5	54
Kinder, La., U.S.	D3	111
Kindia, Gui.	D2	50
Kindu, D.R.C.	D5	54
Kinešma, Russia	C7	22
King, N.C., U.S.	A2	126
King, Wi., U.S.	D4	142
King, co., Tx., U.S.	C2	136
King, co., Wa., U.S.	B3	140
King and Queen, co., Va., U.S.	C6	139
Kingaroy, Austl.	F5	62
King City, Ca., U.S.	D3	98
King City, Mo., U.S.	A3	118
King Cove, Ak., U.S.	E7	95
Kingfield, Me., U.S.	D2	112
Kingfisher, Ok., U.S.	B4	129
Kingfisher, co., Ok., U.S.	B3	129
King George, co., Va., U.S.	B5	139
Kingisepp, Russia	G13	10
King Island, i., Austl.	H3	62
King Island, i., B.C., Can.	C4	85
King Lear Peak, mtn., Nv., U.S.	B3	121
King Leopold Ranges, mts., Austl.	D3	60
Kingman, Az., U.S.	B1	96
Kingman, Ks., U.S.	E5	109
Kingman, co., Ks., U.S.	E5	109
King Mountain, mtn., Or., U.S.	D8	130
King Mountain, mtn., Or., U.S.	E3	130
Kingombe, D.R.C.	D5	54
King Peak, mtn., Ca., U.S.	B1	98
Kings, Ms., U.S.	C3	117
Kings, co., Ca., U.S.	D4	98
Kings, co., N.Y., U.S.	E7	125
Kings, stm., Ar., U.S.	A2	97
Kings, stm., Ca., U.S.	D4	98
Kings, stm., Nv., U.S.	B3	121
King Salmon, Ak., U.S.	D8	95
Kingsburg, Ca., U.S.	D4	98
Kingsbury, co., S.D., U.S.	C8	134
Kings Canyon National Park, Ca., U.S.	D4	98
Kingsey-Falls, P.Q., Can.	D5	90
Kingsford, Mi., U.S.	C2	115
Kingsland, Ga., U.S.	F5	103
Kingsland, Tx., U.S.	D3	136
Kingsley, Ia., U.S.	B2	108
Kingsley, Mi., U.S.	D5	115
King's Lynn, Eng., U.K.	D7	12
Kings Mountain, N.C., U.S.	B1	126
King Sound, strt., Austl.	D3	60
Kings Peak, mtn., Ut., U.S.	C5	137
King's Point, Nf., Can.	D3	88
Kingsport, Tn., U.S.	C11	135
Kingston, On., Can.	C8	89
Kingston, Jam.	B4	80
Kingston, Ga., U.S.	B2	103
Kingston, Id., U.S.	B2	105
Kingston, Ma., U.S.	C6	114
Kingston, N.H., U.S.	E4	122
Kingston, N.Y., U.S.	D6	125
Kingston, Oh., U.S.	C3	128
Kingston, Ok., U.S.	D5	129
Kingston, Pa., U.S.	D10	131
Kingston, R.I., U.S.	F3	132
Kingston, Tn., U.S.	D9	135
Kingston Springs, Tn., U.S.	A4	135
Kingston upon Hull, Eng., U.K.	D6	12
Kingstown see Dún Laoghaire, Ire.	A3	12
Kingstown, St. Vin.	C7	80
Kingstown, Md., U.S.	B5	113
Kingstree, S.C., U.S.	D8	133
Kingsville, On., Can.	E2	89
Kingsville, Md., U.S.	B5	113
Kingsville (North Kingsville), Oh., U.S.	A5	128
Kingsville Naval Air Station, mil., Tx., U.S.	F4	136
King William, co., Va., U.S.	C5	139
King William's Town, S. Afr.	E4	56
Kingwood, W.V., U.S.	B5	141
Kinistino, Sk., Can.	E3	91
Kinkaid Lake, res., Il., U.S.	F4	106
Kinkala, Congo	D2	54
Kinloch, Mo., U.S.	f13	118
Kinmundy, Il., U.S.	E5	106
Kinnaird Head, c., Scot., U.K.	B6	12
Kinnelon, N.J., U.S.	B4	123
Kinney, co., Tx., U.S.	E2	136
Kinsey, Al., U.S.	D4	94
Kinshasa, D.R.C.	D3	54
Kinsley, Ks., U.S.	E4	109
Kinston, N.C., U.S.	B5	126
Kintampo, Ghana	E4	50
Kintyre, pen., Scot., U.K.	C4	12
Kinyeti, mtn., Sudan	J11	48
Kinzia, D.R.C.	D3	54
Kiowa, Ks., U.S.	E5	109
Kiowa, Ok., U.S.	C6	129
Kiowa, co., Co., U.S.	C8	99
Kiowa, co., Ks., U.S.	E4	109
Kiowa, co., Ok., U.S.	C2	129
Kiowa Creek, stm., Ok., U.S.	A1	129
Kiparissiakós Kólpos, b., Grc.	F8	18
Kipembawe, Tan.	E6	54
Kipengere Range, mts., Tan.	E6	54
Kipili, Tan.	E6	54
Kipini, Kenya	D8	54
Kipnuk, Ak., U.S.	C7	95
Kipushi, D.R.C.	F5	54
Kirbyville, Tx., U.S.	D6	136
Kirensk, Russia	D12	26
Kirgiz Range, mts., Asia	A2	40
Kiri, D.R.C.	D3	54
Kiribati, ctry., Oc.	E12	58
Kiribati, is., Kir.	D11	58
Kırıkhan, Tur.	D7	44
Kırıkkale, Tur.	C5	44
Kirinyaga (Kenya, Mount), mtn., Kenya	D7	54
Kiriši, Russia	C5	22
Kiritimati (Christmas Island), atoll, Kir.	D14	58
Kırkağaç, Tur.	C2	44
Kirkcaldy, Scot., U.K.	B5	12
Kirkenes, Nor.	B14	10
Kirkjubæjarklaustur, Ice.	m19	10a
Kirkland, Il., U.S.	A5	106
Kirkland, Wa., U.S.	B3	140
Kirkland Lake, On., Can.	o19	89
Kirklareli, Tur.	B2	44
Kirklin, In., U.S.	D5	107
Kirkpatrick, Mount, mtn., Ant.	E22	67
Kirksville, Mo., U.S.	A5	118
Kirkwall, Scot., U.K.	A5	12
Kirkwood, S. Afr.	E4	56
Kirkwood, De., U.S.	B3	101
Kirkwood, Il., U.S.	C2	106
Kirkwood, Mo., U.S.	f13	118
Kirov, Russia	B13	20
Kirov, Russia	D6	26
Kirovabad see Gäncä, Azer.	B12	44
Kirovakan see Vanadzor, Arm.	B11	44
Kirovohrad, Ukr.	E12	20
Kirovsk, Russia	A5	22
Kirovsk, Turk.	C5	42
Kirovskij, Russia	D17	26
Kirovskij, Russia	A2	31
Kirs, Russia	C9	22
Kirsanov, Russia	D7	22
Kırşehir, Tur.	C6	44
Kırthar Range, mts., Pak.	E9	42
Kirtland, N.M., U.S.	A1	124
Kirtland Air Force Base, mil., N.M., U.S.	k7	124
Kiruna, Swe.	C9	10
Kirwin Reservoir, res., Ks., U.S.	C4	109
Kisangani, D.R.C.	C5	54
Kisar, Pulau, i., Indon.	E7	36
Kisaran, Indon.	C1	36
Kishangarh Bās, India	D2	40
Kishi, Nig.	E5	50
Kishinev see Chişinău, Mol.	F10	20
Kishiwada, Japan	D3	31
Kishwaukee, stm., Il., U.S.	A5	106
Kisii, Kenya	D6	54
Kisiju, Tan.	E7	54
Kiska Island, i., Ak., U.S.	E3	95
Kiskunfélegyháza, Hung.	F5	20
Kiskunhalas, Hung.	F5	20
Kislovodsk, Russia	B4	42
Kismaayo, Som.	D8	54
Kissidougou, Gui.	E2	50
Kissimmee, Fl., U.S.	D5	102
Kissimmee, stm., Fl., U.S.	E5	102
Kissimmee, Lake, l., Fl., U.S.	E5	102
Kississing Lake, l., Mb., Can.	B1	86
Kistler, W.V., U.S.	D3	141
Kisumu, Kenya	D6	54
Kisvárda, Hung.	E7	20
Kita, Mali	D3	50
Kitaibaraki, Japan	C4	31
Kitakyūshū, Japan	E14	28
Kitale, Kenya	C7	54
Kitami, Japan	A4	31
Kit Carson, co., Co., U.S.	B8	99
Kitchener, On., Can.	D4	89
Kíthira, i., Grc.	F9	18
Kíthnos, i., Grc.	F10	18
Kitimat, B.C., Can.	B3	85
Kitsap, co., Wa., U.S.	B3	140
Kitscoty, Ab., Can.	C5	84
Kittanning, Pa., U.S.	E2	131
Kittatinny Mountain, mtn., U.S.	B2	123
Kittery, Me., U.S.	E2	112
Kittery Point, Me., U.S.	E2	112
Kittitas, Wa., U.S.	C5	140
Kittitas, co., Wa., U.S.	B4	140
Kitts, Ky., U.S.	D6	110
Kittson, co., Mn., U.S.	B2	116
Kitty Hawk, N.C., U.S.	A7	126
Kitty Hawk Bay, b., N.C., U.S.	A7	126
Kitui, Kenya	D7	54
Kitwe, Zam.	A4	56
Kiunga, Kenya	D8	54
Kiviõli, Est.	G12	10
Kivu, Lac, l., Afr.	D5	54
Kizёma, Russia	B7	22
Kızılcahamam, Tur.	B5	44
Kızılırmak, stm., Tur.	B6	44
Kızıltepe, Tur.	D9	44
Kizljar, Russia	B5	42
Kizyl-Atrek, Turk.	C6	42
Kjusjur, Russia	B14	26
Kjustendil, Bul.	C9	18
Klabat, Gunung, vol., Indon.	C7	36
Kladno, Czech Rep.	D3	20
Klagenfurt, Aus.	G14	12
Klaipėda, Lith.	I9	10
Klamath, co., Or., U.S.	E5	130
Klamath, stm., U.S.	B2	98
Klamath Falls, Or., U.S.	E5	130
Klamath Mountains, mts., U.S.	E2	130
Klang, Malay.	C2	36
Klatovy, Czech Rep.	E2	20
Klawer, S. Afr.	E2	56
Klawock, Ak., U.S.	D13	95
Kleberg, co., Tx., U.S.	F4	136
Kletna, Russia	C12	20
Klickitat, Wa., U.S.	D4	140
Klickitat, co., Wa., U.S.	D4	140
Klickitat, stm., Wa., U.S.	C4	140
Klimpfjäll, Swe.	D6	10
Klin, Russia	C6	22
Klincy, Russia	C12	20
Klipplaat, S. Afr.	E3	56
Ključevskaja Sopka, vulkan, vol., Russia	D18	26
Kłobuck, Pol.	D5	20
Kłodzko, Pol.	D4	20
Klondike, hist. reg., Yk., Can.	F12	82
Klondike Gold Rush National Historical Park, Ak., U.S.	k22	95
Kluczbork, Pol.	D5	20
Klutina Lake, l., Ak., U.S.	g19	95
Knapp Creek, stm., W.V., U.S.	C5	141
Knee Lake, l., Mb., Can.	B4	86
Kneža, Bul.	C10	18
Knife, stm., N.D., U.S.	B3	127
Knightdale, N.C., U.S.	B4	126
Knight Inlet, b., B.C., Can.	D5	85
Knight Island, i., Ak., U.S.	g18	95
Knightstown, In., U.S.	E6	107
Knightsville, In., U.S.	E3	107
Knightville Reservoir, res., Ma., U.S.	B2	114
Knittelfeld, Aus.	G14	12
Knob Noster, Mo., U.S.	C4	118
Knollwood, W.V., U.S.	m12	141
Knossós, hist., Grc.	G10	18
Knott, co., Ky., U.S.	C6	110
Knox, In., U.S.	B4	107
Knox, Pa., U.S.	D2	131
Knox, co., Il., U.S.	B3	106
Knox, co., In., U.S.	G3	107
Knox, co., Ky., U.S.	D6	110
Knox, co., Me., U.S.	D4	112
Knox, co., Mo., U.S.	A5	118
Knox, co., Ne., U.S.	B8	120
Knox, co., Oh., U.S.	B3	128
Knox, co., Tn., U.S.	C10	135
Knox, co., Tx., U.S.	C3	136
Knox, Cape, c., B.C., Can.	B1	85
Knox City, Tx., U.S.	C3	136
Knox Coast, Ant.	C15	67
Knoxville, Ia., U.S.	C4	108
Knoxville, Il., U.S.	C3	106
Knoxville, Tn., U.S.	D10	135
Knysna, S. Afr.	E3	56
Kōbe, Japan	E15	28
København (Copenhagen), Den.	I5	10
Koblenz, Ger.	E10	12
Kobroor, Pulau, i., Indon.	H9	32
Kobryn, Bela.	C8	20
Kobuk, stm., Ak., U.S.	B8	95
Kobuk Valley National Park, Ak., U.S.	B8	95
Kočani, Mac.	D9	18
Kočevo, Russia	C9	22
Kochi (Cochin), India	H3	40
Kōchi, Japan	E14	28
Koch Peak, mtn., Mt., U.S.	E5	119
Kodaikānal, India	G3	40
Kodiak, Ak., U.S.	D9	95
Kodiak Island, i., Ak., U.S.	D9	95
Kodok, Sudan	B6	54
Koës, Nmb.	D2	56
Kofa Mountains, mts., Az., U.S.	D2	96
Köflach, Aus.	G14	12
Koforidua, Ghana	E4	50
Kōfu, Japan	D15	28

Name	Map Ref.	Page
Kogaluk, stm., Nf., Can.	g9	88
Køge, Den.	I5	10
Kohala Mountains, mts., Hi., U.S.	C6	104
Kohāt, Pak.	D10	42
Kohīma, India	D6	40
Kohler, Wi., U.S.	E6	142
Kohtla-Järve, Est.	G12	10
Koihoa, India	H6	40
Koindu, S.L.	E2	50
Kojgorodok, Russia	B9	22
Kojonup, Austl.	G2	60
Kokand, Uzb.	E9	26
Kokanee Glacier Provincial Park, B.C., Can.	E9	85
Kokčetav, Kaz.	D8	26
Kokemäki, Fin.	F10	10
Kokenau, Indon.	G10	32
Kokkola, Fin.	E10	10
Kokoda, Pap. N. Gui.	H12	32
Koko Head, c., Hi., U.S.	B4	104
Kokolik, stm., Ak., U.S.	B7	95
Kokomo, In., U.S.	D5	107
Koko Nor see Qinghai Hu, l., China	D8	28
Kokosing, stm., Oh., U.S.	B3	128
Kokstad, S. Afr.	E4	56
Kola, Russia	B15	10
Kolaka, Indon.	D6	36
Kola Peninsula see Kol'skij poluostrov, pen., Russia	C5	26
Kolār Gold Fields, India	G3	40
Kolbio, Kenya	D8	54
Kolda, Sen.	D2	50
Kolding, Den.	I3	10
Kole, D.R.C.	D4	54
Kolea, Alg.	I8	16
Kolguev, ostrov, i., Russia	C6	26
Kolhāpur, India	F2	40
Kolka, Lat.	H10	10
Kolmogorovo, Russia	D11	26
Köln (Cologne), Ger.	E10	12
Koło, Pol.	C5	20
Koloa, Hi., U.S.	B2	104
Kołobrzeg, Pol.	B3	20
Kolokani, Mali	D3	50
Kolomna, Russia	D5	26
Kolonia, Micron.	D9	58
Kolonodale, Indon.	D6	36
Kolpaševo, Russia	D10	26
Kolpino, Russia	C5	22
Kol'skij poluostrov, pen., Russia	C5	26
Kolwezi, D.R.C.	F5	54
Kolyma, stm., Russia	C17	26
Kolymskaja, Russia	C17	26
Komandorskie ostrova, is., Russia	D18	26
Komandorski Islands see Komandorskie ostrova, is., Russia	D18	26
Komárno, Slvk.	F5	20
Komatipoort, S. Afr.	D5	56
Kome Island, i., Ug.	D6	54
Komi, state, Russia	C7	26
Komló, Hung.	F5	20
Kommunarsk see Alchevs'k, Ukr.	E15	20
Kommunizma, pik, mtn., Taj.	F9	26
Komodo, Pulau, i., Indon.	E5	36
Komoé, stm., Afr.	E4	50
Komotiní, Grc.	D10	18
Komsomolec, Kaz.	D11	22
Komsomolec, ostrov, i., Russia	A11	26
Komsomol'sk-na-Amure, Russia	D15	26
Konahuanui, Puu, mtn., Hi., U.S.	g10	104
Konārak, hist., India	F5	40
Konawa, Ok., U.S.	C5	129
Kondagaon, India	F4	40
Kondinin, Austl.	G2	60
Kondoa, Tan.	D7	54
Kondopoga, Russia	C5	26
Kondūz, Afg.	C9	42
Koné, N. Cal.	I8	62a
Kong, stm., Asia	C5	34
Kongolo, D.R.C.	E5	54
Kongor, Sudan	B6	54
Kongsvinger, Nor.	F5	10
Kongur Shan, mtn., China	D3	28
Königsberg see Kaliningrad, Russia	D4	26
Konin, Pol.	C5	20
Konna, Mali	D4	50
Konomoc, Lake, res., Ct., U.S.	D7	100
Konoša, Russia	C6	26
Konotop, Ukr.	D12	20
Konstanz, Ger.	G11	12
Kontagora, Nig.	D6	50
Kontcha, Cam.	B2	54
Kon Tum, Viet.	D5	34
Konya, Tur.	D5	44
Konza, Kenya	D7	54
Konžakovskij Kamen', gora, mtn., Russia	C10	22
Koochiching, co., Mn., U.S.	B4	116
Kookynie, Austl.	F3	60
Koolau Range, mts., Hi., U.S.	f10	104
Koontz Lake, In., U.S.	B5	107
Kooskia, Id., U.S.	C3	105
Kootenai, co., Id., U.S.	B2	105
Kootenay Lake, l., B.C., Can.	E9	85
Kootenay National Park, B.C., Can.	D9	85
Kópasker, Ice.	k20	10a
Kópavogur, Ice.	I18	10a
Kopejsk, Russia	C11	22
Kopet Mountains, mts., Asia	C7	42
Köping, Swe.	G6	10
Koppang, Nor.	F4	10
Koppel, Pa., U.S.	E1	131
Koprivnica, Cro.	A6	18
Korab (Korabit, Maja e), mtn., Eur.	D8	18
Korabit, Maja e (Korab), mtn., Eur.	D8	18
Korāput, India	F4	40
Korba, India	E4	40
Korbol, Chad	D8	50
Korçë, Alb.	D8	18
Korea, North, ctry., Asia	C13	28
Korea, South, ctry., Asia	D10	28
Korea Bay, b., Asia	D12	28
Korea Strait, strt., Asia	E13	28
Korenovsk, Russia	A3	42
Korf, Russia	C18	26
Korfovskij, Russia	A3	31
Korhogo, C. Iv.	E3	50
Korinthiakós Kólpos, b., Grc.	E9	18
Kórinthos, Grc.	F9	18
Kōriyama, Japan	C4	31
Korjakskaja Sopka, vulkan, vol., Russia	D17	26
Korjakskoe nagor'e, mts., Russia	C18	26
Korjažma, Russia	B8	22
Korkino, Russia	D11	22
Korkuteli, Tur.	D4	44
Korla, China	C5	28
Korliki, Russia	C10	26
Kornat, Otok, i., Cro.	C5	18
Korogwe, Tan.	E7	54
Koronadal, Phil.	E8	34
Koronis, Lake, l., Mn., U.S.	E4	116
Koror, Palau	E9	32
Koro Sea, Fiji	F12	58
Korosten', Ukr.	D10	20
Korostyshiv, Ukr.	D10	20
Korovin Volcano, vol., Ak., U.S.	E5	95
Korsakov, Russia	E16	26
Korsnäs, Fin.	E9	10
Kos, i., Grc.	F11	18
Koš-Agač, Russia	D10	26
Koščagyl, Kaz.	A6	42
Kościan, Pol.	C4	20
Kościerzyna, Pol.	B4	20
Kosciusko, Ms., U.S.	B4	117
Kosciusko, co., In., U.S.	B6	107
Kosciusko, Mount, mtn., Austl.	H4	62
Koshkonong, Lake, l., Wi., U.S.	F5	142
Košice, Slvk.	E6	20
Kosju, Russia	A10	22
Koslan, Russia	B8	22
Kosovska Mitrovica, Yugo.	C8	18
Kossou, Lac de, res., C. Iv.	E3	50
Kossuth, co., Ia., U.S.	A3	108
Kostiantynivka, Ukr.	E14	·20
Kostopil', Ukr.	D8	20
Kostroma, Russia	C7	22
Kostrzyn, Pol.	C3	20
Koszalin, Pol.	B4	20
Kőszeg, Hung.	F4	20
Kota, India	D3	40
Kotaagung, Indon.	E2	36
Kotabaru see Jayapura, Indon.	G11	32
Kotabaru, Indon.	G6	32
Kota Belud, Malay.	B5	36
Kota Bharu, Malay.	B2	36
Kotabumi, Indon.	D2	36
Kota Kinabalu, Malay.	B5	36
Kotamobagu, Indon.	C6	36
Koteľnič, Russia	C8	22
Koteľnikovo, Russia	E7	22
Koteľnyj, ostrov, i., Russia	B15	26
Kotido, Ug.	C6	54
Kotka, Fin.	F12	10
Kotlas, Russia	C6	26
Kotlik, Ak., U.S.	C7	95
Kotovs'k, Ukr.	F10	20
Kotri, Pak.	E2	42
Kottagūdem, India	F4	40
Kottayam, India	H3	40
Kotte see Sri Jayawardenepura, Sri L.	H4	40
Kotto, stm., C.A.R.	B4	54
Kotuj, stm., Russia	C12	26
Kotzebue, Ak., U.S.	B7	95
Kotzebue Sound, strt., Ak., U.S.	B7	95
Kouchibouguac National Park, N.B., Can.	C5	87
Koudougou, Burkina	D4	50
Kouki, C.A.R.	B3	54
Koulamoutou, Gabon	D2	54
Koulikoro, Mali	D3	50
Koumac, N. Cal.	I8	62a
Koumbia, Gui.	D2	50
Koumra, Chad	E8	50
Koundâra, Gui.	D2	50
Kounradskij, Kaz.	B2	28
Kountze, Tx., U.S.	D5	136
Kourou, Fr. Gu.	B9	70
Kouroussa, Gui.	D3	50
Kousséri, Cam.	D8	50
Koussi, Emi, mtn., Chad	C8	50
Koutiala, Mali	D3	50
Kouts, In., U.S.	B3	107
Kouvola, Fin.	F12	10
Kovdozero, ozero, res., Russia	C15	10
Kovel', Ukr.	D8	20
Kovrov, Russia	C7	22
Kowloon see Jiulong, China	E9	30
Koyukuk, stm., Ak., U.S.	B8	95
Kozan, Tur.	D6	44
Kozáni, Grc.	D8	18
Kozel'sk, Russia	B13	20
Kozhikode (Calicut), India	G3	40
Koziatyn, Ukr.	E10	20
Kozlu, Tur.	B4	44
Kpalimé, Togo	E5	50
Kra, Isthmus of, Asia	D3	34
Krâchéh, Camb.	D5	34
Kragerø, Nor.	G3	10
Kraguievac, Yugo.	B8	18
Kraków, Pol.	D5	20
Kralendijk, Neth. Ant.	C6	80
Kraljevo, Yugo.	C8	18
Kramators'k, Ukr.	E14	20
Kramfors, Swe.	E7	10
Kranj, Slvn.	A5	18
Kraśnik, Pol.	D7	20
Krasnoarmiis'k, Ukr.	E14	20
Krasnodar, Russia	E5	26
Krasnogorsk, Russia	B16	28
Krasnohrad, Ukr.	E13	20
Krasnojarsk, Russia	D11	26
Krasnoperekops'k, Ukr.	G12	20
Krasnosel'kup, Russia	C10	26
Krasnoturjinsk, Russia	C11	22
Krasnoufimsk, Russia	C10	22
Krasnoural'sk, Russia	D8	26
Krasnovišersk, Russia	B10	22
Krasnovodsk see Turkmenbaši, Turk.	E7	26
Krasnoyarsk see Krasnojarsk, Russia	D11	26
Krasnoznamenskoje, Kaz.	D8	26
Krasnyi Luch, Ukr.	E15	20
Krasnystaw, Pol.	D7	20
Krasyliv, Ukr.	E9	20
Krebs, Ok., U.S.	C6	129
Kremenchug Reservoir see Kremenchuts'ke vodoskhovyshche, res., Ukr.	E12	20
Kremenchuk, Ukr.	E12	20
Kremenchuts'ke vodoskhovyshche, res., Ukr.	E12	20
Kremenets', Ukr.	D8	20
Kremmling, Co., U.S.	A4	99
Kretinga, Lith.	I9	10
Kreuztal, Ger.	E11	12
Kribi, Cam.	C1	54
Krishna, stm., India	F3	40
Krishnanagar, India	E5	40
Kristiansand, Nor.	G3	10
Kristianstad, Swe.	I6	10
Kristiansund, Nor.	E2	10
Kristiinankaupunki, Fin.	E9	10
Kristineberg, Swe.	D8	10
Kristinehamn, Swe.	G6	10
Kríti (Crete), i., Grc.	G10	18
Kritikón Pélagos, Grc.	G10	18
Krjukovo, Russia	C17	26
Krk, Otok, i., Cro.	B5	18
Krnov, Czech Rep.	D4	20
Kroměříž, Czech Rep.	E4	20
Krŏng Kaôh Kŏng, Camb.	D4	34
Kronštadt, Russia	B4	22
Kroonstad, S. Afr.	D4	56
Kropotkin, Russia	A4	42
Krosno, Pol.	E6	20
Krotoszyn, Pol.	D4	20
Krotz Springs, La., U.S.	D4	111
Krugersdorp, S. Afr.	D4	56
Krui, Indon.	E2	36
Krung Thep (Bangkok), Thai.	D4	34
Kruševac, Yugo.	C8	18
Kruzof Island, i., Ak., U.S.	m21	95
Kryčaŭ, Bela.	C11	20
Krymsk, Russia	G14	20
Kryms'ki hory, mts., Ukr.	G13	20
Kryms'kyi pivostriv (Crimean Peninsula), pen., Ukr.	G12	20
Kryvyi Rih, Ukr.	F12	20
Ksar-el-Kebir, Mor.	J4	16
Ksenevka, Russia	A11	28
Kšenskij, Russia	D14	20
Kuala Kangsar, Malay.	C2	36
Kualakapuas, Indon.	D4	36
Kuala Krai, Malay.	B2	36
Kuala Lipis, Malay.	C2	36
Kuala Lumpur, Malay.	C2	36
Kuala Pilah, Malay.	C2	36
Kuala Terengganu, Malay.	B2	36
Kuantan, Malay.	C2	36
Kuban', stm., Russia	E6	26
Kuching, Malay.	C4	36
Kuçovë, Alb.	D8	18
Kudat, Malay.	B5	36
Kudus, Indon.	E4	36
Kudymkar, Russia	C9	22
Kuee Ruins, hist., Hi., U.S.	D6	104
Kufstein, Aus.	G13	12
Kühdasht, Iran	F12	44
Kuito, Ang.	F3	54
Kujawy, reg., Pol.	C5	20
Kujbyšev see Samara, Russia	D7	26
Kujbyšev, Russia	D9	26
Kujbyševskoe vodohranilišče, res., Russia	D8	22
Kujgan, Kaz.	A10	42
Kujū-san, vol., Japan	D2	31
Kukawa, Nig.	D7	50
Kukes, Alb.	C8	18
Kula, Tur.	C3	44
Kula, Hi., U.S.	C5	104
Kula Kangri, mtn., Bhu.	D6	40
Kuldīga, Lat.	H9	10
Kule, Bots.	C3	56
Kulebaki, Russia	C7	22
Kuljab, Taj.	F8	26
Kulmbach, Ger.	E12	12
Kuloj, Russia	B7	22
Kulpmont, Pa., U.S.	E9	131
Kul'sary, Kaz.	E7	26
Kulu, Tur.	C5	44
Kulumadau, Pap. N. Gui.	H13	32
Kumagaya, Japan	C3	31
Kumai, Indon.	D4	36
Kumai, Teluk, b., Indon.	D4	36
Kumamoto, Japan	E14	28
Kumanovo, Mac.	C8	18
Kumasi, Ghana	E4	50
Kumba, Cam.	C1	54
Kumbakonam, India	G3	40
Kume-jima, i., Japan	A9	31
Kuminskij, Russia	C12	22
Kumluca, Tur.	D4	44
Kumo, Nig.	E7	50
Kumta, India	G2	40
Kumukahi, Cape, c., Hi., U.S.	D7	104
Kuna, Id., U.S.	F2	105
Kunašir, ostrov, i., Russia	E16	26
Kunda, Est.	G12	10
Kundāpura, India	G2	40
Kundur, Pulau, i., Indon.	C2	36
Kunene (Cunene), stm., Afr.	B1	56
Kunghit Island, i., B.C., Can.	C2	85
Kungrad, Uzb.	B7	42
Kungur, Russia	C10	22
Kunhing, Myan.	B3	34
Kunlun Shan, mts., China	D5	28
Kunming, China	F8	28
Kununurra, Austl.	D4	60
Kunya, Nig.	D6	50
Kuopio, Fin.	E12	10
Kupang, Indon.	F6	36
Kup'ians'k, Ukr.	E14	20
Kupreanof Island, i., Ak., U.S.	m23	95
Kuqa, China	C4	28
Kuqa, China	C4	28
Kür, stm., Asia	C13	44
Kurashiki, Japan	D2	31
Kuraymah, Sudan	G11	48
Kurčatov, Russia	D13	20
Kürdämir, Azer.	B13	44
Kurdistan, hist. reg., Asia	D10	44
Kure, Japan	D2	31
Kure Island, i., Hi., U.S.	k12	104
Kurejka, stm., Russia	C10	26
Kuresaare, Est.	G10	10
Kurgan, Russia	D8	26
Kurgan-Tjube, Taj.	C9	42
Kuril Islands see Kuril'skie ostrova, is., Russia	E16	26
Kuril'sk, Russia	B17	28
Kuril'skie ostrova (Kuril Islands), is., Russia	E16	26
Kuril Trench	A7	144
Kurmuk, Sudan	H11	48
Kurnool, India	F3	40
Kursk, Russia	D5	26
Kurtalan, Tur.	D9	44
Kurtamyš, Russia	D11	22
Kurtistown, Hi., U.S.	D6	104
Kuruman, S. Afr.	D3	56
Kuruman, stm., S. Afr.	D3	56
Kurume, Japan	D2	31
Kurumkan, Russia	D13	26
Kurunegala, Sri L.	H4	40
Kuşadası, Tur.	D2	44
Kuşadası Körfezi, b., Tur.	D2	44
Kuščevskaja, Russia	F15	20
Kuş Gölü, l., Tur.	B2	44
Kushiro, Japan	C16	28
Kushtī, Sudan	H11	48
Kut, Ko, i., Thai.	D4	34
Kütahya, Tur.	C3	44
Kutaisi, Geor.	A10	44
Kutch see Kachchh, Gulf of, b., India	E1	40
Kutch, Gulf of see Kachchh, Gulf of, b., India	E1	40
Kutch, Rann of, reg., Asia	E1	40
Kutina, Cro.	B6	18
Kutno, Pol.	C5	20
Kutu, D.R.C.	D3	54
Kutztown, Pa., U.S.	E10	131
Kuujjuaq, P.Q., Can.	g13	90
Kuusamo, Fin.	D13	10
Kuusankoski, Fin.	F12	10
Kuvango, Ang.	A2	56
Kuwait see Al-Kuwayt, Kuw.	E5	42
Kuwait, ctry., Asia	E5	42
Kuybyshev see Kujbyšev, Russia	D9	26
Kuybyshev see Samara, Russia	D7	26
Kuybyshev Reservoir see Kujbyševskoe vodohranilišče, res., Russia	D8	22
Kuz'movka, Russia	C11	26
Kuzneck, Russia	D6	26
Kuzomen', Russia	A6	22
Kvænangen, b., Nor.	A9	10
Kvaløya, i., Nor.	B8	10
Kvareli, Geor.	B11	44
Kwa, stm., D.R.C.	D3	54
Kwakoegron, Sur.	B8	70
Kwamouth, D.R.C.	D3	54
Kwando (Cuando), stm., Afr.	B1	56
Kwangju, S. Kor.	D13	28
Kwango (Cuango), stm., Afr.	D3	54
Kwangsi Chuang see Guangxi Zhuangzu Zizhiqu, state, China	G9	28
Kwekwe, Zimb.	B4	56
Kwenge, stm., Afr.	E3	54
Kwethluk, Ak., U.S.	C7	95
Kwidzyn, Pol.	C5	20
Kwigillingok, Ak., U.S.	D7	95
Kwilu (Cuilo), stm., Afr.	D3	54
Kyaikto, Myan.	C3	34
Kyaukki, Myan.	C3	34
Kyaukme, Myan.	B3	34
Kyaukpyu, Myan.	C2	34
Kyaukse, Myan.	B3	34
Kyauktaw, Myan.	B2	34
Kyaunggon, Myan.	C3	34
Kyiv (Kiev), Ukr.	D11	20
Kyïvs'ke vodoskhovyshche, res., Ukr.	D11	20
Kyle, Tx., U.S.	E4	136
Kyoga, Lake, l., Ug.	C6	54
Kyŏngju, S. Kor.	C1	31
Kyŏngsŏng-ŭp, N. Kor.	B1	31
Kyōto, Japan	D15	28
Kyrgyzstan, ctry., Asia	A2	40
Kyštovka, Russia	D9	26
Kyštym, Russia	C11	22
Kyuquot Sound, strt., B.C., Can.	E4	85
Kyūshū, i., Japan	E14	28
Kyushu-Palau Ridge	G16	64
Kyyiv see Kyïv, Ukr.	D11	20
Kyyjärvi, Fin.	E11	10
Kyzyl, Russia	D11	26
Kyzylkum, des., Asia	B8	42
Kyzyl-Orda, Kaz.	E8	26
Kzyltu, Kaz.	D9	26

L

Name	Map Ref.	Page
Laascaanood, Som.	I14	48
La Asunción, Ven.	C7	80
Laau Point, c., Hi., U.S.	B4	104
Laayoune see El Aaiún, W. Sah.	A2	50
Labadieville, La., U.S.	E5	111
La Bañeza, Spain	F4	16
La Barca, Mex.	C4	78
La Barge, Wy., U.S.	D2	143
La Barge Creek, stm., Wy., U.S.	D2	143
La Baule-Escoublac, Fr.	D5	16
Labé, Gui.	D2	50
Labe, stm., Eur.	E14	12
La Belle, Fl., U.S.	F5	102
La Belle, Mo., U.S.	A6	118
Labette, co., Ks., U.S.	E8	109
Labinsk, Russia	B4	42
Labis, Malay.	C2	36
Laboulaye, Arg.	E5	72
Labrador, reg., Nf., Can.	g9	88
Labrador Basin	B28	144
Labrador City, Nf., Can.	h8	88
Labrador Sea, N.A.	F29	82
Lábrea, Braz.	E7	70
Labuan, Malay.	B5	36
Labuan, Pulau, i., Malay.	B5	36
Labuha, Indon.	G8	32
Labuhanbajo, Indon.	E5	36
Labytnangi, Russia	A12	22
Laç, Alb.	D7	18
La Canada Flintridge, Ca., U.S.	m12	98
La Carlota, Arg.	E5	72
La Carlota, Phil.	D8	34
La Carolina, Spain	H5	16
Lac-Bouchette, P.Q., Can.	A5	90
Lac-Brome, P.Q., Can.	D5	90
Laccadive, Minicoy and Amīndīvi Islands see Lakshadweep, prov., India	G2	40
Laccadive Islands see Lakshadweep, is., India	G2	40
Lac-Carré, P.Q., Can.	C3	90

Name — Map Ref. — Page

Lac Courte Oreilles Indian Reservation, Wi., U.S. C2 142
Lac du Bonnet, Mb., Can. D3 86
Lac du Flambeau, Wi., U.S. B4 142
Lac du Flambeau Indian Reservation, Wi., U.S. C3 142
La Ceiba, Hond. B2 80
La Center, Ky., U.S. e9 110
Lac-Etchemin, P.Q., Can. C7 90
Lacey, Wa., U.S. B3 140
La Chaux-de-Fonds, Switz. A1 18
Lachine, P.Q., Can. D4 90
La Chorrera, Col. D5 70
La Chorrera, Pan. D3 80
Lachute, P.Q., Can. D3 90
La Citadelle, hist., Haiti B5 80
Lackawanna, N.Y., U.S. C2 125
Lackawanna, co., Pa., U.S. D10 131
Lackland Air Force Base, mil., Tx., U.S. k7 136
Lac La Biche, Ab., Can. B5 84
Lac la Hache, B.C., Can. D7 85
Laclede, co., Mo., U.S. D5 118
Lac-Mégantic, P.Q., Can. D7 90
Lacolle, P.Q., Can. D4 90
La Columna see Bolívar, Pico, mtn., Ven. B5 70
Lacombe, Ab., Can. C4 84
Lacombe, La., U.S. D6 111
Lacon, Il., U.S. B4 106
La Concepción, Pan. D3 80
La Concepción, Ven. C5 80
Laconia, N.H., U.S. C4 122
Laconia, Gulf of 20 Lakonikós Kólpos, b., Grc. F9 18
La Conner, Wa., U.S. A3 140
Lacoochee, Fl., U.S. D4 102
La Coruña see A Coruña, Spain F2 16
Lac qui Parle, co., Mn., U.S. F2 116
Lac qui Parle, stm., Mn., U.S. F2 116
La Creek Lake, l., S.D., U.S. D4 134
La Crescent, Mn., U.S. G7 116
La Crete, Ab., Can. f7 84
La Crosse, In., U.S. B4 107
La Crosse, Ks., U.S. D4 109
La Crosse, Wi., U.S. E2 142
La Crosse, co., Wi., U.S. E2 142
La Crosse, stm., Wi., U.S. E3 142
La Cygne, Ks., U.S. D9 109
Ladākh Range, mts., Asia C3 40
Ladd, Il., U.S. B4 106
Ladies Island, i., S.C., U.S. G6 133
La Digue, i., Sey. h13 57b
Lādīz, Iran E8 42
Ladoga, In., U.S. E4 107
Ladoga, Lake see Ladožskoe ozero, l., Russia C5 26
La Dorada, Col. D5 80
Ladožskoe ozero, l., Russia C5 26
Ladson, S.C., U.S. F7 133
Ladybrand, S. Afr. D4 56
Lady Lake, Fl., U.S. D5 102
Lady Laurier, Mount, mtn., B.C., Can. A6 85
Ladysmith, B.C., Can. E6 85
Ladysmith, S. Afr. D4 56
Ladysmith, Wi., U.S. C2 142
Lae, Pap. N. Gui. H12 32
La Encantada, Mex. B4 78
Læsø, i., Den. H4 10
La Esperanza, Hond. C2 80
La Estrada see A Estrada, Spain F2 16
La Farge, Wi., U.S. E3 142
Lafayette, Al., U.S. C4 94
Lafayette, Co., U.S. B5 99
Lafayette, Ga., U.S. B1 103
Lafayette, In., U.S. D4 107
Lafayette, La., U.S. D3 111
Lafayette, N.C., U.S. B3 126
Lafayette, Or., U.S. B3 130
La Fayette, R.I., U.S. E4 132
Lafayette, Tn., U.S. A5 135
Lafayette, co., Ar., U.S. D2 97
Lafayette, co., Fl., U.S. C3 102
Lafayette, co., La., U.S. D3 111
Lafayette, co., Mo., U.S. B4 118
Lafayette, co., Ms., U.S. A4 117
Lafayette, co., Wi., U.S. F3 142
Lafayette, Mount, mtn., N.H., U.S. B3 122
La Feria, Tx., U.S. F4 136
Lafia, Nig. E6 50
Lafiagi, Nig. E6 50
Lafitte, La., U.S. k11 111
La Flèche, Fr. D6 16
La Follette, Tn., U.S. C9 135
La Fontaine, In., U.S. C6 107
Lafourche, La., U.S. E5 111
Lafourche, co., La., U.S. E5 111
La France, S.C., U.S. B2 133
La Galite, i., Tun. F2 18
Lagarto, Braz. D4 74
Lagawe, Phil. C8 34
Lågen, stm., Nor. F3 10
Lages, Braz. D7 72
Laghouat, Alg. D5 48
Lago, Mount, mtn., Wa., U.S. A5 140
Lagoa da Prata, Braz. F2 74
Lago da Pedra, Braz. B2 74
La Gomera, i., Spain A1 50
Lagonoy Gulf, b., Phil. D8 34
Lagos, Nig. E5 50
Lagos, Port. I2 16
Lagos de Moreno, Mex. C4 78
La Gouèra, W. Sah. B1 50
La Grande, Or., U.S. B8 130
La Grande, stm., P.Q., Can. h11 90
La Grande Deux, Réservoir, res., P.Q., Can. h11 90
Lagrange, Austl. D3 60
La Grange, Ga., U.S. C1 103
La Grange, Il., U.S. B6 106
Lagrange, In., U.S. A7 107
La Grange, Ky., U.S. B4 110
La Grange, Mo., U.S. A6 118
La Grange, N.C., U.S. B5 126
Lagrange, Oh., U.S. A3 128
La Grange, Tx., U.S. E4 136
Lagrange, co., In., U.S. A7 107
La Grange Park, Il., U.S. k9 106
La Gran Sabana, pl., Ven. B7 70
La Guadeloupe (Saint-Evariste), P.Q., Can. D7 90
La Guajira, Península de, pen., S.A. A5 70
La Guardia, Bol. B5 72
La Guardia see A Guardia, Spain G2 16
Laguna, Braz. D8 72
Laguna, N.M., U.S. B2 124
Laguna Beach, Ca., U.S. F5 98
Laguna Dam, U.S. E1 96
Laguna Indian Reservation, N.M., U.S. C2 124
La Habana (Havana), Cuba A3 80
La Habra, Ca., U.S. n13 98
Lahad Datu, Malay. C5 36
Lahad Datu, Telukan, b., Malay. C5 36
Lahaina, Hi., U.S. C5 104
La Harpe, Il., U.S. C3 106
La Harpe, Ks., U.S. E8 109
Lahat, Indon. D2 36
La Have, stm., N.S., Can. E5 87
Lahdenpohja, Russia F14 10
Lāhījān, Iran C6 42
Lahoma, Ok., U.S. A3 129
Lahontan Reservoir, res., Nv., U.S. D2 121
Lahore, Pak. D10 42
Lahti, Fin. F11 10
Laï, Chad E8 50
Lai Chau, Viet. B4 34
Laie, Hi., U.S. B4 104
Lai-hka, Myan. B3 34
Laingsburg, S. Afr. E3 56
Laingsburg, Mi., U.S. F6 115
Lainioälven, stm., Swe. B9 10
Lais, Indon. D2 36
Laisamis, Kenya C7 54
Laiwu, China B4 30
Laiwui, Indon. G8 32
Laiyang, China B5 30
Laizhou Wan, b., China D11 28
La Jara, Co., U.S. D5 99
La Jolla, Point, c., Ca., U.S. o15 98
La Junta, Co., U.S. D7 99
Lakatoro, Vanuatu k9 62a
Lake, co., Ca., U.S. C2 98
Lake, co., Co., U.S. B4 99
Lake, co., Fl., U.S. D5 102
Lake, co., Il., U.S. A6 106
Lake, co., In., U.S. B3 107
Lake, co., Mi., U.S. E5 115
Lake, co., Mn., U.S. C7 116
Lake, co., Mt., U.S. C2 119
Lake, co., Oh., U.S. A4 128
Lake, co., Or., U.S. E6 130
Lake, co., S.D., U.S. C8 134
Lake, co., Tn., U.S. A2 135
Lake Alfred, Fl., U.S. D5 102
Lake Andes, S.D., U.S. D7 134
Lake Ariel, Pa., U.S. D11 131
Lake Arrowhead, Ca., U.S. E5 98
Lake Arthur, La., U.S. D3 111
Lakeba, i., Fiji m11 63b
Lake Benton, Mn., U.S. F2 116
Lake Bluff, Il., U.S. A6 106
Lake Butler, Fl., U.S. B4 102
Lake Cargelligo, Austl. G4 62
Lake Charles, La., U.S. D2 111
Lake Chelan National Recreation Area, Wa., U.S. A5 140
Lake City, Ar., U.S. B5 97
Lake City, Fl., U.S. B4 102
Lake City, Ia., U.S. B3 108
Lake City, Mi., U.S. D5 115
Lake City, Mn., U.S. F6 116
Lake City, Pa., U.S. B1 131
Lake City, S.C., U.S. D8 133
Lake City, Tn., U.S. C9 135
Lake Clark National Park, Ak., U.S. C9 95
Lake Cowichan, B.C., Can. g11 85
Lake Creek, stm., Wa., U.S. B7 140
Lake Crystal, Mn., U.S. F4 116
Lake Delta, N.Y., U.S. B5 125
Lake Delton, Wi., U.S. E4 142
Lake District, reg., Eng., U.K. C5 12
Lake Elsinore, Ca., U.S. F5 98
Lake Erie Beach, N.Y., U.S. C1 125
Lakefield, On., Can. C6 89
Lakefield, Mn., U.S. G3 116
Lake Forest, Il., U.S. A6 106
Lake Fork, stm., Ut., U.S. C5 137
Lake Geneva, Wi., U.S. F5 142
Lake Hamilton, Ar., U.S. g7 97
Lake Havasu City, Az., U.S. C1 96
Lake Helen, Fl., U.S. D5 102
Lakehurst, N.J., U.S. C4 123
Lakehurst Naval Air Station, mil., N.J., U.S. C4 123
Lake in the Hills, Il., U.S. h8 106
Lake Jackson, Tx., U.S. r14 136
Lake Katrine, N.Y., U.S. D7 125
Lake King, Austl. G2 60
Lakeland, Fl., U.S. D5 102
Lakeland, Ga., U.S. E3 103
Lake Linden, Mi., U.S. A2 115
Lake Louise, Ab., Can. D2 84
Lake Magdalene, Fl., U.S. o11 102
Lake Mary, Fl., U.S. D5 102
Lake Mead National Recreation Area, U.S. H7 121
Lake Meredith National Recreation Area, Tx., U.S. B2 136
Lake Mills, Ia., U.S. A4 108
Lake Mills, Wi., U.S. E5 142
Lakemore, Oh., U.S. A4 128
Lake Mountain, mtn., Wy., U.S. E6 143
Lake Nebagamon, Wi., U.S. B2 142
Lake Odessa, Mi., U.S. F5 115
Lake of the Woods, co., Mn., U.S. B4 116
Lake Orion, Mi., U.S. F7 115
Lake Oswego, Or., U.S. B4 130
Lake Ozark, Mo., U.S. C5 118
Lake Park, Fl., U.S. F6 102
Lake Park, Ia., U.S. A2 108
Lake Park, Mn., U.S. D2 116
Lake Placid, Fl., U.S. E5 102
Lake Placid, N.Y., U.S. A7 125
Lake Pontchartrain Causeway, La., U.S. h11 111
Lakeport, Ca., U.S. C2 98
Lake Preston, S.D., U.S. C8 134
Lake Providence, La., U.S. B4 111
Lake Range, mts., Nv., U.S. C2 121
Lakes Entrance, Austl. H4 62
Lake Shore, Md., U.S. B5 113
Lakeshore, Ms., U.S. E4 117
Lakeside, Az., U.S. C6 96
Lakeside, Ca., U.S. F5 98
Lakeside, Ct., U.S. D3 100
Lakeside, Mt., U.S. B2 119
Lakeside, Oh., U.S. A3 128
Lakeside, Or., U.S. D2 130
Lakeside Park, Ky., U.S. h13 110
Lake Station, In., U.S. A3 107
Lake Station, Ok., U.S. A5 129
Lake Stevens, Wa., U.S. A3 140
Lake Superior Provincial Park, On., Can. p18 89
Lake Swamp, stm., S.C., U.S. D8 133
Lake Tansi Village, Tn., U.S. D8 135
Lake Valley, val., Nv., U.S. E7 121
Lake View, Ia., U.S. B2 108
Lakeview, Mi., U.S. E5 115
Lakeview, Oh., U.S. B2 128
Lakeview, Or., U.S. E6 130
Lake View, S.C., U.S. C9 133
Lake Villa, Il., U.S. h8 106
Lake Village, Ar., U.S. D4 97
Lake Village, In., U.S. B3 107
Lakeville, Ct., U.S. B2 100
Lakeville, In., U.S. A5 107
Lakeville, Ma., U.S. C6 114
Lakeville, Mn., U.S. F5 116
Lake Waccamaw, N.C., U.S. C4 126
Lake Wales, Fl., U.S. E5 102
Lakewood, Ca., U.S. n12 98
Lakewood, Co., U.S. B5 99
Lakewood, Ia., U.S. f8 108
Lakewood, Il., U.S. D5 106
Lakewood, N.J., U.S. C4 123
Lakewood, N.Y., U.S. C1 125
Lakewood, Oh., U.S. A4 128
Lakewood, Wa., U.S. B3 140
Lake Worth, Fl., U.S. F6 102
Lake Worth Inlet, b., Fl., U.S. F7 102
Lake Zurich, Il., U.S. h8 106
Lakhdaria, Alg. I8 16
Lakhīmpur, India D4 40
Lakin, Ks., U.S. E2 109
Lakonikós Kólpos, b., Grc. F9 18
Lakota, N.D., U.S. A7 127
Laksefjorden, b., Nor. A12 10
Lakshadweep, prov., India G2 40
Lakshadweep, is., India G2 40
Lakshadweep Sea, Asia G2 40
Lalara, Gabon C2 54
Lalībela, Eth. H12 48
La Libertad, Guat. B1 80
La Línea de la Concepción, Spain I4 16
Lalitpur, India E3 40
La Loche see Churchill, stm., Can. G21 82
La Luz, N.M., U.S. E4 124
La Malbaie, P.Q., Can. B7 90
La Mancha, reg., Spain H5 16
La Manche see English Channel, strt., Eur. C5 16
Lamap, Vanuatu k9 62a
Lamar, Ar., U.S. B2 97
Lamar, Co., U.S. C8 99
Lamar, Mo., U.S. D3 118
Lamar, Pa., U.S. D7 131
Lamar, S.C., U.S. C7 133
Lamar, co., Al., U.S. B1 94
Lamar, co., Ga., U.S. C2 103
Lamar, co., Ms., U.S. D4 117
Lamar, co., Tx., U.S. C5 136
Lamar, stm., Wy., U.S. B2 143
La Mauricie, Parc National de, P.Q., Can. C5 90
Lamb, co., Tx., U.S. B1 136
Lambaréné, Gabon D2 54
Lambayeque, Peru E4 70
Lambert, Ms., U.S. A3 117
Lambert Glacier, Ant. D11 67
Lamberton, Mn., U.S. F3 116
Lambert's Bay, S. Afr. E2 56
Lambertville, Mi., U.S. G7 115
Lambertville, N.J., U.S. C3 123
Lame Deer, Mt., U.S. E10 119
Lamèque, N.B., Can. B5 87
Lamèque, Île, i., N.B., Can. B5 87
La Mesa, Ca., U.S. F5 98
La Mesa, N.M., U.S. E3 124
Lamesa, Tx., U.S. C2 136
Lamía, Grc. E9 18
Lamoille, Nv., U.S. C6 121
Lamoille, co., Vt., U.S. B3 138
Lamoille, stm., Vt., U.S. B3 138
La Moine, stm., Il., U.S. C3 106
Lamon Bay, b., Phil. D8 34
Lamoni, Ia., U.S. D4 108
Lamont, Ab., Can. C4 84
Lamont, Ca., U.S. E4 98
La Monte, Mo., U.S. C4 118
La Motte, Isle, i., Vt., U.S. B2 138
La Moure, N.D., U.S. C7 127
La Moure, co., N.D., U.S. C7 127
Lampang, Thai. C3 34
Lampasas, Tx., U.S. D3 136
Lampasas, co., Tx., U.S. D3 136
Lampazos de Naranjo, Mex. B4 78
Lamphun, Thai. C3 34
Lampman, Sk., Can. H4 91
Lamprey, stm., N.H., U.S. D4 122
Lamu, Kenya D8 54
Lanai, i., Hi., U.S. C4 104
Lanai City, Hi., U.S. C5 104
Lanaihale, mtn., Hi., U.S. C5 104
Lanark, On., Can. C8 89
Lanark, Il., U.S. A4 106
Lanark, W.V., U.S. D3 141
Lanbi Kyun, i., Myan. D3 34
Lancang see Mekong, stm., Asia A3 34
Lancaster, On., Can. B10 89
Lancaster, Eng., U.K. C5 12
Lancaster, Ca., U.S. E4 98
Lancaster, Ky., U.S. C5 110
Lancaster, Mo., U.S. A5 118
Lancaster, N.H., U.S. B3 122
Lancaster, N.Y., U.S. C2 125
Lancaster, Oh., U.S. C3 128
Lancaster, Pa., U.S. F9 131
Lancaster, S.C., U.S. B6 133
Lancaster, Tx., U.S. n10 136
Lancaster, Wi., U.S. F3 142
Lancaster, co., Ne., U.S. D9 120
Lancaster, co., Pa., U.S. G9 131
Lancaster, co., S.C., U.S. B6 133
Lancaster, co., Va., U.S. C6 139
Lance Creek, stm., Wy., U.S. C8 143
Lanchow see Lanzhou, China D8 28
Lanciano, Italy C5 18
Lancun, China B5 30
Lândana, Ang. E2 54
Land Between the Lakes, U.S. f9 110
Landeck, Aus. G12 12
Landegode, Nor. C6 10
Lander, Wy., U.S. D4 143
Lander, co., Nv., U.S. C4 121
Landerneau, Fr. C4 16
Landes, reg., Fr. E6 16
Landess, In., U.S. C6 107
Landis, N.C., U.S. B2 126
Lando, S.C., U.S. B5 133
Landrum, S.C., U.S. A3 133
Land's End, c., Eng., U.K. E4 12
Lands End, c., R.I., U.S. F5 132
Landshut, Ger. F13 12
Landskrona, Swe. I5 10
Lane, co., Ks., U.S. D3 109
Lane, co., Or., U.S. C4 130
La Negra, Chile C3 72
Lanesboro, Mn., U.S. G7 116
Lanett, Al., U.S. C4 94
Langdon, N.D., U.S. A7 127
Langeland, i., Den. I4 10
Langeloth, Pa., U.S. F1 131
Langfang, China B4 30
Langhorne, Pa., U.S. F12 131
Langjökull, Ice. I20 10a
Langkawi, Pulau, i., Malay. B1 36
Langlade, co., Wi., U.S. C4 142
Langley, B.C., Can. f13 85
Langley, S.C., U.S. E4 133
Langley, Wa., U.S. A3 140
Langley Air Force Base, mil., Va., U.S. h15 139
Langley Park, Md., U.S. f9 113
Langøya, i., Nor. B6 10
Langres, Fr. D9 16
Langsa, Indon. C1 36
Lang Son, Viet. B5 34
Langston, Ok., U.S. B4 129
Languedoc, hist. reg., Fr. F8 16
L'Anguille, stm., Ar., U.S. B5 97
Langzhong, China E9 28
Lanham, Md., U.S. C4 113
Lanier, co., Ga., U.S. E3 103
Länkäran, Azer. C13 44
Lannion, Fr. C5 16
Lannon, Wi., U.S. m11 142
L'Annonciation, P.Q., Can. C3 90
Lanping, China A3 34
Lansdale, Pa., U.S. F11 131
Lansdowne, Md., U.S. B4 113
L'Anse, Mi., U.S. B2 115
L'Anse-au-Loup, Nf., Can. C3 88
L'Anse Indian Reservation, Mi., U.S. B2 115
Lansford, Pa., U.S. E10 131
Lanshan, China D3 30
Lansing, Ia., U.S. A6 108
Lansing, Il., U.S. B6 106
Lansing, Ks., U.S. C9 109
Lansing, Mi., U.S. F6 115
Lantana, Fl., U.S. F6 102
Lanxi, China F11 28
Lanzarote, i., Spain A2 50
Lanzhou, China D8 28
Laoag, Phil. C8 34
Laoang, Phil. D9 34
Lao Cai, Viet. B4 34
Laoha, stm., China C12 28
Laohekou, China E10 28
Laon, Fr. C8 16
La Orchila, Isla, i., Ven. C6 80
La Oroya, Peru F4 70
Laos, ctry., Asia B3 32
La Palma, Pan. D4 80
La Palma, i., Spain A1 50
La Paragua, Ven. B7 70
La Paz, Arg. E6 72
La Paz, Bol. B4 72
La Paz, Mex. C2 78
La Paz, co., Az., U.S. D2 96
Lapeer, Mi., U.S. E7 115
Lapeer, co., Mi., U.S. E7 115
Lapel, In., U.S. D6 107
La Perouse Strait, strt., Asia B16 28
La Pine, Or., U.S. D5 130
Lapinlahti, Fin. E12 10
La Place, La., U.S. h11 111
Lapland (Lappland), hist. reg., Eur. B8 10
La Plata, Arg. F6 72
La Plata, Md., U.S. C4 113
La Plata, Mo., U.S. A5 118
La Plata, co., Co., U.S. D3 99
La Plata Mountains, mts., Co., U.S. D3 99
La Plata Peak, mtn., Co., U.S. B4 99
La Platte, stm., Vt., U.S. C2 138
La Pocatière, P.Q., Can. B7 90
Laporte, Co., U.S. A5 99
La Porte, In., U.S. A4 107
La Porte, Tx., U.S. r14 136
La Porte, co., In., U.S. A4 107
La Porte City, Ia., U.S. B5 108
Lappeenranta, Fin. F13 10
Lappland (Lapland), hist. reg., Eur. B8 10
La Prairie, P.Q., Can. D4 90
La Pryor, Tx., U.S. E3 136
Laptev Sea see Laptevyh, more, Russia B14 26
Laptevyh, more, Russia B14 26
La Push, Wa., U.S. B1 140
Lapwai, Id., U.S. C2 105
La Quiaca, Arg. C4 72
L'Aquila, Italy C4 18
Lār, Iran E6 42
Larache, Mor. C3 48
Laramie, Wy., U.S. E7 143
Laramie, co., Wy., U.S. E8 143
Laramie, stm., U.S. E7 143
Laramie Mountains, mts., Wy., U.S. D7 143
Laramie Peak, mtn., Wy., U.S. D7 143
Larantuka, Indon. E6 36
Lärbro, Swe. H8 10
Larchmont, N.Y., U.S. h13 125
Larchwood, Ia., U.S. A1 108
Laredo, Spain F5 16
Laredo, Tx., U.S. F3 136
Largo, Fl., U.S. E4 102
Largo, Cañon, val., N.M., U.S. A2 124
Largo, Key, i., Fl., U.S. G6 102
Larimer, co., Co., U.S. A5 99
Larimore, N.D., U.S. B8 127
La Rioja, Arg. D4 72
La Rioja, reg., Spain F5 16
Lárisa, Grc. E9 18
Lārkāna, Pak. E9 42
Lark Harbour, Nf., Can. D2 88
Larkspur, Ca., U.S. h7 98
Larksville, Pa., U.S. n17 131
Larnaca see Lárnax, Cyp. E5 44
Lárnax, Cyp. E5 44
Larne, N. Ire., U.K. C4 12
Larned, Ks., U.S. D4 109

| | Map
Ref. | Page |
| Name | Ref. | Page |

La Rochelle, Fr. D6 16
La Roche-sur-Yon, Fr. D6 16
La Roda, Spain H5 16
La Romana, Dom. Rep. . . . B6 80
Larose, La., U.S. E5 111
Larrimah, Austl. D5 60
Larsen Ice Shelf, Ant. C34 67
Larue, co., Ky., U.S. C4 110
Larvik, Nor. G4 10
LaSalle, P.Q., Can. q19 90
La Salle, Co., U.S. A6 99
La Salle, Il., U.S. B4 106
La Salle, co., Il., U.S. B4 106
La Salle, co., La., U.S. . . . C3 111
La Salle, co., Tx., U.S. . . . E3 136
Las Animas, Co., U.S. C7 99
Las Animas, co., Co., U.S. D6 99
La Sarre, P.Q., Can. k11 90
Las Casitas, mtn., Mex. . . . C3 78
Las Choapas, Mex. D6 78
La Scie, Nf., Can. D4 88
Las Cruces, N.M., U.S. . . . E3 124
La Selle, Morne, mtn., Haiti B5 80
La Serena, Chile C2 69
La Serena, reg., Spain . . . H4 16
La Seyne-sur-Mer, Fr. . . . F9 16
Las Flores, Arg. F6 72
Lāsh-e Joveyn, Afg. D8 42
Las Heras, Arg. G3 69
Lashio, Myan. B3 34
Lashkar Gāh, Afg. D8 42
Las Margaritas, Mex. D6 78
Las Minas, Cerro, mtn.,
Hond. C2 80
La Solana, Spain H5 16
Las Palmas de Gran Canaria,
Spain A1 50
La Spezia, Italy B2 18
Las Piedras, Ur. E6 72
Las Plumas, Arg. F3 69
Las Rosas, Mex. D6 78
Lassen, co., Ca., U.S. B3 98
Lassen Peak, vol., Ca., U.S. B3 98
Lassen Volcanic National
Park, Ca., U.S. B3 98
L'Assomption, P.Q., Can. . D4 90
Las Tablas, Pan. D3 80
Last Mountain Lake, l., Sk.,
Can. F3 91
Lastoursville, Gabon D2 54
Las Tunas, Cuba A4 80
Las Varas, Mex. B3 78
Las Varas, Mex. C3 78
Las Vegas, N.M., U.S. B4 124
Las Vegas, Nv., U.S. G6 121
Latah, co., Id., U.S. C2 105
Latakia see Al-Lādhiqīyah,
Syria E6 44
Lathrop, Mo., U.S. B3 118
Latimer, co., Ok., U.S. . . . C6 129
Latina, Italy D4 18
Laton, Ca., U.S. D4 98
La Tortuga, Isla, i., Ven. . . C6 80
Latouche Treville, Cape, c.,
Austl. D3 60
Latour Peak, mtn., Id., U.S. B2 105
Latrobe, Pa., U.S. F3 131
Latta, S.C., U.S. C9 133
La Tuque, P.Q., Can. B5 90
Lātūr, India F3 40
Latvia, ctry., Eur. H11 10
Lauderdale, Ms., U.S. C5 117
Lauderdale, co., Al., U.S. . A2 94
Lauderdale, co., Ms., U.S. . C5 117
Lauderdale, co., Tn., U.S. . B2 135
Lauderdale Lakes, Fl., U.S. r13 102
Laughlin, Nv., U.S. H7 121
Laughlin Air Force Base,
mil., Tx., U.S. E2 136
Laughlin Peak, mtn., N.M.,
U.S. A5 124
Laughlintown, Pa., U.S. . . F3 131
Launceston, Austl. I4 62
Launching Point, c., P.E.,
Can. C7 87
La Unión, Chile F2 69
La Unión, El Sal. C2 80
La Unión, Spain I6 16
Laurel, De., U.S. F3 101
Laurel, Fl., U.S. E4 102
Laurel, Md., U.S. B4 113
Laurel, Ms., U.S. D4 117
Laurel, Mt., U.S. E8 119
Laurel, Ne., U.S. B8 120
Laurel, Va., U.S. C5 139
Laurel, co., Ky., U.S. C5 110
Laurel, stm., Ky., U.S. . . . D5 110
Laurel Bay, S.C., U.S. G6 133
Laurel Creek, stm., W.V.,
U.S. n14 141
Laurel Creek, stm., W.V.,
U.S. m12 141
Laureldale, Pa., U.S. F10 131
Laurel Fork, stm., W.V.,
U.S. C5 141
Laurel Hill, N.C., U.S. C3 126
Laurel River Lake, res., Ky.,
U.S. D5 110
Laurence G. Hanscom Air
Force Base, mil., Ma.,
U.S. g10 114
Laurence Harbor, N.J., U.S. C4 123
Laurens, Ia., U.S. B3 108
Laurens, S.C., U.S. C3 133
Laurens, co., Ga., U.S. . . . D4 103

Laurens, co., S.C., U.S. . . . C4 133
Laurentides, P.Q., Can. . . . D4 90
Laurentides, Parc Provincial
des, P.Q., Can. B6 90
Lau Ridge K21 64
Laurier, P.Q., Can. C6 90
Laurierville, P.Q., Can. . . . C6 90
Laurinburg, N.C., U.S. C3 126
Laurium, Mi., U.S. A2 115
Lausanne, Switz. A1 18
Laut, Pulau, i., Indon. C3 36
Laut, Pulau, i., Indon. D5 36
Laut, Selat, strt., Indon. . . D5 36
Lautaro, Chile E2 69
Lauzon (part of Lévis-
Lauzon), P.Q., Can. C6 90
Lava Beds National
Monument, Ca., U.S. . . . B3 98
Lavaca, Ar., U.S. B1 97
Lavaca, co., Tx., U.S. E4 136
Laval, P.Q., Can. D4 90
Laval, Fr. C6 16
La Vale, Md., U.S. k13 113
La Vall d'Uixó, Spain H6 16
Lavaltrie, P.Q., Can. D4 90
Laveen, Az., U.S. m8 96
La Vega, Dom. Rep. B5 80
L'Avenir, P.Q., Can. D5 90
La Vergne, Tn., U.S. A5 135
La Verkin, Ut., U.S. F2 137
La Verne, Ca., U.S. m13 98
Laverne, Ok., U.S. A2 129
La Veta, Co., U.S. D5 99
La Victoria, Ven. C6 80
La Vila Joiosa, Spain H6 16
La Vista, Ne., U.S. g12 120
Lavonia, Ga., U.S. B3 103
Lavon Lake, res., Tx., U.S. m10 136
Lavras, Braz. F2 74
Lavumisa, Swaz. D5 56
Lawai, Hi., U.S. B2 104
Lawn, Nf., Can. E4 88
Lawra, Ghana D4 50
Lawrence, In., U.S. E5 107
Lawrence, Ks., U.S. D8 109
Lawrence, Ma., U.S. A5 114
Lawrence, Mi., U.S. F4 115
Lawrence, N.Y., U.S. k13 125
Lawrence, co., Al., U.S. . . A2 94
Lawrence, co., Ar., U.S. . . A4 97
Lawrence, co., Il., U.S. . . . E6 106
Lawrence, co., In., U.S. . . G4 107
Lawrence, co., Ky., U.S. . . B7 110
Lawrence, co., Mo., U.S. . . D4 118
Lawrence, co., Ms., U.S. . . D3 117
Lawrence, co., Oh., U.S. . . D3 128
Lawrence, co., Pa., U.S. . . E1 131
Lawrence, co., Tn., U.S. . . B4 135
Lawrenceburg, In., U.S. . . F8 107
Lawrenceburg, Ky., U.S. . . B5 110
Lawrenceburg, Tn., U.S. . . B4 135
Lawrence Park, Pa., U.S. . . B1 131
Lawrenceville, Ga., U.S. . . C3 103
Lawrenceville, Il., U.S. . . . E6 106
Lawrenceville, Va., U.S. . . D5 139
Lawson, Mo., U.S. B3 118
Lawsonia, Md., U.S. E6 113
Lawtell, La., U.S. D3 111
Lawton, Mi., U.S. F5 115
Lawton, Ok., U.S. C3 129
Lawz, Jabal al-, mtn., Sau.
Ar. E3 42
Laxå, Swe. G6 10
Lay Lake, res., Al., U.S. . . . B3 94
Laysan Island, i., Hi., U.S. . k13 104
Layton, Ut., U.S. B4 137
Lazarev, Russia D16 26
Lázaro Cárdenas, Mex. . . . D4 78
Lazo, Russia B2 31
Leachville, Ar., U.S. B5 97
Lead, S.D., U.S. C2 134
Leadbetter Point, c., Wa.,
U.S. C1 140
Leadville, Co., U.S. B4 99
Leadwood, Mo., U.S. D7 118
Leaf, stm., Ms., U.S. D5 117
Leaf Rapids, Mb., Can. . . . A1 86
Leake, co., Ms., U.S. C4 117
Leakesville, Ms., U.S. D5 117
Lealman, Fl., U.S. p10 102
Leamington, On., Can. . . . E2 89
Leary, Ga., U.S. E2 103
Leatherman Peak, mtn., Id.,
U.S. E5 105
Leavenworth, Ks., U.S. . . . C9 109
Leavenworth, Wa., U.S. . . B5 140
Leavenworth, co., Ks., U.S. C8 109
Leavittsburg, Oh., U.S. . . . A5 128
Leawood, Ks., U.S. D9 109
Lebanon, De., U.S. A5 101
Lebanon, Il., U.S. E4 106
Lebanon, In., U.S. D5 107
Lebanon, Ky., U.S. C4 110
Lebanon, Mo., U.S. D5 118
Lebanon, N.H., U.S. C1 122
Lebanon, Oh., U.S. C1 128
Lebanon, Or., U.S. C4 130
Lebanon, Pa., U.S. F9 131
Lebanon, Tn., U.S. A5 135
Lebanon, Va., U.S. f9 139
Lebanon, co., Pa., U.S. . . . F8 131
Lebanon, ctry., Asia E6 44
Lebanon Junction, Ky., U.S. C4 110

Lebanon Mountains see
Lubnān, Jabal, mts.,
Leb. F6 44
Lebedjan', Russia C15 20
Lebedyn, Ukr. D13 20
Lebesby, Nor. A12 10
Lebjaže, Kaz. D9 26
Lebo, Ks., U.S. D8 109
Lębork, Pol. B4 20
Lebu, Chile E2 69
Lecce, Italy D7 18
Lecco, Italy B2 18
Le Center, Mn., U.S. F5 116
Lechang, China D3 30
Le Claire, Ia., U.S. C7 108
Lecompte, La., U.S. C3 111
Lecompton, Ks., U.S. C8 109
Le Creusot, Fr. D9 16
Łęczyca, Pol. C5 20
Ledjanaja, gora, mtn., Russia C19 26
Ledo, India D7 40
Ledu, China B1 30
Leduc, Ab., Can. C4 84
Lee, Ma., U.S. B1 114
Lee, co., Al., U.S. C4 94
Lee, co., Ar., U.S. C5 97
Lee, co., Fl., U.S. F5 102
Lee, co., Ga., U.S. E2 103
Lee, co., Ia., U.S. D6 108
Lee, co., Il., U.S. B4 106
Lee, co., Ky., U.S. C6 110
Lee, co., Ms., U.S. A5 117
Lee, co., N.C., U.S. B3 126
Lee, co., S.C., U.S. C7 133
Lee, co., Tx., U.S. D4 136
Lee, co., Va., U.S. f8 139
Lee, Lake, l., Ms., U.S. . . . B3 117
Leechburg, Pa., U.S. E2 131
Leech Lake, l., Mn., U.S. . . C4 116
Leech Lake Indian
Reservation, Mn., U.S. . . C4 116
Lee Creek, stm., U.S. B1 97
Leeds, Eng., U.K. D6 12
Leeds, Al., U.S. B3 94
Leelanau, co., Mi., U.S. . . . D5 115
Leelanau, Lake, l., Mi., U.S. C5 115
Lee Park, Pa., U.S. n17 131
Leer, Ger. D10 12
Leesburg, Fl., U.S. D5 102
Leesburg, Ga., U.S. E2 103
Leesburg, Oh., U.S. C2 128
Leesburg, Va., U.S. A5 139
Lees Summit, Mo., U.S. . . C3 118
Leesville, La., U.S. C2 111
Leesville, S.C., U.S. D4 133
Leesville Lake, res., Va.,
U.S. C3 139
Leeton, Austl. G4 62
Leeton, Mo., U.S. C4 118
Leetonia, Oh., U.S. B5 128
Leetsdale, Pa., U.S. h13 131
Leeuwarden, Neth. D9 12
Leeuwin, Cape, c., Austl. . . G1 60
Leeward Islands, is., N.A. . . E12 76
Leflore, co., Ms., U.S. B3 117
Le Flore, co., Ok., U.S. . . . C7 129
Lega Hida, Eth. B8 54
Legal, Ab., Can. C4 84
Leganés, Spain G5 16
Legaspi, Phil. D8 34
Leghorn see Livorno, Italy . C3 18
Legnica, Pol. D4 20
Le Grand, Ca., U.S. D3 98
Le Grand, Ia., U.S. B5 108
Leh, India C3 40
Le Havre, Fr. C7 16
Lehi, Ut., U.S. C4 137
Lehigh, co., Pa., U.S. E10 131
Lehigh, stm., Pa., U.S. . . . E10 131
Lehigh Acres, Fl., U.S. . . . F5 102
Lehighton, Pa., U.S. E10 131
Lehua Island, i., Hi., U.S. . . A1 104
Lehututu, Bots. C3 56
Leicester, Eng., U.K. D6 12
Leicester, Ma., U.S. B4 114
Leiden, Neth. D9 12
Leighton, Al., U.S. A2 94
Leinster, hist. reg., Ire. . . . D3 12
Leipsic, De., U.S. D3 101
Leipsic, Oh., U.S. A2 128
Leipsic, stm., De., U.S. . . . C3 101
Leipzig, Ger. E13 12
Leiria, Port. H2 16
Leisler, Mount, mtn., Austl. E4 60
Leisure City, Fl., U.S. s13 102
Leitchfield, Ky., U.S. C3 110
Leiyang, China D3 30
Leizhou Bandao, pen.,
China E3 30
Leka, Nor. D4 10
Leland, Il., U.S. B5 106
Leland, Ms., U.S. B3 117
Leleiwi Point, c., Hi., U.S. . D7 104
Leling, China B4 30
Leli Shan, mtn., China . . . E4 28
Le Mans, Fr. C7 16
Le Mars, Ia., U.S. B1 108
Lema Shilindi, Eth. C8 54
Lemesós, Cyp. E5 44
Lemhi, co., Id., U.S. E4 105
Lemhi, stm., Id., U.S. E5 105
Lemhi Pass, Id., U.S. E5 105
Lemhi Range, mts., Id., U.S. E5 105
Lemmon, S.D., U.S. B3 134

Lemmon, Mount, mtn., Az.,
U.S. E5 96
Lemmon Valley, Nv., U.S. . D2 121
Lemnos see Límnos, i., Grc. E10 18
Lemon, Lake, l., In., U.S. . . F5 107
Lemon Fair, stm., Vt., U.S. . C2 138
Lemon Grove, Ca., U.S. . . . o15 98
Lemont, Il., U.S. B5 106
Lemont, Pa., U.S. E6 131
Lemonweir, stm., Wi., U.S. D3 142
Lemoore, Ca., U.S. D4 98
Lemoore Naval Air Station,
mil., Ca., U.S. D4 98
Lempa, stm., N.A. C2 80
Lem Peak, mtn., Id., U.S. . . E5 105
Lena, Il., U.S. A4 106
Lena, stm., Russia B14 26
Lenawee, co., Mi., U.S. . . . G6 115
Lenghu, China D6 28
Leninakan see Gjumri, Arm. B10 44
Lenin Peak, mtn., Asia B2 40
Leninsk, Kaz. E8 26
Leninsk-Kuzneckij, Russia . D10 26
Leninskoe, Russia E15 26
Lennonville, Austl. F2 60
Lennox, S.D., U.S. D9 134
Lennox, co., N.C., U.S. . . . B5 126
Lenoir, N.C., U.S. B1 126
Lenoir, co., N.C., U.S. B5 126
Lenoir City, Tn., U.S. D9 135
Lenore Lake, l., Sk., Can. . . E3 91
Lenore Lake, l., Wa., U.S. . B6 140
Lenox, Ga., U.S. E3 103
Lenox, Ia., U.S. D3 108
Lenox, Ma., U.S. B1 114
Lens, Fr. B8 16
Lensk, Russia C13 26
Lentini, Italy F5 18
Léo, Burkina D4 50
Leo, In., U.S. B7 107
Leoben, Aus. G14 12
Leominster, Ma., U.S. A4 114
León, Mex. C4 78
León, Nic. C2 80
León, Spain F4 16
Leon, Ia., U.S. D4 108
Leon, Ks., U.S. E7 109
Leon, co., Fl., U.S. B2 102
Leon, co., Tx., U.S. D4 136
Leonard, Tx., U.S. C4 136
Leonardo, N.J., U.S. C4 123
Leonardtown, Md., U.S. . . . D4 113
Leonia, N.J., U.S. h9 123
Leonora, Austl. F3 60
Leonville, La., U.S. D4 111
Leopold and Astrid Coast,
Ant. C13 67
Léopoldville see Kinshasa,
D.R.C. D3 54
Leoti, Ks., U.S. D2 109
Lepanto, Ar., U.S. B5 97
Lepar, Pulau, i., Indon. . . . D3 36
Lepe, Spain I3 16
Lepel', Bela. B10 20
Leping, China D4 30
L'Épiphanie, P.Q., Can. . . . D4 90
Lepsy, Kaz. B3 28
Le Puy, Fr. E8 16
Le Roy, Il., U.S. C5 106
Le Roy, Mn., U.S. G6 116
Le Roy, N.Y., U.S. C3 125
Lerwick, Scot., U.K. h19 12a
Léry, P.Q., Can. q19 90
Lery, Lake, l., La., U.S. . . . k12 111
Leskovac, Yugo. C8 18
Leslie, Mi., U.S. F6 115
Leslie, S.C., U.S. B6 133
Leslie, co., Ky., U.S. C6 110
Lesosibirsk, Russia D11 26
Lesotho, ctry., Afr. D4 56
Lesozavodsk, Russia B14 28
Les Sables-d'Olonne, Fr. . . D6 16
Lesser Antilles, is. I12 76
Lesser Caucasus, mts., Asia B11 44
Lesser Khingan Range see
Xiao Hinggan Ling,
mts., China A1 31
Lesser Slave Lake, l., Ab.,
Can. B3 84
Lesser Sunda Islands see
Tenggara, Nusa, is.,
Indon. E5 36
Lester Prairie, Mn., U.S. . . F4 116
Le Sueur, Mn., U.S. F5 116
Le Sueur, co., Mn., U.S. . . F5 116
Lešukonskoe, Russia B8 22
Lésvos, i., Grc. E10 18
Leszno, Pol. D4 20
Letcher, co., Ky., U.S. C7 110
Lethbridge, Ab., Can. E4 84
Lethbridge, Nf., Can. D5 88
Lethem, Guy. C8 70
Leti, Kepulauan, is., Indon. E7 36
Leticia, Col. D6 70
Leting, China B4 30
Letlhakane, Bots. C3 56
Letsôk-aw Kyun, i., Myan. . D3 34
Levádhia, Grc. E9 18

Levanger, Nor. E4 10
Levelland, Tx., U.S. C1 136
Leveque, Cape, c., Austl. . . D3 60
Levice, Slvk. E5 20
Levin, N.Z. p14 63c
Levisa Fork, stm., U.S. C7 110
Lévis [-Lauzon], P.Q., Can. . C6 90
Levittown, N.Y., U.S. E7 125
Levittown, Pa., U.S. F12 131
Levkás, i., Grc. E8 18
Levy, co., Fl., U.S. C4 102
Levy Lake, l., Fl., U.S. C4 102
Lewes, De., U.S. E5 101
Lewes and Rehoboth Canal,
De., U.S. F5 101
Lewis, co., Id., U.S. C2 105
Lewis, co., Ky., U.S. B6 110
Lewis, co., Mo., U.S. A6 118
Lewis, co., N.Y., U.S. B5 125
Lewis, co., Tn., U.S. B4 135
Lewis, co., W.V., U.S. C4 141
Lewis, co., Wa., U.S. C3 140
Lewis, stm., Wa., U.S. C4 140
Lewis, stm., Wy., U.S. B2 143
Lewis, Isle of, i., Scot., U.K. A3 12
Lewis, Mount, mtn., Nv.,
U.S. C5 121
Lewis and Clark, co., Mt.,
U.S. C4 119
Lewis and Clark Cavern,
Mt., U.S. D5 119
Lewis and Clark Lake, res.,
U.S. E8 134
Lewisburg, Ky., U.S. D3 110
Lewisburg, Oh., U.S. C1 128
Lewisburg, Pa., U.S. E8 131
Lewisburg, Tn., U.S. B5 135
Lewisburg, W.V., U.S. D4 141
Lewis Creek, stm., Vt., U.S. C2 138
Lewis Lake, l., Wy., U.S. . . B2 143
Lewisport, Ky., U.S. C3 110
Lewisporte, Nf., Can. D4 88
Lewis Smith Lake, res., Al.,
U.S. B2 94
Lewiston, Id., U.S. C1 105
Lewiston, Me., U.S. D2 112
Lewiston, Mn., U.S. G7 116
Lewiston, N.Y., U.S. B1 125
Lewiston, Ut., U.S. B4 137
Lewiston Peak, mtn., Ut.,
U.S. C3 137
Lewiston Woodville, N.C.,
U.S. A5 126
Lewistown, Il., U.S. C3 106
Lewistown, Mt., U.S. C7 119
Lewistown, Pa., U.S. E6 131
Lewisville, Ar., U.S. D2 97
Lewisville, Tx., U.S. C4 136
Lewisville Lake, res., Tx.,
U.S. C4 136
Lexington, Al., U.S. A2 94
Lexington, Il., U.S. C5 106
Lexington, Ky., U.S. B5 110
Lexington, Ma., U.S. B5 114
Lexington, Mi., U.S. E8 115
Lexington, Mo., U.S. B4 118
Lexington, Ms., U.S. B3 117
Lexington, N.C., U.S. B2 126
Lexington, Ne., U.S. D6 120
Lexington, Oh., U.S. B3 128
Lexington, Ok., U.S. B4 129
Lexington, S.C., U.S. D5 133
Lexington, Tn., U.S. B3 135
Lexington, Va., U.S. C3 139
Lexington, co., S.C., U.S. . . D5 133
Lexington Park, Md., U.S. . . D5 113
Leye, China E2 30
Leyte, i., Phil. D9 34
Lezhë, Alb. D7 18
L'gov, Russia D13 20
Lhasa, China F6 28
Lhazê, China D5 40
Lhokseumawe, Indon. B1 36
Lhorong, China E7 28
L'Hospitalet de Llobregat,
Spain G8 16
Lhünzê, China D6 40
Liancheng, China A7 34
Lianga, Phil. E9 34
Lianjiang, China E3 30
Lianxian, China G10 28
Lianyungang, China E11 28
Liao, stm., China C12 28
Liaocheng, China B4 30
Liaodong Bandao, pen.,
China D12 28
Liaodong Bay see Liaodong
Wan, b., China C12 28
Liaodong Wan, b., China . . C12 28
Liaoning, state, China C12 28
Liaotung, Gulf of see
Liaodong Wan, b.,
China C12 28
Liaotung Bay see Liaodong
Wan, b., China C12 28
Liaoyang, China A5 30
Liaoyuan, China C13 28
Liard, stm., Can. F15 82
Libagon, Phil. D9 34
Libby, Mt., U.S. B1 119
Libenge, D.R.C. C3 54
Liberal, Ks., U.S. E3 109
Liberal, Mo., U.S. D3 118
Liberec, Czech Rep. D3 20
Liberia, C.R. C2 80

Name	Map Ref.	Page

Liberia, ctry., Afr. . . . . E3 . . 50
Liberty, In., U.S. . . . . E8 . . 107
Liberty, Ky., U.S. . . . . C5 . . 110
Liberty, Mo., U.S. . . . . B3 . . 118
Liberty, Ms., U.S. . . . . D3 . . 117
Liberty, N.C., U.S. . . . . B3 . . 126
Liberty, N.Y., U.S. . . . . D6 . . 125
Liberty, S.C., U.S. . . . . B2 . . 133
Liberty, Tx., U.S. . . . . D5 . . 136
Liberty, co., Fl., U.S. . . . . . B2 . . 102
Liberty, co., Ga., U.S. . . . . . E5 . . 103
Liberty, co., Mt., U.S. . . . . . B5 . . 119
Liberty, co., Tx., U.S. . . . . . D5 . . 136
Liberty Center, Oh., U.S. . . . A1 . . 128
Liberty Lake, Wa., U.S. . . . g14 . . 140
Liberty Lake, res., Md., U.S. B4 . . 113
Libertyville, Il., U.S. . . . . . . A6 . . 106
Lībīyah, Aṣ-Ṣaḥrāʾ al-
(Libyan Desert), des.,
Afr. . . . . E9 . . 48
Libo, China . . . . D2 . . 30
Libourne, Fr. . . . . E6 . . 16
Libreville, Gabon . . . . C1 . . 54
Libuse, La., U.S. . . . . C3 . . 111
Libya, ctry., Afr. . . . . E8 . . 48
Libyan Desert see Lībīyah,
Aṣ-Ṣaḥrāʾ al-, des., Afr. E9 . . 48
Licancábur, Cerro, vol., S.A. C4 . . 72
Lice, Tur. . . . . C9 . . 44
Lichinga, Moz. . . . . A6 . . 56
Lichuan, China . . . . C2 . . 30
Lichuan, China . . . . D4 . . 30
Lick Creek, stm., Tn., U.S. . C11 . . 135
Licking, Mo., U.S. . . . . D6 . . 118
Licking, co., Oh., U.S. . . . . . B3 . . 128
Licking, stm., Ky., U.S. . . . . B6 . . 110
Lida, Bela. . . . . C8 . . 20
Lida, Lake, l., Mn., U.S. . . . D3 . . 116
Liden, Swe. . . . . E7 . . 10
Lidgerwood, N.D., U.S. . . . . C8 . . 127
Lidköping, Swe. . . . . G5 . . 10
Lido di Ostia, Italy . . . . D4 . . 18
Lidzbark Warmiński, Pol. . . B6 . . 20
Liebig, Mount, mtn., Austl. . E5 . . 60
Liechtenstein, ctry., Eur. . . . A2 . . 18
Liège, Bel. . . . . E9 . . 12
Lienz, Aus. . . . . G13 . . 12
Liepāja, Lat. . . . . H9 . . 10
Lièvre, Rivière du, stm.,
P.Q., Can. . . . . D2 . . 90
Lifou, i., N. Cal. . . . . I9 . . 62a
Lighthouse Inlet, b., S.C.,
U.S. . . . . k12 . . 133
Lighthouse Point, c., Fl.,
U.S. . . . . C2 . . 102
Lighthouse Point, c., La.,
U.S. . . . . E3 . . 111
Lighthouse Point, c., Mi.,
U.S. . . . . C5 . . 115
Lightning Creek, stm., Wy.,
U.S. . . . . C8 . . 143
Ligonier, In., U.S. . . . . B6 . . 107
Ligonier, Pa., U.S. . . . . F3 . . 131
Ligurian Apennines see
Appennino Ligure, mts.,
Italy . . . . B2 . . 18
Ligurian Sea, Eur. . . . . C2 . . 18
Lihue, Hi., U.S. . . . . B2 . . 104
Lijiang, China . . . . F8 . . 28
Likasi, D.R.C. . . . . F5 . . 54
Likati, D.R.C. . . . . C4 . . 54
Lilbourn, Mo., U.S. . . . . . . E8 . . 118
Lilburn, Ga., U.S. . . . . h8 . . 103
Lille, Fr. . . . . B8 . . 16
Lillebælt, strt., Den. . . . . . . I3 . . 10
Lillehammer, Nor. . . . . F4 . . 10
Lillesand, Nor. . . . . G3 . . 10
Lillestrøm, Nor. . . . . G4 . . 10
Lillian, Al., U.S. . . . . E2 . . 94
Lillington, N.C., U.S. . . . . . B4 . . 126
Lillinonah, Lake, l., Ct., U.S. C2 . . 100
Lillooet, B.C., Can. . . . . . . D7 . . 85
Lillooet, stm., B.C., Can. . . D6 . . 85
Lilly, Pa., U.S. . . . . F4 . . 131
Lilly Fork, stm., W.V., U.S. . m13 . . 141
Lilly Grove, W.V., U.S. . . . D3 . . 141
Lilongwe, Mwi. . . . . A5 . . 56
Liloy, Phil. . . . . E8 . . 34
Lily, Ky., U.S. . . . . C5 . . 110
Lima, Peru . . . . F4 . . 70
Lima, N.Y., U.S. . . . . C3 . . 125
Lima, Oh., U.S. . . . . B1 . . 128
Lima Reservoir, res., Mt.,
U.S. 119
Limay Mahuida, Arg. . . . . . F4 . . 72
Limbe, Cam. . . . . C1 . . 54
Limbé, Haiti . . . . B5 . . 80
Limeira, Braz. . . . . F2 . . 74
Limerick, Ire. . . . . D2 . . 12
Limestone, Me., U.S. . . . . . B5 . . 112
Limestone, co., Al., U.S. . . . A2 . . 94
Limestone, co., Tx., U.S. . . . D4 . . 136
Limestone Point, pen., Mb.,
Can. . . . . C2 . . 86
Limfjorden, l., Den. . . . . . . H3 . . 10
Limingen, l., Nor. . . . . D5 . . 10
Limmen Bight, b., Austl. . . . C6 . . 60
Límnos, i., Grc. . . . . E10 . . 18
Limoges, On., Can. . . . . . . B9 . . 89
Limoges, Fr. . . . . E7 . . 16
Limón, Hond. . . . . B2 . . 80
Limon, Co., U.S. . . . . B7 . . 99
Limoux, Fr. . . . . F8 . . 16
Limpopo, stm., Afr. . . . . . . C5 . . 56

Lin'an, China . . . . C4 . . 30
Linapacan Strait, strt., Phil. . D7 . . 34
Linares, Chile . . . . E2 . . 69
Linares, Mex. . . . . C5 . . 78
Linares, Spain . . . . H5 . . 16
Lincoln, Arg. . . . . E5 . . 72
Lincoln, On., Can. . . . . D5 . . 89
Lincoln, Eng., U.K. . . . . . . D6 . . 12
Lincoln, Al., U.S. . . . . B3 . . 94
Lincoln, Ar., U.S. . . . . B1 . . 97
Lincoln, Ca., U.S. . . . . C3 . . 98
Lincoln, De., U.S. . . . . E4 . . 101
Lincoln, Id., U.S. . . . . F6 . . 105
Lincoln, Il., U.S. . . . . C4 . . 106
Lincoln, Ks., U.S. . . . . C5 . . 109
Lincoln, Ma., U.S. . . . . g10 . . 114
Lincoln, Me., U.S. . . . . C4 . . 112
Lincoln, Mo., U.S. . . . . C4 . . 118
Lincoln, Ne., U.S. . . . . D9 . . 120
Lincoln, N.H., U.S. . . . . B3 . . 122
Lincoln, co., Ar., U.S. . . . . . D4 . . 97
Lincoln, co., Co., U.S. . . . . . C7 . . 99
Lincoln, co., Ga., U.S. . . . . . C4 . . 103
Lincoln, co., Id., U.S. . . . . . G4 . . 105
Lincoln, co., Ks., U.S. . . . . . C5 . . 109
Lincoln, co., Ky., U.S. . . . . . C5 . . 110
Lincoln, co., La., U.S. . . . . . B3 . . 111
Lincoln, co., Me., U.S. . . . . . D3 . . 112
Lincoln, co., Mn., U.S. . . . . F2 . . 116
Lincoln, co., Mo., U.S. . . . . B7 . . 118
Lincoln, co., Ms., U.S. . . . . . D3 . . 117
Lincoln, co., Mt., U.S. . . . . . B1 . . 119
Lincoln, co., N.C., U.S. . . . . B1 . . 126
Lincoln, co., Ne., U.S. . . . . . D5 . . 120
Lincoln, co., N.M., U.S. . . . . D4 . . 124
Lincoln, co., Nv., U.S. . . . . . F6 . . 121
Lincoln, co., Ok., U.S. . . . . . B5 . . 129
Lincoln, co., Or., U.S. . . . . . C3 . . 130
Lincoln, co., S.D., U.S. . . . . D9 . . 134
Lincoln, co., Tn., U.S. . . . . . B5 . . 135
Lincoln, co., W.V., U.S. . . . . C2 . . 141
Lincoln, co., Wa., U.S. . . . . B7 . . 140
Lincoln, co., Wi., U.S. . . . . . C4 . . 142
Lincoln, co., Wy., U.S. . . . . . D2 . . 143
Lincoln, Mount, mtn., Co.,
U.S. . . . . B4 . . 99
Lincoln Acres, Ca., U.S. . . . o15 . . 98
Lincoln City, Or., U.S. . . . . C3 . . 130
Lincoln Hav see Lincoln
Sea, N.A. . . . . B28 . . 82
Lincoln Heights, Oh., U.S. . o13 . . 128
Lincoln Park, Co., U.S. . . . . C5 . . 99
Lincoln Park, Ga., U.S. . . . . D2 . . 103
Lincoln Park, Mi., U.S. . . . . p15 . . 115
Lincoln Park, N.J., U.S. . . . B4 . . 123
Lincoln Sea, N.A. . . . . B28 . . 82
Lincolnshire, Il., U.S. . . . . . h9 . . 106
Lincoln Tomb State
Memorial, hist., Il., U.S. D4 . . 106
Lincolnton, Ga., U.S. . . . . . C4 . . 103
Lincolnton, N.C., U.S. . . . . B1 . . 126
Lincolnville, S.C., U.S. . . . . h11 . . 133
Lincolnwood, Il., U.S. . . . . h9 . . 106
Lincroft, N.J., U.S. . . . . C4 . . 123
Lindale, Ga., U.S. . . . . B1 . . 103
Lindale, Tx., U.S. . . . . C5 . . 136
Linden, Guy. . . . . B8 . . 70
Linden, Al., U.S. . . . . C2 . . 94
Linden, In., U.S. . . . . D4 . . 107
Linden, Mi., U.S. . . . . F7 . . 115
Linden, N.J., U.S. . . . . k8 . . 123
Linden, Tn., U.S. . . . . B4 . . 135
Linden, Tx., U.S. . . . . C5 . . 136
Lindenhurst, Il., U.S. . . . . . h8 . . 106
Lindenhurst, N.Y., U.S. . . . n15 . . 125
Lindenwold, N.J., U.S. . . . . D3 . . 123
Lindesberg, Swe. . . . . G6 . . 10
Lindesnes, c., Nor. . . . . H2 . . 10
Lindi, Tan. . . . . E7 . . 54
Lindon, Ut., U.S. . . . . C4 . . 137
Lindsay, On., Can. . . . . C6 . . 89
Lindsay, Ca., U.S. . . . . D4 . . 98
Lindsay, Ok., U.S. . . . . C4 . . 129
Lindsborg, Ks., U.S. . . . . . . D6 . . 109
Lindstrom, Mn., U.S. . . . . . E6 . . 116
Line Islands, is., Oc. . . . . . E14 . . 58
Linesville, Pa., U.S. . . . . . . C1 . . 131
Lineville, Al., U.S. . . . . B4 . . 94
Linfen, China . . . . D10 . . 28
Lingao, China . . . . F2 . . 30
Lingayen, Phil. . . . . C8 . . 34
Lingayen Gulf, b., Phil. . . . . C8 . . 34
Lingen, Ger. . . . . D10 . . 12
Lingga, Kepulauan, is.,
Indon. . . . . D3 . . 36
Lingga, Pulau, i., Indon. . . . D2 . . 36
Lingle, Wy., U.S. . . . . D8 . . 143
Linglestown, Pa., U.S. . . . . F8 . . 131
Lingqiu, China . . . . B3 . . 30
Lingshan, China . . . . E2 . . 30
Lingshui, China . . . . F3 . . 30
Linguère, Sen. . . . . C1 . . 50
Lingyuan, China . . . . A4 . . 30
Linhai, China . . . . F12 . . 28
Linhares, Braz. . . . . C7 . . 74
Linhe, China . . . . C9 . . 28
Linière, P.Q., Can. . . . . C7 . . 90
Linköping, Swe. . . . . G6 . . 10
Linkou, China . . . . B14 . . 28
Linn, co., Ia., U.S. . . . . B6 . . 108
Linn, co., Ks., U.S. . . . . D9 . . 109
Linn, co., Mo., U.S. . . . . . . B4 . . 118
Linn, co., Or., U.S. . . . . C4 . . 130
Lino Lakes, Mn., U.S. . . . . . m12 . . 116

Linqing, China . . . . B4 . . 30
Linquan, China . . . . C4 . . 30
Linru, China . . . . E10 . . 28
Lins, Braz. . . . . F2 . . 74
Lintan, China . . . . C1 . . 30
Linthicum Heights, Md.,
U.S. . . . . B4 . . 113
Linton, In., U.S. . . . . F3 . . 107
Linton, N.D., U.S. . . . . C5 . . 127
Linwood, N.J., U.S. . . . . . . E3 . . 123
Linxi, China . . . . C11 . . 28
Linxia, China . . . . D8 . . 28
Linyi, China . . . . D11 . . 28
Linyi, China . . . . B4 . . 30
Linz, Aus. . . . . F14 . . 12
Lion, Golfe du, b., Fr. . . . . . F9 . . 16
Lion, Gulf of see Lion,
Golfe du, b., Fr. . . . . . . F9 . . 16
Lipa, Phil. . . . . D8 . . 34
Lipeck, Russia . . . . D5 . . 26
Lipova, Rom. . . . . F6 . . 20
Lipscomb, Al., U.S. . . . . . . B3 . . 94
Lipscomb, co., Tx., U.S. . . . A2 . . 136
Lipu, China . . . . E3 . . 30
Lira, Ug. . . . . C6 . . 54
Lisala, D.R.C. . . . . C4 . . 54
Lisboa (Lisbon), Port. . . . . . H2 . . 16
Lisbon see Lisboa, Port. . . . H2 . . 16
Lisbon, Ia., U.S. . . . . C6 . . 108
Lisbon, Md., U.S. . . . . B3 . . 113
Lisbon, Me., U.S. . . . . D2 . . 112
Lisbon, N.D., U.S. . . . . C8 . . 127
Lisbon, N.H., U.S. . . . . B3 . . 122
Lisbon, Oh., U.S. . . . . B5 . . 128
Lisbon Center, Me., U.S. . . . f7 . . 112
Lisbon Falls, Me., U.S. . . . . D2 . . 112
Lisburne, Cape, c., Ak., U.S. B6 . . 95
Lishui, China . . . . F11 . . 28
Lisianski Island, i., Hi., U.S. k13 . . 104
Lisieux, Fr. . . . . C7 . . 16
Liski, Russia . . . . D5 . . 26
Lisle, Il., U.S. . . . . k8 . . 106
L'Islet-sur-Mer, P.Q., Can. . B7 . . 90
L'Isle-Verte, P.Q., Can. . . . . A8 . . 90
Lismore, Austl. . . . . F5 . . 62
Listowel, On., Can. . . . . D4 . . 89
Litang, China . . . . E8 . . 28
Litang, China . . . . G9 . . 28
Litchfield, Ct., U.S. . . . . . . C3 . . 100
Litchfield, Il., U.S. . . . . D4 . . 106
Litchfield, Mi., U.S. . . . . . . F6 . . 115
Litchfield, Mn., U.S. . . . . . . E4 . . 116
Litchfield, co., Ct., U.S. . . . B2 . . 100
Litchfield Park, Az., U.S. . . m8 . . 96
Lithgow, Austl. . . . . G5 . . 62
Lithia Springs, Ga., U.S. . . . h7 . . 103
Lithonia, Ga., U.S. . . . . C2 . . 103
Lithuania, ctry., Eur. . . . . . B7 . . 20
Lititz, Pa., U.S. . . . . F9 . . 131
Litovko, Russia . . . . B15 . . 28
Little, stm., Ct., U.S. . . . . . C7 . . 100
Little, stm., Ky., U.S. . . . . . D2 . . 110
Little, stm., La., U.S. . . . . . C3 . . 111
Little, stm., N.C., U.S. . . . . B3 . . 126
Little, stm., Ok., U.S. . . . . . B5 . . 129
Little, stm., S.C., U.S. . . . . . C2 . . 133
Little, stm., Tn., U.S. . . . . . n14 . . 135
Little, stm., Va., U.S. . . . . . D7 . . 129
Little, stm., Va., U.S. . . . . . D2 . . 139
Little, stm., Vt., U.S. . . . . . C3 . . 138
Little, stm., U.S. . . . . B5 . . 97
Little Acres, Az., U.S. . . . . . D5 . . 96
Little Andaman, i., India . . . G6 . . 40
Little Arkansas, stm., Ks.,
U.S. . . . . D6 . . 109
Little Belt see Lillebælt, strt.,
Den. . . . . I3 . . 10
Little Belt Mountains, mts.,
Mt., U.S. . . . . D6 . . 119
Little Bighorn, stm., U.S. . . E9 . . 119
Little Black, stm., Me., U.S. A3 . . 112
Little Blue, stm., In., U.S. . . H5 . . 107
Little Blue, stm., U.S. . . . . . B4 . . 120
Little Bow, stm., Ab., Can. . D4 . . 84
Little Cacapon, stm., W.V.,
U.S. . . . . B6 . . 141
Little Catalina, Nf., Can. . . . D5 . . 88
Little Cayman, i., Cay. Is. . . B3 . . 80
Little Cedar, stm., Ia., U.S. . A5 . . 108
Little Churchill, stm., Mb.,
Can. . . . . A4 . . 86
Little Chute, Wi., U.S. . . . . D5 . . 142
Little Coal, stm., W.V., U.S. C3 . . 141
Little Colorado, stm., Az.,
U.S. . . . . B4 . . 96
Little Compton, R.I., U.S. . . E6 . . 132
Little Creek, De., U.S. . . . . D4 . . 101
Little Creek Naval
Amphibious Base, mil.,
Va., U.S. . . . . k15 . . 139
Little Creek Peak, mtn., Ut.,
U.S. . . . . F3 . . 137
Little Current, On., Can. . . . B3 . . 89
Little Diomede Island, i.,
Ak., U.S. . . . . B6 . . 95
Little Egg Harbor, b., N.J.,
U.S. . . . . D4 . . 123
Little Egg Inlet, b., N.J., U.S. E4 . . 123
Little Falls, Mn., U.S. . . . . . E4 . . 116
Little Falls, N.J., U.S. . . . . . B4 . . 123
Little Falls, N.Y., U.S. . . . . B6 . . 125
Little Ferry, N.J., U.S. . . . . h8 . . 123
Littlefield, Tx., U.S. . . . . . . C1 . . 136
Little Fishing Creek, stm.,
W.V., U.S. . . . . h9 . . 141

Littlefork, Mn., U.S. . . . . . . B5 . . 116
Little Fork, stm., Mn., U.S. . B5 . . 116
Little Goose Creek, stm.,
Wy., U.S. . . . . B6 . . 143
Little Gunpowder Falls,
stm., Md., U.S. . . . . A4 . . 113
Little Humboldt, stm., Nv.,
U.S. . . . . B4 . . 121
Little Inagua, i., Bah. . . . . . D10 . . 76
Little Kanawha, stm., W.V.,
U.S. . . . . C4 . . 141
Little Karroo, plat., S. Afr. . E3 . . 56
Little Lake, Mi., U.S. . . . . . B3 . . 115
Little Lake, l., La., U.S. . . . E5 . . 111
Little Lynches, stm., S.C.,
U.S. . . . . C7 . . 133
Little Manatee, stm., Fl.,
U.S. . . . . p11 . . 102
Little Mecatina, stm., Can. . h9 . . 88
Little Miami, stm., Oh., U.S. C1 . . 128
Little Minch, The, strt.,
Scot., U.K. . . . . B3 . . 12
Little Missouri, stm., Ar.,
U.S. . . . . D2 . . 97
Little Missouri, stm., U.S. . . B7 . . 92
Little Muddy, stm., Il., U.S. E4 . . 106
Little Muddy, stm., N.D.,
U.S. . . . . A2 . . 127
Little Namaqualand, hist.
reg., S. Afr. . . . . D2 . . 56
Little Nicobar, i., India . . . . H6 . . 40
Little Osage, stm., U.S. . . . . E9 . . 109
Little Otter Creek, stm., Vt.,
U.S. . . . . C2 . . 138
Little Owyhee, stm., U.S. . . B5 . . 121
Little Pee Dee, stm., S.C.,
U.S. . . . . C9 . . 133
Little Powder, stm., U.S. . . . F11 . . 119
Little Red, stm., Ar., U.S. . . B4 . . 97
Little River, co., Ar., U.S. . . D1 . . 97
Little River Inlet, b., S.C.,
U.S. . . . . D10 . . 133
Little Rock, Ar., U.S. . . . . . C3 . . 97
Little Rock, stm., U.S. . . . . . A1 . . 108
Little Rock Air Force Base,
mil., Ar., U.S. . . . . C3 . . 97
Little Sable Point, c., Mi.,
U.S. . . . . E4 . . 115
Little Salt Lake, l., Ut., U.S. F3 . . 137
Little Sandy, stm., Ky., U.S. B6 . . 110
Little Sandy Creek, stm.,
Wy., U.S. . . . . D3 . . 143
Little Sebago Lake, l., Me.,
U.S. . . . . g7 . . 112
Little Silver, N.J., U.S. . . . . C4 . . 123
Little Sioux, stm., U.S. . . . . B2 . . 108
Little Sioux, West Fork,
stm., Ia., U.S. . . . . B2 . . 108
Little Smoky, stm., Ab., Can. B2 . . 84
Little Snake, stm., U.S. . . . . A2 . . 99
Little Spokane, stm., Wa.,
U.S. . . . . B8 . . 140
Littletown, Pa., U.S. . . . . . . G7 . . 131
Little Tallapoosa, stm., U.S. B4 . . 94
Little Tenmile Creek, stm.,
W.V., U.S. . . . . k10 . . 141
Little Tennessee, stm., U.S. . D9 . . 135
Littleton, Co., U.S. . . . . B6 . . 99
Littleton, Ma., U.S. . . . . f10 . . 114
Littleton, Me., U.S. . . . . B5 . . 112
Littleton, N.C., U.S. . . . . . . A5 . . 126
Littleton, N.H., U.S. . . . . . . B3 . . 122
Littleville, Al., U.S. . . . . . . A2 . . 94
Little Wabash, stm., Il., U.S. E5 . . 106
Little Walnut, stm., Ks., U.S. g13 . . 109
Little White, stm., S.D., U.S. D5 . . 134
Little Wolf, stm., Wi., U.S. . D4 . . 142
Little Wood, stm., Id., U.S. . F4 . . 105
Little Zab, stm., Asia . . . . . E10 . . 44
Liucheng, China . . . . G9 . . 28
Liuzhou, China . . . . G9 . . 28
Live Oak, Ca., U.S. . . . . C3 . . 98
Live Oak, Fl., U.S. . . . . B4 . . 102
Live Oak, co., Tx., U.S. . . . . E3 . . 136
Livermore, Ca., U.S. . . . . . . h9 . . 98
Livermore, Ky., U.S. . . . . . . C2 . . 110
Livermore, Mount, mtn.,
Tx., U.S. . . . . o12 . . 136
Livermore Falls, Me., U.S. . D2 . . 112
Liverpool, Eng., U.K. . . . . . D5 . . 12
Livingston, Guat. . . . . B2 . . 80
Livingston, Al., U.S. . . . . . . C1 . . 94
Livingston, Ca., U.S. . . . . . D3 . . 98
Livingston, Il., U.S. . . . . . . E4 . . 106
Livingston, La., U.S. . . . . . . D5 . . 111
Livingston, Mt., U.S. . . . . . . E6 . . 119
Livingston, N.J., U.S. . . . . . B4 . . 123
Livingston, Tn., U.S. . . . . . . C8 . . 135
Livingston, Tx., U.S. . . . . . . D5 . . 136
Livingston, co., Il., U.S. . . . C5 . . 106
Livingston, co., Ky., U.S. . . e9 . . 110
Livingston, co., La., U.S. . . D5 . . 111
Livingston, co., Mi., U.S. . . F7 . . 115
Livingston, co., Mo., U.S. . . B4 . . 118
Livingston, co., N.Y., U.S. . C3 . . 125
Livingston, Lake, res., Tx.,
U.S. . . . . D5 . . 136
Livingstone, Zam. . . . . B4 . . 56
Livingstone Falls, wtfl., Afr. E2 . . 54
Livingstonia, Mwi. . . . . A5 . . 56
Livny, Russia . . . . C14 . . 20
Livonia, La., U.S. . . . . D4 . . 111
Livonia, Mi., U.S. . . . . F7 . . 115
Livorno, Italy . . . . C3 . . 18
Liwale, Tan. . . . . E7 . . 54

Liwonde, Mwi. . . . . B6 . . 56
Lixi, China . . . . F10 . . 28
Lixian, China . . . . D3 . . 30
Lizard Head Pass, Co., U.S. D3 . . 99
Lizard Head Peak, mtn.,
Wy., U.S. . . . . D3 . . 143
Lizella, Ga., U.S. . . . . D3 . . 103
Ljahovskie ostrova, is.,
Russia . . . . B15 . . 26
Ljubercy, Russia . . . . C6 . . 22
Ljubljana, Slvn. . . . . A5 . . 18
Ljudinovo, Russia . . . . C13 . . 20
Ljungby, Swe. . . . . H5 . . 10
Ljusdal, Swe. . . . . F7 . . 10
Ljusnan, stm., Swe. . . . . . . E6 . . 10
Ljusterö, stm., Swe. . . . . . . G8 . . 10
Llancanelo, Laguna, l., Arg. F4 . . 72
Llano, Tx., U.S. . . . . D3 . . 136
Llano, co., Tx., U.S. . . . . . . D3 . . 136
Llano, stm., Tx., U.S. . . . . . D3 . . 136
Llano Estacado see
Estacado, Llano, pl.,
U.S. . . . . C1 . . 136
Llanos, pl., S.A. . . . . B6 . . 70
Lleida, Spain . . . . G7 . . 16
Llera de Canales, Mex. . . . . C5 . . 78
Lloyd, Ky., U.S. . . . . B7 . . 110
Lloydminster, Ab., Can. . . . C5 . . 84
Lloyds, stm., Nf., Can. . . . . D3 . . 88
Llucmajor, Spain . . . . H8 . . 16
Llullaillaco, Volcán, vol.,
S.A. . . . . C4 . . 72
Loami, Il., U.S. . . . . D4 . . 106
Loange, stm., Afr. . . . . E3 . . 54
Lobamba, Swaz. . . . . D5 . . 56
Lobatse, Bots. . . . . D4 . . 56
Lobelville, Tn., U.S. . . . . . . B4 . . 135
Lobería, Arg. . . . . F6 . . 72
Lobito, Ang. . . . . F2 . . 54
Lobos, Cay, i., Bah. . . . . . . A4 . . 80
Lobster Lake, l., Me., U.S. . C3 . . 112
Lobva, Russia . . . . C11 . . 22
Locarno, Switz. . . . . A2 . . 18
Loch Raven Reservoir, res.,
Md., U.S. . . . . B4 . . 113
Lochsa, stm., Id., U.S. . . . . C3 . . 105
Lockeport, N.S., Can. . . . . . F4 . . 87
Lockesburg, Ar., U.S. . . . . . D1 . . 97
Lockhart, Tx., U.S. . . . . E4 . . 136
Lock Haven, Pa., U.S. . . . . . D7 . . 131
Lockland, Oh., U.S. . . . . . . o13 . . 128
Lockney, Tx., U.S. . . . . B2 . . 136
Lockport, Il., U.S. . . . . B5 . . 106
Lockport, La., U.S. . . . . E5 . . 111
Lockport, N.Y., U.S. . . . . . . B2 . . 125
Lockwood, Mo., U.S. . . . . . D4 . . 118
Lockwood, Mt., U.S. . . . . . . E8 . . 119
Loc Ninh, Viet. . . . . D5 . . 34
Locust, N.C., U.S. . . . . B2 . . 126
Locust Fork, stm., Al., U.S. . B3 . . 94
Locust Grove, Ga., U.S. . . . C2 . . 103
Locust Grove, Ok., U.S. . . . A6 . . 129
Lodejnoe Pole, Russia . . . . B5 . . 22
Lodgepole Creek, stm., U.S. C3 . . 120
Lodi, Italy . . . . B2 . . 18
Lodi, Ca., U.S. . . . . C3 . . 98
Lodi, N.J., U.S. . . . . h8 . . 123
Lodi, Oh., U.S. . . . . A3 . . 128
Lodi, Wi., U.S. . . . . E4 . . 142
Lodja, D.R.C. . . . . D4 . . 54
Lodore, Canyon of, val.,
Co., U.S. . . . . A2 . . 99
Lodwar, Kenya . . . . C7 . . 54
Łódź, Pol. . . . . D5 . . 20
Loei, Thai. . . . . C4 . . 34
Lofoten, is., Nor. . . . . B5 . . 10
Lofoten Basin . . . . D21 . . 144
Loga, Niger . . . . D5 . . 50
Logan, Ia., U.S. . . . . C2 . . 108
Logan, Ks., U.S. . . . . C2 . . 109
Logan, N.M., U.S. . . . . B6 . . 124
Logan, Oh., U.S. . . . . C3 . . 128
Logan, Ut., U.S. . . . . B4 . . 137
Logan, W.V., U.S. . . . . D3 . . 141
Logan, co., Ar., U.S. . . . . . . B2 . . 97
Logan, co., Co., U.S. . . . . . A7 . . 99
Logan, co., Il., U.S. . . . . . . C4 . . 106
Logan, co., Ks., U.S. . . . . . . D2 . . 109
Logan, co., Ky., U.S. . . . . . . D3 . . 110
Logan, co., N.D., U.S. . . . . . C6 . . 127
Logan, co., Ne., U.S. . . . . . C5 . . 120
Logan, co., Oh., U.S. . . . . . B2 . . 128
Logan, co., Ok., U.S. . . . . . B4 . . 129
Logan, co., W.V., U.S. . . . . D3 . . 141
Logan, Mount, mtn., Yk.,
Can. . . . . F11 . . 82
Logan, Mount, mtn., Wa.,
U.S. . . . . A5 . . 140
Logandale, Nv., U.S. . . . . . G7 . . 121
Logan Martin Lake, res., Al.,
U.S. . . . . B3 . . 94
Logan Pass, Mt., U.S. . . . . . B2 . . 119
Logansport, In., U.S. . . . . . . C5 . . 107
Logansport, La., U.S. . . . . . C2 . . 111
Loganville, Ga., U.S. . . . . . C3 . . 103
Loganville, Pa., U.S. . . . . . . G8 . . 131
Loggieville, N.B., Can. . . . . B4 . . 87
Log Lane Village, Co., U.S. A7 . . 99
Logone, stm., Afr. . . . . B3 . . 54
Logroño, Spain . . . . F5 . . 16
Løgstør, Den. . . . . H3 . . 10
Loi-kaw, Myan. . . . . C3 . . 34
Loimaa, Fin. . . . . F10 . . 10
Loire, stm., Fr. . . . . D6 . . 16

Name	Map Ref.	Page

Loja, Ec. D4 70
Loja, Spain I4 16
Lokandu, D.R.C. D5 54
Lokan tekojärvi, res., Fin. . . C12 10
Lokichokio, Kenya C6 54
Lokoja, Nig. E6 50
Lokolama, D.R.C. D3 54
Lola, Gui. F3 50
Lola, Mount, mtn., Ca., U.S. C3 98
Loliondo, Tan. D7 54
Lolland, i., Den. I4 10
Lolo, Mt., U.S. D2 119
Lolo Pass, U.S. C4 105
Lom, Bul. C9 18
Lomami, stm., D.R.C. C4 54
Lomas de Zamora, Arg. . . . E6 72
Lombard, Il., U.S. k8 106
Lomblen, Pulau, i., Indon. . . E6 36
Lombok, i., Indon. E5 36
Lombok, Selat, strt., Indon. E5 36
Lomé, Togo E5 50
Lomela, D.R.C. D4 54
Lomié, Cam. C2 54
Lomira, Wi., U.S. E5 142
Lomonosov, Russia G13 10
Lomonosov Ridge E8 144
Lompoc, Ca., U.S. E3 98
Lom Sak, Thai. C4 34
Łomża, Pol. C7 20
Lonaconing, Md., U.S. k13 113
Loncoche, Chile E2 69
London, On., Can. E3 89
London, Eng., U.K. E6 12
London, Ar., U.S. B2 97
London, Ky., U.S. C5 110
London, Oh., U.S. C2 128
Londonderry, N. Ire., U.K. . . C3 12
Londonderry, N.H., U.S. . . . E4 122
Londonderry, Cape, c.,
Austl. C4 60
Londonderry, Isla, i., Chile . I2 69
Londontown, Md., U.S. C4 113
Londrina, Braz. F1 74
Lone Grove, Ok., U.S. C4 129
Lone Mountain, mtn., Nv.,
U.S. E4 121
Lone Pine, Ca., U.S. D4 98
Lone Tree, Ia., U.S. C6 108
Long, co., Ga., U.S. E5 103
Longa, proliv, strt., Russia . . B19 26
Long Bar Harbor, Md., U.S. . B5 113
Long Beach, Ca., U.S. F4 98
Long Beach, In., U.S. A4 107
Long Beach, Md., U.S. D5 113
Long Beach, Ms., U.S. g7 117
Long Beach, N.Y., U.S. E7 125
Long Beach, Wa., U.S. C1 140
Longboat Key, Fl., U.S. q10 102
Longboat Key, i., Fl., U.S. . . E4 102
Longboat Pass, strt., Fl., U.S. q10 102
Long Branch, N.J., U.S. C5 123
Longbranch, Wa., U.S. B3 140
Long Creek Mountain, mtn.,
Wy., U.S. D5 143
Longde, China B2 30
Longford, Ire. D3 12
Long Grove, Ia., U.S. C7 108
Long Harbour [-Mount
Arlington Heights], Nf.,
Can. E5 88
Longhua, China A4 30
Longiram, Indon. D5 36
Long Island, i., Bah. D10 76
Long Island, i., N.S., Can. . . E3 87
Long Island, i., Ma., U.S. . . . g12 114
Long Island, i., Me., U.S. . . . g7 112
Long Island, i., N.Y., U.S. . . E7 125
Long Island Sound, strt.,
U.S. E7 125
Longjiang, China B12 28
Long Key, i., Fl., U.S. H6 102
Long Lake, Wi., U.S. h8 106
Long Lake, l., Me., U.S. A4 112
Long Lake, l., Me., U.S. D2 112
Long Lake, l., Mi., U.S. D5 115
Long Lake, l., Mi., U.S. C7 115
Long Lake, l., Mn., U.S. D4 116
Long Lake, l., N.D., U.S. . . . C6 127
Long Lake, l., N.Y., U.S. . . . B6 125
Long Lake, l., Wa., U.S. f10 140
Long Lake, l., Wi., U.S. C2 142
Longli, China F9 28
Longling, China B3 34
Longmeadow, Ma., U.S. . . . B2 114
Longmen, China B6 34
Longmont, Co., U.S. A5 99
Longnan, China E3 30
Long Point, c., Mb., Can. . . . C2 86
Long Point, pen., On., Can. E4 89
Long Pond, res., Fl., U.S. . . . C4 102
Long Prairie, Mn., U.S. E4 116
Longquan, China D4 30
Long Range Mountains,
mts., Nf., Can. D3 88
Longreach, Austl. E3 62
Longshan, China D2 30
Longs Peak, mtn., Co., U.S. . A5 99
Long Strait see Longa,
proliv, strt., Russia B19 26
Longueuil, P.Q., Can. D4 90
Long View, N.C., U.S. B1 126
Longview, Tx., U.S. C5 136
Longview, Wa., U.S. C3 140
Longxi, China E8 28
Longxian, China C2 30

Long Xuyen, Viet. D5 34
Longyan, China D4 30
Longzhou, China G9 28
Lonoke, Ar., U.S. C4 97
Lonoke, co., Ar., U.S. C4 97
Lonsdale, Mn., U.S. F5 116
Lonsdale, R.I., U.S. B4 132
Lons-le-Saunier, Fr. D9 16
Loogootee, In., U.S. G4 107
Lookout, Ky., U.S. C7 110
Lookout, Cape, c., N.C.,
U.S. C6 126
Lookout, Point, c., Mi., U.S. d7 115
Lookout Mountain, Tn., U.S. h11 135
Lookout Mountain, mtn.,
Or., U.S. C6 130
Lookout Mountain, mtn.,
U.S. D8 135
Lookout Pass, U.S. B3 105
Lookout Point Lake, res.,
Or., U.S. D4 130
Loongana, Austl. G4 60
Loon Lake, Wa., U.S. A8 140
Loon Lake, l., Me., U.S. B3 112
Loop Creek, stm., W.V.,
U.S. m13 141
Loosahatchie, stm., Tn.,
U.S. B2 135
Lop, China B4 40
Lopatka, mys, c., Russia . . . D17 26
Lop Buri, Thai. D4 34
Lopez, Cap, c., Gabon D1 54
Lopez Island, i., Wa., U.S. . . A3 140
Lop Nor (Lop Nur), l., China C6 28
Lop Nur (Lop Nor), l., China C6 28
Lopphavet, Nor. A9 10
Lora, Hāmūn-i-, l., Asia . . . E8 42
Lorain, Oh., U.S. A3 128
Lorain, co., Oh., U.S. A3 128
Loramie, Lake, res., Oh.,
U.S. B1 128
Lorca, Spain I6 16
Lord Howe Rise K19 64
Lordsburg, N.M., U.S. E1 124
Loreauville, La., U.S. D4 111
Lorenzo, Tx., U.S. C2 136
Loreto, Braz. E10 70
Loreto, Mex. B2 78
Lorette, Mb., Can. E3 86
Loretteville, P.Q., Can. C6 90
Loretto, Ky., U.S. C4 110
Loretto, Pa., U.S. F4 131
Loretto, Tn., U.S. B4 135
Lorica, Col. B4 70
Lorient, Fr. D5 16
L'Orignal, On., Can. B10 89
Loris, S.C., U.S. C10 133
Lorn, Firth of, b., Scot., U.K. B4 12
Lorne, Austl. H3 62
Lorne, N.B., Can. B3 87
Lorraine, hist. reg., Fr. C9 16
Los, Îles de, is., Gui. E2 50
Los Alamos, N.M., U.S. B3 124
Los Alamos, co., N.M., U.S. . B3 124
Los Altos, Ca., U.S. k8 98
Los Angeles, Ca., U.S. E4 98
Los Angeles, co., Ca., U.S. . . E4 98
Los Angeles Aqueduct, Ca.,
U.S. E4 98
Los Banos, Ca., U.S. D3 98
Los Blancos, Arg. C5 72
Los Fresnos, Tx., U.S. F4 136
Los Gatos, Ca., U.S. D2 98
Los Lunas, N.M., U.S. C3 124
Los Mochis, Mex. B3 78
Los Pinos, stm., Co., U.S. . . . D3 99
Los Ranchos de
Albuquerque, N.M.,
U.S. B3 124
Los Roques, Islas, is., Ven. . C6 80
Lost, stm., In., U.S. G4 107
Lost, stm., W.V., U.S. B6 141
Lost, stm., Wa., U.S. A5 140
Lost Creek, stm., Wy., U.S. . D4 143
Lost Peak, mtn., Ut., U.S. . . F2 137
Lost Ranger Peak, mtn., Co.,
U.S. A4 99
Lost River Glacial Caverns,
N.H., U.S. B3 122
Lost River Range, mts., Id.,
U.S. E5 105
Lost Trail Pass, U.S. D5 105
Losuia, Pap. N. Gui. H13 32
Los Vilos, Chile D2 69
Lot, stm., Fr. E7 16
Lota, Chile F3 72
Lotawana, Lake, res., Mo.,
U.S. k11 118
Lotbinière, P.Q., Can. C6 90
Loto, D.R.C. D4 54
Lotung, Tai. E5 30
Louang Namtha, Laos B4 34
Louangphrabang, Laos C4 34
Loubomo, Congo D2 54
Loudon, Tn., U.S. D9 135
Loudon, co., Tn., U.S. D9 135
Loudonville, Oh., U.S. B3 128
Loudoun, co., Va., U.S. A5 139
Louga, Sen. C1 50
Louhi, Russia A5 22
Louisa, Ky., U.S. B7 110
Louisa, Va., U.S. B4 139
Louisa, co., Ia., U.S. C6 108
Louisa, co., Va., U.S. C5 139

Louisa, Lake, l., Fl., U.S. . . . D5 102
Louisbourg, N.S., Can. D10 87
Louisburg, Ks., U.S. D9 109
Louisburg, N.C., U.S. A4 126
Louisdale, N.S., Can. D8 87
Louise, Lake, l., Ak., U.S. . . . f18 95
Louise Island, i., B.C., Can. . C2 85
Louiseville, P.Q., Can. C5 90
Louisiana, Mo., U.S. B6 118
Louisiana, state, U.S. C3 111
Louisiana Point, c., La., U.S. E2 111
Louis Trichardt, S. Afr. C4 56
Louisville, Al., U.S. D4 94
Louisville, Co., U.S. B5 99
Louisville, Ga., U.S. C4 103
Louisville, Il., U.S. E5 106
Louisville, Ky., U.S. B4 110
Louisville, Ms., U.S. B4 117
Louisville, Ne., U.S. D9 120
Louisville, Oh., U.S. B4 128
Louisville Ridge L22 64
Louis-XIV, Pointe, c., P.Q.,
Can. h11 90
Loum, Cam. C1 54
Loup, co., Ne., U.S. C6 120
Loup, stm., Ne., U.S. C8 120
Loup City, Ne., U.S. C7 120
Lourdes, Nf., Can. D2 88
Lourdes, Fr. F6 16
Lourenço Marques see
Maputo, Moz. D5 56
Louviers, Co., U.S. B6 99
Love, co., Ok., U.S. D4 129
Loveč, Bul. C10 18
Loveland, Co., U.S. A5 99
Loveland, Oh., U.S. n13 128
Loveland Park, Oh., U.S. . . . C1 128
Loveland Pass, Co., U.S. . . . B5 99
Lovell, Wy., U.S. B4 143
Lovelock, Nv., U.S. C3 121
Lovely, Ky., U.S. C7 110
Lovenia, Mount, mtn., Ut.,
U.S. C5 137
Love Point, c., Md., U.S. . . . B5 113
Loves Park, Il., U.S. A4 106
Lovettsville, Va., U.S. A5 139
Loving, N.M., U.S. E5 124
Loving, co., Tx., U.S. D1 136
Lovington, Il., U.S. D5 106
Lovington, N.M., U.S. E6 124
Lóvua, Ang. E4 54
Lowden, Ia., U.S. C7 108
Lowell, Ar., U.S. A1 97
Lowell, In., U.S. B3 107
Lowell, Ma., U.S. A5 114
Lowell, Mi., U.S. F5 115
Lowell, N.C., U.S. B1 126
Lowell, Or., U.S. D4 130
Lowell, Vt., U.S. E3 138
Lowell, Lake, res., Id., U.S. . F2 105
Lowellville, Oh., U.S. A5 128
Lower Arrow Lake, res.,
B.C., Can. E8 85
Lower Brule Indian
Reservation, S.D., U.S. . . C6 134
Lower California see Baja
California, pen., Mex. . B2 78
Lower Hutt, N.Z. p14 63c
Lower Klamath Lake, l., Ca.,
U.S. B3 98
Lower Matecumbe Key, i.,
Fl., U.S. H6 102
Lower New York Bay, b.,
N.J., U.S. B4 123
Lower Otay Lake, res., Ca.,
U.S. o16 98
Lower Paia, Hi., U.S. C5 104
Lower Red Lake, l., Mn.,
U.S. C3 116
Lower Rice Lake, l., Mn.,
U.S. C3 116
Lower Salmon Dam, Id.,
U.S. G4 105
Lower Trajan's Wall, hist.,
Eur. G10 20
Lower West Pubnico, N.S.,
Can. F4 87
Lowestoft, Eng., U.K. D7 12
Lowndes, co., Al., U.S. C3 94
Lowndes, co., Ga., U.S. F3 103
Lowndes, co., Ms., U.S. B5 117
Lowry City, Mo., U.S. C4 118
Lowville, N.Y., U.S. B5 125
Loxley, Al., U.S. E2 94
Loxton, Austl. G3 62
Loyal, Wi., U.S. D3 142
Loyall, Ky., U.S. D6 110
Loyalsock Creek, stm., Pa.,
U.S. D8 131
Loyalty Islands see Loyauté,
Îles, is., N. Cal. I9 62a
Loyauté, Îles, is., N. Cal. . . . I9 62a
Loznica, Yugo. B7 18
Lozova, Ukr. E14 20
Lualaba, stm., D.R.C. D5 54
Lua Makika, crat., Hi., U.S. . C5 104
Lu'an, China C4 30
Luan, stm., China C11 28
Luanda, Ang. E2 54
Luang, Thale, l., Thai. E4 34
Luanginga, stm., Afr. A3 56
Luangwa, stm., Afr. A5 56
Luanping, China A4 30
Luanshya, Zam. A4 56
Luan Toro, Arg. F4 72

Luapula, stm., Afr. A4 56
Luau, Ang. F4 54
Luba, Eq. Gui. C1 54
Lubang Islands, is., Phil. . . . D8 34
Lubango, Ang. A1 56
Lubbock, Tx., U.S. C2 136
Lubbock, co., Tx., U.S. C2 136
Lubec, Me., U.S. D6 112
Lübeck, Ger. D12 12
Lubefu, D.R.C. D4 54
Lubin, Pol. D4 20
Lublin, Pol. D7 20
Lubnān, Jabal, mts., Leb. . . . F6 44
Lubny, Ukr. D12 20
Lubudi, D.R.C. F5 54
Lubuklinggau, Indon. D2 36
Lubumbashi, D.R.C. F5 54
Lubutu, D.R.C. D5 54
Lucama, N.C., U.S. B4 126
Lucapa, Ang. E4 54
Lucas, co., Ia., U.S. C4 108
Lucas, co., Oh., U.S. A2 128
Lucasville, Oh., U.S. D3 128
Lucca, Italy C3 18
Luce, co., Mi., U.S. B5 115
Lucedale, Ms., U.S. E5 117
Lucena, Phil. D8 34
Lucena, Spain I4 16
Lučenec, Slvk. E5 20
Lucera, Italy D5 18
Lucerne see Luzern, Switz. . A2 18
Lucerne, Ca., U.S. C2 98
Lucerne, Lake see
Vierwaldstätter See, l.,
Switz. A2 18
Lucernemines, Pa., U.S. . . . E3 131
Lucerne Valley, Ca., U.S. . . . E5 98
Luceville, P.Q., Can. A9 90
Lucira, Ang. A1 56
Luck, Wi., U.S. C1 142
Luckenwalde, Ger. E13 12
Lucknow, On., Can. D3 89
Lucknow, India D4 40
Lucky Peak Lake, res., Id.,
U.S. F3 105
Luçon, Fr. D6 16
Lucusse, Ang. A3 56
Lüda see Dalian, China D12 28
Lüderitz, Nmb. D2 56
Ludhiāna, India C3 40
Ludington, Mi., U.S. E4 115
Ludlow, Ky., U.S. h13 110
Ludlow, Ma., U.S. B3 114
Ludlow, Vt., U.S. E3 138
Ludogorie, reg., Bul. C11 18
Ludowici, Ga., U.S. E5 103
Ludvika, Swe. F6 10
Ludwigsburg, Ger. F11 12
Ludwigslust, Ger. D12 12
Luebo, D.R.C. E4 54
Luena, Ang. F3 54
Luena, D.R.C. E5 54
Lueyang, China C2 30
Lufeng, China E4 30
Lufkin, Tx., U.S. D5 136
Luga, Russia C4 22
Lugano, Switz. A2 18
Luganville, Vanuatu k9 62a
Lugards Falls, wtfl, Kenya . . D7 54
Lugela, Moz. B6 56
Lugo, Italy B3 18
Lugo, Spain F3 16
Lugoff, S.C., U.S. C6 133
Lugoj, Rom. G6 20
Lugovoj, Kaz. B10 42
Luhans'k, Ukr. E15 20
Luiana, stm., Afr. A3 56
Luik see Liège, Bel. D8 20
Luishia, D.R.C. F5 54
Luiza, D.R.C. E4 54
Lukachukai, Az., U.S. A6 96
Luke Air Force Base, mil.,
Az., U.S. D3 96
Lukenie, stm., D.R.C. D3 54
Lukojanov, Russia D7 22
Lukolela, D.R.C. D3 54
Lukolela, D.R.C. E4 54
Lukula, D.R.C. E2 54
Lukulu, Zam. A3 56
Lula, Ga., U.S. B3 103
Lula, D.R.C. D5 54
Luleå, Swe. D10 10
Luleälven, stm., Swe. C9 10
Lüleburgaz, Tur. B2 44
Luliang, China D1 30
Lüliang Shan, mts., China . . D10 28
Luling, La., U.S. k11 111
Luling, Tx., U.S. E4 136
Lulua, stm., D.R.C. E4 54
Lumana, D.R.C. D5 54
Lumbala N'guimbo, Ang. . . . A3 56
Lumber, stm., U.S. C9 133
Lumber City, Ga., U.S. E4 103
Lumberport, W.V., U.S. B4 141
Lumberton, Ms., U.S. D4 117
Lumberton, N.C., U.S. C3 126
Lumbo, Moz. B7 56
Lumby, B.C., Can. D8 85
Lumding, India D6 40
Lummi Indian Reservation,
Wa., U.S. A3 140
Lumpkin, Ga., U.S. D2 103
Lumpkin, co., Ga., U.S. B2 103
Lumsden, Nf., Can. D5 88
Lumut, Tanjung, c., Indon. . . D3 36
Luna, co., N.M., U.S. E2 124
Luna Pier, Mi., U.S. G7 115

Lund, Swe. I5 10
Lund, Nv., U.S. E6 121
Lundar, Mb., Can. D2 86
Lundazi, Zam. A5 56
Lüneburg, Ger. D12 12
Lunenburg, Ma., U.S. A4 114
Lunenburg, co., Va., U.S. . . . D4 139
Lunéville, Fr. C10 16
Lungué-Bungo
(Lungwebungu), stm.,
Afr. A2 56
Lungwebungu (Lungué-
Bungo), stm., Afr. A3 56
Luninec, Bela. C9 20
Luobei, China A2 31
Luochuan, China B2 30
Luoding, China E3 30
Luohe, China E10 28
Luotian, China C4 30
Luoyang, China E10 28
Luoyuan, China D6 30
Luozi, D.R.C. E2 54
Lupanshui, China D1 30
Lupeni, Rom. G7 20
Luputa, D.R.C. E4 54
Luqu, China E8 28
Luray, Va., U.S. B4 139
Lure, Lake, res., N.C., U.S. . . f10 126
Luremo, Ang. E3 54
Lúrio, Moz. A7 56
Lúrio, stm., Moz. A6 56
Lusaka, Zam. B4 56
Lusambo, D.R.C. D4 54
Lusanga, D.R.C. D3 54
Lusangi, D.R.C. D5 54
Lusby, Md., U.S. D5 113
Luseland, Sk., Can. E1 91
Lushnjë, Alb. D7 18
Lushoto, Tan. D7 54
Lüshun, China D12 28
Lusk, Wy., U.S. D8 143
Luther, Ok., U.S. B4 129
Lutherstadt Eisleben, Ger. . . E12 12
Luthersadt Wittenberg,
Ger. E13 12
Luthersville, Ga., U.S. C2 103
Lutherville-Timonium, Md.,
U.S. B4 113
Luton, Eng., U.K. E6 12
Łutselk'e, N.T., Can. F17 82
Luts'k, Ukr. D8 20
Luttrell, Tn., U.S. C10 135
Lutz, Fl., U.S. D4 102
Lutzow-Holm Bay, b., Ant. . . C8 67
Luuq, Som. J13 48
Luverne, Al., U.S. D3 94
Luverne, Mn., U.S. G2 116
Luwingu, Zam. A4 56
Luwuk, Indon. D6 36
Luxapallila Creek, stm., U.S. B5 117
Luxembourg, Lux. F9 12
Luxembourg, ctry., Eur. . . . C10 16
Luxemburg, Wi., U.S. D6 142
Luxi, China G7 28
Luxomni, Ga., U.S. h8 103
Luxor see El-Uqsor, Egypt . . E11 48
Luxora, Ar., U.S. B6 97
Luza, Russia B8 22
Luzern, Switz. A2 18
Luzerne, Pa., U.S. n17 131
Luzerne, co., Pa., U.S. D9 131
Luzhai, China E2 30
Luzhou, China F9 28
Luziânia, Braz. E2 74
Luzilândia, Braz. B3 74
Luzon, i., Phil. C8 34
Luzon Strait, strt., Asia B8 34
L'viv, Ukr. E8 20
L'vov see L'viv, Ukr. E8 20
Lyallpur see Faisalabad, Pak. D10 42
Lycksele, Swe. D8 10
Lycoming, co., Pa., U.S. D7 131
Lycoming Creek, stm., Pa.,
U.S. D7 131
Lydenburg, S. Afr. D5 56
Lyell, Mount, mtn., Can. . . . D2 84
Lyford, Tx., U.S. F4 136
Lykens, Pa., U.S. E8 131
Lyle, Wa., U.S. D4 140
Lyman, S.C., U.S. B3 133
Lyman, Wy., U.S. E2 143
Lyman, co., S.D., U.S. D6 134
Lyman Lake, res., Az., U.S. . . C6 96
Lyme Bay, b., Eng., U.K. . . . E5 12
Lynch, Ky., U.S. D7 110
Lynchburg, Oh., U.S. C2 128
Lynchburg, Tn., U.S. B5 135
Lynchburg, Va., U.S. C3 139
Lynches, stm., S.C., U.S. . . . D8 133
Lynden, Wa., U.S. A3 140
Lynde Point, c., Ct., U.S. . . . D6 100
Lyndhurst, N.J., U.S. h8 123
Lyndhurst, Oh., U.S. g9 128
Lyndon, Ks., U.S. D8 109
Lyndon, Ky., U.S. g11 110
Lyndon B. Johnson National
Historical Site, hist.,
Tx., U.S. D3 136
Lyndon B. Johnson Space
Center, sci., Tx., U.S. . . . r14 136
Lyndonville, Vt., U.S. B4 138
Lyndora, Pa., U.S. E2 131
Lyngen, b., Nor. B9 10

Name	Map Ref.	Page
Lynn, Al., U.S.	A2	94
Lynn, In., U.S.	D8	107
Lynn, Ma., U.S.	B6	114
Lynn, co., Tx., U.S.	C2	136
Lynn, Lake, res., W.V., U.S.	B5	141
Lynn Canal, b., Ak., U.S.	k22	95
Lynnfield, Ma., U.S.	f11	114
Lynn Garden, Tn., U.S.	C11	135
Lynn Haven, Fl., U.S.	u16	102
Lynnhaven Roads, b., Va., U.S.	k15	139
Lynnville, In., U.S.	H3	107
Lynnwood, Wa., U.S.	B3	140
Lynwood, Ca., U.S.	n12	98
Lyon, Fr.	E9	16
Lyon, co., Ia., U.S.	A1	108
Lyon, co., Ks., U.S.	D7	109
Lyon, co., Ky., U.S.	C1	110
Lyon, co., Mn., U.S.	F3	116
Lyon, co., Nv., U.S.	D2	121
Lyons, Co., U.S.	A5	99
Lyons, Ga., U.S.	D4	103
Lyons, Il., U.S.	k9	106
Lyons, In., U.S.	G3	107
Lyons, Ks., U.S.	D5	109
Lyons, Mi., U.S.	F6	115
Lyons, Ne., U.S.	C9	120
Lyons, N.Y., U.S.	B3	125
Lyons, Or., U.S.	C4	130
Lysekil, Swe.	G4	10
Lyster Station, P.Q., Can.	C6	90
Lys'va, Russia	D7	26
Lysychans'k, Ukr.	E15	20
Lytle, Tx., U.S.	E3	136
Lyubotyn, Ukr.	E13	20

M

Name	Map Ref.	Page
Maalaea Bay, b., Hi., U.S.	C5	104
Ma'ān, Jord.	D3	42
Ma'anshan, China	C4	30
Maarianhamina, Fin.	F8	10
Ma'arrat an-Nu'mān, Syria	E7	44
Maas (Meuse), stm., Eur.	B9	16
Maastricht, Neth.	E9	12
Mabank, Tx., U.S.	C4	136
Mabel, Mn., U.S.	G7	116
Maben, Ms., U.S.	B4	117
Mableton, Ga., U.S.	h7	103
Mabote, Moz.	C5	56
Mabscott, W.V., U.S.	D3	141
Mabton, Wa., U.S.	C5	140
Mača, Russia	D13	26
Macaé, Braz.	F3	74
Macaíba, Braz.	C4	74
Macapá, Braz.	A1	74
Macará, Ec.	D4	70
Macau, Braz.	C4	74
Macau, Macau	B5	34
Macau, dep., Asia	E3	30
MacClenny, Fl., U.S.	B4	102
MacDill Air Force Base, mil., Fl., U.S.	E4	102
MacDonnell Ranges, mts., Austl.	E5	60
MacDowell Reservoir, res., N.H., U.S.	E2	122
Macedonia, Oh., U.S.	A4	128
Macedonia, hist. reg., Eur.	D9	18
Macedonia, ctry., Eur.	D8	18
Maceió, Braz.	C4	74
Macenta, Gui.	E3	50
Macerata, Italy	C4	18
Maces Bay, b., N.B., Can.	D3	87
MacGregor, Mb., Can.	E2	86
Machado, stm., Braz.	E7	70
Machakos, Kenya	D7	54
Machala, Ec.	D4	70
Macheke, Zimb.	B5	56
Macheng, China	C3	30
Machias, Me., U.S.	D5	112
Machias, stm., Me., U.S.	D5	112
Machias, stm., Me., U.S.	B4	112
Machias Bay, b., Me., U.S.	D5	112
Machias Lakes, l., Me., U.S.	C5	112
Machilīpatnam, India	F4	40
Machiques, Ven.	A5	70
Macho, Arroyo del, val., N.M., U.S.	C4	124
Machupicchu, Peru	F5	70
Machupicchu, hist., Peru	A3	72
Mackay, Austl.	E4	62
Mackay, Lake, l., Austl.	E4	60
MacKenzie, B.C., Can.	B6	85
Mackenzie, stm., N.T., Can.	E13	82
Mackenzie Bay, b., Can.	E12	82
Mackenzie Mountains, mts., Can.	F14	82
Mackinac, co., Mi., U.S.	B5	115
Mackinac, Straits of, strt., Mi., U.S.	C6	115
Mackinac Bridge, Mi., U.S.	C6	115
Mackinac Island, i., Mi., U.S.	C6	115
Mackinaw, Il., U.S.	C4	106
Mackinaw, stm., Il., U.S.	C4	106
Mackinaw City, Mi., U.S.	C6	115
Mackinnon Road, Kenya	D7	54
Maclean, Austl.	F5	62
Maclear, S. Afr.	H5	56
Macleod, Lake, l., Austl.	E1	60
Maclovio Herrera, Mex.	B3	78
Macomb, Il., U.S.	C3	106
Macomb, co., Mi., U.S.	F8	115
Macomer, Italy	D2	18
Mâcon, Fr.	D9	16
Macon, Ga., U.S.	D3	103
Macon, Il., U.S.	D5	106
Macon, Mo., U.S.	B5	118
Macon, Ms., U.S.	B5	117
Macon, co., Al., U.S.	C4	94
Macon, co., Ga., U.S.	D2	103
Macon, co., Il., U.S.	D4	106
Macon, co., Mo., U.S.	B5	118
Macon, co., N.C., U.S.	f9	126
Macon, co., Tn., U.S.	A5	135
Macon, Bayou, stm., U.S.	B4	111
Macoupin, co., Il., U.S.	D4	106
Macquarie Island, i., Austl.	J23	4
Macquarie Ridge	N18	64
MacTier, On., Can.	B5	89
Macungie, Pa., U.S.	E10	131
Macuspana, Mex.	D6	78
Mad, stm., Ca., U.S.	B2	98
Mad, stm., Ct., U.S.	B3	100
Mad, stm., N.H., U.S.	C3	122
Mad, stm., Oh., U.S.	C2	128
Mad, stm., Vt., U.S.	C3	138
Madagascar, ctry., Afr.	B8	56
Madagascar Basin	K8	64
Madagascar Plateau	L7	64
Madame, Isle, i., N.S., Can.	D9	87
Madang, Pap. N. Gui.	H12	32
Madaoua, Niger	D6	50
Madawaska, Me., U.S.	A4	112
Madawaska, stm., Can.	B9	90
Madawaska, stm., On., Can.	B7	89
Madawaska Lake, l., Me., U.S.	A4	112
Madaya, Myan.	B3	34
Madeira, Oh., U.S.	o13	128
Madeira, stm., S.A.	E7	70
Madeira, Arquipélago da, is., Port.	D1	48
Madeira Islands see Madeira, Arquipélago da, is., Port.	D1	48
Madeleine, Îles de la, is., P.Q., Can.	B8	87
Madelia, Mn., U.S.	F4	116
Madeline Island, i., Wi., U.S.	B3	142
Maden, Tur.	C8	44
Madera, Mex.	B3	78
Madera, Ca., U.S.	D3	98
Madera, co., Ca., U.S.	D4	98
Madera see Madeira, stm., S.A.	E7	70
Madhya Pradesh, prov., India	E3	40
Madill, Ok., U.S.	C5	129
Madimba, D.R.C.	D3	54
Madingo-Kayes, Congo	D2	54
Madingou, Congo	D2	54
Madirovalo, Madag.	B8	56
Madison, Al., U.S.	A3	94
Madison, Ar., U.S.	B5	97
Madison, Ct., U.S.	D5	100
Madison, Fl., U.S.	B3	102
Madison, Ga., U.S.	C3	103
Madison, Il., U.S.	E3	106
Madison, In., U.S.	G7	107
Madison, Ks., U.S.	D7	109
Madison, Me., U.S.	D3	112
Madison, Mn., U.S.	E2	116
Madison, Ms., U.S.	C3	117
Madison, N.C., U.S.	A3	126
Madison, Ne., U.S.	C8	120
Madison, N.J., U.S.	B4	123
Madison, Oh., U.S.	A4	128
Madison, S.D., U.S.	D8	134
Madison, W.V., U.S.	C3	141
Madison, Wi., U.S.	E4	142
Madison, co., Al., U.S.	A3	94
Madison, co., Ar., U.S.	B2	97
Madison, co., Fl., U.S.	B3	102
Madison, co., Ga., U.S.	B3	103
Madison, co., Ia., U.S.	C3	108
Madison, co., Id., U.S.	F7	105
Madison, co., Il., U.S.	E4	106
Madison, co., In., U.S.	D6	107
Madison, co., Ky., U.S.	C5	110
Madison, co., La., U.S.	B4	111
Madison, co., Mo., U.S.	D7	118
Madison, co., Ms., U.S.	C4	117
Madison, co., Mt., U.S.	E5	119
Madison, co., N.C., U.S.	f10	126
Madison, co., Ne., U.S.	C8	120
Madison, co., N.Y., U.S.	C5	125
Madison, co., Oh., U.S.	C2	128
Madison, co., Tn., U.S.	B3	135
Madison, co., Tx., U.S.	D5	136
Madison, co., Va., U.S.	B4	139
Madison, stm., Mt., U.S.	E5	119
Madison Heights, Mi., U.S.	o15	115
Madison Heights, Va., U.S.	C3	139
Madison Lake, Mn., U.S.	F5	116
Madison Range, mts., Mt., U.S.	E5	119
Madisonville, Ky., U.S.	C2	110
Madisonville, La., U.S.	D5	111
Madisonville, Tn., U.S.	D9	135
Madisonville, Tx., U.S.	D5	136
Madoc, On., Can.	C7	89
Mado Gashi, Kenya	C7	54
Madoi, China	E7	28
Madona, Lat.	H12	10
Madrakah, Ra's al-, c., Oman	G7	38
Madras see Chennai, India	G4	40
Madras, Or., U.S.	C5	130
Madras see Tamil Nādu, prov., India	G3	40
Madre, Laguna, b., Tx., U.S.	F4	136
Madre, Laguna, l., Mex.	B5	78
Madre, Sierra, mts., Phil.	C8	34
Madre de Dios, stm., S.A.	F6	70
Madre de Dios, Isla, i., Chile	H1	69
Madre del Sur, Sierra, mts., Mex.	D5	78
Madre Occidental, Sierra, mts., Mex.	B3	78
Madre Oriental, Sierra, mts., Mex.	C4	78
Madrid, Spain	G5	16
Madrid, Ia., U.S.	C4	108
Madura, i., Indon.	E4	36
Madura, Selat, strt., Indon.	E4	36
Madurai, India	H3	40
Maebashi, Japan	D15	28
Mae Hong Son, Thai.	C3	34
Mae Sariang, Thai.	C3	34
Maeser, Ut., U.S.	C6	137
Mae Sot, Thai.	C3	34
Maestra, Sierra, mts., Cuba	B4	80
Maevatanana, Madag.	B8	56
Maéwo, i., Vanuatu	k9	62a
Mafeteng, Leso.	D4	56
Mafia Island, i., Tan.	E7	54
Mafra, Braz.	B7	72
Magadan, Russia	D17	26
Magadi, Kenya	D7	54
Magallanes, Estrecho de (Magellan, Strait of), strt., S.A.	H2	69
Magangué, Col.	B5	70
Magaria, Niger	D6	50
Magazine, Ar., U.S.	B2	97
Magazine Mountain, mtn., Ar., U.S.	B2	97
Magdagači, Russia	D14	26
Magdalena, Bol.	F7	70
Magdalena, N.M., U.S.	C2	124
Magdalena, stm., Col.	D5	80
Magdalena, stm., Mex.	A2	78
Magdalena, Isla, i., Chile	E2	69
Magdalena de Kino, Mex.	A2	78
Magdalena Mountains, mts., N.M., U.S.	D2	124
Magdeburg, Ger.	D12	12
Magee, Ms., U.S.	D4	117
Magelang, indon.	E4	36
Magellan, Strait of see Magallanes, Estrecho de, strt., S.A.	H2	69
Maggie Creek, stm., Nv., U.S.	C5	121
Maggiore, Lago, l., Eur.	B2	18
Maghâgha, Egypt	F10	14
Maghama, Maur.	C2	50
Magic Reservoir, res., Id., U.S.	F4	105
Maglie, Italy	D7	18
Magna, Ut., U.S.	C3	137
Magnetawan, stm., On., Can.	B4	89
Magnitogorsk, Russia	D7	26
Magnolia, Ar., U.S.	D2	97
Magnolia, Ky., U.S.	C4	110
Magnolia, Ms., U.S.	D3	117
Magnolia, N.C., U.S.	C4	126
Magnolia, Oh., U.S.	B4	128
Magoffin, co., Ky., U.S.	C6	110
Magog, P.Q., Can.	D5	90
Magothy River, b., Md., U.S.	B4	113
Magrath, Ab., Can.	E4	84
Magruder Mountain, mtn., Nv., U.S.	F4	121
Magway, Myan.	B2	34
Mahābād, Iran	C5	42
Mahābaleshwar, India	F2	40
Mahabe, Madag.	B8	56
Mahābhārat Lek, mts., Nepal	D4	40
Mahabo, Madag.	C7	56
Mahačkala, Russia	E6	26
Mahagi, D.R.C.	C6	54
Mahajanga, Madag.	B8	56
Mahakam, stm., Indon.	C5	36
Mahalapye, Bots.	C4	56
Mahānadi, stm., India	E4	40
Mahanoro, Madag.	B8	56
Mahanoy City, Pa., U.S.	E9	131
Mahārāshtra, prov., India	C3	40
Maha Sarakham, Thai.	C4	34
Mahaska, co., Ia., U.S.	C5	108
Mahbūbnagar, India	F3	40
Mahd adh-Dhahab, Sau. Ar.	F4	38
Mahdia, Tun.	G3	18
Mahe, India	G3	40
Mahé, i., Sey.	h13	57b
Mahébourg, Mrts.	g10	57a
Mahenge, Tan.	E7	54
Maheshāna, India	I2	40
Mahi, stm., India	I2	40
Mahilëŭ, Bela.	C11	20
Mahmūdābād, India	A5	56
Mahnomen, Mn., U.S.	C3	116
Mahnomen, co., Mn., U.S.	C3	116
Mahogany Mountain, mtn., Or., U.S.	D9	130
Mahomet, Il., U.S.	C5	106
Mahón see Maó, Spain	H9	16
Mahone Bay, N.S., Can.	E5	87
Mahoning, co., Oh., U.S.	B5	128
Mahoning, stm., U.S.	A5	128
Mahopac, N.Y., U.S.	D7	125
Mahuva, India	E2	40
Mahwah, N.J., U.S.	A4	123
Maicao, Col.	C5	80
Maiden, N.C., U.S.	B1	126
Maidstone Lake, l., Vt., U.S.	B5	138
Maiduguri, Nig.	D7	50
Maili, Hi., U.S.	g9	104
Maili Point, c., Hi., U.S.	g9	104
Main, stm., Ger.	F11	12
Main Channel, strt., On., Can.	B3	89
Mai-Ndombe, Lac, l., D.R.C.	D3	54
Maine, hist. reg., Fr.	C6	16
Maine, state, U.S.	C3	112
Maine, Gulf of, b., N.A.	C14	92
Mainland, i., Scot., U.K.	A5	12
Mainland, i., Scot., U.K.	h19	12a
Main Pass, strt., La., U.S.	E6	111
Mainz, Ger.	E11	12
Maio, i., C.V.	g10	50a
Maipú, Arg.	F6	72
Maiquetía, Ven.	A6	70
Maíz, Islas del, is., Nic.	C3	80
Maize, Ks., U.S.	g12	109
Maizuru, Japan	C3	31
Maja, stm., Russia	C15	26
Majene, Indon.	D5	36
Majī, Eth.	B7	54
Majkop, Russia	E6	26
Major, co., Ok., U.S.	A3	129
Majorca see Mallorca, i., Spain	H8	16
Majuro, atoll, Marsh. Is.	D11	58
Maka, Sen.	D2	50
Makabana, Congo	D2	54
Makaha, Hi., U.S.	g9	104
Makaha Point, c., Hi., U.S.	A2	104
Makah Indian Reservation, Wa., U.S.	A1	140
Makahuena Point, c., Hi., U.S.	B2	104
Makakilo City, Hi., U.S.	g9	104
Makapuu Head, c., Hi., U.S.	B4	104
Makarakomburu, Mount, mtn., Sol. Is.	B6	62
Makarov, Russia	B16	28
Makarov Basin	E34	144
Makarska, Russia	E5	36
Makasar see Ujungpandang, Indon.	E5	36
Makasar, Selat (Makassar Strait), strt., Indon.	D5	36
Makassar Strait see Makasar, Selat, strt., Indon.	D5	36
Makat, Kaz.	E7	26
Makawao, Hi., U.S.	C5	104
Makaweli, Hi., U.S.	B2	104
Makeni, S.L.	E2	50
Makgadikgadi, pl., Bots.	C4	56
Makiïvka, Ukr.	E14	20
Makindu, Kenya	D7	54
Makkah, Sau. Ar.	F3	38
Makó, Hung.	F6	20
Makokou, Gabon	C2	54
Makoua, Congo	D3	54
Makrān Coast, Asia	E7	42
Mākū, Iran	C11	44
Makumbi, D.R.C.	E4	54
Makurdi, Nig.	E6	50
Makushin Volcano, vol., Ak., U.S.	E6	95
Mala, Peru	A2	72
Malabar, Fl., U.S.	D6	102
Malabar Coast, India	G2	40
Malabo, Eq. Gui.	C1	54
Malacca see Melaka, Malay.	C2	36
Malacca, Strait of, strt., Asia	C1	36
Malad City, Id., U.S.	G6	105
Maladzečna, Bela.	B9	20
Málaga, Col.	D5	80
Málaga, Spain	I4	16
Malagarasi, Tan.	C6	54
Malaimbandy, Madag.	C8	56
Malaja Kuril'skaja Grjada, is., Russia	B5	31
Malajaroslavec, Russia	B14	20
Malaja Višera, Russia	C5	22
Malakāl, Sudan	I11	48
Malakoff, Tx., U.S.	C4	136
Malakula, i., Vanuatu	I9	62a
Malambo, Col.	C5	80
Malang, Indon.	E4	36
Malanje, Ang.	E3	54
Malanville, Benin	D5	50
Mälaren, l., Swe.	G7	10
Malargüe, Arg.	F4	72
Malartic, P.Q., Can.	k11	90
Malaspina Glacier, Ak., U.S.	D11	95
Malatya, Tur.	C8	44
Mala Vyska, Ukr.	E11	20
Malawi, ctry., Afr.	A5	56
Malawi, Lake see Nyasa, Lake, l., Afr.	F6	54
Malaya see Semenanjung Malaysia, hist. reg., Malay.	C2	36
Malaybalay, Phil.	E9	34
Malāyer, Iran	D5	42
Malay Peninsula, pen., Asia	B2	36
Malaysia, ctry., Asia	C4	36
Malazgirt, Tur.	C10	44
Malbaie, stm., P.Q., Can.	B7	90
Malbork, Pol.	C5	20
Malbrán, Arg.	D5	72
Malcolm, Austl.	F3	60
Malden, Ma., U.S.	B5	114
Malden, Mo., U.S.	E8	118
Malden, W.V., U.S.	m12	141
Malden, i., Kir.	E14	58
Maldives, ctry., Asia	I10	24
Maldonado, Ur.	E7	72
Mālegaon, India	E2	40
Malek Kandī, Iran	D12	44
Malema, Moz.	A6	56
Malha Wells, Sudan	G10	48
Malheur, co., Or., U.S.	D9	130
Malheur, stm., Or., U.S.	D9	130
Malheur Lake, l., Or., U.S.	D8	130
Mali, Gui.	D2	50
Mali, ctry., Afr.	C4	50
Malibu, Ca., U.S.	m11	98
Malin, Or., U.S.	E5	130
Malindi, Kenya	D8	54
Malinga, Congo	D2	54
Malka, Russia	D17	26
Malkara, Tur.	B2	44
Mallawi, Egypt	F10	14
Malletts Bay, b., Vt., U.S.	B2	138
Mallorca (Majorca), i., Spain	H8	16
Malmberget, Swe.	C9	10
Malmesbury, S. Afr.	E2	56
Malmö, Swe.	I5	10
Malmstrom Air Force Base, mil., Mt., U.S.	C5	119
Maloelap, atoll, Marsh. Is.	D11	58
Malolos, Phil.	D8	34
Malone, N.Y., U.S.	f10	125
Maloney Reservoir, res., Ne., U.S.	C5	120
Malonga, D.R.C.	F4	54
Malošujka, Russia	B6	22
Malöy, Nor.	F1	10
Malpelo, Isla de, i., Col.	C3	70
Malpeque Bay, b., P.E., Can.	C6	87
Malta, Il., U.S.	B5	106
Malta, Mt., U.S.	B9	119
Malta, ctry., Eur.	G5	18
Maltahöhe, Nmb.	C2	56
Maluku (Moluccas), is., Indon.	D7	36
Maluku, Laut (Molucca Sea), Indon.	C7	36
Malumfashi, Nig.	D6	50
Mālvan, India	F2	40
Malvern, Ar., U.S.	C3	97
Malvern, Ia., U.S.	D2	108
Malvern, Oh., U.S.	B4	128
Malvern, Pa., U.S.	o19	131
Malverne, N.Y., U.S.	k13	125
Malyj Enisej, stm., Russia	A7	28
Malyn, Ukr.	D10	20
Mama, Russia	D13	26
Mamala Bay, b., Hi., U.S.	g10	104
Mamallapuram, hist., India	G4	40
Mamaroneck, N.Y., U.S.	h13	125
Mamburao, Phil.	D8	34
Mamfe, Cam.	B1	54
Mammoth, Az., U.S.	E5	96
Mammoth Cave National Park, Ky., U.S.	C4	110
Mammoth Lakes, Ca., U.S.	D4	98
Mammoth Spring, Ar., U.S.	A4	97
Mamoré, stm., S.A.	F6	70
Mamou, Gui.	D2	50
Mamou, La., U.S.	D3	111
Mamoudzou, May.	A8	56
Mampikony, Madag.	B8	56
Mamuju, Indon.	D5	36
Man, C. Iv.	E3	50
Man, W.V., U.S.	D3	141
Manacapuru, Braz.	D7	70
Manacor, Spain	H8	16
Manado, Indon.	C6	36
Managua, Nic.	C2	80
Managua, Lago de, l., Nic.	C2	80
Manakara, Madag.	C8	56
Manāli, India	C3	40
Manama see Al-Manāmah, Bahr.	E6	42
Manam Island, i., Pap. N. Gui.	G12	32
Manana Island, i., Hi., U.S.	g11	104
Mananara Avaratra, Madag.	B8	56
Mananjary, Madag.	C8	56
Manankoro, Mali	D3	50
Manantico Creek, stm., N.J., U.S.	E3	123
Mana Point, c., Hi., U.S.	A2	104
Manas, China	C5	28
Manas Hu, l., China	B5	28
Manasquan, N.J., U.S.	C4	123
Manasquan, stm., N.J., U.S.	C4	123
Manassa, Co., U.S.	D5	99
Manassas, Va., U.S.	B5	139
Manassas National Battlefield Park, Va., U.S.	g11	139
Manassas Park, Va., U.S.	g11	139
Manatee, co., Fl., U.S.	E4	102
Manatee, stm., Fl., U.S.	E4	102
Manatuto, Indon.	E7	36
Manaus, Braz.	D7	70
Manavgat, Tur.	D4	44

Name	Map Ref.	Page
Manawa, Wi., U.S.	D5	142
Manbij, Syria	D7	44
Mancelona, Mi., U.S.	D5	115
Manchester, Eng., U.K.	D5	12
Manchester, Ct., U.S.	B5	100
Manchester, Ga., U.S.	D2	103
Manchester, Ia., U.S.	B6	108
Manchester, Ky., U.S.	C6	110
Manchester, Ma., U.S.	A6	114
Manchester, Md., U.S.	A4	113
Manchester, Me., U.S.	D3	112
Manchester, Mi., U.S.	F6	115
Manchester, Mo., U.S.	f12	118
Manchester, N.H., U.S.	E4	122
Manchester, N.Y., U.S.	C3	125
Manchester, Oh., U.S.	D2	128
Manchester, Pa., U.S.	F8	131
Manchester, Tn., U.S.	B5	135
Manchester, Vt., U.S.	E2	138
Manchester Center, Vt., U.S.	E2	138
Manchuria, hist. reg., China	B13	28
Mancos, Co., U.S.	D2	99
Mancos, stm., U.S.	D2	99
Manda, Tan.	F6	54
Mandabe, Madag.	C7	56
Manda Island, i., Kenya	D8	54
Mandal, Nor.	G2	10
Mandalay, Myan.	B3	34
Mandalgovĭ, Mong.	B9	28
Mandalī, Iraq	D5	42
Mandalya, Gulf of see Güllük Körfezi, b., Tur.	D2	44
Mandan, N.D., U.S.	C5	127
Mandar, Teluk, b., Indon.	D5	36
Mandara Mountains, mts., Afr.	A2	54
Mandeb, Bab el, strt.	H4	38
Mandera, Kenya	C8	54
Mandeville, Jam.	B4	80
Mandeville, Ar., U.S.	D2	97
Mandeville, La., U.S.	D5	111
Mandimba, Moz.	A6	56
Mandioli, Pulau, i., Indon.	D7	36
Mandla, India	E4	40
Mandritsara, Madag.	B8	56
Mandsaur, India	E3	40
Manduria, Italy	D6	18
Māndvi, India	E1	40
Mandya, India	G3	40
Manendragarh, India	E4	40
Manfalūt, Egypt	E11	48
Manfredonia, Italy	D5	18
Manfredonia, Golfo di, b., Italy	D6	18
Manga, Braz.	D3	74
Manga, reg., Niger	D7	50
Mangabeiras, Chapada das, hills, Braz.	C2	74
Mangai, D.R.C.	D3	54
Mangalia, Rom.	H10	20
Mangalore, India	G2	40
Mangchang, China	F9	28
Mange, China	C4	40
Manggar, Indon.	D3	36
Mangkalihat, Tanjung, c., Indon.	C5	36
Mangnai, China	D6	28
Mangochi, Mwi.	A6	56
Mangoky, stm., Madag.	C7	56
Mangole, Pulau, i., Indon.	D7	36
Mangum, Ok., U.S.	C2	129
Manhattan, Ks., U.S.	C7	109
Manhattan, Mt., U.S.	E5	119
Manhattan Beach, Ca., U.S.	n12	98
Manhattan Island, i., N.Y., U.S.	h13	125
Manheim, Pa., U.S.	F9	131
Manhuaçu, Braz.	F3	74
Manica, Moz.	B5	56
Manicoré, Braz.	E7	70
Manicouagan, Réservoir, res., P.Q., Can.	h13	90
Manignan, C. Iv.	D3	50
Manila, Phil.	D8	34
Manila, Ar., U.S.	B5	97
Manilla, Ia., U.S.	C2	108
Manipur, prov., India	D6	40
Manisa, Tur.	C2	44
Manistee, Mi., U.S.	D4	115
Manistee, co., Mi., U.S.	D4	115
Manistee, stm., Mi., U.S.	D5	115
Manistique, Mi., U.S.	C4	115
Manistique, stm., Mi., U.S.	B4	115
Manistique Lake, l., Mi., U.S.	B5	115
Manito, Il., U.S.	C4	106
Manitoba, prov., Can.	C3	86
Manitoba, Lake, l., Mb., Can.	D2	86
Manitou, Mb., Can.	E2	86
Manitou Springs, Co., U.S.	C6	99
Manitowoc, Wi., U.S.	D6	142
Manitowoc, co., Wi., U.S.	D6	142
Manitowoc, stm., Wi., U.S.	h10	142
Maniwaki, P.Q., Can.	C2	90
Manizales, Col.	B4	70
Manja, Madag.	C7	56
Manjakandriana, Madag.	B8	56
Manjimup, Austl.	G2	60
Mānjra, stm., India	F3	40
Mankanza, D.R.C.	C3	54
Mankato, Ks., U.S.	C5	109
Mankato, Mn., U.S.	F5	116
Manlius, N.Y., U.S.	C5	125
Manly, Ia., U.S.	A4	108
Manmād, India	E2	40
Manna, Indon.	D2	36
Mannar, Gulf of, b., Asia	H3	40
Mannford, Ok., U.S.	A5	129
Mannheim, Ger.	F11	12
Manning, Ab., Can.	A2	84
Manning, Ia., U.S.	C2	108
Manning, S.C., U.S.	D7	133
Mannington, W.V., U.S.	B4	141
Manns Creek, stm., W.V., U.S.	n14	141
Mannville, Ab., Can.	C5	84
Manokin, stm., Md., U.S.	D6	113
Manokotak, Ak., U.S.	D8	95
Manokwari, Indon.	D8	36
Manomet, Ma., U.S.	C6	114
Manomet Point, c., Ma., U.S.	C6	114
Manono, D.R.C.	E5	54
Manor, Tx., U.S.	D4	136
Manouane, Lac, l., P.Q., Can.	h12	90
Manresa, Spain	G7	16
Mansa, Zam.	A4	56
Manseau, P.Q., Can.	C5	90
Mansfield, Eng., U.K.	D6	12
Mansfield, Ar., U.S.	B1	97
Mansfield, Il., U.S.	C5	106
Mansfield, La., U.S.	B2	111
Mansfield, Ma., U.S.	B5	114
Mansfield, Mo., U.S.	D5	118
Mansfield, Oh., U.S.	B3	128
Mansfield, Pa., U.S.	C7	131
Mansfield, Tx., U.S.	n9	136
Mansfield, Mount, mtn., Vt., U.S.	B3	138
Mansfield Center, Ct., U.S.	B7	100
Mansfield Hollow Lake, res., Ct., U.S.	B7	100
Mansôa, Gui.-B.	D1	50
Manson, Ia., U.S.	B3	108
Manson, Wa., U.S.	B5	140
Mansonville, P.Q., Can.	D5	90
Mansura, La., U.S.	C3	111
Manta, Ec.	D2	70
Mantachie, Ms., U.S.	A5	117
Manteca, Ca., U.S.	D3	98
Manteno, Il., U.S.	B6	106
Manteo, N.C., U.S.	B7	126
Manti, Ut., U.S.	D4	137
Mantiqueira, Serra da, mts., Braz.	F2	74
Manton, Mi., U.S.	D5	115
Mantorville, Mn., U.S.	F6	116
Mántova, Italy	B3	18
Mantua, Oh., U.S.	A4	128
Mantua, Ut., U.S.	B4	137
Manturovo, Russia	C7	22
Mäntyluoto, Fin.	F9	10
Manuae, atoll, Cook Is.	F14	58
Manui, Pulau, i., Indon.	D6	36
Manukau, N.Z.	o13	63c
Manumuskin, stm., N.J., U.S.	E3	123
Manus Island, i., Pap. N. Gui.	G12	32
Manvel, Tx., U.S.	r14	136
Manville, N.J., U.S.	B3	123
Manville, R.I., U.S.	B4	132
Many, La., U.S.	C2	111
Manyara, Lake, l., Tan.	D7	54
Many Farms, Az., U.S.	A6	96
Manyoni, Tan.	E6	54
Manzanillo, Cuba	A4	80
Manzanillo, Mex.	D4	78
Manzanillo Bay, b., N.A.	A5	80
Manzano Mountains, mts., N.M., U.S.	C3	124
Manzano Peak, mtn., N.M., U.S.	C3	124
Manzhouli, China	B11	28
Manzini, Swaz.	D5	56
Mao, Chad	D8	50
Mao, Dom. Rep.	B5	80
Maó, Spain	H9	16
Maoke, Pegunungan, mts., Indon.	G10	32
Maoming, China	G10	28
Mapastepec, Mex.	D6	78
Mapi, Indon.	H10	32
Mapinhane, Moz.	C6	56
Maple, stm., Ia., U.S.	B2	108
Maple, stm., N.D., U.S.	C8	127
Maple, stm., U.S.	A7	134
Maple Bluff, Wi., U.S.	E4	142
Maple Grove, Mn., U.S.	m12	116
Maple Heights, Oh., U.S.	h9	128
Maple Lake, Mn., U.S.	E5	116
Maple Plain, Mn., U.S.	m11	116
Maple Shade, N.J., U.S.	D2	123
Maplesville, Al., U.S.	C3	94
Mapleton, Ia., U.S.	B2	108
Mapleton, Mn., U.S.	G5	116
Mapleton, N.D., U.S.	C8	127
Mapleton, Or., U.S.	C3	130
Mapleton, Ut., U.S.	C4	137
Maple Valley, Wa., U.S.	f11	140
Mapleville, R.I., U.S.	B2	132
Maplewood, Mn., U.S.	n12	116
Maplewood, Mo., U.S.	f13	118
Maplewood, N.J., U.S.	B4	123
Maputo, Moz. •	D5	56
Maqteïr, reg., Maur.	B2	50
Maquela do Zombo, Ang.	E3	54
Maquinchao, Arg.	F3	69
Maquoketa, Ia., U.S.	B7	108
Maquoketa, stm., Ia., U.S.	B6	108
Maquoketa, North Fork, stm., Ia., U.S.	B7	108
Marabá, Braz.	C2	74
Maracá, Ilha de, i., Braz.	C9	70
Maracaibo, Ven.	A5	70
Maracaibo, Lago de, l., Ven.	B5	70
Maracaju, Braz.	C6	72
Maracás, Braz.	D3	74
Maracay, Ven.	A6	70
Marādah, Libya	E8	48
Maradi, Niger	D6	50
Marāgheh, Iran	C5	42
Marahuaca, Cerro, mtn., Ven.	C6	70
Marais des Cygnes, stm., U.S.	D8	109
Marajó, Baía de, b., Braz.	B2	74
Marajó, Ilha de, i., Braz.	B2	74
Maralal, Kenya	C7	54
Marampa, S.L.	E2	50
Marana, Az., U.S.	E4	96
Marand, Iran	C5	42
Maranguape, Braz.	B4	74
Maranhão, state, Braz.	B2	74
Maranhão, stm., Braz.	A8	72
Marañón, stm., Peru	D5	70
Marathon, Fl., U.S.	H5	102
Marathon, Wi., U.S.	D4	142
Marathon, co., Wi., U.S.	D4	142
Marawi, Phil.	E8	34
Marbella, Spain	I4	16
Marble, Mn., U.S.	C5	116
Marble, N.C., U.S.	f9	126
Marble Bar, Austl.	E2	60
Marble Canyon, val., Az., U.S.	A4	96
Marble Falls, Tx., U.S.	D3	136
Marble Hall, S. Afr.	C4	56
Marblehead, Ma., U.S.	B6	114
Marble Hill, Mo., U.S.	D8	118
Marbleton, Wy., U.S.	D2	143
Marburg, Ger.	E11	12
Marbury, Md., U.S.	C3	113
Marceline, Mo., U.S.	B5	118
Marcellus, Mi., U.S.	F5	115
March Air Force Base, mil., Ca., U.S.	F5	98
Marche, hist. reg., Fr.	D7	16
Mar Chiquita, Laguna, l., Arg.	E5	72
Marco, Fl., U.S.	G5	102
Marcus, Ia., U.S.	B2	108
Marcus Baker, Mount, mtn., Ak., U.S.	g18	95
Marcus Hook, Pa., U.S.	G11	131
Marcus Island see Minami-Tori-shima, i., Japan	F18	64
Marcy, Mount, mtn., N.Y., U.S.	A7	125
Mardān, Pak.	D10	42
Mar del Plata, Arg.	F6	72
Mardin, Tur.	D9	44
Maré, i., N. Cal.	I9	62a
Mareeba, Austl.	D4	62
Marengo, Ia., U.S.	C5	108
Marengo, Il., U.S.	A5	106
Marengo, In., U.S.	H5	107
Marengo, co., Al., U.S.	C2	94
Marfa, Tx., U.S.	o12	136
Margaret, Al., U.S.	B3	94
Margaret River, Austl.	G1	60
Margarita, Isla de, i., Ven.	A7	70
Margate, Fl., U.S.	F6	102
Margate City, N.J., U.S.	E3	123
Margherita Peak, mtn., Afr.	C5	54
Margilan, Uzb.	B10	42
Margrethe, Lake, l., Mi., U.S.	D6	115
Marha, Russia	C14	26
Marhanets', Ukr.	F13	20
María, Îles, is., Fr. Poly.	G14	58
María Elena, Chile	B3	69
Maria Island, i., Austl.	C6	60
Mariakani, Kenya	D7	54
Marian, Lake, l., Fl., U.S.	E5	102
Mariana Islands, is., Oc.	C11	32
Mariana Ridge	G17	64
Mariana Trench	G17	64
Marianna, Ar., U.S.	C5	97
Marianna, Fl., U.S.	B1	102
Marias, stm., Mt., U.S.	B4	119
Marias Pass, Mt., U.S.	B3	119
Mariato, Punta, c., Pan.	D3	80
Maribor, Slvn.	A5	18
Maricopa, Az., U.S.	E3	96
Maricopa, Ca., U.S.	E4	98
Maricopa, co., Az., U.S.	D3	96
Maricopa Mountains, mts., Az., U.S.	m7	96
Marie Byrd Land, reg., Ant.	D29	67
Marie-Galante, i., Guad.	B7	80
Mariemont, Oh., U.S.	o13	128
Mariental, Nmb.	C2	56
Marienville, Pa., U.S.	D3	131
Maries, co., Mo., U.S.	C6	118
Mariestad, Swe.	G5	10
Marietta, Ga., U.S.	C2	103
Marietta, Oh., U.S.	C4	128
Marietta, Ok., U.S.	D4	129
Marietta, S.C., U.S.	A2	133
Marieville, P.Q., Can.	D4	90
Marijampolė, Lith.	I10	10
Marij El, state, Russia	D6	26
Marília, Braz.	F2	74
Marimba, Ang.	E3	54
Marin, co., Ca., U.S.	C2	98
Mar'ina Horka, Bela.	C10	20
Marinduque, i., Phil.	D8	34
Marine, Il., U.S.	E4	106
Marine City, Mi., U.S.	F8	115
Marine On St. Croix, Mn., U.S.	E6	116
Marinette, Wi., U.S.	C6	142
Marinette, co., Wi., U.S.	C5	142
Maringá, Braz.	F1	74
Maringouin, La., U.S.	D4	111
Marion, Al., U.S.	C2	94
Marion, Ar., U.S.	B5	97
Marion, Ia., U.S.	B6	108
Marion, Il., U.S.	F5	106
Marion, In., U.S.	C6	107
Marion, Ks., U.S.	D6	109
Marion, Ky., U.S.	e9	110
Marion, La., U.S.	B3	111
Marion, Mi., U.S.	D5	115
Marion, Ms., U.S.	C5	117
Marion, N.C., U.S.	B1	126
Marion, Oh., U.S.	B2	128
Marion, Pa., U.S.	G6	131
Marion, S.C., U.S.	C9	133
Marion, S.D., U.S.	D8	134
Marion, Va., U.S.	f10	139
Marion, Wi., U.S.	D5	142
Marion, co., Al., U.S.	A2	94
Marion, co., Ar., U.S.	A3	97
Marion, co., Fl., U.S.	C4	102
Marion, co., Ga., U.S.	D2	103
Marion, co., Ia., U.S.	C4	108
Marion, co., Il., U.S.	E4	106
Marion, co., In., U.S.	E5	107
Marion, co., Ks., U.S.	D6	109
Marion, co., Ky., U.S.	C4	110
Marion, co., Mo., U.S.	B6	118
Marion, co., Ms., U.S.	D4	117
Marion, co., Oh., U.S.	B2	128
Marion, co., Or., U.S.	C4	130
Marion, co., S.C., U.S.	C9	133
Marion, co., Tn., U.S.	D8	135
Marion, co., Tx., U.S.	C5	136
Marion, co., W.V., U.S.	B4	141
Marion, Lake, res., S.C., U.S.	E7	133
Marion Reef, rf., Austl.	D5	62
Marion Station, Md., U.S.	D6	113
Marionville, Mo., U.S.	D4	118
Mariposa, Ca., U.S.	D3	98
Mariposa, co., Ca., U.S.	D3	98
Mariscal Estigarribia, Para.	C5	72
Marissa, Il., U.S.	E4	106
Maritime Alps, mts., Eur.	B1	18
Maritime Atlas see Atlas Tellien, mts., Alg.	D4	14
Mariupol', Ukr.	F14	20
Märjamaa, Est.	G11	10
Marka, Som.	J13	48
Märkāpur, India	F3	40
Markdale, On., Can.	C4	89
Marked Tree, Ar., U.S.	B5	97
Markesan, Wi., U.S.	E5	142
Markham, On., Can.	D5	89
Markham, Il., U.S.	k9	106
Markham, Tx., U.S.	E4	136
Markit, China	B3	40
Markland Lock and Dam, U.S.	B5	110
Markle, In., U.S.	C7	107
Markovo, Russia	C19	26
Marks, Russia	D8	22
Marks, Ms., U.S.	A3	117
Marksville, La., U.S.	C3	111
Mark Twain Lake, res., Mo., U.S.	B6	118
Marlboro, N.Y., U.S.	D6	125
Marlboro, Va., U.S.	n17	139
Marlboro, co., S.C., U.S.	B8	133
Marlborough, Ct., U.S.	C6	100
Marlborough, Ma., U.S.	B4	114
Marlborough, N.H., U.S.	E2	122
Marlette, Mi., U.S.	E7	115
Marley, Md., U.S.	B4	113
Marlin, Tx., U.S.	D4	136
Marlinton, W.V., U.S.	C4	141
Marlow, Ok., U.S.	C4	129
Marlowe, W.V., U.S.	B7	141
Marlton, N.J., U.S.	D3	123
Marmande, Fr.	E7	16
Marmara, Sea of see Marmara Denizi, Tur.	B3	44
Marmara Denizi, Tur.	B3	44
Marmaris, Tur.	D3	44
Marmet, W.V., U.S.	C3	141
Marmora, On., Can.	C7	89
Marne, stm., Fr.	C8	16
Maroa, Il., U.S.	C5	106
Maroa, Ven.	C6	70
Maroantsetra, Madag.	B8	56
Maromandia, Madag.	A8	56
Maromokotro, mtn., Madag.	A8	56
Marondera, Zimb.	B5	56
Maroni, stm., S.A.	C9	70
Maros, Indon.	E5	36
Maroua, Cam.	A2	54
Marovoay, Madag.	B8	56
Marowijne see Maroni, stm., S.A.	C9	70
Marquesas Islands see Marquises, Îles, is., Fr. Poly.	E16	58
Marquesas Keys, is., Fl., U.S.	H4	102
Marquette, Mi., U.S.	B3	115
Marquette, co., Mi., U.S.	B3	115
Marquette, co., Wi., U.S.	E4	142
Marquette Heights, Il., U.S.	C4	106
Marquises, Îles, is., Fr. Poly.	E16	58
Marrah, Jabal, hill, Sudan	H9	48
Marrakech, Mor.	D3	48
Marrero, La., U.S.	E5	111
Marromeu, Moz.	B6	56
Mars, Pa., U.S.	E1	131
Marsá al-Burayqah, Libya	D8	48
Marsabit, Kenya	C7	54
Marsala, Italy	F4	18
Marseille, Fr.	F9	16
Marseilles, Il., U.S.	B5	106
Marshall, Sk., Can.	D1	91
Marshall, Lib.	E2	50
Marshall, Ar., U.S.	B3	97
Marshall, Il., U.S.	D6	106
Marshall, Mi., U.S.	F6	115
Marshall, Mn., U.S.	F3	116
Marshall, Mo., U.S.	B4	118
Marshall, N.C., U.S.	f10	126
Marshall, Tx., U.S.	C5	136
Marshall, Va., U.S.	B5	139
Marshall, Wi., U.S.	E4	142
Marshall, co., Al., U.S.	A3	94
Marshall, co., Ia., U.S.	C4	108
Marshall, co., Il., U.S.	B4	106
Marshall, co., In., U.S.	B5	107
Marshall, co., Ks., U.S.	C7	109
Marshall, co., Ky., U.S.	f9	110
Marshall, co., Mn., U.S.	B2	116
Marshall, co., Ms., U.S.	A4	117
Marshall, co., Ok., U.S.	C5	129
Marshall, co., S.D., U.S.	B8	134
Marshall, co., Tn., U.S.	B5	135
Marshall, co., W.V., U.S.	B4	141
Marshall Islands, ctry., Oc.	C10	58
Marshall Islands. is., Marsh. Is.	F24	4
Marshallton, De., U.S.	B3	101
Marshalltown, Ia., U.S.	B5	108
Marshallville, Ga., U.S.	D3	103
Marshes Siding, Ky., U.S.	D5	110
Marshfield, Ma., U.S.	B6	114
Marshfield, Mo., U.S.	D5	118
Marshfield, Wi., U.S.	D3	142
Marshfield Hills, Ma., U.S.	B6	114
Marsh Fork, stm., W.V., U.S.	n13	141
Mars Hill, Me., U.S.	B5	112
Mars Hill, N.C., U.S.	f10	126
Marsh Island, i., La., U.S.	E4	111
Marsh Lake, res., Mn., U.S.	E2	116
Marsh Peak, mtn., Ut., U.S.	C6	137
Marshville, N.C., U.S.	C2	126
Marsing, Id., U.S.	F2	105
Märsta, Swe.	G7	10
Marston, Mo., U.S.	E8	118
Mart, Tx., U.S.	D4	136
Martaban, Gulf of, b., Myan.	C3	34
Martapura, Indon.	D2	36
Martapura, Indon.	D4	36
Marthasville, Mo., U.S.	C6	118
Martha's Vineyard, i., Ma., U.S.	D6	114
Martí, Cuba	A4	80
Martigny, Switz.	A1	18
Martigues, Fr.	F9	16
Martin, Slvk.	E5	20
Martin, Ky., U.S.	C7	110
Martin, S.D., U.S.	D4	134
Martin, Tn., U.S.	A3	135
Martin, co., Fl., U.S.	E6	102
Martin, co., In., U.S.	G4	107
Martin, co., Ky., U.S.	C7	110
Martin, co., Mn., U.S.	G4	116
Martin, co., N.C., U.S.	B5	126
Martin, co., Tx., U.S.	C2	136
Martinez, Ca., U.S.	C2	98
Martinez, Ga., U.S.	C4	103
Martínez de la Torre, Mex.	C5	78
Martinique, dep., N.A.	F12	76
Martinique Passage, strt., N.A.	B7	80
Martin Lake, res., Al., U.S.	C4	94
Martin Point, c., Ak., U.S.	A11	95
Martinsburg, Pa., U.S.	F5	131
Martinsburg, W.V., U.S.	B7	141
Martins Ferry, Oh., U.S.	B5	128
Martinsville, Il., U.S.	D6	106
Martinsville, In., U.S.	F5	107
Martinsville, Va., U.S.	D3	139
Marton, N.Z.	p14	63c
Martos, Spain	I5	16
Martti, Fin.	C13	10
Martuni, Arm.	B11	44
Marutea, atoll, Fr. Poly.	F15	58
Marv Dasht, Iran	D6	42
Marvell, Ar., U.S.	C5	97
Marvine, Mount, mtn., Ut., U.S.	E4	137
Mary, Turk.	F8	26

Name	Map Ref.	Page
Mary, Lake, I., Mn., U.S.	E3	116
Mary, Lake, I., Ms., U.S.	D2	117
Maryborough, Austl.	F5	62
Maryborough, Austl.	H3	62
Maryland, state, U.S.	B4	113
Maryland City, Md., U.S.	B4	113
Maryland Heights, Mo., U.S.	f13	118
Maryland Point, c., Md., U.S.	D3	113
Marys, stm., Nv., U.S.	B6	121
Marys Peak, mtn., Or., U.S.	C3*	130
Marystown, Nf., Can.	E4	88
Marysville, Ca., U.S.	C3	98
Marysville, Ks., U.S.	C7	109
Marysville, Mi., U.S.	F8	115
Marysville, Oh., U.S.	B2	128
Marysville, Pa., U.S.	F8	131
Marysville, Wa., U.S.	A3	140
Maryville, Mo., U.S.	A3	118
Maryville, Tn., U.S.	D10	135
Masai Steppe, plat., Tan.	D7	54
Masaka, Ug.	D6	54
Masalembu Besar, Pulau, i., Indon.	E4	36
Masallı, Azer.	C13	44
Masan, S. Kor.	D13	28
Masasi, Tan.	F7	54
Masaya, Nic.	C2	80
Masbate, Phil.	D8	34
Masbate, i., Phil.	D8	34
Mascarene Basin	J8	64
Mascarene Islands, is., Afr.	g10	57a
Mascarene Plateau	I8	64
Mascasín, Arg.	E4	72
Mascoma, stm., N.H., U.S.	C2	122
Mascoma Lake, I., N.H., U.S.	C2	122
Mascot, Tn., U.S.	C10	135
Mascouche, P.Q., Can.	D4	90
Mascoutah, Il., U.S.	E4	106
Maseru, Leso.	C6	56
Mashapaug Pond, I., Ct., U.S.	A7	100
Mashava, Zimb.	B5	56
Mashhad, Iran	C7	42
Mashra'ar Raqq, Sudan	I10	48
Masi-Manimba, D.R.C.	D3	54
Masindi, Ug.	C6	54
Maṣīrah, i., Oman	F7	38
Maṣīrah, Khalīj, b., Oman	G7	38
Masjed-e Soleymān, Iran	D5	42
Maskinongé, P.Q., Can.	C4	90
Mason, Mi., U.S.	F6	115
Mason, Nv., U.S.	E2	121
Mason, Oh., U.S.	C1	128
Mason, Tx., U.S.	D3	136
Mason, W.V., U.S.	B2	141
Mason, co., Il., U.S.	C4	106
Mason, co., Ky., U.S.	B6	110
Mason, co., Mi., U.S.	D4	115
Mason, co., Tx., U.S.	D3	136
Mason, co., W.V., U.S.	C3	141
Mason, co., Wa., U.S.	B2	140
Mason City, Ia., U.S.	A4	108
Mason City, Il., U.S.	C4	106
Masontown, Pa., U.S.	G2	131
Masontown, W.V., U.S.	B5	141
Masqaṭ, Oman	F7	38
Massa, Italy	B2	18
Massabesic Lake, I., N.H., U.S.	E4	122
Massac, co., Il., U.S.	F5	106
Massachusetts, state, U.S.	B4	114
Massachusetts Bay, b., Ma., U.S.	B6	114
Massacre Lake, I., Nv., U.S.	B2	121
Massangena, Moz.	C5	56
Massapoag Lake, I., Ma., U.S.	h11	114
Massasecum, Lake, I., N.H., U.S.	D3	122
Massawa see Mitsiwa, Erit.	G12	48
Massena, N.Y., U.S.	f10	125
Massenya, Chad	D8	50
Masset, B.C., Can.	C1	85
Massey, On., Can.	A2	89
Massillon, Oh., U.S.	B4	128
Massina, reg., Mali	C4	50
Massinga, Moz.	C6	56
Massive, Mount, mtn., Co., U.S.	B4	99
Maşṭağa, Azer.	B14	44
Masterton, N.Z.	p14	63c
Mastic Beach, N.Y., U.S.	n16	125
Mastung, Pak.	E9	42
Masuda, Japan	D2	31
Masuria see Mazury, reg., Pol.	C6	20
Masury, Oh., U.S.	A5	128
Masvingo, Zimb.	B5	56
Matadi, D.R.C.	E2	54
Matagalpa, Nic.	C2	80
Matagorda, co., Tx., U.S.	E5	136
Matagorda Bay, b., Tx., U.S.	E4	136
Matagorda Island, i., Tx., U.S.	E4	136
Matagorda Peninsula, pen., Tx., U.S.	E5	136
Matala, Ang.	A2	56
Matale, Sri L.	H4	40
Matam, Sen.	C2	50
Matamoras, Pa., U.S.	D12	131
Matamoros, Mex.	B4	78
Matamoros, Mex.	B5	78
Matane, P.Q., Can.	k13	90
Matanuska, stm., Ak., U.S.	g18	95
Matanzas, Cuba	A3	80
Matanzas Inlet, b., Fl., U.S.	C5	102
Matapan, Cape see Taínaron, Ákra, c., Grc.	F9	18
Matara, Sri L.	H4	40
Mataram, Indon.	E5	36
Mataranka, Austl.	C5	60
Mataró, Spain	G8	16
Matatīla Dam, India	D3	40
Matawan, N.J., U.S.	C4	123
Matehuala, Mex.	C4	78
Matera, Italy	D6	18
Matewan, W.V., U.S.	D2	141
Mather, Pa., U.S.	G1	131
Mather Peaks, mts., Wy., U.S.	B5	143
Mathews, La., U.S.	E5	111
Mathews, Va., U.S.	C6	139
Mathews, co., Va., U.S.	C6	139
Mathews, Lake, I., Ca., U.S.	n14	98
Mathis, Tx., U.S.	E4	136
Mathiston, Ms., U.S.	B4	117
Mathura, India	D3	40
Mati, Phil.	E9	34
Matinicus Island, i., Me., U.S.	E3	112
Mato, Cerro, mtn., Ven.	B6	70
Matoaca, Va., U.S.	n18	139
Mato Grosso, Braz.	E5	68
Mato Grosso, state, Braz.	F8	70
Mato Grosso, Planalto do, plat., Braz.	F8	70
Mato Grosso do Sul, state, Braz.	B6	72
Matosinhos, Port.	G2	16
Maṭraḥ, Oman	F7	42
Matsqui, B.C., Can.	f13	85
Matsue, Japan	D14	28
Matsumoto, Japan	C3	31
Matsuyama, Japan	E14	28
Mattamiscontis Lake, I., Me., U.S.	C4	112
Mattamuskeet, Lake, I., N.C., U.S.	B6	126
Mattapoisett, Ma., U.S.	C6	114
Mattaponi, stm., Va., U.S.	C5	139
Mattawa, On., Can.	A6	89
Mattawamkeag, Me., U.S.	C4	112
Mattawamkeag, stm., Me., U.S.	C4	112
Mattawamkeag Lake, I., Me., U.S.	C4	112
Matterhorn (Cervino), mtn., Eur.	A1	18
Matterhorn, mtn., Nv., U.S.	B6	121
Matteson, Il., U.S.	k9	106
Matthews, Mo., U.S.	E8	118
Matthews, N.C., U.S.	B2	126
Matthew Town, Bah.	A5	80
Mattituck, N.Y., U.S.	n16	125
Mattoon, Il., U.S.	D5	106
Mattoon, Lake, res., Il., U.S.	D5	106
Mattydale, N.Y., U.S.	B4	125
Matunuck, R.I., U.S.	G3	132
Maturín, Ven.	B7	70
Matveev Kurgan, Russia	F15	20
Maúa, Moz.	A6	56
Maubeuge, Fr.	B8	16
Maud, Ok., U.S.	B5	129
Mauganj, India	E4	40
Maugansville, Md., U.S.	A2	113
Maug Islands, is., N. Mar. Is.	C12	32
Maui, co., Hi., U.S.	B5	104
Maui, i., Hi., U.S.	C6	104
Mauldin, S.C., U.S.	B3	133
Maumee, Oh., U.S.	A2	128
Maumee, stm., U.S.	A2	128
Maumee Bay, b., U.S.	G7	115
Maumelle, Lake, res., Ar., U.S.	C3	97
Maumere, Indon.	E6	36
Maun, Bots.	B3	56
Mauna Kea, vol., Hi., U.S.	D6	104
Maunaloa, Hi., U.S.	B4	104
Mauna Loa, vol., Hi., U.S.	D6	104
Maunalua Bay, b., Hi., U.S.	g10	104
Maunawili, Hi., U.S.	g10	104
Maupihaa, atoll, Fr. Poly.	F14	58
Maurepas, Lake, I., La., U.S.	D5	111
Maurice, Ia., U.S.	B1	108
Maurice, stm., N.J., U.S.	E2	123
Mauritania, ctry., Afr.	C2	50
Mauritius, ctry., Afr.	f10	57a
Mauritius, i., Mrts.	G11	52
Maury, co., Tn., U.S.	B4	135
Maury City, Tn., U.S.	B2	135
Maury Island, i., Wa., U.S.	f11	140
Mauston, Wi., U.S.	E3	142
Maverick, co., Tx., U.S.	E2	136
Mavinga, Ang.	B3	56
Mawlaik, Myan.	B2	34
Mawlamyine, Myan.	C3	34
Maxinkuckee, Lake, I., In., U.S.	B5	107
Maxixe, Moz.	C6	56
Max Meadows, Va., U.S.	D2	139
Maxton, N.C., U.S.	C3	126
Maxville, On., Can.	B10	89
Maxwell, Ia., U.S.	C4	108
Maxwell Acres, W.V., U.S.	g8	141
Maxwell Air Force Base, mil., Al., U.S.	C3	94
Mayaguana, i., Bah.	D10	76
Mayaguana Passage, strt., Bah.	A5	80
Mayagüez, P.R.	B6	80
Mayang, China	D2	30
Mayenne, Fr.	C6	16
Mayer, Az., U.S.	C3	96
Mayerthorpe, Ab., Can.	C3	84
Mayes, co., Ok., U.S.	A6	129
Mayesville, S.C., U.S.	D7	133
Mayfield, Ky., U.S.	f9	110
Mayfield, Pa., U.S.	C10	131
Mayfield Heights, Oh., U.S.	A4	128
Mayfield Lake, res., Wa., U.S.	C3	140
Mayflower, Ar., U.S.	C3	97
Mayking, Ky., U.S.	C7	110
Maymyo, Myan.	B3	34
Maynard, Ma., U.S.	B5	114
Maynardville, Tn., U.S.	C10	135
Mayne, B.C., Can.	g12	85
Mayo, Md., U.S.	C4	113
Mayo, S.C., U.S.	A4	133
Mayo, stm., Mex.	B3	78
Mayodan, N.C., U.S.	A3	126
Mayo Ndaga, Nig.	E7	50
Mayon Volcano, vol., Phil.	D8	34
Mayotte, dep., Afr.	A8	56
May Park, Or., U.S.	B8	130
Mayport Naval Station, mil., Fl., U.S.	B5	102
Maysville, Ga., U.S.	B3	103
Maysville, Ky., U.S.	B6	110
Maysville, Mo., U.S.	B3	118
Maysville, N.C., U.S.	C5	126
Maysville, Ok., U.S.	C4	129
Mayumba, Gabon	D2	54
Mayville, Mi., U.S.	E7	115
Mayville, N.D., U.S.	B8	127
Mayville, N.Y., U.S.	C1	125
Mayville, Wi., U.S.	E5	142
Maywood, Il., U.S.	k9	106
Maywood, N.J., U.S.	h8	123
Mazabuka, Zam.	B4	56
Mazamet, Fr.	F8	16
Mazara del Vallo, Italy	F4	18
Mazār-e Sharīf, Afg.	C9	42
Mazaruni, stm., Guy.	D7	80
Mazatlán, Mex.	C3	78
Mazatzal Mountains, mts., Az., U.S.	C4	96
Mazatzal Peak, mtn., Az., U.S.	C4	96
Mažeikiai, Lith.	H10	10
Mazeppa, Mn., U.S.	F6	116
Mazomanie, Wi., U.S.	E4	142
Mazon, Il., U.S.	B5	106
Mazury, reg., Pol.	C6	20
Mazyr, Bela.	C10	20
Mbabane, Swaz.	D5	56
M'bahiakro, C. Iv.	E4	50
Mbaïki, C.A.R.	C3	54
Mbaké, Sen.	D1	50
Mbala, Zam.	E6	54
Mbale, Ug.	C6	54
Mbalmayo, Cam.	C2	54
Mbamba Bay, Tan.	F6	54
Mbandaka, D.R.C.	C3	54
Mbanga, Cam.	C1	54
M'banza Congo, Ang.	E2	54
Mbanza-Ngungu (Thysville), D.R.C.	E2	54
Mbarara, Ug.	D6	54
Mbeya, Tan.	E6	54
Mbigou, Gabon	D2	54
Mbinda, Congo	D2	54
Mbini, Eq. Gui.	C1	54
Mboi, D.R.C.	E4	54
Mboki, C.A.R.	B5	54
Mbouda, Cam.	B2	54
Mbour, Sen.	D1	50
Mbout, Maur.	C2	50
Mbuji-Mayi, D.R.C.	E4	54
McAdam, N.B., Can.	D2	87
McAdoo, Pa., U.S.	E9	131
McAfee Peak, mtn., Nv., U.S.	B6	121
McAlester, Ok., U.S.	C6	129
McAlester, Lake, res., Ok., U.S.	B6	129
McAllen, Tx., U.S.	F3	136
McAlmont, Ar., U.S.	h10	97
McAlpine, Md., U.S.	B4	113
McAlpine Lock and Dam, U.S.	H6	107
McArthur, Oh., U.S.	C3	128
McBee, S.C., U.S.	C7	133
McCall, Id., U.S.	E2	105
McCalla, Al., U.S.	g6	94
McCamey, Tx., U.S.	D1	136
McCammon, Id., U.S.	G6	105
McCandless, Pa., U.S.	h13	131
McCartney Mountain, mtn., Mt., U.S.	E4	119
McCaysville, Ga., U.S.	B2	103
McChord Air Force Base, mil., Wa., U.S.	f11	140
McClain, co., Ok., U.S.	C4	129
McCleary, Wa., U.S.	B2	140
McClintock, Mount, mtn., Ant.	D20	67
McCloud, Ca., U.S.	B2	98
McClure, Pa., U.S.	E7	131
McClusky, N.D., U.S.	B5	127
McColl, S.C., U.S.	B8	133
McComas, W.V., U.S.	D3	141
McComb, Ms., U.S.	D3	117
McComb, Oh., U.S.	A2	128
McCone, co., Mt., U.S.	C11	119
McConnell Air Force Base, mil., Ks., U.S.	g12	109
McConnellsburg, Pa., U.S.	G6	131
McConnelsville, Oh., U.S.	C4	128
McCook, Ne., U.S.	D5	120
McCook, co., S.D., U.S.	D8	134
McCordsville, In., U.S.	E6	107
McCormick, S.C., U.S.	D3	133
McCormick, co., S.C., U.S.	D3	133
McCracken, co., Ky., U.S.	e9	110
McCreary, Mb., Can.	D2	86
McCreary, co., Ky., U.S.	D5	110
McCrory, Ar., U.S.	B4	97
McCulloch, co., Tx., U.S.	D3	136
McCullough Mountain, mtn., Nv., U.S.	H6	121
McCurtain, co., Ok., U.S.	C7	129
McDermitt, Nv., U.S.	B4	121
McDonald, co., Mo., U.S.	E3	118
McDonough, Ga., U.S.	C2	103
McDonough, co., Il., U.S.	C3	106
McDougall, Mount, mtn., Wy., U.S.	D2	143
McDowell, Ky., U.S.	C7	110
McDowell, co., N.C., U.S.	f10	126
McDowell, co., W.V., U.S.	D3	141
McDowell Mountains, mts., Az., U.S.	k9	96
McDowell Peak, mtn., Az., U.S.	k9	96
McDuffie, co., Ga., U.S.	C4	103
McElroy Creek, stm., W.V., U.S.	k9	141
Mcensk, Russia	C14	20
McEwen, Tn., U.S.	A4	135
McFarland, Ca., U.S.	E4	98
McFarland, Wi., U.S.	E4	142
McGehee, Ar., U.S.	D4	97
McGill, Nv., U.S.	D7	121
McGrath, Ak., U.S.	C8	95
McGregor, Ia., U.S.	A6	108
McGregor, Tx., U.S.	D4	136
McGregor, stm., B.C., Can.	B7	85
McGregor Lake, I., Ab., Can.	D4	84
McGuire, Mount, mtn., Id., U.S.	D4	105
McGuire Air Force Base, mil., N.J., U.S.	C3	123
McHenry, Il., U.S.	A5	106
McHenry, Md., U.S.	k12	113
McHenry, co., Il., U.S.	A5	106
McHenry, co., N.D., U.S.	A4	127
Mchinji, Mwi.	A5	56
McIntosh, Mn., U.S.	C3	116
McIntosh, co., Ga., U.S.	E5	103
McIntosh, co., N.D., U.S.	C6	127
McIntosh, co., Ok., U.S.	B6	129
McKean, co., Pa., U.S.	C4	131
McKee, Ky., U.S.	C6	110
McKeesport, Pa., U.S.	F2	131
McKees Rocks, Pa., U.S.	F1	131
McKenzie, Tn., U.S.	A3	135
McKenzie, co., N.D., U.S.	B2	127
McKenzie, stm., Or., U.S.	C4	130
McKinley, co., N.M., U.S.	B1	124
McKinley, Mount, mtn., Ak., U.S.	C9	95
McKinleyville, Ca., U.S.	B1	98
McKinney, Tx., U.S.	C4	136
McKinney, Lake, I., Ks., U.S.	E2	109
McKittrick Summit, mtn., Ca., U.S.	E4	98
McLaughlin, S.D., U.S.	B5	134
McLean, Il., U.S.	C4	106
McLean, Va., U.S.	g12	139
McLean, co., Il., U.S.	C4	106
McLean, co., Ky., U.S.	C2	110
McLean, co., N.D., U.S.	B4	127
McLeansboro, Il., U.S.	E5	106
McLennan, Ab., Can.	B2	84
McLennan, co., Tx., U.S.	D4	136
McLeod, co., Mn., U.S.	F4	116
M'Clintock Channel, strt., N.T., Can.	D19	82
McLoud, Ok., U.S.	B4	129
McLoughlin, Mount, mtn., Or., U.S.	D4	130
McLouth, Ks., U.S.	C8	109
McMechen, W.V., U.S.	B4	141
McMillan, Lake, res., N.M., U.S.	E5	124
McMinn, co., Tn., U.S.	D9	135
McMinnville, Or., U.S.	B3	130
McMinnville, Tn., U.S.	D8	135
McMullen, co., Tx., U.S.	E3	136
McMurdo Sound, strt., Ant.	B3	67
McNairy, co., Tn., U.S.	B3	135
McNary Dam, U.S.	B7	130
McNeil, Ar., U.S.	D2	97
McNeil, Mount, mtn., B.C., Can.	B2	85
McNeil Island, i., Wa., U.S.	f10	140
McNeill, Ms., U.S.	E4	117
McPherson, Ks., U.S.	D6	109
McPherson, co., Ks., U.S.	D6	109
McPherson, co., Ne., U.S.	C4	120
McPherson, co., S.D., U.S.	B6	134
McQueeney, Tx., U.S.	h7	136
McRae, Ar., U.S.	B4	97
McRae, Ga., U.S.	D4	103
McRoberts, Ky., U.S.	C7	110
McSherrystown, Pa., U.S.	G7	131
Mdandu, Tan.	E6	54
Mead, Wa., U.S.	B8	140
Mead, Lake, res., U.S.	A1	96
Meade, Ks., U.S.	E3	109
Meade, co., Ks., U.S.	E3	109
Meade, co., Ky., U.S.	C3	110
Meade, co., S.D., U.S.	C3	134
Meade, stm., Ak., U.S.	B8	95
Meaden Peak, mtn., Co., U.S.	A3	99
Meade Peak, mtn., Id., U.S.	G7	105
Meadow, stm., W.V., U.S.	C4	141
Meadow Creek, stm., W.V., U.S.	n14	141
Meadow Lands, Pa., U.S.	F1	131
Meadow Valley Wash, val., Nv., U.S.	F7	121
Meadowview, Va., U.S.	f10	139
Meadville, Pa., U.S.	C1	131
Meaford, On., Can.	C4	89
Meagher, co., Mt., U.S.	D6	119
Meander Creek Reservoir, res., Oh., U.S.	A5	128
Meaux, Fr.	C5	16
Mebane, N.C., U.S.	A3	126
Mecca see Makkah, Sau. Ar.	F3	38
Mecca, Ca., U.S.	F5	98
Mechanic Falls, Me., U.S.	D2	112
Mechanicsburg, Oh., U.S.	B2	128
Mechanicsburg, Pa., U.S.	F7	131
Mechanicsville, Ia., U.S.	C6	108
Mechanicsville, Md., U.S.	D4	113
Mechanicsville, Va., U.S.	C5	139
Mechanicville, N.Y., U.S.	C7	125
Mechant, Lake, I., La., U.S.	E4	111
Mecklenburg, co., N.C., U.S.	B2	126
Mecklenburg, co., Va., U.S.	D4	139
Mecklenburg, hist. reg., Ger.	D12	12
Mecklenburg Bay see Mecklenburger Bucht, b., Ger.	C12	12
Mecklenburger Bucht, b., Ger.	C12	12
Mecosta, co., Mi., U.S.	E5	115
Mecúfi, Moz.	A7	56
Medan, Indon.	C1	36
Medanosa, Punta, c., Arg.	G3	69
Medaryville, In., U.S.	B4	107
Meddybumps Lake, I., Me., U.S.	C5	112
Medellín, Col.	B4	70
Médenine, Tun.	B8	50
Mederdra, Maur.	C1	50
Medfield, Ma., U.S.	h10	114
Medford, Ma., U.S.	B5	114
Medford, Mn., U.S.	F5	116
Medford, Ok., U.S.	A4	129
Medford, Or., U.S.	E4	130
Medford, Wi., U.S.	C3	142
Medford Lakes, N.J., U.S.	D3	123
Medgidia, Rom.	G10	20
Media, Pa., U.S.	G11	131
Mediapolis, Ia., U.S.	C6	108
Mediaș, Rom.	F8	20
Medical Lake, Wa., U.S.	B8	140
Medicine Bow, Wy., U.S.	E6	143
Medicine Bow, stm., Wy., U.S.	E6	143
Medicine Bow Mountains, mts., U.S.	E6	143
Medicine Bow Peak, mtn., Wy., U.S.	E6	143
Medicine Hat, Ab., Can.	D5	84
Medicine Lodge, Ks., U.S.	E5	109
Medicine Lodge, stm., U.S.	E4	109
Medina see Al-Madīnah, Sau. Ar.	F3	38
Medina, N.Y., U.S.	B2	125
Medina, Oh., U.S.	A4	128
Medina, Tn., U.S.	B3	135
Medina, Wa., U.S.	e11	140
Medina, co., Oh., U.S.	A4	128
Medina, co., Tx., U.S.	E3	136
Medina, stm., Tx., U.S.	k7	136
Medina del Campo, Spain	G4	16
Medinīpur, India	E4	40
Mediterranean Sea	D5	14
Mediterraneo, Mar see Mediterranean Sea	D5	14
Mednogorsk, Russia	D10	22
Mednyj, ostrov, i., Russia	D18	26
Medora, In., U.S.	G5	107
Médouneu, Gabon	C2	54
Medvežegorsk, Russia	B5	22
Medveži ostrova, is., Russia	B18	26
Medway, Ma., U.S.	B5	114
Medway, Me., U.S.	C4	112
Medway, stm., N.S., Can.	E5	87
Meekatharra, Austl.	E2	60
Meeker, Co., U.S.	A3	99
Meeker, Ok., U.S.	B5	129
Meeker, co., Mn., U.S.	E4	116
Meelpaeg Lake, res., Nf., Can.	D3	88
Meerut, India	D3	40
Meeteetse, Wy., U.S.	A3	143
Mēga, Eth.	C7	54
Mégantic, Lac, I., P.Q., Can.	D7	90
Mégantic, Mont, mtn., P.Q., Can.	D6	90
Meggett, S.C., U.S.	F7	133

Name	Map Ref.	Page
Meghālaya, prov., India	D6	40
Meghri, Arm.	C12	44
Meharry, Mount, mtn., Austl.	H20	4
Meherrin, stm., U.S.	A4	126
Mehlville, Mo., U.S.	f13	118
Mehtarlām, Afg.	D10	42
Meia Meia, Tan.	E7	54
Meiganga, Cam.	B2	54
Meigs, Ga., U.S.	E2	103
Meigs, co., Oh., U.S.	C3	128
Meigs, co., Tn., U.S.	D9	135
Meiktila, Myan.	B3	34
Meiningen, Ger.	E12	12
Meishan, China	C1	30
Meitan, China	D2	30
Meizhou, China	G11	28
Mejillones, Chile	B2	69
Mékambo, Gabon	C2	54
Mek'elē, Eth.	H12	48
Mékhé, Sen.	C1	50
Meknès, Mor.	D3	48
Mekong, stm., Asia	D5	34
Mékôngk see Mekong, stm., Asia	D5	34
Melaka, Malay.	C2	36
Melanesia, is., Oc.	E10	58
Melbourne, Austl.	H4	62
Melbourne, Ar., U.S.	A4	97
Melbourne, Fl., U.S.	D6	102
Melbourne, Ia., U.S.	C4	108
Melbourne, Ky., U.S.	h14	110
Melbourne Beach, Fl., U.S.	D6	102
Melcher, Ia., U.S.	C4	108
Melchor Múzquiz, Mex.	B4	78
Melenki, Russia	C7	22
Meleuz, Russia	D10	22
Mélèzes, Rivière aux, stm., P.Q., Can.	g12	90
Melfi, Chad	D8	50
Melilla, Sp. N. Afr.	J5	16
Melipilla, Chile	E3	72
Melita, Mb., Can.	E1	86
Melitopol', Ukr.	F13	20
Mellen, Wi., U.S.	B3	142
Mellette, co., S.D., U.S.	D5	134
Melo, Ur.	E7	72
Melocheville, P.Q., Can.	q19	90
Melos see Mílos, i., Grc.	F10	18
Melrhir, Chott, l., Alg.	D6	48
Melrose, Austl.	F3	60
Melrose, Ct., U.S.	C4	102
Melrose, Ma., U.S.	B5	114
Melrose, Mn., U.S.	E4	116
Melrose, N.M., U.S.	C6	124
Melton Hill Lake, res., Tn., U.S.	D9	135
Meluco, Moz.	A6	56
Melun, Fr.	C8	16
Melvern Lake, res., Ks., U.S.	D8	109
Melville, La., U.S.	D4	111
Melville, Cape, c., Austl.	C3	62
Melville, Lake, l., Nf., Can.	B2	88
Melville Island, i., Austl.	C5	60
Melville Sound, strt., N.T., Can.	E18	82
Melvin, Ky., U.S.	C7	110
Memboro, Indon.	E5	36
Memel see Klaipėda, Lith.	I9	10
Memmingen, Ger.	G11	12
Mempawah, Indon.	C3	36
Memphis, Fl., U.S.	p10	102
Memphis, Mi., U.S.	F8	115
Memphis, Mo., U.S.	A5	118
Memphis, Tn., U.S.	B2	135
Memphis, Tx., U.S.	B2	136
Memphis Naval Air Station, mil., Tn., U.S.	B2	135
Mena, Ukr.	D12	20
Mena, Ar., U.S.	C1	97
Menahga, Mn., U.S.	D3	116
Ménaka, Mali	C5	50
Menan, Id., U.S.	F7	105
Menands, N.Y., U.S.	C7	125
Menard, Tx., U.S.	D3	136
Menard, co., Il., U.S.	C4	106
Menard, co., Tx., U.S.	D3	136
Menasha, Wi., U.S.	D5	142
Mende, Fr.	E8	16
Mendeleyev Ridge	E4	144
Mendenhall, Ms., U.S.	D4	117
Mendham, N.J., U.S.	B3	123
Mendī, Eth.	B7	54
Mendi, Pap. N. Gui.	H11	32
Mendocino, co., Ca., U.S.	C2	98
Mendocino Fracture Zone	E23	64
Mendon, Il., U.S.	C2	106
Mendon, Mi., U.S.	F5	115
Mendon, Ut., U.S.	B4	137
Mendota, Ca., U.S.	D3	98
Mendota, Il., U.S.	B4	106
Mendota, Lake, l., Wi., U.S.	E4	142
Mendoza, Arg.	E4	72
Mene Grande, Ven.	D5	80
Menemen, Tur.	C2	44
Mengcheng, China	C4	30
Menggala, Indon.	D3	36
Menghai, China	B4	34
Mengjiawan, China	B2	30
Mengzi, China	G8	28
Menifee, co., Ky., U.S.	C6	110
Menindee, Austl.	G3	62
Menlo Park, Ca., U.S.	k8	98
Menno, S.D., U.S.	D8	134
Menominee, Mi., U.S.	C3	115
Menominee, co., Mi., U.S.	C3	115
Menominee, co., Wi., U.S.	C5	142
Menominee, stm., U.S.	C6	142
Menominee Indian Reservation, Wi., U.S.	C5	142
Menomonee, stm., Wi., U.S.	m11	142
Menomonee Falls, Wi., U.S.	E5	142
Menomonie, Wi., U.S.	D2	142
Menongue, Ang.	A2	56
Menor, Mar, b., Spain	I6	16
Menorca (Minorca), i., Spain	G9	16
Mentawai, Kepulauan, is., Indon.	D1	36
Mentawai, Selat, strt., Indon.	D1	36
Mentone, In., U.S.	B5	107
Mentor, Oh., U.S.	A4	128
Mentor-on-the-Lake, Oh., U.S.	A4	128
Menzel Bourguiba, Tun.	F2	18
Menzies, Austl.	F3	60
Meoqui, Mex.	B3	78
Meppen, Ger.	D10	12
Mequinenza, Embalse de, res., Spain	G6	16
Mequon, Wi., U.S.	E6	142
Merambéllou, Kólpos, b., Grc.	G10	18
Meramec, stm., Mo., U.S.	C7	118
Merano, Italy	A3	18
Merasheen Island, i., Nf., Can.	E4	88
Merauke, Indon.	H11	32
Meraux, La., U.S.	k12	111
Mercāra, India	G3	40
Merced, Ca., U.S.	D3	98
Merced, co., Ca., U.S.	D3	98
Merced, stm., Ca., U.S.	D3	98
Mercedes, Arg.	D6	72
Mercedes, Tx., U.S.	F4	136
Mercedes, Ur.	E6	72
Mercer, Pa., U.S.	D1	131
Mercer, Wi., U.S.	B3	142
Mercer, co., Il., U.S.	B3	106
Mercer, co., Ky., U.S.	C5	110
Mercer, co., Mo., U.S.	A4	118
Mercer, co., N.D., U.S.	B4	127
Mercer, co., N.J., U.S.	C3	123
Mercer, co., Oh., U.S.	B1	128
Mercer, co., Pa., U.S.	D1	131
Mercer, co., W.V., U.S.	D3	141
Mercer Island, Wa., U.S.	B3	140
Mercer Island, i., Wa., U.S.	e11	140
Mercersburg, Pa., U.S.	G6	131
Mercerville, N.J., U.S.	C3	123
Mercier, P.Q., Can.	D4	90
Meredith, N.H., U.S.	C3	122
Meredith, Lake, l., Co., U.S.	C7	99
Meredith, Lake, res., Tx., U.S.	B2	136
Meredosia, Il., U.S.	D3	106
Meredosia Lake, l., Il., U.S.	D3	106
Mereeg, Som.	J14	48
Merefa, Ukr.	E14	20
Merenkurkku (Norra Kvarken), strt., Eur.	E9	10
Mergui, Myan.	D3	34
Mergui Archipelago, is., Myan.	D3	34
Meriç (Évros) (Marica), stm., Eur.	D11	18
Mérida, Mex.	C7	78
Mérida, Spain	H3	16
Mérida, Ven.	B5	70
Mérida, Cordillera de, mts., Ven.	B5	70
Meriden, Ct., U.S.	C4	100
Meriden, Ks., U.S.	C8	109
Meridian, Id., U.S.	F2	105
Meridian, Ms., U.S.	C5	117
Meridian, Pa., U.S.	E2	131
Meridian, Tx., U.S.	D4	136
Meridian Hills, In., U.S.	k10	107
Meridian Naval Air Station, mil., Ms., U.S.	C5	117
Meridianville, Al., U.S.	A3	94
Merikarvia, Fin.	F9	10
Merín, Laguna see Mirim, Lagoa, b., S.A.	E7	72
Meriwether, co., Ga., U.S.	C2	103
Merkel, Tx., U.S.	C2	136
Merlin, On., Can.	E2	89
Mermentau, La., U.S.	D3	111
Mermentau, stm., La., U.S.	E3	111
Meron, Har, mtn., Isr.	F6	44
Meron, Mount see Meron, Har, mtn., Isr.	F6	44
Merredin, Austl.	G2	60
Merriam, Ks., U.S.	k16	109
Merrick, co., Ne., U.S.	C7	120
Merrickville, On., Can.	C9	89
Merrill, Ia., U.S.	B1	108
Merrill, Mi., U.S.	E6	115
Merrill, Or., U.S.	E5	130
Merrill, Wi., U.S.	C4	142
Merrillville, In., U.S.	B3	107
Merrimac, Ma., U.S.	A5	114
Merrimack, N.H., U.S.	E4	122
Merrimack, co., N.H., U.S.	D3	122
Merrimack, stm., U.S.	A5	114
Merritt, B.C., Can.	D7	85
Merritt Island, Fl., U.S.	D6	102
Merritt Reservoir, res., Ne., U.S.	B5	120
Merrymeeting Lake, l., N.H., U.S.	D4	122
Merryville, La., U.S.	D2	111
Mersa Matruh, Egypt	D10	48
Mersing, Malay.	C2	36
Merthyr Tydfil, Wales, U.K.	E5	12
Merton, Wi., U.S.	m11	142
Meru, Kenya	C7	54
Merwin, Lake, res., Wa., U.S.	C3	140
Merzifon, Tur.	B6	44
Mesa, Az., U.S.	D4	96
Mesa, co., Co., U.S.	C2	99
Mesabi Range, hills, Mn., U.S.	C6	116
Mesa Mountain, mtn., Co., U.S.	D4	99
Mesa Verde National Park, Co., U.S.	D2	99
Mescalero, N.M., U.S.	D4	124
Mescalero Indian Reservation, N.M., U.S.	D4	124
Meschede, Ger.	E11	12
Meshgīn Shahr, Iran	C12	44
Mesilla, N.M., U.S.	E3	124
Mesolóngion, Grc.	E8	18
Mesopotamia, hist. reg., Asia	D4	42
Mesquite, N.M., U.S.	E3	124
Mesquite, Nv., U.S.	G7	121
Mesquite, Tx., U.S.	n10	136
Messalonskee Lake, l., Me., U.S.	D3	112
Messina, Italy	E5	18
Messina, S. Afr.	C5	56
Messina, Stretto di, strt., Italy	E5	18
Messiniakós Kólpos, b., Grc.	F9	18
Mestghanem, Alg.	C4	48
Mestre, Italy	B4	18
Meta, stm., S.A.	B5	70
Métabetchouan, P.Q., Can.	A6	90
Métabetchouane, stm., P.Q., Can.	A5	90
Metairie, La., U.S.	k11	111
Metamora, Il., U.S.	C4	106
Metán, Arg.	D5	72
Metapán, El Sal.	C2	80
Metapontum, hist., Italy	D6	18
Metcalfe, On., Can.	B9	89
Metcalfe, Ms., U.S.	B2	117
Metcalfe, co., Ky., U.S.	C4	110
Metedeconk, North Branch, stm., N.J., U.S.	C4	123
Metedeconk, South Branch, stm., N.J., U.S.	C3	123
Meteghan, N.S., Can.	E3	87
Meteghan River, N.S., Can.	E3	87
Metéora, Grc.	E8	18
Meteor Crater, crat., Az., U.S.	C4	96
Methow, stm., Wa., U.S.	A5	140
Methuen, Ma., U.S.	A5	114
Metlakatla, Ak., U.S.	D13	95
Metonga, Lake, l., Wi., U.S.	C5	142
Metro, Indon.	E3	36
Metropolis, Il., U.S.	F5	106
Mettawee, stm., U.S.	E2	138
Metter, Ga., U.S.	D4	103
Metuchen, N.J., U.S.	B4	123
Metz, Fr.	C10	16
Metzger, Or., U.S.	h12	130
Meulaboh, Indon.	C1	36
Meuse (Maas), stm., Eur.	C9	16
Mexia, Tx., U.S.	D4	136
Mexia, Lake, res., Tx., U.S.	D4	136
Mexiana, Ilha, i., Braz.	A2	74
Mexicali, Mex.	A1	78
Mexican Basin	F4	66
Mexico, In., U.S.	C5	107
Mexico, Me., U.S.	D2	112
Mexico, Mo., U.S.	B6	118
México, state, Mex.	D4	78
Mexico, ctry., N.A.	C4	78
Mexico, Gulf of, b., N.A.	F10	92
Mexico City see Ciudad de México, Mex.	D5	78
Meyersdale, Pa., U.S.	G3	131
Meyísti, i., Grc.	F12	18
Meymaneh, Afg.	C8	42
Mezcala, Mex.	D5	78
Mezdurečenskij, Russia	C12	22
Mezen', Russia	C6	26
Mezen', stm., Russia	C6	26
Mezenskaja guba, b., Russia	A7	22
Mezőtúr, Hung.	F6	20
Mfangano Island, i., Kenya	D6	54
Mgeta, Tan.	E7	54
M'Goun, Irhil, mtn., Mor.	E2	14
Mhow, India	D6	40
Miahuatlán de Porfirio Díaz, Mex.	D5	78
Miajadas, Spain	H4	16
Miaméré, C.A.R.	B3	54
Miami, Az., U.S.	D5	96
Miami, Fl., U.S.	G6	102
Miami, Ok., U.S.	A7	129
Miami, co., In., U.S.	C5	107
Miami, co., Ks., U.S.	D9	109
Miami, co., Oh., U.S.	B1	128
Miami Beach, Fl., U.S.	G6	102
Miami Canal, Fl., U.S.	F6	102
Miami International Airport, Fl., U.S.	G6	102
Miamisburg, Oh., U.S.	C1	128
Miami Shores, Fl., U.S.	G6	102
Miami Springs, Fl., U.S.	G6	102
Mianchi, China	C3	30
Miandrivazo, Madag.	B8	56
Mīāndoāb, Iran	D12	44
Mianeh, Iran	C5	42
Mianning, China	A4	34
Mianus Reservoir, res., U.S.	E1	100
Miānwāli, Pak.	D10	42
Mianyang, China	E8	28
Mianzhu, China	C1	30
Miass, Russia	D8	26
Mica Mountain, mtn., Az., U.S.	E5	96
Micco, Fl., U.S.	E6	102
Miccosukee, Lake, res., Fl., U.S.	B2	102
Michalovce, Slvk.	E6	20
Michelson, Mount, mtn., Ak., U.S.	B11	95
Michie, Tn., U.S.	B3	135
Michigamme, Lake, l., Mi., U.S.	B2	115
Michigamme Reservoir, res., Mi., U.S.	B2	115
Michigan, state, U.S.	E6	115
Michigan, stm., Co., U.S.	A4	99
Michigan, Lake, l., U.S.	C10	92
Michigan Center, Mi., U.S.	F6	115
Michigan City, In., U.S.	A4	107
Michigan Island, i., Wi., U.S.	B3	142
Michoacán, state, Mex.	D4	78
Micronesia, is., Oc.	C9	58
Micronesia, Federated States of, ctry., Oc.	D8	58
Mičurinsk, Russia	C16	20
Mid-Atlantic Ridge	F9	66
Middelburg, S. Afr.	E3	56
Middelburg, S. Afr.	D4	56
Middelfart, Den.	I3	10
Middle, stm., Ia., U.S.	C3	108
Middle, stm., Mn., U.S.	B2	116
Middle America Trench	G28	64
Middle Andaman, i., India	G6	40
Middleboro (Middleborough Center), Ma., U.S.	C6	114
Middlebourne, W.V., U.S.	B4	141
Middleburg, Fl., U.S.	B5	102
Middleburg, Pa., U.S.	E7	131
Middleburg Heights, Oh., U.S.	h9	128
Middlebury, Ct., U.S.	C3	100
Middlebury, In., U.S.	A6	107
Middlebury, Vt., U.S.	C2	138
Middle Caicos, i., T./C. Is.	B8	80
Middlefield, Ct., U.S.	C5	100
Middlefield, Oh., U.S.	A4	128
Middle Island Creek, stm., W.V., U.S.	B3	141
Middle Nodaway, stm., Ia., U.S.	C3	108
Middle Park, val., Co., U.S.	A4	99
Middle Patuxent, stm., Md., U.S.	B4	113
Middleport, N.Y., U.S.	B2	125
Middleport, Oh., U.S.	C3	128
Middle Raccoon, stm., Ia., U.S.	C3	108
Middle River, Md., U.S.	B5	113
Middlesboro, Ky., U.S.	D6	110
Middlesbrough, Eng., U.K.	C6	12
Middlesex, N.C., U.S.	B4	126
Middlesex, N.J., U.S.	B4	123
Middlesex, co., Ct., U.S.	D5	100
Middlesex, co., Ma., U.S.	A5	114
Middlesex, co., N.J., U.S.	C4	123
Middlesex, co., Va., U.S.	C6	139
Middlesex Fells Reservation, Ma., U.S.	g11	114
Middleton, N.S., Can.	E4	87
Middleton, Id., U.S.	F2	105
Middleton, Ma., U.S.	A5	114
Middleton, Wi., U.S.	E4	142
Middletown, Ca., U.S.	C2	98
Middletown, Ct., U.S.	C5	100
Middletown, De., U.S.	C3	101
Middletown, In., U.S.	D6	107
Middletown, Ky., U.S.	g11	110
Middletown, Md., U.S.	B2	113
Middletown, N.J., U.S.	C4	123
Middletown, N.Y., U.S.	D6	125
Middletown, Oh., U.S.	C1	128
Middletown, Pa., U.S.	F8	131
Middletown, R.I., U.S.	E5	132
Middletown, Va., U.S.	A4	139
Middleville, Mi., U.S.	F5	115
Midfield, Al., U.S.	g7	94
Mid-Indian Basin	I10	64
Mid-Indian Ridge	I9	64
Midland, On., Can.	C5	89
Midland, Mi., U.S.	E6	115
Midland, N.C., U.S.	B2	126
Midland, Pa., U.S.	E1	131
Midland, Tx., U.S.	D1	136
Midland, co., Mi., U.S.	E6	115
Midland, co., Tx., U.S.	D1	136
Midland City, Al., U.S.	D4	94
Midland Park, Ks., U.S.	g12	109
Midland Park, N.J., U.S.	B4	123
Midland Park, S.C., U.S.	k11	133
Midlothian, Il., U.S.	k9	106
Midlothian, Tx., U.S.	C4	136
Midongy Atsimo, Madag.	C8	56
Mid-Pacific Mountains	F18	64
Midvale, Ut., U.S.	C4	137
Midville, Ga., U.S.	D4	103
Midway, B.C., Can.	E8	85
Midway, De., U.S.	F5	101
Midway, Ky., U.S.	B5	110
Midway, Pa., U.S.	G7	131
Midway, Ut., U.S.	C4	137
Midway Islands, dep., Oc.	B12	58
Midwest, Wy., U.S.	C6	143
Midwest City, Ok., U.S.	B4	129
Midyat, Tur.	D9	44
Międzyrzecz, Pol.	C3	20
Miekojärvi, l., Fin.	C11	10
Mielec, Pol.	D6	20
Mieres, Spain	F4	16
Mifflin, co., Pa., U.S.	E6	131
Mifflinburg, Pa., U.S.	E7	131
Mifflinville, Pa., U.S.	D9	131
Miguel Alemán, Presa, res., Mex.	D5	78
Miguel Auza, Mex.	C4	78
Mihajlov, Russia	B15	20
Mihajlovka, Russia	D6	26
Mikasa, Japan	C16	28
Mikíni, hist., Grc.	F9	18
Mikindani, Tan.	F8	54
Mikkeli, Fin.	F12	10
Míkonos, i., Grc.	F10	18
Mikumi, Tan.	E7	54
Mikun', Russia	B9	22
Milaca, Mn., U.S.	E5	116
Milagro, Ec.	D4	70
Milam, co., Tx., U.S.	D4	136
Milan see Milano, Italy	B2	18
Milan, Ga., U.S.	D3	103
Milan, Il., U.S.	B3	106
Milan, In., U.S.	F7	107
Milan, Mi., U.S.	F7	115
Milan, Mo., U.S.	A4	118
Milan, N.M., U.S.	B2	124
Milan, Oh., U.S.	A3	128
Milan, Tn., U.S.	B3	135
Milange, Moz.	B6	56
Milano (Milan), Italy	B2	18
Milâs, Tur.	D2	44
Milazzo, Italy	E5	18
Milbank, S.D., U.S.	B9	134
Mildmay, On., Can.	C3	89
Mildura, Austl.	G3	62
Mile, China	G8	28
Milesburg, Pa., U.S.	E6	131
Miles City, Mt., U.S.	D11	119
Milestone, Sk., Can.	G3	91
Milet (Miletus), hist., Tur.	D2	44
Miletus see Milet, hist., Tur.	D2	44
Milford, Ct., U.S.	E3	100
Milford, De., U.S.	E4	101
Milford, Ia., U.S.	A2	108
Milford, Il., U.S.	C6	106
Milford, In., U.S.	B6	107
Milford, Ma., U.S.	B4	114
Milford, Me., U.S.	D4	112
Milford, Mi., U.S.	F7	115
Milford, Ne., U.S.	D8	120
Milford, N.H., U.S.	E3	122
Milford, Oh., U.S.	C1	128
Milford, Pa., U.S.	D12	131
Milford, Ut., U.S.	E2	137
Milford Haven, Wales, U.K.	E4	12
Milford Lake, res., Ks., U.S.	C6	109
Milford Station, N.S., Can.	D6	87
Milḥ, Baḥr al-, res., Iraq	F10	44
Mililani Town, Hi., U.S.	g9	104
Milk, stm., N.A.	B6	92
Mil'kovo, Russia	D17	26
Milk River, Ab., Can.	E4	84
Mill, stm., Ma., U.S.	h9	114
Millard, co., Ut., U.S.	D2	137
Millau, Fr.	E8	16
Millbrae, Ca., U.S.	h8	98
Millbrook, On., Can.	C6	89
Millbrook, Al., U.S.	C3	94
Mill Brook, stm., Vt., U.S.	B5	138
Millburn, N.J., U.S.	B4	123
Millbury, Ma., U.S.	B4	114
Millbury, Oh., U.S.	e7	128
Mill City, Or., U.S.	C4	130
Millcreek, Ut., U.S.	C4	137
Mill Creek, W.V., U.S.	C5	141
Mill Creek, stm., N.J., U.S.	D4	123
Mill Creek, stm., Oh., U.S.	B2	128
Mill Creek, stm., Tn., U.S.	g10	135
Mill Creek, stm., W.V., U.S.	m13	141
Mill Creek, stm., W.V., U.S.	C3	141
Millcreek Township, Pa., U.S.	B1	131
Milledgeville, Ga., U.S.	C3	103
Milledgeville, Il., U.S.	B4	106
Mille Îles, Rivière des, stm., P.Q., Can.	p19	90
Mille Lacs, co., Mn., U.S.	E5	116
Mille Lacs Indian Reservation, Mn., U.S.	D5	116
Mille Lacs Lake, l., Mn., U.S.	D5	116
Millen, Ga., U.S.	D5	103
Miller, S.D., U.S.	C7	134
Miller, co., Ar., U.S.	D2	97
Miller, co., Ga., U.S.	E2	103
Miller, co., Mo., U.S.	C5	118
Miller, Mount, mtn., Ak., U.S.	C11	95
Millerovo, Russia	E7	22
Miller Peak, mtn., Az., U.S.	F5	96
Miller Run, stm., Vt., U.S.	B4	138

Name	Map Ref.	Page
Millers, stm., Ma., U.S.	A3	114
Millersburg, In., U.S.	A6	107
Millersburg, Ky., U.S.	B5	110
Millersburg, Oh., U.S.	B4	128
Millersburg, Pa., U.S.	E8	131
Millersport, Oh., U.S.	C3	128
Millersville, Pa., U.S.	F9	131
Millet, Ab., Can.	C4	84
Mill Hall, Pa., U.S.	D7	131
Millicent, Austl.	H3	62
Milliken, Co., U.S.	A6	99
Millington, Mi., U.S.	E7	115
Millington, Tn., U.S.	B2	135
Millinocket, Me., U.S.	C4	112
Millinocket Lake, l., Me., U.S.	C4	112
Millinocket Lake, l., Me., U.S.	B4	112
Millis, Ma., U.S.	B5	114
Millport, Al., U.S.	B1	94
Millry, Al., U.S.	D1	94
Mills, Wy., U.S.	D6	143
Mills, co., Ia., U.S.	C2	108
Mills, co., Tx., U.S.	D3	136
Millsboro, De., U.S.	F4	101
Millsboro, Pa., U.S.	G1	131
Millstadt, Il., U.S.	E3	106
Millstone, stm., N.J., U.S.	C4	123
Milltown, In., U.S.	H5	107
Milltown, N.J., U.S.	C4	123
Milltown, Wi., U.S.	C1	142
Milltown [-Head of Bay d'Espoir], Nf., Can.	E4	88
Millvale, Pa., U.S.	k14	131
Mill Valley, Ca., U.S.	D2	98
Millville, Ma., U.S.	B4	114
Millville, N.J., U.S.	E2	123
Millville, Pa., U.S.	D9	131
Millville, Ut., U.S.	B4	137
Millville Lake, N.H., U.S.	E4	122
Millwood, Wa., U.S.	g14	140
Millwood Lake, res., Ar., U.S.	D1	97
Milner Dam, Id., U.S.	G5	105
Milnor, N.D., U.S.	C8	127
Milo, Ia., U.S.	C4	108
Milo, Me., U.S.	C4	112
Mílos, Grc.	F10	18
Mílos, i., Grc.	F10	18
Milparinka, Austl.	F3	62
Milroy, In., U.S.	F7	107
Milroy, Pa., U.S.	E6	131
Milstead, Ga., U.S.	C3	103
Milton, On., Can.	D5	89
Milton, De., U.S.	E4	101
Milton, Fl., U.S.	u14	102
Milton, In., U.S.	E7	107
Milton, Ma., U.S.	B5	114
Milton, N.H., U.S.	D5	122
Milton, Pa., U.S.	D8	131
Milton, Vt., U.S.	B2	138
Milton, W.V., U.S.	C2	141
Milton, Wa., U.S.	f11	140
Milton, Wi., U.S.	F5	142
Milton, Lake, l., Oh., U.S.	A4	128
Miltona, Lake, l., Mn., U.S.	D3	116
Milton-Freewater, Or., U.S.	B8	130
Milton Keynes, Eng., U.K.	D6	12
Milton Reservoir, res., Co., U.S.	A6	99
Milverton, On., Can.	D4	89
Milwaukee, Wi., U.S.	E6	142
Milwaukee, co., Wi., U.S.	E6	142
Milwaukee, stm., Wi., U.S.	m12	142
Milwaukie, Or., U.S.	B4	130
Mims, Fl., U.S.	D6	102
Min, stm., China	F8	28
Min, stm., China	D4	30
Mina, Nv., U.S.	E3	121
Mīnā' al-Aḥmadī, Kuw.	E5	42
Mīnāb, Iran	E7	42
Minahasa, pen., Indon.	C6	36
Minami-Tori-shima, i., Japan	F18	64
Minas, Ur.	E6	72
Minas Basin, b., N.S., Can.	D5	87
Minas Channel, strt., N.S., Can.	D5	87
Minas Gerais, state, Braz.	E2	74
Minatare, Ne., U.S.	C2	120
Minatitlán, Mex.	D6	78
Minbya, Myan.	B2	34
Minco, Ok., U.S.	B4	129
Mindanao, i., Phil.	E8	34
Mindanao Sea see Bohol Sea, Phil.	E8	34
Mindelo, C.V.	g10	50a
Minden, Ger.	D11	12
Minden, La., U.S.	B2	111
Minden, Ne., U.S.	D7	120
Minden, Nv., U.S.	E2	121
Minden, W.V., U.S.	D3	141
Mindoro, i., Phil.	D8	34
Mindoro Strait, strt., Phil.	D8	34
Mine Hill, N.J., U.S.	B3	123
Mineiros, Braz.	B7	72
Mineola, N.Y., U.S.	E7	125
Mineola, Tx., U.S.	C5	136
Miner, Mo., U.S.	E8	118
Miner, co., S.D., U.S.	D8	134
Mineral, co., Co., U.S.	D4	99
Mineral, co., Mt., U.S.	C1	119
Mineral, co., Nv., U.S.	E3	121
Mineral, co., W.V., U.S.	B6	141
Mineral Point, Wi., U.S.	F3	142
Mineral Springs, Ar., U.S.	D2	97
Mineral Wells, Tx., U.S.	C3	136
Minersville, Pa., U.S.	E9	131
Minersville, Ut., U.S.	E3	137
Minerva, Oh., U.S.	B4	128
Minetto, N.Y., U.S.	B4	125
Minfeng, China	D4	28
Mingäçevir, Azer.	B12	44
Mingäçevir su anbarı, res., Azer.	B12	44
Mingechaur Reservoir see Mingäçevir su anbarı, res., Azer.	B12	44
Mingenew, Austl.	F2	60
Mingo, co., W.V., U.S.	D2	141
Mingo Junction, Oh., U.S.	B5	128
Minho (Miño), stm., Eur.	G2	16
Minicoy Island, i., India	H2	40
Minidoka, co., Id., U.S.	G5	105
Minidoka Dam, Id., U.S.	G5	105
Minier, Il., U.S.	C4	106
Minisink Island, i., N.J., U.S.	A3	123
Minitonas, Mb., Can.	C1	86
Minle, China	D8	28
Minna, Nig.	E6	50
Minneapolis, Ks., U.S.	C6	109
Minneapolis, Mn., U.S.	F5	116
Minnedosa, Mb., Can.	D2	86
Minnedosa, stm., Mb., Can.	D1	86
Minnehaha, co., S.D., U.S.	D9	134
Minneola, Ks., U.S.	E3	109
Minneota, Mn., U.S.	F3	116
Minnesota, state, U.S.	E4	116
Minnesota, stm., Mn., U.S.	F2	116
Minnesota Lake, Mn., U.S.	G5	116
Minnetonka, Mn., U.S.	n12	116
Minnetonka, Lake, l., Mn., U.S.	n11	116
Minnewaska, Lake, l., Mn., U.S.	E3	116
Miño (Minho), stm., Eur.	F3	16
Minocqua, Wi., U.S.	C4	142
Minonk, Il., U.S.	C4	106
Minooka, Il., U.S.	B5	106
Minot, N.D., U.S.	A4	127
Minot Air Force Base, mil., N.D., U.S.	A4	127
Minqin, China	B1	30
Minqing, China	D4	30
Minquadale, De., U.S.	i7	101
Minsk, Bela.	B9	20
Minster, Oh., U.S.	B1	128
Mint Hill, N.C., U.S.	B2	126
Minto, N.B., Can.	C3	87
Minturn, Co., U.S.	B4	99
Minusinsk, Russia	D11	26
Minute Man National Historical Park, Ma., U.S.	g10	114
Minvoul, Gabon	C2	54
Minxian, China	E8	28
Minya see El-Minya, Egypt	E11	48
Mio, Mi., U.S.	D6	115
Mīrābād, Afg.	D8	42
Mirabel, P.Q., Can.	D3	90
Mirabella, Gulf of see Merambéllou, Kólpos, b., Grc.	G10	18
Mirador, Braz.	E11	70
Miraflores, Col.	B5	70
Miraj, India	F2	40
Miramar, Fl., U.S.	s13	102
Miramar Naval Air Station, mil., Ca., U.S.	F5	98
Miramichi Bay, b., N.B., Can.	B5	87
Miranda, stm., Braz.	B6	72
Miranda de Ebro, Spain	F5	16
Mirbāṭ, Oman	G6	38
Miri, Malay.	C4	36
Miria, Niger	D6	50
Mirim, Lagoa (Merín, Laguna), b., S.A.	E7	72
Mirnyj, Russia	C13	26
Mīrpur, Pak.	D10	42
Mīrpur Khās, Pak.	E9	42
Mirror Lake, l., N.H., U.S.	C4	122
Mirtóön Pélagos, Grc.	F9	18
Mirzāpur, India	D4	40
Miscouche, P.E., Can.	C6	87
Miscou Island, i., N.B., Can.	B5	87
Miscou Point, c., N.B., Can.	A5	87
Misenheimer, N.C., U.S.	B2	126
Mishan, China	B14	28
Mishawaka, In., U.S.	A5	107
Misheguk Mountain, mtn., Ak., U.S.	B7	95
Mishicot, Wi., U.S.	D6	142
Miskitos, Cayos, is., Nic.	C3	80
Miskolc, Hung.	E6	20
Misool, Pulau, i., Indon.	D8	36
Mişrātah, Libya	D8	48
Missaukee, co., Mi., U.S.	D5	115
Missaukee, Lake, l., Mi., U.S.	D5	115
Mission, Ks., U.S.	m16	109
Mission, S.D., U.S.	D5	134
Mission, Tx., U.S.	F3	136
Mission Range, mts., Mt., U.S.	C3	119
Mission Viejo, Ca., U.S.	n13	98
Missisquoi, stm., Vt., U.S.	B3	138
Missisquoi Bay, b., Vt., U.S.	A2	138
Mississauga, On., Can.	D5	89
Mississinewa, stm., U.S.	D7	107
Mississinewa Lake, res., In., U.S.	C6	107
Mississippi, co., Ar., U.S.	B5	97
Mississippi, co., Mo., U.S.	E8	118
Mississippi, state, U.S.	C4	117
Mississippi, stm., U.S.	E9	92
Mississippi Delta, La., U.S.	E6	111
Mississippi Sound, strt., U.S.	E5	117
Mississippi State, Ms., U.S.	B5	117
Missoula, Mt., U.S.	D2	119
Missoula, co., Mt., U.S.	D2	119
Missouri, state, U.S.	C5	118
Missouri, stm., U.S.	D9	92
Missouri City, Tx., U.S.	r14	136
Missouri Valley, Ia., U.S.	C2	108
Mistassini, Lac, l., P.Q., Can.	h12	90
Mistassini, stm., P.Q., Can.	h12	90
Misti, Volcán, vol., Peru	G5	70
Mita, Punta de, c., Mex.	C3	78
Mitchell, Austl.	F4	62
Mitchell, On., Can.	D3	89
Mitchell, Il., U.S.	E3	106
Mitchell, In., U.S.	G5	107
Mitchell, Ne., U.S.	C2	120
Mitchell, S.D., U.S.	D7	134
Mitchell, co., Ga., U.S.	E2	103
Mitchell, co., Ia., U.S.	A5	108
Mitchell, co., Ks., U.S.	C5	109
Mitchell, co., N.C., U.S.	e10	126
Mitchell, co., Tx., U.S.	C2	136
Mitchell, stm., Austl.	D3	62
Mitchell, Lake, l., Mi., U.S.	D5	115
Mitchell, Lake, res., Al., U.S.	C3	94
Mitchell, Mount, mtn., N.C., U.S.	f10	126
Mitchell Island, i., La., U.S.	E6	111
Mitchellville, Ia., U.S.	C4	108
Mitilíni, Grc.	E11	18
Mitkof Island, i., Ak., U.S.	m23	95
Mito, Japan	C4	31
Mitsiwa, Erit.	G12	48
Mitú, Col.	C5	70
Mitumba, Monts, mts., D.R.C.	E5	54
Mitwaba, D.R.C.	E5	54
Mitzic, Gabon	C2	54
Miyake-jima, i., Japan	E15	28
Miyako, Japan	D16	28
Miyako-jima, i., Japan	B9	34
Miyakonojō, Japan	E14	28
Miyazaki, Japan	E14	28
Miyazu, Japan	D15	28
Miyoshi, Japan	D2	31
Miyun, China	A4	30
Mīzan Teferī, Eth.	B7	54
Mizdah, Libya	D7	48
Mizen Head, c., Ire.	E2	12
Mizhi, China	B3	30
Mizoram, prov., India	E6	40
Mizusawa, Japan	C4	31
Mjakit, Russia	C17	26
Mjölby, Swe.	G6	10
Mjøsa, l., Nor.	F4	10
Mkalama, Tan.	D6	54
Mkokotoni, Tan.	D7	54
Mladá Boleslav, Czech Rep.	D3	20
Mlanje Peak see Sapitwa, mtn., Mwi.	B6	56
Mława, Pol.	C6	20
Mmabatho, S. Afr.	D4	56
Moab, Ut., U.S.	E6	137
Moala, i., Fiji	m10	63b
Moamba, Moz.	D5	56
Moanda, Gabon	D2	54
Moapa River Indian Reservation, Nv., U.S.	G7	121
Moba, D.R.C.	E5	54
Mobaye, C.A.R.	C4	54
Moberly, Mo., U.S.	B5	118
Mobile, Al., U.S.	E1	94
Mobile, co., Al., U.S.	E1	94
Mobile, stm., Al., U.S.	E1	94
Mobile Bay, b., Al., U.S.	E1	99
Mobridge, S.D., U.S.	B5	134
Mobutu Sese Seko, Lac see Albert, Lake, l., Afr.	C6	54
Moca, Dom. Rep.	B5	80
Mocanaqua, Pa., U.S.	D9	131
Moc Chau, Viet.	B4	34
Mocha see Al-Mukhā, Yemen	H4	38
Mochudi, Bots.	C4	56
Mocksville, N.C., U.S.	B2	126
Moclips, Wa., U.S.	B1	140
Môco, Morro de, mtn., Ang.	D3	54
Mococa, Braz.	F2	74
Moctezuma, Mex.	B3	78
Model Reservoir, res., Co., U.S.	D6	99
Módena, Italy	B3	18
Modesto, Ca., U.S.	D3	98
Modoc, co., Ca., U.S.	B3	98
Modowi, Indon.	G9	32
Moe, Austl.	H4	62
Moen-jo-Daro, hist., Pak.	E9	42
Moenkopi, Az., U.S.	A4	96
Moffat, co., Co., U.S.	A2	99
Moffat Tunnel, Co., U.S.	B5	99
Mogadishu see Muqdisho, Som.	J14	48
Mogadore, Oh., U.S.	A4	128
Mogaung, Myan.	A3	34
Mogincual, Moz.	B7	56
Mogoča, Russia	D13	26
Mogogh, Sudan	B6	54
Mogok, Myan.	B3	34
Mogollon Mountains, mts., N.M., U.S.	D1	124
Mogollon Rim, clf, Az., U.S.	C5	96
Mogotón, Pico, mtn., N.A.	F7	76
Mogzon, Russia	A10	28
Mohall, N.D., U.S.	A4	127
Mohammed, Râs, c., Egypt	F10	14
Mohave, co., Az., U.S.	B1	96
Mohave, Lake, res., U.S.	H7	121
Mohave Mountains, mts., Az., U.S.	C1	96
Mohave Valley, Az., U.S.	C1	96
Mohawk, N.Y., U.S.	C5	125
Mohawk, stm., N.H., U.S.	g7	122
Mohawk, stm., N.Y., U.S.	C6	125
Mohawk Lake, l., N.J., U.S.	A3	123
Mohawk Mountains, mts., Az., U.S.	E2	96
Mohe, China	A12	28
Mohican, stm., Oh., U.S.	B3	128
Mohns Ridge	D23	144
Mohnton, Pa., U.S.	F10	131
Mohnyin, Myan.	B3	34
Mohyliv-Podil's'kyi, Ukr.	E9	20
Mo i Rana, Nor.	C6	10
Moisie, P.Q., Can.	h8	88
Mojave, Ca., U.S.	E4	98
Mojave, stm., Ca., U.S.	E5	98
Mojave Desert, des., Ca., U.S.	E5	98
Mojo, Eth.	B7	54
Mojynty, Kaz.	E9	26
Mokapu Peninsula, pen., Hi., U.S.	g10	104
Mokapu Point, c., Hi., U.S.	g11	104
Mokelumne, stm., Ca., U.S.	C3	98
Mokena, Il., U.S.	k9	106
Mokhotlong, Leso.	D4	56
Moknine, Tun.	C5	48
Moko Manu, i., Hi., U.S.	g11	104
Mokolo, Cam.	A2	54
Mokp'o, S. Kor.	E13	28
Mola di Bari, Italy	D6	18
Molalla, Or., U.S.	B4	130
Moldavia, hist. reg., Rom.	F9	20
Moldavia see Moldova, ctry., Eur.	F10	20
Molde, Nor.	E2	10
Moldova, ctry., Eur.	F10	20
Moldoveanu, Vârful, mtn., Rom.	G8	20
Molepolole, Bots.	C4	56
Molfetta, Italy	D6	18
Moline, Il., U.S.	B3	106
Moline, Mi., U.S.	F5	115
Molino, Fl., U.S.	u14	102
Mollendo, Peru	G5	70
Molokai, i., Hi., U.S.	B5	104
Molokai Fracture Zone	F24	64
Molokini, i., Hi., U.S.	C5	104
Molopo, stm., Afr.	D3	56
Molotov see Perm', Russia	D7	26
Moloundou, Cam.	C3	54
Molson Lake, l., Mb., Can.	C3	86
Moluccas see Maluku, is., Indon.	D7	36
Molucca Sea see Maluku, Laut, Indon.	C7	36
Moma, Moz.	B6	56
Mombasa, Kenya	D7	54
Mombetsu, Japan	C16	28
Momence, Il., U.S.	B6	106
Mompós, Col.	D5	80
Momskij hrebet, mts., Russia	C16	26
Møn, i., Den.	I5	10
Mona, Isla de, i., P.R.	B6	80
Monaca, Pa., U.S.	E1	131
Monaco, ctry., Eur.	C1	18
Monadnock, Mount, mtn., N.H., U.S.	E2	122
Monadnock Mountain, mtn., Vt., U.S.	B5	138
Monahans, Tx., U.S.	D1	136
Mona Passage, strt., N.A.	B6	80
Mona Quimbondo, Ang.	E3	54
Monarch Mills, S.C., U.S.	B4	133
Monarch Pass, Co., U.S.	C4	99
Monashee Mountains, mts., B.C., Can.	D8	85
Monastir, Tun.	C5	48
Monção, Braz.	D10	70
Mončegorsk, Russia	C15	10
Mönchengladbach, Ger.	E10	12
Moncks Corner, S.C., U.S.	E7	133
Monclova, Mex.	B4	78
Moncton, N.B., Can.	C5	87
Mondjamboli, D.R.C.	C4	54
Mondovi, Wi., U.S.	D2	142
Monee, Il., U.S.	B6	106
Monessen, Pa., U.S.	F2	131
Monett, Mo., U.S.	E4	118
Monette, Ar., U.S.	B5	97
Monfalcone, Italy	B4	18
Monforte de Lemos, Spain	F3	16
Mongalla, Sudan	B6	54
Mongo, Chad	D8	50
Mongol Altayn nuruu, mts., Asia	B6	28
Mongolia, ctry., Asia	B8	28
Mongonu, Nig.	D7	50
Mongu, Zam.	B3	56
Monhegan Island, i., Me., U.S.	E3	112
Monida Pass, U.S.	E6	105
Moniteau, co., Mo., U.S.	C5	118
Monitor Range, mts., Nv., U.S.	E5	121
Monitor Valley, val., Nv., U.S.	D5	121
Monmouth, Il., U.S.	C3	106
Monmouth, Or., U.S.	C3	130
Monmouth, co., N.J., U.S.	C4	123
Monmouth Beach, N.J., U.S.	C5	123
Monmouth Mountain, mtn., B.C., Can.	D6	85
Mono, co., Ca., U.S.	D4	98
Monocacy, stm., Md., U.S.	B3	113
Mono Lake, l., Ca., U.S.	D4	98
Monomonac, Lake, l., U.S.	E3	122
Monomoy Island, i., Ma., U.S.	C7	114
Monomoy Point, c., Ma., U.S.	C7	114
Monon, In., U.S.	C4	107
Monona, Ia., U.S.	A6	108
Monona, Wi., U.S.	E4	142
Monona, co., Ia., U.S.	B1	108
Monona, Lake, l., Wi., U.S.	E4	142
Monongahela, Pa., U.S.	F2	131
Monongahela, stm., U.S.	G2	131
Monongalia, co., W.V., U.S.	B4	141
Monopoli, Italy	D6	18
Monor, Hung.	F5	20
Monroe, Ga., U.S.	C3	103
Monroe, Ia., U.S.	C4	108
Monroe, In., U.S.	C8	107
Monroe, La., U.S.	B3	111
Monroe, Mi., U.S.	G7	115
Monroe, N.C., U.S.	C2	126
Monroe, N.Y., U.S.	D6	125
Monroe, Oh., U.S.	C1	128
Monroe, Ut., U.S.	E3	137
Monroe, Wa., U.S.	B4	140
Monroe, Wi., U.S.	F4	142
Monroe, co., Al., U.S.	D2	94
Monroe, co., Ar., U.S.	C4	97
Monroe, co., Fl., U.S.	G5	102
Monroe, co., Ga., U.S.	D3	103
Monroe, co., Ia., U.S.	D5	108
Monroe, co., Il., U.S.	E3	106
Monroe, co., In., U.S.	F4	107
Monroe, co., Ky., U.S.	D4	110
Monroe, co., Mi., U.S.	G7	115
Monroe, co., Mo., U.S.	B5	118
Monroe, co., Ms., U.S.	B5	117
Monroe, co., N.Y., U.S.	B3	125
Monroe, co., Oh., U.S.	C4	128
Monroe, co., Pa., U.S.	D11	131
Monroe, co., Tn., U.S.	D9	135
Monroe, co., W.V., U.S.	D4	141
Monroe, co., Wi., U.S.	E3	142
Monroe Center, Ct., U.S.	D3	100
Monroe City, Mo., U.S.	B6	118
Monroe Lake, res., In., U.S.	F5	107
Monroe Peak, De., U.S.	h7	101
Monroeville, Al., U.S.	D2	94
Monroeville, In., U.S.	C8	107
Monroeville, Oh., U.S.	A3	128
Monroeville, Pa., U.S.	k14	131
Monrovia, Lib.	E2	50
Monrovia, Ca., U.S.	m13	98
Monrovia, In., U.S.	E5	107
Monson, Ma., U.S.	B3	114
Mönsterås, Swe.	H7	10
Montague, P.E., Can.	C7	87
Montague, Ca., U.S.	B2	98
Montague, Mi., U.S.	E4	115
Montague, Tx., U.S.	C4	136
Montague Island, i., Ak., U.S.	D10	95
Montague Peak, mtn., Ak., U.S.	g18	95
Montague Strait, strt., Ak., U.S.	h18	95
Mont Alto, Pa., U.S.	G6	131
Montana, Bul.	C9	18
Montana, state, U.S.	D7	119
Montargis, Fr.	C8	16
Montauban, Fr.	E8	16
Montauk, N.Y., U.S.	m17	125
Montbard, Fr.	D9	16
Montbéliard, Fr.	D10	16
Mont Belvieu, Tx., U.S.	E5	136
Montblanc, Spain	G7	16
Montcalm, co., Mi., U.S.	E5	115
Montceau-les-Mines, Fr.	D9	16
Montchanin, De., U.S.	h7	101
Montclair, Ca., U.S.	m13	98
Montclair, N.J., U.S.	A4	123
Mont Clare, Pa., U.S.	o19	131
Mont-de-Marsan, Fr.	F6	16
Monteagle, Tn., U.S.	D8	135
Monte Alegre, Braz.	D9	70
Monte Azul, Braz.	E3	74
Montebello, P.Q., Can.	D3	90
Montebello, Ca., U.S.	m12	98
Montecarlo, Arg.	D7	72
Monte Caseros, Arg.	E6	72
Monte Comán, Arg.	E4	72
Montecristo, Isola di, i., Italy	C3	18
Montego Bay, Jam.	B4	80
Montegut, La., U.S.	E5	111

Name	Map Ref.	Page

Montélimar, Fr. E9 16
Montello, Nv., U.S. B7 121
Montello, Wi., U.S. E4 142
Montemorelos, Mex. B5 78
Montenegro see Crna Gora,
state, Yugo. C7 18
Monte Patria, Chile E3 72
Montepuez, Moz. A6 56
Montepulciano, Italy C3 18
Monte Quemado, Arg. D5 72
Monterey, Ca., U.S. D3 98
Monterey, Tn., U.S. C8 135
Monterey, co., Ca., U.S. . . D3 98
Monterey Bay, b., Ca., U.S. D2 98
Monterey Park, Ca., U.S. . m12 98
Montería, Col. B4 70
Montero, Bol. B5 72
Monterrey, Mex. B5 78
Montesano, Wa., U.S. C2 140
Montes Claros, Braz. E3 74
Montevallo, Al., U.S. B3 94
Montevideo, Mn., U.S. F3 116
Montevideo, Ur. E5 72
Monte Vista, Co., U.S. D4 99
Montezuma, Ga., U.S. D2 103
Montezuma, Ia., U.S. C5 108
Montezuma, In., U.S. E3 107
Montezuma, Ks., U.S. E3 109
Montezuma, co., Co., U.S. . D2 99
Montezuma Castle National
Monument, Az., U.S. C4 96
Montezuma Peak, mtn., Az.,
U.S. D3 96
Montgomery see Sāhīwāl,
Pak. D10 42
Montgomery, Al., U.S. C3 94
Montgomery, Il., U.S. B5 106
Montgomery, La., U.S. C3 111
Montgomery, Mn., U.S. F5 116
Montgomery, N.Y., U.S. . . . D6 125
Montgomery, Oh., U.S. . . . o13 128
Montgomery, Pa., U.S. D8 131
Montgomery, W.V., U.S. . . . C3 141
Montgomery, co., Al., U.S. . C3 94
Montgomery, co., Ar., U.S. . C2 97
Montgomery, co., Ga., U.S. D4 103
Montgomery, co., Ia., U.S. . C2 108
Montgomery, co., Il., U.S. . D4 106
Montgomery, co., In., U.S. . D4 107
Montgomery, co., Ks., U.S. . E8 109
Montgomery, co., Ky., U.S. . B6 110
Montgomery, co., Md., U.S. B3 113
Montgomery, co., Mo., U.S. C6 118
Montgomery, co., Ms., U.S. B4 117
Montgomery, co., N.C., U.S. B3 126
Montgomery, co., N.Y., U.S. C6 125
Montgomery, co., Oh., U.S. . C1 128
Montgomery, co., Pa., U.S. F11 131
Montgomery, co., Tn., U.S. . A4 135
Montgomery, co., Tx., U.S. . D5 136
Montgomery, co., Va., U.S. . C2 139
Montgomery City, Mo., U.S. C6 118
Monticello, Ar., U.S. D4 97
Monticello, Fl., U.S. B3 102
Monticello, Ga., U.S. C3 103
Monticello, Ia., U.S. B6 108
Monticello, Il., U.S. C5 106
Monticello, In., U.S. C4 107
Monticello, Ky., U.S. D5 110
Monticello, Mn., U.S. E5 116
Monticello, Ms., U.S. D3 117
Monticello, N.Y., U.S. D6 125
Monticello, Ut., U.S. F6 137
Monticello, Wi., U.S. F4 142
Mont-Joli, P.Q., Can. A9 90
Mont-Laurier, P.Q., Can. . . C2 90
Montluçon, Fr. D8 16
Montmagny, P.Q., Can. . . . C7 90
Montmorenci, S.C., U.S. . . D4 133
Montmorency, co., Mi., U.S. C6 115
Monto, Austl. E5 62
Montoro, Spain H4 16
Montour, co., Pa., U.S. . . . D8 131
Montour Falls, N.Y., U.S. . . C4 125
Montoursville, Pa., U.S. . . . D8 131
Montpelier, Id., U.S. G7 105
Montpelier, In., U.S. C7 107
Montpelier, Oh., U.S. A1 128
Montpelier, Vt., U.S. C3 138
Montpellier, Fr. F8 16
Montréal, P.Q., Can. D4 90
Montreal, Wi., U.S. B3 142
Montréal, Île de, i., P.Q.,
Can. q19 90
Montreal Lake, l., Sk., Can. C3 91
Montréal-Nord, P.Q., Can. . p19 90
Montreat, N.C., U.S. f10 126
Montreux, Switz. A1 18
Mont-Rolland, P.Q., Can. . . D3 90
Montrose, B.C., Can. E9 85
Montrose, Scot., U.K. B5 12
Montrose, Al., U.S. E2 94
Montrose, Co., U.S. C3 99
Montrose, Ia., U.S. D6 108
Montrose, Mi., U.S. E7 115
Montrose, Pa., U.S. C10 131
Montrose, Va., U.S. m18 139
Montrose, co., Co., U.S. . . C2 99
Mont-Royal, P.Q., Can. . . . p19 90
Mont-Saint-Michel, Le, Fr. . C6 16
Montserrat, dep., N.A. E12 76
Montserrat, Monasterio de,
Spain G7 16

Mont-Tremblant, Parc
Provincial du, P.Q.,
Can. C3 90
Montvale, N.J., U.S. A4 123
Montville, Ct., U.S. D7 100
Monument, Co., U.S. B6 99
Monument Beach, Ma., U.S. C6 114
Monument Peak, mtn., Co.,
U.S. B3 99
Monument Peak, mtn., Id.,
U.S. G4 105
Monument Valley, val., Az.,
U.S. A5 96
Monywa, Myan. B2 34
Monza, Italy B2 18
Monze, Zam. B4 56
Monzón, Spain G7 16
Moodus, Ct., U.S. D6 100
Moodus Reservoir, res., Ct.,
U.S. C6 100
Moody, Tx., U.S. D4 136
Moody, co., S.D., U.S. C9 134
Moon Lake, l., Ms., U.S. . . A3 117
Moora, Austl. G2 60
Moorcroft, Wy., U.S. B8 143
Moore, Ok., U.S. B4 129
Moore, co., N.C., U.S. B3 126
Moore, co., Tn., U.S. B5 135
Moore, co., Tx., U.S. B2 136
Moore, Lake, l., Austl. F2 60
Moore Dam, U.S. B3 122
Moorefield, W.V., U.S. B6 141
Moore Haven, Fl., U.S. . . . F5 102
Mooreland, Ok., U.S. A2 129
Moore Reservoir, res., U.S. B3 122
Moores Creek National
Military Park, N.C., U.S. C4 126
Moores Hill, In., U.S. F7 107
Moorestown, N.J., U.S. . . . D3 123
Mooresville, In., U.S. E5 107
Mooresville, N.C., U.S. . . . B2 126
Moorhead, Mn., U.S. D2 116
Moorhead, Ms., U.S. B3 117
Mooringsport, La., U.S. . . . B2 111
Moorreesburg, S. Afr. E2 56
Moose, stm., N.H., U.S. . . . B4 122
Moose, stm., N.Y., U.S. . . . B5 125
Moose, stm., Vt., U.S. B5 138
Moosehead Lake, l., Me.,
U.S. C3 112
Moose Jaw, stm., Sk., Can. G3 91
Moose Lake, Mb., Can. . . . C1 86
Moose Lake, Mn., U.S. . . . D6 116
Moose Lake, l., Wi., U.S. . . B2 142
Mooseleuk Stream, stm.,
Me., U.S. B4 112
Mooselookmeguntic Lake,
l., Me., U.S. D2 112
Moose Mountain Creek,
stm., Sk., Can. H4 91
Moose Mountain Provincial
Park, Sk., Can. H4 91
Moosic, Pa., U.S. m18 131
Moosup, Ct., U.S. C8 100
Moosup, stm., U.S. C1 132
Mopang Lake, l., Me., U.S. D5 112
Mopti, Mali D4 50
Moquegua, Peru G5 70
Mora, Cam. D7 50
Mora, Spain H5 16
Mora, Swe. F6 10
Mora, Mn., U.S. E5 116
Mora, N.M., U.S. B4 124
Mora, co., N.M., U.S. A5 124
Mora, stm., N.M., U.S. . . . B5 124
Morādābād, India D3 40
Morafenobe, Madag. B7 56
Moramanga, Madag. B8 56
Morant Cays, is., Jam. B4 80
Moratuwa, Sri L. H3 40
Morava, hist. reg., Czech
Rep. E4 20
Moravia, Ia., U.S. D5 108
Morawa, Austl. F2 60
Morawhanna, Guy. B8 70
Moray Firth, b., Scot., U.K. B5 12
Morbi, India E2 40
Morden, Mb., Can. E2 86
Mordovia see Mordovija,
state, Russia D6 26
Mordovija, state, Russia . . D6 26
Mordvinia see Mordovija,
state, Russia D6 26
Moreau, stm., S.D., U.S. . . B3 134
Moreauville, La., U.S. C4 111
Morecambe Bay, b., Eng.,
U.K. D5 12
Moree, Austl. F4 62
Morehead, Ky., U.S. B6 110
Morehead City, N.C., U.S. . C6 126
Morehouse, Mo., U.S. E8 118
Morehouse, co., La., U.S. . B4 111
Morelia, Mex. D4 78
Morelos, state, Mex. D5 78
Morena, Sierra, mts., Spain H4 16
Morenci, Az., U.S. D6 96
Morenci, Mi., U.S. G6 115
Moresby Island, i., B.C.,
Can. C2 85
Moreton Island, i., Austl. . . F5 62
Morey, Lake, l., Vt., U.S. . . D4 138
Morey Peak, mtn., Nv., U.S. E5 121
Morgan, Mn., U.S. F4 116
Morgan, Ut., U.S. B4 137
Morgan, co., Al., U.S. A3 94

Morgan, co., Co., U.S. . . . A7 99
Morgan, co., Ga., U.S. . . . C3 103
Morgan, co., Il., U.S. D3 106
Morgan, co., In., U.S. F5 107
Morgan, co., Ky., U.S. C6 110
Morgan, co., Mo., U.S. . . . C5 118
Morgan, co., Oh., U.S. C4 128
Morgan, co., Tn., U.S. C9 135
Morgan, co., Ut., U.S. B4 137
Morgan, co., W.V., U.S. . . . B6 141
Morgan City, La., U.S. E4 111
Morganfield, Ky., U.S. C2 110
Morgan Hill, Ca., U.S. D3 98
Morgan Island, i., S.C., U.S. G6 133
Morgan Point, c., Ct., U.S. . E4 100
Morganton, N.C., U.S. B1 126
Morgantown, In., U.S. F5 107
Morgantown, Ky., U.S. . . . C3 110
Morgantown, Ms., U.S. . . . D2 117
Morgantown, Tn., U.S. D8 135
Morgantown, W.V., U.S. . . B5 141
Morganza, La., U.S. D4 111
Morghāb (Murgab), stm.,
Asia C8 42
Moriah, Mount, mtn., Nv.,
U.S. D7 121
Moriarty, N.M., U.S. C3 124
Moriki, Nig. D6 50
Morinville, Ab., Can. C4 84
Morioka, Japan D16 28
Morlaix, Fr. C5 16
Morley, Mo., U.S. D8 118
Mormon Peak, mtn., Nv.,
U.S. G7 121
Morning Sun, Ia., U.S. C6 108
Mornington Island, i., Austl. D2 62
Morobe, Pap. N. Gui. H12 32
Morocco, In., U.S. C3 107
Morocco, ctry., Afr. D3 48
Morogoro, Tan. E7 54
Moro Gulf, b., Phil. E8 34
Morombe, Madag. C7 56
Morón, Arg. E6 72
Morón, Cuba A4 80
Mörön, Mong. B8 28
Morondava, Madag. C7 56
Morón de la Frontera, Spain I4 16
Moroni, Com. A7 56
Moroni, Ut., U.S. D4 137
Morotai, i., Indon. C7 36
Moroto, Ug. C6 54
Morozovsk, Russia E7 22
Morrill, Ne., U.S. C2 120
Morrill, co., Ne., U.S. C2 120
Morrilton, Ar., U.S. B3 97
Morrinhos, Braz. E2 74
Morris, Mb., Can. E3 86
Morris, Al., U.S. B3 94
Morris, Il., U.S. B5 106
Morris, Mn., U.S. E3 116
Morris, Ok., U.S. B6 129
Morris, co., Ks., U.S. D7 109
Morris, co., N.J., U.S. B3 123
Morris, co., Tx., U.S. C5 136
Morrisburg, On., Can. C9 89
Morris Island, i., S.C., U.S. F8 133
Morris Jesup, Kap, c., Grnld. B33 82
Morrison, Il., U.S. B4 106
Morrison, Ok., U.S. A4 129
Morrison, co., Mn., U.S. . . D4 116
Morrison City, Tn., U.S. . . . C11 135
Morrisonville, Il., U.S. D4 106
Morrisonville, N.Y., U.S. . . f11 125
Morris Plains, N.J., U.S. . . B4 123
Morristown, In., U.S. E6 107
Morristown, Mn., U.S. F5 116
Morristown, N.J., U.S. B4 123
Morristown, Tn., U.S. C10 135
Morristown National
Historical Park, N.J.,
U.S. B3 123
Morrisville, N.Y., U.S. C5 125
Morrisville, Pa., U.S. F12 131
Morrisville, Vt., U.S. B3 138
Morro Bay, Ca., U.S. E3 98
Morro do Chapéu, Braz. . . D3 74
Morrow, Ga., U.S. C2 103
Morrow, Oh., U.S. C1 128
Morrow, co., Oh., U.S. B3 128
Morrow, co., Or., U.S. B7 130
Morrumbala, Moz. B6 56
Morrumbene, Moz. C6 56
Moršansk, Russia D7 22
Morse, La., U.S. D3 111
Morse Reservoir, res., In.,
U.S. D5 107
Morses Creek, stm., N.J.,
U.S. k8 123
Mortes, stm., Braz. F9 70
Morton, Il., U.S. C4 106
Morton, Ms., U.S. C4 117
Morton, Tx., U.S. C1 136
Morton, Wa., U.S. C3 140
Morton, co., Ks., U.S. E2 109
Morton, co., N.D., U.S. . . . C4 127
Morton Grove, Il., U.S. . . . h9 106
Morton Pass, Wy., U.S. . . . E7 143
Mortons Gap, Ky., U.S. . . . C2 110
Morwell, Austl. H4 62
Moscow see Moskva, Russia D5 26
Moscow, Id., U.S. C2 105
Moscow, Pa., U.S. m18 131
Moscow Mills, Mo., U.S. . . C7 118
Mosel (Moselle), stm., Eur. B10 16
Moselle, Ms., U.S. D4 117

Moselle (Mosel), stm., Eur. C10 16
Moses Coulee, val., Wa.,
U.S. B6 140
Moses Lake, Wa., U.S. . . . B6 140
Moses Lake, l., Wa., U.S. . . B6 140
Mosheim, Tn., U.S. C11 135
Moshi, Tan. D7 54
Mosinee, Wi., U.S. D4 142
Mosjøen, Nor. D5 10
Moskva (Moscow), Russia . D5 26
Mosquero, Col. B2 74
Mosquera, Col. C4 70
Mosquito Creek Lake, res.,
Oh., U.S. A5 128
Mosquito Lagoon, b., Fl.,
U.S. D6 102
Mosquitos, Golfo de los, b.,
Pan. D3 80
Moss, Nor. G4 10
Mossaka, Congo D3 54
Moss Bluff, La., U.S. D2 111
Mosselbaai, S. Afr. E3 56
Mossman, Austl. D4 62
Mossoró, Braz. C4 74
Moss Point, Ms., U.S. E5 117
Most, Czech Rep. D2 20
Mostar, Bos. C6 18
Møsting, Kap, c., Grnld. . . . F32 82
Mosul see Al-Mawṣil, Iraq . C4 42
Møsvatnet, l., Nor. G3 10
Mot'a, Eth. A7 54
Motagua, stm., N.A. B2 80
Motala, Swe. G6 10
Motherwell, Scot., U.K. . . . C5 12
Motley, co., Tx., U.S. B2 136
Motril, Spain I5 16
Mott, N.D., U.S. C3 127
Motueka, N.Z. p13 63c
Motyklejka, Russia D16 26
Mouaskar, Alg. D4 14
Moudjéria, Maur. C2 50
Mouila, Gabon D2 54
Moulins, Fr. D8 16
Moulouya, Oued, stm.,
Mor. D4 48
Moulton, Al., U.S. A2 94
Moulton, Ia., U.S. D5 108
Moultrie, Ga., U.S. E3 103
Moultrie, co., Il., U.S. D5 106
Moultrie, Lake, res., S.C.,
U.S. E7 133
Mounana, Gabon D2 54
Mound, Mn., U.S. n11 116
Mound Bayou, Ms., U.S. . . B3 117
Mound City, Il., U.S. F4 106
Mound City, Ks., U.S. D9 109
Mound City, Mo., U.S. A2 118
Mound City Group National
Monument, Oh., U.S. . . C2 128
Moundou, Chad E8 50
Moundridge, Ks., U.S. D6 109
Mounds, Il., U.S. F4 106
Mounds, Ok., U.S. B5 129
Moundsville, W.V., U.S. . . . B4 141
Moundville, Al., U.S. C2 94
Mountainair, N.M., U.S. . . . C3 124
Mountainaire, Az., U.S. . . . B4 96
Mountain Brook, Al., U.S. . g7 94
Mountain City, Ga., U.S. . . B3 103
Mountain City, Nv., U.S. . . B6 121
Mountain City, Tn., U.S. . . C12 135
Mountain Fork, stm., U.S. . C7 129
Mountain Grove, Mo., U.S. D5 118
Mountain Home, Ar., U.S. . A3 97
Mountain Home, Id., U.S. . F3 105
Mountain Home Air Force
Base, mil., Id., U.S. . . . F3 105
Mountain Iron, Mn., U.S. . . C6 116
Mountain Lake, Mn., U.S. . G4 116
Mountain Lake Park, Md.,
U.S. m12 113
Mountain Nile see Jabal,
Bahr al-, stm., Sudan . . I11 48
Mountain Pine, Ar., U.S. . . C2 97
Mountainside, N.J., U.S. . . B4 123
Mountain View, Ar., U.S. . . B3 97
Mountain View, Ca., U.S. . . k8 98
Mountain View, Mo., U.S. . D6 118
Mountain View, N.M., U.S. C3 124
Mountain View, Ok., U.S. . B3 129
Mountain View, Wy., U.S. . E2 143
Mountain Village, Ak., U.S. C7 95
Mount Airy, Md., U.S. B3 113
Mount Airy, N.C., U.S. A2 126
Mount Albert, On., Can. . . . C5 89
Mount Angel, Or., U.S. . . . B4 130
Mount Arlington, N.J., U.S. B3 123
Mount Augustus, Austl. . . . E2 60
Mount Ayr, Ia., U.S. D3 108
Mount Barker, Austl. G2 60
Mount Carmel, Il., U.S. . . . E6 106
Mount Carmel, Oh., U.S. . . o13 128
Mount Carmel, Pa., U.S. . . E9 131
Mount Carmel [-Mitchell's
Brook-Saint
Catherine's], Nf., Can. . E5 88
Mount Carroll, Il., U.S. . . . A4 106
Mount Clare, W.V., U.S. . . B4 141
Mount Clemens, Mi., U.S. . F8 115
Mount Desert Island, i.,
Me., U.S. D4 112
Mount Dora, Fl., U.S. D5 102

Moselle (Mosel), stm., Eur. C10 16
Mount Forest, On., Can. . . D4 89
Mount Gambier, Austl. . . . H3 62
Mount Gay, W.V., U.S. . . . D2 141
Mount Gilead, N.C., U.S. . . B3 126
Mount Gilead, Oh., U.S. . . B3 128
Mount Hagen, Pap. N. Gui. H11 32
Mount Healthy, Oh., U.S. . . o12 128
Mount Holly, N.C., U.S. . . . B1 126
Mount Holly, N.J., U.S. . . . D3 123
Mount Holly Springs, Pa.,
U.S. F7 131
Mount Hope, Ks., U.S. . . . E6 109
Mount Hope, W.V., U.S. . . D3 141
Mount Hope, stm., Ct., U.S. B7 100
Mount Hope Bay, b., U.S. . D6 132
Mount Horeb, Wi., U.S. . . . E4 142
Mount Ida, Ar., U.S. C2 97
Mount Isa, Austl. E2 62
Mount Jackson, Va., U.S. . B4 139
Mount Jewett, Pa., U.S. . . . C4 131
Mount Joy, Pa., U.S. F9 131
Mount Juliet, Tn., U.S. . . . A5 135
Mount Kisco, N.Y., U.S. . . . D7 125
Mount Lebanon, Pa., U.S. . F1 131
Mount Magnet, Austl. F2 60
Mount Morris, Il., U.S. . . . A4 106
Mount Morris, Mi., U.S. . . . E7 115
Mount Morris, N.Y., U.S. . . C3 125
Mount Olive, Al., U.S. B3 94
Mount Olive, Il., U.S. D4 106
Mount Olive, Ms., U.S. . . . D4 117
Mount Olive, N.C., U.S. . . . B4 126
Mount Olive, Tn., U.S. n14 135
Mount Orab, Oh., U.S. . . . C2 128
Mount Pearl, Nf., Can. . . . E5 88
Mount Penn, Pa., U.S. F10 131
Mount Pleasant, Ia., U.S. . D6 108
Mount Pleasant, Mi., U.S. . E6 115
Mount Pleasant, N.C., U.S. B2 126
Mount Pleasant, Pa., U.S. . F2 131
Mount Pleasant, S.C., U.S. F8 133
Mount Pleasant, Tn., U.S. . B4 135
Mount Pleasant, Tx., U.S. . C5 136
Mount Pleasant, Ut., U.S. . D4 137
Mount Pocono, Pa., U.S. . . D11 131
Mount Prospect, Il., U.S. . . A6 106
Mount Pulaski, Il., U.S. . . . C4 106
Mountrail, co., N.D., U.S. . A3 127
Mount Rainier, Md., U.S. . . f9 113
Mount Rainier National
Park, Wa., U.S. C4 140
Mount Revelstoke National
Park, B.C., Can. D8 85
Mount Riddock, Austl. E5 60
Mount Rogers National
Recreation Area, Va.,
U.S. D1 139
Mount Roskill, N.Z. o13 63c
Mount Rushmore National
Memorial, hist., S.D.,
U.S. D2 134
Mount Savage, Md., U.S. . . k13 113
Mount Shasta, Ca., U.S. . . B2 98
Mount Sterling, Il., U.S. . . . D3 106
Mount Sterling, Ky., U.S. . . B6 110
Mount Sterling, Oh., U.S. . . C2 128
Mount Uniacke, N.S., Can. . E6 87
Mount Union, Pa., U.S. . . . F6 131
Mount Vernon, Austl. E2 60
Mount Vernon, Al., U.S. . . . D1 94
Mount Vernon, Ga., U.S. . . D4 103
Mount Vernon, Ia., U.S. . . . C6 108
Mount Vernon, Il., U.S. . . . E5 106
Mount Vernon, In., U.S. . . . I2 107
Mount Vernon, Ky., U.S. . . C5 110
Mount Vernon, Mo., U.S. . . D4 118
Mount Vernon, N.Y., U.S. . . h13 125
Mount Vernon, Oh., U.S. . . B3 128
Mount Vernon, Tx., U.S. . . C5 136
Mount Vernon, Wa., U.S. . . A3 140
Mount View, R.I., U.S. D4 132
Mount Washington, Ky.,
U.S. B4 110
Mount Wolf, Pa., U.S. F8 131
Mount Zion, Il., U.S. D5 106
Moura, Braz. D7 70
Moussa 'Ali, mtn., Afr. H4 38
Moussoro, Chad D8 50
Moutong, Indon. C6 36
Moville, Ia., U.S. B1 108
Moweaqua, Il., U.S. D4 106
Mower, co., Mn., U.S. G6 116
Moxee City, Wa., U.S. C5 140
Moyale, Kenya C7 54
Moyamba, S.L. E2 50
Moyen Atlas, mts., Mor. . . . E3 14
Moyo, Pulau, i., Indon. . . . E5 36
Moyobamba, Peru E4 70
Moyock, N.C., U.S. A6 126
Moyu, China B7 40
Mozambique, ctry., Afr. . . . B5 56
Mozambique Channel, strt.,
Afr. B7 56
Mozambique Plateau L6 64
Mozdok, Russia B4 42
Mpala, D.R.C. E5 54
Mpanda, Tan. E6 54
Mpika, Zam. A5 56
Mporokoso, Zam. E6 54
Mpulungu, Zam. E6 54
Mpwapwa, Tan. E7 54
Mscislau, Bela. C11 20
M'Sila, Alg. J9 16
Mtubatuba, S. Afr. D5 56
Mtwara, Tan. F8 54

Name	Map Ref.	Page

Muanda, D.R.C. E2 54
Muang Hôngsa, Laos C4 34
Muang Khammouan, Laos . C4 34
Muang Khôngxédôn, Laos . C5 34
Muang Không, Laos D5 34
Muang Ngoy, Laos B4 34
Muang Pak-Lay, Laos C4 34
Muang Pakxan, Laos C4 34
Muang Phalan, Laos C5 34
Muang Sing, Laos B4 34
Muang Thadua, Laos C4 34
Muang Vangviang, Laos . . . C4 34
Muang Xaignabouri, Laos . . C4 34
Muar, Malay. C2 36
Muaraenim, Indon. D2 36
Muarasiberut, Indon. G2 32
Mubende, Ug. C6 54
Mubi, Nig. D7 50
Muchinga Mountains, mts.,
  Zam. A5 56
Muckleshoot Indian
  Reservation, Wa., U.S. . f11 140
Mucojo, Moz. A7 56
Muconda, Ang. F4 54
Mucujê, Braz. F11 70
Mud, stm., Ky., U.S. C3 110
Mud, stm., Mn., U.S. . . . B3 116
Mud, stm., W.V., U.S. . . . C2 141
Mudanjiang, China C13 28
Mud Creek, stm., Ok., U.S. C4 129
Muddy Boggy Creek, stm.,
  Ok., U.S. C6 129
Muddy Creek, stm., Ut.,
  U.S. E4 137
Muddy Creek, stm., Wy.,
  U.S. C4 143
Muddy Creek, stm., Wy.,
  U.S. E5 143
Muddy Creek, stm., Wy.,
  U.S. E2 143
Muddy Creek, stm., Wy.,
  U.S. D6 143
Muddy Mountains, mts.,
  Nv., U.S. G7 121
Muddy Peak, mtn., Nv.,
  U.S. G7 121
Mudgee, Austl. G4 62
Mud Lake, l., Me., U.S. . . A4 112
Mud Lake, l., Nv., U.S. . . F4 121
Mueda, Moz. A6 56
Muenster, Tx., U.S. C4 136
Mufulira, Zam. A4 56
Muğla, Tur. D3 44
Muhlenberg, co., Ky., U.S. C2 110
Mühlhausen, Ger. E12 12
Muhu, l., Est. C10 10
Muié, Ang. A3 56
Muirkirk, Md., U.S. B4 113
Muir Woods National
  Monument, Ca., U.S. . . h7 98
Muja, Russia D13 26
Mujnak, Uzb. B7 42
Mukacheve, Ukr. E7 20
Mukah, Malay. C4 36
Mukden see Shenyang,
  China C12 28
Mukilteo, Wa., U.S. B3 140
Mukinbudin, Austl. F3 60
Mukomuk, Indon. D2 36
Mukry, Turk. C9 42
Mukwonago, Wi., U.S. F5 142
Mula, Spain H6 16
Mulberry, Ar., U.S. B1 97
Mulberry, Fl., U.S. E4 102
Mulberry, In., U.S. D4 107
Mulberry, N.C., U.S. A1 126
Mulberry, stm., Ar., U.S. . B1 97
Mulberry Fork, stm., Al.,
  U.S. B3 94
Muldraugh, Ky., U.S. C4 110
Muldrow, Ok., U.S. B7 129
Muleshoe, Tx., U.S. B1 136
Mulgrave, N.S., Can. D8 87
Mulhacén, mtn., Spain I5 16
Mulhouse, Fr. D10 16
Mull, Island of, i., Scot.,
  U.K. B3 12
Mullan, Id., U.S. B3 105
Mullan Pass, Mt., U.S. . . D4 119
Mullens, W.V., U.S. D3 141
Muller, Pegunungan, mts.,
  Indon. C4 36
Mullet Key, i., Fl., U.S. . . p10 102
Mullett Lake, l., Mi., U.S. C6 115
Mullewa, Austl. F2 60
Mullica, stm., N.J., U.S. . D3 123
Mullins, S.C., U.S. C9 133
Mulongo, D.R.C. E5 54
Multān, Pak. D10 42
Multnomah, co., Or., U.S. B4 130
Mulvane, Ks., U.S. E6 109
Mumbai (Bombay), India . . F2 40
Mumbwa, Zam. A4 56
Mummy Range, mts., Co.,
  U.S. A5 99
Mun, stm., Thai. C4 34
Muna, Mex. C7 78
Muna, Pulau, i., Indon. . . D6 36
München (Munich), Ger. . . F12 12
Muncie, In., U.S. D7 107
Muncy, Pa., U.S. D8 131
Munday, Tx., U.S. C3 136
Mundelein, Il., U.S. A5 106
Münden, Ger. E11 12
Mundrabilla, Austl. G4 60

Munford, Al., U.S. B4 94
Munford, Tn., U.S. B2 135
Munfordville, Ky., U.S. . . . C4 110
Mungbere, D.R.C. C5 54
Munger, India D5 40
Munhall, Pa., U.S. k14 131
Munhango, Ang. F3 54
Munich see München, Ger. F12 12
Munising, Mi., U.S. B4 115
Münster, Ger. E10 12
Munster, In., U.S. A2 107
Munster, hist. reg., Ire. . . D2 12
Munsungan Lake, l., Me.,
  U.S. B3 112
Muntok, Indon. D3 36
Munuscong Lake, l., Mi.,
  U.S. B6 115
Muojärvi, l., Fin. D13 10
Muonio, Fin. C10 10
Muqdisho, Som. J14 48
Mur (Mura), stm., Eur. . . F3 20
Mura (Mur), stm., Eur. . . F4 20
Muradiye, Tur. C10 44
Murakami, Japan C3 31
Murana, Indon. D8 36
Muraši, Russia C8 22
Murat, stm., Tur. C9 44
Murchison, stm., Austl. . . F1 60
Murchison Falls see
  Kabalega Falls, wtfl, Ug. C6 54
Murcia, Spain I6 16
Murderkill, stm., De., U.S. D4 101
Murdo, S.D., U.S. D5 134
Mureș, stm., Eur. G7 20
Muret, Fr. F7 16
Murewa, Zimb. B5 56
Murfreesboro, Ar., U.S. . . . C2 97
Murfreesboro, N.C., U.S. . . A5 126
Murfreesboro, Tn., U.S. . . . B5 135
Murgab, Taj. F9 26
Murgab (Morghāb), stm.,
  Asia C8 42
Muriaé, Braz. F3 74
Müritz, l., Ger. D13 12
Murmansk, Russia C5 26
Murom, Russia D6 26
Muroran, Japan C16 28
Muroto, Japan D2 31
Murphy, Mo., U.S. g13 118
Murphy, N.C., U.S. f8 126
Murphy Island, i., S.C., U.S. E9 133
Murphysboro, Il., U.S. F4 106
Murray, Ia., U.S. C4 108
Murray, Ky., U.S. f9 110
Murray, Ut., U.S. C4 137
Murray, co., Ga., U.S. . . . B2 103
Murray, co., Mn., U.S. . . . F3 116
Murray, co., Ok., U.S. . . . C4 129
Murray, stm., Austl. H3 62
Murray, Lake, l., Pap. N.
  Gui. H11 32
Murray, Lake, res., Ok., U.S. C4 129
Murray, Lake, res., S.C.,
  U.S. C5 133
Murray Bridge, Austl. H2 62
Murray Fracture Zone . . . E24 64
Murray Head, c., P.E., Can. C7 87
Murraysburg, S. Afr. E3 56
Murrayville, Ga., U.S. B3 103
Murree, Pak. C2 40
Murrells Inlet, S.C., U.S. . . D9 133
Murrells Inlet, b., S.C., U.S. D10 133
Murrumbidgee, stm., Austl. G4 62
Murrupula, Moz. B6 56
Mursala, Pulau, i., Indon. . C1 36
Murua Island, i., Pap. N.
  Gui. H13 32
Murud, Gunong, mtn.,
  Malay. C5 36
Murukta, Russia C12 26
Murwāra, India E4 40
Murwillumbah, Austl. F5 62
Murzuq, Libya E7 48
Murzūq, Idhān, des., Libya B7 50
Muş, Tur. C9 44
Musa Alī Terara see Moussa
  ʿAli, mtn., Afr. H4 38
Musāʿid, Libya E9 14
Musala, mtn., Bul. C9 18
Musan-ŭp, N. Kor. B1 31
Musayʿīd, Qatar F6 42
Muscat see Masqaṭ, Oman F7 38
Muscat and Oman see
  Oman, ctry., Asia G7 38
Muscatatuck, stm., In., U.S. G5 107
Muscatine, Ia., U.S. C6 108
Muscatine, co., Ia., U.S. . . C6 108
Muscle Shoals, Al., U.S. . . A2 94
Musclow, Mount, mtn.,
  B.C., Can. C4 85
Muscoda, Wi., U.S. E3 142
Muscogee, co., Ga., U.S. . D2 103
Musconetcong, stm., N.J.,
  U.S. B4 123
Muscooten Bay, l., Il., U.S. C3 106
Muse, Pa., U.S. F1 131
Musgrave Harbour, Nf.,
  Can. D5 88
Musgravetown, Nf., Can. . . D5 88
Mushie, D.R.C. D3 54
Mushin, Nig. E5 50
Musi, stm., Indon. D2 36
Musicians Seamounts . . . E22 64
Muskeg Bay, b., Mn., U.S. B3 116

Muskeget Island, i., Ma.,
  U.S. D7 114
Muskego, Wi., U.S. F5 142
Muskego Lake, l., Wi., U.S. n11 142
Muskegon, Mi., U.S. E4 115
Muskegon, co., Mi., U.S. . E4 115
Muskegon, stm., Mi., U.S. E4 115
Muskegon Heights, Mi.,
  U.S. E4 115
Muskegon Lake, l., Mi., U.S. E4 115
Muskingum, co., Oh., U.S. B4 128
Muskingum, stm., Oh., U.S. C4 128
Muskogee, Ok., U.S. B6 129
Muskogee, co., Ok., U.S. . B6 129
Musoma, Tan. D6 54
Musquacook Lakes, l., Me.,
  U.S. B3 112
Musquodoboit Harbour,
  N.S., Can. E6 87
Mussau Island, i., Pap. N.
  Gui. G12 32
Musselshell, co., Mt., U.S. D8 119
Musselshell, stm., Mt., U.S. D9 119
Mussende, Ang. F3 54
Mussuma, Ang. A3 56
Mustafakemalpaşa, Tur. . . . C3 44
Mustahīl, Eth. B8 54
Mustang, Ok., U.S. B4 129
Mustinka, stm., Mn., U.S. E2 116
Muswellbrook, Austl. G5 62
Mut, Tur. D5 44
Mutare, Zimb. B5 56
Mutoraj, Russia C12 26
Mutsamudu, Com. A7 56
Mutshatsha, D.R.C. F4 54
Mutsu, Japan C16 28
Mutsu-wan, b., Japan . . . B4 31
Mutton Mountains, mts.,
  Or., U.S. C5 130
Muxima, Ang. E2 54
Muyinga, Bdi. D6 54
Muyumba, D.R.C. E5 54
Muzaffarābād, Pak. D10 42
Muzaffargarh, Pak. D10 42
Muzaffarnagar, India D3 40
Muzaffarpur, India D5 40
Muži, Russia C8 26
Muzon, Cape, c., Ak., U.S. n23 95
Muztag, mtn., China D5 28
Mvuma, Zimb. B5 56
Mwadui, Tan. D6 54
Mwali, l., Com. A7 56
Mwanza, Tan. D6 54
Mweka, D.R.C. D4 54
Mwene-Ditu, D.R.C. E4 54
Mwenezi, Zimb. C5 56
Mweru, Lake, l., Afr. E5 54
Mwinilunga, Zam. A3 56
Myakka, stm., Fl., U.S. . . E4 102
Myanaung, Myan. C3 34
Myanmar (Burma), ctry.,
  Asia B3 34
Myaungmya, Myan. C2 34
Myerstown, Pa., U.S. F9 131
Myingyan, Myan. B3 34
Myitkyinā, Myan. A3 34
Myittha, Myan. B3 34
Mykolaïv, Ukr. F11 20
Mymensingh, Bngl. E6 40
Mynaral, Kaz. A10 42
Mýrdalsjökull, Ice. m19 10a
Myrhorod, Ukr. E12 20
Myrtle Beach, S.C., U.S. . . D10 133
Myrtle Grove, Fl., U.S. . . . u14 102
Myrtle Point, Or., U.S. . . . D2 130
Mysore, India G3 40
Mysore see Karnātaka,
  prov., India G3 40
Mystic, Ct., U.S. D8 100
Mystic Lakes, l., Ma., U.S. g11 114
Mys Vhodnoj, Russia B10 26
Mys Želanija, Russia B8 26
Myszków, Pol. D5 20
My Tho, Viet. D5 34
Mzimba, Mwi. A5 56
Mzuzu, Mwi. A5 56

N

Naalehu, Hi., U.S. D6 104
Naberežnye Čelny, Russia . D7 26
Nabeul, Tun. C7 48
Nabire, Indon. G10 32
Nabī Shuʿayb, Jabal an-,
  mtn., Yemen G4 38
Nabnasset, Ma., U.S. A5 114
Nābulus, W.B. F6 44
Nacala-a-Velha, Moz. A7 56
Naches, stm., Wa., U.S. . . C5 140
Nachingwea, Tan. F7 54
Náchod, Czech Rep. D4 20
Nachuge, India G6 40
Nacimiento, Lake, res., Ca.,
  U.S. E3 98
Naco, Az., U.S. F6 96
Nacogdoches, Tx., U.S. . . . D5 136
Nacogdoches, co., Tx., U.S. D5 136
Nacozari de García, Mex. . . A3 78
Nadiād, India E2 40
Nador, Mor. J5 16
Nadvirna, Ukr. E8 20
Nadym, Russia C9 26
Nafada, Nig. D7 50
Nafī, Sau. Ar. E4 42

Naga, Phil. D8 34
Nāgāland, prov., India . . . D6 40
Nagano, Japan D15 28
Nagaoka, Japan D15 28
Nagaon, India D6 40
Nāgappattinam, India . . . G3 40
Nagasaki, Japan E13 28
Nāgaur, India E3 40
Nagda, India E3 40
Nāgercoil, India H3 40
Nago, Japan A9 34
Nagoya, Japan D15 28
Nāgpur, India E3 40
Nagqu, China E6 28
Nags Head, N.C., U.S. B7 126
Nagykanizsa, Hung. F4 20
Naha, Japan A9 34
Nahāvand, Iran E13 44
Nahe, China B12 28
Nahmakanta Lake, l., Me.,
  U.S. C3 112
Nahodka, Russia E15 26
Nahunta, Ga., U.S. E5 103
Nain, Nf., Can. g9 88
Nairobi, Kenya D7 54
Naivasha, Kenya D7 54
Najafābād, Iran B6 42
Najd, hist. reg., Sau. Ar. . . E4 38
Nájera, Spain F5 16
Najin, N. Kor. C14 28
Nakano-shima, i., Japan . . E1 31
Nakhichevan see Naxçıvan,
  Azer. C11 44
Nakhon Pathom, Thai. . . . D4 34
Nakhon Phanom, Thai. . . . C4 34
Nakhon Ratchasima, Thai. . D4 34
Nakhon Sawan, Thai. C4 34
Nakhon Si Thammarat, Thai. E3 34
Nakina, On., Can. o18 89
Nakło nad Notecią, Pol. . . C4 20
Naknek, Ak., U.S. D8 95
Naknek Lake, l., Ak., U.S. D8 95
Nakskov, Den. I4 10
Nakuru, Kenya D7 54
Nakusp, B.C., Can. D9 85
Nalʹčik, Russia E6 26
Nalgonda, India F3 40
Nallıhan, Tur. B4 44
Nālūt, Libya D7 48
Namak, daryācheh-ye, l.,
  Iran D6 42
Namanga, Kenya D7 54
Namangan, Uzb. E9 26
Namanock Island, i., N.J.,
  U.S. A3 123
Namapa, Moz. A6 56
Namarrói, Moz. B6 56
Namatanai, Pap. N. Gui. . . E9 58
Nambour, Austl. F5 62
Nam Co, l., China E6 28
Namekagon, stm., Wi., U.S. B2 142
Namekagon Lake, l., Wi.,
  U.S. B2 142
Namen see Namur, Bel. . . E9 12
Nametil, Moz. B6 56
Namhkam, Myan. B3 34
Namib Desert, des., Nmb. . B1 56
Namibe, Ang. B1 56
Namibia, ctry., Afr. C2 56
Namīn, Iran C13 44
Namjagbarwa Feng, mtn.,
  China F7 28
Namlea, Indon. D7 36
Nam Ngum Reservoir, res.,
  Laos C4 34
Nampa, Id., U.S. F2 105
Nampula, Moz. B6 56
Namsang, Myan. B3 34
Namsos, Nor. D4 10
Namtu, Myan. B3 34
Namur, Bel. E9 12
Namutoni, Nmb. B2 56
Namwala, Zam. B4 56
Nan, Thai. C4 34
Nanaimo, B.C., Can. E5 85
Nanakuli, Hi., U.S. B3 104
Nanao, Japan D15 28
Nancha, China A1 31
Nanchang, China F11 28
Nancheng, China D4 30
Nanchong, China E9 28
Nancy, Fr. C10 16
Nanda Devi, mtn., India . . . C3 40
Nānded, India F3 40
Nandurbār, India E2 40
Nandyāl, India F3 40
Nanfeng, China D4 30
Nanga-Eboko, Cam. C2 54
Nanga Parbat, mtn., Pak. . . C10 42
Nangatayap, Indon. D4 36
Nangong, China B4 30
Nanjing, China E11 28
Nankang, China G9 28
Nanking see Nanjing, China E11 28
Nanle, China B4 30
Nanning, China G9 28
Nannup, Austl. G2 60
Nanping, China F11 28
Nansei-shotō (Ryukyu
  Islands), is., Japan . . . A9 34

Nansemond, stm., Va., U.S. k14 139
Nansen Basin E21 144
Nansen Cordillera E22 144
Nan Shan see Qilian Shan,
  mts., China D7 28
Nantes, Fr. D6 16
Nanticoke, On., Can. E4 89
Nanticoke, Pa., U.S. D10 131
Nanticoke, stm., U.S. . . . D6 113
Nanton, Ab., Can. D4 84
Nantong, China E12 28
Nantucket, Ma., U.S. D7 114
Nantucket, co., Ma., U.S. . D7 114
Nantucket Island, i., Ma.,
  U.S. D7 114
Nantucket Sound, strt., Ma.,
  U.S. C7 114
Nantulo, Moz. A6 56
Nantuxent Point, c., N.J.,
  U.S. E2 123
Nanty Glo, Pa., U.S. F4 131
Nanuet, N.Y., U.S. g12 125
Nanuque, Braz. E3 74
Nanusa, Kepulauan, is.,
  Indon. C7 36
Nanxiong, China F10 28
Nanyang, China E10 28
Nanyuki, Kenya C7 54
Nanzhao, China C3 30
Naoma, W.V., U.S. n13 141
Naomi Peak, mtn., Ut., U.S. B4 137
Napa, Ca., U.S. C2 98
Napa, co., Ca., U.S. C2 98
Napanee, On., Can. C8 89
Napatree Point, c., R.I., U.S. G1 132
Napavine, Wa., U.S. C3 140
Napè, Laos C5 34
Naperville, Il., U.S. B5 106
Napier, N.Z. o14 63c
Napier Mountains, mts.,
  Ant. C10 67
Napierville, P.Q., Can. . . . D4 90
Naples see Napoli, Italy . . D5 18
Naples, Fl., U.S. F5 102
Naples, Tx., U.S. C5 136
Naples, Ut., U.S. C6 137
Napo, stm., S.A. D5 70
Napoleon, N.D., U.S. C6 127
Napoleon, Oh., U.S. A1 128
Napoleonville, La., U.S. . . . E4 111
Napoli (Naples), Italy D5 18
Napoli, Golfo di, b., Italy . D5 18
Nappanee, In., U.S. B5 107
Naqadeh, Iran D11 44
Nara, Japan E15 28
Nara, Mali C3 50
Naracoorte, Austl. H3 62
Naramata, B.C., Can. E8 85
Naranja, Fl., U.S. G6 102
Narasapur, India F4 40
Narathiwat, Thai. E4 34
Nārāyanganj, Bngl. E6 40
Narberth, Pa., U.S. p20 131
Narbonne, Fr. F8 16
Narʹjan-Mar, Russia C7 26
Narmada, stm., India E2 40
Nārnaul, India D3 40
Narodnaja, gora, hills,
  Russia C8 26
Naro-Fominsk, Russia B14 20
Narooma, Austl. H5 62
Narrabri, Austl. G4 62
Narragansett, R.I., U.S. . . F4 132
Narragansett Bay, b., R.I.,
  U.S. E5 132
Narraguagus, stm., Me., U.S. D5 112
Narrandera, Austl. G4 62
Narrogin, Austl. G2 60
Narromine, Austl. G4 62
Narrows, Va., U.S. C2 139
Narsaq, Grnld. F30 82
Narva, Est. G13 10
Narvik, Nor. B10 10
Naryn, stm., Asia A3 40
Naryn, Kyrg. E9 26
Narynkol, Kaz. C4 28
Näsåker, Swe. E7 10
Nasca, Peru F5 70
Naselle, Wa., U.S. C2 140
Nash, Tx., U.S. C5 136
Nash, co., N.C., U.S. A4 126
Nashawena Island, i., Ma.,
  U.S. D6 114
Nāshik, India E2 40
Nash Stream, stm., N.H.,
  U.S. A4 122
Nashua, Ia., U.S. B5 108
Nashua, N.H., U.S. E4 122
Nashua, stm., U.S. E3 122
Nashville, Ar., U.S. D2 97
Nashville, Ga., U.S. E3 103
Nashville, Il., U.S. E4 106
Nashville, In., U.S. F5 107
Nashville, Mi., U.S. F5 115
Nashville, N.C., U.S. B5 126
Nashville, Tn., U.S. A5 135
Nashwauk, Mn., U.S. C5 116
Nāṣir, Sudan I11 48
Nasīrābād, India D2 40
Nasīrābād, Pak. E9 42
Naskaupi, stm., Nf., Can. . g9 88
Nassau, Bah. D9 76
Nassau, co., Fl., U.S. B5 102
Nassau, co., N.Y., U.S. . . E7 125
Nassau, stm., Fl., U.S. . . . k8 102

Name	Map Ref.	Page
Nassau Island, i., Cook Is.	F13	58
Nassau Sound, b., Fl., U.S.	B5	102
Nasser, Lake, res., Afr.	F11	48
Nässjö, Swe.	H6	10
Nasukoan Mountain, mtn., Mt., U.S.	B2	119
Nata, Bots.	C4	56
Natal, Braz.	E7	74
Natalbany, La., U.S.	D5	111
Natalia, Tx., U.S.	E3	136
Natashquan, stm., Can.	h9	88
Natchaug, stm., Ct., U.S.	B7	100
Natchez, Ms., U.S.	D2	117
Natchitoches, La., U.S.	C2	111
Natchitoches, co., La., U.S.	C2	111
Natick, Ma., U.S.	h11	114
National City, Ca., U.S.	F5	98
Natitingou, Benin	D5	50
Natividade, Braz.	F10	70
Natron, Lake, l., Afr.	D7	54
Natrona, co., Wy., U.S.	D5	143
Natrona Heights, Pa., U.S.	E2	131
Natuna Besar, i., Indon.	C3	36
Natuna Besar, Kepulauan, is., Indon.	C3	36
Natuna Selatan, Kepulauan, is., Indon.	C3	36
Natural Bridge, Ut., U.S.	F3	137
Natural Bridge, Va., U.S.	C3	139
Natural Bridges National Monument, U.S.	F6	137
Naturaliste, Cape, c., Austl.	G1	60
Nau, Cap de la, c., Spain	H7	16
Naugatuck, Ct., U.S.	D3	100
Naugatuck, stm., Ct., U.S.	D3	100
Nauru, ctry., Oc.	E10	58
Naushon Island, i., Ma., U.S.	D6	114
Nautilus Park, Ct., U.S.	D7	100
Nautla, Mex.	C5	78
Nauvoo, Il., U.S.	C2	106
Navadwip, India	E5	40
Navahrudak, Bela.	C8	20
Navajo, co., Az., U.S.	B5	96
Navajo Dam, N.M., U.S.	A2	124
Navajo Indian Reservation, U.S.	A4	96
Navajo Mountain, mtn., Ut., U.S.	F5	137
Navajo National Monument, Az., U.S.	A5	96
Navajo Reservoir, res., U.S.	A2	124
Navan, On., Can.	B9	89
Navapolack, Bela.	B10	20
Navarin, mys, c., Russia	C19	26
Navarino, Isla, i., Chile	I3	69
Navarra, hist. reg., Spain	F6	16
Navarre, Oh., U.S.	B4	128
Navarro, co., Tx., U.S.	D4	136
Navasota, Tx., U.S.	D4	136
Navassa Island, i., N.A.	B4	80
Navlja, Russia	C13	20
Navoi, Uzb.	E8	26
Navojoa, Mex.	B3	78
Navsāri, India	E2	40
Nawābshāh, Pak.	E9	42
Nawiliwili Bay, b., Hi., U.S.	B2	104
Naxçivan, Azer.	C11	44
Naxi, China	D2	30
Náxos, Grc.	F10	18
Náxos, i., Grc.	F10	18
Nayarit, state, Mex.	C4	78
Naylor, Mo., U.S.	E7	118
Nayoro, Japan	C16	28
Nazaré, Braz.	D4	74
Nazaré, Port.	H2	16
Nazareth see Nazerat, Isr.	D3	42
Nazareth, Pa., U.S.	E11	131
Nazas, Mex.	B4	78
Nazas, stm., Mex.	B4	78
Nazca Ridge	K5	66
Naze, Japan	F13	28
Naze, The see Lindesnes, c., Nor.	H2	10
Nazerat, Isr.	D3	42
Nazilli, Tur.	D3	44
Nazko, stm., B.C., Can.	C6	85
Nazran', Russia	A11	44
Nazrēt, Eth.	B7	54
Nazwá, Oman	F7	42
N'dalatando, Ang.	E2	54
Ndélé, C.A.R.	B4	54
Ndendé, Gabon	D2	54
N'Djamena, Chad	D8	50
Ndjolé, Gabon	D2	54
Ndola, Zam.	A4	56
Neagh, Lough, l., N. Ire., U.K.	C3	12
Neah Bay, Wa., U.S.	A1	140
Néa Páfos, Cyp.	B4	44
Neápolis, Grc.	F9	18
Near Islands, is., Ak., U.S.	E2	95
Nebitdag, Turk.	F7	26
Neblina, Pico da, mtn., S.A.	C6	70
Nebo, Mount, mtn., Ut., U.S.	D4	137
Nebraska, state, U.S.	C6	120
Nebraska City, Ne., U.S.	D10	120
Nechako, stm., B.C., Can.	C5	85
Neches, stm., Tx., U.S.	D5	136
Necker Island, i., Hi., U.S.	m15	104
Necochea, Arg.	F6	72
Nederland, Co., U.S.	B5	99
Nederland, Tx., U.S.	E6	136
Nêdong, China	F6	28
Nédroma, Alg.	J6	16
Nedrow, N.Y., U.S.	C4	125
Needham, Ma., U.S.	g11	114
Needle Mountain, mtn., Wy., U.S.	B3	143
Needles, Ca., U.S.	E6	98
Needville, Tx., U.S.	r14	136
Neenah, Wi., U.S.	D5	142
Neepawa, Mb., Can.	D2	86
Neffs, Oh., U.S.	B5	128
Neffsville, Pa., U.S.	F9	131
Neftçala, Azer.	C13	44
Negage, Ang.	E3	54
Negaunee, Mi., U.S.	B3	115
Negēlē, Eth.	B7	54
Negley, Oh., U.S.	B5	128
Negombo, Sri L.	H3	40
Negritos, Peru	D3	70
Negro, stm., Arg.	F4	69
Negro, stm., S.A.	D7	70
Negros, i., Phil.	E8	34
Neguac, N.B., Can.	B4	87
Nehalem, stm., Or., U.S.	A3	130
Nehbandān, Iran	D7	42
Neiges, Piton des, mtn., Reu.	g10	57a
Neijiang, China	D2	30
Neill Point, c., Wa., U.S.	f11	140
Neillsville, Wi., U.S.	D3	142
Nei Monggol Zizhiqu (Inner Mongolia), prov., China	C10	28
Neisse see Nysa, Pol.	D4	20
Neiva, Col.	C4	70
Nejd see Najd, hist. reg., Sau. Ar.	E4	38
Nek'emtē, Eth.	B7	54
Nekoosa, Wi., U.S.	D4	142
Nelidovo, Russia	C5	22
Neligh, Ne., U.S.	B7	120
Nel'kan, Russia	D15	26
Nellis Air Force Base, mil., Nv., U.S.	G6	121
Nellore, India	G4	40
Nel'ma, Russia	E15	26
Nelson, B.C., Can.	E9	85
Nelson, N.Z.	p13	63c
Nelson, Ne., U.S.	D7	120
Nelson, co., Ky., U.S.	C4	110
Nelson, co., N.D., U.S.	B7	127
Nelson, co., Va., U.S.	C4	139
Nelson, stm., Mb., Can.	A4	86
Nelson, Cape, c., Austl.	H3	62
Nelsonville, Oh., U.S.	C3	128
Nelspruit, S. Afr.	D5	56
Néma, Maur.	C3	50
Nemacolin, Pa., U.S.	G2	131
Nemadji, stm., U.S.	B1	142
Nemaha, co., Ks., U.S.	C7	109
Nemaha, co., Ne., U.S.	D10	120
Neman (Nemunas), stm., Eur.	B7	20
Nembe, Nig.	F6	50
Nemunas (Neman), stm., Eur.	B7	20
Nemuro, Japan	C17	28
Nenana, Ak., U.S.	C10	95
Nendo, i., Sol. Is.	F10	58
Neodesha, Ks., U.S.	E8	109
Neoga, Il., U.S.	D5	106
Neola, Ia., U.S.	C2	108
Neola, Ut., U.S.	C5	137
Neopit, Wi., U.S.	D5	142
Neosho, Mo., U.S.	E3	118
Neosho, co., Ks., U.S.	E8	109
Neosho, stm., Ok., U.S.	A6	129
Nepal, ctry., Asia	D4	40
Nepālganj, Nepal	D4	40
Nepaug Reservoir, res., Ct., U.S.	B3	100
Nepean, On., Can.	h12	89
Nepewassi Lake, l., On., Can.	A4	89
Nephi, Ut., U.S.	D4	137
Nepisiguit, stm., N.B., Can.	B3	87
Nepisiguit Bay, b., N.B., Can.	B4	87
Neponset, stm., Ma., U.S.	h11	114
Neptune, N.J., U.S.	C4	123
Neptune Beach, Fl., U.S.	B5	102
Neptune City, N.J., U.S.	C4	123
Nerčinsk, Russia	A11	28
Nerčinskij Zavod, Russia	D13	26
Nerehta, Russia	C7	22
Neriquinha, Ang.	B3	56
Nescopeck, Pa., U.S.	D9	131
Neshanic, stm., N.J., U.S.	C3	123
Neshoba, co., Ms., U.S.	C4	117
Neskaupstaður, Ice.	l22	10a
Nesna, Nor.	C5	10
Nesowadnehunk, l., Me., U.S.	B3	112
Nesquehoning, Pa., U.S.	E10	131
Ness, co., Ks., U.S.	D4	109
Ness, Loch, l., Scot., U.K.	B4	12
Ness City, Ks., U.S.	D4	109
Néstos, stm., Eur.	D10	18
Netanya, Isr.	D2	42
Netcong, N.J., U.S.	B3	123
Netherlands, ctry., Eur.	D9	12
Netherlands Antilles, dep., N.A.	F11	76
Netherlands Guiana see Suriname, ctry., S.A.	C8	70
Nettie, W.V., U.S.	C4	141
Nett Lake, l., Mn., U.S.	B5	116
Nett Lake Indian Reservation, Mn., U.S.	B6	116
Nettleton, Ms., U.S.	A5	117
Neubrandenburg, Ger.	D13	12
Neuchâtel, Switz.	A1	18
Neuchâtel, Lac de, l., Switz.	A1	18
Neufchâtel-en-Bray, Fr.	C7	16
Neumarkt in der Oberpfalz, Ger.	F12	12
Neumünster, Ger.	C12	12
Neuquén, Arg.	E3	69
Neuruppin, Ger.	D13	12
Neuse, stm., N.C., U.S.	B6	126
Neustrelitz, Ger.	D13	12
Neuville, P.Q., Can.	C6	90
Nevada, Ia., U.S.	B4	108
Nevada, Mo., U.S.	D3	118
Nevada, co., Ar., U.S.	D2	97
Nevada, co., Ca., U.S.	C3	98
Nevada, state, U.S.	D5	121
Nevada, Sierra, mts., Ca., U.S.	D4	98
Nevada City, Ca., U.S.	C3	98
Nevado, Cerro, mtn., Arg.	F4	72
Nevado, Cerro, mtn., Col.	C5	70
Nevel', Russia	A10	22
Nevel'sk, Russia	E16	26
Never, Russia	D14	26
Nevers, Fr.	D8	16
Neversink, stm., N.Y., U.S.	D6	125
Nevinnomyssk, Russia	B4	42
Nevis, i., St. K./N.	B7	80
Nevis, Ben, mtn., Scot., U.K.	B4	12
Nevjansk, Russia	C11	22
Nevşehir, Tur.	C6	44
New, stm., Az., U.S.	k8	96
New, stm., N.C., U.S.	C5	126
New, stm., U.S.	C3	141
Newala, Tan.	F7	54
New Albany, In., U.S.	H6	107
New Albany, Ms., U.S.	A4	117
New Albany, Oh., U.S.	k11	128
New Amsterdam, Guy.	B8	70
Newark, Ar., U.S.	B4	97
Newark, Ca., U.S.	h8	98
Newark, De., U.S.	B3	101
Newark, Il., U.S.	B5	106
Newark, N.J., U.S.	B4	123
Newark, N.Y., U.S.	B3	125
Newark, Oh., U.S.	B3	128
Newark Bay, b., N.J., U.S.	k8	123
Newark Lake, l., Nv., U.S.	D6	121
New Athens, Il., U.S.	E4	106
New Augusta, Ms., U.S.	D4	117
Newaygo, Mi., U.S.	E5	115
Newaygo, co., Mi., U.S.	E5	115
New Baden, Il., U.S.	E4	106
New Baltimore, Mi., U.S.	F8	115
New Bedford, Ma., U.S.	C6	114
New Bedford, Pa., U.S.	D1	131
Newberg, Or., U.S.	B4	130
New Berlin, Il., U.S.	D4	106
New Berlin, Wi., U.S.	n11	142
New Bern, N.C., U.S.	B5	126
Newberry, Fl., U.S.	C4	102
Newberry, Mi., U.S.	B5	115
Newberry, S.C., U.S.	C4	133
Newberry, co., S.C., U.S.	C4	133
New Bethlehem, Pa., U.S.	D3	131
New Bloomfield, Pa., U.S.	F7	131
New Boston, Mi., U.S.	p15	115
New Boston, Oh., U.S.	D3	128
New Boston, Tx., U.S.	C5	136
New Braunfels, Tx., U.S.	E3	136
New Bremen, Oh., U.S.	B1	128
New Brighton, Mn., U.S.	m12	116
New Brighton, Pa., U.S.	E1	131
New Britain, Ct., U.S.	C4	100
New Britain, i., Pap. N. Gui.	H13	32
New Brockton, Al., U.S.	D4	94
New Brunswick, N.J., U.S.	C4	123
New Brunswick, prov., Can.	C3	87
New Buffalo, Mi., U.S.	G4	115
Newburg, Wi., U.S.	E5	142
Newburgh, On., Can.	C8	89
Newburgh, In., U.S.	I3	107
Newburgh, N.Y., U.S.	D6	125
Newburgh Heights, Oh., U.S.	h9	128
Newburyport, Ma., U.S.	A6	114
New Caledonia, dep., Oc.	l9	62a
New Caledonia Basin	K19	64
New Canaan, Ct., U.S.	E2	100
New Carlisle, In., U.S.	A4	107
New Carlisle, Oh., U.S.	C1	128
Newcastle, Austl.	G5	62
Newcastle, N.B., Can.	C4	87
Newcastle, On., Can.	D6	89
Newcastle, S. Afr.	D4	56
New Castle, Al., U.S.	B3	94
New Castle, Co., U.S.	B3	99
New Castle, De., U.S.	B3	101
New Castle, In., U.S.	E7	107
New Castle, Ky., U.S.	B4	110
Newcastle, Ok., U.S.	B4	129
New Castle, Pa., U.S.	D1	131
Newcastle, Wy., U.S.	C8	143
Newcastle upon Tyne, Eng., U.K.	C6	12
Newcastle Waters, Austl.	D5	60
New City, N.Y., U.S.	D6	125
Newcomerstown, Oh., U.S.	B4	128
New Concord, Oh., U.S.	C4	128
New Cumberland, Pa., U.S.	F8	131
New Cumberland, W.V., U.S.	A4	141
Newdegate, Austl.	G2	60
New Delhi, India	D3	40
New Ellenton, S.C., U.S.	E4	133
Newellton, La., U.S.	B4	111
New England, N.D., U.S.	C3	127
Newenham, Cape, c., Ak., U.S.	D7	95
New Fairfield, Ct., U.S.	D2	100
Newfane, N.Y., U.S.	B2	125
Newfields, N.H., U.S.	D5	122
New Florence, Mo., U.S.	C6	118
Newfound Gap, U.S.	f9	126
Newfound Lake, l., N.H., U.S.	C3	122
Newfoundland, prov., Can.	D4	88
Newfoundland, i., Nf., Can.	D3	88
Newfoundland Basin	D9	66
New Franklin, Mo., U.S.	B5	118
New Freedom, Pa., U.S.	G8	131
New Georgia Sound, strt., Sol. Is.	B6	62
New Germany, N.S., Can.	E6	87
New Glarus, Wi., U.S.	F4	142
New Guinea, i.	G11	32
Newhall, Ia., U.S.	B6	108
New Hampshire, state, U.S.	C3	122
New Hampton, Ia., U.S.	A5	108
New Hanover, co., N.C., U.S.	C5	126
New Hanover, i., Pap. N. Gui.	G13	32
New Harbour, Nf., Can.	E5	88
New Harmony, In., U.S.	H2	107
New Hartford, Ct., U.S.	B4	100
New Hartford, Ia., U.S.	B5	108
New Haven, Ct., U.S.	D4	100
New Haven, In., U.S.	B7	107
New Haven, Ky., U.S.	C4	110
New Haven, Mo., U.S.	C6	118
New Haven, W.V., U.S.	C3	141
New Haven, co., Ct., U.S.	D4	100
New Haven, stm., Vt., U.S.	C2	138
New Haven Harbor, b., Ct., U.S.	E4	100
New Hazelton, B.C., Can.	B4	85
New Hebrides see Vanuatu, ctry., Oc.	F10	58
New Hebrides, i., Vanuatu	F10	58
New Hebrides Trench	K19	64
New Holland, Ga., U.S.	B3	103
New Holland, Pa., U.S.	F9	131
New Holstein, Wi., U.S.	E5	142
New Hope, Al., U.S.	A3	94
New Hope, Ky., U.S.	C4	110
New Hope, Mn., U.S.	m12	116
New Hope, Pa., U.S.	F12	131
New Hudson, Mi., U.S.	o14	115
New Iberia, La., U.S.	D4	111
Newington, Ct., U.S.	C5	100
New Inlet, b., N.C., U.S.	D5	126
New Ireland, i., Pap. N. Gui.	G13	32
New Jersey, state, U.S.	C4	123
New Johnsonville, Tn., U.S.	A4	135
New Kensington, Pa., U.S.	E2	131
New Kent, co., Va., U.S.	C5	139
Newkirk, Ok., U.S.	A4	129
New Kowloon see Xinjiulong, China	E3	30
New Laguna, N.M., U.S.	B2	124
New Lake, l., N.C., U.S.	B6	126
New Lenox, Il., U.S.	B6	106
New Lexington, Oh., U.S.	C3	128
New Lisbon, Wi., U.S.	E3	142
New Liskeard, On., Can.	p20	89
Newllano, La., U.S.	C2	111
New London, Ct., U.S.	D7	100
New London, Ia., U.S.	D6	108
New London, Mn., U.S.	E4	116
New London, Mo., U.S.	B6	118
New London, N.H., U.S.	D3	122
New London, Oh., U.S.	A3	128
New London, Wi., U.S.	D5	142
New London, co., Ct., U.S.	C7	100
New London Submarine Base, mil., Ct., U.S.	D7	100
New Madison, Oh., U.S.	C1	128
New Madrid, Mo., U.S.	E8	118
New Madrid, co., Mo., U.S.	E8	118
Newman, Austl.	E2	60
Newman, Ca., U.S.	D3	98
Newman, Il., U.S.	D6	106
New Manchester, W.V., U.S.	e8	141
Newman Grove, Ne., U.S.	C8	120
Newman Lake, l., Wa., U.S.	B8	140
Newmanstown, Pa., U.S.	F9	131
Newmarket, On., Can.	C5	89
New Market, Al., U.S.	A3	94
New Market, In., U.S.	E4	107
Newmarket, N.H., U.S.	D5	122
New Market, Va., U.S.	B4	139
New Martinsville, W.V., U.S.	B4	141
New Matamoras, Oh., U.S.	C4	128
New Mexico, state, U.S.	C3	124
New Miami, Oh., U.S.	C1	128
New Milford, Ct., U.S.	C2	100
New Milford, N.J., U.S.	h8	123
New Milford, Pa., U.S.	C10	131
Newnan, Ga., U.S.	C2	103
Newnans Lake, l., Fl., U.S.	C4	102
New Norfolk, Austl.	I4	59
New Orleans, La., U.S.	E5	111
New Orleans Naval Air Station, mil., La., U.S.	k11	111
New Oxford, Pa., U.S.	G7	131
New Palestine, In., U.S.	E6	107
New Paltz, N.Y., U.S.	D6	125
New Paris, In., U.S.	B6	107
New Paris, Oh., U.S.	C1	128
New Philadelphia, Oh., U.S.	B4	128
New Philadelphia, Pa., U.S.	E9	131
New Plymouth, N.Z.	o13	63c
New Plymouth, Id., U.S.	F2	105
New Point Comfort, c., Va., U.S.	C6	139
Newport, Wales, U.K.	E5	12
Newport, Ar., U.S.	B4	97
Newport, De., U.S.	B3	101
Newport, In., U.S.	E3	107
Newport, Ky., U.S.	A5	110
Newport, Me., U.S.	D3	112
Newport, Mi., U.S.	G7	115
Newport, Mn., U.S.	n13	116
Newport, N.C., U.S.	C6	126
Newport, N.H., U.S.	D2	122
Newport, Oh., U.S.	C4	128
Newport, Or., U.S.	C2	130
Newport, Pa., U.S.	F7	131
Newport, R.I., U.S.	F5	132
Newport, Tn., U.S.	D10	135
Newport, Vt., U.S.	B4	138
Newport, Wa., U.S.	A8	140
Newport, co., R.I., U.S.	E5	132
Newport Beach, Ca., U.S.	n13	98
Newport News, Va., U.S.	D6	139
New Port Richey, Fl., U.S.	D4	102
New Prague, Mn., U.S.	F5	116
New Preston, Ct., U.S.	C2	100
New Providence, N.J., U.S.	B4	123
New Providence, i., Bah.	C9	76
New Richland, Mn., U.S.	G5	116
New Richmond, P.Q., Can.	A4	87
New Richmond, Oh., U.S.	D1	128
New Richmond, Wi., U.S.	C1	142
New River Inlet, b., N.C., U.S.	C5	126
New Roads, La., U.S.	D4	111
New Rochelle, N.Y., U.S.	E7	125
New Rockford, N.D., U.S.	B6	127
Newry, N. Ire., U.K.	C3	12
New Salem, N.D., U.S.	C4	127
New Sarpy, La., U.S.	k11	111
New Schwabenland, reg., Ant.	D5	67
New Sharon, Ia., U.S.	C5	108
New Siberian Islands see Novosibirskie ostrova, is., Russia	B16	26
New Site, Al., U.S.	B4	94
New Smyrna Beach, Fl., U.S.	C6	102
New South Wales, state, Austl.	G4	62
New Straitsville, Oh., U.S.	C3	128
New Tazewell, Tn., U.S.	C10	135
Newton, Al., U.S.	D4	94
Newton, Ga., U.S.	E2	103
Newton, Ia., U.S.	C4	108
Newton, Il., U.S.	E5	106
Newton, Ks., U.S.	D6	109
Newton, Ma., U.S.	B5	114
Newton, Ms., U.S.	C4	117
Newton, N.C., U.S.	B1	126
Newton, N.J., U.S.	A3	123
Newton, Tx., U.S.	D6	136
Newton, Ut., U.S.	B4	137
Newton, co., Ar., U.S.	B2	97
Newton, co., Ga., U.S.	C3	103
Newton, co., In., U.S.	B3	107
Newton, co., Mo., U.S.	E3	118
Newton, co., Ms., U.S.	C4	117
Newton, co., Tx., U.S.	D6	136
Newton Falls, Oh., U.S.	A5	128
Newton Lake, res., Il., U.S.	E5	106
Newtown, Ct., U.S.	D2	100
Newtown, Oh., U.S.	C1	128
Newtown Square, Pa., U.S.	p20	131
New Ulm, Mn., U.S.	F4	116
New Vienna, Oh., U.S.	C2	128
Newville, Pa., U.S.	F7	131
New Washington, In., U.S.	G6	107
New Washington, Oh., U.S.	B3	128
New Waterford, Oh., U.S.	B5	128
New Westminster, B.C., Can.	E6	85
New Whiteland, In., U.S.	E5	107
New Wilmington, Pa., U.S.	D1	131
New Windsor, Il., U.S.	B3	106
New Windsor, Md., U.S.	A3	113
New Windsor, N.Y., U.S.	D6	125
New World Island, i., Nf., Can.	D4	88
New York, N.Y., U.S.	E7	125
New York, co., N.Y., U.S.	k13	125
New York, state, U.S.	C6	125
New York Mills, Mn., U.S.	D3	116
New Zealand, ctry., Oc.	H10	58

Name	Map Ref.	Page
Neyrīz, Iran	E6	42
Neyshābūr, Iran	C7	42
Nezahualcóyotl, Presa, res., Mex.	D6	78
Nez Perce, co., Id., U.S.	C2	105
Nez Perce Indian Reservation, Id., U.S.	C2	105
Ngabé, Congo	D3	54
Ngangala, Sudan	C6	54
Ngangla Ringco, l., China	E4	28
Ngaoundéré, Cam.	B2	54
Ngeaur, i., Palau	E9	32
Ngidinga, D.R.C.	E3	54
Ngoring Hu, l., China	E7	28
Ngouri, Chad	D8	50
Nguigmi, Niger	D7	50
Nguru, Nig.	D7	50
Nha Trang, Viet.	D5	34
Nhill, Austl.	H3	62
Nhoma, stm., Afr.	B2	56
Niafounké, Mali	C4	50
Niagara, Wi., U.S.	C6	142
Niagara, co., N.Y., U.S.	B2	125
Niagara Falls, On., Can.	D5	89
Niagara Falls, N.Y., U.S.	B1	125
Niagara-on-the-Lake, On., Can.	D5	89
Niah, Malay.	C4	36
Niakaramandougou, C. Iv.	E3	50
Niamey, Niger	D5	50
Niangara, D.R.C.	C5	54
Niangua, stm., Mo., U.S.	D5	118
Nia-Nia, D.R.C.	C5	54
Niantic, Ct., U.S.	D7	100
Nias, Pulau, i., Indon.	C1	36
Niatupo, Pan.	D4	80
Nibley, Ut., U.S.	B4	137
Nicaragua, ctry., N.A.	F7	76
Nicaragua, Lago de, l., Nic.	C2	80
Nicatous Lake, l., Me., U.S.	C4	112
Nice, Fr.	F10	16
Niceville, Fl., U.S.	u15	102
Nichinan, Japan	E14	28
Nicholas, co., Ky., U.S.	B6	110
Nicholas, co., W.V., U.S.	C4	141
Nicholas Channel, strt., N.A.	A3	80
Nicholasville, Ky., U.S.	C5	110
Nicholls, Ga., U.S.	E4	103
Nichols Hills, Ok., U.S.	B4	129
Nicholson, Ms., U.S.	E4	117
Nickajack Lake, res., Tn., U.S.	D8	135
Nickel Centre, On., Can.	p19	89
Nickerson, Ks., U.S.	D5	109
Nicobar Islands, is., India	H6	40
Nicolet, P.Q., Can.	C5	90
Nicolet, stm., P.Q., Can.	C5	90
Nicolet, Lake, l., Mi., U.S.	B6	115
Nicollet, Mn., U.S.	F4	116
Nicollet, co., Mn., U.S.	F4	116
Nicoma Park, Ok., U.S.	B4	129
Nicosia, Cyp.	E5	44
Nicoya, Golfo de, b., C.R.	D2	80
Nicoya, Península de, pen., C.R.	D2	80
Nidzica, Pol.	C6	20
Niellé, C. Iv.	E3	50
Nienburg, Ger.	D11	12
Nieuw Amsterdam, Sur.	B8	70
Nieuw Nickerie, Sur.	B8	70
Nigadoo, N.B., Can.	B4	87
Niğde, Tur.	D6	44
Niger, ctry., Afr.	C6	50
Niger, stm., Afr.	E6	50
Nigeria, ctry., Afr.	E6	50
Nihoa, i., Hi., U.S.	m15	104
Niigata, Japan	D15	28
Niihama, Japan	D2	31
Niihau, i., Hi., U.S.	B1	104
Nijmegen, Neth.	E10	12
Nikel', Russia	B14	10
Nikishka, Ak., U.S.	g16	95
Nikkō, Japan	D15	28
Nikol'sk, Russia	D8	22
Nikol'sk, Russia	D6	26
Nikopol', Ukr.	F13	20
Niksar, Tur.	B7	44
Nīkshahr, Iran	E8	42
Nikšić, Yugo.	C7	18
Nila, Pulau, i., Indon.	E7	36
Niland, Ca., U.S.	F6	98
Nile, stm., Afr.	E11	48
Niles, Il., U.S.	h9	106
Niles, Mi., U.S.	G4	115
Niles, Oh., U.S.	A5	128
Nīmach, India	E2	40
Nimba, Mount, mtn., Afr.	E3	50
Nîmes, Fr.	F9	16
Nimrod Lake, res., Ar., U.S.	C2	97
Nimule, Sudan	J11	48
Nine Degree Channel, strt., India	H2	40
Nine Mile Creek, stm., Ut., U.S.	D5	137
Ninemile Point, c., Mi., U.S.	C6	115
Ninetyeast Ridge	J11	64
Ninety Mile Beach, Austl.	H4	62
Ninety Six, S.C., U.S.	C3	133
Nineveh see Nīnawá, hist., Iraq	C4	42
Ning'an, China	B1	31
Ningbo, China	F12	28
Ningcheng, China	C11	28
Ningde, China	D4	30
Ningdu, China	F11	28
Ninghai, China	D5	30
Ninghua, China	D4	30
Ningi, Nig.	D6	50
Ningming, China	E2	30
Ningnan, China	A4	34
Ningshan, China	C2	30
Ningsia Hui Autonomous Region see Ningxia Huiza Zizhiqu, prov., China	D9	28
Ningxia Huiza Zizhiqu, prov., China	D9	28
Ningxiang, China	D3	30
Ninh Binh, Viet.	B5	34
Ninigo Group, is., Pap. N. Gui.	G11	32
Ninigret Pond, l., R.I., U.S.	G2	132
Ninilchik, Ak., U.S.	C9	95
Ninnescah, stm., Ks., U.S.	E6	109
Ninohe, Japan	B4	31
Niobrara, co., Wy., U.S.	C8	143
Niobrara, stm., U.S.	B7	120
Nioki, D.R.C.	D3	54
Niono, Mali	D3	50
Nioro du Sahel, Mali	C3	50
Niort, Fr.	D6	16
Niota, Tn., U.S.	D9	135
Nipigon, Lake, l., On., Can.	o17	89
Nipissing, Lake, l., On., Can.	A5	89
Nipomo, Ca., U.S.	E3	98
Nipple Mountain, mtn., Co., U.S.	D2	99
Niquero, Cuba	A4	80
Nirmal, India	F3	40
Niš, Yugo.	C8	18
Niscemi, Italy	F5	18
Niskayuna, N.Y., U.S.	C7	125
Nisqually, stm., Wa., U.S.	C3	140
Nisswa, Mn., U.S.	D4	116
Nistru (Dniester) (Dnister), stm., Eur.	F10	20
Niterói, Braz.	F3	74
Nitra, Slvk.	E5	20
Nitro, W.V., U.S.	C3	141
Niue, dep., Oc.	F13	58
Niuke, China	C4	40
Niulakita, i., Tuvalu	E11	58
Niverville, Mb., Can.	E3	86
Niwot, Co., U.S.	A5	99
Nixa, Mo., U.S.	D4	118
Nixon, Nv., U.S.	D2	121
Nixon, Tx., U.S.	E4	136
Nizāmābād, India	F3	40
Nizhyn, Ukr.	D11	20
Nizip, Tur.	D7	44
Nižneangarsk, Russia	D12	26
Nižnee Kujto, ozero, l., Russia	D14	10
Nižnekamsk, Russia	C9	22
Nižneudinsk, Russia	D11	26
Nižnevartovsk, Russia	C9	26
Nižnij Novgorod (Gor'kij), Russia	D6	26
Nižnij Tagil, Russia	D8	26
Nižnjaja Peša, Russia	A8	22
Nižnjaja Tunguska, stm., Russia	C11	26
Njandoma, Russia	C6	26
Njazidja, i., Com.	A7	56
Njinjo, Tan.	E7	54
Njombe, Tan.	E6	54
Njuhča, Russia	B8	22
Njurba, Russia	C13	26
Njuvčim, Russia	B9	22
Nkambe, Cam.	B2	54
Nkawkaw, Ghana	E4	50
Nkhata Bay, Mwi.	A5	56
Nkhotakota, Mwi.	A5	56
Nkongsamba, Cam.	C1	54
Noākhāli, Bngl.	E6	40
Noank, Ct., U.S.	D8	100
Noatak, Ak., U.S.	B7	95
Noatak, stm., Ak., U.S.	B7	95
Nobel, On., Can.	B4	89
Nobeoka, Japan	D2	31
Noble, Ok., U.S.	B4	129
Noble, co., In., U.S.	B7	107
Noble, co., Oh., U.S.	C4	128
Noble, co., Ok., U.S.	A4	129
Nobles, co., Mn., U.S.	G3	116
Noblesville, In., U.S.	D6	107
Nocatee, Fl., U.S.	E5	102
Nocona, Tx., U.S.	C4	136
Nodaway, co., Mo., U.S.	A3	118
Nodaway, stm., U.S.	A2	118
Noel, Mo., U.S.	E3	118
Nogales, Mex.	A2	78
Nogales, Az., U.S.	F5	96
Nogent-le-Rotrou, Fr.	C7	16
Noginsk, Russia	C6	22
Nohar, India	D2	40
Noirmoutier, Île de, i., Fr.	D5	16
Nokaneng, Bots.	B3	56
Nokia, Fin.	F10	10
Nokomis, Fl., U.S.	E4	102
Nokomis, Il., U.S.	D4	106
Nokomis, Lake, res., Wi., U.S.	C4	142
Nokuku, Vanuatu	j9	62a
Nola, C.A.R.	C3	54
Nolan, co., Tx., U.S.	C2	136
Nolichucky, stm., Tn., U.S.	C10	135
Nolin, stm., Ky., U.S.	C3	110
Nolin Lake, res., Ky., U.S.	C3	110
Nolinsk, Russia	C9	22
Nomans Land, i., Ma., U.S.	D6	114
Nome, Ak., U.S.	C6	95
Nominingue, P.Q., Can.	C2	90
Nong'an, China	C13	28
Nong Khai, Thai.	C4	34
Nonquit Pond, l., R.I., U.S.	E6	132
Nooksack, North Fork, stm., Wa., U.S.	A4	140
Nooksack, South Fork, stm., Wa., U.S.	A3	140
Noonkanbah, Austl.	D3	60
Noorvik, Ak., U.S.	B7	95
Nootka Sound, strt., B.C., Can.	E4	85
No Point, Point, c., Md., U.S.	D5	113
Noquebay, Lake, l., Wi., U.S.	C6	142
Nóqui, Ang.	E2	54
Noranda (part of Rouyn-[Noranda]), P.Q., Can.	k11	89
Nora Springs, Ia., U.S.	A5	108
Norborne, Mo., U.S.	B4	118
Norco, La., U.S.	E5	111
Norcross, Ga., U.S.	C2	103
Nordaustlandet, i., Nor.	A4	4
Norden, Ger.	D10	12
Nordenham, Ger.	D11	12
Nordenšel'da, arhipelag, is., Russia	B11	26
Nordfjordeid, Nor.	F2	10
Nordhausen, Ger.	E12	12
Nordkapp, c., Nor.	A11	10
Nord-Ostsee-Kanal, Ger.	C11	12
Nordre Strømfjord, b., Grnld.	E29	82
Nordvik, Russia	B13	26
Norfolk, Ct., U.S.	B3	100
Norfolk, Ne., U.S.	B8	120
Norfolk, N.Y., U.S.	f9	125
Norfolk, Va., U.S.	D6	139
Norfolk, co., Ma., U.S.	B5	114
Norfolk Island, dep., Oc.	G10	58
Norfolk Naval Base, mil., Va., U.S.	k15	139
Norfolk Naval Shipyard, mil., Va., U.S.	k15	139
Norfolk Ridge	K19	64
Norfork Dam, Ar., U.S.	A3	97
Norfork Lake, res., U.S.	A3	97
Noril'sk, Russia	C10	26
Norland, Fl., U.S.	s13	102
Norlina, N.C., U.S.	A4	126
Normal, Il., U.S.	C5	106
Norman, Ok., U.S.	B4	129
Norman, co., Mn., U.S.	C2	116
Norman, Lake, res., N.C., U.S.	B2	126
Normandie, hist. reg., Fr.	C6	16
Normandie, Collines de, hills, Fr.	C6	16
Normandy, Mo., U.S.	f13	118
Normandy see Normandie, hist. reg., Fr.	C6	16
Normandy, Hills of see Normandie, Collines de, hills, Fr.	C6	16
Norman Park, Ga., U.S.	E3	103
Normanton, Austl.	D3	62
Norphlet, Ar., U.S.	D3	97
Ñorquinco, Arg.	F2	69
Norra Kvarken (Merenkurkku), strt., Eur.	E9	10
Norrbotten, hist. reg., Swe.	C10	10
Nørresundby, Den.	H3	10
Norridge, Il., U.S.	k9	106
Norridgewock, Me., U.S.	D3	112
Norris, S.C., U.S.	B2	133
Norris, Tn., U.S.	C9	135
Norris Arm, Nf., Can.	D4	88
Norris City, Il., U.S.	F5	106
Norris Dam, Tn., U.S.	C9	135
Norris Lake, res., Tn., U.S.	C10	135
Norris Point, Nf., Can.	D3	88
Norristown, Pa., U.S.	F11	131
Norrköping, Swe.	G7	10
Norrtälje, Swe.	G8	10
Norseman, Austl.	G3	60
Norsjö, Swe.	D8	10
Norsk, Russia	D15	26
North, S.C., U.S.	D5	133
North, stm., Al., U.S.	B2	94
North, stm., Ia., U.S.	f8	108
North, stm., Ma., U.S.	h12	114
North, stm., W.V., U.S.	B6	141
North, Cape, c., N.S., Can.	B9	87
North Adams, Ma., U.S.	A1	114
North Albany, Or., U.S.	k11	130
North American Basin	E7	66
North Amherst, Ma., U.S.	B2	114
Northampton, Austl.	F1	60
Northampton, Eng., U.K.	D6	12
Northampton, Ma., U.S.	B2	114
Northampton, Pa., U.S.	E11	131
Northampton, co., N.C., U.S.	A5	126
Northampton, co., Pa., U.S.	E11	131
Northampton, co., Va., U.S.	C7	139
North Andaman, i., India	G6	40
North Andover, Ma., U.S.	A5	114
North Anna, stm., Va., U.S.	B5	139
North Anson, Me., U.S.	D3	112
North Apollo, Pa., U.S.	E2	131
North Arapaho Peak, mtn., Co., U.S.	A5	99
North Arlington, N.J., U.S.	h8	123
North Atlanta, Ga., U.S.	h8	103
North Attleboro, Ma., U.S.	C5	114
North Augusta, S.C., U.S.	D4	133
North Aurora, Il., U.S.	k8	106
North Australian Basin	J14	64
North Baltimore, Oh., U.S.	A2	128
North Bay, On., Can.	A5	89
North Beach, Md., U.S.	C4	113
North Belmont, N.C., U.S.	B1	126
North Bend, Ne., U.S.	C9	120
North Bend, Or., U.S.	D2	130
North Bend, Wa., U.S.	B4	140
North Bennington, Vt., U.S.	F2	138
North Bergen, N.J., U.S.	h8	123
North Berwick, Me., U.S.	E2	112
North Billerica, Ma., U.S.	A5	114
Northborough, Ma., U.S.	B4	114
North Branch, Mi., U.S.	E7	115
North Branch, Mn., U.S.	E6	116
North Branch, N.H., U.S.	D3	122
North Branch, N.J., U.S.	B3	123
North Branford, Ct., U.S.	D4	100
Northbridge, Ma., U.S.	B4	114
Northbrook, Il., U.S.	h9	106
North Brookfield, Ma., U.S.	B3	114
North Brunswick, N.J., U.S.	C4	123
North Caicos, i., T./C. Is.	A5	80
North Caldwell, N.J., U.S.	B4	123
North Canadian, stm., Ok., U.S.	A5	129
North Canton, Ct., U.S.	B2	103
North Canton, Oh., U.S.	B4	128
North Cape, c., P.E., Can.	B6	87
North Cape, c., N.Z.	n13	63c
North Cape see Nordkapp, c., Nor.	A11	10
North Cape May, N.J., U.S.	F3	123
North Carolina, state, U.S.	B3	126
North Cascades National Park, Wa., U.S.	A4	140
North Channel, strt., On., Can.	A2	89
North Channel, strt., U.K.	C4	12
North Charleston, S.C., U.S.	F8	133
North Chicago, Il., U.S.	A6	106
North Clarendon, Vt., U.S.	D3	138
Northcliffe, Austl.	G2	60
North College Hill, Oh., U.S.	o12	128
North Conway, N.H., U.S.	B4	122
North Corbin, Ky., U.S.	D5	110
North Crossett, Ar., U.S.	D4	97
North Cyprus, ctry., Asia	E5	44
North Dakota, state, U.S.	B5	127
North Dartmouth, Ma., U.S.	C6	114
North Eagle Butte, S.D., U.S.	B4	134
North East, Md., U.S.	A6	113
North East, Pa., U.S.	B2	131
Northeast, stm., Md., U.S.	A6	113
Northeast Cape, c., Ak., U.S.	C6	95
Northeast Cape Fear, stm., N.C., U.S.	C5	126
Northeast Harbor, Me., U.S.	D4	112
North Easton, Ma., U.S.	B5	114
Northeast Pond, l., N.H., U.S.	D5	122
North Edisto, stm., S.C., U.S.	k11	133
North English, Ia., U.S.	C5	108
North English, stm., Ia., U.S.	C5	108
North Enid, Ok., U.S.	A4	129
Northern Cheyenne Indian Reservation, Mt., U.S.	E10	119
Northern Cook Islands, is., Cook Is.	F13	58
Northern Donets, stm., Eur.	E15	20
Northern Dvina see Severnaja Dvina, stm., Russia	C6	26
Northern Indian Lake, l., Mb., Can.	A3	86
Northern Ireland, prov., N. Ire., U.K.	C3	12
Northern Mariana Islands, dep., Oc.	C9	58
Northern Sporades see Vórioi Sporádhes, is., Grc.	E10	18
Northern Territory, ter., Austl.	D5	60
North Falmouth, Ma., U.S.	C6	114
Northfield, Mn., U.S.	F5	116
Northfield, N.H., U.S.	D3	122
Northfield, N.J., U.S.	E3	123
Northfield, Oh., U.S.	h9	128
Northfield, Vt., U.S.	C3	138
Northfield Falls, Vt., U.S.	C3	138
North Fiji Basin	J20	64
North Flinders Range, mts., Austl.	G2	62
North Fond du Lac, Wi., U.S.	E5	142
Northford, Ct., U.S.	D4	100
North Fork Reservoir, res., Or., U.S.	B4	130
North Fort Myers, Fl., U.S.	F5	102
North Fox Island, i., Mi., U.S.	C5	115
Northglenn, Co., U.S.	B6	99
North Gower, On., Can.	B9	89
North Grafton, Ma., U.S.	B4	114
North Grosvenordale, Ct., U.S.	B8	100
North Gulfport, Ms., U.S.	E4	117
North Haledon, N.J., U.S.	B4	123
North Hampton, N.H., U.S.	E5	122
North Hartland Reservoir, res., Vt., U.S.	D4	138
North Hatley, P.Q., Can.	D6	90
North Haven, Ct., U.S.	D4	100
North Head, N.B., Can.	E3	87
North Hero Island, i., Vt., U.S.	B2	138
North Horn Lake, l., Tn., U.S.	e8	135
North Industry, Oh., U.S.	B4	128
North Inlet, b., S.C., U.S.	E9	133
North Island, i., N.Z.	o14	63c
North Island, i., S.C., U.S.	E9	133
North Island Naval Air Station, mil., Ca., U.S.	o15	98
North Islands, is., La., U.S.	E7	111
North Judson, In., U.S.	B4	107
North Kansas City, Mo., U.S.	h10	118
North Kingstown, R.I., U.S.	E4	132
North Kingsville, Oh., U.S.	A5	128
North La Junta, Co., U.S.	C7	99
Northlake, Il., U.S.	k9	106
North Lakhimpur, India	D6	40
North Laramie, stm., Wy., U.S.	D7	143
North Las Vegas, Nv., U.S.	G6	121
North La Veta Pass, Co., U.S.	D5	99
North Lewisburg, Oh., U.S.	B2	128
North Liberty, Ia., U.S.	C6	108
North Liberty, In., U.S.	A5	107
North Lima, Oh., U.S.	B5	128
North Little Rock, Ar., U.S.	C3	97
North Logan, Ut., U.S.	B4	137
North Loon Mountain, mtn., Id., U.S.	D3	105
North Magnetic Pole	D33	144
North Mamm Peak, mtn., Co., U.S.	B3	99
North Manchester, In., U.S.	C6	107
North Manitou Island, i., Mi., U.S.	C4	115
North Mankato, Mn., U.S.	F4	116
North Miami, Fl., U.S.	G6	102
North Miami Beach, Fl., U.S.	s13	102
North Middletown, Ky., U.S.	B5	110
North Moose Lake, l., Mb., Can.	B1	86
North Mountain, mtn., Pa., U.S.	D9	131
North Muskegon, Mi., U.S.	E4	115
North Myrtle Beach, S.C., U.S.	D10	133
North Naples, Fl., U.S.	F5	102
North New River Canal, Fl., U.S.	F6	102
North Ogden, Ut., U.S.	B4	137
North Olmsted, Oh., U.S.	h9	128
North Ossetia see Severnaja Osetija, state, Russia	E6	26
North Palisade, mtn., Ca., U.S.	D4	98
North Park, Il., U.S.	A4	106
North Park, val., Co., U.S.	A4	99
North Pass, strt., La., U.S.	E7	111
North Pembroke, Ma., U.S.	B6	114
North Plainfield, N.J., U.S.	B4	123
North Plains, Or., U.S.	B4	130
North Plains, pl., N.M., U.S.	C1	124
North Platte, Ne., U.S.	C5	120
North Platte, stm., U.S.	C7	92
North Point, c., Md., U.S.	B5	113
North Point, c., Mi., U.S.	C7	115
North Pole	E12	144
Northport, Al., U.S.	B2	94
North Prairie, Wi., U.S.	F5	142
North Providence, R.I., U.S.	C4	132
North Raccoon, stm., Ia., U.S.	C3	108
North Reading, Ma., U.S.	f11	114
North Richland Hills, Tx., U.S.	n9	136
Northridge, Oh., U.S.	C2	128
North Ridgeville, Oh., U.S.	A3	128
North Royalton, Oh., U.S.	h9	128
North Rustico, P.E., Can.	C6	87
North Salem, N.H., U.S.	E4	122
North Salt Lake, Ut., U.S.	C4	137
North Santee, stm., S.C., U.S.	E9	133
North Saskatchewan, stm., Can.	H18	82
North Schell Peak, mtn., Nv., U.S.	D7	121
North Scituate, Ma., U.S.	h12	114
North Sea, Eur.	D6	6
North Shore City, N.Z.	o13	63c
North Shoshone Peak, mtn., Nv., U.S.	D4	121

Name	Map Ref.	Page

North Siberian Lowland see Severo-Sibirskaja nizmennost', pl., Russia — B11 — 26
North Sioux City, S.D., U.S. — E9 — 134
North Skunk, stm., Ia., U.S. — C5 — 108
North Springfield, Vt., U.S. — E3 — 138
North Springfield Reservoir, res., Vt., U.S. — E4 — 138
North Star, De., U.S. — A3 — 101
North Stradbroke Island, i., Austl. — F5 — 62
North Stratford, N.H., U.S. — A3 — 122
North Sudbury, Ma., U.S. — g10 — 114
North Swanzey, N.H., U.S. — E2 — 122
North Syracuse, N.Y., U.S. — B4 — 125
North Taranaki Bight, b., N.Z. — o13 — 63c
North Tarrytown, N.Y., U.S. — D7 — 125
North Terre Haute, In., U.S. — E3 — 107
North Thompson, stm., B.C., Can. — D8 — 85
North Tonawanda, N.Y., U.S. — B2 — 125
North Troy, Vt., U.S. — B4 — 138
North Tunica, Ms., U.S. — A3 — 117
North Twin Lake, l., Wi., U.S. — B4 — 142
Northumberland, Pa., U.S. — E8 — 131
Northumberland, co., Pa., U.S. — D8 — 131
Northumberland, co., Va., U.S. — C6 — 139
Northumberland Strait, strt., Can. — C6 — 87
North Umpqua, stm., Or., U.S. — D3 — 130
North Uxbridge, Ma., U.S. — B4 — 114
Northvale, N.J., U.S. — g9 — 123
North Vancouver, B.C., Can. — E6 — 85
North Vassalboro, Me., U.S. — D3 — 112
North Vernon, In., U.S. — F6 — 107
Northville, Mi., U.S. — p15 — 115
North Wales, Pa., U.S. — F11 — 131
North Walpole, N.H., U.S. — D2 — 122
North Warren, Pa., U.S. — C3 — 131
North Webster, In., U.S. — B6 — 107
North West Cape, c., Austl. — E1 — 60
Northwest Miramichi, stm., N.B., Can. — B3 — 87
Northwest Pacific Basin — E18 — 64
Northwest Territories, ter., Can. — E15 — 82
North Wildwood, N.J., U.S. — E3 — 123
North Wilkesboro, N.C., U.S. — A1 — 126
North Windham, Ct., U.S. — C7 — 100
North Windham, Me., U.S. — E2 — 112
Northwood, Ia., U.S. — A4 — 108
Northwood, N.D., U.S. — B8 — 127
North Woodstock, N.H., U.S. — B3 — 122
North York, On., Can. — D5 — 89
North York, Pa., U.S. — G8 — 131
Norton, N.B., Can. — D4 — 87
Norton, Ks., U.S. — C4 — 109
Norton, Ma., U.S. — C5 — 114
Norton, Oh., U.S. — A4 — 128
Norton, Va., U.S. — f9 — 139
Norton, co., Ks., U.S. — C4 — 109
Norton Bay, b., Ak., U.S. — C7 — 95
Norton Pond, l., Vt., U.S. — B5 — 138
Norton Reservoir, res., Ks., U.S. — C8 — 109
Norton Shores, Mi., U.S. — E4 — 115
Norton Sound, strt., Ak., U.S. — C6 — 95
Nortonville, Ks., U.S. — C8 — 109
Nortonville, Ky., U.S. — C2 — 110
Norvegia, Cape, c., Ant. — D3 — 67
Norwalk, Ca., U.S. — n12 — 98
Norwalk, Ct., U.S. — E2 — 100
Norwalk, Ia., U.S. — C4 — 108
Norwalk, Oh., U.S. — A3 — 128
Norwalk, stm., Ct., U.S. — E2 — 100
Norwalk Islands, is., Ct., U.S. — E2 — 100
Norway, Me., U.S. — D2 — 112
Norway, Mi., U.S. — C3 — 115
Norway, ctry., Eur. — B9 — 8
Norway House, Mb., Can. — C3 — 86
Norway Lake, l., Mn., U.S. — E3 — 116
Norwegian Basin — C23 — 144
Norwegian Sea, Eur. — I22 — 10a
Norwich, Eng., U.K. — D7 — 12
Norwich, Ct., U.S. — C7 — 100
Norwich, N.Y., U.S. — C5 — 125
Norwich, Vt., U.S. — D4 — 138
Norwood, On., Can. — C7 — 89
Norwood, Ma., U.S. — B5 — 114
Norwood, Mn., U.S. — F5 — 116
Norwood, N.C., U.S. — B2 — 126
Norwood, N.J., U.S. — h9 — 123
Norwood, N.Y., U.S. — f10 — 125
Norwood, Oh., U.S. — o13 — 128
Norwood, Pa., U.S. — p20 — 131
Norwoodville, Ia., U.S. — e8 — 108
Noshiro, Japan — D13 — 28
Nosivka, Ukr. — D11 — 20
Nossob, stm., Afr. — C2 — 56
Nosy-Varika, Madag. — F9 — 56
Notasulga, Al., U.S. — C4 — 94
Notch Peak, mtn., Ut., U.S. — D2 — 137
Noteć, stm., Pol. — C4 — 20

Notodden, Nor. — G3 — 10
Noto-hantō, pen., Japan — C3 — 31
Notre Dame, Monts, mts., P.Q., Can. — k13 — 90
Notre Dame Bay, b., Nf., Can. — D4 — 88
Notre Dame de Lourdes, Mb., Can. — E2 — 86
Notre-Dame-du-Lac, P.Q., Can. — B9 — 90
Nottawasaga Bay, b., On., Can. — C4 — 89
Nottoway, stm., Va., U.S. — h11 — 90
Nottingham, Eng., U.K. — D6 — 12
Nottoway, co., Va., U.S. — C4 — 139
Nottoway, stm., Va., U.S. — D5 — 139
Nouâdhibou, Maur. — B1 — 50
Nouâdhibou, Râs, c., Afr. — B1 — 50
Nouakchott, Maur. — C1 — 50
Nouâmghâr, Maur. — C1 — 50
Nouméa, N. Cal. — I9 — 62a
Noupoort, S. Afr. — E3 — 56
Nouveau-Brunswick see New Brunswick, prov., Can. — C3 — 87
Nouvelle-Calédonie, i., N. Cal. — I9 — 62a
Nova Caipemba, Ang. — E2 — 54
Nova Friburgo, Braz. — F3 — 74
Nova Iguaçu, Braz. — F3 — 74
Novaja Kazanka, Kaz. — E8 — 22
Novaja Sibir', ostrov, i., Russia — B17 — 26
Novaja Zemlja, is., Russia — B7 — 26
Nova Kakhovka, Ukr. — F12 — 20
Nova Lima, Braz. — F3 — 74
Nova Lisboa see Huambo, Ang. — F3 — 54
Nova Mambone, Moz. — C6 — 56
Novara, Italy — B2 — 18
Nova Scotia, prov., Can. — D6 — 87
Novato, Ca., U.S. — C2 — 98
Nova Venécia, Braz. — E3 — 74
Novaya Zemlya see Novaja Zemlja, is., Russia — B7 — 26
Nova Zagora, Bul. — C11 — 18
Nové Zámky, Slvk. — E5 — 20
Novgorod, Russia — D5 — 26
Novhorod-Sivers'kyi, Ukr. — D12 — 20
Novi, Mi., U.S. — p15 — 115
Novikovo, Russia — A4 — 31
Novi Ligure, Italy — B2 — 18
Novi Pazar, Bul. — C11 — 18
Novi Pazar, Yugo. — C8 — 18
Novi Sad, Yugo. — B7 — 18
Novo Aripuanã, Braz. — E7 — 70
Novoazovs'k, Ukr. — F15 — 20
Novočerkassk, Russia — E7 — 22
Novodvinsk, Russia — B7 — 22
Novo Hamburgo, Braz. — D7 — 72
Novohrad-Volyns'kyi, Ukr. — D9 — 20
Novokazalinsk, Kaz. — E8 — 26
Novokujbyševsk, Russia — D8 — 22
Novokuzneck, Russia — D10 — 26
Novomihajlovskij, Russia — G15 — 20
Novomoskovsk, Russia — D5 — 26
Novomoskovs'k, Ukr. — E13 — 20
Novomyrhorod, Ukr. — E11 — 20
Novorossijsk, Russia — E5 — 26
Novošahtinsk, Russia — F15 — 20
Novosergievka, Russia — D9 — 22
Novosibirsk, Russia — D10 — 26
Novosibirskie ostrova, is., Russia — B16 — 26
Novotroick, Russia — D10 — 22
Novotroickoe, Kaz. — B10 — 42
Novotroïts'ke, Ukr. — F13 — 20
Novoukraïnka, Ukr. — E11 — 20
Novouzensk, Russia — D8 — 22
Novovjatsk, Russia — C8 — 22
Novovolyns'k, Ukr. — D8 — 20
Novozybkov, Russia — C11 — 20
Novyi Buh, Ukr. — F12 — 20
Novyj Oskol, Russia — D14 — 20
Novyj Port, Russia — C9 — 26
Novyj Uzen', Kaz. — E7 — 26
Nowa Ruda, Pol. — D4 — 20
Nowata, Ok., U.S. — A6 — 129
Nowata, co., Ok., U.S. — A6 — 129
Nowood, stm., Wy., U.S. — B5 — 143
Nowra, Austl. — G5 — 62
Nowshāk, mtn., Asia — B2 — 40
Nowy Dwór Mazowiecki, Pol. — C6 — 20
Nowy Sącz, Pol. — E6 — 20
Noxon Reservoir, res., Mt., U.S. — C1 — 119
Noxontown Lake, res., De., U.S. — C3 — 101
Noxubee, co., Ms., U.S. — B5 — 117
Noxubee, stm., U.S. — B5 — 117
Noyes Island, i., Ak., U.S. — n22 — 95
Nsanje, Mwi. — B6 — 56
Nsawam, Ghana — E4 — 50
Nsukka, Nig. — E6 — 50
Nsuta, Ghana — E4 — 50
Ntomba, Lac, l., D.R.C. — D3 — 54
Nūbah, Jibāl an-, mts., Sudan — A6 — 54
Nubanusit Lake, l., N.H., U.S. — E2 — 122
Nubian Desert, des., Sudan — F11 — 48
Nuckolls, co., Ne., U.S. — D7 — 120
Nucla, Co., U.S. — C2 — 99
Nueces, co., Tx., U.S. — F4 — 136

Nueces, stm., Tx., U.S. — E3 — 136
Nueltin Lake, l., Can. — F20 — 82
Nueva Antioquia, Col. — D6 — 80
Nueva Gerona, Cuba — A3 — 80
Nueva Imperial, Chile — E2 — 69
Nueva Italia de Ruiz, Mex. — D4 — 78
Nueva Rosita, Mex. — B4 — 78
Nueve de Julio, Arg. — F5 — 72
Nuevitas, Cuba — A4 — 80
Nuevo, Cayo, i., Mex. — C6 — 78
Nuevo, Golfo, b., Arg. — F4 — 69
Nuevo Casas Grandes, Mex. — A3 — 78
Nuevo Laredo, Mex. — B5 — 78
Nuevo León, state, Mex. — B5 — 78
Nui, atoll, Tuvalu — E11 — 58
Nuku'alofa, Tonga — G12 — 58
Nukus, Uzb. — E7 — 26
Nulato, Ak., U.S. — C8 — 95
Nulhegan, stm., Vt., U.S. — B5 — 138
Nullagine, Austl. — E3 — 60
Nullarbor, Austl. — G5 — 60
Nullarbor Plain, pl., Austl. — G4 — 60
Numan, Nig. — E7 — 50
Numancia, hist., Spain — G5 — 16
Numazu, Japan — D3 — 31
Nunivak Island, i., Ak., U.S. — D6 — 95
Nunjiang, China — B13 — 28
Nuoro, Italy — D2 — 18
Nuremberg, Pa., U.S. — E9 — 131
Nurmes, Fin. — E13 — 10
Nürnberg, Ger. — F12 — 12
Nusaybin, Tur. — D9 — 44
Nu Shan, mts., China — F7 — 28
Nushki, Pak. — E9 — 42
Nutley, N.J., U.S. — B4 — 123
Nutter Fort, W.V., U.S. — k10 — 141
Nutting Lake, Ma., U.S. — f10 — 114
Nuuanu Pali, Hi., U.S. — g10 — 104
Nuuk see Godthåb, Grnld. — F29 — 82
Nyabing, Austl. — G2 — 60
Nyack, N.Y., U.S. — D7 — 125
Nyaingêntanglha Shan, mts., China — E6 — 28
Nyakanazi, Tan. — D6 — 54
Nyala, Sudan — H10 — 48
Nyamlell, Sudan — B5 — 54
Nyanza-Lac, Bdi. — D5 — 54
Nyasa, Lake (Malaŵi, Lake), l., Afr. — F6 — 54
Nyasaland see Malawi, ctry., Afr. — A5 — 56
Nyaunglebin, Myan. — C3 — 34
Nyborg, Den. — I4 — 10
Nybro, Swe. — H6 — 10
Nyda, Russia — C9 — 26
Nye, co., Nv., U.S. — E5 — 121
Nyeri, Kenya — D7 — 54
Nyimba, Zam. — A5 — 56
Nyingchi, China — D6 — 40
Nyíregyháza, Hung. — F6 — 20
Nykøbing, Den. — I4 — 10
Nyköping, Swe. — G7 — 10
Nylstroom, S. Afr. — C4 — 56
Nynäshamn, Swe. — G7 — 10
Nyngan, Austl. — G4 — 62
Nyš, Russia — D16 — 26
Nysa, Pol. — D4 — 20
Nyssa, Or., U.S. — D9 — 130
Nyunzu, D.R.C. — E5 — 54
Nzébéla, Gui. — E3 — 50
Nzérékoré, Gui. — E3 — 50
N'zeto, Ang. — E2 — 54
Nzwani, i., Com. — A7 — 56

O

Oahe, Lake, res., U.S. — B7 — 92
Oahe Dam, S.D., U.S. — C5 — 134
Oahu, i., Hi., U.S. — B4 — 104
Oak Bay, B.C., Can. — h12 — 85
Oak Bluffs, Ma., U.S. — D6 — 114
Oak Creek, Co., U.S. — A4 — 99
Oak Creek, Wi., U.S. — n12 — 142
Oakdale, Ca., U.S. — D3 — 98
Oakdale, Ga., U.S. — h8 — 103
Oakdale, La., U.S. — D3 — 111
Oakdale, Pa., U.S. — k13 — 131
Oakes, N.D., U.S. — C7 — 127
Oakfield, N.Y., U.S. — B2 — 125
Oakfield, Wi., U.S. — E5 — 142
Oak Forest, Il., U.S. — k9 — 106
Oak Grove, Ky., U.S. — D2 — 110
Oak Grove, La., U.S. — B4 — 111
Oak Grove, Or., U.S. — B4 — 130
Oak Harbor, Oh., U.S. — A2 — 128
Oak Harbor, Wa., U.S. — A3 — 140
Oak Hill, Mi., U.S. — D4 — 115
Oak Hill, Oh., U.S. — D3 — 128
Oak Hill, W.V., U.S. — D3 — 141
Oak Hill, Ma., U.S. — f9 — 114
Oakhurst, Ok., U.S. — A5 — 129
Oak Island, i., Wi., U.S. — B3 — 142
Oak Lake, l., Mb., Can. — E1 — 86
Oakland, Ca., U.S. — D2 — 98
Oakland, Ia., U.S. — C2 — 108
Oakland, Il., U.S. — D5 — 106
Oakland, Md., U.S. — m12 — 113
Oakland, Me., U.S. — D3 — 112
Oakland, Ne., U.S. — C9 — 120
Oakland, N.J., U.S. — A4 — 123
Oakland, Or., U.S. — D3 — 130
Oakland, R.I., U.S. — B2 — 132
Oakland, co., Mi., U.S. — F7 — 115
Oakland City, In., U.S. — H3 — 107

Oakland Park, Fl., U.S. — r13 — 102
Oak Lawn, Il., U.S. — B6 — 106
Oaklawn, Ks., U.S. — g12 — 109
Oakley, Id., U.S. — G5 — 105
Oakley, Ks., U.S. — C3 — 109
Oakman, Al., U.S. — B2 — 94
Oakmont, Pa., U.S. — E2 — 131
Oak Mountain, mtn., Ga., U.S. — D2 — 103
Oak Orchard, De., U.S. — F5 — 101
Oak Park, Il., U.S. — B6 — 106
Oak Park, Mi., U.S. — p15 — 115
Oak Ridge, N.C., U.S. — A3 — 126
Oak Ridge, Tn., U.S. — C9 — 135
Oak Ridge Reservoir, res., N.J., U.S. — A3 — 123
Oakton, Va., U.S. — g12 — 139
Oaktown, In., U.S. — G3 — 107
Oak Valley, N.J., U.S. — D2 — 123
Oakville, On., Can. — D5 — 89
Oakville, Mo., U.S. — g13 — 118
Oakwood, Ga., U.S. — B3 — 103
Oakwood, Il., U.S. — C6 — 106
Oakwood, Oh., U.S. — C1 — 128
Oamaru, N.Z. — q13 — 63c
Oaxaca, state, Mex. — D5 — 78
Oaxaca de Juárez, Mex. — D5 — 78
Ob', stm., Russia — B9 — 26
Oban, Scot., U.K. — B4 — 12
Ob Bay see Obskaja guba, b., Russia — C9 — 26
Obed, stm., Tn., U.S. — C9 — 135
Oberlin, Ks., U.S. — C3 — 109
Oberlin, La., U.S. — D3 — 111
Oberlin, Oh., U.S. — A3 — 128
Obetz, Oh., U.S. — m11 — 128
Obi, Kepulauan, is., Indon. — D7 — 36
Obi, Pulau, i., Indon. — D7 — 36
Obi, Selat, strt., Indon. — D7 — 36
Óbidos, Braz. — D8 — 70
Obihiro, Japan — C16 — 28
Obion, Tn., U.S. — A2 — 135
Obion, co., Tn., U.S. — A2 — 135
Obion, stm., Tn., U.S. — A2 — 135
Oblong, Il., U.S. — D6 — 106
Obluče, Russia — B14 — 28
Obninsk, Russia — B14 — 20
Obo, C.A.R. — B5 — 54
Obojan', Russia — D14 — 20
O'Brien, co., Ia., U.S. — A2 — 108
Obščij syrt, mts., Eur. — D9 — 22
Observation Peak, mtn., Ca., U.S. — B3 — 98
Obskaja guba, b., Russia — C9 — 26
Obuasi, Ghana — E4 — 50
Obudu, Nig. — E6 — 50
Ocala, Fl., U.S. — C4 — 102
Očamčira, Geor. — A9 — 44
Ocaña, Col. — B5 — 70
Ocaña, Spain — H5 — 16
Occidental, Cordillera, mts., Col. — E4 — 80
Occidental, Cordillera, mts., Peru — E4 — 70
Ocean, co., N.J., U.S. — D4 — 123
Oceana, W.V., U.S. — D3 — 141
Oceana, co., Mi., U.S. — E4 — 115
Oceana Naval Air Station, mil., Va., U.S. — k15 — 139
Ocean Bluff, Ma., U.S. — B6 — 114
Ocean City, Fl., U.S. — u15 — 102
Ocean City, Md., U.S. — D7 — 113
Ocean City, N.J., U.S. — E3 — 123
Ocean Grove, Ma., U.S. — C5 — 114
Ocean Island see Banaba, i., Kir. — E10 — 58
Ocean Park, Wa., U.S. — C1 — 140
Oceanport, N.J., U.S. — C4 — 123
Oceanside, Ca., U.S. — F5 — 98
Ocean Springs, Ms., U.S. — E5 — 117
Ocean [Township], N.J., U.S. — C4 — 123
Ocean View, De., U.S. — F5 — 101
Ocheda Lake, l., Mn., U.S. — G3 — 116
Ocheyedan, stm., Ia., U.S. — A2 — 108
Ochiltree, co., Tx., U.S. — A2 — 136
Ochlockonee, stm., Fl., U.S. — B2 — 102
Ochoco Lake, res., Or., U.S. — C6 — 130
Ocilla, Ga., U.S. — E3 — 103
Ockelbo, Swe. — F7 — 10
Ocmulgee, stm., Ga., U.S. — D3 — 103
Ocoa, Bahía de, b., Dom. Rep. — B5 — 80
Ocoee, Fl., U.S. — D5 — 102
Ocoee, Lake, res., Tn., U.S. — D9 — 135
Oconee, co., Ga., U.S. — C3 — 103
Oconee, co., S.C., U.S. — B1 — 133
Oconee, stm., Ga., U.S. — C3 — 103
Oconee, Lake, res., Ga., U.S. — C3 — 103
Oconomowoc, Wi., U.S. — E5 — 142
Oconto, Wi., U.S. — D6 — 142
Oconto, co., Wi., U.S. — D5 — 142
Oconto, stm., Wi., U.S. — D5 — 142
Oconto Falls, Wi., U.S. — D5 — 142
Ocosingo, Mex. — D6 — 78
Ocotal, Nic. — C2 — 80
Ocotlán, Mex. — C4 — 78
Ocracoke Inlet, b., N.C., U.S. — B6 — 126
Ocracoke Island, i., N.C., U.S. — B7 — 126

October Revolution Island see Oktjabr'skoj Revoljucii, ostrov, i., Russia — B11 — 26
Octoraro Creek, stm., U.S. — A5 — 113
Ocumare del Tuy, Ven. — C6 — 80
Oda, Ghana — E4 — 50
Oda, Jabal, mtn., Sudan — F12 — 48
Odebolt, Ia., U.S. — B2 — 108
Odell, Il., U.S. — B5 — 106
Odell, Or., U.S. — B5 — 130
Odell Lake, l., Or., U.S. — E5 — 130
Odem, Tx., U.S. — F4 — 136
Odemira, Port. — I2 — 16
Ödemiş, Tur. — C2 — 44
Odendaalsrus, S. Afr. — D4 — 56
Odense, Den. — I4 — 10
Odenton, Md., U.S. — B4 — 113
Odenville, Al., U.S. — B3 — 94
Oder, stm., Eur. — C3 — 20
Odesa, Ukr. — F11 — 20
Odessa, On., Can. — C8 — 89
Odessa see Odesa, Ukr. — F11 — 20
Odessa, De., U.S. — C3 — 101
Odessa, Mo., U.S. — C4 — 118
Odessa, Tx., U.S. — D1 — 136
Odessa, Wa., U.S. — B7 — 140
Odienné, C. Iv. — E3 — 50
Odin, Il., U.S. — E4 — 106
Odon, In., U.S. — G4 — 107
O'Donnell, Tx., U.S. — C2 — 136
Odorheiu Secuiesc, Rom. — F8 — 20
Oeiras, Braz. — C3 — 74
Oelwein, Ia., U.S. — B6 — 108
Oenpelli, Austl. — C5 — 60
Of, Tur. — B9 — 44
O'Fallon, Il., U.S. — E4 — 106
O'Fallon, Mo., U.S. — f12 — 118
Ofanto, stm., Italy — D5 — 18
Offa, Nig. — E5 — 50
Offenburg, Ger. — F10 — 12
Offutt Air Force Base, mil., Ne., U.S. — g3 — 120
Ofotfjorden, b., Nor. — B7 — 10
Ogaden, reg., Afr. — I14 — 48
Ogallala, Ne., U.S. — C4 — 120
Ogasawara-guntō, is., Japan — F16 — 64
Ogbomosho, Nig. — E5 — 50
Ogden, Ia., U.S. — B3 — 108
Ogden, Ks., U.S. — C7 — 109
Ogden, Ut., U.S. — B4 — 137
Ogden, Mount, mtn., N.A. — k23 — 95
Ogdensburg, N.J., U.S. — A3 — 123
Ogdensburg, N.Y., U.S. — f9 — 125
Ogeechee, stm., Ga., U.S. — D5 — 103
Ogemaw, co., Mi., U.S. — D6 — 115
Ogle, co., Il., U.S. — A4 — 106
Oglesby, Il., U.S. — B4 — 106
Oglethorpe, Ga., U.S. — D2 — 103
Oglethorpe, co., Ga., U.S. — C3 — 103
Oglethorpe, Mount, mtn., Ga., U.S. — B2 — 103
Ogoja, Nig. — E6 — 50
Ogooué, stm., Afr. — D2 — 54
Ogre, Lat. — H11 — 10
Ogunquit, Me., U.S. — E2 — 112
Ogurdžaly, ostrov, i., Turk. — C6 — 42
Oha, Russia — D16 — 26
Ohanet, Alg. — E6 — 48
Ohatchee, Al., U.S. — B3 — 94
Ohio, co., In., U.S. — G7 — 107
Ohio, co., Ky., U.S. — C3 — 110
Ohio, co., W.V., U.S. — A4 — 141
Ohio, state, U.S. — B3 — 128
Ohio, stm., U.S. — D10 — 92
Ohio Brush Creek, stm., Oh., U.S. — D2 — 128
Ohio City, Oh., U.S. — B1 — 128
Ohio Peak, mtn., Co., U.S. — C3 — 99
Ohioville, Pa., U.S. — E1 — 131
Ohoopee, stm., Ga., U.S. — D4 — 103
Ohotsk, Russia — D16 — 26
Ohrid, Mac. — D8 — 18
Ohrid, Lake, l., Eur. — C8 — 14
Oiapoque, Braz. — C9 — 70
Oiapoque (Oyapok), stm., S.A. — C9 — 70
Oil City, La., U.S. — B2 — 111
Oil City, Pa., U.S. — D2 — 131
Oil Creek, stm., Pa., U.S. — C2 — 131
Oildale, Ca., U.S. — E4 — 98
Oil Springs, On., Can. — E2 — 89
Oilton, Ok., U.S. — A5 — 129
Oise, stm., Eur. — C8 — 16
Ōita, Japan — E14 — 28
Ojai, Ca., U.S. — E4 — 98
Ojinaga, Mex. — B4 — 78
Ojmjakon, Russia — C16 — 26
Ojocaliente, Mex. — C4 — 78
Ojos del Salado, Cerro see Ojos del Salado, Nevado, mtn., S.A. — D4 — 72
Ojos del Salado, Nevado, mtn., S.A. — D4 — 72
Oka, stm., Russia — D6 — 26
Okaba, Indon. — H10 — 32
Okahandja, Nmb. — C2 — 56
Okaloosa, co., Fl., U.S. — u15 — 102
Okamanpeedan Lake, l., U.S. — A3 — 108
Okanagan Falls, B.C., Can. — E8 — 85
Okanagan Lake, l., B.C., Can. — D8 — 85
Okanagan Landing, B.C., Can. — D8 — 85

Name	Map Ref.	Page
Okanogan, Wa., U.S.	A6	140
Okanogan, co., Wa., U.S.	A5	140
Okāra, Pak.	D10	42
Okarche, Ok., U.S.	B4	129
Okatibee Reservoir, res., Ms., U.S.	C5	117
Okaukuejo, Nmb.	B2	56
Okavango (Cubango), stm., Afr.	B3	56
Okawville, Il., U.S.	E4	106
Okaya, Japan	C3	31
Okayama, Japan	E14	28
Okazaki, Japan	D3	31
Okeechobee, Fl., U.S.	E6	102
Okeechobee, co., Fl., U.S.	E6	102
Okeechobee, Lake, l., Fl., U.S.	F6	102
Okeene, Ok., U.S.	A3	129
Okefenokee Swamp, sw., U.S.	F4	103
Okemah, Ok., U.S.	B5	129
Okene, Nig.	E6	50
Okfuskee, co., Ok., U.S.	B5	129
Okhotsk see Ohotsk, Russia	D16	26
Okhotsk, Sea of, Asia	D16	26
Okhotsk Basin	B7	144
Okhtyrka, Ukr.	D13	20
Okinawa, Japan	g6	31a
Okinawa-jima, i., Japan	A9	34
Okinawa-shotō, is., Japan	g6	31a
Okino-Erabu-shima, i., Japan	A9	34
Okino-Tori-shima, i., Japan	G15	28
Oki-shotō, is., Japan	D14	28
Okitipupa, Nig.	E5	50
Oklahoma, co., Ok., U.S.	B4	129
Oklahoma, state, U.S.	B4	129
Oklahoma City, Ok., U.S.	B4	129
Oklawaha, Fl., U.S.	C5	102
Oklawaha, stm., Fl., U.S.	C5	102
Oklawaha, Lake, res., Fl., U.S.	C5	102
Okmulgee, Ok., U.S.	B6	129
Okmulgee, co., Ok., U.S.	B5	129
Okoboji, Ia., U.S.	A2	108
Okobojo Creek, stm., S.D., U.S.	C5	134
Okolona, Ky., U.S.	g11	110
Okolona, Ms., U.S.	B5	117
Okondja, Gabon	D2	54
Okotoks, Ab., Can.	D4	84
Oktibbeha, co., Ms., U.S.	B5	117
Oktjabr'sk, Kaz.	E7	26
Oktjabr'skij, Russia	D9	22
Oktjabr'skoe, Russia	B12	22
Oktjabr'skoj Revoljucii, ostrov, i., Russia	B11	26
Oktwin, Myan.	C3	34
Okushiri-tō, i., Japan	C15	28
Ola, Ar., U.S.	B2	97
Ólafsfjördur, Ice.	k19	10a
Olancha Peak, mtn., Ca., U.S.	D4	98
Olanchito, Hond.	B2	80
Öland, i., Swe.	H7	10
Olanta, S.C., U.S.	D8	133
Olathe, Co., U.S.	C3	99
Olathe, Ks., U.S.	D9	109
Olavarría, Arg.	F5	72
Olbia, Italy	D2	18
Olcott, N.Y., U.S.	B2	125
Old Bahama Channel, strt., N.A.	A4	80
Old Bridge, N.J., U.S.	C4	123
Old Castile see Castilla la Vieja, hist. reg., Spain	G5	16
Oldenburg, Ger.	D11	12
Oldenburg, In., U.S.	F7	107
Oldenburg in Holstein, Ger.	C12	12
Old Faithful Geyser, Wy., U.S.	B2	143
Old Forge, Pa., U.S.	D10	131
Old Fort, N.C., U.S.	f10	126
Oldham, co., Ky., U.S.	B4	110
Oldham, co., Tx., U.S.	B1	136
Old Harbor, Ak., U.S.	D9	95
Old Hickory Lake, res., Tn., U.S.	A5	135
Oldman, stm., Ab., Can.	E4	84
Old Man of the Mountain, N.H., U.S.	B3	122
Oldmans Creek, stm., N.J., U.S.	D2	123
Old Orchard Beach, Me., U.S.	E2	112
Old Perlican, Nf., Can.	D5	88
Old Point Comfort, c., Va., U.S.	h15	139
Old Rhodes Key, i., Fl., U.S.	G6	102
Old River Lake, l., Ar., U.S.	k10	97
Olds, Ab., Can.	D3	84
Old Saybrook, Ct., U.S.	D6	100
Oldsmar, Fl., U.S.	o10	102
Old Tampa Bay, b., Fl., U.S.	p10	102
Old Tappan, N.J., U.S.	g9	123
Old Tate, Bots.	C4	56
Old Topsail Inlet, b., N.C., U.S.	C5	126
Old Town, Me., U.S.	D4	112
Old Wives Lake, l., Sk., Can.	G2	91
Olean, N.Y., U.S.	C2	125
O'Leary, P.E., Can.	C5	87
Olëkma, stm., Russia	C14	26
Olekminsk, Russia	C14	26
Oleksandriia, Ukr.	E12	20
Olenegorsk, Russia	B15	10
Olenëk, Russia	C13	26
Olenëk, stm., Russia	B13	26
Olenëkskij zaliv, b., Russia	B14	26
Olentangy, stm., Oh., U.S.	B3	128
Oléron, Île d', i., Fr.	F6	16
Olevsk, Ukr.	D9	20
Ol'ga, Russia	E15	26
Ölgiy, Mong.	B6	28
Olhão, Port.	I3	16
Olifants (Elefantes), stm., Afr.	C4	56
Olifants, stm., Nmb.	C2	56
Olifantshoek, S. Afr.	D3	56
Ólimbos, mtn., Cyp.	E5	44
Ólimbos, Óros, mtn., Grc.	D9	18
Olin, Ia., U.S.	B6	108
Olinda, Braz.	C5	74
Olive Branch, Ms., U.S.	A4	117
Olive Hill, Ky., U.S.	B6	110
Olivehurst, Ca., U.S.	C3	98
Oliveira, Braz.	F3	74
Oliver, B.C., Can.	E8	85
Oliver, Pa., U.S.	G2	131
Oliver, co., N.D., U.S.	B4	127
Oliver Dam, i., U.S.	C5	94
Oliver Springs, Tn., U.S.	C9	135
Olivet, Mi., U.S.	F6	115
Olivia, Mn., U.S.	F4	116
Oljutorskij, mys, c., Russia	D19	26
Olla, La., U.S.	C3	111
Ollagüe, Chile	B3	69
Olmito, Tx., U.S.	F4	136
Olmos, Peru	E4	70
Olmos Park, Tx., U.S.	k7	136
Olmsted, co., Mn., U.S.	G6	116
Olmsted Falls, Oh., U.S.	h9	128
Olney, Il., U.S.	E5	106
Olney, Md., U.S.	B3	113
Olney, Tx., U.S.	C3	136
Olomouc, Czech Rep.	E4	20
Olonec, Russia	B5	22
Olongapo, Phil.	D8	34
Oloron-Sainte-Marie, Fr.	F6	16
Olot, Spain	F8	16
Olovjannaja, Russia	A11	28
Olsztyn, Pol.	C6	20
Olteniţa, Rom.	G9	20
Olton, Tx., U.S.	B1	136
Olustee, Ok., U.S.	C2	129
Olympia, Wa., U.S.	B3	140
Olympic Mountains, mts., Wa., U.S.	B2	140
Olympic National Park, Wa., U.S.	B2	140
Olympus see Ólimbos, mtn., Cyp.	E5	44
Olympus, Mount see Ólimbos, Óros, mtn., Grc.	D9	18
Olympus, Mount, mtn., Wa., U.S.	B2	140
Olyphant, Pa., U.S.	D10	131
Omagh, N. Ire., U.K.	C3	12
Omaha, Ne., U.S.	C10	120
Omaha Indian Reservation, Ne., U.S.	B9	120
Omak, Wa., U.S.	A6	140
Omak Lake, l., Wa., U.S.	A6	140
Oman, ctry., Asia	G7	38
Oman, Gulf of, b., Asia	F7	42
Omar, W.V., U.S.	D3	141
Omarama, N.Z.	p12	63c
Omaruru, Nmb.	C2	56
Omatako, stm., Nmb.	B2	56
Ombai, Selat, strt., Indon.	E7	36
Omboué, Gabon	D1	54
Omčak, Russia	C16	26
Omdurman see Umm Durmān, Sudan	G11	48
Omega, Ga., U.S.	E3	103
Omemee, On., Can.	C6	89
Omerville, P.Q., Can.	D5	90
Ometepe, Isla de, i., Nic.	C2	80
Ometepec, Mex.	D5	78
Omineca, stm., B.C., Can.	B5	85
Omineca Mountains, mts., B.C., Can.	A4	85
Ōmiya, Japan	C3	31
Ommaney, Cape, c., Ak., U.S.	D12	95
Omolon, stm., Russia	C17	26
Ompompanoosuc, stm., Vt., U.S.	D4	138
Omro, Wi., U.S.	D5	142
Omsk, Russia	D9	26
Omsukčan, Russia	C17	26
Ōmuda (Ōmuta), Japan	E14	28
Ōmura, Japan	D1	31
Ōmuta (Ōmuda), Japan	E14	28
Omutninsk, Russia	C9	22
Onaga, Ks., U.S.	C7	109
Onalaska, Wa., U.S.	C3	140
Onalaska, Wi., U.S.	E2	142
Onamia, Mn., U.S.	D5	116
Onancock, Va., U.S.	C7	139
Onarga, Il., U.S.	C6	106
Onawa, Ia., U.S.	B1	108
Onawa, Lake, l., Me., U.S.	C3	112
Onaway, Mi., U.S.	C6	115
Ondangwa, Nmb.	B2	56
Ondjiva, Ang.	B2	56
Ondo, Nig.	E5	50
Öndörhaan, Mong.	B10	28
Oneco, Fl., U.S.	E4	102
Onega, Russia	C5	26
Onega, stm., Russia	B6	22
Onega, Lake see Onežskoe ozero, l., Russia	C5	26
Onega Bay see Onežskaja guba, b., Russia	B6	22
One Hundred Fifty Mile House, B.C., Can.	C7	85
One Hundred Mile House, B.C., Can.	D7	85
Oneida, Ky., U.S.	C6	110
Oneida, N.Y., U.S.	B5	125
Oneida, Oh., U.S.	C1	128
Oneida, Tn., U.S.	C9	135
Oneida, co., Id., U.S.	G6	105
Oneida, co., N.Y., U.S.	B5	125
Oneida, co., Wi., U.S.	C4	142
Oneida Lake, l., N.Y., U.S.	B5	125
O'Neill, Ne., U.S.	B7	120
Onekotan, ostrov, i., Russia	E17	26
Oneonta, Al., U.S.	B3	94
Oneonta, N.Y., U.S.	C5	125
Oneşti, Rom.	F9	20
Onežskaja guba, b., Russia	B6	22
Onežskoe ozero, l., Russia	C5	26
Ongole, India	F4	40
Onida, S.D., U.S.	C5	134
Onitsha, Nig.	E6	50
Onondaga, co., N.Y., U.S.	C4	125
Onondaga Indian Reservation, N.Y., U.S.	C4	125
Onota Lake, l., Ma., U.S.	B1	114
Onoway, Ab., Can.	C3	84
Onseepkans, S. Afr.	D2	56
Onset, Ma., U.S.	C6	114
Onslow, Austl.	E1	60
Onslow, co., N.C., U.S.	C5	126
Onslow Bay, b., N.C., U.S.	C5	126
Onsted, Mi., U.S.	F6	115
Ontario, Ca., U.S.	E5	98
Ontario, Oh., U.S.	B3	128
Ontario, Or., U.S.	C10	130
Ontario, co., N.Y., U.S.	C3	125
Ontario, prov., Can.	C6	89
Ontario, Lake, l., N.A.	C12	92
Ontinyent, Spain	H6	16
Ontonagon, Mi., U.S.	m12	115
Ontonagon, co., Mi., U.S.	m12	115
Ontonagon Indian Reservation, Mi., U.S.	B1	115
Oodnadatta, Austl.	F2	62
Ooldea, Austl.	G5	60
Oolitic, In., U.S.	G4	107
Oologah, Ok., U.S.	A6	129
Oologah Lake, res., Ok., U.S.	A6	129
Ooltewah, Tn., U.S.	D8	135
Oostburg, Wi., U.S.	E6	142
Oostende, Bel.	E8	12
Ootsa Lake, l., B.C., Can.	C4	85
Opala, D.R.C.	D4	54
Opa-Locka, Fl., U.S.	s13	102
Opava, Czech Rep.	E4	20
Opelika, Al., U.S.	C4	94
Opelousas, La., U.S.	D3	111
Opequon Creek, stm., W.V., U.S.	B6	141
Opobo, Nig.	F6	50
Opočka, Russia	H13	10
Opole, Pol.	D4	20
Opotiki, N.Z.	o14	63c
Opp, Al., U.S.	D3	94
Oppdal, Nor.	E3	10
Oppelo, Ar., U.S.	B3	97
Opportunity, Wa., U.S.	B8	140
Optima Reservoir, res., Ok., U.S.	e9	129
Opuwo, Nmb.	B1	56
Oquawka, Il., U.S.	C3	106
Oracle, Az., U.S.	E5	96
Oradea, Rom.	F6	20
Oradell, N.J., U.S.	h8	123
Oradell Reservoir, res., N.J., U.S.	h9	123
Orai, India	D3	40
Oraibi, Az., U.S.	B5	96
Oran see Wahran, Alg.	C4	48
Oran, Mo., U.S.	D8	118
Oran, Sebkha d', l., Alg.	J6	16
Orange, Austl.	G4	62
Orange, Fr.	E9	16
Orange, Ca., U.S.	n13	98
Orange, Ct., U.S.	D3	100
Orange, Ma., U.S.	A3	114
Orange, N.J., U.S.	B4	123
Orange, Tx., U.S.	D6	136
Orange, Va., U.S.	B4	139
Orange, co., Ca., U.S.	F5	98
Orange, co., Fl., U.S.	D5	102
Orange, co., In., U.S.	G4	107
Orange, co., N.C., U.S.	A3	126
Orange, co., N.Y., U.S.	D6	125
Orange, co., Tx., U.S.	D6	136
Orange, co., Va., U.S.	B4	139
Orange (Oranje), stm., Afr.	D2	56
Orange, Cabo, c., Braz.	C9	70
Orange Beach, Al., U.S.	E2	94
Orangeburg, S.C., U.S.	E6	133
Orangeburg, co., S.C., U.S.	E6	133
Orange City, Fl., U.S.	D5	102
Orange City, Ia., U.S.	B1	108
Orange Grove, Ms., U.S.	E5	117
Orange Grove, Tx., U.S.	F4	136
Orange Park, Fl., U.S.	B5	102
Orangeville, On., Can.	D4	89
Orangeville, Ut., U.S.	D4	137
Orange Walk, Belize	B2	80
Oranienburg, Ger.	D13	12
Oranje see Orange, stm., Afr.	D2	56
Oranjemund, Nmb.	D2	56
Oranjestad, Aruba	C6	80
Orbetello, Italy	C3	18
Orbost, Austl.	H4	62
Orcas Island, i., Wa., U.S.	A3	140
Orchard City, Co., U.S.	C3	99
Orchard Homes, Mt., U.S.	D2	119
Orchard Park, N.Y., U.S.	C2	125
Orchards, Wa., U.S.	D3	140
Orchard Valley, Wy., U.S.	E8	143
Orcutt, Ca., U.S.	E3	98
Ord, Ne., U.S.	C7	120
Ord, Mount, mtn., Austl.	D4	60
Ordway, Co., U.S.	C7	99
Ordzhonikidze see Vladikavkaz, Russia	E6	26
Ordzhonikidze see Yenakiieve, Ukr.	E15	20
Ordžonikidzeabad, Taj.	C9	42
Oreana, Il., U.S.	D5	106
Oregon, Il., U.S.	A4	106
Oregon, Mo., U.S.	B2	118
Oregon, Oh., U.S.	A2	128
Oregon, Wi., U.S.	F4	142
Oregon, co., Mo., U.S.	E6	118
Oregon, state, U.S.	C6	130
Oregon Caves National Monument, Or., U.S.	E2	130
Oregon City, Or., U.S.	B4	130
Oregon Inlet, b., N.C., U.S.	B7	126
Orehovo-Zuevo, Russia	C5	26
Orel, Russia	D5	26
Orem, Ut., U.S.	C4	137
Ore Mountains see Erzgebirge, mts., Eur.	E9	8
Orenburg, Russia	D7	26
Orense, Arg.	F6	72
Orestiás, Grc.	D11	18
Orfanoú, Kólpos, b., Grc.	D9	18
Orfordville, Wi., U.S.	F4	142
Organ Mountains, mts., N.M., U.S.	E3	124
Organ Pipe Cactus National Monument, Az., U.S.	E3	96
Orgūn, Afg.	D9	42
Orhei, Mol.	F10	20
Orhon, stm., Mong.	A9	28
Oriental, N.C., U.S.	B6	126
Oriental, Cordillera, mts., Col.	D5	80
Oriental, Cordillera, mts., Peru	F5	70
Orikhiv, Ukr.	F13	20
Orillia, On., Can.	C5	89
Orinoco, stm., S.A.	B6	70
Oriola, Spain	H6	16
Orion, Il., U.S.	B3	106
Orissa, prov., India	E4	40
Oristano, Italy	E2	18
Oristano, Golfo di, b., Italy	E2	18
Orivesi, Fin.	F11	10
Oriximiná, Braz.	D8	70
Orizaba, Mex.	D5	78
Orkney, S. Afr.	D4	56
Orkney Islands, is., U.K.	A5	12
Orland, Ca., U.S.	C2	98
Orlando, Fl., U.S.	D5	102
Orland Park, Il., U.S.	k9	106
Orléanais, hist. reg., Fr.	C7	16
Orléans, Fr.	D7	16
Orleans, Ma., U.S.	C7	114
Orleans, Vt., U.S.	B4	138
Orleans, co., La., U.S.	E6	111
Orleans, co., N.Y., U.S.	B2	125
Orleans, co., Vt., U.S.	B4	138
Orléans, Île d', i., P.Q., Can.	C6	90
Orlik, Russia	A7	28
Orman Dam, S.D., U.S.	C2	134
Ormāra, Pak.	E8	42
Ormoc, Phil.	D8	34
Ormond Beach, Fl., U.S.	C5	102
Ormstown, P.Q., Can.	D3	90
Örnsköldsvik, Swe.	E8	10
Orocué, Col.	C5	70
Orofino, Id., U.S.	C2	105
Oroluk, atoll, Micron.	D9	3
Oromocto, N.B., Can.	D3	87
Oromocto Lake, l., N.B., Can.	D2	87
Oron, Nig.	F6	50
Orono, Me., U.S.	D4	112
Oronoco, Mn., U.S.	F6	116
Oroquieta, Phil.	E8	34
Orosei, Golfo di, b., Italy	E2	18
Oroville, Ca., U.S.	C3	98
Oroville, Wa., U.S.	A6	140
Oroville, Lake, res., Ca., U.S.	C3	98
Orrick, Mo., U.S.	B3	118
Orrville, Oh., U.S.	B4	128
Orša, Bela.	B11	20
Orsk, Russia	D7	26
Ortaca, Tur.	D3	44
Ortegal, Cabo, c., Spain	F3	16
Orting, Wa., U.S.	B3	140
Ortiz, Mex.	B2	78
Ortonville, Mi., U.S.	F7	115
Ortonville, Mn., U.S.	E2	116
Orto-Tokoj, Kyrg.	A3	40
Orūmīyeh, Iran	C5	42
Orūmīyeh, Daryācheh-ye, l., Iran	C5	42
Oruro, Bol.	B4	72
Orwell, Oh., U.S.	A5	128
Orwigsburg, Pa., U.S.	E9	131
Oš, Kyrg.	E9	26
Osa, Península de, pen., C.R.	D3	80
Osage, Ia., U.S.	A5	108
Osage, Wy., U.S.	C8	143
Osage, co., Ks., U.S.	D8	109
Osage, co., Mo., U.S.	C6	118
Osage, co., Ok., U.S.	A5	129
Osage, stm., Mo., U.S.	C3	118
Osage Beach, Mo., U.S.	C5	118
Osage City, Ks., U.S.	D8	109
Ōsaka, Japan	E15	28
Osakis, Mn., U.S.	E3	116
Osakis, Lake, l., Mn., U.S.	E3	116
Osawatomie, Ks., U.S.	D9	109
Osborne, Ks., U.S.	C5	109
Osborne, co., Ks., U.S.	C5	109
Osburn, Id., U.S.	B3	105
Osceola, Ar., U.S.	B6	97
Osceola, Ia., U.S.	C4	108
Osceola, In., U.S.	A5	107
Osceola, Mo., U.S.	C4	118
Osceola, Ne., U.S.	C8	120
Osceola, Wi., U.S.	C1	142
Osceola, co., Fl., U.S.	E5	102
Osceola, co., Ia., U.S.	A2	108
Osceola, co., Mi., U.S.	E5	115
Osceola Mills, Pa., U.S.	E5	131
Oscoda, Mi., U.S.	D7	115
Oscoda, co., Mi., U.S.	D6	115
Oscura Mountains, mts., N.M., U.S.	D3	124
Osgood, In., U.S.	F7	107
Oshawa, On., Can.	D6	89
Ō-shima, i., Japan	D3	31
Oshkosh, Ne., U.S.	C3	120
Oshkosh, Wi., U.S.	D5	142
Oshnovīyeh, Iran	D11	44
Oshogbo, Nig.	E5	50
Oshtorīnān, Iran	E13	44
Oshwe, D.R.C.	D3	54
Osijek, Cro.	B7	18
Oskaloosa, Ia., U.S.	C5	108
Oskaloosa, Ks., U.S.	C8	109
Oskarshamn, Swe.	H7	10
Oskū, Iran	D12	44
Oslo, Nor.	G4	10
Oslofjorden, b., Nor.	G4	10
Osmānābād, India	F3	40
Osmancık, Tur.	B6	44
Osmaniye, Tur.	D7	44
Osmond, Ne., U.S.	B8	120
Osnabrück, Ger.	D11	12
Osorno, Chile	F2	69
Osoyoos, B.C., Can.	E8	85
Osoyoos Lake, l., Wa., U.S.	A6	140
Osprey, Fl., U.S.	E4	102
Ossa, Mount, mtn., Austl.	I4	62
Ossabaw Island, i., Ga., U.S.	E5	103
Osseo, Mn., U.S.	m12	116
Osseo, Wi., U.S.	D2	142
Ossian, Ia., U.S.	A6	108
Ossian, In., U.S.	C7	107
Ossining, N.Y., U.S.	D7	125
Ossipee, stm., U.S.	C5	122
Ossipee Lake, l., N.H., U.S.	C4	122
Ossora, Russia	D18	26
Ostaškov, Russia	C5	22
Östersund, Swe.	E6	10
Osterville, Ma., U.S.	C7	114
Ostfriesische Inseln, is., Ger.	D10	12
Ostrava, Czech Rep.	E5	20
Ostróda, Pol.	C5	20
Ostrogožsk, Russia	D15	26
Ostroh, Ukr.	D9	20
Ostrołęka, Pol.	C7	20
Ostrov, Russia	H13	10
Ostrowiec Świętokrzyski, Pol.	D6	20
Ostrów Mazowiecka, Pol.	C6	20
Ostrów Wielkopolski, Pol.	D4	20
Ostuni, Italy	D6	18
Ōsumi-shotō, is., Japan	J3	31
Osuna, Spain	I4	16
Oswegatchie, stm., N.Y., U.S.	f9	125
Oswego, Il., U.S.	B5	106
Oswego, Ks., U.S.	E8	109
Oswego, N.Y., U.S.	B4	125
Oswego, co., N.Y., U.S.	B4	125
Oswego, stm., N.J., U.S.	D4	123
Oswego, stm., N.Y., U.S.	B4	125
Otanmäki, Fin.	D12	10
Otaru, Japan	C16	28
Otava, Fin.	F12	10
Otavi, Nmb.	B2	56
Oteen, N.C., U.S.	f10	126
Otero, co., Co., U.S.	D7	99

Name	Map Ref.	Page

Otero, co., N.M., U.S. E3 124
Othello, Wa., U.S. C6 140
Otis Orchards, Wa., U.S. . . g14 140
Otis Reservoir, res., Ma.,
   U.S. B1 114
Otisville, Mi., U.S. E7 115
Otjikondo, Nmb. B2 56
Otjiwarongo, Nmb. C2 56
Otoe, co., Ne., U.S. D9 120
Otra, stm., Nor. G2 10
Otradnyj, Russia D9 22
Ótranto, Italy D7 18
Otranto, Strait of, strt., Eur. C7 18
Otsego, Mi., U.S. F5 115
Otsego, co., Mi., U.S. C6 115
Otsego, co., N.Y., U.S. C5 125
Otsego Lake, l., N.Y., U.S. . C6 125
Õtsu, Japan C3 31
Ottauquechee, stm., Vt.,
   U.S. D4 138
Ottawa, On., Can. B9 89
Ottawa, Il., U.S. B5 106
Ottawa, Ks., U.S. D8 109
Ottawa, Oh., U.S. A1 128
Ottawa, co., Ks., U.S. C6 109
Ottawa, co., Mi., U.S. F4 115
Ottawa, co., Oh., U.S. A2 128
Ottawa, co., Ok., U.S. A6 129
Ottawa, stm., Can. I24 82
Ottawa, stm., Oh., U.S. . . . e6 128
Ottawa Hills, Oh., U.S. . . . e6 128
Ottenby, Swe. H7 10
Otterbein, In., U.S. D3 107
Otter Brook, stm., N.H.,
   U.S. E2 122
Otter Brook Lake, res.,
   N.H., U.S. E2 122
Otter Creek, stm., Ut., U.S. E4 137
Otter Creek, stm., Vt., U.S. C2 138
Otter Creek Reservoir, res.,
   Ut., U.S. E4 137
Otter Islands, is., S.C., U.S. m11 133
Otter Tail, co., Mn., U.S. . . D3 116
Otter Tail, stm., Mn., U.S. . D2 116
Otter Tail Lake, l., Mn., U.S. D3 116
Otterville, On., Can. E4 89
Ottumwa, Ia., U.S. C5 108
Otway, Cape, c., Austl. . . . H3 62
Otwock, Pol. C6 20
Ouachita, co., Ar., U.S. . . . D3 97
Ouachita, co., La., U.S. . . . B3 111
Ouachita, Lake, res., Ar.,
   U.S. C2 97
Ouachita Mountains, mts.,
   U.S. E9 92
Ouadda, C.A.R. B4 54
Ouagadougou, Burkina . . . D4 50
Ouahigouya, Burkina D4 50
Ouahran see Wahran, Alg. . C4 48
Oualâta, Maur. C3 50
Ouallam, Niger D5 50
Ouallene, Alg. F5 48
Ouanda Djallé, C.A.R. B4 54
Ouangolodougou, C. Iv. . . . E3 50
Ouarâne, reg., Maur. B2 50
Ouarzazate, Mor. D3 48
Oubangui (Ubangi), stm.,
   Afr. D3 54
Oudtshoorn, S. Afr. E3 56
Oued Rhiou, Alg. J7 16
Oued-Zem, Mor. E2 14
Ouellé, C. Iv. E4 50
Ouémé, stm., Benin E5 50
Ouessant, Île d', i., Fr. . . . C4 16
Ouesso, Congo C3 54
Ouezzane, Mor. D3 48
Ouham, stm., Afr. B3 54
Ouidah, Benin E5 50
Oujda, Mor. D4 48
Oulu, Fin. D11 10
Oulujärvi, l., Fin. D12 10
Oulujoki, stm., Fin. D12 10
Oum-Chalouba, Chad G9 48
Oumé, C. Iv. E3 50
Ounianga Kébir, Chad G9 48
Ouray, Co., U.S. C3 99
Ouray, co., Co., U.S. C3 99
Ouray, Mount, mtn., Co.,
   U.S. C4 99
Ourense, Spain F3 16
Ouricuri, Braz. C3 74
Ourinhos, Braz. F2 74
Ouro Preto, Braz. F3 74
Outagamie, co., Wi., U.S. . D5 142
Outardes Quatre, Réservoir,
   res., P.Q., Can. h13 90
Outer Hebrides, is., Scot.,
   U.K. B3 12
Outer Island, i., Wi., U.S. . . A3 142
Outer Santa Barbara
   Passage, strt., Ca., U.S. F4 98
Outjo, Nmb. C2 56
Outpost Mountain, mtn.,
   Ak., U.S. B9 95
Outremont, P.Q., Can. p19 90
Ouvéa, i., N. Cal. I9 62a
Ouyen, Austl. H3 62
Ovalle, Chile D2 69
Overbrook, Ks., U.S. D8 109
Overgaard, Az., U.S. C5 96
Overland, Mo., U.S. f13 118
Overland Park, Ks., U.S. . . m16 109
Overlea, Md., U.S. B4 113
Overton, Nv., U.S. G7 121
Overton, Tx., U.S. C5 136

Overton, co., Tn., U.S. C8 135
Ovett, Ms., U.S. D4 117
Ovid, Mi., U.S. E6 115
Oviedo, Spain F4 16
Ovoot, Mong. B10 28
Ovruch, Ukr. D10 20
Owando, Congo D3 54
Owasco Lake, l., N.Y., U.S. C4 125
Owasso, Ok., U.S. A6 129
Owatonna, Mn., U.S. F5 116
Owego, N.Y., U.S. C4 125
Owen, Wi., U.S. D3 142
Owen, co., In., U.S. F4 107
Owen, co., Ky., U.S. B5 110
Owen, Lake, l., Wi., U.S. . . B2 142
Owen, Mount, mtn., Co.,
   U.S. C3 99
Owendo, Gabon C1 54
Owens, stm., Ca., U.S. . . . D4 98
Owensboro, Ky., U.S. C2 110
Owens Cross Roads, Al.,
   U.S. A3 94
Owens Lake, l., Ca., U.S. . . D5 98
Owensville, In., U.S. H2 107
Owensville, Mo., U.S. C6 118
Owensville, Oh., U.S. C1 128
Owenton, Ky., U.S. B5 110
Owerri, Nig. E6 50
Owings Mills, Md., U.S. . . . B4 113
Owingsville, Ky., U.S. B6 110
Owl Creek, stm., Wy., U.S. C4 143
Owl Creek Mountains, mts.,
   Wy., U.S. C4 143
Owo, Nig. E6 50
Owosso, Mi., U.S. E6 115
Owsley, co., Ky., U.S. C6 110
Owyhee, Nv., U.S. B5 121
Owyhee, co., Id., U.S. G2 105
Owyhee, stm., U.S. E9 130
Owyhee, Lake, res., Or.,
   U.S. D9 130
Owyhee Dam, Or., U.S. . . . D9 130
Owyhee Mountains, mts.,
   U.S. G2 105
Oxbow Dam, U.S. E2 105
Oxelösund, Swe. G7 10
Oxford, N.S., Can. D6 87
Oxford, Eng., U.K. E6 12
Oxford, Al., U.S. B4 94
Oxford, Ct., U.S. D3 100
Oxford, Ga., U.S. C3 103
Oxford, Ia., U.S. C6 108
Oxford, In., U.S. C3 107
Oxford, Ks., U.S. E6 109
Oxford, Ma., U.S. B4 114
Oxford, Md., U.S. C5 113
Oxford, Me., U.S. D2 112
Oxford, Mi., U.S. F7 115
Oxford, Ms., U.S. A4 117
Oxford, N.C., U.S. A4 126
Oxford, Ne., U.S. D6 120
Oxford, N.Y., U.S. C5 125
Oxford, Oh., U.S. C1 128
Oxford, Pa., U.S. G10 131
Oxford, co., Me., U.S. D2 112
Oxford Lake, l., Mb., Can. . B4 86
Oxford Peak, mtn., Id., U.S. G6 105
Oxnard, Ca., U.S. E4 98
Oxon Hill, Md., U.S. f9 113
Oxus see Amu Darya, stm.,
   Asia B8 42
Oyama, B.C., Can. D8 85
Oyapak (Oiapoque), stm.,
   S.A. C9 70
Oyem, Gabon C2 54
Oyen, Ab., Can. D5 84
Oyo, Nig. E5 50
Oyster Bay, N.Y., U.S. E7 125
Oyster Keys, is., Fl., U.S. . . G6 102
Ozamiz, Phil. E8 34
Ozark, Al., U.S. D4 94
Ozark, Ar., U.S. B2 97
Ozark, Mo., U.S. D4 118
Ozark, co., Mo., U.S. E5 118
Ozark Plateau, plat., U.S. . D9 92
Ozark Reservoir, res., Ar.,
   U.S. B1 97
Ozarks, Lake of the, res.,
   Mo., U.S. C5 118
Ozaukee, co., Wi., U.S. . . . E6 142
Ôzd, Hung. E6 20
Ozernovskij, Russia D17 26
Ozërnyj, Russia D11 22
Ozette Lake, l., Wa., U.S. . . A1 140
Ozieri, Italy D2 18
Ozinki, Russia D8 22
Ozona, Fl., U.S. o10 102
Ozona, Tx., U.S. D2 136
Ozurgeti, Geor. B10 44

P

Paarl, S. Afr. E2 56
Paauilo, Hi., U.S. C6 104
Pabianice, Pol. D5 20
Pābna, Bngl. E5 40
Pacajus, Braz. B4 74
Pacasmayo, Peru E4 70
Pace, Fl., U.S. u14 102
Pachacamac, hist., Peru . . A2 72
Pachaug Pond, l., Ct., U.S. C8 100

Pachino, Italy F5 18
Pachuca de Soto, Mex. . . . C5 78
Pacific, Mo., U.S. C7 118
Pacific, Wa., U.S. f11 140
Pacific, co., Wa., U.S. C2 140
Pacifica, Ca., U.S. h8 98
Pacific-Antarctic Ridge . . . O22 64
Pacific Beach, Wa., U.S. . . B1 140
Pacific City, Or., U.S. B3 130
Pacific Creek, stm., Wy.,
   U.S. D3 143
Pacific Grove, Ca., U.S. . . . D3 98
Pacific Ocean E20 64
Pacific Palisades, Hi., U.S. g10 104
Pacific Ranges, mts., B.C.,
   Can. D4 85
Pacific Rim National Park,
   B.C., Can. E5 85
Pack Monadnock Mountain,
   mtn., N.H., U.S. E3 122
Packwood, Wa., U.S. C4 140
Pacolet, S.C., U.S. B4 133
Pacolet, stm., S.C., U.S. . . A4 133
Pacolet Mills, S.C., U.S. . . B4 133
Pactola Reservoir, res., S.D.,
   U.S. C2 134
Padang, Indon. D2 36
Padangpanjang, Indon. . . . D2 36
Padangsidempuan, Indon. . C1 36
Paddock Lake, Wi., U.S. . . n11 142
Paden City, W.V., U.S. . . . B4 141
Paderborn, Ger. E11 12
Padma see Ganges, stm.,
   Asia D5 40
Pádova, Italy B3 18
Padrauna, India D4 40
Padre Island, i., Tx., U.S. . . F4 136
Padre Island National
   Seashore, Tx., U.S. . . . F4 136
Padua see Pádova, Italy . . B3 18
Paducah, Ky., U.S. e9 110
Paducah, Tx., U.S. B2 136
Paektu, Mount, mtn., Asia . C13 28
Paektu-san see Paektu,
   Mount, mtn., Asia C13 28
Paestum, hist., Italy D5 18
Pafúri, Moz. C5 56
Pag, Otok, i., Cro. B5 18
Pagadian, Phil. E8 34
Pagai Selatan, Pulau, i.,
   Indon. D2 36
Pagai Utara, Pulau, i.,
   Indon. D2 36
Pagalu see Annobón, i., Eq.
   Gui. C1 52
Pagan, i., N. Mar. Is. C12 32
Pagasitikós Kólpos, b., Grc. E9 18
Page, Az., U.S. A4 96
Page, W.V., U.S. C3 141
Page, co., Ia., U.S. D2 108
Page, co., Va., U.S. B4 139
Pageland, S.C., U.S. B7 133
Pagoda Peak, mtn., Co.,
   U.S. A3 99
Pago Pago, Am. Sam. F12 58
Pagosa Springs, Co., U.S. . D3 99
Paguate, N.M., U.S. B2 124
Pahala, Hi., U.S. D6 104
Pahang, stm., Malay. C2 36
Pahoa, Hi., U.S. D7 104
Pahokee, Fl., U.S. F6 102
Pahrump, Nv., U.S. G6 121
Pahute Mesa, mtn., Nv.,
   U.S. F5 121
Paia, Hi., U.S. C5 104
Paide, Est. G11 10
Päijänne, l., Fin. F11 10
Pailolo Channel, strt., Hi.,
   U.S. B5 104
Painan, Indon. D2 36
Paincourtville, La., U.S. . . . k9 111
Painesville, Oh., U.S. A4 128
Paint, stm., Mi., U.S. B2 115
Paint Creek, stm., Oh., U.S. C2 128
Paint Creek, stm., W.V.,
   U.S. m13 141
Paint Creek, North Fork,
   stm., Oh., U.S. C2 128
Paint Creek Lake, res., Oh.,
   U.S. C2 128
Painted Desert, des., Az.,
   U.S. B4 96
Painted Post, N.Y., U.S. . . C3 125
Painted Rock Reservoir,
   res., Az., U.S. D3 96
Paintsville, Ky., U.S. C7 110
Paisley, On., Can. C3 89
Pajala, Swe. C10 10
Pakaraima Mountains, mts.,
   S.A. E7 80
Pakistan, ctry., Asia E9 42
Pakistan, East see
   Bangladesh, ctry., Asia B2 34
Pakokku, Myan. B3 34
Pakowki Lake, l., Ab., Can. E5 84
Pak Phanang, Thai. E4 34
Paks, Hung. F5 20
Pakxé, Laos C5 34
Pala, Chad E7 50
Palacios, Tx., U.S. E4 136
Palana, Russia D17 26
Palangkaraya, Indon. D4 36
Palani, India G3 40
Pālanpur, India E2 40
Palaoa Point, c., Hi., U.S. . C4 104

Palapye, Bots. C4 56
Palatine, Il., U.S. A5 106
Palatka, Fl., U.S. C5 102
Palau, ctry., Oc. F10 32
Palau Islands, is., Palau . . E9 32
Palaw, Myan. D3 34
Palawan, i., Phil. E7 34
Palawan Passage, strt., Phil. E7 34
Pālayankottai, India H3 40
Paldiski, Est. G11 10
Palembang, Indon. D2 36
Palencia, Spain F4 16
Palenque, hist., Mex. D6 78
Palermo, Italy E4 18
Palestine, Ar., U.S. C5 97
Palestine, Il., U.S. D6 106
Palestine, Tx., U.S. D5 136
Palestine, hist. reg., Asia . . G6 44
Palestine, Lake, res., Tx.,
   U.S. C5 136
Paletwa, Myan. B2 34
Pālghāt, India G3 40
Pāli, India D2 40
Palikea, mtn., Hi., U.S. . . . g9 104
Palisade, Co., U.S. B2 99
Palisades Park, N.J., U.S. . h8 123
Palisades Reservoir, res.,
   U.S. F7 105
Pālitāna, India E2 40
Palk Strait, strt., Asia H3 40
Palliser, Cape, c., N.Z. . . . p14 63c
Palma, Moz. A7 56
Palma del Río, Spain I4 16
Palma de Mallorca, Spain . H8 16
Palmares, Braz. C4 74
Palmas, Braz. F10 70
Palma Soriano, Cuba A4 80
Palm Bay, Fl., U.S. D6 102
Palm Beach, Fl., U.S. F6 102
Palm Beach, co., Fl., U.S. . F6 102
Palmdale, Ca., U.S. E4 98
Palmeira das Missões, Braz. D7 72
Palmeira dos Índios, Braz. . C4 74
Palmer, Ak., U.S. C10 95
Palmer, Ma., U.S. B3 114
Palmer, Mi., U.S. B3 115
Palmer, Ne., U.S. D4 117
Palmer, Ne., U.S. C7 120
Palmer, Tn., U.S. D8 135
Palmer, Tx., U.S. n10 136
Palmer Lake, Co., U.S. . . . B6 99
Palmer Land, reg., Ant. . . . D34 67
Palmerston, On., Can. D4 89
Palmerston, atoll, Cook Is. . F13 58
Palmerston North, N.Z. . . . p14 63c
Palmerton, Pa., U.S. E10 131
Palmetto, Fl., U.S. E4 102
Palmetto, Ga., U.S. C2 103
Palm Harbor, Fl., U.S. o10 102
Palmi, Italy E5 18
Palmira, Col. C4 70
Palms, Isle of, i., S.C., U.S. F8 133
Palm Springs, Ca., U.S. . . . F5 98
Palmyra see Tudmur, Syria E8 44
Palmyra, In., U.S. H5 107
Palmyra, Mo., U.S. B6 118
Palmyra, N.J., U.S. C2 123
Palmyra, N.Y., U.S. B3 125
Palmyra, Pa., U.S. F8 131
Palmyra, Wi., U.S. F5 142
Palmyra, hist., Syria E8 44
Palo Alto, Ca., U.S. D2 98
Palo Alto, co., Ia., U.S. . . . A3 108
Paloich, Sudan H11 48
Palomar Mountain, mtn.,
   Ca., U.S. F5 98
Palomas Mountains, mts.,
   Az., U.S. D2 96
Palo Pinto, co., Tx., U.S. . . C3 136
Palopo, Indon. D6 36
Palo Santo, Arg. D6 72
Palos Park, Il., U.S. k9 106
Palos Verdes Estates, Ca.,
   U.S. n12 98
Palourde, Lake, l., La., U.S. k9 111
Palouse, Wa., U.S. C8 140
Palouse, stm., Wa., U.S. . . C7 140
Palu, Indon. D5 36
Palu, Tur. C8 44
Pamekasan, Indon. E4 36
Pamiers, Fr. F7 16
Pamir, mts., Asia B2 40
Pamlico, co., N.C., U.S. . . . B6 126
Pamlico, stm., N.C., U.S. . . B6 126
Pamlico Sound, strt., N.C.,
   U.S. B6 126
Pampa, Tx., U.S. B2 136
Pampa, reg., Arg. F5 72
Pampa del Infierno, Arg. . . D5 72
Pampas, Peru A3 72
Pamplico, S.C., U.S. . . . . . ● .D8 133
Pamplona, Col. B5 70
Pamplona, Spain F6 16
Pamunkey, stm., Va., U.S. . C5 139
Pana, Il., U.S. D4 106
Panaca, Nv., U.S. F7 121
Panache, Lake, l., On., Can. A3 89
Panaji, India F2 40
Panamá, Pan. D4 80
Panama, Ok., U.S. B7 129
Panama, ctry., N.A. I11 75
Panamá, Bahía de, b., Pan. D4 80
Panamá, Canal de, Pan. . . D4 80
Panamá, Golfo de, b., Pan. D4 80

Panama, Gulf of see
   Panamá, Golfo de, b.,
   Pan. D4 80
Panamá, Istmo de, Pan. . . D4 80
Panama Basin H30 64
Panama Canal see Panamá,
   Canal de, Pan. D4 80
Panama City see Panamá,
   Pan. D4 80
Panama City, Fl., U.S. u16 102
Panama City Beach, Fl., U.S. u16 102
Panamint Range, mts., Ca.,
   U.S. D5 98
Panay, i., Phil. D8 34
Pancake Range, mts., Nv.,
   U.S. E6 121
Pančevo, Yugo. B8 18
Pandharpur, India F3 40
Pandora, Oh., U.S. B2 128
Panfilov, Kaz. E9 26
Pangala, Congo D2 54
Pangani, Tan. E7 54
Pangburn, Ar., U.S. B4 97
Pangi, D.R.C. D5 54
Pangkajene, Indon. D5 36
Pangkalanbuun, Indon. . . . D4 36
Pangkalpinang, Indon. D3 36
Pango Aluquem, Ang. E2 54
Panguitch, Ut., U.S. F3 137
Pangutaran Group, is., Phil. E7 34
Paniau, mtn., Hi., U.S. . . . B1 104
Panié, Mont, mtn., N. Cal. . I8 62a
Panīpat, India D3 40
Panj see Amu Darya, stm.,
   Asia B8 42
Panjang, Indon. E3 36
Panjgūr, Pak. E8 42
Pankshin, Nig. E6 50
Panna, India E4 40
Pannawonica, Austl. E2 60
Panola, co., Ms., U.S. A3 117
Panola, co., Tx., U.S. C5 136
Panora, Ia., U.S. C3 108
Pantar, Pulau, i., Indon. . . . E6 36
Pantelleria, Isola di, i., Italy F3 18
Pánuco, Mex. C5 78
Pánuco, stm., Mex. C5 78
Panxian, China F8 28
Panyam, Nig. E6 50
Panyu, China B6 34
Paola, Italy E5 18
Paola, Ks., U.S. D9 109
Paoli, In., U.S. G5 107
Paoli, Pa., U.S. o20 131
Paonia, Co., U.S. C3 99
Pápa, Hung. F4 20
Papagayo, Golfo de, b.,
   C.R. C2 80
Papago Indian Reservation,
   Az., U.S. E3 96
Papaikou, Hi., U.S. D6 104
Papantla de Olarte, Mex. . . C5 78
Papawai Point, c., Hi., U.S. C5 104
Papeete, Fr. Poly. F15 58
Papenburg, Ger. D10 12
Paphos see Néa Páfos, Cyp. E5 44
Papigochic, stm., Mex. . . . B3 78
Papillion, Ne., U.S. C9 120
Papineauville, P.Q., Can. . . D2 90
Paposo, Chile A2 72
Papua, Gulf of, b., Pap. N.
   Gui. H11 32
Papua New Guinea, ctry.,
   Oc. H11 32
Papun, Myan. C3 34
Pará see Belém, Braz. B2 74
Pará, state, Braz. E9 70
Parabel', Russia D10 26
Paraburdoo, Austl. E2 60
Paracatu, Braz. E2 74
Paracel Islands (Xisha
   Qundao), is., China . . . C6 34
Parachute, Co., U.S. B2 99
Paraćin, Yugo. C8 18
Paracuru, Braz. B4 74
Paradis, La., U.S. k11 111
Paradise, Ca., U.S. C3 98
Paradise, Nv., U.S. G6 121
Paradise, stm., Nf., Can. . . B3 88
Paradise Hills, N.M., U.S. . B3 124
Paradise Valley, Az., U.S. . k9 96
Paradise Valley, Nv., U.S. . B4 121
Pāradwīp, India E5 40
Paragould, Ar., U.S. A5 97
Paraguai (Paraguay), stm.,
   S.A. B6 72
Paraguaná, Península de,
   pen., Ven. C6 80
Paraguay, ctry., S.A. C6 72
Paraguay (Paraguai), stm.,
   S.A. C6 72
Paraíba, state, Braz. C4 74
Paraíba do Sul, stm., Braz. F3 74
Parakou, Benin E5 50
Paramaribo, Sur. B8 70
Paramirim, Braz. F11 70
Paramount, Md., U.S. A2 113
Paramus, N.J., U.S. h8 123
Paramušir, ostrov, i., Russia D17 26
Paraná, Arg. E5 72
Paraná, Braz. F10 70
Paraná, state, Braz. C7 72
Paraná, stm., Braz. F5 68
Paraná, stm., S.A. E6 72

Name	Map Ref.	Page
Paranaguá, Braz.	D8	72
Paranaíba, Braz.	E2	74
Paranapanema, stm., Braz.	C7	72
Paranavaí, Braz.	C7	72
Parang, Phil.	E8	34
Parangaba, Braz.	B4	74
Paranhos, Braz.	C6	72
Paray-le-Monial, Fr.	D9	16
Pārbati, stm., India	D3	40
Parbhani, India	F3	40
Parchment, Mi., U.S.	F5	115
Pardeeville, Wi., U.S.	E4	142
Pardo, stm., Braz.	F2	74
Pardubice, Czech Rep.	E3	20
Parecis, Braz.	A6	72
Parecis, Chapada dos, mts., Braz.	A6	72
Paren', Russia	C18	26
Parepare, Indon.	D5	36
Paria, stm., U.S.	A4	96
Paria, Gulf of, b.	C7	80
Pariaman, Indon.	D2	36
Parigi, Indon.	D6	36
Parika, Guy.	B8	70
Paris, On., Can.	D4	89
Paris, Fr.	C8	16
Paris, Ar., U.S.	B2	97
Paris, Il., U.S.	D6	106
Paris, Ky., U.S.	B5	110
Paris, Mo., U.S.	B5	118
Paris, Tn., U.S.	A3	135
Paris, Tx., U.S.	C5	136
Paris Peak, mtn., Id., U.S.	G7	105
Parita, Bahía de, b., Pan.	D3	80
Park, co., Co., U.S.	B5	99
Park, co., Mt., U.S.	E6	119
Park, co., Wy., U.S.	B3	143
Park, stm., N.D., U.S.	A8	127
Park City, Ks., U.S.	g12	109
Park City, Ut., U.S.	C4	137
Parkdale, P.E., Can.	C6	87
Parke, co., In., U.S.	E3	107
Parker, Az., U.S.	C1	96
Parker, Co., U.S.	B6	99
Parker, Fl., U.S.	u16	102
Parker, S.D., U.S.	D8	134
Parker, co., Tx., U.S.	C4	136
Parker City, In., U.S.	D7	107
Parker Dam, U.S.	C1	96
Parkersburg, Ia., U.S.	B5	108
Parkersburg, W.V., U.S.	B3	141
Parkers Prairie, Mn., U.S.	D3	116
Parkes, Austl.	G4	62
Parkesburg, Pa., U.S.	G10	131
Park Falls, Wi., U.S.	C3	142
Park Forest, Il., U.S.	B6	106
Park Hall, Md., U.S.	D5	113
Parkhill, On., Can.	D3	89
Park Hills, Ky., U.S.	h13	110
Parkin, Ar., U.S.	B5	97
Parkland, Wa., U.S.	f11	140
Park Layne, Oh., U.S.	C1	128
Park Range, mts., Co., U.S.	A4	99
Park Rapids, Mn., U.S.	D3	116
Park Ridge, Il., U.S.	B6	106
Park Ridge, N.J., U.S.	g8	123
Park River, N.D., U.S.	A8	127
Parkrose, Or., U.S.	B4	130
Parksley, Va., U.S.	C7	139
Parkston, S.D., U.S.	D8	134
Parksville, B.C., Can.	E5	85
Parkville, Md., U.S.	B4	113
Parkville, Mo., U.S.	B3	118
Parkwater, Wa., U.S.	g14	140
Parkwood, N.C., U.S.	A6	126
Parlākimidi, India	F4	40
Parle, Lac qui, l., Mn., U.S.	E3	116
Parlier, Ca., U.S.	D4	98
Parma, Italy	B3	18
Parma, Id., U.S.	F2	105
Parma, Mi., U.S.	F6	115
Parma, Mo., U.S.	E8	118
Parma, Oh., U.S.	A4	128
Parmachenee Lake, l., Me., U.S.	C2	112
Parma Heights, Oh., U.S.	h9	128
Parmer, co., Tx., U.S.	B1	136
Parnaguá, Braz.	F11	70
Parnaíba, Braz.	B3	74
Parnaíba, stm., Braz.	B3	74
Parnassós, mtn., Grc.	E9	18
Pärnu, Est.	G11	10
Paro, Bhu.	D16	26
Paromaj, Russia	D16	26
Parowan, Ut., U.S.	F3	137
Par Pond, res., S.C., U.S.	D5	133
Parral, Chile	F3	72
Parramatta, Austl.	G5	62
Parramore Island, i., Va., U.S.	C7	139
Parras de la Fuente, Mex.	B4	78
Parrish, Al., U.S.	B2	94
Parrsboro, N.S., Can.	D5	87
Parry, Mount, mtn., B.C., Can.	C3	85
Parry Sound, On., Can.	B4	89
Parshall, N.D., U.S.	B3	127
Parsons, Ks., U.S.	E8	109
Parsons, Tn., U.S.	B3	135
Parsons, W.V., U.S.	B5	141
Parsonsburg, Md., U.S.	D7	113
Parthenay, Fr.	F6	16
Partille, Swe.	H5	10
Partizansk, Russia	B2	31
Partridge Point, c., Nf., Can.	C3	88
Paru, stm., Braz.	D9	70
Paru de Oeste, stm., Braz.	C8	70
Pārvatīpuram, India	F4	40
Paryang, China	C4	40
Parys, S. Afr.	D4	56
Pasadena, Nf., Can.	D3	88
Pasadena, Ca., U.S.	E4	98
Pasadena, Md., U.S.	B4	113
Pasadena, Tx., U.S.	r14	136
Pascagoula, Ms., U.S.	E5	117
Pascagoula, stm., Ms., U.S.	E5	117
Pascagoula Bay, b., Ms., U.S.	f8	117
Paşcani, Rom.	F9	20
Pasco, Wa., U.S.	C6	140
Pasco, co., Fl., U.S.	D4	102
Pascoag, R.I., U.S.	B2	132
Pascoag Reservoir, res., R.I., U.S.	B2	132
Pascua, Isla de (Easter Island), i., Chile	K28	64
Pasinler, Tur.	B9	44
Pasir Mas, Malay.	B2	36
Pasni, Pak.	E8	42
Paso de los Libres, Arg.	D6	72
Paso de los Toros, Ur.	E6	72
Paso Robles, Ca., U.S.	E3	98
Pasque Island, i., Ma., U.S.	D6	114
Pasquotank, co., N.C., U.S.	A6	126
Passaic, N.J., U.S.	B4	123
Passaic, co., N.J., U.S.	A4	123
Passaic, stm., N.J., U.S.	h8	123
Passamaquoddy Bay, b., Me., U.S.	C6	112
Passau, Ger.	F13	12
Pass Christian, Ms., U.S.	E4	117
Passero, Capo, c., Italy	F5	18
Passo Fundo, Braz.	D7	72
Passos, Braz.	F2	74
Passumpsic, stm., Vt., U.S.	C4	138
Pastavy, Bela.	B9	20
Pastaza, stm., S.A.	D4	70
Pasto, Col.	C4	70
Pastora Peak, mtn., Az., U.S.	A6	96
Pasuruan, Indon.	E4	36
Pasvalys, Lith.	H11	10
Patadkal, hist., India	F3	40
Patagonia, Az., U.S.	F5	96
Patagonia, reg., Arg.	F3	69
Pātan, India	E2	40
Patapsco, stm., Md., U.S.	B4	113
Pataskala, Oh., U.S.	C3	128
Patchet Brook Reservoir, res., R.I., U.S.	E6	132
Patchogue, N.Y., U.S.	n15	125
Pategi, Nig.	E6	50
Pate Island, i., Kenya	D8	54
Paternà, Italy	F5	18
Paternò, Italy	F5	18
Paterson, N.J., U.S.	B4	123
Pathānkot, India	C3	40
Pathein, Myan.	C2	34
Pathfinder Reservoir, res., Wy., U.S.	D6	143
Patiāla, India	C3	40
Patience Island, i., R.I., U.S.	D5	132
Patman, Lake, res., Tx., U.S.	C5	136
Patna, India	D5	40
Patnos, Tur.	C10	44
Pato Branco, Braz.	D7	72
Patoka, In., U.S.	H2	107
Patoka, stm., In., U.S.	H2	107
Patoka Lake, res., In., U.S.	H4	107
Patos, Braz.	C4	74
Patos, Lagoa dos, b., Braz.	E7	72
Patos de Minas, Braz.	E2	74
Patquía, Arg.	D4	72
Pátrai, Grc.	E8	18
Patraïkós Kólpos, b., Grc.	E8	18
Patrick, co., Va., U.S.	D2	139
Patrick Air Force Base, mil., Fl., U.S.	D6	102
Patrocínio, Braz.	E2	74
Pattani, Thai.	E4	34
Patten, Me., U.S.	C4	112
Patterson, Ga., U.S.	E4	103
Patterson, La., U.S.	E4	111
Patterson Creek, stm., W.V., U.S.	B5	141
Patton, Pa., U.S.	E4	131
Patuākhāli, Bngl.	E6	40
Patuca, stm., Hond.	B3	80
Patuxent, stm., Md., U.S.	D4	113
Patuxent Naval Air Test Center, mil., Md., U.S.	D5	113
Pátzcuaro, Mex.	D4	78
Pau, Fr.	F6	16
Paul, Id., U.S.	G5	105
Paulding, Oh., U.S.	A1	128
Paulding, co., Ga., U.S.	C2	103
Paulding, co., Oh., U.S.	A1	128
Paulina, La., U.S.	h10	111
Paulina Mountains, mts., Or., U.S.	D5	130
Paulina Peak, mtn., Or., U.S.	E5	130
Paulins Kill, stm., N.J., U.S.	A3	123
Paulistana, Braz.	E11	70
Paullina, Ia., U.S.	B2	108
Paulo Afonso, Braz.	C4	74
Paulsboro, N.J., U.S.	D2	123
Pauls Valley, Ok., U.S.	C4	129
Paungde, Myan.	C3	34
Pāveh, Iran	E12	44
Pavia, Italy	B2	18
Pavilion Key, i., Fl., U.S.	G5	102
Pāvilosta, Lat.	H9	10
Pavlodar, Kaz.	D9	26
Pavlof Volcano, vol., Ak., U.S.	D7	95
Pavlohrad, Ukr.	E13	20
Pavlovo, Russia	C7	22
Pavo, Ga., U.S.	F3	103
Pawcatuck, Ct., U.S.	D8	100
Pawcatuck, stm., R.I., U.S.	G1	132
Paw Creek, N.C., U.S.	B2	126
Pawhuska, Ok., U.S.	A5	129
Pawling, N.Y., U.S.	D7	125
Pawnee, Il., U.S.	D4	106
Pawnee, Ok., U.S.	A5	129
Pawnee, co., Ks., U.S.	D4	109
Pawnee, co., Ne., U.S.	D9	120
Pawnee, co., Ok., U.S.	A5	129
Pawnee, stm., Ks., U.S.	D3	109
Pawnee City, Ne., U.S.	D9	120
Pawpaw, Il., U.S.	B5	106
Paw Paw, Mi., U.S.	F5	115
Paw Paw, stm., Mi., U.S.	F4	115
Pawpaw Creek, stm., W.V., U.S.	h10	141
Pawtuckaway Pond, l., N.H., U.S.	D4	122
Pawtucket, R.I., U.S.	C4	132
Pawtuxet, stm., R.I., U.S.	C4	132
Paxton, Il., U.S.	C5	106
Paxton, Ma., U.S.	B4	114
Payakumbuh, Indon.	D2	36
Payeti, Indon.	E6	36
Payette, Id., U.S.	E2	105
Payette, co., Id., U.S.	E2	105
Payette, North Fork, stm., Id., U.S.	E2	105
Payette, South Fork, stm., Id., U.S.	E3	105
Payette Lake, res., Id., U.S.	E3	105
Payne, Oh., U.S.	A1	128
Payne, co., Ok., U.S.	A4	129
Payne, Lac, l., Can.	G25	82
Paynes Find, Austl.	F2	60
Paynesville, Mn., U.S.	E4	116
Paysandú, Ur.	E6	72
Payson, Az., U.S.	C4	96
Payson, Il., U.S.	D2	106
Payson, Ut., U.S.	C4	137
Pazar, Tur.	B9	44
Pazarcık, Tur.	D7	44
Pazarcik, Tur.	C11	10
Pazardžik, Bul.	C10	18
Paz de Río, Col.	D5	80
Pea, stm., Al., U.S.	D3	94
Peabody, Ks., U.S.	D6	109
Peabody, Ma., U.S.	A6	114
Peabody, stm., N.H., U.S.	B4	122
Peace, stm., Can.	D8	75
Peace, stm., Fl., U.S.	E5	102
Peace Dale, R.I., U.S.	F3	132
Peace River, Ab., Can.	A2	84
Peach, co., Ga., U.S.	D3	103
Peacham Pond, res., Vt., U.S.	C4	138
Peach Point, c., Ma., U.S.	f12	114
Peach Springs, Az., U.S.	B2	96
Peak Hill, Austl.	F2	60
Peaks Island, i., Me., U.S.	g7	112
Peale, Mount, mtn., Ut., U.S.	E6	137
Pea Patch Island, i., De., U.S.	B3	101
Pea Ridge, Ar., U.S.	A1	97
Pea Ridge National Military Park, Ar., U.S.	A1	97
Pearisburg, Va., U.S.	C2	139
Pearl, Ms., U.S.	C3	117
Pearl, stm., U.S.	D3	117
Pearland, Tx., U.S.	r14	136
Pearl and Hermes Reef, rf., Hi., U.S.	k12	104
Pearl City, Hi., U.S.	B4	104
Pearl Harbor, b., Hi., U.S.	B3	104
Pearl Harbor Naval Station, mil., Hi., U.S.	g10	104
Pearlington, Ms., U.S.	E4	117
Pearl River, La., U.S.	D6	111
Pearl River, N.Y., U.S.	g12	125
Pearl River, co., Ms., U.S.	E4	117
Pearsall, Tx., U.S.	E3	136
Pearson, Ga., U.S.	E4	103
Peary Land, reg., Grnld.	B32	82
Pease, stm., Tx., U.S.	B3	136
Pebane, Moz.	B6	56
Peç, Yugo.	C8	18
Pecatonica, Il., U.S.	A4	106
Pecatonica, stm., U.S.	A4	106
Pecatonica, East Branch, stm., Wi., U.S.	F4	142
Pečenga, Russia	C5	26
Pechora see Pečora, Russia	C7	26
Pechora see Pečora, stm., Russia	C7	26
Pechora Bay see Pečorskaja guba, b., Russia	A9	22
Peckerwood Lake, res., Ar., U.S.	C4	97
Pečora, Russia	C7	26
Pečora, stm., Russia	C7	26
Pečorskaja guba, b., Russia	A9	22
Pečorskoe more, Russia	C7	26
Pecos, N.M., U.S.	B4	124
Pecos, Tx., U.S.	D1	136
Pecos, co., Tx., U.S.	D1	136
Pecos, stm., U.S.	E7	92
Pecos National Monument, N.M., U.S.	B4	124
Pécs, Hung.	F5	20
Peculiar, Mo., U.S.	C3	118
Peddocks Island, i., Ma., U.S.	g12	114
Pedernales, Ven.	D7	80
Pedra Azul, Braz.	E3	74
Pedreiras, Braz.	B3	74
Pedro Afonso, Braz.	E10	70
Pedro II, Braz.	B3	74
Pedro Juan Caballero, Para.	C6	72
Peebles, Oh., U.S.	D2	128
Peekskill, N.Y., U.S.	D7	125
Peel, stm., Can.	E13	82
Pegasus Bay, b., N.Z.	p13	63c
Pegram, Tn., U.S.	A4	135
Pehuajó, Arg.	F5	72
Peikang, Tai.	E5	30
Peipus, Lake, l., Eur.	G12	10
Peixian, China	C4	30
Pekalongan, Indon.	E3	36
Pekanbaru, Indon.	C2	36
Pekin, Il., U.S.	C4	106
Pekin, In., U.S.	G5	107
Peking see Beijing, China	D11	28
Pelagie, Isole, is., Italy	G4	28
Pelahatchie, Ms., U.S.	C4	117
Pelee Island, i., On., Can.	F2	89
Peleng, Pulau, i., Indon.	D6	36
Pelham, On., Can.	D5	89
Pelham, Al., U.S.	B3	94
Pelham, Ga., U.S.	E2	103
Pelham, N.H., U.S.	E4	122
Pelham Manor, N.Y., U.S.	h13	125
Pelican Bay, b., Mb., Can.	C1	86
Pelican Lake, l., Mb., Can.	C1	86
Pelican Lake, l., Mn., U.S.	E5	116
Pelican Lake, l., Mn., U.S.	B6	116
Pelican Lake, l., Mn., U.S.	D3	116
Pelican Lake, l., Mn., U.S.	D4	116
Pelican Lake, l., Wi., U.S.	C4	142
Pelican Mountain, mtn., Ab., Can.	B4	84
Pelican Rapids, Mn., U.S.	D2	116
Pella, Ia., U.S.	C5	108
Pell City, Al., U.S.	B3	94
Pell Lake, Wi., U.S.	n11	142
Pello, Fin.	C11	10
Peloponnesus see Pelopónnisos, pen., Grc.	F8	18
Pelopónnisos, pen., Grc.	F8	18
Pelotas, Braz.	E7	72
Pelton, Lake, l., La., U.S.	E5	111
Pemadumcook Lake, l., Me., U.S.	C3	112
Pematangsiantar, Indon.	C1	36
Pemba, Moz.	A7	56
Pemba, i., Tan.	E7	54
Pemberton, Austl.	G2	60
Pemberville, Oh., U.S.	A2	128
Pembina, N.D., U.S.	A8	127
Pembina, co., N.D., U.S.	A8	127
Pembina, stm., Ab., Can.	C3	84
Pembroke, On., Can.	B7	89
Pembroke, Wales, U.K.	E4	12
Pembroke, Ga., U.S.	D5	103
Pembroke, Ky., U.S.	D2	110
Pembroke, Ma., U.S.	B6	114
Pembroke, N.C., U.S.	C3	126
Pembroke, Va., U.S.	C2	139
Pembroke Pines, Fl., U.S.	r13	102
Pemigewasset, stm., N.H., U.S.	C3	122
Pemiscot, co., Mo., U.S.	E8	118
Penang see George Town, Malay.	B2	36
Peñaranda de Bracamonte, Spain	G4	16
Peñarroya-Pueblonuevo, Spain	H4	16
Penas, Golfo de, b., Chile	G1	69
Penasco, N.M., U.S.	A4	124
Peñasco, Río, stm., N.M., U.S.	E4	124
Penbrook, Pa., U.S.	F8	131
Pendembu, S.L.	E2	50
Pendembu, S.L.	E2	50
Pender, Ne., U.S.	B9	120
Pender, co., N.C., U.S.	C4	126
Pendleton, In., U.S.	E6	107
Pendleton, Or., U.S.	B8	130
Pendleton, co., Ky., U.S.	B5	110
Pendleton, co., W.V., U.S.	C5	141
Pend Oreille, co., Wa., U.S.	A8	140
Pend Oreille, Lake, l., Id., U.S.	A2	105
Pend Oreille, Mount, mtn., Id., U.S.	A2	105
Penedo, Braz.	D4	74
Penetanguishene, On., Can.	C5	89
Penglai, China	D12	28
Pengshui, China	F9	28
Pengxian, China	C1	30
Penhold, Ab., Can.	C4	84
Peniche, Port.	H2	16
Penida, Nusa, i., Indon.	E5	36
Pennant Point, c., N.S., Can.	E6	87
Pennask Mountain, mtn., B.C., Can.	E7	85
Pennell, Mount, mtn., Ut., U.S.	F5	137
Penneru, stm., India	G3	40
Penn Hills, Pa., U.S.	k14	131
Pennington, co., Mn., U.S.	B2	116
Pennington, co., S.D., U.S.	D2	134
Pennington Gap, Va., U.S.	f8	139
Pennsauken, N.J., U.S.	D2	123
Pennsboro, W.V., U.S.	B4	141
Pennsburg, Pa., U.S.	F11	131
Penns Grove, N.J., U.S.	D2	123
Pennsville, N.J., U.S.	D1	123
Pennsylvania, state, U.S.	E7	131
Pennville, In., U.S.	D7	107
Penn Yan, N.Y., U.S.	C3	125
Penobscot, co., Me., U.S.	C4	112
Penobscot, stm., Me., U.S.	C4	112
Penobscot Bay, b., Me., U.S.	D3	112
Penobscot Lake, l., Me., U.S.	C2	112
Penong, Austl.	G5	60
Penonomé, Pan.	D3	80
Penrhyn, atoll, Cook Is.	E14	58
Penrith, Austl.	G5	62
Penrith, Eng., U.K.	C5	12
Pensacola, Fl., U.S.	u14	102
Pensacola Bay, b., Fl., U.S.	u14	102
Pensacola Dam, Ok., U.S.	A6	129
Pensacola Mountains, mts., Ant.	E36	67
Pentagon Mountain, mtn., Mt., U.S.	C3	119
Pentecost Island see Pentecôte, i., Vanuatu	k9	62a
Pentecôte, i., Vanuatu	k9	62a
Penticton, B.C., Can.	E8	85
Pentland Firth, strt., Scot., U.K.	A5	12
Pentwater, Mi., U.S.	E4	115
Penza, Russia	D6	26
Penzance, Eng., U.K.	E4	12
Penžinskaja guba, b., Russia	C18	26
Peonan Point, c., Mb., Can.	D2	86
Peoria, Az., U.S.	D3	96
Peoria, Il., U.S.	C4	106
Peoria, co., Il., U.S.	C4	106
Peoria Heights, Il., U.S.	C4	106
Peotone, Il., U.S.	B6	106
Pepacton Reservoir, res., N.Y., U.S.	C6	125
Pepeekeo, Hi., U.S.	D6	104
Pepin, Wi., U.S.	D1	142
Pepin, co., Wi., U.S.	D2	142
Pepin, Lake, l., U.S.	D1	142
Pepperell, Ma., U.S.	A4	114
Pequannock, N.J., U.S.	B4	123
Pequest, stm., N.J., U.S.	B2	123
Pequop Mountains, mts., Nv., U.S.	C7	121
Pequot Lakes, Mn., U.S.	D4	116
Perabumulih, Indon.	D2	36
Percival Lakes, l., Austl.	E3	60
Percy, Il., U.S.	E4	106
Perdido, Al., U.S.	D2	94
Perdido, stm., U.S.	E2	94
Perdido Bay, b., Al., U.S.	E2	94
Perdido, Col.	C4	70
Pereira, Col.	C4	70
Pereislav-Khmel'nyts'kyi, Ukr.	D11	20
Pergamino, Arg.	E5	72
Pergamum, hist., Tur.	C2	44
Perham, Mn., U.S.	D3	116
Perico, Arg.	C4	72
Pericos, Mex.	B3	78
Peridot, Az., U.S.	D5	96
Périgueux, Fr.	E7	16
Perijá, Serranía de, mts., S.A.	G10	76
Perkasie, Pa., U.S.	F11	131
Perkins, Ok., U.S.	B4	129
Perkins, co., Ne., U.S.	D4	120
Perkins, co., S.D., U.S.	B3	134
Perkinston, Ms., U.S.	E4	117
Perlas, Archipiélago de las, is., Pan.	D4	80
Perlas, Laguna de, b., Nic.	C3	80
Perm', Russia	D7	26
Pernambuco, state, Braz.	C4	74
Pernik, Bul.	C9	18
Perpignan, Fr.	F8	16
Perquimans, co., N.C., U.S.	A6	126
Perrine, Fl., U.S.	G6	102
Perris, Ca., U.S.	F5	98
Perro, Laguna del, l., N.M., U.S.	C4	124
Perrot, Île, i., P.Q., Can.	q19	90
Perry, Fl., U.S.	B3	102
Perry, Ga., U.S.	D3	103
Perry, Ia., U.S.	C3	108
Perry, Ks., U.S.	C8	109
Perry, Mi., U.S.	F6	115
Perry, Mo., U.S.	B6	118
Perry, N.Y., U.S.	C2	125
Perry, Oh., U.S.	A4	128
Perry, Ok., U.S.	A4	129
Perry, Ut., U.S.	B3	137
Perry, co., Al., U.S.	C2	94
Perry, co., Ar., U.S.	C3	97
Perry, co., Il., U.S.	E4	106

Name	Map Ref.	Page
Perry, co., In., U.S.	H4	107
Perry, co., Ky., U.S.	C6	110
Perry, co., Mo., U.S.	D8	118
Perry, co., Ms., U.S.	D4	117
Perry, co., Oh., U.S.	C3	128
Perry, co., Pa., U.S.	F7	131
Perry, co., Tn., U.S.	B4	135
Perry Hall, Md., U.S.	B5	113
Perry Lake, res., Ks., U.S.	C8	109
Perryman, Md., U.S.	B5	113
Perrysburg, Oh., U.S.	A2	128
Perry Stream, stm., N.H., U.S.	f7	122
Perry's Victory and International Peace Memorial, hist., Oh., U.S.	A2	128
Perryton, Tx., U.S.	A2	136
Perryville, Ar., U.S.	B3	97
Perryville, Ky., U.S.	C5	110
Perryville, Md., U.S.	A5	113
Perryville, Mo., U.S.	D8	118
Pershing, co., Nv., U.S.	C3	121
Persia see Iran, ctry., Asia	D6	42
Persian Gulf (The Gulf), b., Asia	E6	42
Person, co., N.C., U.S.	A3	126
Perth, Austl.	G2	60
Perth, On., Can.	C8	89
Perth, Scot., U.K.	B5	12
Perth Amboy, N.J., U.S.	B4	123
Perth-Andover, N.B., Can.	D10	87
Perth Basin	K13	64
Peru, Il., U.S.	B4	106
Peru, In., U.S.	C5	107
Peru, Ne., U.S.	D10	120
Peru, N.Y., U.S.	f11	125
Peru, ctry., S.A.	E4	70
Peru Basin	J5	66
Peru-Chile Trench	J6	66
Perugia, Italy	C4	18
Peruíbe, Braz.	C8	72
Pervari, Tur.	D10	44
Pervomais'k, Ukr.	E11	20
Pervoural'sk, Russia	D7	26
Pesaro, Italy	C4	18
Pescara, Italy	C5	18
Peshastin, Wa., U.S.	B5	140
Peshāwar, Pak.	D10	42
Peshtigo, Wi., U.S.	C6	142
Peshtigo, stm., Wi., U.S.	C5	142
Pesqueira, Braz.	C4	74
Pessac, Fr.	E6	16
Pěstraja Dresva, Russia	C17	26
Petaḥ Tiqwa, Isr.	F6	44
Petal, Ms., U.S.	D4	117
Petaluma, Ca., U.S.	C2	98
Petatlán, Mex.	D4	78
Petawawa, On., Can.	B7	89
Petawawa, stm., On., Can.	A6	89
Petenwell Lake, res., Wi., U.S.	D4	142
Peterborough, Austl.	G2	62
Peterborough, On., Can.	C6	89
Peterborough, Eng., U.K.	D6	12
Peterborough, N.H., U.S.	E3	122
Peterhead, Scot., U.K.	B6	12
Peter I Island, i., Ant.	C31	67
Peter Pond Lake, l., Sk., Can.	m7	91
Petersburg, Ak., U.S.	D13	95
Petersburg, Il., U.S.	C4	106
Petersburg, In., U.S.	H3	107
Petersburg, Mi., U.S.	G7	115
Petersburg, Oh., U.S.	B5	128
Petersburg, Tx., U.S.	C2	136
Petersburg, Va., U.S.	C5	139
Petersburg, W.V., U.S.	B5	141
Peters Creek, stm., W.V., U.S.	m14	141
Peterson, Al., U.S.	B2	94
Peterson Field, mil., Co., U.S.	C6	99
Petersville, Al., U.S.	A2	94
Peter the Great Bay see Petra Velikogo, zaliv, b., Russia	C14	28
Pétion-Ville, Haiti	B5	80
Petit Bois Island, i., Ms., U.S.	E5	117
Petitcodiac, N.B., Can.	D4	87
Petitcodiac, stm., N.B., Can.	C5	87
Petite Amite, stm., La., U.S.	h10	111
Petite Rivière Noire, Piton de la, mtn., Mrts.	g10	57a
Petit Jean, stm., Ar., U.S.	B2	97
Petit Lac Des Allemands, l., La., U.S.	k11	111
Petit Lake, l., La., U.S.	k12	111
Petit-Rocher, N.B., Can.	B4	87
Petitsikapau Lake, l., Nf., Can.	g8	88
Peto, Mex.	C7	78
Petoskey, Mi., U.S.	C6	115
Petra see Al-Batrā', hist., Jord.	D3	42
Petra Velikogo, zaliv, b., Russia	C14	28
Petrič, Bul.	D9	18
Petrified Forest National Park, Az., U.S.	B6	96
Petrila, Rom.	G7	20
Petrodvorec, Russia	G13	10
Petrograd see Sankt-Peterburg, Russia	D5	26

Name	Map Ref.	Page
Petrolândia, Braz.	C4	74
Petroleum, co., Mt., U.S.	C8	119
Petrolia, On., Can.	E2	89
Petrolina, Braz.	C3	74
Petropavlovsk, Kaz.	D8	26
Petropavlovsk-Kamčatskij, Russia	D17	26
Petrópolis, Braz.	F3	74
Petros, Tn., U.S.	C9	135
Petroşani, Rom.	G7	20
Petrovsk, Russia	D8	22
Petrozavodsk, Russia	C5	26
Pettaquamscutt Lake Shores, R.I., U.S.	F4	132
Pettingell Peak, mtn., Co., U.S.	B5	99
Pettis, co., Mo., U.S.	C4	118
Pevek, Russia	C19	26
Pevely, Mo., U.S.	g13	118
Pewaukee, Wi., U.S.	E5	142
Pewaukee Lake, l., Wi., U.S.	m11	142
Pewee Valley, Ky., U.S.	B4	110
Pha-an, Myan.	C3	34
Phalaborwa, S. Afr.	C5	56
Phalodi, India	D2	40
Phangan, Ko, i., Thai.	E4	34
Phangnga, Thai.	E3	34
Phanom Dongrak Range, mts., Asia	D4	34
Phan Rang, Viet.	D5	34
Phan Si Pan see Fan Si Pan, mtn., Viet.	B4	34
Phan Thiet, Viet.	D5	34
Pharr, Tx., U.S.	F3	136
Phatthalung, Thai.	E4	34
Phayao, Thai.	C3	34
Phelps, Ky., U.S.	C7	110
Phelps, N.Y., U.S.	C3	125
Phelps, Wi., U.S.	B4	142
Phelps, co., Mo., U.S.	D6	118
Phelps, co., Ne., U.S.	D6	120
Phelps Lake, l., N.C., U.S.	B6	126
Phenix City, Al., U.S.	C4	94
Phetchabun, Thai.	C4	34
Phetchaburi, Thai.	D3	34
Phibun Mangsahan, Thai.	C5	34
Phichit, Thai.	C4	34
Philadelphia, Ms., U.S.	C4	117
Philadelphia, Pa., U.S.	G11	131
Philadelphia, co., Pa., U.S.	G12	131
Philadelphia Naval Shipyard, mil., Pa., U.S.	P21	131
Phil Campbell, Al., U.S.	A2	94
Philip, S.D., U.S.	C4	134
Philippeville see Skikda, Alg.	C6	48
Philippi, W.V., U.S.	B4	141
Philippi see Fílippoi, hist., Grc.	D10	18
Philippine Basin	G15	64
Philippines, ctry., Asia	C8	34
Philippine Sea	H16	24
Philippine Trench	H15	64
Philippopolis see Plovdiv, Bul.	C10	18
Philipsburg, Mt., U.S.	D3	119
Philipsburg, Pa., U.S.	E5	131
Philleo Lake, l., Wa., U.S.	h14	140
Phillips, Me., U.S.	D2	112
Phillips, Tx., U.S.	B2	136
Phillips, Wi., U.S.	C3	142
Phillips, co., Ar., U.S.	C5	97
Phillips, co., Co., U.S.	A8	99
Phillips, co., Ks., U.S.	C4	109
Phillips, co., Mt., U.S.	B8	119
Phillips Brook, stm., N.H., U.S.	A4	122
Phillipsburg, Ks., U.S.	C4	109
Phillipsburg, N.J., U.S.	B2	123
Philmont, N.Y., U.S.	C7	125
Philo, Il., U.S.	C5	106
Philomath, Or., U.S.	C3	130
Philpott Reservoir, res., Va., U.S.	D2	139
Phitsanulok, Thai.	C4	34
Phnom Penh see Phnum Pénh, Camb.	D4	34
Phnum Pénh (Phnom Penh), Camb.	D4	34
Phoenix, Az., U.S.	D3	96
Phoenix, Il., U.S.	k9	106
Phoenix, N.Y., U.S.	B4	125
Phoenix, Or., U.S.	E4	130
Phoenix Islands, is., Kir.	E12	58
Phoenixville, Pa., U.S.	F10	131
Phon, Thai.	C4	34
Phôngsali, Laos	B4	34
Phrae, Thai.	C4	34
Phra Nakhon Si Ayutthaya, Thai.	D4	34
Phuket, Thai.	E3	34
Phuket, Ko, i., Thai.	E3	34
Phumĭ Chhŭk, Camb.	D4	34
Phumĭ Kâmpóng Srâlau, Camb.	D5	34
Phumĭ Kaôh Kŏng, Camb.	D4	34
Phu Quoc, Dao, i., Viet.	D4	34
Piacenza, Italy	B2	18
Pianosa, Isola, i., Italy	C3	18
Piatra-Neamţ, Rom.	F9	20
Piatt, co., Il., U.S.	D5	106
Piauí, state, Braz.	C3	74
Piave, stm., Italy	A4	18
Píbor Post, Sudan	I11	48
Picacho, Az., U.S.	E4	96
Picardie, hist. reg., Fr.	C8	16

Name	Map Ref.	Page
Picardy see Picardie, hist. reg., Fr.	C8	16
Picayune, Ms., U.S.	E4	117
Piccadilly, Nf., Can.	D2	88
Pichanal, Arg.	A5	72
Picher, Ok., U.S.	A7	129
Pichilemu, Chile	E3	72
Pickaway, co., Oh., U.S.	C2	128
Pickens, Ms., U.S.	C4	117
Pickens, S.C., U.S.	B2	133
Pickens, co., Al., U.S.	B1	94
Pickens, co., Ga., U.S.	B2	103
Pickens, co., S.C., U.S.	B2	133
Pickerel Lake, l., Wi., U.S.	C5	142
Pickering, On., Can.	D5	89
Pickerington, Oh., U.S.	C3	128
Pickett, co., Tn., U.S.	C8	135
Pickwick Lake, res., U.S.	A6	117
Pickworth Point, c., Ma., U.S.	f12	114
Pico de Orizaba, Volcán, vol., Mex.	D5	78
Pico Rivera, Ca., U.S.	n12	98
Picos, Braz.	C3	74
Picton, On., Can.	D7	89
Pictou Island, i., N.S., Can.	D7	87
Picture Butte, Ab., Can.	E4	84
Pictured Rocks National Lakeshore, Mi., U.S.	B4	115
Pidurutalagala, mtn., Sri L.	H4	40
Piedecuesta, Col.	D5	80
Piedmont, Al., U.S.	B4	94
Piedmont, Ca., U.S.	h8	98
Piedmont, Mo., U.S.	D7	118
Piedmont, Ok., U.S.	B4	129
Piedmont, S.C., U.S.	B3	133
Piedmont, W.V., U.S.	B5	141
Piedmont Lake, res., Oh., U.S.	B4	128
Piedra, stm., Co., U.S.	D3	99
Piedras Blancas, Point, c., Ca., U.S.	E3	98
Piedras Negras, Guat.	B1	80
Piedras Negras, Mex.	B4	78
Pieksämäki, Fin.	E12	10
Pielinen, l., Fin.	E13	10
Pierce, Co., U.S.	A6	99
Pierce, Id., U.S.	C3	105
Pierce, Ne., U.S.	B8	120
Pierce, co., Ga., U.S.	E4	103
Pierce, co., N.D., U.S.	A5	127
Pierce, co., Ne., U.S.	B8	120
Pierce, co., Wa., U.S.	C3	140
Pierce, co., Wi., U.S.	D1	142
Pierce, Lake, l., Fl., U.S.	E5	102
Pierce City, Mo., U.S.	E3	118
Pierceton, In., U.S.	B6	107
Pierre, S.D., U.S.	C5	134
Pierrefonds, P.Q., Can.	q19	90
Pierre Part, La., U.S.	k9	111
Pierreville, P.Q., Can.	C5	90
Pierson, Fl., U.S.	C5	102
Pierz, Mn., U.S.	E4	116
Pieštany, Slvk.	E4	20
Pietarsaari, Fin.	E10	10
Pietermaritzburg, S. Afr.	D5	56
Pietersburg, S. Afr.	C4	56
Piet Retief, S. Afr.	D5	56
Pigeon, Mi., U.S.	E7	115
Pigeon, stm., In., U.S.	A6	107
Pigeon, stm., Mn., U.S.	h10	116
Pigeon, stm., Wi., U.S.	k10	142
Pigeon, stm., U.S.	f9	126
Pigeon Cove, Ma., U.S.	A6	114
Pigeon Forge, Tn., U.S.	D10	135
Pigeon Point, c., Mn., U.S.	h10	116
Pigg, stm., Va., U.S.	D3	139
Piggott, Ar., U.S.	A5	97
Pigüé, Arg.	F5	72
Pihlajavesi, l., Fin.	F13	10
Pihtipudas, Fin.	E11	10
Pijijiapan, Mex.	D6	78
Pike, co., Al., U.S.	D4	94
Pike, co., Ar., U.S.	C2	97
Pike, co., Ga., U.S.	C2	103
Pike, co., Il., U.S.	D2	106
Pike, co., In., U.S.	H3	107
Pike, co., Ky., U.S.	C7	110
Pike, co., Mo., U.S.	B6	118
Pike, co., Ms., U.S.	D3	117
Pike, co., Oh., U.S.	C2	128
Pike, co., Pa., U.S.	D11	131
Pike, stm., Wi., U.S.	C6	142
Pike Island Dam, U.S.	f8	141
Pike Lake, Mn., U.S.	D6	116
Pikes Peak, mtn., Co., U.S.	C5	99
Piketberg, S. Afr.	E2	56
Piketon, Oh., U.S.	C2	128
Pikeville, Ky., U.S.	C7	110
Pikeville, Tn., U.S.	D8	135
Piła, Pol.	C4	20
Pilcomayo, stm., S.A.	C5	72
Pilībhīt, India	D3	40
Pillar Point, c., Ca., U.S.	k7	98
Pílos, Grc.	F8	18
Pilot Grove, Mo., U.S.	C5	118
Pilot Knob, Mo., U.S.	D7	118
Pilot Knob, mtn., Id., U.S.	D3	105
Pilot Mound, Mb., Can.	E2	86
Pilot Mountain, N.C., U.S.	A2	126
Pilot Peak, mtn., Nv., U.S.	B7	121
Pilot Peak, mtn., Nv., U.S.	E4	121
Pilot Peak, mtn., Wy., U.S.	B3	143
Pilot Point, Tx., U.S.	C4	136

Name	Map Ref.	Page
Pilot Range, mts., Nv., U.S.	B7	121
Pilot Rock, Or., U.S.	B8	130
Pilot Station, Ak., U.S.	C7	95
Pilsen see Plzeň, Czech Rep.	E2	20
Pima, Az., U.S.	E6	96
Pima, co., Az., U.S.	E3	96
Pimmit Hills, Va., U.S.	g12	139
Pinal, co., Az., U.S.	E4	96
Pinaleno Mountains, mts., Az., U.S.	E5	96
Pinal Mountains, mts., Az., U.S.	D5	96
Pinang see George Town, Malay.	B2	36
Pınarbaşı, Tur.	C7	44
Pinar del Río, Cuba	A3	80
Pinardville, N.H., U.S.	E3	122
Pincher Creek, Ab., Can.	E4	84
Pinckard, Al., U.S.	D4	94
Pinckney, Mi., U.S.	F7	115
Pinckney Island, i., S.C., U.S.	G6	133
Pinckneyville, Il., U.S.	E4	106
Pinconning, Mi., U.S.	E7	115
Pindaré-Mirim, Braz.	B2	74
Píndhos Óros, mts., Grc.	E8	18
Pindus Mountains see Píndhos Óros, mts., Grc.	E8	18
Pine, Az., U.S.	C4	96
Pine, co., Mn., U.S.	D6	116
Pine, stm., Mi., U.S.	D7	115
Pine, stm., Mi., U.S.	D5	115
Pine, stm., N.H., U.S.	C4	122
Pine, stm., Wi., U.S.	C5	142
Pine, stm., Wi., U.S.	C4	142
Pine Barrens, reg., N.J., U.S.	D3	123
Pine Bluff, Ar., U.S.	C3	97
Pinebluff, N.C., U.S.	B3	126
Pine Bluffs, Wy., U.S.	E8	143
Pine Bridge, Ct., U.S.	D3	100
Pine Castle, Fl., U.S.	D5	102
Pine City, Mn., U.S.	E6	116
Pine Creek, Austl.	C5	60
Pine Creek, stm., Nv., U.S.	C5	121
Pine Creek, stm., Pa., U.S.	C6	131
Pine Creek, stm., Wa., U.S.	B8	140
Pine Creek Lake, res., Ok., U.S.	C6	129
Pinedale, Wy., U.S.	D3	143
Pine Falls, Mb., Can.	D3	86
Pine Forest Range, mts., Nv., U.S.	B3	121
Pine Grove, Pa., U.S.	E9	131
Pine Grove Mills, Pa., U.S.	E6	131
Pine Hill, N.J., U.S.	D3	123
Pinehouse Lake, Sk., Can.	B2	91
Pinehouse Lake, l., Sk., Can.	B2	91
Pinehurst, Ma., U.S.	f11	114
Pinehurst, N.C., U.S.	B3	126
Pine Island, Mn., U.S.	F6	116
Pine Island, i., Fl., U.S.	F4	102
Pine Island Sound, strt., Fl., U.S.	F4	102
Pine Key, i., Fl., U.S.	p10	102
Pine Knot, Ky., U.S.	D5	110
Pine Lake, Ga., U.S.	h8	103
Pine Lake, l., In., U.S.	A4	107
Pine Lake, l., Wi., U.S.	C5	142
Pine Lawn, Mo., U.S.	f13	118
Pine Level, N.C., U.S.	B4	126
Pine Mountain, Ga., U.S.	D2	103
Pine Mountain, mtn., Or., U.S.	D6	130
Pine Mountain, mtn., Wy., U.S.	E3	143
Pine Point, Me., U.S.	E2	112
Pine Prairie, La., U.S.	D3	111
Pine Ridge, S.D., U.S.	D3	134
Pine Ridge Indian Reservation, S.D., U.S.	D3	134
Pine River, Mn., U.S.	D4	116
Pines, Isle of see Juventud, Isla de la, i., Cuba	A3	80
Pines, Lake O' the, res., Tx., U.S.	C5	136
Pinesdale, Mt., U.S.	D2	119
Pinetops, N.C., U.S.	B5	126
Pinetown, S. Afr.	D5	56
Pine Valley, val., Ut., U.S.	E2	137
Pineville, Ky., U.S.	D6	110
Pineville, La., U.S.	C3	111
Pineville, N.C., U.S.	B2	126
Pineville, W.V., U.S.	D3	141
Pinewood, S.C., U.S.	D7	133
Piney Creek, stm., W.V., U.S.	n13	141
Piney Fork, stm., W.V., U.S.	h9	141
Piney Point, Md., U.S.	D4	113
Piney View, W.V., U.S.	n13	141
Pingdu, China	B4	30
Pingelly, Austl.	G2	60
Pingjiang, China	F10	28
Pingle, China	E3	30
Pingliang, China	D9	28
Pingluo, China	B2	30
Pingquan, China	C11	28
Pingtan, China	D4	30
P'ingtung, Tai.	E5	30
Pingwu, China	E8	28

Name	Map Ref.	Page
Pingxiang, China	G9	28
Pingxiang, China	F10	28
Pingyang, China	D5	30
Pingyao, China	B3	30
Pingyin, China	B4	30
Pinheiro, Braz.	B2	74
Pini, Pulau, i., Indon.	C1	36
Pinjarra, Austl.	G2	60
Pinjug, Russia	B8	22
Pinnacles National Monument, Ca., U.S.	D3	98
Pinole, Ca., U.S.	h8	98
Pinopolis Dam, S.C., U.S.	E8	133
Pinos, Mount, mtn., U.S.	E4	98
Pinrang, Indon.	D5	36
Pins, Île des, i., N. Cal.	I9	62a
Pins, Pointe aux, c., On., Can.	E3	89
Pinsk, Bela.	C9	20
Pinsk Marshes see Polesye, reg., Eur.	D8	20
Pinson, Al., U.S.	f7	94
Pinta, Isla, i., Ec.	C1	70
Pinta, Sierra, mts., Az., U.S.	E2	96
Pintados, Chile	C4	72
Pintwater Range, mts., Nv., U.S.	G6	121
Pioche, Nv., U.S.	F7	121
Piombino, Italy	C3	18
Pioneer, Oh., U.S.	A1	128
Pioneer Mountains, mts., Id., U.S.	F5	105
Pioneer Mountains, mts., Mt., U.S.	E3	119
Pioner, ostrov, i., Russia	B10	26
Piotrków Trybunalski, Pol.	D5	20
Pīpār, India	D2	40
Pipe Spring National Monument, Az., U.S.	A3	96
Pipestem Creek, stm., N.D., U.S.	B6	127
Pipestone, Mn., U.S.	G2	116
Pipestone, co., Mn., U.S.	F2	116
Pipestone National Monument, Mn., U.S.	G2	116
Pipestone Pass, Mt., U.S.	E4	119
Pipmuacan, Réservoir, res., P.Q., Can.	k12	90
Piqua, Oh., U.S.	B1	128
Piracicaba, Braz.	F2	74
Piracuruca, Braz.	B3	74
Piraeus see Piraiévs, Grc.	E9	18
Piraiévs, Grc.	E9	18
Piranhas, Braz.	E1	74
Pīrān Shahr, Iran	D11	44
Pirapora, Braz.	E3	74
Pires do Rio, Braz.	E2	74
Piripiri, Braz.	B3	74
Pirot, Yugo.	C9	18
Pīr Panjāl Range, mts., Asia	E2	28
Pirtleville, Az., U.S.	F6	96
Piru, Indon.	D7	36
Pisa, Italy	C3	18
Pisagua, Chile	A2	69
Piscataqua, stm., N.H., U.S.	D5	122
Piscataquis, co., Me., U.S.	C3	112
Piscataquis, stm., Me., U.S.	C3	112
Piscataquog, stm., N.H., U.S.	D3	122
Piscataway, N.J., U.S.	B4	123
Pisco, Peru	F4	70
Piseco Lake, l., N.Y., U.S.	B6	125
Písek, Czech Rep.	E3	20
Pisgah, Al., U.S.	A4	94
Pisgah, Mt., U.S.	n13	128
Pisgah, Mount, mtn., Wy., U.S.	B8	143
Pisgah Forest, N.C., U.S.	f10	126
Pishan, China	D3	28
Pismo Beach, Ca., U.S.	E3	98
Pisticci, Italy	D6	18
Pistoia, Italy	C3	18
Pistolet Bay, b., Nf., Can.	C4	88
Pit, stm., Ca., U.S.	B3	98
Pita, Gui.	D2	50
Pitcairn, Pa., U.S.	k14	131
Pitcairn, dep., Oc.	K26	64
Piteå, Swe.	D9	10
Piteälven, stm., Swe.	C8	10
Piteşti, Rom.	G8	20
Pithara, Austl.	G2	60
Pitkin, co., Co., U.S.	B4	99
Pitkjaranta, Russia	B5	22
Pitman, N.J., U.S.	D2	123
Pitt, co., N.C., U.S.	B5	126
Pitt Island, i., B.C., Can.	C3	85
Pittsboro, In., U.S.	E5	107
Pittsboro, N.C., U.S.	B3	126
Pittsburg, Ca., U.S.	g9	98
Pittsburg, Ks., U.S.	E9	109
Pittsburg, Ky., U.S.	C5	110
Pittsburg, Tx., U.S.	C5	136
Pittsburg, co., Ok., U.S.	C6	129
Pittsburgh, Pa., U.S.	F1	131
Pittsfield, Il., U.S.	D3	106
Pittsfield, Ma., U.S.	B1	114
Pittsfield, Me., U.S.	D3	112
Pittsfield, N.H., U.S.	D4	122
Pittsford, Vt., U.S.	D2	138
Pittston, Pa., U.S.	D10	131
Pittsville, Md., U.S.	D7	113
Pittsville, Wi., U.S.	D3	142
Pittsylvania, co., Va., U.S.	D3	139

Name	Map Ref.	Page
Pium, Braz.	F10	70
Piura, Peru	E3	70
Piute, co., Ut., U.S.	E3	137
Piute Peak, mtn., Ca., U.S.	E4	98
Piute Reservoir, res., Ut., U.S.	E3	137
Pivdennyi Buh, stm., Ukr.	F11	20
Pixley, Ca., U.S.	E4	98
Pjandž, stm., Asia	B1	40
Pjaozero, ozero, l., Russia	D14	10
Pjasina, stm., Russia	B10	26
Pjatigorsk, Russia	B4	42
Placentia, Nf., Can.	E5	88
Placentia Bay, b., Nf., Can.	E4	88
Placer, co., Ca., U.S.	C3	98
Placer Mountain, mtn., N.M., U.S.	k8	124
Placerville, Ca., U.S.	C3	98
Placetas, Cuba	A4	80
Placid, Lake, l., Fl., U.S.	E5	102
Placid, Lake, l., N.Y., U.S.	f11	125
Placitas, N.M., U.S.	B3	124
Plain City, Oh., U.S.	B2	128
Plain City, Ut., U.S.	B3	137
Plain Dealing, La., U.S.	B2	111
Plainfield, Ct., U.S.	C8	100
Plainfield, Il., U.S.	B5	106
Plainfield, In., U.S.	E5	107
Plainfield, N.J., U.S.	B4	123
Plainfield, Vt., U.S.	C4	138
Plainfield, Wi., U.S.	D4	142
Plains, Ga., U.S.	D2	103
Plains, Ks., U.S.	E3	109
Plains, Mt., U.S.	C2	119
Plains, Pa., U.S.	n17	131
Plains, Tx., U.S.	C1	136
Plainview, Ar., U.S.	C2	97
Plainview, Mn., U.S.	F6	116
Plainview, Ne., U.S.	B8	120
Plainview, Tx., U.S.	B2	136
Plainville, Ct., U.S.	C4	100
Plainville, Ks., U.S.	C4	109
Plainville, Ma., U.S.	B5	114
Plainwell, Mi., U.S.	F5	115
Plaistow, N.H., U.S.	E4	122
Plampang, Indon.	E5	36
Planeta Rica, Col.	D4	80
Plankinton, S.D., U.S.	D7	134
Plano, Il., U.S.	B5	106
Plano, Tx., U.S.	C4	136
Plantagenet, On., Can.	B9	89
Plantation, Fl., U.S.	r13	102
Plant City, Fl., U.S.	D4	102
Plantersville, Al., U.S.	C3	94
Plantersville, Ms., U.S.	A5	117
Plantsite, Az., U.S.	D6	96
Plantsville, Ct., U.S.	C4	100
Plaquemine, La., U.S.	D4	111
Plaquemines, co., La., U.S.	E6	111
Plasencia, Spain	G3	16
Plaster Rock, N.B., Can.	C2	87
Plata, Río de la, est., S.A.	E6	72
Plate, Île, i., Sey.	i13	57b
Plato, Col.	B5	70
Platte, S.D., U.S.	D7	134
Platte, co., Mo., U.S.	B3	118
Platte, co., Ne., U.S.	C8	120
Platte, co., Wy., U.S.	D7	143
Platte, stm., Mn., U.S.	E4	116
Platte, stm., Ne., U.S.	D6	120
Platte, stm., U.S.	B3	118
Platte City, Mo., U.S.	B3	118
Platteville, Co., U.S.	A6	99
Platteville, Wi., U.S.	F3	142
Plattsburg, Mo., U.S.	B3	118
Plattsburgh, N.Y., U.S.	f11	125
Plattsmouth, Ne., U.S.	D10	120
Plauen, Ger.	E12	12
Plavsk, Russia	C14	20
Playas Lake, l., N.M., U.S.	F2	124
Playgreen Lake, l., Mb., Can.	B6	86
Play Ku, Viet.	D5	34
Pleasant, stm., Me., U.S.	C3	112
Pleasant, Lake, res., Az., U.S.	D3	96
Pleasant Gap, Pa., U.S.	E6	131
Pleasant Garden, N.C., U.S.	B3	126
Pleasant Grove, Al., U.S.	g7	94
Pleasant Grove, Ut., U.S.	C4	137
Pleasant Hill, Ca., U.S.	h8	98
Pleasant Hill, Ia., U.S.	e8	108
Pleasant Hill, Il., U.S.	D3	106
Pleasant Hill, La., U.S.	C2	111
Pleasant Hill, Mo., U.S.	C3	118
Pleasant Hill, Oh., U.S.	B1	128
Pleasant Lake, In., U.S.	A7	107
Pleasant Lake, l., Me., U.S.	C5	112
Pleasant Lake, l., N.H., U.S.	D4	122
Pleasanton, Ca., U.S.	h9	98
Pleasanton, Ks., U.S.	D9	109
Pleasanton, Tx., U.S.	E3	136
Pleasant Prairie, Wi., U.S.	n12	142
Pleasants, co., W.V., U.S.	B3	141
Pleasant Valley, Ia., U.S.	g11	108
Pleasant Valley, Mo., U.S.	h11	118
Pleasant View, Ut., U.S.	B3	137
Pleasantville, Ia., U.S.	C4	108
Pleasantville, N.J., U.S.	E3	123
Pleasantville, N.Y., U.S.	D7	125
Pleasantville, Oh., U.S.	C3	128
Pleasure Beach, Ct., U.S.	D7	100
Pleasure Ridge Park, Ky., U.S.	g11	110
Pleasureville, Ky., U.S.	B4	110
Plenty, Bay of, b., N.Z.	o14	63c
Plentywood, Mt., U.S.	B12	119
Pleseck, Russia	C6	26
Plessisville, P.Q., Can.	C6	90
Pleszew, Pol.	D4	20
Pleven, Bul.	C10	18
Pljussa, Russia	G13	10
Płock, Pol.	C5	20
Ploiești, Rom.	G9	20
Plomosa Mountains, mts., Az., U.S.	D1	96
Plonge, Lac la, l., Sk., Can.	B2	91
Płońsk, Pol.	C6	20
Plovdiv, Bul.	C10	18
Plover, Wi., U.S.	D4	142
Plover, stm., Wi., U.S.	D4	142
Plum, Pa., U.S.	k14	131
Plumas, co., Ca., U.S.	B3	98
Plum Coulee, Mb., Can.	E3	86
Plumerville, Ar., U.S.	B3	97
Plum Island, i., Ma., U.S.	A6	114
Plummer, Id., U.S.	B2	105
Plumsteadville, Pa., U.S.	F11	131
Plumtree, Zimb.	C4	56
Plunge, Lith.	I9	10
Plutarco Elías Calles, Presa, res., Mex.	B3	78
Plymouth, Monts.	B7	80
Plymouth, Eng., U.K.	E4	12
Plymouth, Ct., U.S.	C3	100
Plymouth, Fl., U.S.	D5	102
Plymouth, In., U.S.	B5	107
Plymouth, Ma., U.S.	C6	114
Plymouth, Mi., U.S.	p15	115
Plymouth, Mn., U.S.	m12	116
Plymouth, N.C., U.S.	B6	126
Plymouth, N.H., U.S.	C3	122
Plymouth, Oh., U.S.	A3	128
Plymouth, Pa., U.S.	D10	131
Plymouth, Wi., U.S.	E6	142
Plymouth, co., Ia., U.S.	B1	108
Plymouth, co., Ma., U.S.	C6	114
Plymouth Bay, b., Ma., U.S.	C6	114
Plzeň, Czech Rep.	E2	20
Pô, Burkina	D4	50
Po, stm., Italy	B3	18
Po, stm., Va., U.S.	B5	139
Pobè, Benin	E5	50
Pobeda, gora, mtn., Russia	C16	26
Pobedy, Peak, mtn., Asia	B11	42
Pocahontas, Ar., U.S.	A5	97
Pocahontas, Ia., U.S.	B3	108
Pocahontas, Il., U.S.	E4	106
Pocahontas, co., Ia., U.S.	B3	108
Pocahontas, co., W.V., U.S.	C4	141
Pocasset, Ma., U.S.	C6	114
Pocatalico, W.V., U.S.	C3	141
Pocatalico, stm., W.V., U.S.	C3	141
Pocatello, Id., U.S.	G6	105
Poček, Russia	C12	20
Počinok, Russia	B12	20
Poções, Braz.	D3	74
Pocola, Ok., U.S.	B7	129
Pocomoke, stm., Md., U.S.	D7	113
Pocomoke City, Md., U.S.	D6	113
Pocomoke Sound, strt., Md., U.S.	E6	113
Poconé, Braz.	B6	72
Pocono Mountains, hills, Pa., U.S.	E11	131
Pocono Pines, Pa., U.S.	D11	131
Poços de Caldas, Braz.	F2	74
Pocotopaug Lake, res., Ct., U.S.	C6	100
Podgorica, Yugo.	C7	18
Podkamennaja Tunguska, Russia	C10	26
Podkamennaja Tunguska, stm., Russia	C11	26
Podol'sk, Russia	C6	22
Podor, Sen.	C2	50
Podporože, Russia	B5	22
Pofadder, S. Afr.	D2	56
Poge, Cape, c., Ma., U.S.	D7	114
Pograničnyj, Russia	C14	28
Pohénégamook, P.Q., Can.	B8	90
Pohjanmaa, reg., Fin.	D11	10
Pohnpei, i., Micron.	D9	58
Pohue Bay, b., Hi., U.S.	E6	104
Pohvistnevo, Russia	D9	22
Poinsett, co., Ar., U.S.	B5	97
Poinsett, Cape, c., Ant.	C16	67
Poinsett, Lake, l., Fl., U.S.	D6	102
Poinsett, Lake, l., S.D., U.S.	C8	134
Point Clear, Al., U.S.	E2	94
Pointe a la Hache, La., U.S.	E6	111
Pointe-à-Pitre, Guad.	B7	80
Pointe-au-Pic, P.Q., Can.	B7	90
Pointe-Calumet, P.Q., Can.	p19	90
Pointe-Claire, P.Q., Can.	D4	90
Pointe Coupee, co., La., U.S.	D4	111
Pointe-des-Cascades, P.Q., Can.	q19	90
Point Edward, On., Can.	D2	89
Pointe-Noire, Congo	D2	54
Pointe-Verte, N.B., Can.	B4	87
Point Fortin, Trin.	C7	80
Point Hope, Ak., U.S.	B6	95
Point Imperial, mtn., Az., U.S.	A4	96
Point Judith Pond, l., R.I., U.S.	F4	132
Point Leamington, Nf., Can.	D4	88
Point Marion, Pa., U.S.	G2	131
Point Mugu Naval Air Station, mil., Ca., U.S.	E4	98
Point of Rocks, Md., U.S.	B2	113
Point Pelee National Park, On., Can.	F2	89
Point Pleasant, N.J., U.S.	C4	123
Point Pleasant, W.V., U.S.	C2	141
Point Pleasant Beach, N.J., U.S.	C4	123
Point Reyes National Seashore, Ca., U.S.	C2	98
Point Roberts, Wa., U.S.	A2	140
Poipu, Hi., U.S.	B2	104
Poison Creek, stm., Wy., U.S.	C5	143
Poisson Blanc, Lac du, res., P.Q., Can.	C2	90
Poitiers, Fr.	D7	16
Poitou, hist. reg., Fr.	D6	16
Poivre Atoll, i., Sey.	i12	57b
Pojarkovo, Russia	B13	28
Pokaran, India	D2	40
Pokegama Lake, l., Mn., U.S.	C5	116
Pokegama Lake, l., Wi., U.S.	C2	142
Pokharā, Nepal	D4	40
Polacca, Az., U.S.	B5	96
Polack, Bela.	B10	20
Pola de Lena, Spain	F4	16
Pola de Siero, Spain	F4	16
Poland, ctry., Eur.	C5	20
Polar Bear Provincial Park, On., Can.	n18	89
Polatlı, Tur.	C5	44
Polecat Creek, stm., Ok., U.S.	B5	129
Pol-e Khomrī, Afg.	C9	42
Polesye, reg., Eur.	D8	20
Polewali, Indon.	F6	36
Policastro, Golfo di, b., Italy	E5	18
Pólis, Cyp.	E5	44
Poljarnyj, Russia	B15	10
Polk, Pa., U.S.	D2	131
Polk, co., Ar., U.S.	C1	97
Polk, co., Fl., U.S.	E5	102
Polk, co., Ga., U.S.	C1	103
Polk, co., Ia., U.S.	C4	108
Polk, co., Mn., U.S.	C2	116
Polk, co., Mo., U.S.	D4	118
Polk, co., N.C., U.S.	f10	126
Polk, co., Ne., U.S.	C8	120
Polk, co., Or., U.S.	C3	130
Polk, co., Tn., U.S.	D9	135
Polk, co., Tx., U.S.	D5	136
Polk, co., Wi., U.S.	C1	142
Polk City, Fl., U.S.	D5	102
Polk City, Ia., U.S.	C4	108
Pol'kino, Russia	B11	26
Pollāchi, India	G3	40
Pollença, Spain	H8	16
Polo, Il., U.S.	B4	106
Polohy, Ukr.	F14	20
Polonnaruwa, Sri L.	H4	40
Polonne, Ukr.	D9	20
Polson, Mt., U.S.	C2	119
Poltava, Ukr.	E13	20
Põltsamaa, Est.	G12	10
Polunočnoe, Russia	B11	22
Polynesia, is., Oc.	I23	64
Pombal, Braz.	C4	74
Pomerania, hist. reg., Eur.	C4	20
Pomeroy, Ia., U.S.	B3	108
Pomeroy, Oh., U.S.	C3	128
Pomeroy, Wa., U.S.	C8	140
Pomme de Terre, stm., Mn., U.S.	E3	116
Pomme de Terre, stm., Mo., U.S.	D4	118
Pomme de Terre Lake, res., Mo., U.S.	D4	118
Pomona, Ca., U.S.	m13	98
Pomona, Ks., U.S.	D8	109
Pomona Lake, res., Ks., U.S.	D7	109
Pompano Beach, Fl., U.S.	F6	102
Pompei, Italy	D5	18
Pompéu, Braz.	E6	74
Pompton Lakes, N.J., U.S.	A4	123
Ponaganset, stm., R.I., U.S.	C2	132
Ponaganset Reservoir, res., R.I., U.S.	B2	132
Ponape see Pohnpei, i., Micron.	D9	58
Ponca, Ne., U.S.	B9	120
Ponca City, Ok., U.S.	A4	129
Ponca Creek, stm., U.S.	A6	120
Ponca Indian Reservation, Ne., U.S.	B7	120
Ponce, P.R.	B6	80
Ponce de Leon Bay, b., Fl., U.S.	G5	102
Ponce de Leon Inlet, b., Fl., U.S.	C6	102
Poncha Pass, Co., U.S.	C4	99
Ponchatoula, La., U.S.	D5	111
Pond, stm., Ky., U.S.	C2	110
Pond Creek, Ok., U.S.	A3	129
Pondera, co., Mt., U.S.	B4	119
Pond Fork, stm., W.V., U.S.	D3	141
Pondicherry, India	G3	40
Pone Island, i., Md., U.S.	D5	113
Ponferrada, Spain	F3	16
Ponoi, Russia	C6	26
Ponoka, Ab., Can.	C4	84
Ponta Delgada, Port.	F7	46
Ponta Grossa, Braz.	D8	72
Pontalina, Braz.	E2	74
Ponta Porã, Braz.	H8	70
Pontarlier, Fr.	D10	16
Pontchartrain, Lake, l., La., U.S.	D5	111
Ponteix, Sk., Can.	H2	91
Ponte Nova, Braz.	F3	74
Pontevedra, Spain	F2	16
Ponte Vedra Beach, Fl., U.S.	B5	102
Pontiac, Il., U.S.	C5	106
Pontiac, Mi., U.S.	F7	115
Pontianak, Indon.	C3	36
Pontine Islands see Ponziane, Isole, is., Italy	D4	18
Pontoosuc Lake, l., Ma., U.S.	B1	114
Pontotoc, Ms., U.S.	A4	117
Pontotoc, co., Ms., U.S.	A4	117
Pontotoc, co., Ok., U.S.	C5	129
Pont-Rouge, P.Q., Can.	C6	90
Pontus Mountains see Doğu Karadeniz Dağları, mts., Tur.	B8	44
Pontypool, On., Can.	C6	89
Ponziane, Isole, is., Italy	D4	18
Poole, Eng., U.K.	E5	12
Pooler, Ga., U.S.	D5	103
Pooles Island, i., Md., U.S.	B5	113
Poolesville, Md., U.S.	B3	113
Poopó, Bol.	B4	72
Poopó, Lago, l., Bol.	B4	72
Popayán, Col.	C4	70
Pope, co., Ar., U.S.	B2	97
Pope, co., Il., U.S.	F5	106
Pope, co., Mn., U.S.	E3	116
Pope Air Force Base, mil., N.C., U.S.	B3	126
Poplar, Mt., U.S.	B11	119
Poplar, stm., Can.	C3	86
Poplar, stm., Mn., U.S.	C2	116
Poplar Bluff, Mo., U.S.	E7	118
Poplar Island, i., Md., U.S.	C5	113
Poplarville, Ms., U.S.	E4	117
Popocatépetl, Volcán, vol., Mex.	D5	78
Popokabaka, D.R.C.	E3	54
Popondetta, Pap. N. Gui.	H12	32
Popovo, Bul.	C11	18
Popple, stm., Wi., U.S.	C5	142
Poprad, Slvk.	E6	20
Poquonock, Ct., U.S.	B5	100
Poquonock Bridge, Ct., U.S.	D7	100
Poquoson, Va., U.S.	C6	139
Porangatu, Braz.	D2	74
Porbandar, India	E1	40
Porcher Island, i., B.C., Can.	C2	85
Porcupine, stm., N.A.	E11	82
Porcupine Mountains, mts., Mi., U.S.	m12	115
Pordenone, Italy	B4	18
Pori, Fin.	F9	10
Porirua, N.Z.	p13	63c
Porlamar, Ven.	A7	70
Poronaisk, Russia	E16	26
Porpoise Bay, b., Ant.	C17	67
Porsanger, b., Nor.	A11	10
Porsgrunn, Nor.	G3	10
Portachuelo, Bol.	B5	72
Port Adelaide, Austl.	G2	62
Portadown, N. Ire., U.K.	C2	12
Portage, In., U.S.	A3	107
Portage, Mi., U.S.	F5	115
Portage, Pa., U.S.	F4	131
Portage, Wi., U.S.	E4	142
Portage, co., Oh., U.S.	A4	128
Portage, co., Wi., U.S.	D4	142
Portage, stm., Oh., U.S.	B2	128
Portage Bay, b., Mb., Can.	D2	86
Portage Head, c., Wa., U.S.	A1	140
Portage Lake, l., Me., U.S.	B4	112
Portage Lakes, Oh., U.S.	B4	128
Portage la Prairie, Mb., Can.	E2	86
Portageville, Mo., U.S.	E8	118
Port Alberni, B.C., Can.	E5	85
Portalegre, Port.	H3	16
Portales, N.M., U.S.	C6	124
Port Alfred, S. Afr.	E4	56
Port Alice, B.C., Can.	D4	85
Port Allegany, Pa., U.S.	C5	131
Port Allen, La., U.S.	D4	111
Port Angeles, Wa., U.S.	A2	140
Port Antonio, Jam.	B4	80
Port Aransas, Tx., U.S.	F4	136
Port Arthur see Lüshun, China	D12	28
Port Arthur, Tx., U.S.	E6	136
Port Augusta, Austl.	G2	62
Port au Port Bay, b., Nf., Can.	D2	88
Port au Port [West-Aguathuna-Felix Cove], Nf., Can.	D2	88
Port au Prince Peninsula, pen., Nf., Can.	D2	88
Port au Prince, Haiti	B5	80
Port-Cartier-Ouest, P.Q., Can.	k13	90
Port Chalmers, N.Z.	q13	63c
Port Charlotte, Fl., U.S.	F4	102
Port Chester, N.Y., U.S.	E7	125
Port Clinton, Oh., U.S.	A3	128
Port Colborne, On., Can.	E5	89
Port Coquitlam, B.C., Can.	E6	85
Port Deposit, Md., U.S.	A5	113
Port Dickinson, N.Y., U.S.	C5	125
Port Edward, B.C., Can.	B2	85
Port Edward, S. Afr.	E5	56
Port Edwards, Wi., U.S.	D4	142
Port Elgin, On., Can.	C3	89
Port Elizabeth, S. Afr.	E4	56
Porter, In., U.S.	A3	107
Porter, Tx., U.S.	D5	136
Porter, co., In., U.S.	B3	107
Porter Creek, stm., W.V., U.S.	m13	141
Porterdale, Ga., U.S.	C3	103
Porterville, Ca., U.S.	D4	98
Port Ewen, N.Y., U.S.	D7	125
Port Fairy, Austl.	H3	62
Port Gamble Indian Reservation, Wa., U.S.	B3	140
Port-Gentil, Gabon	D1	54
Port Gibson, Ms., U.S.	D3	117
Port-Harcourt, Nig.	F6	50
Port Hedland, Austl.	E2	60
Port Hood, N.S., Can.	C8	87
Port Hope, On., Can.	D6	89
Port Hope Simpson, Nf., Can.	B3	88
Port Hueneme, Ca., U.S.	E4	98
Port Huron, Mi., U.S.	F8	115
Portimão, Port.	I2	16
Port Isabel, Tx., U.S.	F4	136
Port Jefferson, N.Y., U.S.	n15	125
Port Jervis, N.Y., U.S.	D6	125
Port Lairge see Waterford, Ire.	D3	12
Portland, Austl.	H3	62
Portland, Ct., U.S.	C5	100
Portland, In., U.S.	D8	107
Portland, Me., U.S.	E2	112
Portland, Mi., U.S.	F6	115
Portland, N.D., U.S.	B8	127
Portland, Or., U.S.	B4	130
Portland, Tn., U.S.	A5	135
Portland, Tx., U.S.	F4	136
Portland, Cape, c., Austl.	I4	62
Portland Inlet, b., B.C., Can.	B2	85
Port Laoise, Ire.	D3	12
Port Lavaca, Tx., U.S.	E4	136
Port Lincoln, Austl.	G2	62
Port Loko, S.L.	E2	50
Port Louis, Mrts.	f10	57a
Port Ludlow, Wa., U.S.	B3	140
Port Macquarie, Austl.	G5	62
Port Madison Indian Reservation, Wa., U.S.	B3	140
Port McNeill, B.C., Can.	D4	85
Port McNicoll, On., Can.	C5	89
Port Monmouth, N.J., U.S.	C4	123
Port Moresby, Pap. N. Gui.	H12	32
Port Morien, N.S., Can.	C10	87
Port Neches, Tx., U.S.	E6	136
Portneuf, P.Q., Can.	C6	90
Port Nolloth, S. Afr.	D2	56
Porto, Port.	G2	16
Porto Alegre, Braz.	E7	72
Porto Amboim, Ang.	F2	54
Portobelo, Pan.	D4	80
Porto de Moz, Braz.	D9	70
Porto Esperança, Braz.	G8	70
Porto Esperidião, Braz.	G8	70
Portoferraio, Italy	C3	18
Port of Spain, Trin.	C7	80
Portola, Ca., U.S.	C3	98
Porto Murtinho, Braz.	H8	70
Porto Nacional, Braz.	D2	74
Porto-Novo, Benin	E5	50
Port Orange, Fl., U.S.	C6	102
Port Orchard, Wa., U.S.	B3	140
Port Orford, Or., U.S.	E2	130
Porto Santana, Braz.	B1	74
Porto Santo, i., Port.	D1	48
Porto Seguro, Braz.	E4	74
Porto Torres, Italy	D2	18
Porto-Vecchio, Fr.	D2	18
Porto Velho, Braz.	E7	70
Portoviejo, Ec.	D3	70
Port Penn, De., U.S.	B3	101
Port Phillip Bay, b., Austl.	H3	62
Port Richey, Fl., U.S.	D4	102
Port Rowan, On., Can.	E4	89
Port Royal, S.C., U.S.	G6	133
Port Royal Island, i., S.C., U.S.	G6	133
Port Royal Sound, strt., S.C., U.S.	G6	133
Port Said see Būr Sa'īd, Egypt	E10	48
Port Saint Joe, Fl., U.S.	C1	102
Port Saint Johns, S. Afr.	E4	56
Port Saint Lucie, Fl., U.S.	E6	102
Port Salerno, Fl., U.S.	E6	102
Port Saunders, Nf., Can.	C3	88
Port Shepstone, S. Afr.	E5	56
Portsmouth, Eng., U.K.	E6	12
Portsmouth, N.H., U.S.	D5	122
Portsmouth, Oh., U.S.	D3	128
Portsmouth, R.I., U.S.	E6	132

Name	Map Ref.	Page
Portsmouth, Va., U.S.	D6	139
Portsmouth Naval Shipyard, mil., Me., U.S.	D5	122
Port Stanley, On., Can.	E3	89
Port Stanley see Stanley, Falk. Is.	H5	69
Port Sudan see Būr Sūdān, Sudan	G12	48
Port Sulphur, La., U.S.	E6	111
Port Talbot, Wales, U.K.	E5	12
Porttipahdan tekojärvi, l., Fin.	B12	10
Port Townsend, Wa., U.S.	A3	140
Portugal, ctry., Eur.	G3	16
Port Union, Nf., Can.	D5	88
Port Vila, Vanuatu	k9	62a
Port Washington, N.Y., U.S.	h13	125
Port Washington, Wi., U.S.	E6	142
Port Wentworth, Ga., U.S.	D5	103
Porum, Ok., U.S.	B6	129
Porvenir, Chile	H2	69
Porvoo, Fin.	F11	10
Posadas, Arg.	D6	72
Posen see Poznań, Pol.	C4	20
Posen, Il., U.S.	k9	106
Poset, Russia	E15	26
Posey, co., In., U.S.	H2	107
Poseyville, In., U.S.	H2	107
Posio, Fin.	C13	10
Poso, Indon.	D6	36
Posse, Braz.	D2	74
Post, Tx., U.S.	C2	136
Post Falls, Id., U.S.	B2	105
Postmasburg, S. Afr.	D3	56
Postville, Ia., U.S.	A6	108
Potawatomi Indian Reservation, Ks., U.S.	C8	109
Potchefstroom, S. Afr.	D4	56
Poteau, Ok., U.S.	B7	129
Poteau, stm., U.S.	B7	129
Poteet, Tx., U.S.	E3	136
Potenza, Italy	D5	18
Potgietersrus, S. Afr.	C4	56
Poth, Tx., U.S.	E3	136
Potholes Reservoir, res., Wa., U.S.	B6	140
Poti, Geor.	A9	44
Potiskum, Nig.	D7	50
Potlatch, Id., U.S.	C2	105
Potomac, Md., U.S.	B3	113
Potomac, stm., U.S.	D4	113
Potomac Heights, Md., U.S.	C3	113
Potomac Park, Md., U.S.	k13	113
Potosí, Bol.	B4	72
Potosi, Mo., U.S.	D7	118
Potsdam, Ger.	D13	12
Potsdam, N.Y., U.S.	f10	125
Pottawatomie, co., Ks., U.S.	C7	109
Pottawatomie, co., Ok., U.S.	B4	129
Pottawattamie, co., Ia., U.S.	C2	108
Potter, co., Pa., U.S.	C6	131
Potter, co., S.D., U.S.	B6	134
Potter, co., Tx., U.S.	B2	136
Potter Valley, Ca., U.S.	C2	98
Potts Creek, stm., U.S.	C2	139
Pottstown, Pa., U.S.	F10	131
Pottsville, Ar., U.S.	B2	97
Pottsville, Pa., U.S.	E9	131
Pouce Coupe, B.C., Can.	B7	85
Pouch Cove, Nf., Can.	E5	88
Poughkeepsie, N.Y., U.S.	D7	125
Poulan, Ga., U.S.	E3	103
Poulsbo, Wa., U.S.	B3	140
Poultney, Vt., U.S.	D2	138
Poultney, stm., Vt., U.S.	D2	138
Pound, Va., U.S.	e9	139
Pound Gap, U.S.	C7	110
Pouso Alegre, Braz.	F2	74
Poûthisăt, Camb.	D4	34
Póvoa de Varzim, Port.	G2	16
Povungnituk, P.Q., Can.	f11	90
Powassan, On., Can.	A5	89
Poway, Ca., U.S.	F5	98
Powder, stm., Or., U.S.	C9	130
Powder, stm., U.S.	B6	92
Powder, Middle Fork, stm., Wy., U.S.	C6	143
Powder, North Fork, stm., Wy., U.S.	C6	143
Powder, South Fork, stm., Wy., U.S.	C6	143
Powder River, co., Mt., U.S.	E11	119
Powder River Pass, Wy., U.S.	B5	143
Powder Springs, Ga., U.S.	h8	103
Powell, Oh., U.S.	B2	128
Powell, Tn., U.S.	m13	135
Powell, Wy., U.S.	B4	143
Powell, co., Ky., U.S.	C6	110
Powell, co., Mt., U.S.	D4	119
Powell, stm., U.S.	C10	135
Powell, Lake, res., U.S.	D5	92
Powell, Lake, res., U.S.	F5	137
Powell, Mount, mtn., Co., U.S.	B4	99
Powell, Mount, mtn., N.M., U.S.	B1	124
Powell Butte, Or., U.S.	C5	130
Powell Park, reg., Co., U.S.	A2	99
Powell River, B.C., Can.	E5	85
Powellton, W.V., U.S.	C3	141
Power, co., Id., U.S.	G5	105
Powers, Or., U.S.	E2	130
Powerview, Mb., Can.	D3	86
Poweshiek, co., Ia., U.S.	C5	108
Powhatan, Va., U.S.	C5	139
Powhatan, co., Va., U.S.	C5	139
Powhatan Point, Oh., U.S.	C5	128
Poxoréu, Braz.	G9	70
Poyang Hu, l., China	F11	28
Poyang Lake see Poyang Hu, l., China	F11	28
Poygan, Lake, l., Wi., U.S.	D5	142
Poynette, Wi., U.S.	E4	142
Požarevac, Yugo.	B8	18
Poza Rica, Mex.	C5	78
Požega, Cro.	B6	18
Poznań, Pol.	C4	20
Pozo Redondo Mountains, mts., Az., U.S.	E3	96
Pozuelos, Ven.	C7	80
Prachuap Khiri Khan, Thai.	D3	34
Prado, Braz.	G12	70
Prague see Praha, Czech Rep.	D3	20
Prague, Ok., U.S.	B5	129
Praha (Prague), Czech Rep.	D3	20
Praia, C.V.	h10	50a
Prainha Nova, Braz.	E7	70
Prairie, co., Ar., U.S.	C4	97
Prairie, co., Mt., U.S.	D11	119
Prairie, co., Mn., U.S.	C5	116
Prairie, stm., Wi., U.S.	C4	142
Prairie City, Ia., U.S.	C4	108
Prairie City, Or., U.S.	C8	130
Prairie Creek Reservoir, res., In., U.S.	D7	107
Prairie Dog Creek, stm., U.S.	C5	109
Prairie du Chien, Wi., U.S.	E2	142
Prairie du Sac, Wi., U.S.	E4	142
Prairie Grove, Ar., U.S.	B1	97
Prairies, Rivière des, stm., P.Q., Can.	p19	90
Prairie View, Tx., U.S.	D5	136
Prairie Village, Ks., U.S.	m16	109
Praslin, i., Sey.	h13	57b
Pratāpgarh, India	E2	40
Pratas Island see Tungsha Tao, i., Tai.	E4	30
Prater Mountain, mtn., Wy., U.S.	C2	143
Prato, Italy	C3	18
Pratt, Ks., U.S.	E5	109
Pratt, co., Ks., U.S.	E5	109
Prattville, Al., U.S.	C3	94
Praya, Indon.	E5	36
Preble, co., Oh., U.S.	C1	128
Prečistoe, Russia	B12	20
Premont, Tx., U.S.	F3	136
Prentiss, Ms., U.S.	D4	117
Prentiss, co., Ms., U.S.	A5	117
Prenzlau, Ger.	D13	12
Preparis Island, i., Myan.	D2	34
Preparis North Channel, strt., Myan.	C2	34
Preparis South Channel, strt., Myan.	D2	34
Přerov, Czech Rep.	E4	20
Prescott, On., Can.	C9	89
Prescott, Ar., U.S.	D2	97
Prescott, Az., U.S.	C3	96
Prescott, Wi., U.S.	D1	142
Presho, S.D., U.S.	D5	134
Presidencia Roque Sáenz Peña, Arg.	C4	69
Presidente Dutra, Braz.	C3	74
Presidente Epitácio, Braz.	F1	74
Presidente Prudente, Braz.	F1	74
Presidential Range, mts., N.H., U.S.	B4	122
Presidio, Tx., U.S.	p12	136
Presidio, co., Tx., U.S.	o12	136
Prešov, Slvk.	E6	20
Prespa, Lake, l., Eur.	D8	18
Presque Isle, Me., U.S.	B5	112
Presque Isle, co., Mi., U.S.	C6	115
Prestea, Ghana	E4	50
Preston, Eng., U.K.	D5	12
Preston, Ia., U.S.	B7	108
Preston, Id., U.S.	G7	105
Preston, Mn., U.S.	G6	116
Preston, co., W.V., U.S.	B5	141
Preston Peak, mtn., Ca., U.S.	B2	98
Prestonsburg, Ky., U.S.	C7	110
Presumpscot, stm., Me., U.S.	g7	112
Pretoria, S. Afr.	D4	56
Prettyboy Reservoir, res., Md., U.S.	A4	113
Pretty Prairie, Ks., U.S.	E5	109
Préveza, Grc.	E8	18
Prewitt Reservoir, res., Co., U.S.	A7	99
Pribilof Islands, is., Ak., U.S.	D5	95
Příbram, Czech Rep.	E3	20
Price, Ut., U.S.	D5	137
Price, co., Wi., U.S.	C3	142
Price, stm., Ut., U.S.	D5	137
Price Inlet, b., S.C., U.S.	k12	133
Prichard, Al., U.S.	E1	94
Prieska, S. Afr.	D3	56
Priest Lake, l., Id., U.S.	A2	105
Priest Rapids Dam, Wa., U.S.	C6	140
Priest Rapids Lake, res., Wa., U.S.	C6	140
Priest River, Id., U.S.	A2	105
Prievidza, Slvk.	E5	20
Prijedor, Bos.	B6	18
Prilep, Mac.	D8	18
Prim, Point, c., P.E., Can.	C6	87
Primghar, Ia., U.S.	A2	108
Primorsk, Russia	F13	10
Primorsko-Ahtarsk, Russia	F15	20
Primrose, Il., U.S.	B3	132
Primrose Lake, l., Can.	H18	82
Prince, Lake, res., Va., U.S.	k14	139
Prince Albert National Park, Sk., Can.	C2	91
Prince Charles Mountains, mts., Ant.	D11	67
Prince Edward, co., Va., U.S.	C4	139
Prince Edward Island, prov., Can.	C6	87
Prince Edward Island National Park, P.E., Can.	C6	87
Prince Edward Islands, is., S. Afr.	N13	46
Prince Frederick, Md., U.S.	C4	113
Prince George, B.C., Can.	C6	85
Prince George, co., Va., U.S.	C5	139
Prince Georges, co., Md., U.S.	C4	113
Prince of Wales, Cape, c., Ak., U.S.	B6	95
Prince of Wales Island, i., Austl.	C3	62
Prince of Wales Island, i., Ak., U.S.	n23	95
Prince Olav Coast, is., Ant.	C9	67
Prince Rupert, B.C., Can.	B2	85
Princes Lakes, In., U.S.	F5	107
Princess Anne, Md., U.S.	D6	113
Princess Astrid Coast, Ant.	B5	67
Princess Martha Coast, Ant.	D3	67
Princess Ragnhild Coast, Ant.	D7	67
Princess Royal Channel, strt., B.C., Can.	C3	85
Princess Royal Island, i., B.C., Can.	C3	85
Princeton, B.C., Can.	E7	85
Princeton, Fl., U.S.	G6	102
Princeton, Ia., U.S.	C7	108
Princeton, Il., U.S.	B4	106
Princeton, In., U.S.	H2	107
Princeton, Ky., U.S.	C2	110
Princeton, Me., U.S.	C5	112
Princeton, Mn., U.S.	E5	116
Princeton, Mo., U.S.	A4	118
Princeton, N.C., U.S.	B4	126
Princeton, N.J., U.S.	C3	123
Princeton, W.V., U.S.	D3	141
Princeton, Wi., U.S.	E4	142
Princeton, Mount, mtn., Co., U.S.	C4	99
Princeville, P.Q., Can.	C6	90
Princeville, Il., U.S.	C4	106
Princeville, N.C., U.S.	B5	126
Prince William, co., Va., U.S.	B5	139
Prince William Sound, strt., Ak., U.S.	g18	95
Prinzapolka, Nic.	C3	80
Prior Lake, Mn., U.S.	F5	116
Priozersk, Russia	F14	10
Pripet (Pryp'yat') (Pripjat'), stm., Eur.	C9	20
Pripet Marshes, reg., Eur.	C10	20
Pripyat see Pripet, stm., Eur.	C9	20
Priština, Yugo.	C8	18
Pritchards Island, i., S.C., U.S.	G6	133
Pritzwalk, Ger.	D13	12
Privas, Fr.	E9	16
Privolžskaja vozvyšennosť, plat., Russia	D6	26
Prizren, Yugo.	C8	18
Probolinggo, Indon.	E4	36
Proctor, Mn., U.S.	D6	116
Proctor, Vt., U.S.	D2	138
Proctor Lake, res., Tx., U.S.	C3	136
Proctorsville, Vt., U.S.	E3	138
Proddatūr, India	E4	40
Progreso, Mex.	C7	78
Prohladnyj, Russia	F7	22
Prokopevsk, Russia	D10	26
Prokuplje, Yugo.	C8	18
Proletarskij, Russia	D13	20
Prome, Myan.	C3	34
Promontory Mountains, mts., Ut., U.S.	B3	137
Prophetstown, Il., U.S.	B4	106
Propriá, Braz.	D4	74
Proserpine, Austl.	C3	62
Prospect, Ct., U.S.	D4	100
Prospect, Ky., U.S.	g11	110
Prospect, Oh., U.S.	B2	128
Prospect, Or., U.S.	E4	130
Prospect, Pa., U.S.	E1	131
Prospect Hill, mtn., Or., U.S.	k11	130
Prospect Park, N.J., U.S.	B4	123
Prospect Park, Pa., U.S.	p20	131
Prosperidad, Phil.	E9	34
Prosperity, S.C., U.S.	C4	133
Prosperity, W.V., U.S.	n13	141
Prosser, Wa., U.S.	C6	140
Protection, Ks., U.S.	E4	109
Provadija, Bul.	C11	18
Provence, hist. reg., Fr.	F9	16
Providence, Ky., U.S.	C2	110
Providence, R.I., U.S.	C4	132
Providence, Ut., U.S.	B4	137
Providence, co., R.I., U.S.	C2	132
Providence, stm., R.I., U.S.	C5	132
Providence Point, c., R.I., U.S.	D5	132
Providencia, Isla de, i., Col.	C3	80
Providenija, Russia	C20	26
Province Lake, l., N.H., U.S.	C5	122
Provincetown, Ma., U.S.	B7	114
Provins, Fr.	C8	16
Provo, Ut., U.S.	C4	137
Provo, stm., Ut., U.S.	C4	137
Provost, Ab., Can.	C5	84
Prowers, co., Co., U.S.	D8	99
Prudence Island, i., R.I., U.S.	E5	132
Prudentópolis, Braz.	D7	72
Prudenville, Mi., U.S.	D6	115
Prudhoe Bay, Ak., U.S.	A10	95
Prudhoe Bay, b., Ak., U.S.	A10	95
Prut, stm., Eur.	G10	20
Pružany, Bela.	C8	20
Pryluky, Ukr.	D12	20
Prymors'k, Ukr.	F14	20
Pryor, Mt., U.S.	E8	119
Pryor, Ok., U.S.	A6	129
Pryor Mountains, mts., Mt., U.S.	E8	119
Pryp'yat' (Pripet) (Pripjat'), stm., Eur.	D8	20
Przasnysz, Pol.	C6	20
Przemyśl, Pol.	E7	20
Psël (Ps'ol), stm., Eur.	D13	20
Pskov, Russia	D4	26
Pskov, Lake, l., Eur.	G13	10
Ps'ol (Psël), stm., Eur.	D13	20
Ptolemaís, Grc.	D8	18
Pucallpa, Peru	E5	70
Pucheng, China	F11	28
Puckaway Lake, l., Wi., U.S.	E4	142
Pudož, Russia	B6	22
Pudukkottai, India	G3	40
Puebla, state, Mex.	D5	78
Puebla de Zaragoza, Mex.	D5	78
Pueblo, Co., U.S.	C6	99
Pueblo, co., Co., U.S.	C6	99
Pueblo Mountain, mtn., Or., U.S.	E8	130
Pueblo Mountains, mts., Or., U.S.	E8	130
Pueblo Reservoir, res., Co., U.S.	C6	99
Puente Genil, Spain	I4	16
Pueo Point, c., Hi., U.S.	B1	104
Puerco, stm., U.S.	C6	96
Puerco, Rio, stm., N.M., U.S.	B2	124
Puerto Acosta, Bol.	B4	72
Puerto Ángel, Mex.	D5	78
Puerto Armuelles, Pan.	D3	80
Puerto Asís, Col.	C4	70
Puerto Ayacucho, Ven.	B6	70
Puerto Baquerizo Moreno, Ec.	D2	70
Puerto Barrios, Guat.	B2	80
Puerto Bermúdez, Peru	F5	70
Puerto Berrío, Col.	B5	70
Puerto Bolívar, Col.	C5	80
Puerto Boyacá, Col.	D5	80
Puerto Cabello, Ven.	A6	70
Puerto Cabezas, Nic.	C3	80
Puerto Carreño, Col.	B6	70
Puerto Chicama, Peru	E4	70
Puerto Cortés, Hond.	B2	80
Puerto Cumarebo, Ven.	A6	70
Puerto de la Cruz, Spain	A1	50
Puerto del Rosario, Spain	A2	50
Puerto Deseado, Arg.	G3	69
Puerto Esperanza, Arg.	D7	72
Puerto Guaraní, Para.	C6	72
Puerto Inírida, Col.	E6	80
Puerto Juárez, Mex.	C7	78
Puerto la Cruz, Ven.	A7	70
Puerto Leguízamo, Col.	D5	70
Puerto Libertad, Mex.	B2	78
Puerto Limón, C.R.	C3	80
Puertollano, Spain	H4	16
Puerto Lobos, Arg.	F3	69
Puerto Madryn, Arg.	F3	69
Puerto Maldonado, Peru	F6	70
Puerto Montt, Chile	F2	69
Puerto Morazán, Nic.	C2	80
Puerto Nariño, Col.	D6	80
Puerto Natales, Chile	H2	69
Puerto Padre, Cuba	A4	80
Puerto Páez, Ven.	B6	70
Puerto Peñasco, Mex.	A2	78
Puerto Plata, Dom. Rep.	B5	80
Puerto Princesa, Phil.	E7	34
Puerto Rico, Bol.	F6	70
Puerto Rico, dep., N.A.	B6	80
Puerto Rico Trench	G7	66
Puerto San José, Guat.	C1	80
Puerto San Julián, Arg.	G3	69
Puerto Santa Cruz, Arg.	H3	69
Puerto Sastre, Para.	C6	72
Puerto Suárez, Bol.	B6	72
Puerto Vallarta, Mex.	C3	78
Puerto Villamil, Ec.	D1	70
Puerto Wilches, Col.	B5	70
Puerto Ybapobó, Para.	C6	72
Pugačov, Russia	D8	22
Puget Sound, strt., Wa., U.S.	B3	140
Puget Sound Naval Shipyard, mil., Wa., U.S.	e10	140
Pugwash, N.S., Can.	D6	87
Puhi, Hi., U.S.	B2	104
Pukalani, Hi., U.S.	C5	104
Pukaskwa National Park, On., Can.	o18	89
Pukch'ŏng-ŭp, N. Kor.	C13	28
Pukeashun Mountain, mtn., B.C., Can.	D8	85
Pukou, China	C4	30
Pula, Cro.	B4	18
Pulaski, N.Y., U.S.	B4	125
Pulaski, Tn., U.S.	B4	135
Pulaski, Va., U.S.	C2	139
Pulaski, Wi., U.S.	D5	142
Pulaski, co., Ar., U.S.	C3	97
Pulaski, co., Ga., U.S.	D3	103
Pulaski, co., Il., U.S.	F4	106
Pulaski, co., In., U.S.	B4	107
Pulaski, co., Ky., U.S.	C5	110
Pulaski, co., Mo., U.S.	D5	118
Pulaski, co., Va., U.S.	C2	139
Putawy, Pol.	D7	20
Pulicat Lake, l., India	G4	40
Pullman, Wa., U.S.	C8	140
Pumphrey, Md., U.S.	h11	113
Puná, Isla, i., Ec.	D3	70
Punakha, Bhu.	D5"	40
Punata, Bol.	B4	72
Pune, India	F2	40
Pungo Lake, l., N.C., U.S.	B6	126
Punia, D.R.C.	D5	54
Punjab, prov., India	C3	40
Punjab, prov., Pak.	D11	42
Puno, Peru	G5	70
Punta, Cerro de, mtn., P.R.	B6	80
Punta Alta, Arg.	F5	72
Punta Arenas, Chile	H2	69
Punta de Díaz, Chile	D3	72
Punta del Este, Ur.	F7	72
Punta Delgada, Arg.	F4	69
Punta Gorda, Fl., U.S.	F4	102
Punta Gorda, Bahía de, b., Nic.	C3	80
Puntarenas, C.R.	C2	80
Punto Fijo, Ven.	A5	70
Punxsutawney, Pa., U.S.	E4	131
Puolanka, Fin.	D12	10
Puqi, China	F10	28
Puquio, Peru	F5	70
Purcell, Ok., U.S.	B4	129
Purcellville, Va., U.S.	A5	139
Purdy, Mo., U.S.	E4	118
Purgatoire, stm., Co., U.S.	D7	99
Purgatoire Peak, mtn., Co., U.S.	D5	99
Puri, India	F5	40
Pūrnia, India	D5	40
Purus (Purús), stm., S.A.	D7	70
Purvis, Ms., U.S.	D4	117
Purwakarta, Indon.	E3	36
Purwokerto, Indon.	E3	36
Pusan, S. Kor.	D13	28
Pushaw Lake, l., Me., U.S.	D4	112
Pushkar, India	F4	40
Pushmataha, co., Ok., U.S.	C6	129
Puškin, Russia	G15	10
Putao, Myan.	A3	34
Putaruru, N.Z.	o14	63c
Putian, China	D4	30
Puting, Tanjung, c., Indon.	D4	36
Putnam, Ct., U.S.	B8	100
Putnam, co., Fl., U.S.	C5	102
Putnam, co., Ga., U.S.	C3	103
Putnam, co., Il., U.S.	B4	106
Putnam, co., In., U.S.	E4	107
Putnam, co., Mo., U.S.	A4	118
Putnam, co., N.Y., U.S.	D7	125
Putnam, co., Oh., U.S.	B1	128
Putnam, co., Tn., U.S.	C8	135
Putnam, co., W.V., U.S.	C3	141
Putney, Ga., U.S.	E2	103
Putney, Vt., U.S.	F3	138
Putorana, plato, plat., Russia	C11	26
Puttalam, Sri L.	H3	40
Puttgarden, Ger.	C12	12
Putumayo (Içá), stm., S.A.	D5	70
Putussibau, Indon.	C4	36
Puukohola Heiau National Historic Site, hist., Hi., U.S.	D6	104
Puula, l., Fin.	F12	10
Puxico, Mo., U.S.	E7	118
Puyallup, Wa., U.S.	B3	140
Puyallup, stm., Wa., U.S.	C3	140
Puyang, China	B3	30
Pweto, D.R.C.	E5	54
Pyandzh see Amu Darya, stm., Asia	B8	42
Pyapon, Myan.	C3	34
Pyhäjoki, Fin.	D11	10
Pyhäselkä, l., Fin.	E13	10
Pyinmana, Myan.	C3	34

Name	Map Ref.	Page

Pyles Fork, stm., W.V., U.S. **h10** 141
Pymatuning Reservoir, res., U.S. **C1** 131
P'yŏngyang, N. Kor. **D13** 28
Pyramid Lake, l., Nv., U.S. . **C2** 121
Pyramid Lake Indian Reservation, Nv., U.S. . **D2** 121
Pyramid Mountains, mts., N.M., U.S. **E1** 124
Pyramid Peak, mtn., N.M., U.S. **E1** 124
Pyramid Peak, mtn., Wy., U.S. **C2** 143
Pyrenees, mts., Eur. **F7** 16
Pyriatyn, Ukr. **D12** 20
Pyu, Myan. **C3** 34

Q

Qaanaaq see Thule, Grnld. **C26** 82
Qacentina, Alg. **C6** 48
Qā'emshahr, Iran **C6** 42
Qā'en, Iran **D7** 42
Qaidam Pendi, China **D6** 28
Qalāt, Afg. **D9** 42
Qal'at Bīshah, Sau. Ar. **G4** 38
Qal'at Sukkar, Iraq **G12** 44
Qal'eh-ye Now, Afg. **D8** 42
Qallābāt, Sudan **H3** 38
Qamar, Ghubbat al-, b., Yemen **G6** 38
Qamar Bay see Qamar, Ghubbat al-, b., Yemen **G6** 38
Qamdo, China **E7** 28
Qandahār, Afg. **D9** 42
Qandala, Som. **H5** 38
Qardho, Som. **I14** 48
Qareh Sū, stm., Iran **C12** 44
Qasr el-Boukhari, Alg. **J8** 16
Qasr Farâfra, Egypt **E10** 48
Qatanā, Syria **F7** 44
Qatar, ctry., Asia **E6** 42
Qattâra, Munkhafad el-, depr., Egypt **E10** 48
Qattara Depression see Qattâra, Munkhafad el-, depr., Egypt **E10** 48
Qazimämmäd, Azer. **B13** 44
Qazvīn, Iran **C5** 42
Qena, Egypt **E11** 48
Qeydār, Iran **D13** 44
Qianwei, China **D1** 30
Qianxi, China **D2** 30
Qianyang, China **D3** 30
Qiemo, China **D5** 28
Qigong, China **A4** 34
Qijiang, China **D2** 30
Qilian Shan, mts., China . . **D7** 28
Qimen, China **D4** 30
Qingdao, China **D12** 28
Qinghai, state, China **D7** 28
Qinghai Hu, l., China **D8** 28
Qingjiang, China **E11** 28
Qinglong, China **A4** 30
Qinglong, China **D2** 30
Qingshen, China **D1** 30
Qingtang, China **G10** 28
Qingyang, China **D9** 28
Qingyuan, China **E3** 30
Qing Zang Gaoyuan (Tibet, Plateau of), plat., China **E4** 28
Qinhuangdao, China **D11** 28
Qin Ling, mts., China **E9** 28
Qinxian, China **B3** 30
Qinzhou, China **E2** 30
Qionghai, China **F3** 30
Qionglai, China **E8** 28
Qiongzhong, China **H9** 28
Qiongzhou Haixia, strt., China **G9** 28
Qiqihar, China **B12** 28
Qiryat Shemona, Isr. **F6** 44
Qishn, Yemen **G6** 38
Qitai, China **C5** 28
Qiyang, China **D3** 30
Qobustan, Azer. **B13** 44
Qogir Feng see K2, mtn., Asia **B3** 40
Qom, Iran **D6** 42
Qomolangma Feng see Everest, Mount, mtn., Asia **D5** 40
Qomsheh, Iran **D6** 42
Qorveh, Iran **E12** 44
Quabbin Reservoir, res., Ma., U.S. **B3** 114
Quaddick Reservoir, res., Ct., U.S. **B8** 100
Quail Oaks, Va., U.S. **n18** 139
Quaker Hill, Ct., U.S. **D7** 100
Quakertown, Pa., U.S. . . . **F11** 131
Qualicum Beach, B.C., Can. **E5** 85
Quanah, Tx., U.S. **B3** 136
Quang Ngai, Viet. **C5** 34
Quannapowitt, Lake, l., Ma., U.S. **f11** 114
Quantico, Va., U.S. **B5** 139
Quantico Marine Corps Air Station, mil., Va., U.S. . **B5** 139
Quanzhou, China **G11** 28
Quanzhou, China **D3** 30
Quapaw, Ok., U.S. **A7** 129
Qu'Appelle, Sk., Can. **G4** 91
Qu'Appelle, stm., Can. . . . **G4** 91
Quarryville, Pa., U.S. **G9** 131

Quartu Sant'Elena, Italy . . . **E2** 18
Quartz Mountain, mtn., Or., U.S. **D4** 130
Quartzsite, Az., U.S. **D1** 96
Quassapaug, Lake, l., Ct., U.S. **C3** 100
Quatsino Sound, strt., B.C., Can. **D3** 85
Quay, co., N.M., U.S. **C6** 124
Quba, Azer. **B13** 44
Qūchān, Iran **C7** 42
Queanbeyan, Austl. **H4** 62
Québec, P.Q., Can. **C6** 90
Quebec, prov., Can. **C5** 90
Quechee, Vt., U.S. **D4** 138
Queen, stm., R.I., U.S. **E3** 132
Queen Annes, co., Md., U.S. **B5** 113
Queen Bess, Mount, mtn., B.C., Can. **D5** 85
Queen Charlotte, B.C., Can. **C1** 85
Queen Charlotte Islands, is., B.C., Can. **C1** 85
Queen Charlotte Mountains, mts., B.C., Can. **C1** 85
Queen Charlotte Sound, strt., B.C., Can. **H14** 82
Queen Charlotte Strait, strt., B.C., Can. **D4** 85
Queen City, Mo., U.S. **A5** 118
Queen City, Tx., U.S. **C5** 136
Queen Creek, Az., U.S. . . . **m9** 96
Queen Mary Coast, Ant. . . **C14** 67
Queen Maud Land, reg., Ant. **D4** 67
Queen Maud Mountains, mts., Ant. **E25** 67
Queens, co., N.Y., U.S. **E7** 125
Queensland, state, Austl. . . **E3** 62
Queenstown, Austl. **I4** 62
Queenstown, S. Afr. **E4** 56
Quela, Ang. **E3** 54
Quelimane, Moz. **B6** 56
Querétaro, Mex. **C4** 78
Querétaro, state, Mex. **C5** 78
Queshan, China **C3** 30
Quesnel, B.C., Can. **C6** 85
Quesnel, stm., B.C., Can. . . **C6** 85
Quesnel Lake, l., B.C., Can. **C7** 85
Questa, N.M., U.S. **A4** 124
Quetico Provincial Park, On., Can. **o17** 89
Quetta, Pak. **D9** 42
Quevedo, Ec. **D4** 70
Quezon City, Phil. **D8** 34
Quibala, Ang. **F3** 54
Quibdó, Col. **B4** 70
Quicksand Pond, l., R.I., U.S. **E6** 132
Quiculungo, Ang. **E3** 54
Quidnessett, R.I., U.S. **E4** 132
Quidnick, R.I., U.S. **D3** 132
Quidnick Reservoir, res., R.I., U.S. **D2** 132
Quila, Mex. **C3** 78
Quilcene, Wa., U.S. **B3** 140
Quileute Indian Reservation, Wa., U.S. **B1** 140
Quillota, Chile **D2** 69
Quilon, India **H3** 40
Quimaria, Ang. **E2** 54
Quimilí, Arg. **D5** 72
Quimper, Fr. **D4** 16
Quimperlé, Fr. **D5** 16
Quinault, stm., Wa., U.S. . . **B1** 140
Quinault, Lake, l., Wa., U.S. **B2** 140
Quinault Indian Reservation, Wa., U.S. **B1** 140
Quince Mil, Peru **F5** 70
Quincy, Ca., U.S. **C3** 98
Quincy, Fl., U.S. **B2** 102
Quincy, Il., U.S. **D2** 106
Quincy, Ma., U.S. **B5** 114
Quincy, Mi., U.S. **G6** 115
Quincy, Wa., U.S. **B6** 140
Quincy Bay, b., Ma., U.S. . **g12** 114
Quinebaug, Ct., U.S. **A8** 100
Quinebaug, stm., Ct., U.S. . **C8** 100
Quinhagak, Ak., U.S. **D7** 95
Quinlan, Tx., U.S. **C4** 136
Quinn, stm., Nv., U.S. **B3** 121
Quinn Canyon Range, mts., Nv., U.S. **F6** 121
Quinnesec, Mi., U.S. **C3** 115
Quinnipiac, stm., Ct., U.S. . **D4** 100
Quintana Roo, state, Mex. . **D7** 78
Quinter, Ks., U.S. **C3** 109
Quinton, Ok., U.S. **B6** 129
Quirinópolis, Braz. **E3** 74
Quissanga, Moz. **A7** 56
Quiterajo, Moz. **A7** 56
Quitman, Ar., U.S. **B3** 97
Quitman, Ga., U.S. **F3** 103
Quitman, Ms., U.S. **C5** 117
Quitman, Tx., U.S. **C5** 136
Quitman, co., Ga., U.S. . . . **E1** 103
Quitman, co., Ms., U.S. . . . **A3** 117
Quito, Ec. **D4** 70
Quixadá, Braz. **B4** 74
Quixeramobim, Braz. **C4** 74
Qujing, China **F8** 28
Qumarlêb, China **E7** 28
Qunayyin, Sabkhat al-, l., Libya **E8** 14

Quonnipaug Lake, l., Ct., U.S. **D5** 100
Quonochontaug, R.I., U.S. . **G2** 132
Quonochontaug Pond, l., R.I., U.S. **G2** 132
Quonset Point, c., R.I., U.S. **E4** 132
Quseir, Egypt **E11** 48
Qutdligssat, Grnld. **D29** 82
Quthing, Leso. **E4** 56
Qüxü, China **D6** 40
Quy Nhon, Viet. **D5** 34
Quzhou, China **F11** 28

R

Raab see Győr, Hung. **F4** 20
Raahe, Fin. **D11** 10
Rab, Otok, i., Cro. **B5** 18
Raba, Indon. **E5** 36
Rába, stm., Eur. **F4** 20
Rabat, Mor. **D3** 48
Rabaul, Pap. N. Gui. **G13** 32
Rabbit Creek, stm., S.D., U.S. **B3** 134
Rabbit Ears Pass, Co., U.S. **A4** 99
Rabi, i., Fiji **m11** 63b
Rābigh, Sau. Ar. **F3** 38
Râbniţa, Mol. **F10** 20
Rabun, co., Ga., U.S. **B3** 103
Rabun Bald, mtn., Ga., U.S. **B3** 103
Rabyānah, Ramlat, des., Libya **F8** 48
Raccoon Creek, stm., Oh., U.S. **D3** 128
Raccourci Island, i., La., U.S. **D4** 111
Race, Cape, c., Nf., Can. . . **E5** 88
Raceland, Ky., U.S. **B7** 110
Raceland, La., U.S. **E5** 111
Race Point, c., Ma., U.S. . . **B7** 114
Rach Gia, Viet. **E4** 34
Racine, W.V., U.S. **C3** 141
Racine, Wi., U.S. **F6** 142
Racine, co., Wi., U.S. **F5** 142
Racine Dam, U.S. **C3** 141
Rădăuţi, Rom. **F8** 20
Radcliff, Ky., U.S. **C4** 110
Radford, Va., U.S. **C2** 139
Radom, Pol. **D6** 20
Radomsko, Pol. **D5** 20
Radomyshl', Ukr. **D10** 20
Rãe Bareli, India **D4** 40
Raeford, N.C., U.S. **C3** 126
Rafaela, Arg. **E5** 72
Rafah, Gaza Str. **G6** 44
Rafhā', Sau. Ar. **E4** 38
Rafsanjān, Iran **D7** 42
Raft, stm., Id., U.S. **G5** 105
Raft River Mountains, mts., Ut., U.S. **B2** 137
Raga, Sudan **I10** 48
Ragay Gulf, b., Phil. **D8** 34
Ragged Island, i., Me., U.S. **E4** 112
Ragged Island Range, is., Bah. **D9** 76
Ragged Lake, l., Me., U.S. . **C3** 112
Ragged Top Mountain, mtn., Wy., U.S. **E7** 143
Ragland, Al., U.S. **B3** 94
Ragusa, Italy **F5** 18
Rahīmyār Khān, Pak. **E10** 42
Rahway, N.J., U.S. **B4** 123
Rahway, stm., N.J., U.S. . . . **k7** 123
Rāichūr, India **F3** 40
Raiganj, India **D5** 40
Raigarh, India **E4** 40
Railroad Valley, val., Nv., U.S. **E6** 121
Rainbow Bridge National Monument, Ut., U.S. . . **F5** 137
Rainbow Falls, wtfl, Tn., U.S. **D10** 135
Rainbow Flowage, res., Wi., U.S. **C4** 142
Rainbow Lake, l., Me., U.S. **C3** 112
Rainelle, W.V., U.S. **D4** 141
Rainier, Or., U.S. **A4** 130
Rainier, Wa., U.S. **C3** 140
Rainier, Mount, mtn., Wa., U.S. **C4** 140
Rains, co., Tx., U.S. **C5** 136
Rainsville, Al., U.S. **A4** 94
Rainy Lake, l., Mn., U.S. . . **B5** 116
Rainy River, On., Can. . . . **o16** 89
Raipur, India **E4** 40
Rājahmundry, India **F4** 40
Rajang, stm., Malay. **C4** 36
Rājapalaiyam, India **H3** 40
Rājasthān, prov., India **D2** 40
Rajčihinsk, Russia **E14** 26
Rāj Gangpur, India **E4** 40
Rājkot, India **E2** 40
Rāj Nāndgaon, India **E4** 40
Rājshāhi, Bngl. **E5** 40
Rakhiv, Ukr. **E8** 20
Rakvere, Est. **G12** 10
Raleigh, Ms., U.S. **C4** 117
Raleigh, N.C., U.S. **B4** 126
Raleigh, W.V., U.S. **n13** 141
Raleigh, co., W.V., U.S. . . . **D3** 141
Raleigh Bay, b., N.C., U.S. . **C6** 126
Ralls, Tx., U.S. **C2** 136
Ralls, co., Mo., U.S. **B6** 118
Ralston, Ne., U.S. **g12** 120

Ralston Valley, val., Nv., U.S. **E4** 121
Ramah, N.M., U.S. **B1** 124
Ramah Indian Reservation, N.M., U.S. **C1** 124
Ramapo, stm., N.J., U.S. . . **A4** 123
Ramblewood, N.J., U.S. . . . **D3** 123
Rambouillet, Fr. **C7** 16
Ramea, Nf., Can. **E3** 88
Rāmeswaram, India **H3** 40
Rāmhormoz, Iran **D5** 42
Ramm, Jabal, mtn., Jord. . . **E3** 42
Râmnicu Sărat, Rom. **G9** 20
Râmnicu Vâlcea, Rom. **G8** 20
Ramona, Ca., U.S. **F5** 98
Rampart Range, mts., Co., U.S. **B5** 99
Rāmpur, India **D3** 40
Ramree Island, i., Myan. . . **C2** 34
Ramsay, Mi., U.S. **n12** 115
Ramsele, Swe. **E7** 10
Ramseur, N.C., U.S. **B3** 126
Ramsey, Il., U.S. **D4** 106
Ramsey, N.J., U.S. **A4** 123
Ramsey, co., Mn., U.S. . . . **E5** 116
Ramsey, co., N.D., U.S. . . . **A7** 127
Ramsgate, Eng., U.K. **E7** 12
Ramshorn Peak, mtn., Mt., U.S. **E5** 119
Ramshorn Peak, mtn., Wy., U.S. **C3** 143
Ramu, Kenya **C8** 54
Rāna Pratāp Sāgar, res., India **D2** 40
Rancagua, Chile **D2** 69
Rancharia, Braz. **F1** 74
Rancheria Rock, mtn., Or., U.S. **C6** 130
Ranchester, Wy., U.S. **B5** 143
Rānchi, India **E5** 40
Ranchos de Taos, N.M., U.S. **A4** 124
Rancocas Creek, stm., N.J., U.S. **C3** 123
Rand, W.V., U.S. **C3** 141
Randall, co., Tx., U.S. **B2** 136
Randallstown, Md., U.S. . . **B4** 113
Randers, Den. **H4** 10
Randijaure, l., Swe. **C8** 10
Randle, Wa., U.S. **C4** 140
Randleman, N.C., U.S. . . . **B3** 126
Randolph, Ma., U.S. **B5** 114
Randolph, Me., U.S. **D3** 112
Randolph, Ne., U.S. **B8** 120
Randolph, Vt., U.S. **D3** 138
Randolph, Wi., U.S. **E5** 142
Randolph, co., Al., U.S. . . . **B4** 94
Randolph, co., Ar., U.S. . . . **A4** 97
Randolph, co., Ga., U.S. . . **E2** 103
Randolph, co., Il., U.S. . . . **E4** 106
Randolph, co., In., U.S. . . . **D7** 107
Randolph, co., Mo., U.S. . . **B5** 118
Randolph, co., N.C., U.S. . . **B3** 126
Randolph, co., W.V., U.S. . **C5** 141
Randolph Air Force Base, mil., Tx., U.S. **h7** 136
Randolph Hills, Md., U.S. . . **B3** 113
Random Island, i., Nf., Can. **D5** 88
Random Lake, Wi., U.S. . . . **E6** 142
Randsfjorden, l., Nor. **F4** 10
Rāngāmāti, Bngl. **E6** 40
Rangeley, Me., U.S. **D2** 112
Rangeley Lake, l., Me., U.S. **D2** 112
Rangely, Co., U.S. **A2** 99
Ranger, Tx., U.S. **C3** 136
Ranger Lake, l., N.M., U.S. **D6** 124
Rangoon see Yangon, Myan. **C3** 34
Rangpur, Bngl. **D5** 40
Rānībennur, India **G3** 40
Rankin, Pa., U.S. **k14** 131
Rankin, co., Ms., U.S. **C4** 117
Rann of Kutch see Kutch, Rann of, reg., Asia **E1** 40
Ranohira, Madag. **C8** 56
Ranong, Thai. **E3** 34
Ransiki, Indon. **D8** 36
Ransom, co., N.D., U.S. . . . **C8** 127
Ranson, W.V., U.S. **B7** 141
Rantauprapat, Indon. **C1** 36
Rantoul, Il., U.S. **C5** 106
Raohe, China **A2** 31
Raoul, Ga., U.S. **B3** 103
Rapallo, Italy **B2** 18
Rapid, stm., Mn., U.S. **B4** 116
Rapid City, S.D., U.S. **C2** 134
Rapides, co., La., U.S. **C3** 111
Rapid River, Mi., U.S. **C4** 115
Rapids City, Il., U.S. **B3** 106
Rappahannock, co., Va., U.S. **B4** 139
Rappahannock, stm., Va., U.S. **B5** 139
Raquette, stm., N.Y., U.S. . **f10** 125
Raquette Lake, l., N.Y., U.S. **B6** 125
Raraka, atoll, Fr. Poly. . . . **F15** 58
Raritan, N.J., U.S. **B3** 123
Raritan, stm., N.J., U.S. . . . **C4** 123
Raritan Bay, b., N.J., U.S. . **C4** 123
Rarotonga, i., Cook Is. . . **G14** 58
Ra's al-Khaymah, U.A.E. . . **E7** 42
Ras Dashen Terara, mtn., Eth. **H12** 48
Rashid, Egypt **E10** 14
Rasht, Iran **C5** 42
Rassua, ostrov, i., Russia . **E17** 26

Ratangarh, India **D2** 40
Rāth, India **D3** 40
Rathbun Lake, res., Ia., U.S. **D5** 108
Rathdrum, Id., U.S. **B2** 105
Rat Islands, is., Ak., U.S. . . **E3** 95
Ratlām, India **E3** 40
Ratnāgiri, India **F2** 40
Ratnapura, Sri L. **H4** 40
Raton, N.M., U.S. **A5** 124
Raton Pass, N.M., U.S. . . . **A5** 124
Rattlesnake Creek, stm., Oh., U.S. **C2** 128
Rattlesnake Creek, stm., Wa., U.S. **C6** 140
Rättvik, Swe. **F6** 10
Raub, Malay. **C2** 36
Rauch, Arg. **F6** 72
Rauma, Fin. **F9** 10
Raurkela, India **E5** 40
Ravalli, co., Mt., U.S. **D2** 119
Raven, Va., U.S. **e10** 139
Ravena, N.Y., U.S. **C7** 125
Ravenel, S.C., U.S. **k11** 133
Ravenna, Italy **B4** 18
Ravenna, Ky., U.S. **C6** 110
Ravenna, Mi., U.S. **E5** 115
Ravenna, Ne., U.S. **C7** 120
Ravenna, Oh., U.S. **A4** 128
Raven Park, reg., Co., U.S. . **A2** 99
Ravensburg, Ger. **G11** 12
Ravensthorpe, Austl. **G3** 60
Ravenswood, W.V., U.S. . . **C3** 141
Rāvi, stm., Asia **C2** 40
Ravnina, Turk. **C8** 42
Rawaki, atoll, Kir. **E12** 58
Rāwalpindi, Pak. **D10** 42
Rawdon, P.Q., Can. **C4** 90
Rawhide Creek, stm., Wy., U.S. **D8** 143
Rawlings, Md., U.S. **k13** 113
Rawlinna, Austl. **G4** 60
Rawlins, Wy., U.S. **E5** 143
Rawlins, co., Ks., U.S. **C2** 109
Rawson, Arg. **F3** 69
Ray, N.D., U.S. **A2** 127
Ray, co., Mo., U.S. **B3** 118
Ray, Cape, c., Nf., Can. . . . **E2** 88
Raya, Bukit, mtn., Indon. . . **C4** 36
Rāyachoti, India **G3** 40
Rāyadurg, India **G3** 40
Ray City, Ga., U.S. **E3** 103
Raymond, Ab., Can. **E4** 84
Raymond, Il., U.S. **D4** 106
Raymond, Mn., U.S. **E3** 116
Raymond, Ms., U.S. **C3** 117
Raymond, N.H., U.S. **D4** 122
Raymond, Wa., U.S. **C2** 140
Raymondville, Tx., U.S. . . . **F4** 136
Raymore, Sk., Can. **F3** 91
Raymore, Mo., U.S. **C3** 118
Rayne, La., U.S. **D3** 111
Raynham, Ma., U.S. **C5** 114
Raynham Center, Ma., U.S. **C5** 114
Rayong, Thai. **D4** 34
Raytown, Mo., U.S. **h11** 118
Rayville, La., U.S. **B4** 111
Razdol'noe, Russia **B2** 31
Razgrad, Bul. **C11** 18
Ré, Île de, i., Fr. **D6** 16
Reader, W.V., U.S. **B4** 141
Reading, Eng., U.K. **E6** 12
Reading, Ma., U.S. **A5** 114
Reading, Mi., U.S. **G6** 115
Reading, Oh., U.S. **C1** 128
Reading, Pa., U.S. **F10** 131
Readlyn, Ia., U.S. **B5** 108
Reagan, co., Tx., U.S. **D2** 136
Real, co., Tx., U.S. **E3** 136
Real, Cordillera, mts., S.A. . **G6** 70
Realicó, Arg. **F5** 72
Reamstown, Pa., U.S. **F9** 131
Rebiana Sand Sea see Rabyānah, Ramlat, des., Libya **F8** 48
Rebun-tō, i., Japan **B16** 28
Recherche, Archipelago of the, is., Austl. **G3** 60
Recife, Braz. **C5** 74
Reconquista, Arg. **D6** 72
Rector, Ar., U.S. **A5** 97
Rèčyča, Bela. **C11** 20
Red, stm., Asia **B4** 34
Red, stm., N.A. **B8** 92
Red, stm., Ky., U.S. **C6** 110
Red, stm., Tn., U.S. **A4** 135
Red, stm., U.S. **E9** 92
Red Bank, N.J., U.S. **C4** 123
Red Bank, Tn., U.S. **D8** 135
Red Bay, Al., U.S. **A1** 94
Redberry Lake, l., Sk., Can. **E2** 91
Redbird, Oh., U.S. **A4** 128
Red Bird, stm., Ky., U.S. . . **C6** 110
Red Bluff, Ca., U.S. **B2** 98
Red Bluff Lake, res., U.S. . **o12** 136
Red Boiling Springs, Tn., U.S. **C8** 135
Red Bud, Il., U.S. **E4** 106
Red Butte, mtn., Ut., U.S. . **B2** 137
Red Cedar, stm., Wi., U.S. . **C2** 142
Red Cedar Lake, l., Wi., U.S. **C2** 142
Redcliff, Ab., Can. **D5** 84
Redcliffe, Austl. **F5** 62

Name	Map Ref.	Page

Redcliffe, Mount, mtn., Austl. ... **F3** 60
Red Cliff Indian Reservation, Wi., U.S. **B2** 142
Red Cloud, Ne., U.S. ... **D7** 120
Redcloud Peak, mtn., Co., U.S. ... **D3** 99
Red Deer, Ab., Can. ... **C4** 84
Red Deer, stm., Can. ... **D4** 84
Red Deer, stm., Can. ... **E4** 91
Redding, Ca., U.S. ... **B2** 98
Redding, Ct., U.S. ... **D2** 100
Redeye, stm., Mn., U.S. ... **D3** 116
Redfield, Ar., U.S. ... **C3** 97
Redfield, Ia., U.S. ... **C3** 108
Redfield, S.D., U.S. ... **C7** 134
Redford, Mi., U.S. ... **F7** 115
Redgranite, Wi., U.S. ... **D4** 142
Red Hook, N.Y., U.S. ... **C7** 125
Red Indian Lake, l., Nf., Can. ... **D3** 88
Red Jacket, W.V., U.S. ... **D2** 141
Redkey, In., U.S. ... **D7** 107
Redlake, Mn., U.S. ... **C3** 116
Red Lake, co., Mn., U.S. ... **C2** 116
Red Lake, l., Az., U.S. ... **B1** 96
Red Lake, stm., Mn., U.S. ... **C2** 116
Red Lake Falls, Mn., U.S. ... **C2** 116
Red Lake Indian Reservation, Mn., U.S. **B3** 116
Redlands, Ca., U.S. ... **E5** 98
Red Lion, Pa., U.S. ... **G8** 131
Red Lodge, Mt., U.S. ... **E7** 119
Red Mill Pond, l., De., U.S. **E5** 101
Redmond, Or., U.S. ... **C5** 130
Redmond, Ut., U.S. ... **E4** 137
Redmond, Wa., U.S. ... **e11** 140
Red Mountain, mtn., Ca., U.S. ... **B2** 98
Red Mountain, mtn., Mt., U.S. ... **C4** 119
Red Mountain Pass, Co., U.S. ... **D3** 99
Red Oak, Ga., U.S. ... **h7** 103
Red Oak, Ia., U.S. ... **D2** 108
Red Oak, Ok., U.S. ... **C6** 129
Red Oak, Tx., U.S. ... **n10** 136
Red Oaks, La., U.S. ... **h9** 111
Redon, Fr. ... **D5** 16
Redondo, Wa., U.S. ... **f11** 140
Redondo Beach, Ca., U.S. **n12** 98
Redoubt Volcano, vol., Ak., U.S. ... **g15** 95
Red Peak, mtn., Co., U.S. **B4** 99
Red River, co., La., U.S. ... **B2** 111
Red River, co., Tx., U.S. ... **C5** 136
Red Rock, stm., Mt., U.S. **F4** 119
Red Rock, Lake, res., Ia., U.S. ... **C4** 108
Redruth, Eng., U.K. ... **E4** 12
Red Sea ... **F3** 38
Red Springs, N.C., U.S. ... **C3** 126
Red Table Mountain, mts., Co., U.S. ... **B4** 99
Redwater, Ab., Can. ... **C4** 84
Redwater, stm., Mt., U.S. **C11** 119
Red Willow, co., Ne., U.S. **D5** 120
Redwillow, stm., Can. ... **B7** 85
Red Wing, Mn., U.S. ... **F6** 116
Redwood, co., Mn., U.S. **F3** 116
Redwood, stm., Mn., U.S. **F3** 116
Redwood City, Ca., U.S. ... **D2** 98
Redwood Falls, Mn., U.S. **F3** 116
Redwood National Park, Ca., U.S. ... **B2** 98
Redwood Valley, Ca., U.S. **C2** 98
Ree, Lough, l., Ire. ... **D2** 12
Reed City, Mi., U.S. ... **E5** 115
Reedley, Ca., U.S. ... **D4** 98
Reedsburg, Wi., U.S. ... **E3** 142
Reeds Peak, mtn., N.M., U.S. ... **D2** 124
Reedsport, Or., U.S. ... **D2** 130
Reedsville, Pa., U.S. ... **E6** 131
Reedsville, Wi., U.S. ... **D6** 142
Reedy, stm., S.C., U.S. ... **C3** 133
Reedy Lake, l., Fl., U.S. ... **E5** 102
Reefton, N.Z. ... **p13** 63c
Reelfoot Lake, l., Tn., U.S. **A2** 135
Reese, Mi., U.S. ... **E7** 115
Reese, stm., Nv., U.S. ... **C4** 121
Reese Air Force Base, mil., Tx., U.S. ... **C1** 136
Reeves, co., Tx., U.S. ... **o13** 136
Reform, Al., U.S. ... **B1** 94
Refugio, Tx., U.S. ... **E4** 136
Refugio, co., Tx., U.S. ... **E4** 136
Regensburg, Ger. ... **F12** 12
Reggâne, Alg. ... **E4** 48
Reggio di Calabria, Italy ... **E5** 18
Reggio nell'Emilia, Italy ... **B3** 18
Reghin, Rom. ... **F8** 20
Regina, Sk., Can. ... **G3** 91
Régina, Fr. Gu. ... **C9** 70
Regina Beach, Sk., Can. ... **G3** 91
Registro, Braz. ... **C8** 72
Regozero, Russia ... **D14** 10
Rehoboth, Nmb. ... **C2** 56
Rehoboth Bay, b., De., U.S. **F5** 101
Rehoboth Beach, De., U.S. **F5** 101
Reid, Mount, mtn., Ak., U.S. **n24** 95
Reidland, Ky., U.S. ... **e9** 110
Reidsville, Ga., U.S. ... **D4** 103
Reidsville, N.C., U.S. ... **A3** 126
Reigate, Eng., U.K. ... **E6** 12

Reims, Fr. ... **C9** 16
Reinbeck, Ia., U.S. ... **B5** 108
Reindeer Island, i., Mb., Can. ... **C3** 86
Reindeer Lake, l., Can. ... **G19** 82
Reisterstown, Md., U.S. ... **B4** 113
Reliance, Wy., U.S. ... **E3** 143
Remada, Tun. ... **D7** 48
Remanso, Braz. ... **C3** 74
Rembang, Indon. ... **E4** 36
Remington, In., U.S. ... **C3** 107
Remiremont, Fr. ... **C10** 16
Remmel Dam, Ar., U.S. ... **g8** 97
Remsen, Ia., U.S. ... **B2** 108
Rena, Nor. ... **F4** 10
Rend Lake, res., Il., U.S. ... **E5** 106
Rendsburg, Ger. ... **C11** 12
Renforth, N.B., Can. ... **D7** 87
Renfrew, On., U.S. ... **B8** 89
Rengat, Indon. ... **D2** 36
Rengo, Chile ... **E3** 72
Reng Tläng, mtn., Asia ... **B2** 34
Rennes, Fr. ... **C6** 16
Reno, Nv., U.S. ... **D2** 121
Reno, co., Ks., U.S. ... **E5** 109
Reno, Lake, l., Mn., U.S. ... **E3** 116
Reno Hill, mtn., Wy., U.S. **D6** 143
Renovo, Pa., U.S. ... **D6** 131
Renqiu, China ... **B4** 30
Rensselaer, In., U.S. ... **C3** 107
Rensselaer, N.Y., U.S. ... **C7** 125
Rensselaer, co., N.Y., U.S. **C7** 125
Renton, Wa., U.S. ... **B3** 140
Renville, Mn., U.S. ... **F3** 116
Renville, co., Mn., U.S. ... **F4** 116
Renville, co., N.D., U.S. ... **A4** 127
Reo, Indon. ... **E6** 36
Repentigny, P.Q., Can. ... **D4** 90
Repetek, Turk. ... **C8** 42
Republic, Mi., U.S. ... **B3** 115
Republic, Mo., U.S. ... **D4** 118
Republic, Pa., U.S. ... **G2** 131
Republic, Wa., U.S. ... **A7** 140
Republic, co., Ks., U.S. ... **C6** 109
Republican, stm., U.S. ... **C8** 92
Republican, stm., U.S. ... **C6** 109
Republic of Korea see Korea, South, ctry., Asia **D10** 28
Reşadiye, Tur. ... **B7** 44
Reserve, La., U.S. ... **h10** 111
Resistencia, Arg. ... **D6** 72
Reşiţa, Rom. ... **G6** 20
Resolute, N.T., Can. ... **D20** 82
Resolution Island, i., N.Z. ... **q12** 63c
Reston, Mb., Can. ... **E1** 86
Reston, Va., U.S. ... **B5** 139
Réthimnon, Grc. ... **G10** 18
Réthimnon, Grc. ... **G10** 18
Réunion, dep., Afr. ... **g10** 57a
Reus, Spain ... **G7** 16
Reutlingen, Ger. ... **F11** 12
Revelo, Ky., U.S. ... **D5** 110
Revelstoke, B.C., Can. ... **D8** 85
Revelstoke, Lake, res., B.C., Can. ... **D8** 85
Reventazón, Peru ... **E3** 70
Revere, Ma., U.S. ... **g11** 114
Revillagigedo, Islas, is., Mex. **D2** 78
Revillagigedo Island, i., Ak., U.S. ... **n24** 95
Revin, Fr. ... **C9** 16
Rewa, India ... **E4** 40
Rex, Ga., U.S. ... **h8** 103
Rexburg, Id., U.S. ... **F7** 105
Rexton, N.B., Can. ... **C5** 87
Rey, Isla del, i., Pan. ... **D4** 80
Reyes, Point, c., Ca., U.S. **C2** 98
Reyhanlı, Tur. ... **D7** 44
Reykjanes Ridge ... **B26** 144
Reykjavík, Ice. ... **l18** 10a
Reynolds, Ga., U.S. ... **D2** 103
Reynolds, co., Mo., U.S. ... **D6** 118
Reynoldsburg, Oh., U.S. ... **C3** 128
Reynoldsville, Pa., U.S. ... **D4** 131
Reynosa, Mex. ... **D5** 78
Rezé, Fr. ... **D6** 16
Rēzekne, Lat. ... **H12** 10
Rhaetian Alps, mts., Eur. ... **A2** 18
Rhea, co., Tn., U.S. ... **D9** 135
Rheims see Reims, Fr. ... **C9** 16
Rheine, Ger. ... **D10** 12
Rhinebeck, N.Y., U.S. ... **D7** 125
Rhinelander, Wi., U.S. ... **C4** 142
Rhir, Cap, c., Mor. ... **D2** 48
Rho, Italy ... **B2** 18
Rhode Island, state, U.S. ... **D3** 132
Rhode Island, l., R.I., U.S. ... **E5** 132
Rhode Island Sound, strt., U.S. ... **F5** 132
Rhodes see Ródhos, i., Grc. **G12** 18
Rhodesia see Zimbabwe, ctry., Afr. ... **B4** 56
Rhodes Peak, mtn., Id., U.S. **C4** 105
Rhodes' Tomb, hist., Zimb. **C4** 56
Rhodope Mountains, mts., Eur. ... **D10** 18
Rhône, stm., Eur. ... **E9** 16
Riachão do Jacuípe, Braz. ... **D4** 74
Rialto, Ca., U.S. ... **m14** 98
Riau, Kepulauan, is., Indon. **C2** 36
Riaza, Spain ... **C9** 16
Ribáuè, Moz. ... **A6** 56
Ribe, Den. ... **I3** 10
Ribeira do Pombal, Braz. ... **D4** 74
Ribeira Grande, C.V. ... **g9** 50a

Ribeirão, Braz. ... **C4** 74
Ribeirão Preto, Braz. ... **F2** 74
Riberalta, Bol. ... **F6** 70
Rib Lake, Wi., U.S. ... **C3** 142
Riccione, Italy ... **B4** 18
Rice, Mn., U.S. ... **E4** 116
Rice, co., Ks., U.S. ... **D5** 109
Rice, co., Mn., U.S. ... **F5** 116
Riceboro, Ga., U.S. ... **E5** 103
Rice Lake, Wi., U.S. ... **C2** 142
Rice Lake, l., On., Can. ... **C6** 89
Rice Lake, l., Mn., U.S. ... **D5** 116
Riceville, Ia., U.S. ... **A5** 108
Rich, co., Ut., U.S. ... **B4** 137
Rich, Cape, c., On., Can. ... **C4** 89
Richards Bay, b., S. Afr. ... **D5** 56
Richardson, Tx., U.S. ... **n10** 136
Richardson, co., Ne., U.S. **D10** 120
Richardson Lakes, l., Me., U.S. ... **D2** 112
Richard Toll, Sen. ... **C1** 50
Richardton, N.D., U.S. ... **C3** 127
Rich Creek, Va., U.S. ... **C2** 139
Riche, Pointe, c., Nf., Can. ... **C3** 88
Richfield, Mn., U.S. ... **F5** 116
Richfield, Ut., U.S. ... **E3** 137
Richford, Vt., U.S. ... **B3** 138
Rich Hill, Mo., U.S. ... **C3** 118
Richibucto, N.B., Can. ... **C5** 87
Richland, Ga., U.S. ... **D2** 103
Richland, Mo., U.S. ... **D5** 118
Richland, Wa., U.S. ... **C6** 140
Richland, co., Il., U.S. ... **E5** 106
Richland, co., La., U.S. ... **B4** 111
Richland, co., Mt., U.S. ... **C12** 119
Richland, co., N.D., U.S. ... **C8** 127
Richland, co., Oh., U.S. ... **B3** 128
Richland, co., S.C., U.S. ... **D6** 133
Richland, co., Wi., U.S. ... **E3** 142
Richland Balsam, mtn., N.C., U.S. ... **f10** 126
Richland Center, Wi., U.S. **E3** 142
Richland Creek, stm., Tn., U.S. ... **B5** 135
Richlands, N.C., U.S. ... **C5** 126
Richlands, Va., U.S. ... **e10** 139
Richlandtown, Pa., U.S. ... **F11** 131
Richmond, Austl. ... **E3** 62
Richmond, B.C., Can. ... **E6** 85
Richmond, P.Q., Can. ... **D5** 90
Richmond, N.Z. ... **p13** 63c
Richmond, Ca., U.S. ... **D2** 98
Richmond, Il., U.S. ... **A5** 106
Richmond, In., U.S. ... **E8** 107
Richmond, Ky., U.S. ... **C5** 110
Richmond, Me., U.S. ... **D3** 112
Richmond, Mi., U.S. ... **F8** 115
Richmond, Mn., U.S. ... **E4** 116
Richmond, Mo., U.S. ... **B4** 118
Richmond, Tx., U.S. ... **E5** 136
Richmond, Ut., U.S. ... **B4** 137
Richmond, Va., U.S. ... **C5** 139
Richmond, Vt., U.S. ... **C3** 138
Richmond, co., Ga., U.S. ... **C4** 103
Richmond, co., N.C., U.S. **B3** 126
Richmond, co., N.Y., U.S. ... **E6** 125
Richmond, co., Va., U.S. ... **C6** 139
Richmond Heights, Fl., U.S. **s13** 102
Richmond Heights, Mo., U.S. ... **f13** 118
Richmond Hill, On., Can. ... **D5** 89
Richmond Hill, Ga., U.S. ... **E5** 103
Richmond National Battlefield Park, Va., U.S. ... **n18** 139
Rich Square, N.C., U.S. ... **A5** 126
Richthofen, Mount, mtn., Co., U.S. ... **A5** 99
Richton, Ms., U.S. ... **D5** 117
Richwood, Oh., U.S. ... **B2** 128
Richwood, W.V., U.S. ... **C4** 141
Rickman, Tn., U.S. ... **C8** 135
Riddle, Or., U.S. ... **E3** 130
Riddle Mountain, mtn., Or., U.S. ... **D8** 130
Rideau, stm., On., Can. ... **B9** 89
Ridgecrest, Ca., U.S. ... **E5** 98
Ridge Farm, Il., U.S. ... **D6** 106
Ridgefield, Ct., U.S. ... **D2** 100
Ridgefield, N.J., U.S. ... **h8** 123
Ridgefield, Wa., U.S. ... **D3** 140
Ridgefield Park, N.J., U.S. **B4** 123
Ridgeland, Ms., U.S. ... **C3** 117
Ridgeland, S.C., U.S. ... **G6** 133
Ridgeley, W.V., U.S. ... **B6** 141
Ridgely, Md., U.S. ... **C6** 113
Ridgely, Tn., U.S. ... **A2** 135
Ridge Spring, S.C., U.S. ... **D4** 133
Ridgetop, Tn., U.S. ... **A5** 135
Ridgetown, On., Can. ... **E3** 89
Ridgeview, W.V., U.S. ... **C3** 141
Ridgeville, In., U.S. ... **D7** 107
Ridgeville, S.C., U.S. ... **E7** 133
Ridgeway, Va., U.S. ... **D3** 139
Ridgewood, N.J., U.S. ... **B4** 123
Ridgway, Il., U.S. ... **F5** 106
Ridgway, Pa., U.S. ... **D4** 131
Riding Mountain National Park, Mb., Can. ... **D1** 86
Ridley Park, Pa., U.S. ... **p20** 131
Rieti, Italy ... **C4** 18
Riesa, Ger. ... **E13** 12
Rieti, Italy ... **C4** 18
Rif, mts., Mor. ... **E3** 14
Riffe Lake, res., Wa., U.S. **C3** 140
Rifle, Co., U.S. ... **B3** 99

Rifle, stm., Mi., U.S. ... **D6** 115
Rift Valley, val., Afr. ... **C6** 54
Rīga, Lat. ... **H11** 10
Riga, Gulf of, b., Eur. ... **G10** 10
Rigaud, P.Q., Can. ... **D3** 90
Rigby, Id., U.S. ... **F7** 105
Rīgestān, reg., Afg. ... **D9** 42
Rigo, Pap. N. Gui. ... **H12** 32
Riihimäki, Fin. ... **F11** 10
Riiser-Larsen Peninsula, pen., Ant. ... **C8** 67
Rijeka, Cro. ... **B5** 18
Riley, Ks., U.S. ... **C7** 109
Riley, co., Ks., U.S. ... **C7** 109
Riley, Mount, mtn., N.M., U.S. ... **F2** 124
Rimbey, Ab., Can. ... **C3** 84
Rimersburg, Pa., U.S. ... **D3** 131
Rimini, Italy ... **B4** 18
Rimouski, P.Q., Can. ... **A9** 90
Rimouski, stm., P.Q., Can. ... **A9** 90
Rimouski-Est, P.Q., Can. ... **A9** 90
Rimrock Lake, res., Wa., U.S. ... **C4** 140
Rinca, Pulau, i., Indon. ... **E5** 36
Rincon, Ga., U.S. ... **D5** 103
Rincón del Bonete, Lago Artificial de, res., Ur. ... **E6** 72
Rincón de Romos, Mex. ... **C4** 78
Rincon Mountains, mts., Az., U.S. ... **E5** 96
Ringdove, Vanuatu ... **k9** 62a
Ringgold, Ga., U.S. ... **B1** 103
Ringgold, La., U.S. ... **B2** 111
Ringgold, co., Ia., U.S. ... **D3** 108
Ringim, Nig. ... **D6** 50
Ringkøbing, Den. ... **H3** 10
Ringkøbing Fjord, b., Den. ... **I3** 10
Ringling, Ok., U.S. ... **C4** 129
Ringvassøya, i., Nor. ... **B8** 10
Ringwood, N.J., U.S. ... **A4** 123
Rinjani, Gunung, vol., Indon. ... **E5** 36
Rio, Fl., U.S. ... **E6** 102
Rio, Wi., U.S. ... **E4** 142
Rio Arriba, co., N.M., U.S. **A2** 124
Riobamba, Ec. ... **D4** 70
Rio Blanco, co., Co., U.S. **B2** 99
Rio Branco, Braz. ... **E6** 70
Rio Bravo, Mex. ... **B5** 78
Rio Claro, Braz. ... **F2** 74
Río Colorado, Arg. ... **E4** 69
Río Cuarto, Arg. ... **E5** 72
Rio de Janeiro, Braz. ... **F3** 74
Rio de Janeiro, state, Braz. **F3** 74
Rio Dell, Ca., U.S. ... **B1** 98
Río Gallegos, Arg. ... **H3** 69
Río Grande, Arg. ... **H3** 69
Rio Grande, Braz. ... **E7** 72
Rio Grande, Mex. ... **C4** 78
Rio Grande, Oh., U.S. ... **D3** 128
Rio Grande, co., Co., U.S. **D4** 99
Rio Grande (Bravo), stm., N.A. ... **F7** 92
Rio Grande City, Tx., U.S. **F3** 136
Rio Grande do Norte, state, Braz. ... **E12** 70
Rio Grande do Sul, state, Braz. ... **D7** 72
Rio Grande Reservoir, res., Co., U.S. ... **D3** 99
Ríohacha, Col. ... **A5** 70
Río Hato, Pan. ... **D3** 80
Rio Hondo, Tx., U.S. ... **F4** 136
Rio Largo, Braz. ... **C4** 74
Riom, Fr. ... **E8** 16
Río Mayo, Arg. ... **G2** 69
Ríonegro, Col. ... **D5** 80
Rio Negro, Pantanal do, sw., Braz. ... **G8** 70
Rio Rancho, N.M., U.S. ... **B3** 124
Rio Real, Braz. ... **D4** 74
Ríosucio, Col. ... **D4** 80
Río Tercero, Arg. ... **E5** 72
Rio Tinto, Braz. ... **C4** 74
Rio Verde, Braz. ... **E1** 74
Ríoverde, Mex. ... **C5** 78
Rio Verde de Mato Grosso, Braz. ... **B7** 72
Rio Vista, Ca., U.S. ... **C3** 98
Ripley, Ms., U.S. ... **A5** 117
Ripley, Oh., U.S. ... **D2** 128
Ripley, Tn., U.S. ... **B2** 135
Ripley, W.V., U.S. ... **C3** 141
Ripley, co., In., U.S. ... **F7** 107
Ripley, co., Mo., U.S. ... **E7** 118
Ripon, Eng., U.K. ... **C6** 12
Ripon, Wi., U.S. ... **E5** 142
Rippowam, stm., Ct., U.S. **E1** 100
Ririe Lake, res., Id., U.S. ... **F7** 105
Rishiri-tō, i., Japan ... **B16** 28
Rishon LeẔiyyon, Isr. ... **G6** 44
Rising Sun, De., U.S. ... **D3** 101
Rising Sun, In., U.S. ... **G8** 107
Rising Sun, Md., U.S. ... **A5** 113
Rison, Ar., U.S. ... **D3** 97
Ristijärvi, Fin. ... **D13** 10
Ritchie, co., W.V., U.S. ... **B3** 141
Ritter, Mount, mtn., Ca., U.S. ... **D4** 98
Rittman, Oh., U.S. ... **B4** 128
Ritzville, Wa., U.S. ... **B7** 140
Riva del Garda, Italy ... **B3** 18
Rivanna, stm., Va., U.S. ... **C4** 139
Rivas, Nic. ... **C2** 80

Rivera, Ur. ... **E6** 72
Riverbank, Ca., U.S. ... **D3** 98
River Bourgeois, N.S., Can. **D9** 87
River Cess, Lib. ... **E3** 50
Riverdale, Ca., U.S. ... **D4** 98
Riverdale, Il., U.S. ... **k9** 106
Riverdale, Md., U.S. ... **C4** 113
River Edge, N.J., U.S. ... **h8** 123
River Falls, Al., U.S. ... **D3** 94
River Falls, Wi., U.S. ... **D1** 142
River Forest, Il., U.S. ... **k9** 106
River Grove, Il., U.S. ... **k9** 106
Riverhead, N.Y., U.S. ... **n16** 125
River Hebert, N.S., Can. ... **D5** 87
River Heights, Ut., U.S. ... **B4** 137
River Hills, Wi., U.S. ... **m12** 142
River Pines, Ma., U.S. ... **f10** 114
River Ridge, La., U.S. ... **k11** 111
River Road, Or., U.S. ... **C3** 130
River Rouge, Mi., U.S. ... **p15** 115
Rivers, Mb., Can. ... **D1** 86
Riversdale, S. Afr. ... **E3** 56
Riverside, Al., U.S. ... **B3** 94
Riverside, Ca., U.S. ... **F5** 98
Riverside, Ia., U.S. ... **C6** 108
Riverside, Il., U.S. ... **k9** 106
Riverside, N.J., U.S. ... **C3** 123
Riverside, Pa., U.S. ... **E8** 131
Riverside, co., Ca., U.S. ... **F5** 98
Riverside Reservoir, res., Co., U.S. ... **A6** 99
Riverton, Mb., Can. ... **D3** 86
Riverton, N.Z. ... **q12** 63c
Riverton, Il., U.S. ... **D4** 106
Riverton, Ks., U.S. ... **E9** 109
Riverton, N.J., U.S. ... **C3** 123
Riverton, Ut., U.S. ... **C4** 137
Riverton, Vt., U.S. ... **C3** 138
Riverton, Wy., U.S. ... **C4** 143
Riverton Heights, Wa., U.S. **f11** 140
River Vale, N.J., U.S. ... **h8** 123
Riverview, Fl., U.S. ... **p11** 102
Riverview, Mi., U.S. ... **p15** 115
Rivesville, W.V., U.S. ... **B4** 141
Riviera Beach, Fl., U.S. ... **F6** 102
Riviera Beach, Md., U.S. ... **B4** 113
Rivière-du-Loup, P.Q., Can. **B8** 90
Rivière-Verte, N.B., Can. ... **B1** 87
Rivne, Ukr. ... **D9** 20
Rivoli, Italy ... **B1** 18
Riyadh see Ar-Riyāḍ, Sau. Ar. ... **F5** 38
Rizhao, China ... **D11** 28
Rjazan', Russia ... **D6** 26
Rjažsk, Russia ... **C16** 20
Rjukan, Nor. ... **G3** 10
Roachdale, In., U.S. ... **E4** 107
Road Town, Br. Vir. Is. ... **B7** 80
Roane, co., Tn., U.S. ... **D9** 135
Roane, co., W.V., U.S. ... **C3** 141
Roan Mountain, Tn., U.S. ... **C11** 135
Roanne, Fr. ... **D8** 16
Roanoke, Al., U.S. ... **B4** 94
Roanoke, Il., U.S. ... **C4** 106
Roanoke, In., U.S. ... **C7** 107
Roanoke, Tx., U.S. ... **m9** 136
Roanoke, Va., U.S. ... **C3** 139
Roanoke, co., Va., U.S. ... **C2** 139
Roanoke see Staunton, stm., U.S. ... **D12** 92
Roanoke, stm., U.S. ... **A5** 126
Roanoke Island, i., N.C., U.S. ... **B7** 126
Roanoke Rapids, N.C., U.S. **A5** 126
Roanoke Rapids Lake, res., U.S. ... **A5** 126
Roaring Fork, stm., Co., U.S. **C4** 99
Roaring Spring, Pa., U.S. ... **F5** 131
Roatán, Isla de, i., Hond. ... **B2** 80
Robbins, Il., U.S. ... **k9** 106
Robbins, N.C., U.S. ... **B3** 126
Robbinsdale, Mn., U.S. ... **m12** 116
Robbinsville, N.C., U.S. ... **f9** 126
Robe, Austl. ... **H2** 62
Robersonville, N.C., U.S. ... **B5** 126
Roberta, Ga., U.S. ... **D2** 103
Robert Lee, Tx., U.S. ... **D2** 136
Roberts, Wi., U.S. ... **C1** 142
Roberts, co., S.D., U.S. ... **B8** 134
Roberts, co., Tx., U.S. ... **B2** 136
Roberts, Point, c., Wa., U.S. **A2** 140
Robert's Arm, Nf., Can. ... **D4** 88
Roberts Creek Mountain, mtn., Nv., U.S. ... **D5** 121
Robertsdale, Al., U.S. ... **E2** 94
Robert S. Kerr Reservoir, res., Ok., U.S. ... **B6** 129
Roberts Mountain, mtn., Ak., U.S. ... **C6** 95
Roberts Mountain, mtn., Wy., U.S. ... **D3** 143
Robertson, co., Ky., U.S. ... **B5** 110
Robertson, co., Tn., U.S. ... **A5** 135
Robertson, co., Tx., U.S. ... **D4** 136
Robertsonville, P.Q., Can. ... **C6** 90
Roberval, P.Q., Can. ... **A5** 90
Robeson, co., N.C., U.S. ... **C3** 126
Robins, In., U.S. ... **B6** 108
Robinson, Il., U.S. ... **D6** 106
Róbinson Crusoe, Isla, i., Chile ... **E2** 72

Name	Map Ref.	Page

Name	Map Ref.	Page
Robinson Fork, stm., W.V., U.S.	k9	141
Robinson Fork, stm., W.V., U.S.	m14	141
Robinvale, Austl.	G3	62
Roblin, Mb., Can.	D1	86
Roboré, Bol.	B6	72
Robson, Mount, mtn., B.C., Can.	C8	85
Robstown, Tx., U.S.	F4	136
Roca Partida, Isla, i., Mex.	D2	78
Rocha, Ur.	E7	72
Rochefort, Fr.	E6	16
Rochelle, Ga., U.S.	E3	103
Rochelle, Il., U.S.	B4	106
Rochelle Park, N.J., U.S.	h8	123
Rochester, Il., U.S.	D4	106
Rochester, In., U.S.	B5	107
Rochester, Mi., U.S.	F7	115
Rochester, Mn., U.S.	F6	116
Rochester, N.H., U.S.	D5	122
Rochester, N.Y., U.S.	B3	125
Rochester, Pa., U.S.	E1	131
Rochester, Vt., U.S.	D3	138
Rochester, Wa., U.S.	C2	140
Rochester, Wi., U.S.	n11	142
Rock, co., Mn., U.S.	G2	116
Rock, co., Ne., U.S.	B6	120
Rock, co., Wi., U.S.	F4	142
Rock, stm., U.S.	B3	106
Rock, stm., U.S.	A1	108
Rockall, i., Scot., U.K.	D3	6
Rockall Rise	B24	144
Rockaway, N.J., U.S.	B3	123
Rockaway, Or., U.S.	B3	130
Rockbridge, co., Va., U.S.	C3	139
Rockcastle, co., Ky., U.S.	C5	110
Rockcastle, stm., Ky., U.S.	C5	110
Rockcliffe Park, On., Can.	h12	89
Rock Creek, Mn., U.S.	E6	116
Rock Creek, stm., Nv., U.S.	C5	121
Rock Creek, stm., Or., U.S.	B6	130
Rock Creek, stm., Wa., U.S.	B8	140
Rock Creek, stm., Wa., U.S.	D5	140
Rock Creek, stm., Wy., U.S.	E6	143
Rock Creek, stm., U.S.	B3	113
Rock Creek, stm., U.S.	h14	140
Rock Creek Butte, mtn., Or., U.S.	C8	130
Rockdale, Il., U.S.	B5	106
Rockdale, Md., U.S.	B4	113
Rockdale, Tx., U.S.	D4	136
Rockdale, co., Ga., U.S.	C3	103
Rockefeller Plateau, plat., Ant.	E27	67
Rockfall, Ct., U.S.	C5	100
Rock Falls, Il., U.S.	B4	106
Rockford, Ia., U.S.	A5	108
Rockford, Il., U.S.	A4	106
Rockford, Mi., U.S.	E5	115
Rockford, Mn., U.S.	E5	116
Rockford, Oh., U.S.	B1	128
Rockford, Tn., U.S.	D10	135
Rock Hall, Md., U.S.	B5	113
Rockhampton, Austl.	E5	62
Rockhampton Downs, Austl.	D6	60
Rock Hill, S.C., U.S.	B5	133
Rockingham, Austl.	G2	60
Rockingham, N.C., U.S.	C3	126
Rockingham, co., N.C., U.S.	A3	126
Rockingham, co., N.H., U.S.	D4	122
Rockingham, co., Va., U.S.	B4	139
Rock Island, P.Q., Can.	D5	90
Rock Island, Il., U.S.	B3	106
Rock Island, co., Il., U.S.	B3	106
Rock Island, i., Fl., U.S.	C3	102
Rock Island, i., Wi., U.S.	C7	142
Rock Lake, l., Wa., U.S.	B8	140
Rockland, On., Can.	B9	89
Rockland, Ma., U.S.	B6	114
Rockland, Me., U.S.	D3	112
Rockland, co., N.Y., U.S.	D6	125
Rockledge, Fl., U.S.	D6	102
Rockledge, Pa., U.S.	o20	131
Rocklin, Ca., U.S.	C3	98
Rckmart, Ga., U.S.	B1	103
Rock Mountain, mtn., Co., U.S.	D3	99
Rockport, In., U.S.	I3	107
Rockport, Ma., U.S.	A6	114
Rockport, Me., U.S.	D3	112
Rock Port, Mo., U.S.	A2	118
Rockport, Tx., U.S.	F4	136
Rock Rapids, Ia., U.S.	A1	108
Rock River, Wy., U.S.	E7	143
Rocksprings, Tx., U.S.	D2	136
Rock Springs, Wy., U.S.	E3	143
Rockstone, Guy.	B8	70
Rockton, Il., U.S.	A4	106
Rock Valley, Ia., U.S.	A1	108
Rockville, In., U.S.	E3	107
Rockville, Md., U.S.	B3	113
Rockville Centre, N.Y., U.S.	n15	125
Rockwall, Tx., U.S.	C4	136
Rockwall, co., Tx., U.S.	C4	136
Rockwell, Ia., U.S.	B4	108
Rockwell, N.C., U.S.	B2	126
Rockwell City, Ia., U.S.	B3	108
Rockwell Park, N.C., U.S.	B2	126
Rockwood, Mi., U.S.	F7	115
Rockwood, P.Q., Can.	G3	131
Rockwood, Tn., U.S.	D9	135
Rocky, stm., N.C., U.S.	B2	126
Rocky, stm., S.C., U.S.	C2	133

Name	Map Ref.	Page
Rocky, East Branch, stm., Oh., U.S.	h9	128
Rocky, West Branch, stm., Oh., U.S.	h9	128
Rocky Boys Indian Reservation, Mt., U.S.	B7	119
Rocky Ford, Co., U.S.	C7	99
Rocky Fork Lake, l., Oh., U.S.	C2	128
Rocky Harbour, Nf., Can.	D3	88
Rocky Hill, Ct., U.S.	C5	100
Rocky Lake, l., Me., U.S.	D5	112
Rocky Mount, N.C., U.S.	B5	126
Rocky Mount, Va., U.S.	D3	139
Rocky Mountain, mtn., Mt., U.S.	C4	119
Rocky Mountain House, Ab., Can.	C3	84
Rocky Mountain National Park, Co., U.S.	A5	99
Rocky Mountains, mts., N.A.	B5	92
Rocky Ripple, In., U.S.	k10	107
Rocky River, Oh., U.S.	A4	128
Rocky Top, mtn., Or., U.S.	C4	130
Roddickton, Nf., Can.	C3	88
Rodeo, Arg.	E4	72
Roderfield, W.V., U.S.	D3	141
Rodez, Fr.	E8	16
Ródhos, Grc.	F12	18
Ródhos (Rhodes), i., Grc.	G12	18
Rodney, On., Can.	E3	89
Rodney, Cape, c., Ak., U.S.	C6	95
Rodney Village, De., U.S.	D3	101
Rodrigues, i., Mrts.	F12	52
Roebourne, Austl.	E2	60
Roebuck, S.C., U.S.	B4	133
Roeland Park, Ks., U.S.	k16	109
Roeselare, Bel.	E8	12
Roff, Ok., U.S.	C5	129
Roger Mills, co., Ok., U.S.	B2	129
Rogers, Ar., U.S.	A1	97
Rogers, Mn., U.S.	E5	116
Rogers, Tx., U.S.	D4	136
Rogers, co., Ok., U.S.	A6	129
Rogers, Mount, mtn., Va., U.S.	f10	139
Rogers City, Mi., U.S.	C7	115
Rogers Lake, res., Ct., U.S.	D6	100
Rogers Pass, Mt., U.S.	C4	119
Rogersville, N.B., Can.	C4	87
Rogersville, Al., U.S.	A2	94
Rogersville, Mo., U.S.	D4	118
Rogersville, Tn., U.S.	C10	135
Rogue, stm., Or., U.S.	E2	130
Rogue River, Or., U.S.	E3	130
Rohri, Pak.	E9	42
Rohtak, India	D3	40
Roi Et, Thai.	C4	34
Rokan, stm., Indon.	C2	36
Roland, Ia., U.S.	B4	108
Roland, Ok., U.S.	B7	129
Roland, Lake, res., Md., U.S.	g11	113
Rolette, N.D., U.S.	A6	127
Rolette, co., N.D., U.S.	A6	127
Rolfe, Ia., U.S.	B3	108
Rolla, Mo., U.S.	D6	118
Rolla, N.D., U.S.	A6	127
Rollingbay, Wa., U.S.	e10	140
Rolling Fork, Ms., U.S.	C3	117
Rolling Fork, stm., Ar., U.S.	C1	97
Rolling Fork, stm., Ky., U.S.	C4	110
Rolling Meadows, Il., U.S.	h8	106
Rollingstone, Mn., U.S.	F7	116
Rollinsford, N.H., U.S.	D5	122
Rolvsøya, i., Nor.	A10	10
Roma, Austl.	F4	62
Roma (Rome), Italy	D4	18
Roma, Tx., U.S.	F3	136
Romain, Cape, c., S.C., U.S.	F9	133
Roman, Rom.	F9	20
Romanche Gap	I12	66
Romang, Pulau, i., Indon.	E7	36
Romania, ctry., Eur.	F8	20
Roman Nose Mountain, mtn., Or., U.S.	D3	130
Romano, Cape, c., Fl., U.S.	G5	102
Romano, Cayo, i., Cuba	A4	80
Romans-sur-Isère, Fr.	E9	16
Romanzof, Cape, c., Ak., U.S.	C6	95
Romanzof Mountains, mts., Ak., U.S.	B11	95
Rome see Roma, Italy	D4	18
Rome, Ga., U.S.	B1	103
Rome, Il., U.S.	C4	106
Rome, N.Y., U.S.	B5	125
Rome City, In., U.S.	B7	107
Romeo, Mi., U.S.	F7	115
Romeoville, Il., U.S.	k8	106
Romney, W.V., U.S.	B6	141
Romny, Ukr.	D12	20
Romorantin-Lanthenay, Fr.	D7	16
Romulus, Mi., U.S.	p15	115
Ronan, Mt., U.S.	C2	119
Roncador, Serra do, plat., Braz.	D1	74
Ronceverte, W.V., U.S.	D4	141
Ronda, Spain	I4	16
Rondônia, state, Braz.	F7	70
Rondonópolis, Braz.	G9	70
Rong'an, China	D2	30
Rongcheng, China	B5	30
Ronge, Lac la, l., Sk., Can.	B3	91

Name	Map Ref.	Page
Rongelap, atoll, Marsh. Is.	C10	58
Rongjiang, China	D2	30
Rongxian, China	E3	30
Rønne, Den.	I6	10
Ronneby, Swe.	H6	10
Ronne Ice Shelf, Ant.	D34	67
Roodhouse, Il., U.S.	D3	106
Rooks, co., Ks., U.S.	C4	109
Roosevelt, Ut., U.S.	C5	137
Roosevelt, co., Mt., U.S.	B11	119
Roosevelt, co., N.M., U.S.	C6	124
Roosevelt, stm., Braz.	E7	70
Roosevelt Island, i., Ant.	D24	67
Roosevelt Park, Mi., U.S.	E4	115
Root, stm., Mn., U.S.	G7	116
Root, stm., Wi., U.S.	n12	142
Roper, N.C., U.S.	B6	126
Roper Valley, Austl.	C5	60
Ropi, Fin.	B9	10
Roraima, state, Braz.	C7	70
Roraima, Mount, mtn., S.A.	B7	70
Røros, Nor.	E4	10
Rosamond, Ca., U.S.	E4	98
Rosario, Arg.	E5	72
Rosário, Braz.	B3	74
Rosario, Mex.	C3	78
Rosario, Para.	C6	72
Rosario de la Frontera, Arg.	D5	72
Rosário do Sul, Braz.	E6	72
Rosário Oeste, Braz.	F8	70
Roscoe, Il., U.S.	A5	106
Roscoe, Tx., U.S.	C2	136
Roscommon, Ire.	D2	12
Roscommon, Mi., U.S.	D6	115
Roscommon, co., Mi., U.S.	D6	115
Rose, Mount, mtn., Nv., U.S.	D2	121
Roseau, Dom.	B7	80
Roseau, Mn., U.S.	B3	116
Roseau, co., Mn., U.S.	B3	116
Roseau, South Fork, stm., Mn., U.S.	B3	116
Rose-Blanche [-Harbour le Cou], Nf., Can.	E2	88
Roseboro, N.C., U.S.	C4	126
Rosebud, S.D., U.S.	D5	134
Rosebud, Tx., U.S.	D4	136
Rosebud, co., Mt., U.S.	D10	119
Rosebud Indian Reservation, S.D., U.S.	D5	134
Roseburg, Or., U.S.	D3	130
Rosedale, In., U.S.	E3	107
Rosedale, Md., U.S.	g11	113
Rosedale, Ms., U.S.	B2	117
Rose Hill, Ks., U.S.	E6	109
Rose Hill, N.C., U.S.	C4	126
Rose Hill, Va., U.S.	f8	139
Roseland, Fl., U.S.	E6	102
Roseland, In., U.S.	A5	107
Roseland, La., U.S.	D5	111
Roseland, Oh., U.S.	B3	128
Roselle, Il., U.S.	k8	106
Roselle, N.J., U.S.	k7	123
Roselle Park, N.J., U.S.	k7	123
Rosemère, P.Q., Can.	p19	90
Rosemount, Mn., U.S.	F5	116
Rosenberg, Tx., U.S.	E5	136
Rosendale, Wi., U.S.	E5	142
Rosenheim, Ger.	G13	12
Rose Peak, mtn., Az., U.S.	D6	96
Rosepine, La., U.S.	D2	111
Rose Point, c., B.C., Can.	B2	85
Roseto, Pa., U.S.	E11	131
Rosetta see Rashid, Egypt.	E10	14
Roseville, Ca., U.S.	C3	98
Roseville, Il., U.S.	C3	106
Roseville, Mi., U.S.	o16	115
Roseville, Mn., U.S.	m12	116
Roseville, Oh., U.S.	C3	128
Rosewood Heights, Il., U.S.	E3	106
Rosiclare, Il., U.S.	F5	106
Roşiori de Vede, Rom.	G8	20
Roskilde, Den.	I5	10
Roslavl', Russia	C12	20
Roslyn, Wa., U.S.	B4	140
Roslyn Heights, N.Y., U.S.	h13	125
Ross, Oh., U.S.	C1	128
Ross, co., Oh., U.S.	C2	128
Rossano, Italy	E6	18
Ross Barnett Reservoir, res., Ms., U.S.	C3	117
Rossburn, Mb., Can.	D1	86
Ross Dam, Wa., U.S.	A4	140
Rossford, Oh., U.S.	A2	128
Ross Ice Shelf, Ant.	E23	67
Rossignol, Lake, l., N.S., Can.	E4	87
Ross Island, i., Ant.	D22	67
Ross Island, i., Mb., Can.	B3	86
Ross Lake National Recreation Area, Wa., U.S.	A5	140
Rossland, B.C., Can.	E9	85
Rosso, Maur.	C1	50
Rossoš', Russia	D15	20
Ross Sea, Ant.	D24	67
Røssvatnet, l., Nor.	D5	10
Rossville, Ga., U.S.	B1	103
Rossville, Il., U.S.	C6	106
Rossville, In., U.S.	D4	107
Rossville, Ks., U.S.	C8	109

Name	Map Ref.	Page
Roswell, Ga., U.S.	B2	103
Roswell, N.M., U.S.	D5	124
Rota, i., N. Mar. Is.	D12	32
Rotan, Tx., U.S.	C2	136
Rothesay, N.B., Can.	D4	87
Rothschild, Wi., U.S.	D4	142
Rothsville, Pa., U.S.	F9	131
Rotorua, N.Z.	o14	63c
Rotterdam, Neth.	E9	12
Rotterdam, N.Y., U.S.	C6	125
Roubaix, Fr.	B8	16
Rouen, Fr.	C7	16
Rouge, stm., P.Q., Can.	D3	90
Rough, stm., Ky., U.S.	C3	110
Rough River Lake, res., Ky., U.S.	C3	110
Rouiba, Alg.	I8	16
Roulette, Pa., U.S.	C5	131
Round Island, i., Ms., U.S.	g8	117
Round Lake, Il., U.S.	h8	106
Round Lake Beach, Il., U.S.	h8	106
Round Mountain, Nv., U.S.	E4	121
Round Rock, Tx., U.S.	D4	136
Roundup, Mt., U.S.	D8	119
Round Valley Indian Reservation, Ca., U.S.	C2	98
Round Valley Reservoir, res., N.J., U.S.	B3	123
Rouses Point, N.Y., U.S.	f11	125
Routt, co., Co., U.S.	A3	99
Rouyn [-Noranda], P.Q., Can.	k11	90
Rouzerville, Pa., U.S.	G6	131
Rovaniemi, Fin.	C11	10
Rovereto, Italy	B3	18
Rovigo, Italy	B3	18
Rovuma (Ruvuma), stm., Afr.	F8	54
Rowan, co., Ky., U.S.	B6	110
Rowan, co., N.C., U.S.	B2	126
Rowland, N.C., U.S.	C3	126
Rowlesburg, W.V., U.S.	B5	141
Roxas, Phil.	D8	34
Roxboro, N.C., U.S.	A4	126
Roxburgh, N.Z.	q12	63c
Roxton Falls, P.Q., Can.	D5	90
Roxton Pond, P.Q., Can.	D5	90
Roy, Ut., U.S.	B3	137
Royal, stm., Me., U.S.	g7	112
Royal Center, In., U.S.	C4	107
Royale, Isle, i., Mi., U.S.	h9	115
Royal Gorge, val., Co., U.S.	C5	99
Royal Oak, Mi., U.S.	F7	115
Royal Pines, N.C., U.S.	f10	126
Royalton, Il., U.S.	F4	106
Royalton, Mn., U.S.	E4	116
Royan, Fr.	E6	16
Royersford, Pa., U.S.	F10	131
Royerton, In., U.S.	D7	107
Royse City, Tx., U.S.	C4	136
Royston, B.C., Can.	E5	85
Royston, Ga., U.S.	B3	103
Rtiščevo, Russia	D7	22
Ruacana Falls, wtfl, Afr.	B1	56
Ruapehu, Mount, vol., N.Z.	o14	63c
Rubcovsk, Russia	D10	26
Rubidoux, Ca., U.S.	n14	98
Rubondo Island, i., Tan.	D6	54
Ruby Dome, mtn., Nv., U.S.	C6	121
Ruby Lake, l., Nv., U.S.	C6	121
Ruby Mountains, mts., Nv., U.S.	C6	121
Ruby Range, mts., Co., U.S.	C3	99
Ruby Range, mts., Mt., U.S.	E4	119
Rūdbār, Afg.	D8	42
Rudnja, Russia	B11	20
Rudnyj, Kaz.	D8	26
Rudolf, Lake (Turkana, Lake), l., Afr.	C7	54
Rudyard, Mi., U.S.	B6	115
Rufiji, stm., Tan.	E7	54
Rufino, Arg.	E5	72
Rufisque, Sen.	D1	50
Rufus Woods Lake, res., Wa., U.S.	A6	140
Rugby, N.D., U.S.	A6	127
Rügen, i., Ger.	C13	12
Ruhengeri, Rw.	D5	54
Rui'an, China	F12	28
Ruidoso, N.M., U.S.	D4	124
Ruidoso Downs, N.M., U.S.	D4	124
Ruijin, China	F11	28
Ruiz, Mex.	C3	78
Ruki, stm., D.R.C.	B3	54
Rukwa, Lake, l., Tan.	E6	54
Ruleville, Ms., U.S.	B3	117
Rum, stm., Mn., U.S.	D5	116
Ruma, Yugo.	B7	18
Rumbek, Sudan	I10	48
Rum Cay, i., Bah.	D10	76
Rum Creek, stm., W.V., U.S.	n12	141
Rumford, Me., U.S.	D2	112
Rum Jungle, Austl.	C5	60
Rumoi, Japan	C16	28
Rumphi, Mwi.	A5	56
Rumson, N.J., U.S.	C4	123
Rumstick Point, c., R.I., U.S.	D5	132
Runan, China	E10	28
Rundu, Nmb.	B2	56
Runge, Tx., U.S.	E4	136
Rungwa, Tan.	E6	54
Runnels, co., Tx., U.S.	D3	136
Runnemede, N.J., U.S.	D2	123

Name	Map Ref.	Page
Ruoqiang, China	D5	28
Rupat, Pulau, i., Indon.	C2	36
Rupert, Id., U.S.	G5	105
Rupert, W.V., U.S.	D4	141
Rupert, Rivière de, stm., P.Q., Can.	h11	90
Rural Hall, N.C., U.S.	A2	126
Rural Retreat, Va., U.S.	D1	139
Rurrenabaque, Bol.	A4	72
Rusagonis, N.B., Can.	D3	87
Rusape, Zimb.	B5	56
Ruse, Bul.	C11	18
Rush, co., In., U.S.	E6	107
Rush, co., Ks., U.S.	D4	109
Rush, stm., Mn., U.S.	F4	116
Rush, stm., Wi., U.S.	D1	142
Rush City, Mn., U.S.	E6	116
Rush Creek, stm., Oh., U.S.	B2	128
Rush Creek, stm., Ok., U.S.	C4	129
Rushford, Mn., U.S.	G7	116
Rush Lake, l., Mn., U.S.	D3	116
Rush Lake, l., Mn., U.S.	E5	116
Rush Lake, l., Wi., U.S.	E5	142
Rushmere, Va., U.S.	h14	139
Rush Springs, Ok., U.S.	C4	129
Rushville, Il., U.S.	C3	106
Rushville, In., U.S.	E7	107
Rushville, Ne., U.S.	B3	120
Rusk, Tx., U.S.	D5	136
Rusk, co., Tx., U.S.	C5	136
Rusk, co., Wi., U.S.	C2	142
Ruskin, Fl., U.S.	E4	102
Russas, Braz.	B4	74
Russell, Mb., Can.	D1	86
Russell, On., Can.	B9	89
Russell, Ks., U.S.	D5	109
Russell, Ky., U.S.	B7	110
Russell, Pa., U.S.	C3	131
Russell, co., Al., U.S.	C4	94
Russell, co., Ks., U.S.	D5	109
Russell, co., Ky., U.S.	D4	110
Russell, co., Va., U.S.	f9	139
Russell, Mount, mtn., Ak., U.S.	f16	95
Russell Cave National Monument, Al., U.S.	A4	94
Russell Fork, stm., U.S.	C7	110
Russell Springs, Ky., U.S.	C4	110
Russellville, Al., U.S.	A2	94
Russellville, Ar., U.S.	B2	97
Russellville, Ky., U.S.	D3	110
Russellville, Mo., U.S.	C5	118
Russellville, Tn., U.S.	C10	135
Russia, ctry., Eur.	C11	26
Russian, stm., Ca., U.S.	C2	98
Russiaville, In., U.S.	D5	107
Russkaja Gavan', Russia	B8	26
Rustavi, Geor.	B11	44
Rustburg, Va., U.S.	C3	139
Rustenburg, S. Afr.	D4	56
Ruston, La., U.S.	B3	111
Ruston, Wa., U.S.	B3	140
Rutana, Bdi.	D6	54
Ruteng, Indon.	E6	36
Ruth, Nv., U.S.	D6	121
Rutherford, N.J., U.S.	B4	123
Rutherford, Tn., U.S.	A3	135
Rutherford, co., N.C., U.S.	B1	126
Rutherford, co., Tn., U.S.	B5	135
Rutherfordton, N.C., U.S.	B1	126
Ruthven, Ia., U.S.	A3	108
Rutland, Ma., U.S.	B4	114
Rutland, Vt., U.S.	D3	138
Rutland, co., Vt., U.S.	D2	138
Rutledge, Ga., U.S.	C3	103
Rutledge, Tn., U.S.	C10	135
Rutog, China	C3	40
Rutshuru, D.R.C.	D5	54
Ruvuma (Rovuma), stm., Afr.	F8	54
Ruy Barbosa, Braz.	D3	74
Ruzaevka, Russia	D7	22
Rwanda, ctry., Afr.	D5	54
Ryan, Ok., U.S.	C4	129
Ryan Peak, mtn., Id., U.S.	F4	105
Rybače, Russia	E10	26
Rybačij, poluostrov, pen., Russia	B15	10
Rybinsk, Russia	D5	26
Rybinskoe vodohranilišče, res., Russia	D5	26
Rybinsk Reservoir see Rybinskoe vodohranilišče, res., Russia	D5	26
Rybnik, Pol.	D5	20
Rycroft, Ab., Can.	B1	84
Rye, N.H., U.S.	D5	122
Rye, N.Y., U.S.	h13	125
Rye Beach, N.H., U.S.	E5	122
Rye Patch Dam, Nv., U.S.	C3	121
Rye Patch Reservoir, res., Nv., U.S.	C3	121
Ryl'sk, Russia	D13	20
Ryukyu Islands see Nansei-shotō, is., Japan	A9	34
Ryukyu Trench	F15	64
Rzeszów, Pol.	D7	20
Ržev, Russia	D5	26

S

Name	Map Ref.	Page
Saarbrücken, Ger.	F10	12
Saaremaa, i., Est.	G10	10
Saarijärvi, Fin.	E11	10

Name	Map Ref.	Page

Saarlouis, Ger. **F10**   12
Saatlı, Azer. **C13**   44
Saba, i., Neth. Ant. **B7**   80
Šabac, Yugo. **B7**   18
Sabadell, Spain **G8**   16
Sabah, hist. reg., Malay. . **B5**   36
Sabana, Archipiélago de, is.,
    Cuba **A3**   80
Sabanalarga, Col. **C5**   80
Sabattus, Me., U.S. **D2**   112
Sāberī, Hāmūn-e, l., Asia . **D8**   42
Sabetha, Ks., U.S. **C8**   109
Sabhā, Libya **E7**   48
Sabi (Save), stm., Afr. . . . **B5**   56
Sabillasville, Md., U.S. . . . **A3**   113
Sabina, Oh., U.S. **C2**   128
Sabinal, Tx., U.S. **E3**   136
Sabinal, Cayo, i., Cuba . . **A4**   80
Sabinas, Mex. **B4**   78
Sabinas Hidalgo, Mex. . . . **B4**   78
Sabine, co., La., U.S. **C2**   111
Sabine, co., Tx., U.S. **D6**   136
Sabine, stm., U.S. **E9**   92
Sabine, stm., U.S. **D6**   136
Sabine Lake, l., U.S. **E2**   111
Sabine Pass, strt., U.S. . . . **E2**   111
Sabirabad, Azer. **B13**   44
Sable, Cape, c., Fl., U.S. . . **G5**   102
Sable Island, i., N.S., Can. . **F10**   87
Sabrina Coast, Ant. **C16**   67
Sabula, Ia., U.S. **B7**   108
Şabyā, Sau. Ar. **G4**   38
Sabzevār, Iran **C7**   42
Sac, co., Ia., U.S. **B2**   108
Sac, stm., Mo., U.S. **D4**   118
Sacajawea, Lake, res., Wa.,
    U.S. **C7**   140
Sacajawea Peak, mtn., Or.,
    U.S. **B9**   130
Sacandaga Lake, l., N.Y.,
    U.S. **B6**   125
Sac and Fox Indian
    Reservation, Ia., U.S. . . **C5**   108
Sacaton, Az., U.S. **D4**   96
Sac City, Ia., U.S. **B2**   108
Săcele, Rom. **G8**   20
Sachse, Tx., U.S. **n10**   136
Sachsen, hist. reg., Ger. . . **E13**   12
Sachuest Point, c., R.I., U.S. **F6**   132
Sackville, N.B., Can. **D5**   87
Saco, Me., U.S. **E2**   112
Saco, stm., U.S. **E2**   112
Saco, East Branch, stm.,
    N.H., U.S. **B4**   122
Sacramento, Ca., U.S. . . . **C3**   98
Sacramento, co., Ca., U.S. . **C3**   98
Sacramento, stm., Ca., U.S. **C3**   98
Sacramento, stm., N.M.,
    U.S. **E4**   124
Sacramento Mountains,
    mts., N.M., U.S. **E4**   124
Sacramento Valley, val., Ca.,
    U.S. **C2**   98
Sacré-Coeur-Saguenay,
    P.Q., Can. **A8**   90
Sacred Heart, Mn., U.S. . . **F3**   116
Şa'dah, Yemen **G4**   38
Saddle, mtn., N.J., U.S. . . . **h8**   123
Saddleback Mountain, mtn.,
    Az., U.S. **k8**   96
Saddle Brook, N.J., U.S. . . **h8**   123
Saddlebunch Keys, is., Fl.,
    U.S. **H5**   102
Saddle Mountain, mtn., Or.,
    U.S. **B3**   130
Saddle Mountains, mts.,
    Wa., U.S. **C5**   140
Saddle River, N.J., U.S. . . . **A4**   123
Sa Dec, Viet. **D5**   34
Sado, i., Japan **D15**   28
Sado-kaikyō, strt., Japan . . **C3**   31
Šadrinsk, Russia **D8**   26
Saegertown, Pa., U.S. **C1**   131
Safāga, Egypt **E11**   48
Safety Harbor, Fl., U.S. . . . **E4**   102
Säffle, Swe. **G5**   10
Safford, Az., U.S. **E6**   96
Safi, Mor. **D3**   48
Safonovo, Russia **B12**   22
Safonovo, Russia **A8**   22
Safranbolu, Tur. **B5**   44
Saga, China **F5**   28
Saga, Japan **D2**   31
Sagadahoc, co., Me., U.S. . **E3**   112
Sagaing, Myan. **B3**   34
Sagamore Hills, Oh., U.S. . **n9**   128
Saganaga Lake, l., Mn., U.S. **B7**   116
Sāgar, India **E3**   40
Sagarmāthā see Everest,
    Mount, mtn., Asia **D5**   40
Sagay, Phil. **D8**   32
Sag Harbor, N.Y., U.S. . . . **m16**   125
Saginaw, Mi., U.S. **E7**   115
Saginaw, Tx., U.S. **n9**   136
Saginaw, co., Mi., U.S. . . . **E6**   115
Saginaw Bay, b., Mi., U.S. . **E7**   115
Sagiz, Kaz. **E10**   22
Saglek Bay, b., Nf., Can. . . **f9**   88
Sagonar, Russia **A6**   28
Saguache, co., Co., U.S. . . **C4**   99
Sagua de Tánamo, Cuba . . **A4**   80
Sagua la Grande, Cuba . . . **A3**   80
Saguaro Lake, res., Az., U.S. **k10**   96

Saguaro National
    Monument (Tucson
    Mountain Section), Az.,
    U.S. **E4**   96
Saguaro National
    Monument, Az., U.S. . . **E5**   96
Saguenay, stm., P.Q., Can. **A7**   90
Sagunt, Spain **H6**   16
Sahagún, Col. **D4**   80
Sahalin, ostrov, i., Russia . **D16**   26
Sahara, des., Afr. **F6**   48
Sahāranpur, India **D3**   40
Sahel see Sudan, reg., Afr. **H8**   48
Sāhīwāl, Pak. **D10**   42
Sāhīwāl, Pak. **D10**   42
Şahneh, Iran **E12**   44
Šahrisabz, Uzb. **F8**   26
Šahty, Russia **E5**   26
Sahuaripa, Mex. **B3**   78
Sahuarita, Az., U.S. **F5**   96
Šahunja, Russia **C8**   22
Sa Huynh, Viet. **D5**   34
Saibai Island, i., Austl. . . . **B3**   62
Saïda, Alg. **E4**   14
Saidpur, Bngl. **D5**   40
Saidu, Pak. **D10**   42
Saigon see Thanh Pho Ho
    Chi Minh, Viet. **D5**   34
Saiki, Japan **D2**   31
Šaim, Russia **B11**   22
Saimaa, l., Fin. **F13**   10
Sā'īn Dezh, Iran **D12**   44
Saint Adolphe, Mb., Can. . **E3**   86
Sainte-Agathe, P.Q., Can. . **C6**   90
Sainte-Agathe-des-Monts,
    P.Q., Can. **C3**   90
Saint-Aimé (Massueville),
    P.Q., Can. **D5**   90
Saint-Alban, P.Q., Can. . . **C5**   90
Saint Alban's, Nf., Can. . . . **E4**   88
Saint Albans, Vt., U.S. . . . **B2**   138
Saint Albans, W.V., U.S. . . **C3**   141
Saint Albans Bay, b., Vt.,
    U.S. **B2**   138
Saint Albert, Ab., Can. . . . **C4**   84
Saint-Amand-Montrond, Fr. **D8**   16
Saint-Ambroise, P.Q., Can. **A6**   90
Saint-André-Avellin, P.Q.,
    Can. **D2**   90
Saint-André-Est, P.Q., Can. **D3**   90
Saint Andrew Bay, b., Fl.,
    U.S. **u16**   102
Saint Andrews, N.B., Can. . **D2**   87
Saint Andrews, Scot., U.K. . **B5**   12
Saint Andrews, S.C., U.S. . **C5**   133
Saint Andrews, S.C., U.S. . **F7**   133
Saint Anne, Il., U.S. **B6**   106
Sainte-Anne-de-Beaupré,
    P.Q., Can. **B7**   90
Sainte-Anne [-de-Bellevue],
    P.Q., Can. **q19**   90
Sainte Anne-de-Madawaska,
    N.B., Can. **B1**   87
Sainte Anne-des-Chênes,
    Mb., Can. **E3**   86
Saint-Anselme, P.Q., Can. . **C7**   90
Saint Ansgar, Ia., U.S. . . . **A5**   108
Saint Anthony, Nf., Can. . . **C4**   88
Saint Anthony, Id., U.S. . . **F7**   105
Saint Antoine, N.B., Can. . **C5**   87
Saint-Apollinaire, P.Q., Can. **C6**   90
Saint Arnaud, Austl. **H3**   62
Saint Arthur, N.B., Can. . . **B3**   87
Saint-Aubert, P.Q., Can. . . **B7**   90
Saint Augustin, stm., Can. . **C2**   88
Saint Augustine, Fl., U.S. . **C5**   102
Saint Austell, Eng., U.K. . . **E4**   12
Saint-Avold, Fr. **C10**   16
Saint Basile, N.B., Can. . . **B1**   87
Saint-Basile [-Sud], P.Q.,
    Can. **C6**   90
Saint-Bernard, P.Q., Can. . **C6**   90
Saint Bernard, Al., U.S. . . . **A3**   94
Saint Bernard, La., U.S. . . . **E6**   111
Saint Bernard, Oh., U.S. . . **o13**   128
Saint Bernard, co., La., U.S. **E6**   111
Saint Bernice, In., U.S. . . . **E2**   107
Saint Bride, Mount, mtn.,
    Ab., Can. **D3**   84
Saint Bride's, Nf., Can. . . . **E4**   88
Saint-Brieuc, Fr. **C5**   16
Saint-Bruno, P.Q., Can. . . **A6**   90
Saint-Casimir, P.Q., Can. . **C5**   90
Saint Catharines, On., Can. **D5**   89
Saint Catherine, Lake, l., Vt.,
    U.S. **E2**   138
Saint Catherines Island, i.,
    Ga., U.S. **E5**   103
Saint-Célestin (Annaville),
    P.Q., Can. **C5**   90
Saint-Césaire, P.Q., Can. . **D4**   90
Saint-Chamond, Fr. **E9**   16
Saint-Charles, P.Q., Can. . **C7**   90
Saint Charles, Il., U.S. . . . **B5**   106
Saint Charles, Mi., U.S. . . **E6**   115
Saint Charles, Mn., U.S. . . **G6**   116
Saint Charles, Mo., U.S. . . **C7**   118
Saint Charles, co., La., U.S. **E5**   111
Saint Charles, co., Mo., U.S. **C7**   118
Saint Christopher (Saint
    Kitts), i., St. K./N. **B7**   80
Saint Christopher and Nevis
    see Saint Kitts and
    Nevis, ctry., N.A. **E12**   76

Saint-Chrysostome, P.Q.,
    Can. **D4**   90
Saint Clair, Mi., U.S. **F8**   115
Saint Clair, Mn., U.S. **F5**   116
Saint Clair, Mo., U.S. **C6**   118
Saint Clair, Pa., U.S. **E9**   131
Saint Clair, co., Al., U.S. . . **B3**   94
Saint Clair, co., Il., U.S. . . **E3**   106
Saint Clair, co., Mi., U.S. . **F8**   115
Saint Clair, co., Mo., U.S. . **C4**   118
Saint Clair Shores, Mi., U.S. **p16**   115
Saint Clairsville, Oh., U.S. . **B5**   128
Saint Claude, Mb., Can. . . **E2**   86
Saint Cloud, Fl., U.S. **D5**   102
Saint Cloud, Mn., U.S. . . . **E4**   116
Saint-Coeur-de-Marie, P.Q.,
    Can. **A6**   90
Saint-Constant, P.Q., Can. **q19**   90
Sainte-Croix, P.Q., Can. . . **C6**   90
Saint Croix, co., Wi., U.S. . **C1**   142
Saint Croix, i., V.I.U.S. . . . **B7**   80
Saint Croix, stm., U.S. . . . **C1**   142
Saint Croix, stm., U.S. . . . **D1**   142
Saint Croix Falls, Wi., U.S. . **C1**   142
Saint Croix Stream, stm.,
    Me., U.S. **B4**   112
Saint-Damase, P.Q., Can. . **D4**   90
Saint David, Az., U.S. **F5**   96
Saint-David-de-
    l'Auberivière, P.Q.,
    Can. **n17**   90
Saint-Denis, P.Q., Can. . . **D4**   90
Saint-Denis, Reu. **g10**   57a
Saint-Dié, Fr. **C10**   16
Saint-Dizier, Fr. **C9**   16
Saint-Dominique, P.Q., Can. **D5**   90
Saint Edward, Ne., U.S. . . **C8**   120
Saint Eleanor's, P.E., Can. . **C6**   87
Saint Elias, Cape, c., Ak.,
    U.S. **D11**   95
Saint Elias, Mount, mtn.,
    N.A. **F11**   82
Saint-Élie, Fr. Gu. **C9**   70
Saint Elmo, Al., U.S. **E1**   94
Saint Elmo, Il., U.S. **D5**   106
Saint-Éphrem [-de-Tring],
    P.Q., Can. **C7**   90
Saint-Étienne, Fr. **E9**   16
Saint-Eustache, P.Q., Can. **D4**   90
Saint-Félicien, P.Q., Can. . **A5**   90
Saint-Félix-de-Valois, P.Q.,
    Can. **C4**   90
Saint-Ferdinand
    (Bernierville), P.Q.,
    Can. **C6**   90
Saint-Ferréol [-les-Neiges],
    P.Q., Can. **B7**   90
Saint-Flavien, P.Q., Can. . **C6**   90
Sainte-Foy, P.Q., Can. . . . **n17**   90
Saint Francis, Ks., U.S. . . . **C2**   109
Saint Francis, Mn., U.S. . . **E5**   116
Saint Francis, S.D., U.S. . . **D5**   134
Saint Francis, Wi., U.S. . . . **n12**   142
Saint Francis, co., Ar., U.S. **B5**   97
Saint Francis, stm., U.S. . . **A5**   97
Saint Francis, Cape, c., Nf.,
    Can. **E5**   88
Saint Francis, Cape, c., S.
    Afr. **E3**   56
Saint Francisville, Il., U.S. . **E6**   106
Saint Francisville, La., U.S. . **D4**   111
Saint Francois, co., Mo.,
    U.S. **D7**   118
Saint-François, stm., P.Q.,
    Can. **D5**   90
Saint-François, Lac, l., P.Q.,
    Can. **D6**   90
Saint Francois Mountains,
    hills, Mo., U.S. **D7**   118
Saint Froid Lake, l., Me.,
    U.S. **B4**   112
Saint-Fulgence, P.Q., Can. **A7**   90
Saint-Gabriel, P.Q., Can. . **C4**   90
Saint-Gaudens, Fr. **F7**   16
Saint-Gédéon, P.Q., Can. . **D7**   90
Sainte Genevieve, Mo., U.S. **D7**   118
Sainte Genevieve, co., Mo.,
    U.S. **D7**   118
Saint George, Austl. **F4**   62
Saint George, On., Can. . . **D4**   89
Saint George, S.C., U.S. . . **E6**   133
Saint George, Ut., U.S. . . . **F2**   137
Saint George, Cape, c., Nf.,
    Can. **D2**   88
Saint George, Cape, c., Fl.,
    U.S. **C1**   102
Saint George Island, i., Ak.,
    U.S. **D6**   95
Saint George Island, i., Fl.,
    U.S. **C2**   102
Saint George's, Nf., Can. . **D2**   88
Saint-Georges, P.Q., Can. . **C5**   90
Saint-Georges, Fr. Gu. . . . **C9**   70
Saint George's, Gren. . . . **C7**   80
Saint-Georges, De., U.S. . . **B3**   101
Saint George's Bay, b., Nf.,
    Can. **D2**   88
Saint Georges Bay, b., N.S.,
    Can. **D8**   87
Saint-Georges, Channel,
    strt., Eur. **B3**   16
Saint-Georges-Ouest (part
    of Ville-Saint-Georges),
    P.Q., Can. **C7**   90

Saint-Gervais, P.Q., Can. . **C7**   90
Saint-Gilles, P.Q., Can. . . . **C6**   90
Saint Gotthard Pass see San
    Gottardo, Passo del,
    Switz. **A2**   18
Saint-Grégoire (Larochelle),
    P.Q., Can. **C5**   90
Saint-Guillaume-d'Upton,
    P.Q., Can. **D5**   90
Saint Helen, Lake, l., Mi.,
    U.S. **D6**   115
Saint Helena, Ca., U.S. . . . **C2**   98
Saint Helena, co., La., U.S. **D5**   111
Saint Helena, dep., Afr. . . **K9**   46
Saint Helena Island, i., S.C.,
    U.S. **G6**   133
Saint Helena Sound, strt.,
    S.C., U.S. **G7**   133
Saint Helens, Or., U.S. . . . **B4**   130
Saint Helens, Mount, vol.,
    Wa., U.S. **C3**   140
Saint Helier, Jersey **F5**   12
Saint Henry, Oh., U.S. . . . **B1**   128
Saint-Honoré, P.Q., Can. . **D7**   90
Saint-Hubert, P.Q., Can. . . **q20**   90
Saint-Hubert-de-
    Témiscouata, P.Q.,
    Can. **B8**   90
Saint-Hyacinthe, P.Q., Can. **D5**   90
Saint Ignace, Mi., U.S. . . . **C6**   115
Saint Ignatius, Mt., U.S. . . **C2**   119
Saint Isidore de Prescott,
    On., Can. **B10**   89
Saint Jacobs, On., Can. . . **D4**   89
Saint Jacques, N.B., Can. . **B1**   87
Saint Jacques, P.Q., Can. . **D4**   90
Saint James, Mn., U.S. . . . **G4**   116
Saint James, Mo., U.S. . . . **D6**   118
Saint James, co., La., U.S. **D5**   111
Saint James, Cape, c., B.C. **D2**   85
Saint James City, Fl., U.S. . **F4**   102
Saint-Jean, stm., P.Q., Can. **A7**   90
Saint-Jean, Lac, l., P.Q.,
    Can. **A5**   90
Saint Jean Baptiste, Mb.,
    Can. **E3**   86
Saint-Jean-Chrysostome,
    P.Q., Can. **o17**   90
Saint-Jean-d'Angély, Fr. . . **E6**   16
Saint-Jean-sur-Richelieu,
    P.Q., Can. **D4**   90
Saint-Jérôme, P.Q., Can. . **D3**   90
Saint Jo, Tx., U.S. **C4**   136
Saint-Joachim, P.Q., Can. . **B7**   90
Saint Joe, stm., Id., U.S. . . **B3**   105
Saint John, N.B., Can. . . . **D3**   87
Saint John, In., U.S. **B3**   107
Saint John, Ks., U.S. **E5**   109
Saint John, i., V.I.U.S. **B7**   80
Saint John, stm., N.A. . . . **B14**   92
Saint John, Cape, c., Nf.,
    Can. **D4**   88
Saint John Bay, b., Nf., Can. **C3**   88
Saint John's, Antig. **B7**   80
Saint John's, Nf., Can. . . . **E5**   88
Saint Johns, Az., U.S. **C6**   96
Saint Johns, Mi., U.S. . . . **F6**   115
Saint Johns, co., Fl., U.S. . **C5**   102
Saint Johns, stm., Fl., U.S. . **B5**   102
Saint Johnsbury, Vt., U.S. . **C4**   138
Saint Johnsville, N.Y., U.S. **B6**   125
Saint John the Baptist, co.,
    La., U.S. **D5**   111
Saint Jones, stm., De., U.S. **D4**   101
Saint Joseph, N.B., Can. . . **D5**   87
Saint Joseph, Il., U.S. **C5**   106
Saint Joseph, La., U.S. . . . **C4**   111
Saint Joseph, Mi., U.S. . . . **F4**   115
Saint Joseph, Mn., U.S. . . **E4**   116
Saint Joseph, Mo., U.S. . . **B3**   118
Saint Joseph, Tn., U.S. . . . **B4**   135
Saint Joseph, co., In., U.S. **A5**   107
Saint Joseph, co., Mi., U.S. **G5**   115
Saint Joseph, stm., U.S. . . **F5**   115
Saint-Joseph, Lac, l., P.Q.,
    Can. **n16**   90
Saint Joseph, Lake, l., On.,
    Can. **o17**   89
Saint Joseph Bay, b., Fl.,
    U.S. **C1**   102
Saint-Joseph-de-Beauce,
    P.Q., Can. **C7**   90
Saint Joseph Point, c., Fl.,
    U.S. **v16**   102
Saint Joseph Sound, strt.,
    Fl., U.S. **o10**   102
Saint-Jovite, P.Q., Can. . . **C3**   90
Saint-Junien, Fr. **E7**   16
Saint Kitts see Saint
    Christopher, i., St.
    K./N. **B7**   80
Saint Kitts and Nevis, ctry.,
    N.A. **E12**   76
Saint-Lambert, P.Q., Can. . **p19**   90
Saint Landry, co., La., U.S. **D3**   111
Saint Laurent du Maroni, Fr.
    Gu. **B9**   70
Saint Lawrence, Nf., Can. . **E4**   88
Saint Lawrence, co., N.Y.,
    U.S. **A5**   125
Saint Lawrence, stm., N.A. **B14**   92

Saint Lawrence, Cape, c.,
    N.S., Can. **B9**   87
Saint Lawrence, Gulf of, b.,
    Can. **I27**   82
Saint Lawrence Island, i.,
    Ak., U.S. **C5**   95
Saint Lawrence Islands
    National Park, On.,
    Can. **C9**   89
Saint Léonard, N.B., Can. . **B2**   87
Saint-Léonard [-d'Aston],
    P.Q., Can. **C5**   90
Saint-Liboire, P.Q., Can. . . **D5**   90
Saint-Lô, Fr. **C6**   16
Saint-Louis, Sen. **C1**   50
Saint Louis, Mi., U.S. **E6**   115
Saint Louis, Mo., U.S. . . . **C7**   118
Saint Louis, co., Mn., U.S. . **C6**   116
Saint Louis, co., Mo., U.S. . **C7**   118
Saint Louis, stm., U.S. . . . **D6**   116
Saint-Louis, Lac, l., P.Q.,
    Can. **q19**   90
Saint Louis Bay, b., Ms.,
    U.S. **f7**   117
Saint-Louis-de-Gonzague,
    P.Q., Can. **D3**   90
Saint-Louis-de-Kent, N.B.,
    Can. **C5**   87
Saint-Louis-du-Ha! Ha!,
    P.Q., Can. **B8**   90
Saint Louis Park, Mn., U.S. **n12**   116
Saint-Luc, P.Q., Can. **D4**   90
Saint Lucia, ctry., N.A. . . . **F12**   76
Saint Lucia, Lake, l., S. Afr. **D5**   56
Saint Lucia Channel, strt.,
    N.A. **C7**   80
Saint Lucie, co., Fl., U.S. . . **E6**   102
Saint Lucie Canal, Fl., U.S. **F6**   102
Saint Lucie Inlet, b., Fl.,
    U.S. **E6**   102
Sainte-Madeleine, P.Q.,
    Can. **D4**   90
Saint Magnus Bay, b., Scot.,
    U.K. **h19**   12a
Saint Malo, Mb., Can. . . . **E3**   86
Saint-Malo, Fr. **C6**   16
Saint-Malo, Golfe de, b., Fr. **C5**   16
Saint-Marc, Haiti **B5**   80
Saint-Marc [-des-Carrières],
    P.Q., Can. **C5**   90
Saint Margaret Bay, b., Nf.,
    Can. **C3**   88
Sainte-Marguerite, stm.,
    P.Q., Can. **A7**   90
Sainte-Marie, P.Q., Can. . . **C6**   90
Sainte Marie, Nosy, i.,
    Madag. **B8**   56
Saint Maries, Id., U.S. . . . **B2**   105
Sainte-Marthe, P.Q., Can. . **D3**   90
Saint Martin, co., La., U.S. **D4**   111
Saint-Martin, i., N.A. **B7**   80
Saint Martin, Lake, l., Mb.,
    Can. **D2**   86
Saint Martin Island, i., Mi.,
    U.S. **C4**   115
Saint Martinville, La., U.S. . **D4**   111
Saint Mary, co., La., U.S. . **E4**   111
Saint Mary-of-the-Woods,
    In., U.S. **E3**   107
Saint Mary Peak, mtn.,
    Austl. **G2**   62
Saint Marys, Austl. **I4**   62
Saint Marys, Nf., Can. . . . **E5**   88
Saint Marys, On., Can. . . . **D3**   89
Saint Marys, Ak., U.S. . . . **C7**   95
Saint Marys, Ga., U.S. . . . **F5**   103
Saint Marys, In., U.S. **A5**   107
Saint Marys, Ks., U.S. . . . **C7**   109
Saint Marys, Oh., U.S. . . . **B1**   128
Saint Marys, Pa., U.S. . . . **D4**   131
Saint Marys, W.V., U.S. . . . **B3**   141
Saint Marys, co., Md., U.S. **D5**   113
Saint Marys, stm., N.S., Can. **D8**   87
Saint Marys, stm., Md., U.S. **D5**   113
Saint Marys, stm., U.S. . . . **F5**   103
Saint Marys, stm., U.S. . . . **C8**   107
Saint Mary's, Cape, c., Nf.,
    Can. **E4**   88
Saint Mary's Bay, b., Nf.,
    Can. **E5**   88
Saint Marys Bay, b., N.S.,
    Can. **E3**   87
Saint Marys City, Md., U.S. **D5**   113
Saint Matthew Island, i.,
    Ak., U.S. **C5**   95
Saint Matthews, Ky., U.S. . **B4**   110
Saint Matthews, S.C., U.S. **D6**   133
Saint-Maurice, stm., P.Q.,
    Can. **B5**   90
Saint Michael, Mn., U.S. . . **E5**   116
Saint Michaels, Md., U.S. . **C5**   113
Saint-Michel [-de-
    Bellechasse], P.Q., Can. **C7**   90
Saint-Nazaire, Fr. **D5**   16
Saint-Nicolas, P.Q., Can. . **o17**   90
Saint-Odilon, P.Q., Can. . . **C7**   90
Saint-Omer, Fr. **B8**   16
Saint-Ours, P.Q., Can. . . . **D4**   90
Saint-Pacôme, P.Q., Can. . **B8**   90
Saint-Pamphile, P.Q., Can. **C8**   90
Saint Paris, Oh., U.S. **B2**   128
Saint-Pascal, P.Q., Can. . . **B8**   90
Saint Paul, Ab., Can. **B5**   84
Saint-Paul, Reu. **g10**   57a
Saint Paul, Ak., U.S. **D5**   95

Name	Map Ref.	Page

Saint Paul, In., U.S. **F6** 107
Saint Paul, Ks., U.S. **E8** 109
Saint Paul, Mn., U.S. **F5** 116
Saint Paul, Mo., U.S. **f12** 118
Saint Paul, Ne., U.S. **C7** 120
Saint Paul, Va., U.S. **f9** 139
Saint Paul Island, i., Ak.,
  U.S. **D5** 95
Saint Paul Park, Mn., U.S. . **n12** 116
Saint Pauls, N.C., U.S. **C4** 126
Sainte-Perpétue-de-L'Islet,
  P.Q., Can. **B8** 90
Saint Peter, Mn., U.S. **F5** 116
Saint Peter Port, Guernsey . **F5** 12
Saint Peters, N.S., Can. .. **D9** 87
Saint Peters, Mo., U.S. **C7** 118
Saint Petersburg see Sankt-
  Peterburg, Russia **D5** 26
Saint Petersburg, Fl., U.S. .. **E4** 102
Saint Petersburg Beach, Fl.,
  U.S. **p10** 102
Saint Phillips Island, i., S.C.,
  U.S. **G6** 133
Saint-Pie, P.Q., Can. **D5** 90
Saint-Pierre, Reu. **g10** 57a
Saint-Pierre, St. P./M. ... **E3** 88
Saint-Pierre, i., Sey. **i12** 57b
Saint-Pierre, Lac, l., P.Q.,
  Can. **C5** 90
Saint Pierre and Miquelon,
  dep., N.A. **I28** 82
Saint Pierre-Jolys, Mb., Can. **E3** 86
Saint-Prime, P.Q., Can. .. **A5** 90
Saint Quentin, N.B., Can. .. **B2** 87
Saint-Quentin, Fr. **C8** 16
Saint-Raphaël, P.Q., Can. .. **C7** 90
Saint-Raphaël, Fr. **F10** 16
Saint-Raymond, P.Q., Can. . **C6** 90
Saint-Rédempteur, P.Q.,
  Can. **o17** 90
Saint Regis, Mt., U.S. **C1** 119
Saint Regis, West Branch,
  stm., N.Y., U.S. **f10** 125
Saint-Rémi, P.Q., Can. .. **D4** 90
Saint-Romuald, P.Q., Can. . **C6** 90
Saint Rose, La., U.S. **k11** 111
Sainte Rose du Lac, Mb.,
  Can. **D2** 86
Saintes, Fr. **E6** 16
Saint Sauveur, N.B., Can. .. **B4** 87
Saint-Sauveur-des-Monts,
  P.Q., Can. **D3** 90
Saint-Siméon, P.Q., Can. . **B8** 90
Saint Simons Island, Ga.,
  U.S. **E5** 103
Saint Simons Island, i., Ga.,
  U.S. **E5** 103
Saint Stephen, N.B., Can. . **D2** 87
Saint Stephen, S.C., U.S. .. **E8** 133
Saint Tammany, co., La.,
  U.S. **D5** 111
Sainte-Thècle, P.Q., Can. .. **C5** 90
Sainte-Thérèse, P.Q., Can. . **D4** 90
Saint Thomas, On., Can. .. **E3** 89
Saint Thomas, i., V.I.U.S. .. **B6** 80
Saint Timothée, P.Q., Can. . **q18** 90
Saint-Tite, P.Q., Can. .. **C5** 90
Saint-Tropez, Fr. **F10** 16
Sainte-Véronique, P.Q.,
  Can. **C3** 90
Saint-Victor, P.Q., Can. . **C7** 90
Saint Vincent, i., St. Vin. ... **C7** 80
Saint Vincent and the
  Grenadines, ctry., N.A. **F12** 76
Saint Vincent Island, i., Fl.,
  U.S. **C1** 102
Saint Vincent Passage, strt.,
  N.A. **C7** 80
Saint Vincent's [-Saint
  Stephens-Peter's River],
  Nf., Can. **E5** 88
Saint Walburg, Sk., Can. .. **D1** 91
Saint-Zacharie, P.Q., Can. . **C7** 90
Saipan, i., N. Mar. Is. ... **C12** 32
Sajama, Nevado, mtn., Bol. **B4** 72
Sakakawea, Lake, res., N.D.,
  U.S. **B3** 127
Sakania, D.R.C. **F5** 54
Sakarya, Tur. **B4** 44
Sakarya, stm., Tur. **B4** 44
Sakata, Japan **D15** 28
Sakété, Benin **E5** 50
Sakha [see Jakutija, state,
  Russia **C14** 26
Sakhalin see Sahalin, ostrov,
  i., Russia **D16** 26
Sakon Nakhon, Thai. **C4** 34
Sakonnet, stm., R.I., U.S. .. **E6** 132
Sakonnet Point, c., R.I., U.S. **F6** 132
Sakrivier, S. Afr. **E3** 56
Saky, Ukr. **G12** 20
Sal, i., C.V. **g10** 50a
Sal, Point, c., Ca., U.S. .. **E3** 98
Sala, Swe. **G7** 10
Salaberry-de-Valleyfield,
  P.Q., Can. **D3** 90
Salacgrīva, Lat. **H11** 10
Sala Consilina, Italy **D5** 18
Salada, Laguna, l., Mex. .. **A1** 78
Saladillo, Ar. **F6** 72
Salado, stm., Arg. **F4** 72
Salado, stm., Arg. **F3** 72
Salado, stm., Arg. **D5** 72
Salado, stm., Mex. **B5** 78
Salado, Rio, stm., N.M., U.S. **C2** 124

Salaga, Ghana **E4** 50
Salal, Chad **D8** 50
Salālah, Oman **G6** 38
Salamanca, Mex. **C4** 78
Salamanca, Spain **G4** 16
Salamanca, N.Y., U.S. **C2** 125
Salamís, i., Grc. **F9** 18
Salamis, hist., N. Cyp. **E5** 44
Salamīyah, Syria **E7** 44
Salamonie, stm., In., U.S. .. **C6** 107
Salamonie Lake, res., In.,
  U.S. **C6** 107
Salavat, Russia **D7** 26
Salawati, i., Indon. **D8** 36
Sala y Gómez, Isla, i., Chile **K28** 64
Sala y Gomez Ridge **K28** 64
Saldanha, S. Afr. **E2** 56
Saldus, Lat. **H10** 10
Sale, Austl. **H4** 62
Salé, Mor. **E2** 14
Sale Creek, Tn., U.S. **D8** 135
Salehard, Russia **C8** 26
Salem, India **G3** 40
Salem, Ar., U.S. **A4** 97
Salem, Il., U.S. **E5** 106
Salem, In., U.S. **G5** 107
Salem, Ky., U.S. **e9** 110
Salem, Ma., U.S. **A6** 114
Salem, Mo., U.S. **D6** 118
Salem, N.H., U.S. **E4** 122
Salem, N.J., U.S. **D2** 123
Salem, Oh., U.S. **B5** 128
Salem, Or., U.S. **C4** 130
Salem, S.D., U.S. **D8** 134
Salem, Ut., U.S. **C4** 137
Salem, Va., U.S. **C2** 139
Salem, W.V., U.S. **B4** 141
Salem, Wi., U.S. **n11** 142
Salem, co., N.J., U.S. ... **D2** 123
Salem, stm., N.J., U.S. ... **D2** 123
Salem, Lake, l., Vt., U.S. .. **B4** 138
Salerno, Italy **D5** 18
Salerno, Golfo di, b., Italy .. **D5** 18
Salgótarján, Hung. **E5** 20
Salgueiro, Braz. **C4** 74
Salida, Co., U.S. **C5** 99
Salihli, Tur. **C3** 44
Salihorsk, Bela. **C9** 20
Salima, Mwi. **A5** 56
Salina, Ks., U.S. **D6** 109
Salina, Ok., U.S. **A6** 129
Salina, Ut., U.S. **E4** 137
Salina Cruz, Mex. **D5** 78
Salinas, Braz. **E3** 74
Salinas, Ec. **D3** 70
Salinas, Ca., U.S. **D3** 98
Salinas, stm., N.A. **B1** 80
Salinas, stm., Ca., U.S. .. **D3** 98
Salinas de Hidalgo, Mex. .. **C4** 78
Salinas Peak, mtn., N.M.,
  U.S. **D3** 124
Salinas Pueblo Missions
  National Monument,
  N.M., U.S. **C3** 124
Saline, Mi., U.S. **F7** 115
Saline, co., Ar., U.S. **C3** 97
Saline, co., Il., U.S. **F5** 106
Saline, co., Ks., U.S. **D6** 109
Saline, co., Mo., U.S. **B4** 118
Saline, co., Ne., U.S. **D8** 120
Saline, stm., Ar., U.S. **C1** 97
Saline, stm., Ar., U.S. **D4** 97
Saline, stm., Ks., U.S. **C3** 109
Saline, North Fork, stm., Il.,
  U.S. **F5** 106
Saline Lake, res., La., U.S. .. **C3** 111
Salineville, Oh., U.S. **B5** 128
Salinópolis, Braz. **B2** 74
Salisbury, Austl. **G2** 62
Salisbury, N.B., Can. **C4** 87
Salisbury, Ct., U.S. **B2** 100
Salisbury, Ma., U.S. **A6** 114
Salisbury, Md., U.S. **D6** 113
Salisbury, Mo., U.S. **B5** 118
Salisbury, N.C., U.S. **B2** 126
Salisbury see Harare, Zimb. **B5** 56
Salish Mountains, mts., Mt.,
  U.S. **B2** 119
Salkehatchie, stm., S.C.,
  U.S. **E5** 133
Salla, Fin. **C13** 10
Sallisaw, Ok., U.S. **B7** 129
Salluit, P.Q., Can. **f11** 90
Salmãs, Iran **C11** 44
Salmo, B.C., Can. **E9** 85
Salmon, Id., U.S. **D5** 105
Salmon, stm., N.B., Can. .. **C4** 87
Salmon, stm., Id., U.S. ... **D3** 105
Salmon Creek, Wa., U.S. .. **D3** 140
Salmon Creek Reservoir,
  res., Id., U.S. **G4** 105
Salmon Falls, stm., U.S. .. **D5** 122
Salmon Falls Creek, stm.,
  U.S. **G4** 105
Salmon Mountains, mts.,
  Ca., U.S. **B2** 98
Salmon Point, c., On., Can. **D7** 89
Salmon River Mountains,
  mts., Id., U.S. **E3** 105
Salmon River Reservoir,
  res., N.Y., U.S. **B5** 125
Salo, Fin. **F10** 10
Salò, Italy **B3** 18
Salome, Az., U.S. **D2** 96
Salon-de-Provence, Fr. .. **F9** 16

Salonika see Thessaloníki,
  Grc. **D9** 18
Salonika, Gulf of see
  Thermaïkós Kólpos, b.,
  Grc. **D9** 18
Salonta, Rom. **F6** 20
Sal'sk, Russia **E7** 22
Salt, stm., Az., U.S. **D4** 96
Salt, stm., Ky., U.S. **C4** 110
Salt, stm., Mo., U.S. **B6** 118
Salta, Arg. **A3** 72
Salt Creek, stm., N.M., U.S. **D5** 124
Salt Creek, stm., Oh., U.S. .. **C3** 128
Salt Creek, stm., Wy., U.S. .. **C6** 143
Salter Path, N.C., U.S. **C6** 126
Salt Fork Lake, res., Oh.,
  U.S. **B4** 128
Saltillo, Mex. **B4** 78
Saltillo, Ms., U.S. **A5** 117
Salt Lake, co., Ut., U.S. ... **C3** 137
Salt Lake, l., Hi., U.S. ... **g10** 104
Salt Lake, l., N.M., U.S. ... **E6** 124
Salt Lake City, Ut., U.S. .. **C4** 137
Salto, Ur. **E6** 72
Salton Sea, l., Ca., U.S. ... **F5** 98
Saltonstall, l., Ct., U.S. **D4** 100
Salt Point, c., Ca., U.S. ... **C2** 98
Salt River Indian
  Reservation, Az., U.S. . **k9** 96
Salt River Range, mts., Wy.,
  U.S. **D2** 143
Saltsburg, Pa., U.S. **F3** 131
Salt Springs, Fl., U.S. **C5** 102
Saltville, Va., U.S. **f10** 139
Salt Wells Creek, stm., Wy.,
  U.S. **E4** 143
Saluda, S.C., U.S. **C4** 133
Saluda, co., S.C., U.S. ... **C4** 133
Saluda, stm., S.C., U.S. .. **C4** 133
Saluda Dam, S.C., U.S. .. **C5** 133
Salūm, Egypt **D10** 48
Sālūr, India **F4** 40
Salvador, Braz. **B4** 74
Salvador, El see El Salvador,
  ctry., N.A. **C2** 80
Salvador, Lake, l., La., U.S. **E5** 111
Salween, stm., Asia **G7** 28
Salyan, Azer. **C13** 44
Salyān, Nepal **D4** 40
Salyersville, Ky., U.S. ... **C6** 110
Salzburg, Aus. **G13** 12
Salzgitter, Ger. **D12** 12
Samah, Libya **F7** 14
Samālūt, Egypt **F10** 14
Samana Cay, i., Bah. **A5** 80
Samandağı, Tur. **D6** 44
Samar, i., Phil. **D9** 34
Samara (Kujbyšev), Russia . **D7** 26
Samarai, Pap. N. Gui. .. **I13** 32
Samarinda, Indon. **D5** 36
Samarkand, Uzb. **F8** 26
Sāmarrā', Iraq **D4** 42
Samar Sea, Phil. **D8** 34
Şamaxi, Azer. **B13** 44
Samba Caju, Ang. **E3** 54
Sambalpur, India **E4** 40
Sambas, Indon. **C3** 36
Sambava, Madag. **A9** 56
Sambhal, India **D3** 40
Sāmbhar, India **D3** 40
Sambir, Ukr. **E7** 20
Samboja, Indon. **D5** 36
Samborombón, Bahía, b.,
  Arg. **F6** 72
Samch'ŏk, S. Kor. **D13** 28
Same, Tan. **D7** 54
Samfya, Zam. **A4** 56
Samho, N. Kor. **D13** 28
Sammamish, Lake, l., Wa.,
  U.S. **e11** 140
Samoa, ctry., Oc. **F12** 58
Samoa Islands, is., Oc. ... **F12** 58
Samoded, Russia **B7** 22
Sámos, i., Grc. **F11** 18
Samoset, Fl., U.S. **q10** 102
Samothrace see Samothráki,
  i., Grc. **D10** 18
Samothráki, i., Grc. **D10** 18
Sampit, Indon. **D4** 36
Sampit, stm., S.C., U.S. .. **E9** 133
Sampit, Teluk, b., Indon. .. **D4** 36
Sampson, co., N.C., U.S. .. **B4** 126
Sam Rayburn Reservoir,
  res., Tx., U.S. **D5** 136
Samsang, China **C4** 40
Samson, Al., U.S. **D3** 94
Sam Son, Viet. **C5** 34
Samsun, Tur. **B7** 44
Samtredia, Geor. **A10** 44
Samuels, l., Id., U.S. **A5** 105
Samui, Ko, i., Thai. ... **E4** 34
Samur, stm. **B13** 44
Samut Prakan, Thai. ... **D4** 34
Samut Songkhram, Thai. .. **D4** 34
San, Mali **D4** 50
Şan'ā', Yemen **G4** 38
Sanaba, Burkina **E4** 50
Sanaga, stm., Cam. ... **C2** 54
San Agustín, Cape, c., Phil. **E9** 34
San Agustin, Plains of, pl.,
  N.M., U.S. **C2** 124
Sanak Islands, is., Ak., U.S. **E7** 95
San Ambrosio, Isla, i., Chile **H7** 2
Sanana, Pulau, i., Indon. .. **D7** 36
Sanandaj, Iran **C5** 42

San Andreas, Ca., U.S. ... **C3** 98
San Andrés, Col. **A3** 70
San Andres, Isla de, i., Col. **A3** 70
San Andres Mountains,
  mts., N.M., U.S. **E3** 124
San Andres Peak, mtn.,
  N.M., U.S. **E3** 124
San Andrés Tuxtla, Mex. .. **D5** 78
San Angelo, Tx., U.S. ... **D2** 136
San Anselmo, Ca., U.S. .. **h7** 98
San Antonio, Chile **E3** 72
San Antonio, Tx., U.S. ... **E3** 136
San Antonio, Cabo, c., Arg. **F6** 72
San Antonio, Cabo de, c.,
  Cuba **A2** 80
San Antonio Bay, b., Tx.,
  U.S. **E4** 136
San Antonio de los Baños,
  Cuba **A3** 80
San Antonio Mountain,
  mtn., N.M., U.S. **A3** 124
San Antonio Oeste, Arg. .. **F4** 69
San Augustine, Tx., U.S. .. **D5** 136
San Augustine, co., Tx., U.S. **D5** 136
San Benedetto del Tronto,
  Italy **C4** 18
San Benedicto, Isla, i., Mex. **D2** 78
San Benito, Guat. **B2** 80
San Benito, Tx., U.S. ... **F4** 136
San Benito, co., Ca., U.S. .. **D3** 98
San Benito Mountain, mtn.,
  Ca., U.S. **D3** 98
San Bernardino, Ca., U.S. .. **E5** 98
San Bernardino, co., Ca.,
  U.S. **E5** 98
San Blas, Cape, c., Fl., U.S. **v16** 102
San Borja, Bol. **A4** 72
Sanborn, Ia., U.S. **A2** 108
Sanborn, co., S.D., U.S. .. **D7** 134
Sanbornville, N.H., U.S. .. **C4** 122
San Bruno, Ca., U.S. ... **D2** 98
San Carlos, Arg. **D4** 72
San Carlos, Chile **E2** 69
San Carlos, Phil. **D8** 34
San Carlos, Phil. **C8** 34
San Carlos, Az., U.S. ... **D5** 96
San Carlos, Ven. **D6** 80
San Carlos de Bolívar, Arg. **F5** 72
San Carlos del Zulia, Ven. . **B5** 70
San Carlos de Río Negro,
  Ven. **C6** 70
San Carlos Indian
  Reservation, Az., U.S. . **D5** 96
San Carlos Lake, res., Az.,
  U.S. **D5** 96
Sánchez, Dom. Rep. ... **B6** 80
San Clemente, Ca., U.S. .. **F5** 98
San Clemente Island, i., Ca.,
  U.S. **F4** 98
San Cristóbal, Arg. **E5** 72
San Cristóbal, Dom. Rep. . **B5** 80
San Cristóbal, Ven. **B5** 70
San Cristóbal, Isla, i., Ec. .. **D2** 70
San Cristóbal de las Casas,
  Mex. **D6** 78
Sancti Spíritus, Cuba **A4** 80
Sancy, Puy de, mtn., Fr. .. **E8** 16
Sandakan, Malay. **B5** 36
Sandaré, Mali **D2** 50
Sand Creek, stm., Wy., U.S. **C7** 143
Sandefjord, Nor. **G4** 10
Sanders, Az., U.S. **B6** 96
Sanders, co., Mt., U.S. .. **C1** 119
Sanderson, Tx., U.S. .. **D1** 136
Sandersville, Ga., U.S. .. **D4** 103
Sandersville, Ms., U.S. .. **D4** 117
Sand Hill, Ma., U.S. .. **h13** 114
Sand Hill, stm., Mn., U.S. . **C2** 116
Sandia Crest, mtn., N.M. .. **k8** 124
Sandia Indian Reservation,
  N.M., U.S. **k7** 124
Sandia Mountains, mts.,
  N.M., U.S. **k8** 124
San Diego, Ca., U.S. ... **F5** 98
San Diego, Tx., U.S. ... **F3** 136
San Diego, co., Ca., U.S. .. **F5** 98
San Diego, stm., Ca., U.S. **o15** 98
San Diego, Cabo, c., Arg. . **H3** 69
San Diego Naval Station,
  mil., Ca., U.S. **o15** 98
San Diego Naval Training
  Center, mil., Ca., U.S. . **o15** 98
Sand Island, i., Hi., U.S. .. **g10** 104
Sand Island, i., Wi., U.S. .. **B3** 142
Sand Key, i., Fl., U.S. ... **E4** 102
Sandlick Creek, stm., W.V.,
  U.S. **n13** 141
Sandnes, Nor. **G1** 10
Sandoa, D.R.C. **E4** 54
Sandoval, Il., U.S. **E4** 106
Sandoval, co., N.M., U.S. . **B2** 124
Sandoway, Myan. **C2** 34
Sand Point, Ak., U.S. ... **D7** 95
Sandpoint, Id., U.S. ... **A2** 105
Sands Key, i., Fl., U.S. ... **s3** 102
Sandspring, Ok., U.S. .. **A5** 129
Sandston, Va., U.S. ... **m18** 139
Sandstone, Austl. **F2** 60
Sandstone, Mn., U.S. .. **D6** 116
Sandusky, Mi., U.S. ... **E8** 115
Sandusky, Oh., U.S. ... **A3** 128

Sandusky, co., Oh., U.S. .. **A2** 128
Sandusky, stm., Oh., U.S. . **B2** 128
Sandvika, Nor. **G4** 10
Sandviken, Swe. **F7** 10
Sandwich, Il., U.S. **B5** 106
Sandwich, Ma., U.S. ... **C7** 114
Sandwich Bay, b., Nf., Can. **B3** 88
Sandy, Or., U.S. **B4** 130
Sandy, Ut., U.S. **C4** 137
Sandy, stm., Me., U.S. .. **D2** 112
Sandy Cape, c., Austl. ... **E5** 62
Sandy Creek, stm., Oh.,
  U.S. **B4** 128
Sandy Creek, stm., Ok.,
  U.S. **C2** 129
Sandy Hook, Ct., U.S. ... **D2** 100
Sandy Hook, spit, N.J., U.S. **C5** 123
Sandy Island, i., S.C., U.S. **D9** 133
Sandykači, Turk. **F8** 26
Sandy Lake, l., Nf., Can. .. **D3** 88
Sandy Lake, l., On., Can. . **n16** 89
Sandy Neck, pen., Ma., U.S. **C7** 114
Sandy Point, c., R.I., U.S. . **h7** 132
Sandy Springs, Ga., U.S. .. **h8** 103
Sandy Springs, S.C., U.S. . **B2** 133
Sandyville, Md., U.S. ... **A4** 113
San Felipe, Chile **E3** 72
San Felipe, Col. **C6** 70
San Felipe, Mex. **A2** 78
San Felipe, Ven. **A6** 70
San Felipe Indian
  Reservation, N.M., U.S. **k8** 124
San Felipe Pueblo, N.M.,
  U.S. **B3** 124
San Fernando, Chile **D2** 69
San Fernando, Mex. **C5** 78
San Fernando, Phil. **C8** 34
San Fernando, Phil. **C8** 34
San Fernando, Spain **I3** 16
San Fernando, Trin. **C7** 80
San Fernando, Ca., U.S. . **m12** 98
San Fernando de Apure,
  Ven. **B6** 70
San Fernando de Atabapo,
  Ven. **C6** 70
San Fernando del Valle de
  Catamarca, Arg. **D4** 72
Sanford, Co., U.S. **D5** 99
Sanford, Fl., U.S. **D5** 102
Sanford, Me., U.S. **E2** 112
Sanford, Mi., U.S. **E6** 115
Sanford, N.C., U.S. **B3** 126
Sanford, Mount, mtn., Ak.,
  U.S. **C11** 95
San Francisco, Arg. **E5** 72
San Francisco, Ca., U.S. .. **D2** 98
San Francisco, co., Ca., U.S. **D2** 98
San Francisco, stm., U.S. .. **D6** 124
San Francisco Bay, b., Ca.,
  U.S. **h8** 98
San Francisco del Oro, Mex. **B3** 78
San Francisco del Rincón,
  Mex. **C4** 78
San Francisco de Macorís,
  Dom. Rep. **B5** 80
San Gabriel Mountains,
  mts., Ca., U.S. **m12** 98
Sangamner, India **F2** 40
Sangamon, co., Il., U.S. .. **D4** 106
Sangamon, stm., Il., U.S. .. **C3** 106
Sangar, Russia **C14** 26
Sange, D.R.C. **E5** 54
Sanger, Ca., U.S. **D4** 98
Sanger, Tx., U.S. **C4** 136
Sanggau, Indon. **C4** 36
Sangha, stm., Afr. **D3** 54
Sangihe, Kepulauan, is.,
  Indon. **C7** 36
Sangihe, Pulau, i., Indon. . **C7** 36
San Gil, Col. **B5** 70
San Giovanni in Fiore, Italy **E6** 18
Sangiyn Dalay, Mong. ... **C9** 28
Sāngli, India **F2** 40
Sangmélima, Cam. **C2** 54
San Gorgonio Mountain,
  mtn., Ca., U.S. **E5** 98
San Gottardo, Passo del,
  Switz. **A2** 18
Sanibel, Fl., U.S. **F4** 102
Sanibel Island, i., Fl., U.S. . **F4** 102
San Ignacio, Mex. **B2** 78
San Ignacio, Para. **D6** 72
San Ignacio de Moxo, Bol. **A4** 72
San Ignacio de Velasco, Bol. **G7** 70
Sanilac, co., Mi., U.S. ... **E8** 115
San Isidro, Arg. **E6** 72
San Jacinto, Col. **D4** 80
San Jacinto, Ca., U.S. ... **F5** 98
San Jacinto, co., Tx., U.S. . **D5** 136
San Jacinto, stm., Tx., U.S. **r14** 136
San Javier, Bol. **B5** 72
San Joaquín, Bol. **F7** 70
San Joaquin, co., Ca., U.S. **D3** 98
San Joaquin, stm., Ca., U.S. **D3** 98
San Joaquin Valley, val.,
  Ca., U.S. **D3** 98
San Jorge, Arg. **E5** 72
San Jorge, Golfo, b., Arg. . **G3** 69
San José, C.R. **D3** 80
San Jose, Ca., U.S. **D3** 98
San José, Isla, i., Mex. ... **C2** 78
San José de Chiquitos, Bol. **B5** 72
San José de Guanipa, Ven. **D7** 80
San José de Jáchal, Arg. .. **E4** 72
San José de las Lajas, Cuba **A3** 80

Name	Map Ref.	Page

San José del Cabo, Mex. . . **C3** 78
San José del Guaviare, Col. **C5** 70
San Jose Island, i., Tx., U.S. **E4** 136
San Juan, Arg. **E4** 72
San Juan, P.R. **B6** 80
San Juan, Tx., U.S. **F3** 136
San Juan, co., Co., U.S. . . . **D3** 99
San Juan, co., N.M., U.S. . . **A1** 124
San Juan, co., Ut., U.S. . . . **F5** 137
San Juan, co., Wa., U.S. . . . **A2** 140
San Juan, stm., N.A. **F8** 76
San Juan Bautista, Para. . . **D6** 72
San Juan Capistrano, Ca.,
  U.S. **F5** 98
San Juan de Colón, Ven. . . **D5** 80
San Juan de la Maguana,
  Dom. Rep. **B5** 80
San Juan del Norte, Nic. . . **C3** 80
San Juan de los Morros,
  Ven. **D6** 80
San Juan del Sur, Nic. . . . **C2** 80
San Juan Island, i., Wa.,
  U.S. **A2** 140
San Juan Mountains, mts.,
  Co., U.S. **D3** 99
San Justo, Arg. **E5** 72
Sankt Gallen, Switz. **A2** 18
Sankt-Peterburg (Saint
  Petersburg), Russia . . . **D5** 26
Sankt Pölten, Aus. **F14** 12
Sankuru, stm., D.R.C. . . . **D4** 54
San Lázaro, Cabo, c., Mex. . **C2** 78
San Leandro, Ca., U.S. . . . **h8** 98
Şanlıurfa, Tur. **D8** 44
San Lorenzo, Arg. **E5** 72
San Lorenzo, Bol. **C5** 72
San Lorenzo, Ec. **C4** 70
San Lorenzo, Cabo, c., Ec. . **D3** 70
Sanlúcar de Barrameda,
  Spain **I3** 16
San Lucas, Bol. **C4** 72
San Lucas, Mex. **C3** 78
San Lucas, Cabo, c., Mex. . **C3** 78
San Luis, Arg. **E4** 72
San Luis, Guat. **B2** 80
San Luis, Az., U.S. **E1** 96
San Luis, Co., U.S. **D5** 99
San Luis, Point, c., Ca., U.S. **E3** 98
San Luis Obispo, Ca., U.S. . **E3** 98
San Luis Obispo, co., Ca.,
  U.S. **E3** 98
San Luis Pass, strt., Tx., U.S. **r14** 136
San Luis Peak, mtn., Co.,
  U.S. **D4** 99
San Luis Potosí, Mex. **C4** 78
San Luis Potosí, state, Mex. **C4** 78
San Luis Río Colorado, Mex. **A2** 78
San Luis Valley, val., Co.,
  U.S. **D4** 99
San Manuel, Az., U.S. **E5** 96
San Marcos, Tx., U.S. **E4** 136
San Marcos, stm., Tx., U.S. **h8** 136
San Marino, Ca., U.S. **m12** 98
San Marino, ctry., Eur. . . . **C4** 18
San Martín, Arg. **E4** 72
San Martín, Col. **E5** 80
San Martín, Lago, l., S.A. . **G2** 69
San Martín de los Andes,
  Arg. **F2** 69
San Mateo, Ca., U.S. **D2** 98
San Mateo, co., Ca., U.S. . **D2** 98
San Mateo Mountains, mts.,
  N.M., U.S. **B2** 124
San Mateo Mountains, mts.,
  N.M., U.S. **D2** 124
San Matías, Golfo, b., Arg. . **F4** 69
Sanmenxia, China **E10** 28
San Miguel, El Sal. **C2** 80
San Miguel, co., Co., U.S. . **D2** 99
San Miguel, co., N.M., U.S. **B5** 124
San Miguel, stm., Co., U.S. **C2** 99
San Miguel, Golfo de, b.,
  Pan. **D4** 80
San Miguel de Tucumán,
  Arg. **D4** 72
San Miguel Island, i., Ca.,
  U.S. **E3** 98
San Miguel Mountains, mts.,
  Co., U.S. **D2** 99
Sanming, China **D4** 30
Sannār, Sudan **H11** 48
San Nicolás, Peru **B2** 72
San Nicolás de los Arroyos,
  Arg. **E5** 72
San Nicolás de los Garza,
  Mex. **B4** 78
San Nicolas Island, i., Ca.,
  U.S. **F4** 98
Sânnicolau Mare, Rom. . . **F6** 20
Sannikova, proliv, strt.,
  Russia **B15** 26
Sanok, Pol. **E7** 20
San Pablo, Phil. **D8** 34
San Pablo Bay, b., Ca., U.S. **g8** 98
San Patricio, co., Tx., U.S. **E4** 136
San Pedro, Arg. **C5** 72
San Pedro, Arg. **E6** 72
San-Pédro, C. Iv. **F3** 50
San Pedro, stm., N.A. . . . **A2** 96
San Pedro, stm., Az., U.S. . **E5** 96
San Pedro Bay, b., Ca., U.S. **n12** 98
San Pedro de las Colonias,
  Mex. **B4** 78
San Pedro de Macorís,
  Dom. Rep. **B6** 80

San Pedro de Ycuamandiyú,
  Para. **C6** 72
San Pedro Peaks, mts.,
  N.M., U.S. **A3** 124
San Pedro Sula, Hond. . . . **B2** 80
Sanpete, co., Ut., U.S. . . . **D4** 137
San Pietro, Isola di, i., Italy **E2** 18
Sanpoil, stm., Wa., U.S. . . **A7** 140
San Quintín, Cabo, c., Mex. **A1** 78
San Rafael, Arg. **E4** 72
San Rafael, Ca., U.S. **D2** 98
San Rafael, N.M., U.S. . . . **B2** 124
San Rafael, Ven. **C5** 80
San Rafael, stm., Ut., U.S. . **D5** 137
San Rafael Knob, mtn., Ut.,
  U.S. **E5** 137
San Rafael Mountains, mts.,
  Ca., U.S. **E4** 98
San Ramon, Ca., U.S. **h9** 98
San Ramón de la Nueva
  Orán, Arg. **C5** 72
San Remo, Italy **C1** 18
San Roque, Punta, c., Mex. **B2** 78
San Saba, Tx., U.S. **D3** 136
San Saba, co., Tx., U.S. . . **D3** 136
San Salvador, El Sal. **C2** 80
San Salvador, i., Bah. **D10** 76
San Salvador de Jujuy, Arg. **C4** 72
Sansanné-Mango, Togo . . **D5** 50
San Sebastián see Donostia,
  Spain **F6** 16
San Severo, Italy **D5** 18
San Simon, stm., Az., U.S. . **E6** 96
Santa Ana, Bol. **A4** 72
Santa Ana, El Sal. **C1** 80
Santa Ana, Mex. **A2** 78
Santa Ana, Ca., U.S. **F5** 98
Santa Ana, stm., Ca., U.S. . **n13** 98
Santa Ana Indian
  Reservation, N.M., U.S. **h7** 124
Santa Ana Mountains, mts.,
  Ca., U.S. **n13** 98
Santa Anna, Tx., U.S. **D3** 136
Santa Bárbara, Hond. **B2** 80
Santa Bárbara, Mex. **B3** 78
Santa Barbara, Ca., U.S. . . **E4** 98
Santa Bárbara, Ven. **D5** 80
Santa Barbara, co., Ca., U.S. **E3** 98
Santa Barbara Channel, strt.,
  Ca., U.S. **E3** 98
Santa Barbara Island, i., Ca.,
  U.S. **F4** 98
Santa Catalina, Gulf of, b.,
  Ca., U.S. **F5** 98
Santa Catalina Island, i., Ca.,
  U.S. **F4** 98
Santa Catalina Mountains,
  mts., Az., U.S. **E5** 96
Santa Catarina, state, Braz. **D7** 72
Santa Catarina, Ilha de, i.,
  Braz. **D8** 72
Santa Clara, Cuba **A3** 80
Santa Clara, Ca., U.S. . . . **D2** 98
Santa Clara, Ut., U.S. . . . **F2** 137
Santa Clara, co., Ca., U.S. . **D3** 98
Santa Clara, stm., Ca., U.S. **E4** 98
Santa Claus, In., U.S. **H4** 107
Santa Cruz, Phil. **D8** 34
Santa Cruz, Ca., U.S. **D2** 98
Santa Cruz, N.M., U.S. . . . **B3** 124
Santa Cruz, co., Az., U.S. . **F5** 96
Santa Cruz, co., Ca., U.S. . **D2** 98
Santa Cruz, stm., Az., U.S. . **E4** 96
Santa Cruz, Isla, i., Ec. . . . **D1** 70
Santa Cruz de la Palma,
  Spain **A1** 50
Santa Cruz de la Sierra, Bol. **B5** 72
Santa Cruz del Quiché,
  Guat. **B1** 80
Santa Cruz del Sur, Cuba . **A4** 80
Santa Cruz de Tenerife,
  Spain **A1** 50
Santa Cruz do Sul, Braz. . . **D7** 72
Santa Cruz Island, i., Ca.,
  U.S. **F4** 98
Santa Cruz Islands, is., Sol.
  Is. **F10** 58
Santa Elena, Arg. **E6** 72
Santa Fe, Arg. **E5** 72
Santa Fe, N.M., U.S. **B4** 124
Santa Fe, Tx., U.S. **r14** 136
Santa Fe, co., N.M., U.S. . **B3** 124
Santa Fe, stm., N.M., U.S. **h8** 124
Santa Fe Baldy, mtn., N.M.,
  U.S. **B4** 124
Santa Fé do Sul, Braz. . . . **F1** 74
Santa Filomena, Braz. . . . **E10** 70
Santa Helena, Braz. **B2** 74
Santa Helena de Goiás,
  Braz. **E1** 74
Santai, China **E9** 28
Santa Inés, Isla, i., Chile . . **H2** 69
Santa Isabel, Arg. **F4** 72
Santa Isabel, i., Sol. Is. . . **B6** 62
Santa Isabel see Malabo, Eq.
  Gui. **C1** 54
Santa Lucia Range, mts.,
  Ca., U.S. **E3** 98
Santa Magdalena, Isla, i.,
  Mex. **B2** 78
Santa Margarita, Ca., U.S. . **E3** 98
Santa Margarita, Isla, i.,
  Mex. **C2** 78
Santa Maria, Braz. **D7** 72
Santa Maria, Ca., U.S. . . . **E3** 98

Santa Maria, i., Vanuatu . . . **j9** 62a
Santa Maria, stm., Az., U.S. **C2** 96
Santa Maria, Cabo de, c.,
  Ang. **A1** 56
Santa María, Isla, i., Ec. . . **D1** 70
Santa Maria Mountains,
  mts., Az., U.S. **C3** 96
Santa Marta, Col. **A5** 70
Santa Monica, Ca., U.S. . . **m12** 98
Santana, Braz. **D3** 74
Santana do Livramento,
  Braz. **E6** 72
Santander, Phil. **E8** 34
Santander, Spain **F5** 16
Santanilla, Islas, is., Hond. **B3** 80
Sant'Antioco, Italy **E2** 18
Sant'Antioco, Isola di, i.,
  Italy **E2** 18
Sant Antoni de Portmany,
  Spain **H7** 16
Santa Paula, Ca., U.S. . . . **E4** 98
Santaquin, Ut., U.S. **D4** 137
Santarém, Braz. **D9** 70
Santarém, Port. **H2** 16
Santa Rita, Hond. **B2** 80
Santa Rita, Ven. **C5** 80
Santa Rosa, Arg. **F5** 72
Santa Rosa, Braz. **D7** 72
Santa Rosa, Ec. **D4** 70
Santa Rosa, Ca., U.S. **C2** 98
Santa Rosa, N.M., U.S. . . . **C5** 124
Santa Rosa, Ven. **D6** 80
Santa Rosa, co., Fl., U.S. . . **u14** 102
Santa Rosa de Copán,
  Hond. **C2** 80
Santa Rosa Island, i., Ca.,
  U.S. **F3** 98
Santa Rosa Island, i., Fl.,
  U.S. **u14** 102
Santa Rosalía, Mex. **B2** 78
Santa Rosa Range, mts.,
  Nv., U.S. **B4** 121
Šantarskie ostrova, is.,
  Russia **D15** 26
Santa Sylvina, Arg. **D5** 72
Santa Vitória do Palmar,
  Braz. **E7** 72
Santa Ynez, Ca., U.S. **E3** 98
Santee, Ca., U.S. **o16** 98
Santee, stm., S.C., U.S. . . **E8** 133
Santee Dam, S.C., U.S. . . **E7** 133
Santee Indian Reservation,
  Ne., U.S. **B8** 120
Sant Feliu de Guíxols, Spain **G8** 16
Santiago, Braz. **D7** 72
Santiago, Chile **D2** 69
Santiago, Mex. **C3** 78
Santiago, Pan. **D3** 80
Santiago, i., C.V. **h10** 50a
Santiago, Isla, i., Ec. **D1** 70
Santiago de Compostela,
  Spain **F2** 16
Santiago de Cuba, Cuba . . **B4** 80
Santiago del Estero, Arg. . **D5** 72
Santiago de los Caballeros,
  Dom. Rep. **B5** 80
Santiago Ixcuintla, Mex. . . **C3** 78
Santiago Jamiltepec, Mex. **D5** 78
Santiago Papasquiaro, Mex. **B3** 78
Santiago Peak, mtn., Ca.,
  U.S. **n13** 98
Santiago Reservoir, res., Ca.,
  U.S. **n13** 98
Santiam Pass, Or., U.S. . . . **C4** 130
Sant Jordi, Golf de, b.,
  Spain **G7** 16
Santo Amaro, Braz. **D4** 74
Santo André, Braz. **F2** 74
Santo Ângelo, Braz. **D7** 72
Santo Antão, i., C.V. **g10** 50a
Santo Antônio de Jesus,
  Braz. **D4** 74
Santo Antônio do Içá, Braz. **D6** 70
Santo Domingo, Dom. Rep. **B6** 80
Santo Domingo see
  Hispaniola, i., N.A. . . . **A5** 80
Santo Domingo Indian
  Reservation, N.M., U.S. **h8** 124
Santo Domingo Pueblo,
  N.M., U.S. **B3** 124
Santorini see Thíra, i., Grc. **F10** 18
Santos, Braz. **F2** 74
Santos Dumont, Braz. . . . **F3** 74
Santo Tomé de Guayana
  see Ciudad Guayana,
  Ven. **B7** 70
San Valentín, Monte, mtn.,
  Chile **G2** 69
San Vicente, El Sal. **C2** 80
San Vicente de Cañete,
  Peru **F4** 70
San Vicente del Caguán,
  Col. **C5** 70
San Vicente Reservoir, res.,
  Ca., U.S. **o16** 98
San Xavier Indian
  Reservation, Az., U.S. . **E4** 96
Sanya, China **H9** 28
Sanyuan, China **E9** 28
Sanza Pombo, Ang. **B3** 54
São Bento, Braz. **D9** 70
São Borja, Braz. **D6** 72
São Carlos, Braz. **F2** 74
São Domingos, Braz. **A8** 72

São Domingos, Gui.-B. . . . **D1** 50
São Francisco, Braz. **E3** 74
São Francisco, stm., Braz. . **C4** 74
São Francisco do Sul, Braz. **D8** 72
São Gabriel, Braz. **E7** 72
Sao Hill, Tan. **E7** 54
São João da Barra, Braz. . . **F3** 74
São João da Boa Vista, Braz. **F2** 74
São João de Madeira, Port. **G2** 16
São João Del Rei, Braz. . . **F3** 74
São João do Araguaia, Braz. **E10** 70
São Jorge, i., Port. **F7** 46
São José, Braz. **D8** 72
São José do Rio Preto, Braz. **F2** 74
São José dos Campos, Braz. **F3** 74
São Leopoldo, Braz. **D7** 72
São Lourenço, Pantanal de,
  sw., Braz. **G8** 70
São Lourenço do Sul, Braz. **E7** 72
São Luís, Braz. **B3** 74
São Luís Gonzaga, Braz. . . **D7** 72
São Manuel, stm., Braz. . . **E8** 70
São Mateus, Braz. **E4** 74
São Miguel, i., Port. **F7** 46
São Miguel do Araguaia,
  Braz. **D1** 74
Saona, Isla, i., Dom. Rep. . **B6** 80
Saône, stm., Fr. **D9** 16
São Nicolau, i., C.V. **g10** 50a
São Paulo, Braz. **F2** 74
São Paulo, state, Braz. . . . **C7** 72
São Paulo de Olivença,
  Braz. **D6** 70
São Raimundo Nonato,
  Braz. **C3** 74
São Roque, Cabo de, c.,
  Braz. **C4** 74
São Sebastião, Braz. **F2** 74
São Sebastião, Ilha de, i.,
  Braz. **F2** 74
São Sebastião do Paraíso,
  Braz. **F2** 74
São Simão, Represa de, res.,
  Braz. **B7** 72
São Tomé, S. Tom./P. . . . **C1** 54
São Tomé, i., S. Tom./P. . . **C1** 54
São Tomé, Cabo de, c.,
  Braz. **F3** 74
Sao Tome and Principe,
  ctry., Afr. **C1** 54
São Vicente, Braz. **F2** 74
São Vicente, i., C.V. **g9** 50a
São Vicente, Cabo de, c.,
  Port. **I2** 16
Sapé, Braz. **C4** 74
Sapele, Nig. **E6** 50
Sapelo Island, i., Ga., U.S. **E5** 103
Sapitwa, mtn., Mwi. **B6** 56
Sappa Creek, stm., U.S. . . **E5** 120
Sapphire Mountains, mts.,
  Mt., U.S. **D3** 119
Sappington, Mo., U.S. . . . **f13** 118
Sapporo, Japan **C16** 28
Sapulpa, Ok., U.S. **B5** 129
Sapwe, D.R.C. **F5** 54
Saqqez, Iran **C5** 42
Sarāb, Iran **C5** 42
Saraburi, Thai. **D4** 34
Saragossa see Zaragoza,
  Spain **G6** 16
Sarajevo, Bos. **C7** 18
Sarakhs, Iran **C8** 42
Saraktaš, Russia **D10** 22
Saraland, Al., U.S. **E1** 94
Saranac, Mi., U.S. **F5** 115
Saranac, stm., N.Y., U.S. . . **F11** 125
Saranac Lake, N.Y., U.S. . . **f10** 125
Saranac Lakes, l., N.Y., U.S. **f10** 125
Sarandë, Alb. **E8** 18
Sārangarh, India **E4** 40
Saranpaul', Russia **B11** 22
Saransk, Russia **D6** 26
Sarapul, Russia **D7** 26
Sarasota, Fl., U.S. **E4** 102
Sarasota, co., Fl., U.S. . . . **E4** 102
Sarasota Bay, b., Fl., U.S. . **E4** 102
Saratoga, Ca., U.S. **k8** 98
Saratoga, Tx., U.S. **D5** 136
Saratoga, Wy., U.S. **E6** 143
Saratoga, co., N.Y., U.S. . . **B7** 125
Saratoga Lake, l., N.Y., U.S. **C7** 125
Saratoga National Historical
  Park, N.Y., U.S. **B7** 125
Saratoga Springs, N.Y., U.S. **B7** 125
Saratov, Russia **D6** 26
Saratov Reservoir see
  Saratovskoe
  vodohranilišče, res.,
  Russia **D8** 22
Saratovskoe vodohranilišče,
  res., Russia **D8** 22
Saravan, Laos **C5** 34
Sarawak, hist. reg., Malay. **C4** 36
Saray, Tur. **B2** 44
Saraya, Gui. **D2** 50
Sarayköy, Tur. **D3** 44
Sarcoxie, Mo., U.S. **D3** 118
Sardārshahr, India **D2** 40
Sar Dasht, Iran **D11** 44
Sardegna (Sardinia), i., Italy **D2** 18
Sardinia see Sardegna, i.,
  Italy **D2** 18
Sardis, Ga., U.S. **D5** 103
Sardis, Ms., U.S. **A4** 117
Sardis Lake, res., Ms., U.S. **A4** 117

Sarek, mtn., Swe. **C7** 10
Sar-e Pol, Afg. **C9** 42
Sarepta, La., U.S. **B2** 111
Sargent, Ga., U.S. **C2** 103
Sargent, Ne., U.S. **C6** 120
Sargent, co., N.D., U.S. . . **C8** 127
Sargodha, Pak. **D10** 42
Sarh, Chad **B3** 54
Sārī, Iran **C6** 42
Sarigan, i., N. Mar. Is. . . . **C12** 32
Sarıkamış, Tur. **B10** 44
Sarıkaya, Tur. **C6** 44
Sarikei, Malay. **C4** 36
Sarīr, Libya **F8** 14
Sariwŏn, N. Kor. **D13** 28
Sarıyar Barajı, res., Tur. . . . **C4** 44
Sarja, Russia **D6** 26
Şarkikaraağaç, Tur. **C4** 44
Şarkışla, Tur. **C7** 44
Şarköy, Tur. **B2** 44
Sarmi, Indon. **G10** 32
Särna, Swe. **F5** 10
Sarnia, On., Can. **E2** 89
Sarny, Ukr. **D9** 20
Saronic Gulf see Saronikós
  Kólpos, b., Grc. **F9** 18
Saronikós Kólpos, b., Grc. . **F9** 18
Saros Körfezi, b., Tur. **B2** 44
Sarpy, co., Ne., U.S. **C9** 120
Sarreguemines, Fr. **C10** 16
Sartell, Mn., U.S. **E4** 116
Sartène, Fr. **D2** 18
Šārur, Azer. **C11** 44
Sarus see Seyhan, stm., Tur. **D6** 44
Saryg-Sep, Russia **D11** 26
Sarykamyšskoe ozero, l.,
  Asia **B7** 42
Saryozek, Kaz. **E9** 26
Sarysu, stm., Kaz. **E8** 26
Sary-Taš, Kyrg. **A2** 40
Sasabeneh, Eth. **B8** 54
Sāsārām, India **E4** 40
Sasebo, Japan **D1** 31
Saskatchewan, prov., Can. **E3** 91
Saskatchewan, stm., Can. . **H19** 82
Saskylah, Russia **B13** 26
Sasovo, Russia **B16** 20
Sassafras, stm., Md., U.S. . **B5** 113
Sassafras Mountain, mtn.,
  U.S. **A2** 133
Sassandra, C. Iv. **E3** 50
Sassandra, stm., C. Iv. . . . **E3** 50
Sassari, Italy **D2** 18
Sassnitz, Ger. **C13** 12
Satah Mountain, mtn., B.C.,
  Can. **C5** 85
Sata-misaki, c., Japan . . . **D2** 31
Satanta, Ks., U.S. **E3** 109
Satilla, stm., Ga., U.S. . . . **E5** 103
Satka, Russia **D10** 22
Satluj see Sutlej, stm., Asia **D2** 40
Satna, India **E4** 40
Sátoraljaújhely, Hung. . . . **E6** 20
Sātpura Range, mts., India **E3** 40
Satsuma, Al., U.S. **E1** 94
Satu Mare, Rom. **F7** 20
Satun, Thai. **E3** 34
Satus Creek, stm., Wa., U.S. **C5** 140
Sauceda Mountains, mts.,
  Az., U.S. **E3** 96
Sauðárkrókur, Ice. **I19** 10a
Saudi Arabia, ctry., Asia . . **F4** 38
Saufley Field Naval Air
  Station, mil., Fl., U.S. . . **u14** 102
Saugatuck, Mi., U.S. **F4** 115
Saugatuck, stm., Ct., U.S. . **D2** 100
Saugatucket, stm., R.I., U.S. **F4** 132
Saugatuck Reservoir, res.,
  Ct., U.S. **D2** 100
Saugerties, N.Y., U.S. . . . **C7** 125
Saugus, Ma., U.S. **B5** 114
Saugus, stm., Ma., U.S. . . **g11** 114
Sauk, co., Wi., U.S. **E4** 142
Sauk, stm., Mn., U.S. . . . **E4** 116
Sauk, stm., Wa., U.S. . . . **A4** 140
Sauk Centre, Mn., U.S. . . **E4** 116
Sauk City, Wi., U.S. **E4** 142
Sauk Rapids, Mn., U.S. . . **E4** 116
Saukville, Wi., U.S. **E6** 142
Saül, Fr. Gu. **C9** 70
Saulnierville, N.S., Can. . . **E3** 87
Sault-au-Mouton, P.Q., Can. **A8** 90
Sault Sainte Marie, On.,
  Can. **p18** 89
Sault Sainte Marie, Mi., U.S. **B6** 115
Saumarez Reef, rf., Austl. . **E5** 62
Saumlaki, Indon. **B8** 36
Saumur, Fr. **D6** 16
Saunders, co., Ne., U.S. . . **C9** 120
Saunderstown, R.I., U.S. . . **E4** 132
Saurimo, Ang. **C4** 54
Sausalito, Ca., U.S. **D2** 98
Sava, stm., Eur. **G5** 20
Savage, Md., U.S. **B4** 113
Savage, stm., Md., U.S. . . **k12** 113
Savage River Reservoir, res.,
  Md., U.S. **k12** 113
Savai'i, i., Samoa **F12** 58
Savalou, Benin **E5** 50
Savanna, Il., U.S. **A3** 106
Savanna, Ok., U.S. **C6** 129
Savannah, Ga., U.S. **D5** 103
Savannah, Mo., U.S. **B3** 118

Name	Map Ref.	Page

Savannah, Tn., U.S. **B3** 135
Savannah, stm., U.S. **E11** 92
Savannah, stm., U.S. **F5** 133
Savannah River Plant, sci., S.C., U.S. **E4** 133
Savannakhét, Laos **C4** 34
Savanna Lake, l., Md., U.S. **D6** 113
Savanna-la-Mar, Jam. **B4** 80
Savaştepe, Tur. **C2** 44
Savè, Benin **E5** 50
Save (Sabi), stm., Afr. . . . **C5** 56
Sāveh, Iran **C6** 42
Savelugu, Ghana **E4** 50
Saverne, Fr. **C10** 16
Saville Dam, Ct., U.S. . . . **B4** 100
Savitaipale, Fin. **F12** 10
Savona, Italy **B2** 18
Savonlinna, Fin. **F13** 10
Savoonga, Ak., U.S. **C5** 95
Savoy, Il., U.S. **C5** 106
Savu Sea see Sawu, Laut, Indon. **E6** 36
Sawāi Mādhopur, India . . . **D3** 40
Sawākin, Sudan **G12** 48
Sawankhalok, Thai. **C3** 34
Sawatch Range, mts., Co., U.S. **B4** 99
Sawdā', Jabal as-, hills, Libya **F7** 14
Sawdā', Qurnat as-, mtn., Leb. **E7** 44
Sawnee Mountain, mtn., Ga., U.S. **B2** 103
Sawtooth Mountains, mts., Id., U.S. **F4** 105
Sawtooth National Recreation Area, Id., U.S. **E3** 105
Sawu, Laut (Savu Sea), Indon. **E6** 36
Sawu, Pulau, i., Indon. . . . **F6** 36
Sawyer, co., Wi., U.S. **C2** 142
Sawyerville, P.Q., Can. . . . **D6** 90
Saxonburg, Pa., U.S. **E2** 131
Saxtons, stm., Vt., U.S. . . . **E3** 138
Saxtons River, Vt., U.S. . . . **E3** 138
Sayan Mountains, mts., Asia **D11** 26
Saybrook, Il., U.S. **C5** 106
Saybrook Manor, Ct., U.S. . **D6** 100
Şaydā, Leb. **F6** 44
Saydel, Ia., U.S. **e8** 108
Sayhūt, Yemen **G6** 38
Saylac, Som. **H4** 38
Saylesville, R.I., U.S. **B4** 132
Saylorsburg, Pa., U.S. . . . **E11** 131
Saylorville, Ia., U.S. **e8** 108
Saylorville Lake, res., Ia., U.S. **C4** 108
Saynshand, Mong. **C10** 28
Sayre, Al., U.S. **B3** 94
Sayre, Ok., U.S. **B2** 129
Sayre, Pa., U.S. **C8** 131
Sayreville, N.J., U.S. **C4** 123
Sayula, Mex. **D4** 78
Sayville, N.Y., U.S. **n15** 125
Saywūn, Yemen **G5** 38
Sba, Alg. **F3** 14
Scalp Level, Pa., U.S. **F4** 131
Scanlon, Mn., U.S. **D6** 116
Scapegoat Mountain, mtn., Mt., U.S. **C3** 119
Scappoose, Or., U.S. **B4** 130
Scarborough, On., Can. . . **m15** 89
Scarborough, Trin. **C7** 80
Scarborough, Eng., U.K. . . **C6** 12
Scarborough, Me., U.S. . . . **E2** 112
Scarbro, W.V., U.S. **n13** 141
Scarsdale, N.Y., U.S. **h13** 125
Ščekino, Russia **C14** 20
Ščerbakovo, Russia **C18** 26
Schaefferstown, Pa., U.S. . **F9** 131
Schaller, Ia., U.S. **B2** 108
Schaumburg, Il., U.S. **h8** 106
Schell Creek Range, mts., Nv., U.S. **D7** 121
Schenectady, N.Y., U.S. . . **C7** 125
Schenectady, co., N.Y., U.S. **C6** 125
Schererville, In., U.S. **B3** 107
Schertz, Tx., U.S. **h7** 136
Schiller Park, Il., U.S. . . . **k9** 106
Schio, Italy **B3** 18
Schleicher, co., Tx., U.S. . . **D2** 136
Schleswig, Ger. **C11** 12
Schleswig, Ia., U.S. **B2** 108
Schley, co., Ga., U.S. **D2** 103
Schofield, Wi., U.S. **D4** 142
Schofield Barracks, mil., Hi., U.S. **g9** 104
Schoharie, co., N.Y., U.S. . . **C6** 125
Schoharie Creek, stm., N.Y., U.S. **C6** 125
Schoodic Lake, l., Me., U.S. **C4** 112
Schoolcraft, Mi., U.S. **F5** 115
Schoolcraft, co., Mi., U.S. . **B4** 115
Schroon Lake, l., N.Y., U.S. **B7** 125
Schulenburg, Tx., U.S. . . . **E4** 136
Schulter, Ok., U.S. **B6** 129
Schurz, Nv., U.S. **E3** 121
Schuyler, Ne., U.S. **C8** 120
Schuyler, co., Il., U.S. . . . **C3** 106
Schuyler, co., Mo., U.S. . . . **A5** 118
Schuyler, co., N.Y., U.S. . . **C4** 125
Schuylkill, co., Pa., U.S. . . **E9** 131
Schuylkill, stm., Pa., U.S. . **F10** 131
Schuylkill Haven, Pa., U.S. . **E9** 131

Schwaben, hist. reg., Ger. . **F11** 12
Schwarzwald (Black Forest), mts., Ger. **F11** 12
Schwedt, Ger. **D14** 12
Schwerin, Ger. **D12** 12
Schwyz, Switz. **A2** 18
Sciacca, Italy **F4** 18
Science Hill, Ky., U.S. **C5** 110
Ščigry, Russia **D14** 20
Scilly, Isles of, is., Eng., U.K. **F3** 12
Scio, Or., U.S. **C4** 130
Scioto, co., Oh., U.S. **D3** 128
Scioto, stm., Oh., U.S. . . . **B2** 128
Scituate, Ma., U.S. **B6** 114
Scituate Reservoir, res., R.I., U.S. **C3** 132
Scobey, Mt., U.S. **B11** 119
Scofield Reservoir, res., Ut., U.S. **D4** 137
Scotch Plains, N.J., U.S. . . **B4** 123
Scotia, Ca., U.S. **B1** 98
Scotia, N.Y., U.S. **C7** 125
Scotia Ridge **N8** 66
Scotia Sea **B36** 67
Scotland, On., Can. **D4** 89
Scotland, S.D., U.S. **D8** 134
Scotland, prov., U.K. **B5** 12
Scotland, co., Mo., U.S. . . . **A5** 118
Scotland, co., N.C., U.S. . . **C3** 126
Scotland Neck, N.C., U.S. . **A5** 126
Scotlandville, La., U.S. . . . **D4** 111
Scotrun, Pa., U.S. **D11** 131
Scottstown, P.Q., Can. . . . **D6** 90
Scott, La., U.S. **D3** 111
Scott, co., Ar., U.S. **C1** 97
Scott, co., Ia., U.S. **C7** 108
Scott, co., Il., U.S. **D3** 106
Scott, co., In., U.S. **G6** 107
Scott, co., Ks., U.S. **D3** 109
Scott, co., Ky., U.S. **B5** 110
Scott, co., Mn., U.S. **F5** 116
Scott, co., Mo., U.S. **D8** 118
Scott, co., Ms., U.S. **C4** 117
Scott, co., Tn., U.S. **C9** 135
Scott, co., Va., U.S. **f9** 139
Scott, Cape, c., B.C., Can. . **D3** 85
Scott, Mount, mtn., Or., U.S. **E4** 130
Scott Air Force Base, mil., Il., U.S. **E4** 106
Scott City, Ks., U.S. **D3** 109
Scott City, Mo., U.S. **D8** 118
Scottdale, Ga., U.S. **h8** 103
Scottdale, Pa., U.S. **F2** 131
Scott Mountain, mtn., Id., U.S. **E3** 105
Scott Peak, mtn., Id., U.S. . **E6** 105
Scott Reef, rf., Austl. **C3** 60
Scott Reservoir, res., N.C., U.S. **A1** 126
Scottsbluff, Ne., U.S. **C2** 120
Scotts Bluff, co., Ne., U.S. . **C2** 120
Scotts Bluff National Monument, Ne., U.S. . **C2** 120
Scottsboro, Al., U.S. **A3** 94
Scottsburg, In., U.S. **G6** 107
Scottsdale, Az., U.S. **D4** 96
Scottsville, Ky., U.S. **D3** 110
Scottsville, N.Y., U.S. **B3** 125
Scottville, Mi., U.S. **E4** 115
Scraggly Lake, l., Me., U.S. . **B4** 112
Scranton, Ks., U.S. **D8** 109
Scranton, Pa., U.S. **D10** 131
Scranton, S.C., U.S. **D8** 133
Screven, Ga., U.S. **E4** 103
Screven, co., Ga., U.S. . . . **D5** 103
Scribner, Ne., U.S. **C9** 120
Ščučinsk, Kaz. **D8** 26
Scugog, Lake, l., On., Can. . **C6** 89
Scurry, co., Tx., U.S. **C2** 136
Scutari see Shkodër, Alb. . . **C7** 18
Scutari, Lake, l., Eur. **C7** 18
Scyros see Skíros, i., Grc. . **E10** 18
Seaboard, N.C., U.S. **A5** 126
Seabreeze, De., U.S. **F5** 101
Seabrook, N.H., U.S. **E5** 122
Seabrook, Tx., U.S. **r14** 136
Seabrook Island, i., S.C., U.S. **F7** 133
Seadrift, Tx., U.S. **E4** 136
Seaford, De., U.S. **F3** 101
Seaford, Va., U.S. **h15** 139
Seaforth, On., Can. **D3** 89
Seagoville, Tx., U.S. **n10** 136
Seagraves, Tx., U.S. **C1** 136
Sea Islands, is., U.S. **E11** 92
Sea Isle City, N.J., U.S. . . . **E3** 123
Seal Cove, Nf., Can. **D3** 88
Seal Point, c., P.E., Can. . . **C5** 87
Seal Rock, Or., U.S. **C2** 130
Sealy, Tx., U.S. **E4** 136
Seaman, Oh., U.S. **D2** 128
Seaman Range, mts., Nv., U.S. **F6** 121
Searchlight, Nv., U.S. **H7** 121
Searcy, Ar., U.S. **B4** 97
Searcy, co., Ar., U.S. **B3** 97
Searles Lake, l., Ca., U.S. . **E5** 98
Searsport, Me., U.S. **D4** 112
Seaside, Or., U.S. **B3** 130
Seat Pleasant, Md., U.S. . . **C4** 113
Seattle, Wa., U.S. **B3** 140
Seattle-Tacoma International Airport, Wa., U.S. . . . **f11** 140
Seaview, Wa., U.S. **C1** 140

Sebago Lake, Me., U.S. . . . **E2** 112
Šebalino, Russia **D10** 26
Sebangka, Pulau, i., Indon. . **C2** 36
Sebastian, Fl., U.S. **E6** 102
Sebastian, co., Ar., U.S. . . **B1** 97
Sebastian, Cape, c., Or., U.S. **E2** 130
Sebastian Inlet, b., Fl., U.S. **E6** 102
Sebastián Vizcaíno, Bahía, b., Mex. **B2** 78
Sebasticook Lake, l., Me., U.S. **D3** 112
Sebec Lake, l., Me., U.S. . . **C3** 112
Sebeka, Mn., U.S. **D3** 116
Šebekino, Russia **D14** 20
Sebeş, Rom. **G7** 20
Sebewaing, Mi., U.S. **E7** 115
Şebinkarahisar, Tur. **B8** 44
Seboeis, stm., Me., U.S. . . **B4** 112
Seboeis Lake, l., Me., U.S. . **C4** 112
Seboomook Lake, l., Me., U.S. **C3** 112
Sebree, Ky., U.S. **C2** 110
Sebring, Fl., U.S. **E5** 102
Sebring, Oh., U.S. **B4** 128
Secaucus, N.J., U.S. **h8** 123
Sechelt, B.C., Can. **E6** 85
Sechura, Bahía de, b., Peru **E3** 70
Second Lake, l., N.H., U.S. . **f7** 122
Second Mesa, Az., U.S. . . . **B5** 96
Secret Lake, l., R.I., U.S. . . **E4** 132
Section, Al., U.S. **A4** 94
Security, Co., U.S. **C6** 99
Seda, China **E8** 28
Sedalia, Mo., U.S. **C4** 118
Sedan, Fr. **C9** 16
Sedan, Ks., U.S. **E7** 109
Sedgewick, Ab., Can. **C5** 84
Sedgewick, Mount, mtn., N.M., U.S. **B1** 124
Sedgwick, Ks., U.S. **E6** 109
Sedgwick, co., Co., U.S. . . **A8** 99
Sedgwick, co., Ks., U.S. . . **E6** 109
Sédhiou, Sen. **D1** 50
Sedley, Va., U.S. **D6** 139
Sedona, Az., U.S. **C4** 96
Sedro Woolley, Wa., U.S. . . **A3** 140
Seekonk, Ma., U.S. **C5** 114
Seekonk, stm., R.I., U.S. . . **C4** 132
Seeley, Ca., U.S. **F6** 98
Seeley Lake, Mt., U.S. . . . **C3** 119
Seelyville, In., U.S. **F3** 107
Şefaatli, Tur. **C6** 44
Sefadu, S.L. **E2** 50
Seferihisar, Tur. **C2** 44
Segamat, Malay. **C2** 36
Segesta, hist., Italy **F4** 18
Segeža, Russia **C5** 26
Ségou, Mali **D3** 50
Segovia, Spain **G4** 16
Seguam Island, i., Ak., U.S. **E5** 95
Seguam Pass, strt., Ak., U.S. **E5** 95
Séguédine, Niger **B7** 50
Séguéla, C. Iv. **E3** 50
Seguin, Tx., U.S. **E4** 136
Segura, stm., Spain **I6** 16
Seiling, Ok., U.S. **A3** 129
Seinäjoki, Fin. **E10** 10
Seine, stm., Fr. **C7** 16
Seine, Baie de la, b., Fr. . . **C6** 16
Sejm, stm., Eur. **D12** 20
Sejmčan, Russia **C17** 26
Şeki, Azer. **B12** 44
Sekiu, Wa., U.S. **A1** 140
Sekondi-Takoradi, Ghana . **F4** 50
Selah, Wa., U.S. **C5** 140
Selaru, Pulau, i., Indon. . . **E8** 36
Selatan, Tanjung, c., Indon. **D4** 36
Selayar, Pulau, i., Indon. . . **E6** 36
Selby, S.D., U.S. **B5** 134
Selbyville, De., U.S. **G5** 101
Selçuk, Tur. **D2** 44
Seldovia, Ak., U.S. **D9** 95
Selebi-Phikwe, Bots. **C4** 56
Selenge, D.R.C. **D3** 54
Selenge, stm., Asia **E12** 26
Sélibabi, Maur. **C2** 50
Seligman, Az., U.S. **B3** 96
Šelihova, zaliv, b., Russia . **C17** 26
Selinsgrove, Pa., U.S. . . . **E8** 131
Seljord, Nor. **G3** 10
Selkirk, Mb., Can. **D3** 86
Selkirk, On., Can. **D3** 89
Sellersburg, In., U.S. **H6** 107
Sellersville, Pa., U.S. . . . **F11** 131
Sells, Az., U.S. **F4** 96
Selma, Al., U.S. **C2** 94
Selma, Ca., U.S. **D4** 98
Selma, In., U.S. **D7** 107
Selma, N.C., U.S. **B4** 126
Selmer, Tn., U.S. **B3** 135
Selvagens, Ilhas, is., Port. . **D1** 48
Selvas, for., Braz. **E6** 70
Selway, stm., Id., U.S. . . . **C3** 105
Selwyn Lake, l., Can. **G15** 82
Selwyn Mountains, mts., Can. **F13** 82
Selwyn Range, mts., Austl. . **E3** 62
Semara, W. Sah. **A2** 50
Semarang, Indon. **E4** 36
Semenanjung Malaysia, hist. reg., Malay. **C2** 36
Semenivka, Ukr. **C12** 20
Semenov, Russia **C7** 22

Semey see Semipalatinsk, Kaz. **D10** 26
Semiluki, Russia **D15** 20
Seminoe Mountains, mts., Wy., U.S. **D6** 143
Seminoe Reservoir, res., Wy., U.S. **D6** 143
Seminole, Ok., U.S. **B5** 129
Seminole, Tx., U.S. **C1** 136
Seminole, co., Fl., U.S. . . . **D5** 102
Seminole, co., Ga., U.S. . . **F2** 103
Seminole, co., Ok., U.S. . . **B5** 129
Seminole, Lake, res., U.S. . **F2** 103
Semipalatinsk, Kaz. **D10** 26
Semisopochnoi Island, i., Ak., U.S. **E3** 95
Semitau, Indon. **C4** 36
Semmes, Al., U.S. **E1** 94
Semnān, Iran **C6** 42
Senachwine Lake, l., Il., U.S. **B4** 106
Senador Pompeu, Braz. . . **C4** 74
Senaki, Geor. **A10** 44
Sena Madureira, Braz. . . . **E6** 70
Senanga, Zam. **B3** 56
Senath, Mo., U.S. **E7** 118
Senatobia, Ms., U.S. **A4** 117
Sendai, Japan **D16** 28
Sendelingsdrif, Nmb. **D2** 56
Seneca, Il., U.S. **B5** 106
Seneca, Ks., U.S. **C7** 109
Seneca, Mo., U.S. **E3** 118
Seneca, Pa., U.S. **D2** 131
Seneca, S.C., U.S. **B2** 133
Seneca, co., N.Y., U.S. . . . **C4** 125
Seneca, co., Oh., U.S. . . . **A2** 128
Seneca Falls, N.Y., U.S. . . . **C4** 125
Seneca Lake, l., N.Y., U.S. . **C4** 125
Senecaville Lake, res., Oh., U.S. **C4** 128
Sénéégal, stm., Afr. **C2** 50
Senegal, ctry., Afr. **D1** 50
Senekal, S. Afr. **D4** 56
Senftenberg, Ger. **E13** 12
Senhor do Bonfim, Braz. . . **D3** 74
Senica, Slvk. **E4** 20
Senigallia, Italy **C4** 18
Senja, i., Nor. **B7** 10
Šenkursk, Russia **B7** 22
Senneterre, P.Q., Can. . . **k11** 90
Senoia, Ga., U.S. **C2** 103
Senqu see Orange, stm., Afr. **D2** 56
Sens, Fr. **C8** 16
Senta, Yugo. **B8** 18
Sentinel, Ok., U.S. **B2** 129
Seoni, India **E3** 40
Seoul see Sŏul, S. Kor. . . **D13** 28
Sepanjang, Pulau, i., Indon. **E5** 36
Sepik, stm., Pap. N. Gui. . **G11** 32
Sepulga, stm., Al., U.S. . . **D3** 94
Sequatchie, co., Tn., U.S. . **D8** 135
Sequatchie, stm., Tn., U.S. . **D8** 135
Sequim, Wa., U.S. **A2** 140
Sequoia National Park, Ca., U.S. **D4** 98
Sequoyah, co., Ok., U.S. . . **B7** 129
Šerabad, Uzb. **C9** 42
Serafimovič, Russia **E7** 22
Seram (Ceram), i., Indon. . **D7** 36
Seram, Laut (Ceram Sea), Indon. **D7** 36
Serang, Indon. **E3** 36
Serasan, Pulau, i., Indon. . . **C3** 36
Serasan, Selat, strt., Indon. **C3** 36
Serbia see Srbija, prov., Yugo. **B8** 18
Serdobsk, Russia **D7** 22
Sered', Slvk. **E4** 20
Şereflikoçhisar, Tur. **C5** 44
Seremban, Malay. **C2** 36
Serengeti Plain, pl., Tan. . . **D6** 54
Serenje, Zam. **A5** 56
Sergač, Russia **C8** 22
Sergeant Bluff, Ia., U.S. . . **B1** 108
Sergeevka, Russia **B2** 31
Sergeja Kirova, ostrova, is., Russia **B10** 26
Sergiev Posad, Russia . . . **D5** 26
Serginskij, Russia **C8** 26
Sergipe, state, Braz. **D4** 74
Seria, Bru. **C4** 36
Serian, Malay. **C4** 36
Sérifos, i., Grc. **F10** 18
Şerik, Tur. **D4** 44
Serlovaja Gora, Russia . . . **A11** 28
Serov, Russia **D8** 26
Serowe, Bots. **C4** 56
Serpa, Port. **I3** 16
Serpiente, Boca de la, strt. . **D7** 80
Serpuhov, Russia **B14** 20
Serra do Navio, Braz. **C9** 70
Sérrai, Grc. **D9** 18
Serra Talhada, Braz. **C4** 74
Serrezuela, Arg. **E4** 72
Serrinha, Braz. **D4** 74
Sertânia, Braz. **C4** 74
Sêrtar, China **E7** 28
Sese Islands, is., Ug. **D6** 54
Sesfontein, Nmb. **B1** 56
Sesheke, Zam. **B3** 56
Sesser, Il., U.S. **E4** 106
Sestroreck, Russia **F13** 10
Sète, Fr. **F8** 16

Sete Lagoas, Braz. **E3** 74
Seth, W.V., U.S. **C3** 141
Sétif, Alg. **C6** 48
Seto-naikai, Japan **E14** 28
Setté Cama, Gabon **D1** 54
Setúbal, Port. **H2** 16
Setúbal, Baía de, b., Port. . **H2** 16
Seul, Lac, l., On., Can. . . **o16** 89
Seul Choix Point, c., Mi., U.S. **C5** 115
Sevan, Arm. **B11** 44
Sevana Lich, l., Arm. . . . **B11** 44
Sevastopol', Ukr. **G12** 20
Seven Devils Lake, res., Ar., U.S. **D4** 97
Seven Devils Mountains, mts., Id., U.S. **D2** 105
Seven Hills, Oh., U.S. . . . **h9** 128
Seven Mile Beach, N.J., U.S. **E3** 123
Severn, Md., U.S. **B4** 113
Severn, stm., On., Can. . **n17** 89
Severn, stm., U.K. **D5** 12
Severnaja Dvina, stm., Russia **C6** 26
Severnaja Osetija, state, Russia **E6** 26
Severnaja Sos'va, stm., Russia **B11** 22
Severnaja Zemlja, is., Russia **B12** 26
Severna Park, Md., U.S. . . **B4** 113
Severn River, b., Md., U.S. . **B4** 113
Severnye uvaly, hills, Russia **D6** 26
Severodvinsk, Russia **C5** 26
Severo-Enisejskij, Russia . **C11** 26
Severomorsk, Russia . . . **B15** 10
Severo-Sibirskaja nizmennost', pl., Russia **B11** 26
Severoural'sk, Russia . . . **B11** 22
Sevier, co., Ar., U.S. **D1** 97
Sevier, co., Tn., U.S. . . . **D10** 135
Sevier, co., Ut., U.S. **E4** 137
Sevier, stm., Ut., U.S. . . . **D3** 137
Sevier Bridge Reservoir, res., Ut., U.S. **D4** 137
Sevier Lake, l., Ut., U.S. . . **E2** 137
Sevierville, Tn., U.S. . . . **D10** 135
Sevilla, Col. **E4** 80
Sevilla (Seville), Spain . . . **I4** 16
Seville see Sevilla, Spain . . **I4** 16
Seville, Oh., U.S. **A4** 128
Sewanee, Tn., U.S. **D8** 135
Seward, Ak., U.S. **C10** 95
Seward, Ne., U.S. **D8** 120
Seward, co., Ks., U.S. . . . **E3** 109
Seward, co., Ne., U.S. . . . **D8** 120
Seward Peninsula, pen., Ak., U.S. **B7** 95
Sewickley, Pa., U.S. **E1** 131
Sexsmith, Ab., Can. **B1** 84
Seychelles, ctry., Afr. . . . **i12** 57b
Seychelles, is., Afr. **h13** 57b
Seydişehir, Tur. **D4** 44
Seydisfjördur, Ice. **I21** 10a
Seyhan, stm., Tur. **D6** 44
Seyhan Baraji, res., Tur. . . **D6** 44
Seymour, Austl. **H4** 62
Seymour, Ct., U.S. **D3** 100
Seymour, In., U.S. **G6** 107
Seymour, Mo., U.S. **D5** 118
Seymour, Tx., U.S. **C3** 136
Seymour, Wi., U.S. **D5** 142
Seymour Inlet, b., B.C., Can. **D4** 85
Seymour Johnson Air Force Base, mil., N.C., U.S. . . **B5** 126
Seymour Lake, l., Vt., U.S. . **B4** 138
Seymourville, La., U.S. . . . **h9** 111
Sfântu Gheorghe, Rom. . . **G8** 20
Sfax, Tun. **D7** 48
's-Gravenhage (The Hague), Neth. **D8** 12
Shaanxi, state, China **D9** 28
Shabbona, Il., U.S. **B5** 106
Shabeelle (Shebelē Wenz, Wabē), stm., Afr. **C8** 54
Shabunda, D.R.C. **D5** 54
Shache, China **D3** 28
Shackelford, co., Tx., U.S. . **C3** 136
Shackleton Ice Shelf, Ant. . **C14** 67
Shackleton Range, mts., Ant. **E2** 67
Shadehill Dam, S.D., U.S. . **B3** 134
Shadehill Reservoir, res., S.D., U.S. **B3** 134
Shadow Mountain National Recreation Area, Co., U.S. **A4** 99
Shady Cove, Or., U.S. . . . **E4** 130
Shady Side, Md., U.S. . . . **C4** 113
Shadyside, Oh., U.S. **C5** 128
Shady Spring, W.V., U.S. . . **D3** 141
Shafer, Lake, l., In., U.S. . . **C4** 107
Shafer Butte, mtn., Id., U.S. **F2** 105
Shafter, Ca., U.S. **E4** 98
Shaftsbury, Vt., U.S. **E2** 138
Shag Rocks, rock, S. Geor. . **H8** 69
Shah Alam, Malay. **C2** 36
Shahdol, India **E4** 40
Shāhjahānpur, India **D3** 40
Shāhpura, India **D2** 40
Shahr-e Kord, Iran **D6** 42
Shahr-e Rey, Iran **C6** 42
Shājāpur, India **E3** 40
Shakawe, Bots. **B3** 56

Name	Map Ref.	Page
Shaker Heights, Oh., U.S.	**A4**	128
Shaki, Nig.	**E5**	50
Shakopee, Mn., U.S.	**F5**	116
Shala Hāyk', l., Eth.	**B7**	54
Shallotte, N.C., U.S.	**D4**	126
Shallotte Inlet, b., N.C., U.S.	**D4**	126
Shallowater, Tx., U.S.	**C2**	136
Shām, Jabal ash-, mtn., Oman	**F7**	38
Shambe, Sudan	**B6**	54
Shambu, Eth.	**B7**	54
Shamokin, Pa., U.S.	**E8**	131
Shamokin Dam, Pa., U.S.	**E8**	131
Shamrock, Tx., U.S.	**B2**	136
Shamva, Zimb.	**B5**	56
Shandī, Sudan	**G11**	48
Shandong, state, China	**D11**	28
Shandong Bandao, pen., China	**D12**	28
Shangcai, China	**C3**	30
Shangcheng, China	**C4**	30
Shangchuan Dao, i., China	**E3**	30
Shangdu, China	**A3**	30
Shanghai, China	**E12**	28
Shanghang, China	**D4**	30
Shangqiu, China	**E11**	28
Shangrao, China	**F11**	28
Shangxian, China	**E10**	28
Shangzhi, China	**B13**	28
Shanhaiguan, China	**A4**	30
Shannock, R.I., U.S.	**F2**	132
Shannon, Ga., U.S.	**B1**	103
Shannon, Il., U.S.	**A4**	106
Shannon, Ms., U.S.	**A5**	117
Shannon, co., Mo., U.S.	**D6**	118
Shannon, co., S.D., U.S.	**D3**	134
Shannon, stm., Ire.	**D2**	12
Shannon, Lake, l., Wa., U.S.	**A4**	140
Shannontown, S.C., U.S.	**D7**	133
Shantou, China	**G11**	28
Shantung Peninsula see Shandong Bandao, pen., China	**D12**	28
Shanxi, state, China	**D10**	28
Shanxian, China	**C4**	30
Shanyin, China	**B3**	30
Shaoguan, China	**G10**	28
Shaowu, China	**F11**	28
Shaoxing, China	**E12**	28
Shaoyang, China	**F10**	28
Shaqrā', Sau. Ar.	**E5**	38
Shaqrā', Yemen	**H5**	38
Shara, gora, mtn., Asia	**A10**	44
Shark Bay, b., Austl.	**F1**	60
Sharkey, co., Ms., U.S.	**C3**	117
Shark Point, c., Fl., U.S.	**H5**	102
Sharm El Sheikh, Egypt	**E11**	48
Sharon, Ct., U.S.	**B2**	100
Sharon, Ma., U.S.	**B5**	114
Sharon, Pa., U.S.	**D1**	131
Sharon, Tn., U.S.	**A3**	135
Sharon, Wi., U.S.	**F5**	142
Sharon Hill, Pa., U.S.	**p20**	131
Sharon Park, Oh., U.S.	**n12**	128
Sharon Springs, Ks., U.S.	**D2**	109
Sharonville, Oh., U.S.	**n13**	128
Sharp, co., Ar., U.S.	**A4**	97
Sharpe, Lake, res., S.D., U.S.	**C6**	134
Sharpes, Fl., U.S.	**D6**	102
Sharpley, De., U.S.	**h7**	101
Sharpsburg, Md., U.S.	**B2**	113
Sharpsburg, N.C., U.S.	**B5**	126
Sharpsburg, Pa., U.S.	**k14**	131
Sharpsville, In., U.S.	**D5**	107
Sharpsville, Pa., U.S.	**D1**	131
Sharptown, Md., U.S.	**C6**	113
Shashe, stm., Afr.	**C4**	56
Shashemenē, Eth.	**B7**	54
Shashi, China	**E10**	28
Shasta, co., Ca., U.S.	**B3**	98
Shasta, Mount, vol., Ca., U.S.	**B2**	98
Shasta Lake, res., Ca., U.S.	**B2**	98
Shattuck, Ok., U.S.	**A2**	129
Shaw, Ms., U.S.	**B3**	117
Shaw Air Force Base, mil., S.C., U.S.	**D7**	133
Shawano, Wi., U.S.	**D5**	142
Shawano, co., Wi., U.S.	**D5**	142
Shawano Lake, l., Wi., U.S.	**D5**	142
Shawinigan, P.Q., Can.	**C5**	90
Shawinigan-Sud, P.Q., Can.	**C5**	90
Shawnee, Ks., U.S.	**k16**	109
Shawnee, Ok., U.S.	**B5**	129
Shawnee, co., Ks., U.S.	**D8**	109
Shawneetown, Il., U.S.	**F5**	106
Shawsheen, stm., Ma., U.S.	**f11**	114
Shay Gap, Austl.	**E3**	60
Shaykh, Jabal ash- see Hermon, Mount, mtn., Asia	**F6**	44
Shaykh Sa'd, Iraq	**F12**	44
Shaykh 'Uthmān, Yemen	**H5**	38
Shebelē Wenz, Wabē (Shabeelle), stm., Afr.	**B8**	54
Sheberghān, Afg.	**C9**	42
Sheboygan, Wi., U.S.	**E6**	142
Sheboygan, co., Wi., U.S.	**E6**	142
Sheboygan, stm., Wi., U.S.	**k10**	142
Sheboygan Falls, Wi., U.S.	**E6**	142
Shediac, N.B., Can.	**C5**	87
Sheenjek, stm., Ak., U.S.	**B11**	95
Sheep Mountain, mtn., Az., U.S.	**E1**	96
Sheep Mountain, mtn., Wy., U.S.	**B5**	143
Sheep Mountain, mtn., Wy., U.S.	**C2**	143
Sheep Peak, mtn., Nv., U.S.	**G6**	121
Sheep Range, mts., Nv., U.S.	**G6**	121
Sheet Harbour, N.S., Can.	**E7**	87
Sheffield, Eng., U.K.	**D6**	12
Sheffield, Al., U.S.	**A2**	94
Sheffield, Ia., U.S.	**B4**	108
Sheffield, Il., U.S.	**B4**	106
Sheffield, Pa., U.S.	**C3**	131
Sheffield Lake, Oh., U.S.	**A3**	128
Shehong, China	**C2**	30
Sheila, N.B., Can.	**B5**	87
Shekhūpura, Pak.	**D10**	42
Shelagyote Peak, mtn., B.C., Can.	**B4**	85
Shelbiana, Ky., U.S.	**C7**	110
Shelbina, Mo., U.S.	**B5**	118
Shelburn, In., U.S.	**F3**	107
Shelburne, On., Can.	**C4**	89
Shelburne Falls, Ma., U.S.	**A2**	114
Shelburne Pond, l., Vt., U.S.	**C2**	138
Shelby, Al., U.S.	**B3**	94
Shelby, Ia., U.S.	**C2**	108
Shelby, In., U.S.	**B3**	107
Shelby, Mi., U.S.	**E4**	115
Shelby, Ms., U.S.	**B3**	117
Shelby, Mt., U.S.	**B5**	119
Shelby, N.C., U.S.	**B1**	126
Shelby, Ne., U.S.	**C8**	120
Shelby, Oh., U.S.	**B3**	128
Shelby, co., Al., U.S.	**B3**	94
Shelby, co., Ia., U.S.	**C2**	108
Shelby, co., Il., U.S.	**D5**	106
Shelby, co., In., U.S.	**E6**	107
Shelby, co., Ky., U.S.	**B4**	110
Shelby, co., Mo., U.S.	**B5**	118
Shelby, co., Oh., U.S.	**B1**	128
Shelby, co., Tn., U.S.	**B2**	135
Shelby, co., Tx., U.S.	**D5**	136
Shelbyville, Il., U.S.	**D5**	106
Shelbyville, In., U.S.	**F6**	107
Shelbyville, Ky., U.S.	**B4**	110
Shelbyville, Tn., U.S.	**B5**	135
Shelbyville, Lake, res., Il., U.S.	**D5**	106
Sheldon, Ia., U.S.	**A2**	108
Sheldon, Il., U.S.	**C6**	106
Sheldon, Tx., U.S.	**r14**	136
Shelekhov, Gulf of see Šelihova, zaliv, b., Russia	**C17**	26
Shelikof Strait, strt., Ak., U.S.	**D9**	95
Shell Creek, stm., Wy., U.S.	**B5**	143
Shell Creek, stm., U.S.	**A2**	99
Shelley, Id., U.S.	**F6**	105
Shellharbour, Austl.	**G5**	62
Shell Lake, Wi., U.S.	**C2**	142
Shell Lake, l., Mn., U.S.	**D3**	116
Shell Lake, l., Wi., U.S.	**C2**	142
Shellman, Ga., U.S.	**E2**	103
Shell Rock, Ia., U.S.	**B5**	108
Shell Rock, stm., Ia., U.S.	**B5**	108
Shellsburg, Ia., U.S.	**B6**	108
Shelly Mountain, mtn., Id., U.S.	**F5**	105
Shelter Island, N.Y., U.S.	**m16**	125
Shelton, Ct., U.S.	**D3**	100
Shelton, Ne., U.S.	**D7**	120
Shelton, Wa., U.S.	**B2**	140
Shemya Air Force Base, mil., Ak., U.S.	**E2**	95
Shenandoah, Ia., U.S.	**D2**	108
Shenandoah, Pa., U.S.	**E9**	131
Shenandoah, Va., U.S.	**B4**	139
Shenandoah, co., Va., U.S.	**B4**	139
Shenandoah, stm., U.S.	**A5**	139
Shenandoah, North Fork, stm., Va., U.S.	**B4**	139
Shenandoah, South Fork, stm., Va., U.S.	**B4**	139
Shenandoah Mountain, mtn., U.S.	**B3**	139
Shenandoah National Park, Va., U.S.	**B4**	139
Shenango River Lake, res., U.S.	**D1**	131
Shendam, Nig.	**E6**	50
Shenipsit Lake, l., Ct., U.S.	**B6**	100
Shenmu, China	**B3**	30
Shenqiu, China	**C4**	30
Shenxian, China	**B4**	30
Shenyang, China	**C12**	28
Shenzhen, China	**E3**	30
Shepaug, stm., Ct., U.S.	**C2**	100
Shepaug Dam, Ct., U.S.	**D2**	100
Shepaug Reservoir, res., Ct., U.S.	**C2**	100
Shepetivka, Ukr.	**D9**	20
Shepherd, Mi., U.S.	**E6**	115
Shepherd, Tx., U.S.	**D5**	136
Shepherdstown, W.V., U.S.	**B7**	141
Shepherdsville, Ky., U.S.	**C4**	110
Sheppard Air Force Base, mil., Tx., U.S.	**C3**	136
Shepparton, Austl.	**H4**	62
Sherborn, Ma., U.S.	**h10**	114
Sherbro Island, i., S.L.	**E2**	50
Sherbrooke, P.Q., Can.	**D6**	90
Sherburn, Mn., U.S.	**G4**	116
Sherburne, co., Mn., U.S.	**E5**	116
Sheridan, Ar., U.S.	**C3**	97
Sheridan, Il., U.S.	**B5**	106
Sheridan, In., U.S.	**D5**	107
Sheridan, Mi., U.S.	**E5**	115
Sheridan, Mt., U.S.	**E4**	119
Sheridan, Or., U.S.	**B3**	130
Sheridan, Wy., U.S.	**B6**	143
Sheridan, co., Ks., U.S.	**C3**	109
Sheridan, co., Mt., U.S.	**B12**	119
Sheridan, co., N.D., U.S.	**B5**	127
Sheridan, co., Ne., U.S.	**B3**	120
Sheridan, co., Wy., U.S.	**B5**	143
Sheridan, Mount, mtn., Wy., U.S.	**B2**	143
Sherman, Tx., U.S.	**C4**	136
Sherman, co., Ks., U.S.	**C2**	109
Sherman, co., Ne., U.S.	**C6**	120
Sherman, co., Or., U.S.	**B6**	130
Sherman, co., Tx., U.S.	**A2**	136
Sherman Reservoir, res., Ne., U.S.	**C7**	120
Sherpur, Bngl.	**D6**	40
Sherrill, N.Y., U.S.	**B5**	125
Sherwood, P.E., Can.	**C6**	87
Sherwood, Ar., U.S.	**C3**	97
Sherwood, Or., U.S.	**h12**	130
Sherwood, Wi., U.S.	**h9**	142
Sherwood Manor, Ct., U.S.	**A5**	100
Sherwood Park, De., U.S.	**i7**	101
Shetek, Lake, l., Mn., U.S.	**G3**	116
Shetland Islands, is., Scot., U.K.	**h19**	12a
Shetucket, stm., Ct., U.S.	**C7**	100
Sheyenne, stm., N.D., U.S.	**C8**	127
Sheyenne Lake, res., N.D., U.S.	**B5**	127
Shiawassee, co., Mi., U.S.	**F6**	115
Shibām, Yemen	**G5**	38
Shicheng, China	**A7**	34
Shickshinny, Pa., U.S.	**D9**	131
Shidao, China	**D12**	28
Shiguaigou, China	**A3**	30
Shijiazhuang, China	**D10**	28
Shikārpur, Pak.	**E9**	42
Shikoku, i., Japan	**E14**	28
Shilabo, Eth.	**B8**	54
Shiliguri, India	**D5**	40
Shillington, Pa., U.S.	**F10**	131
Shillong, India	**D6**	40
Shiloh National Military Park, Tn., U.S.	**B3**	135
Shimla, India	**C3**	40
Shimoga, India	**G3**	40
Shimonoseki, Japan	**E14**	28
Shīndand, Afg.	**D8**	42
Shiner, Tx., U.S.	**E4**	136
Shinglehouse, Pa., U.S.	**C5**	131
Shingū, Japan	**E15**	28
Shinnston, W.V., U.S.	**B4**	141
Shinyanga, Tan.	**D6**	54
Shiocton, Wi., U.S.	**D5**	142
Shiono-misaki, c., Japan	**D3**	31
Shiping, China	**B4**	34
Ship Island, i., Ms., U.S.	**E5**	117
Ship Island Pass, strt., Ms., U.S.	**g7**	117
Shippegan, N.B., Can.	**B5**	87
Shippensburg, Pa., U.S.	**F6**	131
Shiprock, N.M., U.S.	**A1**	124
Ship Rock, mtn., N.M., U.S.	**A1**	124
Shīrāz, Iran	**E6**	42
Shiretoko-misaki, c., Japan	**B5**	31
Shirley, In., U.S.	**E6**	107
Shirley, Ma., U.S.	**A4**	114
Shirley Mountains, mts., Wy., U.S.	**D6**	143
Shīrvān, Iran	**C7**	42
Shishaldin Volcano, vol., Ak., U.S.	**E7**	95
Shishmaref, Ak., U.S.	**B6**	95
Shithāthah, Iraq	**F10**	44
Shively, Ky., U.S.	**B4**	110
Shivpuri, India	**D3**	40
Shizuoka, Japan	**C3**	31
Shkodër, Alb.	**C7**	18
Shoal Creek, stm., U.S.	**B4**	135
Shoal Harbour, Nf., Can.	**D4**	88
Shoal Lake, Mb., Can.	**D1**	86
Shoals, In., U.S.	**G4**	107
Shoals, Isles of, is., Me., U.S.	**E2**	112
Shoalwater, Cape, c., Wa., U.S.	**C1**	140
Shoemakersville, Pa., U.S.	**F10**	131
Shongopovi, Az., U.S.	**B5**	96
Shonto, Az., U.S.	**A5**	96
Shoreham, Mi., U.S.	**F4**	115
Shores Acres, R.I., U.S.	**E4**	132
Shoreview, Mn., U.S.	**m12**	116
Shorewood, Il., U.S.	**k8**	106
Shorewood, Mn., U.S.	**n11**	116
Shorewood, Wi., U.S.	**E6**	142
Short Beach, Ct., U.S.	**D4**	100
Shoshone, Id., U.S.	**G4**	105
Shoshone, co., Id., U.S.	**B2**	105
Shoshone, stm., Wy., U.S.	**B4**	143
Shoshone Falls, wtfl, Id., U.S.	**G4**	105
Shoshone Lake, l., Wy., U.S.	**B2**	143
Shoshone Mountains, mts., Nv., U.S.	**E4**	121
Shoshone Peak, mtn., Nv., U.S.	**G5**	121
Shoshone Range, mts., Nv., U.S.	**C5**	121
Shoshong, Bots.	**C4**	56
Shoshoni, Wy., U.S.	**C4**	143
Shostka, Ukr.	**D12**	20
Shouchang, China	**D4**	30
Shouguang, China	**B4**	30
Shoup, Id., U.S.	**D4**	105
Shouxian, China	**C4**	30
Show Low, Az., U.S.	**C5**	96
Shreve, Oh., U.S.	**B3**	128
Shreveport, La., U.S.	**B2**	111
Shrewsbury, Eng., U.K.	**D5**	12
Shrewsbury, Ma., U.S.	**B4**	114
Shrewsbury, N.J., U.S.	**C4**	123
Shrewsbury, Pa., U.S.	**G8**	131
Shuangcheng, China	**B13**	28
Shuangjiang, China	**B3**	34
Shuangliao, China	**C12**	28
Shuangyashan, China	**B14**	28
Shubenacadie, N.S., Can.	**D6**	87
Shubrâ El-Kheima, Egypt	**E10**	14
Shuksan, Mount, mtn., Wa., U.S.	**A4**	140
Shule, China	**B3**	40
Shullsburg, Wi., U.S.	**F3**	142
Shumagin Islands, is., Ak., U.S.	**E7**	95
Shunde, China	**B6**	34
Shungnak, Ak., U.S.	**B8**	95
Shurugwi, Zimb.	**B5**	56
Shūsh, Iran	**F13**	44
Shūshtar, Iran	**D5**	42
Shuswap Lake, l., B.C., Can.	**D8**	85
Shuyang, China	**C4**	30
Shwebo, Myan.	**B3**	34
Shwenyaung, Myan.	**B3**	34
Shyok, stm., Asia	**C3**	40
Siālkot, Pak.	**D10**	42
Siam see Thailand, ctry., Asia	**C4**	34
Siam, Gulf of see Thailand, Gulf of, b., Asia	**D4**	34
Sian see Xi'an, China	**E9**	28
Siargao Island, i., Phil.	**E9**	34
Šiaškotan, ostrov, i., Russia	**E17**	26
Siau, Pulau, i., Indon.	**C7**	36
Šibaj, Russia	**D10**	22
Šibenik, Cro.	**C5**	18
Siberia see Sibir', reg., Russia	**C12**	26
Siberut, Pulau, i., Indon.	**D1**	36
Sibi, Pak.	**E9**	42
Sibir' (Siberia), reg., Russia	**C12**	26
Sibircevo, Russia	**B2**	31
Sibirjakova, ostrov, i., Russia	**B9**	26
Sibiti, Congo	**D2**	54
Sibiu, Rom.	**G8**	20
Sibley, Ia., U.S.	**A2**	108
Sibley, La., U.S.	**B2**	111
Sibley, co., Mn., U.S.	**F4**	116
Sibolga, Indon.	**C1**	36
Sibsāgar, India	**D6**	40
Sibu, Malay.	**C4**	36
Sibuguey Bay, b., Phil.	**E8**	34
Sibut, C.A.R.	**B3**	54
Sibutu Island, i., Phil.	**F7**	34
Sibuyan Island, i., Phil.	**D8**	34
Sibuyan Sea, Phil.	**D8**	34
Sicamous, B.C., Can.	**D8**	85
Sichuan, prov., China	**E8**	28
Sicilia (Sicily), i., Italy	**F4**	18
Sicily see Sicilia, i., Italy	**F4**	18
Sicily, Strait of, strt.	**F3**	18
Sico Tinto, stm., Hond.	**B2**	80
Sicuani, Peru	**F5**	70
Siddipet, India	**F3**	40
Sidéradougou, Burkina	**D4**	50
Siderno, Italy	**E6**	18
Sidhi, India	**E4**	40
Sîdi Barrâni, Egypt	**D10**	48
Sidi bel Abbès, Alg.	**C4**	48
Sidi-Ifni, Mor.	**E2**	48
Sidley, Mount, mtn., Ant.	**D28**	67
Sidney, B.C., Can.	**E6**	85
Sidney, Ia., U.S.	**D2**	108
Sidney, Il., U.S.	**C5**	106
Sidney, Mt., U.S.	**C12**	119
Sidney, Ne., U.S.	**C3**	120
Sidney, N.Y., U.S.	**C5**	125
Sidney, Oh., U.S.	**B1**	128
Sidney Lanier, Lake, res., Ga., U.S.	**B2**	103
Sidon see Ṣaydā, Leb.	**F6**	44
Sidra, Gulf of see Surt, Khalīj, b., Libya	**D8**	48
Sidrolândia, Braz.	**C6**	72
Siedlce, Pol.	**C7**	20
Siegen, Ger.	**E11**	12
Siena, Italy	**C3**	18
Sieradz, Pol.	**D5**	20
Sierpc, Pol.	**C5**	20
Sierra, co., Ca., U.S.	**C3**	98
Sierra, co., N.M., U.S.	**D2**	124
Sierra Blanca Peak, mtn., N.M., U.S.	**D4**	124
Sierra Estrella, mts., Az., U.S.	**m8**	96
Sierra Gorda, Chile	**C4**	72
Sierra Leone, ctry., Afr.	**E2**	50
Sierra Madre, Ca., U.S.	**m12**	98
Sierra Nevada see Nevada, Sierra, mts., Ca., U.S.	**D4**	98
Sierra Vista, Az., U.S.	**F5**	96
Siesta Key, i., Fl., U.S.	**E4**	102
Sieverodonets'k, Ukr.	**E15**	20
Sífnos, i., Grc.	**F10**	18
Sig, Alg.	**J6**	16
Sighetu Marmaţiei, Rom.	**F7**	20
Sighişoara, Rom.	**F8**	20
Siglan, Russia	**D17**	26
Siglufjörður, Ice.	**k19**	10a
Signal Mountain, Tn., U.S.	**D8**	135
Signal Peak, mtn., Az., U.S.	**D1**	96
Signal Peak, mtn., Ut., U.S.	**F2**	137
Sigourney, Ia., U.S.	**C5**	108
Siguatepeque, Hond.	**C2**	80
Siguiri, Gui.	**D3**	50
Sigulda, Lat.	**H11**	10
Siguri Falls, wtfl, Tan.	**E7**	54
Sihanoukville see Kâmpóng Saôm, Camb.	**D4**	34
Sihote-Alin', mts., Russia	**E15**	26
Siirt, Tur.	**D9**	44
Sīkar, India	**D3**	40
Sikasso, Mali	**D3**	50
Sikeston, Mo., U.S.	**E8**	118
Sikiá, Grc.	**D9**	18
Sikiang see Xi, stm., China	**G10**	28
Sikkim, prov., India	**D5**	40
Šikotan, ostrov, i., Russia	**E16**	26
Siktjah, Russia	**B14**	26
Silao, Mex.	**C4**	78
Silchar, India	**E6**	40
Şile, Tur.	**B3**	44
Siler City, N.C., U.S.	**B3**	126
Silesia, hist. reg., Eur.	**D4**	20
Siletz, Or., U.S.	**C3**	130
Silghāt, India	**D6**	40
Silhouette, i., Sey.	**h13**	57b
Silifke, Tur.	**D5**	44
Siling Co, l., China	**E5**	28
Silistra, Bul.	**B11**	18
Silivri, Tur.	**B3**	44
Siljan, l., Swe.	**F6**	10
Šilka, Russia	**D13**	26
Šilka, stm., Russia	**D13**	26
Silkeborg, Den.	**H3**	10
Sillery, P.Q., Can.	**n17**	90
Sillustani, hist., Peru	**B3**	72
Siloam Springs, Ar., U.S.	**A1**	97
Silovo, Russia	**B16**	20
Silsbee, Tx., U.S.	**D5**	136
Silt, Co., U.S.	**B3**	99
Šilutė, Lith.	**I9**	10
Silvan, Tur.	**C9**	44
Silvassa, India	**E2**	40
Silver Bay, Mn., U.S.	**C7**	116
Silver Bow, co., Mt., U.S.	**E4**	119
Silver City, N.M., U.S.	**E1**	124
Silver City, Nv., U.S.	**D2**	121
Silver Creek, Ne., U.S.	**C8**	120
Silver Creek, N.Y., U.S.	**C1**	125
Silver Creek, stm., Or., U.S.	**D7**	130
Silverdale, Wa., U.S.	**B3**	140
Silver Grove, Ky., U.S.	**h14**	110
Silver Hill, Md., U.S.	**f9**	113
Silver Lake, Ks., U.S.	**C8**	109
Silver Lake, Ma., U.S.	**f11**	114
Silver Lake, Mn., U.S.	**F4**	116
Silver Lake, Wi., U.S.	**F5**	142
Silver Lake, l., De., U.S.	**D3**	101
Silver Lake, l., Ia., U.S.	**A3**	108
Silver Lake, l., Me., U.S.	**C3**	112
Silver Lake, l., N.H., U.S.	**C4**	122
Silver Lake, l., N.H., U.S.	**E2**	122
Silver Lake, l., Or., U.S.	**D7**	130
Silver Lake, l., Wa., U.S.	**g13**	140
Silverpeak, Nv., U.S.	**F4**	121
Silver Peak Range, mts., Nv., U.S.	**F4**	121
Silver Spring, Md., U.S.	**C3**	113
Silver Springs, Nv., U.S.	**D2**	121
Silver Star Mountain, mtn., Wa., U.S.	**A5**	140
Silverthrone Mountain, mtn., B.C., Can.	**D4**	85
Silvertip Mountain, mtn., Mt., U.S.	**C3**	119
Silverton, Co., U.S.	**D3**	99
Silverton, Id., U.S.	**B3**	105
Silverton, N.J., U.S.	**C4**	123
Silverton, Oh., U.S.	**o13**	128
Silverton, Or., U.S.	**C4**	130
Silvies, stm., Or., U.S.	**D7**	130
Silview, De., U.S.	**B3**	101
Silvis, Il., U.S.	**B3**	106
Šimanovsk, Russia	**D14**	26
Simao, China	**G8**	28
Simav, stm., Tur.	**C3**	44
Simba, D.R.C.	**C4**	54
Simcoe, On., Can.	**E4**	89
Simcoe, Lake, l., On., Can.	**C5**	89
Simeulue, Palau, i., Indon.	**C1**	36
Simferopol', Ukr.	**G13**	20
Simití, Col.	**B5**	70
Simi Valley, Ca., U.S.	**E4**	98
Simmesport, La., U.S.	**D4**	111
Simms Stream, stm., N.H., U.S.	**g7**	122
Simonette, stm., Ab., Can.	**B1**	84
Simon's Town, S. Afr.	**E2**	56
Simpson, Pa., U.S.	**C11**	131
Simpson, co., Ky., U.S.	**D3**	110
Simpson, co., Ms., U.S.	**D4**	117
Simpson Creek, stm., W.V., U.S.	**k10**	141
Simpson Desert, des., Austl.	**E6**	60
Simpsonville, Ky., U.S.	**B4**	110
Simpsonville, S.C., U.S.	**B3**	133

Name	Map Ref.	Page
Simsboro, La., U.S.	B3	111
Simsbury, Ct., U.S.	B4	100
Simušir, ostrov, i., Russia	E17	26
Sinabang, Indon.	C1	36
Sinai, pen., Egypt	E11	48
Sinai Peninsula see Sinai, pen., Egypt	E11	48
Sinaloa, state, Mex.	B3	78
Sīnāwin, Libya	D7	48
Sincelejo, Col.	B4	70
Sinclair, Wy., U.S.	E5	143
Sindangbarang, Indon.	E3	36
Sindara, Gabon	D2	54
Sindor, Russia	B9	22
Sinfra, C. Iv.	E3	50
Singalamwe, Nmb.	B3	56
Singapore, Sing.	C2	36
Singapore, ctry., Asia	C2	36
Singaraja, Indon.	H6	32
Singen, Ger.	G11	12
Singida, Tan.	D6	54
Singkaling Hkāmti, Myan.	A3	34
Singkang, Indon.	D6	36
Singkawang, Indon.	C3	36
Singkep, Pulau, i., Indon.	D2	36
Singleton, Austl.	G5	62
Sinjai, Indon.	E6	36
Sinjār, Iraq	D9	44
Sinkāt, Sudan	G12	48
Sinkiang see Xinjiang Uygur Zizhiqu, prov., China	C5	28
Sinnemahoning Creek, stm., Pa., U.S.	D5	131
Sinop, Tur.	A6	44
Sinskoe, Russia	C14	26
Sintang, Indon.	C4	36
Sint Helenabaai, b., S. Afr.	E2	56
Sinton, Tx., U.S.	E4	136
Siocon, Phil.	E8	34
Siófok, Hung.	F5	12
Sion, Switz.	A1	18
Sioux, co., Ia., U.S.	A1	108
Sioux, co., N.D., U.S.	C4	127
Sioux, co., Ne., U.S.	B2	120
Sioux Center, Ia., U.S.	A1	108
Sioux City, Ia., U.S.	B1	108
Sioux Falls, S.D., U.S.	D9	134
Sioux Lookout, On., Can.	o17	89
Sioux Rapids, Ia., U.S.	B2	108
Sipalay, Phil.	E8	34
Siping, China	C12	28
Sipiwesk Lake, l., Mb., Can.	B3	86
Siple, Mount, mtn., Ant.	D28	67
Sipsey, stm., Al., U.S.	B2	94
Sipsey Fork, stm., Al., U.S.	A2	94
Sipura, Pulau, i., Indon.	D1	36
Siquijor Island, i., Phil.	E8	34
Si Racha, Thai.	D4	34
Siracusa, Italy	F5	18
Sirājganj, Bngl.	E5	40
Sir Douglas, Mount, mtn., Can.	D3	84
Sir Edward Pellew Group, is., Austl.	D6	60
Siren, Wi., U.S.	C1	142
Siret, stm., Eur.	G9	20
Sīrjān, Iran	E7	42
Şırnak, Tur.	D10	44
Sirohi, India	E2	40
Sironj, India	E3	40
Síros, i., Grc.	F10	18
Sirsa, India	D3	40
Sir Sandford, Mount, mtn., B.C., Can.	D9	85
Sirte, Gulf of see Surt, Khalīj, b., Libya	D8	48
Sir Wilfrid Laurier, Mount, mtn., B.C., Can.	C8	85
Sisaba, mtn., Tan.	E5	54
Sisak, Cro.	B6	18
Si Sa Ket, Thai.	C4	34
Sishen, S. Afr.	D3	56
Sisian, Arm.	C12	44
Siskiyou, co., Ca., U.S.	B2	98
Siskiyou Mountains, mts., U.S.	F3	130
Siskiyou Pass, Or., U.S.	E4	130
Sisôphŏn, Camb.	D4	34
Sisseton, S.D., U.S.	B8	134
Sisseton Indian Reservation, U.S.	B8	134
Sissiboo, stm., N.S., Can.	E4	87
Sisson Branch Reservoir, res., N.B., Can.	B2	87
Sissonville, W.V., U.S.	C3	141
Sisters, Or., U.S.	C5	130
Sistersville, W.V., U.S.	B4	141
Sītāpur, India	D4	40
Sitasjaure, l., Eur.	C7	10
Sitka, Ak., U.S.	D12	95
Sitka National Historical Park, Ak., U.S.	m22	95
Sitka Sound, strt., Ak., U.S.	m22	95
Sittoung, stm., Myan.	C3	34
Sittwe, Myan.	B2	34
Sivas, Tur.	C7	44
Sivers'kyi Donets' see Northern Donets, stm., Eur.	E14	20
Sivrihisar, Tur.	C4	44
Siwa, Egypt	E10	48
Sixian, China	C8	28
Sixth Cataract, wtfl, Sudan	G11	48
Siyäzän, Azer.	B13	44
Siziwang Qi, China	A3	30
Sjælland, i., Den.	I4	10
Skadovs'k, Ukr.	F12	20
Skærbæk, Den.	I3	10
Skagen, Den.	H4	10
Skagerrak, strt., Eur.	B11	12
Skagit, co., Wa., U.S.	A4	140
Skagway, Ak., U.S.	D12	95
Skamania, co., Wa., U.S.	D3	140
Skanderborg, Den.	H3	10
Skåne, hist. reg., Swe.	I5	10
Skaneateles, N.Y., U.S.	C4	125
Skaneateles Lake, l., N.Y., U.S.	C4	125
Skārdu, Pak.	C11	42
Skarżysko-Kamienna, Pol.	D6	20
Skaudvilė, Lith.	I10	10
Skaw, The see Grenen, c., Den.	H4	10
Skegness, Eng., U.K.	D7	12
Skeleton Lake, l., On., Can.	B5	89
Skellefteå, Swe.	D9	10
Skellefteälven, stm., Swe.	D8	10
Ski, Nor.	G4	10
Skiatook, Ok., U.S.	A5	129
Skiatook Reservoir, res., Ok., U.S.	A5	129
Skien, Nor.	G3	10
Skierniewice, Pol.	D6	20
Skihist Mountain, mtn., B.C., Can.	D7	85
Skikda, Alg.	C6	48
Skillet Fork, stm., Il., U.S.	E5	106
Skive, Den.	H3	10
Sklad, Russia	B14	26
Skokie, Il., U.S.	A6	106
Skokomish Indian Reservation, Wa., U.S.	B2	140
Skópelos, i., Grc.	E9	18
Skopin, Russia	C15	20
Skopje, Mac.	C8	18
Skövde, Swe.	G5	10
Skowhegan, Me., U.S.	D3	112
Skull Valley, val., Ut., U.S.	C3	137
Skull Valley Indian Reservation, Ut., U.S.	C3	137
Skuna, stm., Ms., U.S.	B4	117
Skunk, stm., Ia., U.S.	D6	108
Skvyra, Ukr.	G10	20
Skwentna, stm., Ak., U.S.	g15	95
Skye, Island of, i., Scot., U.K.	B3	12
Skykomish, stm., Wa., U.S.	B4	140
Skyland, N.C., U.S.	f10	126
Skyland, Nv., U.S.	D2	121
Skyline, Al., U.S.	A3	94
Slagnäs, Swe.	D8	10
Slamet, Gunung, vol., Indon.	E3	36
Slancy, Russia	G13	10
Slater, Ia., U.S.	C4	108
Slater, Mo., U.S.	B4	118
Slater, S.C., U.S.	A3	133
Slatersville, R.I., U.S.	A3	132
Slatersville Reservoir, res., R.I., U.S.	B3	132
Slatina, Rom.	G8	20
Slatington, Pa., U.S.	E10	131
Slaton, Tx., U.S.	C2	136
Slaughter, La., U.S.	D4	111
Slautnoe, Russia	C18	26
Slave, stm., Can.	F17	82
Slave Lake, Ab., Can.	B3	84
Slavgorod, Russia	D9	26
Slavjanka, Russia	B2	31
Slavjansk-na-Kubani, Russia	G15	20
Slavonia see Slavonija, hist. reg., Cro.	B6	18
Slavonija, hist. reg., Cro.	B6	18
Slavonski Brod, Cro.	B6	18
Slavuta, Ukr.	D9	20
Slayton, Mn., U.S.	G3	116
Sleeping Bear Dunes National Lakeshore, Mi., U.S.	D4	115
Sleeping Bear Point, c., Mi., U.S.	D4	115
Sleepy Eye, Mn., U.S.	F4	116
Slickville, Pa., U.S.	F2	131
Slidell, La., U.S.	D6	111
Sliderock Mountain, mtn., Mt., U.S.	D3	119
Sligo, Ire.	C2	12
Slinger, Wi., U.S.	E5	142
Slippery Rock, Pa., U.S.	D1	131
Sliven, Bul.	C11	18
Sljudjanka, Russia	D12	26
Sloan, Ia., U.S.	B1	108
Sloan, N.Y., U.S.	C2	125
Slobodskoj, Russia	D7	26
Slobozia, Mol.	F10	20
Slobozia, Rom.	E11	20
Slocomb, Al., U.S.	D4	94
Slonim, Bela.	C8	20
Slope, co., N.D., U.S.	C2	127
Slough, Eng., U.K.	E6	12
Slovakia, ctry., Eur.	F6	20
Slovenia, ctry., Eur.	A5	18
Slov'ians'k, Ukr.	E14	20
Sluch, stm., Ukr.	D9	20
Sluck, Bela.	C9	20
Słupsk, Pol.	B4	20
Smackover, Ar., U.S.	D3	97
Småland, hist. reg., Swe.	H6	10
Small Point, c., Me., U.S.	g8	112
Smallwood Reservoir, res., Nf., Can.	g8	88
Smarhon', Bela.	B9	20
Smederevo, Yugo.	B8	18
Smethport, Pa., U.S.	C5	131
Šmidovič, Russia	B14	28
Šmidta, ostrov, i., Russia	A9	26
Smila, Ukr.	E11	20
Smith, co., Ks., U.S.	C5	109
Smith, co., Ms., U.S.	C4	117
Smith, co., Tn., U.S.	A5	135
Smith, co., Tx., U.S.	C5	136
Smith, stm., Mt., U.S.	D5	119
Smith, stm., U.S.	D3	139
Smith and Sayles Reservoir, res., R.I., U.S.	B2	132
Smith Bay, b., Ak., U.S.	A9	95
Smith Canyon, val., Co., U.S.	D7	99
Smith Center, Ks., U.S.	C5	109
Smithers, B.C., Can.	B4	85
Smithers, W.V., U.S.	C3	141
Smithfield, N.C., U.S.	B4	126
Smithfield, Pa., U.S.	G2	131
Smithfield, Ut., U.S.	B4	137
Smithfield, Va., U.S.	D6	139
Smith Island, i., Va., U.S.	C7	139
Smith Island, i., U.S.	D5	113
Smith Mountain Lake, res., Va., U.S.	C3	139
Smith Peak, mtn., Id., U.S.	A2	105
Smith Point, c., Ma., U.S.	D7	114
Smith Point, c., Va., U.S.	C6	139
Smiths, Al., U.S.	C4	94
Smithsburg, Md., U.S.	A2	113
Smiths Falls, On., Can.	C8	89
Smiths Grove, Ky., U.S.	C3	110
Smithton, Austl.	I4	62
Smithton, Il., U.S.	E4	106
Smithtown, N.Y., U.S.	n15	125
Smithville, Ga., U.S.	E2	103
Smithville, Mo., U.S.	B3	118
Smithville, Ms., U.S.	A5	117
Smithville, Oh., U.S.	B4	128
Smithville, Tn., U.S.	D8	135
Smithville, Tx., U.S.	D4	136
Smithville Lake, res., Mo., U.S.	B3	118
Smoke Creek Desert, des., Nv., U.S.	C2	121
Smokey, Cape, c., N.S., Can.	C9	87
Smokey Dome, mtn., Id., U.S.	F4	105
Smoky, stm., Ab., Can.	B1	84
Smoky Hill, stm., U.S.	D5	109
Smoky Lake, Ab., Can.	B4	84
Smoky Mountains, mts., Id., U.S.	F4	105
Smøla, i., Nor.	E3	10
Smolensk, Russia	D5	26
Smoljan, Bul.	D10	18
Smooth Rock Falls, On., Can.	o19	89
Smoothstone Lake, l., Sk., Can.	C2	91
Smyrna see İzmir, Tur.	C2	44
Smyrna, De., U.S.	C3	101
Smyrna, Ga., U.S.	C2	103
Smyrna, Tn., U.S.	B5	135
Smyrna, stm., De., U.S.	C3	101
Smyth, co., Va., U.S.	f10	139
Snake, stm., Mn., U.S.	B1	116
Snake, stm., Ne., U.S.	B4	120
Snake, stm., Ks., U.S.	C4	92
Snake, stm., U.S.	D5	116
Snake Range, mts., Nv., U.S.	E7	121
Snake River Plain, pl., Id., U.S.	F2	105
Snake River Range, mts., U.S.	C2	143
Sneads, Fl., U.S.	B2	102
Sneedville, Tn., U.S.	C10	135
Snihurivka, Ukr.	F12	20
Snipe Keys, is., Fl., U.S.	H5	102
Snøhetta, mtn., Nor.	E3	10
Snohomish, Wa., U.S.	B3	140
Snohomish, co., Wa., U.S.	A4	140
Snoqualmie, Wa., U.S.	B4	140
Snoqualmie, stm., Wa., U.S.	B4	140
Snoqualmie Pass, Wa., U.S.	B4	140
Snøtinden, mtn., Nor.	C5	10
Snowbank Lake, l., Mn., U.S.	B7	116
Snowdon, mtn., Wales, U.K.	D4	12
Snowdrift see Łutselk'e, N.T., Can.	F17	82
Snowflake, Az., U.S.	C5	96
Snow Hill, Md., U.S.	D7	113
Snow Hill, N.C., U.S.	B5	126
Snowking Mountain, mtn., Wa., U.S.	A4	140
Snow Lake, Mb., Can.	B1	86
Snowmass Mountain, mtn., Co., U.S.	B3	99
Snow Peak, mtn., Wa., U.S.	A7	140
Snowshoe Lake, l., Me., U.S.	B4	112
Snowshoe Peak, mtn., Mt., U.S.	B1	119
Snow Water Lake, l., Nv., U.S.	C7	121
Snowy Mountains, mts., Austl.	H4	62
Snowyside Peak, mtn., Id., U.S.	F4	105
Snyder, Ok., U.S.	C3	129
Snyder, Tx., U.S.	C2	136
Snyder, co., Pa., U.S.	E7	131
Soacha, Col.	E5	80
Soalala, Madag.	B8	56
Soap Lake, Wa., U.S.	B6	140
Sobradinho, Represa de, res., Braz.	D3	74
Sobral, Braz.	B3	74
Socastee, S.C., U.S.	D9	133
Soči, Russia	E5	26
Social Circle, Ga., U.S.	C3	103
Société, Archipel de la (Society Islands), is., Fr. Poly.	F14	58
Society Hill, S.C., U.S.	B8	133
Society Islands see Société, Archipel de la, is., Fr. Poly.	F14	58
Socorro, Col.	B5	70
Socorro, N.M., U.S.	C3	124
Socorro, co., N.M., U.S.	D2	124
Socorro, Isla, i., Mex.	D2	78
Socotra see Suquţrā, i., Yemen	H6	38
Soda Springs, Id., U.S.	G7	105
Soddy-Daisy, Tn., U.S.	D8	135
Söderhamn, Swe.	G7	10
Söderköping, Swe.	G7	10
Södertälje, Swe.	G7	10
Sodo, Eth.	B7	54
Sodus, N.Y., U.S.	B3	125
Soe, Indon.	E6	36
Sofala, Moz.	C5	56
Sofia see Sofija, Bul.	C9	18
Sofija, Bul.	C9	18
Sogamoso, Col.	D5	80
Sognefjorden, b., Nor.	F1	10
Sog Xian, China	E6	28
Sointula, B.C., Can.	D4	85
Soissons, Fr.	C8	16
Sojat, India	D2	40
Šojna, Russia	A7	22
Söke, Tur.	D2	44
Sokodé, Togo	E5	50
Sokol, Russia	C7	22
Sokol, Russia	B14	26
Sokółka, Pol.	C7	20
Sokolo, Mali	D3	50
Sokoto, Nig.	D6	50
Sokoto, stm., Nig.	D5	50
Solai, Kenya	C7	54
Solana, Fl., U.S.	F5	102
Solano, Phil.	C8	34
Solano, co., Ca., U.S.	C3	98
Solāpur, India	F3	40
Soldier, stm., Ia., U.S.	C2	108
Soldier Key, i., Fl., U.S.	s3	102
Soldotna, Ak., U.S.	g16	95
Soledad, Col.	A5	70
Soledad, Ca., U.S.	D3	98
Soledad Díez Gutiérrez, Mex.	C4	78
Solikamsk, Russia	D7	26
Sol'-Ileck, Russia	D10	22
Solimões see Amazon, stm., S.A.	D6	70
Sollefteå, Swe.	E7	10
Sóller, Spain	H8	16
Šologoncy, Russia	C13	26
Solomon, Ks., U.S.	D6	109
Solomon, stm., Ks., U.S.	C6	109
Solomon Basin	I18	64
Solomon Islands, ctry., Oc.	B6	62
Solomons, Md., U.S.	D5	113
Solomon Sea, Oc.	B5	62
Solon, China	B12	28
Solon, Ia., U.S.	C6	108
Solon, Oh., U.S.	A4	128
Solothurn, Switz.	A1	18
Solov'evsk, Russia	A11	28
Solvay, N.Y., U.S.	B4	125
Solway Firth, b., U.K.	C5	12
Solwezi, Zam.	A4	56
Soma, Tur.	C2	44
Somabhula, Zimb.	B4	56
Somalia, ctry., Afr.	I14	46
Somali Basin	H8	64
Sombor, Yugo.	B7	18
Sombrerete, Mex.	C4	78
Sombrero Channel, strt., India	H6	40
Somerdale, N.J., U.S.	D2	123
Somers, Ct., U.S.	B6	100
Somers, Mt., U.S.	B2	119
Somerset, Mb., Can.	E2	86
Somerset, Ky., U.S.	C5	110
Somerset, Ma., U.S.	C5	114
Somerset, N.J., U.S.	B3	123
Somerset, Oh., U.S.	C3	128
Somerset, Tx., U.S.	k7	136
Somerset, Wi., U.S.	C1	142
Somerset, co., Md., U.S.	D6	113
Somerset, co., Me., U.S.	C2	112
Somerset, co., N.J., U.S.	B3	123
Somerset, co., Pa., U.S.	G3	131
Somerset East, S. Afr.	E4	56
Somerset Reservoir, res., Vt., U.S.	E3	138
Somers Point, N.J., U.S.	E3	123
Somersville, Ct., U.S.	B6	100
Somersworth, N.H., U.S.	D5	122
Somerton, Az., U.S.	E1	96
Somervell, co., Tx., U.S.	C4	136
Somerville, Ma., U.S.	B5	114
Somerville, N.J., U.S.	B3	123
Somerville, Tn., U.S.	B2	135
Somerville, Tx., U.S.	D4	136
Somerville Lake, res., Tx., U.S.	D4	136
Somonauk, Il., U.S.	B5	106
Son, stm., India	E4	40
Sønderborg, Den.	I3	10
Søndre Strømfjord, Grnld.	E29	82
Søndre Strømfjord, b., Grnld.	E29	82
Sondrio, Italy	A2	18
Sonepur, India	E4	40
Song, Nig.	E7	50
Song Cau, Viet.	D5	34
Songea, Tan.	F7	54
Songhua, stm., China	B14	28
Songhua Hu, res., China	C13	28
Songkhla, Thai.	E4	34
Songnim, N. Kor.	D13	28
Songololo, D.R.C.	E2	54
Songpan, China	C1	30
Sonīpat, India	D3	40
Sonkël', ozero, l., Kyrg.	A3	40
Son La, Viet.	B4	34
Sonmiāni Bay, b., Pak.	E9	42
Sonneberg, Ger.	E12	12
Sonoma, Ca., U.S.	C2	98
Sonoma, co., Ca., U.S.	C2	98
Sonoma Peak, mtn., Nv., U.S.	C4	121
Sonoma Range, mts., Nv., U.S.	C4	121
Sonora, Ca., U.S.	D3	98
Sonora, Tx., U.S.	D2	136
Sonora, state, Mex.	B2	78
Sonora, stm., Mex.	B2	78
Sonoran Desert, des., N.A.	E5	92
Sonoyta, Mex.	A2	78
Sonqor, Iran	E12	44
Sonsón, Col.	D4	80
Sonsonate, El Sal.	C1	80
Sonsorol Islands, is., Palau	E9	32
Son Tay, Viet.	B5	34
Sonthofen, Ger.	G12	12
Soochow see Suzhou, China	E12	28
Soperton, Ga., U.S.	D4	103
Sophia, W.V., U.S.	D3	141
Sopot, Pol.	B5	20
Sopron, Hung.	F4	20
Sopur, India	C2	40
Sorel, P.Q., Can.	C4	90
Sorgun, Tur.	C6	44
Soria, Spain	G5	16
Soroca, Mol.	E10	20
Sorocaba, Braz.	F2	74
Soročinsk, Russia	D9	22
Sorong, Indon.	D8	36
Soroti, Ug.	C6	54
Sørøya, i., Nor.	A10	10
Sorrento, Italy	D5	111
Sør Rondane Mountains, mts., Ant.	D7	67
Sorsele, Swe.	D7	10
Sorsogon, Phil.	D8	34
Sort, Spain	F7	16
Sortavala, Russia	F14	10
Sosnogorsk, Russia	B9	22
Sosnovka, Russia	A7	22
Sosnovo-Ozërskoe, Russia	A10	28
Sosnowiec, Pol.	D5	20
Sos'va, Russia	B11	22
Sotouboua, Togo	E5	50
Soubré, C. Iv.	E3	50
Soucook, stm., N.H., U.S.	D4	122
Soudan, Mn., U.S.	C6	116
Souderton, Pa., U.S.	F11	131
Souhegan, stm., N.H., U.S.	E3	122
Sŏul (Seoul), S. Kor.	D13	28
Souq Ahras, Alg.	F1	18
Sources, Mont-aux-, mtn., Afr.	D4	56
Soure, Braz.	B2	74
Souris, Mb., Can.	E1	86
Souris, P.E.I., Can.	C7	87
Souris, stm., N.A.	B7	92
Sousa, Braz.	C4	74
Sousse, Tun.	C7	48
South, stm., Ia., U.S.	C4	108
South, stm., N.C., U.S.	C4	126
South Acton, Ma., U.S.	g10	114
South Amboy, N.J., U.S.	C4	123
South America	G9	68
South Amherst, Ma., U.S.	B2	114
South Amherst, Oh., U.S.	A3	128
Southampton, On., Can.	C3	89
Southampton, Eng., U.K.	E6	12
Southampton, N.Y., U.S.	n16	125
Southampton, co., Va., U.S.	D5	139
South Andaman, i., India	G6	40
South Anna, stm., Va., U.S.	C5	139
South Australia, state, Austl.	F5	60
South Australian Basin	L16	64
Southaven, Ms., U.S.	A3	117
South Bald Mountain, mtn., Co., U.S.	A5	99
South Baldy, mtn., N.M., U.S.	D2	124

Name	Map Ref.	Page
South Barre, Vt., U.S.	C3	138
South Bay, Fl., U.S.	F6	102
South Beloit, Il., U.S.	A4	106
South Bend, In., U.S.	A5	107
South Bend, Wa., U.S.	C2	140
South Berwick, Me., U.S.	E2	112
South Bloomfield, Oh., U.S.	C3	128
South Boston, Va., U.S.	D4	139
South Bound Brook, N.J., U.S.	B3	123
South Branch Lake, l., Me., U.S.	C4	112
Southbridge, Ma., U.S.	B3	114
South Bristol, Me., U.S.	E3	112
South Britain, Ct., U.S.	D3	100
South Broadway, Wa., U.S.	C5	140
South Burlington, Vt., U.S.	C2	138
Southbury, Ct., U.S.	D3	100
South Carolina, state, U.S.	D6	133
South Charleston, Oh., U.S.	C2	128
South Charleston, W.V., U.S.	C3	141
South Chicago Heights, Il., U.S.	m9	106
South China Basin	G14	64
South China Sea, Asia	D5	32
South Coffeyville, Ok., U.S.	A6	129
South Congaree, S.C., U.S.	D5	133
South Connellsville, Pa., U.S.	G2	131
South Dakota, state, U.S.	C5	134
South Dartmouth, Ma., U.S.	C6	114
South Daytona, Fl., U.S.	C5	102
South Deerfield, Ma., U.S.	B2	114
South Dennis, Ma., U.S.	C7	114
South Duxbury, Ma., U.S.	B6	114
South East Cape, c., Austl.	I4	62
Southeast Cape, c., Ak., U.S.	C6	95
Southeast Indian Ridge	M13	64
South Easton, Ma., U.S.	B5	114
Southeast Pacific Basin	O25	64
Southeast Pass, strt., La., U.S.	E7	111
South East Point, c., Austl.	H4	62
Southeast Point, c., R.I., U.S.	h7	132
South Elgin, Il., U.S.	B5	106
Southend-on-Sea, Eng., U.K.	E7	12
Southern Alps, mts., N.Z.	p13	63c
Southern Cook Islands, is., Cook Is.	F13	58
Southern Cross, Austl.	G2	60
Southern Indian Lake, l., Mb., Can.	f8	86
Southern Ocean	J19	4
Southern Pines, N.C., U.S.	B3	126
Southern Ute Indian Reservation, Co., U.S.	D2	99
South Euclid, Oh., U.S.	g9	128
Southey, Sk., Can.	G3	91
South Fabius, stm., Mo., U.S.	A5	118
South Fallsburg, N.Y., U.S.	D6	125
Southfield, Mi., U.S.	o15	115
South Fiji Basin	K20	64
South Fork, Pa., U.S.	F4	131
South Fox Island, i., Mi., U.S.	C5	115
South Fulton, Tn., U.S.	A3	135
South Gastonia, N.C., U.S.	B1	126
South Gate, Ca., U.S.	n12	98
Southgate, Ky., U.S.	h14	110
Southgate, Mi., U.S.	p15	115
South Georgia, i., S. Geor.	H9	69
South Glastonbury, Ct., U.S.	C5	100
South Glens Falls, N.Y., U.S.	B7	125
South Grafton, Ma., U.S.	B4	114
South Grand, stm., Mo., U.S.	C3	118
South Hadley, Ma., U.S.	B2	114
South Hadley Falls, Ma., U.S.	B2	114
South Hamilton, Ma., U.S.	A6	114
South Haven, In., U.S.	A3	107
South Haven, Mi., U.S.	F4	115
South Hero Island, i., Vt., U.S.	B2	138
South Hill, Va., U.S.	D4	139
South Hingham, Ma., U.S.	h12	114
South Holland, Il., U.S.	k9	106
South Holston Lake, res., U.S.	A9	135
South Honshu Ridge	E16	64
South Hooksett, N.H., U.S.	D4	122
South Hopkinton, R.I., U.S.	F1	132
South Houston, Tx., U.S.	r14	136
South Hutchinson, Ks., U.S.	f11	109
South Indian Basin	N12	64
South Indian Lake, Mb., Can.	A2	86
Southington, Ct., U.S.	C4	100
South International Falls, Mn., U.S.	B5	116
South Island, i., N.Z.	I10	58
South Island, i., S.C., U.S.	E9	133
South Jacksonville, Il., U.S.	D3	106
South Jordan, Ut., U.S.	C3	137
South Kenosha, Wi., U.S.	F6	142
South Korea see Korea, South, ctry., Asia	D10	28
South Lake Tahoe, Ca., U.S.	C4	98
South Lancaster, Ma., U.S.	B4	114
South Lebanon, Oh., U.S.	C1	128
South Lyon, Mi., U.S.	F7	115

Name	Map Ref.	Page
South Magnetic Pole	C18	67
South Manitou Island, i., Mi., U.S.	C4	115
South Marsh Island, i., Md., U.S.	D5	113
South Miami, Fl., U.S.	G6	102
South Miami Heights, Fl., U.S.	s13	102
South Mills, N.C., U.S.	A6	126
South Milwaukee, Wi., U.S.	F6	142
Southmont, N.C., U.S.	B2	126
South Moose Lake, l., Mb., Can.	C1	86
South Mountain, mtn., Id., U.S.	G2	105
South Mountain, mtn., N.M., U.S.	k8	124
South Mountains, mts., Az., U.S.	m8	96
South Mountains, mts., N.C., U.S.	B1	126
South New River Canal, Fl., U.S.	r3	102
South Ogden, Ut., U.S.	B4	137
Southold, N.Y., U.S.	m16	125
South Orange, N.J., U.S.	B4	123
South Orkney Islands, is., Ant.	C36	67
South Paris, Me., U.S.	D2	112
South Park, val., Co., U.S.	B5	99
South Pass, Wy., U.S.	D4	143
South Pass, strt., La., U.S.	F6	111
South Patrick Shores, Fl., U.S.	D6	102
South Pekin, Il., U.S.	C4	106
South Pittsburg, Tn., U.S.	D8	135
South Plainfield, N.J., U.S.	B4	123
South Platte, stm., U.S.	C7	92
South Point, c., Mi., U.S.	D7	115
South Pole	E35	67
Southport (Gold Coast), Austl.	F5	62
Southport, Fl., U.S.	u16	102
Southport, In., U.S.	E5	107
Southport, N.C., U.S.	D4	126
Southport, N.Y., U.S.	C4	125
South Portland, Me., U.S.	E2	112
South Portsmouth, Ky., U.S.	B6	110
South Range, Mi., U.S.	A2	115
South River, On., Can.	B5	89
South River, N.J., U.S.	C4	123
South River, b., Md., U.S.	C4	113
South Royalton, Vt., U.S.	D3	138
South Saint Paul, Mn., U.S.	n12	116
South Sandwich Islands, is., S. Geor.	B2	67
South Sandwich Trench	N11	66
South San Francisco, Ca., U.S.	h8	98
South Shetland Islands, is., Ant.	B35	67
Southside, Al., U.S.	B3	94
Southside Place, Tx., U.S.	r14	136
South Sioux City, Ne., U.S.	B9	120
South Skunk, stm., Ia., U.S.	C4	108
South Streator, Il., U.S.	B5	106
South Taranaki Bight, b., N.Z.	o13	63c
South Tasman Rise	M17	64
South Toms River, N.J., U.S.	D4	123
South Torrington, Wy., U.S.	D8	143
South Tucson, Az., U.S.	E5	96
South Venice, Fl., U.S.	E4	102
South Ventana Cone, vol., Ca., U.S.	D3	98
South Waverly, Pa., U.S.	C8	131
South Wellfleet, Ma., U.S.	C8	114
South Wellington, B.C., Can.	f12	85
South Wenatchee, Wa., U.S.	B5	140
South West Africa see Namibia, ctry., Afr.	C2	56
South West Cape, c., N.Z.	q12	63c
Southwest Channel, strt., Fl., U.S.	E4	102
South West City, Mo., U.S.	E3	118
Southwest Harbor, Me., U.S.	D4	112
Southwest Head, c., N.B., Can.	E3	87
Southwest Indian Ridge	L8	64
Southwest Miramichi, stm., N.B., Can.	C3	87
Southwest Pacific Basin	L23	64
Southwest Pass, strt., La., U.S.	E3	111
Southwest Pass, strt., La., U.S.	F6	111
Southwest Point, c., R.I., U.S.	h7	132
South Weymouth Naval Air Station, mil., Ma., U.S.	h12	114
South Whitley, In., U.S.	B6	107
South Williamson, Ky., U.S.	C7	110
South Williamsport, Pa., U.S.	D7	131
South Windham, Ct., U.S.	C7	100
South Windham, Me., U.S.	E2	112
South Windsor, Ct., U.S.	B5	100
Southwood Acres, Ct., U.S.	A5	100
South Woodstock, Ct., U.S.	B8	100
South Yarmouth, Ma., U.S.	C7	114
South Zanesville, Oh., U.S.	C3	128
Sovetsk, Russia	I9	10

Name	Map Ref.	Page
Sovetsk, Russia	C8	22
Sovetskaja Gavan', Russia	E16	26
Soviets'kyi, Ukr.	G13	20
Soyo, Ang.	E2	54
Sozh, stm., Eur.	C11	20
Spain, ctry., Eur.	H5	16
Spalding, co., Ga., U.S.	C2	103
Spanaway, Wa., U.S.	B3	140
Spangler, Pa., U.S.	E4	131
Spaniard's Bay, Nf., Can.	E5	88
Spanish Fork, Ut., U.S.	C4	137
Spanish Fort, Al., U.S.	E2	94
Spanish Lake, Mo., U.S.	f13	118
Spanish Peak, mtn., Or., U.S.	C7	130
Spanish Sahara see Western Sahara, dep., Afr.	B2	50
Spanish Town, Jam.	B4	80
Sparks, Ga., U.S.	E3	103
Sparks, Nv., U.S.	D2	121
Sparta, On., Can.	E4	89
Sparta, Ga., U.S.	C4	103
Sparta, Il., U.S.	E4	106
Sparta, Mi., U.S.	E5	115
Sparta, Mo., U.S.	D4	118
Sparta, N.C., U.S.	A1	126
Sparta (Lake Mohawk), N.J., U.S.	A3	123
Sparta, Tn., U.S.	D8	135
Sparta, Wi., U.S.	E3	142
Spartanburg, S.C., U.S.	B4	133
Spartanburg, co., S.C., U.S.	B3	133
Spárti, Grc.	F9	18
Spartivento, Capo, c., Italy	E2	18
Sparwood, B.C., Can.	E10	85
Spassk-Dal'nij, Russia	E15	26
Spavinaw Creek, stm., Ok., U.S.	A7	129
Spear, Cape, c., Nf., Can.	E5	88
Spearfish, S.D., U.S.	C2	134
Spearman, Tx., U.S.	A2	136
Spearville, Ks., U.S.	E4	109
Speed, In., U.S.	H6	107
Speedway, In., U.S.	E5	107
Speke Gulf, b., Tan.	D6	54
Spence Bay see Taloyoak, N.T., Can.	E21	82
Spencer, Ia., U.S.	A2	108
Spencer, In., U.S.	F4	107
Spencer, Ma., U.S.	B4	114
Spencer, N.C., U.S.	B2	126
Spencer, Tn., U.S.	D8	135
Spencer, W.V., U.S.	C3	141
Spencer, Wi., U.S.	D3	142
Spencer, co., In., U.S.	H4	107
Spencer, co., Ky., U.S.	B4	110
Spencer, Cape, c., Austl.	H2	62
Spencer, Cape, c., Ak., U.S.	k21	95
Spencer Gulf, b., Austl.	G2	62
Spencer Lake, l., Me., U.S.	C2	112
Spencerport, N.Y., U.S.	B3	125
Spencerville, Md., U.S.	B4	113
Spencerville, Oh., U.S.	B1	128
Sperry, Ok., U.S.	A6	129
Spesutie Island, i., Md., U.S.	B5	113
Speyer, Ger.	F11	12
Spezia see La Spezia, Italy	B2	18
Spiceland, In., U.S.	E7	107
Spicer, Mn., U.S.	E4	116
Spider Lake, l., Wi., U.S.	B2	142
Spindale, N.C., U.S.	B1	126
Spink, co., S.D., U.S.	C7	134
Spirit Lake, Ia., U.S.	A2	108
Spirit Lake, Id., U.S.	B2	105
Spirit Lake, l., Ia., U.S.	A2	108
Spirit Lake, l., Wa., U.S.	C3	140
Spirit River, Ab., Can.	B1	84
Spirit River Flowage, res., Wi., U.S.	C4	142
Spiro, Ok., U.S.	B7	129
Spišská Nová Ves, Slvk.	E6	20
Spitsbergen, i., Nor.	B3	26
Spittal an der Drau, Aus.	G13	12
Split, Cro.	C6	18
Split, Cape, c., N.S., Can.	D5	87
Split Lake, l., Mb., Can.	A4	86
Split Rock Creek, stm., U.S.	G2	116
Spofford, Lake, l., N.H., U.S.	E2	122
Spokane, Wa., U.S.	B8	140
Spokane, co., Wa., U.S.	B8	140
Spokane, stm., U.S.	B8	140
Spokane, Mount, mtn., Wa., U.S.	B8	140
Spokane Indian Reservation, Wa., U.S.	B8	140
Spoleto, Italy	C4	18
Spoon, stm., Il., U.S.	C3	106
Spooner, Wi., U.S.	C2	142
Spooner Lake, l., Wi., U.S.	C2	142
Spornoe, Russia	C17	26
Spotswood, N.J., U.S.	C4	123
Spotsylvania, co., Va., U.S.	B5	139
Sprague, W.V., U.S.	n13	141
Sprague, stm., Or., U.S.	E5	130
Sprague Lake, l., Wa., U.S.	B7	140
Spratly Islands, is., Asia	E6	34
Spring, stm., Ar., U.S.	A4	97
Spring Arbor, Mi., U.S.	F6	115
Spring Bay, b., Ut., U.S.	B3	137
Springbok, S. Afr.	D2	56
Springboro, Oh., U.S.	C1	128
Spring Brook, stm., Pa., U.S.	n18	131
Spring City, Pa., U.S.	F10	131
Spring City, Tn., U.S.	D9	135
Spring City, Ut., U.S.	D4	137

Name	Map Ref.	Page
Spring Creek, stm., N.D., U.S.	B3	127
Spring Creek, stm., Nv., U.S.	C4	121
Spring Creek, stm., U.S.	D4	120
Springdale, Nf., Can.	D3	88
Springdale, Ar., U.S.	A1	97
Springdale, Oh., U.S.	n13	128
Springdale, Pa., U.S.	E2	131
Springdale, S.C., U.S.	D5	133
Springer, N.M., U.S.	A5	124
Springerville, Az., U.S.	C6	96
Springfield, Co., U.S.	D8	99
Springfield, Fl., U.S.	u16	102
Springfield, Ga., U.S.	D5	103
Springfield, Il., U.S.	D4	106
Springfield, Ky., U.S.	C4	110
Springfield, Ma., U.S.	B2	114
Springfield, Mn., U.S.	F4	116
Springfield, Mo., U.S.	D4	118
Springfield, Ne., U.S.	C9	120
Springfield, N.J., U.S.	B4	123
Springfield, Oh., U.S.	C2	128
Springfield, Or., U.S.	C4	130
Springfield, Pa., U.S.	p20	131
Springfield, S.D., U.S.	E8	134
Springfield, Tn., U.S.	A5	135
Springfield, Va., U.S.	g12	139
Springfield, Vt., U.S.	E4	138
Springfield, Lake, res., Il., U.S.	D4	106
Springfontein, S. Afr.	E4	56
Spring Garden, Guy.	B8	70
Spring Glen, Ut., U.S.	D5	137
Spring Green, Wi., U.S.	E3	142
Spring Grove, Il., U.S.	h8	106
Spring Grove, Mn., U.S.	G7	116
Spring Grove, Pa., U.S.	G8	131
Spring Hill, Fl., U.S.	D4	102
Spring Hill, Ks., U.S.	D9	109
Spring Hill, Tn., U.S.	B5	135
Springhill, La., U.S.	A2	111
Spring Hope, N.C., U.S.	B4	126
Spring Island, i., S.C., U.S.	G6	133
Spring Lake, Mi., U.S.	E4	115
Spring Lake, N.C., U.S.	B4	126
Spring Lake, N.J., U.S.	C4	123
Spring Lake, l., Me., U.S.	C2	112
Spring Lake, res., U.S.	B3	106
Spring Lake Heights, N.J., U.S.	C4	123
Spring Mountains, mts., Nv., U.S.	G6	121
Springport, Mi., U.S.	F6	115
Springs, S. Afr.	D4	56
Springside, Sk., Can.	F4	91
Springsure, Austl.	E4	62
Springvale, Me., U.S.	E2	112
Spring Valley, Ca., U.S.	o16	98
Spring Valley, Il., U.S.	B4	106
Spring Valley, Mn., U.S.	G6	116
Spring Valley, N.Y., U.S.	g12	125
Spring Valley, Wi., U.S.	D1	142
Springville, Al., U.S.	B3	94
Springville, Ia., U.S.	B6	108
Springville, N.Y., U.S.	C2	125
Springville, Ut., U.S.	C4	137
Spruce Fork, stm., W.V., U.S.	m12	141
Spruce Grove, Ab., Can.	C4	84
Spruce Knob, mtn., W.V., U.S.	C6	141
Spruce Knob-Seneca Rocks National Recreation Area, W.V., U.S.	C5	141
Spruce Mountain, mtn., Az., U.S.	C3	96
Spruce Mountain, mtn., Nv., U.S.	C7	121
Spruce Pine, N.C., U.S.	f10	126
Spruce Run Reservoir, res., N.J., U.S.	B3	123
Spur, Tx., U.S.	C2	136
Spurr, Mount, mtn., Ak., U.S.	g15	95
Squam Lake, l., N.H., U.S.	C4	122
Squapan Lake, l., Me., U.S.	B4	112
Square Lake, l., Me., U.S.	A4	112
Squatec, P.Q., Can.	B9	90
Squaw Cap Mountain, mtn., N.B., Can.	B3	87
Squaw Hill, mtn., Wy., U.S.	E7	143
Squaw Peak, mtn., Mt., U.S.	C2	119
Squibnocket Point, c., Ma., U.S.	D6	114
Squillace, Golfo di, b., Italy	E6	18
Squire, W.V., U.S.	D3	141
Srbija (Serbia), prov., Yugo.	B8	18
Srbobran, Yugo.	B7	18
Sredinnyj hrebet, mts., Russia	D17	26
Srednee Kujto, ozero, l., Russia	D14	10
Srednekolymsk, Russia	C17	26
Srednerusskaja vozvyšennost', plat., Russia	D5	26
Srednesibirskoe ploskogor'e, plat., Russia	C12	26
Śrem, Pol.	C4	20
Sremska Mitrovica, Yugo.	B7	18
Sretensk, Russia	D13	26
Sri Jayawardenepura, Sri L.	H4	40
Sríkákulam, India	F4	40
Sri Kālahasti, India	G3	40

Name	Map Ref.	Page
Sri Lanka, ctry., Asia	H4	40
Srīnagar, India	C2	40
Stack Reservoir, res., R.I., U.S.	C3	132
Stade, Ger.	D11	12
Stafford, Eng., U.K.	D5	12
Stafford, Ks., U.S.	E5	109
Stafford, Va., U.S.	B5	139
Stafford, co., Ks., U.S.	D5	109
Stafford, co., Va., U.S.	B5	139
Stafford Pond, l., R.I., U.S.	D6	132
Stafford Springs, Ct., U.S.	B6	100
Staked Plain see Estacado, Llano, pl., U.S.	E7	92
Stakhanov, Ukr.	E15	20
Stalin see Varna, Bul.	C11	18
Stalingrad see Volgograd, Russia	E6	26
Stalinogorsk see Novomoskovsk, Russia	D5	26
Stalinsk see Novokuzneck, Russia	D10	26
Stalowa Wola, Pol.	D7	20
Stambaugh, Mi., U.S.	B2	115
Stamford, Ct., U.S.	E1	100
Stamford, Tx., U.S.	C3	136
Stamford, Vt., U.S.	F2	138
Stamford, Lake, res., Tx., U.S.	C3	136
Stamping Ground, Ky., U.S.	B5	110
Stampriet, Nmb.	C2	56
Stamps, Ar., U.S.	D2	97
Stanaford, W.V., U.S.	D3	141
Stanberry, Mo., U.S.	A3	118
Standerton, S. Afr.	D4	56
Standing Rock Indian Reservation, U.S.	B4	134
Standish, Mi., U.S.	E7	115
Stanfield, Az., U.S.	E3	96
Stanfield, Or., U.S.	B7	130
Stanford, Ky., U.S.	C5	110
Stanhope, N.J., U.S.	B3	123
Stanislaus, co., Ca., U.S.	D3	98
Stanley, Falk. Is.	H5	69
Stanley, N.C., U.S.	B1	126
Stanley, N.C., U.S.	A3	127
Stanley, Va., U.S.	B4	139
Stanley, Wi., U.S.	D3	142
Stanley, co., S.D., U.S.	C5	134
Stanley Falls, wtfl, D.R.C.	A5	54
Stanley Reservoir, res., India	G3	40
Stanleytown, Va., U.S.	D3	139
Stanleyville, N.C., U.S.	A2	126
Stanly, co., N.C., U.S.	B2	126
Stanovoe nagor'e, mts., Russia	D13	26
Stanovoj hrebet, mts., Russia	D14	26
Stanovoy Mountains see Stanovoe nagor'e, mts., Russia	D13	26
Stanstead, P.Q., Can.	D5	90
Stanthorpe, Austl.	F5	62
Stanton, Ia., U.S.	D2	108
Stanton, Ky., U.S.	C6	110
Stanton, Mi., U.S.	E5	115
Stanton, Ne., U.S.	C8	120
Stanton, Tx., U.S.	C2	136
Stanton, co., Ks., U.S.	E2	109
Stanton, co., Ne., U.S.	C8	120
Stantonsburg, N.C., U.S.	B5	126
Stanwood, Ia., U.S.	C6	108
Stanwood, Wa., U.S.	A3	140
Staples, Mn., U.S.	D4	116
Stapleton, Al., U.S.	E2	94
Star, Id., U.S.	F2	105
Star, N.C., U.S.	B3	126
Staraja Russa, Russia	C5	22
Stara Planina (Balkan Mountains), mts., Eur.	C9	18
Stara Zagora, Bul.	C10	18
Starbuck, Mn., U.S.	E3	116
Starbuck, i., Kir.	E14	58
Star City, Ar., U.S.	D4	97
Star City, W.V., U.S.	B5	141
Stargard Szczeciński, Pol.	C3	20
Stargo, Az., U.S.	D6	96
Stark, co., Il., U.S.	B4	106
Stark, co., N.D., U.S.	C3	127
Stark, co., Oh., U.S.	B4	128
Starke, Fl., U.S.	C4	102
Starke, co., In., U.S.	B4	107
Starks, La., U.S.	D2	111
Starkville, Ms., U.S.	B5	117
Star Lake, l., Wi., U.S.	C3	116
Starkweather, N.D., U.S.		
Starobil's'k, Ukr.	E15	20
Starodub, Russia	C12	20
Starogard Gdański, Pol.	C5	20
Star Peak, mtn., Nv., U.S.	C3	121
Starr, co., Tx., U.S.	F3	136
Startex, S.C., U.S.	B3	133
Staryj Oskol, Russia	D5	26
State Center, Ia., U.S.	B4	108
State College, Pa., U.S.	E6	131
Stateline, Nv., U.S.	E2	121
State Line, Pa., U.S.	G6	131
Staten Island see Estados, Isla de los, i., Arg.	H4	69
Staten Island, i., N.Y., U.S.	k12	125
Statenville, Ga., U.S.	F4	103
Statesboro, Ga., U.S.	D5	103
Statesville, N.C., U.S.	B2	126
Statham, Ga., U.S.	C3	103
Statue of Liberty National Monument, N.J., U.S.	k8	123

Name	Map Ref.	Page
Staunton, Il., U.S.	D4	106
Staunton, Va., U.S.	B3	139
Staunton, stm., U.S.	D12	92
Stavanger, Nor.	G1	10
Stavropol see Toljatti, Russia	D6	26
Stavropol', Russia	E6	26
Stawell, Austl.	H3	62
Stayner, On., Can.	C4	89
Stayton, Or., U.S.	C4	130
Steamboat, Nv., U.S.	D2	121
Steamboat Mountain, mtn., Mt., U.S.	C4	119
Steamboat Mountain, mtn., Wy., U.S.	E4	143
Steamboat Springs, Co., U.S.	A4	99
Stearns, Ky., U.S.	D5	110
Stearns, co., Mn., U.S.	E4	116
Stearns Brook, stm., N.H., U.S.	A4	122
Stebbins, Ak., U.S.	C7	95
Steele, Al., U.S.	B3	94
Steele, Mo., U.S.	E8	118
Steele, N.D., U.S.	C6	127
Steele, co., Mn., U.S.	F5	116
Steele, co., N.D., U.S.	B8	127
Steele, Mount, mtn., Wy., U.S.	E6	143
Steeleville, Il., U.S.	E4	106
Steelton, Pa., U.S.	F8	131
Steelville, Mo., U.S.	D6	118
Steens Mountain, mts., Or., U.S.	E8	130
Stefanie, Lake, l., Afr.	C7	54
Steger, Il., U.S.	B6	106
Steilacoom, Wa., U.S.	f10	140
Steinbach, Mb., Can.	E3	86
Steinhatchee, stm., Fl., U.S.	C3	102
Steinkjer, Nor.	E4	10
Steinkopf, S. Afr.	D2	56
Stellenbosch, S. Afr.	E2	56
Stendal, Ger.	D12	12
Stepanakert see Xankändi, Azer.	C12	44
Stephen, Mn., U.S.	B2	116
Stephens, Ar., U.S.	D2	97
Stephens, co., Ga., U.S.	B3	103
Stephens, co., Ok., U.S.	C4	129
Stephens, co., Tx., U.S.	C3	136
Stephens City, Va., U.S.	A4	139
Stephens Lake, res., Mb., Can.	A4	86
Stephenson, Mi., U.S.	C3	115
Stephenson, co., Il., U.S.	A4	106
Stephens Passage, strt., Ak., U.S.	m23	95
Stephenville, Nf., Can.	D2	88
Stephenville, Tx., U.S.	C3	136
Stephenville Crossing, Nf., Can.	D2	88
Sterkstroom, S. Afr.	E4	56
Sterling, Ak., U.S.	g16	95
Sterling, Co., U.S.	A7	99
Sterling, Il., U.S.	B4	106
Sterling, Ks., U.S.	D5	109
Sterling, Ok., U.S.	C3	129
Sterling, Va., U.S.	A5	139
Sterling, co., Tx., U.S.	D2	136
Sterling City, Tx., U.S.	D2	136
Sterling Heights, Mi., U.S.	o15	115
Sterling Reservoir, res., Co., U.S.	A7	99
Sterlington, La., U.S.	B3	111
Sterlitamak, Russia	D7	26
Stettler, Ab., Can.	C4	84
Steuben, co., In., U.S.	A7	107
Steuben, co., N.Y., U.S.	C3	125
Steubenville, Oh., U.S.	B5	128
Stevens, co., Ks., U.S.	E2	109
Stevens, co., Mn., U.S.	E3	116
Stevens, co., Wa., U.S.	A7	140
Stevens Creek Dam, U.S.	k8	98
Stevenson, Al., U.S.	A4	94
Stevenson, Ct., U.S.	D3	100
Stevenson, Wa., U.S.	D4	140
Stevenson Lake, l., Mb., Can.	C4	86
Stevens Pass, Wa., U.S.	B4	140
Stevens Peak, mtn., Id., U.S.	B3	105
Stevens Point, Wi., U.S.	D4	142
Stevensville, Md., U.S.	C5	113
Stevensville, Mi., U.S.	F4	115
Stevensville, Mt., U.S.	D2	119
Stewart, co., Ga., U.S.	D2	103
Stewart, co., Tn., U.S.	A4	135
Stewart Island, i., N.Z.	q12	63c
Stewart Mountain, mtn., Az., U.S.	k9	96
Stewartstown, Pa., U.S.	G8	131
Stewartville, Mo., U.S.	B3	118
Stewartville, Mn., U.S.	G6	116
Stewiacke, N.S., Can.	D6	87
Steyr, Aus.	F14	12
Stigler, Ok., U.S.	B6	129
Stikine, stm., Ak., U.S.	D13	95
Still, stm., Ct., U.S.	B3	100
Stillaguamish, North Fork, stm., Wa., U.S.	A4	140
Stillaguamish, South Fork, stm., Wa., U.S.	A4	140
Stillhouse Hollow Lake, res., Tx., U.S.	D4	136
Stillman Valley, Il., U.S.	A4	106
Stillmore, Ga., U.S.	D4	103
Stillwater, Mn., U.S.	E6	116
Stillwater, Ok., U.S.	A4	129
Stillwater, co., Mt., U.S.	E7	119
Stillwater Range, mts., Nv., U.S.	D3	121
Stillwater Reservoir, res., N.Y., U.S.	B5	125
Stillwater Reservoir, res., R.I., U.S.	B3	132
Stilwell, Ok., U.S.	B7	129
Stimson, Mount, mtn., Mt., U.S.	B3	119
Stine Mountain, mtn., Mt., U.S.	E3	119
Stinking Lake, l., N.M., U.S.	A3	124
Stinnett, Tx., U.S.	B2	136
Štip, Mac.	D9	18
Stirling, Austl.	G2	60
Stirling, Austl.	E5	60
Stirling, Ab., Can.	E4	84
Stirling, On., Can.	C7	89
Stockbridge, Ga., U.S.	C2	103
Stockbridge, Mi., U.S.	F6	115
Stockbridge-Munsee Indian Reservation, Wi., U.S.	D5	142
Stockdale, Tx., U.S.	E4	136
Stockholm, Swe.	G8	10
Stockton, Ca., U.S.	D3	98
Stockton, Il., U.S.	A3	106
Stockton, Ks., U.S.	C4	109
Stockton, Md., U.S.	D7	113
Stockton, Mo., U.S.	D4	118
Stockton Island, i., Wi., U.S.	B3	142
Stockton Lake, res., Mo., U.S.	D4	118
Stoddard, Wi., U.S.	E2	142
Stoddard, co., Mo., U.S.	E8	118
Stœng Trêng, Camb.	D5	34
Stoke-on-Trent, Eng., U.K.	D5	12
Stokes, co., N.C., U.S.	A2	126
Stokesdale, N.C., U.S.	A3	126
Stolbovoj, ostrov, i., Russia	B15	26
Stolin, Bela.	D9	20
Stollings, W.V., U.S.	n12	141
Stone, co., Ar., U.S.	B3	97
Stone, co., Mo., U.S.	E4	118
Stone, co., Ms., U.S.	E4	117
Stoneboro, Pa., U.S.	D1	131
Stone Corral Lake, l., Or., U.S.	E7	130
Stoneham, Ma., U.S.	g11	114
Stonehaven, Scot., U.K.	B5	12
Stonehenge, hist., Eng., U.K.	E6	12
Stone Mountain, Ga., U.S.	C2	103
Stone Mountain, mtn., Ga., U.S.	C2	103
Stones River National Battlefield, hist., Tn., U.S.	B4	135
Stoneville, N.C., U.S.	A3	126
Stonewall, Mb., Can.	D3	86
Stonewall, La., U.S.	B2	111
Stonewall, Ms., U.S.	C5	117
Stonewall, co., Tx., U.S.	C2	136
Stonewood, W.V., U.S.	k10	141
Stoney Creek, On., Can.	D5	89
Stonington, Ct., U.S.	D8	100
Stonington, Il., U.S.	D4	106
Stonington, Me., U.S.	D4	112
Stono, stm., S.C., U.S.	k11	133
Stono Inlet, b., S.C., U.S.	F8	133
Stony Brook, N.Y., U.S.	n15	125
Stony Brook, stm., N.J., U.S.	C3	123
Stony Creek, stm., Va., U.S.	C5	139
Stony Island, i., N.Y., U.S.	B4	125
Stony Plain, Ab., Can.	C3	84
Stony Point, N.C., U.S.	B1	126
Storavan, l., Swe.	D8	10
Storebælt, strt., Den.	I4	10
Storey, co., Nv., U.S.	D2	121
Storlien, Swe.	E5	10
Storm Bay, b., Austl.	I4	62
Storm Lake, Ia., U.S.	B2	108
Storm Lake, l., Ia., U.S.	B2	108
Storm Mountain, mtn., Ak., U.S.	h16	95
Stornoway, Scot., U.K.	A3	12
Storrs, Ct., U.S.	B7	100
Storsjön, l., Swe.	E6	10
Storslett, Nor.	B9	10
Storuman, Swe.	D7	10
Storuman, l., Swe.	D7	10
Story, Wy., U.S.	B6	143
Story, co., Ia., U.S.	B4	108
Story City, Ia., U.S.	B4	108
Stoŭbcy, Bela.	C9	20
Stoughton, Sk., Can.	H4	91
Stoughton, Ma., U.S.	B5	114
Stoughton, Wi., U.S.	F4	142
Stover, Mo., U.S.	C5	118
Stow, Oh., U.S.	A4	128
Stow Creek, stm., N.J., U.S.	E2	123
Stowe, Pa., U.S.	F10	131
Stowe, Vt., U.S.	C3	138
Stoyoma Mountain, mtn., B.C., Can.	E7	85
Strabane, Pa., U.S.	F1	131
Strafford, Pa., U.S.	m20	131
Strafford, co., N.H., U.S.	D4	122
Straffordville, On., Can.	E4	89
Strakonice, Czech Rep.	E2	20
Stralsund, Ger.	C13	12
Strand, S. Afr.	E2	56
Stranraer, Scot., U.K.	C4	12
Strasbourg, Fr.	C10	16
Strasburg, Co., U.S.	B6	99
Strasburg, Oh., U.S.	B4	128
Strasburg, Pa., U.S.	G9	131
Strasburg, Va., U.S.	B4	139
Stratford, On., Can.	D3	89
Stratford, N.Z.	o13	63c
Stratford, Ct., U.S.	E3	100
Stratford, Ia., U.S.	B4	108
Stratford, N.J., U.S.	D2	123
Stratford, Ok., U.S.	C5	129
Stratford, Tx., U.S.	A1	136
Stratford, Wi., U.S.	D3	142
Stratford Point, c., Ct., U.S.	E3	100
Stratham, N.H., U.S.	D5	122
Strathmore, Ab., Can.	D4	84
Strathmore, Ca., U.S.	D4	98
Strathroy, On., Can.	E3	89
Stratton, Co., U.S.	B8	99
Straubing, Ger.	F13	12
Strawberry, stm., Ar., U.S.	A4	97
Strawberry, stm., Ut., U.S.	C5	137
Strawberry Mountain, mtn., Or., U.S.	C8	130
Strawberry Point, Ia., U.S.	B6	108
Strawberry Point, c., Ma., U.S.	B6	114
Strawberry Range, mts., Or., U.S.	C8	130
Strawberry Reservoir, res., Ut., U.S.	C4	137
Streaky Bay, b., Austl.	G5	60
Streator, Il., U.S.	B5	106
Strelka-Čunja, Russia	C12	26
Strimón (Struma), stm., Eur.	D9	18
Strimón, Gulf of see Orfanoú, Kólpos, b., Grc.	D9	18
Stromsburg, Ne., U.S.	C8	120
Strömsund, Swe.	E6	10
Strong, Ar., U.S.	D3	97
Strong, Me., U.S.	D2	112
Strong, stm., Ms., U.S.	C4	117
Strong City, Ks., U.S.	D7	109
Stronghurst, Il., U.S.	C3	106
Strongsville, Oh., U.S.	A4	128
Stroud, Ok., U.S.	B5	129
Stroudsburg, Pa., U.S.	E11	131
Stroudwater, stm., Me., U.S.	g7	112
Strum, Wi., U.S.	D2	142
Struma (Strimón), stm., Eur.	D9	18
Strumica, Mac.	D9	18
Struthers, Oh., U.S.	A5	128
Strydenburg, S. Afr.	D3	56
Stryi, Ukr.	E7	20
Stryker, Oh., U.S.	A1	128
Stuart, Fl., U.S.	E6	102
Stuart, Ia., U.S.	C3	108
Stuart, Ne., U.S.	B6	120
Stuart, Va., U.S.	D2	139
Stuart, Mount, mtn., Wa., U.S.	B5	140
Stuart Lake, l., B.C., Can.	B5	85
Stuarts Draft, Va., U.S.	B3	139
Stull, stm., Can.	B5	86
Stump Lake, l., N.D., U.S.	B7	127
Stump Pond, res., R.I., U.S.	D2	132
Stupino, Russia	B15	20
Sturbridge, Ma., U.S.	B3	114
Sturgeon, Mo., U.S.	B5	118
Sturgeon, stm., Mi., U.S.	B4	115
Sturgeon Bay, Wi., U.S.	D6	142
Sturgeon Bay, b., Mb., Can.	C3	86
Sturgeon Falls, On., Can.	A5	89
Sturgeon Lake, l., On., Can.	C6	89
Sturgis, Sk., Can.	F4	91
Sturgis, Ky., U.S.	e10	110
Sturgis, Mi., U.S.	G5	115
Sturgis, S.D., U.S.	C2	134
Sturtevant, Wi., U.S.	F6	142
Sturt Stony Desert, des., Austl.	F3	62
Stutsman, co., N.D., U.S.	B6	127
Stutterheim, S. Afr.	E4	56
Stuttgart, Ger.	F11	12
Stuttgart, Ar., U.S.	C4	97
Styr, stm., Eur.	D8	20
Suaita, Col.	D5	80
Subei, China	B7	40
Sublette, Ks., U.S.	E3	109
Sublette, co., Wy., U.S.	D2	143
Sublett Range, mts., Id., U.S.	G6	105
Sublimity, Or., U.S.	C4	130
Subotica, Yugo.	A7	18
Sucarnoochee, stm., Al., U.S.	C1	94
Succasunna, N.J., U.S.	B3	123
Suceava, Rom.	F9	20
Sucre, Bol.	B4	72
Sud, Canal du, strt., Haiti	E7	80
Sudan, ctry., Afr.	H10	48
Sudan, reg., Afr.	H8	48
Sudbury, On., Can.	A4	89
Sudbury, Ma., U.S.	B5	114
Sudbury, co., Ma., U.S.	B5	114
Sudbury Center, Ma., U.S.	g10	114
Sudbury Reservoir, res., Ma., U.S.	g10	114
Suez see El-Suweis, Egypt	E11	48
Suez, Gulf of see Suweis, Khalîg el-, b., Egypt	F10	14
Suez Canal see Suweis, Qanâ el-, Egypt	E10	14
Suffern, N.Y., U.S.	D6	125
Suffield, Ct., U.S.	B5	100
Suffolk, Va., U.S.	D6	139
Suffolk, co., Ma., U.S.	B5	114
Suffolk, co., N.Y., U.S.	n15	125
Sugar, stm., N.H., U.S.	D2	122
Sugar, stm., U.S.	F4	142
Sugar City, Id., U.S.	F7	105
Sugarcreek, Pa., U.S.	D2	131
Sugar Creek, Mo., U.S.	h11	118
Sugar Creek, stm., Oh., U.S.	C2	128
Sugar Creek, stm., Pa., U.S.	C8	131
Sugar Grove, Va., U.S.	D1	139
Sugar Hill, Ga., U.S.	B2	103
Sugar Island, i., Mi., U.S.	B6	115
Sugar Land, Tx., U.S.	E5	136
Sugar Loaf, Va., U.S.	C3	139
Sugarloaf Mountain, mtn., Mt., U.S.	C4	119
Sugar Notch, Pa., U.S.	n17	131
Suggi Lake, l., Sk., Can.	C4	91
Suğla Gölü, l., Tur.	D5	44
Suhag, Egypt	E11	48
Suhana, Russia	C13	26
Şuḩār, Oman	F7	38
Sühbaatar, Mong.	A9	28
Suhl, Ger.	E12	12
Suhona, stm., Russia	C6	26
Suhumi, Geor.	A9	44
Suiattle, stm., Wa., U.S.	A4	140
Suichang, China	D4	30
Suichuan, China	D3	30
Suide, China	D10	28
Suijiang, China	D1	30
Suining, China	E9	28
Suining, China	C4	30
Suitland, Md., U.S.	C4	113
Suixi, China	C4	30
Suiyang, China	B2	31
Suizhong, China	C12	28
Suizhou, China	E10	28
Sukabumi, Indon.	E3	36
Sukadana, Indon.	D3	36
Sukaraja, Indon.	D4	36
Sukarnapura see Jayapura, Indon.	G11	32
Sukhothai, Thai.	C3	34
Sukkertoppen, Grnld.	E29	82
Sukkozero, Russia	B5	22
Sukkur, Pak.	E9	42
Sukumo, Japan	D2	31
Sula, Kepulauan, is., Indon.	D7	36
Sulaimān Range, mts., Pak.	E9	42
Sulawesi (Celebes), i., Indon.	D6	36
Sulawesi, Laut see Celebes Sea, Asia	C6	36
Sulechów, Pol.	C3	20
Sullana, Peru	D3	70
Sulligent, Al., U.S.	B1	94
Sullivan, Il., U.S.	D5	106
Sullivan, In., U.S.	F3	107
Sullivan, Mo., U.S.	C6	118
Sullivan, co., In., U.S.	F3	107
Sullivan, co., Mo., U.S.	A4	118
Sullivan, co., N.H., U.S.	D2	122
Sullivan, co., N.Y., U.S.	D6	125
Sullivan, co., Pa., U.S.	D9	131
Sullivan, co., Tn., U.S.	C11	135
Sullivan Lake, l., Ab., Can.	D5	84
Sullivans Island, S.C., U.S.	k12	133
Sully, Ia., U.S.	C5	108
Sully, co., S.D., U.S.	C5	134
Sulmona, Italy	C4	18
Sulphur, La., U.S.	D2	111
Sulphur, Ok., U.S.	C5	129
Sulphur, stm., U.S.	D2	97
Sulphur Spring Range, mts., Nv., U.S.	C5	121
Sulphur Springs, Tx., U.S.	C5	136
Sultan, Wa., U.S.	B4	140
Sultānpur, India	D4	40
Sulu Archipelago, is., Phil.	F7	34
Suluq, Libya	D9	48
Sulu Sea, Asia	E7	34
Sumas, Wa., U.S.	A3	140
Sumatera (Sumatra), i., Indon.	C2	36
Sumatra see Sumatera, i., Indon.	C2	36
Sumba, i., Indon.	F5	36
Sumba, Selat, strt., Indon.	E6	36
Sumbawa, i., Indon.	E5	36
Sumbawa Besar, Indon.	E5	36
Sumbawanga, Tan.	E6	54
Sumbe, Ang.	F2	54
Sumedang, Indon.	E3	36
Šumen, Bul.	C11	18
Sumenep, Indon.	E4	36
Šumerlja, Russia	C8	22
Šumiha, Russia	C11	22
Sumisu-jima, i., Japan	E16	28
Sumiton, Al., U.S.	B2	94
Summerfield, N.C., U.S.	A3	126
Summerford, Nf., Can.	D4	88
Summer Island, i., Mi., U.S.	C4	115
Summer Lake, l., Or., U.S.	E6	130
Summerland, B.C., Can.	E8	85
Summers, co., W.V., U.S.	D4	141
Summerside, P.E., Can.	C6	87
Summersville, W.V., U.S.	C4	141
Summersville Lake, res., W.V., U.S.	C4	141
Summerton, S.C., U.S.	D7	133
Summertown, Tn., U.S.	B4	135
Summerville, Ga., U.S.	B1	103
Summerville, S.C., U.S.	E7	133
Summit, Il., U.S.	k9	106
Summit, Ms., U.S.	D3	117
Summit, N.J., U.S.	B4	123
Summit, Tn., U.S.	h11	135
Summit, co., Co., U.S.	B4	99
Summit, co., Oh., U.S.	A4	128
Summit, co., Ut., U.S.	C5	137
Summit Hill, Pa., U.S.	E10	131
Summit Lake, l., Ia., U.S.	C3	108
Summit Lake Indian Reservation, Nv., U.S.	B2	121
Summit Mountain, mtn., Nv., U.S.	D5	121
Summit Peak, mtn., Co., U.S.	D4	99
Summitville, In., U.S.	D6	107
Sumner, Ia., U.S.	B5	108
Sumner, Il., U.S.	E6	106
Sumner, Wa., U.S.	B3	140
Sumner, co., Ks., U.S.	E6	109
Sumner, co., Tn., U.S.	A5	135
Sumner, Lake, res., N.M., U.S.	C5	124
Sumner Dam, N.M., U.S.	C5	124
Sumner Strait, strt., Ak., U.S.	m23	95
Šumperk, Czech Rep.	E4	20
Sumqayıt, Azer.	B13	44
Sumrall, Ms., U.S.	D4	117
Šumšu, ostrov, i., Russia	D17	26
Sumter, S.C., U.S.	D7	133
Sumter, co., Al., U.S.	C1	94
Sumter, co., Fl., U.S.	D4	102
Sumter, co., Ga., U.S.	D2	103
Sumter, co., S.C., U.S.	D7	133
Sumy, Ukr.	D13	20
Sumzom, China	D7	40
Sun, stm., Mt., U.S.	C4	119
Sunapee, N.H., U.S.	D2	122
Sunapee Lake, l., N.H., U.S.	D2	122
Sunbright, Tn., U.S.	C9	135
Sunbury, Oh., U.S.	B3	128
Sunbury, Pa., U.S.	E8	131
Sunchales, Arg.	E5	72
Suncho Corral, Arg.	D5	72
Sun City, Az., U.S.	k8	96
Suncook, N.H., U.S.	D4	122
Suncook, stm., N.H., U.S.	D4	122
Suncook Lakes, l., N.H., U.S.	D4	122
Sundance, Wy., U.S.	B8	143
Sundance Mountain, mtn., Wy., U.S.	B8	143
Sundarbans, reg., Asia	B1	34
Sunda Shelf	H13	64
Sunda Strait see Sunda, Selat, strt., Indon.	E3	36
Sunderland, On., Can.	C5	89
Sunderland, Eng., U.K.	C6	12
Sundown, Austl.	F5	60
Sundown, Tx., U.S.	C1	136
Sundre, Ab., Can.	D3	84
Sundridge, On., Can.	B5	89
Sundsvall, Swe.	E7	10
Sunflower, Ms., U.S.	B3	117
Sunflower, co., Ms., U.S.	B3	117
Sunflower, Mount, mtn., Ks., U.S.	C2	109
Sungaidareh, Indon.	D2	36
Sungai Kolok, Thai.	E4	34
Sungai Petani, Malay.	B2	36
Sungari see Songhua, stm., China	B14	28
Sungari Reservoir see Songhua Hu, res., China	C13	28
Sungurlu, Tur.	B6	44
Sunland Park, N.M., U.S.	F3	124
Sunlight Creek, stm., Wy., U.S.	B3	143
Sunman, In., U.S.	F7	107
Sunne, Swe.	G5	10
Sunnyside, Nf., Can.	E5	88
Sunnyside, Wa., U.S.	C5	140
Sunnyvale, Ca., U.S.	k8	98
Sun Prairie, Wi., U.S.	E4	142
Sunray, Tx., U.S.	A2	136
Sunset, La., U.S.	D3	111
Sunset, Ut., U.S.	B4	137
Sunset Beach, Hi., U.S.	f9	104
Sunset Crater National Monument, Az., U.S.	B4	96
Sunset Lake, l., Vt., U.S.	D2	138
Sunshine, Austl.	H3	62
Suntar, Russia	C13	26
Suntar-Hajata, hrebet, mts., Russia	C16	26
Suntaug Lake, l., Ma., U.S.	f11	114
Sun Valley, Id., U.S.	F4	105
Sun Valley, Nv., U.S.	D2	121
Sunyani, Ghana	E4	50
Suojarvi, Russia	B5	22
Suomussalmi, Fin.	D13	10
Superior, Az., U.S.	D4	96
Superior, Mt., U.S.	C2	119
Superior, Ne., U.S.	D7	120
Superior, Wi., U.S.	B1	142
Superior, Wy., U.S.	E4	143
Superior, Lake, l., N.A.	B10	92
Superstition Mountains, mts., Az., U.S.	m10	96
Suphan Buri, Thai.	D4	34

Name	Map Ref.	Page

Suquamish, Wa., U.S. B3 140
Suquṭrā, i., Yemen H6 38
Şūr, Leb. F6 44
Şūr, Oman F7 38
Sur, Point, c., Ca., U.S. . . D3 98
Sura, stm., Russia E15 6
Surabaya, Indon. E4 36
Surakarta, Indon. E4 36
Sūrat, India E2 40
Sūratgarh, India D2 40
Surat Thani, Thai. B3 34
Surendranagar, India E2 40
Surfside, Fl., U.S. s13 102
Surfside Beach, S.C., U.S. . D10 133
Surgoinsville, Tn., U.S. . . . C11 135
Surgut, Russia C9 26
Surigao, Phil. E9 34
Surigao Strait, strt., Phil. . E9 34
Surin, Thai. D4 34
Suriname, ctry., S.A. C8 70
Surprise, Az., U.S. k8 96
Surrey, N.D., U.S. A4 127
Surry, co., N.C., U.S. A2 126
Surry, co., Va., U.S. C6 139
Surry Mountain Lake, res.,
  N.H., U.S. D2 122
Surt, Libya D8 48
Surt, Khalīj, b., Libya D8 48
Sürüç, Tur. D8 44
Surulangun, Indon. D2 36
Šuryškary, Russia A12 22
Sūsangerd, Iran G13 44
Susanville, Ca., U.S. B3 98
Suşehri, Tur. B8 44
Susitna, stm., Ak., U.S. . . . C10 95
Susquehanna, Pa., U.S. . . . C10 131
Susquehanna, co., Pa., U.S. C10 131
Susquehanna, stm., U.S. . . A5 113
Susquehanna, West Branch,
  stm., Pa., U.S. D5 131
Sussex, N.B., Can. D4 87
Sussex, N.J., U.S. A3 123
Sussex, Wi., U.S. m11 142
Sussex, co., De., U.S. F4 101
Sussex, co., N.J., U.S. A3 123
Sussex, co., Va., U.S. D5 139
Susuman, Russia C16 26
Susurluk, Tur. C3 44
Sutherland, S. Afr. E3 56
Sutherland, Ia., U.S. B2 108
Sutherland, Ne., U.S. C4 120
Sutherlin, Or., U.S. D3 130
Sutlej (Satluj), stm., Asia . . D2 40
Sutter, co., Ca., U.S. C3 98
Sutter Creek, Ca., U.S. . . . C3 98
Sutton, P.Q., Can. D5 90
Sutton, Ne., U.S. D8 120
Sutton, W.V., U.S. C4 141
Sutton, co., Tx., U.S. D2 136
Sutton Lake, res., W.V., U.S. C4 141
Sutwik Island, i., Ak., U.S. . D8 95
Süüj, Mong. B8 28
Suur Munamägi, hill, Est. . . H12 10
Suva, Fiji F11 58
Suwałki, Pol. B7 20
Suwanee, Ga., U.S. B2 103
Suwannee, co., Fl., U.S. . . . B3 102
Suwannee, stm., U.S. C4 102
Suwannee Sound, strt., Fl.,
  U.S. C3 102
Suwanose-jima, i., Japan . . F14 28
Suwarrow, atoll, Cook Is. . . F13 58
Suweis, Khalīg el- (Suez,
  Gulf of), b., Egypt F10 14
Suweis, Qanâ el- (Suez
  Canal), Egypt E10 14
Suwŏn, S. Kor. D13 28
Suzak, Kaz. B9 42
Suzhou, China E12 28
Suzhou, China E11 28
Svalbard, dep., Nor. D20 144
Svaliava, Ukr. E7 20
Svappavaara, Swe. C9 10
Svatove, Ukr. E15 20
Svay Riêng, Camb. D5 34
Sveg, Swe. E6 10
Švenčionėliai, Lith. I11 10
Svendborg, Den. I4 10
Svensen, Or., U.S. A3 130
Sverdlovsk see Ekaterinburg,
  Russia D8 26
Sverdrup, ostrov, i., Russia . B9 26
Svetlahorsk, Bela. C10 20
Svetlaja, Russia E15 26
Svetlograd, Russia A4 42
Svetlyj, Russia D11 22
Svetlyj, Russia D13 26
Svetogorsk, Russia F13 10
Svetozarevo, Yugo. C8 18
Svirsk, Russia A8 28
Svištov, Bul. C10 18
Svitavy, Czech Rep. E4 20
Svjatoj Nos, mys, c., Russia A7 22
Svjatoj Nos, mys, c., Russia B15 26
Svobodnyj, Russia D14 26
Svolvær, Nor. B6 10
Swabia see Schwaben, hist.
  reg., Ger. F11 12
Swain, co., N.C., U.S. f9 126
Swain Reefs, rf., Austl. . . . E5 62
Swainsboro, Ga., U.S. D4 103
Swakopmund, Nmb. C1 56
Swampscott, Ma., U.S. . . . B6 114
Swan, stm., Can. C1 86
Swan Creek, stm., Oh., U.S. e6 128

Swan Falls, wtfl, Id., U.S. . . F2 105
Swan Hill, Austl. H3 62
Swan Hills, Ab., Can. B3 84
Swan Islands see Santanilla,
  Islas, is., Hond. B3 80
Swan Lake, l., Mb., Can. . . C1 86
Swan Lake, l., Me., U.S. . . . D4 112
Swan Lake, l., Ne., U.S. . . . C3 120
Swannanoa, N.C., U.S. . . . f10 126
Swan Peak, mtn., Mt., U.S. . C3 119
Swan Range, mts., Mt., U.S. C3 119
Swan River, Mb., Can. C1 86
Swansboro, N.C., U.S. C5 126
Swansea, Wales, U.K. E4 12
Swansea, Il., U.S. E4 106
Swanson Lake, res., Ne.,
  U.S. D4 120
Swanton, Oh., U.S. A2 128
Swanton, Vt., U.S. B2 138
Swanzey Center, N.H., U.S. E2 122
Swarthmore, Pa., U.S. p20 131
Swartswood Lake, l., N.J.,
  U.S. A3 123
Swartz Creek, Mi., U.S. . . . F7 115
Swayzee, In., U.S. C6 107
Swaziland, ctry., Afr. D5 56
Swea City, Ia., U.S. A3 108
Sweden, ctry., Eur. E7 10
Swedru, Ghana E4 50
Sweeny, Tx., U.S. r14 136
Sweet Grass, co., Mt., U.S. . E7 119
Sweet Home, Or., U.S. . . . C4 130
Sweetser, In., U.S. C6 107
Sweet Springs, Mo., U.S. . . C4 118
Sweetwater, Tn., U.S. D9 135
Sweetwater, Tx., U.S. C2 136
Sweetwater, co., Wy., U.S. . E3 143
Sweetwater, stm., Wy., U.S. D4 143
Sweetwater Creek, Fl., U.S. p10 102
Sweetwater Creek, stm.,
  U.S. B1 129
Swellendam, S. Afr. E3 56
Swepsonville, N.C., U.S. . . A3 126
Świdwin, Pol. C3 20
Świebodzin, Pol. C3 20
Świecie, Pol. C5 20
Swift, co., Mn., U.S. E3 116
Swift, stm., N.H., U.S. B4 122
Swift Creek, stm., N.C., U.S. B5 126
Swift Creek, stm., Va., U.S. n17 139
Swift Diamond, stm., N.H.,
  U.S. g7 122
Swifton, Ar., U.S. B4 97
Swift Reservoir, res., Wa.,
  U.S. C3 140
Swindon, Eng., U.K. E6 12
Swinomish Indian
  Reservation, Wa., U.S. . . A3 140
Świnoujście, Pol. C3 20
Swisher, Ia., U.S. C6 108
Swisher, co., Tx., U.S. B2 136
Swissvale, Pa., U.S. k14 131
Switzer, W.V., U.S. D3 141
Switzerland, Fl., U.S. m8 102
Switzerland, co., In., U.S. . . G7 107
Switzerland, ctry., Eur. . . . A2 18
Swoyersville, Pa., U.S. . . . D10 131
Syalah, Russia C14 26
Sycamore, Al., U.S. B3 94
Sycamore, Il., U.S. B5 106
Sycamore, Oh., U.S. B2 128
Sycamore Creek, stm.,
  W.V., U.S. m13 141
Sydenham, On., Can. C8 89
Sydney, Austl. G5 62
Sykesville, Md., U.S. B4 113
Sykesville, Pa., U.S. D4 131
Syktyvkar, Russia C7 26
Sylacauga, Al., U.S. B3 94
Sylhet, Bngl. E6 40
Sylt, i., Ger. C11 12
Sylva, N.C., U.S. f9 126
Sylvania, Al., U.S. A4 94
Sylvania, Ga., U.S. D5 103
Sylvania, Oh., U.S. A2 128
Sylvan Lake, Ab., Can. . . . C3 84
Sylvan Lake, Mi., U.S. o15 115
Sylvan Lake, l., In., U.S. . . B7 107
Sylvan Pass, Wy., U.S. . . . B2 143
Sylvester, Ga., U.S. E3 103
Sym, Russia C10 26
Symmes Creek, stm., Oh.,
  U.S. D3 128
Symsonia, Ky., U.S. f9 110
Syracuse, In., U.S. B6 107
Syracuse, Ks., U.S. E2 109
Syracuse, Ne., U.S. D9 120
Syracuse, N.Y., U.S. B4 125
Syracuse, Ut., U.S. B3 137
Syrdarja, Uzb. B9 42
Syr Darya (Syrdarʹja), stm.,
  Asia B9 42
Syria, ctry., Asia E8 44
Syriam, Myan. C3 34
Syrian Desert, des., Asia . . F8 44
Syros see Ermoúpolis, Grc. . F10 18
Sysladobsis Lake, l., Me.,
  U.S. C4 112
Syvash, zatoka, strt., Ukr. . F13 20
Syzranʹ, Russia D6 26
Szamotuły, Pol. C4 20
Szczecin, Pol. C3 20
Szczecinek, Pol. C4 20
Szczytno, Pol. C6 20

Szechwan see Sichuan,
  prov., China E8 28
Szeged, Hung. F6 20
Székesfehérvár, Hung. F5 20
Szekszárd, Hung. F5 20
Szentes, Hung. F6 20
Szolnok, Hung. F6 20
Szombathely, Hung. F4 20

T

Tabar Islands, is., Pap. N.
  Gui. G13 32
Tabarka, Tun. F2 18
Tabasco, state, Mex. D6 78
Tabayin, Myan. B3 34
Tabbys Peak, mtn., Ut., U.S. C3 137
Tabelbala, Alg. E4 48
Taber, Ab., Can. E4 84
Tablas Island, i., Phil. D8 34
Table Head, c., Nf., Can. . . B4 88
Table Mountain, mtn., Az.,
  U.S. E5 96
Table Rock Lake, res., U.S. . E4 118
Table Top, mtn., Az., U.S. . . E3 96
Tábor, Czech Rep. E3 20
Tabor, Russia B17 26
Tabor, Ia., U.S. D2 108
Tabora, Tan. D6 54
Tabor City, N.C., U.S. C4 126
Tabou, C. Iv. F3 50
Tabrīz, Iran C5 42
Tabūk, Sau. Ar. E3 38
Tabuleiro do Norte, Braz. . . C4 74
Täby, Swe. G8 10
Tacloban, Phil. D9 34
Tacna, Peru G5 70
Tacoma, Wa., U.S. B3 140
Taconic Range, mts., U.S. . . A1 114
Tacuarembó, Ur. E6 72
Tacurong, Phil. E8 34
Tademaït, Plateau du, plat.,
  Alg. E5 48
Tadjemout, Alg. A5 50
Tadoussac, P.Q., Can. A8 90
T'aebaek-sanmaek, mts.,
  Asia D13 28
Taegu, S. Kor. D13 28
Taejŏn, S. Kor. D13 28
Tafalla, Spain F6 16
Tafo, Ghana E4 50
Taft, Ca., U.S. E4 98
Taft, Tx., U.S. F4 136
Taganrog, Russia F15 20
Tagânt, reg., Maur. C2 50
Tagaytay, Phil. D8 34
Tagbilaran, Phil. E8 34
Taguke, China E4 28
Tagum, Phil. E9 34
Tagus, stm., Eur. H2 16
Tahan, Gunong, mtn.,
  Malay. C2 36
Tahat, mtn., Alg. F6 48
Tahiataš, Uzb. B7 42
Tahifet, Alg. B6 50
Tahiti, i., Fr. Poly. F15 58
Tahlequah, Ok., U.S. B7 129
Tahoe, Lake, l., U.S. D3 92
Tahoe, Lake, l., U.S. E1 121
Tahoe City, Ca., U.S. C3 98
Tahoka, Tx., U.S. C2 136
Taholah, Wa., U.S. B1 140
Tahoua, Niger D6 50
Tahquamenon, stm., Mi.,
  U.S. B5 115
Tahsis, B.C., Can. E4 85
Tahtā, Egypt F10 14
Tahta-Bazar, Turk. C8 42
Tahtakupyr, Uzb. B8 42
Tahtsa Peak, mtn., B.C.,
  Can. C4 85
Tahulandang, Pulau, i.,
  Indon. C7 36
Tahuna, Indon. C7 36
Taiʹan, China D11 28
Taibai Shan, mtn., China . . C2 30
Taibus Qi, China A4 30
T'aichung, Tai. E5 30
Taigu, China B3 30
Taihang Shan, mts., China . B3 30
Taihape, N.Z. o14 63c
Taihe, China D3 30
Taihu, China C4 30
Tai Hu, l., China E11 28
Taikang, China C4 30
Tailai, China B12 28
Tai Lake see Tai Hu, l.,
  China E11 28
Taimba, Russia C11 26
T'ainan, Tai. E5 30
Taínaron, Ákra, c., Grc. . . . F9 18
Tainaron, Cape see
  Taínaron, Ákra, c., Grc. . F9 18
T'aipei, Tai. D5 30
Taiping, Malay. C2 36
Taisha, Japan C2 31
Taishan, China E3 30
Taishun, China F11 28
Taitao, Península de, pen.,
  Chile G1 69
T'aitung, Tai. E5 30
Taivalkoski, Fin. D13 10
Taiwan, ctry., Asia B8 34
Taiwan Strait, strt., Asia . . E4 30
Taiyuan, China D10 28

Taizhou, China C4 30
Taʹizz, Yemen H4 38
Tajikistan, ctry., Asia B2 40
Tāj Mahal, hist., India D3 40
Tajmyr, ozero, l., Russia . . B12 26
Tajmyr, poluostrov, pen.,
  Russia B12 26
Tajo see Tagus, stm., Eur. . H5 16
Tajšet, Russia D11 26
Tak, Thai. C3 34
Takāb, Iran D12 44
Takalar, Indon. E5 36
Takamatsu, Japan E14 28
Takaoka, Japan C3 31
Takasaki, Japan C3 31
Takatsuki, Japan D3 31
Takêv, Camb. D4 34
Takhli, Thai. C4 34
Takikawa, Japan B4 31
Takla Lake, l., B.C., Can. . . B5 85
Taklimakan Shamo, des.,
  China D4 28
Takoma Park, Md., U.S. . . . f8 113
Taku Glacier, Ak., U.S. . . . k22 95
Takum, Nig. E7 50
Takutea, i., Cook Is. F14 58
Talak, reg., Niger C6 50
Talara, Peru D3 70
Talas, Kyrg. E9 26
Talasea, Pap. N. Gui. H13 32
Talata Mafara, Nig. D6 50
Talaud, Kepulauan, is.,
  Indon. C7 36
Talavera de la Reina, Spain H4 16
Talawdī, Sudan A6 54
Talbot, co., Ga., U.S. D2 103
Talbot, co., Md., U.S. C5 113
Talbot Island, i., Fl., U.S. . . B5 102
Talbot Lake, l., Mb., Can. . . B2 86
Talbotton, Ga., U.S. D2 103
Talca, Chile D2 69
Talcahuano, Chile D2 69
Taldykorgan, Kaz. E9 26
Talent, Or., U.S. E4 130
Talgar, Kaz. B11 42
Taliabu, Pulau, i., Indon. . . D6 36
Taliaferro, co., Ga., U.S. . . C4 103
Talihina, Ok., U.S. C6 129
Talish Mountains see
  Ṭavālesh, Kūhhā-ye,
  mts., Asia D13 44
Taliwang, Indon. E5 36
Talkeetna, Ak., U.S. C10 95
Talkeetna Mountains, mts.,
  Ak., U.S. f17 95
Talladega, Al., U.S. B3 94
Talladega, co., Al., U.S. . . . B3 94
Tall ʻAfar, Iraq D10 44
Tallahassee, Fl., U.S. B2 102
Tallahatchie, co., Ms., U.S. . B3 117
Tallahatchie, stm., Ms., U.S. B3 117
Tallangatta, Austl. H4 62
Tallapoosa, Ga., U.S. C1 103
Tallapoosa, co., Al., U.S. . . C4 94
Tallapoosa, stm., Al., U.S. . C3 94
Tallassee, Al., U.S. C4 94
Talleyville, De., U.S. A3 101
Tallinn, Est. G11 10
Tall Kūjik, Syria D9 44
Tallmadge, Oh., U.S. A4 128
Tallulah, La., U.S. B4 111
Talʹne, Ukr. E11 20
Talok, Indon. C5 36
Tāloqān, Afg. C9 42
Taloyoak, N.T., Can. E21 82
Talquin, Lake, res., Fl., U.S. B2 102
Talsi, Lat. H10 10
Taltal, Chile C2 69
Talu, Indon. C1 36
Taluk, Indon. D2 36
Tama, Ia., U.S. C5 108
Tama, co., Ia., U.S. B5 108
Tamale, Ghana E4 50
Tamalpais, Mount, mtn.,
  Ca., U.S. h7 98
Tamaqua, Pa., U.S. E10 131
Tamaroa, Il., U.S. E4 106
Tamaulipas, state, Mex. . . . C5 78
Tamazulapan del Progreso,
  Mex. D5 78
Tamazunchale, Mex. C5 78
Tambacounda, Sen. D2 50
Tambej, Russia B9 26
Tambelan, Kepulauan, is.,
  Indon. C3 36
Tamberías, Arg. E4 72
Tambohorano, Madag. . . . B7 56
Tambora, Gunung, vol.,
  Indon. E5 36
Tambov, Russia D6 26
Tambura, Sudan I10 48
Tâmchekket, Maur. C2 50
Tame, Col. B5 70
Tamel Aike, Arg. F2 69
Tamenghest, Alg. F6 48
Tamiahua, Mex. C5 78
Tamiahua, Laguna de, l.,
  Mex. C5 78
Tamiami Canal, Fl., U.S. . . G6 102
Tamil Nādu, prov., India . . G3 40
Tam Ky, Viet. C5 34
Tampa, Fl., U.S. E4 102
Tampa Bay, b., Fl., U.S. . . . E4 102
Tampere, Fin. F10 10
Tampico, Mex. C5 78

Tampico, Il., U.S. B4 106
Tam Quan, Viet. D5 34
Tamsagbulag, Mong. B11 28
Tamu, Myan. B2 34
Tamworth, Austl. G5 62
Tana (Teno), stm., Eur. . . . B12 10
Tana, stm., Kenya D7 54
Tanabe, Japan D3 31
Tanafjorden, Nor. A13 10
Tanaga Island, i., Ak., U.S. . E4 95
Tanahbala, Pulau, i., Indon. D1 36
Tanahjampea, Pulau, i.,
  Indon. E5 36
Tanahmasa, Pulau, i., Indon. D1 36
Tanahmerah, Indon. H11 32
Tanami Desert, des., Austl. . C6 60
Tanana, Ak., U.S. B9 95
Tanana, stm., Ak., U.S. . . . C10 95
Tananarive see
  Antananarivo, Madag. . . B8 56
Tanchʹŏn-ŭp, N. Kor. C13 28
Tandag, Phil. E9 34
Ţăndărei, Rom. G9 20
Tandil, Arg. F6 72
Tanega-shima, i., Japan . . . E14 28
Taney, co., Mo., U.S. E4 118
Taneycomo, Lake, res., Mo.,
  U.S. E4 118
Tanezrouft, des., Afr. B4 50
Tanga, Tan. E7 54
Tanganyika see Tanzania,
  ctry., Afr. E6 54
Tanganyika, Lake, l., Afr. . . E5 54
Tanger, Mor. C3 48
Tanggula Shan, mts., China E5 28
Tanghe, China C3 30
Tangier, Va., U.S. C7 139
Tangier Island, i., Va., U.S. . C6 139
Tangier Sound, strt., Md.,
  U.S. D6 113
Tangipahoa, co., La., U.S. . D5 111
Tangipahoa, stm., La., U.S. . D5 111
Tangmai, China C7 40
Tangra Yumco, l., China . . . C5 40
Tangshan, China D11 28
Tangyin, China B3 30
Tangyuan, China A1 31
Tanhoj, Russia A9 28
Tanimbar, Kepulauan, is.,
  Indon. E8 36
Tanjungbalai, Indon. C1 36
Tanjungkarang-Telukbetung,
  Indon. E3 36
Tanjungpandan, Indon. . . . D3 36
Tanjungpinang, Indon. C2 36
Tanjungredep, Indon. C5 36
Tānk, Pak. D10 42
Tanna, i., Vanuatu k9 62a
Tännäs, Swe. E5 10
Tanner, Al., U.S. A3 94
Tannu-Ola Mountains, mts.,
  Asia A6 28
Tanout, Niger C6 50
Tanta, Egypt D11 48
Tan-Tan, Mor. A2 50
Tantoyuca, Mex. C5 78
Tanzania, ctry., Afr. E6 54
Taormina, Italy F5 18
Taos, Mo., U.S. C5 118
Taos, N.M., U.S. A4 124
Taos, co., N.M., U.S. A4 124
Taos Pueblo, N.M., U.S. . . A4 124
Taoudenni, Mali B4 50
Taounate, Mor. E3 14
Taourirt, Mor. E3 14
Tapa, Est. G11 10
Tapachula, Mex. E6 78
Tapajós, stm., Braz. D8 70
Tapaktuan, Indon. C1 36
Taphan Hin, Thai. C4 34
Tāpi, stm., India E2 40
Tappahannock, Va., U.S. . . C6 139
Tappan, N.Y., U.S. g13 125
Tappan, Lake, res., N.J.,
  U.S. g9 123
Tappan, Lake, res., Oh., U.S. B4 128
Tapul Group, is., Phil. D7 34
Tapuruquara, Braz. D6 70
Taqâ, Sudan D5 54
Taqtaʹ Hayyâ, Sudan G12 48
Taquari Novo, stm., Braz. . . G8 70
Tar, stm., N.C., U.S. B5 126
Tara, On., Can. C3 89
Tara, Russia D9 26
Tarabuco, Bol. B5 72
Ṭarābulus (Tripoli), Leb. . . E6 44
Ṭarābulus (Tripoli), Libya . . D7 48
Ṭarābulus (Tripolitania), hist.
  reg., Libya E7 14
Tarakan, Indon. C5 36
Taranaki, Mount (Egmont,
  Mount), vol., N.Z. o13 63c
Tarancón, Spain G5 16
Taranto, Italy D6 18
Taranto, Golfo di, b., Italy . D6 18
Taranto, Gulf of see
  Taranto, Golfo di, b.,
  Italy D6 18
Tarapoto, Peru E4 70
Taraquá, Braz. C6 70
Tarat, Alg. A6 50
Tarauacá, Braz. B2 72
Tarauacá, Braz. E5 70
Tarawa, atoll, Kir. D11 58
Tarazona, Spain G6 16

Name	Map Ref.	Page
Tarbagatay Range, mts., Asia	B4	28
Tarbes, Fr.	F7	16
Tarboro, N.C., U.S.	B5	126
Tarbū, Libya	E8	48
Tarcoola, Austl.	G5	60
Tardoki-Jani, gora, mtn., Russia	B15	28
Taree, Austl.	G5	62
Tareja, Russia	B11	26
Tarentum, Pa., U.S.	E2	131
Tarfaya, Mor.	E2	48
Targhee Pass, U.S.	E7	105
Tărgovište, Bul.	C11	18
Târgoviște, Rom.	G8	20
Târgu Jiu, Rom.	G7	20
Târgu Mureș, Rom.	F8	20
Târgu-Neamț, Rom.	F9	20
Târgu Ocna, Rom.	F9	20
Tarifa, Spain	I4	16
Tariffville, Ct., U.S.	B4	100
Tarija, Bol.	C5	72
Tarim, stm., China	C4	28
Tarim Pendi, China	D4	28
Tariñ Kowt, Afg.	D9	42
Tarkastad, S. Afr.	E4	56
Tarkio, Mo., U.S.	A2	118
Tarko-Sale, Russia	C9	26
Tarkwa, Ghana	E4	50
Tarma, Peru	F4	70
Tarn, stm., Fr.	F7	16
Tärnaby, Swe.	D6	10
Târnăveni, Rom.	F8	20
Tarnobrzeg, Pol.	D6	20
Tarnów, Pol.	E6	20
Tarpey, Ca., U.S.	D4	98
Tarpon, Lake, l., Fl., U.S.	o10	102
Tarpon Springs, Fl., U.S.	D4	102
Tarquinia, Italy	C3	18
Tarragona, Spain	G7	16
Tarrant, Al., U.S.	B3	94
Tarrant, co., Tx., U.S.	C4	136
Tarryall Mountains, mts., Co., U.S.	B5	99
Tarrytown, N.Y., U.S.	D7	125
Tarsus, Tur.	D6	44
Tartagal, Arg.	C5	72
Tărtăr, Azer.	B12	44
Tartu, Est.	G12	10
Țarțūs, Syria	E6	44
Tarutung, Indon.	C1	36
Tasāwah, Libya	A7	50
Tasbuget, Kaz.	B9	42
Taseko Mountain, mtn., B.C., Can.	D6	85
Ṭashk, Daryācheh-ye, l., Iran	E6	42
Tashkent see Taškent, Uzb.	E8	26
Taškent, Uzb.	E8	26
Taškepri, Turk.	C8	42
Taşköprü, Tur.	B6	44
Tasman Basin	M18	64
Tasman Bay, b., N.Z.	p13	63c
Tasmania, state, Austl.	I4	62
Tasmania, i., Austl.	I3	62
Tasman Sea, Oc.	L18	64
Taşova, Tur.	B7	44
Tasso, Tn., U.S.	D9	135
Taštagol, Russia	D10	26
Tata, Hung.	F5	20
Tatarbunary, Ukr.	G10	20
Tatarija, state, Russia	D6	26
Tatarsk, Russia	D9	26
Tatarskij proliv, Russia	E16	26
Tatarstan see Tatarija, state, Russia	D6	26
Tatar Strait see Tatarskij proliv, strt., Russia	E16	26
Tate, Ga., U.S.	B2	103
Tate, co., Ms., U.S.	A4	117
Tateville, Ky., U.S.	D5	110
Tatnam, Cape, c., Mb., Can.	f9	86
Tatta, Pak.	F9	42
Tattnall, co., Ga., U.S.	D4	103
Tatum, N.M., U.S.	D6	124
Tatvan, Tur.	C10	44
Tauá, Braz.	C3	74
Taučik, Kaz.	B6	42
Taujskaja guba, b., Russia	D17	26
Taum Sauk Mountain, mtn., Mo., U.S.	D6	118
Taunggyi, Myan.	B3	34
Taungup, Myan.	C2	34
Taunton, Eng., U.K.	E5	12
Taunton, Ma., U.S.	C5	114
Taunton, co., Ma., U.S.	C5	114
Taupo, N.Z.	o14	63c
Taupo, Lake, l., N.Z.	o14	63c
Tauranga, N.Z.	o14	63c
Taureau, Réservoir, res., P.Q., Can.	C4	90
Taurus Mountains see Toros Dağları, mts., Tur.	D5	44
Țavālesh, Kūhhā-ye, mts., Asia	D13	44
Tavares, Fl., U.S.	D5	102
Tavas, Tur.	D3	44
Tavda, Russia	D8	26
Tavda, stm., Russia	D8	26
Tavernier, Fl., U.S.	G6	102
Taveuni, i., Fiji	m11	63b
Tavșanlı, Tur.	C3	44
Tawakoni, Lake, res., Tx., U.S.	C4	136
Tawas City, Mi., U.S.	D7	115
Tawas Lake, l., Mi., U.S.	D7	115
Tawau, Malay.	C5	36
Tawitawi Group, is., Phil.	E8	34
Tawkar, Sudan	G12	48
Ṭāwūq, Iraq	E11	44
Taxco de Alarcón, Mex.	D5	78
Taxkorgan Tajik Zizhixian, China	B3	40
Taylor, B.C., Can.	A7	85
Taylor, Ar., U.S.	D2	97
Taylor, Az., U.S.	C5	96
Taylor, Mi., U.S.	p15	115
Taylor, Pa., U.S.	D10	131
Taylor, Tx., U.S.	D4	136
Taylor, co., Fl., U.S.	B3	102
Taylor, co., Ga., U.S.	D2	103
Taylor, co., Ia., U.S.	D3	108
Taylor, co., Ky., U.S.	C4	110
Taylor, co., Tx., U.S.	C3	136
Taylor, co., W.V., U.S.	B4	141
Taylor, co., Wi., U.S.	C3	142
Taylor, stm., Co., U.S.	C4	99
Taylor, Mount, mtn., N.M., U.S.	B2	124
Taylor Mill, Ky., U.S.	k14	110
Taylor Mountain, mtn., Id., U.S.	E4	105
Taylor Park Reservoir, res., Co., U.S.	C4	99
Taylors, S.C., U.S.	B3	133
Taylors Falls, Mn., U.S.	E6	116
Taylors Island, i., Md., U.S.	D5	113
Taylorsville, In., U.S.	F6	107
Taylorsville, Ky., U.S.	B4	110
Taylorsville, Ms., U.S.	D4	117
Taylorsville, N.C., U.S.	B1	126
Taylorville, Il., U.S.	D4	106
Taymā', Sau. Ar.	E3	38
Taymyr Peninsula see Tajmyr, poluostrov, pen., Russia	B12	26
Tay Ninh, Viet.	D5	34
Taytay, Phil.	D7	34
Taz, stm., Russia	D9	26
Taza, Mor.	E3	14
Tazewell, Tn., U.S.	C10	135
Tazewell, Va., U.S.	e10	139
Tazewell, co., Il., U.S.	C4	106
Tazewell, co., Va., U.S.	e10	139
Tazovskij, Russia	C9	26
Tbessa, Alg.	C6	48
Tbilisi, Geor.	B11	44
Tchaourou, Benin	E5	50
Tchefuncta, stm., La., U.S.	D5	111
Tchibanga, Gabon	D2	54
Tchula, Ms., U.S.	B3	117
Tczew, Pol.	B5	20
Tea, S.D., U.S.	D9	134
Teague, Tx., U.S.	D4	136
Teakean Butte, mtn., Id., U.S.	C2	105
Teaneck, N.J., U.S.	h8	123
Teapa, Mex.	D6	78
Teaticket, Ma., U.S.	C6	114
Te Awamutu, N.Z.	o14	63c
Tebingtinggi, Indon.	C1	36
Tebingtinggi, Pulau, i., Indon.	C2	36
Téboursouk, Tun.	F2	18
Techlé, W. Sah.	B2	50
Tecka, Arg.	F2	69
Tecomán, Mex.	D4	78
Tecpan de Galeana, Mex.	D4	78
Tecuala, Mex.	C3	78
Tecuci, Rom.	G9	20
Tecumseh, On., Can.	E2	89
Tecumseh, Ks., U.S.	k14	109
Tecumseh, Mi., U.S.	G7	115
Tecumseh, Ne., U.S.	D9	120
Tecumseh, Ok., U.S.	B5	129
Tedžen, Turk.	F8	26
Teeli, Russia	D10	26
Teeswater, On., Can.	C3	89
Tefé, Braz.	D7	70
Tegal, Indon.	E3	36
Tégama, reg., Niger	C6	50
Tegucigalpa, Hond.	C2	80
Tehachapi, Ca., U.S.	E4	98
Tehachapi Mountains, mts., Ca., U.S.	E4	98
Tehama, co., Ca., U.S.	B2	98
Tehrān, Iran	C6	42
Tehuacán, Mex.	D5	78
Tehuantepec, Golfo de, b., Mex.	D6	78
Tehuantepec, Istmo de, Mex.	D6	78
Teide, Pico del, mtn., Spain	A1	50
Teixeira Pinto, Gui.-B.	C1	50
Tejo see Tagus, stm., Eur.	H3	16
Tekamah, Ne., U.S.	C9	120
Tekax, Mex.	C7	78
Tekeli, Kaz.	E9	26
Tekes, China	A4	40
Tekirdağ, Tur.	B2	44
Tekoa, Wa., U.S.	B8	140
Tekonsha, Mi., U.S.	F5	115
Telavi, Geor.	B11	44
Tel Aviv-Yafo, Isr.	D2	42
Teleckoe, ozero, l., Russia	A5	28
Telêmaco Borba, Braz.	C7	72
Telemark, prov., Nor.	G3	10
Telén, Arg.	F4	72
Telescope Peak, mtn., Ca., U.S.	D5	98
Telfair, co., Ga., U.S.	E4	103
Telford, Eng., U.K.	D5	12
Telford, Pa., U.S.	F11	131
Télimélé, Gui.	D2	50
Telkwa, B.C., Can.	B4	85
Tell City, In., U.S.	I4	107
Teller, co., Co., U.S.	C5	99
Tellicherry, India	G3	40
Tellico Plains, Tn., U.S.	D9	135
Telluride, Co., U.S.	D3	99
Telos Lake, l., Me., U.S.	B3	112
Telsen, Arg.	F3	69
Telukbatang, Indon.	D3	36
Teluk Intan, Malay.	C2	36
Tema, Ghana	E5	50
Temax, Mex.	C7	78
Tembilahan, Indon.	D2	36
Temecula, Ca., U.S.	F5	98
Teminabuan, Indon.	D8	36
Temir, Kaz.	E10	22
Temirtau, Kaz.	E9	26
Témiscouata, Lac, l., P.Q., Can.	B9	90
Te-Moak Indian Reservation, Nv., U.S.	C6	121
Temora, Austl.	G4	62
Temosachic, Mex.	B3	78
Tempe, Az., U.S.	D4	96
Temperance, Mi., U.S.	G7	115
Temperance, stm., Mn., U.S.	C8	116
Temple, Ga., U.S.	C1	103
Temple, Ok., U.S.	C3	129
Temple, Pa., U.S.	F10	131
Temple, Tx., U.S.	D4	136
Temple Terrace, Fl., U.S.	o11	102
Temrjuk, Russia	G14	22
Temuco, Chile	E2	69
Tenafly, N.J., U.S.	B5	123
Tenaha, Tx., U.S.	D5	136
Tena Kourou, mtn., Burkina	D4	50
Tenāli, India	F4	40
Tenasserim, Myan.	D3	34
Tendaho, Eth.	H13	48
Ten Degree Channel, strt., India	H6	40
Ténéré, des., Niger	C6	50
Tenerife, i., Spain	A1	50
Tengchong, China	G7	28
Tenggara, Nusa (Lesser Sunda Islands), is., Indon.	E5	36
Tengiz, ozero, l., Kaz.	D8	26
Tengréla, C. Iv.	D3	50
Tengxian, China	B4	30
Tengxian, China	E3	30
Tenino, Wa., U.S.	C3	140
Tenke, D.R.C.	F5	54
Tenkeli, Russia	C16	26
Tenkiller Ferry Lake, res., Ok., U.S.	B6	129
Tenkodogo, Burkina	D4	50
Tenmile, stm., U.S.	B5	132
Tenmile Creek, stm., W.V., U.S.	k10	141
Tenmile Lake, l., Mn., U.S.	D4	116
Tennant Creek, Austl.	D5	60
Tennessee, state, U.S.	B5	135
Tennessee, stm., U.S.	B3	135
Tennessee Pass, Co., U.S.	B4	99
Tennessee Ridge, Tn., U.S.	A4	135
Tennille, Ga., U.S.	D4	103
Teno (Tana), stm., Eur.	B12	10
Tenosique, Mex.	D6	78
Tensas, co., La., U.S.	B4	111
Tensas, stm., La., U.S.	B4	111
Tensaw, stm., Al., U.S.	E2	94
Ten Sleep, Wy., U.S.	B5	143
Tenterfield, Austl.	E5	62
Ten Thousand Islands, is., Fl., U.S.	G5	102
Teófilo Otoni, Braz.	E3	74
Tepa, Indon.	E7	36
Tepehuanes, Mex.	B3	78
Tepic, Mex.	C4	78
Téra, Niger	D5	50
Teramo, Italy	C4	18
Terceira, i., Port.	F7	46
Terek, Russia	A11	44
Terek, stm., Russia	B5	42
Teresina, Braz.	C3	74
Tergüün Bogd uul, mtn., Mong.	C8	28
Termas de Río Hondo, Arg.	D5	72
Terme, Tur.	B7	44
Termez, Uzb.	C9	42
Términos, Laguna de, b., Mex.	D6	78
Ternej, Russia	A3	31
Terneuzen, Neth.	E8	12
Terni, Italy	C4	18
Ternopil', Ukr.	E8	20
Terpenija, mys, c., Russia	E16	26
Terra Alta, W.V., U.S.	B5	141
Terrace, B.C., Can.	B3	85
Terracina, Italy	D4	18
Terra Nova National Park, Nf., Can.	D4	88
Terrassa, Spain	G8	16
Terrebonne, P.Q., Can.	D4	90
Terrebonne, co., La., U.S.	E5	111
Terrebonne Bay, b., La., U.S.	E5	111
Terre Haute, In., U.S.	F3	107
Terre Hill, Pa., U.S.	F9	131
Terrell, Tx., U.S.	C4	136
Terrell, co., Ga., U.S.	E2	103
Terrell, co., Tx., U.S.	D1	136
Terrell Hills, Tx., U.S.	k7	136
Terrenceville, Nf., Can.	E4	88
Terry, Ms., U.S.	C3	117
Terry, Mt., U.S.	D11	119
Terry, co., Tx., U.S.	C1	136
Terrytown, Ne., U.S.	C2	120
Terryville, Ct., U.S.	C3	100
Teruel, Spain	G6	16
Teseney, Erit.	G12	48
Teshekpuk Lake, l., Ak., U.S.	A9	95
Teshio, Japan	B4	31
Tessalit, Mali	B5	50
Tessaoua, Niger	D6	50
Tesuque, N.M., U.S.	B4	124
Tete, Moz.	B5	56
Teteriv, stm., Ukr.	D10	20
Teton, co., Id., U.S.	F7	105
Teton, co., Mt., U.S.	C4	119
Teton, co., Wy., U.S.	C2	143
Teton, stm., Mt., U.S.	C5	119
Teton Pass, Wy., U.S.	C2	143
Teton Range, mts., Wy., U.S.	C2	143
Teton Village, Wy., U.S.	C2	143
Tetouan, Mor.	C3	48
Tetovo, Mac.	C8	18
Teulon, Mb., Can.	D3	86
Teutopolis, Il., U.S.	D5	106
Tevere, stm., Italy	C4	18
Teverya, Isr.	D3	42
Tewksbury, Ma., U.S.	A5	114
Texada Island, i., B.C., Can.	E5	85
Texarkana, Ar., U.S.	D1	97
Texarkana, Tx., U.S.	C5	136
Texas, co., Mo., U.S.	D5	118
Texas, co., Ok., U.S.	e9	129
Texas, state, U.S.	D3	136
Texas City, Tx., U.S.	E5	136
Texhoma, Ok., U.S.	e9	129
Texico, N.M., U.S.	C6	124
Texoma, Lake, res., U.S.	D5	129
Teziutlán, Mex.	D5	78
Tezpur, India	D6	40
Thabana-Ntlenyana, mtn., Leso.	D4	56
Thabazimbi, S. Afr.	C4	56
Thai Binh, Viet.	B5	34
Thailand, ctry., Asia	D4	34
Thailand, Gulf of, b., Asia	D4	34
Thai Nguyen, Viet.	B5	34
Thames, N.Z.	o14	63c
Thames, stm., On., Can.	E3	89
Thames, stm., Eng., U.K.	E7	12
Thames, stm., Ct., U.S.	D7	100
Thamesville, On., Can.	E3	89
Thāna, India	F2	40
Thanh Hoa, Viet.	C5	34
Thanh Pho Ho Chi Minh (Saigon), Viet.	D5	34
Thanjāvūr, India	G3	40
Tharād, India	E2	40
Thar Desert (Great Indian Desert), des., Asia	D2	40
Tharrawaddy, Myan.	C3	34
Tharros, hist., Italy	E2	18
Tharthār, Buḥayrat ath-, res., Iraq	E10	44
Thásos, Grc.	D10	18
Thásos, i., Grc.	D10	18
Thatcher, Az., U.S.	E6	96
Thaton, Myan.	C3	34
Thayer, Mo., U.S.	E6	118
Thayer, co., Ne., U.S.	D8	120
Thayetmyo, Myan.	C3	34
Thayne, Wy., U.S.	C2	143
Thazi, Myan.	B3	34
Thealka, Ky., U.S.	C7	110
The Barrens, plat., Tn., U.S.	B5	135
Thebes see Thívai, Grc.	E9	18
The Dalles, Or., U.S.	B5	130
The Dells, val., Wi., U.S.	E4	142
Thedford, On., Can.	D3	89
Thedford, Ne., U.S.	C5	120
The Everglades, sw., Fl., U.S.	G6	102
The Flat Tops, mts., Co., U.S.	B3	99
The Flume, wtfl, N.H., U.S.	B3	122
The Graves, is., Ma., U.S.	g12	114
The Hague see 's-Gravenhage, Neth.	D8	12
The Heads, c., Or., U.S.	E2	130
The Little Minch see Little Minch, The, strt., Scot., U.K.	B3	12
The Minch, strt., Scot., U.K.	A4	12
The Narrows, strt., Wa., U.S.	f10	140
Theodore, Al., U.S.	E1	94
Theodore Roosevelt Lake, res., Az., U.S.	D4	96
Theodore Roosevelt National Park (North Unit), N.D., U.S.	B2	127
Theodore Roosevelt National Park (South Unit), N.D., U.S.	C2	127
The Pas, Mb., Can.	C1	86
The Plains, Oh., U.S.	C3	128
Theresa, Wi., U.S.	E5	142
Thermaïkós Kólpos, b., Grc.	D9	18
Thermopílai, hist., Grc.	E9	18
Thermopolis, Wy., U.S.	C4	143
Thermopylae see Thermopílai, hist., Grc.	E9	18
The Rockies, mts., Wa., U.S.	C3	140
Thessalía, hist. reg., Grc.	E9	18
Thessalon, On., Can.	p19	89
Thessaloníki (Salonika), Grc.	D9	18
Thessaly see Thessalía, hist. reg., Grc.	E9	18
Thetford Mines, P.Q., Can.	C6	90
The Thimbles, is., Ct., U.S.	E5	100
The Valley, Anguilla	B7	80
The Village, Ok., U.S.	B4	129
The Wash, b., Eng., U.K.	D7	12
Thibodaux, La., U.S.	E5	111
Thief, stm., Mn., U.S.	B2	116
Thief Lake, l., Mn., U.S.	B3	116
Thief River Falls, Mn., U.S.	B2	116
Thielsen, Mount, mtn., Or., U.S.	D4	130
Thiensville, Wi., U.S.	E6	142
Thiès, Sen.	D1	50
Thika, Kenya	D7	54
Thimphu, Bhu.	D5	40
Thingvellir, Ice.	l18	10a
Thio, N. Cal.	l9	62a
Thionville, Fr.	C10	16
Thíra, i., Grc.	F10	18
Third Cataract, wtfl, Sudan	G11	48
Third Lake, l., N.H., U.S.	f7	122
Thisted, Den.	H3	10
Thistilfjördur, b., Ice.	k21	10a
Thívai, Grc.	E9	18
Thjórsá, stm., Ice.	m18	10a
Thomas, Ok., U.S.	B3	129
Thomas, co., Ga., U.S.	F3	103
Thomas, co., Ks., U.S.	C2	109
Thomas, co., Ne., U.S.	C5	120
Thomasboro, Il., U.S.	C5	106
Thomaston, Ct., U.S.	C3	100
Thomaston, Ga., U.S.	D2	103
Thomaston, Me., U.S.	D3	112
Thomaston Reservoir, res., Ct., U.S.	C3	100
Thomasville, Al., U.S.	D2	94
Thomasville, Ga., U.S.	F3	103
Thomasville, N.C., U.S.	B2	126
Thompson, Mb., Can.	B3	86
Thompson, Ct., U.S.	B8	100
Thompson, N.D., U.S.	B8	127
Thompson, stm., U.S.	A4	118
Thompson Falls, Mt., U.S.	C1	119
Thompson Island, i., Ma., U.S.	g11	114
Thompson Lake, l., U.S.	D2	112
Thompson Peak, mtn., Ca., U.S.	B2	98
Thompson Peak, mtn., N.M., U.S.	h9	124
Thompson Reservoir, res., Or., U.S.	E5	130
Thomson, Ga., U.S.	C4	103
Thongwa, Myan.	C3	34
Thonon-les-Bains, Fr.	D10	16
Thonotosassa, Fl., U.S.	D4	102
Thonze, Myan.	C3	34
Thorburn, N.S., Can.	D7	87
Thoreau, N.M., U.S.	B1	124
Thornbury, On., Can.	C4	89
Thorndale, Tx., U.S.	D4	136
Thornton, On., Can.	C5	89
Thorntown, In., U.S.	D4	107
Thorold, On., Can.	D5	89
Thorp, Wi., U.S.	D3	142
Thorsby, Al., U.S.	C3	94
Thorshavn see Tórshavn, Far. Is.	n23	10b
Thórshöfn, Ice.	k21	10a
Thouars, Fr.	D6	16
Thousand Islands, is., N.Y., U.S.	A4	125
Thousand Lake Mountain, mtn., Ut., U.S.	E4	137
Thousand Springs Creek, stm., U.S.	B7	121
Thrace, hist. reg., Eur.	D11	18
Thrakikón Pélagos, Grc.	D10	18
Three Fingered Jack, mtn., Or., U.S.	C5	130
Three Forks, Mt., U.S.	E5	119
Three Hills, Ab., Can.	D4	84
Three Hummock Island, i., Austl.	I4	62
Three Kings Islands, is., N.Z.	n13	63c
Three Lakes, Wi., U.S.	C4	142
Three Mile Plains, N.S., Can.	E5	87
Three Oaks, Mi., U.S.	G4	115
Three Pagodas Pass, Asia	C3	34
Three Points, Cape, c., Ghana	F4	50
Three Rivers, Ma., U.S.	B3	114
Three Rivers, Mi., U.S.	G5	115
Three Rivers, Tx., U.S.	E3	136
Three Sisters, mtn., Or., U.S.	C5	130
Three Springs, Austl.	F2	60
Throckmorton, co., Tx., U.S.	C3	136
Throop, Pa., U.S.	m18	131
Thule (Qaanaaq), Grnld.	C26	82
Thun, Switz.	A1	18
Thunder Bay, On., Can.	o17	89
Thunder Bay, b., Mi., U.S.	D7	115

Name	Map Ref.	Page

Thunder Bay, stm., Mi., U.S. **D6** — 115
Thunderbird, Lake, res., Ok., U.S. **B4** — 129
Thunderbolt, Ga., U.S. **D5** — 103
Thunder Butte Creek, stm., S.D., U.S. **B3** — 134
Thurmont, Md., U.S. **A3** — 113
Thurso, P.Q., Can. **D2** — 90
Thurso, Scot., U.K. **A5** — 12
Thurston, co., Ne., U.S. **B9** — 120
Thurston, co., Wa., U.S. **C2** — 140
Thy, reg., Den. **H3** — 10
Thyolo, Mwi. **B6** — 56
Tianchang, China **C4** — 30
Tiandong, China **E2** — 30
Tianguá, Braz. **B3** — 74
Tianjin, China **D11** — 28
Tianjun, China **D7** — 28
Tianlin, China **E2** — 30
Tianmen, China **E10** — 28
Tianshui, China **E9** — 28
Tiantai, China **F12** — 28
Tianyang, China **E2** — 30
Tianzhu, China **D8** — 28
Tiassalé, C. Iv. **E4** — 50
Tibati, Cam. **B2** — 54
Tiber see Tevere, stm., Italy **C4** — 18
Tiberias see Teverya, Isr. **D3** — 42
Tibesti, mts., Afr. **B8** — 50
Tibet see Xizang Zizhiqu, prov., China **E5** — 28
Tibet, Plateau of see Qing Zang Gaoyuan, plat., China **E4** — 28
Tiburón, Isla, i., Mex. **B2** — 78
Tice, Fl., U.S. **F5** — 102
Tichît, Maur. **C3** — 50
Tickfaw, stm., La., U.S. **C5** — 111
Ticonderoga, N.Y., U.S. **B7** — 125
Ticul, Mex. **C7** — 78
Tidaholm, Swe. **G5** — 10
Tide Head, N.B., Can. **B3** — 87
Tidjikja, Maur. **C2** — 50
Tiébissou, C. Iv. **E3** — 50
Tieli, China **A1** — 31
Tieling, China **C12** — 28
Tien Shan, mts., Asia **C3** — 28
Tientsin see Tianjin, China **D11** — 28
Tierp, Swe. **F7** — 10
Tierra Amarilla, N.M., U.S. **A3** — 124
Tierra Blanca, Mex. **D5** — 78
Tierra de Campos, reg., Spain **F4** — 16
Tierra del Fuego, i., S.A. **H3** — 69
Tietê, stm., Braz. **F1** — 74
Tieton, Wa., U.S. **C5** — 140
Tieton, stm., Wa., U.S. **C4** — 140
Tieton Dam, Wa., U.S. **C4** — 140
Tiffany Mountain, mtn., Wa., U.S. **A6** — 140
Tiffin, Oh., U.S. **A2** — 128
Tiffin, stm., Oh., U.S. **A1** — 128
Tift, co., Ga., U.S. **E3** — 103
Tifton, Ga., U.S. **E3** — 103
Tigard, Or., U.S. **h12** — 130
Tigerton, Wi., U.S. **D4** — 142
Tighina, Mol. **F10** — 20
Tignall, Ga., U.S. **C4** — 103
Tignish, P.E., Can. **C5** — 87
Tigris (Dicle) (Dijlah), stm., Asia **D5** — 42
Tiguentourine, Alg. **F5** — 14
Tihert, Alg. **D4** — 14
Tihoreck, Russia **E6** — 26
Tihvin, Russia **C5** — 22
Tijuana, Mex. **A1** — 78
Tikal, hist., Guat. **B2** — 80
Tīkamgarh, India **E3** — 40
Tikrīt, Iraq **D4** — 42
Tikšeozero, ozero, l., Russia **C15** — 10
Tiksi, Russia **B14** — 28
Tilburg, Neth. **E9** — 12
Tilbury, On., Can. **E2** — 89
Tilden, Il., U.S. **E4** — 106
Tilden, Ne., U.S. **B8** — 120
Tilghman, Md., U.S. **C5** — 113
Tilghman Island, i., Md., U.S. **C5** — 113
Tilimsen, Alg. **D4** — 48
Tillabéri, Niger **D5** — 50
Tillamook, Or., U.S. **B3** — 130
Tillamook, co., Or., U.S. **B3** — 130
Tillanchäng Dwip, i., India **H6** — 40
Tillery, Lake, res., N.C., U.S. **B2** — 126
Tillman, co., Ok., U.S. **C2** — 129
Tillmans Corner, Al., U.S. **E1** — 94
Tillsonburg, On., Can. **E4** — 89
Tílos, i., Grc. **F11** — 18
Tilton, Il., U.S. **C6** — 106
Tilton, N.H., U.S. **D3** — 122
Tiltonsville, Oh., U.S. **B5** — 128
Timanskij krjaž, hills, Russia **C7** — 26
Timaru, N.Z. **p13** — 63c
Timaševsk, Russia **G15** — 20
Timbalier Island, i., La., U.S. **E5** — 111
Timbaúba, Braz. **C4** — 74
Timbedgha, Maur. **C3** — 50
Timberlake, Va., U.S. **C3** — 139
Timberville, Va., U.S. **B4** — 139
Timbuktu see Tombouctou, Mali **C4** — 50
Timimoun, Alg. **E5** — 48
Timirist, Râs, c., Maur. **C1** — 50

Timişoara, Rom. **G6** — 20
Timmins, On., Can. **o19** — 89
Timmonsville, S.C., U.S. **C8** — 133
Timms Hill, hill, Wi., U.S. **C3** — 142
Timon, Braz. **C3** — 74
Timor, i., Indon. **E7** — 36
Timor Sea **F6** — 58
Timošino, Russia **B6** — 22
Timpanogos Cave National Monument, Ut., U.S. **C4** — 137
Timšer, Russia **B9** — 22
Tims Ford Lake, res., Tn., U.S. **B5** — 135
Tinaca Point, c., Phil. **E9** — 34
Tinaquillo, Ven. **C6** — 80
Tindouf, Alg. **E3** — 48
Tinghert, Hamâdat, plat., Afr. **E7** — 48
Tingmerkpuk Mountain, mtn., Ak., U.S. **B7** — 95
Tingo María, Peru **E4** — 70
Tingsryd, Swe. **H6** — 10
Tinian, i., N. Mar. Is. **D12** — 32
Tinker Air Force Base, mil., Ok., U.S. **B4** — 129
Tinley Park, Il., U.S. **k9** — 106
Tinniswood, Mount, mtn., B.C., Can. **D6** — 85
Tinogasta, Arg. **D4** — 72
Tínos, i., Grc. **F10** — 18
Tinsukia, India **D7** — 40
Tintina, Arg. **D5** — 72
Tinton Falls, N.J., U.S. **C4** — 123
Tioga, La., U.S. **C3** — 111
Tioga, N.D., U.S. **A3** — 127
Tioga, co., N.Y., U.S. **C4** — 125
Tioga, co., Pa., U.S. **C7** — 131
Tioga, stm., Pa., U.S. **C7** — 131
Tiogue Lake, res., R.I., U.S. **D3** — 132
Tioman, Pulau, i., Malay. **C2** — 36
Tionesta Creek, stm., Pa., U.S. **C3** — 131
Tionesta Lake, res., Pa., U.S. **D3** — 131
Tioughnioga, stm., N.Y., U.S. **C4** — 125
Tipitapa, Nic. **C2** — 80
Tippah, co., Ms., U.S. **A5** — 117
Tippah, stm., Ms., U.S. **A4** — 117
Tipp City, Oh., U.S. **C1** — 128
Tippecanoe, co., In., U.S. **D4** — 107
Tippecanoe, stm., In., U.S. **C4** — 107
Tipperary, Austl. **C5** — 60
Tipton, Ca., U.S. **D4** — 98
Tipton, Ia., U.S. **C6** — 108
Tipton, In., U.S. **D5** — 107
Tipton, Mo., U.S. **C5** — 118
Tipton, Ok., U.S. **C2** — 129
Tipton, co., In., U.S. **D5** — 107
Tipton, co., Tn., U.S. **B2** — 135
Tipton, Mount, mtn., Az., U.S. **B1** — 96
Tiptonville, Tn., U.S. **A2** — 135
Tirana see Tiranë, Alb. **D7** — 18
Tiranë, Alb. **D7** — 18
Tiraspol, Mol. **F10** — 20
Tire, Tur. **C2** — 44
Tirebolu, Tur. **B8** — 44
Tiree, i., Scot., U.K. **B3** — 12
Tírnavos, Grc. **E9** — 18
Tiruchchirāppalli, India **G3** — 40
Tirunelveli, India **H3** — 40
Tirupati, India **G3** — 40
Tiruppur, India **G3** — 40
Tiruvannāmalai, India **G3** — 40
Tiruvottiyūr, India **G4** — 40
Tisa (Tisza) (Tysa), stm., Eur. **G6** — 20
Tishomingo, Ok., U.S. **C5** — 129
Tishomingo, co., Ms., U.S. **A5** — 117
Tiskilwa, Il., U.S. **B4** — 106
Tista, stm., Asia **A1** — 34
Tisza (Tisa) (Tysa), stm., Eur. **F6** — 20
Titicaca, Lake, l., S.A. **E4** — 68
Titilāgarh, India **E4** — 40
Titograd see Podgorica, Yugo. **C7** — 18
Titonka, Ia., U.S. **A3** — 108
Titov Veles, Mac. **D8** — 18
Titran, Nor. **E3** — 10
Titule, D.R.C. **C5** — 54
Titus, co., Tx., U.S. **C5** — 136
Titusville, Fl., U.S. **D6** — 102
Titusville, Pa., U.S. **C2** — 131
Tivaouane, Sen. **C1** — 50
Tiverton, On., Can. **C3** — 89
Tiverton, R.I., U.S. **D6** — 132
Tizimín, Mex. **C7** — 78
Tizi-Ouzou, Alg. **C5** — 48
Tjeggelvas, l., Swe. **C7** — 10
Tjukalinsk, Russia **D9** — 26
Tjul'gan, Russia **D10** — 22
Tjumen', Russia **D8** — 26
Tkibuli, Geor. **A10** — 44
Tkvarčeli, Geor. **A9** — 44
Tlahualilo de Zaragoza, Mex. **B4** — 78
Tlalnepantla, Mex. **D5** — 78
Tlaquepaque, Mex. **C4** — 78
Tlaxcala, state, Mex. **D5** — 78
Tlaxcala de Xicohténcatl, Mex. **D5** — 78
Tlemsah, Libya **A8** — 50
Tmassah, Libya **A8** — 50
Toamasina, Madag. **B8** — 56
Toano, Va., U.S. **C6** — 139

Toano Range, mts., Nv., U.S. **C7** — 121
Toast, N.C., U.S. **A2** — 126
Toba, Danau, l., Indon. **C1** — 36
Tobacco Root Mountains, mts., Mt., U.S. **E5** — 119
Tobago, i., Trin. **C7** — 80
Toba Inlet, b., B.C., Can. **D5** — 85
Toba Kākar Range, mts., Pak. **D9** — 42
Tobejuba, Isla, i., Ven. **D7** — 80
Tobin, Mount, mtn., Nv., U.S. **C4** — 121
Tobin Lake, l., Sk., Can. **D4** — 91
Tobin Range, mts., Nv., U.S. **C4** — 121
Tobique, stm., N.B., Can. **B2** — 87
Tobol, Kaz. **D11** — 22
Tobol, stm., Asia **D8** — 26
Tobol'sk, Russia **D8** — 26
Tobyhanna, Pa., U.S. **D11** — 131
Tocantínia, Braz. **E10** — 70
Tocantinópolis, Braz. **C2** — 74
Tocantins, state, Braz. **D2** — 74
Tocantins, stm., Braz. **B2** — 74
Toccoa, Ga., U.S. **B3** — 103
Toccoa, stm., Ga., U.S. **B2** — 103
Toccoa Falls, Ga., U.S. **B3** — 103
Tocopilla, Chile **B2** — 69
Todd, co., Ky., U.S. **D2** — 110
Todd, co., Mn., U.S. **D4** — 116
Todd, co., S.D., U.S. **D5** — 134
Tofield, Ab., Can. **C4** — 84
Tofino, B.C., Can. **E5** — 85
Togiak, Ak., U.S. **D7** — 95
Togian, Kepulauan, is., Indon. **D6** — 36
Togo, ctry., Afr. **E5** — 50
Togtoh, China **D3** — 40
Togwotee Pass, Wy., U.S. **C2** — 143
Tohakum Peak, mtn., Nv., U.S. **C2** — 121
Tohatchi, N.M., U.S. **B1** — 124
Tohopekaliga, Lake, l., Fl., U.S. **D5** — 102
Toiyabe Range, mts., Nv., U.S. **D4** — 121
Tok, Ak., U.S. **C11** — 95
Tōkamachi, Japan **C3** — 31
Tokat, Tur. **B7** — 44
Tokelau, dep., Oc. **E12** — 58
Tokmak, Kyrg. **A3** — 40
Tokmak, Ukr. **F13** — 20
Tokoroa, N.Z. **o14** — 63c
Toktogul, Kyrg. **A2** — 40
Tokuno-shima, i., Japan **A9** — 34
Tokushima, Japan **D2** — 31
Tōkyō, Japan **D16** — 28
Tôlañaro, Madag. **D8** — 56
Toledo, Braz. **C7** — 72
Toledo, Spain **H4** — 16
Toledo, Ia., U.S. **B5** — 108
Toledo, Il., U.S. **D5** — 106
Toledo, Oh., U.S. **A2** — 128
Toledo, Or., U.S. **C3** — 130
Toledo Bend Reservoir, res., U.S. **E9** — 92
Toledo Bend Reservoir, res., U.S. **C2** — 111
Toler, Ky., U.S. **C7** — 110
Toliara, Madag. **C7** — 56
Tolima, Nevado del, vol., Col. **C4** — 70
Tolitoli, Indon. **C6** — 36
Toljatti, Russia **D6** — 26
Tol'ka, Russia **C10** — 26
Tolland, Ct., U.S. **B6** — 100
Tolland, co., Ct., U.S. **B6** — 100
Tollesboro, Ky., U.S. **B6** — 110
Tolleson, Az., U.S. **m8** — 96
Tolmezzo, Italy **A4** — 18
Tolo, D.R.C. **D3** — 54
Tolo, Gulf of see Tolo, Teluk, b., Indon. **D6** — 36
Tolo, Teluk, b., Indon. **D6** — 36
Tolono, Il., U.S. **D5** — 106
Tolstoj, mys, c., Russia **D17** — 26
Tolt Reservoir, res., Wa., U.S. **B4** — 140
Tolú, Col. **D4** — 80
Toluca, Il., U.S. **C4** — 106
Toluca de Lerdo, Mex. **D5** — 78
Tomah, Wi., U.S. **E3** — 142
Tomahawk, Wi., U.S. **C4** — 142
Tomahawk Lake, l., Wi., U.S. **C4** — 142
Tomakomai, Japan **C16** — 28
Tomaszów Lubelski, Pol. **E6** — 20
Tomaszów Mazowiecki, Pol. **D6** — 20
Tomball, Tx., U.S. **D5** — 136
Tombe, Sudan **G6** — 54
Tombigbee, stm., U.S. **D1** — 94
Tombouctou, Mali **C4** — 50
Tombstone, Az., U.S. **F5** — 96
Tombua, Ang. **B1** — 56
Tomé, Chile **F3** — 72
Tomé-Açu, Braz. **B2** — 74
Tomelloso, Spain **H5** — 16
Tom Green, co., Tx., U.S. **D2** — 136
Tomini, Indon. **C6** — 36
Tomini, Gulf of see Tomini, Teluk, b., Indon. **D6** — 36
Tomini, Teluk, b., Indon. **D6** — 36
Tom Nevers Head, c., Ma., U.S. **D8** — 114
Tomo, stm., Col. **B6** — 70

Tompkins, co., N.Y., U.S. **C4** — 125
Tompkinsville, Ky., U.S. **D4** — 110
Tom Price, Austl. **E2** — 60
Tomptokan, Russia **D15** — 26
Toms, stm., N.J., U.S. **C4** — 123
Tomsk, Russia **D10** — 26
Toms River, N.J., U.S. **D4** — 123
Tonalá, Mex. **D6** — 78
Tonasket, Wa., U.S. **A6** — 140
Tonawanda Indian Reservation, N.Y., U.S. **B2** — 125
Tondano, Indon. **C6** — 36
Tonekābon, Iran **C6** — 42
Tonga, ctry., Oc. **F12** — 58
Tonganoxie, Ks., U.S. **C8** — 109
Tonga Ridge **J21** — 64
Tongatapu, i., Tonga **G12** — 58
Tonga Trench **K21** — 64
Tongcheng, China **E11** — 28
Tongchuan, China **D9** — 28
Tongguan, China **E10** — 28
Tonghai, China **G8** — 28
Tonghua, China **C13** — 28
Tongjiang, China **C2** — 30
Tongjiang, China **A2** — 31
Tongjosŏn-man, b., N. Kor. **D13** — 28
Tongliao, China **C12** — 28
Tongoy, Chile **D2** — 69
Tongren, China **F9** — 28
Tongren, China **B1** — 30
Tongsa Dzong, Bhu. **D6** — 40
Tongtian, stm., China **E7** — 28
Tongue, stm., Mt., U.S. **E10** — 119
Tongue, stm., Tx., U.S. **p13** — 136
Tongxian, China **D11** — 28
Tongyu, China **C12** — 28
Tongzi, China **F9** — 28
Tonk, India **D3** — 40
Tonkawa, Ok., U.S. **A4** — 129
Tonkin, Gulf of, b., Asia **B5** — 34
Tônlé Sab, Bœng, l., Camb. **D4** — 34
Tonle Sap see Tônlé Sab, Bœng, l., Camb. **D4** — 34
Tonopah, Nv., U.S. **E4** — 121
Tønsberg, Nor. **G4** — 10
Tonstad, Nor. **G2** — 10
Tonto National Monument, Az., U.S. **D4** — 96
Tonto Natural Bridge, Az., U.S. **C4** — 96
Tooele, Ut., U.S. **C3** — 137
Tooele, co., Ut., U.S. **C2** — 137
Toole, co., Mt., U.S. **B5** — 119
Toombs, co., Ga., U.S. **D4** — 103
Toomsboro, Ga., U.S. **D3** — 103
Toora-Hem, Russia **D11** — 26
Toowoomba, Austl. **F5** — 62
Topeka, In., U.S. **A6** — 107
Topeka, Ks., U.S. **C8** — 109
Topock, Az., U.S. **C1** — 96
Topol'čany, Slvk. **E5** — 20
Topolobampo, Mex. **B3** — 78
Topozero, ozero, l., Russia **D14** — 10
Toppenish, Wa., U.S. **C5** — 140
Topsfield, Ma., U.S. **A6** — 114
Topsham, Me., U.S. **E3** — 112
Topton, Pa., U.S. **F10** — 131
Toquima Range, mts., Nv., U.S. **E5** — 121
Tor, Eth. **B6** — 54
Torbalı, Tur. **C2** — 44
Torbat-e Ḥeydarīyeh, Iran **C7** — 42
Torbat-e Jām, Iran **C8** — 42
Torbay, N.f., Can. **E5** — 88
Torbay see Torquay, Eng., U.K. **E5** — 12
Torbert, Mount, mtn., Ak., U.S. **g15** — 95
Torch Lake, l., Mi., U.S. **D5** — 115
Tordesillas, Spain **G4** — 16
Töre, Swe. **D10** — 10
Torez, Ukr. **E15** — 20
Torino (Turin), Italy **B1** — 18
Torit, Sudan **J11** — 48
Tormes, stm., Spain **G4** — 16
Tornado, W.V., U.S. **C3** — 141
Torneälven (Tornionjoki), stm., Eur. **C10** — 10
Torneträsk, l., Swe. **B8** — 10
Torngat Mountains, mts., Can. **f8** — 88
Tornio, Fin. **D11** — 10
Tornionjoki (Torneälven), stm., Eur. **C10** — 10
Tornquist, Arg. **F5** — 72
Toro, Spain **G4** — 16
Toro Peak, mtn., Ca., U.S. **F5** — 98
Tororo, Ug. **C6** — 54
Toronto, On., Can. **D5** — 89
Toronto, Oh., U.S. **B5** — 128
Toronto Lake, res., Ks., U.S. **E7** — 109
Toros Dağları, mts., Tur. **D5** — 44
Torquay, Eng., U.K. **E5** — 12
Torrance, Ca., U.S. **n12** — 98
Torrance, co., N.M., U.S. **C3** — 124
Torrelavega, Spain **F4** — 16
Torremolinos, Spain **I4** — 16
Torrens, Lake, l., Austl. **E7** — 62
Torrent, Spain **H6** — 16
Torreón, Mex. **B4** — 78
Torres, Îles, is., Vanuatu **j9** — 62a
Torres Strait, strt., Oc. **B3** — 62
Torres Vedras, Port. **H2** — 16
Torrington, Ct., U.S. **B3** — 100
Torrington, Wy., U.S. **D8** — 143

Tórtolas, Cerro las, mtn., S.A. **D4** — 72
Tortosa, Spain **G7** — 16
Tortue, Île de la, i., Haiti **A5** — 80
Toruń, Pol. **C5** — 20
Toržok, Russia **C5** — 22
Tostado, Arg. **D5** — 72
Tõstamaa, Est. **G10** — 10
Tosya, Tur. **B5** — 44
Totagatic, stm., Wi., U.S. **B2** — 142
Totana, Spain **I6** — 16
Toteng, Bots. **C3** — 56
Tot'ma, Russia **B7** — 22
Totowa, N.J., U.S. **B4** — 123
Totson Mountain, mtn., Ak., U.S. **C8** — 95
Tottenham (part of Alliston Beeton Tecumseth and Tottenham), On., Can. **C5** — 89
Tottori, Japan **C2** — 31
Touba, C. Iv. **E3** — 50
Toubkal, Jebel, mtn., Mor. **D3** — 48
Touchet, stm., Wa., U.S. **C7** — 140
Toudao see Songhua, stm., China **B14** — 28
Touggourt, Alg. **D6** — 48
Touisset, Ma., U.S. **C5** — 114
Toul, Fr. **C9** — 16
Touliu, Tai. **E5** — 30
Toulon, Fr. **F9** — 16
Toulon, Il., U.S. **B4** — 106
Toulouse, Fr. **F7** — 16
Toumodi, C. Iv. **E3** — 50
Toungoo, Myan. **C3** — 34
Touraine, hist. reg., Fr. **D7** — 16
Tournai, Bel. **E8** — 12
Tours, Fr. **D7** — 16
Toussaint Creek, stm., Oh., U.S. **f7** — 128
Toussidé, Pic, vol., Chad **B8** — 50
Toutle, North Fork, stm., Wa., U.S. **C3** — 140
Touwsrivier, S. Afr. **E3** — 56
Tovarkovskij, Russia **C15** — 20
Tovuz, Azer. **B11** — 44
Towanda, Il., U.S. **C5** — 106
Towanda, Ks., U.S. **E7** — 109
Towanda, Pa., U.S. **C9** — 131
Towanda Creek, stm., Pa., U.S. **C8** — 131
Tower City, Pa., U.S. **E8** — 131
Town Creek, Al., U.S. **A2** — 94
Towner, N.D., U.S. **A5** — 127
Towner, co., N.D., U.S. **A6** — 127
Towns, co., Ga., U.S. **B3** — 103
Townsend, De., U.S. **C3** — 101
Townsend, Mt., U.S. **D5** — 119
Townshend Reservoir, res., Vt., U.S. **E3** — 138
Townsville, Austl. **D4** — 62
Towson, Md., U.S. **B4** — 113
Towuti, Danau, l., Indon. **D6** — 36
Toyama, Japan **D15** — 28
Toyohashi, Japan **D3** — 31
Toyota, Japan **C3** — 31
Tozeur, Tun. **D6** — 48
Trabzon, Tur. **B8** — 44
Tracadie, N.B., Can. **B5** — 87
Tracy, N.B., Can. **D3** — 87
Tracy, P.Q., Can. **C4** — 90
Tracy, Ca., U.S. **D3** — 98
Tracy, Mn., U.S. **F3** — 116
Tracy City, Tn., U.S. **D8** — 135
Tracyton, Wa., U.S. **e10** — 140
Tradewater, stm., Ky., U.S. **C2** — 110
Traer, Ia., U.S. **B5** — 108
Trafford, Pa., U.S. **k14** — 131
Trafford, Lake, l., Fl., U.S. **F5** — 102
Trail, B.C., Can. **E9** — 85
Trail Creek, In., U.S. **A4** — 107
Traill, co., N.D., U.S. **B8** — 127
Trail Ridge, mtn., Fl., U.S. **F4** — 103
Tralee, Ire. **D2** — 12
Tranås, Swe. **G6** — 10
Trancas, Arg. **D4** — 72
Trang, Thai. **E3** — 34
Trangan, Pulau, i., Indon. **E8** — 36
Trani, Italy **D6** — 18
Transantarctic Mountains, mts., Ant. **E32** — 67
Transkei, hist. reg., S. Afr. **E4** — 56
Transylvania, hist. reg., Rom. **F7** — 20
Transylvanian Alps see Carpaţii Meridionali, mts., Rom. **G7** — 20
Trapani, Italy **E4** — 18
Trappe, Md., U.S. **C5** — 113
Trapper Peak, mtn., Mt., U.S. **E2** — 119
Traralgon, Austl. **H4** — 62
Trârza, reg., Maur. **C1** — 50
Trasimeno, Lago, l., Italy **C3** — 18
Travelers Rest, S.C., U.S. **B3** — 133
Traverse, co., Mn., U.S. **E2** — 116
Traverse, Lake, l., U.S. **B9** — 134
Traverse City, Mi., U.S. **D5** — 115
Tra Vinh, Viet. **E5** — 34
Travis, co., Tx., U.S. **D4** — 136
Travis Air Force Base, mil., Ca., U.S. **C2** — 98
Travnik, Bos. **B6** — 18
Tray Mountain, mtn., Ga., U.S. **B3** — 103

Name	Map Ref.	Page

Trayning, Austl. — G2 — 60
Treasure, co., Mt., U.S. — D9 — 119
Treasure Island Naval Station, mil., Ca., U.S. — h8 — 98
Třebíč, Czech Rep. — E3 — 20
Trebišov, Slvk. — E6 — 20
Trego, co., Ks., U.S. — D4 — 109
Treherne, Mb., Can. — E2 — 86
Treinta y Tres, Ur. — E7 — 72
Trelew, Arg. — F3 — 69
Trelleborg, Swe. — I5 — 10
Tremblant, Mont, mtn., P.Q., Can. — C3 — 90
Tremont, Il., U.S. — C4 — 106
Tremont, Pa., U.S. — E9 — 131
Tremonton, Ut., U.S. — B3 — 137
Tremp, Spain — F7 — 16
Trempealeau, Wi., U.S. — D2 — 142
Trempealeau, co., Wi., U.S. — D2 — 142
Trempealeau, stm., Wi., U.S. — D2 — 142
Trenche, stm., P.Q., Can. — B5 — 90
Trenčín, Slvk. — E5 — 20
Trenque Lauquen, Arg. — F5 — 72
Trent, stm., Eng., U.K. — D6 — 12
Trent, stm., B.C., Can. — B5 — 126
Trente et un Milles, Lac des, l., P.Q., Can. — C2 — 90
Trento, Italy — A3 — 18
Trenton, On., Can. — C7 — 89
Trenton, Fl., U.S. — C4 — 102
Trenton, Ga., U.S. — B1 — 103
Trenton, Il., U.S. — E4 — 106
Trenton, Mi., U.S. — F7 — 115
Trenton, Mo., U.S. — A4 — 118
Trenton, Ne., U.S. — D4 — 120
Trenton, N.J., U.S. — C3 — 123
Trenton, Oh., U.S. — C1 — 128
Trenton, Tn., U.S. — B3 — 135
Trepassey, Nf., Can. — E5 — 88
Trepassey Bay, b., Nf., Can. — E5 — 88
Tresckow, Pa., U.S. — E10 — 131
Três Corações, Braz. — F2 — 74
Tres Esquinas, Col. — C4 — 70
Três Lagoas, Braz. — F1 — 74
Tres Marías, Islas, is., Mex. — C3 — 78
Três Marias, Represa de, res., Braz. — E2 — 74
Tres Puntas, Cabo, c., Arg. — G3 — 69
Três Rios, Braz. — F3 — 74
Tres Zapotes, hist., Mex. — D5 — 78
Treutlen, co., Ga., U.S. — D4 — 103
Treviso, Italy — B4 — 18
Trevor, Wi., U.S. — n11 — 142
Trevorton, Pa., U.S. — E8 — 131
Treynor, Ia., U.S. — C2 — 108
Trezevant, Tn., U.S. — A3 — 135
Triadelphia, W.V., U.S. — A4 — 141
Triadelphia Reservoir, res., Md., U.S. — B3 — 113
Triangle, Va., U.S. — B5 — 139
Tribune, Ks., U.S. — D2 — 109
Tricase, Italy — E7 — 18
Trichinopoly see Tiruchchirāppalli, India — G3 — 40
Trichūr, India — G3 — 40
Tri City, Or., U.S. — E3 — 130
Trident Peak, mtn., Nv., U.S. — B3 — 121
Trier, Ger. — F10 — 12
Trieste, Italy — B4 — 18
Trigg, co., Ky., U.S. — D2 — 110
Triglav, mtn., Slvn. — A4 — 18
Trigo Mountains, mts., Az., U.S. — D1 — 96
Tríkala, Grc. — E8 — 18
Trikora, Puncak, mtn., Indon. — G10 — 32
Tri Lakes, In., U.S. — B7 — 107
Trimble, Tn., U.S. — A2 — 135
Trimble, co., Ky., U.S. — B4 — 110
Trimont, Mn., U.S. — G4 — 116
Trincomalee, Sri L. — H4 — 40
Tring Jonction, P.Q., Can. — C6 — 90
Trinidad, Bol. — A5 — 72
Trinidad, Col. — B5 — 70
Trinidad, Cuba — A3 — 80
Trinidad, Co., U.S. — D6 — 99
Trinidad, Tx., U.S. — C4 — 136
Trinidad, Ur. — E6 — 72
Trinidad, i., Trin. — C7 — 80
Trinidad and Tobago, ctry., N.A. — F12 — 76
Trinidad Head, c., Ca., U.S. — B1 — 98
Trinity, Al., U.S. — A2 — 94
Trinity, Tx., U.S. — D5 — 136
Trinity, co., Ca., U.S. — B2 — 98
Trinity, co., Tx., U.S. — D5 — 136
Trinity, stm., Ca., U.S. — B2 — 98
Trinity, stm., Tx., U.S. — D5 — 136
Trinity Bay, b., Nf., Can. — D5 — 88
Trinity Islands, is., Ak., U.S. — D9 — 95
Trinity Mountain, mtn., Id., U.S. — F3 — 105
Trinity Mountains, mts., Ca., U.S. — B2 — 98
Trinity Peak, mtn., Nv., U.S. — C3 — 121
Trinity Range, mts., Nv., U.S. — C3 — 121
Trion, Ga., U.S. — B1 — 103
Tripoli see Ṭarābulus, Leb. — E6 — 44
Tripoli see Ṭarābulus, Libya — D7 — 48
Tripoli, Ia., U.S. — B5 — 108
Trípolis, Grc. — F9 — 18

Tripolitania see Ṭarābulus, hist. reg., Libya — E7 — 14
Tripp, S.D., U.S. — D8 — 134
Tripp, co., S.D., U.S. — D6 — 134
Tripura, prov., India — E6 — 40
Tristan da Cunha Group, is., St. Hel. — M8 — 46
Triumph, La., U.S. — E6 — 111
Trivandrum, India — H3 — 40
Trnava, Slvk. — E4 — 20
Trochu, Ab., Can. — D4 — 84
Troick, Russia — D8 — 26
Troicko-Pečorsk, Russia — B10 — 22
Trois-Pistoles, P.Q., Can. — A8 — 90
Trois-Rivières, P.Q., Can. — C5 — 90
Trois-Rivières-Ouest, P.Q., Can. — C5 — 90
Troïts'ke, Ukr. — F11 — 20
Trollhättan, Swe. — G5 — 10
Tromsø, Nor. — B8 — 10
Trona, Ca., U.S. — E5 — 98
Tronador, Monte, mtn., S.A. — F2 — 69
Trondheim, Nor. — E4 — 10
Trondheimsfjorden, b., Nor. — E4 — 10
Trophy Mountain, mtn., B.C., Can. — D8 — 85
Trotwood, Oh., U.S. — C1 — 128
Troup, co., Ga., U.S. — C1 — 103
Trousdale, co., Tn., U.S. — A5 — 135
Trout, stm., Fl., U.S. — m8 — 102
Trout, stm., Vt., U.S. — B3 — 138
Trout Creek, On., Can. — B5 — 89
Trout Creek Pass, Co., U.S. — C5 — 99
Trout Lake, Wa., U.S. — D4 — 140
Trout Lake, l., On., Can. — o16 — 89
Trout Lake, l., Mn., U.S. — B6 — 116
Trout Lake, l., Wi., U.S. — B4 — 142
Troutman, N.C., U.S. — B2 — 126
Trout Peak, mtn., Wy., U.S. — B3 — 143
Trout River, Nf., Can. — D2 — 88
Troutville, Va., U.S. — C3 — 139
Troy, Al., U.S. — D4 — 94
Troy, Id., U.S. — C2 — 105
Troy, Il., U.S. — E4 — 106
Troy, Ks., U.S. — C8 — 109
Troy, Mi., U.S. — o15 — 115
Troy, Mo., U.S. — C7 — 118
Troy, Mt., U.S. — B1 — 119
Troy, N.C., U.S. — B3 — 126
Troy, N.H., U.S. — E2 — 122
Troy, N.Y., U.S. — C7 — 125
Troy, Oh., U.S. — B1 — 128
Troy, Pa., U.S. — C8 — 131
Troy, Tn., U.S. — A2 — 135
Troy see Truva, hist., Tur. — C2 — 44
Troyes, Fr. — C8 — 16
Troy Peak, mtn., Nv., U.S. — E6 — 121
Trubč'evsk, Russia — C12 — 20
Truchas Peak, mtn., N.M., U.S. — B4 — 124
Trucial States see United Arab Emirates, ctry., Asia — F6 — 42
Truckee, Ca., U.S. — C3 — 98
Truckee, stm., U.S. — D2 — 121
Trujillo, Hond. — B2 — 80
Trujillo, Peru — E4 — 70
Trujillo, Spain — H4 — 16
Trujillo, Ven. — B5 — 70
Truk Islands see Chuuk Islands, is., Micron. — D9 — 58
Truman, Mn., U.S. — G4 — 116
Trumann, Ar., U.S. — B5 — 97
Trumansburg, N.Y., U.S. — C4 — 125
Trumbull, Ct., U.S. — E3 — 100
Trumbull, co., Oh., U.S. — A5 — 128
Trumbull, Mount, mtn., Az., U.S. — A2 — 96
Trussville, Al., U.S. — B3 — 94
Trustom Pond, l., R.I., U.S. — G3 — 132
Truth or Consequences (Hot Springs), N.M., U.S. — D2 — 124
Truva (Troy), hist., Tur. — C2 — 44
Tryon, N.C., U.S. — f10 — 126
Trzcianka, Pol. — C4 — 20
Tsaidam Basin see Qaidam Pendi, China — D6 — 28
Tsala Apopka Lake, l., Fl., U.S. — D4 — 102
Tsaratanana, Madag. — B8 — 56
Tsaratanana, mts., Madag. — A8 — 56
Tsau, Bots. — C3 — 56
Tsavo, Kenya — D7 — 54
Tschida, Lake, res., N.D., U.S. — C4 — 127
Tselinograd see Akmola, Kaz. — D9 — 26
Tses, Nmb. — D2 — 56
Tsévié, Togo — E5 — 50
Tshabong, Bots. — C3 — 56
Tshane, Bots. — C3 — 56
Tshela, D.R.C. — B2 — 54
Tshikapa, D.R.C. — E4 — 54
Tshofa, D.R.C. — E5 — 54
Tshumbe (Chiumbe), stm., Afr. — E4 — 54
Tsimlyansk Reservoir see Cimljanskoe vodohranilišče, res., Russia — E7 — 22
Tsintsabis, Nmb. — B2 — 56
Tsiombe, Madag. — D8 — 56
Tsiroanomandidy, Madag. — B8 — 56
Tsu, Japan — D3 — 31
Tsugaru-kaikyō, strt., Japan — C16 — 28

Tsumeb, Nmb. — B2 — 56
Tsuruoka, Japan — D15 — 28
Tsushima, is., Japan — D1 — 31
Tsuyama, Japan — C2 — 31
Tswaane, Bots. — C3 — 56
Tual, Indon. — G8 — 36
Tualatin, stm., Or., U.S. — h11 — 130
Tuamotu, Îles, is., Fr. Poly. — F15 — 58
Tuamotu Ridge — J24 — 64
Tuangku, Pulau, i., Indon. — C1 — 36
Tuapse, Russia — E5 — 26
Tuba City, Az., U.S. — A4 — 96
Tuban, Indon. — E4 — 36
Tubarão, Braz. — D8 — 72
Tübingen, Ger. — F11 — 12
Ṭubruq, Libya — D9 — 48
Tubuai, i., Fr. Poly. — G15 — 58
Tucacas, Ven. — A6 — 70
Tucannon, stm., Wa., U.S. — C8 — 140
Tucano, Braz. — D4 — 74
Tuckahoe, N.Y., U.S. — h13 — 125
Tuckahoe, stm., N.J., U.S. — E3 — 123
Tuckanarra, Austl. — F2 — 60
Tucker, Ga., U.S. — h8 — 103
Tucker, co., W.V., U.S. — B5 — 141
Tucker Island, i., N.J., U.S. — E4 — 123
Tuckerman, Ar., U.S. — B4 — 97
Tuckernuck Island, i., Ma., U.S. — D7 — 114
Tuckerton, N.J., U.S. — D4 — 123
Tucson, Az., U.S. — E5 — 96
Tucumcari, N.M., U.S. — B6 — 124
Tucumcari Mountain, mtn., N.M., U.S. — B6 — 124
Tucupita, Ven. — B7 — 70
Tucuruí, Braz. — B2 — 74
Tucuruí, Represa de, res., Braz. — B2 — 74
Tudela, Spain — F6 — 16
Tudmur, Syria — E8 — 44
Tugaloo Lake, res., U.S. — B1 — 133
Tugela, stm., S. Afr. — D5 — 56
Tug Fork, stm., U.S. — C2 — 141
Tuguegarao City, Phil. — C8 — 34
Tugur, Russia — D15 — 26
Tujmazy, Russia — D9 — 22
Tukangbesi, Kepulauan, is., Indon. — E6 — 36
Ṭūkrah, Libya — D8 — 14
Tukums, Lat. — H10 — 10
Tukuyu, Tan. — C6 — 54
Tukwila, Wa., U.S. — f11 — 140
Tula, Mex. — C5 — 78
Tula, Russia — D5 — 26
Tulalip Indian Reservation, Wa., U.S. — A3 — 140
Tulancingo, Mex. — C5 — 78
Tulare, Ca., U.S. — D4 — 98
Tulare, co., Ca., U.S. — D4 — 98
Tulare Lake, l., Ca., U.S. — D4 — 98
Tularosa, N.M., U.S. — D3 — 124
Tularosa Mountains, mts., N.M., U.S. — D1 — 124
Tularosa Valley, val., N.M., U.S. — E3 — 124
Tulbagh, S. Afr. — E2 — 56
Tulcán, Ec. — C4 — 70
Tulcea, Rom. — E10 — 20
Tul'chyn, Ukr. — E10 — 20
Tule Lake, sw., Ca., U.S. — B3 — 98
Tule River Indian Reservation, Ca., U.S. — E4 — 98
Tule Valley, val., Ut., U.S. — D2 — 137
Tuli, Zimb. — C4 — 56
Tulia, Tx., U.S. — B2 — 136
Tullahoma, Tn., U.S. — B5 — 135
Tulle, Fr. — E7 — 16
Tully, Austl. — D4 — 62
Tulsa, Ok., U.S. — A6 — 129
Tulsa, co., Ok., U.S. — B6 — 129
Tuluá, Col. — E4 — 80
Tulun, Russia — D12 — 26
Tulungagung, Indon. — E4 — 36
Tumacacori National Monument, Az., U.S. — F4 — 96
Tumaco, Col. — C4 — 70
Tuman-gang (Tumen), stm., Asia — B1 — 31
Tumanovo, Russia — B13 — 20
Tumbarumba, Austl. — H4 — 62
Tumbes, Peru — D3 — 70
Tumble Mountain, mtn., Mt., U.S. — E7 — 119
Tumbler Ridge, B.C., Can. — B7 — 85
Tumen, China — C13 — 28
Tumen (Tuman-gang), stm., Asia — B1 — 31
Tumeremo, Ven. — B7 — 70
Tumkūr, India — G3 — 40
Tumuc-Humac Mountains, mts., S.A. — C8 — 70
Tumut, Austl. — H4 — 62
Tumwater, Wa., U.S. — B3 — 140
Tunceli, Tur. — C8 — 44
Tunduru, Nig. — E6 — 50
Tunga, Nig. — E6 — 50
Tungabhadra, stm., India — F3 — 40
Tungabhadra Reservoir, res., India — F3 — 40
Tungkang, Tai. — E5 — 30
Tungsha Tao (Pratas Island), i., Tai. — E4 — 30
Tuni, India — F4 — 40

Tunis, Tun. — C7 — 48
Tunis, Golfe de, b., Tun. — F3 — 18
Tunis, Gulf of see Tunis, Golfe de, b., Tun. — F3 — 18
Tunisia, ctry., Afr. — D7 — 48
Tunja, Col. — B5 — 70
Tunkhannock, Pa., U.S. — C10 — 131
Tunk Lake, l., Me., U.S. — D4 — 112
Tunnel Hill, Ga., U.S. — B1 — 103
Tunp Range, mts., Wy., U.S. — D2 — 143
Tununak, Ak., U.S. — C6 — 95
Tunuyán, Arg. — E4 — 72
Tunxi, China — D4 — 30
Tuolumne, Ca., U.S. — D3 — 98
Tuolumne, co., Ca., U.S. — C4 — 98
Tuolumne, stm., Ca., U.S. — D3 — 98
Tupã, Braz. — F1 — 74
Tupaciguara, Braz. — E2 — 74
Tupelo, Ms., U.S. — A5 — 117
Tupiza, Bol. — C4 — 72
Tupper Lake, N.Y., U.S. — A6 — 125
Tupper Lake, l., N.Y., U.S. — A6 — 125
Tura, India — D6 — 40
Tura, Russia — C11 — 26
Tura, stm., Russia — D18 — 6
Turan, Russia — A6 — 28
Turan Lowland, pl., Asia — B7 — 42
Ṭurayf, Sau. Ar. — G8 — 44
Turbat, Pak. — E8 — 42
Turbeville, S.C., U.S. — D7 — 133
Turbo, Col. — B4 — 70
Turda, Rom. — F7 — 20
Turgaj, Kaz. — E8 — 26
Turgaj, stm., Kaz. — E8 — 26
Turgajskaja ložbina, reg., Kaz. — D8 — 26
Turgutlu, Tur. — C2 — 44
Turhal, Tur. — B7 — 44
Turia, stm., Spain — H6 — 16
Turin see Torino, Italy — B1 — 18
Turinsk, Russia — C11 — 22
Turkana, Lake see Rudolf, Lake, l., Afr. — C7 — 54
Turkestan, Kaz. — E8 — 26
Turkey, ctry., Asia — C3 — 38
Turkey, stm., Ia., U.S. — B6 — 108
Turkey Creek, stm., Ok., U.S. — A3 — 129
Turkey Point, c., Md., U.S. — B5 — 113
Turkish Republic of Northern Cyprus see North Cyprus, ctry., Asia — C2 — 44
Turkmenbaši, Turk. — E7 — 26
Turkmenistan, ctry., Asia — C7 — 42
Türkoğlu, Tur. — D7 — 44
Turks and Caicos Islands, dep., N.A. — D10 — 76
Turks Islands, is., T./C. Is. — A5 — 80
Turku (Åbo), Fin. — F10 — 10
Turley, Ok., U.S. — A6 — 129
Turlock, Ca., U.S. — D3 — 98
Turnbull, Mount, mtn., Az., U.S. — D5 — 96
Turneffe Islands, is., Belize — B2 — 80
Turner, Or., U.S. — C4 — 130
Turner, co., Ga., U.S. — E3 — 103
Turner, co., S.D., U.S. — D8 — 134
Turners Falls, Ma., U.S. — A2 — 114
Turner Valley, Ab., Can. — D3 — 84
Turnor Lake, l., Sk., Can. — m7 — 91
Turpan, China — C5 — 28
Turpan Pendi, depr., China — C5 — 28
Turquino, Pico, mtn., Cuba — B4 — 80
Turrell, Ar., U.S. — B5 — 97
Turret Peak, mtn., Az., U.S. — C4 — 96
Turnu Măgurele, Rom. — H8 — 20
Turpan, China — C5 — 28
Turtle Creek, Pa., U.S. — k14 — 131
Turtle Flambeau Flowage, res., Wi., U.S. — B3 — 142
Turtle Lake, N.D., U.S. — B5 — 127
Turtle Lake, Wi., U.S. — C1 — 142
Turtle Lake, l., Sk., Can. — D1 — 91
Turtle Mountain Indian Reservation, N.D., U.S. — A6 — 127
Turuhansk, Russia — C10 — 26
Tuscaloosa, Al., U.S. — B2 — 94
Tuscaloosa, co., Al., U.S. — B2 — 94
Tuscarawas, co., Oh., U.S. — B4 — 128
Tuscarawas, stm., Oh., U.S. — B4 — 128
Tuscarora Indian Reservation, N.Y., U.S. — B2 — 125
Tuscarora Mountain, mtn., Pa., U.S. — F6 — 131
Tuscarora Mountains, mts., Nv., U.S. — B5 — 121
Tuscola, Il., U.S. — D5 — 106
Tuscola, co., Mi., U.S. — E7 — 115
Tuscumbia, Al., U.S. — A2 — 94
Tuskegee, Al., U.S. — C4 — 94
Tusket, stm., N.S., Can. — E4 — 87
Tustumena Lake, l., Ak., U.S. — g16 — 95
Tutak, Tur. — C10 — 44
Tuticorin, India — H3 — 40
Tutrakan, Bul. — B11 — 18
Tuttle, Ok., U.S. — B4 — 129
Tuttle Creek Lake, res., Ks., U.S. — C7 — 109
Tuttlingen, Ger. — F11 — 12
Tutuila, i., Am. Sam. — F12 — 58
Tutupaca, Volcán, vol., Peru — G5 — 70
Tututalak Mountain, mtn., Ak., U.S. — B7 — 95
Tutwiler, Ms., U.S. — A3 — 117

Tuva, state, Russia — D11 — 26
Tuvalu, ctry., Oc. — E11 — 58
Ṭuwayq, Jabal, mts., Sau. Ar. — F5 — 38
Tuxedo, N.C., U.S. — f10 — 126
Tuxedo Park, De., U.S. — i7 — 101
Tuxpan, Mex. — C3 — 78
Tuxpan de Rodríguez Cano, Mex. — C5 — 78
Tuxtepec, Mex. — D5 — 78
Tuxtla Gutiérrez, Mex. — D6 — 78
Tuyen Quang, Viet. — B5 — 34
Tuy Hoa, Viet. — D5 — 34
Tūysarkān, Iran — E13 — 44
Tuz, Iraq — E11 — 44
Tuz Gölü, l., Tur. — C4 — 44
Tuzigoot National Monument, Az., U.S. — C4 — 96
Tuzla, Bos. — B7 — 18
Tver', Russia — D5 — 26
Tweed, On., Can. — C7 — 89
Tweedsmuir Provincial Park, B.C., Can. — C4 — 85
Tweedy Mountain, mtn., Mt., U.S. — E4 — 119
Twelvepole Creek, stm., W.V., U.S. — C2 — 141
Twentymile Creek, stm., W.V., U.S. — C3 — 141
Twentynine Palms, Ca., U.S. — E5 — 98
Twentynine Palms Marine Corps Base, mil., Ca., U.S. — E5 — 98
Twiggs, co., Ga., U.S. — D3 — 103
Twillingate, Nf., Can. — D4 — 88
Twin Buttes, mtn., Or., U.S. — C4 — 130
Twin Buttes Reservoir, res., Tx., U.S. — D2 — 136
Twin City, Ga., U.S. — D4 — 103
Twin Creek, stm., Oh., U.S. — C1 — 128
Twin Falls, Id., U.S. — G4 — 105
Twin Falls, co., Id., U.S. — G4 — 105
Twin Knolls, Az., U.S. — m9 — 96
Twin Lakes, Ga., U.S. — F3 — 103
Twin Lakes, Wi., U.S. — F5 — 142
Twin Lakes, l., Ct., U.S. — A2 — 100
Twin Lakes, l., Ia., U.S. — B3 — 108
Twin Lakes, l., Me., U.S. — C4 — 112
Twin Mountains, mtn., Wy., U.S. — E7 — 143
Twin Peaks, mts., Id., U.S. — E4 — 105
Twin Rivers, N.J., U.S. — C4 — 123
Twinsburg, Oh., U.S. — A4 — 128
Twin Valley, Mn., U.S. — C2 — 116
Twisp, Wa., U.S. — A5 — 140
Two Harbors, Mn., U.S. — C7 — 116
Two Hills, Ab., Can. — C5 — 84
Two Mile Beach, N.J., U.S. — F3 — 123
Two Rivers, Wi., U.S. — D6 — 142
Two Rivers, North Branch, stm., Mn., U.S. — B2 — 116
Two Rivers, South Branch, stm., Mn., U.S. — B2 — 116
Tybee Island, Ga., U.S. — D6 — 103
Tygart Lake, res., W.V., U.S. — B5 — 141
Tygart River, Falls of the, wtfl, W.V., U.S. — k10 — 141
Tygart Valley, stm., W.V., U.S. — B4 — 141
Tyger, stm., S.C., U.S. — B4 — 133
Tyler, Mn., U.S. — F2 — 116
Tyler, Tx., U.S. — C5 — 136
Tyler, co., Tx., U.S. — D5 — 136
Tyler, co., W.V., U.S. — B4 — 141
Tyler, Lake, res., Tx., U.S. — C5 — 136
Tyler Branch, stm., Vt., U.S. — B3 — 138
Tyler Heights, W.V., U.S. — C3 — 141
Tylertown, Ms., U.S. — D3 — 117
Tymochtee Creek, stm., Oh., U.S. — B2 — 128
Tynda, Russia — D14 — 26
Tyndall, S.D., U.S. — E8 — 134
Tyndall Air Force Base, mil., Fl., U.S. — u16 — 102
Tyne, stm., Eng., U.K. — C5 — 12
Tyonek, Ak., U.S. — C9 — 95
Tyre see Ṣūr, Leb. — F6 — 44
Tyrifjorden, l., Nor. — F3 — 10
Tyrma, Russia — A14 — 28
Tyrone, N.M., U.S. — E1 — 124
Tyrone, Ok., U.S. — e9 — 129
Tyrone, Pa., U.S. — E5 — 131
Tyronza, Ar., U.S. — B5 — 97
Tyrrell, co., N.C., U.S. — B6 — 126
Tyrrhenian Sea, Eur. — D3 — 18
Tysa (Tisa) (Tisza), stm., Eur. — E7 — 20
Tysnesøya, i., Nor. — G1 — 10
Tzaneen, S. Afr. — C5 — 56

U

Uaupés (Vaupés), stm., S.A. — C6 — 70
Ubá, Braz. — F3 — 74
Ubangi (Oubangui), stm., Afr. — D3 — 54
Ubatã, Braz. — D4 — 74
Ube, Japan — E14 — 28
Úbeda, Spain — I5 — 16
Uberaba, Braz. — E2 — 74
Uberlândia, Braz. — E2 — 74
Ubly, Mi., U.S. — E8 — 115
Ubon Ratchathani, Thai. — C4 — 34
Ubrique, Spain — I4 — 16
Ubundu, D.R.C. — D5 — 54
Učaly, Russia — D10 — 22

Name	Map Ref.	Page

Učami, Russia — C11 — 26
Ucar, Azer. — B12 — 44
Ucayali, stm., Peru — E5 — 70
Uchiura-wan, b., Japan — C16 — 28
Uchiza, Peru — E4 — 70
Učkuduk, Uzb. — B8 — 42
Ucluelet, B.C., Can. — E5 — 85
Ucon, Id., U.S. — F7 — 105
Udagamandalam, India — G3 — 40
Udaipur, India — E2 — 40
Udall, Ks., U.S. — E6 — 109
Uddevalla, Swe. — G4 — 10
Uddjaure, l., Swe. — D7 — 10
Udgīr, India — F3 — 40
Udine, Italy — A4 — 18
Udmurtia see Udmurtija, state, Russia — D7 — 26
Udmurtija, state, Russia — D7 — 26
Udon Thani, Thai. — C4 — 34
Udupi, India — G2 — 40
Ueda, Japan — C3 — 31
Uedinenija, ostrov, i., Russia — B10 — 26
Uele, stm., D.R.C. — C4 — 54
Uel'kal', Russia — C19 — 26
Uelzen, Ger. — D12 — 12
Ufa, Russia — D7 — 26
Uganda, ctry., Afr. — C6 — 54
Ugarit, hist., Syria — E6 — 44
Ugashik Lakes, l., Ak., U.S. — D8 — 95
Uglegorsk, Russia — E16 — 26
Uglič, Russia — C6 — 22
Uherské Hradiště, Czech Rep. — E4 — 20
Uhrichsville, Oh., U.S. — B4 — 128
Uhta, Russia — C7 — 26
Uíge, Ang. — E3 — 54
Uil, Kaz. — E9 — 22
Uinta, co., Wy., U.S. — E2 — 143
Uinta, stm., Ut., U.S. — C5 — 137
Uintah, co., Ut., U.S. — D6 — 137
Uintah and Ouray Indian Reservation, Ut., U.S. — C5 — 137
Uinta Mountains, mts., Ut., U.S. — C5 — 137
Uitenhage, S. Afr. — E4 — 56
Uivak, Cape, c., Nf., Can. — f9 — 88
Ujar, Russia — D11 — 26
Ujelang, atoll, Marsh. Is. — D10 — 58
Ujiji, Tan. — D5 — 54
Ujjain, India — E3 — 40
Ujungpandang, Indon. — E5 — 36
Uka, Russia — D18 — 26
Ukara Island, i., Tan. — D6 — 54
Ukerewe Island, i., Tan. — D6 — 54
Ukiah, Ca., U.S. — C2 — 98
Ukyr, Russia — B9 — 28
Ulaanbaatar (Ulan Bator), Mong. — B9 — 28
Ulaangom, Mong. — B6 — 28
Ulaan-Uul, Mong. — C10 — 28
Ulak Island, i., Ak., U.S. — E4 — 95
Ulan Bator see Ulaanbaatar, Mong. — B9 — 28
Ulan-Ude, Russia — D12 — 26
Ulan Ul Hu, l., China — C6 — 40
Ulchin, S. Kor. — C1 — 31
Ulcinj, Yugo. — D7 — 18
Ulhāsnagar, India — F2 — 40
Uliastay, Mong. — B7 — 28
Ulja, Russia — D16 — 26
Uljanovsk, Russia — D6 — 26
Ullŭng-do, i., S. Kor. — C2 — 31
Ulm, Ger. — F11 — 12
Ulónguè, Moz. — A5 — 56
Ulsan, S. Kor. — C1 — 31
Ulster, co., N.Y., U.S. — D6 — 125
Ulster, hist. reg., Eur. — C3 — 12
Ulu, Indon. — C7 — 36
Ulu, Russia — C14 — 26
Ulúa, stm., Hond. — B2 — 80
Ulubat Gölü, l., Tur. — B3 — 44
Ulundi, S. Afr. — D5 — 56
Ulungur Hu, l., China — B5 — 28
Uluru (Ayers Rock), mtn., Austl. — F5 — 60
Ulverstone, Austl. — I4 — 62
Ulysses, Ks., U.S. — E2 — 109
Umán, Mex. — C7 — 78
Uman', Ukr. — E11 — 20
Umanak, Grnld. — D29 — 82
Umarkot, Pak. — E9 — 42
Umatilla, Fl., U.S. — D5 — 102
Umatilla, Or., U.S. — B7 — 130
Umatilla, co., Or., U.S. — B8 — 130
Umatilla, stm., Or., U.S. — B7 — 130
Umatilla Indian Reservation, Or., U.S. — B8 — 130
Umba, Russia — A5 — 22
Umbagog Lake, l., U.S. — A4 — 122
Umboi Island, i., Pap. N. Gui. — H12 — 32
Umcolcus Lake, l., Me., U.S. — B4 — 112
Umeå, Swe. — E9 — 10
Umeälven, stm., Swe. — D9 — 10
Umm al-'Abīd, Libya — A8 — 50
Umm Durmān, Sudan — G11 — 48
Umm Lajj, Sau. Ar. — E3 — 42
Umnak Island, i., Ak., U.S. — E6 — 95
Umpqua, stm., Or., U.S. — D3 — 130
Umsaskis Lake, l., Me., U.S. — B3 — 112
Umtata, S. Afr. — E4 — 56
Umuarama, Braz. — H9 — 70
Umzinto, S. Afr. — E5 — 56
Unadilla, Ga., U.S. — D3 — 103
Unadilla, stm., N.Y., U.S. — C5 — 125

Unaí, Braz. — E2 — 74
Unalakleet, Ak., U.S. — C7 — 95
Unalaska Island, i., Ak., U.S. — E6 — 95
'Unayzah, Sau. Ar. — E4 — 38
'Unayzah, Jabal, mtn., Asia — F8 — 44
Uncasville, Ct., U.S. — D7 — 100
Uncompahgre, stm., Co., U.S. — C3 — 99
Uncompahgre Mountains, mts., Co., U.S. — C3 — 99
Uncompahgre Peak, mtn., Co., U.S. — C3 — 99
Underwood, Al., U.S. — B3 — 94
Underwood, N.D., U.S. — B4 — 127
Uneča, Russia — C12 — 20
Ungava, Péninsule d', pen., P.Q., Can. — g12 — 90
Ungava Bay, b., Can. — G26 — 82
Ungava Peninsula see Ungava, Péninsule d', pen., P.Q., Can. — F25 — 82
União, Braz. — B3 — 74
Uniãoda Vitória, Braz. — D7 — 72
União dos Palmares, Braz. — C4 — 74
Unicoi, Tn., U.S. — C11 — 135
Unicoi, co., Tn., U.S. — C11 — 135
Unicoi Mountains, mts., U.S. — D9 — 135
Unimak Island, i., Ak., U.S. — D7 — 95
Unimak Pass, strt., Ak., U.S. — E6 — 95
Unión, Arg. — F4 — 72
Union, Ky., U.S. — k13 — 110
Union, Mo., U.S. — C6 — 118
Union, Ms., U.S. — C4 — 117
Union, Or., U.S. — B9 — 130
Union, S.C., U.S. — B4 — 133
Union, Wa., U.S. — B2 — 140
Union, co., Ar., U.S. — D3 — 97
Union, co., Fl., U.S. — B4 — 102
Union, co., Ga., U.S. — B2 — 103
Union, co., Ia., U.S. — C3 — 108
Union, co., Il., U.S. — F4 — 106
Union, co., In., U.S. — E8 — 107
Union, co., Ky., U.S. — C2 — 110
Union, co., La., U.S. — B3 — 111
Union, co., Ms., U.S. — A4 — 117
Union, co., N.C., U.S. — B2 — 126
Union, co., N.J., U.S. — B4 — 123
Union, co., N.M., U.S. — A6 — 124
Union, co., Oh., U.S. — B2 — 128
Union, co., Or., U.S. — B8 — 130
Union, co., Pa., U.S. — E7 — 131
Union, co., S.C., U.S. — B4 — 133
Union, co., S.D., U.S. — E9 — 134
Union, co., Tn., U.S. — C10 — 135
Union, West Branch, stm., Me., U.S. — D4 — 112
Union Beach, N.J., U.S. — C4 — 123
Union Bridge, Md., U.S. — A3 — 113
Union City, Ca., U.S. — h8 — 98
Union City, Ga., U.S. — C2 — 103
Union City, In., U.S. — D8 — 107
Union City, Mi., U.S. — F5 — 115
Union City, N.J., U.S. — h8 — 123
Union City, Oh., U.S. — B1 — 128
Union City, Ok., U.S. — B4 — 129
Union City, Pa., U.S. — C2 — 131
Union City, Tn., U.S. — A2 — 135
Union Flat Creek, stm., Wa., U.S. — C8 — 140
Union Gap, Wa., U.S. — C5 — 140
Union Grove, Wi., U.S. — F5 — 142
Union Lake, l., N.J., U.S. — E2 — 123
Union Pier, Mi., U.S. — G4 — 115
Union Point, Ga., U.S. — C3 — 103
Union Springs, Al., U.S. — C4 — 94
Uniontown, Al., U.S. — C2 — 94
Uniontown, Ky., U.S. — C2 — 110
Uniontown, Oh., U.S. — B4 — 128
Uniontown, Pa., U.S. — G2 — 131
Union Village, R.I., U.S. — B3 — 132
Union Village Reservoir, res., Vt., U.S. — D4 — 138
Unionville, Ct., U.S. — B4 — 100
Unionville, Mo., U.S. — A4 — 118
United Arab Emirates, ctry., Asia — F6 — 42
United Arab Republic see Egypt, ctry., Afr. — E10 — 48
United Kingdom, ctry., Eur. — C6 — 12
United Nations Headquarters, N.Y., U.S. — h12 — 125
United States, ctry., N.A. — D6 — 92
United States Air Force Academy, mil., Co., U.S. — B6 — 99
United States Military Academy, mil., N.Y., U.S. — C6 — 125
United States Naval Academy, mil., Md., U.S. — C4 — 113
Unity Reservoir, res., Or., U.S. — C8 — 130
University City, Mo., U.S. — C7 — 118
University Heights, Ia., U.S. — C6 — 108
University Heights, Oh., U.S. — h9 — 128
University Park, Ia., U.S. — C5 — 108
University Park, N.M., U.S. — E3 — 124
University Park, Tx., U.S. — n10 — 136
University Place, Wa., U.S. — f10 — 140
Unnão, India — D4 — 40
Unuli Horog, China — B6 — 40

Ünye, Tur. — B7 — 44
Unža, stm., Russia — C7 — 22
Upata, Ven. — B7 — 70
Upernavik, Grnld. — D28 — 82
Upington, S. Afr. — D3 — 56
Upland, Ca., U.S. — E5 — 98
Upland, In., U.S. — D7 — 107
Upolu, i., Samoa — F12 — 58
Upolu Point, c., Hi., U.S. — C6 — 104
Upper Ammonoosuc, stm., N.H., U.S. — A4 — 122
Upper Arlington, Oh., U.S. — B2 — 128
Upper Arrow Lake, res., B.C., Can. — D9 — 85
Upperco, Md., U.S. — A4 — 113
Upper Darby, Pa., U.S. — G11 — 131
Upper Greenwood Lake, N.J., U.S. — A4 — 123
Upper Humber, stm., Nf., Can. — D3 — 88
Upper Hutt, N.Z. — p14 — 63c
Upper Iowa, stm., Ia., U.S. — A5 — 108
Upper Island Cove, Nf., Can. — E5 — 88
Upper Klamath Lake, l., Or., U.S. — E4 — 130
Upper Marlboro, Md., U.S. — C4 — 113
Upper New York Bay, b., U.S. — k8 — 123
Upper Red Lake, l., Mn., U.S. — B4 — 116
Upper Saddle River, N.J., U.S. — A4 — 123
Upper Sandusky, Oh., U.S. — B2 — 128
Upper Sheila [Haut Sheila], N.B., Can. — B5 — 87
Upper Volta see Burkina Faso, ctry., Afr. — D4 — 50
Uppland, hist. reg., Swe. — F7 — 10
Uppsala, Swe. — G7 — 10
Upright, Cape, c., Ak., U.S. — C5 — 95
Upshur, co., Tx., U.S. — C5 — 136
Upshur, co., W.V., U.S. — C4 — 141
Upson, co., Ga., U.S. — D2 — 103
Upton, P.Q., Can. — D5 — 90
Upton, Ky., U.S. — C4 — 110
Upton, Ma., U.S. — B4 — 114
Upton, Wy., U.S. — B8 — 143
Upton, co., Tx., U.S. — D2 — 136
Uraj, Russia — B12 — 22
Urakawa, Japan — A4 — 31
Ural, stm. — E9 — 22
Ural Mountains see Ural'skie gory, mts., Russia — D7 — 26
Ural'sk, Kaz. — D7 — 26
Ural'skie gory (Ural Mountains), mts., Russia — D7 — 26
Urania, La., U.S. — C3 — 111
Ura-Tjube, Taj. — C9 — 42
Urbana, Il., U.S. — C5 — 106
Urbana, Oh., U.S. — B2 — 128
Urbancrest, Oh., U.S. — m10 — 128
Urbandale, Ia., U.S. — C4 — 108
Urbino, Italy — C4 — 18
Ures, Mex. — B2 — 78
Urfa see Şanlıurfa, Tur. — D8 — 44
Urgenč, Uzb. — E8 — 26
Ürgüp, Tur. — C6 — 44
Uribia, Col. — A5 — 70
Urjung-Haja, Russia — B13 — 26
Urjupinsk, Russia — D7 — 22
Urla, Tur. — C2 — 44
Urmia see Orūmīyeh, Iran — C5 — 42
Urmia, Lake see Orūmīyeh, Daryācheh-ye, l., Iran — C5 — 42
Uromi, Nig. — E6 — 50
Uroševac, Yugo. — C8 — 18
Urrao, Col. — D4 — 80
Uruapan del Progreso, Mex. — D4 — 78
Uruguai (Uruguay), stm., S.A. — E6 — 72
Uruguaiana, Braz. — D6 — 72
Uruguay, ctry., S.A. — E6 — 72
Uruguay (Uruguai), stm., S.A. — D6 — 72
Ürümqi, China — C5 — 28
Urundi see Burundi, ctry., Afr. — D5 — 54
Urup, ostrov, i., Russia — I17 — 26
Urziceni, Rom. — G9 — 20
Uržum, Russia — C8 — 22
Usa, Japan — D2 — 31
Uşak, Tur. — C3 — 44
Usakos, Nmb. — C2 — 56
Usborne, Mount, mtn., Falk. Is. — H5 — 69
Usedom, i., Eur. — B3 — 20
Ushuaia, Arg. — H3 — 69
Usinsk, Russia — C7 — 26
Usman', Russia — C15 — 20
Usoke, Tan. — E6 — 54
Usole-Sibirskoe, Russia — D12 — 26
Usquepaug, R.I., U.S. — F3 — 132
Ussuri (Wusuli), stm., Asia — E15 — 26
Ussurijsk, Russia — E15 — 26
Ust'-Barguzin, Russia — C19 — 26
Ust'-Belaja, Russia — C19 — 26
Ust'-Čaun, Russia — C4 — 22
Ust'-Cil'ma, Russia — A9 — 22
Ust'-Ilimsk, Russia — D12 — 26
Ústí nad Labem, Czech Rep. — D3 — 20
Ustinov see Iževsk, Russia — D7 — 26
Ustka, Pol. — B4 — 20

Ust'-Kamčatsk, Russia — D18 — 26
Ust'-Kamenogorsk, Kaz. — E10 — 26
Ust'-Koksa, Russia — A5 — 28
Ust'-Kujda, Russia — C15 — 26
Ust'-Kut, Russia — D12 — 26
Ust'-Lyža, Russia — A10 — 22
Ust'-Maja, Russia — C15 — 26
Ust'-Man'ja, Russia — B11 — 22
Ust'-Nera, Russia — C16 — 26
Ust'-Njukža, Russia — D14 — 26
Uštobe, Kaz. — B3 — 28
Ust'-Tym, Russia — D10 — 26
Ust-Urt Plateau, plat., Asia — B7 — 42
Usu, China — C4 — 28
Usulután, El Sal. — C2 — 80
Usumacinta, stm., N.A. — D6 — 78
Ušumun, Russia — A13 — 28
Utah, co., Ut., U.S. — C4 — 137
Utah, state, U.S. — D4 — 137
Utah Lake, l., Ut., U.S. — C4 — 137
Ute Creek, stm., N.M., U.S. — A6 — 124
Ute Mountain Indian Reservation, U.S. — D2 — 99
Utena, Lith. — I11 — 10
Ute Reservoir, res., N.M., U.S. — B6 — 124
Utete, Tan. — E7 — 54
Uthai Thani, Thai. — C4 — 34
Utiariti, Braz. — F8 — 70
Utica, Il., U.S. — B5 — 106
Utica, Mi., U.S. — F7 — 115
Utica, Ms., U.S. — C3 — 117
Utica, Ne., U.S. — D8 — 120
Utica, N.Y., U.S. — B5 — 125
Utica, Oh., U.S. — B3 — 128
Utiel, Spain — H6 — 16
Utikuma Lake, l., Ab., Can. — B3 — 84
Utila, Isla de, i., Hond. — B2 — 80
Utopia, Austl. — E5 — 60
Utrecht, Neth. — D9 — 12
Utrecht, S. Afr. — D5 — 56
Utrera, Spain — I4 — 16
Utsunomiya, Japan — D16 — 28
Uttaradit, Thai. — C4 — 34
Uttar Pradesh, prov., India — D3 — 40
Uusikaupunki, Fin. — F9 — 10
Uvalde, Tx., U.S. — E3 — 136
Uvalde, co., Tx., U.S. — E3 — 136
Uvarovo, Russia — D7 — 22
Uvinza, Tan. — E6 — 54
Uvira, D.R.C. — D5 — 54
Uvs Lake, l., Asia — A6 — 28
Uwajima, Japan — E14 — 28
Uwayl, Sudan — B5 — 54
Uwharrie, stm., N.C., U.S. — B3 — 126
Uxbridge, Ma., U.S. — B4 — 114
Uyo, Nig. — E6 — 50
Uyuni, Bol. — C4 — 72
Uyuni, Salar de, pl., Bol. — C4 — 72
Uzbekistan, ctry., Asia — C8 — 42
Uzhhorod, Ukr. — E7 — 20
Uzlovaja, Russia — C15 — 20
Uzunköprü, Tur. — B2 — 44
Užur, Russia — D11 — 26

V

Vaal, stm., S. Afr. — D4 — 56
Vaaldam, res., S. Afr. — D4 — 56
Vaasa, Fin. — E9 — 10
Vác, Hung. — F5 — 20
Vaca Key, i., Fl., U.S. — H5 — 102
Vacaria, Braz. — D7 — 72
Vacaville, Ca., U.S. — C3 — 98
Vache, Île à, i., Haiti — E11 — 80
Vacherie, La., U.S. — h10 — 111
Vadodara, India — I2 — 40
Vadsø, Nor. — A13 — 10
Vaduz, Liech. — G11 — 12
Vaga, stm., Russia — B7 — 22
Vah, stm., Russia — C9 — 26
Váh, stm., Slvk. — E4 — 20
Vaiden, Ms., U.S. — B4 — 117
Vail, Co., U.S. — B4 — 99
Vajgač, ostrov, i., Russia — B7 — 26
Vākhān, hist. reg., Afg. — C10 — 42
Val-Bélair, P.Q., Can. — n17 — 90
Valcourt, P.Q., Can. — D5 — 90
Valdai Hills see Valdajskaja vozvyšennost', hills, Russia — C5 — 22
Valdaj, Russia — C5 — 22
Valdajskaja vozvyšennost', hills, Russia — C5 — 22
Valday see Valdaj, Russia — C5 — 22
Valdepeñas, Spain — H5 — 16
Valders, Wi., U.S. — D6 — 142
Valdés, Península, pen., Arg. — F4 — 69
Valdese, N.C., U.S. — B1 — 126
Valdez, Ak., U.S. — C10 — 95
Valdivia, Chile — E2 — 69
Val-d'Or, P.Q., Can. — k11 — 90
Valdosta, Ga., U.S. — F3 — 103
Vale, Or., U.S. — D9 — 130
Valemount, B.C., Can. — C8 — 85
Valença, Braz. — D4 — 74
Valença do Piauí, Braz. — E4 — 74
Valence, Fr. — E9 — 16
València, Spain — H6 — 16
Valencia, Ven. — B6 — 70
Valencia, co., N.M., U.S. — C3 — 124
València, Golf de, b., Spain — H7 — 16

Valencia de Alcántara, Spain — H3 — 16
Valencia Heights, S.C., U.S. — D6 — 133
Valenciennes, Fr. — B8 — 16
Valentine, Ne., U.S. — B5 — 120
Valera, Ven. — B5 — 70
Valga, Est. — H12 — 10
Valhalla, N.Y., U.S. — D7 — 125
Valhermoso Springs, Al., U.S. — A3 — 94
Valjevo, Yugo. — B7 — 18
Valkeakoski, Fin. — F11 — 10
Valladolid, Mex. — C7 — 78
Valladolid, Spain — G4 — 16
Vallecito Reservoir, res., Co., U.S. — D3 — 99
Valle de la Pascua, Ven. — B6 — 70
Valledupar, Col. — A5 — 70
Vallée-Jonction, P.Q., Can. — C7 — 90
Vallegrande, Bol. — B5 — 72
Valle Hermoso, Mex. — B5 — 78
Vallejo, Ca., U.S. — C2 — 98
Vallenar, Chile — C2 — 69
Valletta, Malta — G5 — 18
Valley, Ne., U.S. — C9 — 120
Valley, co., Id., U.S. — E3 — 105
Valley, co., Mt., U.S. — B10 — 119
Valley, co., Ne., U.S. — C6 — 120
Valley, stm., Mb., Can. — D1 — 86
Valley Center, Ks., U.S. — E6 — 109
Valley City, N.D., U.S. — C8 — 127
Valley Cottage, N.Y., U.S. — g13 — 125
Valley East, On., Can. — p19 — 89
Valley Falls, Ks., U.S. — C8 — 109
Valley Falls, R.I., U.S. — B4 — 132
Valley Forge, Pa., U.S. — o20 — 131
Valley Mills, Tx., U.S. — D4 — 136
Valley Park, Mo., U.S. — f12 — 118
Valley Springs, S.D., U.S. — D9 — 134
Valley Station, Ky., U.S. — g11 — 110
Valley Stream, N.Y., U.S. — n15 — 125
Valleyview, Ab., Can. — B2 — 84
Valley View, Pa., U.S. — E8 — 131
Valliant, Ok., U.S. — D6 — 129
Valls, Spain — G7 — 16
Vallscreek, W.V., U.S. — D3 — 141
Valmeyer, Il., U.S. — E3 — 106
Valmiera, Lat. — H11 — 10
Valona see Vlorë, Alb. — D7 — 18
Vālpārai, India — G3 — 40
Valparaíso, Chile — D2 — 69
Valparaiso, Fl., U.S. — u15 — 102
Valparaiso, In., U.S. — B3 — 107
Vals, Tanjung, c., Indon. — H10 — 32
Valsbaai, b., S. Afr. — E2 — 56
Valtimo, Fin. — E13 — 10
Valujki, Russia — D15 — 22
Val Verde, Ut., U.S. — C4 — 137
Val Verde, co., Tx., U.S. — E2 — 136
Valverde del Camino, Spain — I3 — 16
Van, Tur. — C10 — 44
Van, Tx., U.S. — C5 — 136
Van, W.V., U.S. — n12 — 141
Vanadzor, Arm. — B11 — 44
Van Alstyne, Tx., U.S. — C4 — 136
Vanavara, Russia — C12 — 26
Van Buren, Ar., U.S. — B1 — 97
Van Buren, In., U.S. — C6 — 107
Van Buren, Me., U.S. — A5 — 112
Van Buren, Mo., U.S. — E6 — 118
Van Buren, co., Ar., U.S. — B3 — 97
Van Buren, co., Ia., U.S. — D6 — 108
Van Buren, co., Mi., U.S. — F4 — 115
Van Buren, co., Tn., U.S. — D8 — 135
Vanč, Taj. — C10 — 42
Vance, co., N.C., U.S. — A4 — 126
Vance Air Force Base, mil., Ok., U.S. — A3 — 129
Vanceboro, N.C., U.S. — B5 — 126
Vanceburg, Ky., U.S. — B6 — 110
Vancleave, Ms., U.S. — E5 — 117
Vancouver, B.C., Can. — E6 — 85
Vancouver, Wa., U.S. — D3 — 140
Vancouver Island, i., B.C., Can. — E4 — 85
Vancouver Island Ranges, mts., B.C., Can. — D4 — 85
Vandalia, Il., U.S. — E4 — 106
Vandalia, Mo., U.S. — B6 — 118
Vandenberg Air Force Base, mil., Ca., U.S. — E3 — 98
Vander, N.C., U.S. — B4 — 126
Vanderbilt Peak, mtn., N.M., U.S. — E1 — 124
Vanderburgh, co., In., U.S. — H2 — 107
Vandergrift, Pa., U.S. — E2 — 131
Vanderhoof, B.C., Can. — C5 — 85
Vanderlin Island, i., Austl. — D2 — 62
Van Diemen Gulf, b., Austl. — C5 — 60
Vänern, l., Swe. — G5 — 10
Vänersborg, Swe. — G5 — 10
Vangaindrano, Madag. — C8 — 56
Van Gölü, l., Tur. — C10 — 44
Van Horn, Tx., U.S. — o12 — 136
Van Horne, Ia., U.S. — B5 — 108
Vanier, On., Can. — h12 — 89
Vanimo, Pap. N. Gui. — G11 — 32
Vanino, Russia — B16 — 28
Vankarem, Russia — C20 — 26
Vankleek Hill, On., Can. — B10 — 89
Van Kull, Kill, stm., N.J., U.S. — k8 — 123
Van Lear, Ky., U.S. — C7 — 110
Van Meter, Ia., U.S. — C4 — 108
Vännäs, Swe. — E8 — 10
Vannes, Fr. — D5 — 16

Name	Map Ref.	Page
Van Rees, Pegunungan, mts., Indon.	G10	32
Vanrhynsdorp, S. Afr.	E2	56
Vansant, Va., U.S.	e9	139
Vanua Lava, i., Vanuatu	j9	62a
Vanua Levu, i., Fiji	F11	58
Vanuatu, ctry., Oc.	F10	58
Van Vleck, Tx., U.S.	r14	136
Van Wert, Oh., U.S.	B1	128
Van Wert, co., Oh., U.S.	B1	128
Vanwyksvlei, S. Afr.	E3	56
Van Zandt, co., Tx., U.S.	C5	136
Vārānasi (Benares), India	D4	40
Varangerfjorden, b., Nor.	A13	10
Varaždin, Cro.	A6	18
Varberg, Swe.	H5	10
Vardaman, Ms., U.S.	B4	117
Vardar (Axiós), stm., Eur.	D9	18
Varde, Den.	I3	10
Vardø, Nor.	A14	10
Varennes, P.Q., Can.	D4	90
Varese, Italy	B2	18
Varginha, Braz.	F2	74
Varina, Va., U.S.	C5	139
Varkaus, Fin.	E12	10
Värmland, hist. reg., Swe.	G5	10
Varna, Bul.	C11	18
Varna, Russia	D11	22
Värnamo, Swe.	H6	10
Varnville, S.C., U.S.	F5	133
Varto, Tur.	C9	44
Várzea Grande, Braz.	B6	72
Vashon, Point, c., Wa., U.S.	e11	140
Vashon Island, i., Wa., U.S.	f11	140
Vaslui, Rom.	F9	20
Vass, N.C., U.S.	B3	126
Vassar, Mi., U.S.	E7	115
Vastenjaure, l., Swe.	C7	10
Västerås, Swe.	G7	10
Västerbotten, hist. reg., Swe.	D8	10
Västerdalälven, stm., Swe.	F5	10
Västervik, Swe.	H7	10
Vasto, Italy	C5	18
Vasylivka, Ukr.	F13	20
Vasyl'kiv, Ukr.	D11	20
Vatican City, ctry., Eur.	D4	18
Vatnajökull, Ice.	I20	10a
Vatomandry, Madag.	B8	56
Vatra Dornei, Rom.	F8	20
Vättern, l., Swe.	G6	10
Vaudreuil, P.Q., Can.	D3	90
Vaughan, On., Can.	D5	89
Vaughn, Mt., U.S.	C5	119
Vaughn, N.M., U.S.	C4	124
Vaukavysk, Bela.	C8	20
Vaupés (Uaupés), stm., S.A.	C5	70
Vauxhall, Ab., Can.	D4	84
Vava'u, i., Tonga	F12	58
Vavoua, C. Iv.	E3	50
Vavuniya, Sri L.	H4	40
Växjö, Swe.	H6	10
Vaygach Island see Vajgač, ostrov, i., Russia	B7	26
Važgort, Russia	B8	22
Veazie, Me., U.S.	D4	112
Veedersburg, In., U.S.	D3	107
Veendam, Neth.	D10	12
Vega, i., Nor.	D4	10
Vegreville, Ab., Can.	C4	84
Veinticinco de Mayo, Arg.	F5	72
Vejle, Den.	I3	10
Vélez-Málaga, Spain	I4	16
Velika Morava, stm., Yugo.	B8	18
Velikie Luki, Russia	D5	26
Velikij Ustjug, Russia	C6	26
Vélingara, Sen.	D2	50
Velletri, Italy	D4	18
Vellore, India	G3	40
Velma, Ok., U.S.	C4	129
Vel'sk, Russia	C6	26
Velva, N.D., U.S.	A5	127
Venado Tuerto, Arg.	E5	72
Venango, co., Pa., U.S.	D2	131
Vendôme, Fr.	D7	16
Veneta, Or., U.S.	C3	130
Venézia (Venice), Italy	B4	18
Venezuela, ctry., S.A.	B6	70
Venezuela, Golfo de, b., S.A.	A5	70
Venezuela, Gulf of see Venezuela, Golfo de, b., S.A.	A5	70
Venezuelan Basin	G7	66
Veniaminof, Mount, mtn., Ak., U.S.	D8	95
Venice see Venézia, Italy	B4	18
Venice, Fl., U.S.	E4	102
Venice, Il., U.S.	E3	106
Venice, Gulf of, b., Eur.	B4	18
Venta, stm., Eur.	H10	10
Ventimiglia, Italy	C1	18
Ventnor City, N.J., U.S.	E4	123
Ventspils, Lat.	H9	10
Ventura (San Buenaventura), Ca., U.S.	E4	98
Ventura, co., Ca., U.S.	E4	98
Vera, Arg.	D5	72
Vera, Spain	I6	16
Veracruz, Mex.	D5	78
Veracruz, state, Mex.	D5	78
Verāval, India	E2	40
Verbania, Italy	B2	18
Vercelli, Italy	B2	18
Verchères, P.Q., Can.	D4	90
Verda, Ky., U.S.	D6	110
Verde, stm., Az., U.S.	C4	96
Verden, Ger.	D11	12
Verdi, Nv., U.S.	D2	121
Verdigre, Ne., U.S.	B7	120
Verdigris, Ok., U.S.	A6	129
Verdigris, stm., U.S.	A6	129
Verdi Peak, mtn., Nv., U.S.	C6	121
Verdun, P.Q., Can.	q19	90
Verdun-sur-Meuse, Fr.	C9	16
Vereeniging, S. Afr.	D4	56
Vereščagino, Russia	C10	26
Vergennes, Vt., U.S.	C2	138
Verhneimbatsk, Russia	C10	26
Verhnemulomskoe vodohranilišče, res., Russia	B14	10
Verhnetulomskij, Russia	B14	10
Verhneural'sk, Russia	D10	22
Verhnij Baskunčak, Russia	E8	22
Verhnij Ufalej, Russia	C11	22
Verhnjaja Amga, Russia	D14	26
Verhnjaja Inta, Russia	A11	22
Verhnjaja Salda, Russia	C11	22
Verhojansk, Russia	C15	26
Verhojanskij hrebet, mts., Russia	C14	26
Verhoture, Russia	C11	22
Verkhoyansk see Verhojansk, Russia	C15	26
Vermilion, Ab., Can.	C5	84
Vermilion, Oh., U.S.	A3	128
Vermilion, co., Il., U.S.	C6	106
Vermilion, co., La., U.S.	E3	111
Vermilion, stm., Ab., Can.	C5	84
Vermilion, stm., Il., U.S.	C5	106
Vermilion, stm., La., U.S.	E3	111
Vermilion, stm., Mn., U.S.	B6	116
Vermilion, stm., Oh., U.S.	A3	128
Vermilion Bay, b., La., U.S.	E3	111
Vermilion Lake, l., Mn., U.S.	C6	116
Vermilion Pass, Can.	D2	84
Vermillion, S.D., U.S.	E9	134
Vermillion, co., In., U.S.	E2	107
Vermillion, East Fork, stm., S.D., U.S.	D8	134
Vermillon, stm., P.Q., Can.	B4	90
Vermont, Il., U.S.	C3	106
Vermont, state, U.S.	D3	138
Vermontville, Mi., U.S.	F5	115
Vernal, Ut., U.S.	C6	137
Vernon, B.C., Can.	D8	85
Vernon, Al., U.S.	B1	94
Vernon, Tx., U.S.	B3	136
Vernon, co., La., U.S.	C2	111
Vernon, co., Mo., U.S.	D3	118
Vernon, co., Wi., U.S.	E3	142
Vernon Hills, Il., U.S.	h9	106
Vernonia, Or., U.S.	B3	130
Vero Beach, Fl., U.S.	E6	102
Véroia, Grc.	D9	18
Verona, On., Can.	C8	89
Verona, Italy	B3	18
Verona, Ms., U.S.	A5	117
Verona, N.J., U.S.	B4	123
Verona, Pa., U.S.	k14	131
Verona, Wi., U.S.	E4	142
Verret, Lake, l., La., U.S.	E4	111
Versailles, Fr.	C8	16
Versailles, In., U.S.	F7	107
Versailles, Ky., U.S.	B5	110
Versailles, Mo., U.S.	C5	118
Versailles, Oh., U.S.	B1	128
Vert, Cap, c., Sen.	D1	50
Vertientes, Cuba	A4	80
Vesele, Ukr.	F13	20
Vešenskaja, Russia	F15	8
Vesoul, Fr.	D10	16
Vestal, N.Y., U.S.	C4	125
Vestavia Hills, Al., U.S.	g7	94
Vesterålen, is., Nor.	B6	10
Vestfjorden, b., Nor.	C5	10
Vestmannaeyjar, Ice.	m18	10a
Vesuvio, vol., Italy	D5	18
Vesuvius see Vesuvio, vol., Italy	D5	18
Veszprém, Hung.	F4	20
Vetlanda, Swe.	H6	10
Vetluga, Russia	C8	22
Vetluga, stm., Russia	C8	22
Vevay, In., U.S.	G7	107
Vezirköprü, Tur.	B6	44
Viacha, Bol.	B4	72
Vian, Ok., U.S.	B7	129
Viana, Braz.	B2	74
Viana do Castelo, Port.	G2	16
Viangchan (Vientiane), Laos	C4	34
Viangphoukha, Laos	B4	34
Viareggio, Italy	C3	18
Viborg, Den.	H3	10
Viborg, S.D., U.S.	D8	134
Vibo Valentia, Italy	E5	18
Viburnum, Mo., U.S.	D6	118
Vic, Spain	G8	16
Vicebsk, Bela.	B11	20
Vicente, Point, c., Ca., U.S.	n12	98
Vicente Guerrero, Presa, res., Mex.	C5	78
Vicenza, Italy	B3	18
Vichada, stm., Col.	C5	70
Vichy, Fr.	F8	16
Vici, Ok., U.S.	A2	129
Vicksburg, Mi., U.S.	F5	115
Vicksburg, Ms., U.S.	C3	117
Vicksburg National Military Park, Ms., U.S.	C3	117
Victor, Ia., U.S.	C5	108
Victor, N.Y., U.S.	C3	125
Victoria see Limbe, Cam.	C1	54
Victoria, B.C., Can.	E6	85
Victoria, Nf., Can.	E5	88
Victoria, Chile	E2	69
Victoria see Xianggang, China	I3	30
Victoria, Gui.	D2	50
Victoria, Sey.	h13	57b
Victoria, Ks., U.S.	D4	109
Victoria, Tx., U.S.	E4	136
Victoria, state, Austl.	H3	62
Victoria, stm., Austl.	D5	60
Victoria, Lake, l., Afr.	D6	54
Victoria, Mount, mtn., Pap. N. Gui.	H12	32
Victoria Falls, wtfl, Afr.	B4	56
Victoria Harbour, On., Can.	C5	89
Victoria Island, i., N.T., Can.	D17	82
Victoria Lake, res., Nf., Can.	D3	88
Victoria Land, reg., Ant.	D21	67
Victoria Nile, stm., Ug.	C6	54
Victoria Peak, mtn., Belize	B2	80
Victoria River Downs, Austl.	D5	60
Victorias, Phil.	D8	34
Victoriaville, P.Q., Can.	C6	90
Victoria West, S. Afr.	E3	56
Victorville, Ca., U.S.	E5	98
Vicuña Mackenna, Arg.	C5	72
Vidalia, Ga., U.S.	D4	103
Vidalia, La., U.S.	C4	111
Vidin, Bul.	C9	18
Vidisha, India	E3	40
Vidor, Tx., U.S.	D5	136
Viedma, Arg.	F4	69
Viedma, Lago, l., Arg.	G2	69
Vienna see Wien, Aus.	F15	12
Vienna, Ga., U.S.	D3	103
Vienna, Il., U.S.	F5	106
Vienna, Mo., U.S.	C6	118
Vienna, Va., U.S.	B5	139
Vienna, W.V., U.S.	B3	141
Vienne, Fr.	E9	16
Vienne, stm., Fr.	D7	16
Vientiane see Viangchan, Laos	C4	34
Vieques, Isla de, i., P.R.	B6	80
Vierwaldstätter See, l., Switz.	A2	18
Vierzon, Fr.	D8	16
Vieste, Italy	D6	18
Vietnam, ctry., Asia	C5	34
Viet Tri, Viet.	B5	34
Vieux Desert, Lac, l., Wi., U.S.	B4	142
Vigan, Phil.	B7	34
Vigo, Spain	F2	16
Vigo, co., In., U.S.	F3	107
Vijayawāda, India	F4	40
Vike, Arm.	C11	44
Viking, Ab., Can.	C5	84
Vikna, Nor.	D4	10
Vikna, i., Nor.	D4	10
Vikramasingapuram, India	H3	40
Vila de Sena, Moz.	B6	56
Vila do Ibo, Moz.	A7	56
Vila Fontes, Moz.	B6	56
Vila Gamito, Moz.	A5	56
Vilagarcía de Arousa, Spain	F2	16
Vilanandro, Tanjona, c., Madag.	B7	56
Vilankulo, Moz.	C6	56
Vilanova i la Geltrú, Spain	G7	16
Vila Real, Port.	G3	16
Vilas, co., Wi., U.S.	B4	142
Vila Velha, Braz.	F3	74
Vilejka, Bela.	B9	20
Vilhelmina, Swe.	D7	10
Vilhena, Braz.	F7	70
Viljandi, Est.	G11	10
Viljuj, stm., Russia	C14	26
Viljujsk, Russia	C14	26
Vil'kickogo, proliv, strt., Russia	B11	26
Villa Ángela, Arg.	D5	72
Villa Bella, Bol.	F6	70
Villacañas, Spain	H5	16
Villacarrillo, Spain	H5	16
Villach, Aus.	G13	12
Villa Dolores, Arg.	E4	72
Villa Grove, Il., U.S.	D5	106
Villaguay, Arg.	E6	72
Villahermosa, Mex.	D6	78
Villaldama, Mex.	D4	78
Villalonga, Arg.	F4	69
Villa María, Arg.	E4	72
Villa Mercedes, Arg.	E4	72
Villa Montes, Bol.	C5	72
Villanueva de la Serena, Spain	H4	16
Villa Ocampo, Arg.	D6	72
Villa Ojo de Agua, Arg.	D5	72
Villa Park, Il., U.S.	k8	106
Villa Rica, Ga., U.S.	C2	103
Villarrica, Chile	E2	69
Villarrica, Para.	D6	72
Villarrobledo, Spain	H5	16
Villas, N.J., U.S.	E3	123
Villa Unión, Mex.	C3	78
Villa Valeria, Arg.	E4	72
Villavicencio, Col.	C5	70
Villefranche-sur-Saône, Fr.	E9	16
Villena, Spain	H6	16
Villeneuve-sur-Lot, Fr.	E7	16
Ville Platte, La., U.S.	D3	111
Ville Saint-Georges, P.Q., Can.	C7	90
Villeurbanne, Fr.	E9	16
Villisca, Ia., U.S.	D3	108
Vilnius, Lith.	I11	10
Vilonia, Ar., U.S.	B3	97
Vimmerby, Swe.	H6	10
Viña del Mar, Chile	D2	69
Vinalhaven, Me., U.S.	D4	112
Vinalhaven Island, i., Me., U.S.	D4	112
Vinaròs, Spain	G7	16
Vincennes, In., U.S.	G2	107
Vincennes Bay, b., Ant.	C15	67
Vincent, Al., U.S.	B3	94
Vindhya Range, mts., India	E3	40
Vine Brook, stm., Ma., U.S.	g11	114
Vine Grove, Ky., U.S.	C4	110
Vineland, N.J., U.S.	E2	123
Vineyard Haven, Ma., U.S.	D6	114
Vineyard Sound, strt., Ma., U.S.	D6	114
Vinh, Viet.	C5	34
Vinh Long, Viet.	D5	34
Vinita, Ok., U.S.	A6	129
Vinson Massif, mtn., Ant.	D32	67
Vinton, Ia., U.S.	B5	108
Vinton, La., U.S.	D2	111
Vinton, Va., U.S.	C3	139
Vinton, co., Oh., U.S.	C3	128
Viola, Il., U.S.	B3	106
Violet, La., U.S.	k12	111
Virac, Phil.	D8	34
Viramgām, India	E2	40
Virandozero, Russia	C14	8
Viranşehir, Tur.	D8	44
Virden, Mb., Can.	E1	86
Virden, Il., U.S.	D4	106
Vire, Fr.	C6	16
Virgin, stm., U.S.	G8	121
Virgin Gorda, i., Br. Vir. Is.	B7	80
Virginia, S. Afr.	D4	56
Virginia, Al., U.S.	g6	94
Virginia, Il., U.S.	D3	106
Virginia, Mn., U.S.	C6	116
Virginia, state, U.S.	C4	139
Virginia Beach, Va., U.S.	D7	139
Virginia City, Nv., U.S.	D2	121
Virginia Peak, mtn., Nv., U.S.	D2	121
Virgin Islands, dep., N.A.	B7	80
Virgin Islands, is., N.A.	E11	76
Viroqua, Wi., U.S.	E3	142
Virovitica, Cro.	B6	18
Virrat, Fin.	E10	10
Virtsu, Est.	G10	10
Virudunagar, India	H3	40
Vis, Otok, i., Cro.	C6	18
Visalia, Ca., U.S.	D4	98
Visayan Sea, Phil.	D8	34
Visby, Swe.	H8	10
Viscount Melville Sound, strt., N.T., Can.	D17	82
Viseu, Port.	G3	16
Vishākhapatnam, India	F4	40
Vista, Ca., U.S.	F5	98
Vistula see Wisła, stm., Pol.	C5	20
Vitarte, Peru	F4	70
Viterbo, Italy	C3	18
Viti Levu, i., Fiji	F11	58
Vitim, Russia	D13	26
Vitim, stm., Russia	D13	26
Vitória, Braz.	F3	74
Vitoria see Gasteiz, Spain	F5	16
Vitória da Conquista, Braz.	D3	74
Vitré, Fr.	C6	16
Vitry-le-François, Fr.	C9	16
Vittoria, Italy	F5	18
Vittorio Veneto, Italy	B4	18
Vivian, La., U.S.	B2	111
Vizianagaram, India	F4	40
Vizinga, Russia	B9	22
Vjatka, stm., Russia	D7	26
Vjatskie Poljany, Russia	C9	22
Vjazemskij, Russia	B14	28
Vjaz'ma, Russia	B13	20
Vladikavkaz, Russia	E6	26
Vladikavkaz see Ordzhonikidze, Ukr.	F13	20
Vladimir, Russia	D6	26
Vladivostok, Russia	E15	26
Vlissingen, Neth.	E8	12
Vlorë, Alb.	D7	18
Vogel Peak see Dimlang, mtn., Nig.	E7	50
Vohimena, Tanjona, c., Madag.	D8	56
Voi, Kenya	D7	54
Voinjama, Lib.	E3	50
Voj-Vož, Russia	B9	22
Volcano, Hi., U.S.	D6	104
Volcano Islands see Kazan-rettō, is., Japan	F17	64
Volga, S.D., U.S.	C9	134
Volga, stm., Russia	E6	26
Volga-Baltic Canal see Volgo-Baltijskij kanal, Russia	B6	22
Volga Plateau see Privolžskaja vozvyšennost', plat., Russia	D6	26
Volgo-Baltijskij kanal, Russia	B6	22
Volgodonsk, Russia	E6	26
Volgograd, Russia	E6	26
Volgograd Reservoir see Volgogradskoe vodohranilišče, res., Russia	D8	22
Volgogradskoe vodohranilišče, res., Russia	D8	22
Volhov, Russia	D12	6
Volksrust, S. Afr.	D4	56
Volnovakha, Ukr.	F14	20
Voločanka, Russia	B11	26
Volodarskoe, Kaz.	D8	26
Volodymyr-Volyns'kyi, Ukr.	D8	20
Vologda, Russia	D6	26
Vólos, Grc.	E9	18
Volos, Gulf of see Pagasitikós Kólpos, b., Grc.	E9	18
Volosovo, Russia	G13	10
Vol'sk, Russia	D6	26
Volta, stm., Ghana	E5	50
Volta Lake, res., Ghana	E5	50
Volta Redonda, Braz.	F3	74
Volterra, Italy	C3	18
Volusia, co., Fl., U.S.	C5	102
Volžsk, Russia	C8	22
Volžskij, Russia	E6	26
Vondrozo, Madag.	C8	56
Von Frank Mountain, mtn., Ak., U.S.	C9	95
Vonore, Tn., U.S.	D9	135
Vordingborg, Den.	I4	10
Vórioi Sporádhes, is., Grc.	E10	18
Vórios Evvoïkós Kólpos, b., Grc.	E9	18
Vorkuta, Russia	C8	26
Vormsi, i., Est.	G10	10
Voronež, Russia	D5	26
Voroshilovsk see Alchevs'k, Ukr.	E15	20
Vorpommern, hist. reg., Ger.	D13	12
Võrtsjärv, l., Est.	G12	10
Võru, Est.	H12	10
Vosges, mts., Fr.	C10	16
Voss, Nor.	F2	10
Vostočno-Sibirskoe more, Russia	B17	26
Vostočnyj Sajan, mts., Russia	D11	26
Vostok, i., Kir.	F14	58
Votkinsk, Russia	D7	26
Votuporanga, Braz.	F2	74
Voyageurs National Park, Mn., U.S.	B5	116
Vožega, Russia	B7	22
Voznesens'k, Ukr.	F11	20
Vraca, Bul.	C9	18
Vrangelja, ostrov, i., Russia	B20	26
Vranje, Yugo.	C8	18
Vrede, S. Afr.	D4	56
Vršac, Yugo.	B8	18
Vryburg, S. Afr.	D3	56
Vryheid, S. Afr.	D5	56
Vsevidof, Mount, mtn., Ak., U.S.	E6	95
Vukovar, Cro.	B7	18
Vulcan, Ab., Can.	D4	84
Vyborg, Russia	C4	26
Vyčegda, stm., Russia	C6	26
Vym', stm., Russia	B9	22
Vyšnij Voločok, Russia	C5	22
Vytegra, Russia	B6	22

W

Wa, Ghana	D4	50
Waajid, Som.	C8	54
Waal, stm., Eur.	E9	12
Waawaea, Puu, mtn., Hi., U.S.	D6	104
Wabag, Pap. N. Gui.	H11	32
Wabana (Bell Island), Nf., Can.	E5	88
Wabasca, Ab., Can.	B4	84
Wabasca, stm., Ab., Can.	f1	84
Wabash, In., U.S.	C6	107
Wabash, co., Il., U.S.	E6	106
Wabash, co., In., U.S.	C6	107
Wabash, stm., U.S.	D10	92
Wabash, stm., U.S.	H2	107
Wabasha, Mn., U.S.	F6	116
Wabasha, co., Mn., U.S.	F6	116
Wabasso, Fl., U.S.	E6	102
Wabasso, Mn., U.S.	F3	116
Wabaunsee, co., Ks., U.S.	D7	109
Wabeno, Wi., U.S.	C5	142
Wabowden, Mb., Can.	B2	86
Wabush, Nf., Can.	h8	88
Waccamaw, stm., U.S.	D9	133
Waccamaw, Lake, l., N.C., U.S.	C4	126
Waccasassa Bay, b., Fl., U.S.	C4	102
Wachusett Mountain, mtn., Ma., U.S.	B4	114
Wachusett Reservoir, res., Ma., U.S.	B4	114
Waco, Tx., U.S.	D4	136

Name	Map Ref.	Page

Waco Lake, res., Tx., U.S. . **D4** 136
Waconda Lake, res., Ks.,
U.S. **C5** 109
Waconia, Mn., U.S. **F5** 116
Waddān, Libya **E8** 48
Waddenzee, strt., Neth. . **D9** 12
Waddi Chappal, Afr. **B2** 54
Waddington, Mount, mtn.,
B.C., Can. **D5** 85
Wadena, Mn., U.S. **D3** 116
Wadena, co., Mn., U.S. . **D4** 116
Wadesboro, N.C., U.S. . . **C2** 126
Wādī Ḥalfāʾ, Sudan **F11** 48
Wading, stm., N.J., U.S. . **D3** 123
Wadley, Ga., U.S. **D4** 103
Wad Madanī, Sudan **H11** 48
Wadmalaw Island, i., S.C.,
U.S. **F7** 133
Wadsworth, Il., U.S. . . . **h9** 106
Wadsworth, Nv., U.S. . . **D2** 121
Wadsworth, Oh., U.S. . . **A4** 128
Wafangdian, China **B5** 30
Wagadugu see
Ouagadougou, Burkina **D4** 50
Wagener, S.C., U.S. . . . **D5** 133
Wagga Wagga, Austl. . . **H4** 62
Wagin, Austl. **G2** 60
Wagner, S.D., U.S. **D7** 134
Wagoner, Ok., U.S. **B6** 129
Wagoner, co., Ok., U.S. . **B6** 129
Wagontire Mountain, mtn.,
Or., U.S. **D7** 130
Waha, Libya **E9** 48
Wahai, Indon. **D7** 36
Wah Cantonment, Pak. . **D10** 42
Wahiawa, Hi., U.S. **B3** 104
Wahiawa Reservoir, res.,
Hi., U.S. **g9** 104
Wahkiakum, co., Wa., U.S. **C2** 140
Wahoo, Ne., U.S. **C9** 120
Wahpeton, N.D., U.S. . . **C9** 127
Wahran, Alg. **C4** 48
Wahweap Creek, stm., Ut.,
U.S. **F4** 137
Waialua, Hi., U.S. **B3** 104
Waialua Bay, b., Hi., U.S. **B3** 104
Waianae, Hi., U.S. **B3** 104
Waianae Range, mts., Hi.,
U.S. **f9** 104
Waidhofen an der Ybbs,
Aus. **G14** 12
Waigeo, Pulau, i., Indon. . **C8** 36
Waikabubak, Indon. **E5** 36
Waikapu, Hi., U.S. **C5** 104
Waikato, stm., N.Z. . . . **o14** 63c
Waikiki Beach, Hi., U.S. . **g10** 104
Wailua, Hi., U.S. **A2** 104
Wailuku, Hi., U.S. **C5** 104
Waimanalo, Hi., U.S. . . **B4** 104
Waimanalo Bay, b., Hi.,
U.S. **g11** 104
Waimate, N.Z. **p13** 63c
Waimea, Hi., U.S. **B2** 104
Waimea, Hi., U.S. **f9** 104
Wainganga, stm., India . . **E3** 40
Waingapu, Indon. **E6** 36
Wainwright, Ab., Can. . . **C5** 84
Wainwright, Ak., U.S. . . **A8** 95
Waipahu, Hi., U.S. **B3** 104
Waipara, N.Z. **p13** 63c
Waipio Acres, Hi., U.S. . **g9** 104
Waipio Peninsula, pen., Hi.,
U.S. **g10** 104
Wairoa, N.Z. **o14** 63c
Waitara, N.Z. **o13** 63c
Waitemata, N.Z. **o13** 63c
Waite Park, Mn., U.S. . . **E4** 116
Waits, stm., Vt., U.S. . . **C4** 138
Waitsburg, Wa., U.S. . . **C7** 140
Wajir, Kenya **C8** 54
Waka, D.R.C. **C4** 54
Waka, Eth. **B7** 54
Wakarusa, In., U.S. . . . **A5** 107
Wakarusa, stm., Ks., U.S. **D8** 109
Wakasa-wan, b., Japan . . **C3** 31
Wakatomika Creek, stm.,
Oh., U.S. **B3** 128
Wakayama, Japan **E15** 28
Wake, co., N.C., U.S. . . **B4** 126
WaKeeney, Ks., U.S. . . **C4** 109
Wakefield, P.Q., Can. . . **D2** 90
Wakefield, Ks., U.S. . . . **C6** 109
Wakefield, Ma., U.S. . . . **B5** 114
Wakefield, Mi., U.S. . . . **n12** 115
Wakefield, Ne., U.S. . . . **B9** 120
Wakefield, R.I., U.S. . . . **F3** 132
Wakefield, Va., U.S. . . . **D6** 139
Wake Forest, N.C., U.S. . **B4** 126
Wake Island, dep., Oc. . . **C10** 58
Wakema, Myan. **C3** 34
Wakeman, Oh., U.S. . . . **A3** 128
Wakkanai, Japan **B16** 28
Waku Kungo, Ang. **F3** 54
Wakulla, co., Fl., U.S. . . **B2** 102
Walachia, hist. reg., Rom. **G8** 20
Walbridge, Oh., U.S. . . . **e6** 128
Wałbrzych, Pol. **D4** 20
Walcott, Ia., U.S. **C7** 108
Walcott, Lake, res., Id., U.S. **G5** 105
Wałcz, Pol. **C4** 20
Walden, On., Can. **A3** 89
Walden, Co., U.S. **A4** 99
Walden, N.Y., U.S. **D6** 125
Waldenburg see Wałbrzych,
Pol. **D4** 20

Walden Ridge, mtn., Tn.,
U.S. **D8** 135
Waldheim, Sk., Can. . . . **E2** 91
Waldo, Ar., U.S. **D2** 97
Waldo, co., Me., U.S. . . **D3** 112
Waldoboro, Me., U.S. . . **D3** 112
Waldo Lake, l., Ma., U.S. **h11** 114
Waldo Lake, l., Or., U.S. **D4** 130
Waldport, Or., U.S. . . . **C2** 130
Waldron, Ar., U.S. **C1** 97
Waldron, In., U.S. **F6** 107
Waldwick, N.J., U.S. . . . **A4** 123
Wales, prov., U.K. **E4** 12
Waleska, Ga., U.S. **B2** 103
Walgett, Austl. **G4** 62
Walgreen Coast, Ant. . . **D30** 67
Walhalla, N.D., U.S. . . . **A8** 127
Walhalla, S.C., U.S. . . . **B1** 133
Walhonding, stm., Oh., U.S.**B3** 128
Walikale, D.R.C. **D5** 54
Walker, Ia., U.S. **B6** 108
Walker, La., U.S. **g10** 111
Walker, Mi., U.S. **E5** 115
Walker, Mn., U.S. **C4** 116
Walker, co., Al., U.S. . . **B2** 94
Walker, co., Ga., U.S. . . **B1** 103
Walker, co., Tx., U.S. . . **D5** 136
Walker, stm., Nv., U.S. . **E3** 121
Walker Lake, l., Nv., U.S. **E3** 121
Walker River Indian
Reservation, Nv., U.S. **D3** 121
Walkersville, Md., U.S. . **B3** 113
Walkerton, On., Can. . . **C3** 89
Walkerton, In., U.S. . . . **B5** 107
Walkertown, N.C., U.S. . **A2** 126
Walkerville, Mt., U.S. . . **D4** 119
Wall, S.D., U.S. **D3** 134
Wallace, Id., U.S. **B3** 105
Wallace, N.C., U.S. . . . **B4** 126
Wallace, co., Ks., U.S. . **D2** 109
Wallaceburg, On., Can. . **E2** 89
Wallace Lake, res., La., U.S.**B2** 111
Walla Walla, Wa., U.S. . **C7** 140
Walla Walla, co., Wa., U.S. **C7** 140
Walla Walla, stm., U.S. . **C7** 140
Walled Lake, Mi., U.S. . **o15** 115
Wallen, In., U.S. **B7** 107
Wallenpaupack, Lake, l.,
Pa., U.S. **D11** 131
Waller, Tx., U.S. **q14** 136
Waller, co., Tx., U.S. . . **E4** 136
Wallingford, Ct., U.S. . . **D4** 100
Wallingford, Vt., U.S. . . **E3** 138
Wallington, N.J., U.S. . . **h8** 123
Wallis, Îles, is., Wal./F. . **F12** 58
Wallis and Futuna, dep.,
Oc. **F12** 58
Wallkill, N.Y., U.S. . . . **D6** 125
Wallkill, stm., N.Y., U.S. **D6** 125
Wall Lake, Ia., U.S. . . . **B2** 108
Wall Lake, l., Ia., U.S. . **B4** 108
Walloomsac, stm., U.S. . **F2** 138
Walloon Lake, l., Mi., U.S. **C6** 115
Wallowa, Or., U.S. **B9** 130
Wallowa, co., Or., U.S. . **B9** 130
Wallowa Mountains, mts.,
Or., U.S. **B9** 130
Wallula, Lake, res., U.S. **C7** 140
Wallum Lake, l., U.S. . . **A1** 132
Walnut, Ia., U.S. **C2** 108
Walnut, Il., U.S. **B4** 106
Walnut, stm., Ks., U.S. . **E6** 109
Walnut Canyon National
Monument, Az., U.S. . **B4** 96
Walnut Cove, N.C., U.S. **A2** 126
Walnut Creek, Ca., U.S. **h8** 98
Walnut Creek, stm., Ks.,
U.S. **D4** 109
Walnut Grove, Al., U.S. . **A3** 94
Walnut Grove, Mn., U.S. **F3** 116
Walnutport, Pa., U.S. . . **E10** 131
Walnut Ridge, Ar., U.S. . **A5** 97
Walpole, Austl. **H2** 60
Walpole, Ma., U.S. . . . **B5** 114
Walpole, N.H., U.S. . . . **D2** 122
Walsall, Eng., U.K. . . . **D6** 12
Walsenburg, Co., U.S. . . **D6** 99
Walsh, Co., U.S. **D8** 99
Walsh, co., N.D., U.S. . . **A8** 127
Walterboro, S.C., U.S. . **F6** 133
Walter F. George Dam, U.S.**D4** 94
Walter F. George Lake, res.,
U.S. **D4** 94
Walters, Ok., U.S. **C3** 129
Walthall, co., Ms., U.S. . **D3** 117
Waltham, Ma., U.S. . . . **B5** 114
Walthill, Ne., U.S. **B9** 120
Walthourville, Ga., U.S. . **E5** 103
Walton, In., U.S. **C5** 107
Walton, Ky., U.S. **B5** 110
Walton, N.Y., U.S. **C5** 125
Walton, co., Fl., U.S. . . **u15** 102
Walton, co., Ga., U.S. . . **C3** 103
Walvis Bay, Nmb. **C1** 56
Walvis Bay, b., Nmb. . . **C1** 56
Walvis Ridge **K14** 66
Walworth, Wi., U.S. . . . **F5** 142
Walworth, co., S.D., U.S. **B5** 134
Walworth, co., Wi., U.S. **F5** 142
Wamac, Il., U.S. **E4** 106
Wamba, D.R.C. **C5** 54
Wamba, Nig. **E6** 50
Wamba, stm., Afr. **E3** 54
Wamego, Ks., U.S. . . . **C7** 109
Wamesit, Ma., U.S. . . . **A5** 114

Wamsutter, Wy., U.S. . . **E5** 143
Wanaka, N.Z. **p12** 63c
Wanamingo, Mn., U.S. . **F6** 116
Wanapum Dam, Wa., U.S. **C6** 140
Wanapum Lake, res., Wa.,
U.S. **B6** 140
Wanaque, N.J., U.S. . . . **A4** 123
Wanaque Reservoir, res.,
N.J., U.S. **A4** 123
Wanatah, In., U.S. **B4** 107
Wanchese, N.C., U.S. . . **B7** 126
Wando, stm., S.C., U.S. . **F8** 133
Wando Woods, S.C., U.S. **k11** 133
Wanfoxia, China **A7** 40
Wanganui, N.Z. **p13** 63c
Wangaratta, Austl. . . . **H4** 62
Wangiwangi, Pulau, i.,
Indon. **E6** 36
Wangqing, China **B1** 31
Wanigela, Pap. N. Gui. . **H12** 32
Wanneroo, Austl. **G2** 60
Wanning, China **F3** 30
Wanxian, China **E9** 28
Wanyuan, China **C2** 30
Wanzai, China **D3** 30
Wapakoneta, Oh., U.S. . **B1** 128
Wapato, Wa., U.S. . . . **C5** 140
Wapawekka Lake, l., Sk.,
Can. **C3** 91
Wapello, Ia., U.S. **C6** 108
Wapello, co., Ia., U.S. . . **C5** 108
Wapiti, stm., Can. **B1** 84
Wappapello, Lake, res.,
Mo., U.S. **D7** 118
Wappingers Falls, N.Y., U.S.**D7** 125
Wapsipinicon, stm., Ia., U.S.**B6** 108
War, W.V., U.S. **D3** 141
Waramaug, Lake, l., Ct.,
U.S. **C2** 100
Warangal, India **F3** 40
Ward, Ar., U.S. **B4** 97
Ward, co., N.D., U.S. . . **A4** 127
Ward, co., Tx., U.S. . . . **D1** 136
Warden, Wa., U.S. . . . **C6** 140
Wardha, India **E3** 40
Ward Mountain, mtn., Mt.,
U.S. **D2** 119
Ware, Ma., U.S. **B3** 114
Ware, co., Ga., U.S. . . . **E4** 103
Ware, stm., Ma., U.S. . . **B3** 114
War Eagle Mountain, mtn.,
Id., U.S. **G2** 105
Wareham, Ma., U.S. . . **C6** 114
Warehouse Point, Ct., U.S. **B5** 100
Waren, Indon. **G10** 32
Ware Shoals, S.C., U.S. . **C3** 133
Warfield, B.C., Can. . . . **E9** 85
Wargla, Alg. **F1** 48
Warialda, Austl. **F5** 62
Warin Chamrap, Thai. . . **C4** 34
Warmbad, Nmb. **D2** 56
Warmbad, S. Afr. **C4** 56
Warminster, Pa., U.S. . . **F11** 131
Warm Springs Indian
Reservation, Or., U.S. **C5** 130
Warm Springs Reservoir,
res., Or., U.S. **D8** 130
Warner, N.H., U.S. . . . **D3** 122
Warner, Ok., U.S. **B6** 129
Warner, stm., N.H., U.S. **D3** 122
Warner Mountains, mts.,
Ca., U.S. **B3** 98
Warner Peak, mtn., Or.,
U.S. **E7** 130
Warner Robins, Ga., U.S. **D3** 103
Warracknabeal, Austl. . . **H3** 62
Warr Acres, Ok., U.S. . . **B4** 129
Warragul, Austl. **H4** 62
Warren, Ar., U.S. **D3** 97
Warren, Il., U.S. **A4** 106
Warren, In., U.S. **C7** 107
Warren, Mi., U.S. **B3** 114
Warren, Mn., U.S. **F7** 115
Warren, Oh., U.S. **B2** 116
Warren, Or., U.S. **A5** 128
Warren, Pa., U.S. **B4** 130
Warren, R.I., U.S. **C3** 131
Warren, Vt., U.S. **D5** 132
Warren, co., Ga., U.S. . . **C3** 138
Warren, co., Ia., U.S. . . **C4** 103
Warren, co., Il., U.S. . . **C4** 108
Warren, co., In., U.S. . . **C3** 106
Warren, co., Ky., U.S. . . **D3** 107
Warren, co., Mo., U.S. . **C3** 110
Warren, co., Ms., U.S. . **C6** 118
Warren, co., N.C., U.S. . **C3** 117
Warren, co., N.J., U.S. . **A4** 126
Warren, co., N.Y., U.S. . **B3** 123
Warren, co., Oh., U.S. . **B7** 125
Warren, co., Pa., U.S. . . **C1** 128
Warren, co., Tn., U.S. . . **C4** 131
Warren, co., Va., U.S. . . **D8** 135
Warren Park, In., U.S. . . **B4** 139
Warren Peaks, mts., Wy., **k10** 107
U.S. **B8** 143
Warrensburg, Il., U.S. . . **D4** 106
Warrensburg, Mo., U.S. . **C4** 118
Warrensburg, N.Y., U.S. **B7** 125
Warrensville Heights, Oh.,
U.S. **h9** 128
Warrenton, S. Afr. . . . **D3** 56
Warrenton, Ga., U.S. . . **C4** 103
Warrenton, Mo., U.S. . . **C6** 118

Warrenton, N.C., U.S. . . **A4** 126
Warrenton, Or., U.S. . . **A3** 130
Warrenton, Va., U.S. . . **B5** 139
Warrenville, Il., U.S. . . . **k8** 106
Warrenville, S.C., U.S. . **D4** 133
Warri, Nig. **E6** 50
Warrick, co., In., U.S. . . **H3** 107
Warrington, Fl., U.S. . . **u14** 102
Warrior, Al., U.S. **B3** 94
Warrior Lake, res., Al., U.S. **C2** 94
Warrnambool, Austl. . . **H3** 62
Warroad, Mn., U.S. . . . **B3** 116
Warsaw see Warszawa, Pol. **C6** 20
Warsaw, Il., U.S. **C2** 106
Warsaw, In., U.S. **B6** 107
Warsaw, Ky., U.S. **B5** 110
Warsaw, Mo., U.S. . . . **C4** 118
Warsaw, N.C., U.S. . . . **B4** 126
Warsaw, N.Y., U.S. . . . **C2** 125
Warsaw, Va., U.S. **C6** 139
Warszawa (Warsaw), Pol. **C6** 20
Wartburg, Tn., U.S. . . . **C9** 135
Warwick, Austl. **F5** 62
Warwick, P.Q., Can. . . . **D6** 90
Warwick, Md., U.S. . . . **B6** 113
Warwick, N.Y., U.S. . . . **D6** 125
Warwick, R.I., U.S. . . . **D4** 132
Wasaga Beach, On., Can. **C4** 89
Wasatch, co., Ut., U.S. . **C4** 137
Wasco, Ca., U.S. **E4** 98
Wasco, co., Or., U.S. . . **B5** 130
Waseca, Mn., U.S. **F5** 116
Waseca, co., Mn., U.S. . **F5** 116
Washakie, co., Wy., U.S. **C5** 143
Washakie Needles, mts.,
Wy., U.S. **C3** 143
Washburn, Ia., U.S. . . . **B5** 108
Washburn, Il., U.S. . . . **C4** 106
Washburn, Me., U.S. . . **B4** 112
Washburn, N.D., U.S. . . **B5** 127
Washburn, Wi., U.S. . . **B3** 142
Washburn, co., Wi., U.S. **C2** 142
Washburn, Mount, mtn.,
Wy., U.S. **B2** 143
Washīm, India **E3** 40
Washington, D.C., U.S. . **C3** 113
Washington, Ga., U.S. . **C4** 103
Washington, Ia., U.S. . . **C6** 108
Washington, Il., U.S. . . **C4** 106
Washington, In., U.S. . . **G3** 107
Washington, Ks., U.S. . **C6** 109
Washington, Ky., U.S. . **B6** 110
Washington, La., U.S. . . **D3** 111
Washington, Mo., U.S. . **C6** 118
Washington, Ms., U.S. . **D2** 117
Washington, N.C., U.S. . **B5** 126
Washington, N.J., U.S. . **B3** 123
Washington, Pa., U.S. . **F1** 131
Washington, Ut., U.S. . **F2** 137
Washington, Va., U.S. . **B4** 139
Washington, Co., U.S. . **B7** 99
Washington, co., Al., U.S. **D1** 94
Washington, co., Ar., U.S. **A1** 97
Washington, co., Co., U.S. **B7** 99
Washington, co., Fl., U.S. **u16** 102
Washington, co., Ga., U.S. **C4** 103
Washington, co., Ia., U.S. **C6** 108
Washington, co., Id., U.S. **E2** 105
Washington, co., Il., U.S. **E4** 106
Washington, co., In., U.S. **G5** 107
Washington, co., Ks., U.S. **C6** 109
Washington, co., Ky., U.S. **C4** 110
Washington, co., La., U.S. **D5** 111
Washington, co., Md., U.S. **A2** 113
Washington, co., Me., U.S. **D5** 112
Washington, co., Mn., U.S. **E6** 116
Washington, co., Mo., U.S. **D7** 118
Washington, co., Ms., U.S. **B3** 117
Washington, co., N.C., U.S. **B6** 126
Washington, co., Ne., U.S. **C9** 120
Washington, co., N.Y., U.S. **B7** 125
Washington, co., Oh., U.S. **C4** 128
Washington, co., Ok., U.S. **A6** 129
Washington, co., Or., U.S. **B3** 130
Washington, co., Pa., U.S. **F1** 131
Washington, co., R.I., U.S. **E2** 132
Washington, co., Tn., U.S. **C11** 135
Washington, co., Tx., U.S. **D4** 136
Washington, co., Ut., U.S. **F2** 137
Washington, co., Va., U.S. **f9** 139
Washington, co., Vt., U.S. **C3** 138
Washington, co., Wi., U.S. **E5** 142
Washington, Lake, l., Fl.,
U.S. **D6** 102
Washington, Lake, l., Mn.,
U.S. **E4** 116
Washington, Lake, l., Ms.,
U.S. **B3** 117
Washington, Lake, l., Wa.,
U.S. **e11** 140
Washington, Mount, mtn.,
N.H., U.S. **B4** 122
Washington Court House,
Oh., U.S. **C2** 128
Washington Island, i., Wi.,
U.S. **C7** 142
Washington Park, Il., U.S. **E3** 106
Washington Terrace, Ut.,
U.S. **B4** 137
Washita, co., Ok., U.S. . **B2** 129
Washita, stm., Ok., U.S. . **C4** 129
Washoe, co., Nv., U.S. . **C2** 121
Washoe City, Nv., U.S. . **D2** 121
Washougal, Wa., U.S. . . **D3** 140
Washow Bay, b., Mb., Can. **D3** 86
Washtenaw, co., Mi., U.S. **F7** 115

Wasilla, Ak., U.S. **C10** 95
Wasior, Indon. **D8** 36
Waskom, Tx., U.S. **C5** 136
Waspam, Nic. **C3** 80
Wasque Point, c., Ma., U.S. **D7** 114
Wassookeag, Lake, l., Me.,
U.S. **C3** 112
Wassuk Range, mts., Nv.,
U.S. **E3** 121
Wataga, Il., U.S. **B3** 106
Watampone, Indon. . . . **D6** 36
Watansopeng, Indon. . . **D5** 36
Watauga, co., N.C., U.S. **A1** 126
Watauga, stm., Tn., U.S. **C12** 135
Watauga Lake, res., Tn.,
U.S. **C12** 135
Watchaug Pond, l., R.I.,
U.S. **F2** 132
Watch Hill Point, c., R.I.,
U.S. **G1** 132
Watchung, N.J., U.S. . . **B4** 123
Waterbury, Ct., U.S. . . **C3** 100
Waterbury, Vt., U.S. . . **C3** 138
Waterbury Center, Vt., U.S. **C3** 138
Waterbury Reservoir, res.,
Vt., U.S. **C3** 138
Wateree, stm., S.C., U.S. **D6** 133
Wateree Lake, res., S.C.,
U.S. **C6** 133
Waterford, Ire. **D3** 12
Waterford, Ct., U.S. . . . **D7** 100
Waterford, N.Y., U.S. . . **C7** 125
Waterford, Pa., U.S. . . **C2** 131
Waterford, Wi., U.S. . . **F5** 142
Waterhen Lake, l., Mb.,
Can. **C2** 86
Waterloo, Bel. **E9** 12
Waterloo, On., Can. . . . **D4** 89
Waterloo, P.Q., Can. . . **D5** 90
Waterloo, Ia., U.S. **B5** 108
Waterloo, Il., U.S. **E3** 106
Waterloo, In., U.S. **B7** 107
Waterloo, N.Y., U.S. . . **C4** 125
Waterloo, Wi., U.S. . . . **E5** 142
Waterman, Il., U.S. . . . **B5** 106
Waterman Reservoir, res.,
R.I., U.S. **B3** 132
Waterproof, La., U.S. . . **C4** 111
Watersmeet, Mi., U.S. . **n12** 115
Waterton Lakes National
Park, Ab., Can. **E3** 84
Watertown, Ct., U.S. . . **C3** 100
Watertown, Ma., U.S. . **g11** 114
Watertown, N.Y., U.S. . **B5** 125
Watertown, S.D., U.S. . **C8** 134
Watertown, Tn., U.S. . . **A5** 135
Watertown, Wi., U.S. . . **E5** 142
Water Valley, Ms., U.S. . **A4** 117
Waterville, Ks., U.S. . . **C7** 109
Waterville, Me., U.S. . . **D3** 112
Waterville, Mn., U.S. . . **F5** 116
Waterville, N.Y., U.S. . . **C5** 125
Waterville, Oh., U.S. . . **A2** 128
Waterville, Wa., U.S. . . **B5** 140
Watervliet, Mi., U.S. . . **F4** 115
Watervliet, N.Y., U.S. . . **C7** 125
Watford, On., Can. . . . **E3** 89
Watford City, N.D., U.S. **B2** 127
Wathena, Ks., U.S. . . . **C9** 109
Watheroo, Austl. **G2** 60
Watkins, Mn., U.S. . . . **E4** 116
Watkins Glen, N.Y., U.S. **C4** 125
Watkinsville, Ga., U.S. . **C3** 103
Watling Island see San
Salvador, i., Bah. . . . **D10** 76
Watonga, Ok., U.S. . . . **B3** 129
Watonwan, co., Mn., U.S. **F4** 116
Watonwan, stm., Mn., U.S. **G4** 116
Watsa, D.R.C. **C5** 54
Watseka, Il., U.S. **C6** 106
Watsontown, Pa., U.S. . **D8** 131
Watsonville, Ca., U.S. . **D3** 98
Watts Bar Dam, Tn., U.S. **D9** 135
Watts Bar Lake, res., Tn.,
U.S. **D9** 135
Wattsville, S.C., U.S. . . **B4** 133
Watubela, Kepulauan, is.,
Indon. **D8** 36
Waubaushene, On., Can. **C5** 89
Waubay, S.D., U.S. . . . **B8** 134
Waubay Lake, l., S.D., U.S. **B8** 134
Wauchope, Austl. **E5** 60
Wauchula, Fl., U.S. . . . **E5** 102
Wauconda, Il., U.S. . . . **h8** 106
Waugh Mountain, mtn., Id.,
U.S. **D4** 105
Waukee, Ia., U.S. **C4** 108
Waukegan, Il., U.S. . . . **A6** 106
Waukesha, Wi., U.S. . . **F5** 142
Waukesha, co., Wi., U.S. **E5** 142
Waukewan, Lake, l., N.H.,
U.S. **C3** 122
Waukomis, Ok., U.S. . . **A4** 129
Waukon, Ia., U.S. **A6** 108
Waunakee, Wi., U.S. . . **E4** 142
Wauneta, Ne., U.S. . . . **D4** 120
Waungumbaug Lake, l., Ct.,
U.S. **B6** 100
Waupaca, Wi., U.S. . . . **D4** 142
Waupaca, co., Wi., U.S. **D5** 142
Waupun, Wi., U.S. . . . **E5** 142
Wauregan, Ct., U.S. . . **C8** 100
Waurika, Ok., U.S. . . . **C4** 129
Waurika Lake, res., Ok.,
U.S. **C3** 129

Name	Map Ref.	Page
Wausau, Wi., U.S.	D4	142
Wausau, Lake, res., Wi., U.S.	D4	142
Wauseon, Oh., U.S.	A1	128
Wautoma, Wi., U.S.	D4	142
Waushara, co., Wi., U.S.	D4	142
Wauwatosa, Wi., U.S.	m12	142
Wave Hill, Austl.	D5	60
Waveland, Ms., U.S.	E4	117
Waverley, N.S., Can.	E6	87
Waverly, Ia., U.S.	B5	108
Waverly, Il., U.S.	D4	106
Waverly, Ks., U.S.	D8	109
Waverly, Mn., U.S.	E5	116
Waverly, Mo., U.S.	B4	118
Waverly, Ne., U.S.	D9	120
Waverly, N.Y., U.S.	C4	125
Waverly, Oh., U.S.	C3	128
Waverly, Tn., U.S.	A4	135
Waverly, Va., U.S.	C5	139
Waverly, W.V., U.S.	B3	141
Waverly Hall, Ga., U.S.	D2	103
Wāw, Sudan	I10	48
Wāw al-Kabīr, Libya	E8	48
Wawanesa, Mb., Can.	E2	86
Wawasee, Lake, l., In., U.S.	B6	107
Wawayanda Lake, l., N.J., U.S.	A4	123
Wawota, Sk., Can.	H4	91
Waxahachie, Tx., U.S.	C4	136
Waxhaw, N.C., U.S.	C2	126
Waycross, Ga., U.S.	E4	103
Wayland, Ia., U.S.	C6	108
Wayland, Ma., U.S.	g10	114
Wayland, Mi., U.S.	F5	115
Wayland, N.Y., U.S.	C3	125
Waylyn, S.C., U.S.	k12	133
Waymart, Pa., U.S.	C11	131
Wayne, Mi., U.S.	p15	115
Wayne, Ne., U.S.	B8	120
Wayne, N.J., U.S.	B4	123
Wayne, W.V., U.S.	C2	141
Wayne, co., Ga., U.S.	E5	103
Wayne, co., Ia., U.S.	D4	108
Wayne, co., Il., U.S.	E5	106
Wayne, co., In., U.S.	E7	107
Wayne, co., Ky., U.S.	D5	110
Wayne, co., Mi., U.S.	F7	115
Wayne, co., Mo., U.S.	D7	118
Wayne, co., Ms., U.S.	D5	117
Wayne, co., N.C., U.S.	B4	126
Wayne, co., Ne., U.S.	B8	120
Wayne, co., N.Y., U.S.	B3	125
Wayne, co., Oh., U.S.	B4	128
Wayne, co., Pa., U.S.	C11	131
Wayne, co., Tn., U.S.	B4	135
Wayne, co., Ut., U.S.	E4	137
Wayne, co., W.V., U.S.	C2	141
Wayne City, Il., U.S.	E5	106
Waynesboro, Ga., U.S.	C4	103
Waynesboro, Ms., U.S.	D5	117
Waynesboro, Pa., U.S.	G6	131
Waynesboro, Tn., U.S.	B4	135
Waynesboro, Va., U.S.	B4	139
Waynesburg, Oh., U.S.	B4	128
Waynesburg, Pa., U.S.	G1	131
Waynesville, Mo., U.S.	D5	118
Waynesville, N.C., U.S.	f10	126
Waynesville, Oh., U.S.	C1	128
Waynetown, In., U.S.	D3	107
Waynewood, Va., U.S.	g12	139
Waynoka, Ok., U.S.	A3	129
Wayzata, Mn., U.S.	n11	116
Waza, Cam.	D7	50
We, Pulau, i., Indon.	B1	36
Weakley, co., Tn., U.S.	A3	135
Weatherford, Ok., U.S.	B3	129
Weatherford, Tx., U.S.	C4	136
Weatherly, Pa., U.S.	E10	131
Weatogue, Ct., U.S.	B4	100
Weaver, Al., U.S.	B4	94
Weaver Mountains, mts., Az., U.S.	C3	96
Weaverville, Ca., U.S.	B2	98
Weaverville, N.C., U.S.	f10	126
Webb, Al., U.S.	D4	94
Webb, Ms., U.S.	B3	117
Webb, co., Tx., U.S.	F3	136
Webb City, Mo., U.S.	D3	118
Webbers Falls, Ok., U.S.	B6	129
Webberville, Mi., U.S.	F6	115
Webb Lake, l., Me., U.S.	D2	112
Weber, co., Ut., U.S.	B4	137
Weber City, Va., U.S.	f9	139
Webster, Ma., U.S.	B4	114
Webster, N.Y., U.S.	B3	125
Webster, Pa., U.S.	F2	131
Webster, S.D., U.S.	B8	134
Webster, co., Ga., U.S.	D2	103
Webster, co., Ia., U.S.	B3	108
Webster, co., Ky., U.S.	C2	110
Webster, co., La., U.S.	B2	111
Webster, co., Mo., U.S.	D5	118
Webster, co., Ms., U.S.	B4	117
Webster, co., Ne., U.S.	D7	120
Webster, co., W.V., U.S.	C4	141
Webster City, Ia., U.S.	B4	108
Webster Groves, Mo., U.S.	f13	118
Webster Reservoir, res., Ks., U.S.	C4	109
Webster Springs, W.V., U.S.	C4	141
Websterville, Vt., U.S.	C4	138
Weda, Indon.	C7	36
Weddell Sea, Ant.	C1	67
Wedgeport, N.S., Can.	F4	87
Wedgewood, Mo., U.S.	f13	118
Wedowee, Al., U.S.	B4	94
Weed, Ca., U.S.	B2	98
Weed Heights, Nv., U.S.	E2	121
Weedon, P.Q., Can.	D6	90
Weedsport, N.Y., U.S.	B4	125
Weedville, Pa., U.S.	D5	131
Weehawken, N.J., U.S.	h8	123
Weeksbury, Ky., U.S.	C7	110
Weeping Water, Ne., U.S.	D9	120
Weichang, China	A4	30
Weiden in der Oberpfalz, Ger.	F12	12
Weifang, China	D11	28
Weihai, China	D12	28
Weimar, Ger.	E12	12
Weimar, Tx., U.S.	E4	136
Weinan, China	E9	28
Weiner, Ar., U.S.	B5	97
Weippe, Id., U.S.	C3	105
Weir, Ks., U.S.	E9	109
Weir, Lake, l., Fl., U.S.	C5	102
Weirsdale, Fl., U.S.	D5	102
Weirton, W.V., U.S.	A4	141
Weiser, Id., U.S.	E2	105
Weiser, stm., Id., U.S.	E2	105
Weishan Hu, l., China	B4	30
Weissenburg in Bayern, Ger.	F11	12
Weissenfels, Ger.	E12	12
Weiss Lake, res., U.S.	A4	94
Weixi, China	A3	34
Weixian, China	B4	30
Wejherowo, Pol.	B5	20
Welbourn Hill, Austl.	F5	60
Welch, W.V., U.S.	D3	141
Welcome, Mn., U.S.	G4	116
Welcome, S.C., U.S.	B3	133
Weld, co., Co., U.S.	A6	99
Weldon, N.C., U.S.	A5	126
Weldon Spring, Mo., U.S.	f12	118
Weleetka, Ok., U.S.	B5	129
Welkʼīte, Eth.	B7	54
Welkom, S. Afr.	D4	56
Welland, On., Can.	E5	89
Wellesley, On., Can.	D4	89
Wellesley, Ma., U.S.	B5	114
Wellesley Islands, is., Austl.	D2	62
Wellford, S.C., U.S.	B3	133
Wellington, Austl.	G4	62
Wellington, On., Can.	D7	89
Wellington, N.Z.	I11	58
Wellington, Co., U.S.	A5	99
Wellington, Ks., U.S.	E6	109
Wellington, Mo., U.S.	B4	118
Wellington, Nv., U.S.	E2	121
Wellington, Oh., U.S.	A3	128
Wellington, Tx., U.S.	B2	136
Wellington, Ut., U.S.	D5	137
Wellington, Isla, i., Chile	G2	69
Wellman, Ia., U.S.	C6	108
Wells, Me., U.S.	E2	112
Wells, Mn., U.S.	G5	116
Wells, Nv., U.S.	B7	121
Wells, co., In., U.S.	C7	107
Wells, co., N.D., U.S.	B6	127
Wells, stm., Vt., U.S.	C4	138
Wellsboro, Pa., U.S.	C7	131
Wellsburg, Ia., U.S.	B5	108
Wellsburg, W.V., U.S.	A4	141
Wellston, Oh., U.S.	C3	128
Wellston, Ok., U.S.	B4	129
Wellsville, Ks., U.S.	D8	109
Wellsville, Mo., U.S.	B6	118
Wellsville, N.Y., U.S.	C3	125
Wellsville, Oh., U.S.	B5	128
Wellsville, Ut., U.S.	B4	137
Wellton, Az., U.S.	E1	96
Wels, Aus.	F13	12
Welsh, La., U.S.	D3	111
Wembley, Ab., Can.	B1	84
Wenatchee, Wa., U.S.	B5	140
Wenatchee, stm., Wa., U.S.	B5	140
Wenatchee Lake, l., Wa., U.S.	B5	140
Wenatchee Mountains, mts., Wa., U.S.	B5	140
Wenchang, China	F3	30
Wenchi, Ghana	E4	50
Wendell, Id., U.S.	G4	105
Wendell, N.C., U.S.	B4	126
Wendeng, China	B5	30
Wendover, Ut., U.S.	C1	137
Wengyuan, China	J3	30
Wenham, Ma., U.S.	A6	114
Wenham Lake, l., Ma., U.S.	f12	114
Wenling, China	D5	30
Wenshan, China	G8	28
Wenshang, China	B4	30
Wensu, China	A4	40
Wentworth, Austl.	G3	62
Wentworth, Lake, l., N.H., U.S.	C4	122
Wentzville, Mo., U.S.	C7	118
Wenzhou, China	F12	28
Weohyakapka, Lake, l., Fl., U.S.	E5	102
Werda, Bots.	D3	56
Weri, Indon.	D8	36
Werribee, Austl.	H3	62
Wesel, Ger.	E10	12
Weser, stm., Ger.	D11	12
Weslaco, Tx., U.S.	F4	136
Wesleyville, Nf., Can.	D5	88
Wesleyville, Pa., U.S.	B2	131
Wessel, Cape, c., Austl.	C6	60
Wessel Islands, is., Austl.	C6	60
Wesserunsett Lake, l., Me., U.S.	D3	112
Wessington Springs, S.D., U.S.	C7	134
Wesson, Ms., U.S.	D3	117
West, Tx., U.S.	D4	136
West, stm., Ct., U.S.	D5	100
West, stm., Ma., U.S.	h9	114
West, stm., Vt., U.S.	E3	138
West Acton, Ma., U.S.	g10	114
West Alexandria, Oh., U.S.	C1	128
West Allis, Wi., U.S.	m11	142
West Alton, Mo., U.S.	f13	118
West Andover, Ma., U.S.	A5	114
West Antarctica, reg., Ant.	E29	67
West Baden Springs, In., U.S.	G4	107
West Baton Rouge, co., La., U.S.	D4	111
West Bay, b., Fl., U.S.	u16	102
West Bay, b., N.C., U.S.	B6	126
West Bay, b., Tx., U.S.	r15	136
West Bend, Ia., U.S.	B3	108
West Bend, Wi., U.S.	E5	142
West Bengal, prov., India	E5	40
West Berlin, N.J., U.S.	D3	123
West Billerica, Ma., U.S.	f10	114
West Blocton, Al., U.S.	B2	94
Westborough, Ma., U.S.	B4	114
West Bountiful, Ut., U.S.	C4	137
West Boylston, Ma., U.S.	B4	114
West Branch, Ia., U.S.	C6	108
West Branch, Mi., U.S.	D6	115
West Branch Reservoir, res., Ct., U.S.	B3	100
West Bridgewater, Ma., U.S.	B5	114
Westbrook, Ct., U.S.	D6	100
Westbrook, Me., U.S.	E2	112
Westbrook, Mn., U.S.	F3	116
West Burlington, Ia., U.S.	D6	108
West Butte, mtn., Mt., U.S.	B5	119
Westby, Wi., U.S.	E3	142
West Cache Creek, stm., Ok., U.S.	C3	129
West Caldwell, N.J., U.S.	B4	123
West Canada Creek, stm., N.Y., U.S.	B6	125
West Cape Howe, c., Austl.	H2	60
West Caroline Basin	H16	64
West Carroll, co., La., U.S.	B4	111
West Carrollton, Oh., U.S.	C1	128
West Carthage, N.Y., U.S.	B5	125
Westchester, Il., U.S.	k9	106
West Chester, Pa., U.S.	G10	131
Westchester, co., N.Y., U.S.	D7	125
West Chicago, Il., U.S.	k8	106
West Chop, c., Ma., U.S.	D6	114
West College Corner, In., U.S.	E8	107
West Columbia, S.C., U.S.	D5	133
West Columbia, Tx., U.S.	E5	136
West Concord, Ma., U.S.	B5	114
West Concord, Mn., U.S.	F6	116
West Concord, N.C., U.S.	B2	126
Westconnaug Reservoir, res., R.I., U.S.	C2	132
West Cote Blanche Bay, b., La., U.S.	E4	111
West Covina, Ca., U.S.	m13	98
West Crossett, Ar., U.S.	D4	97
West Cumberland, Me., U.S.	E2	112
West Dennis, Ma., U.S.	C7	114
West Des Moines, Ia., U.S.	C4	108
West Elk Mountains, mts., Co., U.S.	C3	99
West Elk Peak, mtn., Co., U.S.	C3	99
Westerly, R.I., U.S.	F1	132
Western Australia, state, Austl.	E2	60
Western Desert, des., Egypt	F9	14
Western Dvina (Zapadnaja Dvina), stm., Eur.	C4	22
Western Ghāts, mts., India	F2	40
Westernport, Md., U.S.	m12	113
Western Sahara, dep., Afr.	B2	50
Western Samoa see Samoa, ctry., Oc.	F12	58
Western Sayans see Zapadnyj Sajan, mts., Russia	D11	26
Western Springs, Il., U.S.	k9	106
Westerville, Oh., U.S.	B3	128
West European Basin	D11	66
West Falkland, i., Falk. Is.	H4	69
West Fargo, N.D., U.S.	C9	127
West Feliciana, co., La., U.S.	D4	111
Westfield, N.B., Can.	D3	87
Westfield, In., U.S.	D5	107
Westfield, Ma., U.S.	B2	114
Westfield, N.J., U.S.	B4	123
Westfield, N.Y., U.S.	C1	125
Westfield, Pa., U.S.	C6	131
Westfield, Wi., U.S.	E4	142
Westfield, stm., Ma., U.S.	B2	114
West Fork, Ar., U.S.	B1	97
West Fork, stm., W.V., U.S.	B4	141
West Frankfort, Il., U.S.	F5	106
West Freehold, N.J., U.S.	C4	123
West Friendship, Md., U.S.	B4	113
Westgate, Fl., U.S.	F6	102
West Grand Lake, l., Me., U.S.	C5	112
West Grove, Pa., U.S.	G10	131
West Hanover, Ma., U.S.	h12	114
West Hartford, Ct., U.S.	B4	100
West Haven, Ct., U.S.	D4	100
West Hazleton, Pa., U.S.	E9	131
West Helena, Ar., U.S.	C5	97
West Hill Reservoir, res., Ma., U.S.	B4	114
Westhope, N.D., U.S.	A4	127
West Ice Shelf, Ant.	C13	67
West Indies, is.	D11	76
West Island, i., Ma., U.S.	C6	114
West Jefferson, N.C., U.S.	A1	126
West Jefferson, Oh., U.S.	C2	128
West Jordan, Ut., U.S.	C3	137
West Kingston, R.I., U.S.	F3	132
West Lafayette, In., U.S.	D4	107
West Lafayette, Oh., U.S.	B4	128
Westlake, La., U.S.	D2	111
Westlake, Oh., U.S.	h9	128
West Lake, l., Me., U.S.	C4	112
West Land, Mi., U.S.	F7	115
West Laramie, Wy., U.S.	E7	143
West Lawn, Pa., U.S.	F10	131
West Lebanon, In., U.S.	D3	107
West Liberty, Ia., U.S.	C6	108
West Liberty, Ky., U.S.	C6	110
West Liberty, Oh., U.S.	B2	128
West Liberty, W.V., U.S.	f8	141
West Linn, Or., U.S.	B4	130
Westlock, Ab., Can.	B4	84
West Long Branch, N.J., U.S.	C4	123
West Lorne, On., Can.	E3	89
West Marion, N.C., U.S.	f10	126
West Medway, Ma., U.S.	B5	114
West Memphis, Ar., U.S.	B5	97
West Miami, Fl., U.S.	s13	102
West Middlesex, Pa., U.S.	D1	131
West Mifflin, Pa., U.S.	F2	131
West Milton, Oh., U.S.	C1	128
West Milwaukee, Wi., U.S.	m12	142
Westminster, Ca., U.S.	n12	98
Westminster, Co., U.S.	B5	99
Westminster, Md., U.S.	A4	113
Westminster, S.C., U.S.	B1	133
West Monroe, La., U.S.	B3	111
Westmont, Il., U.S.	k9	106
Westmont, N.J., U.S.	D2	123
Westmont, Pa., U.S.	F4	131
Westmoreland, Tn., U.S.	A5	135
Westmoreland, co., Pa., U.S.	F2	131
Westmoreland, co., Va., U.S.	B6	139
Westmorland, Ca., U.S.	F6	98
West Musquash Lake, l., Me., U.S.	C5	112
West Mystic, Ct., U.S.	D8	100
West Newton, Pa., U.S.	F2	131
West New York, N.J., U.S.	h8	123
West Nicholson, Zimb.	C4	56
West Nishnabotna, stm., Ia., U.S.	C2	108
West Norriton, Pa., U.S.	o20	131
Weston, Ct., U.S.	E2	100
Weston, Ma., U.S.	g10	114
Weston, Mo., U.S.	B3	118
Weston, Oh., U.S.	A2	128
Weston, Or., U.S.	B8	130
Weston, W.V., U.S.	B4	141
Weston, co., Wy., U.S.	C8	143
Weston-super-Mare, Eng., U.K.	E5	12
Westover, Md., U.S.	D6	113
Westover, W.V., U.S.	B5	141
Westover Air Force Base, mil., Ma., U.S.	B2	114
West Palm Beach, Fl., U.S.	F6	102
West Pawlet, Vt., U.S.	E2	138
West Pearl, stm., La., U.S.	D6	111
West Pelzer, S.C., U.S.	B3	133
West Pensacola, Fl., U.S.	u14	102
West Peoria, Il., U.S.	C4	106
Westphalia, Mi., U.S.	F6	115
West Pittsburg, Pa., U.S.	E1	131
West Pittston, Pa., U.S.	m17	131
West Plains, Mo., U.S.	E6	118
West Point, Ca., U.S.	C3	98
West Point, Ga., U.S.	D1	103
West Point, Ia., U.S.	D6	108
West Point, Ky., U.S.	C4	110
West Point, Ms., U.S.	B5	117
West Point, Ne., U.S.	C9	120
West Point, N.Y., U.S.	D7	125
West Point, Va., U.S.	C6	139
West Point, mtn., Ak., U.S.	C11	95
West Point Lake, res., U.S.	C1	103
Westport, On., Can.	C8	89
Westport, Ct., U.S.	E2	100
Westport, In., U.S.	F6	107
Westport, Wa., U.S.	C1	140
West Portsmouth, Oh., U.S.	D2	128
West Quoddy Head, c., Me., U.S.	D6	112
West Reading, Pa., U.S.	F10	131
West Rutland, Vt., U.S.	D2	138
West Saint Paul, Mn., U.S.	n12	116
West Salem, Il., U.S.	E5	106
West Salem, Oh., U.S.	B3	128
West Salem, Wi., U.S.	E2	142
West Scarborough, Me., U.S.	E2	112
West Seneca, N.Y., U.S.	C2	125
West Siberian Lowland see Zapadno-Sibirskaja ravnina, pl., Russia	C9	26
West Simsbury, Ct., U.S.	B4	100
West Slope, Or., U.S.	g12	130
West Spanish Peak, mtn., Co., U.S.	D6	99
West Springfield, Ma., U.S.	B2	114
West Springfield, Va., U.S.	g12	139
West Swanzey, N.H., U.S.	E2	122
West Terre Haute, In., U.S.	F3	107
West Thompson Lake, res., Ct., U.S.	B8	100
West Union, Ia., U.S.	B6	108
West Union, Oh., U.S.	D2	128
West Union, W.V., U.S.	B4	141
West Unity, Oh., U.S.	A1	128
West University Place, Tx., U.S.	r14	136
West Valley City, Ut., U.S.	C4	137
West Vancouver, B.C., Can.	f12	85
West Van Lear, Ky., U.S.	C7	110
West View, Pa., U.S.	h13	131
Westville, Il., U.S.	C6	106
Westville, In., U.S.	A4	107
Westville, N.H., U.S.	E4	122
Westville, N.J., U.S.	D2	123
Westville, Ok., U.S.	A7	129
Westville Lake, res., Ma., U.S.	B3	114
West Virginia, state, U.S.	C4	141
West Walker, stm., U.S.	E2	121
West Wareham, Ma., U.S.	C6	114
West Warwick, R.I., U.S.	D3	132
Westwego, La., U.S.	k11	111
Westwood, Ca., U.S.	B3	98
Westwood, Ks., U.S.	k16	109
Westwood, Ky., U.S.	B7	110
Westwood, Ma., U.S.	B5	114
Westwood, N.J., U.S.	B4	123
Westwood Lakes, Fl., U.S.	s13	102
West Wyalong, Austl.	G4	62
West Wyoming, Pa., U.S.	n17	131
West Yarmouth, Ma., U.S.	C7	114
West Yellowstone, Mt., U.S.	F5	119
West York, Pa., U.S.	G8	131
Wetar, Pulau, i., Indon.	E7	36
Wetar, Selat, strt., Indon.	E7	36
Wetaskiwin, Ab., Can.	C4	84
Wete, Tan.	D7	54
Wethersfield, Ct., U.S.	C5	100
Wet Mountains, mts., Co., U.S.	C5	99
Wetumka, Ok., U.S.	B5	129
Wetumpka, Al., U.S.	C3	94
Wetzel, co., W.V., U.S.	B4	141
Wetzlar, Ger.	E11	12
Wewahitchka, Fl., U.S.	B1	102
Wewak, Pap. N. Gui.	G11	32
Wewoka, Ok., U.S.	B5	129
Wexford, Ire.	D3	12
Wexford, co., Mi., U.S.	D5	115
Weyauwega, Wi., U.S.	D5	142
Weymouth, Eng., U.K.	E5	12
Weymouth, Ma., U.S.	B6	114
Whakatane, N.Z.	o14	63c
Whaleysville, Md., U.S.	D7	113
Whangarei, N.Z.	o13	63c
Wharton, N.J., U.S.	B3	123
Wharton, Tx., U.S.	E4	136
Wharton, co., Tx., U.S.	E4	136
Wharton Basin	J13	64
What Cheer, Ia., U.S.	C5	108
Whatcom, co., Wa., U.S.	A4	140
Whatcom, Lake, l., Wa., U.S.	A3	140
Wheatfield, In., U.S.	B3	107
Wheatland, Ca., U.S.	C3	98
Wheatland, Ia., U.S.	C7	108
Wheatland, Wy., U.S.	D8	143
Wheatland, co., Mt., U.S.	D7	119
Wheatland Reservoir, res., Wy., U.S.	E7	143
Wheatley, On., Can.	E2	89
Wheaton, Il., U.S.	B5	106
Wheaton, Md., U.S.	B3	113
Wheaton, Mn., U.S.	E2	116
Wheaton, Mo., U.S.	E3	118
Wheat Ridge, Co., U.S.	B5	99
Wheelbarrow Peak, mtn., Nv., U.S.	F5	121
Wheeler, Ms., U.S.	A5	117
Wheeler, Tx., U.S.	B2	136
Wheeler, co., Ga., U.S.	D4	103
Wheeler, co., Ne., U.S.	C7	120
Wheeler, co., Or., U.S.	C6	130
Wheeler, co., Tx., U.S.	B2	136
Wheeler Air Force Base, mil., Hi., U.S.	g9	104
Wheeler Lake, res., Al., U.S.	A2	94
Wheeler Peak, mtn., Ca., U.S.	C4	98
Wheeler Peak, mtn., N.M., U.S.	A4	124
Wheeler Peak, mtn., Nv., U.S.	E7	121
Wheelersburg, Oh., U.S.	D3	128
Wheeling, Il., U.S.	h9	106
Wheeling, W.V., U.S.	A4	141
Wheeling Creek, stm., W.V., U.S.	f8	141

Name	Map Ref.	Page

Wheelwright, Ky., U.S......C7 110
Whetstone, stm., U.S.....E2 116
Whidbey Island, i., Wa., U.S........A3 140
Whidbey Island Naval Air Station, mil., Wa., U.S. A3 140
Whigham, Ga., U.S......F2 103
Whiskey Peak, mtn., Wy., U.S........D5 143
Whiskeytown-Shasta-Trinity National Recreation Area, Ca., U.S.....B2 98
Whistler, B.C., Can......D6 85
Whitacres, Ct., U.S.....A5 100
Whitakers, N.C., U.S.....A5 126
Whitbourne, Nf., Can.....E5 88
Whitby, On., Can.......D6 89
Whitchurch-Stouffville, On., Can.......D5 89
White, co., Ar., U.S......B4 97
White, co., Ga., U.S......B3 103
White, co., Il., U.S......E5 106
White, co., In., U.S......C4 107
White, co., Tn., U.S......D8 135
White, stm., Ar., U.S.....D5 96
White, stm., In., U.S.....H2 107
White, stm., Mi., U.S.....E4 115
White, stm., Nv., U.S.....E6 121
White, stm., Tx., U.S.....C2 136
White, stm., Vt., U.S.....D4 138
White, stm., Wa., U.S.....B5 140
White, stm., Wa., U.S.....B4 140
White, stm., U.S........C4 97
White, stm., U.S........D5 134
White, stm., U.S........C7 137
White Bay, b., Nf., Can. . . .D3 88
White Bear, stm., Nf., Can. E3 88
White Bear Lake, Mn., U.S. E5 116
White Bluff, Tn., U.S.....A4 135
White Butte, mtn., N.D., U.S........C2 127
White Castle, La., U.S....D4 111
White Center, Wa., U.S. . .e11 140
White City, Or., U.S......E4 130
White Clay Creek, stm., U.S........A3 120
White Cliffs, Austl.......F3 60
White Cliffs, Austl.......G3 62
White Cloud, Mi., U.S.....E5 115
Whitecourt, Ab., Can.....B3 84
White Creek, stm., U.S....E2 138
Whiteday, stm., W.V., U.S. h10 141
White Deer, Tx., U.S.....B2 136
White Earth Indian Reservation, Mn., U.S. .C3 116
White Earth Lake, l., Mn., U.S........C3 116
Whiteface, stm., Mn., U.S. .C6 116
Whiteface Mountain, mtn., N.Y., U.S........f11 125
Whitefield, N.H., U.S.....B3 122
Whitefish, Mt., U.S......B2 119
Whitefish Bay, Wi., U.S. . .m12 142
Whitefish Bay, b., Mi., U.S. B6 115
Whitefish Lake, l., Mn., U.S.D4 116
Whitefish Range, mts., Mt., U.S........B2 119
Whiteford, Md., U.S......A5 113
White Hall, Al., U.S......C3 94
White Hall, Ar., U.S.....C3 97
White Hall, Il., U.S......D3 106
Whitehall, Mi., U.S.......E4 115
Whitehall, Mt., U.S......E4 119
Whitehall, N.Y., U.S......B7 125
Whitehall, Oh., U.S.....m11 128
Whitehall, Wi., U.S......D2 142
Whitehall Reservoir, res., Ma., U.S........h9 114
Whitehaven, Eng., U.K. . . .C5 12
White Haven, Pa., U.S. . . .D10 131
Whitehorn, Point, c., Wa., U.S........A3 140
Whitehorse, Yk., Can.....F13 82
White Horse, N.J., U.S.....C3 123
Whitehouse, Oh., U.S.....A2 128
White House, Tn., U.S.....A5 135
White Island Shores, Ma., U.S........C6 114
White Knob Mountains, mts., Id., U.S......F5 105
White Lake, l., La., U.S.....E3 111
Whiteman Air Force Base, mil., Mo., U.S......C4 118
White Mesa Natural Bridge, Az., U.S........A4 96
White Mountain Peak, mtn., Ca., U.S........D4 98
White Mountains, mts., N.H., U.S........B3 122
White Mountains, mts., U.S. D4 98
Whitemouth, stm., Mb., Can........E4 86
Whitemouth Lake, l., Mb., Can........E4 86
White Nile see Abyad, Al-Bahr al-, stm., Sudan . H11 48
White Oak, Oh., U.S. . . .o12 128
Whiteoak Creek, stm., Oh., U.S........D2 128
Whiteoak Creek, stm., Tn., U.S........A4 135
White Oak Lake, res., Ar., U.S........D2 97
White Pigeon, Mi., U.S. . .G5 115
White Pine, Mi., U.S. . . .m12 115

White Pine, Tn., U.S......C10 135
White Pine, co., Nv., U.S. . .D6 121
White Plains, Md., U.S.....C4 113
White Plains, N.Y., U.S.....D7 125
Whiteriver, Az., U.S......D6 96
White River Junction, Vt., U.S........D4 138
White Rock, B.C., Can. . . .E6 85
White Russia see Belarus, ctry., Eur.........C9 20
White Salmon, Wa., U.S....D4 140
White Salmon, stm., Wa., U.S........D4 140
White Sands Missile Range, mil., N.M., U.S.....E3 124
White Sands National Monument, N.M., U.S. E3 124
Whitesboro, N.Y., U.S.....B5 125
Whitesboro, Tx., U.S......C4 136
Whitesburg, Ga., U.S......C2 103
Whitesburg, Ky., U.S......C7 110
Whites Creek, stm., Tn., U.S........g10 135
White Sea see Beloe more, Russia........C5 26
Whiteside, co., Il., U.S....B3 106
White Sulphur Springs, Mt., U.S........D6 119
White Sulphur Springs, W.V., U.S.......D4 141
Whitesville, Ky., U.S.....C3 110
White Swan, Wa., U.S. . . .C5 140
White Tank Mountains, mts., Az., U.S......k7 96
Whiteville, N.C., U.S.....C4 126
Whiteville, Tn., U.S......B2 135
White Volta, stm., Afr.....E4 50
Whitewater, Ks., U.S......E6 109
Whitewater, Wi., U.S......F5 142
Whitewater, stm., Ks., U.S. E6 109
Whitewater, stm., U.S.....F7 107
Whitewater Baldy, mtn., N.M., U.S........D1 124
Whitewater Bay, b., Fl., U.S.G6 102
Whitewood, S.D., U.S.....C2 134
Whitewright, Tx., U.S.....C4 136
Whitfield, co., Ga., U.S....B2 103
Whitfield Estates, Fl., U.S. .q10 102
Whiting, Ia., U.S........B1 108
Whiting, In., U.S........A3 107
Whiting, Wi., U.S........D4 142
Whiting Field Naval Air Station, mil., Fl., U.S. .u14 102
Whitinsville, Ma., U.S.....B4 114
Whitley, co., In., U.S......B6 107
Whitley, co., Ky., U.S.....D5 110
Whitley City, Ky., U.S.....D5 110
Whitman, Ma., U.S.......B6 114
Whitman, W.V., U.S......D2 141
Whitman, co., Wa., U.S....B8 140
Whitman Square, N.J., U.S. D2 123
Whitmire, S.C., U.S......B4 133
Whitmore Lake, Mi., U.S. . .p14 115
Whitmore Mountains, mts., Ant........E31 67
Whitmore Village, Hi., U.S. f9 104
Whitney, S.C., U.S......B4 133
Whitney, Tx., U.S.......D4 136
Whitney, Lake, res., Tx., U.S........D4 136
Whitney, Mount, mtn., Ca., U.S........D4 98
Whitney Point Lake, res., N.Y., U.S........C5 125
Whitsunday Island, i., Austl. E4 62
Whittier, Ak., U.S.......C10 95
Whittier, Ca., U.S.......F4 98
Whitwell, Tn., U.S.......D8 135
Whyalla, Austl........G2 62
Wiarton, On., Can......C3 89
Wibaux, Mt., U.S.......D12 119
Wibaux, co., Mt., U.S.....D12 119
Wichita, Ks., U.S........E6 109
Wichita, co., Tx., U.S.....B3 136
Wichita Falls, Tx., U.S....C3 136
Wichita Mountains, mts., Ok., U.S........C3 129
Wick, Scot., U.K........A5 12
Wickenburg, Az., U.S.....D3 96
Wickham, Austl.......E2 60
Wickham, Cape, c., Austl. .H3 62
Wickiup Reservoir, res., Or., U.S........E5 130
Wickliffe, Ky., U.S......f8 110
Wickliffe, Oh., U.S......A4 128
Wicklow, Ire.........D3 12
Wicomico, co., Md., U.S. . .D6 113
Wicomico, stm., Md., U.S. .D6 113
Wiconisco, Pa., U.S......E8 131
Widefield, Co., U.S......C6 99
Widgiemooltha, Austl.....G3 60
Wieluń, Pol.........D5 20
Wien, Aus.........F15 12
Wiener Neustadt, Aus.....G15 12
Wieprz, stm., Pol.......D7 20
Wiesbaden, Ger.......E11 12
Wiggins, Ms., U.S.......E4 117
Wiggins Peak, mtn., Wy., U.S........C3 143
Wight, Isle of, i., Eng., U.K. E6 12
Wikwemikong, On., Can. . .B3 89
Wilbarger, co., Tx., U.S....B3 136
Wilber, Ne., U.S........D9 120
Wilberforce, Oh., U.S.....C2 128

Wilbraham, Ma., U.S......B3 114
Wilbur, Wa., U.S........B7 140
Wilburton, Ok., U.S......C6 129
Wilcannia, Austl........G3 62
Wilcox, Pa., U.S........C4 131
Wilcox, co., Al., U.S......D2 94
Wilcox, co., Ga., U.S......E3 103
Wild, stm., U.S........B4 122
Wild Ammonoosuc, stm., N.H., U.S........B3 122
Wild Branch, stm., Vt., U.S. B4 138
Wilder, Id., U.S........F2 105
Wilder, Vt., U.S........D4 138
Wilder Dam, U.S........C2 122
Wildhorse Creek, stm., Ok., U.S........C4 129
Wild Horse Reservoir, res., Nv., U.S........B6 121
Wildorado, Tx., U.S......B1 136
Wild Rice, stm., Mn., U.S. . .C2 116
Wild Rice, stm., N.D., U.S. . C8 127
Wildwood, Fl., U.S......D4 102
Wildwood, N.J., U.S......F3 123
Wildwood Crest, N.J., U.S. .F3 123
Wilhelm, Mount, mtn., Pap. N. Gui........H12 32
Wilhelmina Peak see Trikora, Puncak, mtn., Indon........G10 32
Wilhelmshaven, Ger......D10 12
Wilkes, co., Ga., U.S......C4 103
Wilkes, co., N.C., U.S.....A1 126
Wilkes-Barre, Pa., U.S.....D10 131
Wilkes Land, reg., Ant.....D16 67
Wilkesboro, N.C., U.S.....A1 126
Wilkin, co., Mn., U.S......D2 116
Wilkinsburg, Pa., U.S.....F2 131
Wilkinson, W.V., U.S.....D3 141
Wilkinson, co., Ga., U.S. . .D3 103
Wilkinson, co., Ms., U.S. . .D2 117
Will, co., Il., U.S.......B6 106
Willacoochee, Ga., U.S....E3 103
Willacy, co., Tx., U.S......F4 136
Willamette, stm., Or., U.S. .C3 130
Willamette Pass, Or., U.S. . D4 130
Willamina, Or., U.S......B3 130
Willapa Bay, b., Wa., U.S. . C1 140
Willard, Mo., U.S.......D4 118
Willard, Oh., U.S.......A3 128
Willard, Ut., U.S........B3 137
Willard Bay, b., Ut., U.S....B3 137
Willards, Md., U.S.......D7 113
Willard Stream, stm., Vt., U.S........B5 138
Willcox, Az., U.S.......E6 96
Willcox Playa, l., Az., U.S. . E5 96
Willemstad, Neth. Ant. . . .C6 80
William Bill Dannelly Reservoir, res., Al., U.S. C2 94
Williams, Az., U.S.......B3 96
Williams, Ca., U.S.......C2 98
Williams, co., N.D., U.S. . . .A2 127
Williams, co., Oh., U.S. . . .A1 128
Williams, stm., Vt., U.S....E3 138
Williams, stm., W.V., U.S. . .C4 141
Williams Bay, Wi., U.S.....F5 142
Williamsburg, Ia., U.S.....C5 108
Williamsburg, In., U.S.....E8 107
Williamsburg, Ky., U.S.....D5 110
Williamsburg, Oh., U.S.....C1 128
Williamsburg, Pa., U.S.....F5 131
Williamsburg, Va., U.S.....C6 139
Williamsburg, co., S.C., U.S.D8 133
Williams Fork, stm., Co., U.S........A3 99
Williams Lake, B.C., Can. . C6 85
Williamson, N.Y., U.S.....B3 125
Williamson, W.V., U.S.....D2 141
Williamson, co., Il., U.S....F4 106
Williamson, co., Tn., U.S. . .B5 135
Williamson, co., Tx., U.S. . .D4 136
Williamsport, In., U.S.....D3 107
Williamsport, Md., U.S.....A2 113
Williamsport, Pa., U.S.....D7 131
Williamston, Mi., U.S.....F6 115
Williamston, N.C., U.S.....B5 126
Williamston, S.C., U.S.....B3 133
Williamstown, Ky., U.S....B5 110
Williamstown, Ma., U.S....A1 114
Williamstown, N.J., U.S. . . .D3 123
Williamstown, Pa., U.S....E8 131
Williamstown, Vt., U.S....C3 138
Williamstown, W.V., U.S. . .B3 141
Williamsville, Il., U.S......D4 106
Williamsville, N.Y., U.S....C2 125
Willimantic, Ct., U.S......C7 100
Willimantic, stm., Ct., U.S. .B6 100
Willimantic Reservoir, res., Ct., U.S........C7 100
Willingboro, N.J., U.S.....C3 123
Willis, Tx., U.S........D5 136
Willis Group, is., Austl.....D5 62
Williston, S. Afr........E3 56
Williston, Fl., U.S.......C4 102
Williston, N.D., U.S......A2 127
Williston, S.C., U.S......E5 133
Williston Lake, res., B.C., Can........B6 85
Willits, Ca., U.S........C2 98
Willmar, Mn., U.S.......E3 116
Willoughby, Oh., U.S.....A4 128
Willoughby, Lake, l., Vt., U.S........B4 138
Willoughby Hills, Oh., U.S. A4 128
Willow, Ak., U.S........g17 95

Willow Creek, stm., Nv., U.S........E5 121
Willow Creek, stm., Ut., U.S........D6 137
Willow Creek, stm., Wy., U.S........C6 143
Willow Grove Naval Air Station, mil., Pa., U.S. F11 131
Willowick, Oh., U.S......A4 128
Willowmore, S. Afr......E3 56
Willow Reservoir, res., Wi., U.S........C3 142
Willow Run, De., U.S.....i7 101
Willow Run, Mi., U.S.....p14 115
Willows, Ca., U.S.......C2 98
Willow Springs, Il., U.S....k9 106
Willow Springs, Mo., U.S. . E6 118
Wilmar, Ar., U.S........D4 97
Wilmerding, Pa., U.S.....k14 131
Wilmette, Il., U.S.......A6 106
Wilmington, De., U.S......B3 101
Wilmington, Il., U.S......B5 106
Wilmington, Ma., U.S.....A5 114
Wilmington, N.C., U.S.....C5 126
Wilmington, Oh., U.S.....C2 128
Wilmington, Vt., U.S......F3 138
Wilmington Manor, De., U.S........i7 101
Wilmore, Ky., U.S.......C5 110
Wilmot, Ar., U.S........D4 97
Wilson, Ar., U.S........B5 97
Wilson, Ks., U.S........D5 109
Wilson, La., U.S........D4 111
Wilson, N.C., U.S.......B5 126
Wilson, Ok., U.S........C4 129
Wilson, Pa., U.S........E11 131
Wilson, Wy., U.S........C2 143
Wilson, co., Ks., U.S......E8 109
Wilson, co., N.C., U.S.....B5 126
Wilson, co., Tn., U.S......A5 135
Wilson, co., Tx., U.S......E3 136
Wilson, Mount, mtn., Az., U.S........B1 96
Wilson, Mount, mtn., Ca., U.S........m12 98
Wilson, Mount, mtn., Co., U.S........D2 99
Wilson, Mount, mtn., Nv., U.S........E7 121
Wilson, Mount, mtn., Or., U.S........B5 130
Wilson Creek, stm., Wa., U.S........B5 140
Wilson Creek, stm., Wa., U.S........B6 140
Wilson Lake, res., Al., U.S. A2 94
Wilson Lake, res., Ks., U.S. D4 109
Wilsons Beach, N.B., Can. . E3 87
Wilsons Promontory, pen., Austl........H4 62
Wilsonville, Al., U.S......B3 94
Wilsonville, Or., U.S.....h12 130
Wilton, Al., U.S........B3 94
Wilton, Ct., U.S........E2 100
Wilton, Ia., U.S........C6 108
Wilton, Me., U.S........D2 112
Wilton, N.D., U.S.......B5 127
Wilton, N.H., U.S.......E3 122
Wiluna, Austl.........F3 60
Wimauma, Fl., U.S......E4 102
Wimico, Lake, l., Fl., U.S. . .C1 102
Winamac, In., U.S.......B4 107
Winburg, S. Afr........D4 56
Wincheck Pond, l., R.I., U.S........E1 132
Winchendon, Ma., U.S....A3 114
Winchester, On., Can.....B9 89
Winchester, Eng., U.K.....E6 12
Winchester, Il., U.S......D3 106
Winchester, In., U.S......D8 107
Winchester, Ks., U.S.....k15 109
Winchester, Ky., U.S.....C5 110
Winchester, Ma., U.S.....g11 114
Winchester, N.H., U.S.....E2 122
Winchester, Nv., U.S.....G6 121
Winchester, Oh., U.S.....D2 128
Winchester, Tn., U.S.....B5 135
Winchester, Va., U.S.....A4 139
Winchester Bay, Or., U.S. . D2 130
Wind, stm., Wa., U.S.....D4 140
Wind, stm., Wy., U.S.....C4 143
Windber, Pa., U.S.......F4 131
Wind Cave National Park, S.D., U.S........D2 134
Winder, Ga., U.S.......C3 103
Windfall, In., U.S.......D6 107
Windgap, Pa., U.S......E11 131
Windham, Ct., U.S......C7 100
Windham, Oh., U.S......A4 128
Windham, co., Ct., U.S....B7 100
Windham, co., Vt., U.S....F3 138
Windhoek, Nmb.......C2 56
Wind Lake, Wi., U.S......F5 142
Wind Lake, l., Wi., U.S.....n11 142
Windmill Point, c., Va., U.S.C6 139
Windom, Mn., U.S......G3 116
Windom Peak, mtn., Co., U.S........D3 99
Window Rock, Az., U.S....B6 96
Wind Point, Wi., U.S.....n12 142
Wind River Indian Reservation, Wy., U.S. C4 143
Wind River Peak, mtn., Wy., U.S........D3 143

Wind River Range, mts., Wy., U.S........C3 143
Windsor (part of Grand Falls-Windsor), Nf., Can........D4 88
Windsor, On., Can......E1 89
Windsor, P.Q., Can......D5 90
Windsor, Co., U.S.......A6 99
Windsor, Ct., U.S.......B5 100
Windsor, Il., U.S........D5 106
Windsor, Mo., U.S.......C4 118
Windsor, N.C., U.S......A6 126
Windsor, Pa., U.S.......G8 131
Windsor, Va., U.S.......D6 139
Windsor, Vt., U.S.......E4 138
Windsor, co., Vt., U.S.....D3 138
Windsor Heights, Ia., U.S. . e8 108
Windsor Locks, Ct., U.S....B5 100
Windward Islands, is., N.A. F12 76
Windward Passage, strt., N.A........E10 76
Windy Hill, S.C., U.S......C8 133
Windy Peak, mtn., Wa., U.S........A6 140
Winefred Lake, l., Ab., Can. B5 84
Winfield, Al., U.S.......B2 94
Winfield, Ia., U.S.......C6 108
Winfield, Ks., U.S.......E7 109
Winfield, Mo., U.S.......C7 118
Winfield, W.V., U.S......C3 141
Wing, stm., Mn., U.S......D3 116
Wingate, N.C., U.S......C2 126
Wingham, On., Can......D3 89
Winifrede, W.V., U.S.....m12 141
Winisk, stm., On., Can.....n18 91
Wink, Tx., U.S.........D1 136
Winkelman, Az., U.S.....E5 96
Winkler, Mb., Can......E3 86
Winkler, co., Tx., U.S.....D1 136
Winlock, Wa., U.S......C3 140
Winn, co., La., U.S......C3 111
Winneba, Ghana.......E4 50
Winnebago, Il., U.S......A4 106
Winnebago, Mn., U.S.....G4 116
Winnebago, Ne., U.S.....B9 120
Winnebago, Wi., U.S.....h8 142
Winnebago, co., Ia., U.S. . .A4 108
Winnebago, co., Il., U.S. . . .A4 106
Winnebago, co., Wi., U.S. . .D5 142
Winnebago, stm., Ia., U.S. . A4 108
Winnebago, Lake, l., Wi., U.S........E5 142
Winnebago Indian Reservation, Ne., U.S. .B9 120
Winneconne, Wi., U.S.....D5 142
Winnemucca, Nv., U.S....C4 121
Winnemucca Lake, l., Nv., U.S........C2 121
Winner, S.D., U.S.......D6 134
Winneshiek, co., Ia., U.S. . .A6 108
Winnetka, Il., U.S.......A6 106
Winnfield, La., U.S......C3 111
Winnibigoshish, Lake, l., Mn., U.S........C4 116
Winnipeg, Mb., Can......E3 86
Winnipeg, stm., Can......D4 86
Winnipeg, Lake, l., Mb., Can........C3 86
Winnipeg Beach, Mb., Can. D3 86
Winnipegosis, Mb., Can. . .D2 86
Winnipegosis, Lake, l., Mb., Can........C2 86
Winnipesaukee, Lake, l., N.H., U.S........C4 122
Winnisquam, N.H., U.S....C3 122
Winnisquam Lake, l., N.H., U.S........C3 122
Winnsboro, La., U.S......B4 111
Winnsboro, S.C., U.S.....C5 133
Winnsboro, Tx., U.S......C5 136
Winnsboro Mills, S.C., U.S. C5 133
Winona, Mn., U.S.......F7 116
Winona, Mo., U.S.......D6 118
Winona, Ms., U.S.......B4 117
Winona, co., Mn., U.S.....F7 116
Winona Lake, In., U.S.....B6 107
Winona Lake, l., Vt., U.S. . .C2 138
Winooski, Vt., U.S.......C2 138
Winooski, stm., Vt., U.S. . .C3 138
Winslow, Az., U.S.......C5 96
Winslow, In., U.S.......H3 107
Winslow, Me., U.S......D3 112
Winsted, Ct., U.S.......B3 100
Winsted, Mn., U.S.......F4 116
Winston, Fl., U.S........D4 102
Winston, Or., U.S.......D3 130
Winston, co., Al., U.S.....A2 94
Winston, co., Ms., U.S....B4 117
Winston-Salem, N.C., U.S. .A2 126
Winter Garden, Fl., U.S....D5 102
Winter Harbor, Me., U.S. . .D4 112
Winter Haven, Fl., U.S.....D5 102
Winter Park, Fl., U.S......D5 102
Winter Park, N.C., U.S....C5 126
Winterport, Me., U.S.....D4 112
Winter Ridge, mtn., Or., U.S........E6 130
Winters, Ca., U.S.......C2 98
Winters, Tx., U.S.......D3 136
Winterset, Ia., U.S......C4 108
Wintersville, Oh., U.S.....B5 128
Winterthur, Switz.......G11 12
Winterton, Nf., Can......E5 88
Winterville, Ga., U.S......C3 103
Winterville, N.C., U.S.....B5 126

Name — Map Ref. — Page

Winthrop, Ia., U.S. B6 108
Winthrop, Ma., U.S. B6 114
Winthrop, Me., U.S. D3 112
Winthrop, Mn., U.S. F4 116
Winthrop, Lake, l., Ma., U.S. h10 114
Winthrop Harbor, Il., U.S. A6 106
Wintinna, Austl. F5 60
Winton, Austl. E3 62
Winton, N.Z. q12 63c
Winton, N.C., U.S. A6 126
Winton Lake, res., Oh., U.S. o12 129
Winyah Bay, b., S.C., U.S. E9 133
Wirt, co., W.V., U.S. B3 141
Wiscasset, Me., U.S. D3 112
Wisconsin, state, U.S. D4 142
Wisconsin, stm., Wi., U.S. E3 142
Wisconsin, Lake, res., Wi., U.S. E4 142
Wisconsin Dells, Wi., U.S. E4 142
Wisconsin Rapids, Wi., U.S. D4 142
Wise, Va., U.S. f9 139
Wise, co., Tx., U.S. C4 136
Wise, co., Va., U.S. e9 139
Wishek, N.D., U.S. C6 127
Wishram, Wa., U.S. D4 140
Wisła, stm., Pol. C5 20
Wismar, Ger. D12 12
Wisner, La., U.S. C4 111
Wisner, Ne., U.S. C9 120
Wissota, Lake, res., Wi., U.S. D2 142
Wister, Ok., U.S. C7 129
Wister Lake, res., Ok., U.S. C7 129
Witbank, S. Afr. D4 56
Withamsville, Oh., U.S. C1 128
Witherspoon, Mount, mtn., Ak., U.S. g18 95
Withlacoochee, stm., Fl., U.S. C4 102
Withlacoochee, stm., U.S. B3 102
Witless Bay, Nf., Can. E5 88
Witt, Il., U.S. D4 106
Wittenberg, Wi., U.S. D4 142
Wittenberge, Ger. D12 12
Wittenoom, Austl. E2 60
Wittlich, Ger. E10 12
Wittman, Md., U.S. C5 113
Wittmann, Az., U.S. D3 96
Witu Islands, is., Pap. N. Gui. G12 32
Wixom, Mi., U.S. o14 115
Wixom Lake, res., Mi., U.S. E6 115
Włocławek, Pol. C5 20
Woburn, Ma., U.S. B5 114
Wodonga, Austl. H4 62
Wokam, Pulau, i., Indon. H9 32
Wolcott, Ct., U.S. C4 100
Wolcott, In., U.S. C3 107
Wolcottville, In., U.S. A7 107
Woleai, atoll, Micron. D8 58
Wolf, stm., Ms., U.S. E4 117
Wolf, stm., Tn., U.S. e9 135
Wolf, stm., Wi., U.S. C5 142
Wolf, Volcán, vol., Ec. C1 70
Wolf Creek, Or., U.S. E3 130
Wolf Creek, stm., W.V., U.S. m13 141
Wolf Creek, stm., U.S. A2 129
Wolf Creek Pass, Co., U.S. D3 99
Wolfe, co., Ky., U.S. C6 110
Wolfeboro, N.H., U.S. C4 122
Wolfeboro Falls, N.H., U.S. C4 122
Wolfe City, Tx., U.S. C4 136
Wolfen, Ger. E13 12
Wolf Lake, Mi., U.S. E4 115
Wolf Lake, l., Il., U.S. k9 106
Wolf Mountain, mtn., Ak., U.S. B9 95
Wolf Point, Mt., U.S. B11 119
Wolfsberg, Aus. G14 12
Wolfsburg, Ger. D12 12
Wolf Swamp, sw., N.C., U.S. C5 126
Wollaston, Islas, is., Chile I3 69
Wollaston Lake, l., Sk., Can. m8 91
Wollongong, Austl. G5 62
Wolmaransstad, S. Afr. D4 56
Wolverhampton, Eng., U.K. D5 12
Woman Lake, l., Mn., U.S. D4 116
Womelsdorf, Pa., U.S. F9 131
Wonder Lake, Il., U.S. A5 106
Wondinong, Austl. F2 60
Wonewoc, Wi., U.S. E3 142
Wŏnsan, N. Kor. D13 28
Wonthaggi, Austl. H4 62
Wood, co., Oh., U.S. A2 128
Wood, co., Tx., U.S. C5 136
Wood, co., W.V., U.S. B3 141
Wood, co., Wi., U.S. D3 142
Wood, stm., Sk., Can. H2 91
Wood, stm., R.I., U.S. F2 132
Wood, stm., Wy., U.S. C3 143
Wood, Mount, mtn., Mt., U.S. E7 119
Woodall Mountain, mtn., Ms., U.S. A5 117
Woodbine, Ga., U.S. F5 103
Woodbine, Ia., U.S. C2 108
Woodbine, Ky., U.S. D5 110
Woodbine, N.J., U.S. E3 123
Woodbridge, Ct., U.S. D3 100
Woodbridge, Va., U.S. B5 139
Woodbridge [Township], N.J., U.S. B4 123
Woodburn, In., U.S. B8 107
Woodburn, Or., U.S. B4 130
Woodbury, Ct., U.S. C3 100
Woodbury, Ga., U.S. D2 103
Woodbury, Mn., U.S. F6 116
Woodbury, N.J., U.S. D2 123
Woodbury, Tn., U.S. B5 135
Woodbury, co., Ia., U.S. B1 108
Woodcliff Lake, N.J., U.S. g8 123
Woodcliff Lake, l., N.J., U.S. g8 123
Wood Dale, Il., U.S. k9 106
Wood End, spit, Ma., U.S. B7 114
Woodfield, S.C., U.S. C6 133
Woodford, co., Il., U.S. C4 106
Woodford, co., Ky., U.S. B5 110
Woodhull, Il., U.S. B3 106
Woodlake, Ca., U.S. D4 98
Woodland, Ca., U.S. C3 98
Woodland, Me., U.S. C5 112
Woodland, N.C., U.S. A5 126
Woodland, Wa., U.S. D3 140
Woodland Acres, Co., U.S. D6 99
Woodland Park, Co., U.S. C5 99
Woodlawn, Ky., U.S. e9 110
Woodlawn, Md., U.S. g10 113
Woodlawn, Oh., U.S. n13 128
Woodlawn, Va., U.S. D2 139
Woodmont, Ct., U.S. E4 100
Woodmoor, Md., U.S. B4 113
Woodridge, Il., U.S. k8 106
Wood-Ridge, N.J., U.S. h8 123
Wood River, Il., U.S. E3 106
Wood River, Ne., U.S. D7 120
Woodroffe, Mount, mtn., Austl. F5 60
Woodruff, S.C., U.S. B3 133
Woodruff, Wi., U.S. C4 142
Woodruff, co., Ar., U.S. B4 97
Woods, co., Ok., U.S. A3 129
Woods, Lake, res., Tn., U.S. B5 135
Woods, Lake of the, l., N.A. B9 92
Woodsboro, Tx., U.S. E4 136
Woods Cross, Ut., U.S. C4 137
Woodsfield, Oh., U.S. C4 128
Woods Hole, Ma., U.S. C6 114
Woodson, Ar., U.S. C3 97
Woodson, co., Ks., U.S. E8 109
Woodstock, N.B., Can. C2 87
Woodstock, On., Can. D4 89
Woodstock, Ga., U.S. B2 103
Woodstock, Il., U.S. A5 106
Woodstock, Md., U.S. B4 113
Woodstock, N.Y., U.S. C6 125
Woodstock, Va., U.S. B4 139
Woodstock, Vt., U.S. D3 138
Woodstown, N.J., U.S. D2 123
Woodsville, N.H., U.S. B2 122
Woodville, Fl., U.S. B2 102
Woodville, Ms., U.S. D2 117
Woodville, Oh., U.S. A2 128
Woodville, Tx., U.S. D5 136
Woodville, Wi., U.S. D1 142
Woodward, Ia., U.S. C4 108
Woodward, Ok., U.S. A2 129
Woodward, co., Ok., U.S. A2 129
Woodworth, La., U.S. C3 111
Woolmarket, Ms., U.S. E5 117
Woolrich, Pa., U.S. D7 131
Woolsey Peak, mtn., Az., U.S. D3 96
Woomera, Austl. G2 62
Woonsocket, R.I., U.S. A3 132
Woonsocket, S.D., U.S. C7 134
Woonsocket Reservoir Number Three, res., R.I., U.S. B3 132
Wooster, Oh., U.S. B4 128
Worcester, S. Afr. E2 56
Worcester, Eng., U.K. D5 12
Worcester, Ma., U.S. B4 114
Worcester, co., Ma., U.S. A3 114
Worcester, co., Md., U.S. D7 113
Worden, Il., U.S. E4 106
Worden Pond, l., R.I., U.S. F3 132
Worland, Wy., U.S. B5 143
Worms, Ger. F11 12
Worth, Il., U.S. k9 106
Worth, co., Ga., U.S. E3 103
Worth, co., Ia., U.S. A4 108
Worth, co., Mo., U.S. A3 118
Worthing, Eng., U.K. E6 12
Worthington, In., U.S. F4 107
Worthington, Ky., U.S. B7 110
Worthington, Mn., U.S. G3 116
Worthington, Oh., U.S. B2 128
Worthington Peak, mtn., Nv., U.S. F6 121
Wosu, Indon. D6 36
Wour, Chad B8 50
Wowoni, Pulau, i., Indon. D6 36
Woy Woy, Austl. G5 62
Wrangel Island see Vrangelja, ostrov, i., Russia B20 26
Wrangell, Ak., U.S. D13 95
Wrangell, Cape, c., Ak., U.S. E2 95
Wrangell, Mount, mtn., Ak., U.S. f19 95
Wrangell Island, i., Ak., U.S. m24 95
Wrangell Mountains, mts., Ak., U.S. C11 95
Wrangell-Saint Elias National Park, Ak., U.S. C11 95
Wrath, Cape, c., Scot., U.K. A4 12
Wray, Co., U.S. A8 99
Wrens, Ga., U.S. C4 103
Wrentham, Ma., U.S. B5 114
Wrexham, Wales, U.K. D5 12
Wright, co., Ia., U.S. B4 108
Wright, co., Mn., U.S. E4 116
Wright, co., Mo., U.S. D5 118
Wright, Mount, mtn., Mt., U.S. C4 119
Wright Brothers National Memorial, hist., N.C., U.S. A7 126
Wright City, Mo., U.S. C8 118
Wright City, Ok., U.S. C6 129
Wright Patman Lake, res., Tx., U.S. A6 78
Wright-Patterson Air Force Base, mil., Oh., U.S. C1 128
Wrightson, Mount, mtn., Az., U.S. F5 96
Wrightstown, N.J., U.S. C3 123
Wrightstown, Wi., U.S. D5 142
Wrightsville, Ar., U.S. C3 97
Wrightsville, Ga., U.S. D4 103
Wrightsville, Pa., U.S. F8 131
Wrightsville Beach, N.C., U.S. C5 126
Wrightsville Reservoir, res., Vt., U.S. C3 138
Wrocław, Pol. D4 20
Wu, stm., China F9 28
Wuchuan, China E3 30
Wuchuan, China A3 30
Wuda, China B2 30
Wudaoliang, China D6 28
Wudi, China B4 30
Wuding, China A4 34
Wudu, China E8 28
Wugang, China F10 28
Wuhai, China D9 28
Wuhan, China E10 28
Wuhe, China C4 30
Wuhu, China E11 28
Wüjang, China E3 28
Wukari, Nig. E6 50
Wuliang Shan, mts., China G8 28
Wuming, China B5 34
Wupatki National Monument, Az., U.S. B4 96
Wuppertal, Ger. E10 12
Wuqi, China B2 30
Wuqing, China B4 30
Wurno, Nig. D6 50
Würzburg, Ger. F12 12
Wushan, China C2 30
Wushenqi, China D9 28
Wusuli (Ussuri), stm., Asia E15 26
Wutai Shan, mtn., China D10 28
Wutongqiao, China F8 28
Wuvulu Island, i., Pap. N. Gui. G11 32
Wuwei, China D8 28
Wuwei, China C4 30
Wuxi, China E12 28
Wuyi Shan, mts., China F11 28
Wuyuan, China C9 28
Wuzhi Shan, mtn., China H9 28
Wuzhong, China D9 28
Wuzhou, China G10 28
Wyaconda, stm., Mo., U.S. A6 118
Wyandot, co., Oh., U.S. B2 128
Wyandotte, Mi., U.S. F7 115
Wyandotte, co., Ks., U.S. C9 109
Wyanet, Il., U.S. B4 106
Wye, stm., U.K. D5 12
Wylie, Lake, res., U.S. A5 133
Wyman Lake, res., Me., U.S. C3 112
Wymore, Ne., U.S. D9 120
Wyndham, Austl. D4 60
Wynndel, B.C., Can. E9 85
Wynne, Ar., U.S. B5 97
Wynnewood, Ok., U.S. C4 129
Wynoochee, stm., Wa., U.S. B2 140
Wyoming, On., Can. E2 89
Wyoming, De., U.S. D3 101
Wyoming, Ia., U.S. B6 108
Wyoming, Il., U.S. B4 106
Wyoming, Mi., U.S. F5 115
Wyoming, Mn., U.S. E6 116
Wyoming, Oh., U.S. o13 128
Wyoming, Pa., U.S. n17 131
Wyoming, R.I., U.S. E2 132
Wyoming, co., N.Y., U.S. C2 125
Wyoming, co., Pa., U.S. D9 131
Wyoming, co., W.V., U.S. D3 141
Wyoming, state, U.S. C5 143
Wyoming Peak, mtn., Wy., U.S. D2 143
Wyoming Range, mts., Wy., U.S. D2 143
Wyomissing, Pa., U.S. F10 131
Wyong, Austl. G5 62
Wysocking Bay, b., N.C., U.S. B7 126
Wythe, co., Va., U.S. D1 139
Wytheville, Va., U.S. D1 139

X

Xaafuun, Raas, c., Som. H15 48
Xaçmaz, Azer. B13 44
Xaidulla, China D3 28
Xainza, China E5 28
Xai-Xai, Moz. D5 56
Xalapa, Mex. D5 78
Xam Nua, Laos B4 34
Xá-Muteba, Ang. E3 54
Xangongo, Ang. B2 56
Xankändi, Azer. C12 44
Xánthi, Grc. D10 18
Xanxerê, Braz. D7 72
Xapuri, Braz. F6 70
Xàtiva, Spain H6 16
Xau, Lake, pl., Bots. C3 56
Xenia, Oh., U.S. C2 128
Xi, stm., China G10 28
Xiachuan Dao, i., China E3 30
Xiamen, China G11 28
Xi'an, China E9 28
Xianfeng, China D2 30
Xiang, stm., China D3 30
Xiangfan, China E10 28
Xianggang (Hong Kong), China E3 30
Xiangkhoang, Laos C4 34
Xiangride, China D7 28
Xiangtan, China F10 28
Xianju, China D5 30
Xianning, China D3 30
Xianyang, China C2 30
Xianyou, China F11 28
Xiaogan, China E10 28
Xiao Hinggan Ling, mts., China A1 31
Xiaojin, China C1 30
Xiapu, China F12 28
Xiayi, China C4 30
Xichang, China F8 28
Xigazê, China F5 28
Ximiao, China C8 28
Xin'anjiang Shuiku, res., China D4 30
Xinavane, Moz. C5 56
Xincai, China C4 30
Xing'an, China F10 28
Xingcheng, China A5 30
Xinghe, China A3 30
Xingren, China D2 30
Xingtai, China D10 28
Xingu, stm., Braz. D9 70
Xingxian, China B3 30
Xingyi, China F8 28
Xinhua, China D3 30
Xining, China D8 28
Xinji, China B4 30
Xinjiang Uygur Zizhiqu (Sinkiang), prov., China C5 28
Xinjin, China C1 30
Xinjin, China B5 30
Xinjiulong (New Kowloon), China E3 30
Xinning, China D3 30
Xinwen, China B4 30
Xinxian, China B3 30
Xinxiang, China D10 28
Xinyang, China E10 28
Xique-Xique, Braz. D3 74
Xisha Qundao (Paracel Islands), is., China C6 34
Xiushan, China D2 30
Xiushui, China D3 30
Xixiang, China C2 30
Xizang Zizhiqu (Tibet), prov., China E5 28
Xuancheng, China E11 28
Xuanhan, China C2 30
Xuanhua, China A4 30
Xuanwei, China D1 30
Xuchang, China E10 28
Xupu, China D3 30
Xuwen, China G10 28
Xuyong, China F9 28
Xuzhou, China E11 28

Y

Yaan, China E8 28
Yablonovy Range see Jablonovyj hrebet, mts., Russia D13 26
Yabrīn, Sau. Ar. F5 42
Yacolt, Wa., U.S. D3 140
Yacuiba, Bol. C5 72
Yādgīr, India F3 40
Yadkin, co., N.C., U.S. A2 126
Yadkin, stm., N.C., U.S. B2 126
Yadkinville, N.C., U.S. A2 126
Yadong, China A1 34
Yafran, Libya E6 14
Yagoua, Cam. A3 54
Yagradagzê Shan, mtn., China D7 28
Yahyalı, Tur. C6 44
Yainax Butte, mtn., Or., U.S. E5 130
Yakima, Wa., U.S. C5 140
Yakima, co., Wa., U.S. C4 140
Yakima, stm., Wa., U.S. C6 140
Yakima Indian Reservation, Wa., U.S. C5 140
Yako, Burkina D4 50
Yakobi Island, i., Ak., U.S. m21 95
Yakoma, D.R.C. C4 54
Yakumo, Japan B3 31
Yaku-shima, i., Japan E14 28
Yakutat, Ak., U.S. D12 95
Yakutat Bay, b., Ak., U.S. D11 95
Yakutia see Jakutija, state, Russia C14 26
Yakutsk see Jakutsk, Russia C14 26
Yakymivka, Ukr. F13 20
Yala, Thai. E4 34
Yale, Mi., U.S. E8 115
Yale, Ok., U.S. A5 129
Yale, Mount, mtn., Co., U.S. C5 99
Yale Lake, res., Wa., U.S. D3 140
Yalgoo, Austl. F2 60
Yalinga, C.A.R. B4 54
Yalobusha, co., Ms., U.S. A4 117
Yalobusha, stm., Ms., U.S. B4 117
Yalong, stm., China E7 28
Yalova, Tur. B3 44
Yalta, Ukr. G13 20
Yalu, stm., Asia C13 28
Yalvaç, Tur. C4 44
Yamachiche, P.Q., Can. C5 90
Yamagata, Japan D16 28
Yamaguchi, Japan D2 31
Yamal Peninsula see Jamal, poluostrov, pen., Russia B8 26
Yambio, Sudan J10 48
Yamdena, Pulau, i., Indon. E8 36
Yamethin, Myan. B3 34
Yamhill, Or., U.S. h11 130
Yamhill, co., Or., U.S. B3 130
Yamoussoukro, C. Iv. E3 50
Yampa, stm., Co., U.S. A2 99
Yampil', Ukr. E10 20
Yamsay Mountain, mtn., Or., U.S. E5 130
Yamuna, stm., India D4 40
Yamunānagar, India C3 40
Yamzho Yumco, l., China F6 28
Yana see Jana, stm., Russia C15 26
Yanam, India F4 40
Yan'an, China D9 28
Yanbuʿ al-Baḥr, Sau. Ar. F3 38
Yancey, co., N.C., U.S. f10 126
Yanceyville, N.C., U.S. A3 126
Yancheng, China E12 28
Yanchi, China D9 28
Yanfolila, Mali D3 50
Yangambi, D.R.C. C4 54
Yangchun, China E3 30
Yanggao, China A3 30
Yangjiang, China G10 28
Yangliuqing, China B4 30
Yangon (Rangoon), Myan. C3 34
Yangquan, China D10 28
Yangshan, China E3 30
Yangshuo, China E3 30
Yangtze see Chang, stm., China E9 28
Yangxian, China C2 30
Yangxin, China D4 30
Yangzhou, China E11 28
Yanji, China C13 28
Yankton, S.D., U.S. E8 134
Yankton, co., S.D., U.S. D8 134
Yanqi, China C5 28
Yantai, China D12 28
Yantic, stm., Ct., U.S. C7 100
Yanting, China C2 30
Yanyuan, China A4 34
Yanzhou, China B4 30
Yaoundé, Cam. C2 54
Yap, i., Micron. E10 32
Yapen, Pulau, i., Indon. G10 32
Yaqui, stm., Mex. B3 78
Yardley, Pa., U.S. F12 131
Yardville, N.J., U.S. C3 123
Yarīm, Yemen H4 38
Yarkand see Shache, China D3 28
Yarkand see Yarkant, stm., China B3 40
Yarkant, stm., China B3 40
Yarloop, Austl. G2 60
Yarmouth, Me., U.S. E2 112
Yarnell, Az., U.S. C3 96
Yaroslavl' see Jaroslavl', Russia D6 26
Yarumal, Col. B4 70
Yass, Austl. G4 62
Yatağan, Tur. D3 44
Yaté, N. Cal. I9 62a
Yates, co., N.Y., U.S. C3 125
Yates Center, Ks., U.S. E8 109
Yates City, Il., U.S. C3 106
Yatsushiro, Japan E14 28
Yatta Plateau, plat., Kenya D7 54
Yavapai, co., Az., U.S. C3 96
Yavarí (Javari), stm., S.A. D5 70
Yavatmāl, India E3 40
Yaví, Cerro, mtn., Ven. B6 70
Yawgoog Pond, l., R.I., U.S. E1 132
Yazd, Iran D6 42
Yazoo, co., Ms., U.S. C3 117
Yazoo, stm., Ms., U.S. C3 117
Yazoo City, Ms., U.S. C3 117
Ye, Myan. C3 34
Yeadon, Pa., U.S. p21 131
Yeagertown, Pa., U.S. E6 131
Yecheng, China D3 28
Yecla, Spain H6 16
Yeeda, Austl. D3 60
Yei, Sudan C6 54
Yélimané, Mali C2 50
Yell, co., Ar., U.S. B2 97
Yellow see Huang, stm., China D11 28
Yellow, stm., In., U.S. B4 107
Yellow, stm., Wi., U.S. C3 142

Name	Map Ref.	Page
Yellow, stm., Wi., U.S.	D3	142
Yellow, stm., U.S.	u15	102
Yellow Creek, stm., Tn., U.S.	A4	135
Yellowhead Pass, Can.	C1	84
Yellowjacket Mountains, mts., Id., U.S.	D4	105
Yellowknife, N.T., Can.	F17	82
Yellow Lake, l., Wi., U.S.	C1	142
Yellow Medicine, co., Mn., U.S.	F2	116
Yellow Sea, Asia	D12	28
Yellow Springs, Oh., U.S.	C2	128
Yellowstone, co., Mt., U.S.	D8	119
Yellowstone, stm., U.S.	D10	119
Yellowstone Lake, l., Wy., U.S.	B2	143
Yellowstone National Park, co., Mt., U.S.	E6	119
Yellowstone National Park, U.S.	B2	143
Yellville, Ar., U.S.	A3	97
Yelm, Wa., U.S.	C3	140
Yemassee, S.C., U.S.	F6	133
Yemen, ctry., Asia	G5	38
Yenagoa, Nig.	F6	50
Yenakiieve, Ukr.	E15	20
Yenangyaung, Myan.	B2	34
Yen Bai, Viet.	B4	34
Yendéré, Burkina	D4	50
Yendi, Ghana	E4	50
Yengisar, China	D3	28
Yenice, stm., Tur.	B5	44
Yenişehir, Tur.	B3	44
Yenisey see Enisej, stm., Russia	C10	26
Yentna, stm., Ak., U.S.	f16	95
Yerevan, Arm.	B11	44
Yerington, Nv., U.S.	E2	121
Yerington Indian Reservation, Nv., U.S.	D2	121
Yerköy, Tur.	C6	44
Yermo, Ca., U.S.	E5	98
Yerupaja, Nevado, mtn., Peru	F4	70
Yerushalayim, Isr.	D3	42
Yeşilhisar, Tur.	C6	44
Yetti, reg., Afr.	A3	50
Yeu, Île d', i., Fr.	D5	16
Yevpatoriia, Ukr.	G12	20
Ygatimí, Para.	C6	72
Yi'an, China	B13	28
Yibin, China	F8	28
Yichang, China	E10	28
Yichuan, China	B3	30
Yichun, China	B13	28
Yichun, China	D3	30
Yidu, China	B4	30
Yidu, China	C3	30
Yilan, China	B13	28
Yıldızeli, Tur.	C7	44
Yiliang, China	G8	28
Yinchuan, China	D9	28
Yingde, China	E3	30
Yingkou, China	C12	28
Yingtan, China	F11	28
Yining, China	C4	28
Yinmabin, Myan.	B2	34
Yirga 'Alem, Eth.	B7	54
Yirol, Sudan	B6	54
Yishan, China	E2	30
Yitulihe, China	A12	28
Yiyang, China	F10	28
Yiyang, China	D4	30
Yizhang, China	D3	30
Yli-Kitka, l., Fin.	C13	10
Yoakum, Tx., U.S.	E4	136
Yoakum, co., Tx., U.S.	C1	136
Yockanookany, stm., Ms., U.S.	C4	117
Yocona, stm., Ms., U.S.	A4	117
Yogyakarta, Indon.	E4	36
Yoho National Park, B.C., Can.	D9	85
Yokadouma, Cam.	C2	54
Yoko, Cam.	B2	54
Yokohama, Japan	D15	28
Yokosuka, Japan	C3	31
Yokote, Japan	C4	31
Yola, Nig.	E7	50
Yolo, co., Ca., U.S.	C2	98
Yom, stm., Thai.	C3	34
Yomba Indian Reservation, Nv., U.S.	D4	121
Yonago, Japan	D14	28
Yoncalla, Or., U.S.	D3	130
Yonezawa, Japan	C3	31
Yong'an, China	F11	28
Yongchang, China	B1	30
Yongchuan, China	D2	30
Yongding, China	E4	30
Yongfeng, China	A7	34
Yongkang, China	D5	30
Yongping, China	A3	34
Yongren, China	F8	28
Yongshan, China	F8	28
Yongxiu, China	D4	30
Yongzhou, China	F10	28
Yonkers, N.Y., U.S.	E7	125
Yonne, stm., Fr.	C8	16
Yopal, Col.	D5	80
Yopurga, China	B3	40
York, Austl.	G2	60
York, On., Can.	D5	89
York, Eng., U.K.	C6	12
York, Al., U.S.	C1	94
York, Me., U.S.	E2	112
York, Ne., U.S.	D8	120
York, Pa., U.S.	G8	131
York, S.C., U.S.	B5	133
York, co., Me., U.S.	E2	112
York, co., Ne., U.S.	D8	120
York, co., Pa., U.S.	G8	131
York, co., S.C., U.S.	A5	133
York, co., Va., U.S.	C6	139
York, stm., On., Can.	B7	89
York, stm., Va., U.S.	C6	139
York, Cape, c., Austl.	C3	62
York, Kap, c., Grnld.	C26	82
York Harbor, Me., U.S.	E2	112
Yorke Peninsula, pen., Austl.	G2	62
Yorklyn, De., U.S.	A3	101
Yorktown, In., U.S.	D7	107
Yorktown, Tx., U.S.	E4	136
Yorktown, Va., U.S.	C6	139
Yorktown Manor, R.I., U.S.	E4	132
Yorkville, Il., U.S.	B5	106
Yorkville, N.Y., U.S.	B5	125
Yorkville, Oh., U.S.	B5	128
Yoro, Hond.	B2	80
Yoron-jima, i., Japan	g6	31a
Yosemite National Park, Ca., U.S.	D4	98
Yos Sudarso, Pulau, i., Indon.	H10	32
Yotaú, Bol.	B5	72
You, stm., China	G9	28
Youbou, B.C., Can.	g11	85
Youghiogheny, stm., U.S.	F2	131
Youghiogheny River Lake, res., U.S.	G3	131
Young, Austl.	G4	62
Young, Az., U.S.	C5	96
Young, co., Tx., U.S.	C3	136
Young Harris, Ga., U.S.	B3	103
Youngs, Lake, l., Wa., U.S.	f11	140
Youngstown, N.Y., U.S.	B1	125
Youngstown, Oh., U.S.	A5	128
Youngsville, La., U.S.	D3	111
Youngsville, Pa., U.S.	C3	131
Youngtown, Az., U.S.	k8	96
Youngwood, Pa., U.S.	F2	131
Youxian, China	D3	30
Youyang, China	F9	28
Yozgat, Tur.	C6	44
Ypacarai, Para.	D6	72
Ypsilanti, Mi., U.S.	F7	115
Yreka, Ca., U.S.	B2	98
Ystad, Swe.	I5	10
Yuanling, China	F10	28
Yuanmou, China	F8	28
Yuba, co., Ca., U.S.	C3	98
Yuba, stm., Ca., U.S.	C3	98
Yuba City, Ca., U.S.	C3	98
Yūbari, Japan	C16	28
Yucatán, state, Mex.	C7	78
Yucatan Channel, strt., N.A.	A2	80
Yucatan Peninsula, pen., N.A.	B2	80
Yucca Lake, l., Nv., U.S.	F5	121
Yucca Mountain, mtn., Nv., U.S.	G5	121
Yucheng, China	B4	30
Yudu, China	D4	30
Yueqing, China	D5	30
Yuexi, China	A4	34
Yueyang, China	F10	28
Yugoslavia, ctry., Eur.	C8	18
Yukon, Ok., U.S.	B4	129
Yukon, ter., Can.	F12	82
Yukon, stm., N.A.	F7	82
Yulee, Fl., U.S.	B5	102
Yulin, China	D9	28
Yulin, China	G10	28
Yuma, Az., U.S.	E1	96
Yuma, Co., U.S.	A8	99
Yuma, co., Az., U.S.	E1	96
Yuma, co., Co., U.S.	A8	99
Yuma Marine Corps Air Station, mil., Az., U.S.	E1	96
Yumbi, D.R.C.	D3	54
Yumbo, Col.	E4	80
Yumen, China	D7	28
Yuncheng, China	D10	28
Yunnan, state, China	G8	28
Yunxian, China	E10	28
Yunxiao, China	E4	30
Yunyang, China	C2	30
Yurimaguas, Peru	E4	70
Yuruá see Juruá, stm., S.A.	E6	70
Yushan, China	D4	30
Yü Shan, mtn., Tai.	E5	30
Yushu, China	E7	28
Yutan, Ne., U.S.	C9	120
Yutian, China	D4	28
Yuyao, China	C5	30
Yvetot, Fr.	C7	16

Z

Name	Map Ref.	Page
Žabasak, Kaz.	D11	22
Zabīd, Yemen	H4	38
Zābol, Iran	D8	42
Zacapa, Guat.	B2	80
Zacapu, Mex.	D4	78
Zacatecas, Mex.	C4	78
Zacatecas, state, Mex.	C4	78
Zachary, La., U.S.	D4	111
Zadar, Cro.	B5	18
Zadoi, China	C7	40
Zadonsk, Russia	C15	20
Zafer Burnu, c., N. Cyp.	E6	44
Zafra, Spain	H3	16
Zagazig, Egypt	E10	14
Zagora, Mor.	E2	14
Zagreb, Cro.	B5	18
Zāgros, Kūhhā-ye (Zagros Mountains), mts., Iran	D6	42
Zagros Mountains see Zāgros, Kūhhā-ye, mts., Iran	D6	42
Zāhedān, Iran	E8	42
Zahīrābād, India	F3	40
Zaḥlah, Leb.	F6	44
Zaire see Congo, Democratic Republic of the, ctry., Afr.	D4	54
Zaïre see Congo, stm., Afr.	D2	54
Zaječar, Yugo.	C9	18
Zajsan, Kaz.	E10	26
Zajsan, ozero, l., Kaz.	E10	26
Zakamensk, Russia	D12	26
Zakho, Iraq	D10	44
Zákinthos, Grc.	F8	18
Zákinthos, i., Grc.	F8	18
Zakopane, Pol.	E6	20
Zakouma, Chad	A3	54
Zalaegerszeg, Hung.	F4	20
Zalău, Rom.	F7	20
Zalishchyky, Ukr.	F4	20
Zamantı, stm., Tur.	D6	44
Zambeze (Zambezi), stm., Afr.	A3	56
Zambezi, Zam.	A3	56
Zambezi (Zambeze), stm., Afr.	B5	56
Zambia, ctry., Afr.	E5	52
Zamboanga, Phil.	E8	34
Zamboanga Peninsula, pen., Phil.	E8	34
Zambrów, Pol.	C7	20
Žâmbuè, Moz.	B5	56
Žambyl, Kaz.	E9	26
Zamora, Spain	G4	16
Zamora de Hidalgo, Mex.	D4	78
Zamość, Pol.	D7	20
Zanaga, Congo	D2	54
Žanatas, Kaz.	B9	42
Zanesville, Oh., U.S.	C4	128
Zanjān, Iran	D1	30
Zante see Zákinthos, i., Grc.	F8	18
Zanthus, Austl.	G3	60
Zanzibar, Tan.	E7	54
Zanzibar, i., Tan.	E7	54
Zanzibar Channel, strt., Tan.	E7	54
Zaozhuang, China	C4	30
Zapadno-Sibirskaja ravnina, pl., Russia	C9	26
Zapadnyj Sajan, mts., Russia	D11	26
Zapala, Arg.	E2	69
Zapata, Tx., U.S.	F3	136
Zapata, co., Tx., U.S.	F3	136
Zapopan, Mex.	C4	78
Zaporizhzhia, Ukr.	F13	20
Zaqatala, Azer.	B12	44
Zara, Tur.	C7	44
Zaragoza, Spain	G6	16
Zarajsk, Russia	B15	20
Zaranj, Afg.	D8	42
Zarasai, Lith.	I12	10
Zárate, Arg.	E6	72
Zarembo Island, i., Ak., U.S.	m23	95
Zarghūn Shahr, Afg.	D9	42
Zaria, Nig.	D6	50
Žarkamys, Kaz.	E10	22
Žarma, Kaz.	B4	28
Žary, Pol.	D3	20
Zāskār Mountains, mts., Asia	C3	40
Zavala, co., Tx., U.S.	E3	136
Zave, Zimb.	B5	56
Zavitinsk, Russia	A13	28
Zawiercie, Pol.	D5	20
Zāwiyat Masūs, Libya	E8	14
Zaysan, Lake see Zajsan, ozero, l., Kaz.	E10	26
Zdolbuniv, Ukr.	D9	20
Zduńska Wola, Pol.	D5	20
Zearing, Ia., U.S.	B4	108
Zebulon, Ga., U.S.	C2	103
Zebulon, N.C., U.S.	B4	126
Zeehan, Austl.	I4	62
Zeeland, Mi., U.S.	F5	115
Zeerust, S. Afr.	D4	56
Zeigler, Il., U.S.	F4	106
Zeja, Russia	D14	26
Zeja, stm., Russia	D14	26
Zejskoe vodohranilišče, res., Russia	D14	26
Zelenogorsk, Russia	F13	10
Zelenokumsk, Russia	B4	42
Železnodorožnyj, Russia	B9	22
Železnogorsk, Russia	C13	20
Železnogorsk-Ilimskij, Russia	D12	26
Zelienople, Pa., U.S.	E1	131
Zell am See, Aus.	G13	12
Zémio, C.A.R.	B5	54
Zenica, Bos.	B6	18
Zenith, Wa., U.S.	f11	140
Zenobia Peak, mtn., Co., U.S.	A2	99
Zenza do Itombe, Ang.	E2	54
Zephyr Cove, Nv., U.S.	E2	121
Zephyrhills, Fl., U.S.	D4	102
Žerdevka, Russia	D7	22
Zestafoni, Geor.	A10	44
Zeya see Zeja, stm., Russia	D14	26
Zeya Reservoir see Zejskoe vodohranilišče, res., Russia	D14	26
Žežkazgan, Kaz.	E8	26
Zgierz, Pol.	D5	20
Zhalun, China	C4	40
Zhangjiakou, China	C10	28
Zhangpu, China	E4	30
Zhangye, China	D8	28
Zhangzhou, China	G11	28
Zhanhua, China	B4	30
Zhanjiang, China	G10	28
Zhao'an, China	G11	28
Zhaoqing, China	G10	28
Zhaotong, China	F8	28
Zhashkiv, Ukr.	E11	20
Zhaxigang, China	E3	28
Zhdanov see Mariupol', Ukr.	F14	20
Zhejiang, state, China	F11	28
Zhenghe, China	D4	30
Zhenglan Qi, China	A4	30
Zhengzhou, China	D10	28
Zhenjiang, China	C4	30
Zhenning, China	D2	30
Zhenping, China	E10	28
Zhenxiong, China	D1	30
Zhenyuan, China	F9	28
Zhidoi, China	C6	40
Zhijiang, China	D2	30
Zhob, Pak.	D9	42
Zhob, stm., Pak.	D9	42
Zhongba, China	E4	28
Zhongdian, China	F7	28
Zhongning, China	D9	28
Zhongshan, China	B6	34
Zhongwei, China	B2	30
Zhongxian, China	C2	30
Zhongxiang, China	E10	28
Zhoushan Qundao, is., China	E12	28
Zhovtneve, Ukr.	F12	20
Zhuanghe, China	B5	30
Zhucheng, China	B4	30
Zhumadian, China	C3	30
Zhuolu, China	A4	30
Zhuozhou, China	D11	28
Zhushan, China	E10	28
Zhuzhou, China	F10	28
Zhytomyr, Ukr.	D10	20
Zia Indian Reservation, N.M., U.S.	h7	124
Zibo, China	D11	28
Ziebach, co., S.D., U.S.	C4	134
Zielona Góra, Pol.	D3	20
Žigalovo, Russia	D12	26
Žigansk, Russia	C14	26
Zigong, China	F8	28
Ziguinchor, Sen.	D1	50
Zihuatanejo, Mex.	D4	78
Zile, Tur.	B6	44
Žilina, Slvk.	E5	20
Zillah, Libya	E8	48
Zillah, Wa., U.S.	C5	140
Zilwaukee, Mi., U.S.	E7	115
Zima, Russia	D12	26
Zimbabwe, ctry., Afr.	B4	56
Zimi, S.L.	E2	50
Zimmerman, Mn., U.S.	E5	116
Zinder, Niger	D6	50
Zion, Il., U.S.	A6	106
Zion National Park, Ut., U.S.	F3	137
Zion Reservoir, res., Az., U.S.	C6	96
Zionsville, In., U.S.	E5	107
Zipaquirá, Col.	D5	80
Zirkel, Mount, mtn., Co., U.S.	A4	99
Zitong, China	C2	30
Zittau, Ger.	E14	12
Zitundo, Moz.	D5	56
Ziway Hāyk', l., Eth.	B7	54
Ziyun, China	D2	30
Zlatoust, Russia	D7	26
Zlītan, Libya	D7	48
Žlobin, Bela.	C11	20
Złotów, Pol.	C4	20
Zmeinogorsk, Russia	A4	28
Znam'ianka, Ukr.	E12	20
Znojmo, Czech Rep.	E4	20
Žodzina, Bela.	B10	20
Zolfo Springs, Fl., U.S.	E5	102
Zomba, Mwi.	B6	56
Zonguldak, Tur.	B4	44
Zouar, Chad	B8	50
Zouérat, Maur.	B2	50
Zrenjanin, Yugo.	B8	18
Žuantobe, Kaz.	B9	42
Zug, Switz.	A2	18
Zugdidi, Geor.	A9	44
Zugspitze, mtn., Eur.	G12	12
Žukovka, Russia	C12	20
Zumbo, Moz.	B5	56
Zumbro, stm., Mn., U.S.	F6	116
Zumbrota, Mn., U.S.	F6	116
Zuni (Zuni Pueblo), N.M., U.S.	B1	124
Zuni, stm., U.S.	C6	96
Zuni Indian Reservation, N.M., U.S.	B1	124
Zuni Mountains, mts., N.M., U.S.	B1	124
Zunyi, China	F9	28
Zūrābād, Iran	C11	44
Zurich, On., Can.	D3	89
Zürich, Switz.	A2	18
Zurich, Lake see Zürichsee, l., Switz.	A2	18
Zürichsee, l., Switz.	A2	18
Zuru, Nig.	D6	50
Zuwārah, Libya	E6	14
Zvishavane, Zimb.	C4	56
Zvolen, Slvk.	E5	20
Zwedru, Lib.	E3	50
Zwickau, Ger.	E13	12
Zwolle, Neth.	D10	12
Zwolle, La., U.S.	C2	111
Žyrardów, Pol.	C6	20
Zyrjanka, Russia	C17	26
Zyrjanovsk, Kaz.	E10	26
Żywiec, Pol.	E5	20